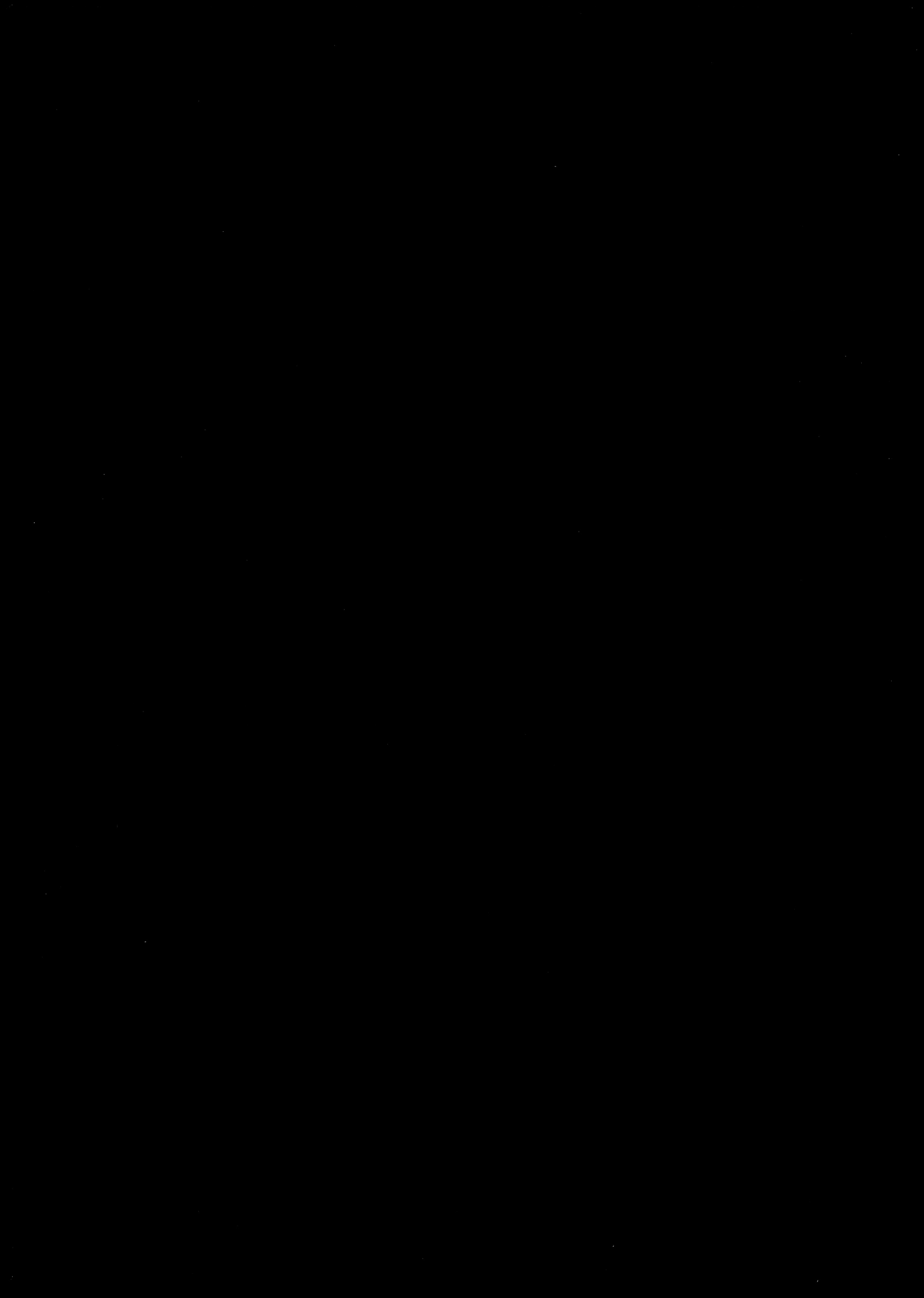

exiles+emigrés

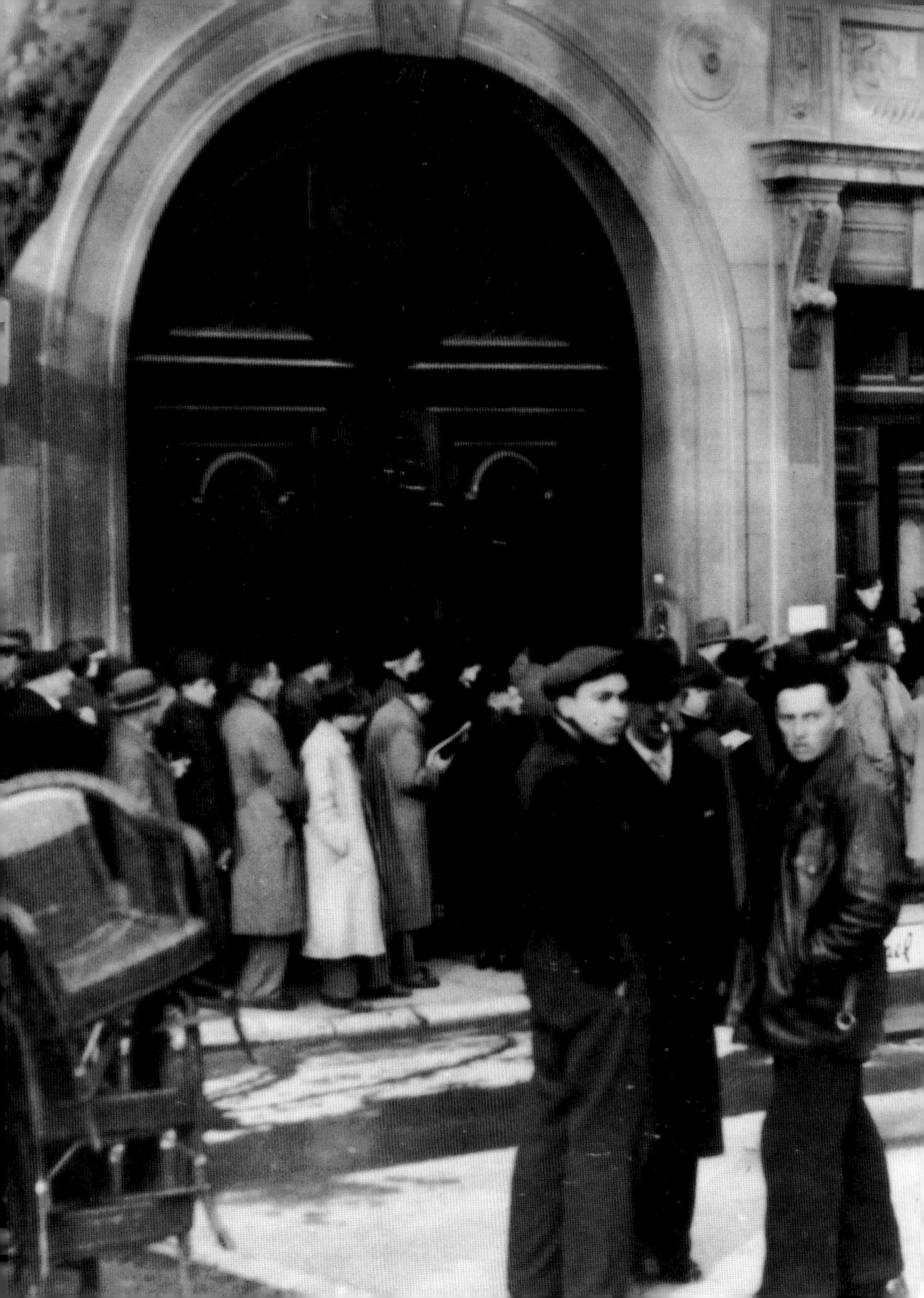

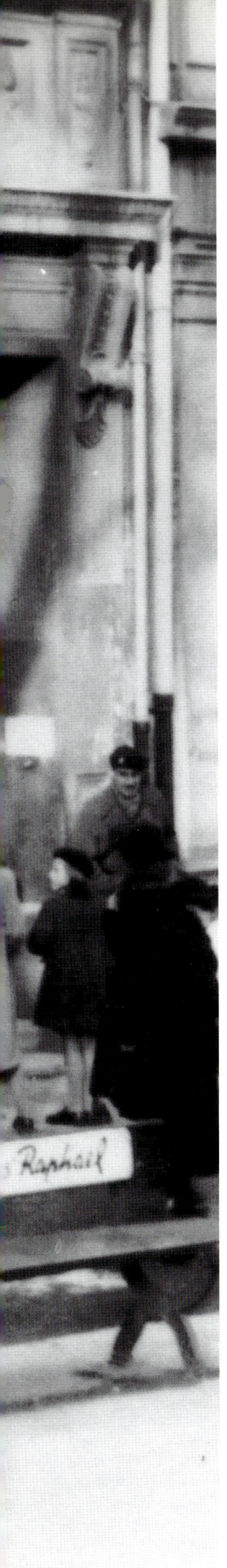

exiles+emigrés

The Flight of European Artists from Hitler

Stephanie Barron

with Sabine Eckmann

contributions by
Matthew Affron
Vivian Endicott Barnett
Elizabeth Kessin Berman
Sheri Bernstein
Barbara Copeland Buenger
Hans Magnus Enzensberger
Romy Golan
Peter Hahn
Keith Holz
Deborah Irmas
Kathleen James
Martin Jay
Stephan Lackner
Karen Michels
Kevin Parker
Franz Schulze
Lawrence Weschler

LOS ANGELES COUNTY MUSEUM OF ART • HARRY N. ABRAMS, INC., PUBLISHERS

Copublished by the Los Angeles County Museum of Art, 5905 Wilshire Boulevard, Los Angeles, California 90036, and Harry N. Abrams, Inc., 100 Fifth Avenue, New York 10011.

© 1997 by Museum Associates, Los Angeles County Museum of Art. All rights reserved. No part of the contents of this book may be reproduced without written permission of the publisher.

This book was published in conjunction with the exhibition *Exiles and Emigrés: The Flight of European Artists from Hitler*, which was organized by the Los Angeles County Museum of Art. It was funded in part by grants from the National Endowment for the Humanities, Helen and Peter Bing, the Righteous Persons Foundation, the National Endowment for the Arts, the Silent Foundation for the Arts, Daniel Greenberg and Susan Steinhauser, and Villa Aurora. It received an indemnity from the Federal Council on the Arts and the Humanities and additional assistance from the Federal Republic of Germany.

International passenger and cargo transportation was provided by Lufthansa German Airlines.

Lufthansa

Exhibition itinerary

Los Angeles County Museum of Art
    February 23–May 11, 1997

Montreal Museum of Fine Arts
    June 19–September 7, 1997

Neue Nationalgalerie, Berlin
    October 9, 1997–January 4, 1998

The essays by Peter Hahn and Karen Michels and the texts by Sabine Eckmann (with the exception of the essays on Lyonel Feininger and George Grosz and the Chronology) were translated from the German by David Britt.

Edited by Karen Jacobson
Designed by Scott Taylor
Production assistance by Theresa Velázquez
Printed by Nissha Printing Co. Ltd.,
Kyoto, Japan

Library of Congress Catalog Card Number:
ISBN: 0-8109-3271-7 (cloth)
ISBN: 0-87587-178-x (paper)

Frontispiece:
Refugees waiting for visas outside the U.S. consulate in Marseilles, 1940–41; photograph by Hiram Bingham.

Right:
Les Milles internment camp, Vichy France, 1940–41.

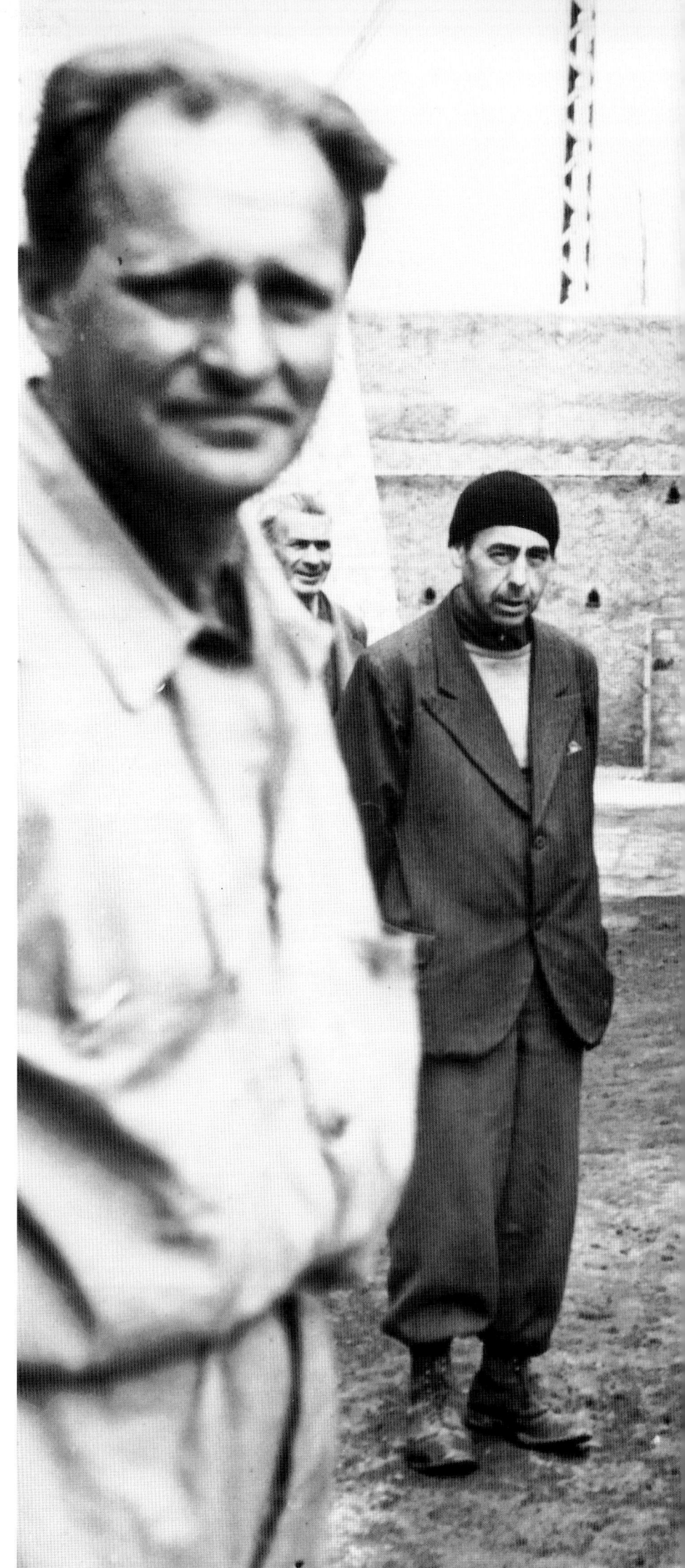

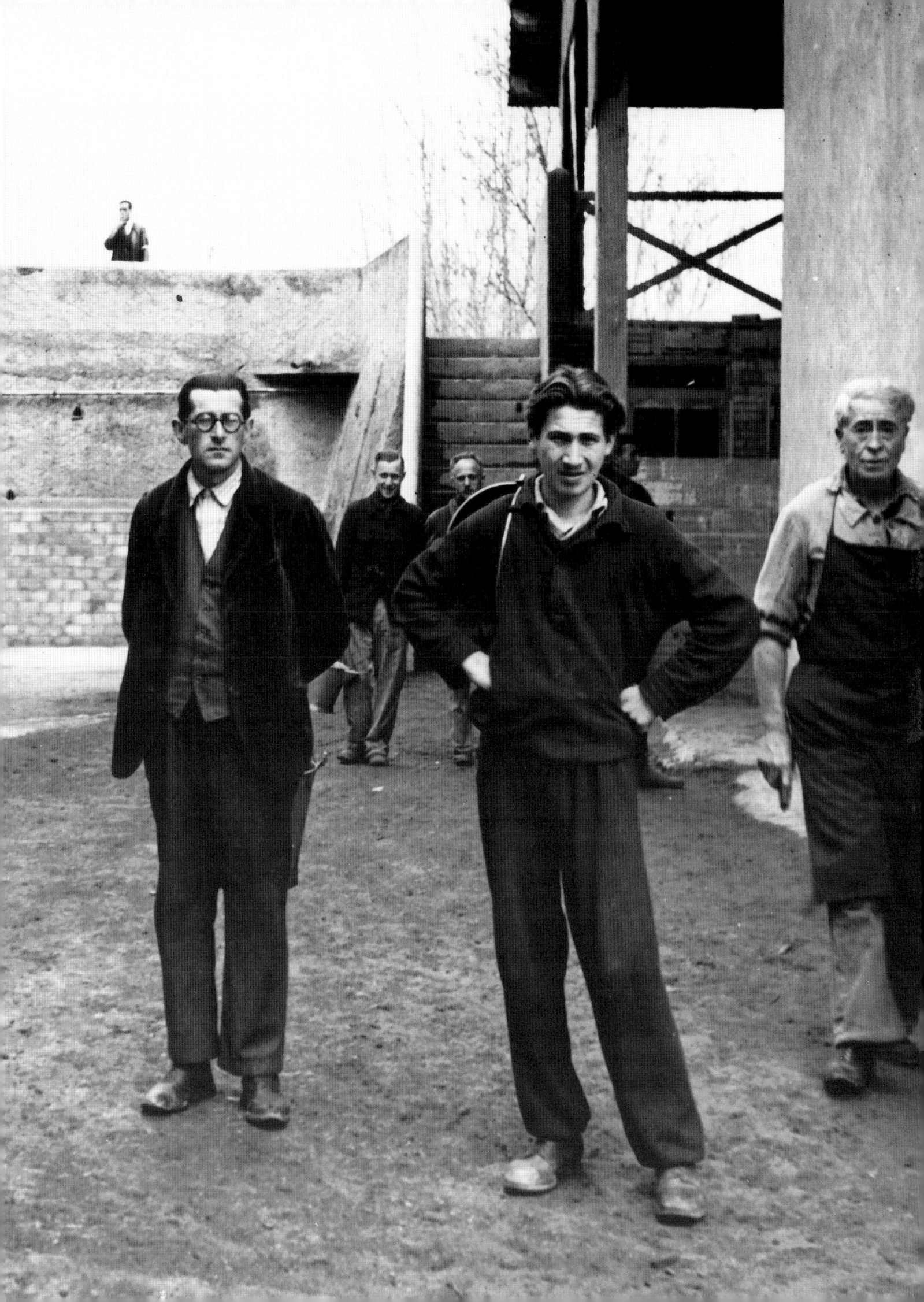

contents

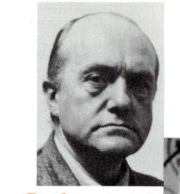
Max Beckmann 58

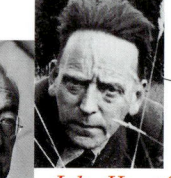
John Heartfield 74

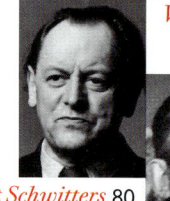
Wassily Kandinsky 68

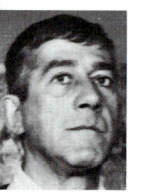
Kurt Schwitters 80

Oskar Kokoschka 86

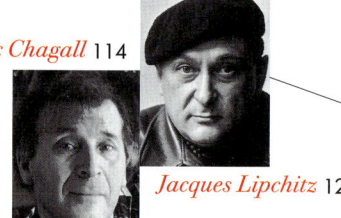
Marc Chagall 114 *Jacques Lipchitz* 120

Yves Tanguy 170

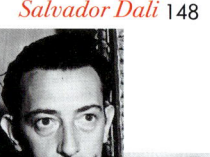
Salvador Dali 148

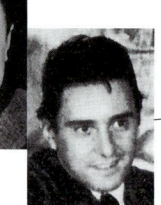
Matta Echaurren 176

André Masson 164

Max Ernst 156

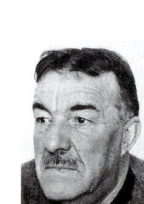
Piet Mondrian 190

Fernand Léger 184

Andreas Feininger 196

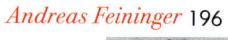
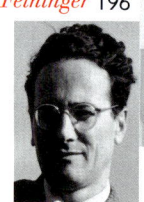
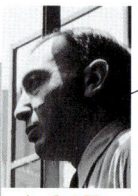
André Kertész 202

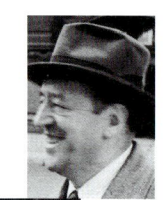
Ludwig Mies van der Rohe 236

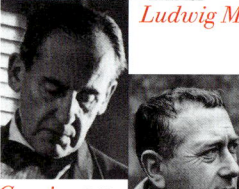
Walter Gropius 242

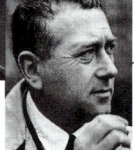
Marcel Breuer 248

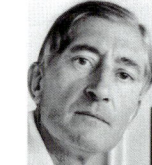
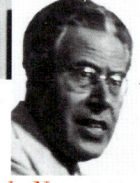
Josef Albers 254

László Moholy-Nagy 262

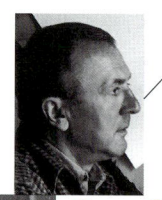
George Grosz 286

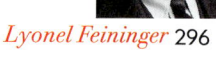
Lyonel Feininger 296

Foreword	8	Graham W. J. Beal
European Artists in Exile: A Reading between the Lines	11	Stephanie Barron
Considering (and Reconsidering) Art and Exile	30	Sabine Eckmann
Scenes from Exile in Western Europe: **The Politics of Individual and Collective Endeavor among German Artists**	43	Keith Holz
Antifascism or Autonomous Art? *Max Beckmann, Wassily Kandinsky, John Heartfield, Kurt Schwitters* *Oskar Kokoschka*	57	Barbara Copeland Buenger Keith Holz
Moral Triage or Cultural Salvage? **The Agendas of Varian Fry and the Emergency Rescue Committee**	99	Elizabeth Kessin Berman
Constructing a New Jewish Identity *Marc Chagall, Jacques Lipchitz*	113	Matthew Affron
On the Passage of a Few Persons through a Rather Brief Period of Time	128	Romy Golan
Surrealism in Exile: Responses to the European Destruction of Humanism *Salvador Dali, Max Ernst, André Masson, Yves Tanguy, Matta Echaurren*	147	Sabine Eckmann
New York's Impact on Modernity *Fernand Léger, Piet Mondrian*	183	Matthew Affron
Experiencing the New World *Andreas Feininger, André Kertész*	195	Deborah Irmas
Bauhaus and Exile: **Bauhaus Architects and Designers between the Old World and the New**	211	Peter Hahn
The Bauhaus Architects and the Rise of Modernism in the United States	225	Franz Schulze
Changing the Agenda: From German Bauhaus Modernism to U.S. Internationalism *Ludwig Mies van der Rohe, Walter Gropius, Marcel Breuer*	235	Kathleen James
Purism and Pragmatism *Josef Albers, László Moholy-Nagy*	253	Sheri Bernstein
Banned German Art: Reception and Institutional Support of Modern German Art **in the United States, 1933–45**	273	Vivian Endicott Barnett
The Loss of Homeland and Cultural Identity *George Grosz, Lyonel Feininger*	285	Sabine Eckmann
Transfer and Transformation: The German Period in American Art History	304	Karen Michels
Art History and Exile: Richard Krautheimer and Erwin Panofsky	317	Kevin Parker
The German Migration: Is There a Figure in the Carpet?	326	Martin Jay
Paradise: The Southern California Idyll of Hitler's Cultural Exiles	341	Lawrence Weschler
Reflections on Exile in France and the United States	363	Stephan Lackner
The Great Migration	374	Hans Magnus Enzensberger
Chronology	386	
Checklist of the Exhibition	401	
Selected Bibliography	408	
Acknowledgments	418	
Lenders to the Exhibition	422	
Index	424	

foreword

It seems impossible today to read any report of world events that does not involve issues related to cultural identity: the migration of a group of people to a new land; the problems associated with sudden demands for minorities to "assimilate"; out-and-out persecution on religious, racial, tribal, national, or political grounds. Whether one lives in Los Angeles or Liverpool, Grozny or Sarajevo, Djakarta or Colombo, these are issues that are all around us.

The exhibition *Exiles and Emigrés: The Flight of European Artists from Hitler* and its catalogue are devoted to a specific time period: the twelve years of National Socialist rule in Germany, from 1933 to 1945. As a prelude to the well-known systematic eradication of millions of Jews and other minorities, this period saw the forced migration of thousands of accomplished and well-regarded professionals, first from Germany and subsequently from the countries of Europe progressively occupied by Hitler's armies. The impact of Hitler's unprecedented assault on the intellectual, artistic, and professional communities of Europe is still being assessed. For the first time in the context of a major museum exhibition in North America, *Exiles and Emigrés* seeks to chart not only the course of the exiles' journeys within Europe and to the United States but also their activities in exile, the characteristics of the work they produced, and the nature of the responses they faced in their host countries.

Over the past fifteen years the Los Angeles County Museum of Art has initiated a number of exhibitions that examined twentieth-century art within a social, historical, and political framework. In 1991 the museum presented *"Degenerate Art": The Fate of the Avant-Garde in Nazi Germany*—organized by Stephanie Barron, LACMA's senior curator of twentieth-century art—which scrutinized the virulent cultural attack mounted by the Nazis. *Exiles and Emigrés*—an exhibition rich in art, documents, narrative, and interpretation—continues this story. Again, the driving force behind the exhibition was Stephanie Barron, and I want to thank her for her immense efforts in organizing such an ambitious project. She was ably assisted in all aspects of the endeavor by Sabine Eckmann, exhibition associate, and to her, also, thanks are due.

We are very pleased that our colleagues Pierre Théberge, director of the Montreal Museum of Fine Arts; Wolf-Dieter Dube, director general of the Staatliche Museen zu Berlin, Preussischer Kulturbesitz; and Peter-Klaus Schuster, director of the Alte Nationalgalerie, Berlin, have enthusiastically joined with us to make a splendid international tour.

Our thanks as well to the National Endowment for the Humanities and the National Endowment for the Arts, our chief sponsors, for without their crucial support this project would have been impossible to realize. The commitment of these federal agencies to projects that examine cultural issues of such importance cannot be too highly praised. The Federal Republic of Germany has provided crucial financial assistance, and we are grateful to Consul General Hans Alard von Rohr and Deputy Consul General Jean-Pierre Rollin in Los Angeles for their help in securing this subvention. We are also grateful to Helen and Peter Bing, the Righteous Persons Foundation, and the Silent Foundation for the Arts; their support underwrote essential research and educational programs, without which this project could not have assumed its present dimensions.

Ultimately the import of an exhibition and its publication lies with the audience. It is our deepest hope that *Exiles and Emigrés: The Flight of European Artists from Hitler*, along with its extensive related programming, will stimulate and enlighten a receptive and inquiring public.

GRAHAM W. J. BEAL
Director and Executive Vice President

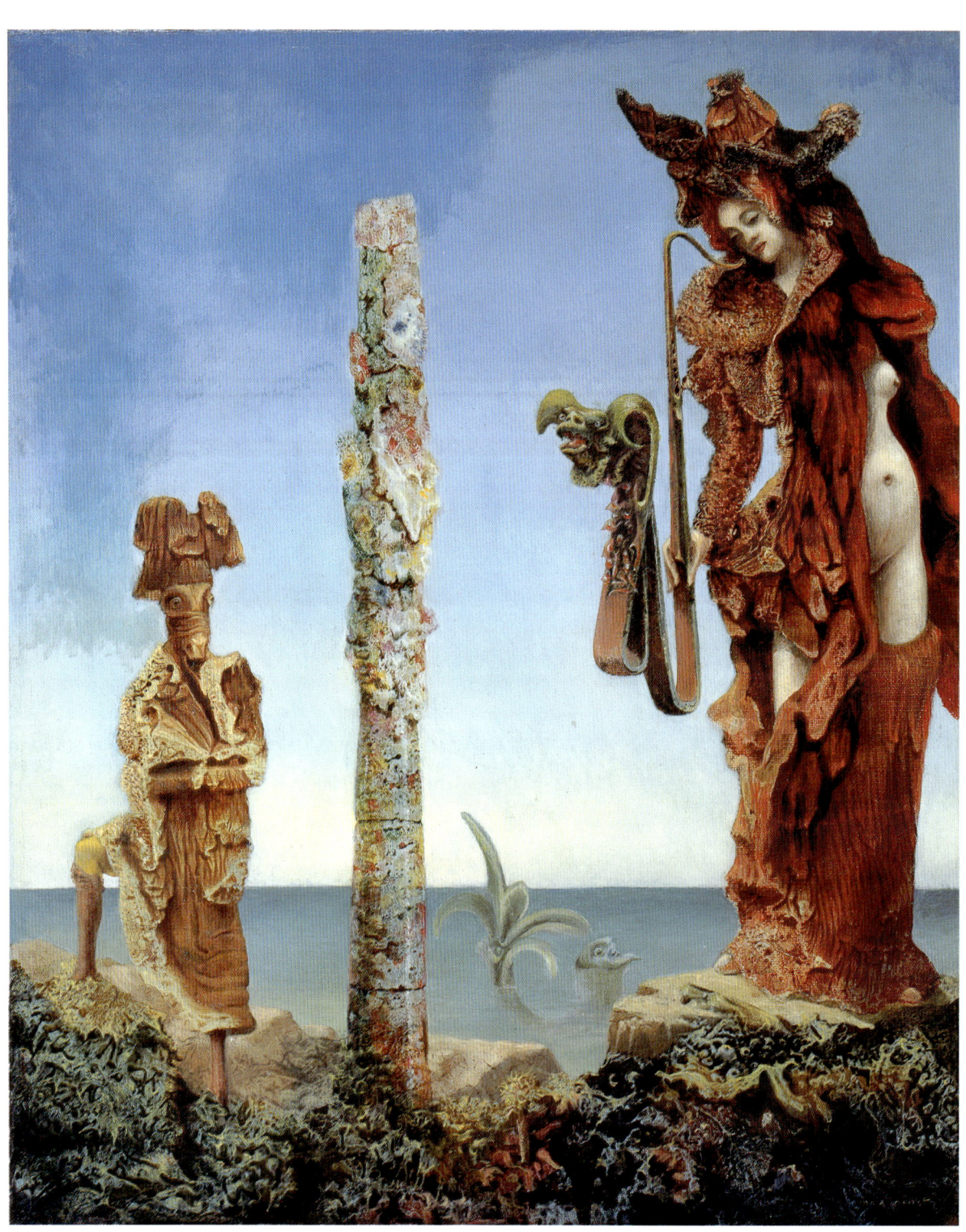

european artists in exile: a reading between the lines

STEPHANIE BARRON

The idea for this exhibition first occurred to me in the early 1980s, when, having recently moved to Los Angeles from New York, I became increasingly aware of the rich constellation of writers, musicians, filmmakers, actors, and individuals associated with the art world who had settled for a time on the shores of the Pacific as a result of the cataclysmic events then unfolding in Nazi Germany. These talented professionals were part of a virtual wave of emigrés who arrived in the United States during the 1930s and 1940s, seeking refuge and opportunity. I wanted to examine this remarkable influx of talent to a city often regarded as lacking international background and to locate Los Angeles in its place alongside New York and Chicago, long celebrated for their hospitality to the refugees. Yet an exhibition must rely upon important works of art, and unfortunately almost no European visual artists settled in Los Angeles during this period. Consequently the project was shelved for several years while I searched for an appropriate approach to this rich topic. The experience of organizing the 1991 exhibition *"Degenerate Art": The Fate of the Avant-Garde in Nazi Germany* made me realize that it might be possible to put together a show that involved art and documentary materials and an examination of social and political conditions if one could assemble works of art that clearly address core issues of exile. Thus, the project began to take its present form.

The first part of *Exiles and Emigrés: The Flight of European Artists from Hitler* seeks to trace the migration within Europe of refugees from Nazi Germany and Austria. In the 1930s and 1940s, with the Nazi occupation of most of Western Europe and the outbreak and escalation of the war, many sought to leave Europe. Those fortunate enough to escape landed in places as far flung as Palestine, Russia, China, South America, and Canada. It was, however, necessary to limit the scope of the project, and the second part of *Exiles and Emigrés* focuses solely on migration to the United States. By a similar logic one could have sought to document the full range of artists in exile, including not only the well-known figures but also those of little renown whose lives and careers were nevertheless profoundly altered by emigration. Instead we chose to concentrate on the careers of twenty-three artists, architects, and photographers who had achieved considerable reputations before emigration. Although the fact that the pre-exile work of these artists is well known makes it easier in some cases to discern the impact of emigration on their works, a decision was made to look exclusively at the work created during the exile period. Despite the reputation of the artists in the exhibition, their activities during this period have generally been overlooked by scholars. For this reason the texts in this catalogue on the individual artists, which are interwoven with the thematic essays, often contain original research that brings to light new aspects of the artists' careers in exile. Of equal importance is the reception of the emigrés by their various host countries. By considering the effect of both government policies toward the exiles and the cultural milieu of the host countries, we can attain a better understanding of the circumstances under which these works were created.

Exiles and Emigrés presents approximately 130 works of art in a variety of mediums as well as publications, photographs, historical

1
Max Ernst, *Napoleon in the Wilderness*, 1941 (cat. no. 33).

documents, ephemera, and a film about American immigration policies during this period. Among the thousands who escaped Nazi Europe, the exhibition focuses on artists who worked in Germany before their emigration—Josef Albers, Max Beckmann, Marcel Breuer, Andreas Feininger, Lyonel Feininger, Walter Gropius, George Grosz, John Heartfield, Wassily Kandinsky, André Kertész, Oskar Kokoschka, Ludwig Mies van der Rohe, László Moholy-Nagy, and Kurt Schwitters—as well as those who worked in France—Marc Chagall, Salvador Dali, Max Ernst, Fernand Léger, Jacques Lipchitz, André Masson, Matta, Piet Mondrian, and Yves Tanguy.

The exhibition and catalogue reexamine the tremendous consequences of the exodus of European artists which followed Hitler's rise to power. From an American perspective this approach, focusing more on the exiles themselves than on their impact on American artists, is a departure from earlier accounts. *Exiles and Emigrés* looks at the work they did in exile, its significance within their own development, and its reception by the American art world. The exhibition and catalogue are organized thematically according to the following topics: the initial flight of refugees from Germany and Austria to Paris, Amsterdam, and London; the escape from Europe and the political and cultural climate encountered by immigrants to the United States in the 1930s and early 1940s; the Parisian exile community in the United States; the American cultural infrastructure; the exiles as teachers; and the American response to modern German art.

The National Socialists' Rise to Power

When Adolf Hitler assumed power in Germany, on January 30, 1933, the National Socialists initiated a policy of racial and political persecution that was directed against all "non-Aryans" as well as those who held views that were politically and philosophically opposed to those of the party. Throughout the 1930s these attacks escalated, from rhetoric to increasingly restrictive laws to physical assaults on both individuals and their property. Jews began to flee Germany soon after the Nazi takeover, and many more began to contemplate leaving. After November 1938, in the wake of Kristallnacht—the "night of broken glass," a pogrom in which almost all of Germany's synagogues and many Jewish-owned businesses were destroyed (see fig. 3)—the need to escape became more urgent.

During this period modern artists, musicians, writers, critics, publishers, museum directors and curators, art historians, theater directors, and actors found themselves under careful scrutiny, even if they were not Jewish, because of their political or aesthetic leanings. By September 1933 propaganda minister Joseph Goebbels had established the Reichskulturkammer (Reich chamber of culture), with seven divisions overseeing the press and all types of artistic production. The Professional Civil Service Restoration Act (*Gesetz zur Wiederherstellung des Berufsbeamtentums*) of April 7, 1933, made it possible for Nazi officials to dismiss non-Aryan government employees, including many academics and museum officials. The purge of "undesirables" from universities, academies, museums, libraries, concert halls, and theaters was thus put into motion.

The first four years of Nazi rule were a time of much internal conflict over what kind of art should be identified with the new Germany. In 1934 there were divergent opinions about what the official Nazi attitude toward modern German art should be. Some saw the work of artists such as Ernst Barlach and Emil Nolde as truly German and Nordic, with roots traceable to the Gothic era. Goebbels, in fact, at first surrounded himself with examples of their art. In contrast, Alfred Rosenberg, chief Nazi theorist and leader of the Kampfbund der deutschen Kultur (Campaign for German culture), argued against modernism, and his view was ultimately embraced by the party.

Goebbels and Rosenberg were also sharply divided in their views of modern architecture. While Nazi writers and polemicists attacked the Bauhaus, the institution most closely identified with modernism, and closed down the progressive school in 1933, they did not attack modern architecture as a whole. As Peter Hahn points out in his essay in this catalogue, although the Nazis excoriated the "architectural bolshevism" of the Bauhaus, they were not opposed to employing former Bauhäuslers if their talents were useful to the Reich, particularly in areas such as product and graphic design and industrial architecture.

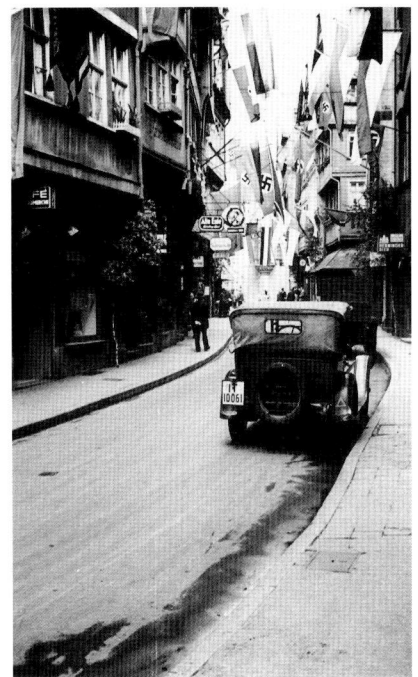

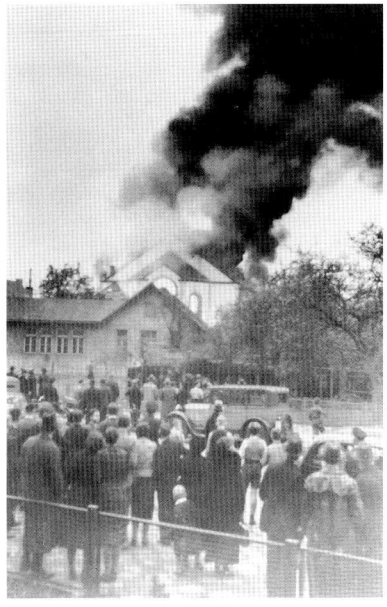

Herbert Bayer, for instance, received several commissions to design propaganda exhibitions after 1933. Both Gropius and Mies, the school's first and final directors, entered architectural competitions sponsored by the National Socialists, although neither received commissions. Affiliation with the Bauhaus was not sufficient grounds for persecution, but most former members found it difficult to obtain work after the school closed.

Many artists and intellectuals determined that—for racial, political, and cultural reasons—emigration was the only possible choice. Jewish artist Jankel Adler—who had been a communist sympathizer and a member of leftist artists groups in Cologne, Berlin, Lodz, and Düsseldorf—was part of this first wave of emigration, fleeing Germany for Paris in 1933. At the time he said that he saw his exile "as an active struggle against the fascist regime in Germany."[1] Hans Feibusch, also Jewish, fled Germany in 1933 for England, a logical destination since his wife was British. Although armed with a letter of recommendation from the head of the Städelsches Kunstinstitut in Frankfurt to the curator of the Tate Gallery in London, he nevertheless found it difficult to make ends meet and supported himself as a book illustrator.[2] George Grosz, John Heartfield, and publisher Wieland Herzfelde (Heartfield's brother)—all vocal opponents of Hitler—were among those who emigrated in 1933 for political reasons. Many who had by chance been abroad when the Nazis came to power watched from a distance what was going on at home and elected to remain away. Heinrich Campendonk was traveling in Norway in 1933 when he learned of his dismissal from the Düsseldorf Academy; he chose to immigrate to Amsterdam.

2
Nazi Germany, 1935; photograph by Varian Fry.

3
Burning of the synagogue in Rostock, Kristallnacht (November 9, 1938).

Only in July of 1937, four years after the Nazis had come to power, did their policy regarding modern art become absolutely clear with the simultaneous opening in Munich of one exhibition that celebrated art glorified by the Reich, the *Große deutsche Kunstausstellung* (Great German art exhibition), and a second that ridiculed modern art, *Entartete Kunst* (Degenerate art) (see fig. 4). Thus, with the formulation of this cultural policy, the National Socialists began to use art to propagate their political ideology. It was no longer possible for artists to operate in a realm discrete from politics, and they were forced to respond.

Those attacked had three choices: to remain at home and stop working in the offending style, to attempt to compromise with the Nazis, or to leave.

Not all artists responded immediately. It was not until 1939, two years after his work had been pilloried in *Entartete Kunst*, that Jewish artist Ludwig Meidner fled to England.[3] Those who chose to stay in Germany—including Willi Baumeister, Otto Dix, Conrad Felixmüller, and Oskar Schlemmer—entered a period known as inner emigration. Ernst Ludwig Kirchner became so despondent that he took his own life. Dix, who moved to Lake Constance, commented that during this period, "I painted landscapes; that was tantamount to emigration."[4] Many artists, such as Karl Schmidt-Rottluff and Erich Heckel, moved to small villages in an attempt to escape the notice of the authorities. Some were erroneously attacked for being Jews; Lyonel Feininger, Karl Hofer, and Paul Klee all had to produce documents proving their Aryan status.

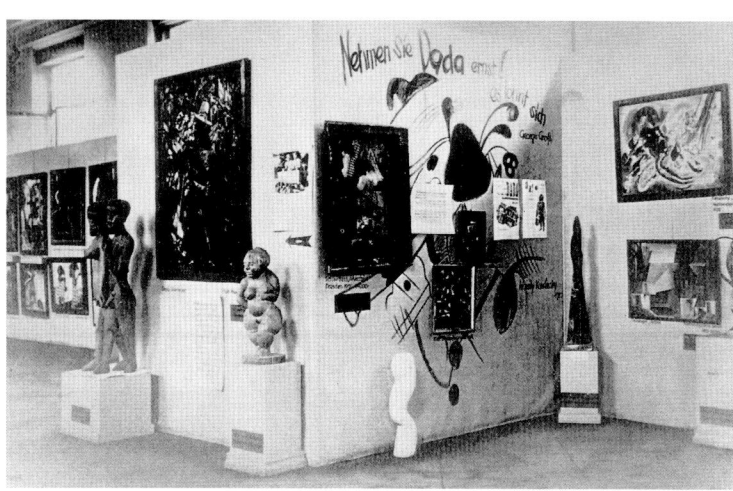

4
Installation view of *Entartete Kunst*, Munich, 1937.

Since 1933 Schlemmer had watched as his work was systematically removed from German museums. He was stunned by the attacks on his work—"I am cut to the quick for the first time by political events," he wrote to his friend Gerhard Marcks[5]—and on several occasions he protested to Goebbels and other Nazi party officials. Nevertheless, in 1934 he entered an official competition to decorate the congress hall of the Deutsches Museum in Munich.[6] As for Marcks, he was never prohibited from working, even after his sculpture was included in *Entartete Kunst*, and he continued to enter public competitions, albeit unsuccessfully. Ewald Mataré continued to receive commissions to decorate churches; only his secular work was attacked. Karl Caspar, though also represented in *Entartete Kunst*, was not immediately dismissed from the Munich Academy.

Throughout the 1930s a great number of artists continued to flee the country: Beckmann to Amsterdam, Rudolf Belling to New York and then Turkey, Lyonel Feininger to New York, Raoul Hausmann to Ibiza, Kandinsky to Paris, Kokoschka to Prague and then London, Schwitters to Norway and then England. Despite the fact that their art had been politicized, many of the emigrés attempted to maintain an apolitical stance.

The Nazi attack on modernism encompassed not only those who made art but also those who wrote about it, organized exhibitions of it, and sold it. Critics, art historians, museum directors and curators, and art dealers were also forced to consider their options. Many, a considerable percentage of whom were Jewish, chose exile. Alexander Dorner, ousted from his post as director of the Provinzialmuseum in Hannover, emigrated in 1937 to the United States, where he was appointed director of the Art Museum of the Rhode Island School of Design. In 1937 Curt Valentin, a well-known art dealer from Berlin, fled to New York, where he established a branch of the Buchholz Gallery, an important nexus of the emigré art world. Art historian Alfred Neumeyer left Germany in 1935 and began teaching at Mills College in Oakland.

Between 1933 and 1935 many Germans continued to believe that things would improve. For this reason the majority of those who emigrated early on initially remained nearby. Many chose places with cultural ties to Germany, such as Czechoslovakia and Switzerland; France, England, and the Netherlands were also common destinations.

France, and especially Paris, had long been a preferred destination for European emigrés. German artists such as Max Ernst and Otto Freundlich had already settled there in the 1920s. By 1936 leftist emigrés in Paris had formed the Kollektiv deutscher Künstler (Collective of German artists), with members Ernst, Freundlich, Gert Wollheim, and the writer and publisher Paul Westheim. In 1938 the Freier Künstlerbund (Free League of artists) mounted a counterexhibition to *Entartete Kunst*. The primary purpose of these groups was to inform the public about opposition to the German government through exhibitions, publications, and educational events.

The situation of German and Austrian emigrés living in France was dependent upon political and economic circumstances. Between 1930 and 1935 France was in the throes of the Depression. Unemployment was high, and emigrants were generally looked upon with suspicion. Although Paris remained the artistic capital, many galleries and publications shut down, collectors sold works, and the art market collapsed. On the political scene fascist and nationalist organizations gained ground, while the middle class remained staunchly anticommunist. With the election in 1936 of Léon Blum as premier a somewhat unified socialist front prevailed. The new government was more tolerant of German refugees than the previous one had been; they were issued identity cards and participated in a government advisory committee on emigration. With Blum's resignation in 1938, however, their situation worsened. His successor, Edouard Daladier, succumbed to British pressure to appease Hitler, signing the Munich Accord in 1938.

With the French and British declaration of war against Germany following the invasion of Poland and the signing of the nonaggression pact between Germany and the Soviet Union, the French government outlawed the Communist party, and the situation for left-wing German emigrés became untenable. All German male refugees between the ages of seventeen and sixty-five were arrested and interned, regardless of their political sympathies or their religion. Although several well-known German refugees were able to obtain their freedom through connections with well-placed Frenchmen, it was only temporary, since by May 1940 those who remained in France were rearrested and deported to detention camps in the south of France. Ernst and fellow German artist Hans Bellmer were among those interned. With France's surrender to Germany and the Occupation, Hitler's anti-Jewish laws were extended to France. By the end of 1941 the deportation of Jews from France to Eastern Europe had begun. One of those deported was Freundlich, who was murdered at the extermination camp at Majdanek in 1943. By 1942 German forces had moved into the south of France as well.

In 1933 approximately six thousand refugees made their way from Germany to Great Britain, a country that had historically welcomed refugees from religious and political persecution. The celebrated Warburg Library, a private art historical research institute in Hamburg, which had come under attack in part because of its high quotient of Jewish scholars, was invited to relocate to London. This provided a haven for dozens of art historians, who exerted

Exile in Europe

a profound impact on British culture. Through 1937, when the number of German immigrants stood at about eleven thousand, emigration procedures were relatively simple; it was sufficient for a British citizen to serve as a guarantor. By 1938, however, the number of Germans and Austrians seeking asylum had increased to seventy thousand in the first half of the year alone. This coincided with massive British unemployment. Because of the troubled economy at home and the rapidly developing international political crisis, the British government began to limit the number of immigrants from Nazi Germany. It became much more difficult to obtain visas and, for those fortunate enough to be admitted, work permits.

In Britain, as in France, following the declaration of war, communists came under suspicion as Nazi sympathizers. As anti-immigrant fervor spread, the government announced restrictions on "enemy aliens." Although many Germans and Austrians were interned, the situation was easier for refugees in Britain than it was for their counterparts in France. In Britain tribunals were set up to review each case. Most of the Jewish refugees were deemed loyal to Britain and thus escaped internment. Of the small number of enemy aliens whose loyalty was suspect, most were deported to Australia or Canada. The remainder, numbering about four thousand, were sent to hastily erected camps on the Isle of Man, where living conditions were relatively comfortable. Heartfield was interned only briefly because of health problems; Schwitters was arrested immediately upon his arrival in England in 1940 and remained in custody for a year and a half.

Although there was little appreciation for German art in England, in 1938 the New Burlington Galleries in London presented the *Exhibition of Twentieth Century German Art* (see fig. 5). Despite its bland title (a reflection of British appeasement policies), the exhibition was a pointed reaction to *Entartete Kunst* and Britain's first comprehensive look at modern German art. London too was home to several exiled artists' groups, including the Free German League of Culture (1938–46), which mounted shows on topics such as English and refugee artists and art in exile.

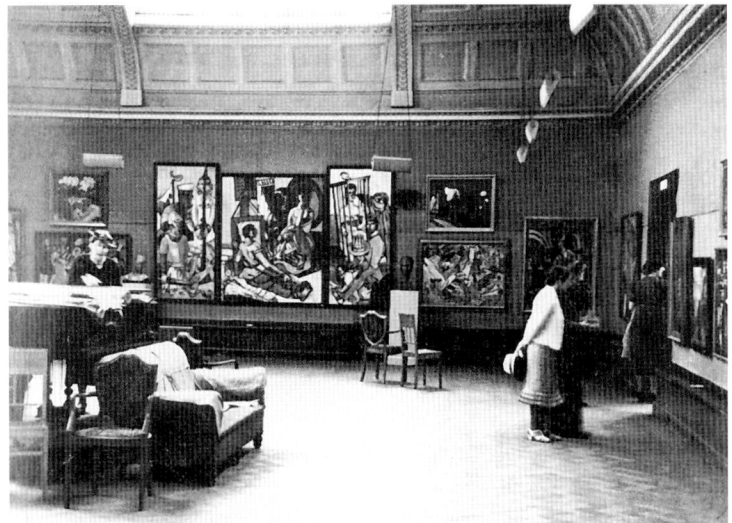

5
Installation view of the *Exhibition of Twentieth Century German Art*, New Burlington Galleries, London, 1938, with works by Max Beckmann, Wassily Kandinsky, and Wilhelm Lehmbruck. Beckmann's triptych *Temptation* (1936–37) can be seen at center; photograph by Ewan Phillips.

The Netherlands provided a sympathetic haven for many German-speaking refugees until its occupation by Germany in 1940. By 1937–38, however, it was becoming increasingly difficult to find refuge there, as regulations for granting political asylum tightened. By the end of 1938 no more visas were being issued, and new identity cards were required of all immigrants. Following the Occupation many refugees desperately sought to escape the Netherlands, and they were usually able to secure the necessary papers. By 1942 the deportation of Jews had begun. Many private citizens in the Netherlands tried to hide and protect Jews, and there was an active Dutch Resistance.

A close-knit community of exiled artists, writers, and musicians blossomed in Amsterdam during the late 1930s. Paul Citroen's private art school, the Nieuwen Kunstschool, attracted a number of German emigrés to its faculty and student body, including former Bauhaus member Hajo Rose. Until the Occupation several German artists were able to find employment and opportunities for exhibition. In 1935 Campendonk obtained a teaching position at the Rijksakademie van beeldende Kunsten. He left the academy following the Occupation and spent the duration of the war in hiding. The abstract painter Friedrich Vordemberge-Gildewart, a friend of Beckmann's, fled to Amsterdam in 1938 by way of Switzerland with his Jewish wife and secured a visa in 1939. He received encouragement from the staff of the Stedelijk Museum and was able to exhibit intermittently, but his existence was generally an isolated and lonely one: "We're pretty much alone here and it takes such an awful amount of effort to keep your head above the water as an artist. I still have to be the driving force, in the circle of artists I know, it is very, very quiet."[7]

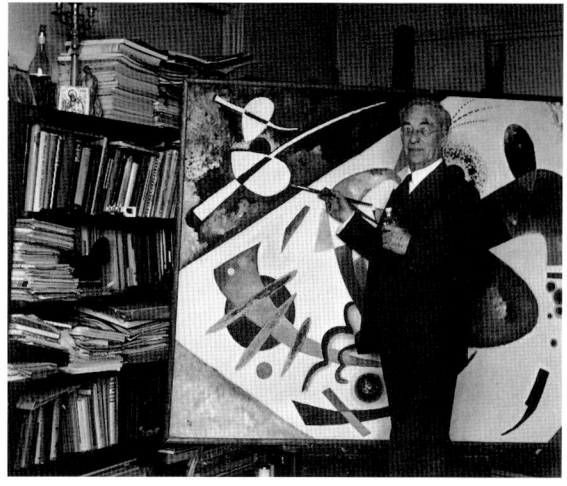

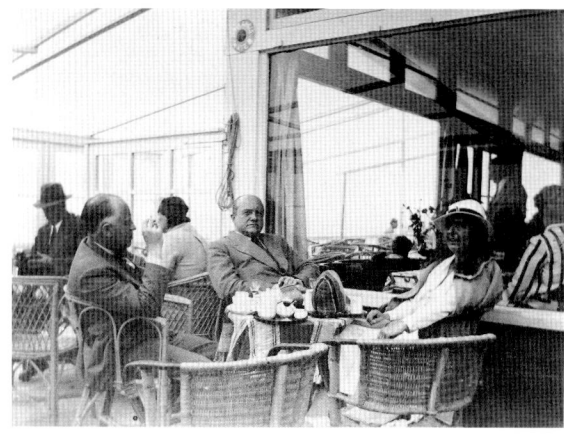

In his essay for this catalogue Keith Holz looks at the activities of exiled artists in Paris, Amsterdam, and London, comparing the attitudes of politically active artists with those of painters who worked independently and attempted to remain aloof from politics. Paintings by Kandinsky, Beckmann, and Kokoschka are examined alongside works by Freundlich, Eugen Spiro, and Heartfield; the latter artists as well as Kokoschka were affiliated with left-wing exiled artists groups that actively opposed the National Socialist regime and its cultural policies. Holz questions why some exiled artists sought to maintain their preflight activity, reputation, and style, while others pursued collaborative ventures, usually political in nature. In considering these projects within the context of this exhibition, Holz looks beyond the conventional fine art media of painting, original prints, and sculpture in order to question the values underlying traditional definitions of modern art and of the modern artist as an autonomous, apolitical creator.

6
Wassily Kandinsky, Paris, 1938; photograph by Josef Breitenbach.

7
Max Beckmann and Hedda Kaulbach, the Netherlands, c. 1939.

Kandinsky (see fig. 6), who claimed that his departure from Germany had nothing to do with politics, did not become involved in any of these collective activities. He remained devoted to abstraction, and his work in exile took on biomorphic characteristics, inspired by his contacts with the surrealists in Paris. Beckmann (see fig. 7), who had fled Germany immediately following the opening of *Entartete Kunst*, produced a large body of work in Amsterdam in which he developed his rich, personal iconography, incorporating references to the political situation into works such as *Birds' Hell* (1938; fig. 36, cat. no. 8). He refused to participate in group exhibitions organized by German exiles in Paris. Although he spoke at the opening of the New Burlington Galleries exhibition, he referred only obliquely to political events. Throughout the war both Beckmann and Kandinsky were able to find supporters and buyers for their work in their new homes and in Germany as well.

In London Kokoschka (see fig. 8) wholeheartedly participated in exiled artists' groups. Because of his Czech citizenship he escaped internment, and he was sought out as a spokesman for Austrian and German exiles, contributing to publications and exhibitions and even donating funds to refugee causes. He created a group of allegorical paintings—including *"Anschluss"—Alice in Wonderland* (1942; fig. 81, cat. no. 85) and *What We Are Fighting For* (1943; fig. 83)—in which he commented on political events.

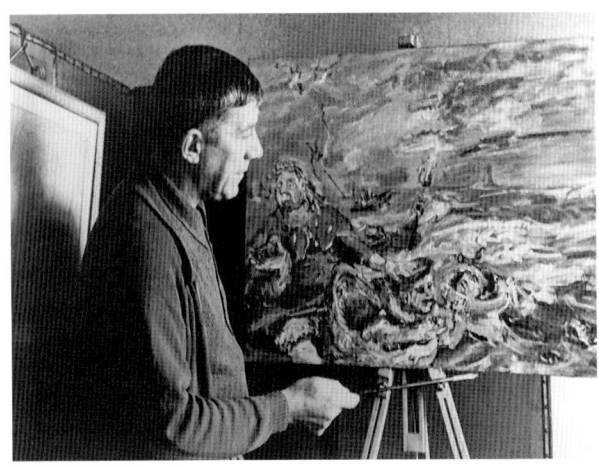

8
Oskar Kokoschka with the painting *Loreley* (cat. no. 84), London, 1942; photograph by Erich Auerbach FRPS.

Heartfield and Schwitters continued their work in England under less than ideal circumstances. Heartfield, who fled occupied Prague for London in 1938, had earned a reputation for mordant political satire. Excluded from the New Burlington Galleries show because of his communist sympathies, he was nevertheless welcomed by many Britons as an antifascist. He was involved with the Artists International Association (AIA) and was a founder of the Free German League of Culture. Although his work in London lacked the incisiveness of his earlier political photomontages (perhaps because he no longer had the sympathetic audience he had enjoyed in Berlin and Prague), he continued to attack the Nazi regime. In *Five Minutes to Twelve* (1942; fig. 60, cat. no. 65), for example, he employed the acerbic style familiar from his illustrations for the periodical *AIZ*, visualizing the panic of Nazi leaders faced with the prospect of a "second front" victory by France and England. Schwitters continued to work on his *Merz* creations in England, and a few of his collages from this period, such as *The Hitler Gang* (c. 1944; fig. 72, cat. no. 130) and *The Wounded Hunter* (1942; fig. 69, cat. no. 128), allude to his exile and the political situation. Briefly associated with the AIA, he stayed away from the Free German League of Culture, believing that it had been tainted by Heartfield's communist sympathies.

The Flight from Europe to the United States

The second, larger wave of emigration took place between 1938 and 1941, in the wake of Kristallnacht; Germany's annexation of Austria and the Sudetenland; and, following the beginning of World War II in September 1939, the occupation of Poland, the Low Countries, and France. America beckoned as a safe haven, but for most of those who sought refuge at this time, it was becoming increasingly difficult to secure passage out of Europe and to find a country willing to extend welcome. Discussions among government officials at the Evian Conference in July 1938—in which the United States, France, Great Britain, and other League of Nations members participated—yielded no resolution to the refugee problem.[8] Stories of the difficulties of obtaining visas, of veiled and overt expressions of anti-Semitism, of ships filled with desperate refugees being turned away after perilously crossing the Atlantic, are unfortunately part of the history of this era (see fig. 9). The United States and Canada closed their doors to the vast majority of the refugees.

Part of the problem was that those seeking asylum in the United States in the 1930s represented the second wave of migration, following the immense influx of unskilled laborers between 1880 and 1924, when half of all those who ever immigrated to the United States arrived. Fears about the changing composition of the American population gave rise to a restrictionist fervor in the early decades of this century. In 1924 Congress adopted the Johnson-Reed Bill, or the National Origins Act, which provided for an annual immigration quota of 164,667 people, or 2 percent of each Caucasian nationality represented in the 1890 U.S. census. Nevertheless, the quotas for German and Austrian immigrants remained unfilled during the 1930s and 1940s.

While most immigration to the United States was strictly regulated by these quotas, a number of "nonquota" immigrants were able to enter the country more freely. This group included academics, their immediate families, and students who intended to study at an accredited American institution. It was this loophole that made possible the widespread immigration of academics. In 1940 the State Department established a procedure for issuing "emergency visitor" visas, which were available to imperiled refugees whose intellectual or cultural achievements or political activities were of interest to the United States. Visa applicants also needed to present appropriate credentials, including proof of employment or evidence of financial support.

Several private organizations were established to assist those seeking asylum in the United States. One of the best known was the Emergency Rescue Committee. Varian Fry, a young journalist with connections to leftist political organizations, was sent to Marseilles in August 1940 to arrange for the escape of the many prominent cultural figures who had been trapped in southern France following the Nazi occupation. The committee's supporters[9] were interested primarily in rescuing these elite figures, whom they feared might be arrested under Article 19 of the Franco-German Armistice, which required the "surrender on demand" to Germany of foreign nationals residing in France. Within the thirteen months that Fry was able to operate in Marseilles, he was responsible for arranging the safe passage (often involving harrowing journeys over the Pyrenees on foot) of several hundred artists, writers, intellectuals, and musicians, including Breton, Chagall, Ernst, Lion Feuchtwanger, Wifredo Lam, Golo Mann, Heinrich Mann, Masson, Remedios Varos, Franz Werfel, and Alma Mahler-Werfel.

Moreover, as Elizabeth Berman discusses in her essay in this volume, Fry also aided less celebrated refugees, many of them Jewish, in escaping Europe. By the time he was expelled from France for his activities, he had assisted, according to his own account, some two thousand individuals, far more than the two hundred he was sent to deliver. Berman provides new information on this important chapter of America's intervention in the refugee crisis, questioning the myths that have surrounded the Emergency Rescue Committee's activities. Fry emerges from her account no less a hero, but one with greater dimension, sensitive to a wider range of concerns, and one who was morally conflicted by his mission of celebrity rescue.

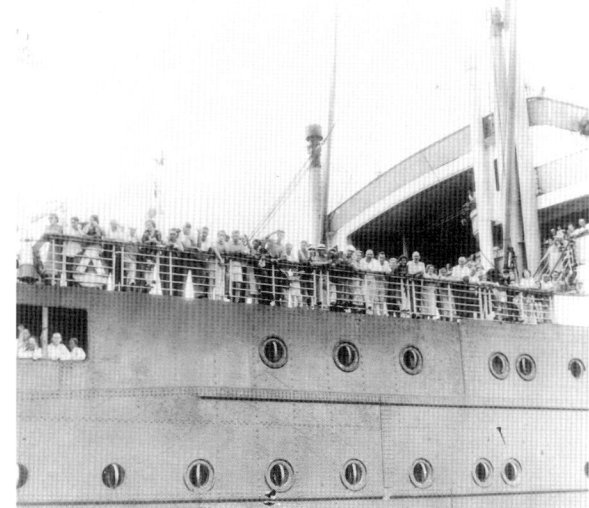

9
The German steamship *Saint Louis* carrying German Jewish refugees denied permission to land in Cuba, June 1, 1939.

Although the refugees from Nazi Germany were often mature, well-educated professionals,[10] general sentiment in Depression-era America was anti-immigrant. Many were fearful that new arrivals would take jobs away from Americans. In a survey published in 1939 in *Fortune*, more than 80 percent of the respondents expressed negative feelings about the admittance of European refugees.[11] Popular magazines and newspapers carried articles critical of the emigrés, which certainly influenced public opinion. In 1940 *Life* published a letter titled "Refugees De Luxe," which described well-to-do refugees taking over expensive hotels, filling fashionable resorts, and dining in expensive restaurants, displaying assertive and flamboyant behavior. Articles with headlines such as "Refugees—Burden or Asset?" "Spies among Refugees," and "Refugee Gold Rush" in *American Magazine* all contributed to the impression that refugees were a problematic issue in America.[12]

The press also published articles that were more sympathetic to the refugees. Pieces written by Fry appeared in *The Nation* and *The New Leader*; in 1942 *The New Republic* published his "Massacre of the Jews." F. Kirchway wrote several pieces for *The Nation*, alerting readers to the plight of refugees and criticizing the inaction of the State Department. *Newsweek*, *Time*, and other publications often focused on the activities of writers and intellectuals. *The New Yorker* regularly reviewed exhibitions of work by emigré artists. "Transplanted Talent" was the title of a 1942 *Art Digest* editorial, while "Hitler's Gift to America" ran in *American Mercury* in 1943. Many local newspapers covered the arrival of famous refugees in New York or on visits to their cities.[13]

In addition to the hostility of Americans, the emigrés faced significant cultural barriers and were hampered by their lack of English. Many of the exiles congregated in enclaves in the Yorkville section of Manhattan's East Side, in rural Connecticut, or in the Pacific Palisades in Los Angeles. Artists gravitated to emigré dealers, such as Karl Nierendorf and Curt Valentin. Differences emerge between the exiles from Germany and those from France. The Germans, who could no longer identify with their homeland, experienced a more traumatic break with their heritage. When the United States entered the war, they were declared enemy aliens. The French exiles generally continued to identify with French culture, and many spent the war years waiting for the German occupation to end, intending to return as soon as possible. In most cases the French artists and intellectuals had left because of their antifascist political beliefs, not out of fear of racial persecution, and many shared an intense anger at the Vichy government and French collaboration.

Safe in New York: The Exile Community from Paris

A number of the artists whom Fry was sent to rescue from occupied France ended up in New York, either with the direct assistance of the Emergency Rescue Committee or through efforts extended by museum directors, supporters, collectors, or other artists. Although some eventually settled elsewhere, surrealists Dali, Ernst, Masson, Matta, and Tanguy; Jewish artists Chagall and Lipchitz; and Léger and Mondrian all initially came to New York City. In this catalogue Romy Golan considers their reception in their new home in "On the Passage of a Few Persons through a Rather Brief Period of Time," drawing attention to the network of relationships among dealers, museum people, and artists in New York, which often benefited the newly arrived artists. Key players included the dealers Julien Levy, Pierre

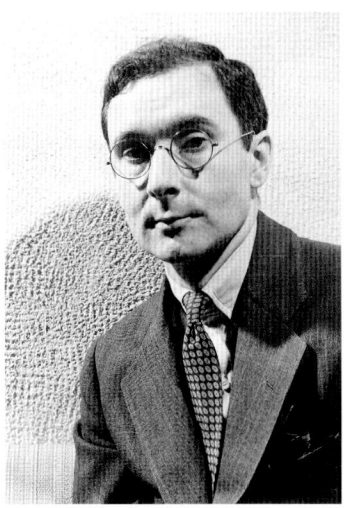

10
Alfred H. Barr Jr., c. 1929–30.

Matisse, Nierendorf, Valentin, Valentine Dudensing, and Peggy Guggenheim, who opened the Art of This Century gallery, as well as museum directors Alfred H. Barr Jr. (see fig. 10) of the Museum of Modern Art and A. Everett "Chick" Austin of the Wadsworth Atheneum in Hartford, Connecticut, and MoMA curator James Thrall Soby. Shortly after their arrival Tanguy, Matta, Mondrian, Masson, and Ernst had solo gallery shows; Tanguy's was followed immediately by his first museum show, in Hartford. The Baltimore Museum of Art presented Masson's work, and the Museum of Modern Art almost immediately exhibited, purchased, or arranged

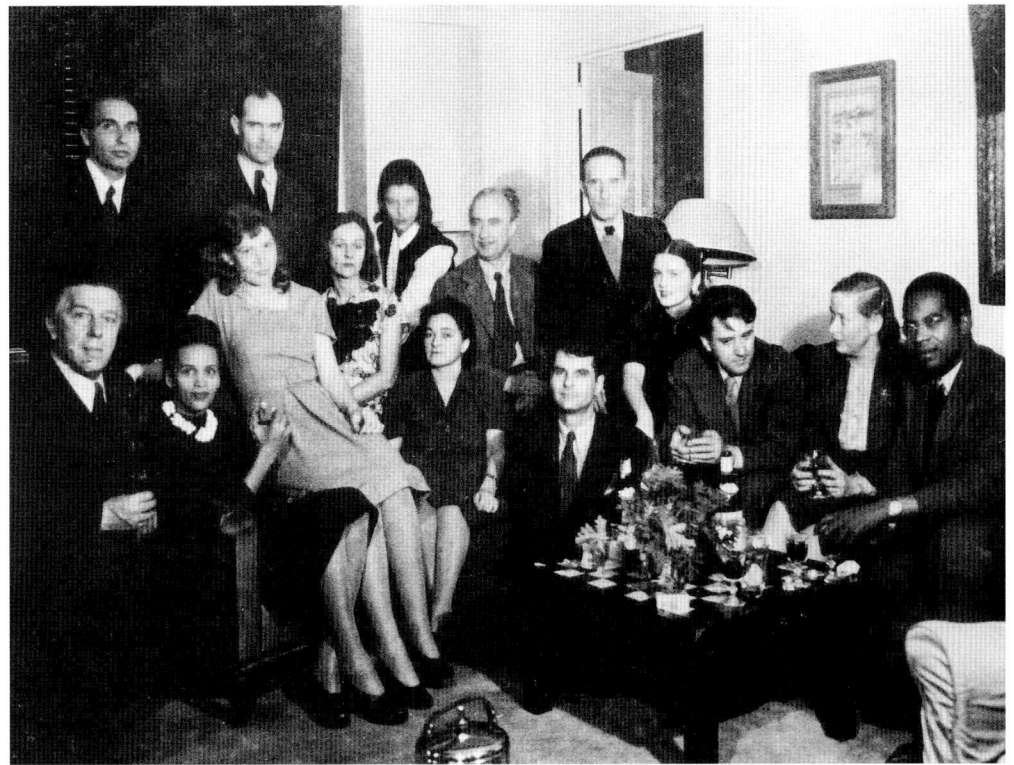

11
A gathering at Pierre Matisse's apartment, 1945 (front row: André Breton, Mrs. Césaire, Jackie Matisse, Elisa Breton, Mrs. Calas, Nicholas Calas, Matta, Teeny Duchamp, Aimé Césaire; back row: Esteban Frances, Denis de Rougemont, Sonia Sekula, Yves Tanguy, Marcel Duchamp, Patricia Matta).

12
Marcel Duchamp at the exhibition *First Papers of Surrealism*, 1942; photograph © 1942 Arnold Newman.

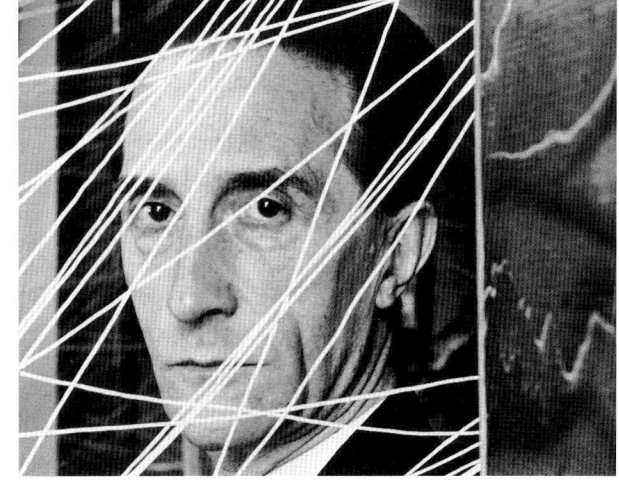

for the donation of works by Dali, Ernst, Kertész, Léger, Masson, Matta, Mondrian, and Tanguy. In architecture too MoMA's championing of the emigré architects from the Bauhaus through exhibitions such as *Bauhaus, 1919–1928*, organized by Walter and Ise Gropius and Herbert Bayer, strongly influenced the reception of modernist architecture.

Although the surrealists arrived in New York intent upon continuing the work in which they had been engaged in Europe, they found it difficult to sustain their collective activities in a new milieu. They lamented the absence of cafés, bars, and other centralized meeting places. Many suffered considerable financial hardship as well.[14] Nevertheless, opportunities were available for the artists to establish themselves in America. Pierre Matisse, son of painter Henri, gave vigorous support to French exile artists (see fig. 11), including their work in the exhibitions *Artists in Exile* (1942), *War and the Artist* (1943), and *Homage to the "Salon d'automne" 1944: Salon de la Libération* (1944). In 1942 the surrealist-oriented magazine *VVV* published its first issue, and in addition to *Artists in Exile*, the *First Papers of Surrealism* exhibition opened, with its provocative installation designed by Marcel Duchamp (see fig. 12)—followed a few days later by the vernissage of Art of This Century (see fig. 13), designed by Frederick Kiesler. Golan recounts that many New York critics were suspicious of these "unholy alliances" among artists, dealers, and museum officials, which in many cases led to the elevation of the artists' reputations, especially when their work was shown or acquired by the influential Museum of Modern Art.

American reaction to the surrealists was not overwhelmingly positive. Some were entertained by their escapades, bizarre dress, parties, and fanciful exhibitions, which were

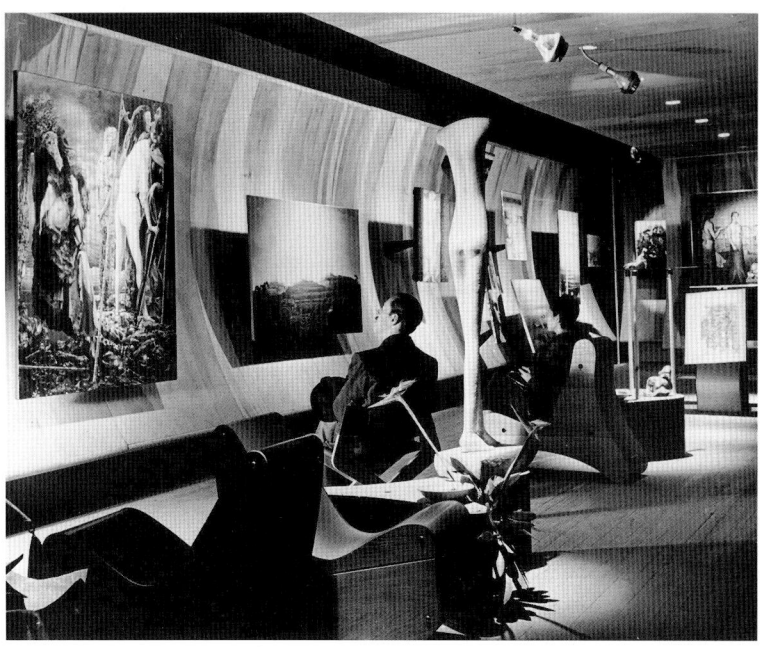

13
The Surrealist Gallery at Peggy Guggenheim's Art of This Century, designed by Frederick Kiesler, 1942.

widely reported in the popular press. Golan and other authors in this catalogue, however, cite sarcastic contemporaneous criticism, on the part of both American and European commentators. In a particularly vitriolic attack entitled "Surrealist Circus," Klaus Mann inveighed against Ernst; his then-wife, Peggy Guggenheim; and the coterie of surrealists, calling them "Nazoid" and linking the nihilism of their art to Hitler's concept of degenerate art. The works the surrealists created in America are both varied and complex. Masson, based in Connecticut, painted dense telluric canvases, semiabstract pictures with references to animals and imagery related to Native American culture. In fact, Native American art and artifacts also fascinated several of the other surrealists, including Breton, Ernst, Matta, Tanguy, and Kurt Seligmann. The dreamscapes of Masson's fellow Connecticut resident Tanguy took on a harsher palette and reflected his sense of America's more expansive spaces. Ernst's surreal foliage and anthropomorphic rock formations hint at decaying landscapes. Matta was impressed by the ever-changing nature of the American landscape and spoke of his desire to show the earth as something terrific, burning, and metamorphic. The countryside Léger found on a visit to Rouses Point, in northern New York—overgrown and littered with fragments of machinery—led to a group of gouaches and paintings; his fascination with skyscrapers, the desert, and the mechanized are all reflected in his exile work. For Mondrian, whose style was well established when he arrived in New York, the city's pace, its architecture, its music, and its diverse population provided fresh inspiration.

For a number of exiles, however, events in Europe were still all too present. Masson produced several politically motivated paintings containing allusions to war, destruction, and violence. His *Oradour* (1944; fig. 152, cat. no. 106), for example, was painted in response to the 1944 German bombing of the French town of Oradour-sur-Glane and the massacre of its population. These representational works were reviewed unfavorably by American critics, however, who preferred his allusive telluric paintings. After 1941 Matta created a group of paintings invoking experiences of captivity, ravaged landscapes and burning skies, and the cruelties of war. Ernst, using his multilayered decalcomania technique, portrayed a ruined world in works such as *Europe after the Rain II* (1940–42; fig. 135), *Napoleon in the Wilderness* (1941; fig. 1, cat. no. 33), and *The Eye of Silence* (1943–44; fig. 141, cat. no. 37).

In examining the work of Chagall and Lipchitz in exile, the exhibition considers how Jewish culture and its symbols were transformed to reflect current relevance. In New York Chagall was understandably preoccupied with the fate of the Eastern European Jews and made several paintings whose titles reflect this concern, including *Ghetto* (renamed *Resistance*) (1937–48; fig. 104, cat. no. 20) and *Persecution* (c. 1941; fig. 99, cat. no. 23). Lipchitz memorialized both "flight" and "arrival" and employed the myth of Prometheus strangling the vulture as a metaphor for the events in Europe in several sculptures that he initiated in the period before and after his passage to New York.

New York and its imposing architecture, distinct neighborhoods, and collision of cultures provided provocative subject matter for emigré photographers Andreas Feininger and André Kertész. Feininger was employed almost immediately upon his arrival in New York by Black Star Pictures and *Life* magazine, and Kertész, who did commercial work for the Keystone Photographic Company, showed at the Julien Levy Gallery and was represented in Beaumont Newhall's survey of photography at the Museum of Modern Art.

The Exile as Teacher

Some professionals—including many artists, musicians, and scholars—managed to gain entrance to the United States through clause 4d of the National Origins Act, which allowed teachers of higher education to be issued "nonquota" visas. A number found positions on the faculties of American universities, despite serious obstacles. During the 1920s and 1930s many of the most prestigious American universities maintained discriminatory admissions and hiring policies that specifically excluded Jews. There tended to be more opportunities for Jews at city- or state-run universities and at schools away from the East Coast, and many of these schools benefited from the influx of gifted foreigners. The European emigrés made tremendous contributions to the fields of physics, literature, sociology, psychology, architecture, music, art, film, and art history in the United States.[15]

Several organizations were active in bringing intellectual refugees to America. The Emergency Committee for Displaced Foreign Scholars found space for two hundred academics; the Rockefeller Foundation supported approximately one hundred scholars, as did the Oberlaender Trust. The emigrés' salaries were funded, at least initially, by the foundations, and many schools welcomed the opportunity to augment their faculties without bearing a financial burden. New York's New School for Social Research offered positions to about seventy-five, and the Institute for Advanced Study in Princeton, New York University, Vassar College, Mount Holyoke College, and the University of Chicago also appointed emigrés to their faculties.

The intellectual emigrés exposed American students to a different style of teaching and fostered the growth of entire disciplines. Art history is one of the fields on which they had an especially profound impact. Most of the emigré art historians did not have international reputations before their emigration; only Erwin Panofsky and Paul Frankl were full professors in Germany. In his essay in this catalogue Kevin Parker focuses on Richard Krautheimer and Panofsky, describing how their experiences as exiles (and, even earlier, as assimilated Jews in Weimar Germany) helped shape their art historical methodology. The impact of the emigrés on the field was not only deep but widespread as well; almost every important American art historian teaching in a university in the 1960s and 1970s had at least one direct encounter with the exile generation of art historians.

Over the past decade a group of scholars at the University of Hamburg, under the direction of Martin Warnke, have conducted a research project on the immigration of German art historians to the United States and Great Britain. The Hamburg project has conducted interviews and collected archival data tracing the careers of Walter Friedlaender, Julius S. Held, Horst W. Janson, Ernst Kitzinger, Jacob Rosenberg, and many others. One of the participants, Karen

Michels, shares the results of that research in this catalogue, questioning the notion of a smooth, one-way transplant of an academic tradition from Germany to the United States.

In the fall of 1933 two schools, one in New York City and the other in North Carolina, opened their doors to faculty who had been displaced from Germany. Perhaps the most influential person to recognize the potential benefit that intellectual refugees from Nazi Germany could provide the United States was Alvin Johnson, founder of the New School for Social Research, an institution devoted to adult education (see figs. 14–15). Even before 1933 he had traveled to Germany with the intention of offering positions in America to certain academics. By the fall of 1933 fourteen of them had accepted his invitation to join a newly constituted, self-governing institute of the New School, the University in Exile. Within the next decade Johnson would attract more than ninety teachers from Germany, Austria, and France, who would offer more than two hundred advanced courses in music, fine and applied arts, psychology, social sciences, and economics.[16] During this period the faculty included Hannah Arendt, Rudolf Arnheim, Hanns Eisler, Erich Fromm, Otto Klemperer, Hans Kohn, Ernst Kris, Claude Lévi-Strauss, Erwin Piscator, Wilhelm Reich, and Max Wertheimer.

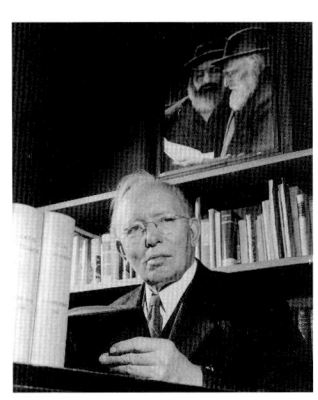

The New School was also important for emigré visual artists. In 1941 the British printmaker Stanley William Hayter moved his print studio, Atelier 17 (formerly in London and Paris), to the school. There Chagall, Ernst, Lipchitz, Masson, and Tanguy experimented with new techniques of intaglio printmaking. In 1940–41 Gordon Onslow Ford, a British emigré artist, gave a series of four lectures on the surrealist movement.[17] Several surrealist installations accompanied the lectures, including an "exquisite corpse" for the public to complete.[18]

The New School was not the only institution to attract influential exiles. During the spring of 1933, as the Bauhaus faced closure, several faculty from Rollins College in Winter Park, Florida, were dismissed over issues of academic freedom.[19] They quickly regrouped, and with financial assistance from several New Yorkers—including Malcolm Forbes, Edward Warburg, and the brother of Katherine S. Dreier—they were able to secure a campus near Asheville, North Carolina, for what became Black Mountain College. One of the organizers contacted Philip Johnson, curator of architecture at the Museum of Modern Art, who arranged for Josef and Anni Albers, who had just lost their positions at the Bauhaus, to join the Black Mountain faculty. The Alberses were instrumental in the formulation of a progressive curriculum emphasizing active learning, the development of creative and problem-solving abilities, and crafts rather than painting and sculpture (see fig. 16).

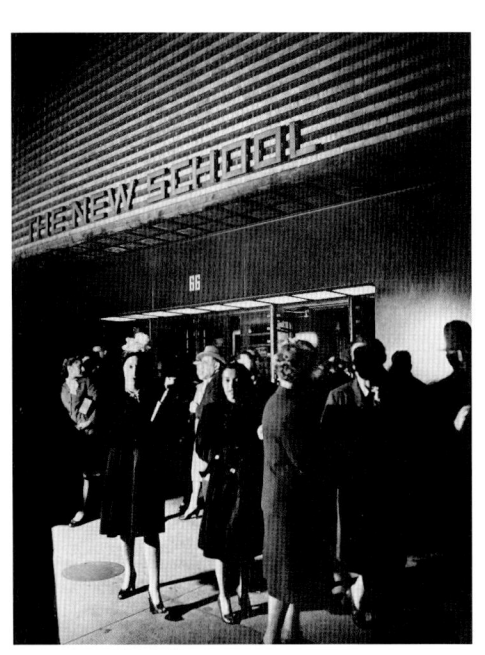

14
Alvin Johnson, director of the New School for Social Research, 1945.

15
New Yorkers taking evening courses at the New School for Social Research, 1940s.

In 1937 Moholy-Nagy opened the New Bauhaus in Chicago, seeking to apply idealistic Bauhaus principles to American design education (see fig. 17). Rather quickly he was forced to redefine his approach to better suit his new environment. The school went through several transformations and was eventually renamed the Institute of Design. Moholy was able to tailor the curriculum to meet the needs of American industry (even developing innovative designs for the military during World War II) and was successful in attracting corporate support.

Other emigrés contributed to the development of new curricula at existing institutions. Four Bauhaus architects were invited to the United States, where they would exert a

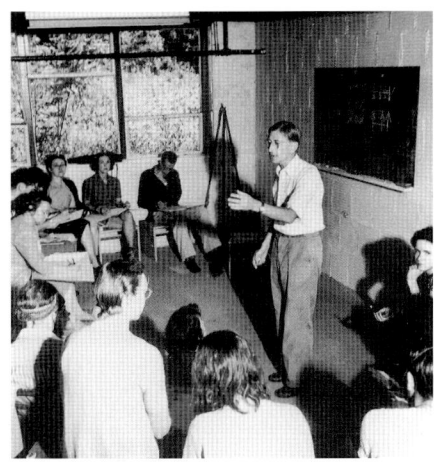
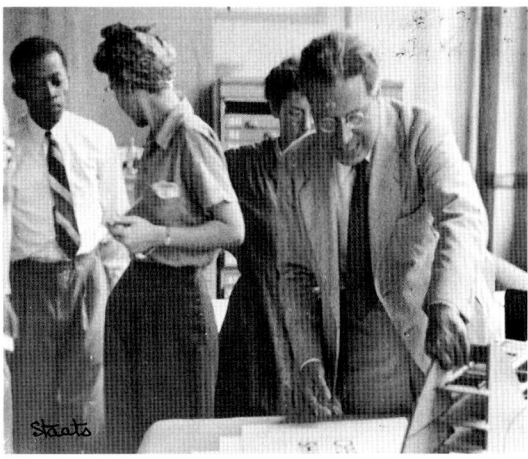

16
Josef Albers's color class at Black Mountain College, summer 1944; photograph by Josef Breitenbach.

17
László Moholy-Nagy teaching in Chicago.

18
Ludwig Mies van der Rohe; Illinois Institute of Technology, Chicago, Illinois, master plan for the campus, aerial view, 1939–41; photomontage; Mies van der Rohe Archive, The Museum of Modern Art, New York.

lasting effect through their teaching and practices. Harvard University appointed Gropius head of its Graduate School of Design, and Breuer also joined the faculty there. Mies van der Rohe and Ludwig Hilberseimer developed a new architectural curriculum for Chicago's Armour Institute of Technology (later the Illinois Institute of Technology) (see fig. 18).

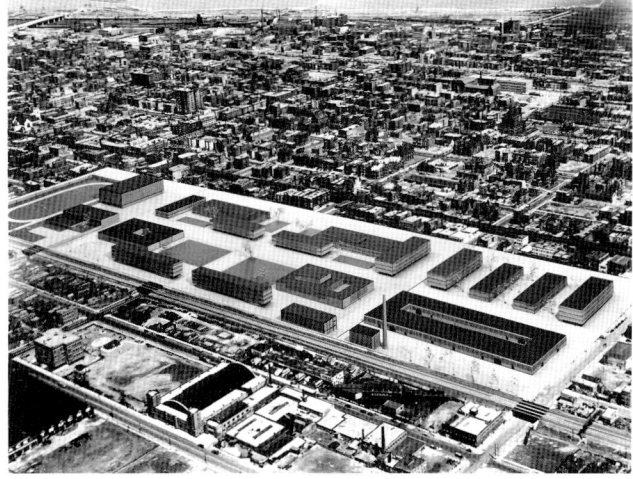

The Bauhaus concept, as it was transplanted to the United States, was fundamentally different from the principles upon which the experimental school had been founded in Weimar in 1919. The guiding principle of the Bauhaus was to unify all aspects of art making—painting, sculpture, handicrafts—as elements of a new kind of art, erasing the division between "high" and decorative art. Explorations of materials, color, and form were important building blocks of the curriculum. The artists and designers of the Bauhaus believed that this new type of art and design would help to create a better society, and they sought commissions to design public buildings and other elements of public life (such as flags and currency). In America, however, the Bauhaus ideas lost their social and political thrust. The emigré teachers in Chicago, Cambridge, and North Carolina who had been committed to progressive architecture and design ideas in Germany were now lionized as upholders of a pure, reductivist style.

Two articles in the present volume are devoted to the Bauhaus architects. In "Bauhaus and Exile: Bauhaus Architects and Designers between the Old World and the New," Peter Hahn reviews the circumstances surrounding the closure of the Bauhaus and discusses the complicated issues of the architects' politics in Germany, their attempts at accommodation with the National Socialist regime, and their emigration. Hahn refutes the notion that the leading members of the Bauhaus went into exile at the time of the Nazi takeover, arguing that the emigration of Gropius, Mies, and others should be seen as professionally motivated. Franz Schulze addresses the activities of Breuer, Gropius, and Mies in the United States, with particular emphasis on their teaching. He examines the different curricula developed by Gropius at Harvard and by Mies at the Armour Institute of Technology. Both men were instrumental in the replacement of the Beaux-Arts principles that had dominated the teaching of architecture in the early part of the century with curricula based on modernist principles.

In addition to those affiliated with the Bauhaus, other European artists played an important role in molding subsequent generations of Americans. Some taught occasionally, such as Léger and Lyonel Feininger, who conducted summer classes at Mills College. Masson participated in the Pontigny-en-Amérique colloquia, held by the French exile community at Mount Holyoke College. Amédée Ozenfant established his own art school, and Grosz taught at the Art Students League.

The American Reception of Banned German Art

The reception accorded the artists whose work was banned by the Nazis was directly related to American attitudes toward Germany and the National Socialists. The American press responded with appropriate invective to the 1937 *Entartete Kunst* show in Munich. Thereafter, the meaning of modern art in America changed, and it was equated with the art of democracy. While many felt sympathy for the persecuted artists and there were efforts to show and support their work, the form that that support took was sometimes problematic. In 1938 the German government sponsored a public sale at the Galerie Fischer in Lucerne of 125 paintings and sculptures that had been confiscated from German public collections. Among the bidders were several American collectors and Valentin, who advised other buyers. Some concern had been expressed in the United States about the morality of buying at the auction since it was assumed that all proceeds would go directly to feed the German war machine. Theodor Fischer assured American buyers that the funds would be used by German museums for new acquisitions; there is no evidence, however, that this is what occurred.[20] Although several paintings and sculptures that had been sold in Lucerne ended up in MoMA's collection, Barr did not bid directly on any work.

Attitudes toward modern German art underwent a shift when the United States entered the war. It became virtually impossible for American institutions to show public support for German art. Some continued their efforts to assist the German exiles, but only those like Grosz, who had become an American citizen, or Lyonel Feininger, an American by birth, were able to exhibit consistently through this period. In this catalogue Vivian Barnett addresses these issues in "Banned German Art: Reception and Institutional Support of Modern German Art in the United States, 1933–45." Barr at the Museum of Modern Art, Neumeyer at Mills College, William R. Valentiner at the Detroit Institute of Arts, Perry Rathbone at the Saint Louis Art Museum, Charles Kuhn at Harvard, James Plaut at the Institute for Modern Art in Boston, emigré dealers Valentin and Nierendorf in New York, and Galka Scheyer in California were among the close-knit group of supporters of German art in America whose activities are charted by Barnett.

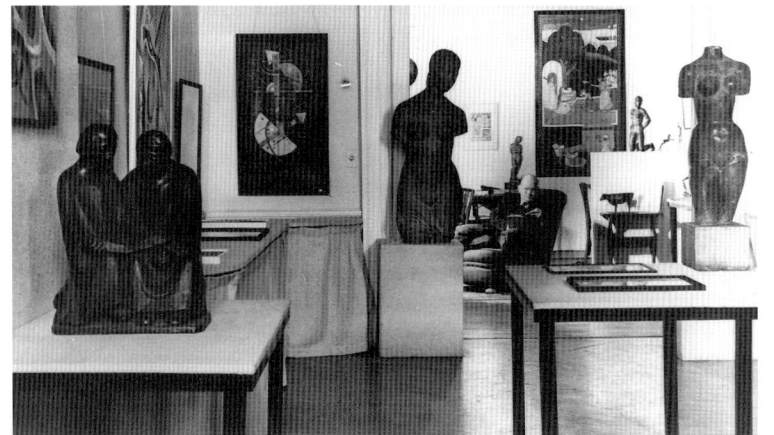

19
The Nierendorf Gallery, New York, with sculptures by Ernst Barlach and Wilhelm Lehmbruck, 1940s.

Barr's enthusiasm for German art during this period stemmed in part from his travels in Germany. In 1933 he had written a series of articles based on his observations during an extended stay in Stuttgart. Had they been published at the time they were written, they would have done much to alert the American public to the National Socialists' intentions. Instead they appeared only in 1945, after Germany's defeat. During this period Barr generally focused on formal issues in his presentations of German art, avoiding discussions of the political and racial implications of Nazi cultural policies. By contrast, Plaut, director of Boston's fledgling Institute of Modern Art, mounted a series of exhibitions of German art in which he clearly acknowledged the political context of his programming.

For Grosz, who arrived a few days before Hitler assumed power, and Feininger—who, though born in America, had spent almost his entire life in Germany—life as an exile in the United States was mixed with internal conflict and feelings of displacement and dissatisfaction. Although Grosz's reputation in America was based on his achievements as a Weimar social critic, even before his exile he had come to distrust the effectiveness of political art and had begun to seek a new identity and purpose. His exile works, such as his self-portrait *Remembering* (1937; fig. 283, cat. no. 54) and his political allegory *Cain or Hitler in Hell* (1945; fig. 286, cat. no. 59), lack the moralizing tone of his German works, instead reflecting his profound disappointment with humanism.

At age sixty-six Feininger found it very difficult to move back to America. He identified deeply with Germany's history and culture. Highly regarded in Germany, he was little known in the United States, and, like other exiles from Germany, he was dependent upon a coterie of supporters: Barr, Neumeyer, Valentin, and Valentiner. Only with the traveling show organized by the Museum of Modern Art in 1944, billed at that sensitive time as the retrospective of an American artist (or at least one indebted to American tradition), did his visibility improve. Although he sought to portray the skyscrapers of Manhattan in a series of pictures evocative of work he had done in Germany (see figs. 291–94, cat. nos. 49–52), he complained that he was not inspired by the American milieu.

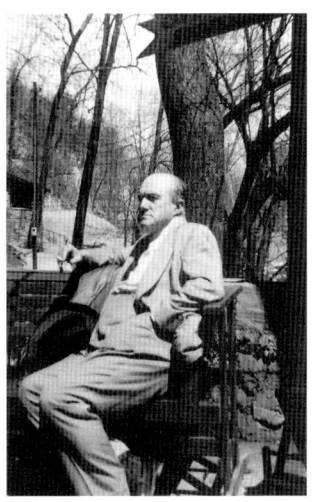

20
Max Beckmann, New York.

Beckmann (see fig. 20) was by far the best known and most widely exhibited German exile artist. Unable to obtain a visa during the war, he was able to emigrate from Amsterdam to the United States only in 1947. He is the only artist represented in this exhibition by works from both his European and American exile phases. In the three years he spent in the United States before his death in 1950, Beckmann produced an astonishing number of vigorous allegorical works containing allusions to his life as an exile and emigré. In paintings such as *The Prodigal Son* (1949; fig. 43, cat. no. 15) and the triptych *The Argonauts* (1949–50; fig. 45, cat. no. 16) he combined his personal iconography with biblical and mythological references invoking his own experiences.

during the years since the war much has been written on the subject of the exile from Nazi Europe. An entire discipline of exile studies, or *Exilforschung*, emerged in Germany, focusing primarily on literature, music, the social sciences, and, to a lesser degree, fine art. In the United States and the two Germanies scholarly approaches to the topic were directly related to prevailing political positions. In this catalogue historian Martin Jay—in "The German Migration: Is There a Figure in the Carpet?"—adroitly analyzes the ways in which the history of the migration has been argued at different times and from different perspectives based on the writer's political sympathies and intentions.

The final three essays in the volume offer more personal views of exile. The firsthand experiences of an exiled German writer in France and the United States are recounted in Stephan Lackner's memoir. Lackner, a writer, left Germany with his family in the early

1930s, but not before forming an enduring friendship with Max Beckmann. Lackner supported the painter during his years in Amsterdam and became a leading Beckmann collector and scholar. He describes his own initial exile in Europe, where he contributed regularly to the exile journal *Das neue Tagebuch* in Paris and met Thomas Mann and Walter Benjamin. After the occupation of Czechoslovakia Lackner emigrated to the United States, ultimately settling in Santa Barbara, California. After America entered the war, he was called up for military duty. He recalls the haunting experience of returning to Germany in an American uniform and participating in the liberation of a concentration camp. After the war he traveled back to Europe, where he encountered a sentiment also described by Jay. Lackner writes, "Many Germans had a nasty resentment against emigrés—as if we had deserted and left them to cope with the tyrannical Nazis and Allied bombs."

Exiles and Emigrés focuses for the most part on the activities of artists in exile in Paris, Amsterdam, London, New York, and Chicago. Los Angeles, however, though not a center for exiled visual artists, did provide a haven in the 1930s and 1940s for many German and Austrian musicians, filmmakers, writers, and intellectuals, among them Theodor W. Adorno, Bertolt Brecht, Lion Feuchtwanger, Max Horkheimer, Otto Klemperer, Erich Korngold, Heinrich and Thomas Mann, Arnold Schoenberg, Igor Stravinsky, Salka Viertel, Bruno Walter, and Franz Werfel. Lawrence Weschler, himself the grandson of Austrian emigré composer Ernst Toch, offers a splendid collage of anecdotes; personal recollections; and excerpts from letters, memoirs, and diaries, which often reveals the poignant and humorous sides of the problems of assimilation addressed elsewhere in this volume.

The final essay, Hans Magnus Enzensberger's "The Great Migration," reflects on the conflicts that have been engendered by migration throughout history. Enzensberger, a German leftist intellectual, traces these conflicts to characteristics of human behavior that transcend geography or historical, political, or economic circumstances. Like many of us, he is disturbed by the recent hate crimes against foreigners in Germany. He points out that Germany is a country that has always been populated by a very mixed people, in part because of its geography, and argues that the blood and race ideologies that have developed there are an attempt to compensate for this heterogeneity. He writes, "[Their] function can only be to prop up, by means of a fiction, an especially fragile national identity"—an observation that is also germane to our own culturally diverse society.

The story of the exile and emigration of European artists during the twelve years of National Socialist rule is a complex and multilayered one, made up of hundreds of individual histories. It is difficult to generalize about the quality of that exile, about the characteristics of the work produced in exile, and about the artists' responses to National Socialism. Each circumstance was different. What emerges clearly from an examination of the works produced during this period, however, is the indelible imprint of exile on the development of twentieth-century art. The issues central to "exile" art in all its myriad forms—the relationship of art and politics; displacement, assimilation, and cultural identity; and the exploration of memory and loss—remain as relevant today as they were half a century ago.

Notes

1 Jankel Adler, in *Literarische Blätter* 38 (1933): 614, quoted in Jürgen Harten, ed., *Jankel Adler, 1895–1949* (Cologne: DuMont, 1985), 29.
2 David Coke, ed., *Hans Feibusch: The Heat of Vision* (London: Lund-Humphries, 1995), 10.
3 Meidner was interned on the Isle of Man until 1941. Following his release, he was able to support himself only by working as a night watchman and by painting portraits of the dead modeled on photographs; see Stephanie Barron et al., *"Degenerate Art": The Fate of the Avant-Garde in Nazi Germany*, exh. cat. (Los Angeles: Los Angeles County Museum of Art, 1991), 299.
4 Hans Kinkel, "Begegnung mit Otto Dix," in *Otto Dix*, exh. cat. (Hannover: Kestner-Gesellschaft, 1987), 21.
5 Schlemmer to Marcks, 7 December 1937, quoted in Karin von Maur, *Oskar Schlemmer Monographie* (Munich: Prestel, 1979), 238.
6 Arnold L. Lehman and Brenda Richardson, eds., *Oskar Schlemmer* (Baltimore: Baltimore Museum of Art, 1986), 204.
7 Vordemberge-Gildewart to Nelly van Doesburg, 17 January 1941, quoted in Dietrich Helms, ed., *Vordemberge-Gildewart: The Complete Works* (Munich: Prestel, 1990), 24.
8 Throughout the conference there was a great effort to avoid using the word *Jew*, and instead *refugee* was used. In his opening remarks, Myron Taylor, the U.S. representative to the talks, acknowledged that there were then six hundred thousand "men and women of every race, creed, and economic condition" in dire need of immediate sanctuary. Nevertheless, he continued, the United States would not change its immigration laws and would continue to accept twenty-seven thousand refugees a year, the quota for Germany and Austria. Not once did Taylor refer to the Jews. See Saul Friedman, *No Haven for the Oppressed: United States Policy toward Jewish Refugees, 1938–1945* (Detroit: Wayne State University Press, 1973), 59.
9 The committee's supporters included Eleanor Roosevelt; media representatives Dorothy Thompson, Elmer Rice, and Raymond Graham Swing, a prominent newscaster; and five university presidents: Robert Hutchins of the University of Chicago, Alvin Johnson of the New School for Social Research, William A. Nielsen of Smith College, George Schuster of Hunter College, and Charles Seymour of Yale University. Europeans Max Ascoli, Klaus and Erika Mann, Jacques Maritain, and Jan Masaryk also assisted the committee in compiling lists of possible candidates for rescue.
10 See Donald Peterson Kent, *The Refugee Intellectual* (New York: Columbia University Press, 1953).
11 See "The Fortune Survey XX," esp. pt. 4, "No Haven for Refugees," pt. 5, "The Jews in America," and pt. 6, "Why Is Anti-Semitism?" in *Fortune*, April 1939, 102–7; "Twelve Artists in U.S. Exile," *Fortune*, December 1941; "Artists in Exile, Artists in Captivity," *Art News* 40 (1–14 November 1941), 24–25.
12 R. Cameron to the editors, *Life*, 22 July 1940, 5; H. Pol, "Spies among Refugees," *Nation*, 167–68; S. F. Porter, "Refugee Gold Rush," *American Magazine*, October 1942, 46–47; K. R. Grossmann, "Refugee—Burden or Asset?" *Nation*, 26 December 1942, 708–10; see also "Impact of Migration Weighed," *Business Week*, 24 April 1943, 72–73.
13 Varian Fry, "The Massacre of the Jews," *New Republic*, 7 December 1942, 728, and 21 December 1942, 815–19; F. Kirchway, "Bargains in Refugees," *Nation*, 5 August 1939, 137–38; idem, "Scandal in the State Department," *Nation*, 19 July 1941, 45; idem, "State Department versus Political Refugees," *Nation*, 28 December 1940, 648–49; Peyton Boswell, "Comments: Transplanted Talent," *Art Digest* 17 (1 November 1942): 3; M. Gumpert, "Hitler's Gift to America," *American Mercury*, July 1943, 49–53; see also I. Lundberg, "Who Are These Refugees?" *Harper's*, January 1942, 164–72; "Persecuting the Refugee," *New Republic*, 18 August 1941, 208; A. Hamilton, "Refugee Scholars in the United States," *American Scholar*, July 1942, 374–78; N. Angell, "Refugees Can Be Assets," *Nation*, 21 September 1940, 236–39; "Saving Writers from Hitler," *Newsweek*, 28 October 1940, 53.
14 For example, in 1940 Pavel Tchelitchev wrote to James Thrall Soby urging him to provide some support for Matta, who had no place to live and no money for food (Tchelitchev to Soby, 2 October 1940, James Thrall Soby Papers, Resource Collections, Getty Research Institute for the History of Art and the Humanities, Los Angeles).
15 See Herbert A. Strauss, ed., *International Biographical Dictionary of Central European Emigrés, 1933–1945*, vol. 2, *The Arts, Sciences, and Literature* (Munich and New York: K. G. Saur, 1983), for a thorough listing of emigrés to America, with brief biographies.
16 During the early 1940s some of the courses offered included a ten-week seminar entitled National Socialist Propaganda, which began with readings of *Mein Kampf* and then studied its current applications; this was at the same time that the Nazis were implementing the "final solution" (New School catalogue, 1943, preserved in scrapbooks at the New School for Social Research, New York). See also Claus-Dieter Krohn, *Intellectuals in Exile: Refugee Scholars and the New School for Social Research*, trans. Rita and Robert Kimber (Amherst: University of Massachusetts Press, 1993).
17 See Colin W. Nettelbeck, "Not under Bushels: The French Mind Abroad," in *Forever French* (New York: Berg, 1991), 88–105.
18 Howard Putzel arranged surrealist games in which the public was invited to participate in executing composite drawings. Sheets of pink paper were fastened to the wall, and the participants were to draw on them "in the split second after a few minutes of complete mental relaxation. Each drawing will be concealed, but for the bottom edge, from the gaze of the next experimenter, and the whole effort will be finally viewed in a surrealist holiday mood; we hope it seems rude to add that a group of drawings by the insane will also be on view" (*Art News* 40 [15 March 1941]: 44–45).
19 For a description the formation of Black Mountain College, see Mary Emma Harris, *The Arts at Black Mountain College* (Cambridge: MIT Press, 1987), 2–7.
20 Alfred Frankfurter, editor of *Art News*, who actually attended and bid at the auction (on behalf of the collector Maurice Wertheim), cabled Fischer weeks before the sale suggesting that he clarify how the proceeds would be used. Fischer responded, both directly to Frankfurter and with a form letter sent to all potential American buyers: "We have been informed by friends that in America there is at present vehement propaganda in order to boycott this sensational public sale, pretending that the proceeds will go to Germany for purposes of armament. This argument is ridiculous and wrong. We therefore wish to state very clearly that all payments are to be addressed to the Galerie Fischer, Lucerne, and that the German Government has nothing to do with it. It was always understood that the funds will be distributed in favour of the German Museums so as to enable them to buy other works of art" (June 1939, copy in the Curt Valentin Papers, Museum of Modern Art Library, New York; original in the Fischer Gallery Archives, Lucerne).

considering
(and reconsidering)
art and exile

SABINE ECKMANN

Since the late 1960s there has been much interest in the complex of themes connected with exile and emigration under the Third Reich. At the same time, however, the activities of visual artists in exile have received relatively little attention, as becomes apparent if we compare the volume of art historical publications in this area with that of, for example, those concerned with literary or intellectual emigrés.[1]

Exiles and Emigrés: The Flight of European Artists from Hitler brings together three strands of exile studies: the exile of German artists within Europe; German artists, architects, and art historians in exile in the United States; and, finally, the American exile of members of the international Paris art scene. Unlike the German artists, many from this third group—such as the Russian Marc Chagall, the Lithuanian Jacques Lipchitz, and the Dutch Piet Mondrian—had acquired the status of foreigners and outsiders long before they arrived in the United States. In the 1920s and 1930s they had been part of an artistic avant-garde that regarded itself as cosmopolitan, and their artistic practice transcended national boundaries, even though, in most cases, their intellectual center of gravity lay within Parisian culture.

Up to now the latter theme has been untouched by German exile studies. In American art history,[2] as well as in general survey projects in Europe,[3] it has been discussed strictly in terms of artistic impact. That is, the influence of "Parisian" artists on the genesis of abstract expressionism has been analyzed, and the international artistic exchanges that took place in New York have been reconstructed, but there has been no attempt to draw parallels to the German emigration. Whereas American scholars have based their analysis of the German emigration on the hypothesis of a successful transplantation of artistic talent, the German literature is dominated by the issue of antifascism. As a result, in analyzing the artists' political views and practices, studies published to date in Germany have shown a bias in favor of either antifascist or autonomous, apolitical positions.[4]

Neither the term *exile* nor the term *emigration* is entirely straightforward in its meaning. Emigration is generally distinguished from exile by the active and voluntary nature of the decision to leave one's native country for political, economic, or religious reasons. In the case of exile the same motivations apply, except that here the state is the active party, compelling the individual to relocate by "deprivation of citizenship, banishment, persecution." Both the exile and the emigré can be clearly distinguished from the migrant, who makes repeated changes of domicile, or the traveler, who usually has a return ticket in hand. As a stronger variant of *exile* we have *flight*, which implies a hasty and enforced departure from the home country in which property is abandoned.[5]

In practice, however, such definitions are not of much use. The same terms have been used in different ways at different times by the individuals concerned, by the country that drove them out, by the host countries, and by historians of exile. Thus, Manfred Briegel notes that in 1936 those who left Germany regarded themselves as emigrés, as did Jewish organizations in Germany, when in fact what was taking place was a forced expulsion. The National Socialist state itself described the expulsion of Jews and political opponents as a voluntary emigration. The word *exile,* as distinct from *emigré,* was employed by the German opposition to indicate membership in its ranks.[6] This is reflected in the reactions of a number of artists, notably Oskar Kokoschka, who described himself as an exile after he decided to speak out against National Socialism.[7] Walter Gropius, by contrast, declined to call himself either an exile or an emigré because he had no desire to be identified with an anti-German position.[8] Others, including André Masson and Yves Tanguy, opposed the term *exile* because they denied their status as victims. In West Germany, after 1945, it was supposed that "exiles" might easily be transformed into "emigrés," since they were now free to return to Germany. Even this brief discussion of terminology reveals the complex nature of this theme, its resistance to simple definitions and interpretations.

German exile studies have generally been structured around either geographical centers of immigrant life or the German cities from which artists fled.[9] The title of Werner Mittenzwei's series *Kunst und Literatur im antifaschistischen Exil, 1933–1945* (Art and literature in antifascist exile, 1933–1945), published in East Germany, is paradigmatic of the East-West divide in exile studies that persisted until the dissolution of the Warsaw Pact and the reunification of the two Germanies in the early 1990s. Sustained by contrary motivations, scholars on both sides examined the exiles' activities in terms of their antifascist involvement (which the East viewed positively and the West, until the 1970s, negatively). Each side used the discipline of exile studies to legitimize a political status quo that still labored under the burden of the Nazi past.[10]

Over the decades the content of the debate has shifted. In West Germany in the 1940s and 1950s the main aim was to rehabilitate what the Nazis had called degenerate art, and—with some exceptions[11]—little attention was paid to the topic of exile as such. In this connection Michael Nungesser has shown that even titles of exhibitions of work by emigré or exiled German artists, such as *Ausgewanderte Maler* (Painters who emigrated),[12] point to the difficulty of dealing with the topic. Such titles imply that the artists left Germany of their own free will, with no explicit reference to the political causes. Along with the systematic rehabilitation of the modernist art that the Nazis had denigrated went an avoidance of the issue of exile. Thus, no one asked how individual artists had reacted to the political ideologization of their works or to National Socialism itself—or indeed why they had chosen to leave Germany or to stay there. Instead, all modernist artists were tagged as victims.

Even today artists' political positions are often a taboo subject in Germany. If we begin to examine those positions, however, we find that, aside from unequivocal antifascist involvement on an artist's part (as exemplified by Käthe Kollwitz and Hans and Lea Grundig), a range of possible attitudes can be identified, both among emigré artists and those who remained in Germany. Many including Lyonel Feininger, Kurt Schwitters, and Max Beckmann—insisted that as artists they were untouched by politics and attempted to salvage their artistic autonomy from a dictatorship that declined to recognize the existence of any such thing.

Other artists, including Emil Nolde and Franz Radziwill, expressed support for National Socialist Germany, a fact that tends to be suppressed or glossed over to this day.[13] Yet others, such as Gropius and Ludwig Mies van der Rohe,[14] were prepared to compromise in order to carry on with their careers—another subject that is often avoided. And there are those—such as Willi Baumeister, Otto Dix, and Conrad Felixmüller—whose positions are hard to determine because they shifted between acquiescence and withdrawal.

In West Germany there was a strong tendency to favor the "pure" and thus apolitical artist in order to buttress a libertarian society that regarded the modernist practice of art as an inherently democratic activity. The apolitical stance has itself been interpreted as a form of resistance, since democracy, unlike communism, theoretically guarantees the autonomy of art.[15] In the East, however, an apolitical art was unacceptable because, as Harald Olbrich has pointed out, the German Democratic Republic aimed at a "self-definition in terms of antifascism," and this entailed the "politicization of art in the direction of an 'aesthetic of resistance.'"[16] Hans-Ernst Mittig emphasized, in the same context, that in the West "the freedom of art and artists from political constraints...was used during the Cold War as a political argument against adversaries in the East."[17]

The volume of published work by art historians on the topics of exile and "inner emigration" began to grow only in the late 1970s. It was prompted by a renewed interest in the cultural politics of the Third Reich,[18] which in turn stemmed from the influence of the student movement of the late 1960s. The debate on the relationship between modernist artists and National Socialism began to come out into the open. The East German art historian Erhard Frommhold—in his controversial essay for the catalogue *Zwischen Widerstand und Anpassung: Kunst in Deutschland, 1933–1945* (Between resistance and acquiescence: Art in Germany, 1933–1945), published in West Germany in 1978[19]—was the first to take a closer look at the political reactions of those artists who remained in Germany in a state of so-called inner emigration. Frommhold did not interpret the alternatives of resistance and conformity as moral norms[20] but set out to characterize the German artistic milieu under the Third Reich by examining political attitudes in relation to the workings of National Socialist ideology. Arguing against an autonomous, self-referential art and attempting to point to the ways in which art is dependent on the external world, he drew connections between artists' political attitudes and their visual practice.

The 1980 exhibition *Widerstand statt Anpassung: Deutsche Kunst im Widerstand gegen den Faschismus* (Resistance instead of acquiescence: German art in resistance to fascism)[21] was devoted exclusively to the antifascist activities of artists in European centers of exile. A pendant to *Zwischen Widerstand und Anpassung*, this exhibition was also based on Frommhold's research[22] and on the practice of exile studies in East Germany. It rehabilitated the emigré artists vis-à-vis the inner emigrants, adding a marked moral undertone to the debate. Three years later the exhibition *Aus Berlin emigriert: Werke Berliner Künstler, die nach 1933 Deutschland verlassen mußten* (Emigrants from Berlin: Works by Berlin artists forced out of Germany after 1933) kept the debate on the same moral and subjective plane.[23] In the catalogue Eberhard Roters begged his readers to ask themselves, "How would I have behaved?" The emigré artists are presented as fellow beings subject to a shared destiny, and their stories are told in such a way as to elicit sympathy.

By contrast, the 1986 Berlin exhibition project *Kunst im Exil in Großbritannien, 1933–1945* (Art in exile in Great Britain, 1933–1945), encyclopedic in its scope, steered clear of moral judgments, approaching the topic from the standpoint of social history. It did not focus exclusively on the issue of antifascism, although Nungesser, in the introduction to the catalogue, drew attention to this complex of issues, stressing that "'Art in resistance' is not identical with 'art in exile.'"[24] Exile art was treated as a heterogeneous phenomenon, and close attention was paid to political, institutional, and social conditions in Britain and to the activities of the exiles themselves.

Werner Haftmann's *Verfemte Kunst: Malerei der inneren und äußeren Emigration* (published in English as *Banned and Persecuted: Dictatorship of Art under Hitler*) remains the most comprehensive survey to date, covering all the major geographic centers of exile as well as the inner emigration. Haftmann, a witness to the cultural policies of the Third Reich, traced the course of the antifascism debate, taking a firm stand against the tendency in exile studies to judge works of art on political grounds. He argued in favor of an autonomous role for the artist, one located outside political reality, sweepingly declaring *all* modernists to be victims of National Socialism. Such a position is problematic in that it does not distinguish between those artists who left Germany more or less voluntarily, because their professional or artistic prospects were better elsewhere, and those, whether Jews or political opponents of Nazism, whose lives were in danger. For Haftmann, however, the issue of artistic quality is paramount: "In its methodology this book constitutes an admonition to those engaged in exile studies not to allow political or sociological inessentials to obscure the true point—the independent achievement of the autonomous artist."[25]

Thus, the relationship between German-speaking art historians and the discipline of exile studies has clearly been a highly conflicted and subjective one. The repression of the entire theme of exile in favor of a rehabilitation of "degenerate art," the moralistic celebration of antifascism in East Germany, and the preference for an autonomous, apolitical art in the West were all devices aimed at political self-justification in relation to the National Socialist past. The exceptions here have been those studies that strive for a critical and historical treatment of the subject, such as *Kunst im Exil in Großbritannien*. *Exiles and Emigrés* is an attempt to build on these. This catalogue seeks to go beyond one-sided proclamations of faith, whether for or against antifascism, and to follow the example of Lutz Winckler by scrutinizing the myths of exile studies and by "historicizing" the theme of exile, that is, by trying to understand it in terms of its own time and the conditions then prevailing.[26]

This approach must also be applied to the myth of antifascism. Accordingly, the individual biographical studies in this catalogue explore artists' reactions to National Socialism and its enforced politicization of their works. In many cases no clear position emerges. Thus, Barbara Copeland Buenger shows how for Beckmann exile gave rise to a conflict between the need for autonomy and the exigencies of current politics. She also analyzes Schwitters's ambivalent position, caught between autonomous artistic production and the inclusion of political commentary. The example of Kokoschka reveals how a consistently independent modernist responded to political circumstances by transforming himself into an active antifascist.

In his essay for the present catalogue, "Scenes from Exile in Western Europe: The Politics of Individual and Collective Endeavor among German Artists," Keith Holz contrasts the alternative positions of antifascism and artistic autonomy among exiled artists in the Netherlands, France, and Great Britain. Within the framework of a political and institutional history of art he contrasts the individual artistic agendas of Beckmann and Kandinsky with the collective involvement of Otto Freundlich, John Heartfield, Kokoschka, and Eugen Spiro with exiled artists' groups. Peter Hahn, in "Bauhaus and Exile: Bauhaus Architects and Designers between the Old World and the New," examines the political attitudes of the leaders of the Bauhaus alongside the National Socialist responses to their work. He questions the notion that the Bauhaus stood for a politically "better" Germany and shows how its overriding artistic goal, the establishment of modernist principles, took precedence over democratic ideals.

American scholars have tended to approach the topic of the exile and emigration of German artists in terms of the thesis of successful cultural transfer. Here, just as in the postwar German states, an important factor is political identity, in this case, that of the United States as a world power. As Martin Jay makes clear in his essay in this catalogue, the American response to German intellectuals in exile is dominated by arguments for and against the "deradicalization" of progressive thinking, notably that of the Frankfurt School. When it comes to visual art, however, those scholars who have managed to look beyond the tired issue of the exiles' impact on American art have concentrated on demonstrating their adaptive capacity. Much attention has been focused on associates of the Bauhaus. While no one has seriously contested the fact that Bauhaus ideas underwent a transformation in the United States, few have expressed regret over the loss of the progressive social agenda that distinguished the work of the Bauhaus in Germany.[27] We are constantly told that in the United States Bauhaus architects, designers, and painters found a country that was more receptive to their artistic creed, modernism, than Germany—even Germany without the all-pervading cultural politics of National Socialism—had ever been.

In her 1968 study of the "intellectual migration," Laura Fermi, herself an immigrant, stated that the emigration "brought to our shores the greatest of Europe, and they heightened the cultural prestige of our country," while emphasizing that the success enjoyed by Bauhaus people in the United States depended on Americans' enthusiasm for technology and on their openness to the immigrants' experimental, antitraditional aims. Her account suggests that the European modernists and America were made for each other.[28]

This simplistic interpretation was taken up in the studies that followed. One year later, in his informative but uncritical essay "The Aftermath of the Bauhaus in America: Gropius, Mies, and Breuer," William H. Jordy described the work of Bauhaus people in America as a postscript, arguing that there was no real continuation of the German Bauhaus. Like Fermi, he concluded that the encounter was a fortunate one for both sides: "The affluence of [American] society and the congeniality of [the immigrants'] work to their new environment were cardinal factors in their success, both economic and architectural."[29]

Fourteen years later, in 1983, Jarrell C. Jackman and Carla M. Borden published a collection of symposium papers under the title *The Muses Flee Hitler: Cultural Transfer and Adaptation, 1930–1945*. Jackman emphasized the immigrants' adaptability and their contribution to American culture, with particular stress on the successful transplantation of the Bauhaus, which "seemed to belong in America."[30] In his contribution to the volume,

"American Skyscrapers and Weimar Modern: Transactions between Fact and Idea," Christian F. Otto maintained Fermi's and Jordy's line that America and the Bauhaus sought and found each other. At the same time, however, he cast doubt on the conventional wisdom by asking what it was that made the United States into a mecca for the Bauhaus architects, why their influence was so great, and why an architecture that was tied to the social and cultural milieu of the Weimar Republic was able to flourish under totally different conditions. Pointing to Philip Johnson's role in promoting Mies and highlighting the influence of the Museum of Modern Art, Otto persuasively suggested that this successful transplantation was not by any means—as has been naively supposed—a coincidence or a stroke of luck.

Several authors of the present catalogue attempt to correct one-sided accounts of the transfer of the Bauhaus. Franz Schulze, in "The Bauhaus Architects and the Rise of Modernism in the United States," points to the American interest in the Bauhaus that existed even before 1933. He shows that Americans invariably sought to purge Bauhaus ideas of their social implications and that Gropius, tied into the institutional structures of Harvard and Boston, met with stiff conservative opposition in pushing through his modernist agenda. The immigrants' interests were by no means identical with the demands of American institutions. In her individual case studies Kathleen James describes Gropius's difficulties in importing his German architecture to the United States and discusses Marcel Breuer's "middle way" of combining American regional traditions with a modern vocabulary. Sheri Bernstein, analyzing the American career of László Moholy-Nagy, shows how this former Bauhaus teacher was forced to compromise in the United States. In his practical work in design education Moholy bowed to the demands of the American corporate world; in his artistic work, by contrast, he withdrew into a subjective language of form.

In a similar vein, Karen Michels presents here the results of empirical research on German emigré art historians, which shows how they were compelled to adapt to the requirements of the American university system. The notion of a linear transplantation of art historical scholarship also turns out to be in need of revision and elaboration.

Unlike the members of the Bauhaus, many of the exiles from the former artistic milieu of Paris were temporary visitors. The majority of them—including André Breton, Fernand Léger, André Masson, and Matta—returned to Europe after the war.[31] Discussion of this topic tends to be dominated by the thesis that their presence in New York was one factor among many that influenced the genesis of the New York school. Artists such as Willem de Kooning, Robert Motherwell, and Jackson Pollock are thought to have absorbed impulses from the "Parisians" before going on to engender an authentically American art of their own. This view has its political motivation: when the Germans occupied Paris in June 1940, the French capital lost its position as the art center of the Western world. It was consequently tempting for Americans to imagine that New York could now secure the same cultural hegemony.[32] The fulfillment of this enterprise was to make history under the banner of the "triumph of American painting." This version of history springs in part from the fact that French artists had no interest in participating in the genesis of an American art. Whereas many German exiles were prepared to give up their identities and become Americans, acculturation had less appeal for the French.[33] Instead, they endeavored—with little success—to implant Paris in New York.[34]

Dore Ashton's 1972 account took a less triumphalist line. Taking up the notion of the American "melting pot," Ashton argued that the enforced immigration of a number of distinguished European painters created a progressive artistic milieu in New York which led to a synthesis of differing practices of art. In her narrative of the transformation of surrealist concepts, their influence on American artists, and the subsequent gradual emergence of the New York school, she emphasized a modernist, evolutionary approach.[35] Other publications on the subject—such as the exhibition catalogues *Paris–New York* and *The Golden Door: Artist-Immigrants of America, 1876–1976*[36]—also stress the productive interchange among artists.

It was Serge Guilbaut, in his 1983 book *How New York Stole the Idea of Modern Art: Abstract Expressionism, Freedom, and the Cold War*, who mounted the first ideological critique of America's cultural objectives.[37] Guilbaut analyzed the controversies aroused by America's ambition to become the capital of the international art scene and the contribution that visual art was expected to make to the country's new status as a world power, showing why a politically neutral art was favored. He questioned the extent of the influence exerted by Parisian artists, showing that interest in their work remained limited because, logically, only an authentically American art could secure cultural leadership. Thus, American artists made selective use of those aspects of European modern art that suited their concerns.

The recent publications by Martica Sawin and Dickran Tashjian on the surrealists and the American avant-garde analyze a wide variety of primary sources to present an image of the period that is rich in cultural cross-references. Both authors take a skeptical view of the notion that the surrealists straightforwardly influenced American artists.[38]

The genesis of abstract expressionism, and the precise part played therein by Parisian artists, is not a central concern of the present volume. Thus, in her contribution, Romy Golan concentrates on the "field of cultural production,"[39] analyzing the rhetoric of the responses to exile both of the host country and the artists themselves. Accounts of individual artists reveal not only how the Europeans were received within the American artistic milieu but also—more importantly—how the multilayered experience of exile was manifested in their art. No unified narrative is possible in such circumstances. Diverse responses to the new culture, to political events in Europe, and to the artists' own cultures led to artistic formulations that dealt with new social utopias (Ernst, Matta, Mondrian), resistance to doctrinaire political regimes (Masson, Matta, Lipchitz), issues of contemporary Jewish identity (Chagall, Lipchitz), retreat into private life (Ernst, Léger, Tanguy), and the conflicts provoked by the artists' own identities as Europeans in an alien North American environment (Salvador Dali, Matta). In answer to Sybil Milton—who posed the question "Is there an exile art or only exile artists?"[40]—it can be said that there is neither a homogeneous exile art nor an array of totally diverse, individual bodies of work by exiled artists.

In addressing the momentous and formative experience of exile, which has left its mark on late twentieth-century postmodernism in particular, the exploration of individual exile identities in this catalogue has been informed by an awareness of North American and British work in the field of postcolonial studies and by the wider discipline of cultural studies, with its concern with displacement, exile, migration, nationalism, cultural hybridity, and complex formulations of identity.[41] This is not the place for a contextual history of these methodologies, though some aspects are relevant to the history of exiled European artists during the 1930s and 1940s. This catalogue is not about the constitution of heterogeneous identities within the structures of the state, its power, and national culture,[42] but about the ways in which individual artists dealt with exile and emigration and their impact on identity. The aim is to uncover those conflicts omitted from previous art historical accounts that emphasize a linear assimilation process.

Here national identity comes into play,[43] in that, for German artists in particular, the lost sense of belonging to a nation and such basic, associated experiences as language, custom (social intercourse), and cultural tradition constituted the fundamental experiences of exile. This becomes apparent in George Grosz's complex dialogue with America and his ultimately unsuccessful attempts to establish an American identity. The American-born Feininger, who had made his artistic career in Germany and whose intellectual ties were with German tradition, was neither able nor willing to reestablish a bond with American culture after his return. The exile experience of loss emerges in these pages—together with the allied sense of memory and the articulation of a lost cultural identity and of a certain "unconnectedness"[44] with the new environment—as central to the work of many artists, among them Chagall, Dali, Feininger, Grosz, André Kertész, Lipchitz, and Tanguy.

Facing death in Nazi-occupied Europe and experiencing anti-Semitic attitudes in exile in the United States, Jews in particular were forced to redefine their identities. In his essay "Art History and Exile: Richard Krautheimer and Erwin Panofsky" Kevin Parker reveals the assimilationist strategies behind the art historical methodologies developed by these two scholars, which he traces to their origins as assimilated Jews in Weimar Germany. Parker argues that in American exile they moved even further in this direction, developing approaches that allowed them to avoid questions of identity or politics. Matthew Affron considers the experiences of the Eastern European Jewish artists Chagall and Lipchitz. In their work these artists not only responded to Nazi atrocities but also expressed allegiance to French culture and attempted to reach a universal audience.

This catalogue not only examines the activities and exile of visual artists and art historians but also analyzes the responses of the host countries, in terms of both the institutional prerequisites for the making of art and the reception accorded it. In order to do this, the authors have confined their examination to a representative selection of visual artists and exile centers and have concentrated on a detailed analysis of a limited body of historical material. This method challenges the received canon of art history, in that the second half of the twentieth century has evaluated many of the artists differently from the way they were judged in the 1930s and 1940s. The surrealists, to take but one example, met with a far from friendly reception from contemporary New York art critics.[45]

Lastly, the importance of the theme of exile to a reconsideration of modernism must not be underestimated. Edward Said regards exile as emblematic of the modern age, not only because the facts of Realpolitik have filled the world with so many migrants and refugees but also because of intellectual demands for the rejection of such notions as domesticity and tradition. The cultural production of exiles and "outsiders" thus plays a defining role in the emergence of a specifically modern culture.[46] And so this catalogue not only interprets aspects of the history of exile in the first half of this century but also rewrites a pivotal period of the history of modernism itself.

Notes

1 See Martin Jay's essay in this catalogue, "The German Migration: Is There a Figure in the Carpet?" Of all the publications enumerated by Jay, only two address the visual arts: Laura Fermi, *Illustrious Immigrants: The Intellectual Migration from Europe, 1930–1941* (Chicago and London: University of Chicago Press, 1968); Jarrell C. Jackman and Carla M. Borden, eds., *The Muses Flee Hitler: Cultural Transfer and Adaptation, 1930–1945* (Washington, D.C.: Smithsonian Institution Press, 1983).

2 E.g., William S. Rubin, *Dada and Surrealist Art* (New York: Harry N. Abrams, 1968), 342–92; Serge Guilbaut, *How New York Stole the Idea of Modern Art: Abstract Expressionism, Freedom, and the Cold War* (Chicago and London: University of Chicago Press, 1983), esp. chap. 2, "The Second World War and the Attempt to Establish an Independent American Art"; Martica Sawin, *Surrealism in Exile and the Beginnings of the New York School* (Cambridge and London: MIT Press, 1995); and Dickran Tashjian, *A Boatload of Madmen: Surrealism and the American Avant-Garde, 1920–1950* (London and New York: Thames and Hudson, 1995).

3 E.g., Laszlo Glozer, ed., *Westkunst: Zeitgenössische Kunst seit 1939*, exh. cat. (Cologne: Museen der Stadt Köln; DuMont, 1981), 101ff.; Robert Motherwell, "Artistes parisiens en exil: New York, 1939–1945," and Daniel Abadie, "Art of This Century," in *Paris–New York: 1908–1968*, exh. cat. (Paris: Musée National d'Art Moderne, Centre Georges Pompidou, 1977; rev. ed., Paris: Gallimard, 1991), 553–69, 618–22; Gail Levin, "Surrealisten in New York und ihr Einfluß auf die amerikanische Kunst," in *Europa/Amerika: Die Geschichte einer künstlerischen Faszination seit 1940*, exh. cat. (Cologne: Museum Ludwig, 1986), 69–79.

4 In this context *autonomous* refers to an understanding of art that rejects all dependence on morality, politics, and religion and regards art as a praxis obeying only its own laws. The notion of art as answerable only to itself was underpinned by Immanuel Kant, who derived the autonomy of art from a priori laws of human reason, and by G. W. F. Hegel, who based the independence of art on the theory of absolute mind. Increasingly since the nineteenth century this ahistorical notion has been called into question; the choice between an autonomous and a politically responsible art is now one that every artist must make individually.

5 These definitions are derived from *Duden: Deutsches Universalwörterbuch*, 1st ed.

6 Manfred Briegel and Wolfgang Frühwald, eds., *Die Erfahrung der Fremde: Kolloquium des Schwerpunktprogrammes "Exilforschung" der deutschen Forschungsgemeinschaft* (Weinheim: VCH, 1988), 6.

7 See Keith Holz's essay on Kokoschka in this catalogue.

8 See Peter Hahn, "Bauhaus and Exile: Bauhaus Architects and Designers between the Old World and the New," in this catalogue.

9 *Aus Berlin emigriert: Werke Berliner Künstler, die nach 1933 Deutschland verlassen mußten*, exh. cat. (Berlin: Berlinische Galerie, 1983); *Kunst im Exil in Großbritannien, 1933–1945*, exh. cat. (Berlin: Neue Gesellschaft für bildende Kunst; Frölich und Kaufmann, 1986); and Werner Mittenzwei, ed., *Kunst und Literatur im antifaschistischen Exil, 1933–1945*, 7 vols. (Leipzig: Philipp Reclam, 1979), which covers the Soviet Union, Switzerland, the United States, Shanghai, Latin America, Czechoslovakia, Great Britain, Scandinavia, Palestine, the Netherlands, Spain, and France.

10 Much the same applies to the historiography of intellectuals in exile, as presented here by Martin Jay.

11 *Ausgewanderte Maler*, exh. cat. (Leverkusen: Städtisches Museum Schloß Morsbroich, 1955).

12 Michael Nungesser, "Die bildenden Künstler im Exil," in *Kunst im Exil in Großbritannien*, 27.

13 There have been some important exceptions. On the manifold and contradictory reception of Nolde's position under the Third Reich, see Monika Hecker, "Ein Leben an der Grenze: Emil Nolde und die NSDAP," *Nordfriesland*, no. 110 (June 1995): 9–15. On Radziwill, see James Van Dyck, "Franz Radziwill, the Art Politics of the National Socialist Regime, and the Question of Resistance in Germany, 1930–1939" (Ph.D. diss., Northwestern University, 1996). Both artists are discussed in *Zwischen Widerstand und Anpassung: Kunst in Deutschland, 1933–1945*, exh. cat. (Berlin: Akademie der Künste, 1978), 214–17, 228–71.

14 See Peter Hahn's essay in this catalogue.

15 "The path of autonomous and self-referential art was of course also a form of resistance to all artistic dictatorship" (Helmut Kohl, foreword to Werner Haftmann, *Verfemte Kunst: Malerei der inneren und äußeren Emigration* [Cologne: DuMont, 1986], unpaginated).

16 Harald Olbrich, "Aspekte der Kunst der dreißiger Jahre," in *Kunst und Kunstkritik der dreißiger Jahre*, ed. Maria Rüger (Dresden: Verlag der Kunst in association with Akademie der Künste der DDR, 1990), 14; idem, "Antifaschistische Kunst in der Emigration," *Wissenschaftliche Zeitschrift der Ernst-Moritz-Arndt-Universität Greifswald: Gesellschafts- und Sprachwissenschaftliche Reihe* 15, no. 4 (1996): 431–46.

17 Hans-Ernst Mittig, "Immer wieder unpolitisches Künstlertum?" in *Kultfigur und Mythenbildung*, ed. Michael Groblowski and Oskar Bätschmann (Berlin: Akademie Verlag, 1993), 152.

18 The reference here is to exhibitions such as *Kunst im dritten Reich: Dokumente der Unterwerfung* (Frankfurter Kunstverein, Frankfurt, 1974) and *Die dreißiger Jahre: Schauplatz Deutschland* (Haus der Kunst, Munich, 1977).

19 See note 13 above; on "inner emigration," see also Berthold Roland, ed., *Abstrakte Maler der inneren Emigration*, exh. cat. (Mainz: Landesmuseum, 1985), and *Ateliergemeinschaft Klosterstraße Berlin: Künstler in der Zeit des Nationalsozialismus, 1933–1945*, exh. cat. (Berlin: Akademie der Künste, 1994).

20 For a detailed and balanced account of political and apolitical attitudes, see also the article written seven years later by Jutta Held, "Widerstand der bildenden Künstler gegen den Faschismus," *Exil*, no. 2 (1985): 47–59. Held goes beyond the scrutiny of individual positions to compare the alternatives of "inner" and "outer" emigration and concludes that artists in exile typically became politicized. She thus contrasts "good," antifascist exile with "bad" (because apolitical) inner emigration; there is some justice in this view, but it has the disadvantage of preventing an examination of the subject in terms of its historical complexities.

21 *Widerstand statt Anpassung: Deutsche Kunst im Widerstand gegen den Faschismus*, exh. cat. (Karlsruhe: Badischer Kunstverein, 1980).

22 Erhard Frommhold, ed., *Kunst im Widerstand: Malerei, Graphik, Plastik, 1922–1945* (Dresden: Verlag der Kunst, 1968).

23 See note 9 above.

24 *Kunst im Exil in Großbritannien*, 28.

25 Haftmann, *Verfemte Kunst*, 19. Haftmann himself participated in the so-called expressionism debate (1933–34), in which he took the side of those who sought to defend expressionism as the future art of the Third Reich. See Stefan Germer, "Kunst der Nation: Zu einem Versuch, die Avantgarde zu nationalisieren," in *Kunst auf Befehl? Dreiunddreißig bis Fünfundvierzig*, ed. Bazon Brock and Achim Preiss (Munich: Klinkhardt und Biermann, 1990), 27, 38–39.

26 Lutz Winckler, "Mythen der Exilforschung?" in *Kulturtransfer im Exil*, ed. Claus-Dieter Krohn, Erwin Rotermund, Lutz Winckler, and Wulf Koepke, vol. 13 of *Exilforschung: Ein internationales Jahrbuch* (1995): 68–81.

27 For an exception, see Alain Findeli, "Design Education and Industry: The Laborious Beginnings of the Institute of Design in Chicago in 1944," *Journal of Design History* 4, no. 2 (1993): 97–113.

28 Fermi, *Illustrious Immigrants*, 233. Terry Smith—in *Making the Modern: Industry, Art, and Design in America* (Chicago and London: University of Chicago Press, 1993)—discusses the phenomenon of the Bauhaus alumni in the context of a comprehensive account of the genesis of modernism in the United States. He qualifies the received notion of the overwhelming importance of the immigrants' contribution by treating their buildings and designs as one possible aspect of modernism among many; see esp. 395–401.

29 William H. Jordy, "The Aftermath of the Bauhaus in America: Gropius, Mies, and Breuer," in *The Intellectual Migration: Europe and America, 1930–1960*, ed. Donald Fleming and Bernard Bailyn (Cambridge: Harvard University Press, 1969), 526.

30 Jackman and Borden, eds., *The Muses Flee Hitler*, 21. This book conducts a critical reassessment of the traditional image of the United States as a country of immigration, the issues raised by the strict curbs on immigration under Roosevelt, and the bias in favor of the European intellectual elite. See esp. Roger Daniels, "American Refugee Policy in Historical Perspective" (61–77), and Cynthia Jaffee McCabe, "'Wanted by the Gestapo: Saved by America'—Varian Fry and the Emergency Rescue Committee" (79–81).

31 See Fermi, *Illustrious Immigrants*, 243ff.

32 Such is the interpretation given in many accounts of the New York school. See Sam Hunter, *American Art in the Twentieth Century* (New York: Harry N. Abrams, 1973); Barbara Rose, *American Art since 1900* (New York: Praeger, 1968); Irving Sandler, *The Triumph of American Painting: A History of Abstract Expressionism* (New York: Praeger, 1970). Sandler's account in particular has been strongly disputed by German art historians: "To this day all interest in this unheard-of chapter, the influence of surrealism, has been repressed.... This is all part of the American claim to artistic hegemony, which has been reformulated since 1945 in ever more aggressive variants. We are faced with a remarkable case of the denial of history.... In a sense, it seems to me that it is part of the apologetics of the New York school to deny the historical evidence. The New York school has sought to define its own identity and uniqueness in terms of a categorical Otherness in relation to Europe" (Werner Spies, in *Max Ernst: Retrospektive*, exh. cat. [Munich: Prestel, 1971], 97).

33 On the German tendency toward assimilation, see my essay on Grosz in this catalogue. By contrast, the French artists more often assumed the role of ambassadors for French culture. This is particularly evident in the case of Masson; see my essay in this catalogue.

34 Going beyond this, Romy Golan, writing in this catalogue, discusses the ways in which the surrealists mythologized and patronized America.

35 Dore Ashton, *Life and Times of the New York School* (New York: Viking Press, 1972), 118.

36 Motherwell, "Artistes parisiens en exil," Abadie, "Art of This Century," and idem, "Mondrian à New York," in *Paris–New York*, 553–69; Cynthia Jaffee McCabe, ed. *The Golden Door: Artist-Immigrants of America, 1876–1976*, exh. cat. (Washington, D.C.: Hirshhorn Museum and Sculpture Garden; Smithsonian Institution Press, 1976).

37 Guilbaut, *How New York*.

38 Sawin, *Surrealism in Exile*; Tashjian, *A Boatload of Madmen*. Tashjian studied the reactions of American artists and intellectuals to the surrealist movement between 1920 and 1950, emphasizing that the "French and American avant-gardes developed at their own paces, making oblique points of contact" and that this was principally because "Surrealism remained primarily European in identity." Against the backdrop of political history Sawin gives a chronological and descriptive account of the surrealist movement between 1938 and 1947. In her view the surrealists provided, at the very least, a stimulus to the American artists.

39 Here Golan is partly following Pierre Bourdieu, who has defined the "field of cultural production" in terms of a number of interacting factors: the production of art, the producers of art, and their strategies and goals; the art world at large (public, publishers, critics, galleries, museums, academies, etc.); see Bourdieu, *The Field of Cultural Production: Essays on Art and Literature*, ed. Randal Johnson (New York: Columbia University Press, 1993), 29–73.

40 Sybil Milton, "Is There an Exile Art or Only Exile Artists?" in *Exil: Literatur und die Künste nach 1933*, Studien zur Literatur der Moderne, no. 17 (Bonn: Bouvier, 1990): 83–89. In a comparison between art made in exile and art made in internment camps, Milton concludes that the latter reveals affinities based on a shared experience, whereas no such features appear in exile art.

41 Recent studies that have been helpful include Angelika Bammer, ed., *Displacements: Cultural Identities in Question* (Bloomington and Indianapolis: Indiana University Press, 1994); Homi K. Bhabha, "Cultural Diversity and Cultural Differences," in *The Postcolonial Studies Reader*, ed. Bill Ashcroft, Gareth Griffiths, and Helen Tiffin (London and New York: Routledge, 1995); idem, *The Location of Culture* (London and New York: Routledge, 1993); idem, "Frontlines/Borderposts," in Bammer, ed., *Displacements*; James Clifford, "Traveling Cultures," in *Cultural Studies*, ed. Lawrence Grossberg, Cary Nelson, and Paula Treichler (London and New York: Routledge, 1993), 96–112; Ian Chambers, *Migrancy, Culture, Identity* (London and New York: Routledge, 1994).

42 See, for example, Benedict Anderson, *Imagined Communities: Reflections on the Origin and Spread of Nationalism* (London and New York: Verso, 1983); Homi K. Bhabha, ed., *Nation and Narration* (New York and London: Routledge, 1990); Frederic Jameson, *Nationalism, Colonialism, and Literature: Modernism and Imperialism* (Belfast: Field Day Pamphlets, 1988).

43 Edward Said lays particular stress on the mutually dependent relationship between exile and nationalism ("Reflections on Exile," in *Out There: Marginalization and Contemporary Cultures*, ed. Russell Ferguson et al. [New York: Museum of Contemporary Art; Cambridge and London: MIT Press, 1990], 359–60).

44 Ibid.

45 See Romy Golan's essay and my essays on the surrealists in this catalogue.

46 Said, "Reflections on Exile," 357.

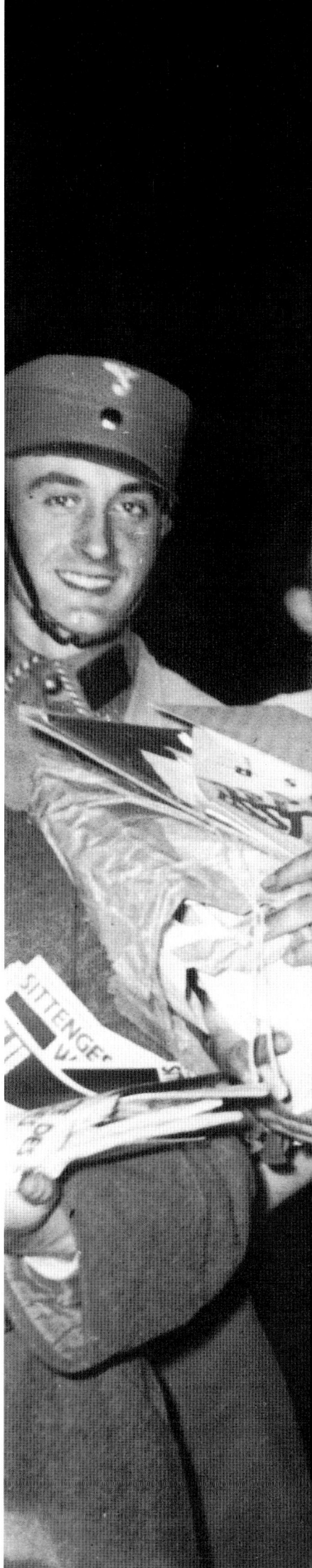

Overleaf left:
Burning of "un-German" literature at the Opernplatz in Berlin, May 10, 1933; Bildarchiv Preussischer Kulturbesitz.

Overleaf right:
Austrian Jews attempting to emigrate, 1938; Österreichische Gesellschaft für Zeitgeschichte, Vienna, Bildarchiv.

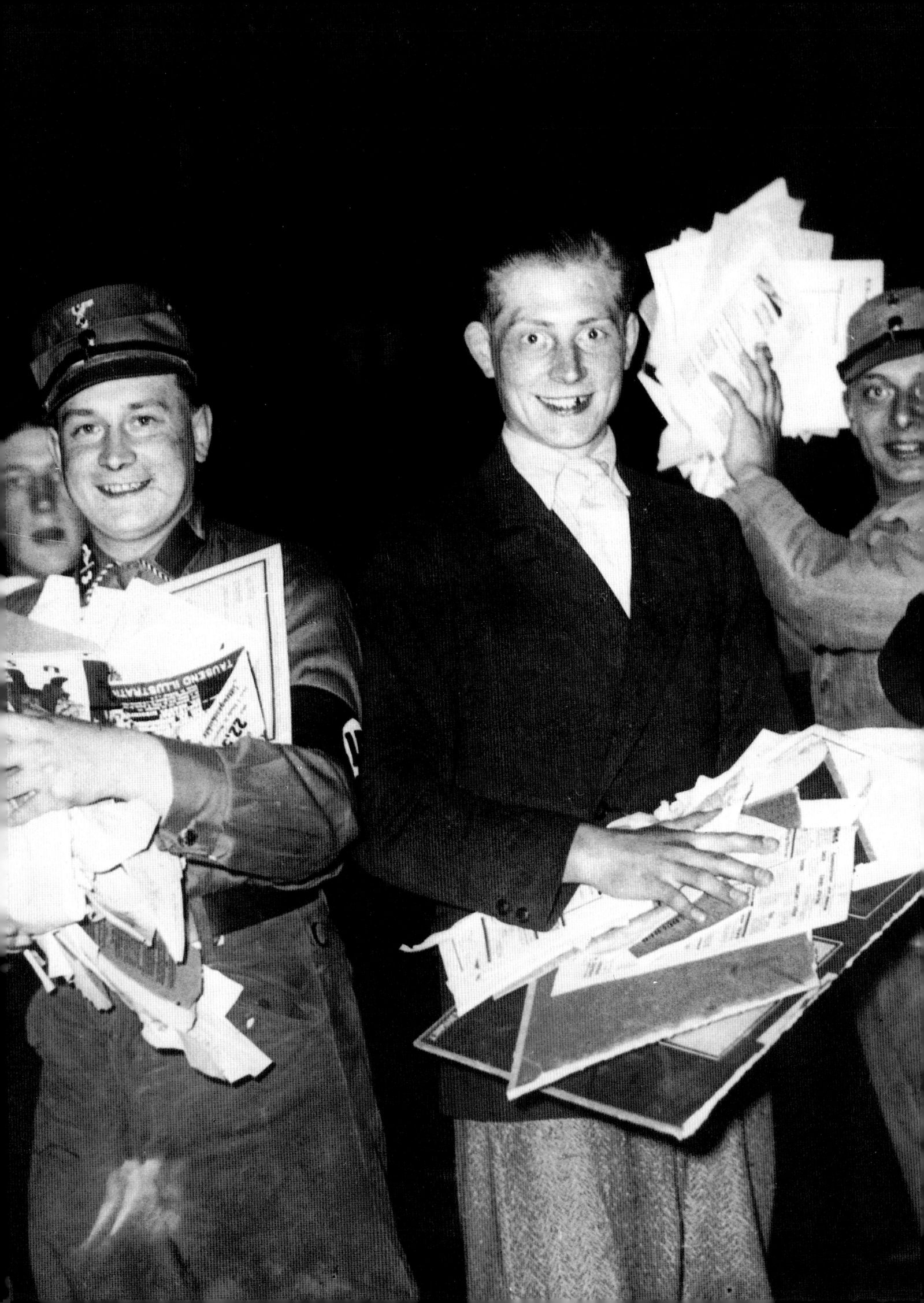

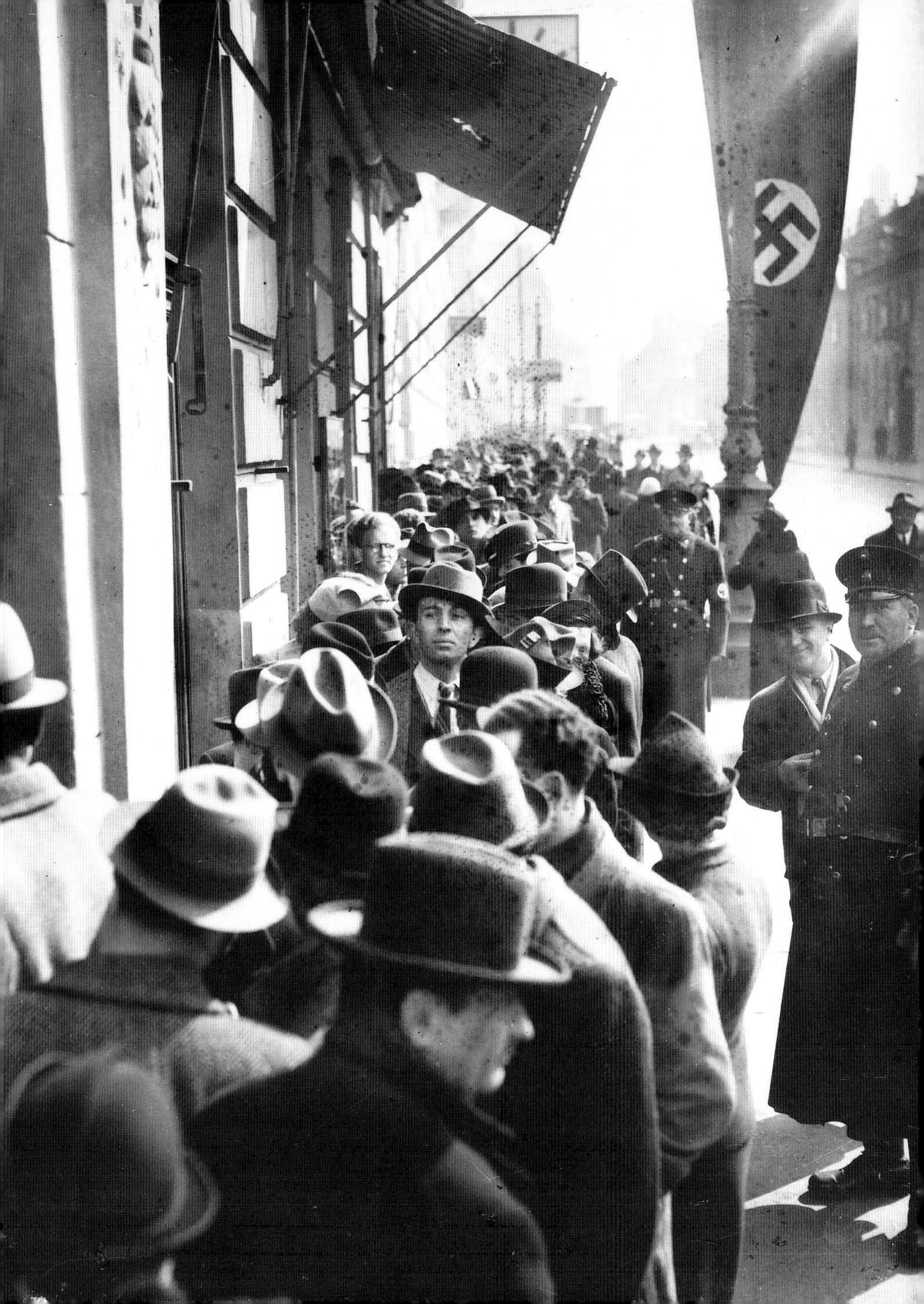

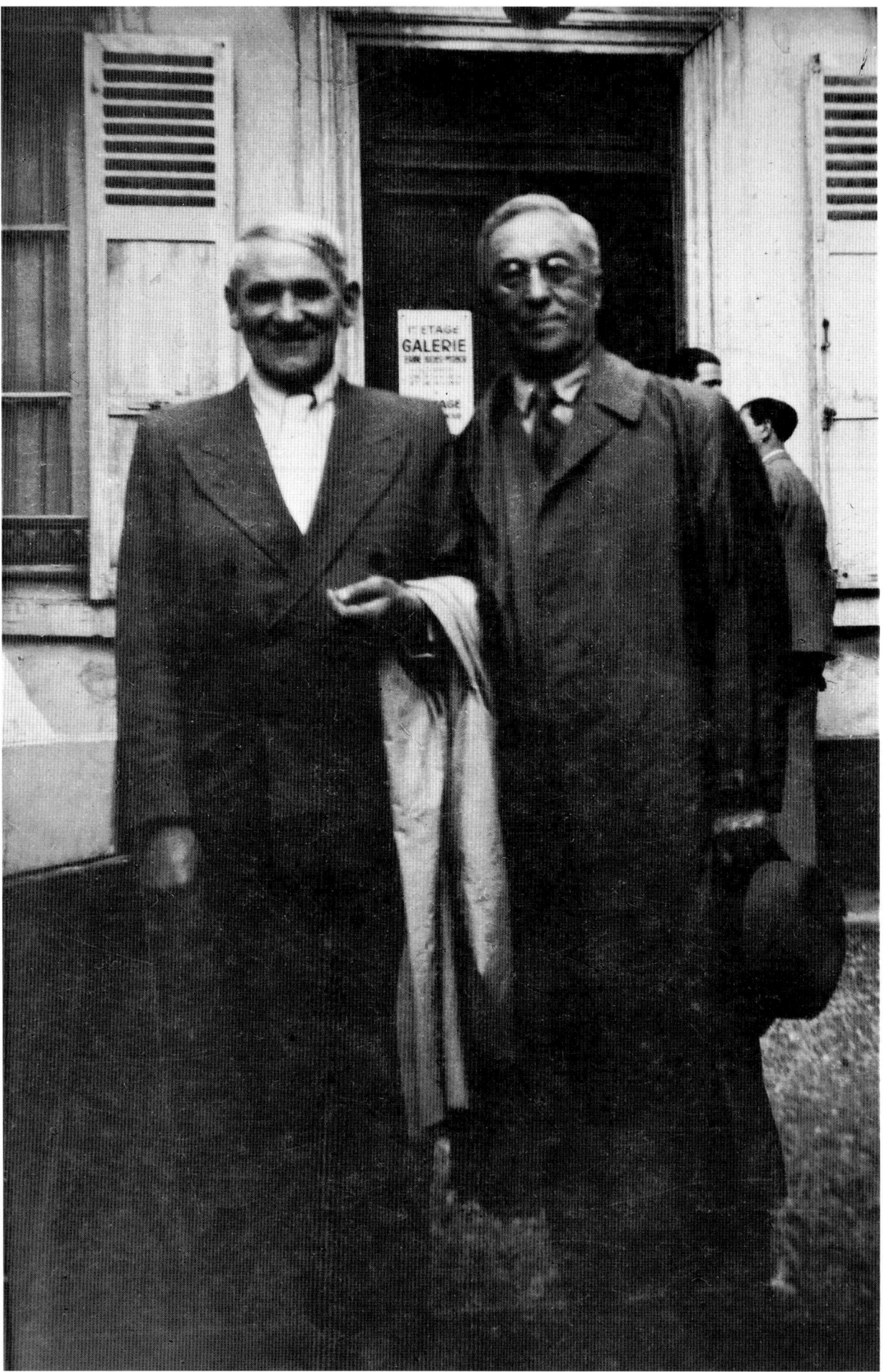

KEITH HOLZ

scenes from exile in western europe:
the politics of individual and collective endeavor among german artists

From metropolitan havens beyond German borders many exiled visual artists and critics stayed abreast of political transformations within Germany. They also experienced the impact of those changes on their host countries as the democratic governments not only adjusted diplomatic agreements with Germany but also passed legislation to regulate immigrants from Central Europe. By 1935, when the Third Reich's viability could no longer be denied, exiles often turned to assessing their position in relation to Germany's past and future. Some sought to reclaim and publicly convey to available audiences a history of Germany and its recent cultural past; others revisited their memories. Some made concrete plans for a Germany liberated from Nazi rule; others dreamed of a better future. Across the geographically dispersed German emigration, many exiles were quick to recognize that not only was Germany's future in jeopardy but the historical representation of its past cultural achievements as well.

With the National Socialist government's internationally publicized opening of the defamatory exhibition *Entartete Kunst* (Degenerate art) in July 1937, the embattled status of modern German art was rendered alarmingly vivid to Germany's art world in exile. In Paris and London counterexhibitions were organized, and new histories of modern German art were fashioned in an effort to rectify the derogatory interpretations of modern art widely publicized by the German government and its supporters.[1] As if to impart historical urgency to their interpretations of German art and culture, many exile responses adopted titles that suggested the daily unfolding of German history. Paradigmatic in this regard was *Germany of Yesterday, Germany of Tomorrow*, the extraordinary effort made by a group of Paris-based artists and scholars, the Deutsches Kulturkartell (German cartel of culture), to present German cultural history at the 1939 New York World's Fair through thirty-three text and picture panels (see fig. 22).

To describe these collaborative picture-text panels as a major achievement of exiled German artists unleashes at least three issues key to an interpretation of the endeavors of German artists in exile. First, it directs art historical inquiry beyond modernism's focus on paintings, fine prints, and sculpture—often embraced without question as "modern German art"—to include that potentially unwieldy expanse of materials often referred to as "visual culture." Second, the visual and documentary evidence of contributions by more than two dozen exiled artists and scholars to these panels attests to the continuation of a legacy of cultural practices and beliefs that valued collective production no less, and sometimes more, than work by individual artists. And, third, the planned presentation of these panels to a large, general public in New York reminds us that scores of artists in exile chose not merely to

21
Otto Freundlich and Wassily Kandinsky at Freundlich's sixtieth birthday celebration, Galerie Jeanne Bucher, Paris, 1938.

43

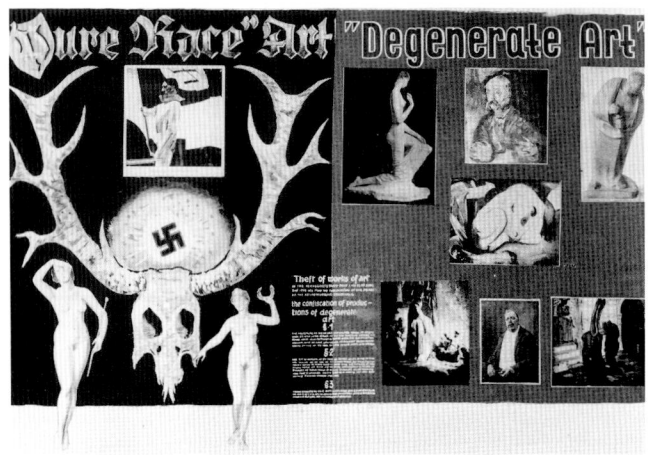

22
"Pure Race" Art / "Degenerate Art," text panel created by German exile artists in Paris for the unrealized exhibition *Germany of Yesterday, Germany of Tomorrow*, planned for the 1939 New York World's Fair; proof print by Josef Breitenbach.

make art for a market of individual art lovers predisposed to solitary habits of contemplative reception, but instead utilized their artistic abilities to educate the masses about the National Socialist government's distortions of German culture as well as its injustices and violations of human rights.

A sustained analysis of these thirty-three panels in relation to other, individually directed efforts by their contributors would clearly dramatize differences between art and visual culture as well as between individual and collective production and practice. Here, however, given this catalogue's focus on the exile production of well-known modernists, it seems more appropriate to examine works by single artists in order to reveal the diversity of artistic practices among the exiles. Such an analysis can also help illuminate the potent values and beliefs underlying individualism and collectivism, values and beliefs that were supported by institutionalized traditions and practices. To this end, a small pastel; a modest, improvised print; and a photomontaged book cover are each compared with an oil painting by one of the emigration's most highly acclaimed modernist artists. The former works were authored by somewhat lesser known artists who were also involved in exiled German artists' groups. Comparison of paintings by Wassily Kandinsky, Max Beckmann, and Oskar Kokoschka with contemporary artworks by Otto Freundlich of the Kollektiv deutscher Künstler, Eugen Spiro of the Freier Künstlerbund, and John Heartfield of the Free German League of Culture focuses attention on the ways in which the exiles' collectivist or individualist aspirations were embodied in their artworks and also clarifies the political importance of such aspirations.

Celebration of Otto Freundlich's sixtieth birthday prompted Kandinsky to travel into Paris from Neuilly on July 10, 1938, for an "Hommage à Freundlich" hosted by Jeanne Bucher, the Paris gallerist who, even during the economically lean early 1930s, had exhibited and supported both artists.[2] Inasmuch as the photograph taken on that occasion (fig. 21) has been used to suggest a commonality between these two senior practitioners and theorists of abstract art from Germany, it is misleading.[3] While they surely felt some sense of camaraderie because of the pillorying their art was receiving in the ongoing "degenerate art" campaign and because of the French government's then-tightening regulation of immigrants,[4] their political positions toward Nazi Germany and their beliefs about the social role of the artist and the significance of their abstract art differed drastically. Letters by each from 1935–36 help elucidate their different interests:

> This time it is the fate of my countrymen, who have been driven from their homeland, which occasions me to write to you. Almost all German artists of worth have fled abroad.... There they live dispersed, and they lack the possibility to show the civilized world that there are German artists who detest this regime of horror and hatred which rules today in Germany. They have banded together into a group of antifascist artists who would like to show through a group exhibition in Paris that the spirit of culture and of art—even amid the difficult conditions of exile—still lives in them [*Freundlich to Othon Friesz, director, Salon des Tuileries*].[5]

The reasons I have not been in Germany for almost two years now have nothing to do with politics but only with art [*Kandinsky to Alexandre Kojève*].⁶

Freundlich, a German Jew who had lived in Paris since 1924, voiced the shared aims of a group of exiled artists seeking to cultivate public opposition to the German government, while Kandinsky sought to safeguard his once-successful German career by denying that his January 1934 departure from Germany was motivated by political (i.e., anti-Nazi) reasons. Christian Derouet has documented occasions when Kandinsky's self-proclaimed position of having "nothing to do with politics" veered toward fascination with and admiration for the new government in Berlin.⁷ While Freundlich was captivated by the revolutionary fervor that gripped the exiled German parties on the left, which in the fall of 1935 coalesced into the German Popular Front against Fascism, Kandinsky's affiliations were with Italian Fascist and futurist artists in Paris and Italy. In addition, Kandinsky favored several independent groups and magazines that supported abstract art, namely, Abstraction-Création, Cercle et carré, *Cahiers d'art, Verve, XXe siècle, Plastique, Axis,* and *Transition*.⁸ By contrast, Freundlich broke with the group Abstraction-Création to devote his energies solely to the development of his art, abstract art he deemed closely tied to the cause of the revolutionary proletariat.⁹ In the months following the formation of the German Popular Front, Freundlich's zeal found institutional expression in the Kollektiv deutscher Künstler (Collective of German artists). His reply to the Kollektiv's fall 1935 founding appeal for members, issued by communist press illustrator and painter Max Lingner and surrealist painter and stage designer Heinz Lohmar, quickly led to his chairmanship of the Kollektiv.

At a time when Kandinsky hoped to travel to Rome for an anticipated Fascist-sponsored exhibition of his art,¹⁰ Freundlich, on December 4, 1935, delivered the keynote speech for the first announced gathering of the Kollektiv deutscher Künstler in Paris. Entitled "German Art Yesterday, Today, and Tomorrow," Freundlich's speech affirmed his belief in the benefits of collective work and action. He contended that abstract art should play an integral role in the revolutionary goals of the Popular Front.¹¹ Having found little support for this view, he resigned the chair prior to March 1936,¹² yet the Kollektiv continued a program of discussion sessions centered upon the artwork and art historical presentations of its members. These meetings continued until early July, shortly after the French Popular Front election victory. Participants in the Kollektiv's lecture-discussion series included architectural critic Roger Ginsburger, painter Gert Wollheim, graphic artist Horst Strempel, and film director Slatan Dudow.¹³ The Kollektiv also issued a modest graphic portfolio simply entitled *Die Mappe* (The portfolio) with contributions by members Max Ernst, Hans (Jean) Kralik, Lingner, and Lohmar.¹⁴

The political differences indicated by Kandinsky's and Freundlich's affiliations with certain artists' groups raise the question of whether politics informed their paintings. Freundlich insisted that they did, while Kandinsky was less forthcoming. Comparison of Freundlich's *Composition* (1933–36; fig. 23) and Kandinsky's *Each for Himself,* painted in April 1934 (fig. 24), suggests some important differences. Freundlich's *Composition,* like numerous similar paintings of the 1930s, gave pictorial form to the aim he articulated for the Kollektiv deutscher Künstler: to advance "without one unit . . . living at the expense of another, or suppressing another."¹⁵ In this pastel, as in most other paintings of these years,

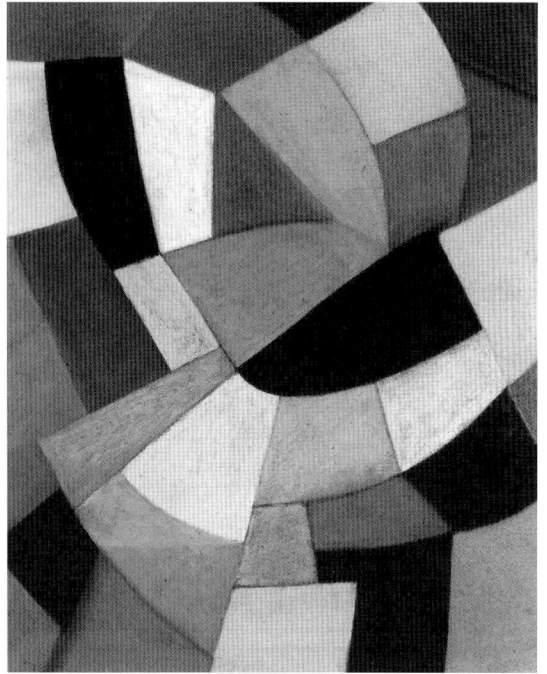
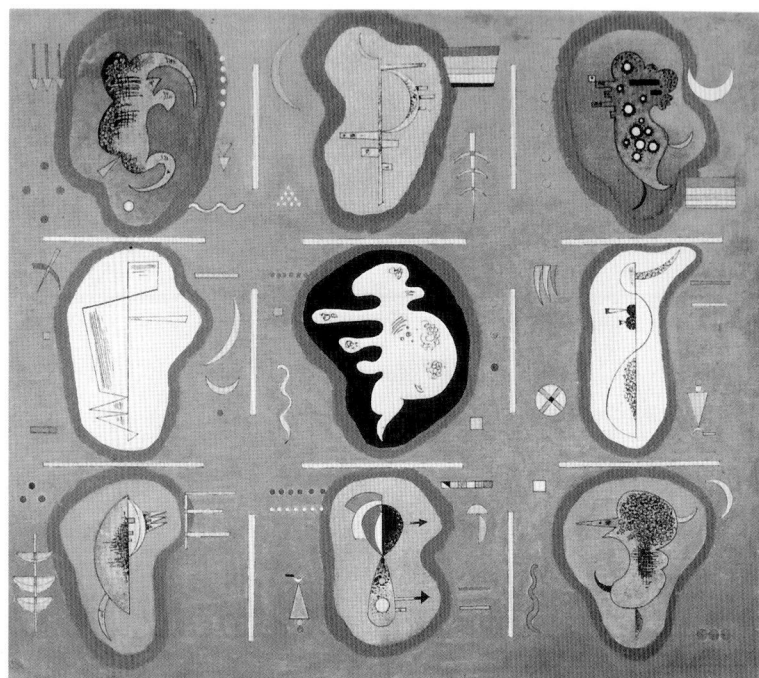

23
Otto Freundlich; *Composition*, 1933–36; pastel on paper; 23½ x 19⅝ in. (59.5 x 50 cm); collection of Franka Berndt, Paris.

24
Wassily Kandinsky; *Each for Himself*, 1934; oil and tempera on canvas; 23⅝ x 28 in. (60 x 71 cm); private collection.

he eradicated figure-ground relationships in order to suppress the dualism he regarded as inherent in easel painting. For Freundlich repudiation of spatial dualism was tantamount to a rejection of one of the a priori conditions for capitalism: the individual possession of things.[16] In comparison, in Kandinsky's *Each for Himself* nine uniquely colored and configured biomorphic cellular shapes float upon a green ground. These irregular forms are pigeonholed within a regular, open grid, each boxed apart from its neighbors. Thus, while *Composition* comprises multicolored units, each delineated by both curved and straight contours to establish the dynamic field that they, and only they, collectively produce, *Each for Himself* aligns individuated and animated shapes within regular columns and rows, ordered and regulated by a standardized, geometric grid. In light of the politicized group allegiances each artist maintained in 1934, one can hardly ignore the political and social implications of these abstract visualizations of individual units: Freundlich's produced their own operative ground of action, while Kandinsky's were subordinated to a pre-existing order.

In contrast to the Kollektiv deutscher Künstler's spirited revival of leftist Weimar Republic artists' collectives during the Popular Front, the Freier Künstlerbund (Free league of artists) was a larger, broader-based coalition of exiled artists founded in September 1937 as a response to *Entartete Kunst*. The group first called itself the Deutscher Künstlerbund, after the alliance of German artists' organizations founded in 1903, but by April 1938—in the wake of Germany's annexation of Austria—it had dropped *Deutscher* and added *Freier*, in part to avoid another "annexation" of its Austrian members.[17] The Künstlerbund benefited from the veteran leadership of Eugen Spiro, an impressionist painter of landscapes and portraits who had formerly chaired the Berlin Secession. Paul Westheim, the art critic, reporter, and former editor of *Das Kunstblatt* (1917–33), served as secretary. In Paris Westheim was art editor of the emigration's daily newspapers, the *Pariser Tageblatt* (1933–36) and the *Pariser Tageszeitung* (1936–40), and continued his prolific outpouring of art reporting and criticism.[18] The painters Victor Tischer and Gert Wollheim, art historian Sabine Spiro, and art critic Herta Wescher rounded out the Künstlerbund's organizing committee.[19] Although its membership represented diverse artistic as well as political orientations and affiliations, the Künstlerbund itself affirmed an "apolitical," independent position, even after joining the umbrella association for Paris-based German cultural organizations, the Deutsches Kulturkartell, in September 1938.[20]

The Künstlerbund functioned as a clearinghouse for artistic and cultural-political information for Paris-based and internationally dispersed exiled artists and as a conduit for information to artists still in Germany. Between autumn 1937 and autumn 1938 it directed its energies into realizing a counterexhibition to *Entartete Kunst*.[21] Although the planning was fraught with practical and political obstacles, *Freie deutsche Kunst* (Free German art) was eventually held in November 1938 at the Paris Maison de la Culture, a meeting hall of the Association des écrivains et artistes révolutionnaires (Association of revolutionary writers and artists; see fig. 25).[22] No obstacle proved greater than the New Burlington Galleries' *Exhibition of Twentieth Century German Art*, which opened in London in July 1938 (see fig. 5).[23] The London exhibition siphoned off Paris-based exile Hugo Simon's large collection of modern German art, which had allegedly been promised to the Künstlerbund.[24]

Not all artists believed that Künstlerbund membership served their best interests. Paul Klee in Switzerland and Josef Albers in North Carolina, for example, were among those who responded with encouraging words but declined invitations to join this artists' group in search of a public. Their decisions were motivated in part by concern about potential retribution against family members still in Germany.[25] Lily Steiner, an Austrian painter in Paris who exhibited frequently in various Paris salons between 1935 and 1938, explained her refusal clearly: "It has always been a principle of mine to join no artists' association; I have previously always rejected this and can consequently, as sorry as I am, this time also not give up my position."[26] This principled stand was presumably derived from the ultimately romantic belief in the sovereign, autonomous artist, hardened in the face of decades of experience with Central European artists' associations. Few were as plainspoken in their denials as Steiner, but others surely shared her socially and institutionally entrenched ideology of the independent artist-agent.

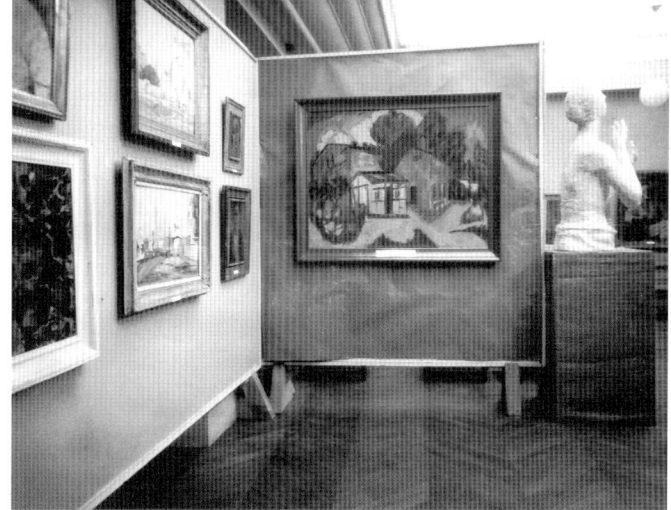

25
The exhibition *Freie deutsche Kunst*, Maison de la Culture, Paris, November 1938; photograph by Josef Breitenbach.

No German artist in exile upheld, even personified, this model more than Max Beckmann. Well before his July 19, 1937, escape from Berlin to Amsterdam, where his wife, Mathilde ("Quappi"), had family, Beckmann had established a highly successful career and reputation in Germany, holding a professorship at the Städelschule in Frankfurt. During the last years of the Weimar Republic he made several extended stays in Paris. In Amsterdam he continued to view Paris as the most important venue for his art, visiting the city in September 1937 and taking an apartment there from October 1938 to May or June 1939 with the aim of relocating.[27] But, following the German invasion of the Netherlands in May 1940, Beckmann was confined to occupied Amsterdam for the duration of the war.[28] Throughout the war he managed to keep producing paintings. Through his son Peter, a German military doctor and ambulance driver, some of his paintings were even conveyed to collectors inside Germany.[29]

A comparison of two portraits completed by August 1938, Eugen Spiro's *Thomas Mann at the Lecture Podium* (fig. 26) and Beckmann's *Self-Portrait with Horn* (fig. 27, cat. no. 10), highlights the artists' different approaches to both art and political engagement in the months preceding the Munich agreement. The Beckmann self-portrait was his second in oil since his escape to Amsterdam. Spiro published Mann's portrait in August in an edition of one hundred prints pulled from an incised wax-coated plate.[30] The Mann print was the first of a series of twelve inserted in the first hundred subscription copies of *Freie Kunst und Literatur* (1938–39). Edited by Westheim, this mimeographed monthly was founded by the Künstlerbund in August 1938 to report art and literary news of concern to the exiles. Representation of Mann underscored the Künstlerbund's solidarity with the German emigration's most distinguished author, who only recently had begun to speak out in the United States against the Nazi government. Mann is presented in public attire, standing over his notes at a lecture podium outfitted with a microphone, a device for amplification or radio transmission. By contrast, Beckmann represented his own likeness within the private space of his studio. Standing in the immediate foreground, the artist's broad frame is clothed in a boldly striped robe. His balding head is framed by a golden, horizontal frame. He looks into the mouthpiece of a horn suspended from his left hand. Whereas Mann is shown speaking, or poised to speak, through a microphone to audiences potentially mass and distant; Beckmann presents himself intent on monitoring, almost measuring, through an age-old horn, his position to the world beyond the studio. With right hand tense, he balances between collecting sonic or visual clues and the possibility of sending them out. But in contrast to the Künstlerbund's agenda and Mann's decisive turn from silence to anti-Nazi opposition, Beckmann's evaluations of the contemporary world, however vigilant or insightful, were never articulated as explicit condemnations of, or operative political alternatives to, Nazi Germany. What Beckmann took in of contemporary political life was instead reiterated in individualistic, cryptic paintings in which his hermetic interpretations of mythology and literature were often enmeshed.

Mann's turn to vocal opposition to Nazism coincided with the New Burlington Galleries' dropping him in spring 1938 from the preliminary list of honorary patrons for *Twentieth Century German Art*.[31] This and other changes—including the substitution of Beckmann for Oskar Kokoschka as the exhibition's visiting artist-speaker—marked the London exhibition committee's change from an anti-Nazi position to one in line with British appeasement policies toward Germany. In a letter drafted by Kokoschka, Spiro and the Künstlerbund protested the change, charging that the committee had capitulated to political pressures.[32]

If opportunity ever fell to Beckmann to lodge a political complaint against the Nazi government, it was his keynote speech for *Twentieth Century German Art*. Instead he offered a mystifying affirmation of the autonomy of the individual artist. Stating up front that he had "passed blindly many things which belong to real and political life,"[33] he came closest to criticizing the Nazi government toward the end of his speech: "The greatest danger which

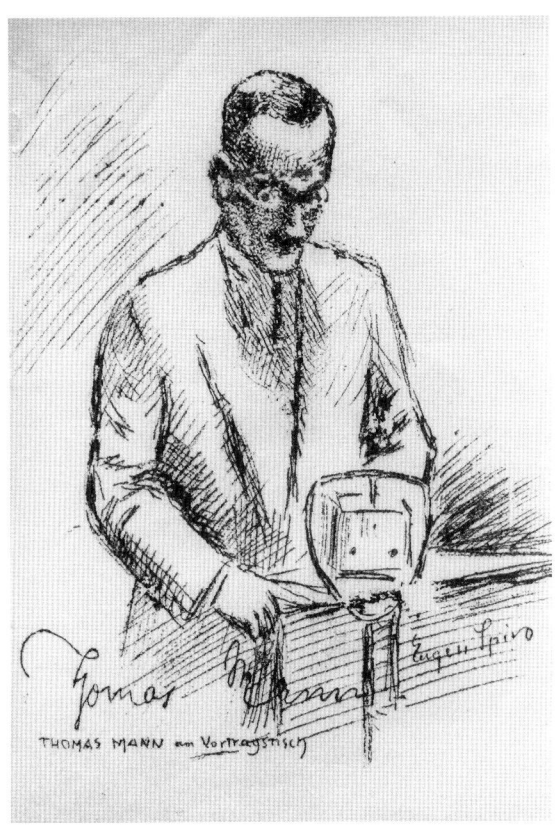 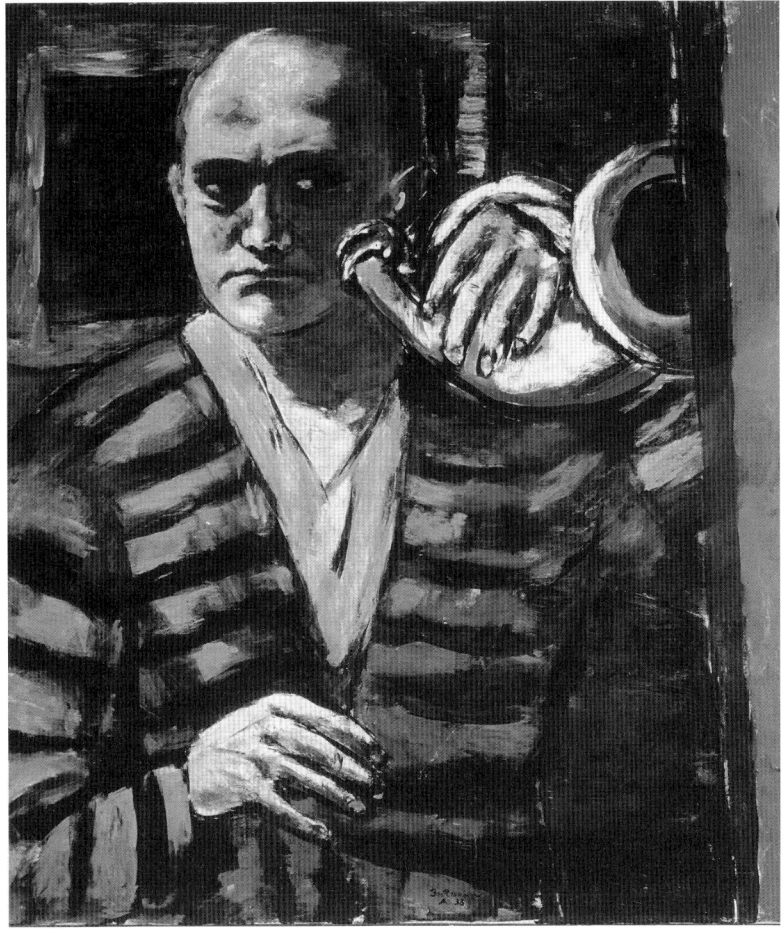

threatens mankind is collectivism. Everywhere attempts are being made to lower the happiness and the way of living of mankind to the level of termites. I am against these attempts with all the strength of my being."³⁴ While avoidance of clear political references was fully in character for Beckmann, his address was made at a time when outspoken statements against the German government were being strongly discouraged in England. The Foreign Office had even resorted to pressuring institutions of the British press to dampen criticisms of Germany.³⁵ Beckmann's audience would have had to strain hard to hear a denunciation of Nazi Germany in this general condemnation of collectivism, never stated more acerbically than above. But his condemnation of collectivism, together with his advocacy of artistic autonomy, may also be construed to have been directed against exiled artists' groups like the Paris Freier Künstlerbund. The previous year, in a letter to his Paris representative, Käthe von Porada, he disparaged the Freier Künstlerbund's exhibition plans and clarified his wish not to lend paintings to its exhibition, writing: "the...exhibition shall surely be overrun by a disagreeable throng of hangers-on, so that one finds oneself in bad company, which is very damaging."³⁶

As Beckmann obviously considered his own artistic endeavors superior to those of the members of the Künstlerbund, questions of art might not even have entered his mind had he learned of *Germany of Yesterday, Germany of Tomorrow,* the historical exhibition assembled by members of the Deutsches Kulturkartell for the 1939 New York World's Fair.³⁷ After the German government declined its right to represent Germany at the fair, these Paris-based exiles channeled their collective energies into constructing a set of thirty-three text

26
Eugen Spiro; *Thomas Mann at the Lecture Podium*, 1938; waxograph; 15¾ x 11¾ in. (40 x 30 cm); from *Freie Kunst und Literatur*, no. 1 (August–September 1938).

27
Max Beckmann, *Self-Portrait with Horn*, 1938 (cat. no. 10).

scenes from exile 49

and picture boards representing past German cultural, educational, and scientific achievements as well as the present government's destruction of those traditions. No fewer than thirty exiled artists and intellectuals—including Max Ernst, Alfred Kantorowicz, Paul Westheim, and Johannes Wüsten—researched and executed the initial design, conceived by Heinz Lohmar and Alfred Hermann.[38] But after timely prompting by the Bureau international des expositions in Paris, the Paris German Embassy filed an official protest against the exiles' enterprise with the bureau. The official objection required the directors of the fair to bar the exiles from representing a nation they did not govern and thereby prevented World's Fair visitors from ever viewing exiled Germany's elaborate construction of German cultural history.[39]

In contrast to the distance Beckmann and Kandinsky maintained toward German exiled artists' groups, Kokoschka took an active role in the London-based Free German League of Culture after his escape from Prague to England in October 1938.[40] From the league's inception in Hampstead in December 1938 until 1946, Kokoschka served as president of its visual arts division and contributed regularly to its many exhibitions, programs, and publications.[41] In Prague he had lent his name to—without joining—the exiled artists of the Oskar-Kokoschka-Bund (mostly leftist graphic artists of the anti-Nazi press) and had served as honorary president of Paris's Freier Künstlerbund, but his engagement with both of those groups paled in comparison to his involvement in the Free German League of Culture. Many of the other artists in the group had also spent the preceding years in Prague until they were forced into a second exile after the Germans marched into Czechoslovakia.[42] Their escape to England had been aided by the Artists' Refugee Committee, a joint effort of the Artists International Association (AIA), the New English Arts Club, and the Royal Academy. The leaders of this committee—Steven Bone, Roland Penrose, and Diana and Fred Uhlman—were among those who had responded to the urgent pleas of the Czech painter Josef Čapek and others to assist in the evacuation of the endangered members of the Oskar-Kokoschka-Bund.[43]

At its largest the Hampstead-based league comprised well over two hundred members. Its size and longevity owed much to the inclusion of British as well as German and Austrian members. There were sections for writers, thespians, musicians, and scholars as well as visual artists. The artists' section included Theo Balden, Siegfried Charoux, Georg Ehrlich, Paula Fischer, René Graetz, John Heartfield, Eugen Hoffmann, Erich Kahn, Oskar Kokoschka, Kurt Lade, Samson Schames, Fred Uhlman, Heinz Worner, and Johannes and Dorothea Wüsten.[44] Their aims included the preservation and advancement of free German culture, correction of the distortions of German culture propagated by the Nazis, and the development of cultural relations with the British.[45] Over the course of the war league artists participated in numerous exhibitions, including *Camp Art in Canada* (1941), the documentary exhibition *Allies inside Germany* (1942), and *For Liberty* (1943).[46]

Upon the outbreak of war the British government classified most German and Austrian refugees as "friendly enemy aliens." By June 1940, however, it initiated mass internments of German and Austrian refugees in British camps and deported many to Canada and Australia. Kurt Schwitters, for example, was interned in the large camp on the Isle of Man.[47] Although

Kokoschka's recently acquired Czech citizenship spared him internment, upon the declaration of war he joined voices with other league executive committee members to underscore to the British public that they were victims of Nazi barbarism and stood with the British on the side of "freedom, culture, and democracy."[48]

Kokoschka's involvement in the league brought him into direct social and working relationships with many leftist artists of the sort he had previously kept some distance from during the Weimar Republic and in Prague, including photomontage artist Heartfield.[49] He also began reckoning with the wartime political situation in essays, speeches, oil paintings, and even a poster for mass distribution.[50] He persistently appealed for an international peace to be secured on the basis of his comprehensive educational philosophy, which he believed could ultimately reform the cognitive bases of international decision making. Many of his views were adapted from writings of the sixteenth-century Moravian pedagogue Johann Amos Comenius, from which he drew his convictions about the importance of educating youth through the various senses.[51]

Distinctive and unprecedented in Kokoschka's painted oeuvre is the series of oil paintings he executed between 1940 and 1943, in which he transposed—however allegorically—pressing contemporary political events onto his canvases (see figs. 28, 79–81, 83, cat. nos. 84–86). By thematizing these events in oil paintings, he undermined his image as the defender of timeless artistic traditions, in particular easel painting, regarded by many in the league as bourgeois. He had become identified with this position because of his notorious 1920 exchange with Heartfield and George Grosz, a debate triggered by an incident in which a Rubens painting in Dresden's Zwinger Gallery was grazed by a stray bullet from street fighting between the Reichswehr and workers. Heartfield and Grosz branded Kokoschka the "Art Scab" (*Der Kunstlump*) and contested his defense of the beauty and spirit of "masterpieces" like the Rubens oil. They took particular offense at his notion of artworks as the "most sacred possessions" (*heiligsten Güter*) of the German people and his implication that the eternal values associated with art were of greater importance than the topical political concerns of contemporary Germans.[52] Thus, Kokoschka's turn to painting contemporary political events in oil begs explanation. Partly it can be seen to have obtained from his league activities and his association with Heartfield and other leftist artists and intellectuals, including Marxist art historian Francis Klingender.

As Robert Radford and Richard Calvocoressi have pointed out, Kokoschka's multi-figure political paintings were also informed by his newfound familiarity with the British caricature traditions of William Hogarth and James Gillray,[53] which facilitated address to British viewers literate in those traditions. He also knew Klingender's writings on caricature and the exhibition he organized in summer 1943 for the AIA, *Hogarth and English Caricature*.[54] From Klingender, Kokoschka would have been exposed to a view that placed caricature on an equal footing with the fine art tradition of oil painting. This view stood in contrast to mainstream British media-supported views, which tended to nudge caricature into the realm of propaganda and elevate the fine arts into the orbit of ideal, eternal values.[55] In that context Kokoschka's political paintings confounded the efforts of major British media and cultural institutions to keep high art on the side of the democratic powers while disparaging the politically directed art of Germany, Italy, and the Soviet Union as mere propaganda.

If Kokoschka's political paintings are responsive to wartime distinctions between art and propaganda, what insights might be disclosed by comparing his *The Red Egg* (fig. 28) with Heartfield's book cover *Freedom Calling: The Story of the Secret German Radio* (fig. 29, cat. no. 60), which represents counterpropaganda in action? In this photomontage Heartfield casts himself in the role of the anti-Nazi radio technician, who operates the dials of a transmitter, sending "underground" radio signals in arcing waves across Germany. A cringing Hitler presses his fingers to his temples in pain, tormented by the three lightning bolts that deliver the voices of freedom that he would prefer the German people not hear. In contrast to the first-person role projected by Heartfield, Kokoschka assumes a removed, third-person relationship to an event. By setting the foreground figures in the Moldau River Valley, complete with Charles Bridge and the castle in the background, Kokoschka again recalls Prague, as in his 1938 *Prague, Nostalgia* (fig. 30). In this recollected setting, he stages the dismemberment of Czechoslovakia in the Munich agreement with caricatures of Hitler, Mussolini, Chamberlain, and Daladier. They are positioned around a table, upon which is a plate holding a red egg. Four forks extend from each of the leaders to the egg, from which the yolk and white have run. Kokoschka lays blame on the four powers, represented by Hitler in a fool's cap, Mussolini with a stupendous face, the French cat under the table, and the British lion resting comfortably upon the signed documents of the Munich agreement, which, in the name of peace, led directly to the dismemberment of Kokoschka's recent

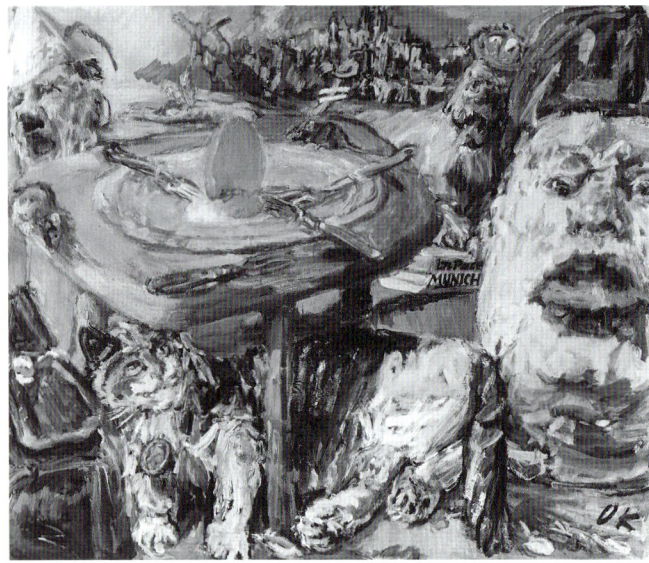

28
Oskar Kokoschka; *The Red Egg*, 1940–41; oil on canvas; 24 x 30 in. (61 x 76 cm); Národní Galerie, Prague.

29
John Heartfield, *Freedom Calling: The Story of the Secret German Radio*, 1939 (cat. no. 60).

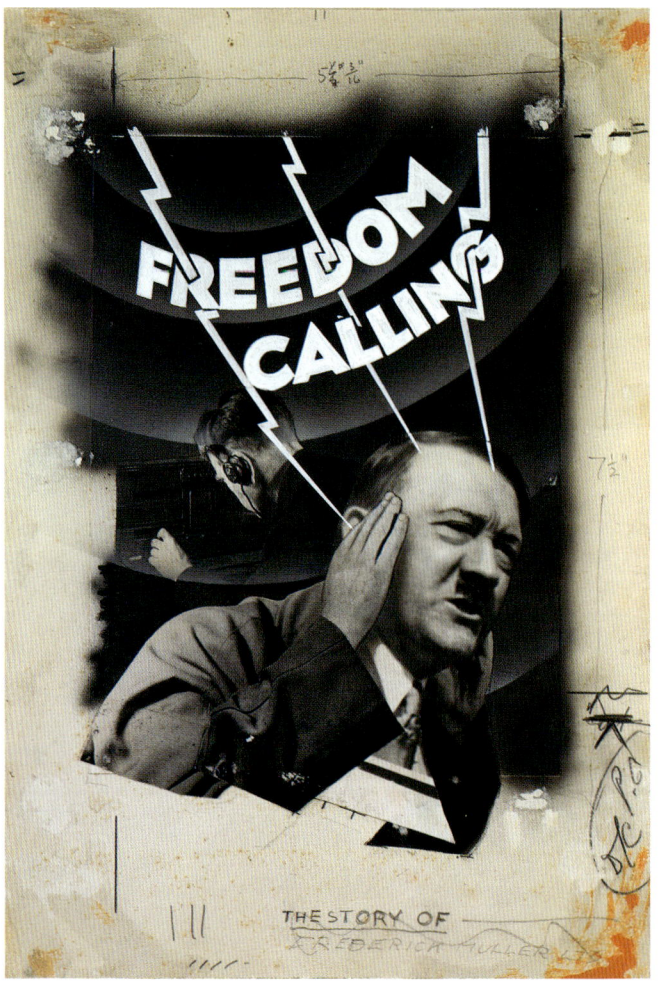

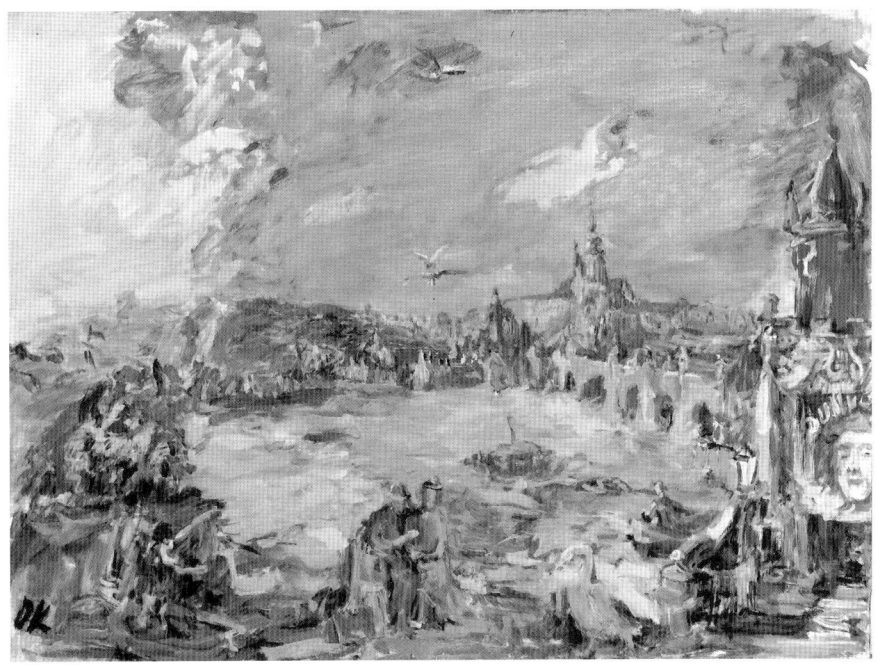

30
Oskar Kokoschka; *Prague, Nostalgia*, 1938; oil on canvas; 22 x 30 in. (56 x 76 cm); private collection, on loan to the Scottish National Gallery of Modern Art, Edinburgh.

home, Czechoslovakia. With a knife in its back, a plucked chicken flies the coop, just like the Czech president and the German exiles now in London.[56]

As much as these two works by Heartfield and Kokoschka differ, especially in terms of medium and iconographic complexity, they each reveal much about the authorial adaptation and symbolic resistance of two recent Central European arrivals to England. Heartfield projected himself into the spatial imaginary of photomontage to identify nostalgically with the underground radio operator, an anti-Nazi propaganda occupation that in England still rivaled in its political efficacy his own recent and trenchant work in Prague as the anti-Nazi photomonteur nonpareil. In *The Red Egg* Kokoschka too expressed nostalgia for Prague, but his adaptation of his oil painting to the language of British caricature also demonstrates his ability to use a new medium to remind the English of their culpability in the diplomatic catastrophe that had occasioned the arrival of thousands of Central European refugees among them.

Consideration of the relationships between the six artists discussed here and the three artists' groups founded in Paris and London by German exiles can tell us much about the allure of both collective and individual endeavor for exiled artists. In general these artists remained on the course that they had embarked upon before their exile, but in the face of a fascist and expansionist Germany that increasingly threatened the countries where they had found asylum, the political implications of the choice between individual and collective endeavor became more urgent. Nevertheless, Beckmann and Kandinsky remained committed to artistic practices that perpetuated the German romantic and bourgeois ideals of individual self-formation. Their continued devotion to art making as a solitary, purely aesthetic activity nearly blinded them at times to the proximity of their own views to the aestheticized politics and depoliticized art of German National Socialism or Italian Fascism, especially as they sought to distance themselves from the overtly politicized cultural activities of German exile groups.

By contrast, both Freundlich and Spiro worked to reimplement possibilities for collective engagement through the formation of artists' groups, groups quite different from each other but similar to ones in which each had been active during the Weimar Republic. Whether due to the deterioration of his health or the loss of the shared German linguistic environment upon which his earlier work depended so heavily, the photomontages that Heartfield produced in London offered little more than a weak reminder of the prolific and politically effective work he had published in the illustrated press in Prague and Berlin prior to October 1938. Of the six artists discussed here, Kokoschka is the only one for whom exile entailed a break with his earlier approach, as what had been merely passive support of exiled artists' groups gave way to activist involvement. In London he also departed from his previous avoidance of politically charged subjects in an unprecedented series of major oil paintings that addressed topical political concerns.

The issues surrounding the choice between individual and collective endeavor were very familiar to those exiles who had worked as artists during the Weimar Republic. During those years such decisions had been recognized as forming the very crux of one's approach to artistic practice. In exile—upon the loss of a shared democratic public sphere (which the Weimar Republic had, however precariously, still enabled), together with the removal of a German government recognized as legitimate by most exiled Germans—artists' choices simply became more consequential politically. Whether it was attachment to traditional art forms or the embrace of mass cultural media, identification with a romantic, bourgeois conception of the self-sufficient, autonomous artist or the partial submersion of the self within collective activity, approaches to artistic production and identity became urgent matters in exile. Yet even when conscious of a responsibility to uphold, represent, or redefine German art in order to counter the representations and claims of the National Socialist government and its adherents, artists exiled from Germany seldom set aside their fundamental disagreements when it came to the organization of artists or the particular ways in which art could be related to politics—or not.

Notes

1 See René Huyghe, ed., *L'Allemagne et l'Europe centrale* (Paris: Alcan, 1935); *Exhibition of Twentieth Century German Art*, exh. cat. (London: New Burlington Galleries, 1938); Peter Thoene [Oto Bihalji-Merin], *Modern German Art*, trans. Charles Fullmann, introduction by Herbert Read (Harmondsworth, England: Penguin, 1938); Hugo Rellstab, "Deutsche und österreichische Künstler in Paris," *Die Zukunft* 2 (26 May 1939): 6. Secondary literature includes Cordula Frowein, "The Exhibition of 20th Century German Art in London 1938—eine Antwort auf die Ausstellung 'Entartete Kunst' in München 1937," in *Exilforschung: Ein internationales Jahrbuch* 2 (1984): 212–37; Stephan Lackner and Helene Adkins, "Exhibition of 20th Century German Art," and Inka Graeve, "Freie deutsche Kunst" and "Rekonstruktion der Ausstellung 'Freie deutsche Kunst' Paris 1938," in *Stationen der Moderne: Die bedeutenden Kunstausstellungen des 20. Jahrhunderts in Deutschland*, exh. cat. (Berlin: Berlinische Galerie, 1988), 314–37, 338–49.

2 Christian Derouet, "Kandinsky in Paris: 1934–1944," trans. Eleanor Levieux, in *Kandinsky in Paris, 1934–1944*, exh. cat. (New York: Solomon R. Guggenheim Museum, 1985), 20.

3 Ibid., 21, fig. 5.

4 On May 2, 1938, the recently elected Daladier government passed a decree that made it more difficult for foreigners to remain legally in France.

5 Freundlich to Othon Friesz, 26 February 1936; reprinted in Uli Bohnen, ed., *Otto Freundlich Schriften: Ein Wegbereiter der gegenstandslosen Kunst* (Cologne: DuMont Buchverlag, 1982), 203.

6 Undated letter [summer 1935] from Kandinsky to Kojève, in Derouet, "Kandinsky in Paris," 20 n. 30.

7 Ibid., 18–21.

8 Ibid., 49–51, 56–57 n. 182.

9 Freundlich to Georges Vantongerloo, November 1934 (Archives et Donation Otto Freundlich, Pontoise, Correspondence with Persons), in Bohnen, ed., *Otto Freundlich Schriften*, 195.

10 Kandinsky to Will Grohmann, 2 December 1935 (Archiv Will Grohmann, Staatsgalerie Stuttgart); cited in Derouet, "Kandinsky in Paris," 50–51 n. 137.

11 *Pariser Tageblatt*, 1 December 1935, 5; and "Bekenntnisse eines revolutionären Malers," November 1935. Dated November 1935 by O.F., and annotated by "J.K.K." (Johanna Klosnick-Kloss). A copy of the manuscript is held in the Archives et Donation Otto Freundlich, Pontoise. A highly edited version appears in Bohnen, *Otto Freundlich Schriften*, 197–202. For a discussion of the textual evidence linking this manuscript to the speech, see the author's "Modern German Art and Its Public in Prague, Paris, and London, 1933–1940" (Ph.D. diss., Northwestern University, 1992), 131–34.

12 Freundlich to M. and Ita Schmidt, 22 February 1936 (Archives et Donation Otto Freundlich, Pontoise, Correspondence with Persons).

13 These meetings were announced in the *Pariser Tageblatt / Tageszeitung* between December 1935 and July 1936.

14 Tanja Frank, "Max Lingner und die deutschen Künstlergruppen im Pariser Exil," in *Max Lingner, 1888–1959: Gemälde, Zeichnungen, Pressegraphik* (Berlin: Nationalgalerie und der Akademie der Künste der DDR, 1988), 29–32.

15 "Bekenntnisse eines revolutionären Malers," 11; and Freundlich to M. and Ita Schmidt (see note 12 above).

16 "Bekenntnisse eines revolutionären Malers," 11–12, 15.

17 Bundesarchiv, Potsdam, Nachlaß Eugen Spiro, Akte 21, Bl. 29rs. On the Paris artists' groups, see Hélène Roussel, "Die emigrierten deutschen Künstler in Frankreich und der Freie Künstlerbund," in *Exilforschung: Ein internationales Jahrbuch* 2 (1984): 173–211.

18 An annotated selection of Westheim's art criticism and reporting from Paris has been collected in Tanja Frank, ed., *Paul Westheim: Kunstkritik aus dem Exil* (Hanau: Müller und Kiepenheuer, 1985).

19 Bundesarchiv, Potsdam, Nachlaß Spiro, Akte 21, Bl. 51; cited in Roussel, "Die emigrierten deutschen Künstler," 189 n. 105.

20 Bundesarchiv, Potsdam, Nachlaß Spiro, Akte 21, Bl. 56; also cited in ibid., 197, 207 n. 148.

21 See the extensive documentation at the Bundesarchiv, Potsdam, Nachlaß Spiro, Akte 21.

22 Graeve, "Freie deutsche Kunst," and "Rekonstruktion der Ausstellung," 314–37, 338–49.

23 Heidrun Schröder-Kehler, "Deutsche Künstler im französischen Exil," in *Widerstand statt Anpassung: Deutsche Kunst im Widerstand gegen den Faschismus, 1933–1945* (Karlsruhe: Badischer Kunstverein; Berlin: Elefanten, 1980), 127–53; Frowein, "The Exhibition of 20th Century German Art"; Roussel, "Die emigrierten deutschen Künstler," 188–89; Cordula Frowein, "Ausstellungsaktivitäten der Exilkünstler," in *Kunst im Exil in Großbritannien, 1933–1945*, exh. cat. (Berlin: Neue Gesellschaft für bildende Kunst, Orangerie des Schlosses Charlottenburg, 1986), 35–48; Lackner and Adkins, "Exhibition of 20th Century German Art," 314–37, 338–49; Holz, "Modern German Art and Its Public," 208–41; and Monica Bohm-Duchen, "The Welcome of Strangers: British Responses to German Art and Artists in the 1930s and 1940s," *AICARC Bulletin*, no. 29–30 (1991): 12–15.

24 Bundesarchiv, Potsdam, Nachlaß Spiro, Akte 21, Bl. 17–18.

25 Klee to Westheim (draft), 25 May 1938 (Felix Klee Archive, Bern); cited in Otto Karl Werckmeister, "Paul Klee in Exile," *Paul Klee in Exile, 1933–1940* (Himeji: City Museum of Art, 1985), 35, 42 n. 52; Klee to Frau Freundlich (copy), May 1938 (Archives et Donation Otto Freundlich, Pontoise); Josef Albers to Herta Wescher, 1 July 1938 (Bundesarchiv, Potsdam, Nachlaß Spiro, Akte 3, Bl. 64).

26 Steiner to Westheim, 20 April 1938 (Bundesarchiv, Potsdam, Nachlaß Spiro, Akte 7, Bl. 6).

27 Peter Rautmann, "Max Beckmann in Paris 1937 bis 1939: Kunst und Gewalt am Vorabend des Zweiten Weltkriegs," *Exilforschung: Ein internationales Jahrbuch* 10 (1992): 12–14.

28 Werner Haftmann, *Banned and Persecuted: Dictatorship of Art under Hitler*, trans. Eileen Martin (Cologne: DuMont, 1986), 47–64.

29 Carla Schulz-Hoffmann and Judith C. Weiss, eds., *Max Beckmann Retrospective*, exh. cat. (Saint Louis: Saint Louis Art Museum; Munich: Prestel Verlag, 1984), 463; see also Barbara C. Buenger's essay on Beckmann in this catalogue.

30 Westheim called this simple intaglio process waxography (*Wachsographie*); Westheim to Spiro, 2 August 1938 (Bundesarchiv, Potsdam, Nachlaß Spiro, Akte 3, Bl. 47).

31 Wollheim and Spiro to Herbert Read, 11 May 1938 (Bundesarchiv, Potsdam, Nachlaß Spiro, Akte 3, Bl. 39).

32 Undated letter of Kokoschka, and redrafted version of Paris FKb. (Bundesarchiv, Potsdam, Nachlaß Spiro, Akte 4, Bl. 105, 105rs, 106).

33 Max Beckmann, "On My Painting," in *Modern Artists on Art*, ed. Robert L. Herbert (Englewood Cliffs, N.J.: Prentice-Hall, 1964), 131.

34 Ibid., 135.

35 Anthony Adamthwaite, "The British Government and the Media, 1937–1938," *Journal of Contemporary History*, no. 18 (1983): 281–97.

36 Beckmann to Käthe von Porada, 30 September 1937 (Archivalien, Deutsches Exilarchiv, 1933–45, Deutsche Bibliothek, Frankfurt a. M.); cited with the official written permission of the Deutsche Bibliothek, Deutsches Exilarchiv 1933–1945.

37 Roussel, "Die emigrierten deutschen Künstler," 199–201; and Holz, "Modern German Art and Its Public," 288–93.

38 Josef Breitenbach Archive, Center for Creative Photography, University of Arizona, Tucson, AG90: 29/38, "L'Exposition 'L'Allemagne telle qu'elle etait hier, telle qu'elle sera demain,'" 1–2.

39 BIE to von Campe, 18 January 1939 and 16 February 1939; German Foreign Office (Berlin) to German Embassy (Paris), 25 February 1939 (Archiv des Auswärtigen Amts, Bonn, Kulturabteilung, Folder: "Botschaft Paris: Internationale Ausstellung New York 1939," unpaginated); and "Wie steht es mit der Amerika-Ausstellung?" *Freie Kunst und Literatur*, no. 5 [March 1939]: unpaginated; and "Deutschland von gestern—Deutschland von morgen," *Freie Kunst und Literatur* [no. 6, April or May 1939]: 5.

40 Ulla Hahn, "Der Freie deutsche Kulturbund in Großbritannien: Eine Skizze seiner Geschichte," in *Antifaschistische Literatur: Programme, Autoren, Werke*, ed. Lutz Winckler, vol. 2 (Kronberg: Scriptor-Verlag, 1977), 131–95; and Ludwig Hoffmann, ed., *Exil in der Tschechoslowakei, in Großbritannien, Skandinavien und Palästina*, vol. 5 of *Kunst und Literatur im antifaschistischen Exil, 1933–1945* (Leipzig: Verlag Philipp Reclam Jun., 1980), 211–302.

41 Secondary literature on Kokoschka in exile in London is extensive; recent contributions include Richard Calvocoressi, "Introduction," in *Oskar Kokoschka, 1886–1980*, exh. cat. (New York: Solomon R. Guggenheim Museum, 1986), 19–21; Robert Radford, "Kokoschka's Political Allegories," *Art Monthly*, no. 97 (June 1986): 3–6; idem, *Art for a Purpose: The Artists' International Association, 1933–1953* (Winchester, Hampshire: Winchester School of Art Press, 1987): 140–47; Diether Schmidt, "Partisan Oskar Kokoschka," in *Kunst im Exil*, 189–94; Johann Holzner, "Ästhetik als Kundgebung gegen die Drosselung der Humanität: Über Oskar Kokoschka," in *Exil: Literatur und die Künste nach 1933*, ed. Alexander Stephan (Bonn: Bouvier, 1990), 40–47; *Drehscheibe Prag: Deutsche Emigranten / Staging Point Prague: German Exiles, 1933–1939* (Munich: Adalbert Stifter Verein, 1989), esp. 131–39, 226–33; and, most recently, Jutta Hülsewig-Johnen, ed., *Oskar Kokoschka: Emigrantenleben Prag und London 1934–1953* (Bielefeld: Kunsthalle Bielefeld and Kerber Verlag, 1994).

42 Keith Holz, "Responses from Bohemia to Degenerate Art, 1937–1938," *Exilforschung: Ein internationales Jahrbuch* 10 (1992): 30–49.

43 Ibid., 43–44, 49 nn. 70–76.

44 Hoffmann, *Exil in der Tschechoslowakei*, 249–52.

45 FGLC Information Sheet; reproduced in Freya Mülhaupt, "Der Lauf der Dinge: Exil und Rückkehr kommunistischer Künstler," in *Kunst im Exil*, 76.

46 Frowein, "Ausstellungsaktivitäten der Exilkünstler," 38–48.

47 Freimut Schwarz, "Kulturarbeit in den englischen Internierungscamps," in *Kunst im Exil*, 283–88.

48 *Times* (London), 5 September 1939.

49 On Heartfield in Prague, see Michael Kresja, "NS-Reaktionen auf Heartfields Arbeit, 1933–1939," in *John Heartfield* (Berlin: Akademie der Künste, 1991), 368–78.

50 Calvocoressi, "Introduction," 19–21, 25 n. 46.

51 E.g., Oskar Kokoschka, "Education To-Morrow," in *Inside Nazi Germany* 1 (November 1939): 14.

52 Beth Lewis, *George Grosz: Art and Politics in the Weimar Period* (Princeton: Princeton University Press, 1971), 93–95.

53 Calvocoressi, "Introduction," 31; Radford, "Kokoschka's Political Allegories," 4, 6; idem, *Art for a Purpose*, 143–46.

54 Calvocoressi, "Introduction," 21; Radford, *Art for a Purpose*, 146.

55 E. H. Gombrich, "Art and Propaganda," *Listener*, 7 December 1939, 1118–20; and Gonda Gore (pseud.), "Art and Propaganda in Nazi Germany," *Studio*, no. 119 (May 1940): 154–59.

56 This reading follows the more extensive iconographical reading by Radford in "Kokoschka's Political Allegories."

31
Max Beckmann, *Self-Portrait with Horn*, 1938 (cat. no. 10).

antifascism or autonomous art?

BARBARA COPELAND BUENGER

max beckmann

wassily kandinsky

john heartfield

kurt schwitters

KEITH HOLZ   **oskar kokoschka**

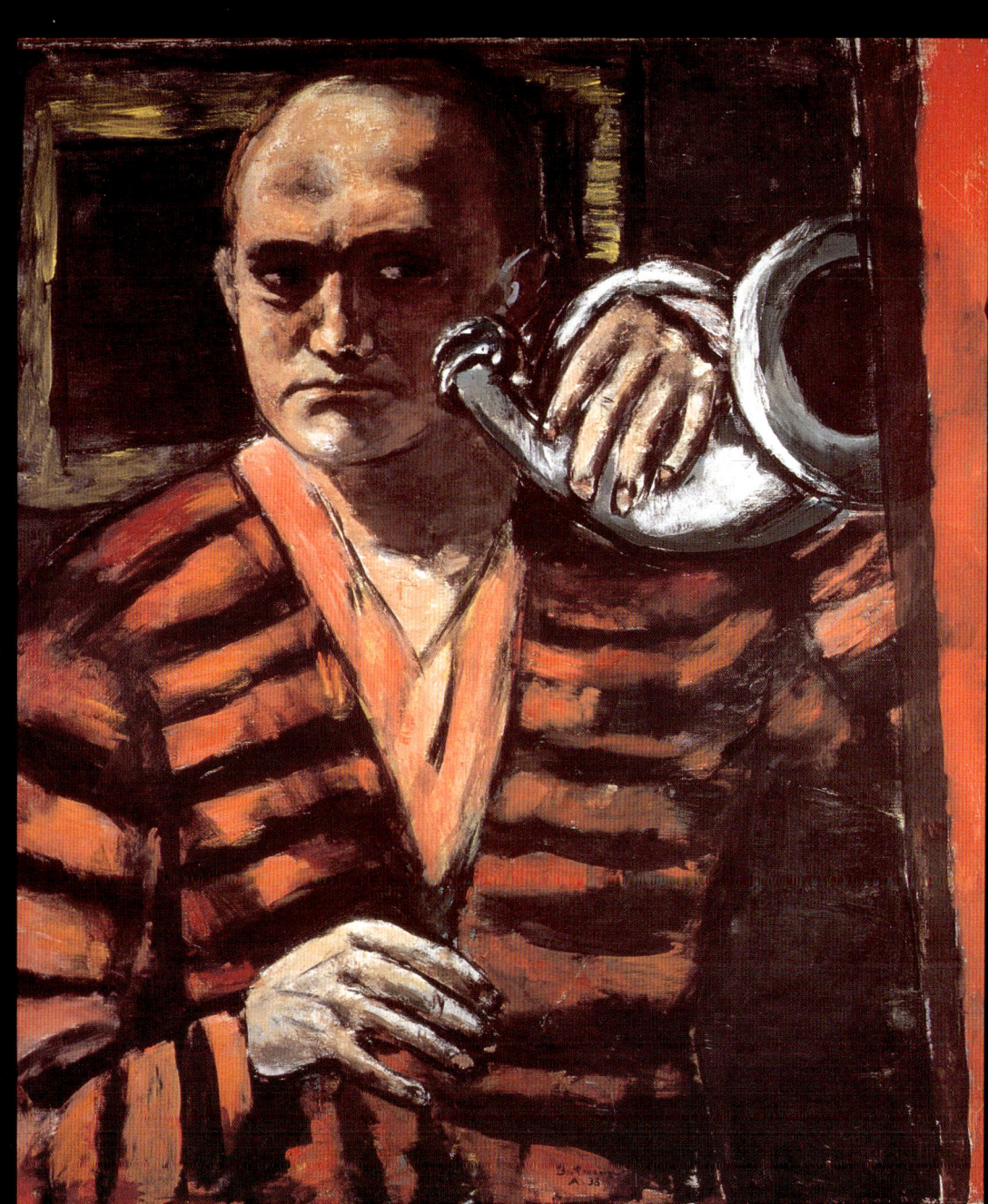

max beckmann in paris, amsterdam, and the united states, 1937–50

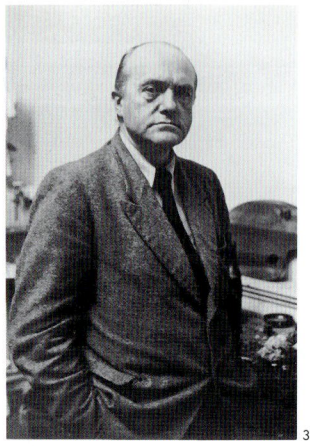

1884	born in Leipzig, Germany
1937	immigrates to the Netherlands (Amsterdam)
1947	immigrates to the U.S. (St. Louis)
1950	dies in New York

After the Nazis fired him from his Frankfurt teaching position in May 1933, Max Beckmann and his wife, Mathilde ("Quappi"), moved to Berlin, hoping to escape Nazi notice in the much larger city. Over the next four years he discussed his options with such persons as the architect Ludwig Mies van der Rohe; the director of the Nationalgalerie, Eberhard Hanfstaengl; and the dealer Karl Buchholz. Beckmann's *The Architect (Two Men)* (1944, fig. 33, cat. no. 12), painted from a photo of Mies with some Bauhaus students,[1] recalls those last years in a Germany in which both had flourished but were also forced to reconsider their positions.

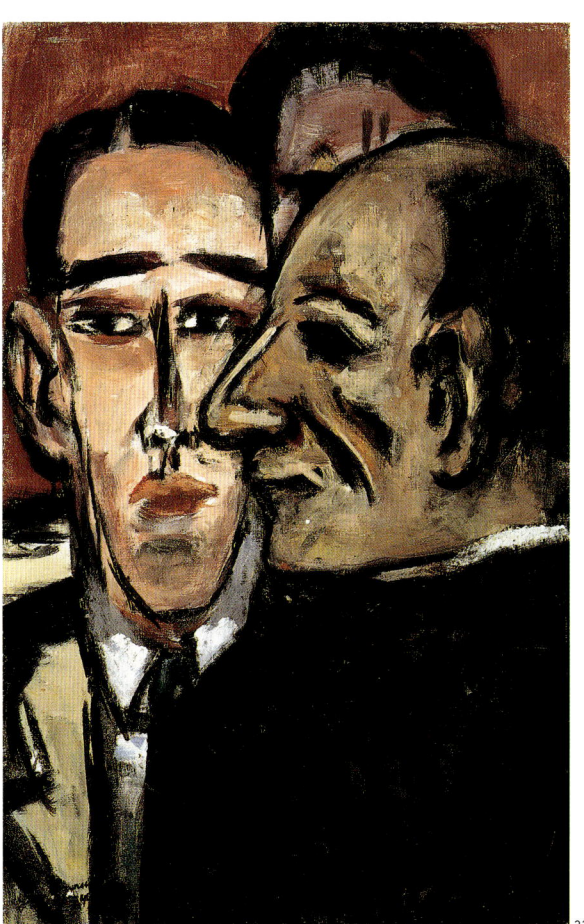

Beckmann felt deeply bound to Germany and had grave doubts about his ability to establish himself elsewhere. The Beckmanns also had many conservative friends—some strongly against, some supporters or members of, the National Socialist party—who worked both within and in spite of the regime to achieve their goals. Lilly von Schnitzler and her I. G. Farben executive husband, Georg von Schnitzler, for instance, held salons for Nazi leaders in their apartment filled with Beckmann's paintings;[2] Buchholz was both a Nazi and a member of the Reichskammer der bildenden Künste, the Nazi-controlled arts organization;[3] and Erhard Göpel, one of Beckmann's chief supporters and friends in the Netherlands, was centrally involved in the acquisition and confiscation of art in Belgium, Holland, and France for Hitler's planned museum in Linz.[4]

The Beckmanns left Germany for Amsterdam on July 19, 1937, the day following the opening of the *Entartete Kunst* (Degenerate art) exhibition in Munich. Beckmann made a short visit to Paris in September 1937, and the couple spent the winter of 1938–39 there, obtaining identity cards that would allow them to stay permanently. Caught in the Netherlands at the outbreak of the war, they remained in Amsterdam for its duration.

In July 1938 Beckmann traveled to London for the opening of the New Burlington Galleries' *Exhibition of Twentieth Century German Art,* where he delivered a lecture entitled "On My Painting," in which he stated that he had never been politically active and stressed the necessity of art's transcendence even in times of turmoil. He also criticized

32
Max Beckmann, Amsterdam, 1938.

33
Max Beckmann, *The Architect (Two Men)*, 1944 (cat. no. 12).

34
Max Beckmann, *Birth*, 1937 (cat. no. 7).

35
Max Beckmann, *Death*, 1938 (cat. no. 9).

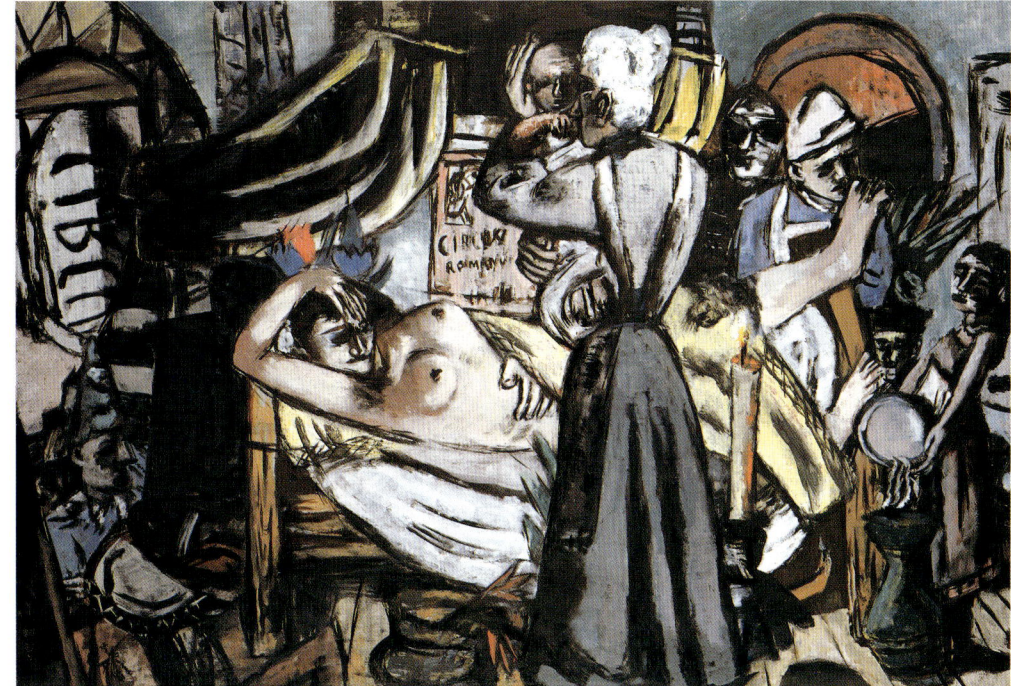

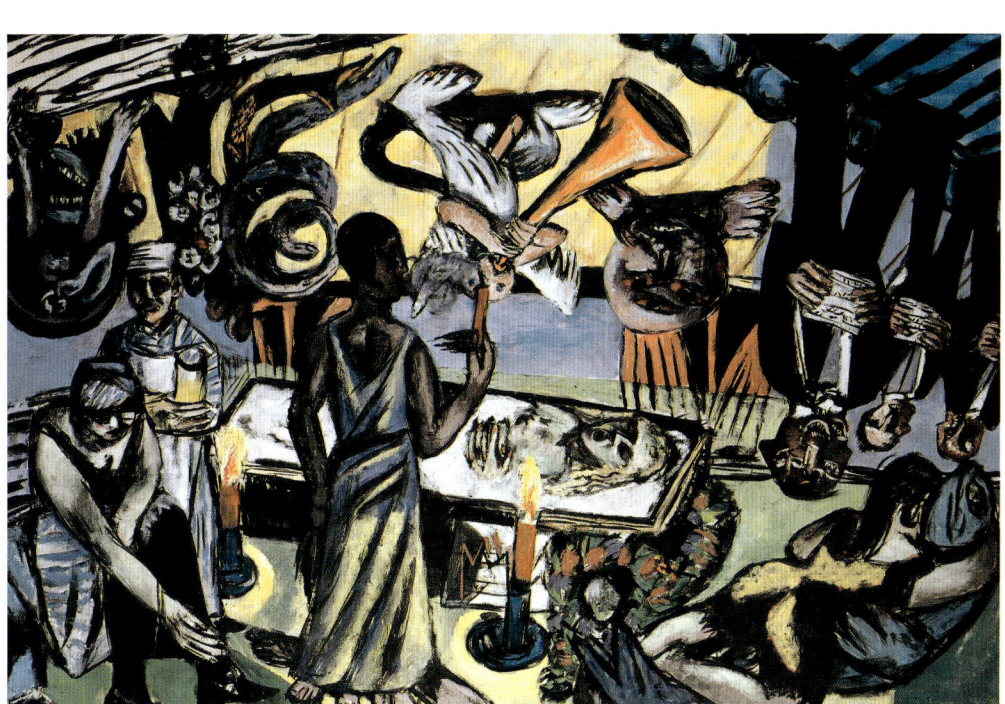

politicized artists who made only "journalistic" art.[5] Though one of his works appeared in the November 1938 show of the antifascist Freier Künstlerbund (Free league of artists) in Paris, he otherwise had little to do with the group.

Beckmann produced three major figural works—the almost identically sized *Birth* (1937; fig. 34, cat. no. 7), *Death* (1938; fig. 35, cat. no. 9), and *Birds' Hell* (1938; fig. 36, cat. no. 8)—in his first eighteen months of exile in Amsterdam and Paris. Like many of the figural works of his exile, they emphasize the contradictions between his desire for an autonomous, transcendent art and the realities of the day. *Birth* and its slightly later counterpart, *Death*, can be read as representations of the symbolic birth and death of the artist or spirit in exile; both include a wide range of imagery that, like his 1938 London talk, speak to the richness and tenacity of life and the imagination even in troubled times. *Birth* shows the fertile, seductive, and mysterious world surrounding a birth

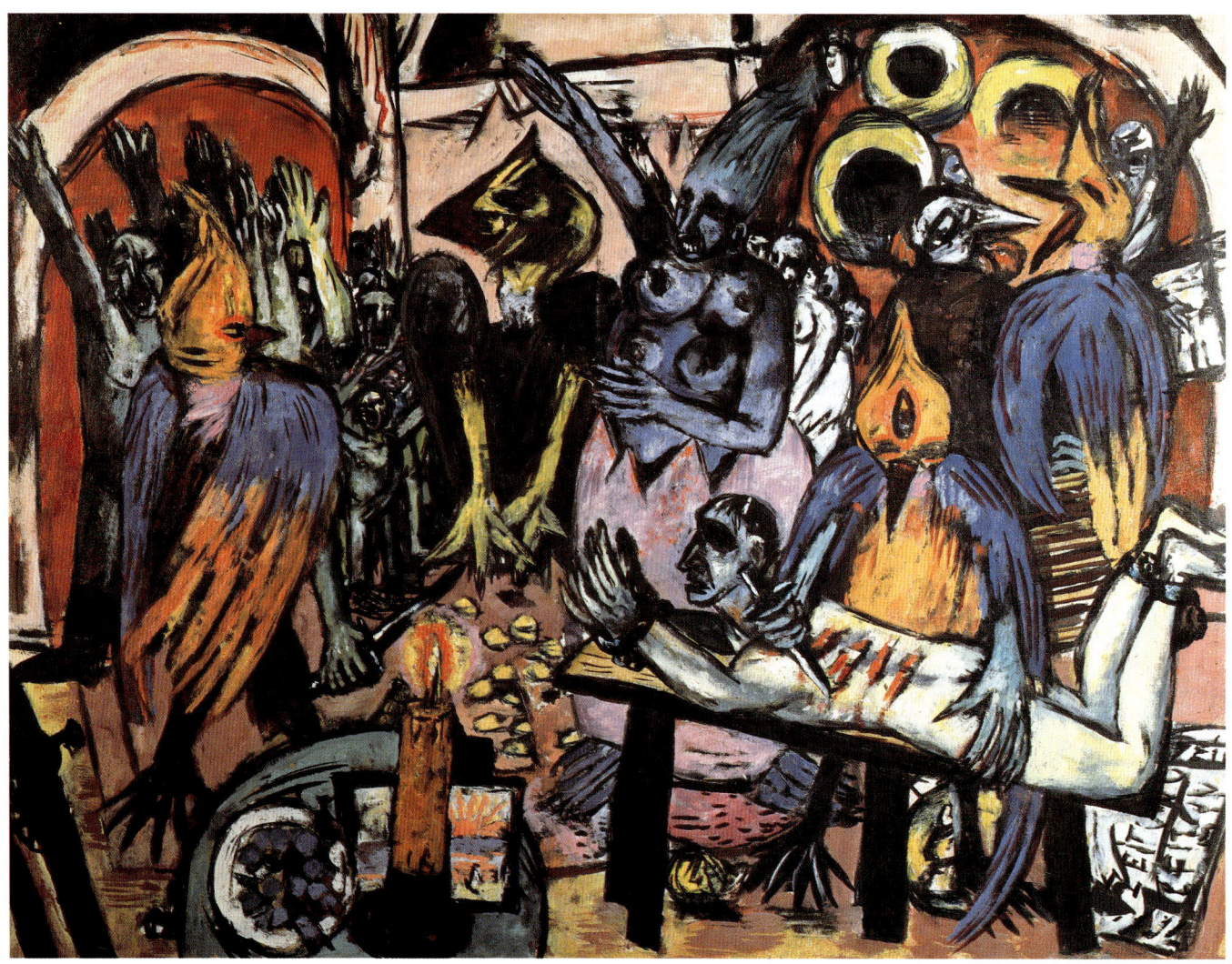

in a gypsy circus wagon; *Death*'s more artificially colored realm—with its phantoms of spirituality, lust, and hell—suggests that even death brings no release from the commotion of life. *Birds' Hell,* begun in Amsterdam but completed in Paris at the end of 1938—the year of the Anschluss, the annexation of Czechoslovakia, and Kristallnacht—is one of Beckmann's few works that explicitly refer to the Nazis; it also reflects on the artist and art.[6]

Overripe fertility goddesses and masses of figures give the Nazi salute to gaudily colored bird overlords and golden coins. The shackled figure on the right is derived from a much older German work, Stefan Lochner's *Martyrdom of Saint Bartholomew,* which portrays the saint who was flayed for refusing to worship idols. Together with a small painting of a sunset, grapes, and a thick, burning candle, the martyr saint—like most of Beckmann's protagonists,

36
Max Beckmann, *Birds' Hell*, 1938 (cat. no. 8).

37
Max Beckmann, *Double Portrait: Curt Valentin and Hanns Swarzenski*, 1946 (cat. no. 14).

38
Max Beckmann, *The Artists with Vegetable*, 1943 (cat. no. 11).

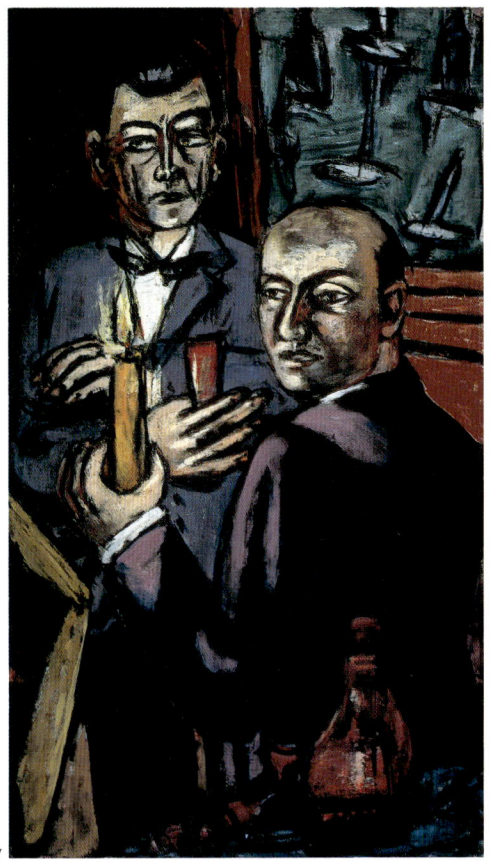

a stand-in for the artist himself—seems to symbolize the hope for artistic transcendence; the garish and claustrophobic surroundings, however, emphatically suggest that hope will be quashed.

Most of the works produced in Beckmann's first two years of exile were taken to New York in 1939 by Stephan Lackner, who also gave him a contract for future works and helped the dealers Curt Valentin and J. B. Neumann promote Beckmann's American reputation. Beckmann continued to sell his works during the war; between 1940 and 1944 more than seventy of his paintings returned to Germany, and others were bought in occupied Holland. These, of course, were not exhibited publicly and were purchased mostly by friends, family, and dealers; Beckmann did receive payment, however, and did not suffer financially.[7]

At least half of those paintings that went to Germany were taken there by his son, Peter, a doctor in the Luftwaffe, who was assisted by Buchholz and the Munich dealer Günther Franke. Göpel, officially employed by the Nazi occupation government and directly responsible to its head, Arthur Seyss-Inquart, had many means to assist Beckmann and prevented his conscription by the military. After Göpel left the Netherlands in the fall of 1944, the Beckmanns were greatly aided by the dealer Helmuth Lütjens, of Paul Cassirer & Co.

The Artists with Vegetable (fig. 38, cat. no. 11)—executed between June 1942 and January 1943 as the Germans suffered "catastrophe after catastrophe"[8] in North Africa and Russia—depicts Beckmann and the younger artists Friedrich Vordemberge-Gildewart

max beckmann   61

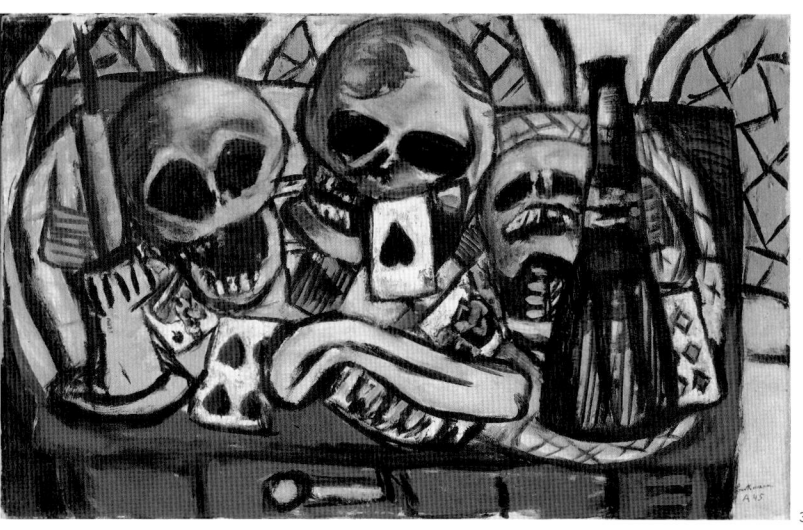

39
Max Beckmann; *Still Life with Death's Heads*, 1945; oil on canvas; 21¾ x 35¼ in. (55.2 x 89.5 cm); Museum of Fine Arts, Boston, gift of Mrs. Culver Orswell.

40
Max Beckmann, *Hotel Lobby*, 1950 (cat. no. 17).

41
The Plaza Hotel, New York, view from Palm Court toward the Fifth Avenue entrance, 1960s.

and Herbert Fiedler and the poet Wolfgang Frommel around a table that holds a large and sensuous, sputtering candle. Following northern traditions, Beckmann showed the figures together but not communicating (these particular individuals never met as a group), each holding an attribute that refers to their common attempt to pursue the life of the spirit. Beckmann's mirror—never devoid of irony—reflects a distorted clown face. The fat carrot held by Vordemberge-Gildewart, a traditional symbol of money and the desire to make it hold out, might also be read more generally as a symbol of wartime deprivations. Fiedler's fish evokes many associations as a symbol of fertility, recognition among believers, arrival into new self-awareness, and a food of sacred meals. Frommel's more indecipherable object might be a "round" that symbolizes the group's unity or his own publishing activities.[9] Whereas both Beckmann and Fiedler continued their artistic work in exile, Vordemberge-Gildewart, an internationally known abstractionist who was married to a Jew, had been forbidden to paint in both Germany and Holland and was forced to work in advertising. Frommel, a conservative follower of poet Stefan George, had promoted an oppositional "third humanism" in Nazi radio broadcasts before he fled Germany in 1937;[10] he supported himself in Amsterdam by working for publishers.

Before, during, and after the war Beckmann's prevailing mood was pessimistic, and his health problems caused him to dwell on himself more than his situation might seem to have warranted. In his diaries he regularly focused on his health, expressed his apprehension about bombers and the destruction of Germany and his concern for his family and friends, and indulged in existential musings. He also noted the substantial Dutch resistance to the Germans, Germany's destruction of the city of Rotterdam, the transports of Jews, and the temporary internment of a few close friends in concentration camps. The diaries—extensively edited by Mathilde Beckmann before their publication—are not without humor, self-criticism, or irony. Beckmann's often grim humor is also reflected in his *Still Life with Death's Heads* (fig. 39), completed in the war's last months (January 20–April 10, 1945). Stimulated by Cézanne's late still lifes of skulls in discrepantly bright surroundings, Beckmann's horribly wounded skulls gape and smile fiercely against lively patterns, noisemakers, and playing cards; a single black heart introduces a particularly cynical note.

Beckmann was hardly less pessimistic or self-centered at the war's end; he made no mention, for instance, of the opening of the concentration camps and declared that the war had ended for him only after he received his

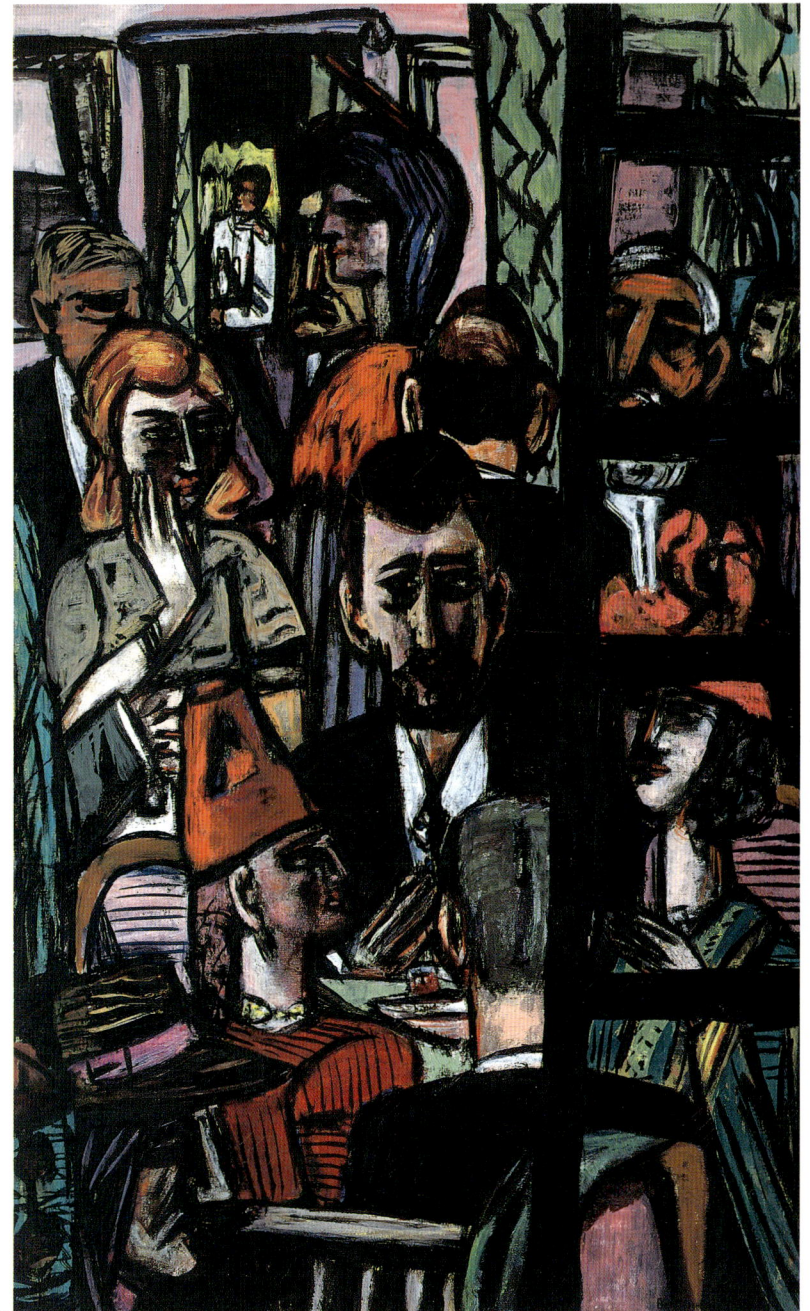

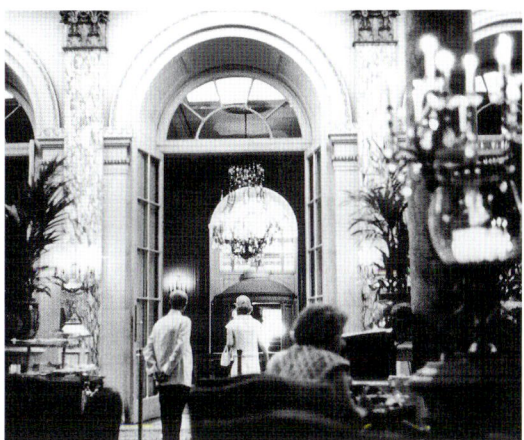

nonenemy papers in August 1946. And not until the close of the war did he declare that he was through with Germany; though several German schools invited him to teach, he stated that he had no desire to return to a country that lay in shambles and was about to be "castrated" by the victorious powers.[11] From September 1947 through June 1949 he taught at Washington University in Saint Louis, where Perry Rathbone was concurrently arranging a huge traveling retrospective for the City Art Museum,[12] and in the autumn of 1949 he began teaching at the Brooklyn Museum Art School. The Beckmanns returned to Amsterdam in the summer of 1948 and spent the subsequent summers at the University of Colorado in Boulder and Mills College in Oakland.

Although the Beckmanns were concerned about leaving Europe for an America that the artist assumed was spiritually impoverished,[13] they adapted gracefully to the fast whirl of their American life and enjoyed a period of real release after their years in the Netherlands. Beckmann worked at a fervent pace, developed many good friendships, and was pleased at the enthusiastic response to his 1948 retrospective but less pleased at his cooler reception from the Museum of Modern Art. The vehement new colorism of his American works was stimulated in part by his renewed access to works of Matisse.[14] Garish American pinks, greens, and oranges distinguish his *Hotel Lobby* (1950; fig. 40, cat. no. 17) from a comparable postwar European subject made only three years earlier, *Café (Hôtel de l'Europe),* which employed a more somber palette. The New York painting frames a diversified crowd in the Plaza Hotel's Palm

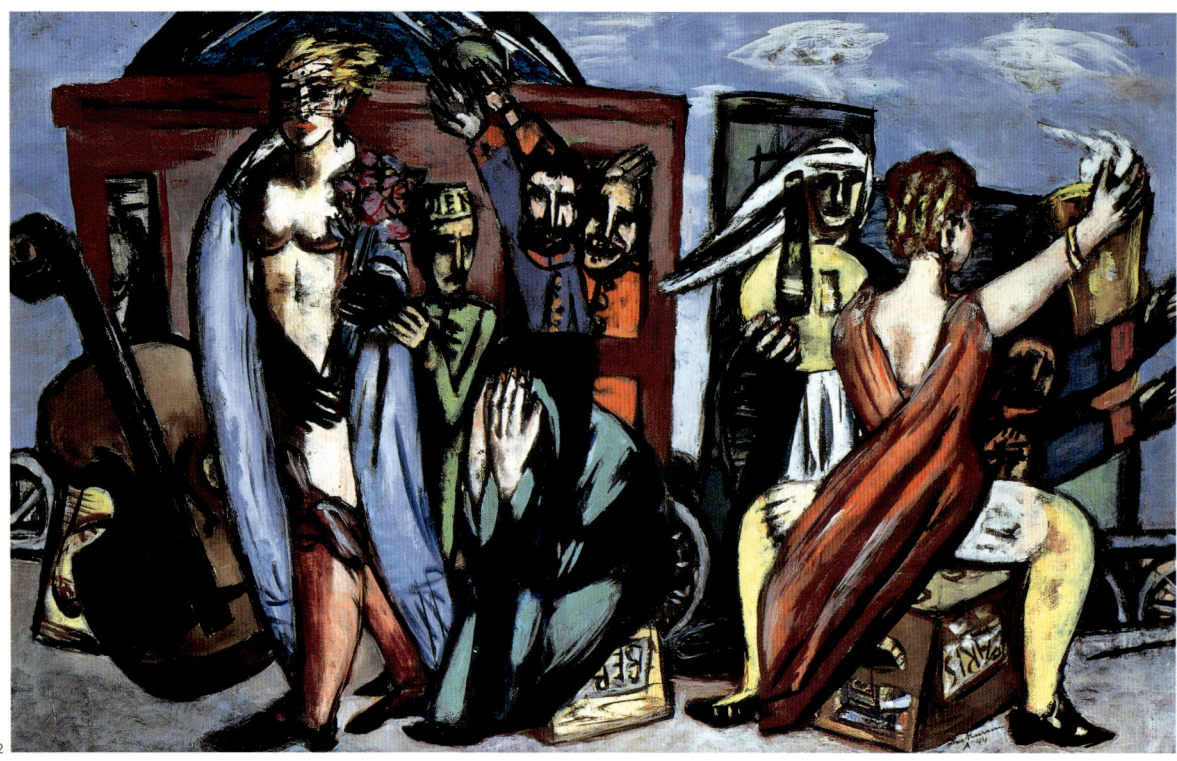

42

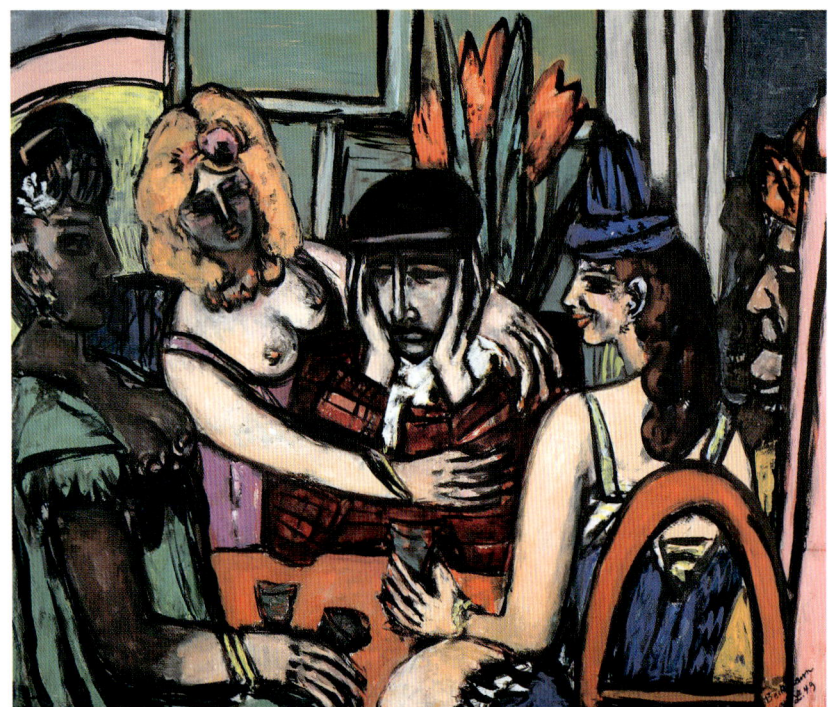

43

Court through one of the trellis doors below the Fifth Avenue entrance arches, but the colors and lattices lock the figures into stagnancy.

After the war Beckmann continued to allegorize his situation as an exile and emigré, as he had in earlier works. In his dreamlike *The Journey* (1944; fig. 42, cat. no. 13), for example, produced as air attacks on Berlin and other German cities escalated, soldiers on a train wave energetically at whores on the railway platform. The whores are identified with Berlin and Paris, the cities of greatest appeal to Beckmann himself, but the *Berlinerin* is joined by a weeping robed woman, a reminder both of the city's destruction and of Beckmann's own inability to journey. *The Prodigal Son* (1949; fig. 43, cat. no. 15), begun in Amsterdam on July 13, 1948, just after Beckmann's first year in the United States, might have been conceived to signal his return to father Europe. The remorseful son holds himself apart from the sinning traditionally associated with the scene; the young, ample-bosomed prostitutes that surround him may symbolize the temptations of America. *The Town (City Night)*,

42
Max Beckmann, *The Journey*, 1944 (cat. no. 13).

43
Max Beckmann, *The Prodigal Son*, 1949 (cat. no. 15).

44
Max Beckmann, *The Town (City Night)*, 1950 (cat. no. 19).

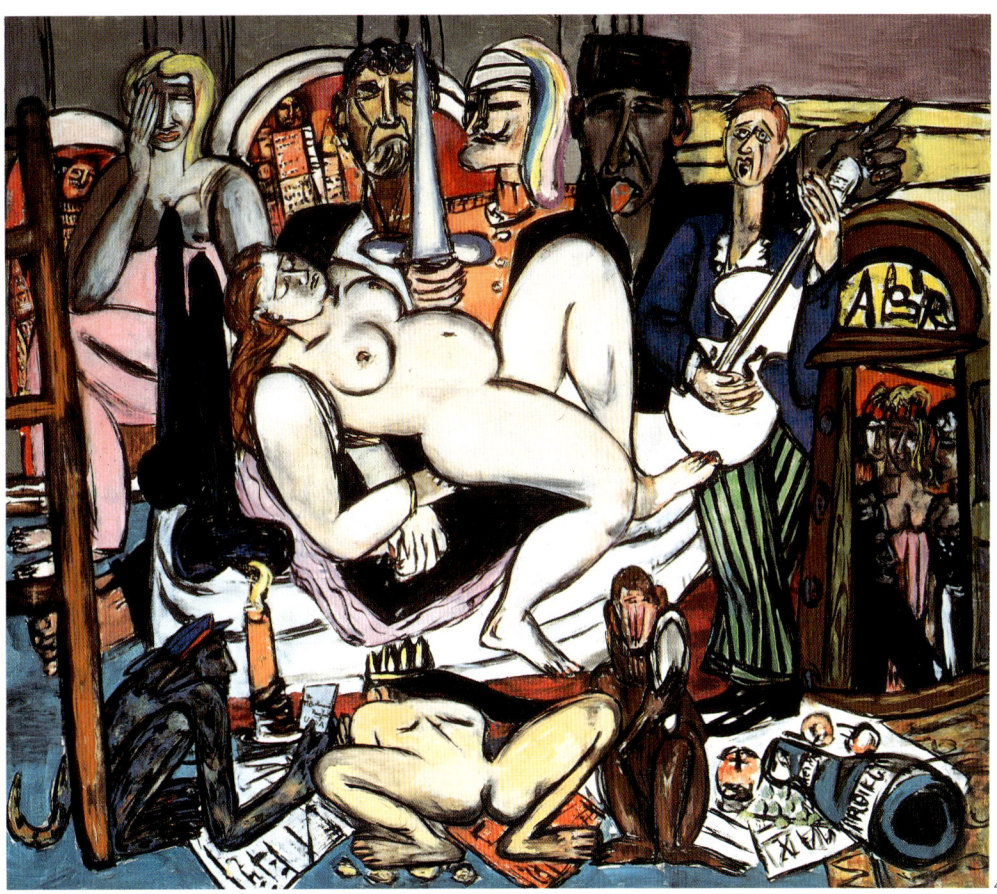

(fig. 44, cat. no. 19), executed in March 1950, directly recalls the man-beasts and the use of a woman as a central allegorical figure in Pieter Brueghel's *Avarice*; the large, bound nude, however, is not a personification of vice, but a figure of beauty sacrificed to greed, lust, and materialism.

Beckmann reflected on his situation and career in grander, more introspective and retrospective fashion in his last triptych, *The Argonauts* (fig. 45, cat. no. 16), begun in Saint Louis in April 1949 and completed in New York on December 26, 1950, the day before his death at the age of sixty-six. The Argonauts' journey had long been associated with the path of the artist (Frommel, who had written a tract on the subject, had called his own Amsterdam group the Argonauts), and all of the artistically inclined figures in the triptych could be said to represent Argonauts. The virile, naked youths in the central panel— who are about to be initiated into the mysteries of an ancient, hermetic world—recall both Beckmann's European mythological themes and the specific subject of his first major work, *Young Men by the Sea* (1905). The asceticism of the youths is contrasted with the sensuous abandon of the contemporary female musicians on the right and with the more troubled demeanor of the painter on the left, modeled

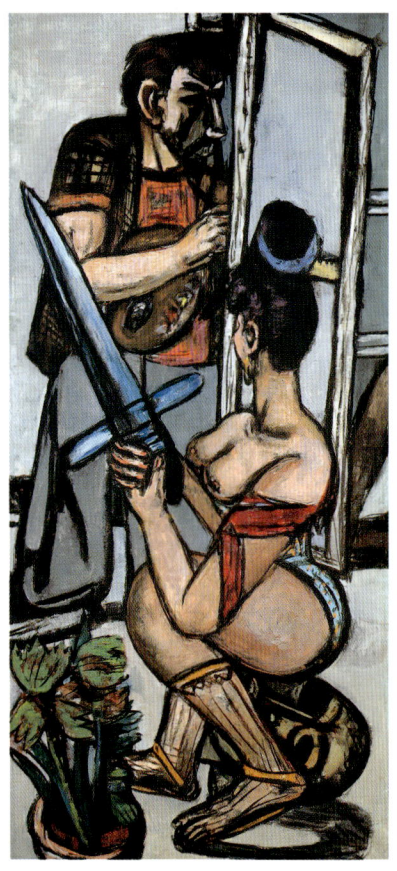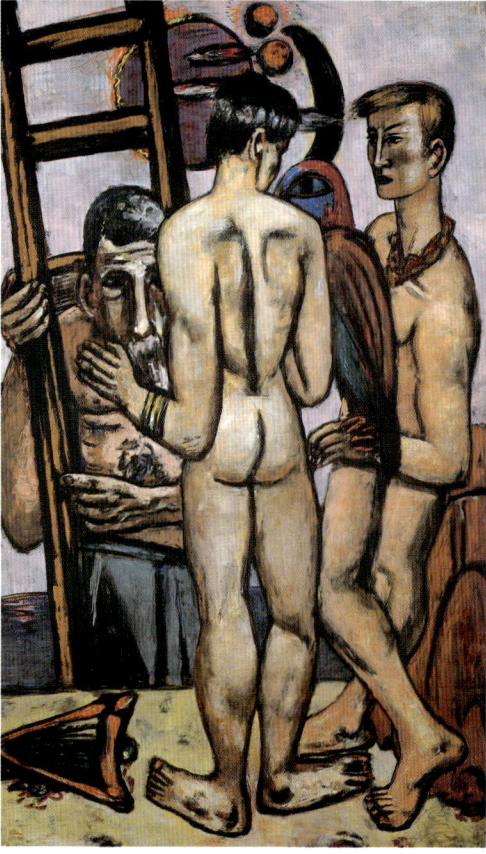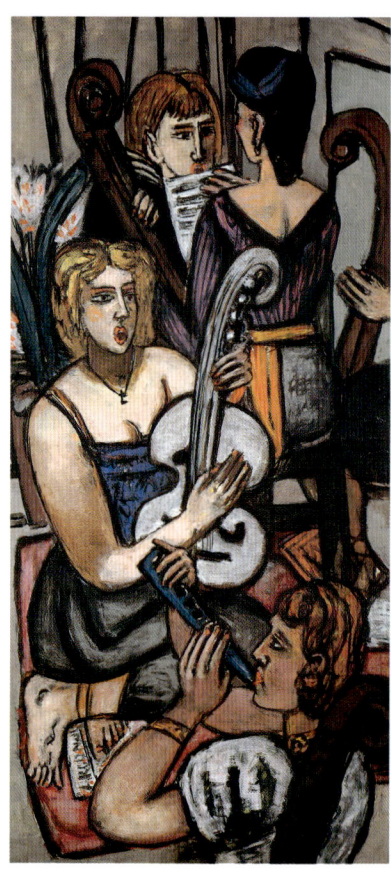

45
Max Beckmann, *The Argonauts*, 1949–50 (cat. no. 16).

directly on a self-portrait by Vincent van Gogh, which Beckmann had seen at the Metropolitan Museum of Art in 1949.[15] As he presented the various stages or alternative forms of creativity, Beckmann ultimately seems to have aligned himself with the troubled, long-wandering Dutch artist, whose diaries he had recently read. The goading, fierce, and sexually attractive Medea-Amazon seems to symbolize the passion and compulsion as well as the sometimes brutal exigencies of art, of which the other Argonauts may not yet be aware.

 The war made great inroads on Beckmann's health and well-being, but he was much better off than most exiles. He had the means, discipline, and support to continue his work, and his years of exile and emigration were some of the most prolific of his career. Since his youth Beckmann had sought to make art that would function both as self-representation and as a symbol of its time; his exile works also refer to himself and the tensions of the day, albeit in languages of allegory, portraiture, landscape, and still life which often initially appear remote from reality. Yet, for all of the seeming aloofness of Beckmann's position, the tensions and contradictions of his life and art profoundly manifest the rich and troubling complexities of reality.

Notes

1 Beckmann had requested a photo of Mies from Curt Valentin in 1939 (Beckmann to Valentin, 19 August 1939, Curt Valentin Papers, Museum of Modern Art Library, New York).

2 Peter Hayes, *Industry and Ideology: I. G. Farben in the Nazi Era* (Cambridge: Cambridge University Press, 1987), 103.

3 Josephine Gabler, "'Vor allem aber, er hat keine Angst, sich durch die Ausstellung zu schaden': Die Buch- und Kunsthandlung Karl Buchholz in Berlin," in *Ateliergemeinschaft Klosterstraße Berlin, 1933–1945*, exh. cat. (Berlin: Akademie der Künste, 1994), 84–95; and Andreas Hüneke, "Einer Legende begegnen," *Bildende Kunst* 45, no. 3 (1991): 54–55.

4 Consolidated Interrogation Reports on the Linz Museum, National Archives, Washington, D.C.; Lynn H. Nicholas, *The Rape of Europa* (New York: Alfred A. Knopf, 1994); and David Roxan and Ken Wanstall, *The Rape of Art* (New York: Coward-McCann, 1965).

5 Beckmann to Stephan Lackner, 29 January 1938, in Stephan Lackner, *Ich erinnere mich gut an Max Beckmann* (Mainz: Florian Kupferberg, 1967), 36–37.

6 The painting was first publicly exhibited in 1945.

7 The known provenance of each of Beckmann's works is listed in Erhard and Barbara Göpel, *Max Beckmann: Katalog der Gemälde*, vol. 1 (Bern: Kornfeld und Cie, 1976).

8 Max Beckmann, 7 October 1942, in *Tagebücher, 1940–1950*, comp. Mathilde Q. Beckmann, ed. Erhard Göpel (Munich: Albert Langen–Georg Müller, 1955), 40.

9 Frommel published his dissertation under a pseudonym: Lothar Helbing, *Der dritte Humanismus* (Berlin: Runde, 1932–35).

10 Michael Philipp, "'Vom Schicksal des deutschen Geistes': Wolfgang Frommels oppositionelle Rundfunkarbeit in den Jahren 1933–1935," *Castrum Peregrini*, nos. 209–10 (1993): 124–40.

11 Max Beckmann, 13 April 1945 and 3 August 1945, *Tagebücher*, 116, 129.

12 *Max Beckmann 1948*, City Art Museum, Saint Louis, 10 May– 28 June 1948. The show subsequently traveled to Baltimore, Cambridge, Detroit, Los Angeles, San Francisco, Minneapolis, and Boulder, Colorado.

13 Max Beckmann, 3 August 1947, *Tagebücher*, 199.

14 See Barbara C. Buenger, *Max Beckmann's Artistic Sources* (Ann Arbor, Mich.: University Microfilms, 1981), 263–74.

15 Ibid., 335.

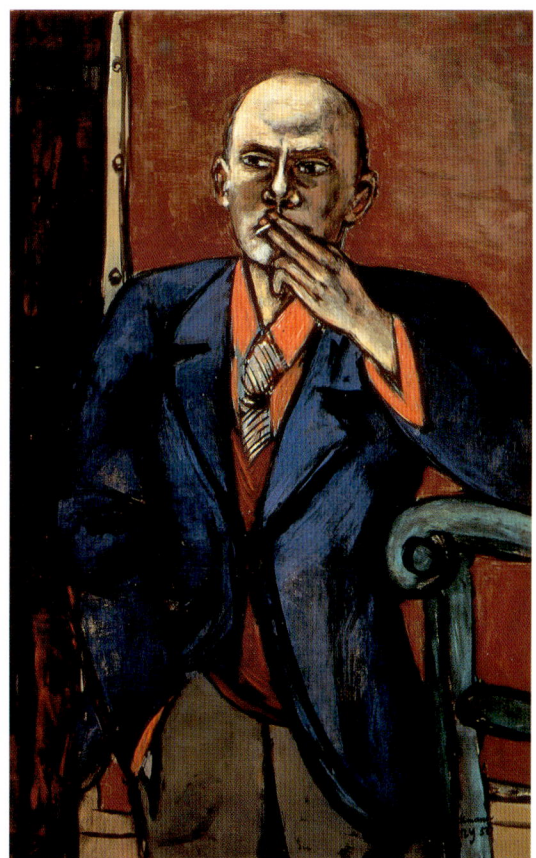

46
Max Beckmann, *Self-Portrait*, 1950 (cat. no. 18).

wassily kandinsky in paris, 1933–44

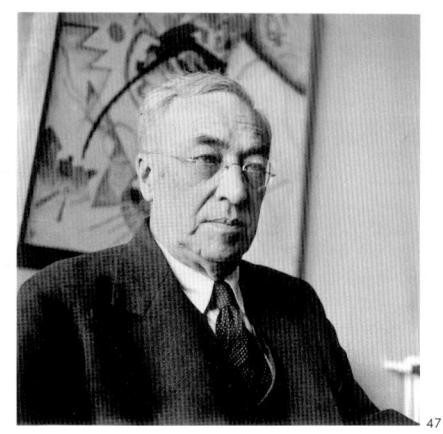

1866	born in Moscow
1933	emigrates from Germany (Berlin) to France (Neuilly-sur-Seine)
1944	dies in Neuilly-sur-Seine

Disturbed by the Reichstag fire, the closing of the Bauhaus, and Hitler's attack on modern artists at the September Nuremberg party congress,[1] Wassily and Nina Kandinsky left Germany for their new apartment in the Paris suburb of Neuilly by the end of 1933. For at least a year they hoped that they might return to Germany, where Kandinsky had enjoyed more than thirty years of fruitful artistic production, but they eventually decided that this was not possible.[2] A committed internationalist who saw abstraction and modernism as paths to a new world, the sixty-eight-year-old Kandinsky entered his Paris exile ready to work and tenaciously continued to champion the liberation of abstraction even as the cosmopolitan Parisian art world increasingly shut down. Throughout his exile his financial well-being, eminence, age, and discipline enabled him to work prolifically and even to challenge himself to move in new directions.

In Paris Kandinsky produced less than half the number of works that he had produced at the Bauhaus over the previous decade, but he was ten years older, lacked the continuous stimulus of the Bauhaus fellowship, and experienced limitations brought on by the Depression, war, and Occupation. Nonetheless, he refused to make his Paris exile a period of retirement. Before the war, with access to international outlets, he worked indefatigably on his art and its promotion and enjoyed exhibitions and publications throughout the world. He was not only acutely and critically attuned to the Parisian scene but also strongly inspired by it.

As an advocate of abstraction, Kandinsky was adamant that art transcend the experience of the material world; his art rarely dealt directly with his personal experience, and it is not surprising that exile never became one of his themes. His exile works demonstrate much continuity with his earlier oeuvre; they reflect his exile experience chiefly as they represent his further development of his abstraction, his receptivity to new sources and stimuli, and his practical responses to material conditions and restrictions. His sudden adoption of a new type of biomorphic figuration—something that had interested colleagues such as Paul Klee and László Moholy-Nagy at the Bauhaus—was also stimulated by surrealism, with which he had long been familiar,[3] as well as by his continuing study of biological illustrations from scientific, philosophic, artistic, and popular publications.[4] Though disappointed by surrealism's politicization and excessive preoccupation with eroticism, automatism, and dreams, Kandinsky was delighted to come into contact with new forms of surrealist biomorphic abstraction and other abstract tendencies. He regularly saw works by and maintained contact with Joan Miró,[5] Jean Arp and Sophie Taeuber-Arp, and even the more distant Klee. Many passages of Kandinsky's works pay undisguised homage to their works.

The identically sized *Balancing Act* (1935; fig. 48, cat. no. 70) and *Brown with Supplement* (1935; fig. 49, cat. no. 71) are typical of these first Paris years, with their bright, new colors—something Kandinsky himself attributed to the colors and light of Paris—and in their musical development of biomorphic and geometric forms. Indeed, a photograph of *Brown with Supplement* in Maurice Barret's "living room of an intellectual" (see fig. 50)—

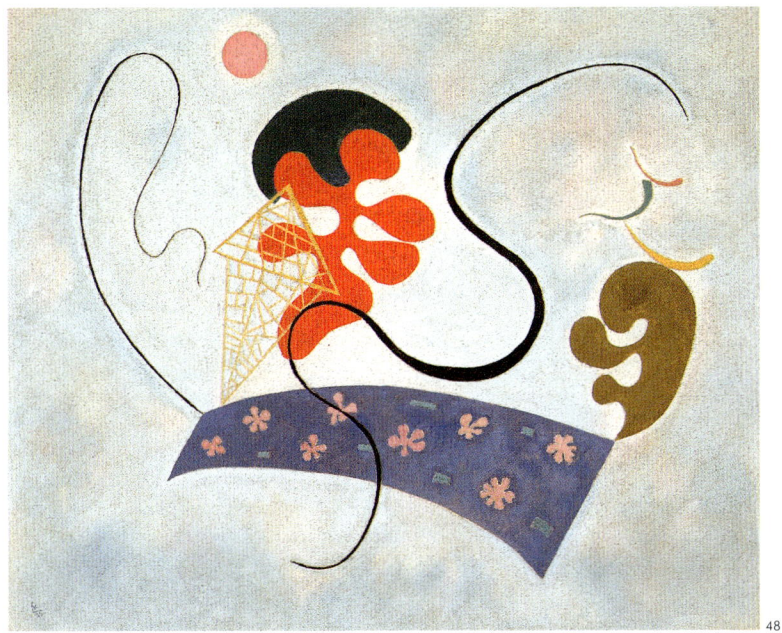

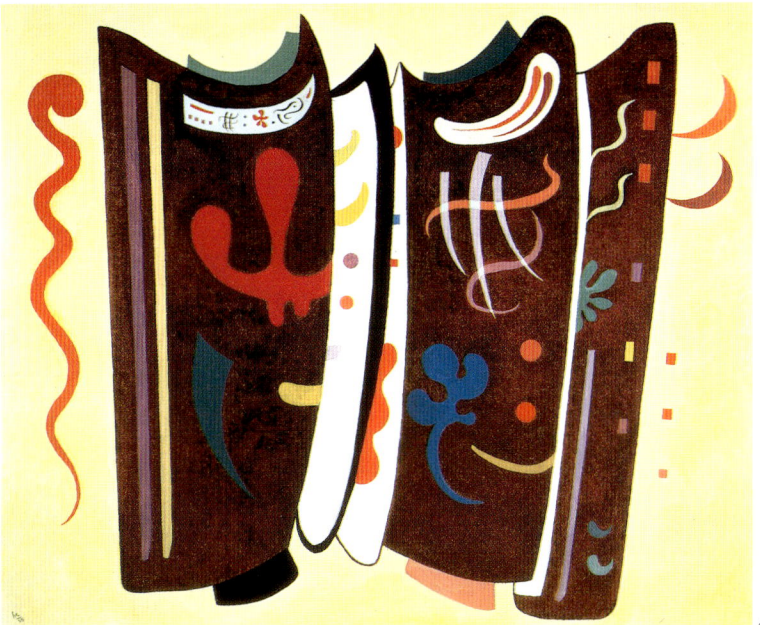

an ensemble possibly designed for the decorative arts exposition in 1935[6]—suggests that Kandinsky had found an ideal home and reception in Paris, but the Parisian scene changed greatly in the following years. As he finally recognized the reality of an art market that had been drastically reduced by the Depression, Kandinsky became increasingly disgruntled by what he saw as the Parisians' general materialism and lack of interest in art, the growing chauvinism in both French art and politics, and the lack of a serious audience for the kinds of abstraction he championed. He felt that his own abstraction was misunderstood not only by the general public but also in leading art circles; in 1937 he even parted ways from his earliest Parisian supporter, Christian Zervos, partly because Zervos considered cubism to be more important than abstraction.

47
Wassily Kandinsky, Paris, 1938; photograph by Josef Breitenbach.

48
Wassily Kandinsky, *Balancing Act*, 1935 (cat. no. 70).

49
Wassily Kandinsky, *Brown with Supplement*, 1935 (cat. no. 71).

50
The "living room of an intellectual," designed by Maurice Barret, c. 1935.

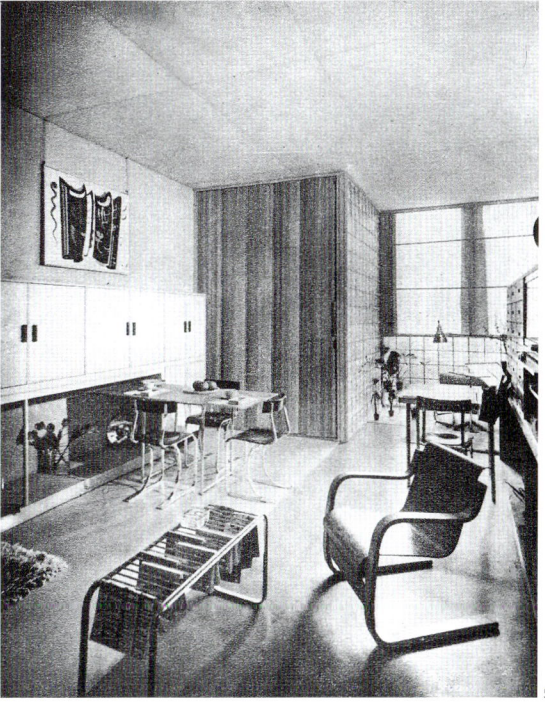

wassily kandinsky   69

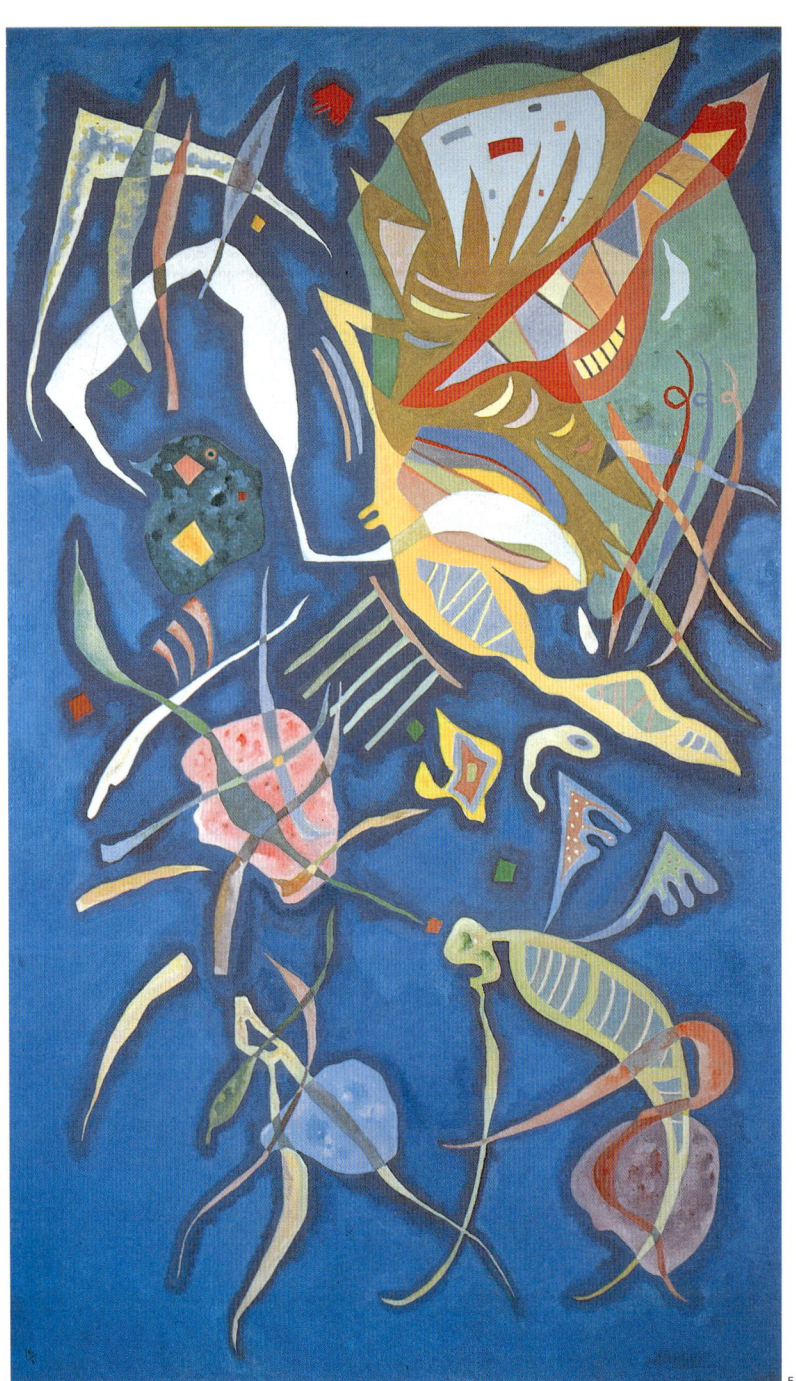

51

Kandinsky turned to the more supportive but much less renowned dealer Jeanne Bucher, who showed many of the international abstractionists with whom he had become associated.

Kandinsky exerted himself considerably to promote abstraction in Paris. Initially involved with the international Abstraction-Création group, he quickly found many in the group too dogmatic and rigidly geometric. Through that group, however, he strengthened his connections with artists such as the Arps and Jean Hélion and came into contact with younger artists such as Hans Hartung and Gualtieri di San Lazerro, whom he encouraged and invited to his studio. He was also attracted to Fernand Léger, who joined him in sponsoring Filippo Tommaso Marinetti's 1935 Paris lecture; André Breton; Alberto Giacometti; and the Italians Alberto Magnelli and Enrico Prampolini. Though he was scorned by many artists in Paris for his support of the fascist Marinetti and the Second Futurists, Kandinsky steadfastly celebrated futurism's abstracting modernism.[7] He maintained contacts with the openly Fascist Galleria del Milione in Milan through 1938 and, like many of his contemporaries, found Italian Fascism not incompatible with modern art and modernism.

Tensions in the political and cultural worlds increasingly affected the artistic sphere. When Kandinsky and Zervos finally fell out in 1937, both were still fighting for the acceptance of modernism in Paris. The official French representation of modern art at the 1937 world's fair, curated by Raymond Escholier for the Petit Palais, *Les maîtres de l'art indépendant, 1895–1937* (The masters of independent art, 1895–1937; June–October

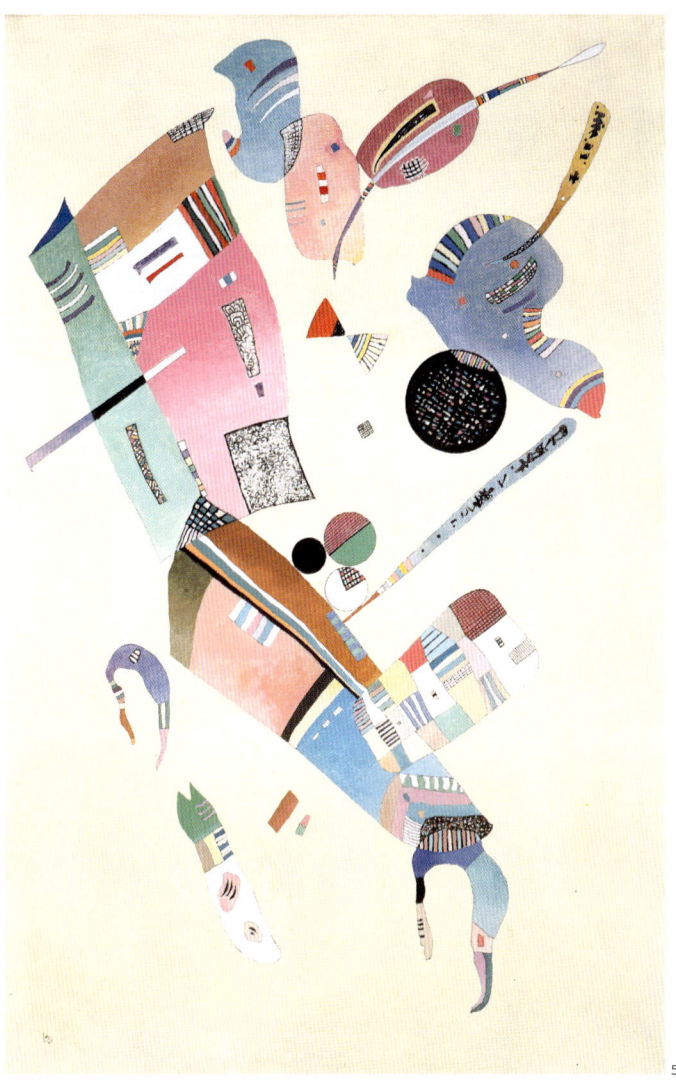

52

51
Wassily Kandinsky, *Grouping*, 1937 (cat. no. 72).

52
Wassily Kandinsky, *Moderation*, 1940 (cat. no. 73).

1937), had initially excluded cubism—long derided as un-French but increasingly championed since the 1930s—and Zervos had successfully intervened for its inclusion. International abstractionists and surrealists who had worked in Paris for shorter periods—and who had made some of the liveliest contributions to the interwar Parisian scene—were excluded from the official French show. André Dézarrois, however, the curator of the Jeu de Paume, quickly developed an international exhibition for that summer, *Origines et développement de l'art international indépendant* (The origins and development of international independent art; July 30–October 31, 1937), and Kandinsky, Magnelli, and Julio González offered both their works and their advice. Kandinsky seems to have played a major role in suggesting possible artists and in writing a text for the catalogue. Yet Dézarrois made critical changes in the catalogue and, like Zervos and others, presented Kandinsky's abstraction as secondary to cubism.

Kandinsky's life, career, and moves had already been affected by politics on many occasions; he was less blind than arrogant toward politics, but they continued to impinge upon his greater visions. Denied his German visa in 1938, he easily obtained the French citizenship that facilitated his generally untroubled existence during the war. With the encouragement of Herbert Read, he refused to exhibit with politicized German refugee artists whose works he did not respect.[8] At the same time he was increasingly disturbed to learn of the Nazis' treatment of "degenerate" artists and in 1938 took steps to assist the German-Jewish refugee Otto Freundlich. Kandinsky clearly recognized the menace of National Socialism by the late 1930s, but he remained an admirer of Germany and Germans. He probably had no compunction about selling his works to uniformed Germans during the Occupation and, in fact, was able on two occasions to exhibit his works in occupied Paris.

As international tensions increased, Kandinsky returned to themes of the thundering collision and creation of worlds, which he had begun to adopt in his Compositions before World War I. In *Grouping* (1937; fig. 51, cat. no. 72) an unruly figuration of irregular and meandering organic forms contrasts with the more dynamic and sharply articulated forms at the upper right, which seem to suggest the birth of a new world or organism. *Moderation* (1940; fig. 52; cat. no. 73), by contrast, presents a gently hovering group of geometrically patterned, swelling organic forms.

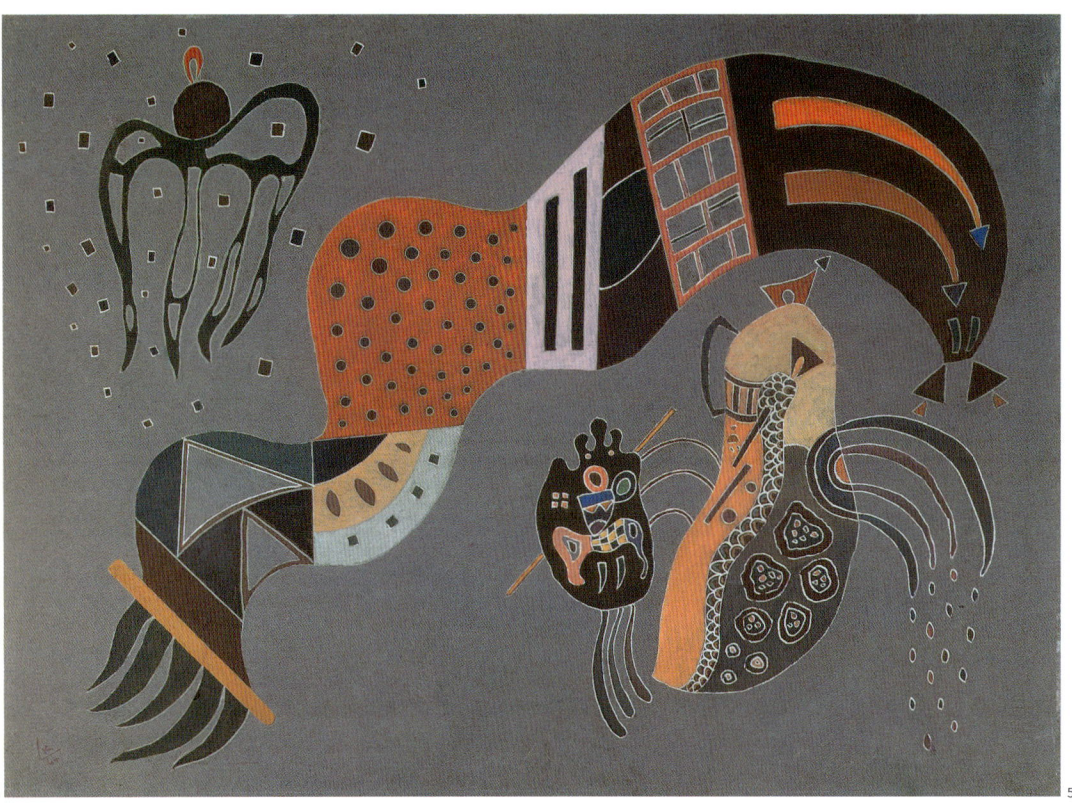

53
Wassily Kandinsky, *Tempered Elan*, 1944 (cat. no. 74).

54
Wassily Kandinsky, *Unfinished Painting*, 1944 (cat. no. 75).

The more tempered structures and moods of the wartime works, with their evocation of primal beginnings and ancient civilizations, promoted quieter contemplation, but these works remained uncompromisingly contemporary in their colors and abstraction. From 1942 on, Kandinsky was forced to work on board or cardboard because he had no more canvas and found it easier to sell smaller works. Most of his wartime works are on cardboard of the same smaller format (16½ x 22⅞ in.). In *Tempered Elan* (1944; fig. 53, cat. no. 74), almost a variation on his dynamic *Dominant Violet* of ten years earlier, a great and ornately patterned salamander hovers over a pair of coupling forms that end in dangling legs and a sprouting medusa. In *Unfinished Painting* (1944; fig. 54, cat. no. 75) an Egyptian abacus with circles and lotus leaves separates two fields of patterned organic forms, some resembling large organisms such as medusae or trunkfish,[9] others reading almost like hieroglyphs.

Like his writings, Kandinsky's later works continued to assert the necessity and victory of abstraction in a world rent by crisis. His newly bright, often gratingly decorative colorism;[10] his flattened bio- and technomorphism; and his increasingly complex spaces can be understood only as challenges to the distracted world of materialism. Though Kandinsky was always interested more in the greater, cosmic concerns of art and the spirit than in contemporary politics, he was not insensitive to his times. He had little tolerance for those who failed to follow or sympathize with him; his increasing withdrawal from the art world and from Paris itself clearly reflected his recognition that he could pursue his form of abstraction only in protected isolation.

Notes

I am grateful to the University of Wisconsin, Madison, for a Hilldale Undergraduate/Faculty Research Grant to work on this topic in collaboration with Sarah E. Fancher.

1 Nina Kandinsky, *Kandinsky und Ich* (Munich: Kindler, 1976), 150–51.

2 Christian Derouet suggests that Kandinsky tried to ingratiate himself with Nazi officials in order to return to Germany ("Kandinsky in Paris: 1934–1944," trans. Eleanor Levieux, in *Kandinsky in Paris, 1934–1944*, exh. cat. [New York: Solomon R. Guggenheim Museum, 1985], 20), but the letter quoted refers only to Kandinsky's desire to retrieve money from a German bank account (Kandinsky to Kojève [n.d., summer 1935], in *Vassily Kandinsky: Correspondances avec Zervos et Kojève* [Paris: Centre Georges Pompidou, 1992], 173).

3 See Derouet, "Kandinsky in Paris," 34, 51.

4 See Vivian Barnett, "Kandinsky and Science: The Introduction of Biological Images in the Paris Period," in *Kandinsky in Paris*, 61–87.

5 See Carolyn Lanchner, *Joan Miró*, exh. cat. (New York: Museum of Modern Art, 1993), 330–35, 439–44.

6 Illustrated in P. D'Uckerman, *L'art dans la vie moderne* (Paris: Flammarion, 1937), 115.

7 See Christian Derouet, "Kandinsky: Diario italiano, 1932–1940," in *Kandinsky a Parigi, 1934–1944*, exh. cat. (Milan: Palazzo Reale, 1985), 71–84.

8 Read to Kandinsky, 9 November 1938, quoted in Derouet, "Kandinsky in Paris," 20.

9 Cf. Ernst Haeckel, *Art Forms in Nature* (New York: Dover Publications, 1974), pl. 42.

10 On Kandinsky's "Necco-Wafer" colorism, see Brooks Adams, "Epic Kandinsky," *Art in America* 83 (July 1995): 45–51, 98–99.

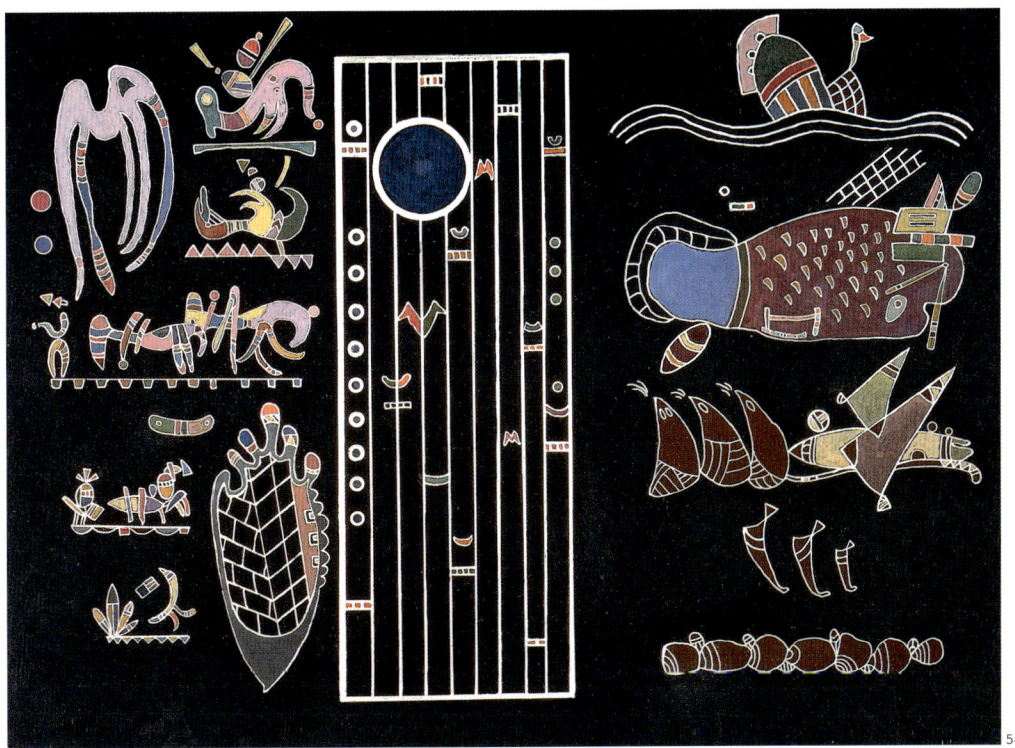

54

john heartfield in london, 1938–45

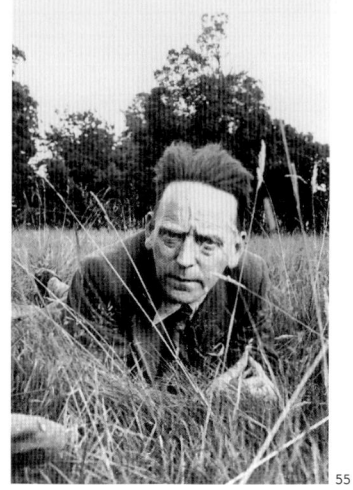

55

1891	born in Berlin
1933	immigrates to Czechoslovakia (Prague)
1938	immigrates to England (London)
1950	returns to Germany (East Berlin)
1968	dies in East Berlin

On December 6, 1938, just two months after the German annexation of Czech territory began and a few months prior to the occupation of Prague, the German communist artist John Heartfield made a quick escape to London with the aid of the Artists' Refugee Committee, formed largely of Artists International Association (AIA) members such as Diana Croft Uhlman and Richard Carline. Heartfield's Prague period had been the most prolific of his career,[1] a time when his work also found recognition abroad. Because his works were so blatantly political, he had been excluded from the July 1938 *Exhibition of Twentieth Century German Art* at London's New Burlington Galleries, yet because so many liberal Britons applauded his antifascism, he arrived in England with a strong network of support.

Within a few weeks of his arrival in London, Heartfield moved into the Hampstead home of Uhlman and her husband, the Stuttgart refugee lawyer-turned-artist, Fred Uhlman. The Uhlmans subsequently moved and left the house in the care of the British Marxist art historian Francis Klingender;[2] Heartfield lived there with Klingender until 1943. In Hampstead he also met Gertrud Feist, who ultimately became his wife, and on January 29, 1943, the couple moved into their own Highgate apartment.

Heartfield quickly became involved with the AIA but gravitated primarily toward communist groups. He helped the Uhlmans found the Free German League of Culture on March 28, 1939, and frequently participated in its meetings and events. Though the group declared itself a "non-partisan refugee organization,"[3] he and other communists soon became its driving force.

Soon after Heartfield's arrival the German emigré editor Stefan Lorant published several of his photomontages in *Lilliput* and commissioned him to make a cover for the *Picture Post* (fig. 56, cat. no. 61). The latter appeared on the September 9, 1939, issue of the London edition, which dealt with the Soviet-German nonaggression pact and Britain's entry into the war. Heartfield reused an earlier montage of Hitler wearing Kaiser Wilhelm II's uniform and moustache. The 1932 montage had been accompanied by Heartfield's punning variation on one of the kaiser's earliest World War I announcements, and the inscription on the kaiser's medal, *pour le mérite,* was revised to read *pour le profite.* In England, however, Heartfield could no longer employ the sophisticated wordplay of his German original; he now introduced a map, placing Hitler's head against Central Europe, to stress the two leaders' similarly belligerent expansionist aims.

Although the *Picture Post* continued to be influenced by German journalism and photography, it never again used a montage on its cover during the war. Perhaps the form was too radically modern and militant for a popular weekly. Lorant himself published no more of Heartfield's works, and the artist's political stance may well have been a contributing factor. The revelation of the Soviet-German nonaggression pact and Britain's entry into the war had aroused great hostility toward German refugees in England; Fred Uhlman, who later spoke with disgust of Heartfield's unquestioning devotion to Stalin, noted that Heartfield

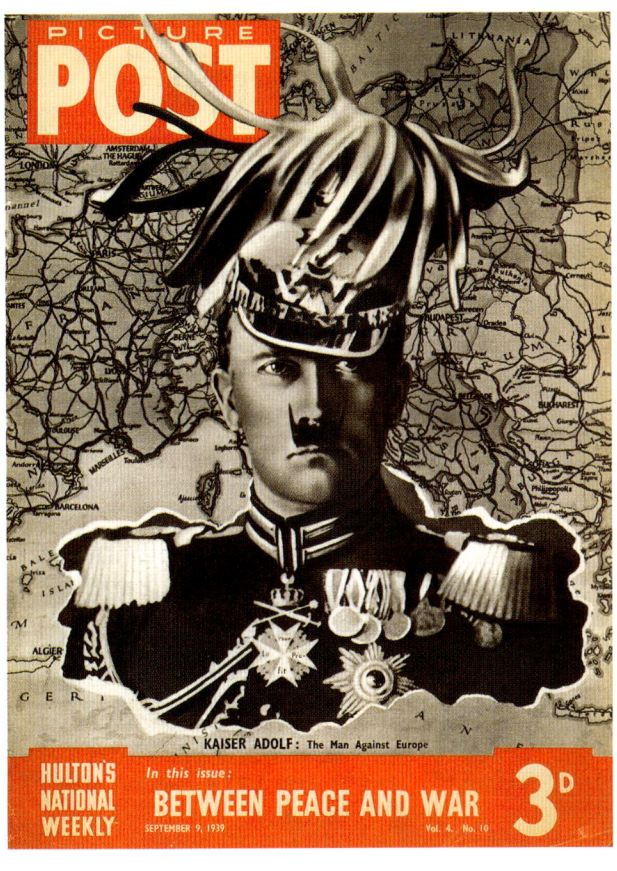

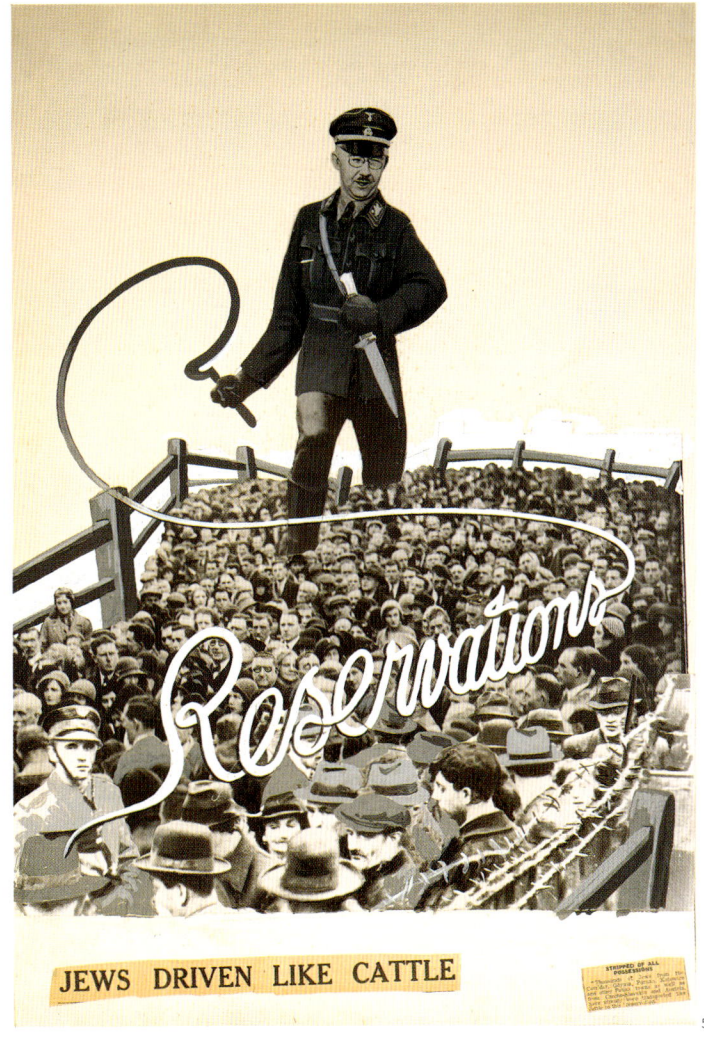

55
John Heartfield, c. 1947.

56
John Heartfield, *Kaiser Adolf: The Man against Europe*, 1939 (cat. no. 61).

57
John Heartfield, *Reservations: Jews Driven like Cattle*, 1939 (cat. no. 62).

and many other German communist refugees had adopted a wait-and-see attitude toward the war, refusing to condemn Stalin.[4]

In the following months Heartfield received only a few commissions. In those he not only continued to excoriate the Nazis and their crimes but, like other German communist refugees, stressed that there were other, respectable Germans—particularly among the working class—who either resisted or were helplessly enchained by the National Socialists. He made several montages for the *Reynolds News*, including *Reservations: Jews Driven like Cattle* in December 1939 (fig. 57, cat. no. 62), but was unhappy that he had no control over their titles, quality of printing, size, or placement in the newspaper and soon canceled the contract.[5] He otherwise worked mostly for communist and anti-Nazi groups. For his December 1939 cover for Jürgen Kuczynski's anonymously published *Freedom Calling: The Story of the Secret German Radio* (fig. 29, cat. no. 60), Heartfield himself posed as the radio operator sending bolts of lightning that strike the head of an exasperated Hitler. Heartfield's cover for the March 1940 issue of *Inside Nazi Germany* (fig. 59, cat. no. 63), a journal published by the Friends of the German People's Front and Group of the German Opposition (to which Kuczynski, Albert Meusel, and Hans Hess contributed), stressed the crushing burden of Nazism on the German people.

Inside Nazi Germany ceased publication with that issue; most of its contributors went into British internment camps after the German invasions of France and Northern Europe. Heartfield, who was given the "C" classification of "refugee from Nazi oppression," became ill and was quickly released from the Huyton camp through the intercession of two members of Parliament, Ellen Wilkensen and Eleanor Rathbone.

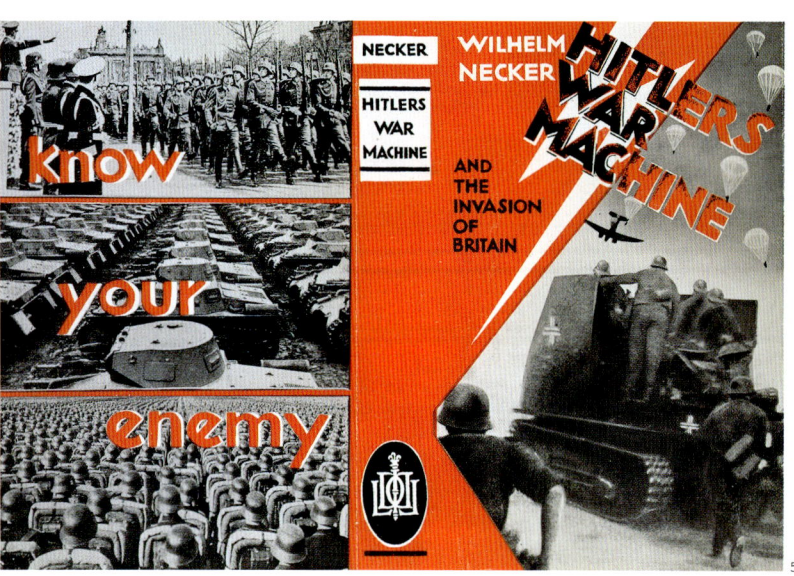

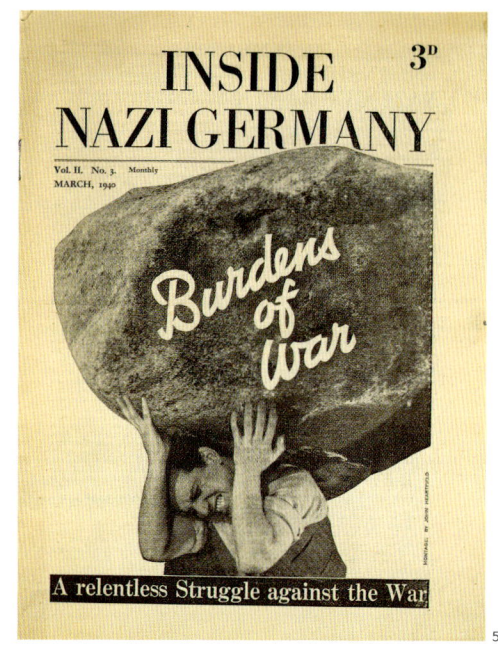

58
John Heartfield, *Hitler's War Machine*, 1941 (cat. no. 64).

59
John Heartfield, *Burdens of War*, 1940 (cat. no. 63).

60
John Heartfield, *Five Minutes to Twelve*, 1942 (cat. no. 65).

61
John Heartfield, *And Yet It Moves!* 1943 (cat. no. 67).

Heartfield found few options open to him following his release and turned to activities such as lecturing to leftist groups; he received permission to work as a freelance cartoonist only in 1943. Already in 1941, however, he began to produce book and pamphlet covers for Lindsay Drummond, who continued to be his chief source of employment throughout his stay in England. The "bourgeois-liberal" Drummond[6] published numerous pamphlets that dealt both with Nazi aggression and the resistance to it, but he also published a wide range of modern literature and, after the war, many volumes on travel, science, art, and music. Heartfield made covers for many different types of Drummond publications—many of them nonpolitical—and felt that he profited from the challenge of adopting a new, more pictorialist realist style for his new audience. In his cover for Wilhelm Necker's *Hitler's War Machine and the Invasion of Britain* (1941; fig. 58, cat. no. 64), however, he used straightforward modernist inflections of typography, diagonals, and perspective to convey a sense of the relentless impetus of the German military.

With the German invasion of the Soviet Union on June 22, 1941, pressure on German refugees in England eased. Refugees redoubled their efforts to distinguish the Germans who had made positive contributions to culture and society and to call for resistance. Heartfield joined the Free German League of Culture in planning the exhibition *Allies inside Germany* (July 3–August 16, 1942),[7] which consisted of twenty-seven panels that traced Hitler's rise to power, elimination of enemies, and victories from 1938 through 1941. The final panels depicted Germans who had made great cultural contributions in the past, contemporary Germans who had been exiled or silenced, German refugees who had helped fight Nazism and joined the Allied war efforts, and German labor.

Five Minutes to Twelve (fig. 60, cat. no. 65), included in the exhibition's sixth panel, was executed in the sharply humorous style of the best of Heartfield's earlier *AIZ* illustrations: the screaming figures of a miniature Goebbels with a huge club foot, Göring, and Hitler pull tautly on a rope to stop the progress of a clock—labeled "Made in France"—toward midnight. The doomsday they feared was a "second front victory" by France and England; in 1942 Stalin insisted that the Allies engage

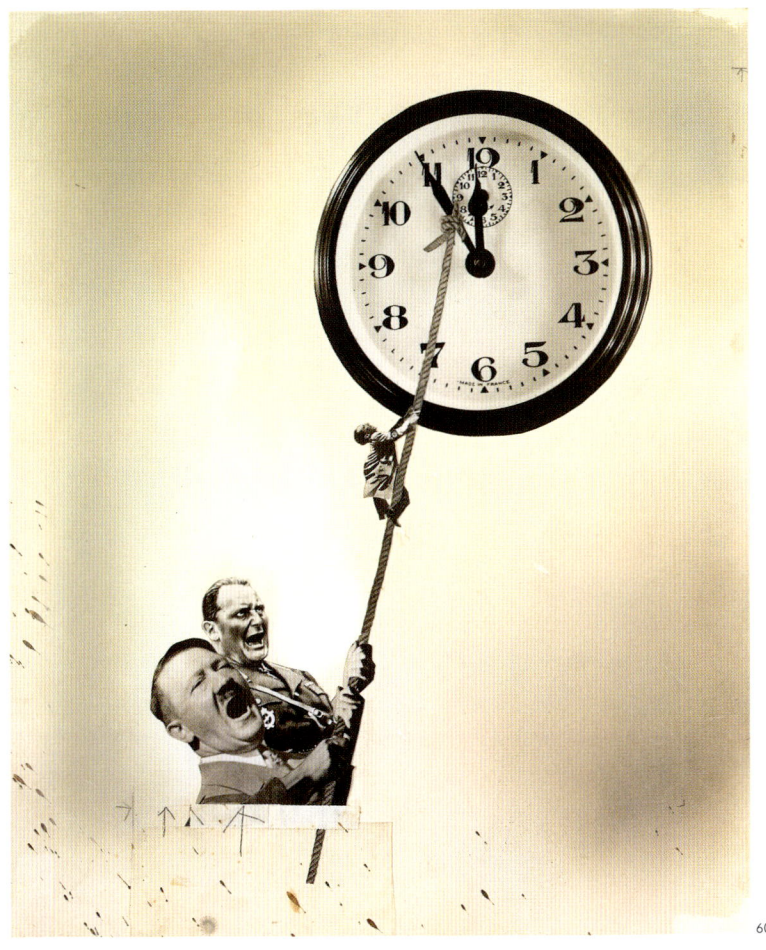

60

a "second front" to relieve the Russian people, but this would not be established until the Normandy invasion of 1944 (the exhibition did not mention Stalin's alliance with Hitler as Britain, France, and Northern Europe fought in 1940). In the same panel, represented in a colossal photo next to a much smaller image of Roosevelt, Stalin is quoted affirming his loyalty to the German people, above clippings that tell of the Germans' wartime suffering and the growing resistance to Hitler.

Heartfield also produced a montage for the cover of the 1943 Free German League of Culture anthology, *Freie deutsche Dichtung* (Free German poetry), titled *And Yet It Moves!* (fig. 61, cat. no. 67). Like the world commandeered by the saber-wielding gorilla-Hitler, free German poetry—symbolically embodied by a twisting, resistant frog in Hitler's hand—still moves. The title, taken from a line supposedly uttered by Galileo during his trial in 1633, had acquired special significance for communists in the Third Reich: in 1933, the three-hundredth anniversary of Galileo's trial, Georgi Dimitrov, the Bulgarian communist accused and acquitted of plotting the Reichstag fire, had quoted the line in his own defense, inspiring Heartfield,[8] Bertolt Brecht,[9] and many others with his dignified resistance.

In 1945 Heartfield executed a few works for the *Soviet War News* and *Soviet News,* but he was otherwise employed chiefly by Drummond, Penguin, and other publishers. Two of his montages were produced for publications that reflected British liberal consideration of the alternatives of the East and West. That for a pamphlet by the distinguished Soviet economist M. I. Bogolepov, *The Soviet*

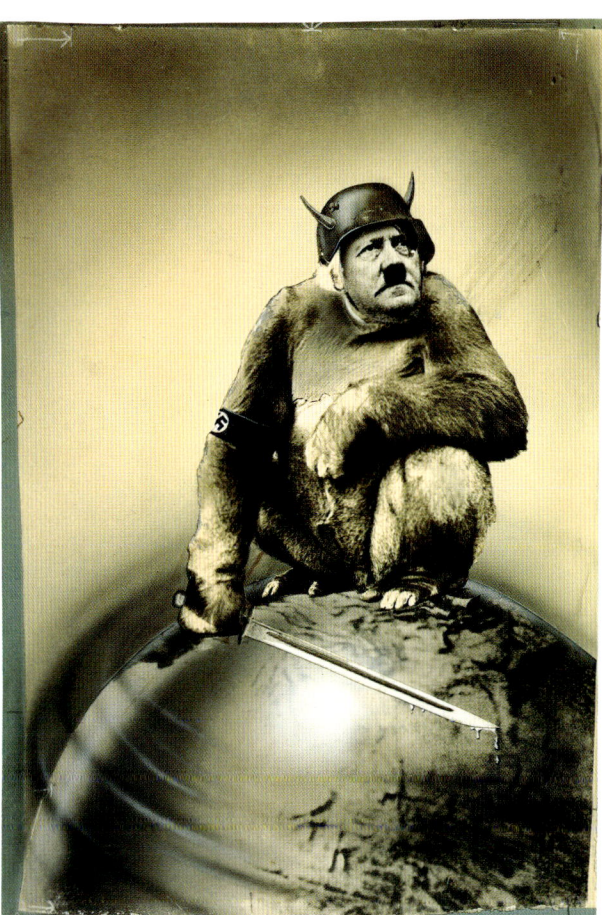

61

john heartfield   77

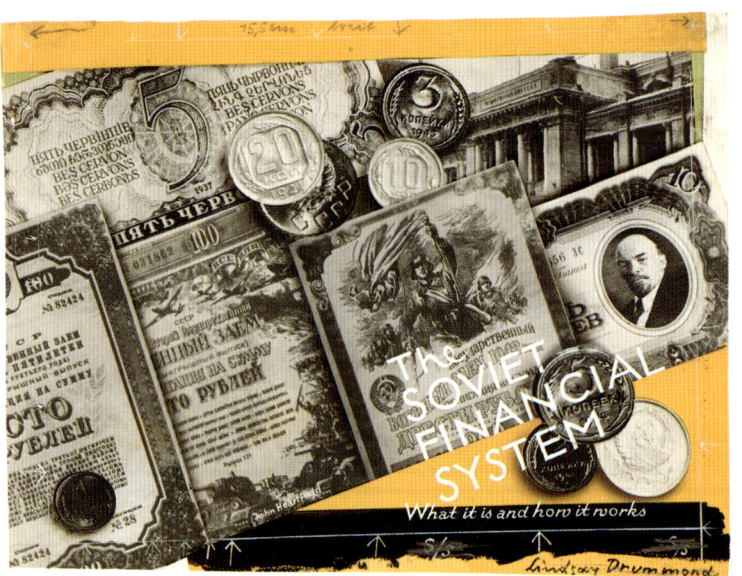 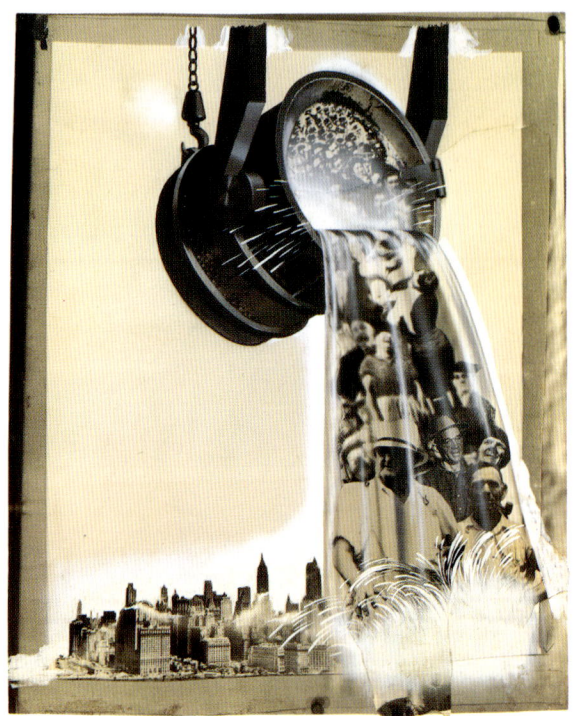

62
John Heartfield, *Soviet Financial System*, 1945 (cat. no. 68).

63
John Heartfield, *American Melting Pot*, 1946 (cat. no. 69).

Financial System: What It Is and How It Works (1945; fig. 62, cat. no. 68), showed a field of Soviet coins and bills whose images of fighting warplanes, heroic troops, and Lenin rise diagonally toward the state bank building, or Gosudarstvennyi Bank, in Moscow.

The montage for Wyndham Lewis's essay "American Melting Pot" (1946; fig. 63, cat. no. 69), included in a volume of miscellany titled *Britain Meets East and West,* published by Contact Books in 1946, depicts a great industrial pot that pours a stream of translucent, molten steel filled with masses of ordinary people before a New York skyline. In the 1920s and 1930s Lewis's books attacking liberal social reforms, speaking favorably of Hitler and Nazism, and championing an authoritarian state modeled on communist Russia, Fascist Italy, and Nazi Germany had made him one of the most hated writers in Britain. He had spent the war in Canada and the United States, however, and greatly modified his views. This essay endorsed an antinationalistic melting pot as the hope for the birth of the new "cosmic man."[10] Heartfield was conceivably brought into the project by Klingender, who also contributed to the volume.

Both in Weimar Germany and in his Prague exile, Heartfield was an antifascist communist activist who reached a broad public through the popular media. In England, more distant from his target, he found it difficult to sustain that attack. He lacked sufficient access to and control of an appropriate journal, not to mention a knowledgeable audience that was responsive to his political message, caustic humor, and language. Further restricted by the war, by his identity as both a German and a communist, and by his poor health, Heartfield had few opportunities to use his art as a political weapon. Out of necessity he undertook many different kinds of work and did not regret those experiences. He was exposed both to a more moderate liberalism and to many other aspects of communism in England and received support and encouragement from bourgeois liberals such as Drummond and Marxists such as Klingender. Unswayed by those alternatives, Heartfield remained convinced that his and Germany's future lay in a new communist republic, and he returned to East Berlin in 1950.

Notes

Anne Grevstad-Nordbrock, a Ph.D. student at the University of Wisconsin, Madison, undertook the initial research, chronology, and analyses on which this essay was based.

1   See David Evans, *John Heartfield: AIZ—Arbeiter-Illustrierte Zeitung—Volks-illustrierte, 1930–38* (New York: Kent Fine Art, 1992).

2   See Fred Uhlman, *Erinnerungen eines Stuttgarter Judens* (Stuttgart: Klett-Cotta, 1992), 152–56.

3   Keith Holz, *Modern German Art and Its Public* (Ann Arbor, Mich.: UMI, 1994), 308.

4   Uhlman, *Erinnerungen eines Stuttgarter Judens,* 156.

5   Gertrud Heartfield, quoted in Roland März, ed., *Der Schnitt entlang der Zeit: Selbstzeugnisse—Erinnerungen—Interpretationen: Eine Dokumentation* (Dresden: VEB Verlag der Kunst, 1981), 422–23.

6   Gertrud Heartfield, quoted in Eckhard Siepmann, ed., *Montage: John Heartfield vom Club Dada zur Arbeiter-Illustrierten Zeitung* (Berlin: Elefanten Presse, 1977), 222–24.

7   See Cordula Frowein, "Ausstellungsaktivitäten der Exilkünstler," in *Kunst in Exil in Großbritannien, 1933–1945,* exh. cat. (Berlin: Neue Gesellschaft für bildende Kunst, Orangerie des Schlosses Charlottenburg, 1986), 39–46.

8   Cf. *AIZ* 12 (16 November 1933): 755.

9   Brecht wrote both a poem on Dimitrov and a series of Galileo plays; see Bärbel Schrader and Günther Klotz, eds., *Bertolt Brecht: Stücke,* vol. 5 of *Bertolt Brecht: Werke* (Berlin, Weimar, and Frankfurt: Aufbau-Verlag and Suhrkamp Verlag, 1988), 331–36. Three of Brecht's poems were included in this issue of *Freie deutsche Dichtung,* 18–24.

10   See Julian Symons, ed., *The Essential Wyndham Lewis* (London: André Deutsch, 1989), 4–10, 115–31.

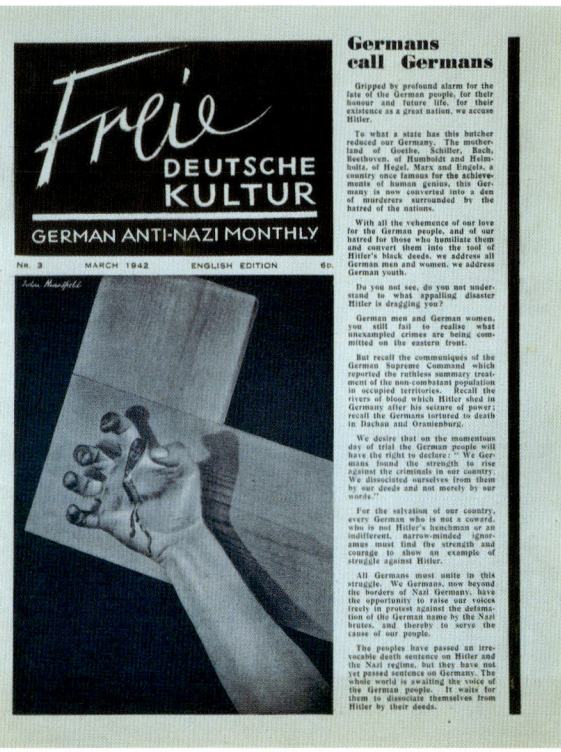

64
John Heartfield, Untitled, 1942 (cat. no. 66).

kurt schwitters in england, 1940–45

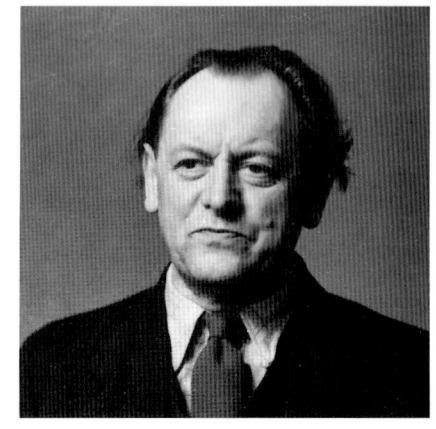

1887	born in Hannover, Germany
1937	immigrates to Norway (Lysaker, Oslo)
1940	immigrates to England (London, Ambleside)
1948	dies in Kendal-Ambleside, England

In his *Merz* collages and constructions Kurt Schwitters spiritedly punctured the fine surface of art, weaving debris and clippings into abstraction. In the late 1910s and early 1920s his works rapidly captivated the international avant-garde but simultaneously antagonized many others, both large art-loving and art-hating publics as well as the leftist Berlin dadaists, who found *Merz* too aesthetic. Schwitters confidently and stubbornly maintained that art should be autonomous and not political, yet he always recognized that it had an uncanny, delightful, and disturbing force that worked in both the public and private spheres.

Since his works had long been attacked, Schwitters had no illusions about where he would stand in a National Socialist regime. After the Nazis took power, he and his family stayed abroad for increasingly long periods, especially in Norway, where they had vacationed since the 1920s. He dreaded emigration from Hannover, where he had long enjoyed considerable spiritual and financial well-being,[1] and he rightly sensed that he would have difficulties in another milieu. Schwitters must have determined to leave by the late autumn of 1936, however, when he would have learned of the scope of the forthcoming "degenerate art" measures. His wife, Helma, the beloved "Anna Blume" of his works and poems, stayed in Hannover to manage the family's properties, which had become their primary source of income;[2] Schwitters and their nineteen-year-old son, Ernst, who was involved in antifascist activities, immigrated to Norway on January 1, 1937.

Schwitters immediately resumed his production of romantic Norwegian landscapes and realistic portraits, a practice he justified because it challenged him to come to terms with natural appearances and was also a source of income. He resumed work on his abstract *Merzbilder,* or collages, as well and on a second, supposedly portable *Merzbau.*[3] He continued his correspondence with a broad network of friends—including Jean Arp and Sophie Taeuber-Arp, Carola Giedion-Welcker, Katherine Dreier, and Kate Steinitz, inviting them to Norway to see his works and requesting their help for an eventual move to the United States, where he assumed he would have no trouble finding support. Nevertheless, he was reluctant to leave Norway even as the Germans arrived; he and Ernst were able to escape to Britain only through Ernst's connections with the Norwegian foreign secretary. Immediately after their arrival in Edinburgh on June 19, 1940, they were arrested and interned as enemy aliens.

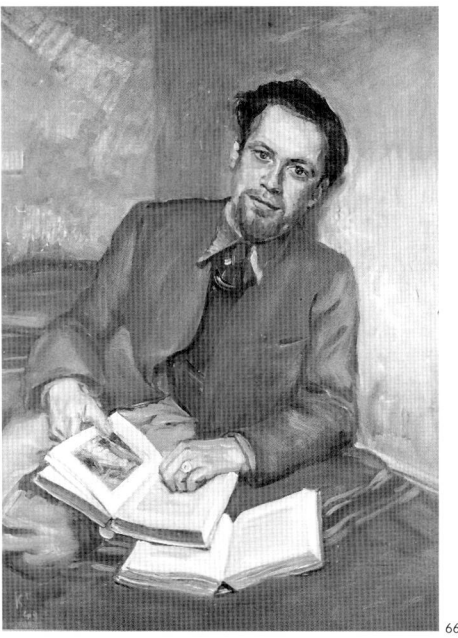

80 buenger

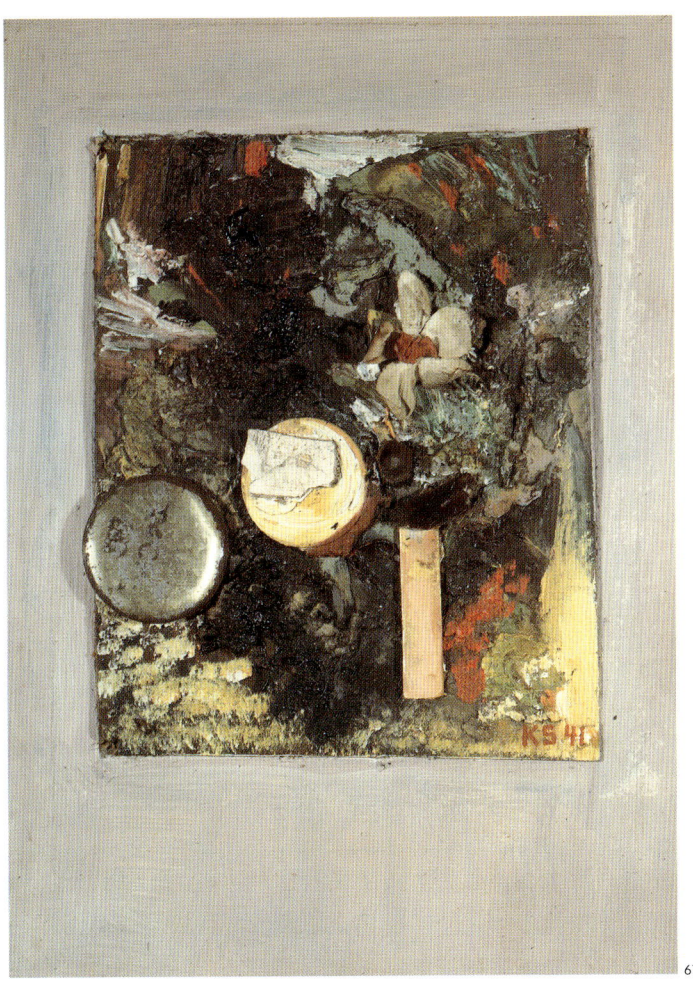

67

65
Kurt Schwitters, London, 1944; photograph by Ernst Schwitters.

66
Kurt Schwitters; *Portrait of Fred Uhlman*, 1945; oil on panel; 40⅛ x 29½ in. (102 x 75 cm); Hatton Gallery, University of Newcastle upon Tyne.

67
Kurt Schwitters, *Small Flower Picture*, 1941 (cat. no. 125).

For reasons that are unknown, Schwitters was held in the Hutchinson Camp at Douglas on the Isle of Man for the unusually long period of one and a half years. His works had been featured in the 1936 *International Surrealist Exhibition* in London and the 1938 *Exhibition of Twentieth Century German Art,* held at London's New Burlington Galleries. British admirers wrote to authorities on his behalf, and he and Ernst protested their internment in a letter to the *New Statesman.* Yet Schwitters had few friends in England, lacked political connections, and was not publicly identified as an antifascist. One can only imagine that his odd artistic preoccupations, scant English, and general intractability aroused concerns about both his politics and his ability to support himself on the outside.

Schwitters readily joined in the Hutchinson activities of newspapers, concerts, readings, lectures, and films. There and throughout his exile he continued to write poetry, prose, and essays and to produce the realistic portraits (see fig. 66) and lush landscapes that constituted his few works that were sold in England during his lifetime. He made between two and three hundred works of art at the camp, now fabricating *Merz* from junk, porridge, linoleum, and paint.[4] *Small Flower Picture* (1941; fig. 67, cat. no. 125), for instance, which combined the "vegetable density"[5] of his earlier abstraction with attached elements of a bouquet, was produced on a piece of linoleum from a camp floor.

After he was finally released from Hutchinson in December 1941, Schwitters joined his son in Bayswater, where he met Edith Thomas, who became his companion at the end of his life; in 1943 he moved into a home in Barnes. Ernst was employed by the Norwegian government in exile, and Schwitters managed the house and garden and painted. Schwitters wrote everyone he knew in search of monetary assistance but experienced financial hardship for the remainder of his life. In January 1944 he suffered a severe stroke, and in 1945 he moved with Thomas to the Lake District. He continued to suffer acute health problems but enjoyed several periods of productivity and recognition after the war. He was heartened to collaborate with the former Berlin dadaist Raoul Hausmann, and a 1947 stipend from the Museum of Modern Art enabled him to undertake his third *Merzbau* in Harry Pierce's barn in Elterwater, a project he had almost completed before his death in January 1948.

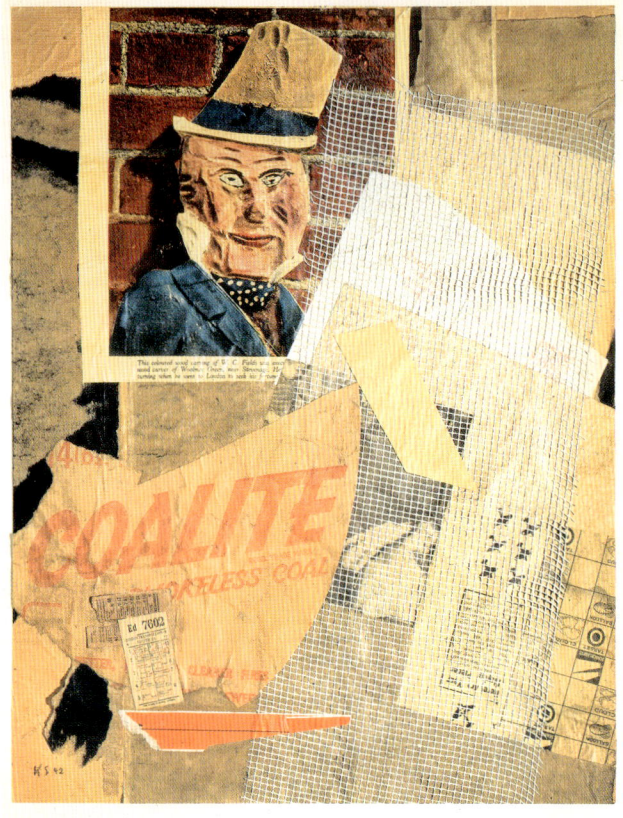

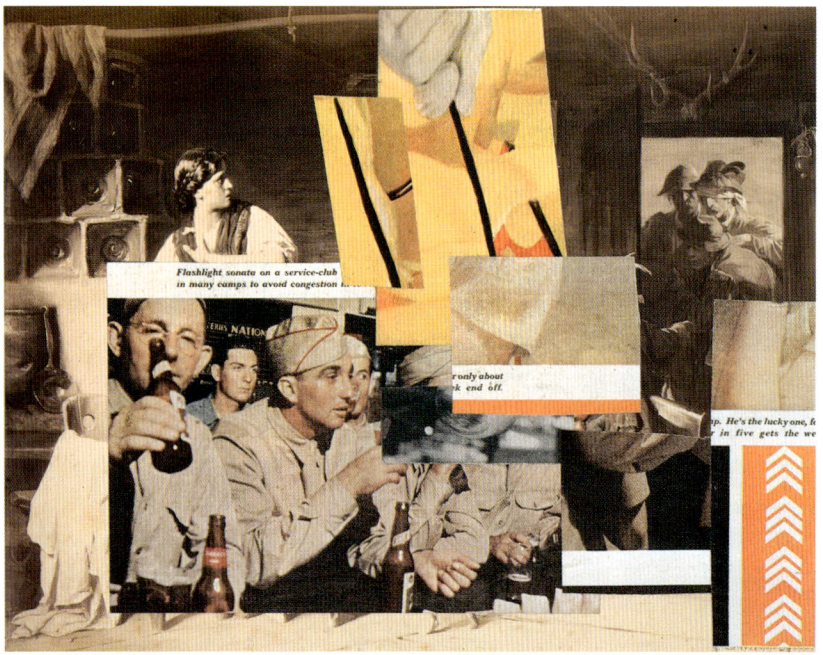

68
Kurt Schwitters, *W. C. Fields*, 1942 (cat. no. 127).

69
Kurt Schwitters, *The Wounded Hunter*, 1942 (cat. no. 128).

Schwitters quickly established contacts with those members of the international avant-garde in London (including Naum Gabo, Barbara Hepworth, E. L. T. Mesens, Lucia Moholy-Nagy, Ben Nicholson, Roland Penrose, Herbert Read, and Stefan and Franciska Themerson) with whom he felt the strongest affinities. His art did not go over well with the public, however, and he received only a single solo show during his exile, at the Modern Art Gallery of Jack Bilbo, a fellow refugee and internee at Hutchinson, in December 1944. Though Schwitters joined the Artists International Association in 1942 and participated in several of its shows, he increasingly maintained his distance both from it and from the Free German League of Culture because of their strongly politicized stances. In 1947 he complained bitterly that John Heartfield had made the league a vassal to communism.[6]

Amid their irony, abstract and idiosyncratic elements, and coded word and pictorial play, Schwitters's exile works contain many references to his times and his situation. In *W. C. Fields* (1942; fig. 68, cat. no. 127) a piece of netting protectively covers a number of images apparently associated with Schwitters and Ernst: a children's war game; an envelope from the Norway House, which then housed the Norwegian Ministry of Defense and might have been where Ernst worked; and a chick that opens its wings. The colored illustration of a wood sculpture of W. C. Fields (who wore the hat shown only in *My Little Chickadee* [1940]), may stand in for Schwitters himself, who would also have identified with the unknown sculptor, who "went to London to seek his fortune." A torn label from the commercial fuel product

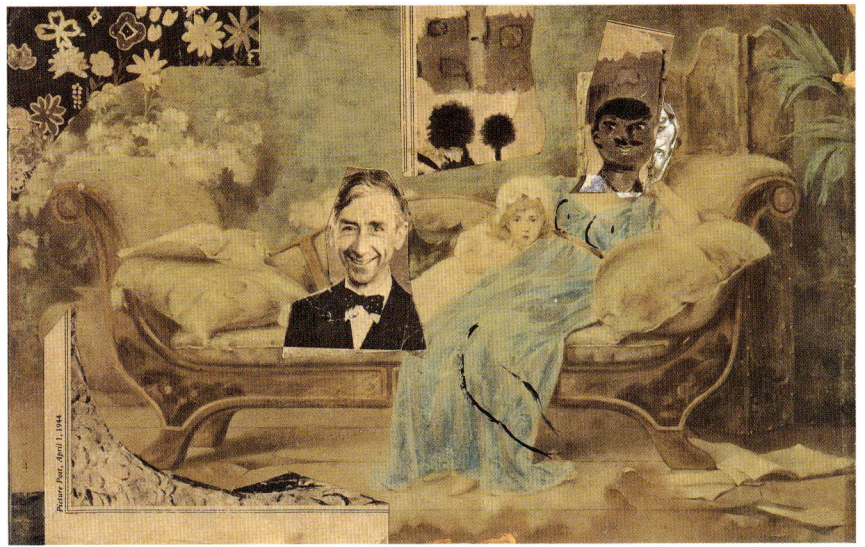
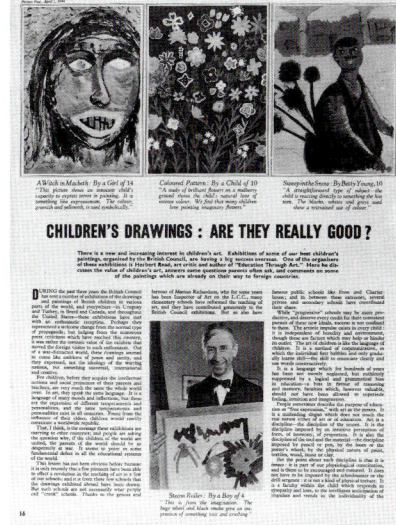

70
Kurt Schwitters, *Collage (Herbert Read)*, 1944 (cat. no. 129).

71
Page from the *Picture Post*, April 1, 1944, showing a photograph of Herbert Read.

"Coalite...okeless coal" and two transit tickets might also refer to their activities: the two escapees from Nazi Germany had come to "co-alight" in London to make "better... cleaner fires."

By 1942 Schwitters had acquired a photogravure portfolio of works by Franz von Defregger (1835–1921), the popular Austrian-German painter of idyllic rural folk scenes, published by the Hanfstaengl art-publishing house in Munich. Schwitters undoubtedly knew that the heir to the Hanfstaengl firm, Ernst ("Putzi") Hanfstaengl, was one of the early wealthy supporters of Hitler and that the German taste for Defregger remained unabated. As a once-successful, internationally known avant-gardist who was now penniless in London, Schwitters was unquestionably aware of the ironies of his creating *Merz* out of Hanfstaengl[7] and Defregger. Indeed, the eight known Defregger collages contain several references to war and exile.[8]

The many images of women in the Defregger collages and other wartime works not only recall Schwitters's and Hannah Höch's earlier preoccupation with feminine subjects but may also refer to the absence of Helma. *The Wounded Hunter* (1942; fig. 69, cat. no. 128) mocked Defregger's melodrama of a wife's shock at her wounded husband's return. The Defregger wife may be a stand-in for Helma and the hunter may represent Schwitters himself, imprisoned or incapacitated in Great Britain. Fragmented images and clichés from the contemporary popular press—a woman's hand with a thin beater; a woman's arm under a short-sleeved blouse; and a group of GIs drinking bottled American beer—obliterate Defregger's crowded domestic scene and suggest both female sensuality and escape. The reconstructed caption below the woman's arm reveals the "hunter's" good fortune: "–p. He's the lucky one, for only about /–r in five gets the week end off."

The small *Collage (Herbert Read)* (1944; fig. 70, cat. no. 129) pays homage to the new friend and critic who would write an introduction to the catalogue of Schwitters's exhibition at Bilbo's. Schwitters enlivened an older, amusingly sentimental representation of a mother and child sitting listlessly, journals flung to the floor, with collaged elements from the April Fool's Day issue of the *Picture Post,* which featured Read, then working on the art of children, and a number of pictures by children (fig. 71).[9] He enlarged and spiced up the scene through his placement of the photos of Read and the children's art and by adding sexual diversity and amplitude to the figure of the reclining woman.

Schwitters produced both the Herbert Read collage and *The Hitler Gang* (c. 1944; fig. 72, cat. no. 130) when he was closely associated with the Themersons, the Polish Dada filmmakers who had just completed a successful experimental film that directly attacked Hitler,

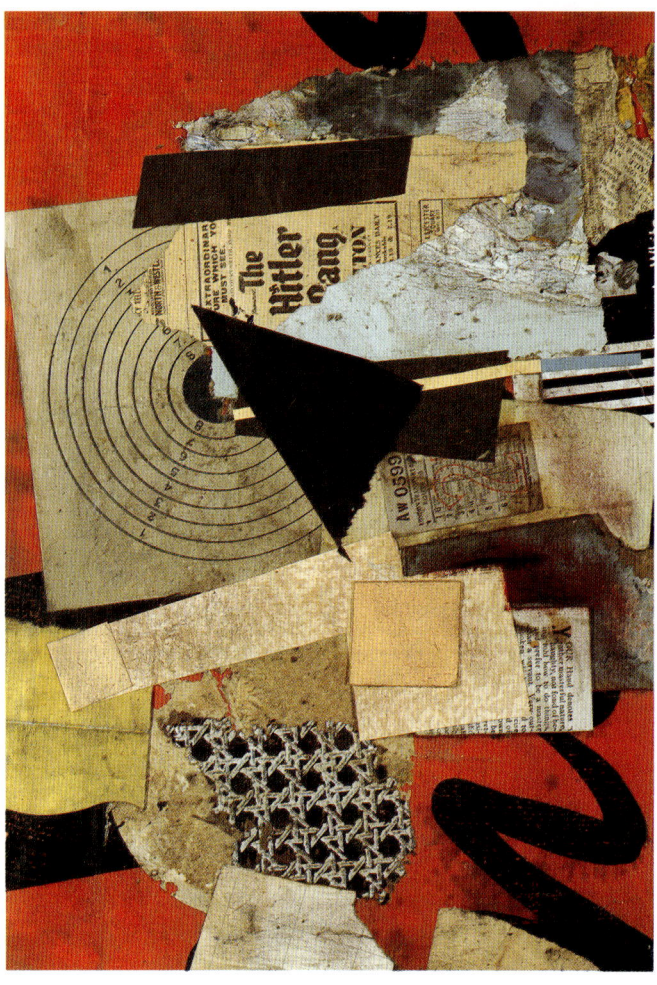

72
Kurt Schwitters, *The Hitler Gang*, c. 1944 (cat. no. 130).

Calling Mr. Smith (1943).[10] Both their film and the renewed German bombing of London might have inspired Schwitters to use his own form of abstraction to take a direct shot at Hitler; *The Hitler Gang* was the only work in which he did so. The title was taken from a newspaper advertisement for John Farrow's 1944 Paramount film, a serious and critical portrayal of the group (including Hanfstaengl) that had supported Hitler's rise to power. Schwitters turned the clipping with the words *The Hitler Gang* on an angle as if he were setting it in his sight and framed it with a real shooting target and ominous abstract elements. He underlined his own command of the situation as an active and insubordinate artist with the accompanying fortune: "your hand denotes a rather masterful nature, haughty, not fond of being told how to do things, and prefer to be a master than servant, very outspoken." The frequently noted piece of chair caning in Schwitters's collage, which recalls Picasso's collage of 1912,[11] not only pays homage to a forerunner of *Merz* but also suggests a steady, even line of shots. More overtly than in the Defregger collages, Schwitters demonstrated that precisely because his art was abstract, difficult, and rebellious, it could be an effective expression of resistance.

Many of Schwitters's abstract *Merz* assemblages and sculptures, including *The Double Picture* (1942; fig. 73, cat. no. 126), initially demand reading solely on a formal level. Both this and *Heavy Relief* (1945) with its substantial plaster and organic or organically suggestive form, closely approach the transformed and abstracted natural motifs in the Elterwater *Merzbau* and his many earlier cosmic abstractions. All, however, emphasize the discrepancy between the components' gritty origins and the more transcendent scope of abstraction, the tug-of-war between art and reality which the artist always sought to articulate.

Schwitters left Germany because of his political and personal needs to continue his work and protect his son. Just as he had in Weimar Germany, he continued to insist that art must be apolitical and serve only the spirit, yet he persisted in making work that got under the skin and hit many of its targets—particularly German complacency, narrow-mindedness, and belligerency. He did not waver from his commitment to art as an autonomous, searching, and utterly human pursuit; even through the protective irony of his *Merz* play, his art speaks with depth and pungency of his difficult exile experience.

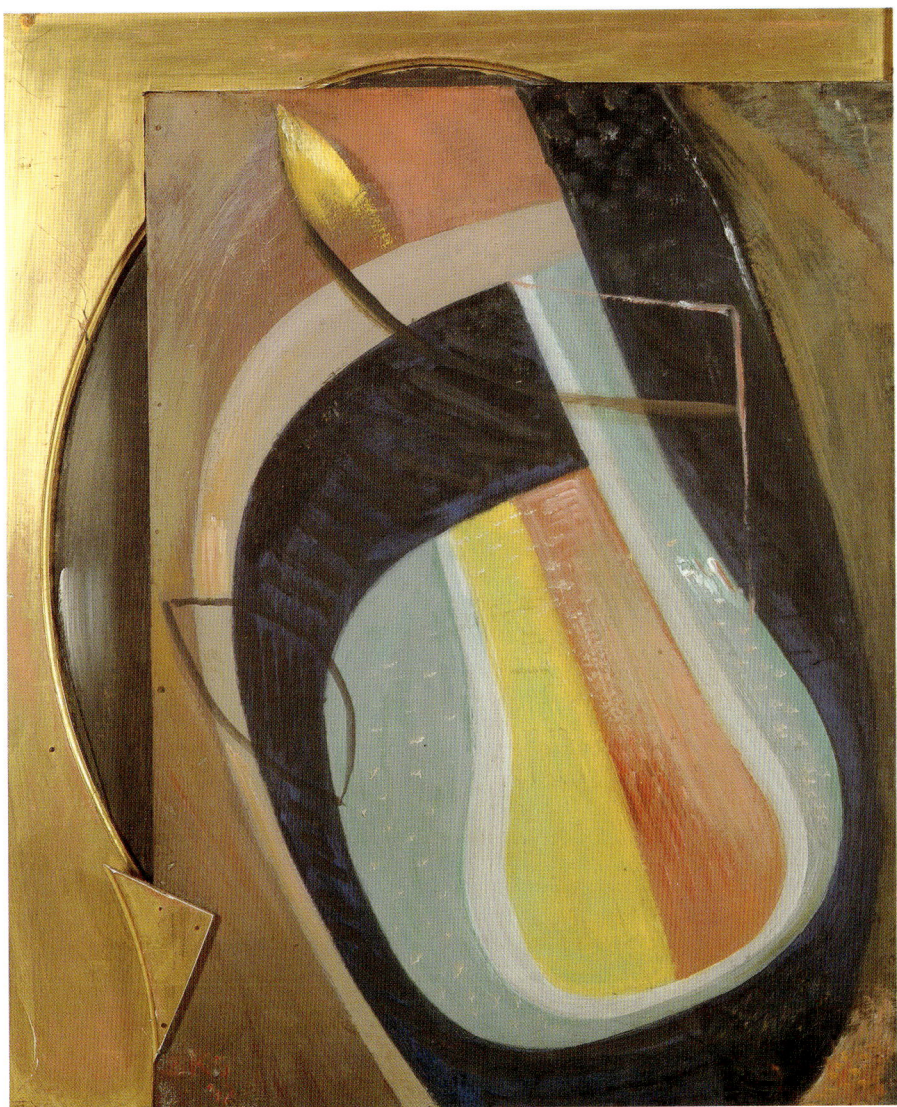

73
Kurt Schwitters, *The Double Picture*, 1942 (cat. no. 126).

Notes

Susan L. Funkenstein, a Ph.D. student at the University of Wisconsin, Madison, undertook the initial research, chronology, and analyses on which this essay was based.

1 Sibyl Moholy-Nagy, *Moholy-Nagy: Experiment in Totality*, 2d ed. (Cambridge: MIT Press, 1969), 98.

2 Although Helma occasionally visited them, she last saw them in 1939 and died of cancer in 1944.

3 Schwitters's first *Merzbau* was an environment of found objects which he constructed in his home in Hannover between 1920 and 1937; it was destroyed by bombing in 1943. He abandoned his second *Merzbau* when he fled Norway in 1940, and it was destroyed by fire in 1951. He was working on a third *Merzbau* at the time of his death.

4 Fred Uhlman, *Erinnerungen eines Stuttgarter Judens* (Stuttgart: Klett-Cotta, 1992), 164–74.

5 John Elderfield, *Kurt Schwitters* (New York: Thames and Hudson, 1985), 217.

6 Schwitters to Carola Giedion-Welcker, 19 August 1947; quoted in *Carola Giedion-Welcker: Schriften, 1926–1971*, ed. Reinhold Hohl (Cologne: DuMont, 1973), 506.

7 Hanfstaengl had himself fled Hitler and Germany in February 1937, an escape that was internationally reported.

8 Another of the collages, for instance, referred to his fellow Hutchinson internee Siegfried Charoux.

9 "Children's Drawings: Are They Really Good?" *Picture Post* 23 (1 April 1944): 16–18.

10 These connections were first suggested in Sarah Wilson, "Kurt Schwitters en Angleterre," in *Kurt Schwitters*, exh. cat. (Paris: Réunion des Musées Nationaux, Editions du Centre Pompidou, 1994), 299.

11 Picasso's *Still Life with Chair Caning* (1912) could have been known to Schwitters only through the reproduction in Alfred H. Barr Jr., *Picasso: Forty Years of His Art* (New York: Museum of Modern Art, 1939), 78, which conceivably could have made its way to one of Schwitters's acquaintances in London.

oskar kokoschka in london, 1938–45

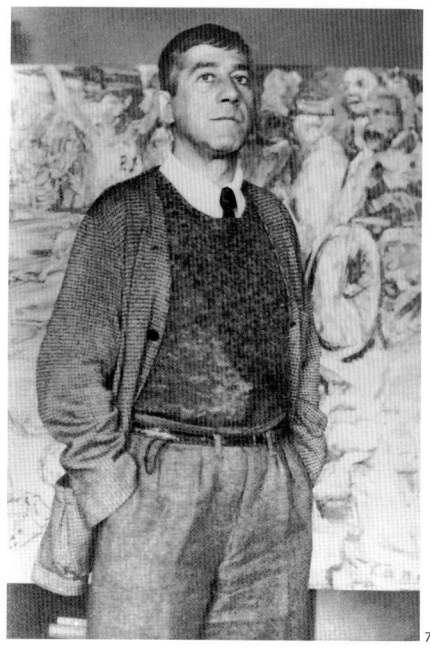

1886	born in Pöchlarn, Austria
1934	immigrates to Czechoslovakia (Prague)
1938	immigrates to England (London)
1953	immigrates to Switzerland (Villenueve)
1980	dies in Villenueve, Switzerland

In October 1934 Oskar Kokoschka quit Vienna for Prague, the capital of the First Czechoslovak Republic.[1] Four years later, following the Munich agreement and the German Wehrmacht's entry into the Sudetenland, he escaped by air to London, where, except for excursions to the countryside and Scotland, he remained for the duration of the war. His relocation to Prague was motivated less by political conditions brought about by the election of Austrofascist Engelbert Dollfuss as chancellor in 1932 than by the desire for an improved market for his pictures.

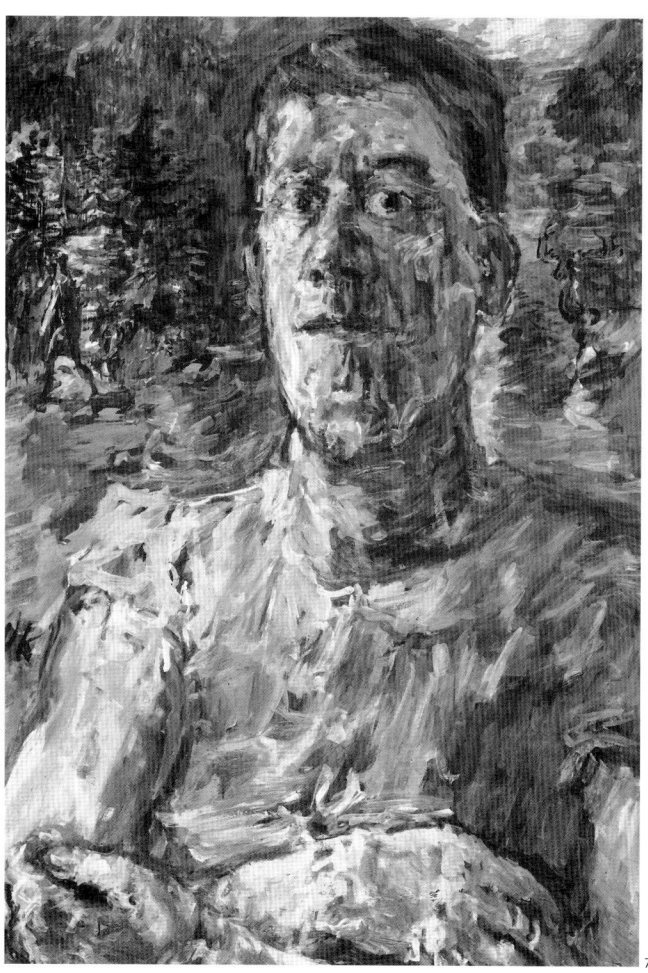

Kokoschka's *Self-Portrait as a Degenerate Artist* (fig. 75),[2] painted in Prague in 1937, is one record of the fifty-year-old artist's timely consideration of how to respond to the German government's "degenerate art" campaign. The campaign began in Munich in July 1937 with the traveling exhibition *Entartete Kunst* (Degenerate art) and also included the confiscation of thousands of artworks from German public collections, including 417 by Kokoschka. The painting's title, together with its depiction of the artist with his exposed arms crossed behind his cupped hand, retains vestiges of the conventional representation of the artist as martyr—that pre-World War I trope of the artist alienated from society which Kokoschka had so productively explored in Vienna and Berlin. Yet in this self-portrait retreat into subjective reflection yields to assertiveness. Set in the immediate foreground, before a wooded mountain landscape with a hunted stag and running man, the artist presents himself as confident, if not defiant, collecting his energies. His attentive visage is modeled by multicolored, abbreviated, and discontinuous brush strokes—this at a moment when Hitler was railing against excesses in facture and color and when exiled leftist artists and intellectuals in Prague were asking whether they must defend expressionism merely because Hitler had defamed it.[3] *Self-Portrait as a Degenerate Artist* marks Kokoschka's transition from exploiting a commercially viable

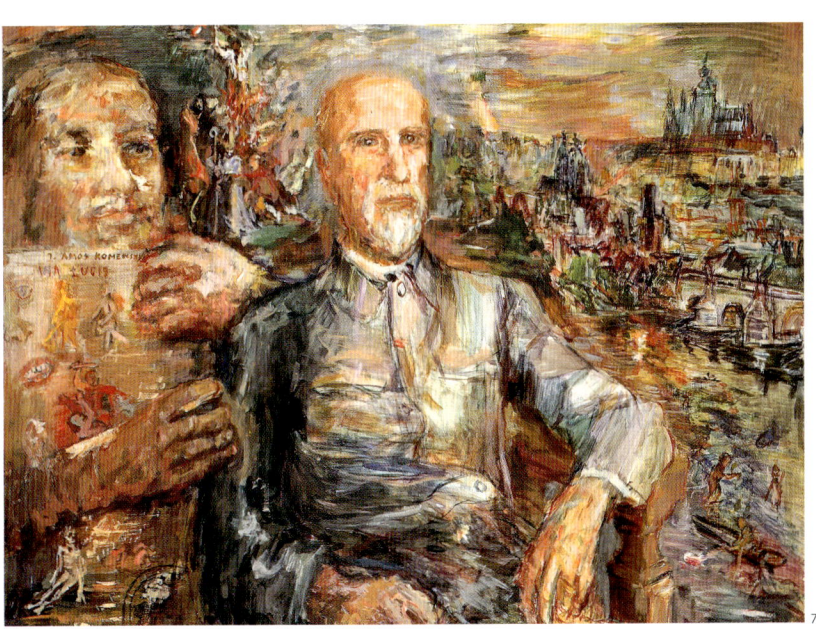

74
Oskar Kokoschka in front of the painting *What We Are Fighting For*, London, 1943.

75
Oskar Kokoschka; *Self-Portrait as a Degenerate Artist*, 1937; oil on canvas; 43¼ x 33½ in. (110 x 85 cm); private collection, on loan to the Scottish National Gallery of Modern Art, Edinburgh.

76
Oskar Kokoschka, *Thomas Garrique Masaryk*, 1936 (cat. no. 82).

77
Installation view of the exhibition *Freie deutsche Kunst*, Paris, November 1938, showing the slashed *Portrait of Robert Freund* by Kokoschka; photograph by Josef Breitenbach.

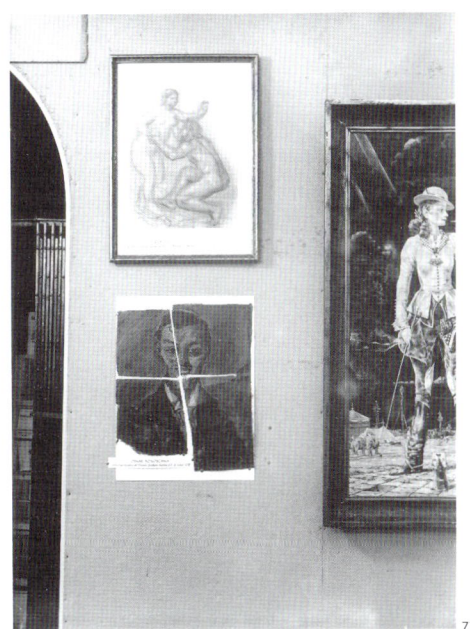

public identity based on martyrdom toward active participation in the anti-Nazi cultural organizations to which he would devote so much of his energy in London.

Unlike Kokoschka's voluntary relocation to Prague, his flight to London was forced. After the annexation of Austria by Germany in March 1938 Central Europe became forbidden terrain for him. The institutional support he had received in Prague was no longer forthcoming in occupied Czechoslovakia. Similarly, in Vienna, where as late as May 1937 Kokoschka's old friend Carl Mopp had realized a retrospective at the Museum für angewandte Kunst und Industrie in honor of Kokoschka's fiftieth birthday,[4] Kokoschka's artwork was exhibited in May and June 1939 in *Entartete Kunst*, which traveled to the Austrian capital.[5] After the Nazis marched into Vienna in 1938, his *Portrait of Robert Freund* of 1910 was slashed by the Gestapo during a house search.[6] With Kokoschka's help the Freier Künstlerbund (Free league of artists) exhibited the mutilated painting in *Freie deutsche Kunst* (Free German art) later that year in Paris as evidence of the Nazis' barbaric treatment of the arts (see fig. 77).[7]

Kokoschka's move from self-absorption to open political engagement—a transformation also undergone by Thomas Mann and many others at this time—was negotiated through a range of involvements with fellow exiles. Kokoschka was sought out by exiled German and Austrian artists' groups in Prague, Paris, and London to serve as their public representative. He allowed the Oskar-Kokoschka-Bund in Prague the use of his name and little else;[8] from Paris's Freier Künstlerbund he

oskar kokoschka

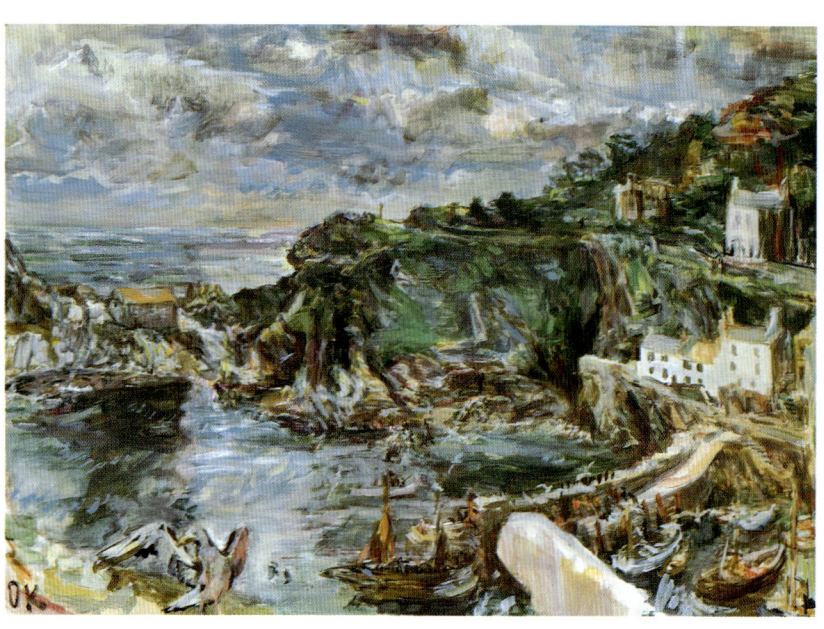

78
Oskar Kokoschka, *Polperro II*, 1939 (cat. no. 83).

accepted an honorary presidency, and he penned several letters on the group's behalf.[9] His commitments in London to the Free German League of Culture and the various cultural groups within the Free Austria Movement, however, were more thoroughgoing. Tracing Kokoschka's transformation from outsider to kingpin of the German and Austrian exile artists groups involves not only tracking his geographic relocations (Vienna-Prague-London and excursions to the English and Scottish countrysides) but also considering his own representations in word and image of his migrant identity, which underwent marked readjustments between 1934 and 1945.

Kokoschka's shifting relationships to his places of residence also point to the difficulty of fitting him into the lexicographic pigeonholes suggested by terms such as *exile* or *emigrant*. The fit of such terms loosens when one asks whether his years in Prague and England comprise experiences so different from his move in 1910 from an intolerant Vienna to Berlin or from his travels between 1927 and 1931 as an itinerant painter producing landscapes to be marketed through his dealer. To adequately describe his early twentieth-century relocations, one would have to draw upon the vocabulary that has recently been brought into currency to describe the contingency of home and the multiple severances from place more common to the refugees, travelers, tourists, migrants, nomads, transients, and displaced persons of the latter part of this century. Moreover, Kokoschka's adoption of guises such as "knight errant,"[10] "happy tramp,"[11] and "emigrant"[12] during earlier phases of his life betrays his own chameleon-like reinventions of his identity amid successive migratory displacements.

On the back of one of his first canvases painted in England, the *Portrait of Michael Croft* (1938–39), Kokoschka added another term: "1939 in dirty exile, ill and poor nobody could pa[i]nt this work, but nobody could value it too, at this dirty time, when they all, every where, are hunting the artist and become slaves themselves." Unlike Kokoschka's earlier shifting self-characterizations, his donning of this last identification, "exile"—in the wake of the annexation of Austria and the Munich Accord—coincided with his adoption of a new approach to political action, namely, working with associations of exiled German and Austrian artists.

Shortly after his arrival in London, in December 1938, Kokoschka assumed the presidency of the visual artists' division of the newly founded Free German League of Culture. He remained head of the artists' section until 1941 and, from summer 1941 to 1946, was president

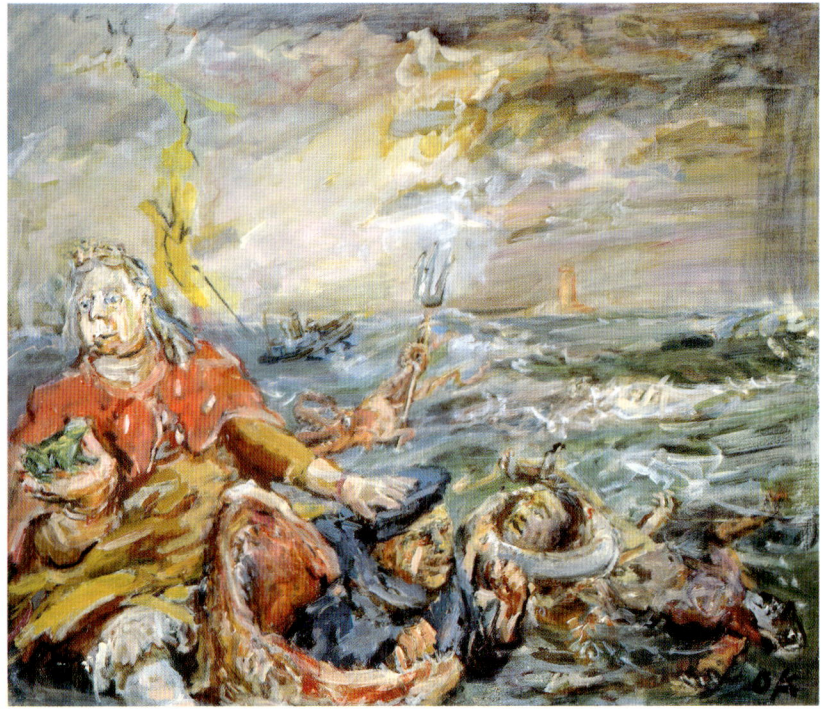

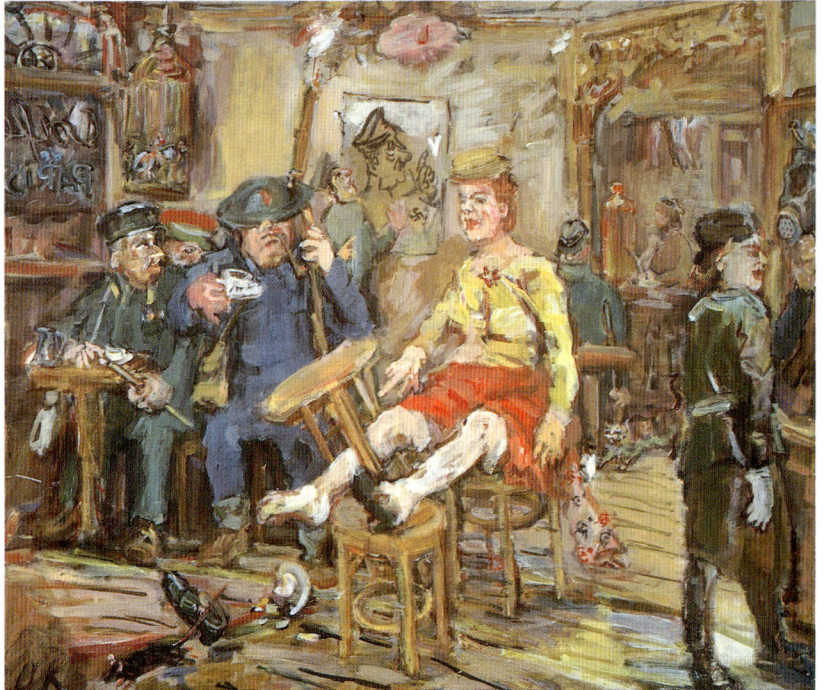

79
Oskar Kokoschka, *Loreley*, 1941–42 (cat. no. 84).

80
Oskar Kokoschka, *Marianne-Maquis*, 1942 (cat. no. 86).

of the entire league. Theo Balden, Georg Ehrlich, John Heartfield, Eugen Hoffmann, Fred Uhlman, and Heinz Worner were among the more than one hundred visual artists in this exile association, which comprised more than twelve hundred members.[13] Kokoschka also contributed to the league's many exhibitions, programs, and publications. The Czech citizenship he had obtained in Prague spared him internment, allowing him to assume a public role as a spokesperson for exiles. He was unwavering in his support of his fellow Austrian and German exiles, who, after the outbreak of the war and the formation of the "second front" in response to Germany's occupation of the Low Countries, were classified as enemy aliens by the British government. He also worked with the Austrian emigrés of London's Free Austria Movement, which unified in December 1941 and included at different times between fifteen and twenty-seven Austrian exile associations, such as the Austrian Centre and the youth group Young Austria.[14] In keeping with his Austrian heritage and German career, Kokoschka lent his support to both German and Austrian exiled artists' groups.

Upon Britain's declaration of war he joined other league executive committee members in underscoring to readers of the *Times* that exiles were victims of Nazi barbarism and stood with the British on the side of "freedom, culture, and democracy."[15] Whether on behalf of his first biographer, Freier Künstlerbund secretary Paul Westheim, who feared blindness as he sought to escape the Continent,[16] or of the thousands of children displaced and orphaned by the war, Kokoschka was always quick to offer assistance by making speeches, organizing exhibitions, or even by donating the proceeds from the sales of his artwork.

Between 1939 and 1943 Kokoschka painted a series of oil paintings that depict recent European political events or situations, including *Loreley* (1941–42; fig. 79, cat. no. 84) and *Marianne-Maquis* (1942; fig. 80, cat. no. 86). Scholars have identified the characters and motifs in these paintings and classified the entire group as political allegories.[17] Although

oskar kokoschka

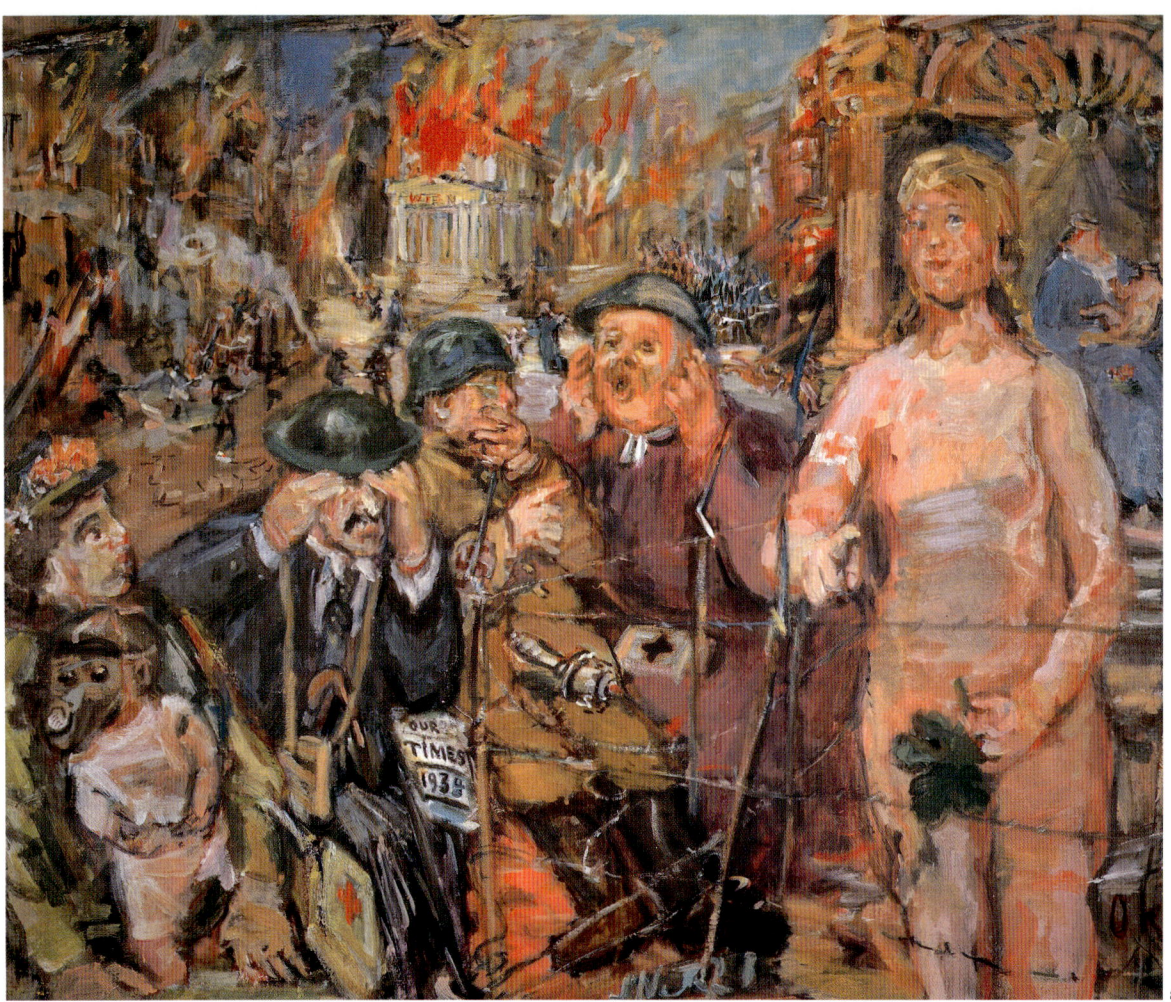

this classification separates these five canvases (the first four of identical size) from others in Kokoschka's oeuvre, it says little about the different modes of address adopted in the paintings. An important clue lies in each painting's temporal relationship to the political events described. For example, the series begins with a transposed memory of a political event that occurred more than a year earlier, *The Red Egg* (1940–41; fig. 28; see my essay in this catalogue for a discussion of this work), and ends with *What We Are Fighting For* (1943; fig. 83), which offers poignant and critical observations on the current political situation. My point can be supported by comparing Kokoschka's refiguration of politics as history in *"Anschluss"—Alice in Wonderland* (1942; fig. 81, cat. no. 85) with the later *What We Are Fighting For*.

In spring 1942 Kokoschka took up the theme of the annexation of his homeland in *"Anschluss"—Alice in Wonderland*. Austria is personified as a large, youthful blonde woman wearing only pigtails and a Red Cross armband. (The figure, usually identified as Naked Truth, covers her sex with an oak leaf.) Penned in by a barbed-wire fence, she is separated by a row of figures from a public square where street fighting is taking place before Vienna's burning Town Hall—reminiscent of the civil uprisings there in 1934. In the left foreground a woman holds a child outfitted with gas mask, and there are three men: Neville Chamberlain, holding his characteristic umbrella and sporting the helmet of a British air-raid warden, and a Nazi soldier with hand-grenade phallus, who points to the third man, a portly bishop, who covers his ears. Continuing in line with these figures, before a damaged baroque altar and behind Austria, a headless Virgin Mary sits in blue robes holding a decapitated Christ child. The three men mime the Chinese apes who can see, speak, and hear no evil—a pointed indictment of the complicity of the British government's

81
Oskar Kokoschka, *"Anschluss"—Alice in Wonderland*, 1942 (cat. no. 85).

82
Caricature by David Low criticizing British internment policies, first published in the *Evening Standard* in 1940 and reprinted in a Free German League of Culture pamphlet of the same year.

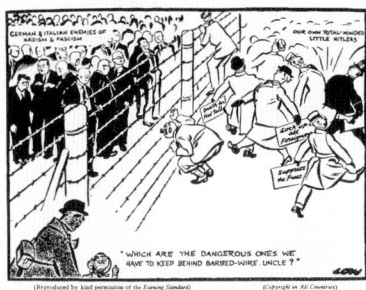

82

appeasement policies, the Nazis, and the Roman Catholic Church in allowing both Austrofascism and Nazism to undermine Austria's independence.

Moreover, to relate this scene to the Anschluss, most scholars have read the date on the paper beneath Chamberlain's elbow as 1938 rather than 1934, despite the rectilinear shape of the upper half of the final digit.[18] The civil strife in the background, however, is more suggestive of the street fighting and the occupation of government buildings that took place in 1934 than of any events accompanying the Anschluss. To accept the earlier date is to admit an expanded historical trajectory for Austria's loss of independence—one that includes the alliance of Austrofascists and clerics in the Vaterländische Front (Fatherland front), thereby broadening the web of those culpable far beyond the British prime minister.

The painting would have had particular resonance for Austrian and German exiles in Great Britain. As refugees whose journey had begun with a flight from Central Europe across the English Channel and whose legal identities had been repeatedly altered by British immigration policies, they would have identified with Lewis Carroll's Alice, who fell down a long rabbit hole only to be repeatedly subjected to apparently arbitrary transformations of scale.[19]

Kokoschka's portrayal of an Austria behind barbed wire was conditioned not only by his knowledge of the internment of Austrians and Germans—as recently as December 1941 he had published an article in London's Austrian exile newspaper calling for the release of Austrians interned in English camps[20]—but also by contemporary press illustrations addressing this topic, such as David Low's political cartoon from 1940, reprinted in a pamphlet of the Free German League of Culture (fig. 82).[21] Low places well-dressed "German and Italian enemies of Nazism & Fascism" on one side of the fence and the British agitators for internment, labeled "our own total-minded little Hitlers," on the other. The internment scene is presented from the viewpoint of a curious child, who asks, "Which are the dangerous ones we have to keep behind barbed wire, Uncle?" By adapting a well-known English children's tale, a manoeuver in keeping with the support he was then giving children's art and relief efforts for war orphans of all nationalities, Kokoschka expanded the potential audience for this painting by enhancing its legibility to those familiar with English literature, and to youth as well.

Such a reading is buttressed when we recall that Kokoschka donated the proceeds from the sale of this very painting to support

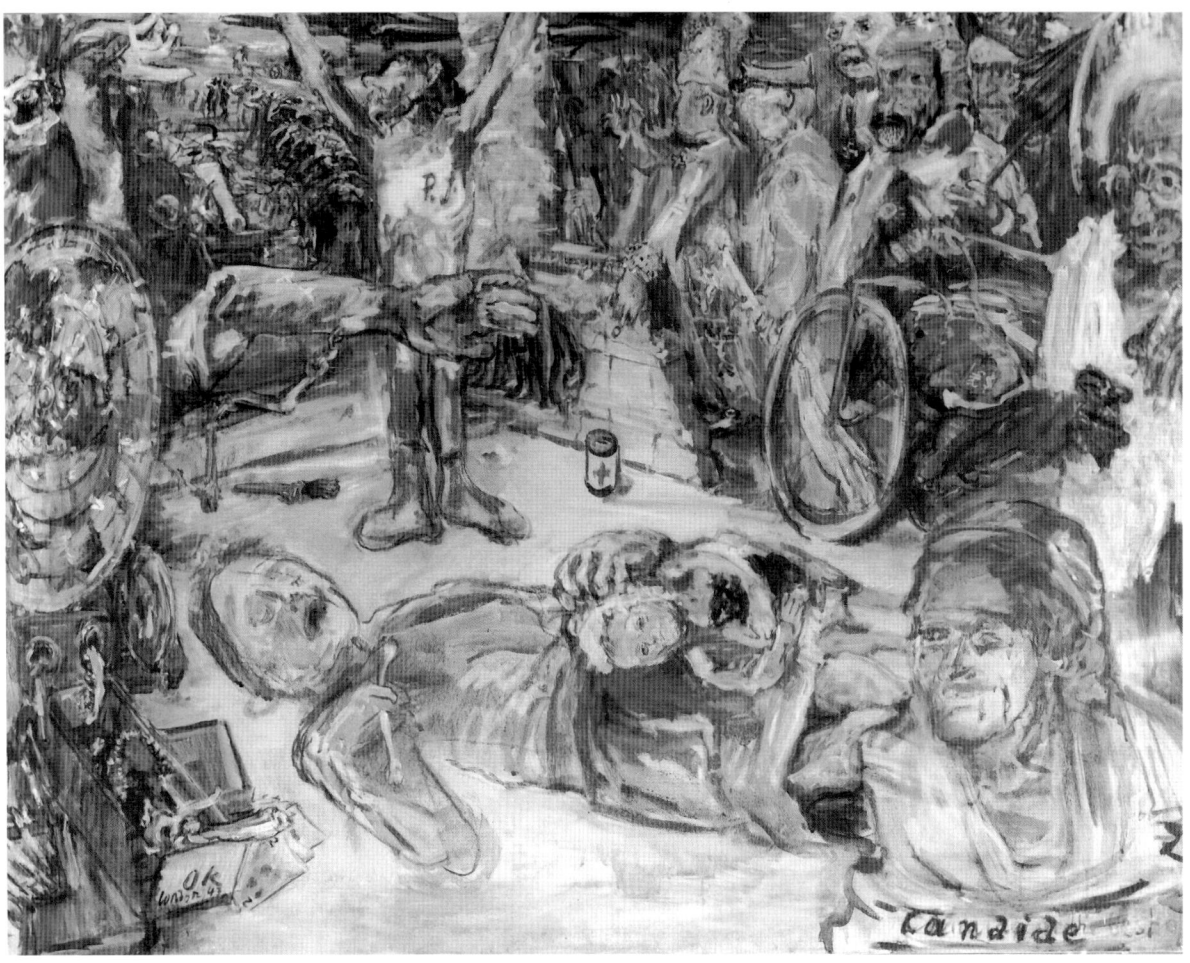

83
Oskar Kokoschka; *What We Are Fighting For*, 1943; oil on canvas; 45⅞ x 59⅞ in. (116.5 x 152 cm); Kunsthaus Zürich.

the education of young Austrians in Great Britain.[22] In December 1941 he signed the "Deklaration österreichischer Vereinigungen in Großbritannien" (Declaration of Austrian associations in Great Britain), endorsing the Austrian people's fight for freedom and expressing support for Britain, the Soviet Union, and their allies. This led to the founding in early 1942 of the Free Austria Movement, which unified the many Austrian exile associations pursuing the common goal of reestablishing a free, independent Austria. Kokoschka served on a committee for Young Austria and held leadership roles in both the Austrian Centre and the Austrian Youth Association. The specific aims of the declaration he signed included the assurance of the Austrian people's right to self-determination, as defined in the Atlantic Charter; that Austrians be allowed to enter the British civil service in order to produce armaments for the Allies; and to bring about a change in their enemy alien status. The first objective listed in the declaration, however, was to press for the British government's nonrecognition of the Anschluss.[23] Thus, *"Anschluss"— Alice in Wonderland* can be seen as advocating the interests of independent Austria in exile.

Kokoschka's last multifigure political allegory was the larger-format *What We Are Fighting For*. It was painted for the Artists International Association exhibition *For Liberty*, held in March 1943 in the improvised basement exhibition space of John Lewis's Oxford Street Department Store in London (and subsequently shown at the AIA's Charlotte Street Centre in London, June 8–28, 1944). The exhibition aimed to involve visual artists in producing propaganda for the Allied war effort, and for that it received strong praise from Britain's minister of information. The main exhibition hall contained four mural-size paintings celebrating the Atlantic Charter's Four Freedoms program,[24] accompanied by a large text panel listing the Four Freedoms: freedom of speech, freedom to worship, freedom from want, and freedom from fear.[25] Kokoschka's painting departed from the exhibition's celebratory tone, instead condemning nationalistically motivated warfare. Like his earlier pictorial and epistolary criticisms of British appeasement politics, this painting refused to comply with the propaganda aims of the Atlantic Charter and the British government.

In the painting's foreground, on the stage of a theater of cruelty, a victorious figure stands, arms aloft, over a supine, defeated figure, who paws a bonneted child, who in turn embraces a black rat.[26] To the left stands a whirling, fanlike war machine, which ingests human limbs and produces ammunition, while a regally clad rabbit rests on its haunches above. In the left background, beneath the warplane along the upper edge, is a sketch that may refer to the recent military reversal at Stalingrad, showing helmeted troops retreating to the left of a tank and prisoners of war, hands atop heads, advancing to the right. Behind the floor in the right background a large group of seven men who have profited from the war stand looking on. They include a bishop dropping a token contribution into a Red Cross box, Marshal Pétain, Bank of England governor and German sympathizer Montague Norman, and German financier Hjalmar Schacht. With the exception of Gandhi—whose "fighting for" Indian independence from British rule Kokoschka admired—before a rickshaw on the far right, the other two figures remain unidentified.

Rather than conforming to British and Allied war aims, Kokoschka's attempt to portray the unfolding global political situation expresses both humanitarian concern and cynical doubt about the repercussions of Allied triumphalism—doubt reinforced by the sardonically grinning bust of Voltaire in the immediate foreground. No concern is figured more prominently here than the fate of European Jewry, with the initials *P.J.*—Perish Judea—emblazoned on, if not carved into, the victor's chest. While financiers and the Catholic Church (and the organizers of the exhibition *For Liberty*) could now exult in turning the military tide against Nazi Germany, *What We Are Fighting For* points to the intertwined interests of Christianity, capital, and nationalism, which the artist viewed as a hindrance to international cooperation and the advancement of pressing humanitarian interests, interests on behalf of which he would continue to work for the remainder of his life.

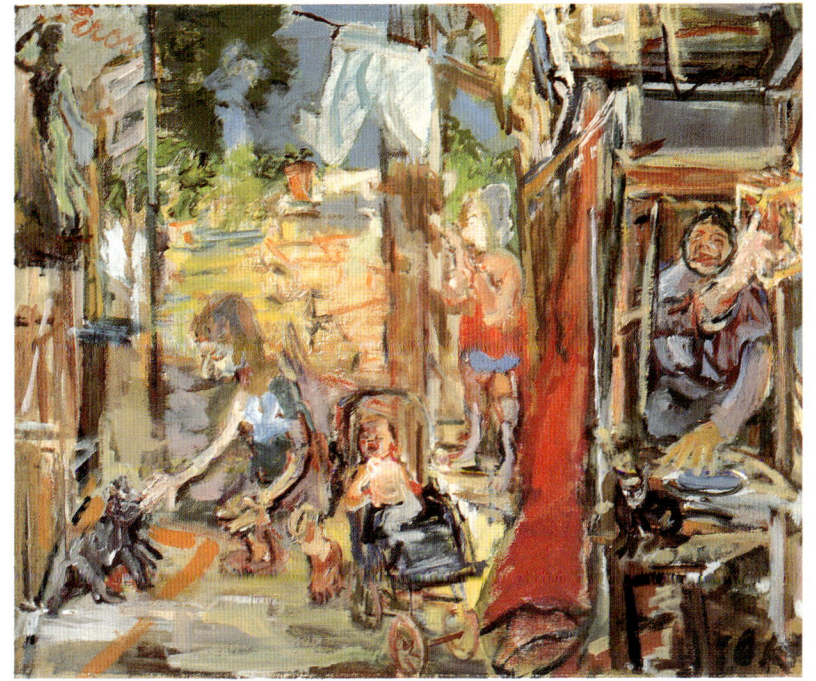

84
Oskar Kokoschka, *Family of Jugglers*, 1946 (cat. no. 87).

Notes

1   In addition to the works listed in the Bibliography, important sources on Kokoschka's years in Prague and London include *Drehscheibe Prag: Deutsche Emigranten / Staging Point Prague: German Exiles, 1933–1939*, exh. cat. (Munich: Sudetendeutsches Haus, 1989), 133–38; Robert Radford, *Art for a Purpose: The Artists' International Association, 1933–1953* (Winchester: Winchester School of Art Press, 1987), 137–47; Werner Haftmann, *Verfemte Kunst: Malerei der inneren und äußeren Emigration in der Zeit des Nationalsozialismus*, ed. Berthold Roland (Cologne: DuMont, 1986), 68–88; Diether Schmidt, "Partisan Oskar Kokoschka," in *Kunst im Exil in Großbritannien, 1933–1945*, exh. cat. (Berlin: Neue Gesellschaft für bildende Kunst, 1986), 189–94; Ludwig Hoffmann, ed., *Exil in der Tschechoslowakei, in Großbritannien, Skandinavien und Palästina*, vol. 5 of *Kunst und Literatur im antifaschistischen Exil, 1933–1945* (Leipzig: Philipp Reclam Jun., 1980), 294–302.

2   My reading derives in part from that of Richard Calvocoressi, in *Oskar Kokoschka* (New York: Rizzoli International, 1992), 20.

3   Ernst Bloch und Hanns Eisler, "Avantgarde-Kunst und Volksfront," *Die neue Weltbühne* 32 (9 December 1937): 1568–73. For more on this debate and artists exiled in Prague, see Keith Holz, "Responses from Bohemia to *Entartete Kunst*, 1937–1938," *Exilforschung: Ein internationales Jahrbuch* 10 (1992): 30–49.

4   "Oskar Kokoschka, Wien 1937," in *Kunst und Diktatur: Architektur, Bildhauerei und Malerei in Österreich, Deutschland, Italien und Sowjetunion, 1922–1956*, exh. cat., ed. Jan Tabor (Baden: Grasl, 1994), vol. 2, 934–35.

5   "Entartete Kunst, Wien 1939," in ibid., 938–39.

6   See the undated letter from Kokoschka (Prague) to Carl Moll (Vienna) in which Kokoschka specified details of the house search and noted that pieces of the painting were then in Prague (*Oskar Kokoschka: Briefe*, ed. Olda Kokoschka und Heinz Spielmann [Düsseldorf: Classen, 1986], vol. 3, 12). For the reception of the quartered portrait in New York in 1943, see "Bericht von Maude Riley in der Zeitschrift 'Art Digest' über eine Oskar Kokoschka-Ausstellung in der Galerie St. Etienne (N.Y.C.), 15.4.1943," Hildegard Bachert collection, Galerie St. Etienne, New York, DOW E 20.213, reprinted in *Österreicher im Exil: USA, 1938–1945: Eine Dokumentation*, vol. 1, Dokumentationsarchiv des österreichischen Widerstandes (Vienna: Österreichischer Bundesverlag, 1995), 404–5.

7   The painting was reproduced many times in the French press in November 1938. See the extensive collection of press clippings about this exhibition, Bundesarchiv Potsdam, Nachlaß Eugen Spiro, Akte 18; Hélène Roussel, "Die emigrierten deutschen Künstler in Frankreich und der Freie Künstlerbund," in *Exilforschung: Ein internationales Jahrbuch* 2 (1984): 194; Inka Graeve, "Freie deutsche Kunst," in *Stationen der Moderne: Die bedeutenden Kunstausstellungen des 20. Jahrhunderts in Deutschland*, exh. cat. (Berlin: Berlinische Galerie, 1988), 338–49; and Keith Holz, "Modern German Art and Its Public in Prague, Paris, and London, 1933–1940" (Ph.D. diss., Northwestern University, 1992), 304–7.

8   Holz, "Responses from Bohemia," 40–43.

9   Draft of letter from Oskar Kokoschka to the London exhibition committee, rewritten by Freier Künstlerbund members in Paris (Bundesarchiv Potsdam, Nachlaß Eugen Spiro, Akte 4, Bl. 105, 106; Kokoschka to Herbert Read, 17 May 1938, in *Briefe*, vol. 3, 66–67).

10   *Knight Errant*, or *Der irrende Ritter*, is the title of a 1915 self-portrait (Solomon R. Guggenheim Museum, New York).

11   Kokoschka to Alfred Neumeyer, published as "A Letter from Oskar Kokoschka," *Magazine of Art* 39 (May 1946): 146, cited by Calvocoressi, *Oskar Kokoschka*, 24 n. 54.

12   *Freie Kunst und Literatur* (Paris), no. 9 ([August] 1939): 2–5; reprinted in Jutta Hülsewig-Johnen, ed., *Oskar Kokoschka—Emigrantenleben—Prag und London, 1934–1953* (Bielefeld: Kerber, 1995), 225–28.

13   This figure is cited in Haftmann, *Verfemte Kunst*, 78. On the Free German League of Culture, see Hoffmann, ed., *Exil in der Tschechoslowakei, in Großbritannien*, 211ff.; Cordula Frowein, "Ausstellungsaktivitäten der Exilkünstler," in *Kunst im Exil*, 35–48; and Ulla Hahn, "Der Freie deutsche Kulturbund in Großbritannien: Eine Skizze seiner Geschichte," in *Antifaschistische Literatur: Programme, Autoren, Werke*, ed. Lutz Winckler, vol. 2 (Kronberg: Scriptor, 1977), 131–95.

14   On Austrian exile associations in Great Britain and Kokoschka's participation in them, see Wolfgang Muchitsch, ed., *Österreicher im Exil: Großbritannien, 1938–1945*, Dokumentationsarchiv des österreichischen Widerstandes (Vienna: Österreichischer Bundesverlag, 1992), 164–74, 283–84, 316–17, 334–37, 364–66, 371–73, 398–99, 440, 471–77.

15   *Times* (London), 5 September 1939, 6c.

16   Kokoschka to American Guild for German Cultural Freedom (New York), 8 March 1940 (EB 70/117, Archivalien, Deutsches Exilarchiv, 1933–1945, Deutsche Bibliothek, Frankfurt a. M.).

17   E.g., Robert Radford, "Kokoschka's Political Allegories," *Art Monthly*, no. 97 (June 1986): 3–6. The question of the series' beginning, or of its discreteness, is problematic. *The Red Egg* might be said to "begin" this "series" because of its use of oil painting to picture multiple figures who represent political leaders. Yet just prior to *The Red Egg*, in *The Crab* (1938–39) Kokoschka introduced into oil painting explicit commentary on recent political events (i.e., British appeasement policies). Similarly, the obviously politically invested *Portrait of Ambassador Ivan Maisky* of 1942–43 suggests further problems in defining a discrete series.

18   *Oskar Kokoschka, 1886–1980*, exh. cat. (London: Tate Gallery, 1986), 321; and Hülsewig-Johnen, ed., *Oskar Kokoschka—Emigrantenleben*, 285.

19 These specific resonances of Lewis Carroll's story are noted in Hülsewig-Johnen, ed., *Oskar Kokoschka—Emigrantenleben*, 285, no. 65, which cites Edwin Lachnit, "Die Macht der Bilder," in *Oskar Kokoschka*, ed. Klaus Albrecht Schröder and Johann Winkler (Munich: Prestel, 1991), 39.

20 "Erklärung zugunsten internierter Emigranten," *Zeitspiegel: Anti-Nazi-Weekly*, no. 51 (22 December 1941), excerpted and annotated in *Oskar Kokoschka: Das schriftliche Werk*, ed. Heinz Spielmann, vol. 3, *Aufsätze, Vorträge, Essays zur Kunst* (Hamburg: Hans Christians, 1975), 353–54.

21 Cartoon with captions reprinted in Gerhard Hirschfeld, "Great Britain and the Emigration from Nazi Germany: An Historical Overview," in *Theatre and Film in Exile: German Artists in Britain, 1933–1945*, ed. Günter Berghaus (Oxford: Berg, 1989), 11.

22 "Erinnerungen von Georg Eisler an dessen Kontakte zu Oskar Kokoschka in London, 1944–1946" (1972), in Muchitsch, ed., *Österreicher im Exil: Großbritannien*, 474.

23 Sculptors Georg Ehrlich and Anna Mahler also signed, as did about thirty individuals and eleven Austrian associations (ibid., 284).

24 The programs, exhibitions, and artworks (which include the well-known series by American illustrator Norman Rockwell) produced internationally to support the Atlantic Charter's program merit further art historical attention.

25 Lynda Morris and Robert Radford, *The Story of the AIA: Artists International Association, 1933–1953*, exh. cat. (Oxford: Museum of Modern Art, 1983), 66–67.

26 My reading relies in part upon the informed readings of Radford, "Kokoschka's Political Allegories," 5–6; idem, *Art for a Purpose*, 136–41; and Haftmann, *Verfemte Kunst*, 85–87.

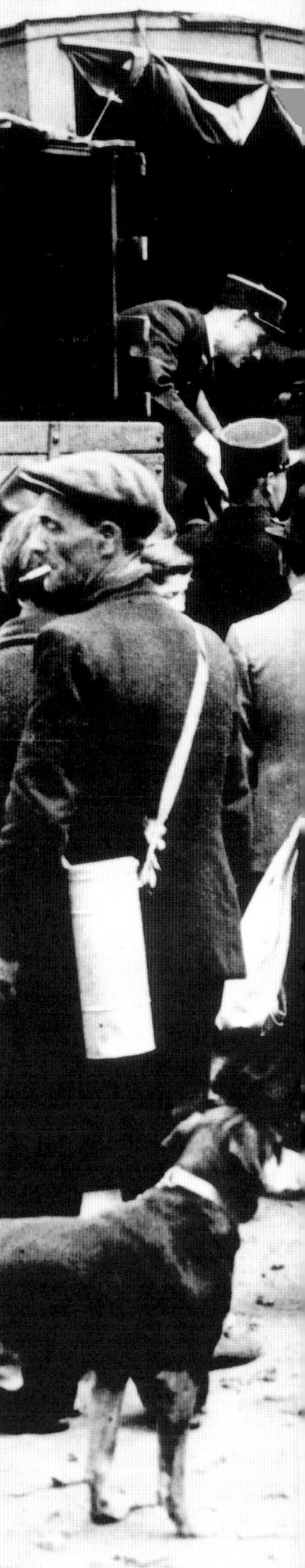

Overleaf left:
French refugees being herded into trucks, which were to convey them to safety.

Overleaf right:
German troops marching into Paris, June 20, 1940.

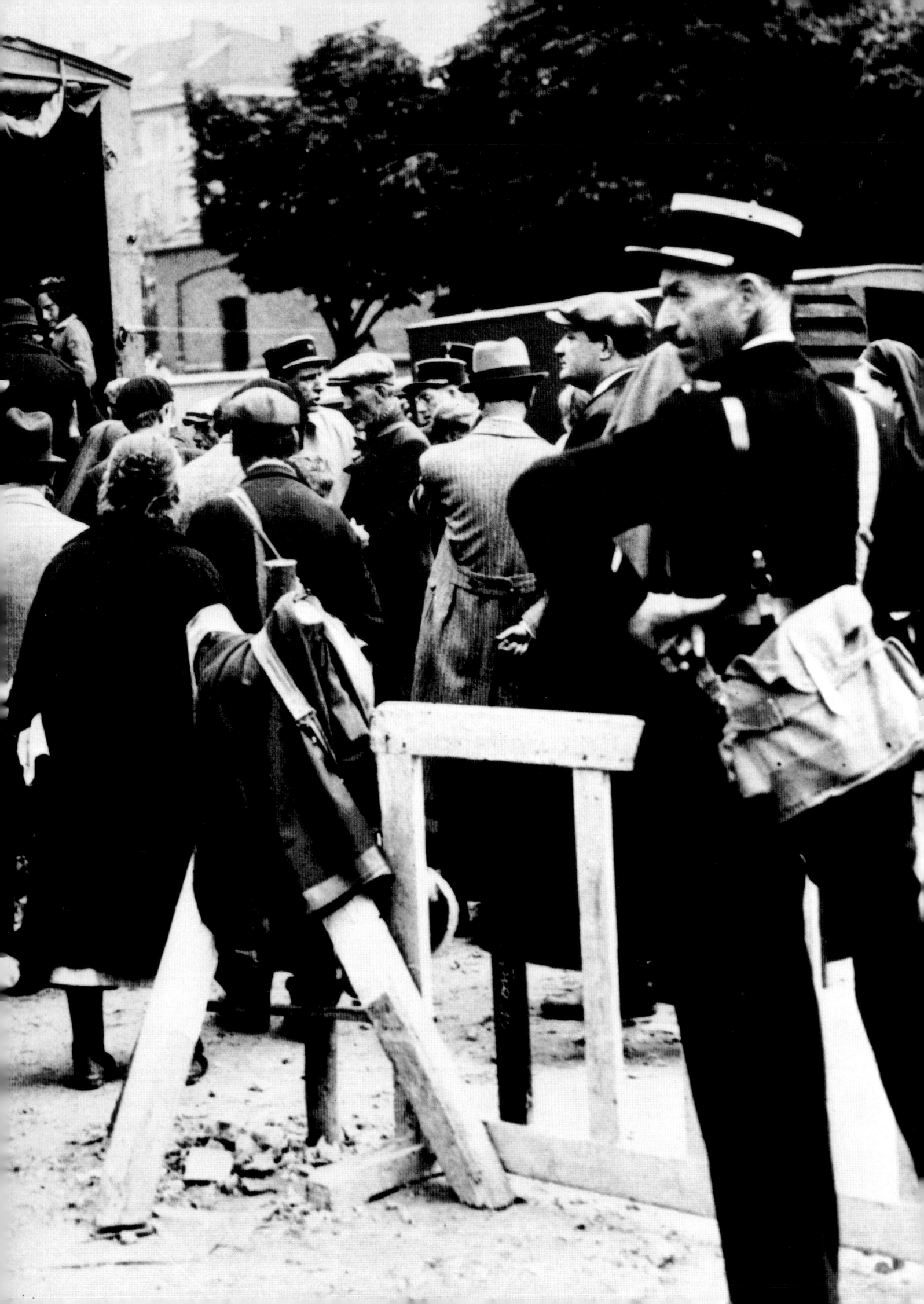

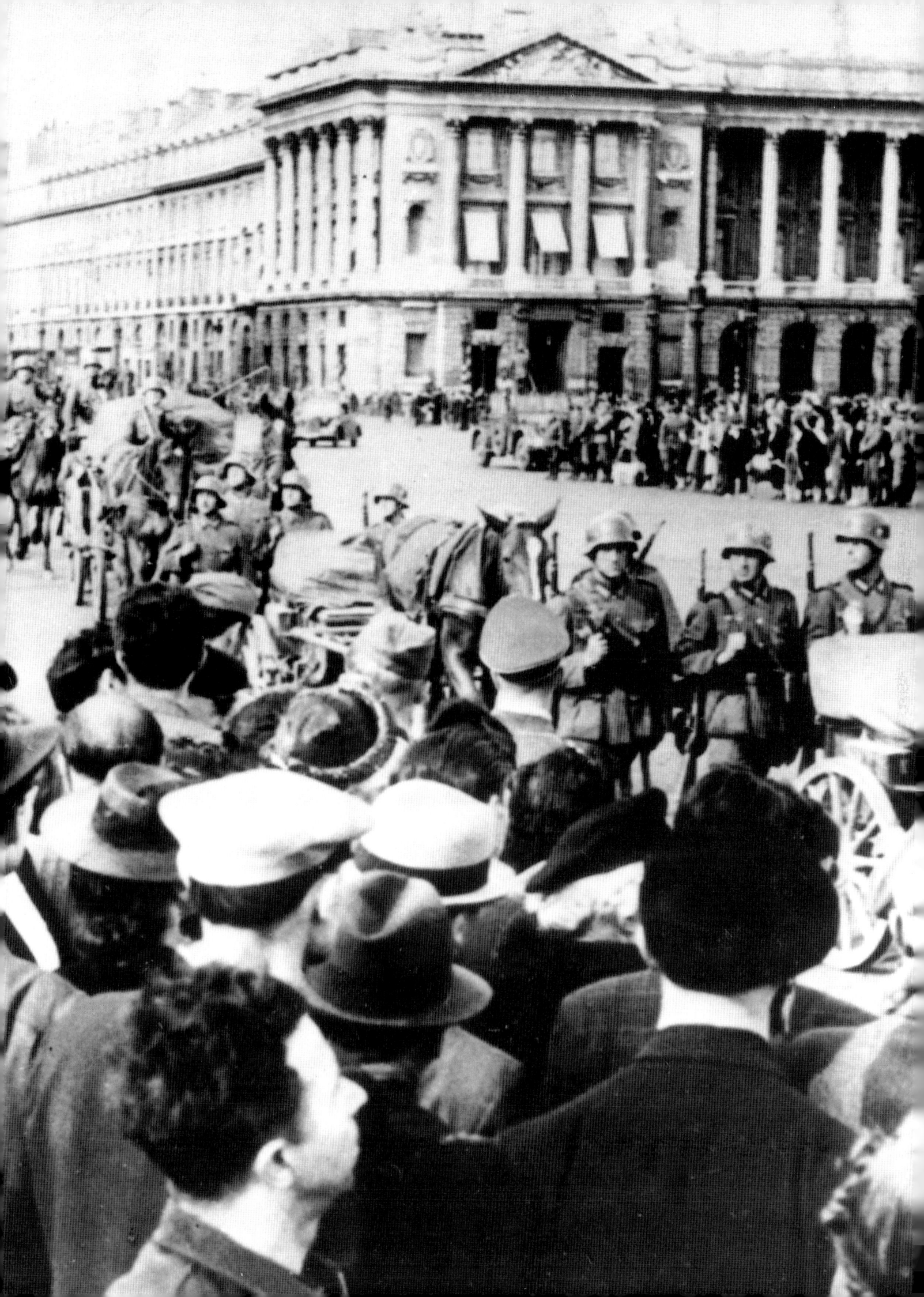

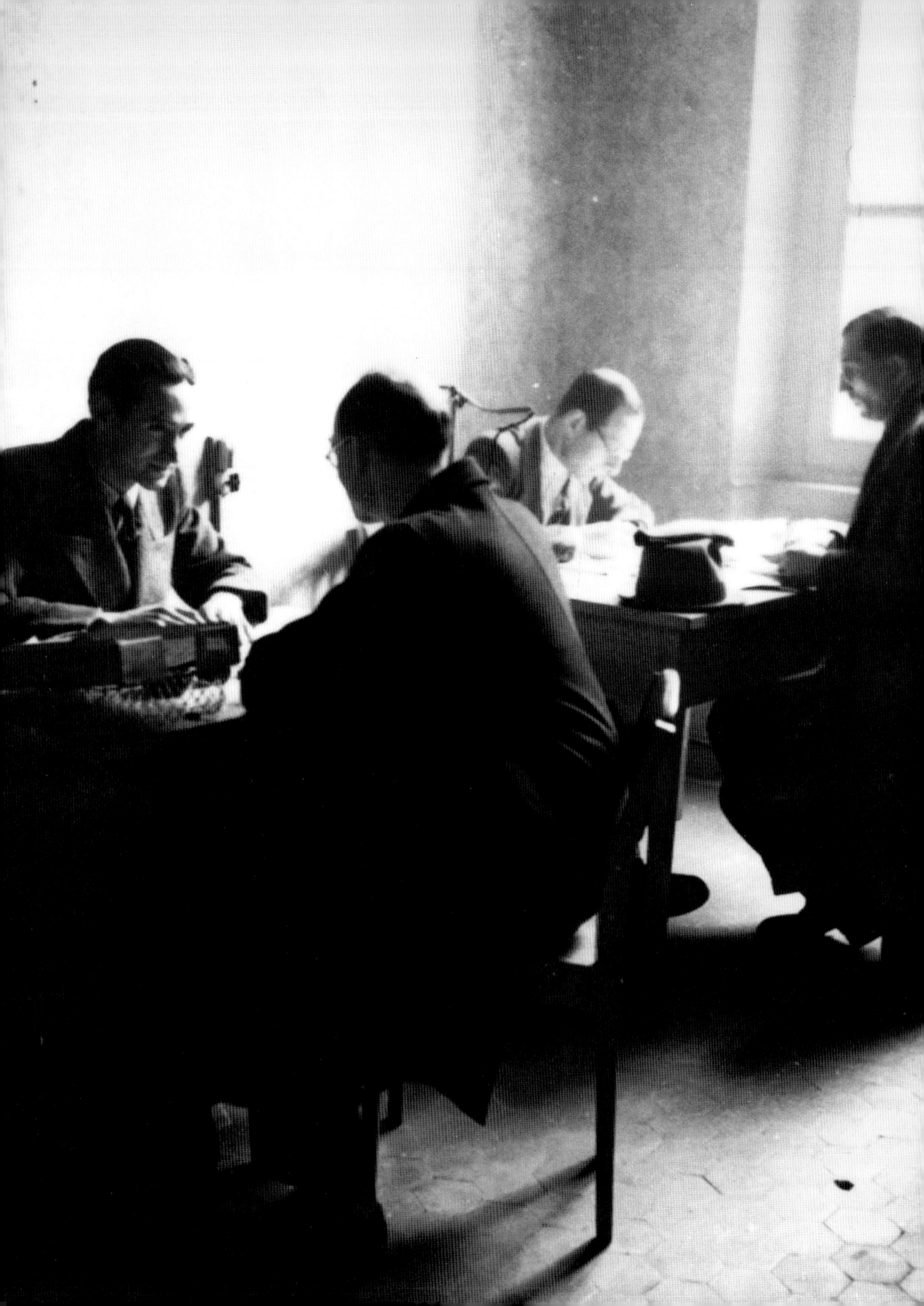

ELIZABETH KESSIN BERMAN

moral triage or cultural salvage?
the agendas of varian fry and
the emergency rescue committee

When it was learned that the armistice which France made with Germany in June, 1940 contained a clause providing for the "surrender on demand" of German refugees, a group of American citizens, who were deeply shocked by this violation of the right of asylum and who believed that democrats should help democrats, regardless of nationality, immediately formed the Emergency Rescue Committee. The sole purpose of the Committee was to bring the political and intellectual refugees out of France before the Gestapo and the Ovra and the Seguridad got them.

After several weeks of searching for a suitable candidate the committee selected me. I had no experience in refugee work, and none in underground work. But I accepted the assignment because, like members of the Committee, I believed in the importance of democratic solidarity.[1]

these words, written by Varian Fry, begin *Surrender on Demand,* his firsthand account of what has come to be regarded as the most successful mission to rescue anti-Nazi artists, writers, intellectuals, scientists, and political refugees during World War II. Fry's book presents a remarkable description of his successes and tells the inspiring, heroic story of how, despite numerous obstacles, he managed to save many endangered leaders of European culture and democracy. Fry's book also reveals, however, that he faced critical dilemmas in engaging in the rescue work his committee commissioned. He had been asked to help a few prominent figures, and it appears that he was profoundly troubled by this limited agenda: "My lists [of refugees] were obviously arbitrary. They had been made up quickly and from memory by people who were thousands of miles away and had little or no idea of what was really going on in France. Some names had been put on them which ought not to have been there. Others had been left off which ought to have been on."[2]

Surrender on Demand was published in late December 1945. Fry, who probably had little choice but to comply with the wishes of his publisher, produced an account that was intended to appeal to a ragged and weary postwar American audience. Instead of recounting in a more precise, critical manner his efforts to expand the committee's agenda, the book often reads like an adventure story. The dramatic escapes of his most famous and admired clients—among them Marc Chagall, Max Ernst, Lion Feuchtwanger, Konrad Heiden, Heinrich Mann, Alma Mahler-Werfel, and Franz Werfel—form the core of the narrative.[3] Fry's personal confrontation with the U.S. government's restrictive wartime policy toward refugees, a topic that he repeatedly addressed in his editorial writings in journals and newspapers during the war, was subtly woven into a series of suspenseful accounts of the escapes of his VIPs. He also played down, quite significantly, the fact that he was able to add to the original lists by stretching to its limit the U.S. government's only means of aiding refugees: the "emergency visitors" visa program, which issued special, limited visas during the war to those who were considered valuable to America because of their cultural, political, or

85
The offices of the Centre Américain de Secours, Marseilles, 1941; photograph by Chaim Lipnitski.

intellectual activities.[4] Moreover, Fry offered only oblique allusions to the issues that ultimately thwarted his mission to rescue those not on his lists, most notably the lack of public support in America for funding the flight of masses of unknown Europeans, who were largely of Jewish descent.

The core of Fry's story begins after his arrival in southern France in August 1940 on his mission to assist about two hundred preselected refugees who were believed to be subject to the terms of Article 19 of the Franco-German armistice, the so-called "surrender on demand" clause. This loosely worded article to the armistice, which had been signed at the very site where the Germans had capitulated to the French at the end of World War I, called for the handover of German prisoners of war and any other foreign nationals specified by the Germans. Taken literally, this signaled the end of safe havens for all political and cultural foes of the Third Reich.[5]

Upon his arrival Fry was besieged by throngs of exiles, including not only political or intellectual refugees but also potential victims of Hitler's anti-Jewish policies. Fry, who had witnessed pogroms on the streets of Berlin in 1935, immediately sensed that the Jewish refugees were in an especially perilous situation. Although the Nazis would not begin to deport Jews to extermination camps until 1942, Jews in Vichy France, like those in other Nazi-controlled territories, were subject to increasingly restrictive and inhumane anti-Jewish laws. Within days Fry acted on his own to expand the number of persons on the Emergency Rescue Committee's lists beyond the small group who had been selected because of their fame or cultural or political importance. Over the course of thirteen months he arranged for the emigration of more than two thousand refugees, far exceeding the original number targeted by the committee.[6] To accomplish this, he hastily organized a new relief bureau in Marseilles, the Centre Américain de Secours (see fig. 85). This ad hoc agency functioned as a front for an elaborate escape organization that included document forgers, black marketeers, smugglers, and peasant mountain guides.[7]

Fry's impromptu and unorthodox relief activities were scrutinized not only by his Vichy adversaries but also by his presumed allies. His aid to prominent political refugees led local French authorities to monitor his daily activities, and eventually, in September 1941, he was forcibly expelled at the Franco-Spanish border. While in Marseilles, however, Fry was troubled by the lack of support he received from local American consular officials, and he continually challenged their sluggish methods of issuing visas. His published account of his conflicts with various diplomatic officials is, however, modest in comparison to the numerous pages of correspondence that document his contentious relationship with American consular representatives. In many letters Fry openly protested the blatant anti-Semitism of consular officials in France. There is no question that the U.S. State Department played an important role in hindering his activities and supported his expulsion from France.[8]

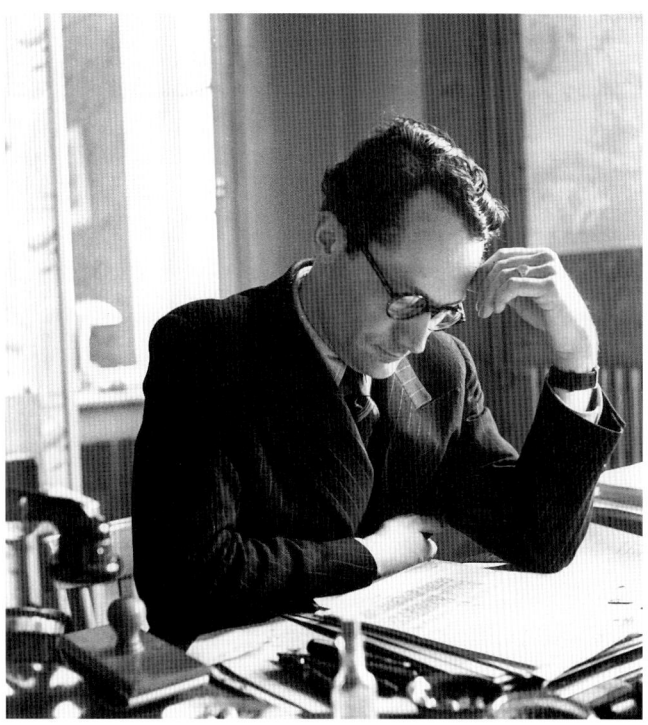

86
Varian Fry in the offices of the Centre Américain de Secours, Marseilles, 1941; photograph by YLLA.

Almost from the start Fry's new and expanded agenda for the rescue of antifascists, most of whom were Jewish, met with reserved opposition from key leaders of the Emergency Rescue Committee. Although he chose to disregard this in his book, he was discharged from the committee within months of his return to New York. The tensions between Fry and the committee emerge early in Fry's personal letters and in the committee's official letters, written while he was in Marseilles. The problems continued to mount throughout his tenure there.[9] Clearly the committee felt compelled to maintain its narrow, selective agenda.

Fry's differences with the Emergency Rescue Committee and his clashes with American and Vichy officials are set out most clearly in the original, unedited manuscript for *Surrender on Demand,* an eight-hundred-page account written shortly after his return in late 1941.[10] In contrast to the dramatic description that introduces this essay, Fry's original manuscript begins with a different version of the origins of the Emergency Rescue Committee. There he describes the committee's founding not as the result of a spontaneous gathering of political and intellectual leaders outraged by Article 19, but as the unexpected outcome of a modest fund-raising luncheon organized by a small group of activists, the American Friends of German Freedom, to find sponsors for the emigration of a few young, radical German and Austrian socialists.

For many years Fry had been an active member of the American Friends of German Freedom, a little-known organization formed in America by the ousted German socialist leader Paul Hagen (also known as Karl Frank) to raise money for the anti-Nazi work of a group called Neu Beginnen (New beginning).[11] After the invasion of Poland, however, as Hitler's armies began to overrun Europe, the group recognized the danger to outspoken opponents of Hitler. Fry writes: "It was no longer a question of financing the underground movement. It was a question now of saving lives of the underground workers. For that, money would be needed—even more money than had been needed for underground work."[12] Hagen wrote biographies of some of the underground workers who had been stationed in France and the Low Countries, and these were sent to sympathetic Americans, accompanied by appeals for funds to save them. The luncheon was conceived as an opportunity to present this appeal publicly to a carefully selected group of potential sponsors.

The luncheon finally took place on June 25, 1940, three days after France signed the armistice with Germany. The "surrender on demand" clause had been featured prominently in newspapers. Shocked by the sudden collapse of the last bastion of cultural and political freedom in continental Europe, the guests, who had originally been solicited to support the rescue of German and Austrian revolutionaries, began to raise the predicament of their own intellectual and political colleagues. Klaus and Erika Mann presented specific examples of the distress calls their father, the refugee writer Thomas Mann, had been getting from well-known writers and cultural figures who had fled to southern France.[13] The assembled group, in a remarkable show of solidarity, decided to aid other celebrated refugees: "Nearly three-thousand dollars was collected. The money had been given to the American Friends of German Freedom, but the audience felt that a new committee should be formed to help not only Paul's comrades, but all the political and intellectual refugees in France whose lives were now in danger. The Emergency Rescue Committee was established that same day."[14]

Several weeks after the luncheon the new committee formed an advisory board to compile lists of candidates for emergency rescue. From Fry's perspective, and no doubt those of the rest of the American Friends of German Freedom, combining the names of these virtually unknown opponents of Hitler with those of some of the most renowned intellectuals remaining in Europe seemed to be the ideal way of achieving the original goals of the American Friends of German Freedom. Figures like Thomas Mann and the French theologian Jacques Maritain gathered to propose names of their own colleagues, meeting with political leaders Joseph Buttinger for the Austrian refugees, J. Alvarez del Vayo for the Spaniards, Jan Masaryk for the Czechs, Max Ascoli for the Italians, and others. Alvin Johnson, the president of the New School for Social Research, also submitted the names of a number of scholars and academics.[15] A key outcome was the decision to send a representative to France to deliver personally the money raised by the committee and to assist the passage of its most distinguished "clients." Fry volunteered for this job, believing that his mission included a program to save not only an impressive collection of European cultural figures but also the uncelebrated political activists supported by the American Friends of German Freedom.[16]

Even before the advisory board met to draw up the names of selected VIPs, the Emergency Rescue Committee had hired a seasoned New York fund-raiser, Harold Oram, to begin a broad fund-raising campaign. Without relying on a specific list, Oram came up with a group of names that he included in the committee's first appeal, a telegram dated July 8, 1940. The name he chose to lead off this plea for support was that of the antifascist best known in America, Pablo Picasso. The telegram was worded concisely: "Making desperate efforts through our State Department and foreign governments to save and transport to this hemisphere Picasso, Franz Werfel, Silone, Antoine de Saint Exupery, Leon [sic] Feuchtwanger, Heinrich Mann and many others of like character..."[17]

Although the committee chose to emphasize artists in its first public fund-raising appeal, Alfred H. Barr Jr., the director of the Museum of Modern Art, who had been one of the most influential advocates for persecuted artists in Europe during the 1930s, was not on the original advisory board. Barr was not present at that fateful luncheon, and his name does not appear among those of its supporters in any of the Emergency Rescue Committee's literature.[18] Although his connections with the committee are not well documented, he nonetheless appears to have been in touch with Fry and other members. Before Fry left for Marseilles, Barr had given him a list of potential candidates for rescue, and this list figures prominently in Fry's account:

> I got out my lists and set about trying to memorize them. There was the list which Mildred Adams had given me in the lobby of the Plaza Hotel. There was the list which Paul had brought to my office. There was Alfred Barr's list of modern artists. There were the lists of Thomas Mann and Pertinax [André Géraud]....
>
> Alfred's list was a list of artists the Museum of Modern Art wanted me to rescue: Picasso, Chagall, Ernst, Arp....
>
> Altogether there were more than two hundred names to be memorized in less than twenty-four hours. Plus a good many addresses.[19]

The complete lists of the committee's two hundred or so candidates for rescue have not survived, probably because Fry himself, as he implies, destroyed them out of fear for his own safety and that of those whom he believed to be sought by the Gestapo, particularly the Austrian and German socialists.[20] One can ascertain the names of at least some of the artists on the list by tracing the ones Fry did contact while in southern France. When he arrived in Marseilles, he immediately wrote to Arp, Chagall, Ernst, and Picasso, as well as to Wassily Kandinsky, Jacques Lipchitz, and Henri Matisse. If these are, in fact, the only names that Barr supplied, Fry was given an extremely short and limited list, which included the artists that Barr himself most admired and those who were best known to the American public.[21]

Of the artists that Fry approached, only Chagall, Lipchitz, and Ernst were in true danger—but not because of their art. Chagall and Lipchitz were subject to the anti-Jewish laws, and Ernst was in danger of deportation because he was a German national living in France as an *apatride*, a stateless refugee. He had already been interned in French detention camps. The others faced the prospect of being deprived of their livelihood because of Hitler's cultural policies, but they were in no political or physical danger.

Following his committee's directions, Fry paid several visits to Chagall at his studio in Gordes and to Matisse in Nice (see figs. 87–88). At each encounter Fry was surprised to learn that he had to spend time convincing the artist to leave France. He reports that Chagall agreed to go only when he realized that he would likely be a victim of the ever-tightening anti-Jewish restrictions in France.[22] In Matisse's case Fry's efforts were fruitless: "[Matisse] saw no reason why, as a Frenchman, he should have to think of going. With all his genius, he was the successful bourgeois at heart, ... proud of his collections of African masks and sculpture, plants and tropical birds. We did all we could to persuade him to leave them, arguing that though he might not be in any personal danger, even as the doyen of that 'degenerate' art the Nazis profess to despise so heartily, he was nevertheless in real danger of starving to death before the war was over. But he refused to be persuaded."[23]

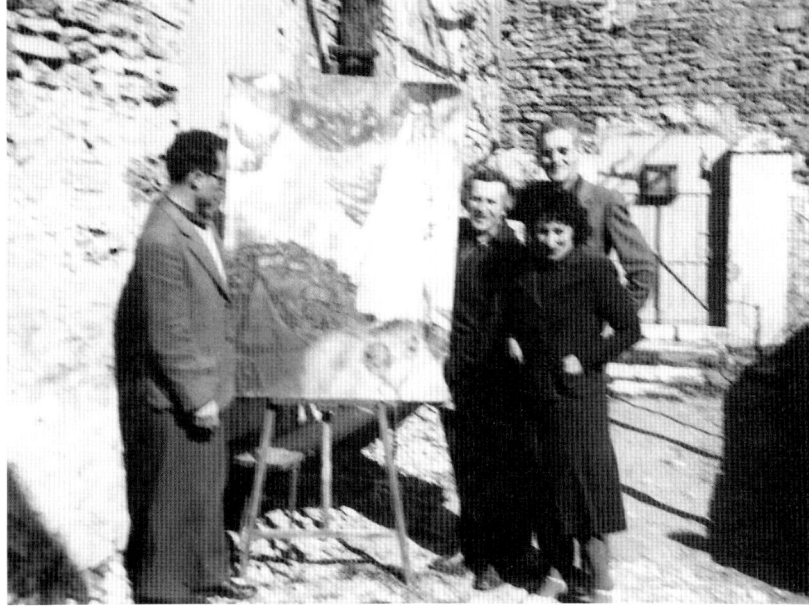

87
Varian Fry (left), Hiram Bingham, and Marc and Bella Chagall at the artist's studio in Gordes, spring 1941.

In fact, everyone else on Barr's list, except for Lipchitz, was reluctant to leave: Picasso repeatedly rejected Fry's persistent appeals, in letters dated as late as July 2, 1941.[24] Jean Arp and Sophie Taeuber-Arp, although willing to accept stipends from the Emergency Rescue Committee, found refuge in Switzerland only in the last days of the Vichy government. The aged Kandinsky also refused the committee's offer to aid his emigration. There were other cultural figures on the committee's lists who rejected Fry's offers of assistance; Pablo Casals, André Gide, and André Malraux are among those mentioned.[25]

Thus, during Fry's earliest days as an agent in Marseilles, he faced problems that he had not anticipated when he accepted the assignment. It was clear that many of the esteemed artists and other distinguished cultural figures on his lists—persons who were critical to his committee's existence and fund-raising efforts—were disinclined to accept exile. At the same time, however, he was continually confronted with numerous unknown refugees who did not figure into the original agenda. Fry wrote:

> Before the end of my first week in Marseille, word had apparently spread all over the unoccupied zone that an American had arrived from New York, like an angel from heaven, with his pockets stuffed with money and passports and a direct connection with the State Department enabling him to get any kind of visa at a moment's notice. I even heard that at Toulouse an enterprising merchant was selling my name and address to the refugees for fifty francs. It wasn't true, of course, that I could get visas quickly—I wish it had been—but the refugees believed it, and they began coming in droves. I was no longer seeing just the people on my lists, but scores who thought they ought to be on them.[26]

Appalled by the prospect of performing triage in the midst of a refugee crisis, Fry began on his own to augment the committee's lists. Setting for himself a clear limit "to be careful not to help a police spy or a fifth columnist, or a communist masquerading as a democrat"—and mindful of the U.S. government's cumbersome and limited emergency visa policy—he set up a quasi-relief organization to review cases of refugees whose political, cultural, or academic backgrounds, no matter how remote, might qualify them to be admitted under an emergency visa.[27] He hired a number of local French resistance workers to review applicants as well as many refugees who eventually earned visas and sponsors to aid their own emigration. Among them were German poet Hans Sahl and political scientist Albert Hirschman. A number of Americans stranded in France also joined the team.

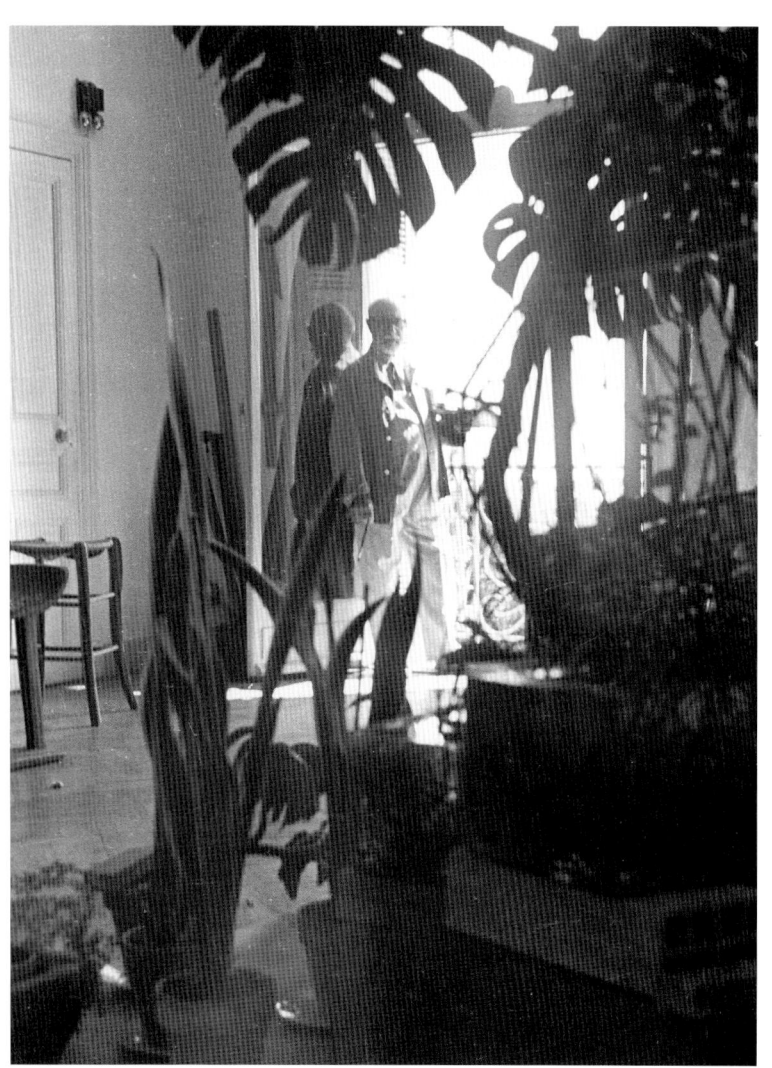

88
Henri Matisse in his studio at Cimiez, 1941; photograph by Varian Fry.

Fry's relief office functioned during the day as an ordinary foreign humanitarian organization extending monetary aid to refugees and appearing to offer general assistance in visa and transit affairs to refugees in Marseilles as well as to many interned in French detention camps in southern France. His office sent names to the New York office, which handled the nightmarish sequence of procedures and corresponding paperwork necessary to complete the visa process. At night, in secluded conferences, Fry's team reviewed cases and conspired to find solutions for each individual through a variety of contrived, illegal escape routes, enabling refugees to avoid having to obtain French exit permits or timed Spanish and Portuguese transit visas. Fry began to cable the names of new clients to his New York office in the hope that they would be added to the original list of two hundred or so.

By the winter of 1940 Fry's Marseilles operation had taken on the cases of many hundreds of refugees. Desperate for money to finance passage for his new clients and suspecting not only the cooperation of the Emergency Rescue Committee but also the effectiveness of its fund-raising tactics, Fry decided to launch his own fund-raising appeal from Marseilles. To accomplish this, he went over the heads of his committee and directly approached people he thought would consider a larger effort; one of those he contacted was Alfred Barr.[28]

Fry apparently did this because, during the period when he was expanding the scope of his work in Marseilles, he was also receiving requests on behalf of artists from Barr and, in particular, his wife, Margaret Scolari Barr. According to the minutes of the October 10, 1940, meeting of the board of trustees of the Museum of Modern Art, Barr himself reported that bringing artists over was not merely a process of making a simple list and awaiting the artist's arrival; it had become a daunting task for him, his wife, and his staff. His office had become very much engaged in the complicated paperwork required to bring the few artists on his original list to America and in raising funds for their passage.[29] Records of the Emergency Rescue Committee show that during the fall of 1940 the Barrs gave their support to other artists whose names were supplied by concerned individuals outside the museum. Kurt Seligmann, the emigré artist who had arrived in New York in 1939, brought to the Barrs' attention the plight of André Masson, who had fled to southern France, as well as those of other artists and writers who had fled Paris, including André Breton, Paul Eluard, Pierre Mabille, and Benjamin Péret.[30]

It appears that there were other artists whose situations were handled by the Barrs as a result of outside petitions brought by personal acquaintances of the refugees. Eugen Spiro, a German academic artist and an acquaintance of Thomas Mann, was also supported by Barr. The French artist Jean Hélion obtained Barr's sponsorship in response to a letter from his American wife, Jean Blair Hélion. Beaumont Newhall, of MoMA's photography department, promoted Camilla Koffler, the photographer who worked under the name YLLA.[31]

Fry's independent plea to Barr for financial help soon came to the attention of the Emergency Rescue Committee, bringing a stern rebuke from Oram, now ensconced as the committee's only fund-raiser. Furious that Fry had tried to sidestep the committee, and sensing that he was too far removed from reality, Oram sent him a sharply worded response that bluntly sums up the pressures that the committee was facing as well as the overwhelming apathy that Americans felt toward Europe's beleaguered victims of Hitler's policies:

> One practical note, if Albert Einstein could be brought to America today we could raise one million within a short time by exhibiting him throughout the country. Casals is probably worth one hundred thousand. Picasso—fifty thousand. *Your trio* brought in thirty five thousand. Since their arrival we have had nothing to offer to the public and they are pretty shopworn by this time. See if you can dig up something big—I know this is a large order in a Europe at war and it may seem ironic that a supposedly intelligent person can find time to think in terms of this equation but the solution of this equation is the solution of our problem of existence, i.e., the possibility of a continued fruitful work.[32]

Oram's allusion to the "trio" is a cryptic reference to the committee's widely publicized rescue of the celebrated writers Lion Feuchtwanger, Heinrich Mann, and Franz Werfel. Their arrival in New York in October 1940 was flaunted in the press and in the committee's own fund-raising literature (see fig. 89).[33] Sensing that the only way to keep his own operation going was to follow Oram's advice, Fry immediately organized his own public relations campaign in Marseilles. Using the most distinguished refugees he could find among the many he now considered his clients, he arranged the well-known series of photographs by YLLA of the major surrealist emigrés Breton, Ernst, Jacqueline Lamba, and Masson (see fig. 90). In time these publicity shots replaced those of the Werfels and the Manns and were featured on a new series of fund-raising brochures.[34]

89
"Wanted by the Gestapo," Emergency Rescue Committee brochure, c. 1940.

90
Max Ernst (far left), Jacqueline Lamba, André Masson, André Breton, and Varian Fry, Marseilles, 1941; photograph by YLLA; Photographic Archives, The Museum of Modern Art, New York. Negative donated by Mrs. Annette R. Fry.

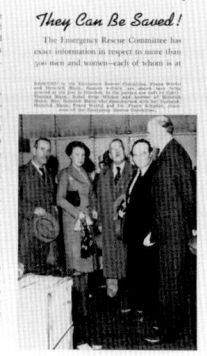
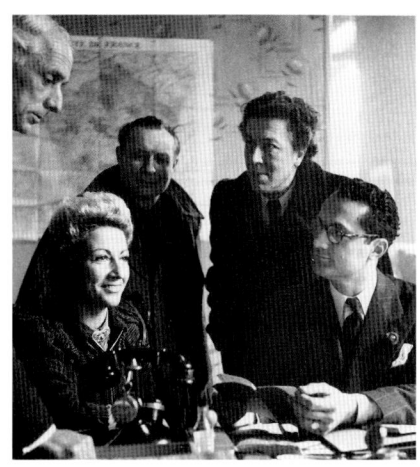

Fry's concern for refugee artists may also have been a direct result of his extraordinary personal connection with certain exiled artists, namely Breton and many of his followers. For a short while, during the winter of 1940–41, Fry's staff quarters at the Villa Air Bel, a retreat outside Marseilles, became a shelter for the exiled Breton and his family (see figs. 91–92). During that winter Breton welcomed to Villa Air Bel members of the surrealist circle who had fled Paris. There they created a remarkable series of artistic and literary works, including several "collective collages" and a card game called *Le jeu de Marseille* (see fig. 93), as well as Breton's poetic work *Fata Morgana,* illustrated by Wifredo Lam.[35] After Breton arrived in New York, he would write of Villa Air Bel as a place where, for a time, artists tried to carry on with their work as the world around them collapsed:

> Towards the end of 1940 and the beginning of '41, many people connected with the surrealist movement in one way or another met or got together in Marseilles. Among these were Victor Brauner, André Breton, René Char, René Daumal, Robert Delanglade, Oscar Dominguez, Marcel Duchamp, Max Ernst, Jacques Hérold (Blumer), Sylvain Itkine, Wifredo Lam, André Masson, Benjamin Péret, and Tristan Tzara. Many of them got together at Château Air-Bel, where they were welcomed graciously by Varian Fry, President of the Emergency Rescue Committee....
>
> Great is the power of defiance, of spite, and also of hope toward and against everything—never did those involved in this react more like children: singing, playing and laughing with the greatest of joy.[36]

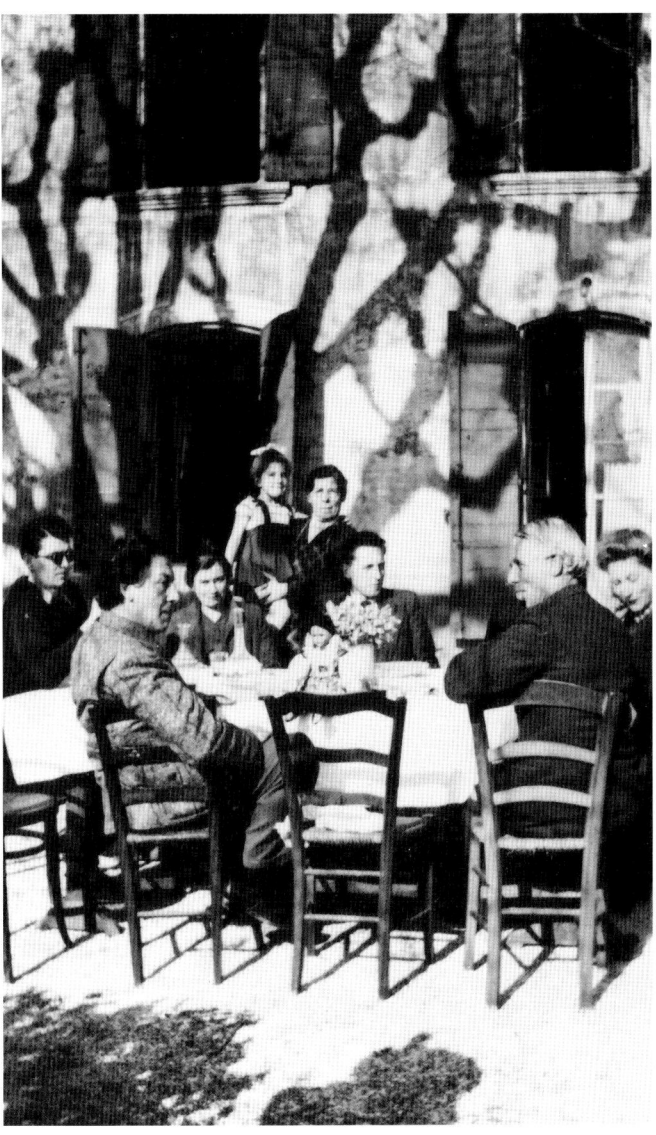

91
Max Ernst, André Breton, Aube Breton, and Emergency Rescue Committee associates (Daniel Bénédite, Jean Gemahling, and others) on the grounds of Villa Air Bel, on the outskirts of Marseilles, c. 1940–41.

92
André Breton in the library of Villa Air Bel, c. 1940–41; photograph by Varian Fry.

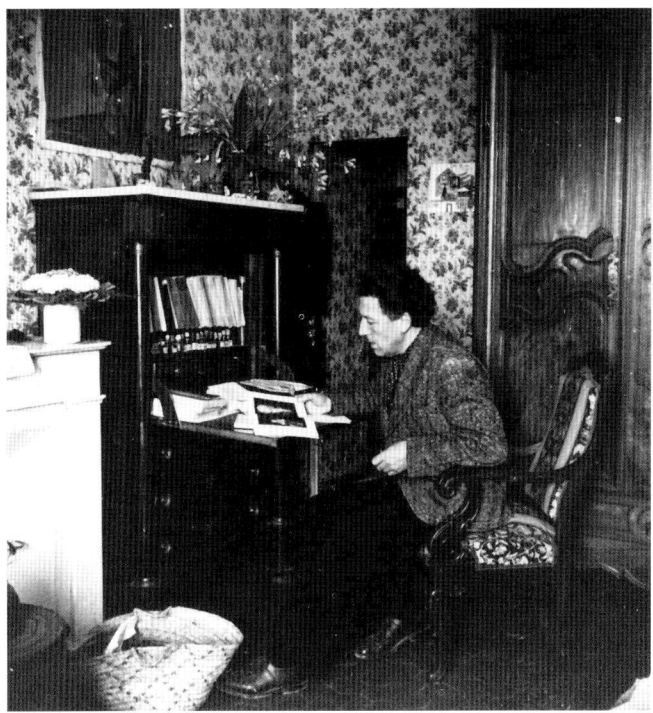

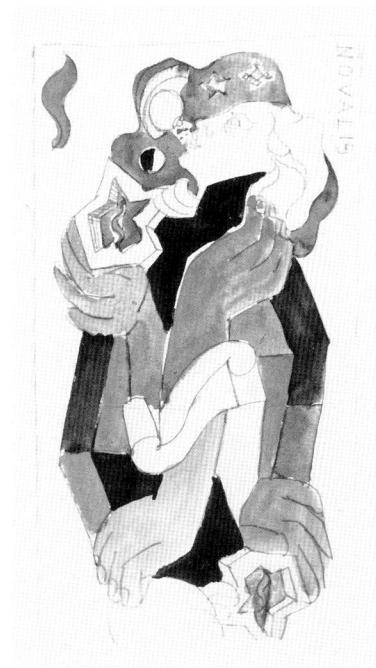

93
André Masson; *Novalis* (maquette for *Le jeu de Marseille*), 1940/41; collection of the children of André Masson

Fry was successful in assisting the emigration of artists such as Breton, Ernst, and Masson, who had established patrons in the United States.[37] Fry was also able to help a few lesser-known members of the surrealist group, such as Lam, Péret, and Péret's companion, Remedios Varos, who left France with visas for destinations in the Caribbean or Mexico (see fig. 94). Others, however, such as Victor Brauner and Jacques Hérold, who as Jews desperately sought to escape France, were unable to get visas because they lacked sponsors. Fry sent several telegrams in January 1941, hoping that the Museum of Modern Art would find patrons who were willing to sign the sponsorship forms required for every applicant. Eventually Brauner's passage was guaranteed by Peggy Guggenheim, who was instrumental in organizing Ernst's passage to America. But no sponsors in the United States were ever identified to support his application for a visa and sign the crucial "affidavit of support," which assured that the applicant would not become a public charge. Brauner remained in hiding throughout the remainder of the war. Hérold, whose work was virtually unknown in New York, never found a sponsor.[38] He survived the war in Marseilles, concealing his Jewish identity. When Fry was finally expelled from France, he carried with him to New York works by Brauner, Dominguez, Hérold, and quite a few "unknowns" and continued, in vain, to search for potential patrons for these artists.[39]

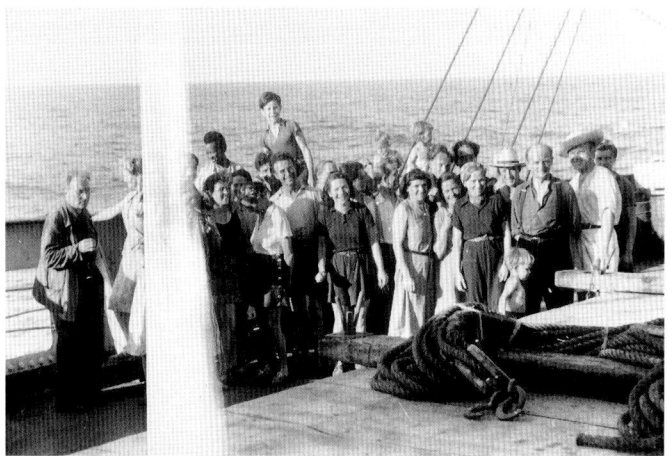

94
Refugees on board a ship, spring 1941, including Victor Serge (far left) and Wifredo Lam (back row, fourth from left).

95
Varian Fry and members of his staff prior to his expulsion, Perpignan, France, August 1941.

Even when Fry knew that his expulsion from France was imminent and his clandestine work doomed, he still devoted a significant portion of his time to trying to save artists and writers, including César Domela, Paul Eluard, Leonor Fini, Otto Freundlich, Georges Hugnet, Alberto Magnelli, Antoine Pevsner, Bernard Reder, Pierre Roy, and Chagall's children. Ever mindful of the committee's agenda, Fry also continued to seek "celebrity" refugees

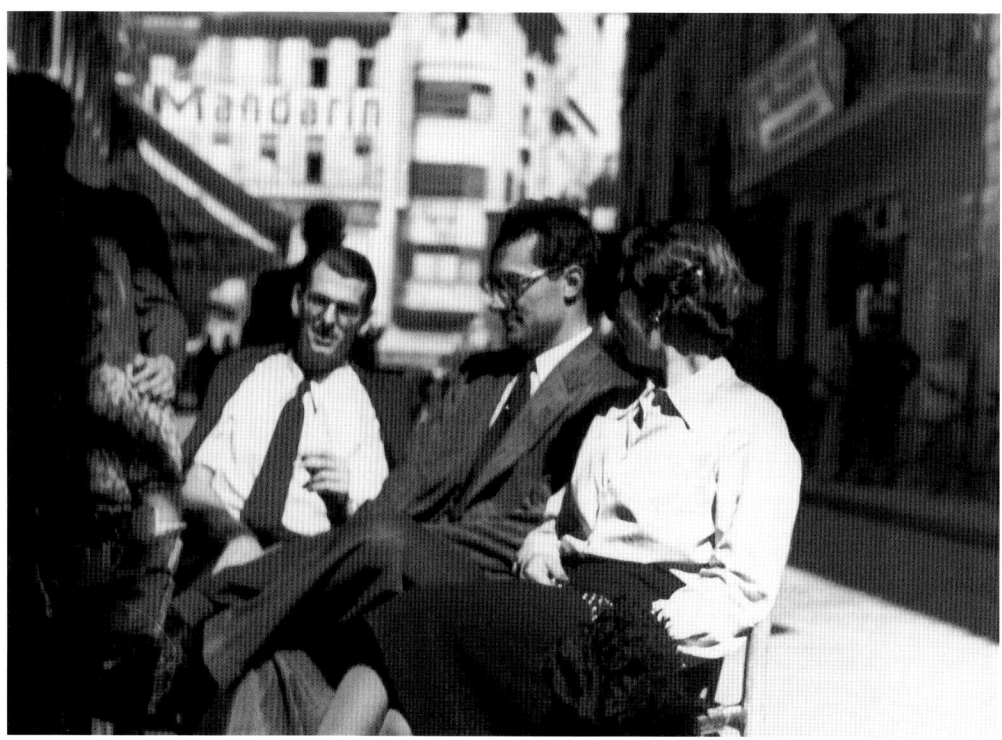

and to encourage their flight to America. In a telegram sent only weeks before he was jailed by the Vichy authorities, he reported to the New York office that Casals and Picasso continued to resist his appeals to leave.[40]

During his stay in France Fry was never completely convinced that the cultural and academic figures were in peril. As he later wrote, "One of our principal difficulties came from the fact that we still had no way of knowing who was really in danger."[41] His attempts to "rescue" prominent figures no doubt detracted from his efforts to save those who were clearly at risk, and in several documented cases (and in many more undocumented ones) this had tragic consequences. Freundlich, a German artist of Jewish descent, got caught in a paper trap that held up his emigration for years. In 1943 he was deported from France to Poland, where he perished at the Majdanek extermination camp.[42] Another well-known case is that of the Jewish art critic Louise Strauss Ernst, the first wife of Max Ernst. Having divorced the painter, she refused to pose as his wife in order to facilitate her emigration, preferring to rely on her own connections in the United States. While waiting for an American visa and a French exit permit to be issued, she was caught in occupied France and later deported to Auschwitz.[43] Among the political refugees were Rudolf Breitscheid and Rudolf Hilferding, ousted leaders of the Social Democratic party, who stood ready to form governments in exile. Despite Fry's efforts, these two were detained under the terms of Article 19 and deported to Germany, where they died. Fry must have suspected the reality of the refugee situation—that only Jews and political foes of Hitler were in mortal danger.

Fry returned to New York in the fall of 1941 with a measure of success. Charged with the rescue of two hundred, he estimated that he had helped more than ten times that number escape Europe, but he was haunted by the knowledge that his work was far from complete. He continued to draw attention to the plight of refugees, especially those of Jewish descent, in his capacity as an editor for *The New Republic* and as a contributor to other political journals. He wrote a series of strongly worded articles criticizing America's short-sighted immigration policy.[44] In these editorials he speaks eloquently of the dangers of selective and restrictive immigration and advocates a much more liberal policy. He stands among the few voices in the American press during this period who charged that the architects and custodians of America's foreign policy were consciously limiting the immigration not only of suspected communists and "fifth columnists" but also of Jews, who happened to number prominently among political and intellectual refugees.[45]

Varian Fry came to be regarded as the "scarlet pimpernel" who, through his courage and defiance of authorities, brought many of this century's important cultural figures and proponents of democracy to safety in the United States during one of the darkest periods of history. In the shadow of his obvious successes, however, he left a paper trail that reveals that saving Europe's cultural giants was not his ultimate—or only—goal. In effect, Fry exploited the well-publicized rescues of a handful of cultural luminaries to help support a broader humanitarian mission. Employed by a committee that depended for its financial support on an American public that was largely indifferent to the fate of the masses of unknown refugees, he responded pragmatically, finding a way to reconcile his own agenda with that of the committee.

Notes

1   From Varian Fry, *Surrender on Demand* (New York: Random House, 1945), ix–x. This article is partially based on research compiled for the exhibition *Assignment: Rescue: The Story of Varian Fry and the Emergency Rescue Committee,* the inaugural special exhibition of the United States Holocaust Memorial Museum, Washington, D.C. (25 June 1993–29 January 1995), directed by Susan W. Morgenstein.

2   Fry, *Surrender on Demand,* 30–31.

3   Other memoirs of Fry's Marseilles work have been written by some of his colleagues, including Mary Jayne Gold, *Crossroads Marseilles, 1940* (New York: Doubleday, 1980), and Daniel Bénédite, *La Filière Marseillaise: Un chemin vers la liberté sous l'occupation* (Paris: Editions Clancier Guénaud, 1984). With regard to Fry's work on behalf of artists, see Cynthia Jaffee McCabe, "'Wanted by the Gestapo, Saved by America'—Varian Fry and the Emergency Rescue Committee," in *The Muses Flee Hitler: Cultural Transfer and Adaptation, 1930–1945,* ed. Jarrell C. Jackman and Carla M. Borden (Washington, D.C.: Smithsonian Institution Press, 1983), 79–91, and, most recently, Martica Sawin, *Surrealism in Exile and the Beginnings of the New York School* (Cambridge: MIT Press, 1995). On Fry's work on behalf of German exiled writers, see Hans-Albert Walter, *Deutsche Exilliteratur, 1933–1950,* vol. 3, *Internierung, Flucht und Lebensbedingungen im Zweiten Weltkrieg* (Stuttgart: J. B. Metzler, 1988), 318ff., and the postscript to the German translation of *Surrender on Demand: Auslieferung auf Verlangen: Die Rettung deutscher Emigranten in Marseille, 1940–41,* trans. Wolfgang Elfe and Jan Hans (Munich: Carl Hanser Verlag, 1986). For a review of Fry's historical papers, see the introduction to Karen Greenberg, ed., *Archives of the Holocaust: An International Collection of Selected Documents,* vol. 5, *Columbia University Library, New York: The Varian Fry Papers* (New York: Garland Publishing, 1990).

4   In short, Fry's work in Marseilles was possible only because of the State Department's policy of issuing "emergency" visas to help alleviate the refugee crisis precipitated by the fall of France. Nonquota emigrants who could prove that they were "political" or "intellectual" refugees were permitted to enter the United States not as immigrants, but as temporary visitors on an emergency visa; see David Wyman, *Paper Walls: America and the Refugee Crisis, 1938–1941* (New York: Pantheon Books, 1985), 137ff., and Henry L. Feingold, *The Politics of Rescue: The Roosevelt Administration and the Holocaust, 1938–1945* (New Brunswick, N.J.: Rutgers University Press, 1970). See also Richard Breitman and Alan M. Kraut, *American Refugee Policy and European Jewry, 1933–1945* (Bloomington: Indiana University Press, 1987).

5   For the full text of Article 19 of the Franco-German Armistice, see Fry, *Surrender on Demand,* ix, n. 1. Article 19, as Fry points out, called for the handover of all German prisoners and German nationals on French soil. It was perceived, especially by Fry's colleagues in the United States, as a legal means of deporting all those blacklisted by the Third Reich, including political and intellectuals opponents of Hitler; see also Wyman, *Paper Walls,* 137–38, and Feingold, *The Politics of Rescue,* 139–40.

6   The actual number ultimately aided by Fry is difficult to determine. A copy of a surviving list entitled "Liste complète des clients du Centre Américain de Secours" (International Rescue Committee Papers, United States Holocaust Memorial Research Institute Archives, Washington, D.C.) lists more than two thousand persons who were registered by Fry's relief agency. This list seems to contain many individuals who were helped only marginally, however, and it does not contain most of Fry's earliest and best-known clients. Fry himself was unclear about his figures and estimated that he and his colleagues met with more than fifteen thousand persons. But, of those seeking aid, only eighteen hundred cases, representing nearly four thousand individuals, were offered relief in some form. See Fry, *Surrender on Demand,* 189.

7   The course Fry followed after his arrival in Marseilles diverges considerably from the Emergency Rescue Committee's mission statement; see Mildred Adams to Varian Fry, 3 August 1940 (Varian Fry Papers, Butler Rare Book and Manuscript Library, Columbia University).

8   For a comprehensive and insightful discussion of Fry's interactions with the U.S. State Department, see Anita Kassof, "The German Refugees and Article 19 of the Franco-German Armistice, 1940–1941" (M.A. thesis, University of Maryland, 1992). Fry's correspondence with the State Department can be found in National Records and Archives Administration, Washington, D.C., General Records of the Department of State (RG 59), and Washington National Records Center, Suitland, Maryland, State Department Diplomatic Post Records (RG 84).

9   Fry left most of his papers and photographs to the Butler Rare Book and Manuscript Library of Columbia University during the 1960s. Many of his letters have been published in Greenberg, ed., *Varian Fry Papers.* Other papers and artworks were donated by Mrs. Annette Riley Fry to the United States Holocaust Memorial Museum and Archives, Washington, D.C. The surviving papers of the New York office of the Emergency Rescue Committee are available in partial form at the State University of New York, Albany, and in the Deutsches Exilarchiv, Frankfurt am Main. The files of Fry's Marseilles office have not been recovered.

10 See Fry's manuscript for *Surrender on Demand,* Varian Fry Papers, Columbia University.

11 See Peter Grasmann, *Sozialdemokraten gegen Hitler, 1933–1945* (Munich: Günter Olzog Verlag, 1976), 115ff. For biographical accounts of the German and Austrian socialist movements in exile, see Ingrid Warburg Spinelli, *Die Dringlichkeit des Mitleids und die Einsamkeit, nein zu sagen* (Hamburg: Doelling und Galitz Verlag, 1990), 165ff., and Muriel Gardiner, *Code Name "Mary": Memoirs of an American Woman in the Austrian Underground* (New Haven and London: Yale University Press, 1983).

12 Fry, manuscript for *Surrender on Demand,* 9.

13 See Spinelli, *Die Dringlichkeit des Mitleids,* 174ff.

14 Fry, manuscript for *Surrender on Demand,* 9–10. See also Frank Kingdon to Benjamin Huebsch, 18 June 1941 (Reinhold Niebuhr Papers, Library of Congress, Manuscript Division, Washington, D.C.). Frank Kingdon, then president of the University of Newark and chairman of the American Friends of German Freedom, assumed the role of president of the Emergency Rescue Committee.

15 There were several organized efforts during the 1930s to come to the aid of Europe's embattled intellectuals. The New School for Social Research worked steadily to encourage the immigration of blacklisted scientists and academics. Other organizations, such as the Rockefeller Foundation and the Emergency Committee in Aid of Displaced German Scholars, tried to find comparable positions for scholars, physicians, and scientists in the States. See Claus-Dieter Krohn, *Intellectuals in Exile: Refugee Scholars and the New School for Social Research* (Amherst: University of Massachusetts Press, 1993), 21ff. For a recent treatment of efforts on behalf of imperiled German writers, see Berthold Werner et al., *Deutsche Intellektuelle im Exil: Ihre Akademie und die "American Guild for German Cultural Freedom": Eine Ausstellung des Deutschen Exilarchivs 1933–1945 der Deutschen Bibliothek, Frankfurt am Main,* Deutsche Bibliothek, Sonderveröffentlichungen, no. 18 (Munich: K. G. Saur, 1993).

16 Fry, manuscript for *Surrender on Demand,* 12. In June 1940 many organizations and citizens' groups were sending lists to the State Department hoping to obtain special visas for endangered refugees. Several smaller labor organizations, such as the German Labor Delegation and the Jewish Labor Committee, had aligned themselves with more influential national organizations such as the American Federation of Labor and the International Ladies Garment Workers Union and together submitted lists of persons requiring immediate emergency visas to the State Department. See, for example, William Green et al. to Cordell Hull, 2 July 1940 (National Archives and Records Administration, RG 59, FW 811.111 Refugees /127). See Jack Jacobs, *Ein Freund in Not: Das jüdische Arbeiterkomitee in New York und die Flüchtlinge aus den deutschsprachigen Ländern, 1933–1945* (Bonn: Forschungsinstitut der Friedrich-Ebert-Stiftung, 1993), 19ff. For other groups that submitted lists to the State Department and the reaction of State to these lists, see Wyman, *Paper Walls,* 137ff. Just a day before the Emergency Rescue Committee's formation at that eventful luncheon, the members of the American Friends of German Freedom, obviously influenced by the actions of colleague labor organizations, had already composed a list of its own. Its list contained more than fifty names of political exiles and was first sent to Eleanor Roosevelt. See Max Ascoli, Karl Frank, J. Alvarez del Vayo, Joseph Buttinger et al. to E. Roosevelt, 24 June 1940, and E. Roosevelt to Berle, 25 June 1940 (National Archives and Records Administration, Washington, D.C., RG 59, FW 811.111 Refugees /139); and Spinelli, *Die Dringlichkeit des Mitleids,* 175–76.

17 Robert J. Horn Papers, United States Holocaust Memorial Research Institute Archives.

18 Barr's activities on behalf of refugee artists prior to 1940 are described in Alice Goldfarb Marquis, *Alfred H. Barr Jr., Missionary for the Modern* (Chicago and New York: Contemporary Books, 1989), 183–87. For Barr's questionable involvement in the early organization of the Emergency Rescue Committee, see the collection of fund-raising brochures in the Harold Oram Papers, Indiana University–Purdue University at Indianapolis, and the article "Group Acts to Save Leaders in Exile," *The New York Times,* 15 August 1940.

19 Fry, manuscript for *Surrender on Demand,* 24.

20 Ibid.

21 Names of artists are gathered from Fry's manuscript and ERC correspondence. See also Barr's letter to Archibald MacLeish: "Our Museum has no official connection with the Committee but the Trustees have given money which has been used by the Committee for the rescue of a half dozen of the most distinguished modern artists living in France" (9 May 1941, Alfred Barr Papers, Museum of Modern Art, New York).

22 See Fry, *Surrender on Demand,* 130, 157, and the manuscript for *Surrender on Demand,* which reports that Fry and others visited the artists in the fall of 1940 and late in the spring of 1941.

23 Fry, *Surrender on Demand,* 157.

24 See the case file of André Masson, Emergency Rescue Committee Papers, State University of New York, Albany.

25 See Fry to Emergency Rescue Committee (telegram), 14 February 1941 (case file of Max Ernst, International Rescue Committee Papers, United States Holocaust Memorial Research Institute Archives).

26 Fry, *Surrender on Demand,* 23–24. The text is also similar in Fry's original manuscript.

27 Ibid., 24.

28 Eileen Fry to Varian Fry, 25 November 1940 and 16 December 1940; Harold Oram to Varian Fry, 22 January 1941; and report of Varian Fry, 24 January 1941 (Varian Fry Papers, Columbia University).

29 See Rona Roob, "From the Archives: Refugee Artists," *MoMA: The Members Quarterly of the Museum of Modern Art,* no. 6 (1991): 18–19, and also, McCabe, "Wanted by the Gestapo," 81. Margaret Scolari Barr was a pivotal figure in the processing of paperwork required for visa application and approval and in raising funds for the refugees' passage.

30 See the case file of André Masson, Emergency Rescue Committee Papers, State University of New York, Albany, and Kurt Seligmann to Margaret Barr, 9 October 1940, Kurt Seligmann Papers, private collection, New York. Thanks are due to Martica Sawin for bringing the Kurt Seligmann Papers to my attention. See also Sawin, *Surrealism in Exile,* 109.

31 See the case files of Eugen Spiro, Jean Hélion, and Camilla Koffler, Emergency Rescue Committee Papers, State University of New York, Albany. Curt Valentin and Kay Sage also appear in the correspondence of the Emergency Rescue Committee files among those who helped find sponsors and financial backing for artists.

32 Oram to Fry, 22 January 1941, Varian Fry Papers, Columbia University.

33 See *New York Times,* 14 October 1940 and 17 October 1940, and *Time,* 11 November 1940. The *Time* article mentions that there were several other groups in New York who were claiming responsibility for the rescue of Feuchtwanger, Mann, and Werfel.

34 Throughout the fall and winter of 1940 the committee held a series of fund-raising events in New York. During the one held on behalf of artists, a sculpture by Jo Davidson was auctioned off. See Edna Albers to Lewis Mumford, 25 November 1940 (Lewis Mumford Papers, University of Pennsylvania), and Harold Oram Papers, Indiana University–Purdue University at Indianapolis. Breton, Chagall, Ernst, Lipchitz, and Masson, who arrived in the spring through Fry's efforts, were individually asked to make public appearances on behalf of stranded colleagues. See Frank Crowninshield to Kurt Seligmann, 11 June 1941 (Kurt Seligmann Papers, private collection, New York), and

Eileen Fry to Saidie A. May, 15 October 1941 (Saidie A. May Papers, Baltimore Museum of Art).

35 For a discussion of the artworks produced at Villa Air Bel, see Sawin, *Surrealism in Exile*, 124ff.

36 André Breton, "Jeu de Marseille," *VVV* 3 (1943): 89–90 (translated by Carole Frankel).

37 Marcel Duchamp received subsistence funds from the committee, and his passage was arranged in late 1942, after Fry had returned to New York.

38 See telegrams dated 14 January 1941 and 2 April 1941 in the case file of Max Ernst, International Rescue Committee Papers, United States Holocaust Memorial Museum Archives. Support for Jacques Hérold was harder to obtain since no sponsors were ever identified in France or the United States. In a very polite letter of rejection, Fry informed Hérold that the New York Committee had not favorably reviewed his candidacy for a visa. See Fry and Bénédite to Hérold, 2 January 1941 (private collection, Paris).

39 Fry brought back with him several paintings and drawings by Brauner, Dominguez, Freundlich, Hérold, Lam, Philippe Hosiasson, Gerta Sauer, and Otto Wols.

40 Fry to Museum of Modern Art (cablegram), 19 April 1941, and Fry to Museum of Modern Art (partially preserved letter), 2 July 1941 (case file of André Masson, Emergency Rescue Committee Papers, State University of New York, Albany). For Pablo Casals, see Fry to Emergency Rescue Committee (copy of cablegram), 14 February 1941 (case file of Max Ernst, International Rescue Committee Papers, United States Holocaust Memorial Research Institute Archives).

41 See Fry, *Surrender on Demand*, 166, and report of Varian Fry, 24 January 1941 (Varian Fry Papers, Columbia University).

42 See the partially preserved letter from Fry to the Museum of Modern Art, 2 July 1941, cited in note 40, and Michèle C. Cone, *Artists under Vichy: A Case of Prejudice and Persecution* (Princeton: Princeton University Press, 1993), 127–29, and *Otto Freundlich et ses amis,* exh. cat. (Pontoise: Musée de Pontoise, 1993).

43 See case file of Max Ernst, International Rescue Committee papers, United States Holocaust Memorial Research Institute Archives.

44 These articles include "France, Once the Haven of Exiles, Becomes Gestapo Mantrap," *New Leader*, 25 April 1942; "Anti-Refugee Consuls Get Power of Life-Death in State Dep't Visa Policy," *New Leader*, 2 May 1942; "Our Consuls at Work," *Nation*, 2 May 1942; "Narrow Gov't Policy Deprives U.S. of Aid, Expert Knowledge of Anti-Fascist Refugees," *New Leader*, 9 May 1942, and perhaps his most poignant, "The Massacre of the Jews," *New Republic*, 21 December 1942.

45 David S. Wyman, *The Abandonment of the Jews: America and the Holocaust, 1941–1945* (New York: Pantheon Books, 1984), 313.

96
Marc Chagall, *Yellow Crucifixion*, 1943 (cat. no. 25).

constructing a new jewish identity

MATTHEW AFFRON

marc chagall
jacques lipchitz

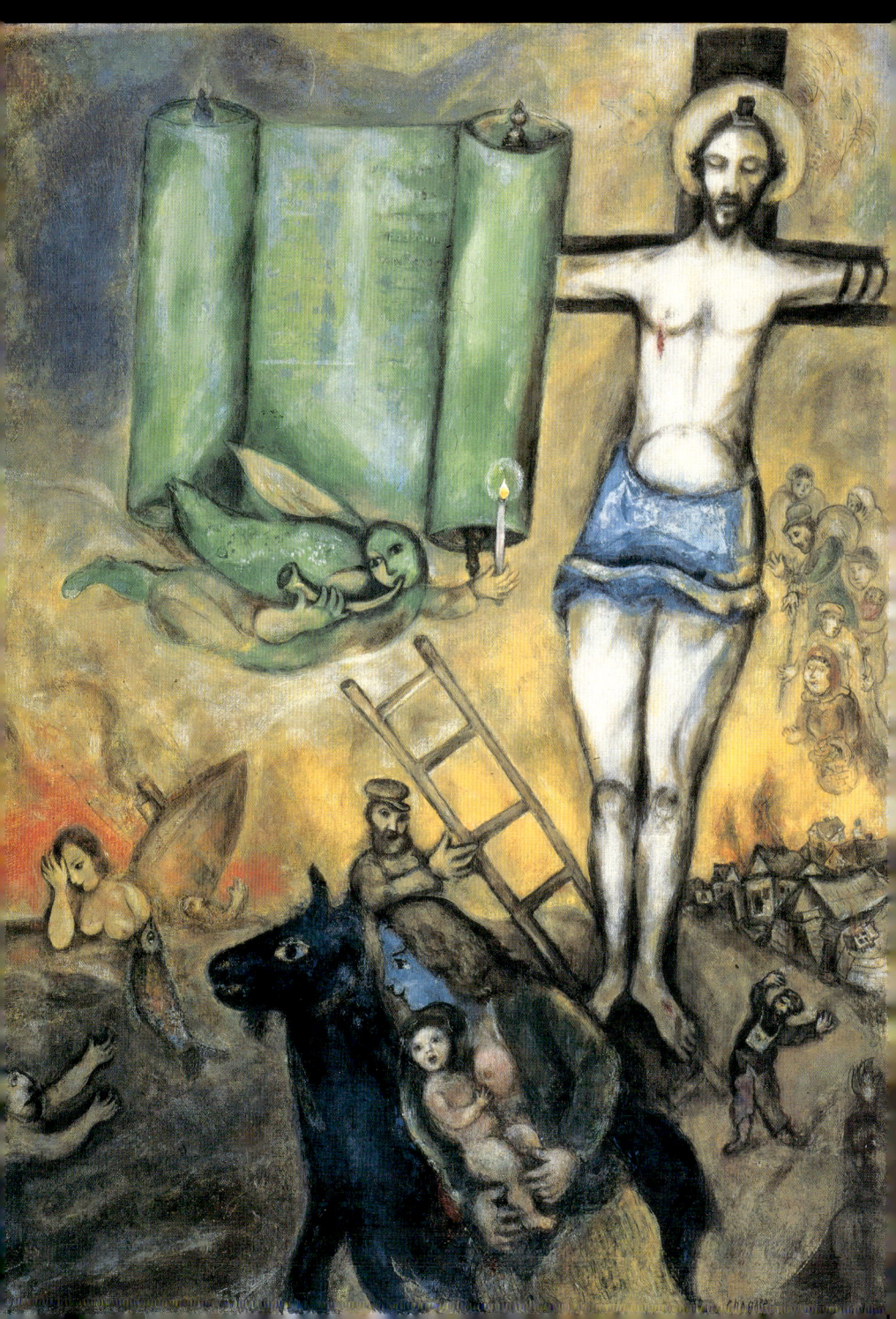

marc chagall in new york, 1941–45

1887	born in Vitebsk, Russia
1941	emigrates from France (Gordes) to the U.S. (New York)
1948	returns to France (Orgeval)
1985	dies in Saint-Paul-de-Vence

97
Marc Chagall, 1941; photograph ©1941 Arnold Newman.

98
Marc Chagall; *White Crucifixion*, 1938; oil on canvas; 60¾ x 55 in. (154.3 x 139.7 cm); The Art Institute of Chicago, gift of Alfred S. Alschuler, 1946.925.

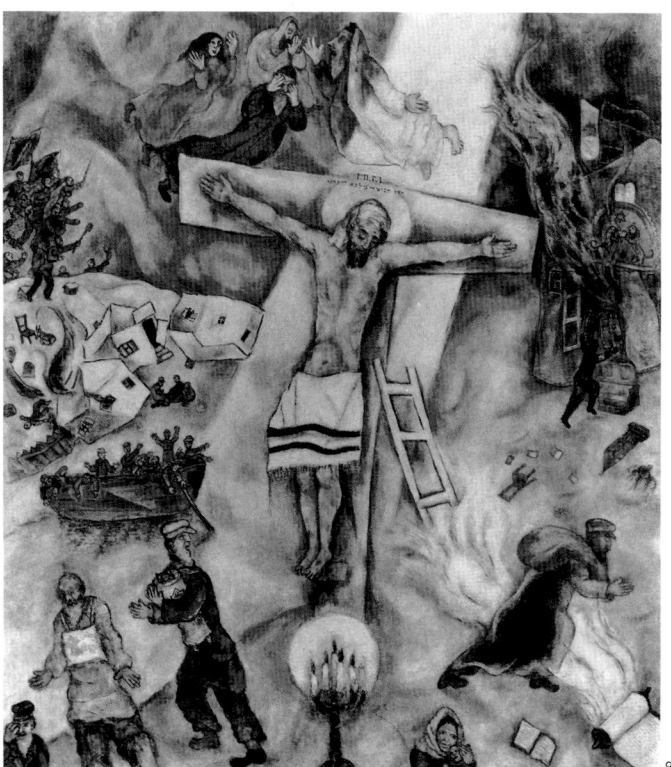

In January 1940, four months after France's entry into World War II, a major exhibition of recent works by Marc Chagall opened in central Paris. This event was the first in an ambitious series of one-artist exhibitions planned by the Galerie "Mai," which hoped, by showing the works of the "most representative" artists of the day, to provide a permanent venue for modernist art during this difficult wartime period.[1] The Chagall show surveyed the major themes of the painter's art, subjects of private sentiment that, having been crafted and reworked over three decades, took on general significance. These forms included lovers and marriage pairs, acrobats and angels, fantastic animals, and memories of the painter's childhood in the Jewish community of the Russian town of Vitebsk. Yet one picture, marked by an extremely grave emotional tone and by its remarkably explicit commentary on the current European political situation, stood out from the group. This was *White Crucifixion* of 1938 (fig. 98).

White Crucifixion, whose subject is the persecution of the Jews in Germany, is anchored symbolically by Chagall's treatment of its principal figure, the crucified Christ. Deviating from the standard representation, Chagall accentuated Jesus' Jewish character. The figure's clothing recalls the traditional Jewish prayer shawl, and the light of a Jewish candelabrum at Jesus' feet complements the heavenly beam that falls from above. The three biblical patriarchs and single matriarch that float in lamentation above Christ's head appear, like the central figure, in Jewish dress. Chagall switches from a biblical register to an entirely different presentation of suffering along the other three edges of the composition. Working now in smaller vignettes that, although inventions, are rich in allusions to contemporary events, the painter depicts a pogrom. Moving clockwise from the upper right in a snowy, nocturnal landscape, a soldier oversees the destruction of a synagogue, Jews flee on land and sea, and a village is annihilated. Although a group of armed peasants appear from over a hill at the upper left, it is not certain that any of the refugees will be saved.[2]

Jewish themes had always been fundamental to the artist. There were, in fact, important antecedents in his work for many of the iconographical elements within *White Crucifixion:* the Wandering Jew, the crucified Christ, and the fleeing mother and child.

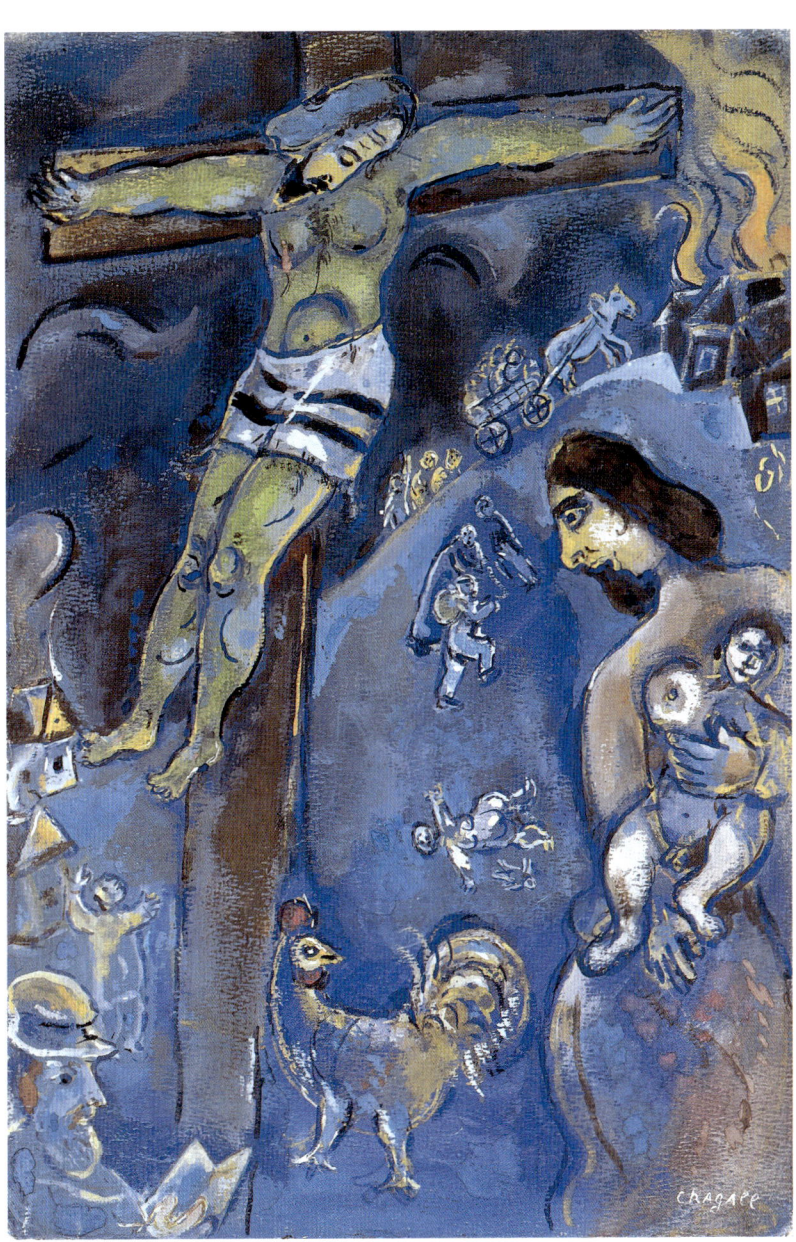

99
Marc Chagall, *Persecution*, c. 1941
(cat. no. 23).

The picture's formal devices were also familiar, as Chagall dispensed with conventional rules of spatial and narrative unity and instead organized his pictures by balancing semiautonomous episodic fragments within a shallow visual setting. Nevertheless, as the Russian painter Alexandre Benois pointed out in reviewing the Galerie "Mai" exhibition for the Parisian periodical *Cahiers d'art,* if *White Crucifixion* was firmly rooted in Chagall's previous work, it brought an uncommon tragic power and polemical charge to the painter's distinctive vision of the world. "It is clear," stated Benois, "that this vision was prompted by events of the past few years, and especially by the untranslatable horror that has engulfed Chagall's coreligionists." He went on to call *White Crucifixion* "a document on the soul of our times."[3]

Benois was correct in seeing this 1938 work as a turning point within Chagall's art. *White Crucifixion* launched an extensive series of images depicting martyrdom, pictures that became primary vehicles of Chagall's artistic response to the Holocaust before and during his exile, which began in May 1941. Some of these works, *Persecution* (c. 1941; fig. 99, cat. no. 23) and *Yellow Crucifixion* (1943; fig. 96, cat. no. 25), for example, hark back to *White Crucifixion* but employ different symbolic forms (drawn from the Old and New Testaments and from contemporary events) surrounding the principal figure. In other cases Chagall found ways to incorporate his self-portrait into the work; he depicted himself in the related guises of painter, witness, and mourner. These images allowed him to place his own evolving situation and private

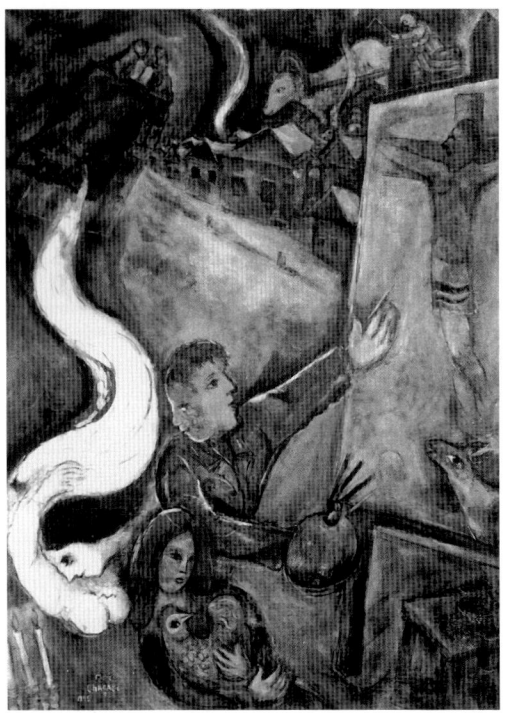 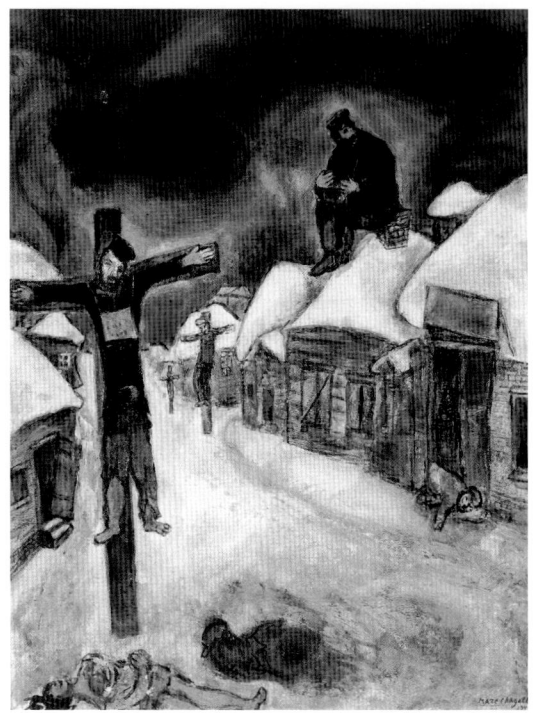

100
Marc Chagall; *The Soul of the City*, 1945; oil on canvas; 42⅛ x 32¼ in. (107 x 82 cm); Musée National d'Art Moderne, Centre Georges Pompidou.

101
Marc Chagall; *The Crucified*, 1944; gouache on paper; 24½ x 18⅝ in. (62.2 x 47.3 cm); Gift of Victoria (Vitya) Babin to America-Israel Cultural Foundation; on permanent loan to the Israel Museum, Jerusalem.

misfortunes in relation to the collective tragedy of war. For instance, in *The Soul of the City* (1945; fig. 100) the artist depicts himself seated at the easel, palette in hand. Janus-faced, he looks toward a large Crucifixion image on one side while simultaneously gazing at a luminous female apparition who descends from the upper left, a vision of the painter's recently deceased wife, Bella. Another form of self-presentation occurs in works such as *The Martyr* (1940–41). Here the setting is not Golgotha, but an Eastern European village, and the sufferer is not Christ, but a contemporary Jew who dies at the stake. Chagall, visible in the lower right hand corner of the image, appears as a spectator.

Presenting a distant but dramatic variation upon the Crucifixion theme, *The Martyr* is one of many images in which Chagall synthesized contemporary subjects, Christian iconography, and Jewish themes. A 1944 gouache entitled *The Crucified* (fig. 101) depicts a devastated Eastern European town, its street lined with crucified Jews. A 1943 canvas entitled *War* features the Wandering Jew, a subject that simultaneously underlined the painter's concern for the fate of his people and served to represent Chagall himself, who had by this time become a refugee.

Chagall found a receptive environment for his work in New York. He quickly formed an association with the art dealer Pierre Matisse, who, because the painter had managed to ship a very considerable number of his own works out of France, was able to open a Chagall retrospective in November 1941. Matisse would exhibit Chagall's work on an almost annual basis until 1947. The painter was also represented in important group shows of New York exile artists, including Matisse's 1942 *Artists in Exile* and the *First Papers of Surrealism* exhibition of the same year. The Museum of Modern Art presented the first comprehensive Chagall exhibition in the United States in 1946.[4]

In discussing his American experience, Chagall presented a set of views that are familiar within the literature of European responses to the United States. He described America as a place of startling vitality, novelty, and size, and he located the signs of those national attributes in the country's natural environment, in the vibrant sensibility of its people, and especially in its skyscrapers. Yet while he looked upon those tall buildings as the authentic expression of a remarkable national spirit, he was able to discern only early indicators of a comparable achievement when he considered

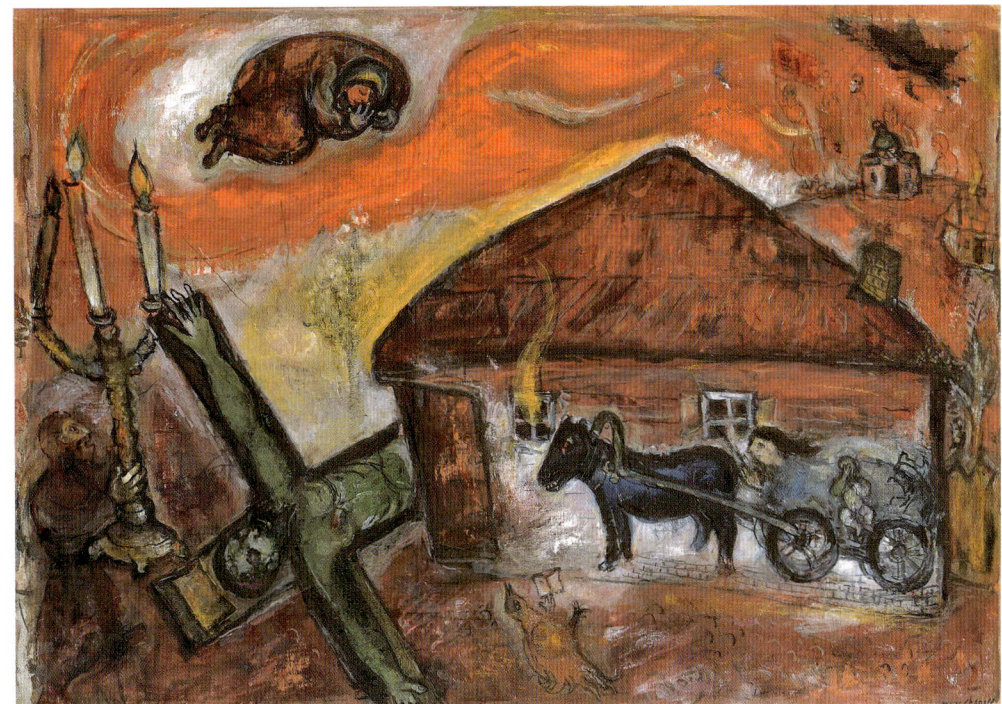

102
Marc Chagall, *Obsession*, 1943 (cat. no. 24).

103
Marc Chagall, *Resurrection*, 1937–48 (cat. no. 21).

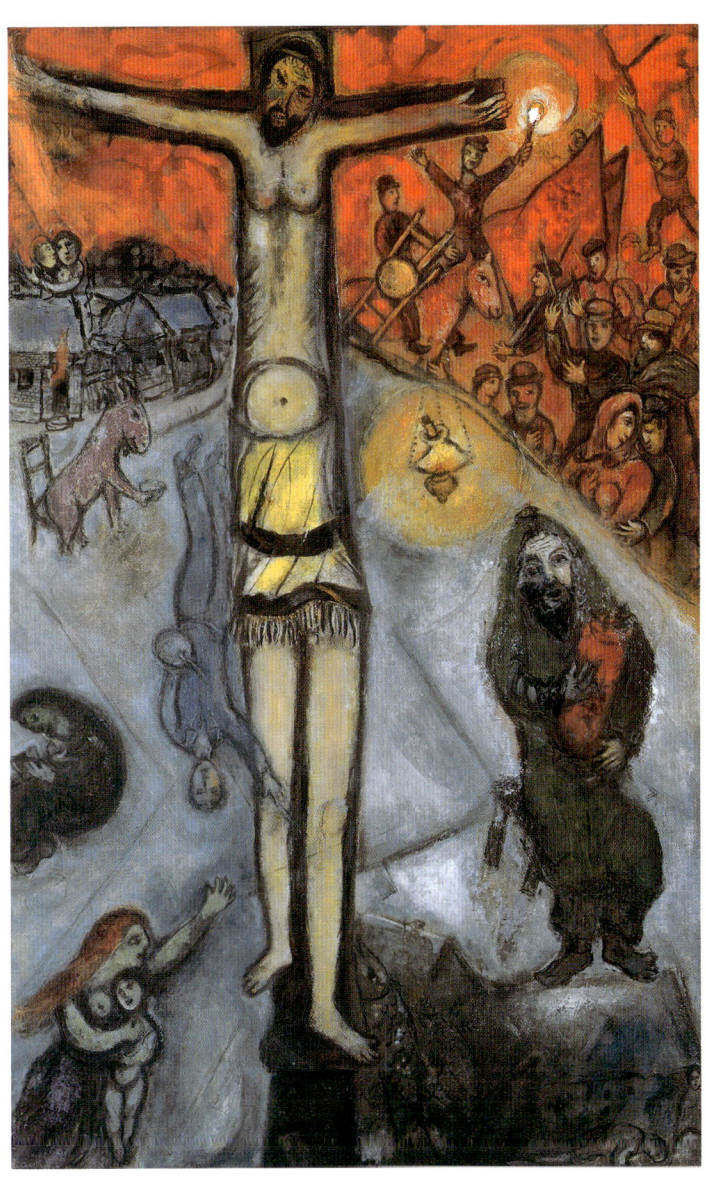

American art.[5] As a consequence he felt unable to transplant himself from the artistic traditions and community of France to American ground. As he explained in late 1944, in an open letter to his Parisian colleagues, "I suffered for having to leave you during that terrible year. It was not my destiny to sacrifice my life to Paris. The enemy was preparing a degrading death for me somewhere in Poland. I took the hospitable hand offered by America."[6] Thus, while in his public statements Chagall often lauded the country of his exile as a place of freedom, he never integrated himself fully into American life. American subjects would not play a significant role in his work, and the twin geographical poles of the painter's modernist sensibility remained strictly Russian and Parisian in nature. This was well understood by American observers such as the artist Louis Lozowick and the critic Harold Rosenberg, who pointed to Chagall's internationalist orientation as a key to the aesthetic and social value of his work, contrasting his art with contemporary forms of cultural nationalism.[7]

In fact, in his paintings and public statements of the American period, as in the poems he wrote during this time, Chagall revealed a constant obsession with the fate of two European populations: the artists of France and

marc chagall 117

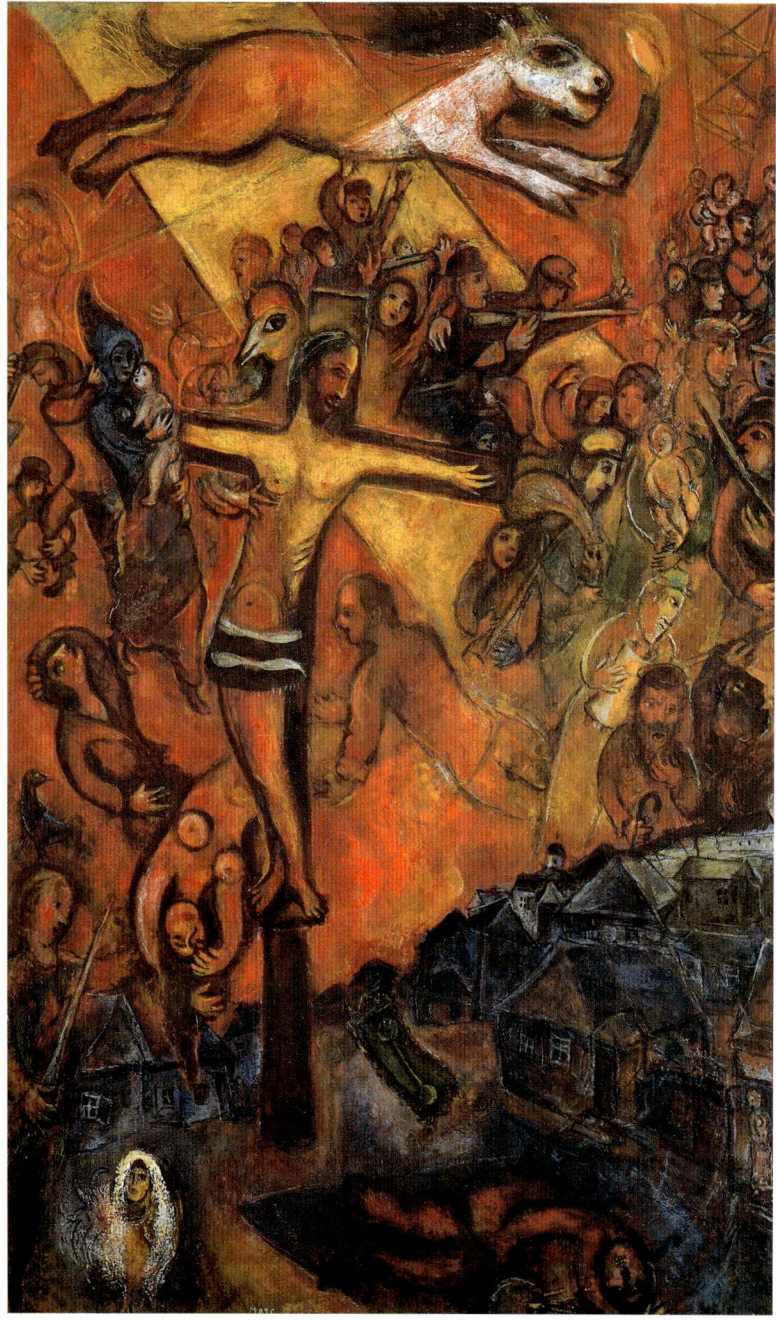

104
Marc Chagall, *Ghetto* (renamed *Resistance*), 1937–48 (cat. no. 20).

the Jews of Eastern Europe. He often referred to the first group in written statements and interviews, urgently expressing the hope that a renaissance in French art would follow the end of hostilities and honoring those artists who had remained in the country. "During these [past] years," he wrote in another 1944 message to the painters of France, "the world anguished over the fate of French civilization and art. The absence of France seemed impossible, inconceivable.... I bow before your combat, your combat against the enemy of Art and of Life."[8] The struggle of the Eastern Europeans, meanwhile, continued to figure strongly as a subject in Chagall's painting. A notable example is *Ghetto* (renamed *Resistance*; fig. 104, cat. no. 20), which he completed in 1948, the year of his return to France. The picture's locale is once again a Jewish ghetto, but its main activity takes place above, in a turbulent red-orange sky. The crucified Christ presides at the center of the scene, surrounded by refugees and by the resistance fighters who have finally arrived to protect them. *Resistance* is essentially hopeful in tone, yet it contains an elegiac dimension. The corpses of some fighters are visible in the foreground. Near the foot of the Cross, either dreaming or fallen like the martyred partisans, lies the painter Chagall.

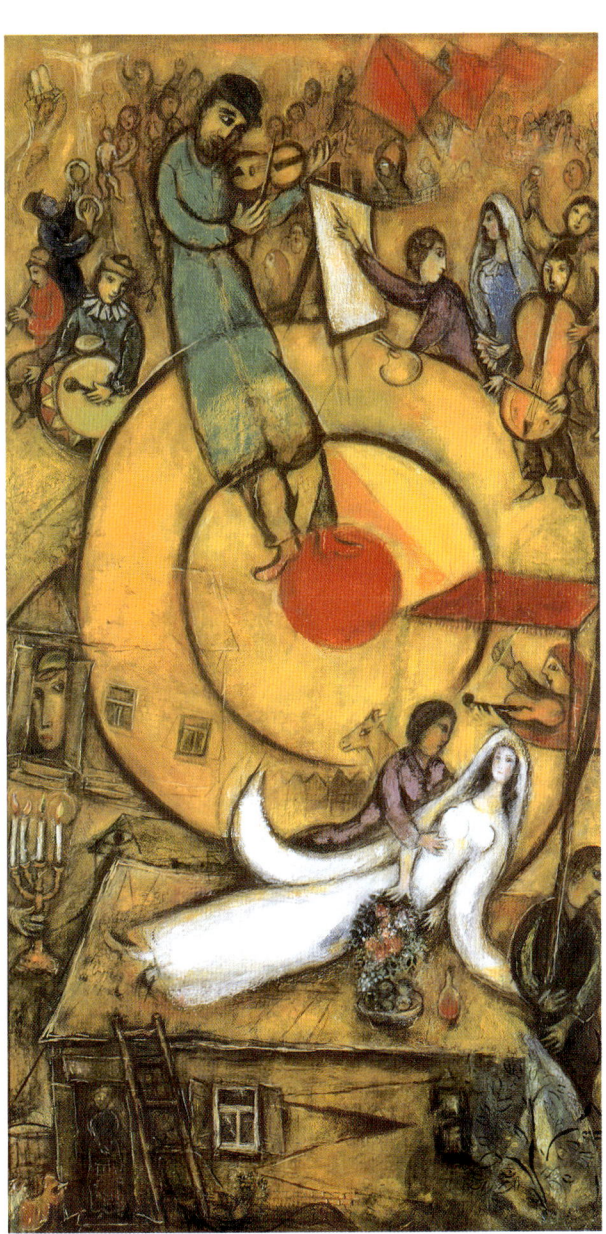

105
Marc Chagall, *Liberation*, 1937–52
(cat. no. 22).

Notes

1   See the editorial note in "Les Expositions," *Cahiers d'art* 15, no. 1–2 (1940): 33. Founded by Yvonne Zervos in 1939, the Galerie "Mai" was shut down before the end of 1940.

2   Ziva Amishai-Maisels provides an extended interpretation of this image in "Chagall's *White Crucifixion*," *Museum Studies* 17, no. 2 (1991): 139–53, 180–81. Regarding the crucified Christ as a symbol in Holocaust art, see idem, "The Jewish Jesus," *Journal of Jewish Art* 9 (1982): 84–104.

3   Alexandre Benois, "Chagall, oeuvres récentes," *Cahiers d'Art* 15, no. 1–2 (1940): 33 (all translations are by the author).

4   See James Johnson Sweeney, *Marc Chagall*, exh. cat. (New York: Museum of Modern Art, 1946).

5   For Chagall's attitudes toward America, see the following statements and interviews: "Marc Chagall nous parle de l'Amérique," *La voix de France*, n.s., no. 17 (15 May 1942): 8; Raymond Abel, "An Interview with Marc Chagall," *The League* 14 (April 1942): 7; and a lecture by Chagall entitled "The Artist," trans. Otto von Simson and George J. McMorrow, in *The Works of the Mind*, ed. Robert B. Heywood (Chicago: University of Chicago Press, 1947), 21.

6   Chagall, "Pour Paris," typescript, September 1944, Chagall scrapbook, vol. 1, Museum of Modern Art Library, New York.

7   See Louis Lozowick, "Marc Chagall," *The Jewish Survey* 1 (January 1942): 16–17, and Harold Rosenberg, "Marc Chagall: Jewish Modernist Master," *Jewish Frontier* 12 (April 1945): 26–33.

8   Marc Chagall, "Message de Marc Chagall aux peintres français," *Le spectateur des arts*, no. 1 (December 1944): 3. See also Chagall's concluding remarks in a 1943 lecture entitled "Quelques impressions sur la peinture," *Renaissance* 2–3 (1944–45): 56–57; and a radio message of October 1944, typescript, Chagall scrapbook, vol. 2, Museum of Modern Art Library, New York.

jacques lipchitz in new york, 1941–45

1891	born in Druskieniki, Lithuania
1941	emigrates from France (Toulouse) to the U.S. (New York)
1973	dies in Capri, Italy

On leaving Europe, I lost everything except my faith. And in the last three years I've begun a new life, from the modeling studio to the casting vat, from the drawing stand to the scaffolding, where in the clay my [sculpted] volumes encounter the light. I struggle on with thirty years of experience, knowing what I want and where I am headed and carrying out as best I can my line of thought—a term I use to avoid the old notion of "ideal," which, though a bit worn, remains beautiful.[1]

Jacques Lipchitz fled Paris in May 1940, after the German invasion of France, and moved to the southern city of Toulouse, in the country's unoccupied zone. As a Jew and an artist well known for his antifascist beliefs, however, he was unable to remain in safety there. In the summer of 1941, with the help of the American Emergency Rescue Committee, he immigrated to New York.

Among the very few sculptures that the artist had in his possession upon arriving in the United States, one acknowledged directly the experience of exile. *Flight* (1940; fig. 107, cat. no. 95), modeled during the Toulouse stopover, depicts a man and a woman on the move, the man's arms raised in a gesture of protection. The two bodies lean forward, establishing a dramatic silhouette; the prevailing sense of dynamism is underscored by the very strong modeling of the work's surface. Lipchitz's free treatment of anatomy only accentuates the impression of emotional urgency. The pair move ahead on three legs, the expressive fusion of two bodies emphasizing the force of their embrace. Although the figures in *Flight* face an uncertain future, a companion piece entitled *Arrival* (1941; fig. 108, cat. no. 96) imagines a happy outcome for them. Here, while the couple continue to strain ever forward, the woman succeeds in lifting a child to safety. Lipchitz conceived *Arrival* soon after his own landing in the United States.

Flight and *Arrival* illustrate Lipchitz's fundamental attitudes toward matters of style and subject in modern sculpture. First, the artist saw the recent history of sculpture as a series of great discoveries leading to the technical and aesthetic liberation of the medium. If Auguste

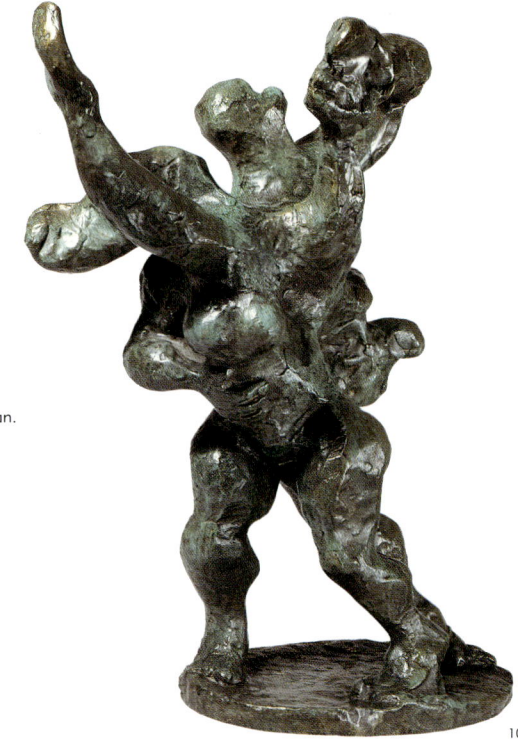

106
Jacques Lipchitz, New York, 1946; photograph © 1946 Arnold Newman.

107
Jacques Lipchitz, *Flight*, 1940 (cat. no. 95).

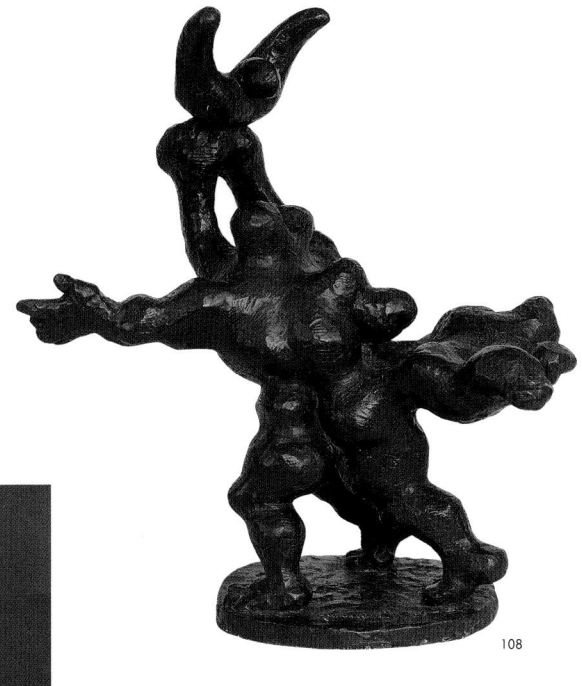

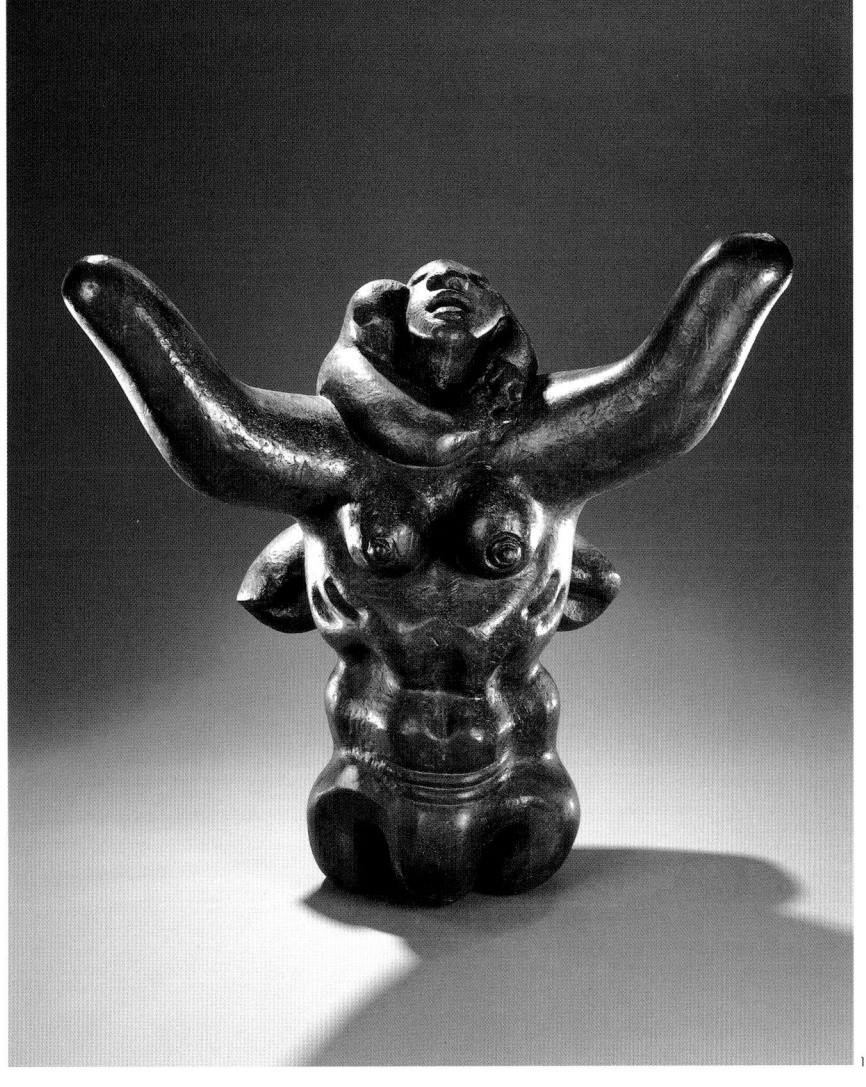

108
Jacques Lipchitz, *Arrival*, 1941
(cat. no. 96).

109
Jacques Lipchitz, *Mother and Child II*,
1941–45 (cat. no. 97).

Rodin, by orchestrating the play of light and shadow upon the object, opened up new possibilities in sculptural expression, the artists of Lipchitz's own cubist generation advanced the art by developing new syntaxes of abstract representation. Lipchitz attached a strong moral and political imperative to this legacy, linking the ideal of creative liberty with the emancipation of the individual and, in allusions to the contemporary European situation, condemning the totalitarian regulation of both art and life. Indeed, he was very concerned with the social and political functions of sculpture. He endeavored to fashion works that might function simultaneously as meditations on the great problems of human existence, as responses to the social and political conflicts of the age, and as deeply felt autobiographical expressions.[2] The theme of the refugee registered in all these ways as he translated his own experience of escape and expatriation, synthetically and symbolically, through the tribulations of a family in *Flight* and *Arrival*.

Both works were included in Lipchitz's first solo exhibition of the exile period, organized by Curt Valentin at the Buchholz Gallery in January–February 1942.[3] This show brought together bronze casts and sketches dating from 1936 to the exhibition's opening, including *Mother and Child*, a work that Lipchitz had conceived during the final Parisian years but did not execute in sculptural terms until after arriving in New York. As in its sequel, *Mother and Child II* (1941–45; fig. 109, cat. no. 97), a woman gestures heavenward, her child clinging to her neck; from its foundation in the truncated base, the mother's form surges upward into arms whose radical simplification establishes the eloquence of the supplicating gesture. The sculpture's monumental and volumetric forms contrast strongly with the expressionist turbulence of *Flight* and *Arrival*, and its effect

jacques lipchitz   **121**

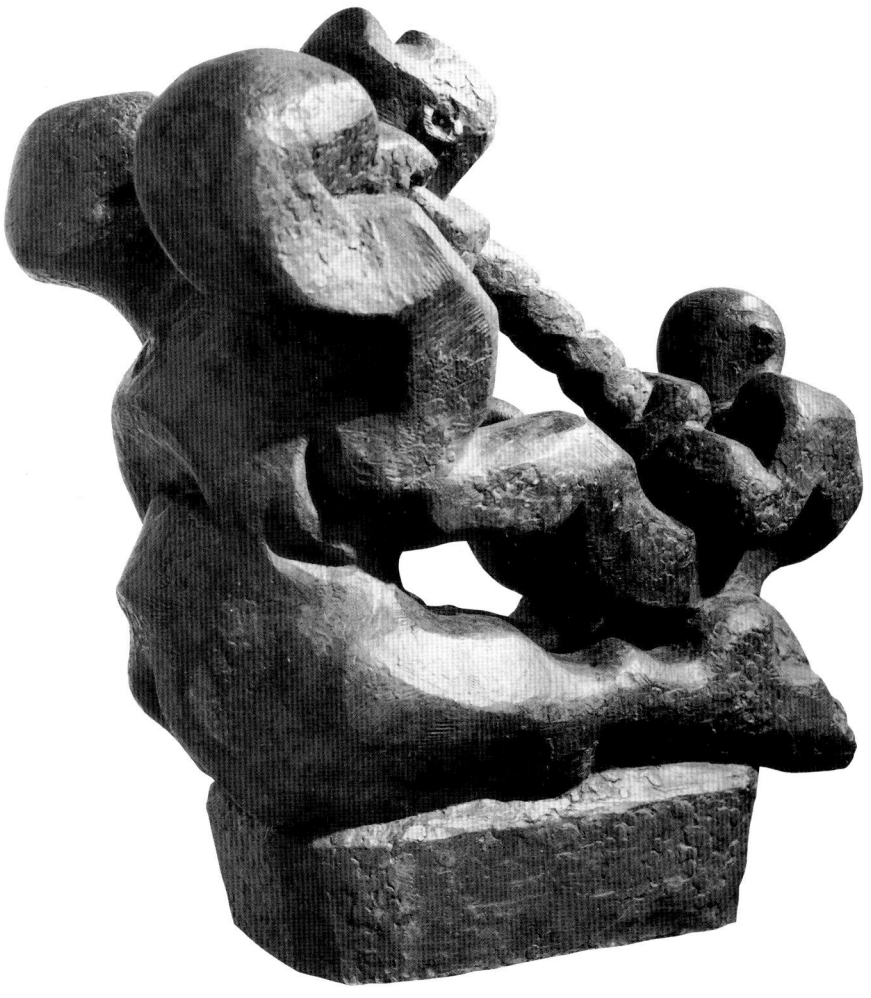

110
Jacques Lipchitz; *David and Goliath*, 1933; bronze; h: 33 in. (83.8 cm); Estate of Jacques Lipchitz, courtesy Marlborough International Fine Art AG.

derives essentially from the dramatic contouring of the heroic body. The abstractness of the mother's body allows Lipchitz to conjure a secondary image within it, as the head of a bull seems to emerge from the contours of torso and upraised arms. This doubling bears upon the ultimate significance of the work, since the effect of pathos is tempered by an underlying sense of power and defiance. As was explained in a Buchholz Gallery press release, "*Mother and Child* . . . reveals the artist's conception of the hope of our age—the form of the bull's head appearing in the clapsed [*sic*] shapes of the mother and child symbolize[s] in this embrace the hope and strength of the Eternal Mother."[4] The fusion of visual metaphors had been an important characteristic of Lipchitz's practice since his days as a cubist. The reuse of this device two decades later demonstrates the underlying continuity of his practice.

The 1942 exhibition revealed another important facet of the emigré sculptor's response to current events: his use of biblical and mythological subjects as vehicles for symbolic reflection on the struggle against tyranny. Lipchitz had first worked in this fashion in the early 1930s, most notably in sculptures of 1933 on the theme of David and Goliath. In one bronze version (fig. 110) Goliath rises up in anguish, straining against the strangulating force of a great noose that David holds fast. Lipchitz made his immediate political concerns fully evident by incising a swastika directly upon the giant's breast. At the same time the sculptor wished to address fundamental themes of good and evil in ways that might communicate a transcendent moral vision. Referring to the *David and Goliath* in 1935, he stated: "I responded in my gut as a Jew on behalf of my scattered and persecuted blood brothers. But this monster that we're killing is not just antisemitism, it is in fact whatever keeps man from walking tall."[5]

Lipchitz made similar use of certain favored mythological subjects. One of these was Prometheus, who fashioned the first man from clay and, defying Jupiter, gave humans the gift of fire. The hero's defense of humanity made him an inspiring symbol of human progress. Lipchitz took up the theme of Prometheus Bound—in

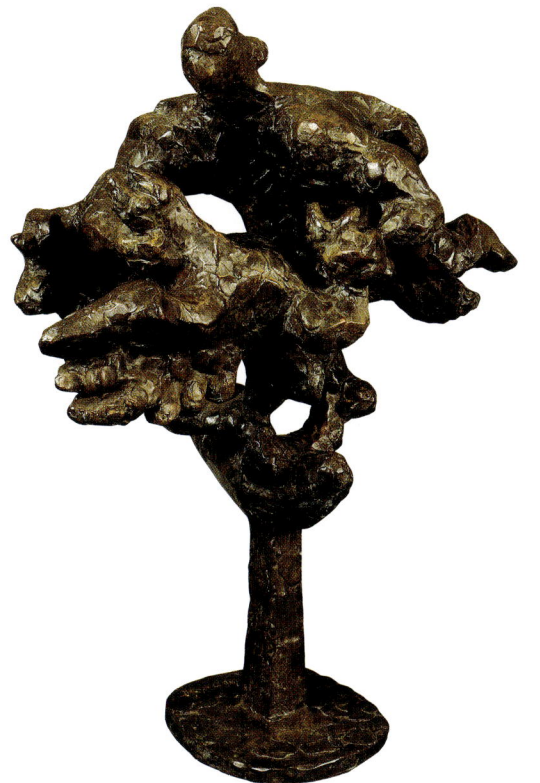
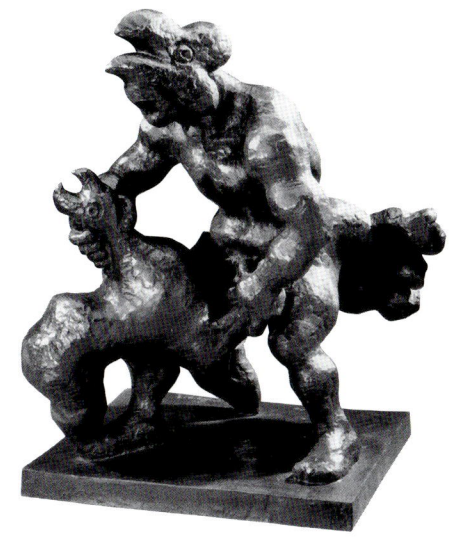

111
Jacques Lipchitz, *Prometheus Strangling the Vulture*, 1943 (cat. no. 99).

112
Jacques Lipchitz; *Prometheus Strangling the Vulture*, 1943; bronze; h: 37½ in. (95.3 cm); location unknown.

which Jupiter punishes the hero by causing him to be chained to a rock and tormented daily by an eagle that picks at his liver—but modified the mythological text in important and immediately recognizable ways. The classical eagle becomes a vulture, and Prometheus, apparently freed from his shackles, is able to resist his attacker.[6] The sculptor embarked on this subject in sketches and models of 1933, already thinking of it as an allegory of active resistance against European totalitarianism. Yet it was not until 1937, when he realized his Prometheus triumphant as a work of public sculpture, that the work's political force became fully apparent. He had been hired by France's left-leaning Popular Front government to create an architectural monument for display at the Palace of Discovery and Invention, a museum of science and technology within the 1937 Paris world's fair. The sculptor made a ten-meter-high plaster version of the *Prometheus,* its unchained protagonist wearing the Phrygian bonnet, a symbol of liberty. Placed over one of the building's entrances, the work performed a powerful symbolic fusion of the social ideal of technical progress and the democratic political program of the Popular Front. Then, after the closing of the fair, the *Prometheus* was moved to a ground-level installation on the Champs-Elysées, where it lost its crucial architectural and symbolic context. Yet the monumental sculpture remained controversial, and in early 1938, after a violent right-wing press campaign, it was destroyed.

Lipchitz continued work on the theme of Prometheus, producing new variations both before and after his emigration (see fig. 111, cat. no. 99). The 1943 *Prometheus Strangling the Vulture* (fig. 112) is in some ways the most unexpected and equivocal of these versions. Here the hero has the head of a rooster, the symbol of France, and becomes in this struggle, however improbably, the morphological double of his antagonist. How do we understand these two substitutions, the metamorphosis of the hero and the replacement of the German eagle with the vulture? Lipchitz seems to suggest that, in order for democratic forces to prevail in occupied France, the country will need first to subdue the evil within itself.[7] We should note that the sculptor made a point of refraining from producing literal readings of his textual sources and always modified them to suit his own specific purposes. Such a case is the 1941 *Rape of Europa*.[8] In a startling deviation from the standard narrative—in which Europa is ravished by Jupiter, who has taken the shape of a white bull—Lipchitz's wartime Europa plunges a

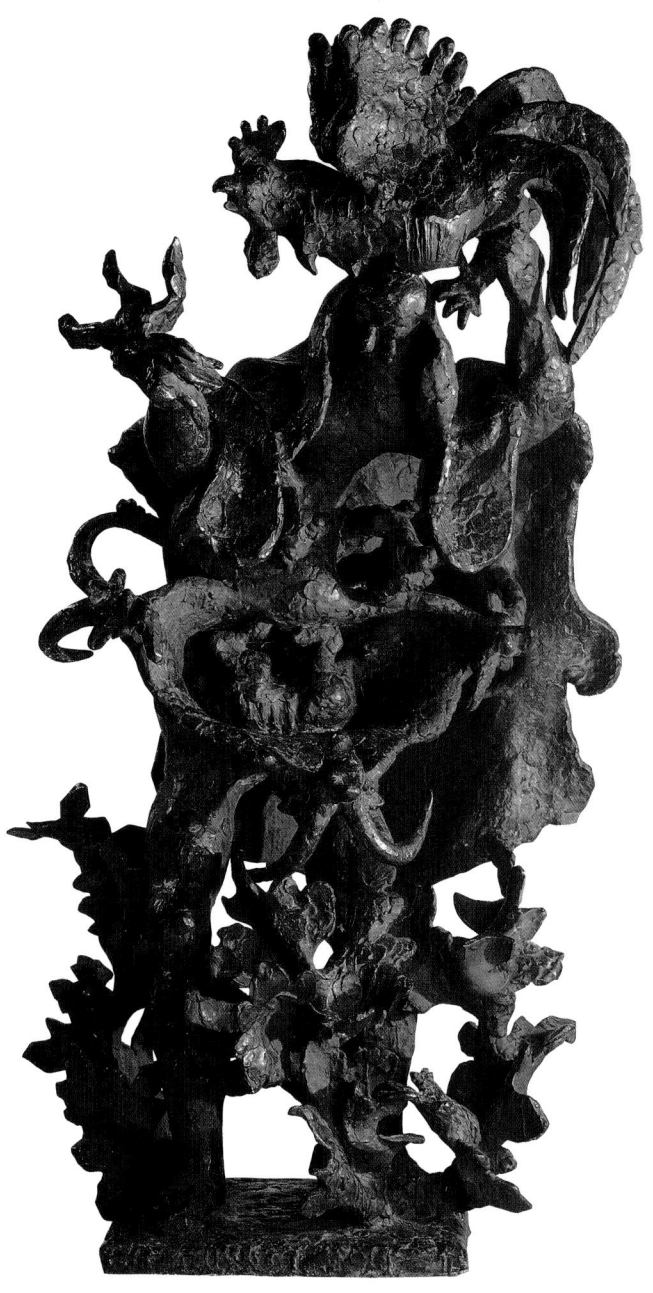

113
Jacques Lipchitz, *The Prayer*, 1943 (cat. no. 98).

knife into the chest of her attacker. The sculptor has transformed the subject into a fantasy on Europe's revolt against tyranny. By allowing his epic protagonist to rise up, once again, against an aggressive force, Lipchitz infuses his sculptural enterprise with distinctly prophetic ambitions.[9]

Lipchitz's sculpture accommodated and in fact depended upon conspicuous forms of philosophical, magical, and mystical idealism. Or—as Maurice Raynal, one of his veteran critics, astutely observed in 1947, soon after seeing Lipchitz's first Parisian exhibition of the postwar period—an overriding sense of metaphysical struggle linked the sculptor's artistic temperament with specific modes of formal experimentation and connected both to a class of fundamental moral concerns.[10] These interrelated factors are expressed with great clarity in two symbolic self-portraits by Lipchitz, *The Pilgrim* (1942) and *The Prayer* (1943; fig. 113, cat. no. 98). The earlier work, a complex exercise in lost-wax casting, offers a particularly agitated treatment of the human form; in an extravagant metamorphosis the body of the traveler seems at once gravely wounded and alive with a dynamic profusion of plant forms. *The Prayer* turns this expressive treatment of the figure into a metaphor for spiritual anguish. This sculpture represents the enactment of an ancient and esoteric ritual; an aged Jew sacrifices a rooster by swinging it violently overhead, symbolically expiating his sins by transferring them to the animal. Conceived, as Lipchitz later said, during the darkest days of the war, this work was offered as a prayer for the Jews of Europe.[11]

After the conclusion of hostilities Lipchitz returned temporarily to France, spending part of the year 1946 in Paris. Disappointed that nothing was the same, he soon decided to return to New York and went on to develop his modernist sculptural reflection on spiritual and humanist themes during nearly three decades of residence in the United States.

Notes

1 Jacques Lipchitz, in Michel Georges-Michel, "De Montparnasse à la 57ème rue," *Pour la victoire*, no. 30 (22 July 1944): 6 (all translations are by the author).

2 Lipchitz takes these positions in many statements and interviews of the 1930s and 1940s; see the artist's response to a questionnaire in *Cahiers d'art* 10, no. 1–4 (1935): 68; James Johnson Sweeney, "An Interview with Jacques Lipchitz," *Partisan Review* 12 (Winter 1945): 83–89; and the statement in "The Ides of Art: Fourteen Sculptors Write," *Tiger's Eye*, no. 4 (June 1948): 80.

3 The Buchholz Gallery gave Lipchitz further solo exhibitions in 1943 and 1944, and Valentin would be Lipchitz's primary agent in New York from 1941 to 1954.

4 Buchholz Gallery press release (1942), cited in Ziva Amishai-Maisels, *Depiction and Interpretation: The Influence of the Holocaust on the Visual Arts* (Oxford: Pergamon Press, 1993), 422 n. 112. On *Mother and Child*, see also Avigdor W. G. Posèq, "Childhood Fantasy into Archetype Icons in Jacques Lipchitz," *Konsthistorisk tidskrift* 60, no. 1 (1991): 42–55; and Michael Parke-Taylor, *Jacques Lipchitz: Mother and Child,* exh. cat. (Regina, Saskatchewan: Norman Mackenzie Art Gallery, University of Regina, 1983).

5 Statement to a French reporter, quoted in E. M. Benson, "Seven Sculptors," *The American Magazine of Art* 28 (August 1935): 458 (translation modified). Regarding this sculpture, see Avigdor W. G. Posèq, "Jacques Lipchitz's *David and Goliath,*" *Source* 8 (Spring 1989): 22–31.

6 Lipchitz discusses this work in "The Story of My Prometheus," *Art in Australia,* ser. 4, no. 6 (June–August 1942): 28–35. For a concise summary of Lipchitz's involvement with the Prometheus theme, see Nicole Barbier, *Lipchitz: Oeuvres de Jacques Lipchitz,* exh. cat. (Paris: Centre Georges Pompidou, Musée National d'Art Moderne, 1978), 80–81.

7 See Amishai-Maisels, *Depiction and Interpretation,* 199–200.

8 See Alan G. Wilkinson, *Jacques Lipchitz: A Life in Sculpture,* exh. cat. (Toronto: Art Gallery of Ontario, 1989), no. 85.

9 For an analysis of Lipchitz's use of mythological themes, see Amishai-Maisels, *Depiction and Interpretation,* 198–202.

10 Maurice Raynal, *Lipchitz* (Paris: Editions Jeanne Bucher, 1947), esp. 17–18. The 1946 exhibition, a career retrospective, was held at the Galerie Maeght in Paris.

11 Lipchitz discusses this work in an interview with Frederick S. Wight, in *Jacques Lipchitz: A Retrospective Selected by the Artist,* exh. cat. (Los Angeles: UCLA Art Galleries, 1963), 12–13.

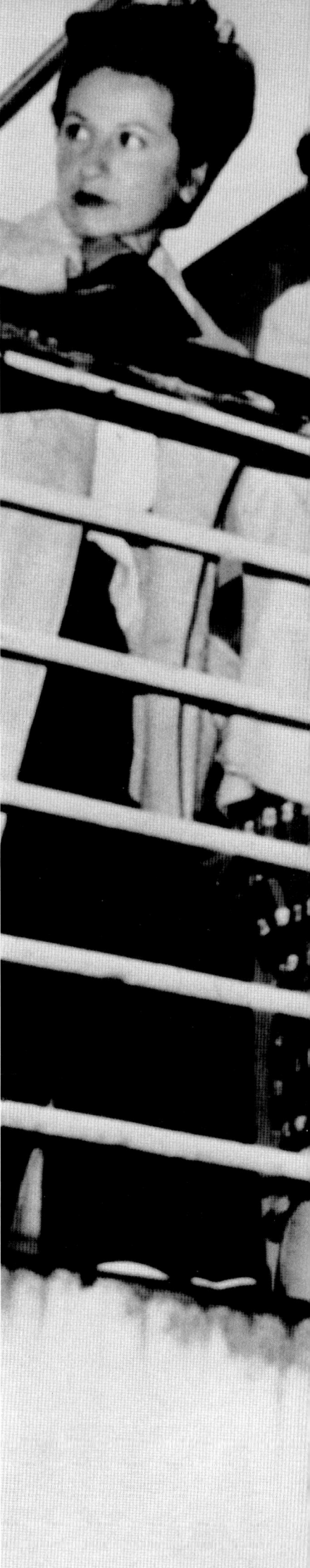

Overleaf left:
European refugees aboard a ship that was denied entry to the United States at New York and to Mexico at Vera Cruz, September 11, 1940.

Overleaf right:
George S. Rublee, center, former director of the Intergovernmental Committee on Political Refugees, arriving in New York on the *Queen Mary,* after concluding unsuccessful negotiations with Germany on the emigration of German Jews, February 23, 1939.

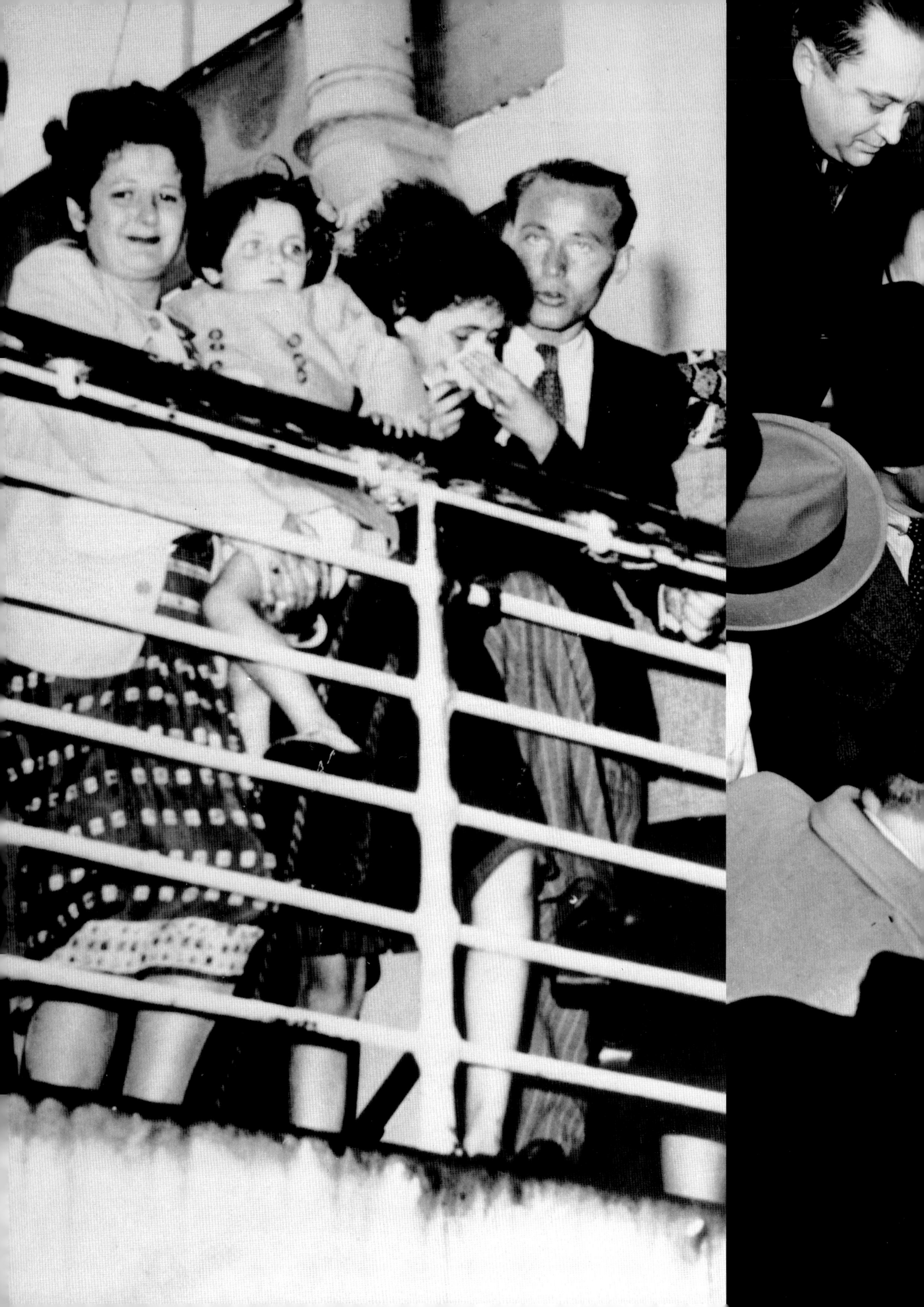

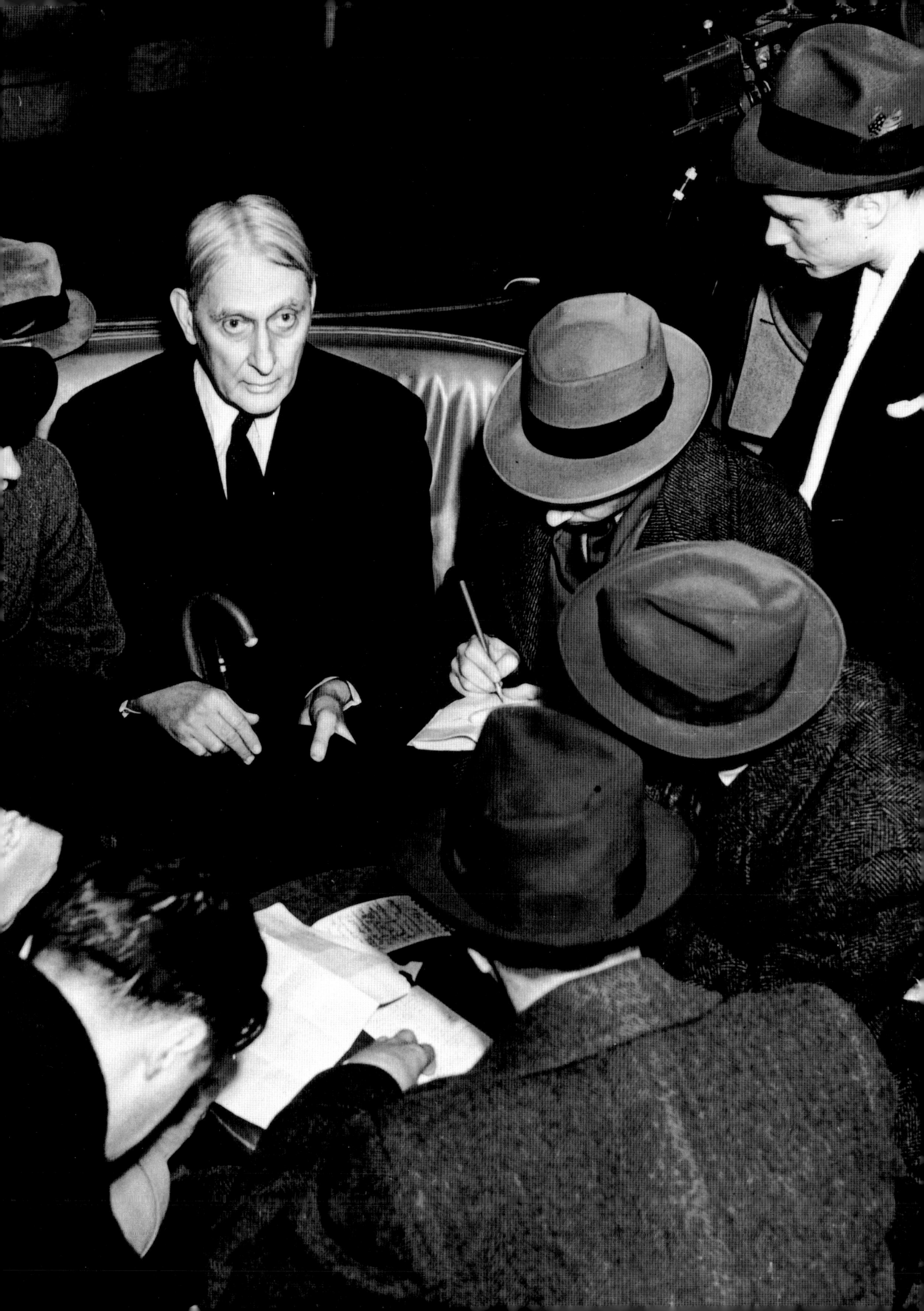

on the passage of a few persons
through a rather brief period of time

ROMY GOLAN

t he passage of Parisian emigrés through New York in the 1940s has hardly gone unremarked in the critical literature.[1] Rather than trying then to recount what befell these exiles abroad, where they went, and who happened to be there, this essay will instead consider the manifold experience of exile; the triangular relationship between artists, dealers, and collectors in New York; the tropes informing the emigrés' mythicized view of America; the masculinization of the discourse surrounding their activity; and, finally, their attempt at legitimization via academia. It will thus focus not so much on the conditions of art production as on the rhetorics of its reception.[2]

Modalities of Exile

In 1946 a special issue of the *Bulletin of the Museum of Modern Art* published cameo profiles and interviews with eleven of the artist-emigrés.[3] Its timing was significant, for it appeared just as many of them were about to decide whether to return to Europe. Each artist's statement reveals a different modality of exile. Some, focusing solely on artistic considerations, avoided the subject altogether. Those who had been in the United States before the war insisted that they had come not as refugees, but by choice. While some hinted that they felt at home in their new environment, others admitted to a sense of alienation. Still others spoke from sites of retrenchment, outside the city, in the countryside. And, lastly, there were those who mourned their double displacement, first from Eastern Europe to Paris and then from Paris to America.

Marcel Duchamp, who since the teens had shuttled between Paris and New York, had nothing much to say about exile. Avoiding the confessional mode of the interview and playing, as it were, a confidence game of his own, he voiced his experience of exile in the most matter-of-fact way: through his works themselves. Five years earlier, on January 17, 1941, Duchamp had sent an "official" request to André Breton, printed in the surrealist-affiliated magazine *View,* to find him an "artistic (sic) mission" in New York. Using a mock blank form of the French government censor (fig. 114), Duchamp wrote after the heading "travaille à" (works at): "ma boîte qui est finie" (my box, which is finished).[4] In June of the following year, he would disembark in New York with *The Box in a Valise* (1941; fig. 115), a leather valise containing miniature replicas of his past oeuvre—a most suitable suitcase for exile.[5]

Fernand Léger, who had come to work in the United States on three separate occasions during the 1930s, likewise made no comments on exile per se but extemporized, as he had earlier, on his love of New York's garishness: "Bad taste is one of the valuable raw materials for the country.... Fourteenth Street may be ruined by the taste of Fifth Avenue; but Avenue B is still rich. And in spite of the fact that people run to good taste as soon as they discover they have bad taste, there will always be another Fourteenth Street or Avenue B while America keeps young."

In contrast, Amédée Ozenfant, who had been visiting the United States in 1938, emphasized that he did not consider himself "a refugee": "I had decided to come here and stay here before the war began.... Already won by what we had seen of America and disgusted by Munich and what had led up to it we decided to remain in America and begin a New Life. I went back to London and Paris to close the doors of my past. Then, February 2, 1939, I reentered as an immigrant.... On June 13, 1944, I received my citizenship papers."

Piet Mondrian, who had died two years earlier, was represented in the MoMA *Bulletin* by comments pertaining strictly to art. Yet in "Mondrian in New York: A Memoir," published eleven years later, one finds painter Carl Holty beginning his piece with the quintessential American tale of immigration: the day spent accompanying Mondrian through what promised to be a long series of bureaucratic hurdles at the Federal Building on Christopher Street, where he had gone to apply for citizenship. When an employee's eyebrow was raised at the name Piet, Holty explained that this was how it was spelled in the entry on the painter in the *Encyclopaedia Britannica,* and the name was allowed to stand. Mondrian said that he had already made enough concessions with his name, having dropped the second *a* from his original surname, Mondriaan, after he moved from Amsterdam to Paris in 1911.[6]

Jean Hélion, the only one of the eleven who actually fought in the war, reiterated the saga recounted in his book *They Shall Not Have Me: The Capture, Forced Labor, and Escape of a Prisoner of War* (1943). Invited by László Moholy-Nagy to teach at the New Bauhaus in Chicago in 1938, Hélion had returned to France as an army volunteer in 1939. Captured by

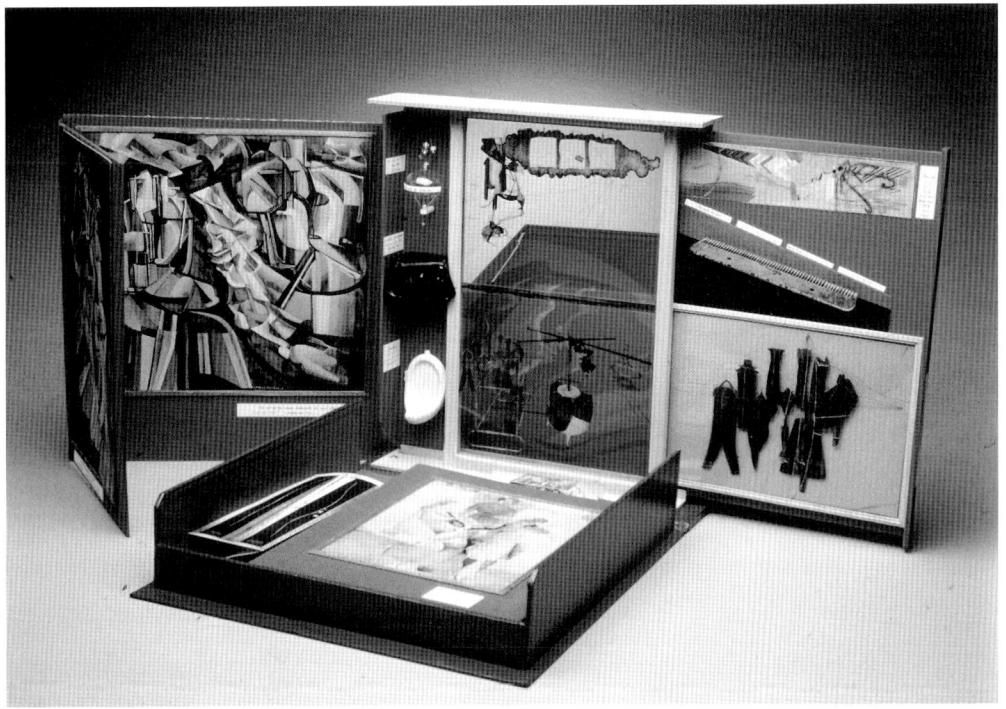

114
Form sent by Marcel Duchamp to André Breton, Paris, 1941; published in *View*, ser. 1, no. 7–8 (October–November 1941): 5.

115
Marcel Duchamp; *The Box in a Valise*, 1941; paper, board, and mixed media; 16⅛ × 14⅞ × 4⅛ in. (41.0 × 37.8 × 10.5 cm); Los Angeles County Museum of Art, gift of the Grinstein family.

the Germans in the summer of 1942 in Pomerania, he spent twenty-two months in prison camps until his escape. After his return to the States in 1943 he devoted most of his time to lecturing, writing, working for the Red Cross, and delivering radio broadcasts. His tone in MoMA's *Bulletin*—like his activities—was purposeful, even spartan.

Max Ernst, who had already lived in voluntary exile as a German expatriate in Paris after joining the surrealist movement in the 1920s, claimed personal detachment: "For me it does not matter whether I work in the United States or Europe. I never lose touch with the world around me. After my arrival in this country, I remained two or three weeks in New York and then began traveling about the country." Yet in Ernst's view—and despite the fact that his own entrance into the New York art scene seemed the most glamorous, thanks largely to his marriage to Peggy Guggenheim—the transplant of European artists to the United States was partly a failure. Unlike Paris, New York had no communal life, no cafés, no communication, and this fostered a sense of loneliness and isolation.

André Masson and Yves Tanguy both spoke from their homes in Connecticut. Masson extravagantly tapped into the romantic myth of the frontier individualist to justify his withdrawal from New York:

> My idea of America, like that of so many French, was, and perhaps still is, rooted in Chateaubriand. Nature: the might of nature—the feeling that nature may one day recover its strength and turn all back to chaos.... There is a rich American mythology awaiting exploitation.... Naturally a city like New York could be stimulating. But I have never been long enough in the city. Perhaps I am temperamentally better fitted to understand the life of the pioneers, their struggle with the elements. In fact I think I understand the life of the past and the problems of the past in the new world better than the city life of the present.

Tanguy, less defensive about his rural residence, focused on exile not as an opportunity for self-definition, but as a locus of emotional refuge: "Of course there is a Paris one always misses. Still, Woodbury fits me perfectly. Here... I scarcely felt touched by the war. It seemed so far away from me. But there is more freedom—more room in this country. That was why I came here.... As early as 1934 I had begun to recognize certain Fascist symptoms in France—in an outbreak here and a squabble there. I almost came out to America with Paalen.[7] Only some difficulties with papers kept me from it."

As Jews, Jacques Lipchitz and Marc Chagall had suffered a double uprooting, first from Lithuania and Russia when they came to Paris around 1910 and then, years later, from there to New York to escape the grip of the Vichy Gestapo. The result was a wistfulness particular to the Jewish experience. For if the etymological root of the word *nostalgia* is the Greek *nostos*—that is, return home—then Jewish nostalgia is the yearning for return to a place of origin that no longer exists. It is a yearning predicated on absence, on the loss of origins. Most striking then, to my mind, is the deep attachment to France expressed in their interviews. Lipchitz describes the moment when, hiding as far as possible beyond the demarcation lines of the "Free Zone"—the part of France left unoccupied by the Germans until 1942— Jews finally realized, by a bitterly ironic twist of history, the "return to the soil" symbolically forbidden them in the xenophobic discourse that surrounded their reception in art magazines throughout the 1920s and 1930s:[8] "In June 1940, on the road to exile our first stop was a delightful village, Castel Moron-sur-Lot.... The news were disastrous, the Germans were already at the gates of Paris. It was the 13th of June. I remember, I was there in that peasant house and I was thinking of my Paris, of what it was going to become, of the terrible sleep filled with nightmares into which it was going to be plunged. And I suddenly felt the need to sing it a lullaby soft and full of hopes.... A year later to the day I arrived to New York and landed June 13, 1941." Chagall ended his interview with a prayer for his second—adopted—motherland: "Let us keep faith, as ever, in the spirit of France. With our whole soul let us look for that rebirth, which will be at the same time that of the whole world."

It is often through intersubjective experience, in odd passages in firsthand accounts by others, that one gains the most insight into exile's toll. Charles Duit, one of Breton's young recruits in America, thus recalls his first visit to the writer in his small apartment on Bleecker Street: "He seemed tired, bitter, alone, terribly alone, bearing that loneliness with the patience of a beast, silent, wrapped in that silence. Like lava in the process of hardening."[9] An anecdote about Tanguy in Julien Levy's memoirs suggests that the artist's own matter-of-fact statements to MoMA masked a deep underlying discontent:

> The first year in Connecticut Kay [Sage] set out to camouflage Yves as a Connecticut country gentleman. Escorting him through Abercrombie and Fitch, she bought him a corduroy hunting cap, a jacket with leather shoulders, leather armpads and other pipings and patches. For Christmas he received a double-barrel shotgun and rifle. Yves was desperately unhappy over all this. A proud and sturdy Breton, he had no picture of himself as a country gentleman. As their evenings in isolation in the country wore on and his inclination to drink crept upon him, his nostalgic drunken stories would more and more turn to his vagabond days as an artist, or he'd recall earlier days as a sailor in the merchant marine.[10]

One of the rallying points in a metropolis, New York, that—according to these interviews—lacked intimacy and communication was, significantly, the Radio Libre at the Voice of America. In March 1942, after America's entry into the war, Pierre Lazareff, the former director of the Parisian daily *France-Soir,* took charge of an evening broadcast of a French bulletin relayed from New York to France via London with the opening phrase "La voix d'Amérique parle aux français" (the Voice of America speaks to the people of France).[11] Breton, in his bitterness, apparently condemned this daily activity as monotonous and servile. Resentful of what he regarded as the program's nationalist propaganda, he saw his own participation as ransom for his freedom in New York.[12] Yet Hélion, Ozenfant, art historians Henri Focillon and Georges Duthuit, anthropologist Claude Lévi-Strauss, Catholic philosopher Jacques Maritain, writer Denis de Rougemont, and countless others all dutifully spoke.

History, as we know, had it both ways. Radio, disseminated to an ever-larger number of households in the 1930s, also served as the most successful, manipulative, and mystificatory weapon of both Hitler and Mussolini.[13] And it was on the radio, his quavering voice repeatedly pledging "j'ai fait don de ma personne à la France" (I have given myself to France), that the octogenarian leader Philippe Pétain—whose motto reiterated precisely the body-voice fusion of the radio affect—sounded most consoling, avuncular, and thus seductive to the French population. Yet it was also via the radio—with its collapse of geographical distance; its visual-auditory confusion, which allowed for a cunningly intimate relation with its auditors; and its unique power of interference in the midst of enemy lines—that the Parisian exiles most convincingly reached back "home."

Unholy Alliances

For all of the alienation evoked by exile, and the lack of communal life for artists in New York, the myth of America as land of eternal youth or second chances, a land where everything is possible, served most of these middle-aged artists well. The Paris art scene, and the position of France by and large in world culture and politics, had been losing ground since 1918.[14] Meanwhile the New York art world had already, by the late 1930s, before the arrival of these exiled Europeans, established its own solid and particularly well orchestrated support structure. The subsequent influx of exiled artists certainly played a significant role in focusing attention on New York as a hub of avant-garde activity. Thus, in a feature article on the Fifty-seventh Street gallery scene published in 1946, *Fortune* reported, as if visiting a foreign land, that "there are curious customs to be observed among the inhabitants of the art district. The French are the model.... The larger part of the New York art boom has been most effulgently a French affair."[15]

Yet I would argue that already in the 1930s such New York dealers as Julien Levy and Pierre Matisse (son of Henri) had a more ambitious and more institutional agenda than their Parisian counterparts ever had. Indeed, in contrast to Paris, where galleries, museums, and collectors seemed to function as autonomous, heterogeneous, and often rival fields, there was a smooth triangulation between them in New York, which—for better or worse—worked wonders. Paris, for all of the museological impetus of its 1937 world's fair, was not to have a legitimate museum of modern art until the 1950s. New York had three by the end of the 1930s: MoMA, the Whitney Museum of American Art, and the Museum of Non-Objective Art (later the Solomon R. Guggenheim Museum), founded in 1929, 1931, and 1939, respectively. And private collections like that of Walter and Louise Arensberg, Katherine S. Dreier's Société Anonyme, and Peggy Guggenheim's Art of This Century gallery, which opened in 1942, were very much conceived as mini-museums. Not by chance, Peggy Guggenheim's advisory team included artists Duchamp, Breton, and Ernst and dealer Howard Putzel, as well as MoMA's Alfred H. Barr Jr., James Thrall Soby, and James Johnson Sweeney.

The smoothness of this triangulation and the particular ease with which the European emigrés, and the surrealists in particular, seemed to fit into what some saw as an unholy alliance was not lost on critics on the political left. Reviewing a show of new acquisitions by MoMA for *The Nation* in 1943, Clement Greenberg remarked: "Their presence [of paintings by Matta and Masson] evidences the extreme sensitivity of the museum to trade winds on Fifty-seventh Street. The museum shows taste in that when it buys the work of inferior artists it at least chooses their best work. But this does not atone for its masochistic fondness for the social and other epigones of the School of Paris."[16] In one of his most violent attacks on the surrealists, whom he and Philip Rahv repeatedly declared "dead upon arrival to New York" in the pages of *Partisan Review,* Greenberg wrote in 1944: "The anti-institutional, antiformal, anti-aesthetic nihilism of the Surrealists has in the end proved a blessing to the restless rich, the expatriates, the aesthetes-flaneurs in general who were repelled by the asceticisms of modern art."[17] Realist artist George Biddle, in "The Surrealists—Isolationists of Art," published in the liberal *New Republic,* similarly commented:

> At this particular moment, critical indeed to American art, a fresh impetus has been given to the always decadent and recently dying movement of Surrealism and the more ingrown of the French Abstractionists.... It has been thrown into high relief by the

publicity methods of certain New York dealers, and also by the official stamp of the Museum of Modern Art, which has given fine exhibitions in many fields but in the domain of painting has a reputation of reediting in de-luxe editions what was *le dernier mot* in Paris twenty years ago.... There is no immediate danger to the Republic from this band of weakened, sapless and occasionally loud-mouthed *homunculi*. Let them play with their melting watch-chains, their rubber snakes and other childish contraptions without much threat of hidden bomb.[18]

The strongest blow against the surrealists came not from an American, but from a fellow European emigré, Klaus Mann (the son of Thomas), in a piece entitled "Surrealist Circus" in the *American Mercury* in 1943. Not mincing words, Mann not only called them "Nazoid"—drawing a direct parallel between Hitler's concept of degenerate art and the irresponsible, mystic, cunning, antiart, anticivilization, nihilism of surrealism—but also described them as whores:

> Millions may die and worlds may crash, but the Breton coterie will be carried to safety and comfort on the wings of benevolent angels. In this case the friendly wings were spread by Peggy Guggenheim. They sheltered not only the surrealist messiah and his prophet, i.e., Breton and Ernst, but a batch of their friends. The party occupied most of the seats and beds in a transatlantic clipper. Shortly after Marshal Pétain signed his agreement with Hitler, the American lady signed a check and the surrealist family rose to the skies. Ernst married Miss Guggenheim and the American phase of Surrealism got off to a start with one of the great American fortunes at its disposal.[19]

Even the critic of a mainstream publication like *Time* magazine seemed unable to refrain from sarcasm: "One could well expect that Surrealism—condemned as arch-degenerate by the Nazis—would go under. Not at all, it simply moved to Manhattan. Today's Surrealism headquarters is a dignified old mansion on Manhattan's fashionable East Side overlooking the East River. The group's financial angel, who lives in the mansion and is married to Surrealist Ernst, is black-haired, husky voiced Peggy Guggenheim, niece of philanthropic Copper Tycoon Solomon Guggenheim."[20]

The vitriol evident in these quotations goes beyond a mere defense mechanism against things foreign or a flexing of muscle on the part of a moralizing left vis-à-vis seduction by the power of money *and* France's fall to fascism—the two being perceived, it seems, as two sides of the same coin.[21] Rather, it is a manifestation of a much older habit on the part of Americans and Germans alike: the feminizing of France. I would argue that the dichotomy between an eternally feminine, capricious, and alluring France versus a masculine, super-industrial, pragmatic America and Germany came to the fore in the interwar period. France contributed to it through its self-feminization as "Le Paris des années folles" ("the Paris of the mad years," the successor to the equally feminized Belle Epoque) and as a pastoral, anti-industrial, neo-feudal, pacifist nation. And at no time was this dichotomy more acute than during the 1940s, when America heralded itself as the savior of a collapsed maiden-nation held "hostage" by the Nazis and of a people who had found refuge in the soft, consoling brand of fascism personified by the elderly Pétain.[22]

Proper Elisions

To be taken seriously and to achieve a successful "graft" onto a puritan America already prone to view art as an escapist, feminine, or all too often homosexual activity,[23] supportive critics and dealers had to ensure the masculinization of the discourse attached to the Parisian exiles. This rhetorical twist is manifest in an article entitled "America's Duty to French Culture," written by poet Archibald MacLeish for the *Saturday Review of Literature* in the fall of 1942. With such exhibitions as *Artists in Exile* at Pierre Matisse's gallery, followed a few months later by *First Papers of Surrealism* and, just a few weeks after, by the opening of Peggy Guggenheim's gallery, this was the year of maximum exposure for the exiles in New York. Yet the fact that it coincided with the drama of America's entry into the war made the art world look ever more escapist.[24]

Despite the egalitarian tone of his opening statement, which bound the survival of French culture to its people, not its libraries, MacLeish immediately went on to condemn French art by referring to the feminization of its reception, if not its production: "During the years between the wars and particularly during the later years between the wars, French art was not a people's art in America but a rich woman's fashion. And when the art of one country becomes a fashionable woman's fashion in another, there is no possibility of communication between the artist of the first country and the people of the second." Clearly the reference here is to the surrealists' hobnobbing with the Parisian aristocracy, abandoning the street for the salon, in the late 1930s. Turned into society events, the openings of the second and third International Surrealist Exhibitions, held in two of the poshest galleries in London and Paris in 1936, were reported in *Vogue* and *Harper's Bazaar* and attended by London's smart set and *le tout Paris*.[25] The pattern would continue in New York, where Elsa Schiaparelli and Peggy Guggenheim were among the sponsors of *First Papers of Surrealism* under the auspices of the Coordinating Council of French Relief Societies. The event, held in the sumptuous surroundings of the Whitelaw Reid mansion at 451 Madison Avenue, was thus turned into an elegant society benefit. The glamorous opening of Art of This Century in Guggenheim's new triplex apartment on Sutton Place followed suit.

It was in his concluding paragraphs that MacLeish effected the required gender switch: "The French artist who exiled himself from France to continue here his war fate, both as a man and as an artist, for a free man's world, will find in America a surging, mounting current of determination and belief to which he can, without reluctance or reserve, commit himself. He will do this as a man, a Frenchman, and an artist.... America has been for many generations in its history the fatherland of all in every country who place freedom first."

Indeed, the elision of the feminine-socialite side of the French art scene had already begun and was best achieved by photography. In his 1941 article "School of Paris Comes to U.S." Sidney Janis made sure, for instance, to portray and photograph each artist (Léger, Mondrian, Ernst, and Matta) alone in his studio next to—or, as the caption on Matta reads, "engulfed" by—his paintings. Most memorable were the group photographs. While the representation of male group formations had been part and parcel of the avant-garde's self-promotion for decades, the body language in photos of the European exiles is particularly telling. The deliberation with which heads and bodies are lined up and turned one way or another in front of the large fireplace in Peggy Guggenheim's apartment is provocative (see fig. 116). The full-frontal stares in George Platt Lynes's more famous photograph—for the catalogue of Pierre Matisse's *Artists in Exile* show—alone seem deliberately confrontational and hence masculine (see fig. 117). But it is through omission that this image's participation in the masculinization of art in exile is most pronounced: the fireplace and domestic (however grand) interior of the Guggenheim photograph are gone, replaced by the public space of the gallery, and gone are Guggenheim and the two women artists, Leonora Carrington and Berenice Abbott.

While the *punctum* of these photographs, in the Barthian sense, is the almost desperate bringing into close formation of people whose lives and sense of direction were in fact disarrayed by a world war—and who never imagined that they would one day find themselves together at such a place and time—the severe, almost corporate, and highly staged quality of these photographs had a definite aim. It was meant to picture for posterity, "for the record," as it were, the transformation of historical happenstance into inevitability for the launching of what some have called the second historical avant-garde.[26]

Indeed, it was Lynes's photo, more than the works hanging on the walls at Matisse's, that held the attention of reviewers. *Newsweek*'s critic read between the lines, noting prosaically that the picture shot by "the crack fashion and portrait photographer George Platt Lynes" gathered men who, before coming from Paris to New York, were originally from

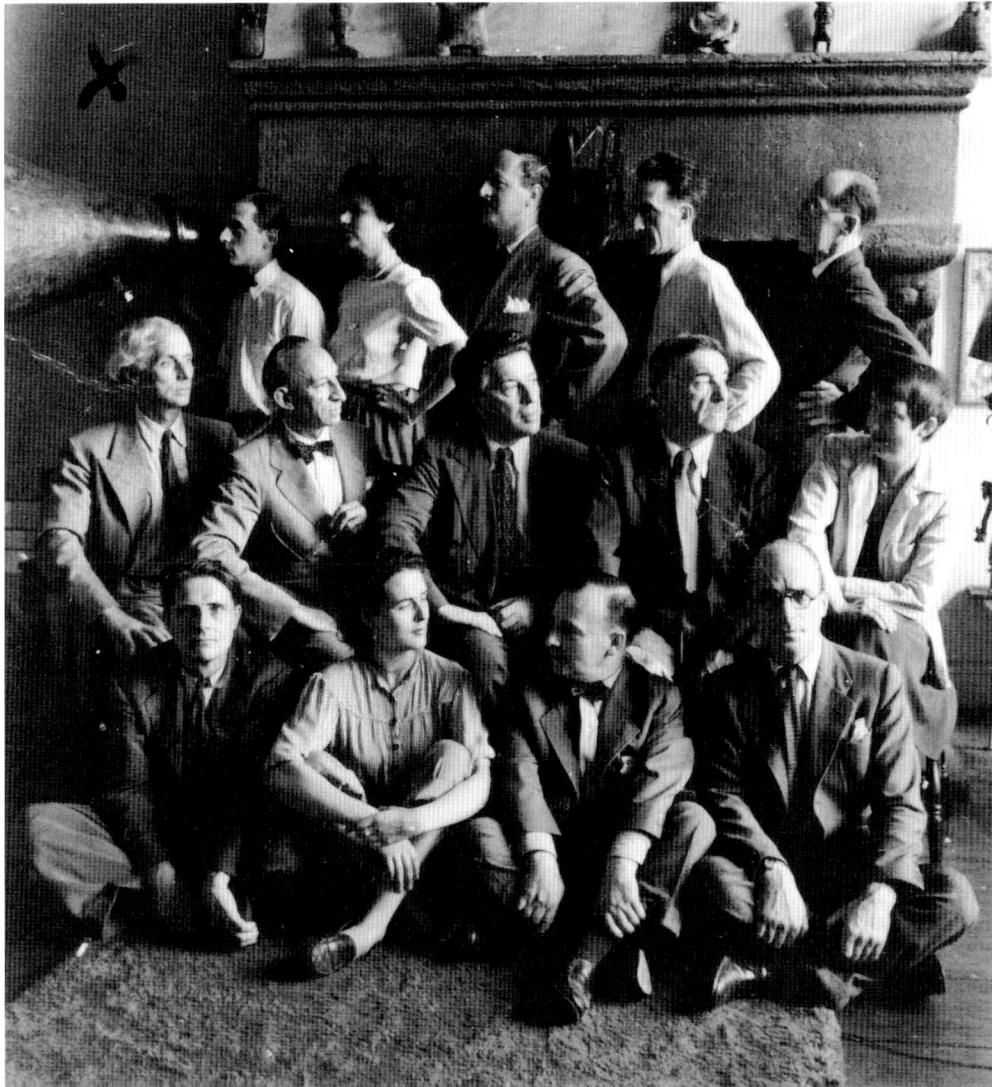

116
Emigrés in Peggy Guggenheim's New York apartment, 1942 (left to right, front row: S. W. Hayter, Leonora Carrington, Frederick Kiesler, Kurt Seligmann; middle row: Max Ernst, Amédée Ozenfant, André Breton, Fernand Léger, Berenice Abbott; back row: Jimmy Ernst, Peggy Guggenheim, John Ferren, Marcel Duchamp, Piet Mondrian); photograph by Hermann Landshoff.

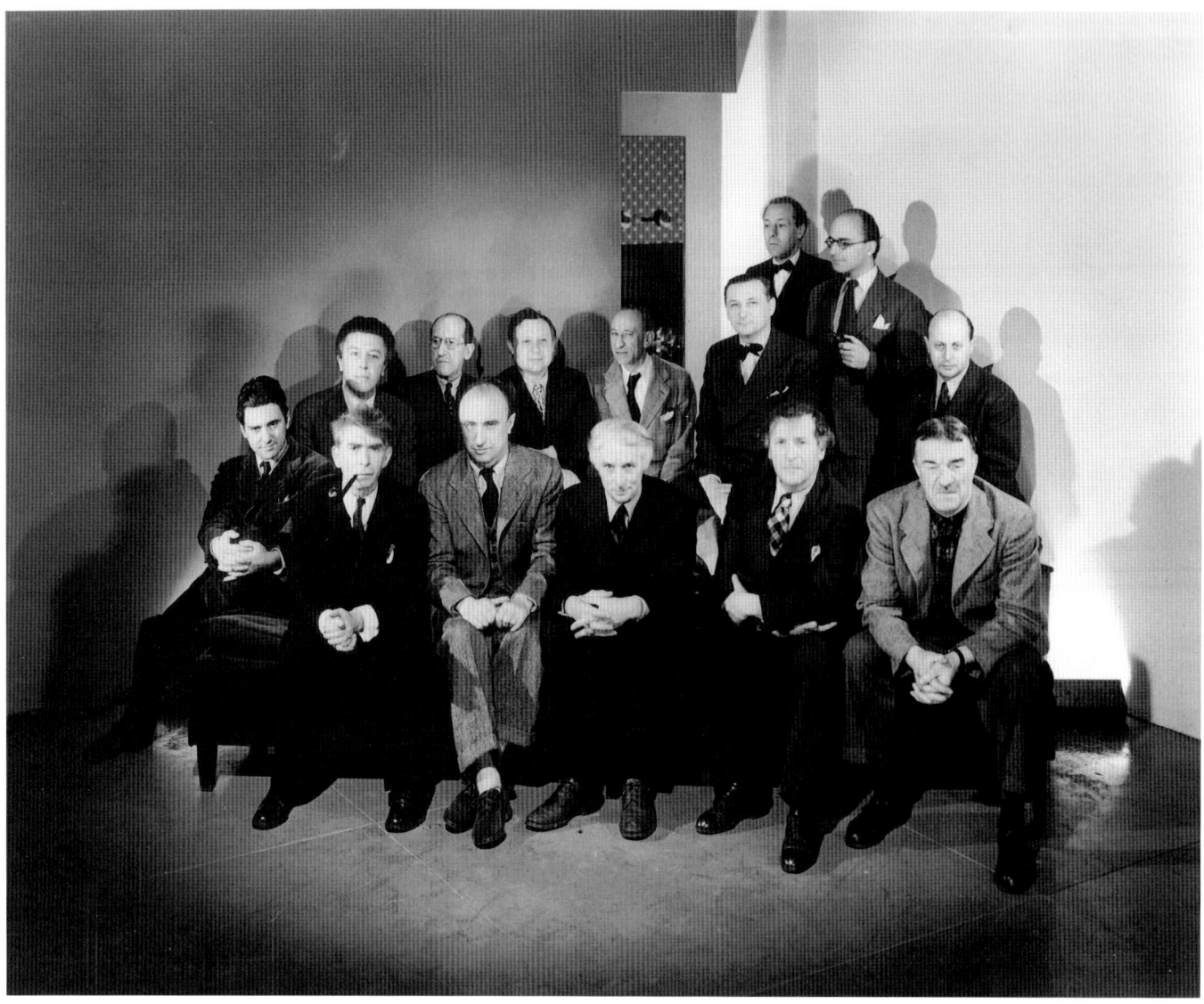

117
Photograph taken on the occasion of the exhibition *Artists in Exile*, Pierre Matisse Gallery, New York, March 1942 (left to right, front row: Matta, Ossip Zadkine, Yves Tanguy, Max Ernst, Marc Chagall, Fernand Léger; back row: André Breton, Piet Mondrian, André Masson, Amédée Ozenfant, Jacques Lipchitz, Pavel Tchelitchev, Kurt Seligmann, Eugene Berman); photograph by George Platt Lynes.

Russia, Holland, Lithuania, Germany, and Switzerland.[27] Poet Rosamund Frost, writing in *Art News,* was positively hyperbolic:

> With this major artistic migration, the largest, we are told since the fall of Constantinople, one side or the other must inevitably dominate.... The thing about travel is that it brings the most unlikely people together. In Paris artists were divided into camps, hermetic cells, each storing up its own brand of honey, of monasticism, of electricity. The fantastic, the Purists, the Surrealists, no matter how inwardly at odds, continued to revolve around their appropriate electrons. Today in America all has changed. The photograph of Artists in Exile in the show's catalogue unites the most diverse factors in the European artistic scene (and represents, incidentally, a diplomatic triumph for Pierre Matisse who posed the subjects at George Platt Lynes' studio one agitated morning).[28]

In retrospect these photos were the forerunners of other still more famous and macho ones: Hans Namuth's photographs of Jackson Pollock truly "engulfed" by his paintings and that of the so-called Irascibles, the abstract expressionists, taken by Nina Leen in the studios of *Life* magazine in 1950 (fig. 118). Here, in the logic of conquest set up by the master narrative of modernism, the European exiles have been replaced nine years later by a new, home-bred generation. Equally male (except for Hedda Sterne), and made to look equally businesslike in their suits and ties, this group is nevertheless more casual, cooler, no longer sitting in rows, but keenly perched on stools.[29]

If the discourse around their work was to be masculinized, Parisian emigré artists concomitantly had to "straighten"—both literally and figuratively—their act. One way out of the feminine, this time in terms of production, was through the rejection of mass culture.[30] Thus, for all his proclaimed love of American "bad taste" in the MoMA *Bulletin,* Léger kept Americana at arm's length. And although it was Mondrian, the Purist of purists and Formalist of formalists, who, ironically enough, engaged most openly with urban culture—living in the thick of things in Midtown (rather than, like most Parisians, in the Village) at 15 East Fifty-ninth Street, going to clubs in Harlem to listen to jazz and ragtime music, dancing the foxtrot at music halls, and introducing their syncopated rhythms into such masterpieces as *Victory Boogie-Woogie* and *Broadway Boogie-Woogie* (figs. 180, 197)—he did so, after all, in the most analogical fashion.[31]

For the surrealists this distancing from mass culture was mostly achieved by a relocation of myth away from urban culture and back into lofty natural and supranatural phenomena, as evidenced in countless articles published in *VVV* and, most notably, in Breton's "Prolegomena to a Third Manifesto of Surrealism or Else" of 1942 and in his *Arcane 17,* illustrated by Matta in 1945.[32] Indeed, surrealism—which, more than any other modern movement, had celebrated the condition of deterritorialization (*dépaysement*)—entered its most esoteric phase during its years in exile. No more drifting for Breton and Ernst around flea markets or, as one might have expected, the dime stores of the Village and the Lower East Side. Visits to dealers of West Coast Indian and Eskimo art in search of the great American primitive replaced those more serendipitous hunts. Although Breton did pair a frame from a Superman comic with Nietzsche's profile in one of the cameo collages illustrating his catalogue essay for *First Papers of Surrealism,* the surrealists refrained from any sustained search for mythical figures in American pulp fiction comparable to Louis Feuillade's *Fantômas* or tabloid heroines like parricide Violette Nozière. Instead, they reveled, as Masson acknowledged in his MoMA interview, in the French image of America as a brave New World where the golden age found refuge.[33] The dithyrambic intensification of vegetation and color in Masson's "telluric paintings," Tanguy's sidereal dreamscapes, Ernst's fantastic foliage and rock formations, and Matta's subaqueous Inscapes all fit this trope of America as an uncultured, mythical place: a promised Land of Cockaigne, source of eternal youth and regeneration. Thus, when, in a special issue of *View* dedicated to surrealism, Charles Henry Ford asked Breton what he thought of his American surroundings, the answer was:

> I like enormously what I have seen on the Hudson and its green islets—the Floating Islands—which doubtless remain something secret and menacing from the books of

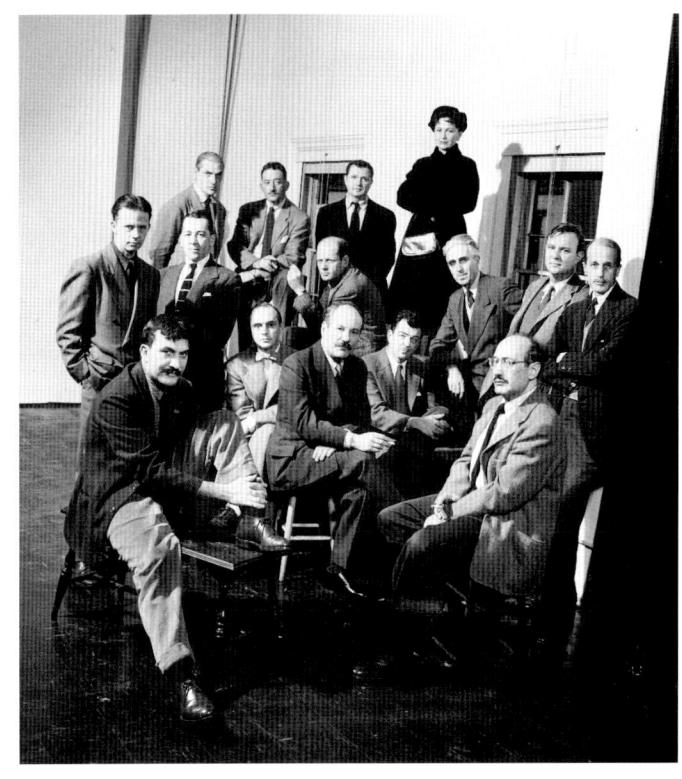

118
"The Irascibles," 1950 (left to right, top row: Willem de Kooning, Adolph Gottlieb, Ad Reinhardt, Hedda Sterne; middle row: Richard Pousette-Dart, William Baziotes, Jackson Pollock, Clyfford Still, Robert Motherwell, Bradley Walker Tomlin; bottom row: Theodoros Stamos, Jimmy Ernst, Barnett Newman, James Brooks, Mark Rothko); photograph by Nina Leen; published in *Life,* 15 January 1951. © Time Inc.

my childhood.... At André Masson's, in the heat of a little wood, it was a wonderful surprise to discover the little "Indian Pipe," so timorous, so ambiguous.... Truly surrealist flora has been enriched, as far as I am concerned, with a new species, shown by Kay and Yves Tanguy: a staghorn fern suspended in its superb turtleshell. But, above all, I have begun my initiation into the mysteries of American butterflies.[34]

Breton's stereotyping, patronizing attitude vis-à-vis an innocent land waiting to be christened by surrealism's founding father was immediately seized upon by Klaus Mann as another excuse to attack surrealism on the basis of gender. Mentioning Breton's exchange "with a young man whose magazine *View* was as cute as can be," he cynically belittled, in one blow, both Breton's preciosity and *View*'s strong homosexual contingent: "There are also edifying passages on the 'truly surrealist flora' of the New York countryside. The nation at large will be thrilled to learn that Breton liked 'enormously' what he had seen on the Hudson and has already begun his 'initiation into the mysteries of American butterflies.'"[35]

Even Duchamp, who since the teens had embraced America as the place of things-as-things rather than things-as-art—that is, the paradise of the readymade—made remarkably few forays into hardware or popular culture during the 1940s. His installation of sixteen miles of string for *First Papers of Surrealism* alluded to, more than anything, the myth of the Minotaur's labyrinth. And his influence in these years—most notably on Matta, who pursued a series of monumental paintings based on the *Large Glass*—was not through mass culture but via arcane literary sources such as Raymond Roussel, the fourth dimension, and the alchemic. In 1946, however, for the cover of Breton's book *Young Cherry Trees Secured against Hares,* Duchamp collaged the author's face onto the Statue of Liberty, which was seen through a benday dot ground (fig. 119). Thus, he paid homage, through France's great gift to America—the colossal beacon of freedom welcoming every European immigrant at the city's harbor—to the founder of surrealism. In proper Duchampian form, however, the image can be seen as both celebratory and subversive, allegorical and gender-bending. For, after all—and unbeknownst to Breton—here is the leonine, arch-male, oft-homophobe (for all of Mann's insinuations of queer preciosity) "pope" of surrealism, not so much androgynous as mascarading in drag as Lady Liberty, paying tribute to America a year after the liberation of France by the GIs.[36]

Indelible Disturbances

No wonder Salvador Dali became a major embarrassment to the emigrés in general and the surrealists in particular during these years in America. Breton had clamorously ousted him from the surrealist movement in 1939 for flirting with fascism, nicknaming him "Avida Dollars" for his eagerness to make money. He was discredited by Nicolas Calas as "anti-Surrealist" on the front page of *View* in 1941[37] and was vilified in countless other articles, including several by Greenberg. And he was conspicuously missing from Peggy Guggenheim's stable of artists and from Sweeney's article for the MoMA *Bulletin*. What made Dali truly anathema was the fact that he came to touch a most sensitive spot: not so much kitsch as that thing called *camp*. What made him such a hard pill to swallow is the fact that, pariah as he may have been for the intellectual elite of the New York art world, Dali was the only emigré artist—and in fact the only artist *tout court,* aside from Pollock—to have two articles devoted to him in *Life* in the 1940s.[38] For indeed it is a well-known fact that, for all

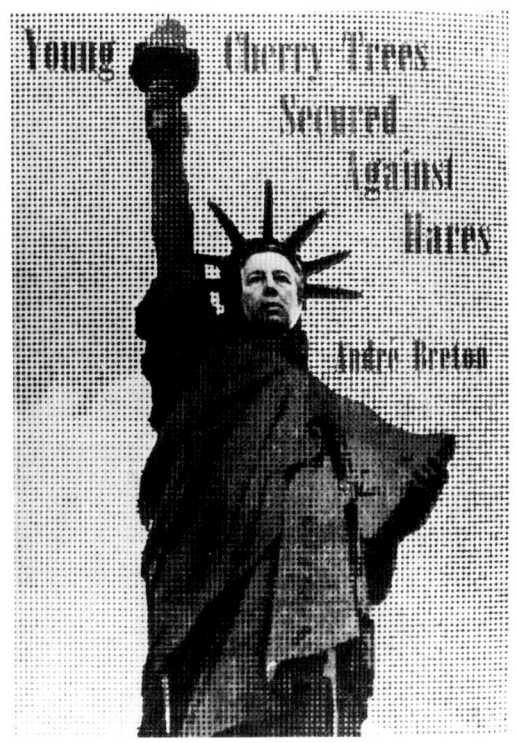 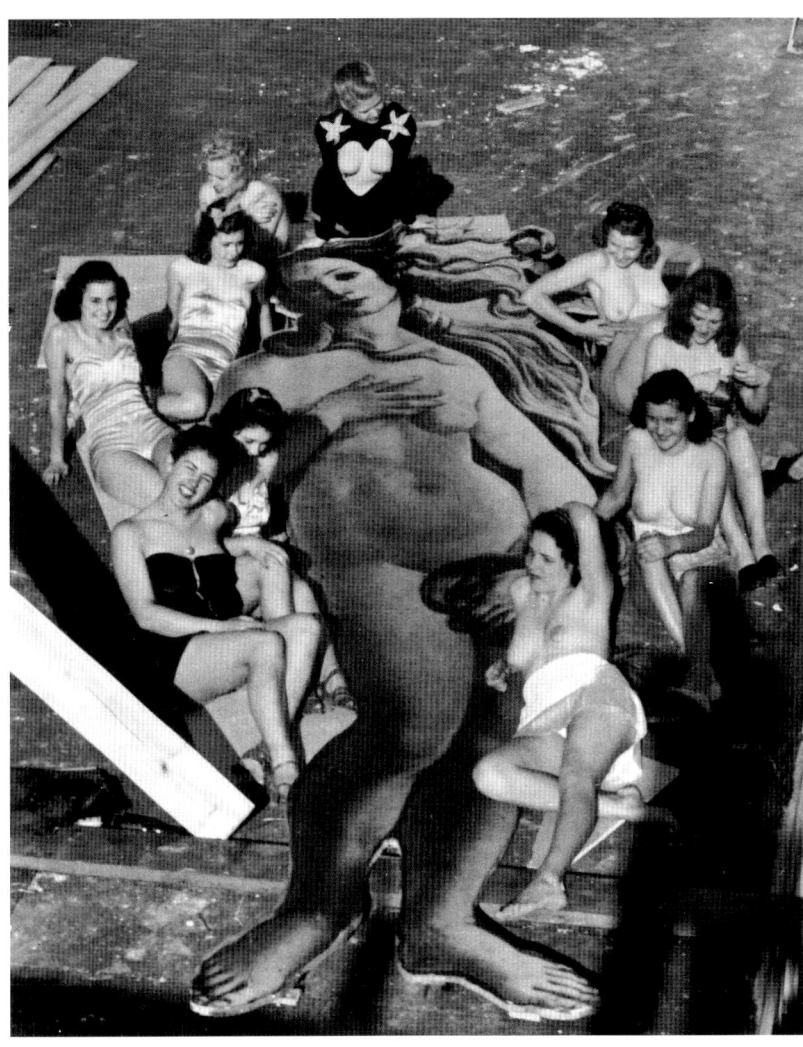

of their professed puritanism, Americans are fascinated by eccentricity and excess. And Winthrop Sargent's profile of Dali in *Life* gave readers their share of excitement:

> For the past ten years—the average American has become increasingly aware of a curious ghostly cast of characters that have leered at him from theater stages, shop windows and the pages and covers of his favorite magazines. They include dismembered arms, female torsos half buried in sand dunes..., tables with beautifully nyloned female legs.... [This] world and its inhabitants have helped advertise Gunther's furs, Ford cars, Wrigley's chewing gum, Schiaparelli's perfume, Gruen watches, the products of the Abbott Laboratories and the Container Corporation of America. They have been reproduced in the window of nearly every smart Fifth Avenue shop.... Surrealism, starting out in one of art's most esoteric ivory towers, wound up a commercial success. The man most responsible for this success is Salvador Dali. His antics have made front-page news for a decade. They have made him a celebrity to millions who have never been next to an art gallery. But his services in bringing the blessing of limp watches and dismembered nymphs to the masses have earned him no credit with his brother Surrealists. To patriarchal Surrealist Max Ernst he is "the bureaucrat and racketeer of Surrealism."

The reference to patriarchy, and the disturbance thereof, is apt. For while Ernst's escapades in high society, involving the exchange of beautiful and powerful women—marrying Peggy Guggenheim while still involved with young Leonora Carrington, then dropping both

119
Marcel Duchamp; cover for André Breton's *Young Cherry Trees Secured against Hares* (View Publications, 1946).

120
Salvador Dali's *Dream of Venus* under construction, New York World's Fair, 1939; photograph attributed to George Platt Lynes.

for Dorothea Tanning—actually boosted his reputation as a grandee of surrealism,[39] Dali's seduction was of a different ilk. Lynes's photographs of Dali with mannequins and lobsters or of Dali's female team posing as muses next to his *Dream of Venus* at the 1939 New York World's Fair (see fig. 120), obviously function on a different register from the photographer's commissioned group portraits. In fact, they are much closer to the mythological photographs Llynes contributed to *View* in those years or to the soft-porn, homoerotic, and camp aesthetic of his main and best "body" of work.[40]

Interestingly, in view of MoMA's reputation for purging modernists of all underbelly activities, the catalogue of Dali's 1941 retrospective, curated by Soby, mentioned the artist's involvement with furniture and with fashion designers Coco Chanel and Elsa Schiaparelli, and the show included five pieces of jewelry designed by Dali in collaboration with the duke of Verdura. Significantly absent from the MoMA show were Dali's society portraits, which had been exhibited a few months earlier at Levy's gallery (more would be shown in 1943 at Knoedler's). Unabashedly kitsch in their parody of both Florentine mannerist portraiture and Dali's own "paranoiac critical method" (which already verged on the simulacrum when the artist introduced it in 1929), these portraits—of Lady Mountbatten; Don Juan Gardenas, Spanish (i.e., Franco's) ambassador to the United States; the Marquis George de Cuevas; Mrs. George Tait II as a sliced bust propped atop an ornate capital; Princess Arthchil Gourielli as a would-be Andromeda tied to a rock; and Mrs. Harrison Williams surrounded by Egyptian and Roman ruins under a spectral psychedelic light—were simply, MoMA-wise, beyond the pale.

Talk of the Town

It was nevertheless under the rubric of sensationalism and more often through the gossip column than the art reviews that the activities of Parisian artists in exile made their way to the American public. The reception of the opening of Art of This Century is a case in point. It was covered not only by the art press and the main New York papers but also by the *Trenton Times,* the *Eagle* (Brooklyn), and—deep in the American heartland—the *Dallas News,* the *Indianapolis Star,* the *Alameda Times Star,* the *Madison State Journal,* the *Times Dispatch* (Richmond, Virginia), and the *Montana Standard.* What struck reviewers most and made for entertaining reading was not the works themselves, which ran the established gamut of European modernism, but the gallery's design. As *Art Digest* put it, "the installation, certainly the most spectacular in town, all but floored the critics." Henry McBride heartily concurred, writing in "New Gallery Ideas" for the *New York Sun* that "frankly, my eyes never bulged further from their sockets than in this show."[41]

Frederick Kiesler, chosen by Guggenheim to design her gallery, was himself a Jewish emigré who had come from Vienna to the United States in 1926. Having previously specialized in the design of theaters, screening rooms, and stage sets, Kiesler, after two years that included a stint as window designer for Saks Fifth Avenue, had embraced the great American message: packaging is as important as contents, and spectacle in the service of selling merchandise is all. In the opening chapter of his book *Contemporary Art Applied to the Store and Its Display* (1930), Kiesler referred to the works of Constantin Brancusi, Paul Klee, Henri Matisse, and Pablo Picasso as models for window display. Capitalizing on the early-twentieth-century modernist strategies of deframing and depedestalization, he argued that the real frame was no longer the one surrounding the canvas or the sculpture's base, but was the shop window.

Although Kiesler never mentioned the gallery space in his book, it was at Guggenheim's that he put to use some of his most "user friendly" devices. In the Surrealist Gallery (see fig. 121) the paintings were hung unframed, held cantilevered on the gallery's curved walls by a system of projecting wooden arms made of sawed-off baseball bats. Biomorphic furniture doubled as sculpture pedestals. The floors were painted turquoise, and the lighting was fluorescent. In the Kinetic Gallery Klee's paintings were displayed on a paternoster, a machine that released them automatically onto a conveyor belt. An invisible light beam controlled their rotation. Each of the seven paintings appeared in the spotlight for ten seconds and disappeared. A visitor who wanted to look longer at any of the paintings could push a button. Opposite this machine was a large wheel. When it was turned by hand, a succession of fourteen different reproductions from Duchamp's *Valise* could be seen through the peephole. The third automated object was a display of Breton's *Portrait of the Actor A. B.* (1941), first shown at Pierre Matisse's, set in a shadow-box construction. When the viewer lifted the lever, the portrait swung around, and the shutter opened to reveal the poem-object within.[42]

The tone of the reviews and their use of slang were in sync with the quirkiness of the installation. The *New York Times* commented on a "piquant event" reminiscent of "a mystery play filled with strange and wonderful gadgets which suspense should not be vitiated by

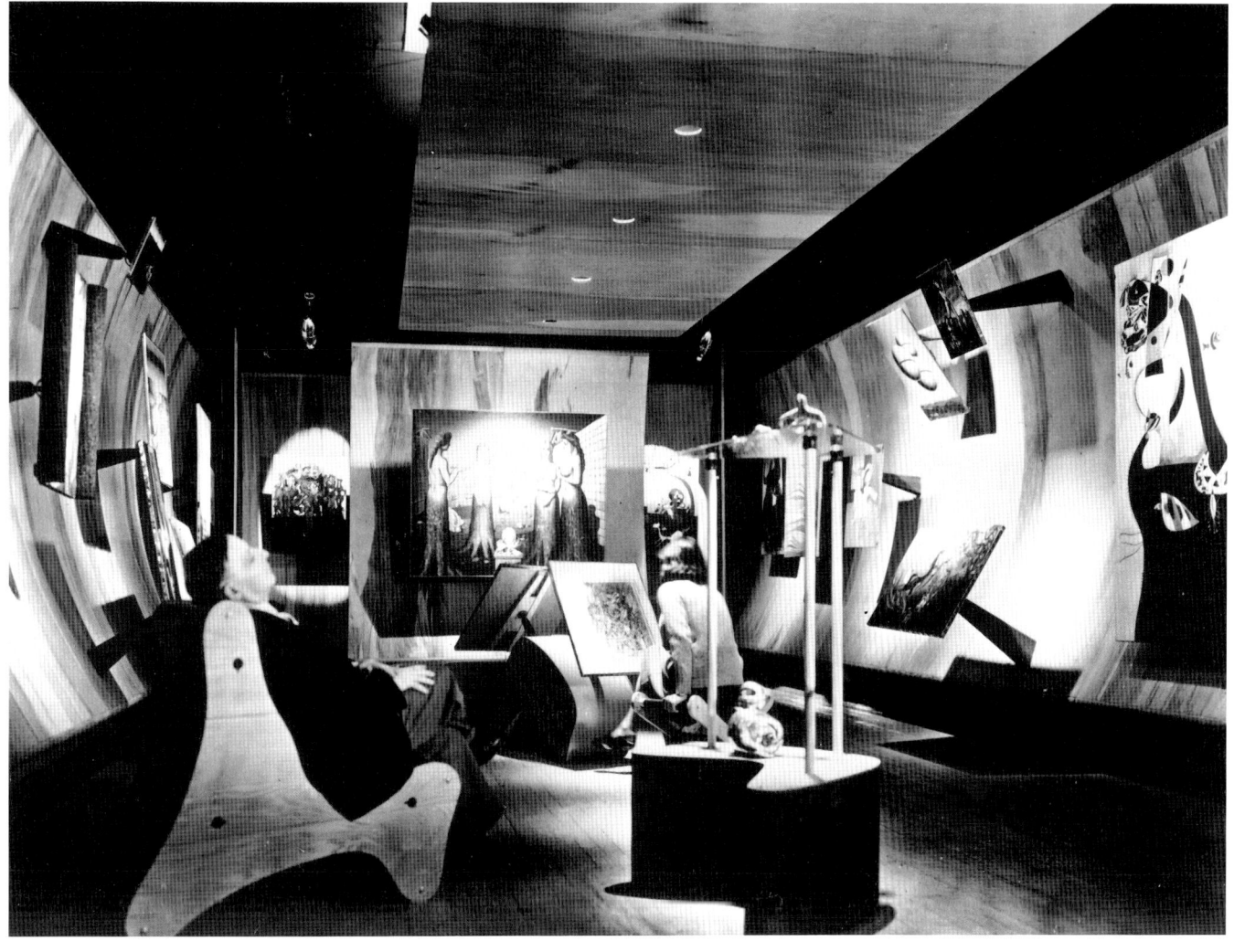

121
The Surrealist Gallery of Peggy Guggenheim's Art of This Century gallery, designed by Frederick Kiesler, 1942 (Kiesler is seated on the "rocker" he designed for the gallery); photograph by Berenice Abbott.

giving away its secrets."⁴³ *Newsweek*'s critic wrote: "Isms rampant: Peggy Guggenheim's dreamworld goes Abstract, Cubist and generally Non-Real. To symbolize her impartiality she wore, on opening night, one abstract earring (a miniature mobile by Alexander Calder), made of metal and wire in constant motion, and one Surrealist earring (a little painting of a pink desert by Yves Tanguy).... One of the galleries was a sort of penny-arcade peep show, except that you didn't need pennies."⁴⁴ "One novel device in the gallery"—wrote the critic of the *New York Journal American*—"is a spiral wheel that enables the visitor to 'thumb' through a series of paintings by looking into a light box." *Time*'s review, entitled "Interiors of Chaos," likened the setting and its contents to Coney Island: "Here are the shadow boxes, peepholes. Another peep show, manipulated by turning a huge ship's wheel, shows a rotating exhibit of reproductions of all the works, including a miniature toilet for men, by screwball Surrealist Marcel Duchamp. Beyond these gadgets mankind swarms into what seems to be a decorated subway. Every two minutes while onlookers enjoy the spectacle, a roar of an approaching train is heard, lights go out on one side of the gallery, pop on at the other."⁴⁵

Homo Academicus

If, after all was said and done, frivolity continued to cast its mark on the American perception of artists in exile, a last and rather shrewd attempt at legitimization during the war years came via what was still a male stronghold in the 1940s: academe. Artists with a didactic leaning—like Hélion, Léger, and Ozenfant—had often lectured in museums and in art schools (generally their own) in Europe,⁴⁶ yet it would be difficult to imagine the surrealists lecturing at the Sorbonne, the Ecole Normale, or any of the "Grandes Ecoles." Indeed, one of the premises of the avant-garde was precisely to work against the grain of such institutions.⁴⁷ Once in America, however, virtually all emigré-artists developed a busy network of relationships with the university system.

The first tie, not too surprisingly, was with the New School for Social Research on Twelfth Street. The school's graduate faculty in the social sciences, established in 1934 for the purpose of welcoming German scholars fleeing Nazism, became in 1940 host to the Ecole Libre des Hautes Etudes, staffed by French and Belgian—and mostly Jewish—professors in exile. Contrary to his expectations, Breton did not get a position at the school—where major figures such as Lévi-Strauss, Maritain, linguist Roman Jakobson, and medievalists Henri Focillon and Gustave Cohen taught—since he couldn't teach in English.⁴⁸ It was thus a young British painter named Gordon Onslow Ford, more academic in style than his contemporary Matta, but not a member of the surrealist old guard, who was asked to give a series of lectures there under the title "Surrealist Painting: An Adventure into Human Consciousness." Stressing image making over textual practice, and focusing as much on the younger generation of artists who had joined the movement in the United States (e.g., William Baziotes, Jimmy Ernst, Boris Mago, Helen Phillips, and Kay Sage) as on its European founding fathers, Ford's account, delivered before American artists and inspirational figures such as Meyer Schapiro, deviated, to Breton's great annoyance, from the master narrative of the movement.

Gathering momentum in 1944–45, the Ecole compiled three issues of a journal entitled *Renaissance*. Published in French and unmistakably academic in its thickness, content, lack of illustrations, and all-male cast, it included contributions by such artists as Masson and Chagall. Significantly these contributions appealed not to the transgressive side of surrealism, but to lofty concepts of restraint and order. In a piece entitled "Unité et variété de la peinture française," Masson stressed the importance of "le fait pictural" over anecdote in paint, thus shielding himself from Greenberg's repeated dismissal of the Pre-Raphaelite—that is, effeminate and fastidious—"over-literariness" of surrealism. Masson's argument was a cautionary one. Stating his preference for concision over abundance, in line with the famous French "sense of measure" represented by Poussin and Seurat, he warned against the dissolving forces of automatism when taken as an end in itself. Automatism had to be kept in check; it had to be followed by discernment. Along the same lines, Chagall wrote in his "Quelques impressions sur la peinture française": "I can do without automatism. As far as I am concerned, I have slept perfectly well without Freud."[49]

More unusual was the Parisian involvement with the American academic elite: the Ivy League. Dealer Julien Levy, Alfred H. Barr Jr. and Henry-Russell Hitchcock at MoMA, and A. Everett ("Chick") Austin at the Wadsworth Atheneum were all products of the fine arts department at Harvard. The more immediate connection, however, was with Yale. On December 10, 1942, Henri Peyre, longtime chair of the French department, invited Breton to speak to Yale undergraduates. The lecture, delivered in French and entitled "La situation du surréalisme entre les deux guerres," would be the only major public address given by Breton in America.[50] Conscious that he was facing young men soon to be drafted, Breton stressed the parallels between this moment and World War I. In defense against the impatient grave diggers who wanted it dead, he presented surrealism as more relevant than ever. Professing it to be the only movement able to claim an unchallenged position in the European avant-garde between the wars, Breton argued that it maintained "une valeur opératoire," an operative value. Moreover, one thing it had *never* compromised on was the meaning of freedom. One senses in Breton's insistence on the affirmative power of youth both an underlying anxiety about the generational gap between speaker and audience and a desperate struggle to maintain his position as a leading European intellectual.

Another Yale connection was Focillon,[51] who was offered a position at Yale in 1933 and shuttled back and forth to Paris in 1938–39 to teach at the Collège de France. A formalist at a time when most medievalists of his generation were concerned with religious and iconographic issues, Focillon was nevertheless an *engagé* intellectual at heart, acutely aware of the ideological bearing that his distinction between Eastern and Western mentalities in the German and French Middle Ages had on contemporary events.[52] What is most interesting about him in the context of this essay is the fact that, instead of spending the war years ensconced in the stacks of Yale's Sterling Library, he engaged—and, paradoxically, more militantly than any of the surrealists—in relentless political activity. Siding with General de Gaulle and refusing to accept France's collapse, Focillon, who died in 1944, spent the last two years of his life speaking for a free France wherever he was invited to do so, from the classroom to Carnegie Hall.[53]

A final rallying point under the mantle of academe was the Pontigny Colloquia, held during summer breaks from 1942 to 1944 at Mount Holyoke College, one of the Seven Sisters, as a kind of spin-off of the Ecole Libre in New York and the offspring—in exile—

of the Entretiens de Pontigny, founded by Paul Desjardins in 1912. Devoted to broad humanist topics such as "Art and Man" or "The Nature of Crisis and the Present Crisis," the conferences involved almost all of the Parisian emigrés. These meetings were probably the most idyllic moments spent by many a French-speaking exile in the United States in the 1940s.[54]

Composed of a mixture of nostalgia for the past and intense engagement with the present, trauma and trivia, worldliness and private misery, exile is a most heterogeneous and fragmented experience. It had, however, in the case of the French in New York, an uninterrupted rhetoric attached to it, which had notably to do with gender. That the compulsion to elide the feminine was such an overarching one—stretching from the specific (the indexical omissions of women from group photographs) to the analogical (the need to distance oneself from kitsch and popular culture), all the way to the realm of national politics (the need to compensate for the feminization of France)—is telling. For, unhinged as exile may be, what this passage of a few Frenchmen through New York provided was the ideological hinge for the two-part Master Narrative of the so-called first (European, pre–World War II) and second (American, post-1945) historical avant-gardes.

Notes

I would like to thank Lesley Baier and Sabine Eckmann for their help while writing this essay.

1 The title of this piece is taken from the French situationists (specifically a film script by Guy Debord of 1959), for, as heirs to the surrealists, they perfected the experience of drift and deterritorialization; see Ken Knabb, ed., *Situationist International Anthology* (Berkeley, Calif.: Bureau of Public Secrets, 1981). On Parisian artists in New York during World War II, see Julien Levy, *Memoir of an Art Gallery, 1931–1948* (New York: Putnam, 1977); Jimmy Ernst, *A Not So Still Life* (New York: St. Martin's Press, 1984); Peggy Guggenheim, *Out of This Century* (New York: Dial Press, 1946); idem, *Confessions of an Art Addict* (New York: Macmillan, 1960); Irving Sandler, *The Triumph of American Painting: A History of Abstract Expressionism* (New York: Praeger, 1970); Serge Guilbaut, *How New York Stole the Idea of Modern Art: Abstract Expressionism, Freedom, and the Cold War* (Chicago: University of Chicago Press, 1983); and, most recently, Dickran Tashjian, *A Boatload of Madmen: Surrealism and the American Avant-Garde, 1920–1950* (New York: Thames and Hudson, 1995), and Martica Sawin, *Surrealism in Exile and the Beginnings of the New York School* (Cambridge: MIT Press, 1995).

2 For a theoretical outline of some of these issues—although not, it should be said, those involving gender—see Pierre Bourdieu, *The Field of Cultural Production: Essays on Art and Literature* (New York: Columbia University Press, 1993).

3 James Johnson Sweeney, ed., "Eleven Europeans in America," *Bulletin of the Museum of Modern Art* 13, no. 4–5 (1946). In addition to the ten artists discussed here, the article included an interview with Kurt Seligmann.

4 "Cords and Concords," *View*, ser. 1, no. 7–8 (October–November 1941): 5.

5 The story goes that Duchamp escaped from occupied France in 1941 with the *Valise*, disguised as a cheese merchant. See Anne D'Harnoncourt and Kynaston McShine, eds., *Marcel Duchamp: A Retrospective Exhibition*, exh. cat. (Philadelphia: Philadelphia Museum of Art, 1973), 23.

6 Carl Holty, "Mondrian in New York: A Memoir," *Arts* 31 (September 1957): 17–21.

7 Wolfgang Paalen had gone from France to British Columbia in 1939 and from there to Mexico, where he published the review *Dyn* (1942–44).

8 See Kenneth E. Silver and Romy Golan, *The Circle of Montparnasse: Jewish Artists in Paris, 1905–1945* (New York: Jewish Museum, 1985); Romy Golan, *Modernity and Nostalgia: French Art and Politics between the Wars* (London and New Haven: Yale University Press, 1995); and Michele Cone, *Artists under Vichy: A Case of Prejudice and Persecution* (Princeton: Princeton University Press, 1993).

9 Charles Duit, *André Breton a-t-il dit passé?* (Paris: Denoël, 1969).

10 Levy, *Memoirs of an Art Gallery*, 267. The misogynist tinge in Levy's quote might have had something to do with Breton's antipathy for Sage as both a moneyed American woman who reversed traditional marital roles by providing Tanguy with financial stability in America and as a mature woman who took her work seriously, refusing to fit into the roles women traditionally played for the surrealists as either young muses, lovers, or lesser artists; see Judith D. Suther, "Separate Studios: Kay Sage and Yves Tanguy," in *Significant Others: Creativity and Intimate Partnership*, ed. Whitney Chadwick and Isabelle de Courtivron (London: Thames and Hudson, 1993), 137–54, and Susan Rubin Suleiman, *Subversive Intent: Gender, Politics, and the Avant-Garde* (Cambridge: Harvard University Press, 1990).

11 See Christian Brochand, *Histoire générale de la radio et de la télévision en France*, vol. 1, *1921–1944* (Paris: Documentation Française, 1994.)

12 See Henri Behar, *André Breton: Le grand indésirable* (Paris: Calman-Levy, 1990), 346.

13 On the orality of fascism, see Alice Yaeger Kaplan, *Reproductions of Banality: Fascism, Literature, and French Intellectual Life* (Minneapolis: University of Minnesota Press, 1986). The psychoanalytic and poststructuralist literature (especially the work of Jacques Derrida) on the power of the voice and on the privileging of speaking over writing is extensive and beyond the scope of this essay.

14 See Golan, *Modernity and Nostalgia*.

15 "57th Street: A Tight Bottleneck for Art in the United States," *Fortune* 34 (September 1946): 145–49.

16 Clement Greenberg, in *Nation*, 9 October 1943, reprinted in *Clement Greenberg: The Collected Essays and Criticism*, ed. John O'Brian (Chicago: University of Chicago Press, 1986), vol. 1, 153–54.

17 Clement Greenberg, "Surrealist Painting," *Nation*, 12 and 19 August 1944, reprinted in ibid., 225–26.

18 George Biddle, "The Surrealists—Isolationists of Art," *New Republic* 105 (27 October 1941): 6.

19 Klaus Mann, "Surrealist Circus," *American Mercury*, February 1943, 174–81. Peyton Boswell, editor of *Art Digest*, reprinted large portions of Mann's article, with not a word of commentary (see *Art Digest* 17 [15 May 1945]: 27). Meanwhile, when Mann enlisted as a volunteer in the American army, his own magazine, *Decision*, published from 1941 to 1942, mounted a veritable crusade against surrealism.

20 "Surrealists in Exile," *Time*, 20 April 1942.

21 For a riveting analysis of the political dimension of the reception of French art in the 1940s (in spite of a slightly paranoid reading of the conspiratorial power struggles at play in the wake of a new world order), see Guilbaut, *How New York*.

22 On France's fear of its perennial German foe and of an almighty America, as well as its various forms of self-feminization during the interwar years and the Vichy regime, see Golan, *Modernity and Nostalgia*.

23 On the gendering of the American avant-garde and, in particular, the fear of homosexuality in art, see especially Jonathan Weinberg, *Speaking for Vice: Homosexuality in the Art of Charles Demuth, Marsden Hartley, and the First American Avant-Garde* (New Haven: Yale University Press, 1993), and Kenneth E. Silver, "Modes of Disclosure: The Construction of Gay Identity and the Rise of Pop Art," in *Hand Painted Pop: American Art in Transition, 1955–62*, exh. cat. (New York: Rizzoli, 1993).

24 Archibald MacLeish, "America's Duty to French Culture," *Saturday Review of Literature* 25 (November 1942): 5–6, 18.

25 See Susan Rabin Suleiman, "Between the Street and the Salon: The Dilemma of Surrealist Politics in the 1930s," *Visual Anthropology Review* 7 (Spring 1991): 39–50.

26 See Peter Bürger, *Theory of the Avant-Garde* (Minneapolis: University of Minnesota Press, 1984).

27 See *Newsweek*, 9 March 1942.

28 Rosamund Frost, "First Fruits of Exile: What Recent Emigré Artists Have Done in America," *Art News* (1942): 23, 32.

29 The photo of "The Irascibles" appeared in *Life* on 15 January 1951.

30 See Andreas Huyssen, "Mass Culture as Woman: Modernism's Other," in *After the Great Divide: Modernism, Mass Culture, Postmodernism* (Bloomington: Indiana University Press, 1986), 44–62.

31 Indeed, as a critic recently mused, had Mondrian survived the war (he was the first of the New York exiles to die there, in 1944), one would like to imagine that he would have stayed in Manhattan and enjoyed the high voltage of the place in his old age. See Simon Schama, "True Grid," *New Yorker*, 9 October 1995, 42–48.

32 See Romy Golan, "Matta, Duchamp et le mythe: Un nouveau paradigme pour la dernière phase du surréalisme," in *Les classiques du XXe siècle: Matta* (Paris: Editions du Centre Pompidou, 1985), and idem, "Mise en suspend de l'incrédulité: Breton et le mythe des Grands Transparents," in *André Breton: La beauté convulsive* (Paris: Editions du Centre Georges Pompidou, 1991).

33 Literary sources for the French mythical construction of America include Chateaubriand's *Mémoires d'outre-tombe* (1849–50), Paul Adam's *Vues d'Amérique ou la Nouvelle Jouvence* (1906), and Paul Morand's *New York* (1930). See also Dominique Jullien, *Récits du Nouveau Monde: Les voyageurs français en Amérique de Chateaubriand à nos jours* (Paris: Nathan, 1992), and Fernando Ainsa, "The Inventions of America: Imaginary Sign of the Discovery and Construction of Utopia," *Diogenes*, no. 145 (Spring 1989): 98–111.

34 "Interview with André Breton," *View* 1 (October–November 1941): 1–2.

35 Mann, "Surrealist Circus," 179. *View*'s homosexual contingent—which included Charles Henry Ford, Parker Tyler, Virgil Thomson, Gertrude Stein, Maya Deren, Jean Cocteau, and the Neo-romantics Eugene Berman, Pavel Tchelitchev, and Christian Bérard—is touched upon by Tashjian in *A Boatload of Madmen*, 157. As Tashjian remarks, it led to tensions between Ford and the homophobic Breton, which explains the latter's aloofness toward the review and his desire to start a magazine of his own, *VVV*. See also Charles Henry Ford, ed., *View: Parade of the Avant-Garde, 1940–1947* (New York: Thunder's Mouth Press, 1991).

36 Breton's book was published in French, with an English translation by Edouard Roditi, by Charles Henry Ford's and Carl Van Vechten's View Editions.

37 Nicolas Calas, "Anti-Surrealist Dali: I Say His Flies Are Ersatz," *View* 1 (June 1941): 1. This attack, it should be said, was probably published under pressure from Breton. Indeed, Ford did not feel free to include his friends Dali and Cocteau in his magazine, knowing that it would alienate Breton.

38 See "*Life* Calls on Salvador Dali," *Life*, 7 April 1941, 98–101; and Winthrop Sargent, "Dali," *Life*, 24 September 1945, 63–66, 68.

39 For an entertaining but dismaying account of Ernst's love affairs, see Susan Rubin Suleiman, "The Bird Superior Meets the Bride of the Wind: Leonora Carrington and Max Ernst," in *Significant Others*, 97–118.

40 For a brief discussion of Lynes in the context of surrealism, see Jeffrey Wechsler, *Surrealism and American Art, 1931–1947*, exh. cat. (New Brunswick, N.J.: Rutgers University Art Gallery, 1976), 48–49; see also James Crump, "Iconography of Desire: George Platt Lynes and Gay Male Visual Culture in Postwar New York," in *George Platt Lynes: Photographs from the Kinsey Institute* (New York: Bullfinch Press, 1993).

41 *New York Sun*, 23 October 1942.

42 See Cynthia Goodman, "The Art of Revolutionary Display Techniques," in *Frederick Kiesler*, exh. cat. (New York: Whitney Museum of American Art, 1989).

43 *New York Times*, 25 October 1942.

44 *Newsweek*, 2 November 1942.

45 "Interiors of Chaos," *Time*, 2 November 1942, 47.

46 Ozenfant opened a school of fine arts at 208 East Twentieth Street, near Gramercy Park.

47 A case in point is Georges Bataille, who set up the subversive and semiautonomous Collège de Sociologie. See Denis Hollier, ed., *The College of Sociology (1937–39)* (Minneapolis: University of Minnesota Press, 1988).

48 After its first two years of existence, the Ecole Libre counted ninety-one professors and one thousand students. See Gustave Cohen, *Lettres aux américains* (Montreal: Editions de l'Arbre, 1942).

49 André Masson, "Unité et variété de la peinture française," *Renaissance* 2–3 (1944–45): 217–23; Marc Chagall, "Quelques impressions sur la peinture française," ibid., 45–57.

50 Published in pamphlet form, it was reprinted in both French and English in *VVV*, nos. 2–3 (1943).

51 Though known as a medieval scholar (in 1925 he replaced France's foremost medievalist, Emile Mâle, as professor at the Sorbonne), Focillon repeatedly ventured into other fields, writing on Piranesi, Cellini, Hokusai, and Buddhist art as well as producing a two-volume book on nineteenth-century painting and one on art and revolution. See Louis Grodecki and Henri Peyre, *Bibliographie Henri Focillon*, Yale Publications in the History of Art, no. 15 (New Haven: Yale University Press, 1963); George Kubler, "Tribute," *College Art Journal* 4 (January 1945): 71–74.

52 The distinction, mostly disparaging of the Orient, is between a sense of fatality, enslavement, and pain versus the constant creativity and democratic worldview of the West. See Focillon's *Pierres de France*, and "L'art allemand depuis 1870," in *Technique et sentiment*, both published in 1919, in the aftermath of World War I; and *Art d'Occident* (1938).

53 See Focillon's *From Paris to the Sea down the River Seine* (New York: Wildenstein Gallery, 1943) and *Témoignage pour la France* (New York: Brentano's, 1945).

54 Breton's name, however, is conspicuously absent. The founders of Pontigny MHC were Gustave Cohen; Helen E. Patch, an American who was head of the French department at Mount Holyoke College; and Jean Wahl, a French poet and philosopher. The meetings did not survive under that name after the Liberation. Their spirit continued, however, in such endeavors as the conferences sponsored by Eleanor Roosevelt. See "Pontigny-en-Amérique," Mount Holyoke Archives. I am thankful to Nadia Margolis for examining the archives.

122
André Masson, *Curtain for a Ceremony*, 1942 (cat. no. 101).

surrealism in exile:
responses to the european
destruction of humanism

SABINE ECKMANN

salvador dali

max ernst

andré masson

yves tanguy

matta echaurren

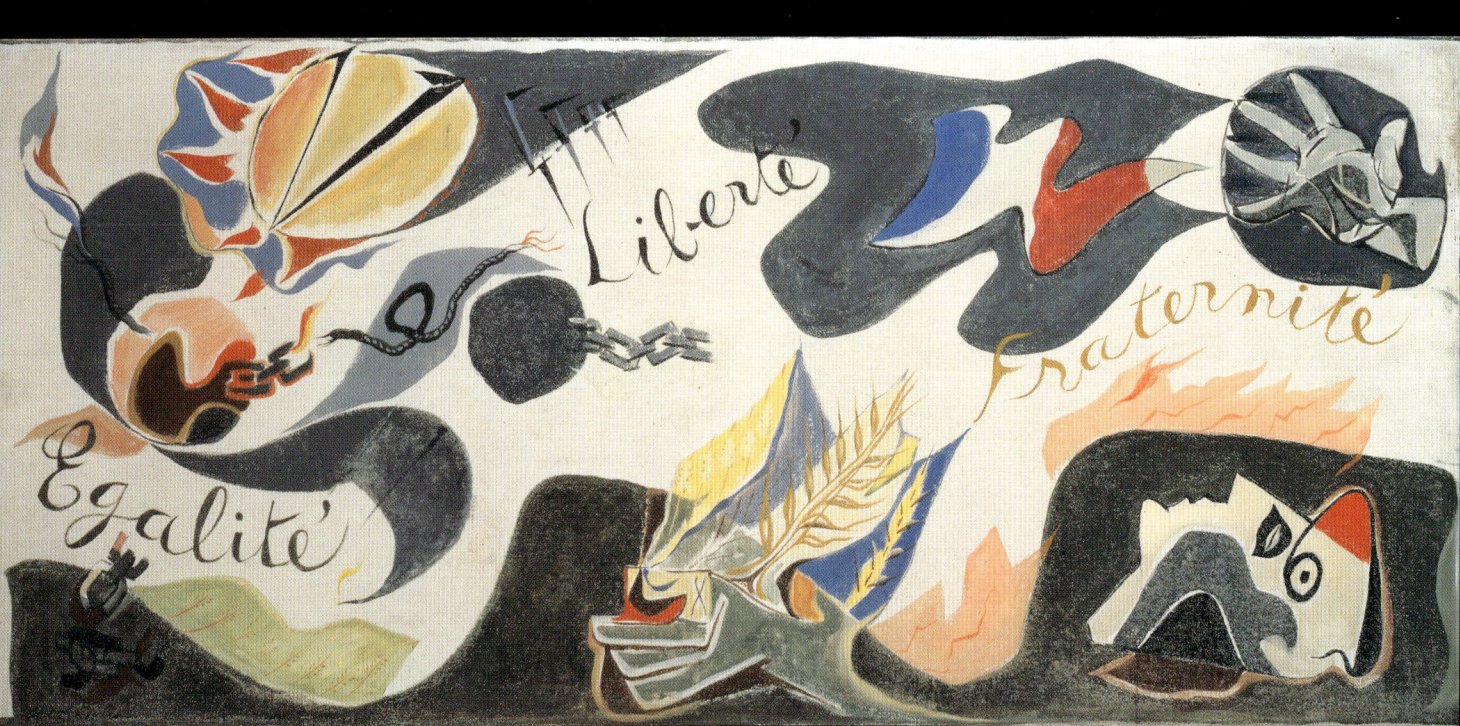

salvador dali
in new york and california,
1940–45

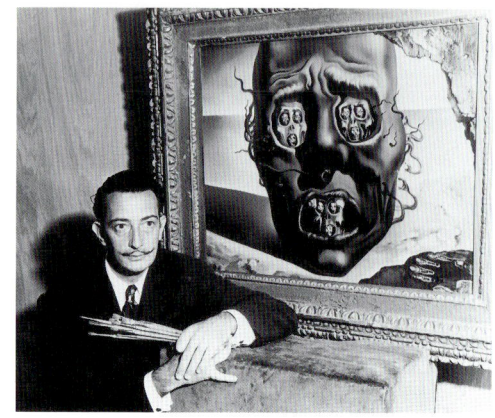

1904	born in Figueras, Spain
1940	emigrates from France (Paris) to the U.S. (New York; Monterey, Calif.)
1948	returns to Spain (Port Lligat)
1989	dies in Figueras

In the United States in the 1930s Salvador Dali was regarded as the most important and influential representative of surrealism.[1] From 1934 onward exhibitions, lectures, and scandalous publicity made him the most popular artistic personality of his generation, whereas in Europe, after the outbreak of World War II, he increasingly felt himself to be under threat of Nazi persecution. And so, on August 8, 1940, Salvador and Gala Dali arrived in New York from Lisbon. On previous visits Dali had come to America voluntarily and for a limited and specific time span; now he faced an uncertain period of exile.

Between 1940 and 1945 Dali increasingly made work to order for the fashion industry, the musical theater, and the movies; he illustrated books and took on portrait commissions from rich and famous personalities. One example is his *Portrait of Isabel Styler-Tas (Melancholy)* (1945; fig. 124, cat. no. 32), in which he presents two images of the sitter. The right-hand side of the picture, modeled on Piero della Francesca's *Battista Sforza, Duchess of Urbino,* shows her in an idealized, classical pose; on the left, her face has been transformed into a surrealist landscape.

Both styles, classical naturalism and surrealist alienation, are characteristic of Dali's painting of this period. The former style attracted the reproach that he had become an academic painter,[2] but that was not all that lay behind his markedly adverse reception from professional critics during his years in America. The critics focused on three themes: his painting, his aggressive marketing of his

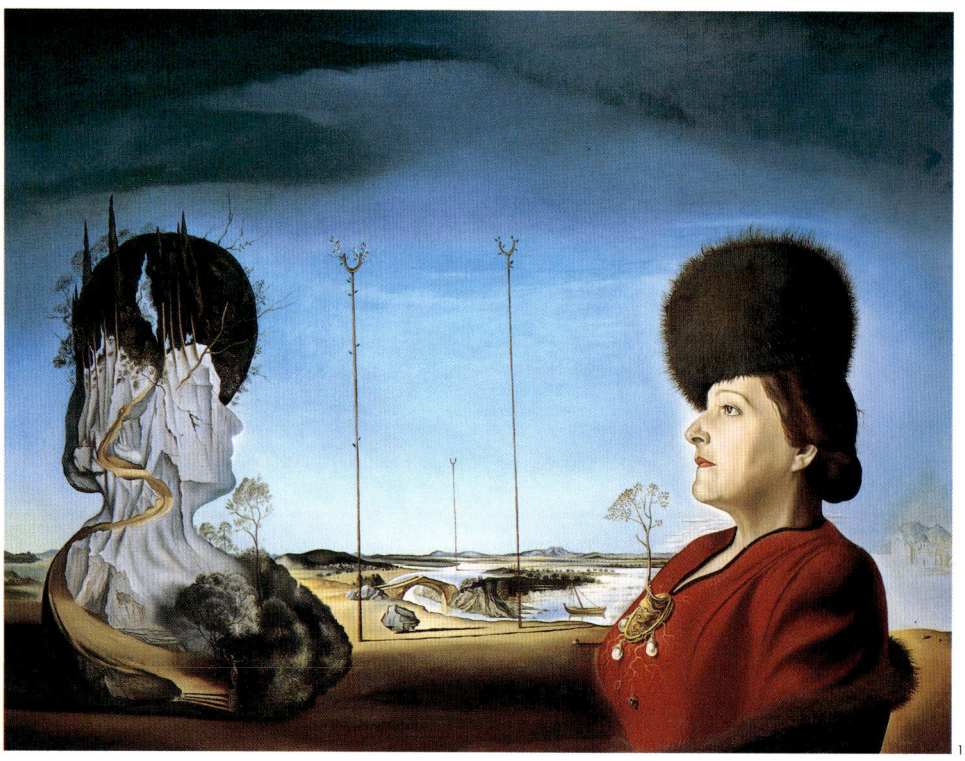

123
Salvador Dali with *Face of War*, Julien Levy Gallery, New York, 1941.

124
Salvador Dali, *Portrait of Isabel Styler-Tas (Melancholy)*, 1945 (cat. no. 32).

125
Salvador Dali; *Slave Market with the Disappearing Bust of Voltaire*, 1940; oil on canvas; 18¼ x 25⅜ in. (46.4 x 64.5 cm); The Salvador Dali Museum, Saint Petersburg, Florida.

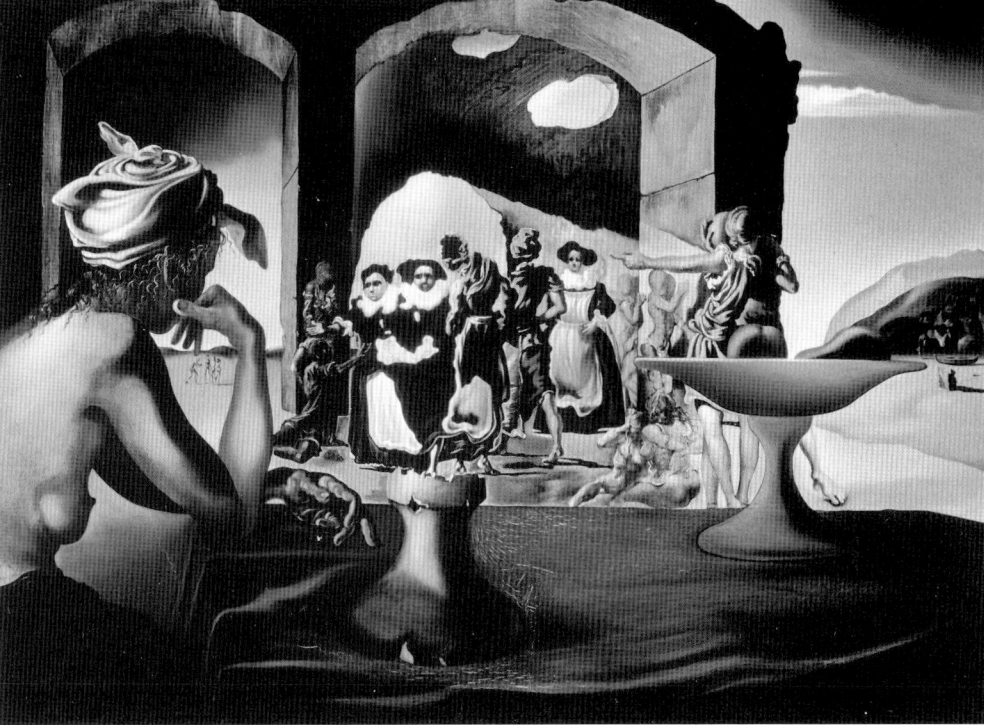

own personality, and his political posture. In an article entitled "Anti-Surrealist Dali," published in *View* magazine in 1941, Nicolas Calas voiced the criticisms of the painter's erstwhile colleagues among the European surrealists. Calas accused him of apostasy because he no longer supported the revolutionary aims of surrealism; because he had rediscovered Spain, Catholicism, and neoclassicism; and because he was trying to paint beautiful forms in the style of an artist like Ingres. To Calas, Dali's realism was decorative and superficial. Instead of creating a new reality, he was producing what Calas called an "atmosphere of technicolor unreality."[3]

André Breton's anagram for Dali's name, "Avida Dollars," summed up the surrealists' attitude toward his commercial successes and the public promotion of his artistic persona, which garnered increasing support and attention from the popular press. The image of the artistic genius as a social outsider, whose talent authorizes him to break through social boundaries and who consequently exerts a fascination without ever having to take responsibility for his actions and statements, was Dali's ideal. He exploited this self-image to build a rapport with the public. In his article "Total Camouflage for Total War," published in *Esquire* in August 1942, he cast doubt on the existence of an objective, rational visual culture—a central tenet of surrealism. He explained to his public how his ambiguous images were created and how they were to be read. For example, in *Slave Market with the Disappearing Bust of Voltaire* (1940; fig. 125) the three figures in the middle ground, framed by a white arch, could be read as a portrait of Voltaire if the white areas were seen as positive forms. Through this object lesson in ambiguity Dali proclaimed his allegiance to a visual culture subject to human control. By so doing, he stood surrealism on its head.

In addition to this kind of direct communication, Dali kept himself in the public eye through professionally orchestrated media

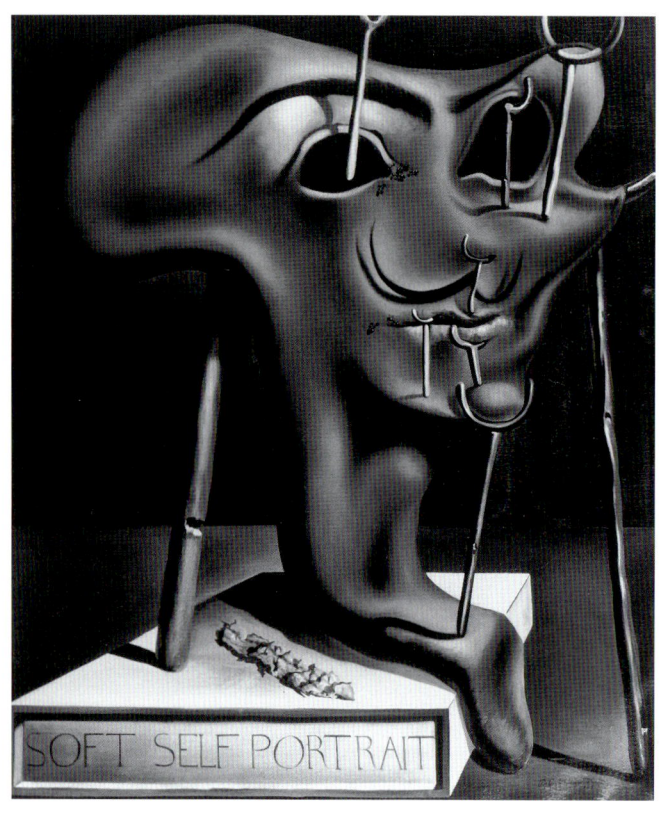

events. The culmination of these activities was his "Surrealistic Night in an Enchanted Forest," which took place at the Hotel Del Monte in Oakland, California, in September 1941. More than a thousand well-known personalities came in costume as their own worst dream.[4] Dali's use of the American mass media to market his persona and his art signals his assimilation into American culture.

In some of his paintings, too, Dali emphasized his own "Americanization." In *Soft Self-Portrait with Fried Bacon* (1941; fig. 126) he combined elements of his surrealist vocabulary—the head shown as boneless, soft matter and the ants that can be seen on the bacon—with a reference to his interest in classical art, in the form of a base for a portrait bust. This

126
Salvador Dali; *Soft Self-Portrait with Fried Bacon*, 1941; oil on canvas; 24⅛ x 20 in. (61.3 x 50.8 cm); Fundació Gala-Salvador Dalí, Figueras.

127
Salvador Dali, *Melancholy Atomic and Uranic Idyll*, 1945 (cat. no. 31).

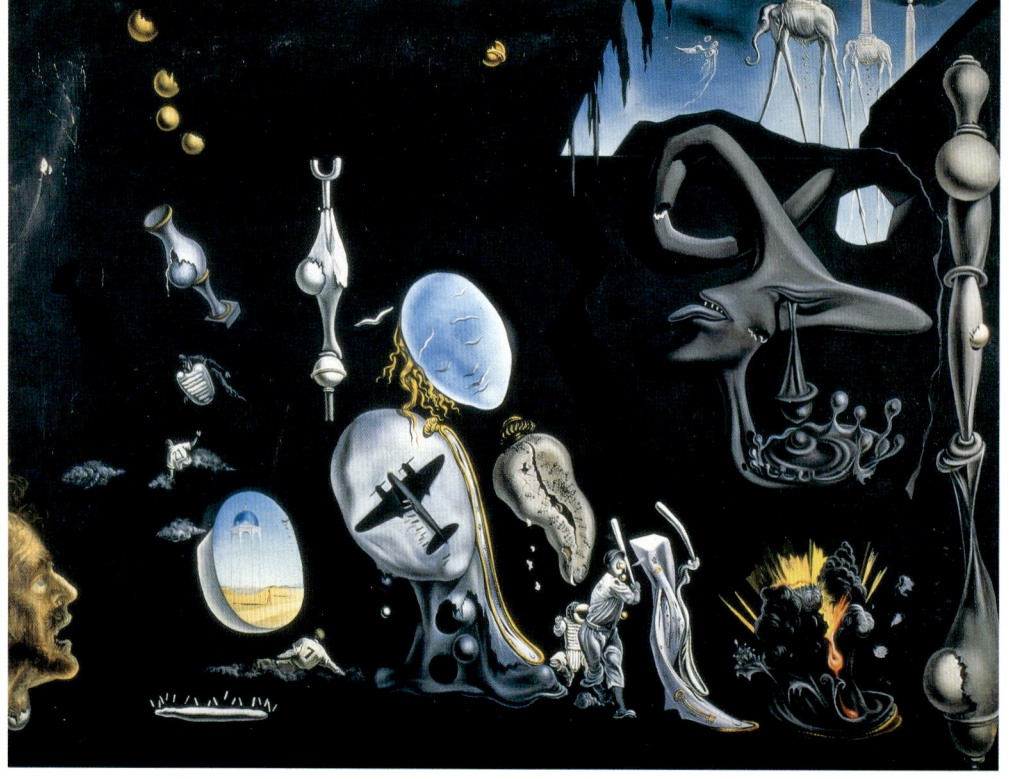

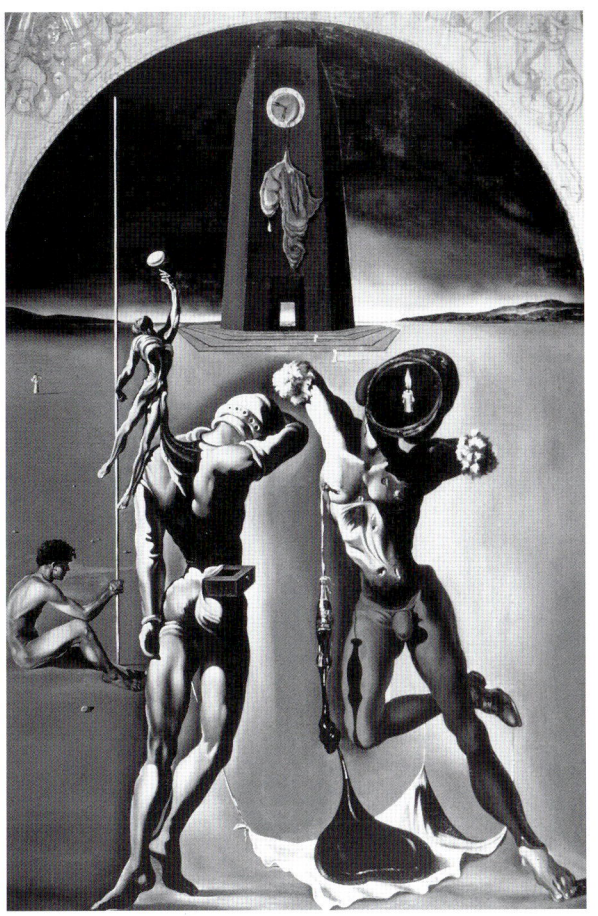 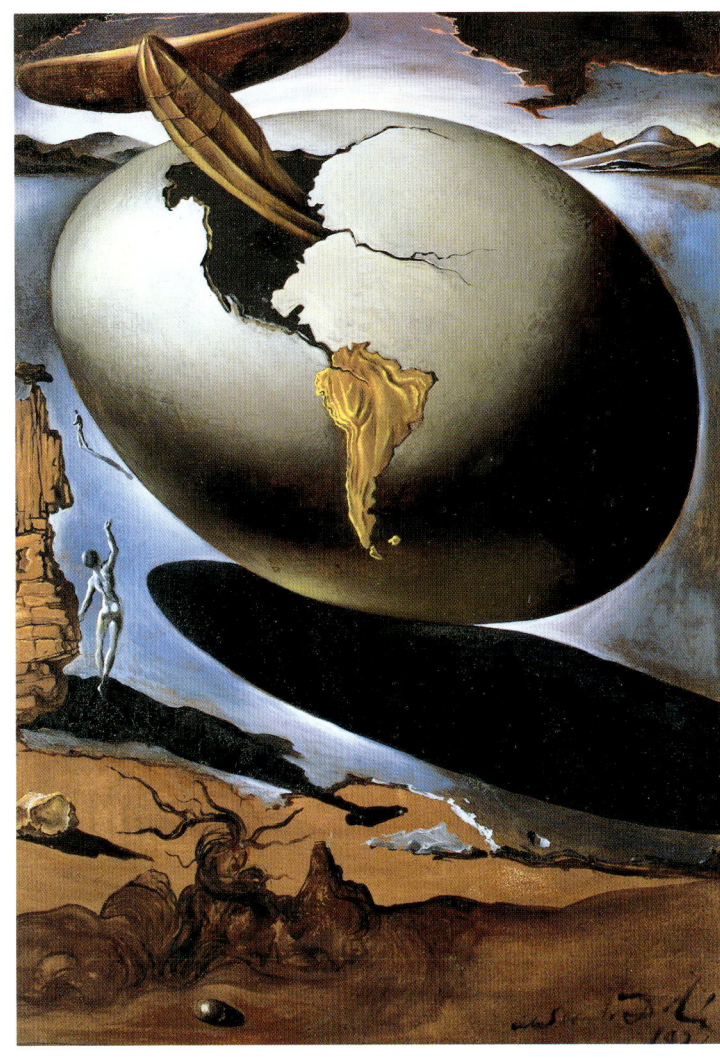

128
Salvador Dali; *Poetry of America—the Cosmic Athletes*, 1943; oil on canvas; 46 x 31 in. (116.8 x 78.7 cm); Fundació Gala-Salvador Dalí, Figueras.

129
Salvador Dali, *Allegory of an American Christmas*, 1943 (cat. no. 28).

amalgam of disparate styles is rounded off by a symbol of American culture, the bacon rasher, which allows him to give visual expression to his newfound identification with his host country.

In *Poetry of America—the Cosmic Athletes* (1943; fig. 128), by contrast, Dali restricted himself to a characterization of the host country. Assorted symbols of American culture—a white and a black football player and a Coca-Cola bottle—appear in a de Chirico–like landscape, framed by a triumphal arch. A critique of elitist, European culture, with its time-honored, traditional definition of art, is implicit in the presentation of "profane" symbols of American popular culture within a triumphal arch. *Allegory of an American Christmas* (1943; fig. 129, cat. no. 28), which was used as an illustration in the December 1943 issue of *Esquire*, also celebrates the New

World. Dali depicts America as a monstrous cocoon with a fragment of an airplane breaking through its surface, thereby paying tribute to the country's commitment to technical progress. The cocoon seems to embody Dali's belief that America would give birth to a new, humane world that would replace the old, war-torn one. Interestingly, in the depiction of the airplane he once again drew on imagery from popular culture to distinguish America from Europe.

All the same, in his 1944 novel *Hidden Faces* Dali expressed a negative view of America: "Its fruit has no flavor, its women have no shame, and its men are without honor."[5] This remark reveals his difficulty in integrating into American culture. One work that addresses the exile's inability to feel at home in the host country, and the degree to which he misses his own culture, is the painting *Honey Is*

salvador dali 151

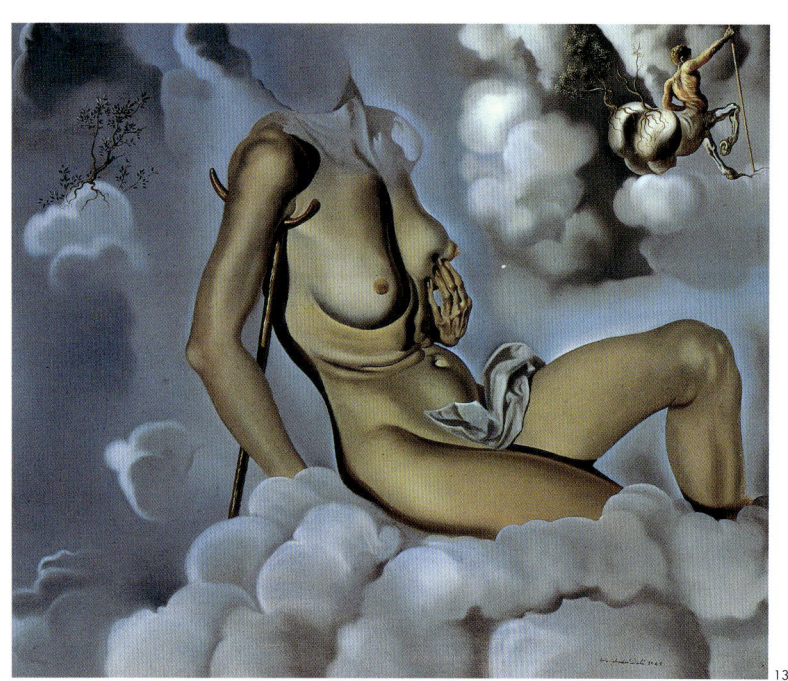

Sweeter than Blood (1941; fig. 130, cat. no. 26). In this work Dali reverts to a theme first treated in 1926, giving visual expression to a saying coined by a fellow Spaniard, Lidia de Cadaqués, in which honey symbolizes erotic fascination and blood stands for ties of kinship. *The Apotheosis of Homer* (1944; fig. 131, cat. no. 29) can also be interpreted as an expression of Dali's repressed desire for his own culture. Various mutated symbols of Mediterranean civilization—a sleeping nude on the right, a plaster bust of Homer with the face of a small child, a stone fragment in the foreground with Hebraic inscriptions, an open sarcophagus with a snake, and the Triumph of Neptune in the background—suggest Dali's nostalgia for traditional "high" European culture.

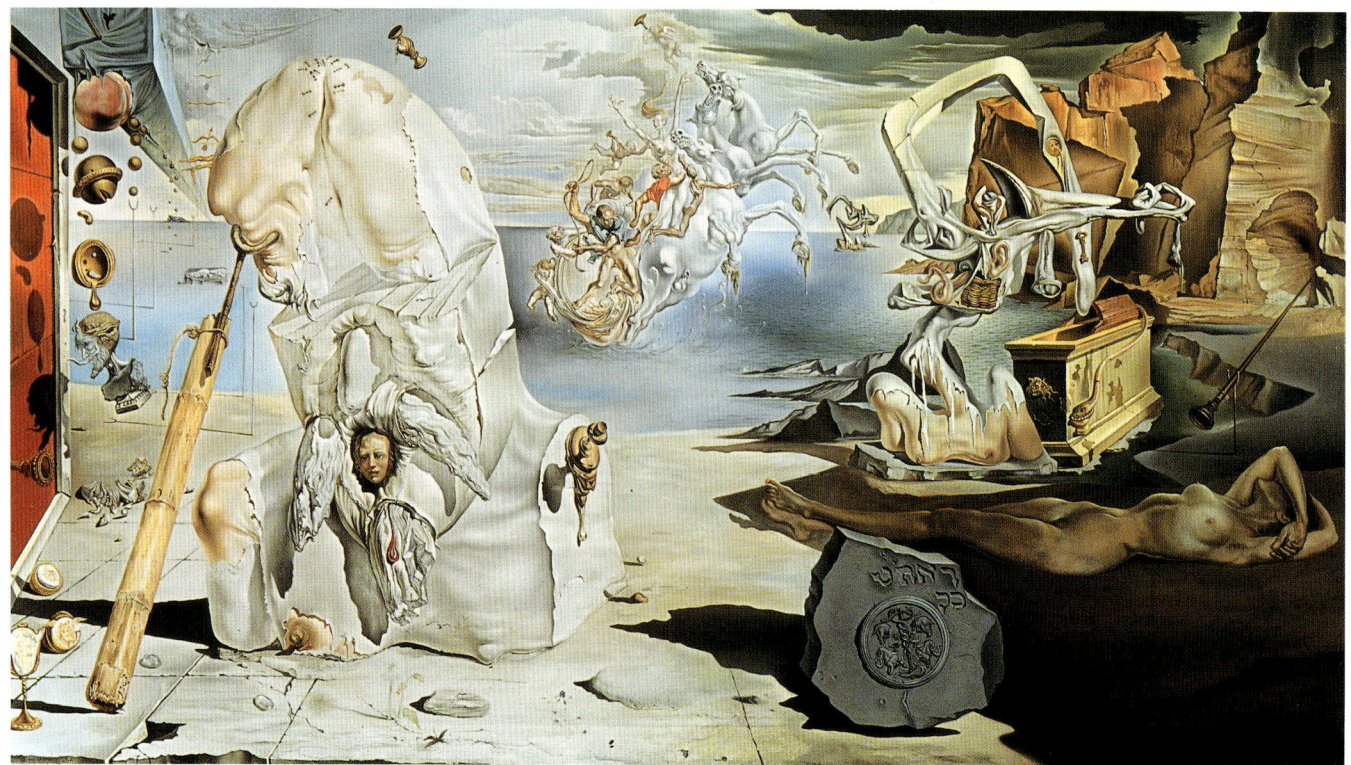

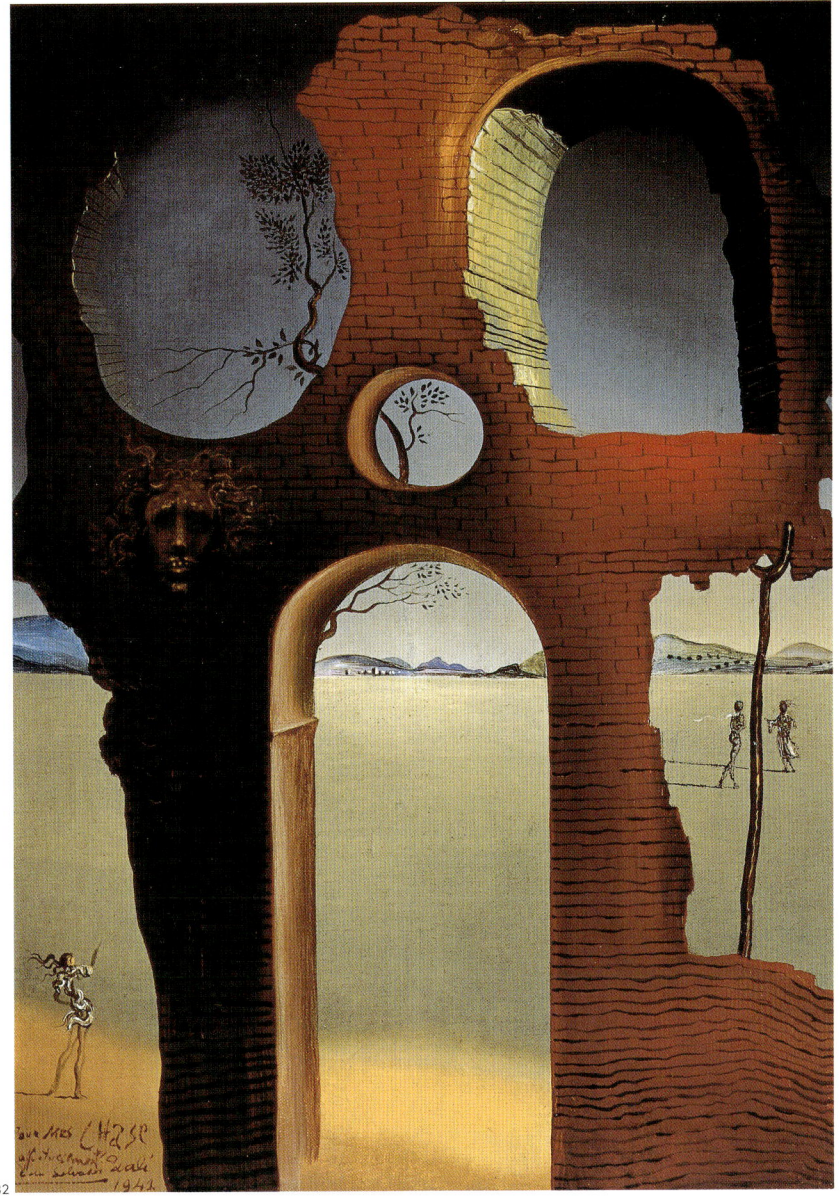

130
Salvador Dali, *Honey Is Sweeter than Blood*, 1941 (cat. no. 26).

131
Salvador Dali, *The Apotheosis of Homer*, 1944 (cat. no. 29).

132
Salvador Dali, *Ruin with Head of Medusa*, 1941 (cat. no. 27).

Even in *Poetry of America* Dali incorporated elements from his native Spain; the landscape in the background looks like Cadaqués and the Cape Creus coastline.[6] He was thus deeply concerned both with his own identity and with his native country, remembering the Spanish landscape and the work he had done there while simultaneously Americanizing that work. In *Poetry of America* American symbols dominate; in *Honey Is Sweeter than Blood* Gala looks like an American pinup girl.

In November 1941 the exhibition *Salvador Dali,* curated by James Thrall Soby, opened at the Museum of Modern Art in New York. Like many other MoMA presentations, the show toured all across America. In 1942 and 1943 it was shown in eight different cities, educating the population at large and enhancing Dali's American reputation still further. At the same time the museum knew full well that it was laying itself open to severe criticism from artistic and intellectual quarters for involvement in quasi-commercial activities. In his catalogue foreword Monroe Wheeler, the director of exhibitions at MoMA, accordingly distanced himself both from the mass-media response to Dali and from Dali's own interpretation of his work—a classic illustration of MoMA's self-image as America's ultimate authority on modern art. Wheeler took pains to explain that the museum wanted to show works of art characteristic of the present day, and Dali's work, in his view, was just that. "We believe," he wrote, "that Dali is an artist of the greatest interest at the moment, and meaningful in this historic sense.... Dali's dream of the present is tragic, and we should not shrink from the shock and pain of it."[7]

It is tempting to see many of Dali's paintings, which take destructiveness, violence, and loss of coherence as their theme, as symbolic of the "age of violence." Dali also made a number of explicit comments on the horrors of his time, however, most manifestly in the painting *Face of War* (see fig. 123), which dates from 1940, shortly after his arrival in the United States. The skull with smaller skulls set within its orifices embodies both the memory of the Spanish Civil War and the violence and horror of World War II, which had just begun. The same is true of *Ruin with Head of Medusa* (1941; fig. 132, cat. no. 27), in which the skull-shaped ruin—Medusa's head as a symbol of disaster—and the vast, uninhabited landscape evoke a postapocalyptic world.[8]

salvador dali 153

The relationship between Dali's work and contemporary reality inspired varying critical responses. The respected art magazine *Art Digest* took much the same view as MoMA; its reviewer of the MoMA exhibition opined that Dali's works would one day stand as testimonies to a "mad, garbled, politically fraudulent, economically cannibalistic era."[9] By contrast, in 1941 Emily Genauer, art critic of the *New York World Telegram,* denounced Dali's work as degenerate. Four years later she changed her mind, having come to believe, after Hiroshima and the end of World War II, that Dali's themes corresponded to reality—and indeed had been overtaken by it.[10] Despite the turnabout in her opinion, Genauer nevertheless continued—consciously or unconsciously—to apply the same National Socialist critical vocabulary to Dali's work, now recognizing it as healthy and logical.

Surprisingly enough, it was on precisely the same grounds that the American left attacked Dali as a fascist. In 1941 the artist Walter Quirt, a dedicated progressive, accused him and his followers of being fascistic and lacking social and political responsibility, charging that, by representing destructive themes in their work, they promoted violence and cruelty.[11] Dali had already come under political attack for his painting *The Enigma of Hitler* (c. 1939) and his declaration of allegiance to Franco's Spain. Although both Breton and Quirt denounced him as a fascist on the strength of that painting, Dali's political position in the 1940s still resists clear definition. In his written statements he retreated to an apolitical stance: "I was definitely not a historic man. On the contrary I felt myself essentially a-historic and a-political."[12]

There are nationalistic allusions in several of Dali's paintings, however, including *Poetry of America, Allegory of an American Christmas,* and *Birth of a Nation (Birth of a New World),* dated 1942, in which he expressed his devotion to America. It remains an open question whether he ever really sympathized with American nationalism or was simply trying to curry favor with the American public. His fondness for the aristocracy, however, and his predilection (observed by Calas) for Catholicism and classical art as monarchical props suggest a reactionary political attitude. Yet neither his paintings nor his writings convey an explicitly fascist position.

Dali's American exile was marked by a barrage of criticism from both the highbrow art critics and the New York surrealists, aimed at his work, his personality, and his political attitudes. Meanwhile Dali kept his distance from the art world and played to a wider public that was not particularly interested in art. By the time he left America in 1948, he no longer had a contract with any art dealer. For all his genius for publicity, and his determined and successful marketing of his own work and personality, he seems to have had an ambivalent relationship with his host country. On the one hand, he made overtures to American culture by incorporating American symbols into his paintings; on the other, he found refuge in his memories and drew themes from his native Spanish culture.

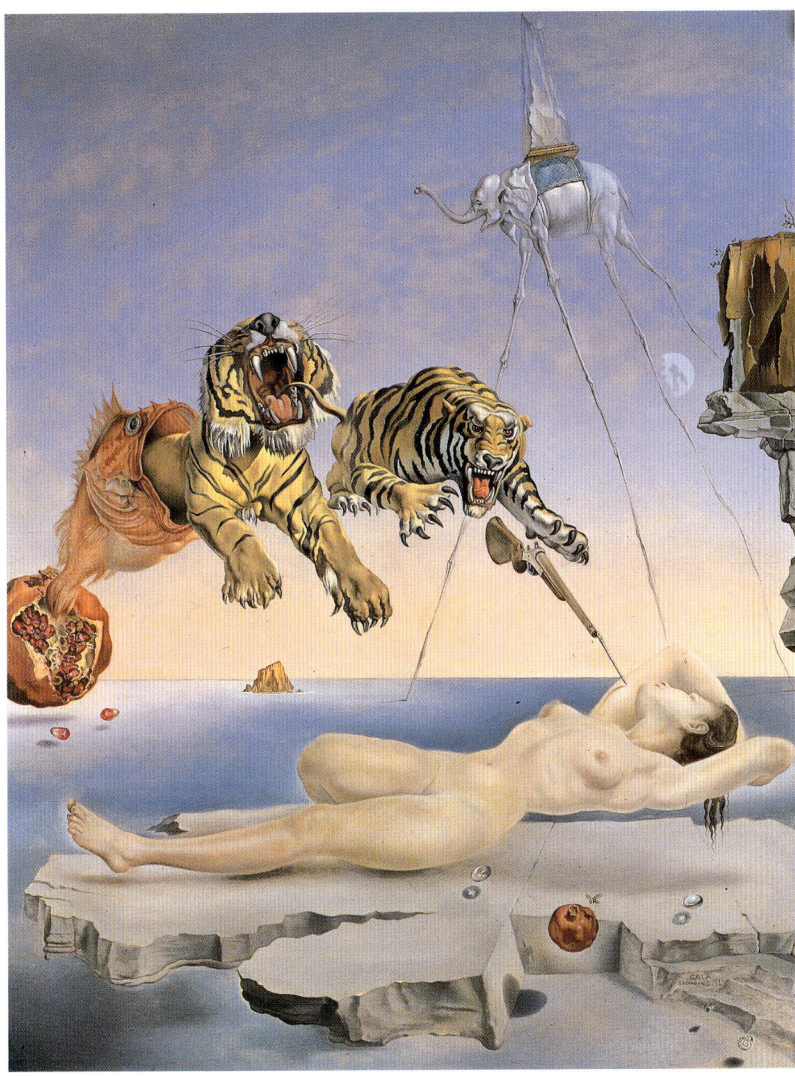

133
Salvador Dali, *Dream Caused by the Flight of a Bee around a Pomegranate a Second before Awakening*, 1944 (cat. no. 30).

Notes

1 Dickran Tashjian, *A Boatload of Madmen: Surrealism and the American Avant-Garde, 1920–1950* (New York: Thames and Hudson, 1995), 50–65, 83–90.
2 D. B., *Art News* 40 (1 January 1942): 21.
3 *View*, ser. 1, no. 6 (June 1941): 1, 3.
4 *Monterey Peninsula Herald*, 1 September 1941, 10, and 3 September 1941, 2.
5 Salvador Dali, *Hidden Faces* (New York: Dial Press, 1944), 334.
6 Robert Descharnes and Gilles Néret, *Salvador Dali, 1904–1989: Oeuvre-Katalog* (Cologne: Taschen, 1994), vol. 2, 374.
7 Monroe Wheeler, in *Salvador Dali*, exh. cat., ed. James Thrall Soby (New York: Museum of Modern Art, 1941), 7–8.
8 *Ruin with Head of Medusa* is dedicated to Edna Woolman Chase, the editor in chief of *Vogue*, for whom Dali worked several times during his exile as a designer of clothing and fashion layouts for the magazine.
9 "Dali and Miro Jar New York with Visions of the Subconscious," *Art Digest* 16 (1 December 1941): 6.
10 Emily Genauer, *New York World Telegram*, 24 November 1945, 5.
11 Walter Quirt, quoted in "Dali a Fascist," *Art Digest* 16 (1 December 1941): 5.
12 Salvador Dali, *The Secret Life of Salvador Dali* (New York: Dial Press, 1942), 357.

max ernst in new york, 1941–45

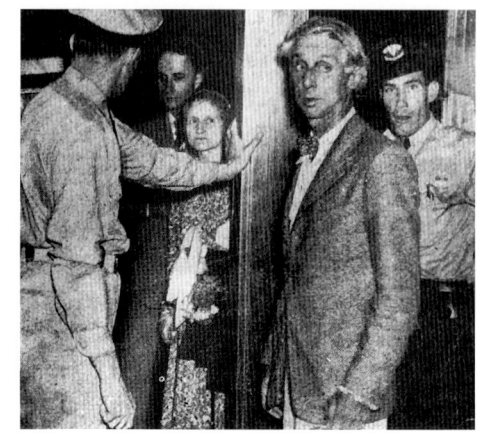

134

1891	born in Brühl, Germany
1941	emigrates from France (Paris) to the U.S. (New York)
1953	returns to France (Paris)
1976	dies in Seillans, France

In an interview with James Johnson Sweeney in New York in 1946 Max Ernst proclaimed his personal adherence to the modernist idea of the autonomy of the individual artist but refused to dwell on the exceptional nature of his own status as an artist banned in Germany and as an exile: "For me it does not matter whether I work in the United States or in Europe."[1] This assertion of the artist's independence from his surroundings and from contemporary political events is contradicted by his own autobiographical notes, which establish connections between his life and political events: "1941:... After Pearl Harbor, short-lived marriage to Miss Peggy Guggenheim.... 1945:... On the day of the collapse of the Third Reich (May 8), opening of an exhibition at the Julien Levy Gallery. No customers, no sales."[2] In fact, Ernst often complained about the poor response to his work in the United States and about his own awkward situation as a political emigré.

Ernst's autobiographical notes are not to be taken all that literally, but it is true that his situation was more difficult than those of the other surrealists. After America's entry into the war in December 1941 he was declared an enemy alien, but he had already experienced problems with immigration officials and had been briefly arrested on his arrival in New York (see fig. 134). Moreover, he had no well-established dealer, such as Pierre Matisse or Curt Valentin, to support him, and by separating from Guggenheim in 1943, he cut himself off from Art of This Century, New York's leading museum-gallery of the avant-garde. And the reception of his work in the 1940s was not all positive, by any means. Clement Greenberg dismissed it as representational and therefore academic, likening his landscapes to picture postcards.[3] Though sometimes hailed in the popular press as "strong, powerful, confident, dramatic,"[4] his work was also described—in terms familiar to him from Nazi Germany—as "perverse, unhealthy, abnormal."[5]

In his writings Ernst never resolved the obvious contradiction between his demand for

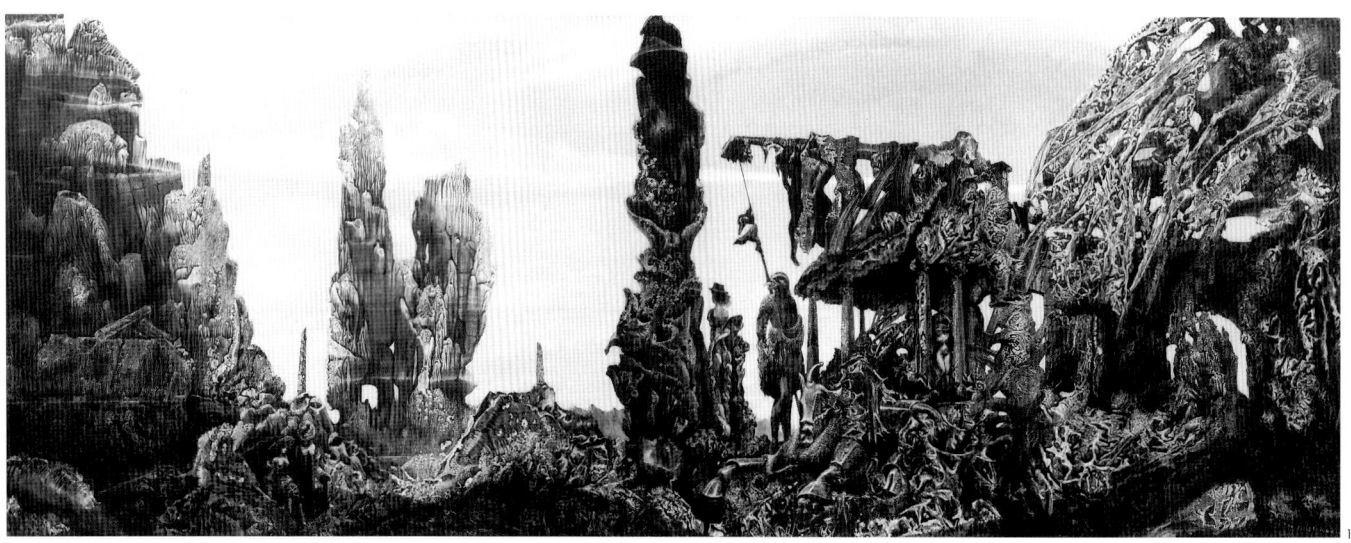

135

134
Max Ernst arrested upon his arrival in New York, July 1941.

135
Max Ernst; *Europe after the Rain II*, 1940–42; oil on canvas; 21½ x 58⅛ in. (54.8 x 147.8 cm); Wadsworth Atheneum, Hartford, The Ella Gallup Sumner and Mary Catlin Sumner Collection Fund.

136
Max Ernst, *The Cocktail Drinker*, 1945 (cat. no. 40).

137
Max Ernst sipping champagne with Pat Sanchez, daughter of a wealthy Cuban sugar planter, in a photograph from an unidentified newspaper.

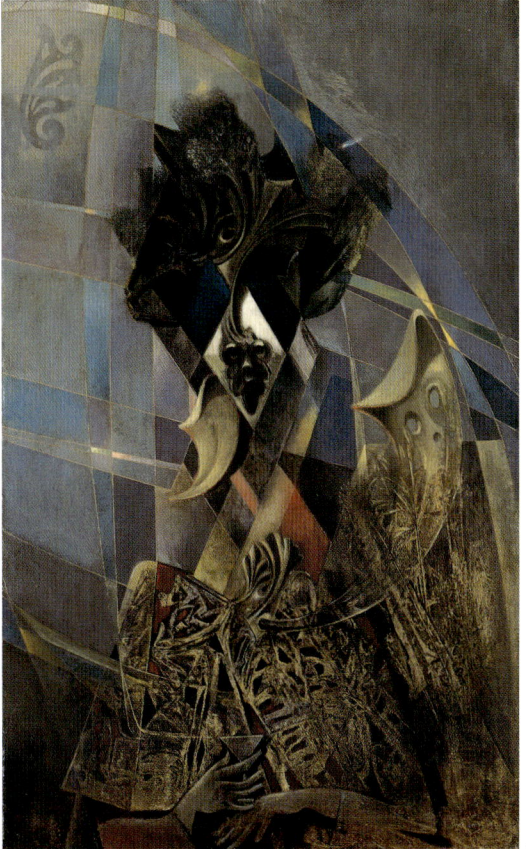

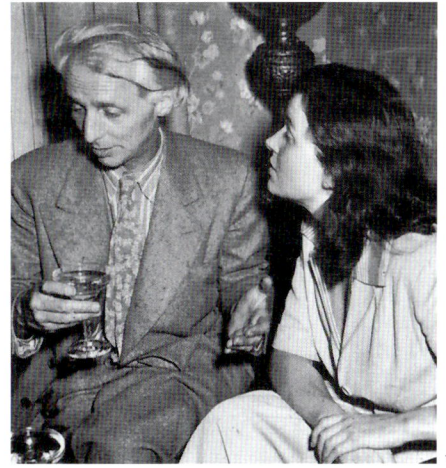

artistic autonomy and the determining effect of social context. He avoided any reference to National Socialism[6] or to his own political position. The American critics, too, did their best to play down the contemporary relevance of Ernst's work. For instance, *Europe after the Rain II* (1940–42; fig. 135), which has gone down in art history as a horrific vision of the destruction of Europe,[7] was interpreted by Rosamund Frost as "the most optimistic commentary on destruction we have seen yet."[8]

When Ernst arrived in New York in 1941, he was received as one of the most celebrated and distinguished representatives of the surrealist movement. His marriage to Peggy Guggenheim further intensified public interest in him as a personality. The fifty-year-old Ernst was best known to the American public through the exhibitions *Newer Super-Realism* (Wadsworth Atheneum, Hartford, 1931) and *Fantastic Art, Dada, Surrealism* (Museum of Modern Art, New York, 1936–37). The first full year of his American exile, 1942, can be regarded as the most active, public portion of his career there. He contributed works to all of the surrealists' major group exhibitions,[9] and a number of solo exhibitions of his work were held. *View* magazine, which was close to the surrealist movement, devoted a special issue to him in April. Together with André Breton, Marcel Duchamp, and David Hare, he founded the magazine *VVV*, which became the forum of surrealism in American exile. In the three remaining years of World War II, Ernst's public profile was markedly lower, with just one individual show each year.[10] Whether voluntarily or not, he had clearly withdrawn from America's public art world.

To a certain degree Ernst's experiences mirror those of the surrealists as a group. After their arrival in New York the surrealists attempted to continue their collective activities and to establish an artistic milieu that resembled that of Paris. One significant reason for their failure to do so was New York's completely different social structure. The city did not offer meeting places (such as cafés or bars) that were conducive to spontaneous gatherings. As Ernst recalled: "During my first months in New York there were many Paris painters here. At first the surrealist group seemed to have real strength; but little by little they began to break up. It was hard to see each other in New York. The café was lacking."[11]

In many of his paintings from this period Ernst provides allusions that cast light on his

max ernst

138
Max Ernst, *Euclid*, 1945 (cat. no. 41).

139
Max Ernst, *Day and Night*, 1941–42; oil on canvas; 44⅛ x 57½ in. (112 x 146 cm); The Menil Collection, Houston.

140
Max Ernst; *Totem and Taboo*, 1941–42; oil on canvas; 28⅜ x 36¼ in. (72 x 92 cm); Staatsgalerie moderner Kunst, Munich; on loan from the Theo Wormland-Stiftung.

141
Max Ernst, *The Eye of Silence*, 1943–44 (cat. no. 37).

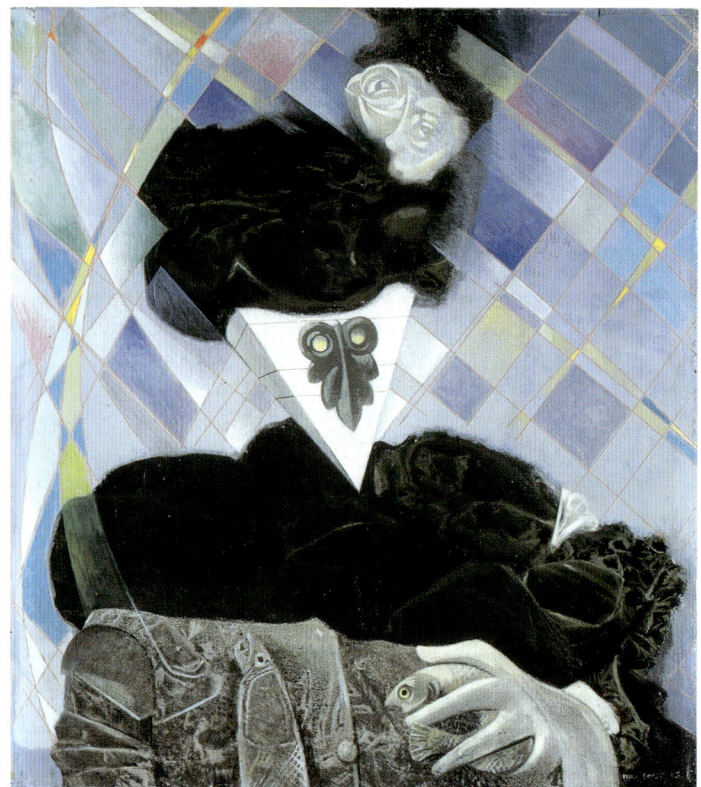

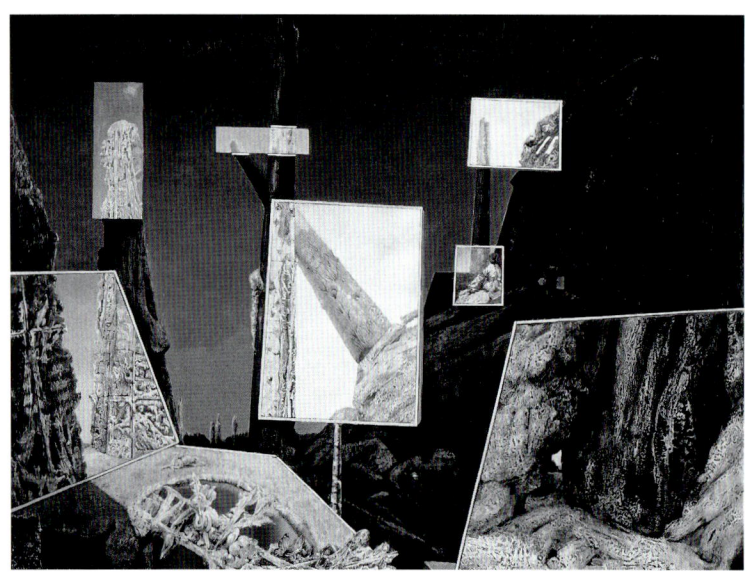

situation as a refugee, an exile, and an alien. *Vox Angelica* (1943) includes a blue rectangular section on which the drip technique has been used to trace a network of parallel lines, like a lattice or a fence. Since the adjacent yellow compartments to the left and right contain identifiable images of the Eiffel Tower and the Empire State Building, Ernst is clearly alluding to his own detention in a succession of concentration camps in France and his escape to America. Again, in *Napoleon in the Wilderness* (1941; fig. 1, cat. no. 33) the female figure holding a saxophone-like object has been seen as a reference to American jazz. Ernst's response to American popular music is more evident in *Day and Night* (1941–42; fig. 139), whose title echoes that of a famous song ("Night and Day") written by Cole Porter, whom Ernst knew. In a self-portrait painted in 1945 (fig. 136, cat. no. 40), Ernst shows himself as a "cocktail drinker"— an allusion to his brief high-society period during his marriage to Guggenheim, as illustrated in a press photograph of the time (fig. 137).

Central to the pictorial language of Ernst's work of the exile period is the decalcomania technique, which he and Hans Bellmer first tried out at Les Milles internment camp in France.[12] *Napoleon in the Wilderness, Day and Night, Totem and Taboo* (1941–42; fig. 140), *Europe after the Rain II, The Eye of Silence* (1943–44; fig. 141, cat. no. 37), and related works all incorporate this technique or imitate it by means of brushwork. Ernst began some of them (including *Europe after the Rain* and *Totem and Taboo*) before he left France. On his arrival in the United States he was thus primarily interested in carrying on with work in progress, and this in itself was an assertion of his autonomy.

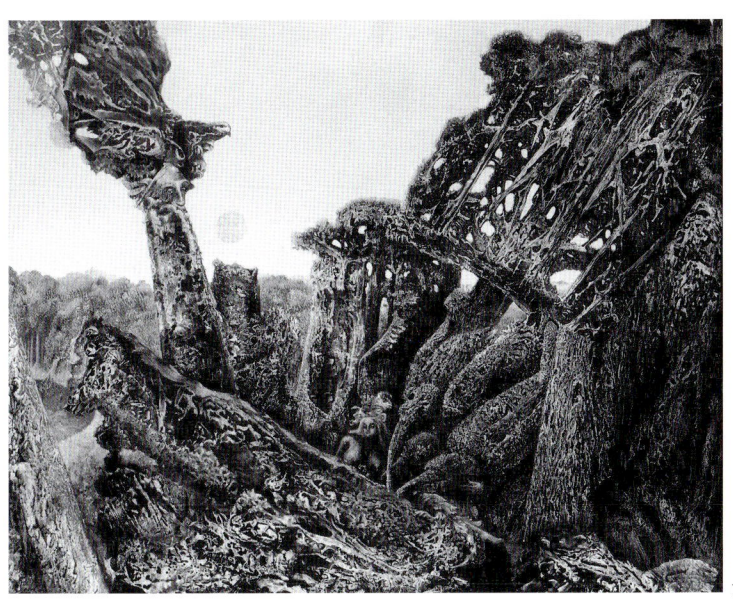

140

Many of the works just mentioned—above all, *Europe after the Rain*—allude to the destruction of Europe. It is noteworthy that in this work, as in many of the other decalcomanias, almost all the human beings shown are women. Depicted alone or in groups, these figures are visualized as dreamy, gentle, sexually appealing, or unreal apparitions—in stark contrast to the man-ravaged landscape. In *Europe after the Rain* we see an androgynous birdman (Ernst) and also a woman, who walks away from us and from the canopy that has collapsed and buried Europa's bull. *Napoleon in the Wilderness* is dominated by the vertical form of a huge, half-clad woman, who is almost twice the size

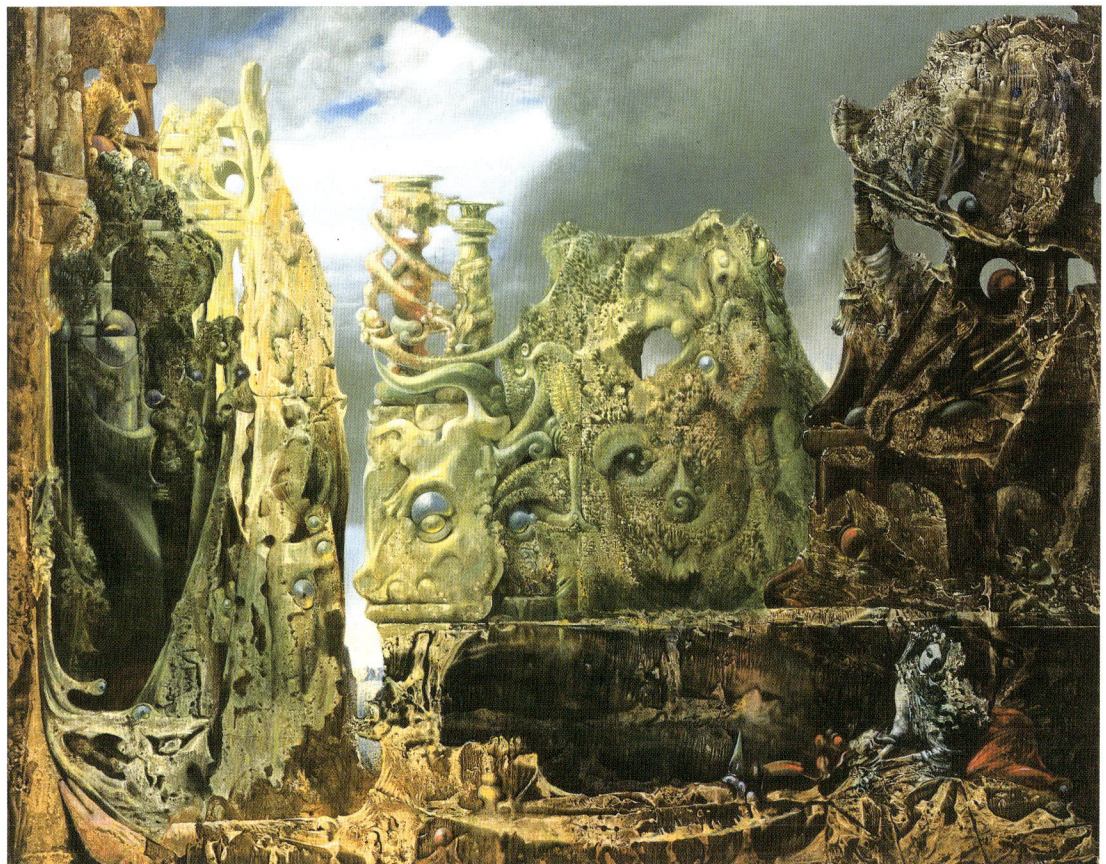

141

142
Max Ernst, *Stolen Mirror*, 1941 (cat. no. 34).

143
Max Ernst; *The Barbarians*, 1937; oil on cardboard; 9½ x 13 in. (24 x 33 cm); The Jacques and Natasha Gelman Collection.

144
Max Ernst, *Painting for Young People*, 1943 (cat. no. 35).

145
Max Ernst, *Painting for Young People*, 1943 (cat. no. 36).

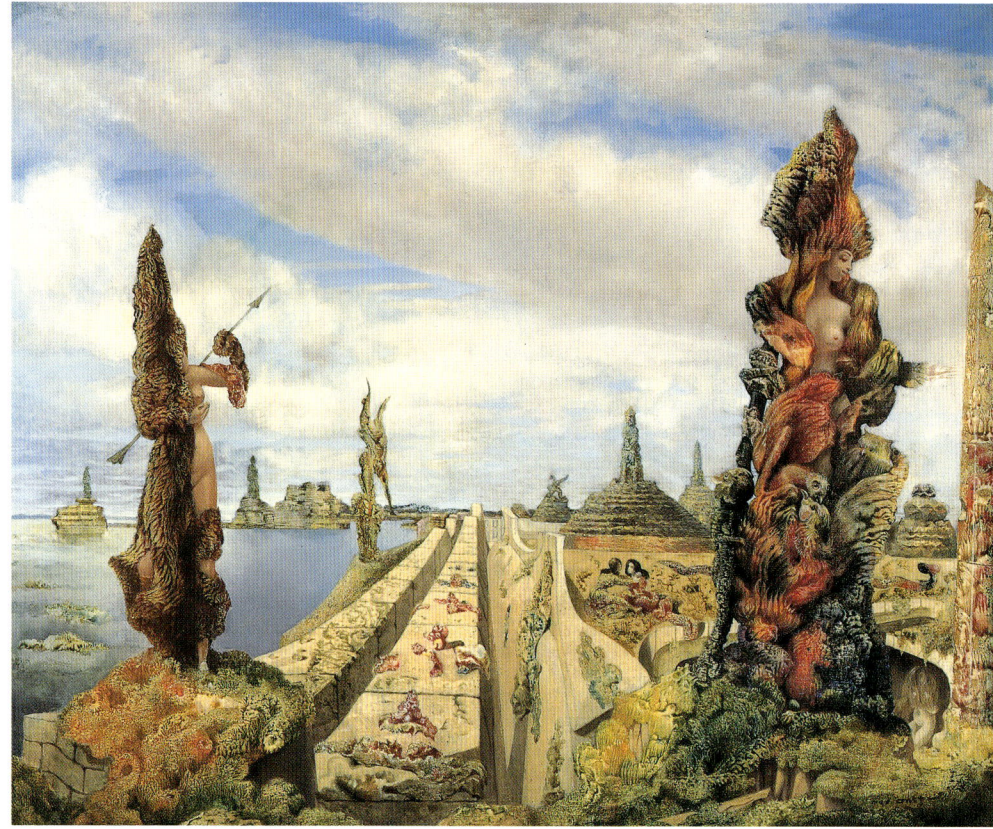

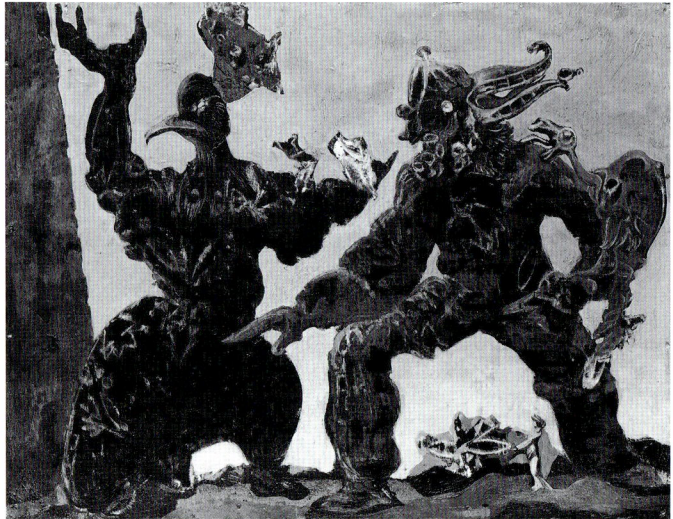

of the birdman (Napoleon or Ernst himself); in *Stolen Mirror* (fig. 142, cat. no. 34), also of 1941, a pair of women, similar to the one in *Napoleon in the Wilderness,* stand in the right and left foreground and lead the viewer into a new, exotic-looking environment. In contrast, in *The Eye of Silence* Ernst depicts a dreaming, innocent-looking woman on a rocklike object, and in *Totem and Taboo* the torso of a blonde woman also suggests a gentler feminine ideal. Thus, Ernst presents two opposing images of women. On the one hand, he associates them with the traditionally male privilege of leadership; on the other, he highlights the conventional idea of women as the "gentle" sex, a quality that he apparently deems necessary for the leaders of a new society. In both depictions he implies that the female sex will create a new social order. The call for matriarchy also became explicit in the writings of Breton's American period; in 1945 he wrote that "the time should come to assert the ideas of woman at the expense of those of man, the bankruptcy of which is today so tumultuously complete."[13]

In his European paintings of the 1930s Ernst often concentrated wholly on violence and destruction, as in *The Barbarians* (1937; fig. 143). In these mostly American works of the 1940s, however, while still showing Europe in ruins, he goes beyond this to point to a society of the future. That society is presented from a very masculine perspective and is seen not in realistic terms—since the women who will presumably form it are depicted as unreal beings—but as a new utopia. This shows, if nothing else, that Ernst's physical remoteness from the German dictatorship and the European war led to a change of theme.

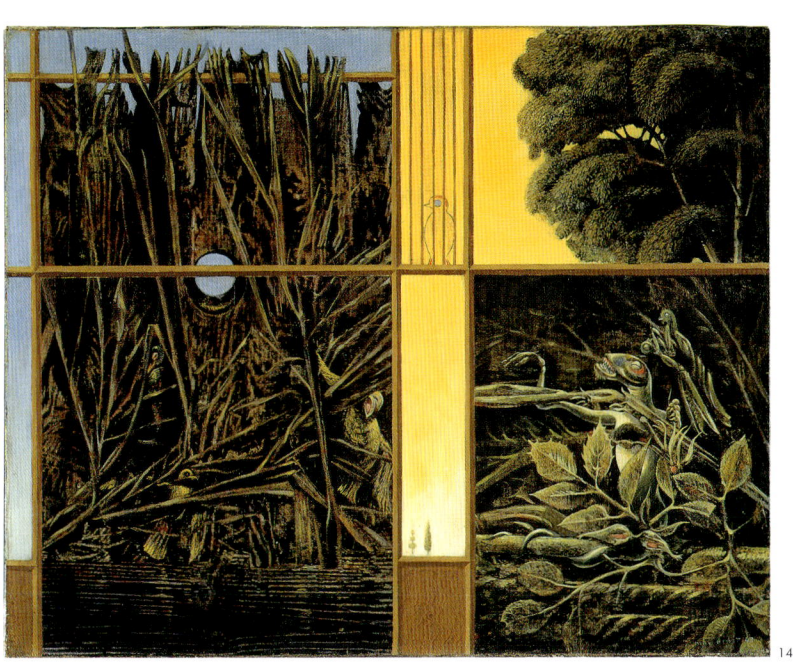

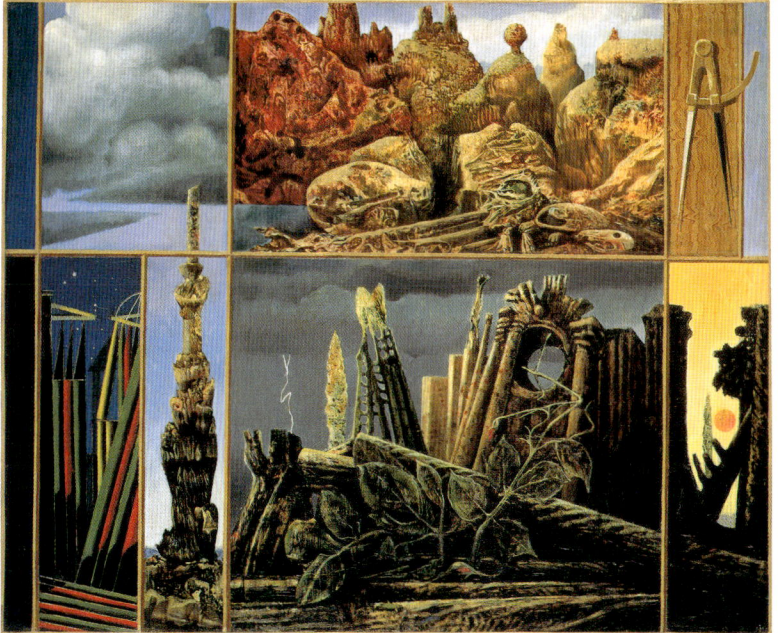

The decalcomania technique generates a visual experience that resists any single interpretation because the landscapes constantly change as the viewer looks at them. The stalactite and stalagmite forms assume new meanings that are not objectifiable. As a contemporary observer pointed out, "[Ernst] specializes in rocks and trees which crawl with half-human forms, so numerous and strange that their very precision makes them hard to see."[14]

In these works, then, Ernst is calling into question the integrity of our visual perception—and doing so more radically than in his collages and frottages. The collages inaugurated a discourse involving various methods of perception; the ambiguous, multilevel connections between the artwork and experiential reality contradict the proclaimed self-referentiality of modernism.[15] The objectively oriented decalcomanias, with their active forms, go beyond this by forcibly manipulating visual experience. First, the forms constantly change, baffling the viewer; second, the objects in the landscapes enforce direct associations with danger, destruction, and visionary experience.[16] This is most evident in *The Eye of Silence*. The title of this fantastic scene incorporating bits of architectural decor and pools of water prompts us to discern eye forms, which pose the question of the relationship between blindness, the visual, and the visionary.

In other paintings, too, Ernst pursues a cultural critique that undermines rationality by disrupting unitary forms of perception. In *Day and Night* (begun before he left France) he spotlights rectangular patches of a decalcomania landscape as pictures in their own right within that very same landscape. He thus presents us with a multiple picture plane that ignores

max ernst 161

146

Max Ernst; *Surrealism and Painting*, 1942; oil on canvas; 77 x 92 in. (195.6 x 233.7 cm); The Menil Collection, Houston.

147

Max Ernst, *An Anxious Friend*, 1944 (cat. no. 38).

148

Max Ernst, *Moonmad*, 1944 (cat. no. 39).

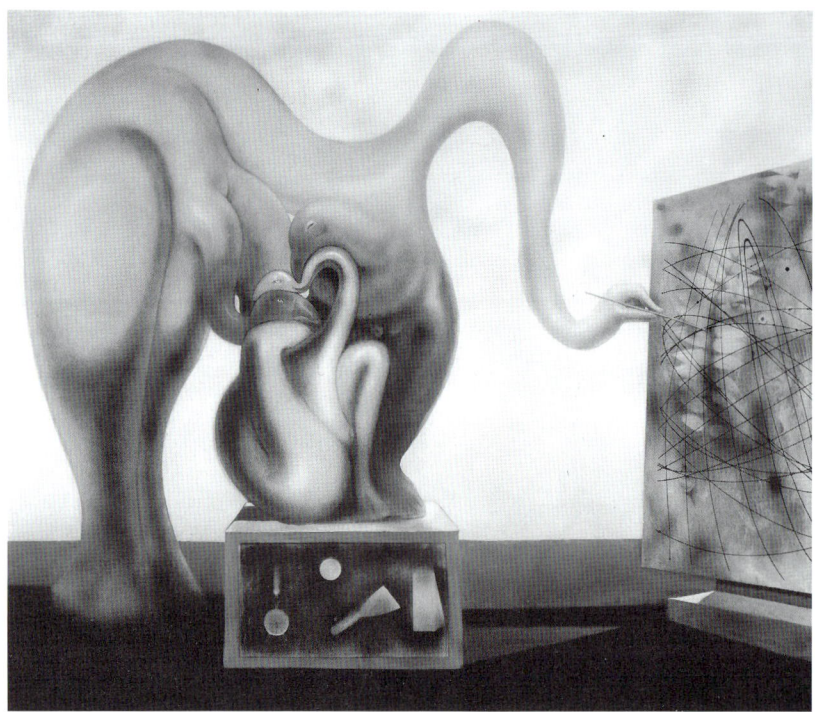

experiential reality, combining disjointed pieces into multiple layers of meaning. In the two versions of *Painting for Young People* (figs. 144–45, cat. nos. 35–36) and *Vox Angelica,* all of 1943,[17] the pictorial field is subdivided by a grid pattern. The surface is broken down into discrete rectangles of assorted sizes, within which Ernst quotes his own paintings—the forests of the 1930s; the menacing landscapes of the 1940s; the experiments with frottage, grattage, and oscillation[18]—and offers autobiographical allusions. Randomly combined, these isolated motifs can be read as a reflection on his previous work and as a quest for an artistic standpoint.

Persecuted and banned by the National Socialists and faced with a disappointing reception in the United States, Ernst withdrew in his American exile to an individualistic, private position. *Surrealism and Painting* (1942; fig. 146) can be perceived as a paradigmatic representation of his exile identity. Ernst portrays himself as a maternal, birdlike figure that appears to enclose smaller figures of birds. The figures seem locked in an embrace that shuts out external reality. Here Ernst underscores the theme of privacy. In his other works he sought to maintain the modernist self-image of the artist as independent of his surroundings, responding to contemporary events with autobiographical allusions and using his involuntary exile to sum up his own work as an artist. In contrast to André Masson, who commented directly on political events in works such as *Oradour* (1944; fig. 152, cat. no. 106), Ernst reacted indirectly. His response to the specific historical situation was a utopian one; by working with forcibly manipulated or dissociated visual perceptions, he presented a generalized critique of civilization as he knew it.

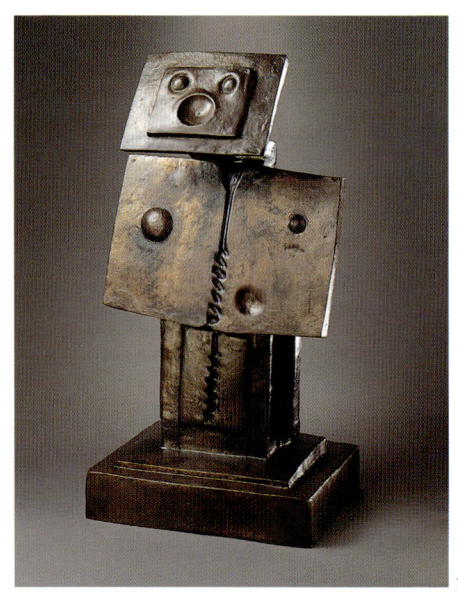

162 eckmann

Notes

1 Quoted in James Johnson Sweeney, ed., "Eleven Europeans in America," *Bulletin of the Museum of Modern Art* 13, no. 4–5 (1946): 16. Ernst, who had been living in Paris since 1922, was pilloried in the Nazis' 1937 exhibition *Entartete Kunst* (Degenerate art), which included two of his works (see Stephanie Barron et al., *"Degenerate Art": The Fate of the Avant-Garde in Nazi Germany*, exh. cat. [Los Angeles: Los Angeles County Museum of Art, 1991], 232). After being held in a number of internment camps in southern France as an enemy alien, he escaped to New York in 1941 with the aid of the Emergency Rescue Committee. Traveling with Peggy Guggenheim, he reached New York on July 14.

2 Werner Spies, ed., *Max Ernst: Retrospektive*, exh. cat. (Munich: Prestel, 1979), 168, 174.

3 Clement Greenberg, "Surrealist Painting," pts. 1, 2, *Nation*, 12 and 19 August 1944, 192ff., 219–20.

4 For example, *Chicago Daily Tribune*, 23 May 1942, 17.

5 *Chicago Sunday Tribune*, 31 May 1942, 4.

6 By contrast, in Paris in the 1930s Ernst adopted an antifascist position; see Jutta Held, "Die Avantgarde in Frankreich in den dreißiger Jahren," in *Kunst und Kunstkritik der dreißiger Jahre*, ed. Maria Rüger (Dresden: Verlag der Kunst, 1990), 37–38.

7 See, for example, Ulrich Bischoff, *Max Ernst, 1891–1976: Jenseits der Malerei* (Cologne: Taschen, 1987), 66.

8 Rosamund Frost, "First Fruits of Exile: What Recent Emigré Artists Have Done in America," *Art News* 41 (March 1942): 23–32.

9 *Artists in Exile*, Pierre Matisse Gallery; *First Papers of Surrealism*, Whitelaw Reid mansion (Coordinating Council of French Relief Societies), New York; and Art of This Century, New York.

10 At the Julien Levy Gallery, New York, in 1943 and 1944; at the Caresse Crosby Gallery, Washington, D.C., in 1945.

11 Quoted in Sweeney, ed., "Eleven Europeans in America," 18.

12 In the decalcomania technique, first used by Oscar Dominguez in 1935, a thin layer of paint is applied to a sheet of paper or other flat surface and then transferred to a canvas. This results in uneven areas of color, which initially suggest stalagmites or stalactites but which, after prolonged viewing, appear to take on the form of animals, human beings, and architectural elements. The art historical literature characterized this effect as metamorphosis. See Günter Metken, "Europa nach dem Regen—Max Ernsts Dekalkomanien und die Tropfsteinhöhlen in Südfrankreich," *Städeljahrbuch* 5 (1975): 287ff.

13 André Breton, in Roszika Parker and Griselda Pollock, *Old Mistresses: Women, Art, and Ideology* (New York: Pantheon Books, 1981), 138; cited here from David Batchelor, Briony Fer, and Paul Wood, *Realism, Rationalism, Surrealism: Art between the Wars* (New Haven and London: Yale University Press, 1993), 171.

14 Alice Bradley Davey, *Chicago Sun*, 31 May 1942.

15 Rosalind Krauss, *The Originality of the Avant-Garde and Other Modernist Myths* (Cambridge and London: MIT Press, 1985), esp. 33ff.

16 See also Martin Jay, *Downcast Eyes: The Denigration of Vision in Twentieth-Century French Thought* (Berkeley, Los Angeles, and London: University of California Press, 1993), esp. 211, 237, 247–48.

17 David Hopkins, "Hermetic and Philosophical Themes in Max Ernst's 'Vox Angelica' and Related Works," *Burlington Magazine* 134 (November 1992): 716–23, esp. 720.

18 In the programmatic image *Surrealism and Painting* (fig. 146) Ernst depicts himself by using the technique of "oscillation" (i.e., drip painting), which had an impact on younger American painters, notably Jackson Pollock.

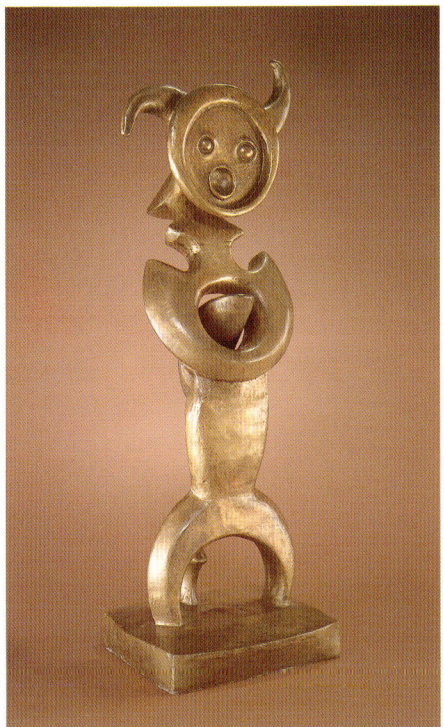

148

andré masson in connecticut, 1941–45

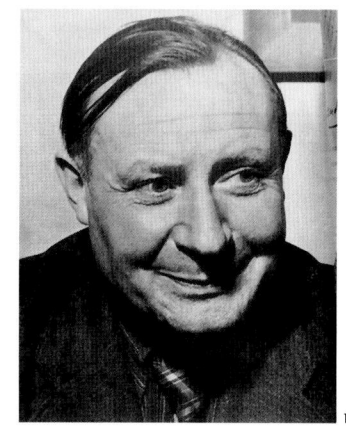
149

1896	born in France (Balagny-sur-Thérain)
1941	immigrates to the U.S. (New York; New Preston, Conn.)
1945	returns to France (Paris)
1987	dies in Paris

André Masson took a long time to decide to go into exile in the United States, even though the undisguised violence and sexuality of his painting, his connections with surrealism and communism, and the Jewish ancestry of his wife, Rose, meant that his family was under imminent threat of Gestapo persecution. As late as the end of 1940 Daniel-Henry Kahnweiler wrote Masson's American patron Saidie A. May (who had offered to pay his passage) that he was not sure Masson really wanted to go to America.[1] The Massons left Europe at the end of March 1941, more than eight months after the German occupation of northern France. They reached New York on May 29, and by the following September Masson had found a house in New Preston, Connecticut, which became his permanent base in the United States. In America, as in France (at Lyons-la-Forêt), Masson preferred rural life to the big city.

Masson in exile not only was highly productive[2] but also made numerous public appearances, so that the contemporary American press image of him as a recluse was only partly accurate: "Since May 1941, he has been in this country and now lives in isolation at New Preston, Conn. The fact that he knows no English further safeguards that isolation in that rural New England neighborhood."[3] True, Masson never did learn English, but his life was not at all isolated. On the contrary, he worked tirelessly to make contemporary French art and culture better known. At the opening of his first museum exhibition, at the Baltimore Museum of Art in October 1941, he gave a lecture entitled "Origines du cubisme et du surréalisme" (The origins of cubism and surrealism). In the same year he went to Boston for a conference of the Emergency Rescue Committee. In 1943 and 1944 he was at Mount Holyoke College for the "Pontigny-en-Amérique" meetings, a continuation (1942–44) of the symposia held between 1910 and 1940 at the Cistercian abbey of Pontigny in Burgundy. In 1944 he organized the art section of the meeting, on the theme "art and crisis."[4]

In his theoretical lectures Masson concentrated on expounding his conception of contemporary art and defining his own position, which can be summarized as follows: The painting is an artifact "created" by an artist and is independent of outward, experiential reality; it contributes to a humane culture by giving visual expression to aspects of humanity that are often subconscious and suppressed, such as the elemental instincts of sexuality and violence. While crediting art with a humanistic function, Masson thus avoided adopting a political posture.

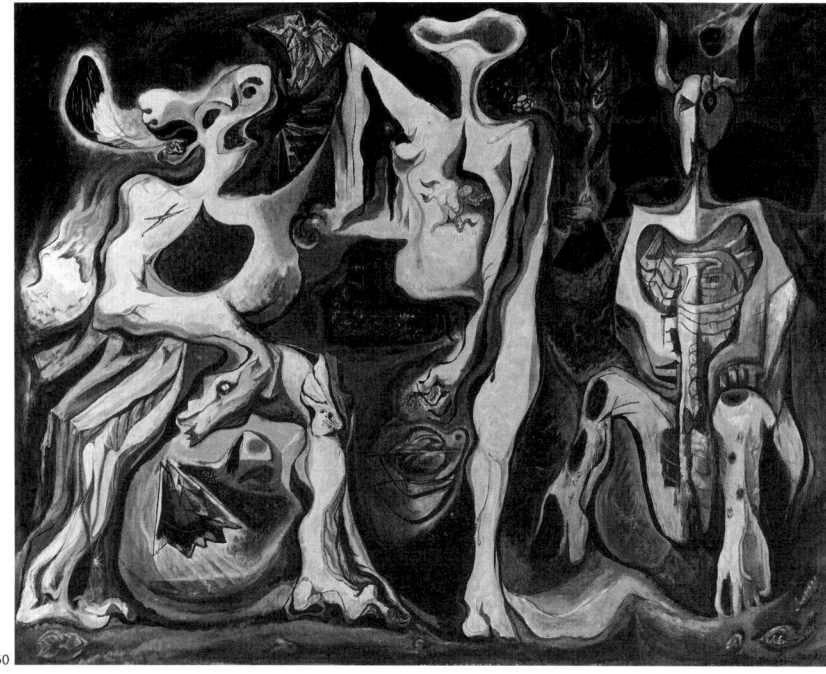
150

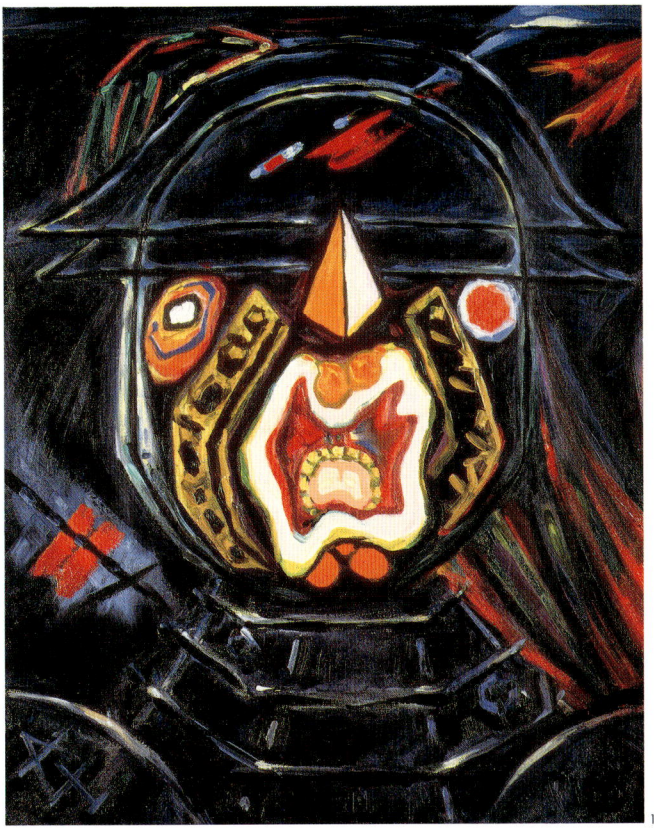
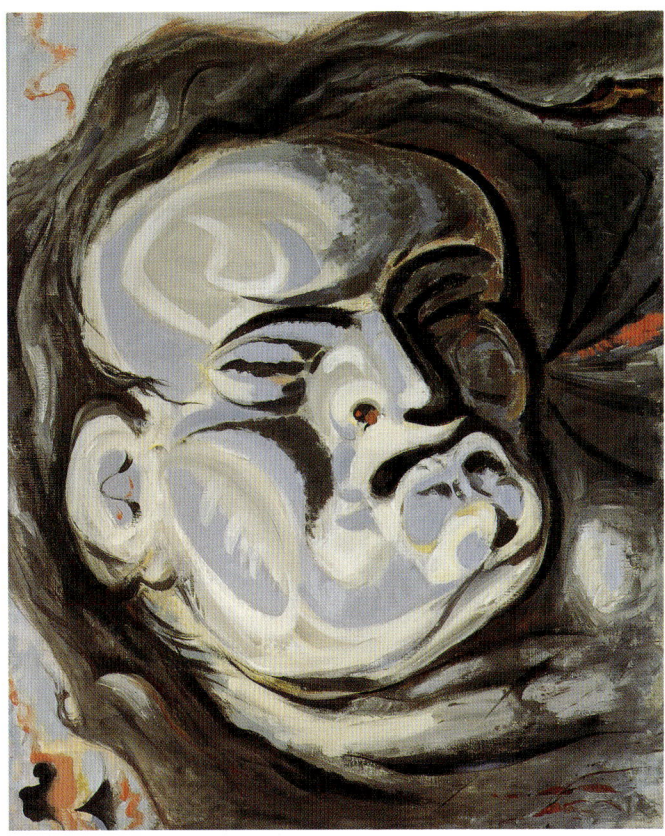

149
André Masson, c. 1942.

150
André Masson; *There Is No Finished World*, 1942; oil on canvas; 53 x 68 in. (134.6 x 172.7 cm); The Baltimore Museum of Art, bequest of Saidie A. May, BMA 1951.333.

151
André Masson, *The German Soldier*, 1941 (cat. no. 100).

152
André Masson, *Oradour*, 1944 (cat. no. 106).

In print, however, Masson did take a position on the cultural policies of dictatorships and the attendant repression of artistic freedom. In "Life and Liberty," published in Australia in 1942, he called upon the artist not to obscure or ignore political realities: "We are living in an extremely disturbed moment of history, and it is not necessary, either, that the painter should conceal the disquietude of his epoch." He went on to condemn the subjugation of the artist by the totalitarian state and the imposition of a state art, but beyond the imperative of freedom of expression he left the choice of themes entirely up to the individual artist.[5] Masson's position was thus an individualistic one; in the name of expressive originality—the quality emphasized in all his theoretical writings and speeches—he resisted any attempt to enlist his work as propaganda for the antifascist cause.

Nevertheless, his American work does reflect his political views. *There Is No Finished World* (1942; fig. 150) can be read as an allusion to the cruelties of the European dictatorships and of Hitler's regime in particular. It cannot, however, be seen exclusively in terms of contemporary events: violence as an extreme, elemental human experience is a principal theme of Masson's work, and this painting contains no direct allusions that might carry the theme further. It belongs, in fact, to the context of the Minotaur myth—the visual evocation of Pasiphaë, Theseus, Daedalus, and the Labyrinth—and to that of violent, erotic imagery in general.[6] A comparable image is the sculpture *Praying Mantis* (1942),[7] an emblematic embodiment of instinctual cruelty with no specific, direct reference to political fact.

There are a number of representational paintings in which Masson depicted the cruelties of war and addressed political resistance. These works, with their overt political motivation, are the only ones in which he worked figuratively; his others are markedly more abstract. *The German Soldier* (1941; fig. 151, cat. no. 100) and *Oradour* (1944; fig. 152, cat. no. 106) are antiwar

andré masson

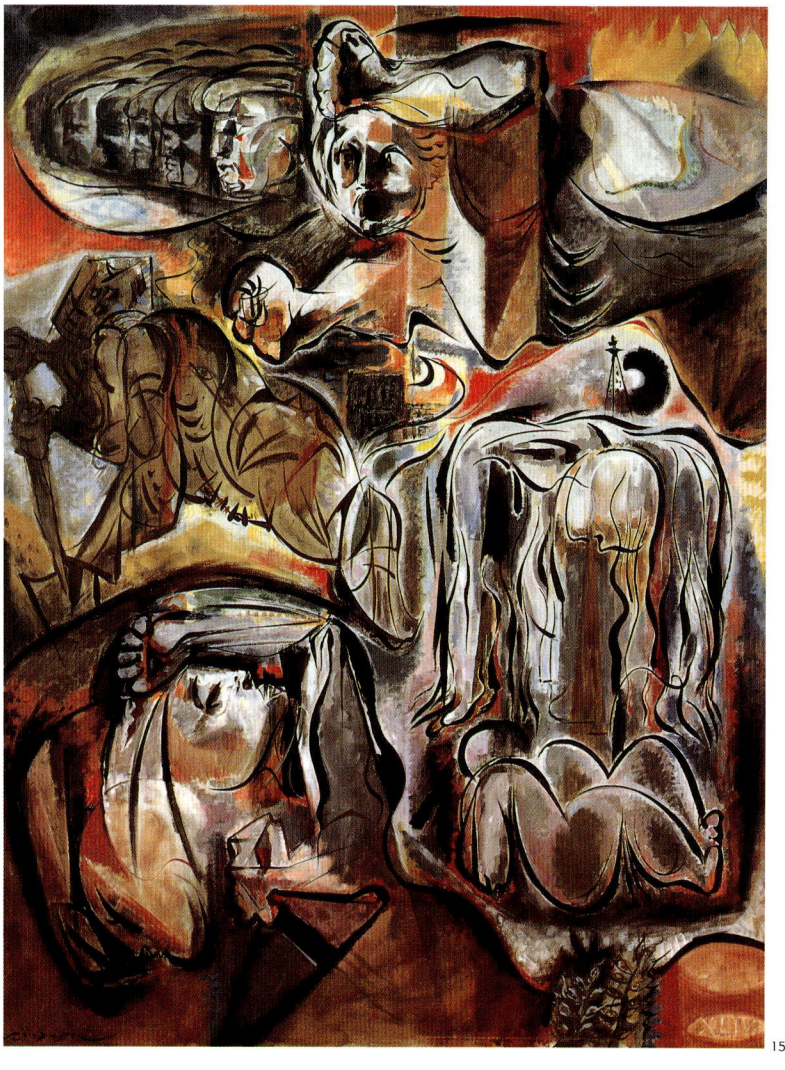

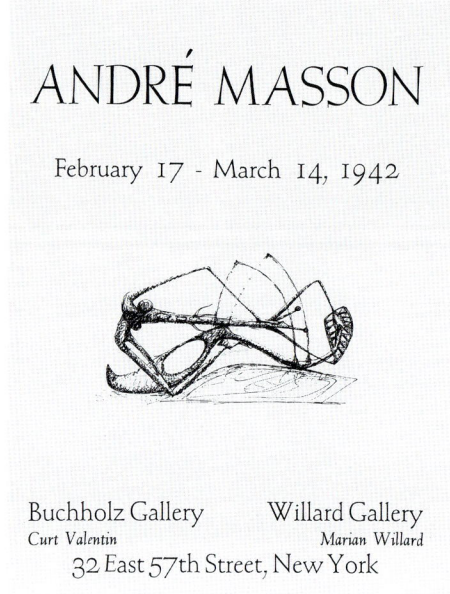

153
André Masson, *The Resistance*, 1944 (cat. no. 107).

154
André Masson, praying mantis design on cover of brochure for the exhibition *André Masson*, Buchholz Gallery and Willard Gallery, New York, 1942.

155
André Masson, *The Seeded Earth*, 1942 (cat. no. 104).

156
André Masson, *The Germ of the Cosmos*, 1942 (cat. no. 102).

paintings featuring barbaric German soldiers. The latter is Masson's response to the destruction of the little town of Oradour-sur-Glane and the massacre of its entire population by the Germans on June 10, 1944—an "act of revenge" against the French Resistance. *The Resistance* (fig. 153, cat. no. 107), also painted in 1944, deals with the same theme. Resistance as such was not an option for Masson in America, and this made him ambivalent toward his own position as an exile. His antiwar paintings and public statements can be seen in part as an alternative form of involvement.

In general the American critics did not like *The Resistance* and the studies for it.[8] Specifically they objected that realism entailed a sacrifice of aesthetic qualities. As Henry McBride wrote, "In the present collection of paintings and drawings he does not get far enough away from the facts for the spectator to revel in the painting as painting."[9]

Before his arrival in the United States, Masson's reputation there rested on two solo exhibitions at the Pierre Matisse Gallery (1933, 1935), plus a number of contributions to thematic shows.[10] Upon Masson's arrival the influential Curt Valentin took over the contract that he had had with Kahnweiler since 1922. The major private collector of his work was May; it was she who donated *There Is No Finished World* to the Baltimore Museum of Art in 1942. After the 1941 museum exhibition in Baltimore, he had solo exhibitions at the Buchholz and Willard (see fig. 154) and Rosenberg Galleries in New York and at the Dwight Art Memorial in South Hadley, Massachusetts, in 1942, 1944, and 1945. He also took part in all of the major group exhibitions of European artists in exile, of surrealists in the United States, and of artists against fascism.[11] From an art-world perspective[12] Masson was therefore one of the European exile artists most in demand, though it must of

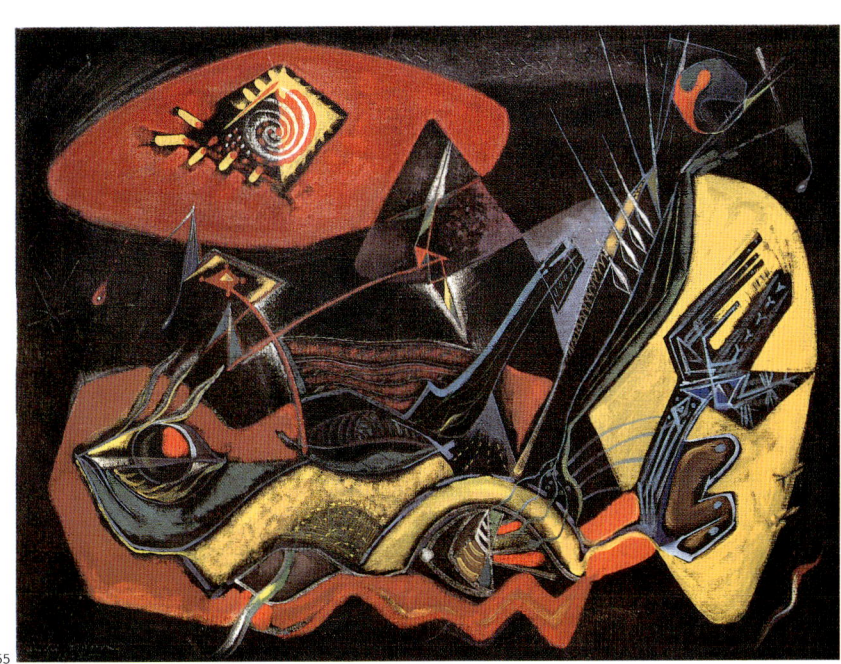

155

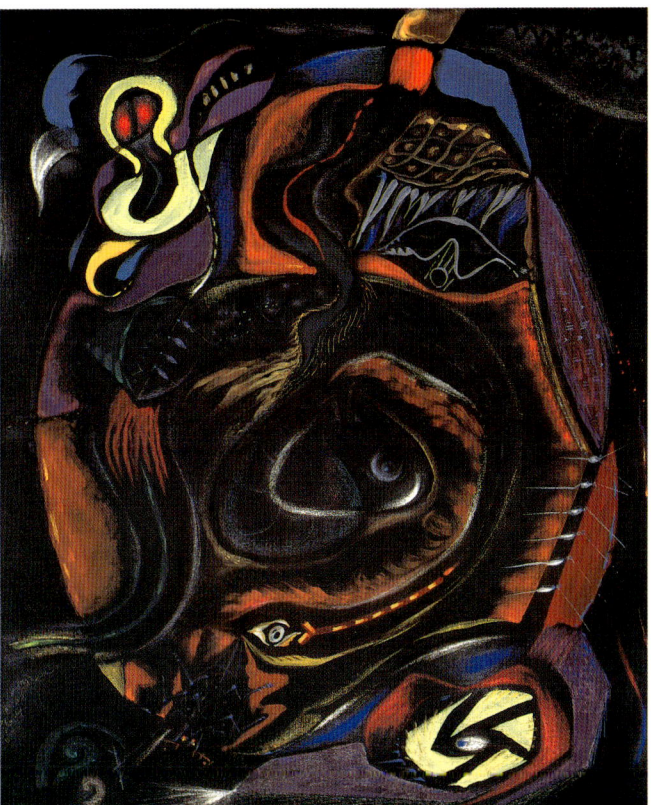

156

course be remembered that he was patronized mainly by the network of European or European-minded dealers, collectors, and curators.

Nevertheless, American press reactions were mostly negative. Emily Genauer, one of the few critics who thought highly of his work, headlined one of her reviews "New Exhibition Honors Transplanted European,"[13] thereby emphasizing his non-American cultural background. Among the few paintings that the American critics liked were the so-called Telluric Landscapes, which can be interpreted as references to the American landscape.[14] Mostly painted in 1942, these tend to be semi-abstract evocations of fragmentary plant and animal forms, mingled with the zoomorphic and anthropomorphic imagery of the Native American cultures of the Northwest Coast. *The Seeded Earth* (fig. 155, cat. no. 104) and *The Germ of the Cosmos* (fig. 156, cat. no. 102) are versions of creation myths, presenting the positive, vitalistic forces of germination and growth; their complementary opposites, destruction and death, complete the telluric concept.

Alongside these paintings indebted to American themes, Masson also worked intensively on the myth of the Minotaur, which had interested him since 1937. This myth—with its themes of irrational forces, violence, and sexuality—was charged with topical relevance in the 1930s and early 1940s by the incalculable menace of authoritarian regimes. In direct—though not readily decipherable—figurative terms, *The Night* (1942; fig. 157, cat. no. 103) and *Pasiphaë* (1943; fig. 158, cat. no. 105) present the sexual act between Pasiphaë and the bull, which led to the birth of the Minotaur, the bull-man.[15]

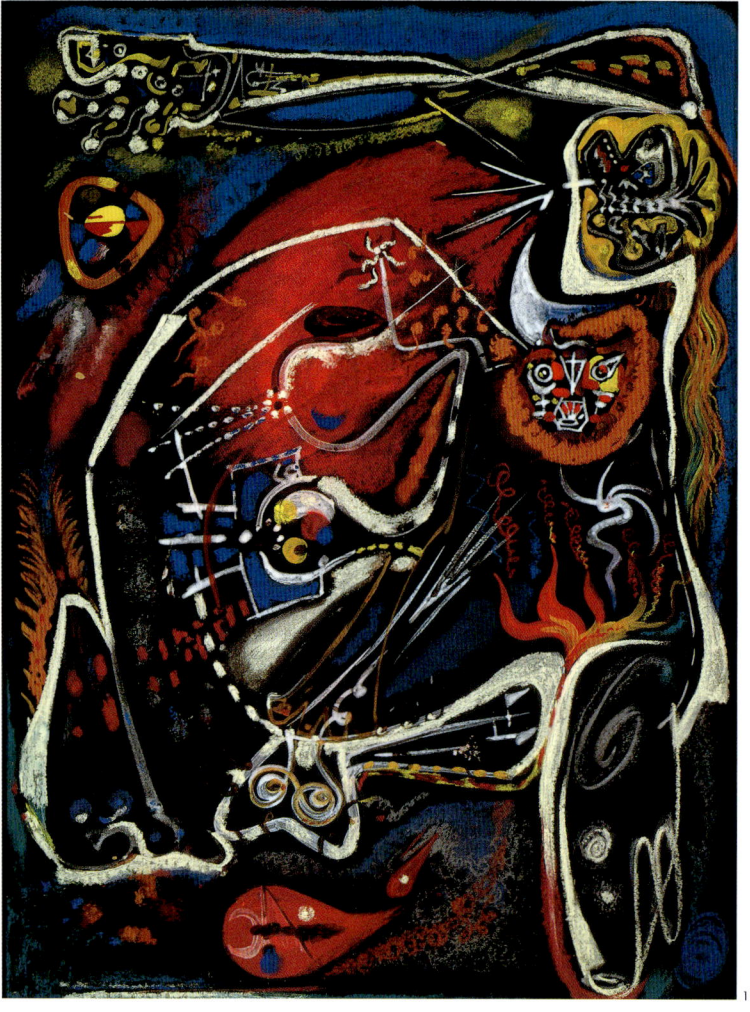

157
André Masson, *The Night*, 1942
(cat. no. 103).

158
André Masson, *Pasiphaë*, 1943
(cat. no. 105).

Among Masson's severest critics were Edward Alden Jewell of the *New York Times* and Clement Greenberg; unlike those critics who condemned his themes (that of the Minotaur, in particular, was an affront to American puritanism), these two concentrated on the formal aspects of his work. Criticizing its abstract qualities, Jewell accused Masson of lacking originality and of using color badly.[16] His caustic tone is echoed in the writing of other critics; for example, the critic of the *Chicago Daily Tribune* wrote, "There are moments in the exhibit when you are under the impression that Walt Disney could make something of Masson." By dismissing Masson's paintings on the grounds that they might have something in common with popular culture, this critic evokes Greenberg's distinction between a self-referential, "pure" advanced art and kitsch.[17]

Greenberg himself focused on different issues in his critique of Masson, however, arguing that surrealism could not be a progressive art movement because of its literary subject matter and its populism. Nevertheless, Masson's paintings based on automatism were among those surrealist works that he found least objectionable. In a review he acknowledged Masson's potential to produce painting of quality, while refusing to acknowledge that he had yet done so: "Masson's failure is in the contemporary grand manner . . . the raging sickness of color, the obtuseness with which he rattles together pigments, design, space—the art nouveau, the hard, machined insensitivity of line in his drawings, and their maladroit literary flourishes."[18]

Greenberg was here following Immanuel Kant, who employed subjective likes and dislikes as valid criteria of art criticism; he comprehensively condemned Masson's work on formal grounds. This antipathy was shared by most other American critics and thus can serve as an index of American artistic taste in the 1940s.

Masson regarded his exile as a transitory phase—as he made clear when, immediately after the surrender of the Third Reich in May 1945, he started making plans for his return to France. In retrospect he described his time in America as a positive experience and refused to use the term *exile* because of its negative connotations: "I chose to leave Europe in order to escape Nazism. But I have never been in exile, for I have always been in sympathy with the world."[19]

Notes

1 Kahnweiler to May, 13 December 1940, Saidie A. May Papers, Baltimore Museum of Art.

2 Between 1941 and 1945—in addition to a very large number of drawings, watercolors, and pastels—he produced more than one hundred paintings, fifty prints, and approximately twelve sculptures. See Doris A. Birmingham, "André Masson in America: The Artist's Achievement in Exile, 1941–1945" (Ph.D. diss., University of Michigan, Ann Arbor, 1976), 40.

3 Henry McBride, *New York Sun*, 20 February 1942.

4 See the Mount Holyoke College Archives.

5 André Masson, "Life and Liberty," *Art in Australia*, 4th ser., no. 5 (March–May 1942): 11.

6 See Lawrence M. Saphire, in *André Masson: Second Surrealist Period, 1937–43*, exh. cat. (New York: Blue Moon Gallery, 1974), 12, 17–18.

7 Like many other surrealists, Masson was particularly fascinated by this insect because the female devours the male after mating.

8 Edward Alden Jewell, *New York Times*, 29 April 1945.

9 Henry McBride, "André Masson's Resistance," *New York Sun*, 28 April 1945.

10 Among these were the following: *Newer Super-Realism*, Wadsworth Atheneum, Hartford, 1931; *Fantastic Art, Dada, Surrealism*, Museum of Modern Art, New York, 1936–37; and *Collection of Saidie A. May*, Baltimore Museum of Art, 1938.

11 Among these were the following: *Artists in Exile*, Pierre Matisse Gallery, New York, 1942; *First Papers of Surrealism*, Whitelaw Reid mansion (Coordinating Council of French Relief Societies), New York, 1942; *Paul Klee, André Masson, and Some Aspects of Ancient and Primitive Sculpture*, Buchholz Gallery, New York, 1943; *War and the Artist*, Pierre Matisse Gallery, 1943; *Europe in America*, Institute of Contemporary Art, Boston, 1943; *Homage to the "Salon d'automne": Salon de la Libération*, Pierre Matisse Gallery, 1944; *European Artists in America*, Whitney Museum of American Art, New York, 1945.

12 The Museum of Modern Art, New York, acquired the painting *Street Singer* (1941) in 1942 and *Leonardo da Vinci and Isabella d'Este* (1942) in 1944.

13 *New York World Telegram*, 28 April 1945.

14 James Johnson Sweeney, ed., "Eleven Europeans in America," *Bulletin of the Museum of Modern Art* 13, no. 4–5 (1946): 3.

15 On the iconography, see Doris A. Birmingham, "Masson's Pasiphae: Eros and Unity of the Cosmos," *Art Bulletin* 49 (June 1987): 279–94.

16 *New York Times*, 22 February 1942.

17 *Chicago Daily Tribune*, 23 May 1942. Greenberg used the term *kitsch* to describe "popular, commercial art and literature with their chromotypes, magazine covers, illustrations, ads, slick and pulp fiction, comics, Tin Pan Alley music, tap dancing, Hollywood movies etc., etc." According to Greenberg, avant-garde art and kitsch, though opposed to each other, can function only in relation to each other and indeed as antithetical elements that control and define each other; see "Avant-Garde and Kitsch" (1939), in Clement Greenberg, *The Collected Essays and Criticism*, ed. John O'Brian, vol. 1, *Perceptions and Judgment, 1939–1944* (Chicago: University of Chicago Press, 1986), esp. 11.

18 Clement Greenberg, *Nation*, 7 March 1942, republished in Greenberg, *Collected Essays and Criticism*, vol. 1, 99.

19 Cleto Polcina, "André Masson by André Masson: An Interview," in *André Masson*, exh. cat. (New York: Arnold Herstand, 1984), unpaginated.

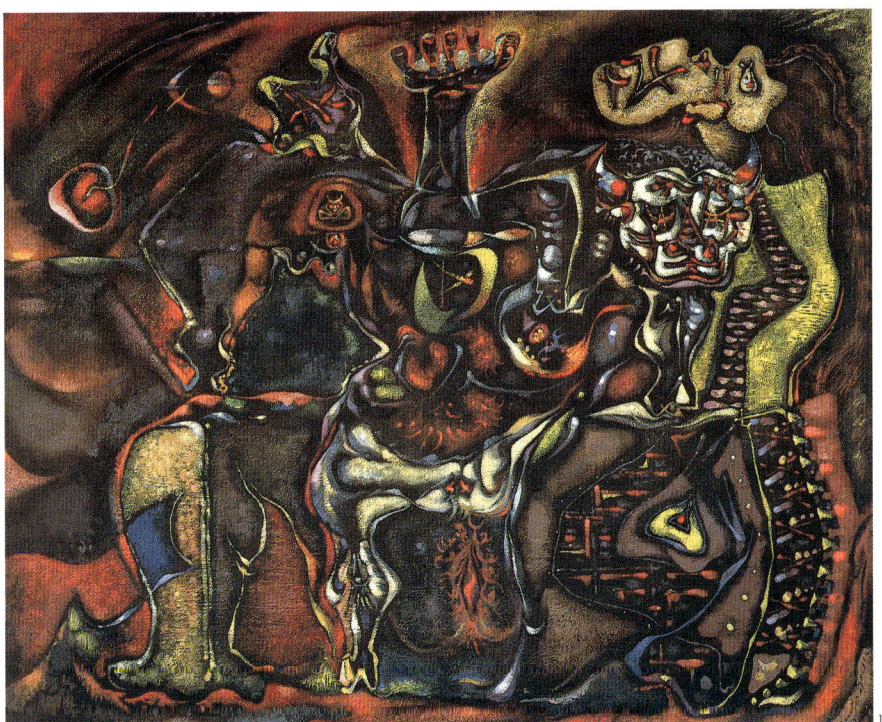

158

yves tanguy in connecticut, 1939–45

1900	born in Paris
1939	immigrates to the U.S. (New York; Woodbury, Conn.)
1955	dies in Woodbury

Even as early as 1934 I had begun to recognize certain fascist symptoms in France—in an outbreak here and a squabble there.... And when I began to see hints of impending trouble in Europe I made up my mind to leave the Old World as early as possible.[1]

Yves Tanguy arrived in the New World on November 1, 1939, shortly after war broke out, with the help of the wealthy American painter Kay Sage, whom he married in 1940.[2] He lived in Greenwich Village in New York in 1939–40 and in the small town of Woodbury, Connecticut, from 1941 onward.

As far as the outward conditions of life were concerned, Tanguy's years in America were his most stable. His marriage made him financially independent for the first time in his career.[3] In terms of public recognition, too, emigration spelled success. In the United States Tanguy was regarded as a well-known contemporary artist, with successful individual and collective exhibitions to his name and important advocates among American dealers and curators.[4] In 1937 Alfred H. Barr Jr. had purchased two paintings of

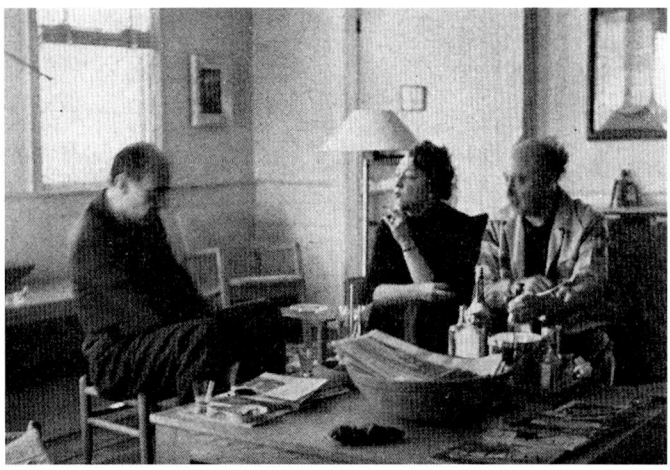

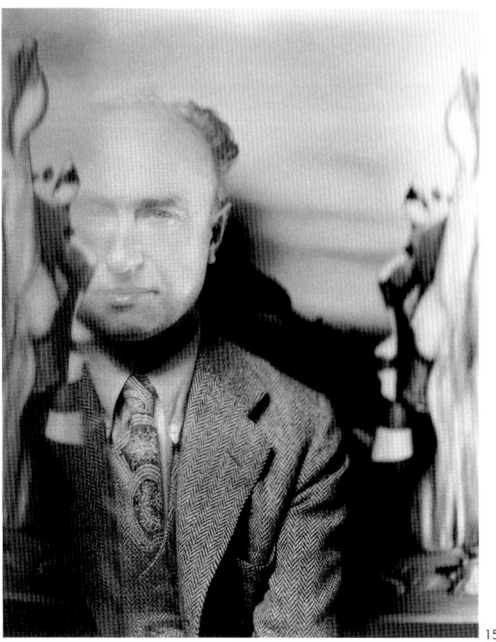

1927, *Mama, Papa Is Wounded* and *Nonessential Lights Off,* for the Museum of Modern Art, and this gave Tanguy a foothold in America's most prestigious modern art institution. In Europe prior to his emigration Tanguy's work had been shown in four solo exhibitions,[5] and he had also participated in a number of surrealist group shows. These exhibitions had established him as an avant-garde figure but had uncovered no market for his work in Europe. To the taciturn Tanguy a move to the United States must therefore have looked promising.

In December 1939, one month after Tanguy's arrival, Pierre Matisse (see fig. 159), his former schoolmate at the Lycée Montaigne in Paris, put on a solo exhibition of the thirty-nine-year-old surrealist's work, showing ten paintings from American collections. One month later, in January 1940, Tanguy had his first museum exhibition. The Wadsworth Atheneum in Hartford, Connecticut—under its innovative director, A. Everett ("Chick") Austin, who was sympathetic to surrealism—organized a show that traveled later that year to the Arts Club of Chicago and the San Francisco Museum of Art.

This splashy debut helped cement Tanguy's standing in the American art world. From 1942 he had a contract with Matisse, who thenceforth regularly showed his work to the New York public. Between 1939 and 1945 he sold a number of paintings. In 1942 Saidie A. May purchased *The Earth and the Air* (1941; fig. 161, cat. no. 131), which she then donated to the Baltimore

159
Yves Tanguy; photograph by George Platt Lynes.

160
Yves Tanguy and Kay Sage with Pierre Matisse.

161
Yves Tanguy, *The Earth and the Air*, 1941 (cat. no. 131).

162
Yves Tanguy, *Indefinite Divisibility*, 1942 (cat. no. 132).

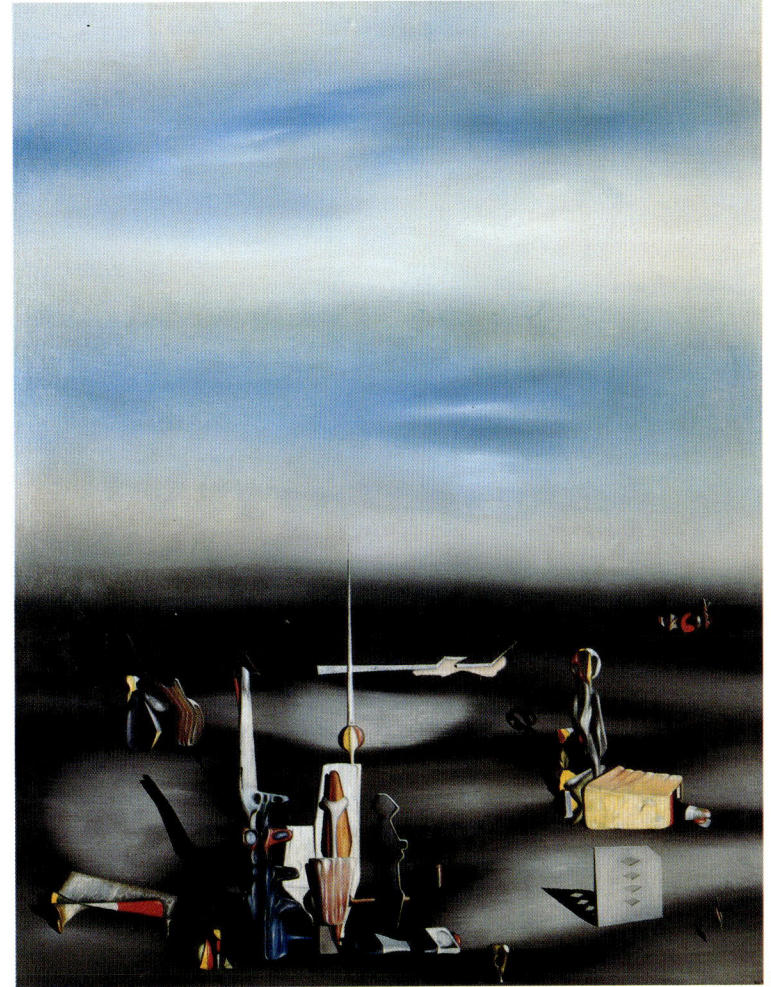

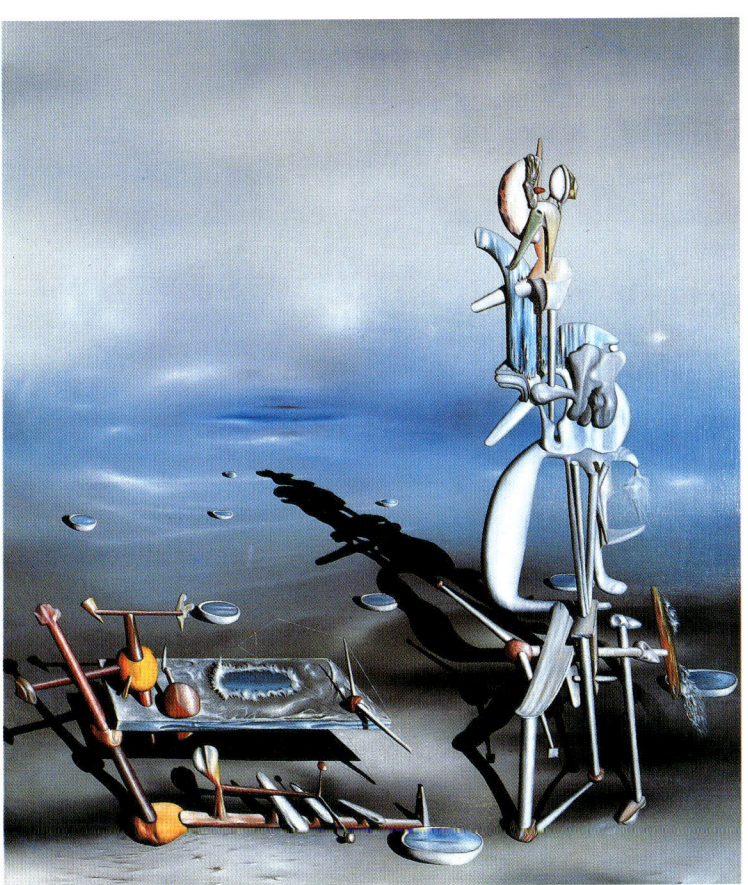

Museum of Art, and in 1945 the Albright Art Gallery in Buffalo, New York, acquired *Indefinite Divisibility* (1942; fig. 162, cat. no. 132). In New York, as in Paris, Tanguy was active in surrealist circles, and he took part in all the major exhibitions of surrealism in exile.⁶

Tanguy received his most extraordinary recognition in May 1942, when the surrealist magazine *View* devoted a whole issue jointly to him and to Pavel Tchelitchev; this also functioned as the catalogue of the Tanguy exhibition at Pierre Matisse (see fig. 163). In this publication Nicolas Calas and André Breton wrote on Tanguy's hermetic landscapes, such as *The Earth and the Air*, which defy a single, rational interpretation. Both related them to the surrealist theme of the subconscious. Calas first drew a connection between Tanguy's unreal landscapes and contemporary reality: "Whatever may be the rational reasons for liking Tanguy, I am convinced that the unconscious ones, fear of death, disillusion provoked by ideological

yves tanguy   **171**

163
Yves Tanguy, cover design for *View*, 2d ser., no. 2 (May 1942).

164
Yves Tanguy, *Slowly toward the North*, 1942 (cat. no. 133).

165
Yves Tanguy, *The Prodigal Son Never Returns II*, 1943 (cat. no. 134).

166
Yves Tanguy, *The Prodigal Son Never Returns III*, 1943 (cat. no. 135).

confusion...force those who do not abandon the struggle to seek for strength in solitude."[7] Thus, Calas did not interpret Tanguy's remote, solitary worlds as escapist, but argued that they afforded "spiritual" sustenance in the face of a reality dominated by dictatorial powers.

Returning to the subject four years later, Calas described Tanguy's paintings as magical icons. He likened the painter's "individual universe" to a kind of post-Christian Golgotha—a place of the skull—and reasserted the works' contemporary function: "His polyhedric constructions...carry us to worlds where we feel...the actuality of dehumanized places."[8]

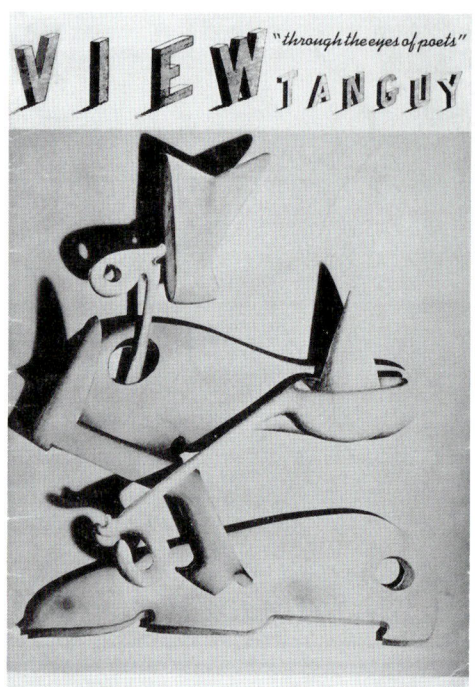

163

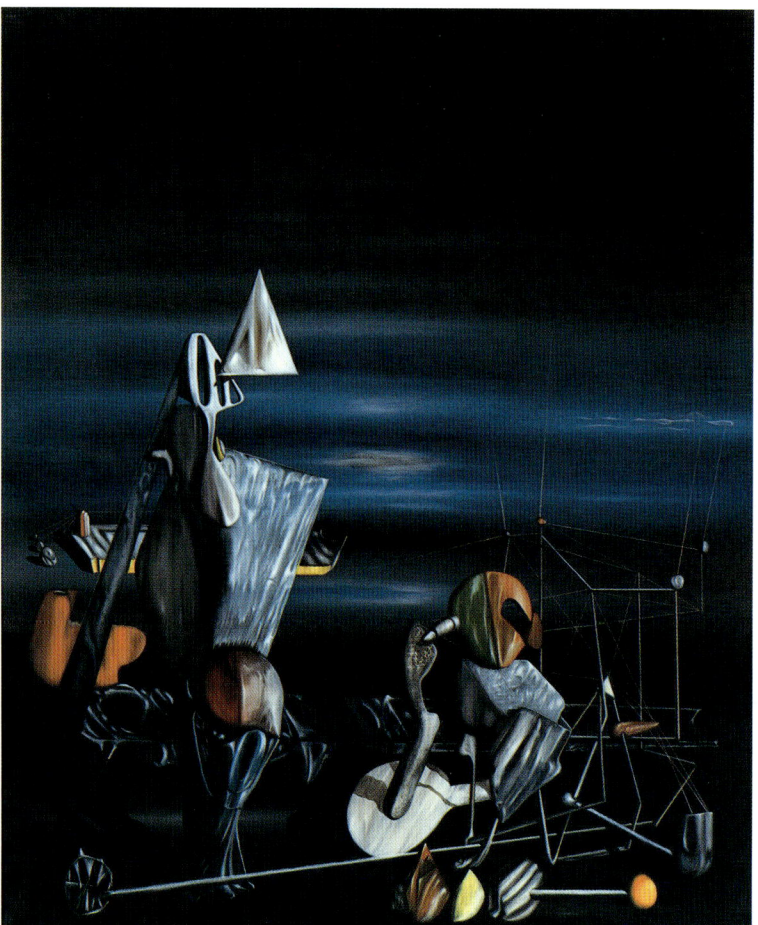

164

Breton, in his 1942 *View* article, described Tanguy's paintings as worlds of total indeterminacy, not subject to any definitive interpretation. He saw them as landscapes of the inner world, revealing the elusive beings, the wraiths, that lurk behind the scenes of life. Their spiritual home, he said, was at Locronan in Brittany and on rue du Château in Paris's fourteenth arrondissement.[9]

Both of these European writers emphasized Tanguy's roots in contemporary European surrealist thinking. While Breton pointed to Tanguy's ties to European geography, Calas brought out the direct connection between the artist's work and contemporary political events, underpinning the topical relevance of surrealism. By contrast, Tanguy's American interpreters tended to concentrate on the formal qualities of the works; without downplaying the surrealist content, they took a more pragmatic line. According to James Johnson Sweeney, the oneiric quality of the paintings was conveyed through a personal and indecipherable system of signs. Avoiding detailed theoretical interpretation *à la* Breton and Calas, he opted for a reading that focused on the outward experience of reality: "For essentially Tanguy's art is an abstract art in the sense that his forms have been stripped of familiar individualizing resemblances to objects in the world of nature."[10] James

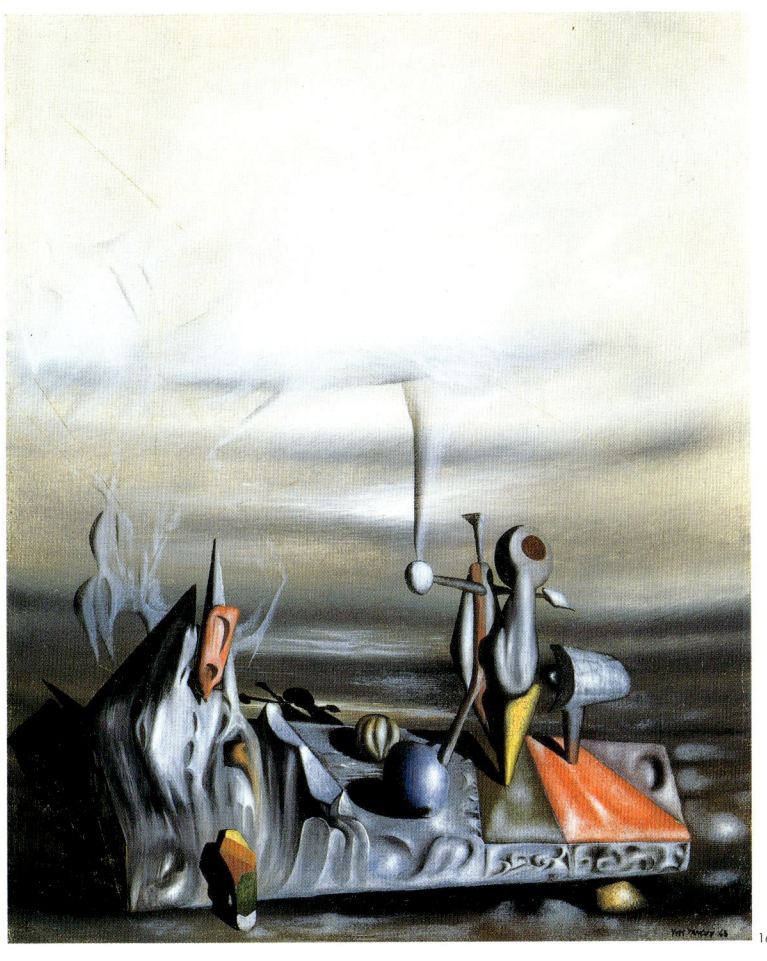

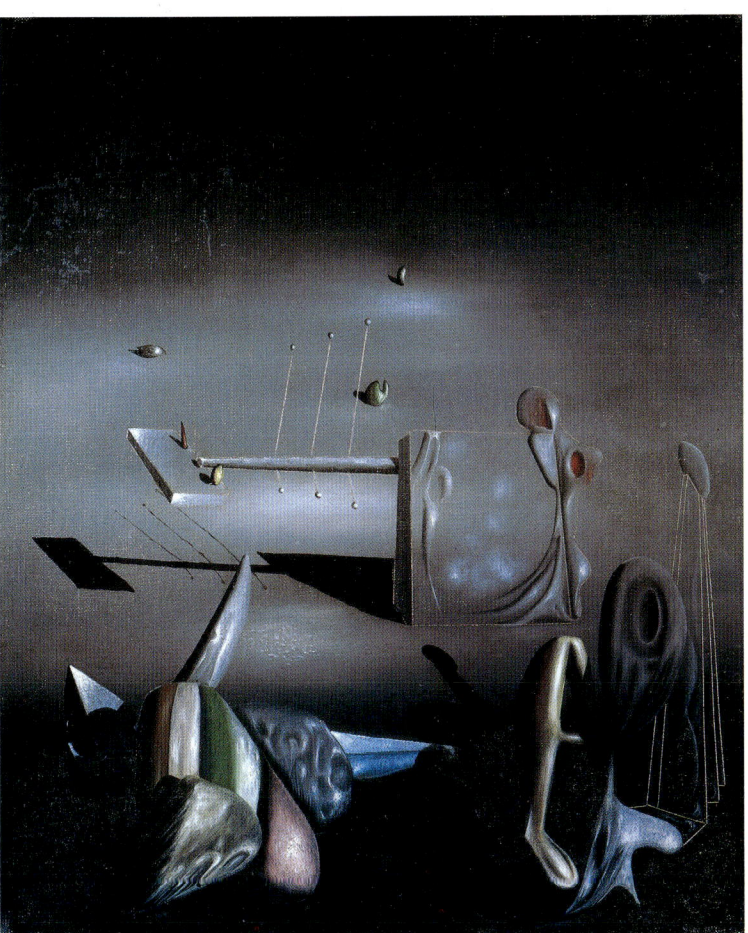

Thrall Soby, one of Tanguy's champions, likewise read his landscapes primarily in formal terms.[11]

In the general press critics also concentrated on formal criteria in their evaluations of Tanguy's work. Such factors as his use of color as texture, the parallels in his work to Mondrian's clear and harmonious planar organization, and his shallow arrays of three-dimensional forms close to the picture plane were stressed in order to establish a positive view of Tanguy as a "pure," modern painter. An exception was Margaret Breuning, for whom Tanguy's art aroused additional associations with current political events. She detected in his paintings a sense of spiritual torment; the shadow of war was present in his imagery, "not in any objective, explicit form, but in an inescapable reflection of the artist's anguish and disillusionment, in the obvious sense of futility of these fantastic shapes to recall a reasonable or happy world."[12]

Observers also recorded stylistic changes in Tanguy's work, principally in his palette and in the scale of his objects.[13] His American work from 1942–43 onward is marked by a strongly vertical alignment of pictorial elements, harsher coloring, foreground marshaling of forms, and monumentalization of the objects, and at least some of this was evident to contemporary critics. Whereas *The Earth and the Air* and *Slowly toward the North* (1942; fig. 164, cat. no. 133) still contain minutely subdivided biomorphic forms, scattered in an endless, empty landscape, the two 1943 paintings *The Prodigal Son Never Returns II* and *The Prodigal Son Never Returns III* (figs. 165–66, cat. nos. 134–35) as well as *Through Birds, through Fire, but Not through Glass* (fig. 167, cat. no. 136), also of 1943, employ large-scale, artificial-looking forms that dominate the

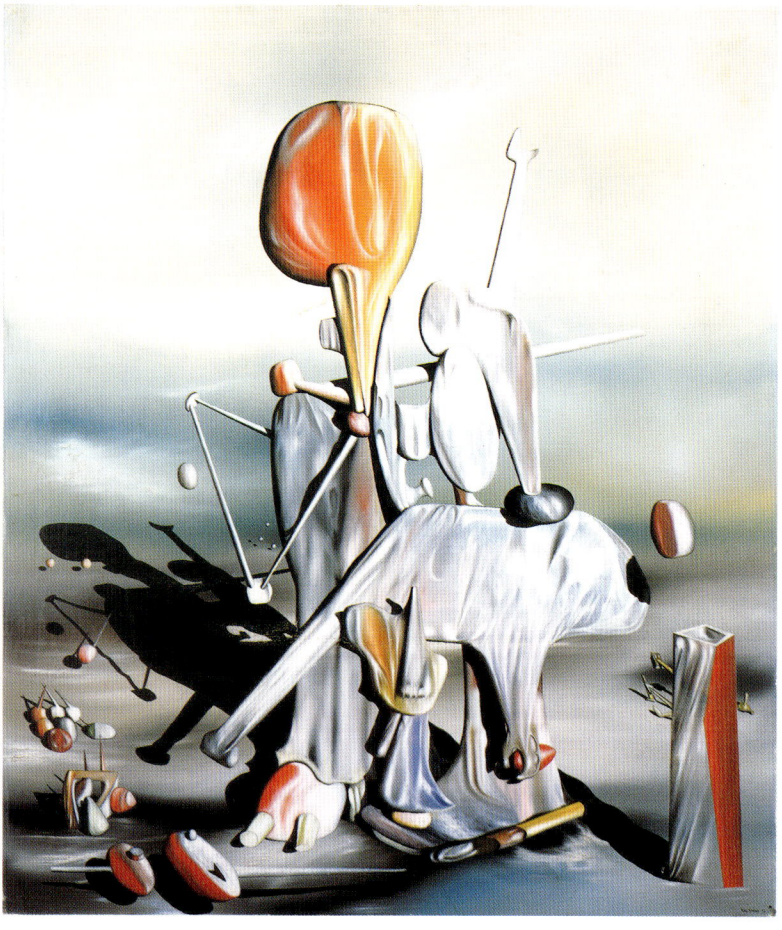

167
Yves Tanguy, *Through Birds, through Fire, but Not through Glass*, 1943 (cat. no. 136).

unchanged, dual-perspective space. In an interview in 1946 Tanguy himself conceded that there had been a change: "Here in the United States the only change I can distinguish in my work is possibly in my palette. What the cause of this intensification of color is I can't say.... Perhaps it is due to the light. I also have the feeling of greater space here, more 'room.'"[14]

Tanguy himself thus attached importance to the changes in his work, both in intensity of color and in spatial relationships; though mostly dismissed as marginal in the literature,[15] these aspects point to the assimilation of the American environment and culture. The unreal-looking objects, hectic colors, and large-scale figurations are not only a response to the unfamiliar North American landscape but an allusion to American popular culture as well. The work of this French emigré thus reflects an ambivalent relationship with his host country; he retained the fundamental pictorial concept of an endless landscape space which he had developed in Europe, while altering a few aspects, albeit decisive ones.

Tanguy's relationship with France and America was a complex one. In America he had found prosperity and recognition, and he liked to stress the advantages of his new home: its remoteness from the European war, its greater freedom, and the better social standing enjoyed by the artist.[16] Nevertheless, his social contacts were largely limited to his fellow surrealists, and he was left in an isolated position when, at the end of the war, most of them returned to France. When Julien Levy visited Tanguy and Sage in 1954—by which time, of course, Tanguy was free to return to France—he inquired into the issue of Tanguy's intellectual and cultural displacement in the United States:

> I pursue my question of why they live in Connecticut.
>
> "Because we have our work to do, ourselves are peaceful, and neighbors are friendly. In our heads we have the Boul' Mich' or the Via Appia."
>
> Kay continues: "Now that we are in Connecticut I don't think that changes anything at all. If I were in China it would be the same. You don't have to think about the surroundings.... Yes, your own memories that you can develop."[17]

These answers, which bear the stamp of a modernist view of artistic autonomy, clearly reflect the psychic defense mechanisms that Tanguy brought into play to minimize the importance of his mental, spiritual, and cultural ties to his native country.[18]

Notes

1. James Johnson Sweeney, interview with Yves Tanguy, in "Eleven Europeans in America," *Bulletin of the Museum of Modern Art* 13, no. 4–5 (1946): 22.

2. On Sage's commitment to helping European artists escape to the Unites States, see Judith D. Suther, "Separate Studios: Kay Sage and Yves Tanguy," in *Significant Others: Creativity and Intimate Partnership,* ed. Whitney Chadwick and Isabelle de Courtivron (New York: Thames and Hudson, 1993), 142–43.

3. Marcel Duhamel, *Raconte pas ta vie* (Paris, 1972), esp. 597.

4. Among these were the following: Stanley Rose Gallery, Hollywood, 1935; Julien Levy Gallery, New York, 1936; *Cubism and Abstract Art,* Museum of Modern Art, New York, 1936; *Fantastic Art, Dada, Surrealism,* Museum of Modern Art, New York, 1936–37.

5. Galerie Surréaliste, Paris, 1927; Galerie Cahiers d'Art, Paris, 1935; Galerie Jeanne Bucher, Paris, 1938; Guggenheim Jeune Gallery, London, 1938.

6. Including *First Papers of Surrealism*, Whitelaw Reid mansion, New York (Coordinating Council of French Relief Societies), 1942, and Peggy Guggenheim's gallery, Art of This Century.

7. Nicolas Calas, "Alone," *View* 2 (May 1942): unpaginated.

8. Nicolas Calas, "Magic Icons," *Horizon* 14 (November 1946): 311.

9. André Breton, "What Tanguy Veils and Reveals," *View* 2 (May 1942): unpaginated. From 1924 through 1929 Tanguy lived on rue du Château, near the Montparnasse train station.

10. James Johnson Sweeney, "Iconographer of Melancholy," *View* 2 (May 1942): unpaginated.

11. James Thrall Soby, "Inland Subconscious: Yves Tanguy," *Magazine of Art* 42 (January 1949): 3–7.

12. Margaret Breuning, "Surrealist Disillusion of Yves Tanguy," *Art Digest* 19 (15 December 1945): 9.

13. Soby, "Inland Subconscious," 6.

14. Ibid., 23.

15. This was emphasized, for instance, by Soby in 1949 (ibid., 6) and in 1955 (*Yves Tanguy*, exh. cat. [New York: Museum of Modern Art, 1955], 18), and Roland Penrose maintained the same interpretation (in *Yves Tanguy: A Retrospective,* exh. cat. [New York: Solomon R. Guggenheim Museum, 1983], 11).

16. Sweeney, in "Eleven Europeans in America," 22–23.

17. Julien Levy, "Tanguy. Connecticut. Sage," *Art News* 53 (October 1954): 25, 26.

18. On the psychic toll that exile exacted on Tanguy, see also Romy Golan's essay in this volume, esp. p. 131.

roberto sebastián matta echaurren
in new york, 1939–45

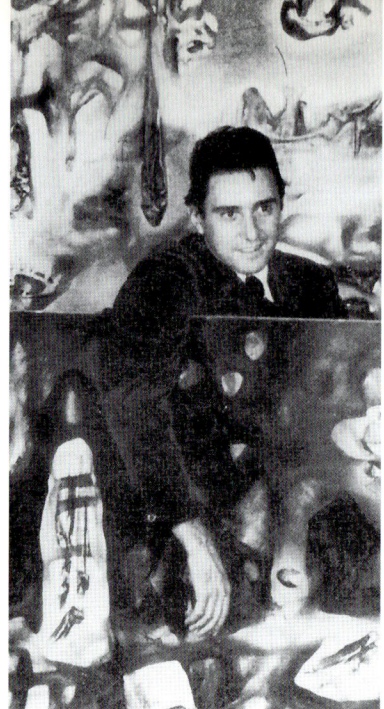

168

1912	born in Chiloé, Chile
1939	emigrates from France (Paris) to the U.S. (New York)
1948	immigrates to Italy (Rome)

Emigration comes from wanting to breathe.[1]

Roberto Sebastián Matta Echaurren holds a unique position among the European surrealists in exile in America. For one thing, he was not of European descent but was a Chilean of Basque stock who had lived in Paris on and off since 1934. For another, unlike most of his fellow surrealists, he had only recently begun to make an artistic career for himself; he had joined the surrealist group in Paris in 1937. In October 1939 he moved to New York because in Europe he felt threatened by the National Socialist regime: "I had signed too many anti-Hitler and anti-Stalin papers not to be persecuted by the SS. The 'resistance' was not yet possible."[2]

Comparatively young (twenty-eight on arrival) and already able to speak English, Matta underwent a very different assimilation process from the other surrealists. Aside from his affiliation with the European and surrealist elite, he also sought out New York artists of his own generation. Of all the exiles, it was Matta who had the closest links with the future abstract expressionists. At a number of gatherings in his Manhattan studio in the winter of 1942–43 he labored to convert William Baziotes, Peter Busa, Erwin Kamrovsky, Robert Motherwell, Jackson Pollock, and others to his own ideas of art and to launch a debate on the potential of automatism for the creation of a new painting.

Matta's own principal artistic concern was to establish a comprehensive "morphology" of the cosmos, and this led him to nonobjective imagery, as in *Theory of Nature's Strategy (Polypsychology)* of c. 1939 (fig. 169, cat. no. 108). He wanted to create an art that would, in a way analogous to science, reveal the constantly shifting existential forms of an object or a phenomenon, depicting the process of change itself. Since he was particularly interested in investigating human existence or aspects of it from within, a number of his Morphologies were given the epithet "psychological."[3]

With his New York colleagues, who had yet to find a public of their own, Matta hoped to form a group that would proclaim a kind of counterinitiative to surrealism. In contrast to surrealism, with its exclusively psychological basis, he was interested in a morphological concept that would also encompass the physical. The group never formed, probably because Matta's own artistic concerns were starting to change. It was in 1943 that he began to pay closer attention to political and social events,

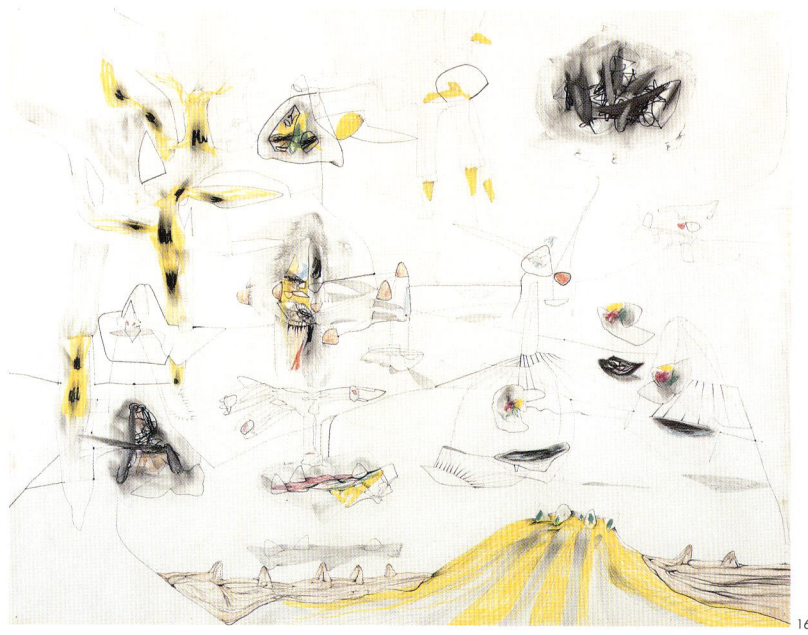

169

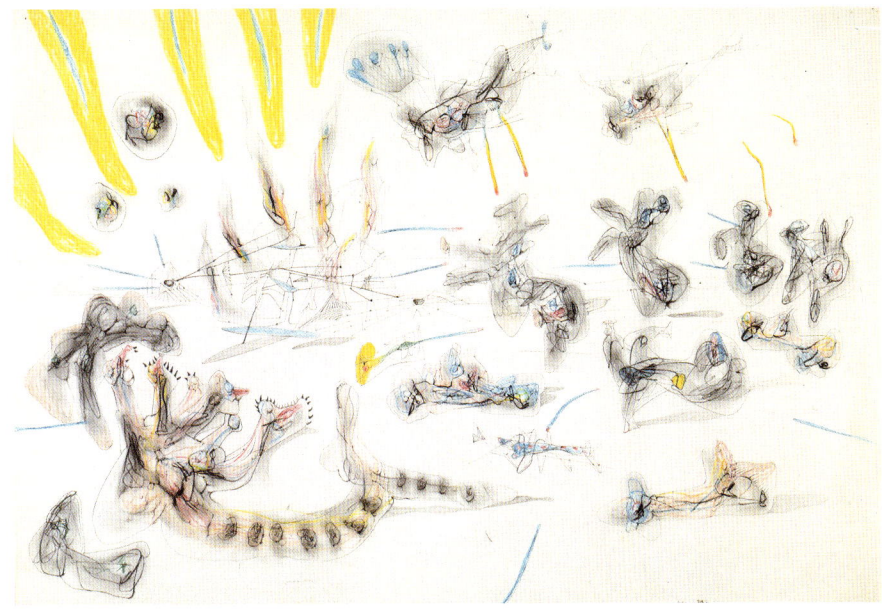

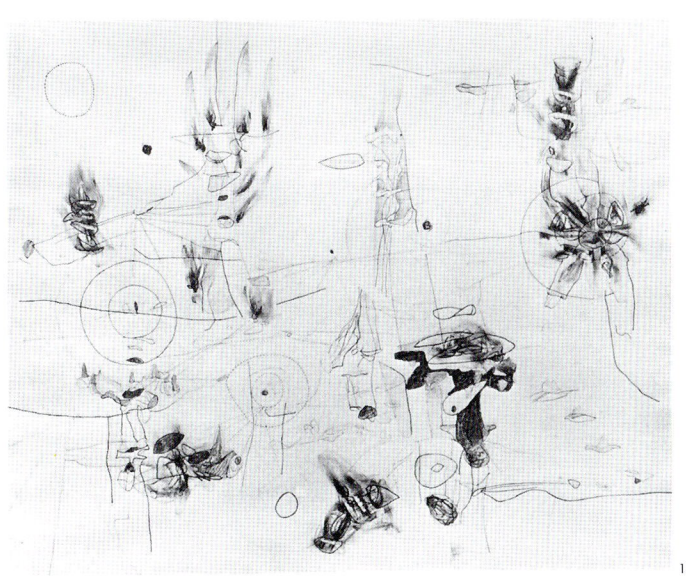

168
Matta in New York, December 1941.

169
Matta Echaurren, *Theory of Nature's Strategy (Polypsychology)*, c. 1939 (cat. no. 108).

170
Matta Echaurren, Untitled, 1940 (cat. no. 109).

171
Matta Echaurren, *The Great Transparent Ones (Los grandes transparentes)*, illustration to André Breton's "Prolegomena to a Third Manifesto of Surrealism or Else," published in VVV (June 1942).

and this ultimately led to visual expressions of the horrors of war: "I wasn't in the war. I felt that I should participate, but being terrifically antimilitarist, I went through a ferocious crisis, so to speak. And then I passed, in my work, to these anthropomorphic things.... It created a very definite divorce.... I became a fellow who wasn't accepted."[4]

It is also possible, however, that Matta changed his approach out of fear of jeopardizing his contacts with the surrealists, who were established artists. He had the most important of the surrealists' mentors on his side, in the person of André Breton. Breton even defended Matta's affinity for science, which was surely incompatible with the surrealists' protest against the rationalism of civilization. Breton saw Matta's imagery as a promising new departure for surrealism, because it gave access to new worlds rooted in the subconscious: "The need to call upon the support of the most modern resources [those of science] simply expresses the aspiration to extend the field of vision."[5]

Together with Breton, Matta elaborated the concept of the "great transparent ones,"[6] which formed the basis of Breton's American "Prolegomena to a Third Manifesto of Surrealism or Else" (see fig. 171). In this manifesto Breton put forth the idea of invisible, transparent beings embodying a new myth, formulated in response to contemporary experiences of inhumanity, war, and destruction. He argued that "man is perhaps not the center, the focus of the universe. One may go so far as to believe that there exist above him... beings whose behavior is alien to him.... It would not be possible... even to succeed in making plausible the complexion and structure of such hypothetical beings, which obscurely manifest themselves to us in fear and the feeling of chance."[7] He thus offered an explanation based on the assumption of an irrational universe, vindicating humankind by implying that the culpability for contemporary events lay beyond the human sphere.

Within the American art world Matta's painting was seen primarily in the context of surrealism in exile[8] but also in relation to Latin American art[9] and to the work of young American artists.[10] His dealers were Julien Levy and the more influential Pierre Matisse. He maintained contacts with the Museum of Modern Art, with Peggy Guggenheim, and with Katherine S. Dreier, with whom he published

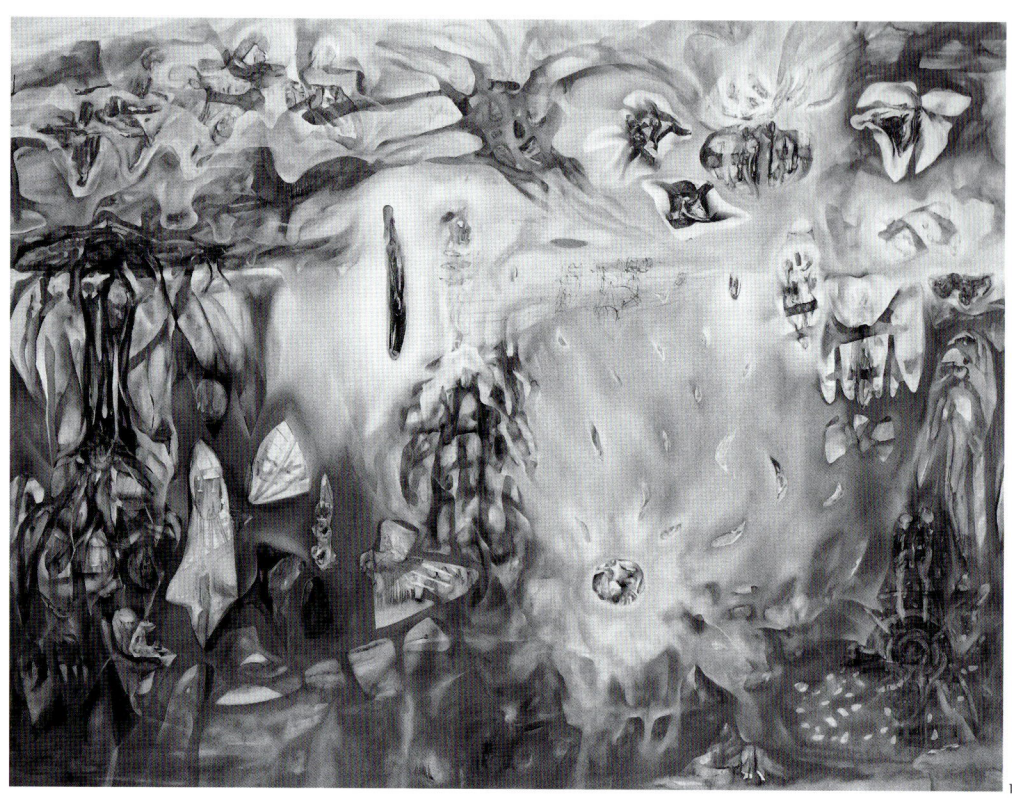

a joint study of Marcel Duchamp in 1944.[11] He had his first, small solo exhibition in the United States at the Julien Levy Gallery in 1940.[12] Pierre Matisse put on the first major Matta exhibition in 1942 and thereafter presented his work annually, a sign that established artistic circles were taking an interest in Matta's art. Matta's work was also shown in 1943 at Peggy Guggenheim's museum-gallery, Art of This Century; in 1944 at the Arts Club of Chicago; and in 1945 at Sidney Janis's newly opened gallery in New York.

The morphological "landscapes" of the first few years of Matta's American exile reveal no dialogue between human being and environment, such as he had called for in his programmatic text "Mathématique sensible—Architecture du temps."[13] Far from it: Morphologies such as *Invasion of the Night* (1941; fig. 173, cat. no. 110) are barely decipherable abstractions. One can distinguish gaseous-looking, fluid, and crystalline forms, embodied in patches of hectic color. A thick impasto has evidently been gouged by a knife; there are also thinly painted areas, producing an uneven and expressive surface. The result is a visual evocation of the battle between chaos and cosmos.[14] These works are denser than Matta's European paintings—a change he attributed to his encounter with the American landscape: "When I arrived in the United States, I started talking about the earth. In these pictures I tried to show not landscape which is 'scenery'—a scene of the earth—but the earth as something terrific, burning, changing, transforming, growing."[15]

These paintings show no discrete, self-sufficient internal surfaces; the forms are amorphous, with no hierarchy and no central focus. As they lack a correlative—that is to say,

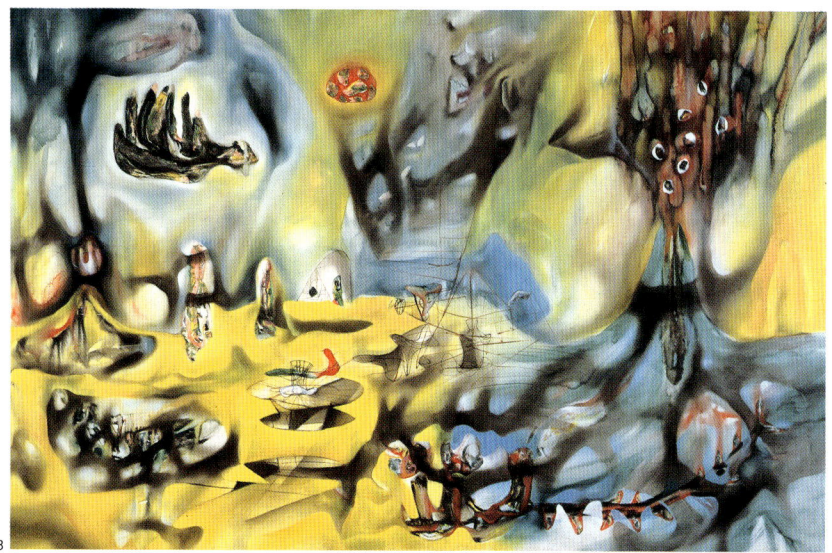

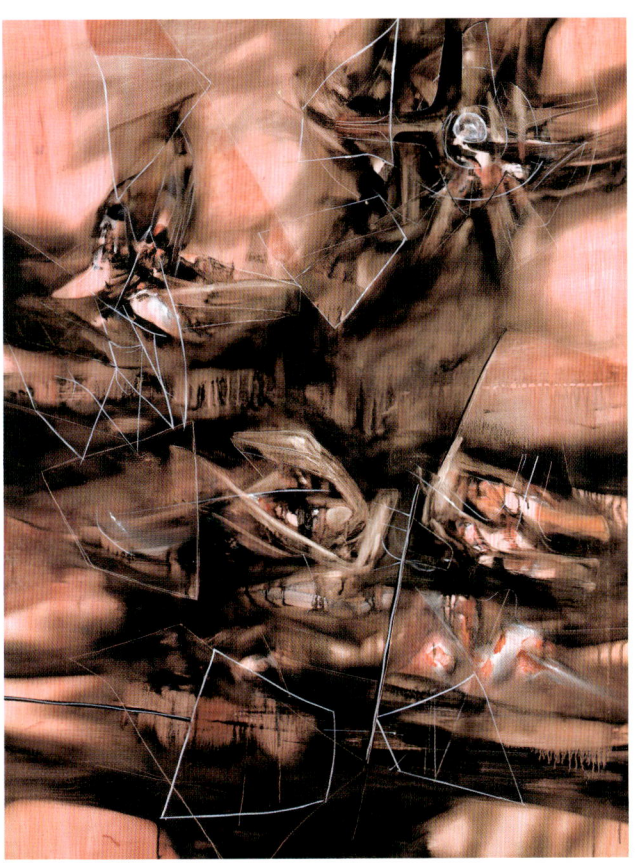

their point of reference is a universe projected by the subjective self—Matta's landscapes can be interpreted in terms of a modernist view of the individual as absolute.

In the years that followed, Matta turned away from this self-referentiality to engage with the political issues of his time. The unprecedentedly large format of *The Earth Is a Man* (1942; fig. 172) springs directly from his social commitment. In Mexico in 1941 he had seen large formats combined with a sociopolitical message in the murals of Diego Rivera, David Alfaro Siqueiros, and José Clemente Orozco. In paintings such as *Locus Solus* (1941–42; fig. 175, cat. no. 111) and *The Year 1944—the Putting to Death of the Father* (1942; fig. 174, cat. no. 113) Matta used concentric lines paralleling the outlines of his amorphous shapes. The resulting patterns look like labyrinths, evoking contemporary associations of captivity and loss of freedom. Duchamp's labyrinthine twine installation for

172
Matta Echaurren; *The Earth Is a Man*, 1942; oil on canvas; 72 x 94 in. (182.9 x 238.8 cm); The Art Institute of Chicago, gift of Mr. and Mrs. Joseph Randall Shapiro, 1992.168.

173
Matta Echaurren, *Invasion of the Night*, 1941 (cat. no. 110).

174
Matta Echaurren, *The Year 1944— the Putting to Death of the Father*, 1942 (cat. no. 113).

175
Matta Echaurren, *Locus Solus*, 1941–42 (cat. no. 111).

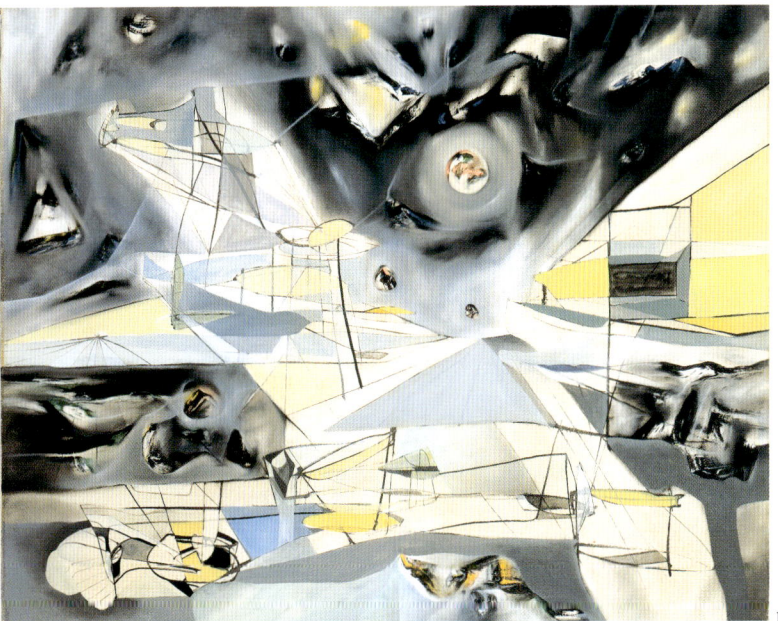

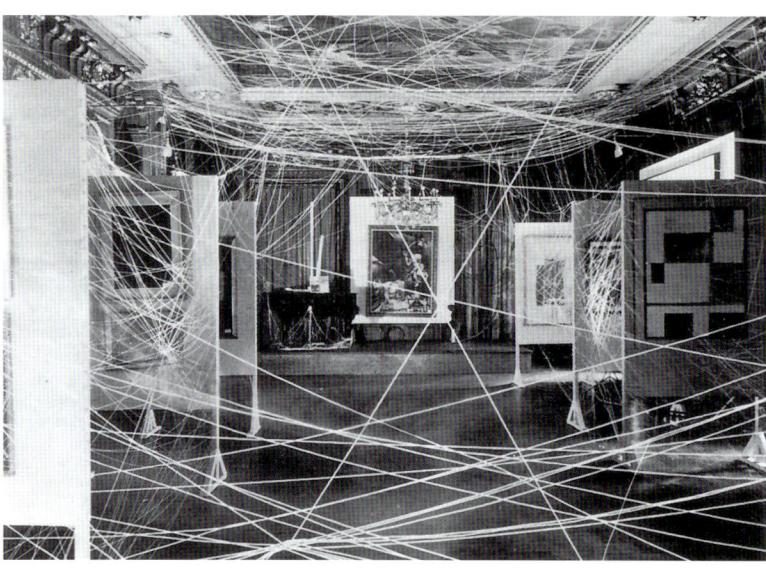

176
Marcel Duchamp, twine installation for the exhibition *First Papers of Surrealism*, Whitelaw Reid mansion, New York, 1942; photograph by John Schiff.

177
Matta Echaurren, *The Disasters of Mysticism*, 1942 (cat. no. 112).

the exhibition *First Papers of Surrealism* in 1942 (see fig. 176) and the same artist's "Large Glass," *The Bride Stripped Bare by Her Bachelors, Even* (to which Matta responded in 1944 with a painting entitled *The Bachelors, Twenty Years After*) inspired Matta to use these lines to suggest multiperspectival spatial systems.[16]

The harsh colors and light of *The Disasters of Mysticism* (1942; fig. 177, cat. no. 112) suggest a burning sky, apparently alluding to the battles of World War II. Such works as *Being With* (1945), *The Thought of a Permanent Table* (1945; fig. 179, cat no. 114), and *A Grave Situation* (1946; fig. 178, cat. no. 115) evoke the cruelties of the war. In the latter work machine forms, a deformed human body, instruments of torture, and automata are set on an open pictorial stage,

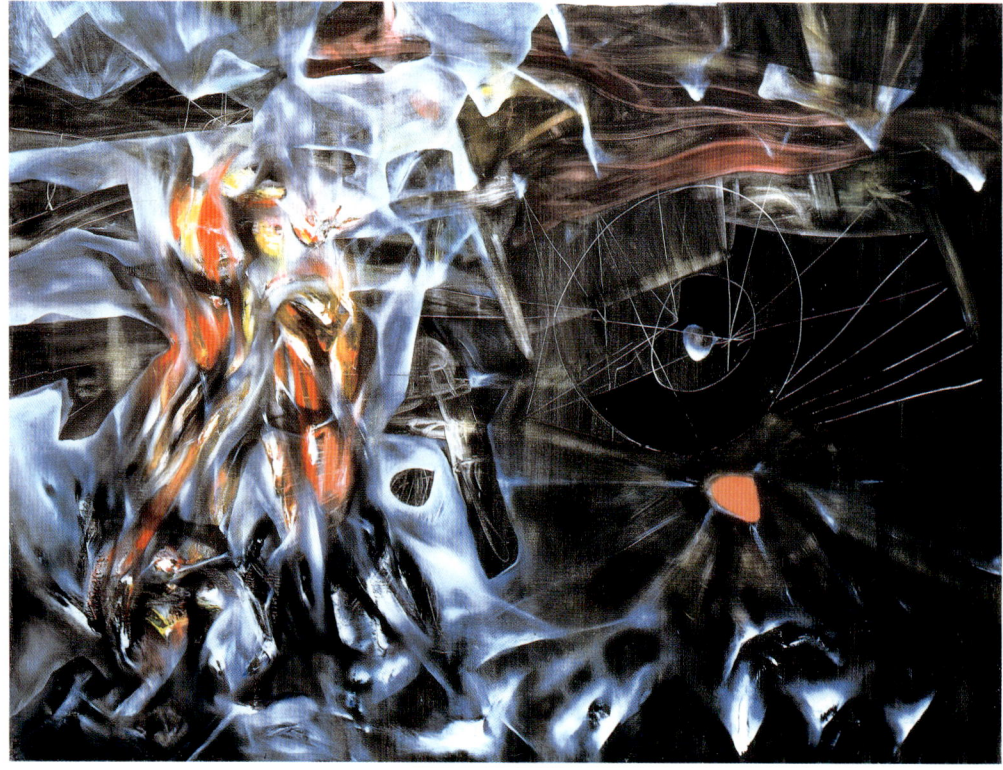

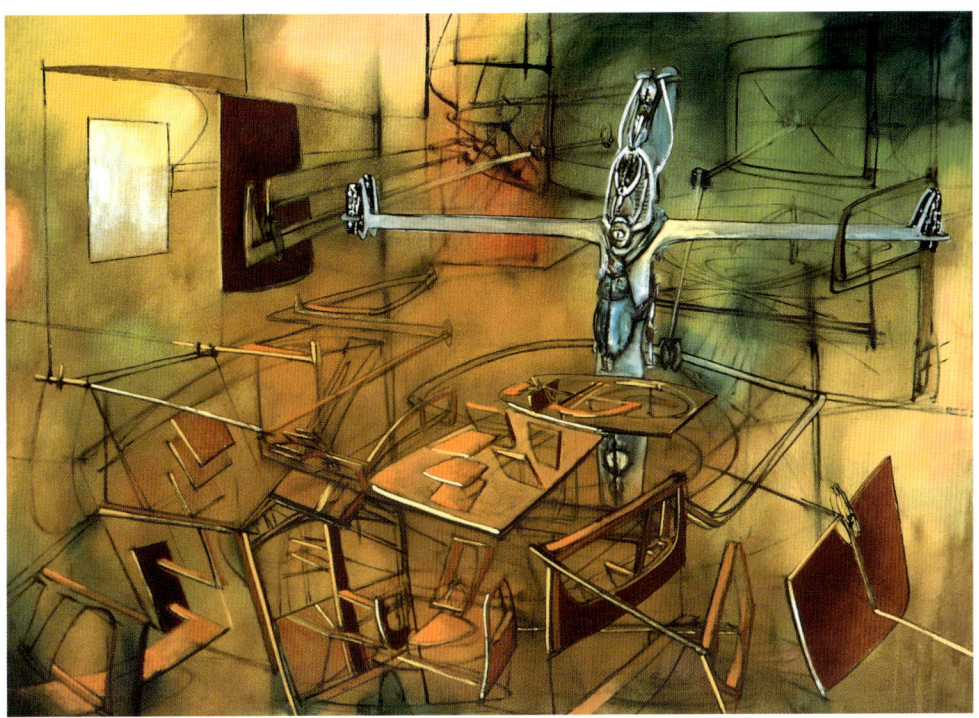

178
Matta Echaurren, *A Grave Situation*, 1946 (cat. no. 115).

made up of tones of gray, brown, and yellow. Breton acknowledged the topical relevance of these images to the horrors of World War II; he also pointed out how Matta had contrasted the death instinct with the positive instinct of eros, thus taking up a major surrealist theme: "During these last few years, the 'death instinct' has permitted itself every use of freedom.... It was essential that this 'death instinct' should be opposed with equally increased vigor by the sexual instinct.... No one else's painting has, so far, shown so clearly and almost analytically [as Matta's] these rival instincts at grips."[17] These paintings are thus about life-creating and life-enhancing forces as well as life-destroying ones; they are not exclusively expressions of the destructiveness of the 1940s. This utopian quality is reinforced by their often monumental scale.

In contemporary American critical writing, Matta's name does not appear as frequently as those of the better-known surrealists. Clement Greenberg curtly dismissed his landscapes of the years 1939–42 as too popular, describing them as "iridescent burlesque-house decorations...which are little more, really, than the comic strip of abstract art."[18] In Sidney Janis, James Thrall Soby, and Rosamund Frost, by contrast, Matta found important advocates. Interestingly, they did not see him primarily as an emigré artist from Europe but drew connections between his use of color and his Latin American origins.[19] Frost alluded to Matta's sociopolitical ambitions, though she found no trace of them in his work. She saw his art as rooted in the realm of pure artistic pleasure: "Although Matta feels that the artist should denounce or accuse rather than decorate or entertain, there is a great deal of visual enjoyment simply in the way he handles his medium."[20]

During his exile in the United States Matta fell between the two stools of young American art and surrealism, as well as between those of self-referential abstraction and political commitment. His outsider status—as a young artist with a new concept within the surrealist group and as a Latin American among Europeans in an alien North American environment—seems to have made it impossible for him to choose one position over the other. Though he differed from many of his colleagues in not insisting on an individualistic self-image, he was the one who found himself isolated. As early as 1944 Frost recognized that Matta "probably...will remain an isolated phenomenon, [the] result of the mingling of the Iberian race, French intellectualism, the American Continent, and the modern age."[21]

Notes

1 Quoted in Valerie Fletcher, *Crosscurrents of Modernism: Four Latin American Pioneers: Diego Rivera, Joaquín Torres-García, Wifredo Lam, Matta,* exh. cat. (Washington, D.C.: Hirshhorn Museum and Sculpture Garden in association with Smithsonian Institution Press, 1992), 231.
2 Sidney Simon, "Concerning the Beginnings of the New York School, 1939–1943: An Interview with Peter Busa and Matta," *Art International* 12 (Summer 1967): 17. This interview is the only source for this information.
3 See also Nancy Miller, "Interview with Matta," in *Matta: The First Decade,* exh. cat. (Waltham, Mass.: Rose Art Museum, Brandeis University, 1982), 11.
4 Simon, "Concerning the Beginnings of the New York School," 18–19.
5 Andre Breton, "Matta" (1944), in *Surrealism and Painting*, trans. Simon Watson Taylor (New York: Harper and Row, 1972), 187.
6 See Miller, "Interview with Matta," 16.
7 Quoted in William Rubin, *Matta,* exh. cat. (New York: Museum of Modern Art, 1957), 7.
8 Among these were *Artists in Exile,* Pierre Matisse Gallery, New York, 1942; *First Papers of Surrealism,* Whitelaw Reid mansion (Coordinating Council of French Relief Societies), New York, 1942; *Europe in America,* Institute of Contemporary Art, Boston, 1943; *The Imagery of Chess,* Julien Levy Gallery, New York, 1945; *European Artists in America,* Whitney Museum of American Art, New York, 1945.

9 At the Art Institute of Chicago in 1941, jointly with Wifredo Lam.
10 For example, *Spring Salon for Young Artists,* Art of This Century, New York, 1943.
11 Katherine Dreier and Matta Echaurren, *Duchamp's Glass… an Analytical Reflection* (New York: Société Anonyme; Museum of Modern Art, 1944).
12 See Simon "Concerning the Beginnings of the New York School," 19.
13 Matta wrote this text at Breton's request and published it in *Minotaure* in Paris in 1938.
14 See *Roberto Sebastian Matta,* exh. cat. (Vienna: Museum des 20. Jahrhunderts, 1963), 36.
15 Miller "Interview with Matta," 12.
16 See Romy Golan, "Matta, Duchamp et le mythe: Un nouveau paradigme pour la dernière phase du surréalisme," in *Matta,* exh. cat. (Paris: Centre Georges Pompidou, Musée national d'art moderne, 1985), 37–51.
17 André Breton, "Three Years Ago" (1944), in *Surrealism and Painting,* 191.

18 Clement Greenberg, "Review of Mondrian's *New York Boogie Woogie* and Other Acquisitions at the Museum of Modern Art," *Nation,* 9 October 1943; reprinted in Greenberg, *The Collected Essays and Criticism,* ed. John O'Brian (Chicago: University of Chicago Press, 1986), 154.
19 Sidney Janis, "School of Paris Comes to U.S.," *Decision,* no. 5–6 (November–December 1941): 95; James Thrall Soby, "Matta Echaurren," *Magazine of Art* 40 (March 1947): 106; Rosamund Frost, "Matta's Third Surrealist Manifesto," *Art News* 43 (February 1944): 18.
20 Frost, "Matta's Third Surrealist Manifesto," 18.
21 Ibid.

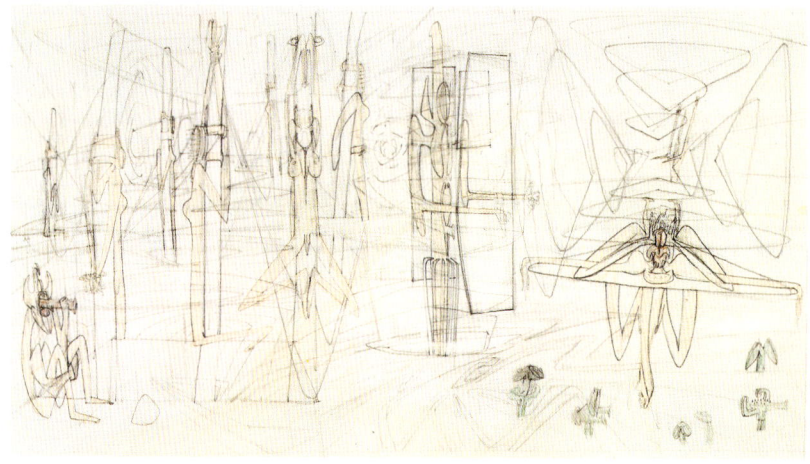

179
Matta Echaurren, *The Thought of a Permanent Table,* 1945 (cat. no. 114).

180
Piet Mondrian; *Victory Boogie-Woogie,* 1942–44; oil and paper on canvas (unfinished); 50 x 50 in. (127 x 127 cm); vertical axis: 70½ in. (179 cm); private collection.

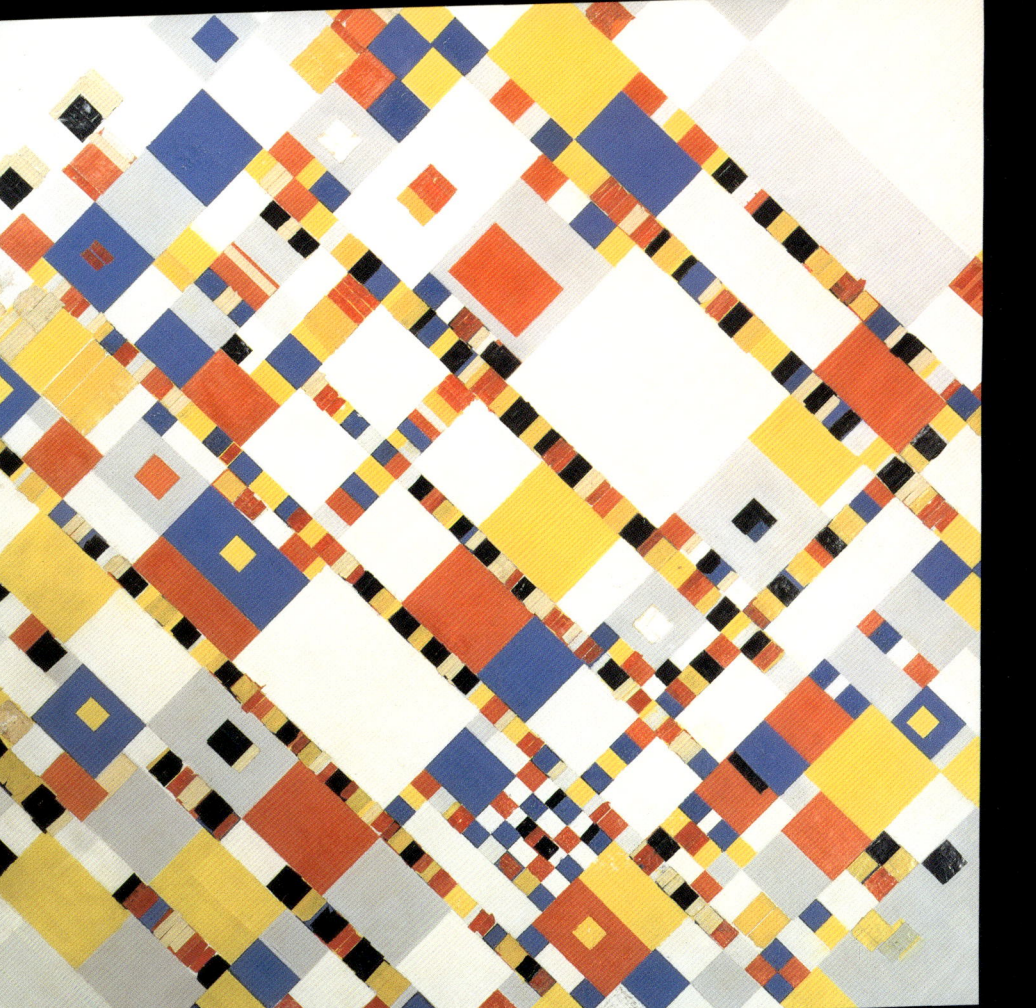

fernand léger in new york, 1940–45

1881	born in Argentan, France
1940	immigrates to the U.S. (New York; New Haven, Conn.; Oakland)
1945	returns to France (Paris)
1955	dies in Gif-sur-Yvette, France

181
Fernand Léger, New York, 1941; photograph ©1941 Arnold Newman.

182
Fernand Léger; *Composition with Two Parrots*, 1935–39; oil on canvas; 157½ x 189 in. (400 x 480 cm); Musée National d'Art Moderne, Centre Georges Pompidou.

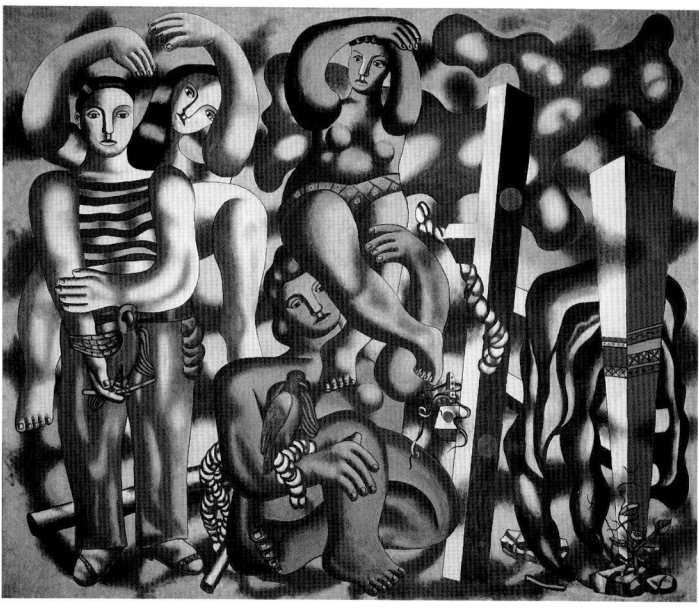

In April 1940 the Parisian public was invited to the studio of the American sculptor Mary Callery to see a recently completed painting by Fernand Léger, the *Composition with Two Parrots* of 1935–39 (fig. 182). This monumental picture, more than twelve feet in width, offered viewers a spectacular example of a prominent modernist painter's work. Four acrobats dominate the left and center portions of the picture, while the remaining section is given over to a simple structure of wooden posts, suggesting a fragment of a circus tent's substructure.[1] Replacing conventional narrative logic, dynamic contrasts of shape, form, and color govern the interaction of figures and objects in the composition. Whereas the wooden planks are rectilinear in contour, rigid in form, and firmly footed in the ground, the acrobats' bodies are rounded and buoyant, eloquent in pose if not in facial expression. While the amorphous yellow-brown background establishes a sober mood, it is strongly accented by vivid red, blue, and green tones in the clothing of two acrobats, in the fabric that drapes over the fence, in the cloud overhead, and in the coloration of the two birds mentioned in the work's title. Under the big top Léger discovered a world whose significant relationships were abstract. At the same time the artist imported from the circus tent a working-class context that, he hoped, would counter the social elitism of his own cultural practice, abstract painting. While a confrontation with popular aesthetics had always been fundamental to Léger's concept of modernist art, that issue acquired new urgency in the mid-1930s, when the *Composition with Two Parrots* was formulated and when he joined other leading cultural figures in supporting the social reforms of France's leftist Popular Front government.[2] Yet by the time the painting was unveiled in the studio of its new owner, several months into the war, the political optimism expressed in it was no longer justified.

Mary Callery took the unusual step of a one-day showing in order to display the *Composition with Two Parrots* in Paris before sending it off, in June, for exhibition in New York. Léger also left Paris that month, just ahead of the German occupation of the city, and joined the migration of many French citizens toward the south of France. The painter gradually made his way to Lisbon in September 1940 and then to New York in early November.[3] Having visited the United States three times during the 1930s, he arrived with considerable knowledge of his new locale and with access to a substantial network of local contacts. He quickly found opportunities for work as a lecturer and teacher, integrated himself into the community of exiled Europeans, and contributed essays to

183
Fernand Léger, *The Divers*, 1942 (cat. no. 89).

184
Fernand Léger, *The Divers II*, 1941–42 (cat. no. 88).

185
Fernand Léger, *The Women Cyclists*, 1944; oil on canvas; 29 x 36 in. (73.6 x 91.4 cm); Washington University Gallery of Art, Saint Louis, gift of Mr. Charles H. Yalem, 1963.

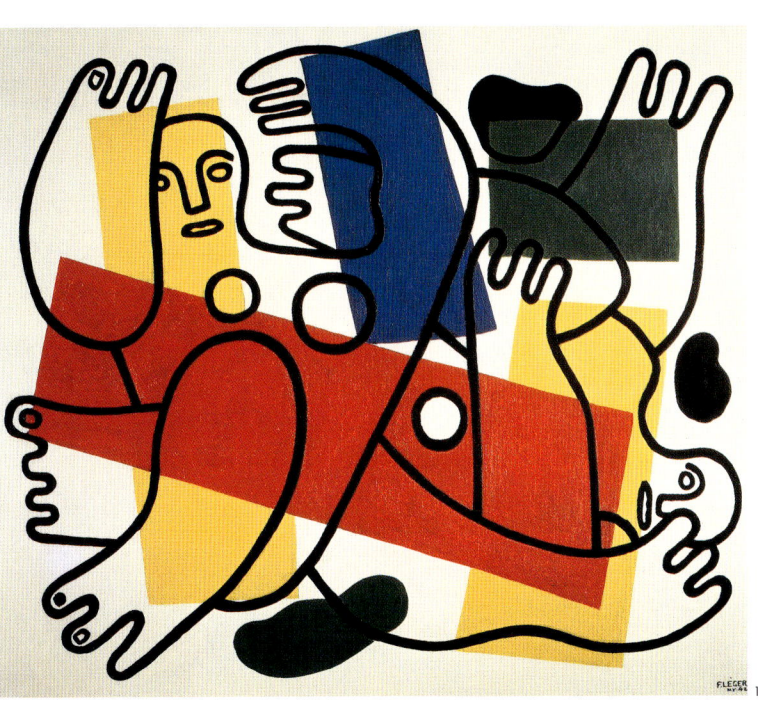

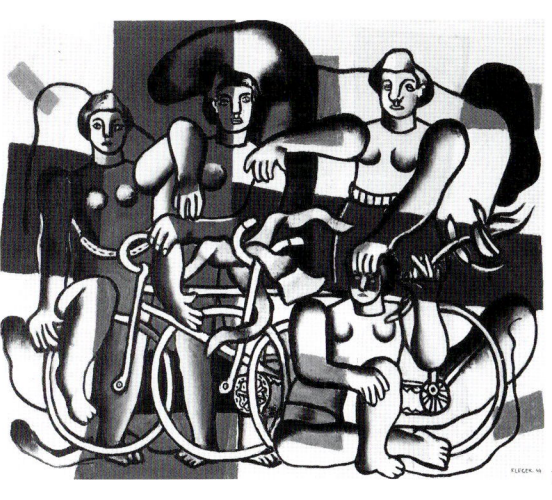

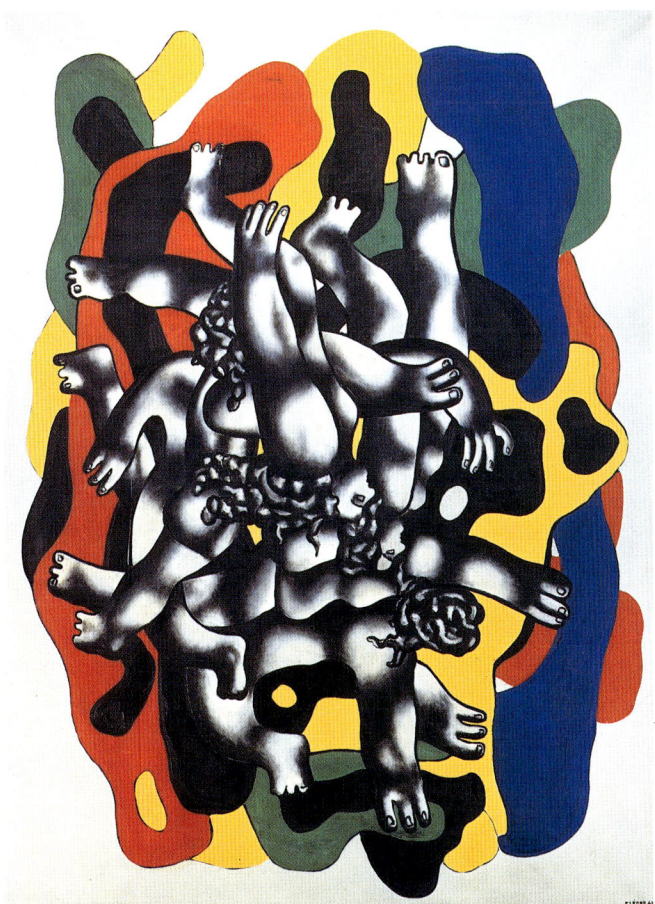

La voix de France, the newspaper of the French expatriate community in New York. The painter was characteristically prolific during his years in exile, and the results of his work were seen in galleries across North America throughout this period.

Composition with Two Parrots, which went on view at the Museum of Modern Art in December 1940, set the tone for much of Léger's American production. The painter continued to experiment with strategies for presenting the human form abstractly, often looking to the world of leisure, sport, and popular entertainment for his themes. *The Divers II* (1941–42; fig. 184, cat. no. 88), for instance, catches a churning mass of muscular, monochromatic bodies in a state of weightlessness against flat but brightly colored background shapes. *The Divers* (1942; fig. 183, cat. no. 89) achieves an alternate effect by reducing the human form to nothing more than a thickly drawn outline. The human body returned to earth in works depicting acrobats, musicians, and female bicyclists. Léger may have regarded *The Women Cyclists* (1944; fig. 185) and related pictures as

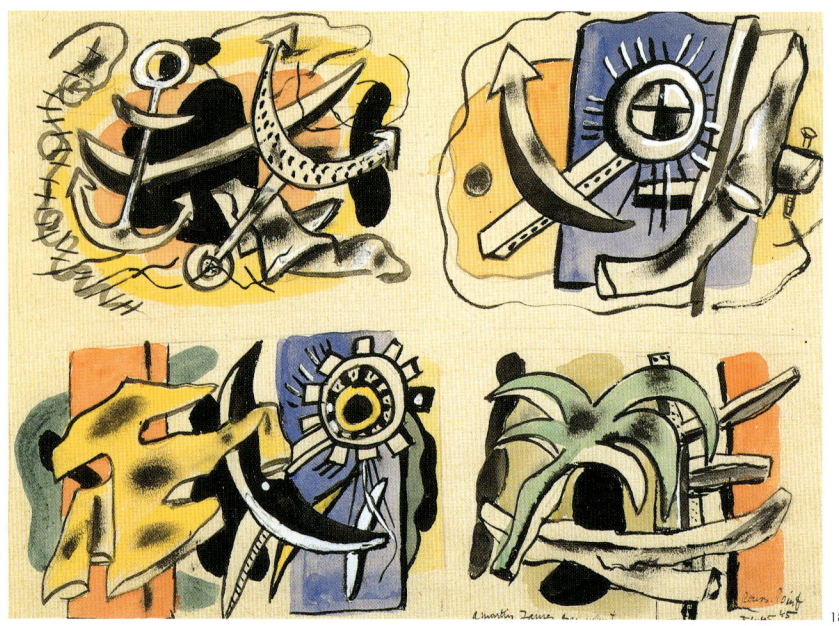
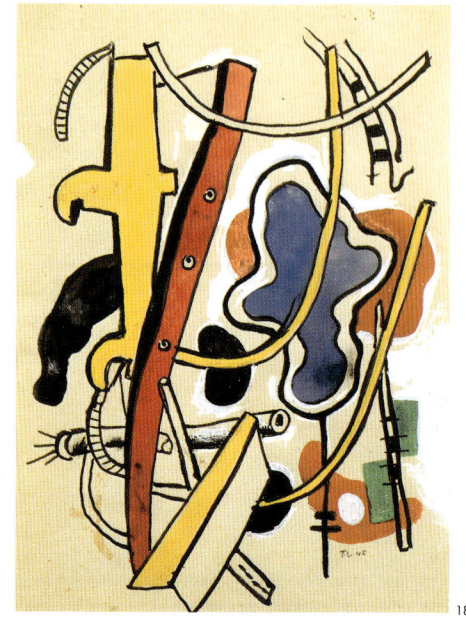

186
Fernand Léger, *Four Composition Studies (Rouses Point)*, 1943–45 (cat. no. 92).

187
Fernand Léger, *Mechanical Fragments* c. 1945 (cat. no. 94).

188
Fernand Léger at Rouses Point, summer 1945.

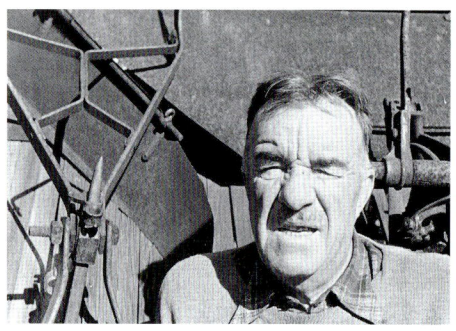

an homage to the energetic character of the American people,[4] but the figure paintings of the exile years rarely present subjects specifically coded as American. In matters of style, however, some of these works did register the impact of a long immersion in the American milieu. *The Divers* and *The Women Cyclists* were based on the interplay of a remarkably economical linear structure and bold overlays of autonomous color. This dissonant technique infused Léger's exile production with a new measure of abstract simplification, purification, and vitality. The painter was eager to credit environmental influence in explaining the transformation. "During these years in America," he explained, "I do feel I have worked with a greater intensity and achieved more expression than in my previous work. In this country there is a definitely romantic atmosphere in the good sense of the word—an increased sense of movement and violence. This is a melodramatic country, for all its clear skies."[5]

A veteran traveler and keen observer of life in foreign places, Léger was very responsive to America's material and psychological dynamism. He valued the country's vigorous, unruly nature as a counterweight to what he saw as French refinement and orderliness. The painter's published travel accounts confirm his fascination with American extremes: from the skyscraper canyons of Wall Street to the vast Midwestern landscape, from the raw nature of the desert Southwest to the mechanized modernity of Los Angeles. "We refugees must become absorbed in this atmosphere," Léger told the readers of *La voix de France*. "[We] must hold fast in this luminous, electric intensity; [in America] life is burned up."[6]

For Léger, confronting the "luminous, electric intensity" of American cities as a painter meant considering the ways in which that intensity might be incorporated into the structure of his artwork. Not only was he alert to the signs of this process in his own painting, he looked for it in the work of his expatriate colleagues. "I think it is entirely normal to take certain influences from one's environment," Léger remarked. "Even Mondrian's latest work in this country, his *Boogie Woogie* compositions, showed the effect of this atmosphere of movement.... This is clearly a powerful country—one feels it at once; one can resist it, but it is very strong."[7]

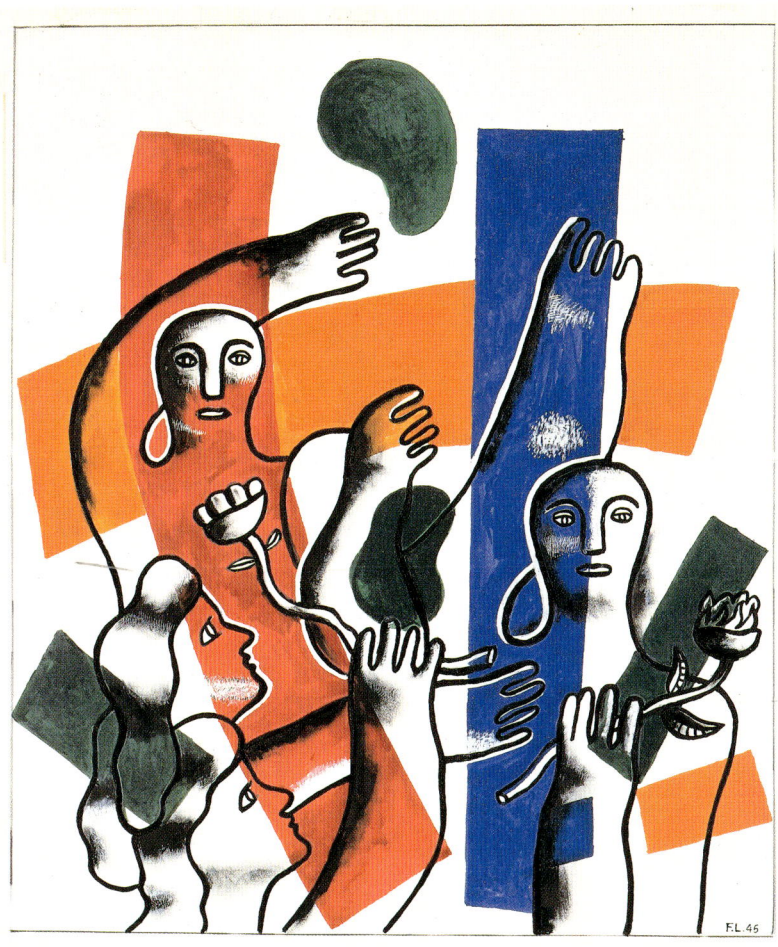

189
Fernand Léger, *France Reborn*, 1945 (cat. no. 93).

190
Fernand Léger; *France Reborn*, 1945; poster for Container Corporation of America; whereabouts unknown.

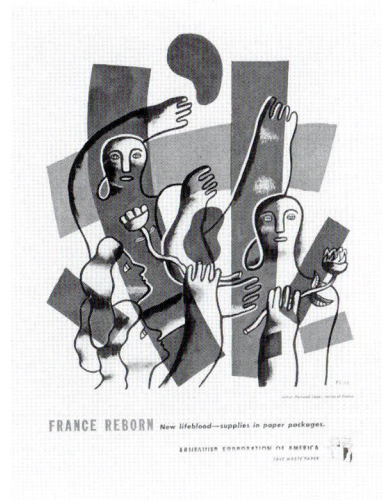

Although the neon lights of Broadway may have been one source for the bright color overlays that Léger introduced into his paintings in 1942, elements of urban subject matter were extremely rare in the painter's exile production.[8] Instead, he engaged most explicitly with the specifics of the American environment in a sequence of landscape studies. Vacationing near the town of Rouses Point in northern New York State in 1943–45, the painter discovered an intriguing site: an overgrown farm whose terrain was littered with discarded agricultural equipment and tools. This locale became the subject of *Four Composition Studies (Rouses Point)* (1943–45; fig. 186, cat. no. 92), one of a series of works in which fragments of machines and organic forms, thrown against areas of color, are transformed into objects of purely visual power. On an abandoned farm Léger located what he took to be the core drama of material and mental existence in America: an essentially romantic exchange between vast natural resources and immense mechanical forces.[9]

Léger's artistic response to the conditions of existence in America excluded, however, any didactic presentation of social or political ideas. The painter acted on his political sympathies by participating in the cultural projects of France Forever, an American support organization for the French Resistance.[10] He came closest to a direct visual comment on the international situation in a 1945 poster design entitled *France Reborn* (fig. 190). This work was commissioned by the Container Corporation of America to publicize that company's contribution to European relief efforts. Léger's watercolor original (fig. 189, cat. no. 93), the basis for the poster, depicts four human figures whose forms intersect

fernand léger **187**

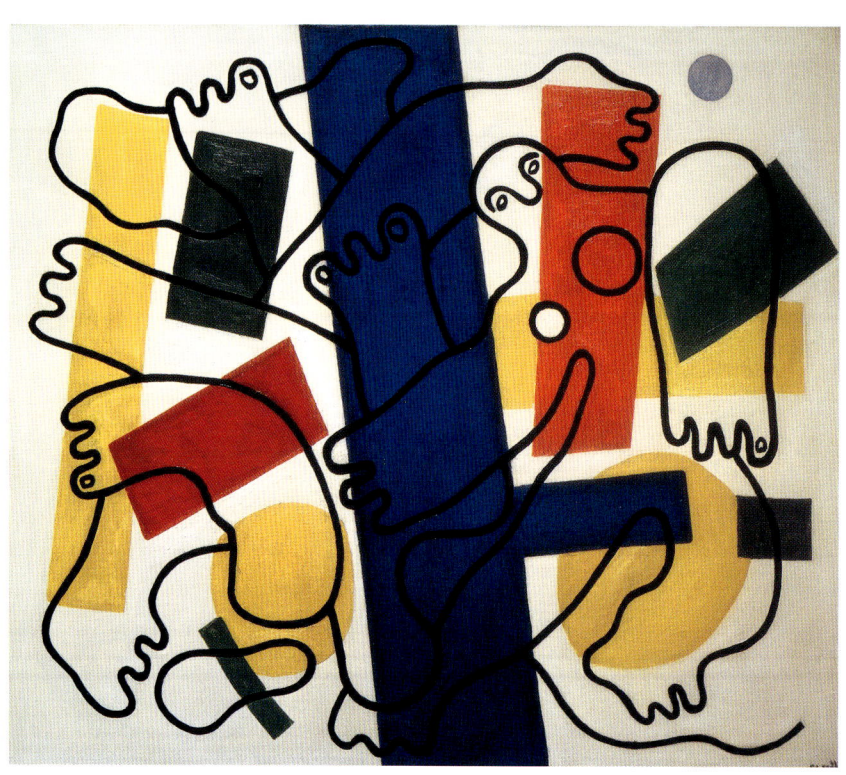

191
Fernand Léger, *Two Acrobats*, 1942–43 (cat. no. 91).

with red, yellow-orange, green, and blue color swatches. A caption reads "France Reborn. New Lifeblood—supplies in paper packages." *France Reborn* was displayed in an exhibition of the Container Corporation's posters, and the show's catalogue provided the following gloss: "In the painting 'France Reborn,' [Léger] has expressed the French peoples' feelings of joy and liberation when Allied armies swept the Germans out. The elevation of the arms, the flowers, the pure colors, all express what the artist calls 'the plastic sign of liberation.'"[11]

Léger's letters of 1945 are our best source for understanding his reflection on the politics of culture during World War II and afterward. In these letters to Nadia Khodossievitch, his Russian-born studio assistant (and subsequently his wife), who had worked with the Resistance, he made clear that he was aware of and somewhat embarrassed by the ambiguities of his own status as exile. "I sense that I have been taken to task here for not being partisan enough. 'France Forever,' but I want you to know that I consider the Resistance to be France's *salvation,* it will be the most beautiful page in our history."[12] He also speculated on the future of modern art in a rebuilding French society. Reacting to the postwar political success of the French parties of the left, he thought back, somewhat nostalgically, to the days of the Popular Front, when he and his colleagues had confronted the question of cultural democratization. "We must once again take up this effort alongside the workers of France," Léger announced, "endeavor to make them understand our art—a fascinating task. The great days of socialism, I believe, have arrived."[13]

Léger joined the French Communist party in a telegram of October 1945 and returned to France at the end of that year. The great project of his postwar career would be a long sequence of images depicting working-class labor and leisure.[14] First, however, he bade farewell to the country of his exile by painting a final American landscape, the brilliantly colored abstraction entitled *Adieu New York*.

Notes

1 Georges Bauquier, a former assistant to Léger, identifies the wooden elements on the right side of the picture as tent pole fragments in *Fernand Léger: Vivre dans le vrai* (Paris: Editions Adrien Maeght, 1987), 159.

2 See Fernand Léger, "The Human Body Considered as an Object" (1945) and "The Circus" (1950), in *Functions of Painting*, ed. Edward F. Fry, trans. Alexandra Anderson (New York: Viking Press, 1973), 132–36, 170–77.

3 On the painter's emigration, see the correspondence reproduced in Bauquier, *Fernand Léger*, 193–203.

4 See Léger's statement in James Johnson Sweeney, ed., "Eleven Europeans in America," *Bulletin of the Museum of Modern Art* 13, nos. 4–5 (1946): 15.

5 Ibid., 13. Commentators on both sides of the Atlantic often made the same judgment in presenting Léger's newest works to their readers. See James Johnson Sweeney, "Léger and the Search for Order," *View* 4 (Summer 1944): 84–87; and Georges Besson, "Fernand Léger," *Pages françaises*, no. 13 (1946): 123–25.

6 Fernand Léger, "Découvrir l'Amérique," *La voix de France*, 15 May 1942, 9 (all translations are by the author). This essay, along with other texts written in America in the early 1940s, is reprinted in Fernand Léger, *Mes voyages* (Paris: Jacques London, 1960; reprint, Geneva: Edito Service; Paris: Diffusion Bibliothèque des Arts, 1976).

7 Léger, in "Eleven Europeans in America," 14–15.

8 Martin James, one of the painter's American friends, reports that Léger credited Broadway's lights as a source for the color planes ("Léger at Rouses Point, 1944: A Memoir," *Burlington Magazine* 130 [April 1988]: 281). The city had been a major theme for Léger before 1925, during his cubist period. *La ville* (1919), the most grandiose of those city compositions, was in New York, having been bought by Albert C. Gallatin for his Museum of Living Art in 1936. Critical reflection on problems of city life and urbanism is abundant in the painter's writings; see, for example, "New York" (1931), in *Functions of Painting*, 84–90.

9 Sigfried Giedion published valuable summaries of talks he had with Léger during the Rouses Point summers; see Giedion's "Léger and America," in *Exhibition of Paintings by Fernand Léger* (Cincinnati: Cincinnati Art Museum, 1944), 2–5; and "Léger in America," *Magazine of Art* 38 (December 1945): 295–99.

10 One such event was *France Fights On*, a 1942 exhibition designed by Pierre Chareau for the New York-based Ecole Libre des Hautes Etudes on the theme of French resistance to the German invasion. See "The Fighting French Exhibit," *France Forever Yearbook* (1943), 117.

11 *Modern Art in Advertising: An Exhibition of Designs for Container Corporation of America* (Chicago: Art Institute of Chicago, 1945), unpaginated. This exhibition catalogue contains an essay by Léger entitled "Relationship between Modern Art and Contemporary Industry," 4–5. On the Container Corporation's advertising program, see National Museum of American Art, *Art, Design, and the Modern Corporation*, exh. cat. (Washington, D.C.: Smithsonian Institution Press, 1985).

12 Léger to Khodossievitch, 19 September 1945, in Bauquier, *Fernand Léger*, 248.

13 Léger to Khodossievitch, 22 August 1945, in ibid., 247; see also the letter of 10 October 1945, in ibid., 251.

14 On Léger's politics, see Sarah Wilson, "Fernand Léger: Art and Politics, 1935–1955," in *Fernand Léger: The Later Years*, exh. cat. (London: Whitechapel Gallery, 1987), esp. 61–73.

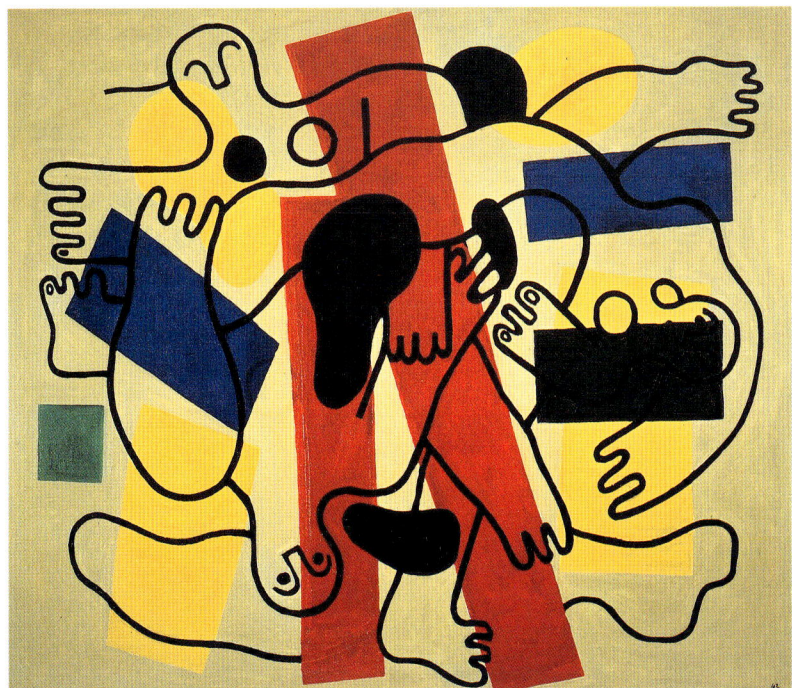

192
Fernand Léger, *The Divers (Red and Black)*, 1942 (cat. no. 90).

piet mondrian in new york, 1940–44

1872	born in Amersfoort, the Netherlands
1938	emigrates from France (Paris) to England (London)
1940	immigrates to the U.S. (New York)
1944	dies in New York

193
Piet Mondrian with *Broadway Boogie-Woogie*, New York, 1944; photograph by Fritz Glarner.

194
Piet Mondrian; *Composition with Red, Yellow, and Blue*, 1935–42; oil on canvas; 39¾ x 20⅛ in. (101 x 51 cm); courtesy Christie's, New York.

In September 1938, alarmed by the imminence of war, Piet Mondrian resolved to leave Europe for more secure surroundings in the United States. The first step in this itinerary involved a move from Paris, the city that had been the Dutch painter's adopted home for more than two decades, to London, where he would remain for two years. By mid-1940, having witnessed the German occupation of Holland and France and anticipating the aerial bombing of the British capital, Mondrian made final preparations for his voyage to America. He reached New York in early October 1940, having forwarded a significant number of notebook drawings and oil paintings.[1]

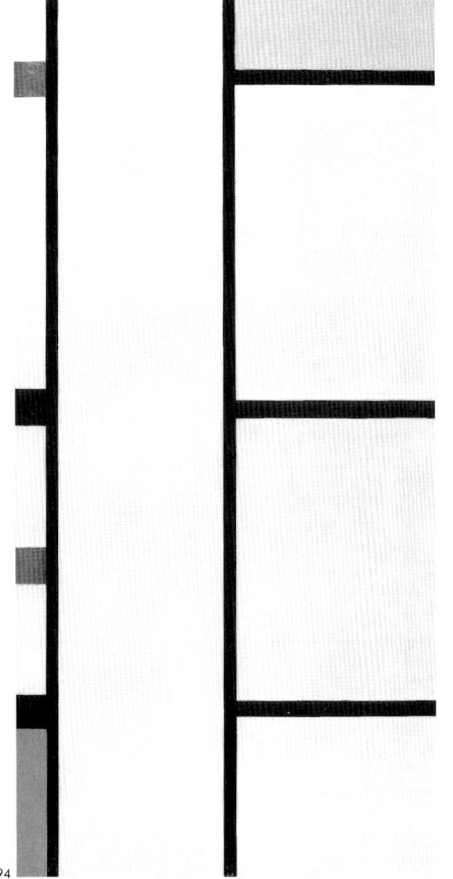

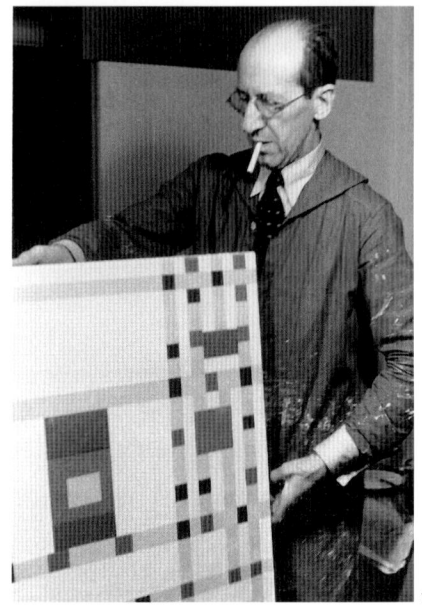

Mondrian made the transition to his new surroundings with relative ease. He found social and artistic companionship with expatriate artists of his own generation (including Max Ernst, László Moholy-Nagy, and Hans Richter) and with a group of younger New York-based abstract painters (Fritz Glarner, Carl Holty, Harry Holtzman, and Charmion von Wiegand).[2] He joined the American Abstract Artists, a New York exhibiting society, in January 1941. Mondrian resumed painting by reworking a group of canvases that had arrived from London, acknowledging the long delay between conception and completion by inscribing two separate dates on them. The painter also began a series of entirely new compositions in whose titles he paid homage to New York, his new hometown. The Valentine Gallery organized a solo exhibition, the first of Mondrian's career, at the beginning of 1942.

Because their production spans the European and North American phases of Mondrian's activity, the double-dated compositions are excellent measures of both long-term trends and new developments in the painter's art. *Composition with Red, Yellow, and Blue* (1935–42; fig. 194) is one such picture. Like all of Mondrian's works after 1920, this painting was constructed from a small set of compositional variables: color planes (in the primary tones of red, yellow, and blue), planes of "noncolor" (white, gray, and black), and black lines that demarcate planes and sometimes subdivide the entire canvas. The expressive effects of this

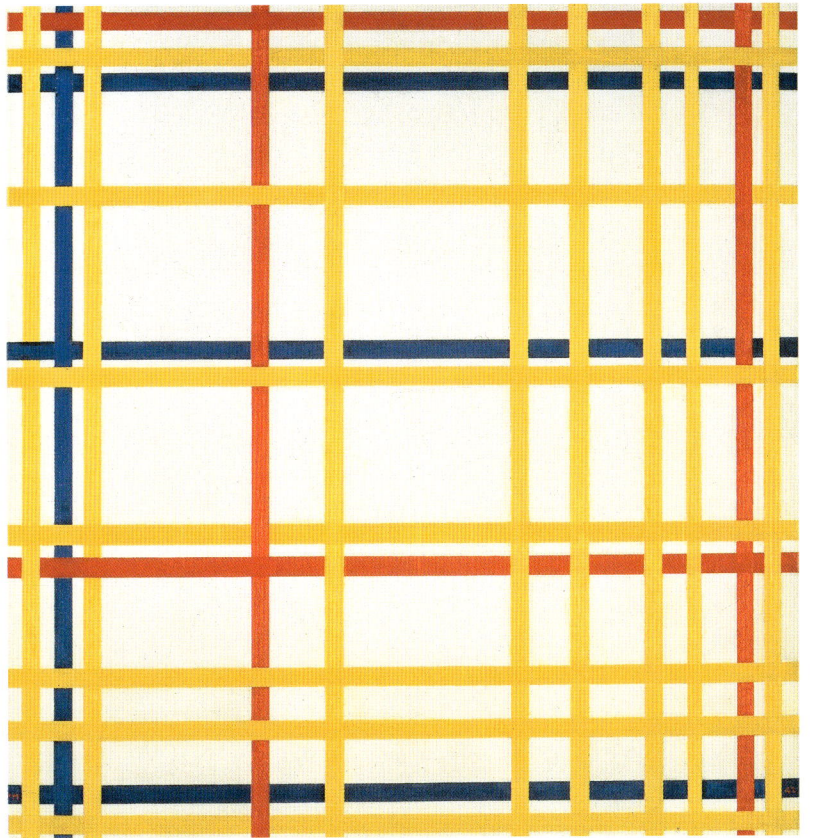

195
Piet Mondrian; *New York City; New York City I*, 1941–42; oil on canvas; 47 x 45 in. (119.3 x 114.2 cm); Musée National d'Art Moderne, Centre Georges Pompidou, Paris.

particular work—its feeling of expansion or focus, equilibrium or dynamism—followed from the relationship of line to plane and the relationship of these to the composition's outer edge. In *Composition with Red, Yellow, and Blue*, rectangular planes of noncolor, separated by black bars of two different widths, establish a rhythmical dialogue across an undivided central channel, while opposing corners of the canvas are marked by fields that contrast with each other in terms of their color (yellow and blue), size, proportion, and horizontal-vertical alignment. Effects of this kind conform to the well-established logic of Mondrian's system.

Like the other double-dated European-American works, however, *Composition with Red, Yellow, and Blue* also bears the mark of an important evolution in the painter's system. The painting's left margin contains two small colored elements, red bars, which were added only during the final phases of work. Since these are not defined by black borders, the bars appear as bits of lines rather than planes. The result is an apparent fusion of color and line, two elements that had generally operated as distinct variables within Mondrian's painting system. This shift in approach had an immediate effect on the character of the painter's work; its repercussions were amply demonstrated in *New York City; New York City I* (1941–42; fig. 195), the only entry in the 1942 Valentine Gallery exhibition that had been conceived and executed entirely on North American soil. *New York City; New York City I* is taken over by colored lines. As the linear weave of red, yellow, and blue grids extends across the canvas, there is a marked intensification in effects of visual dynamism across the length and breadth of the picture and into a shallow optical space.

Neoplasticism, Mondrian's label for his abstract painting style, revealed the underlying logic of such compositions: the expression of abstract, or "new," form in painting. The painter proposed that the elimination of all references to natural forms would produce a distinct transformation in the viewer's subjective response to art. He proposed further that his abstract painting had the power to inspire ever more profound and transcendent aesthetic perceptions. Neoplasticism paved the way for a purification, revitalization, and liberation of human consciousness. Finally, abstract art's emancipatory function was not a matter of aesthetics alone; it had, in fact, broader implications for the evolution of human existence. As Mondrian concluded in an essay that appeared in conjunction with the 1942 Valentine Gallery exhibition, "Because it is free of all utilitarian limitations plastic art must move not only parallel with human progress but must advance ahead of it."[3]

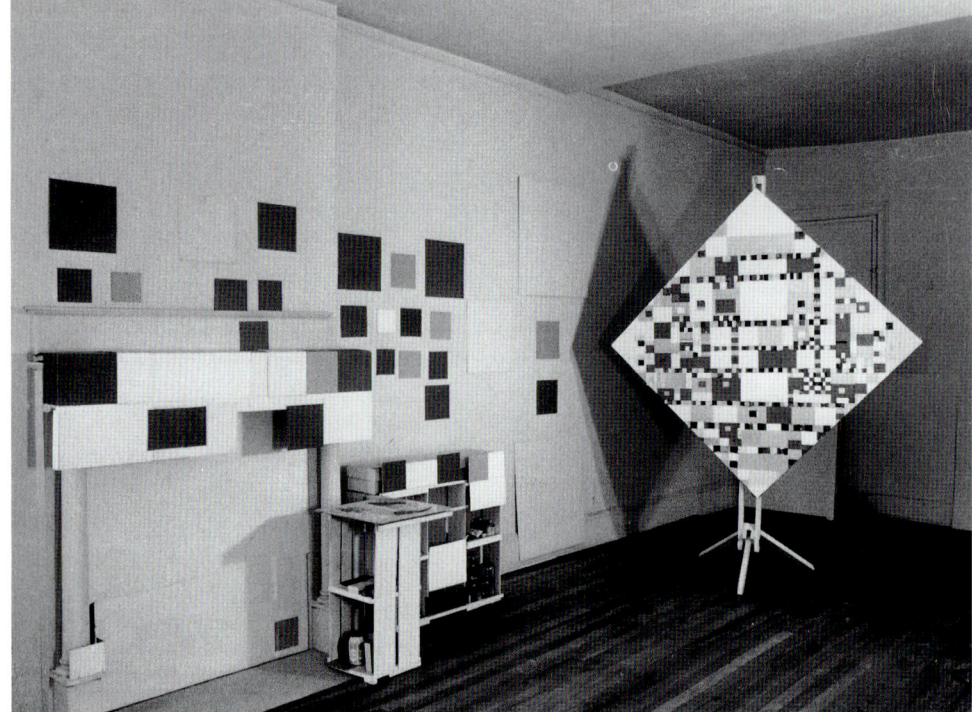

196
Mondrian's studio on East Fifty-ninth Street after the artist's death, showing *Victory Boogie-Woogie*, 1944; photograph by Fritz Glarner.

197
Piet Mondrian; *Broadway Boogie-Woogie*, 1942–43; oil on canvas; 50 x 50 in. (127 x 127 cm); The Museum of Modern Art, New York, given anonymously.

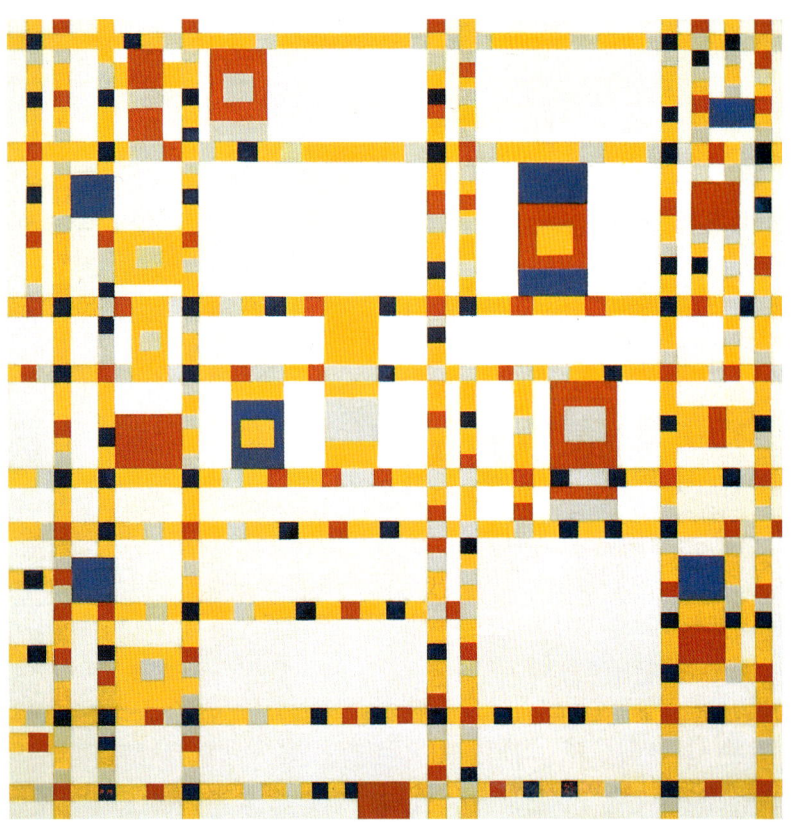

The realization of a neoplastic utopia was, Mondrian admitted, a matter for the distant future. Nevertheless, he did find the incipient signs of a prospective culture of pure form—and thus the promise of a release from regressive ways of perceiving and living—in the culture of the present. The connection was effected through the artist's response to the urban environment in which he thrived. Mechanization, modern architecture, the urban entertainments of jazz and contemporary social dancing all presented gratifying examples of the modernization of consciousness. While his painting style excluded any possibility of depicting these parallel phenomena, Mondrian was willing to refer to them when explaining his artistic ambitions. Boogie-woogie was not simply one of the painter's great passions. It realized effects that were "homogeneous" with his own intentions in painting: the creation of an abstract sensibility through the continuous deployment of pure aesthetic means, in this case musical rhythms. To take another example, in *New York City; New York City I* and related paintings Mondrian in fact sought to communicate "what New York meant to [him]" as he approached the city by boat and there reestablished his existence, without ever actually depicting the modern architecture he so admired.[4]

Whatever the precise nature of those personal meanings, they clearly went well beyond a generic affinity for metropolitan experience. No doubt those meanings were substantially informed by Mondrian's most immediate political circumstances, that is, by his status as an exile. He reflected on the political implications of neoplasticism in "Liberation from Oppression in Art and Life," an essay he conceived while living in London in 1939. In a letter to

Holtzman, Mondrian explained that he had been inspired to write "by impulse of the actual world situation," adding that the essay "would be useful for America too."[5] The lessons of the piece were emphatically idealist in nature. In moral terms, Mondrian argued, modern art functions to "help to unveil the evil of all oppression" and, in a moment of political crisis, provides a site for spiritual struggle against totalitarianism. "Plastic art is a free aspect of life. *Not being bound* by physical or material conditions, it does not tolerate any oppression and can resist it. It is disinterested, its only function is to 'show.' It is up to us to see what it reveals."[6] The essay was completed with Holtzman's assistance during Mondrian's first few weeks in New York. Although it went unpublished during the painter's lifetime, "Liberation" had a public reading in January 1942, during a meeting sponsored by the American Abstract Artists.

The years 1942 and 1943 were a period of intense activity for Mondrian. He began two new compositions, works that would be vehicles of a final evolution within the neoplastic system. The first of these, *Broadway Boogie-Woogie* (1942–43; fig. 197), demonstrates the nature of this last transition. The lattice effect of *New York City; New York City I* and related works disappears as line dissolves into a highly accented structure of colored squares and rectangles. Now broken into particles, the composition achieves a new measure of evanescence; in conceptual terms the emancipation of vision proceeds on its course. *Broadway Boogie-Woogie* was shown at Mondrian's second Valentine Gallery show in March 1943 and was quickly purchased by a collector for the Museum of Modern Art. The painter was soon able to move to expanded quarters, a combined studio and living space that became the final testing ground for the principles of neoplasticism (see fig. 196).

As he had done in previous studios, Mondrian adapted the constructive and compositional principles of his art in appointing his working environment. Rectangular cards of red, yellow, blue, gray, and white were tacked to off-white walls, creating independent and changeable assemblies. While he used these groupings to test compositional ideas for his painting, the cards also had an architectural function; they animated the room's walls in dynamic rhythm. Mondrian's environmental work extended even to the studio's rectilinear, white-painted furniture, much of it fashioned by the painter from salvaged wooden boards. Unifying the plane surfaces of his rooms with their functional furnishings, the painter transformed his environment into a neoplastic construction. The studio was a place in which to work, of course, but it also functioned as the model for a future in which, to borrow Mondrian's terms, painting and architecture would merge and where art would converge with practical existence.[7] Once this new type of spatial harmony was achieved, Mondrian believed, individuals would be free to realize a harmonious and universalized mode of living.[8] It was in his second New York studio that Mondrian worked on his final composition, a canvas whose title looks forward to the eventual triumph of neoplastic culture and to the victory of modernism itself: *Victory Boogie-Woogie* (1943–44; fig. 180).[9] This work remained in the studio, unfinished, at the time of the painter's death on February 1, 1944.

Notes

1 Mondrian's correspondence contains valuable information regarding the stages of his move to New York; see Sophie Bowness, "Mondrian in London: Letters to Ben Nicholson and Barbara Hepworth," *Burlington Magazine* 132 (November 1990): 782–88. See also the comprehensive chronology by Joop Joosten with Angelica Zander Rudenstine, in *Piet Mondrian, 1872–1944*, exh. cat. (Milan: Leonardo Arte, 1994), 72–75. The latter publication is the best source of documentation regarding the works of art discussed here.

2 On Mondrian's American followers, see Nancy J. Troy, *Mondrian and Neo-Plasticism in America*, exh. cat. (New Haven: Yale University Art Gallery, 1979).

3 Piet Mondrian, "Toward the True Vision of Reality" (1941), in *The New Art—The New Life: The Collected Writings of Piet Mondrian*, ed. and trans. Harry Holtzman and Martin James (Boston: G. K. Hall, 1986), 341.

4 See the painter's comments in the "Interview with Mondrian" composed by the curator and critic James Johnson Sweeney from letters sent by Mondrian in 1943, in Mondrian, *The New Art—The New Life,* 357; and in Sidney Janis, "School of Paris Comes to U.S.," *Decision* 2 (November–December 1941): 90. See also the painter's 1927 essay "Jazz and the Neo-Plastic," in *The New Art—The New Life,* 217–22.

5 Mondrian, letter of 13 February 1940; cited in Harry Holtzman, "Mondrian and 'Liberation,'" in *Mondrian: Drawings, Watercolors, New York Paintings,* exh. cat. (Stuttgart: Staatsgalerie Stuttgart, 1980), 24.

6 Piet Mondrian, "Liberation from Oppression in Art and Life" (1939–40), in *The New Art—The New Life,* 320. See also the related essay entitled "A New Religion?" (1938–40), ibid., 318–19.

7 The painter analyzed this distinction in several essays concerning the relation of architecture and painting, including "The Arts and the Beauty of Our Tangible Surroundings" (1923) and "Home—Street—City" (1926), in *The New Art—The New Life,* 189, 205–12.

8 Herbert Henkels traces Mondrian's attitudes toward his working space in "Mondrian in His Studio," trans. Maya von Leeuwen and Hans Nieuweling, in *Mondrian: Drawings, Watercolors, New York Paintings,* 219–85. See also Harry Holtzman, "Piet Mondrian's Environment," in *Mondrian: The Process Works,* exh. cat. (New York: Pace Gallery, 1970): 4–5.

The second New York studio was ultimately dismantled and partly preserved by Holtzman. Surviving elements included pieces of handmade furniture, personal objects, and several groupings of Mondrian's colored wall rectangles, which were eventually mounted, framed, and fixed permanently in the sequences they happened to be in at the time of the painter's death. The conservation of its parts, together with periodic reconstructions of the space, have given Mondrian's final interior a meaning that is both lasting and ambiguous. Attesting to the painter's mode of living and working, the surviving elements have a documentary value. Once removed from the studio, the arrangements of colored cards have been exhibited as if they were works of art in their own right; since the wall arrangements were not meant to be seen as permanent and autonomous compositions, however, this is controversial. On the preservation of the studio, see Harry Holtzman, "Introduction," in *Piet Mondrian: The Wall Works, 1943–44,* exh. cat. (New York: Carpenter and Hochman Gallery, 1984), unpaginated; and Nancy Troy, "To Be Continued: A Note on Some Recent Mondrians," *October,* no. 27 (Winter 1983): 75–80.

9 On the meaning of the title *Victory Boogie-Woogie,* see E. A. Carmean Jr., *Mondrian: The Diamond Compositions,* exh. cat. (Washington, D.C.: National Gallery of Art, 1979), 65–66.

198
André Kertész, *Lost Cloud*, 1937 (cat. no. 80).

experiencing the new world

DEBORAH IRMAS

andreas feininger

andré kertész

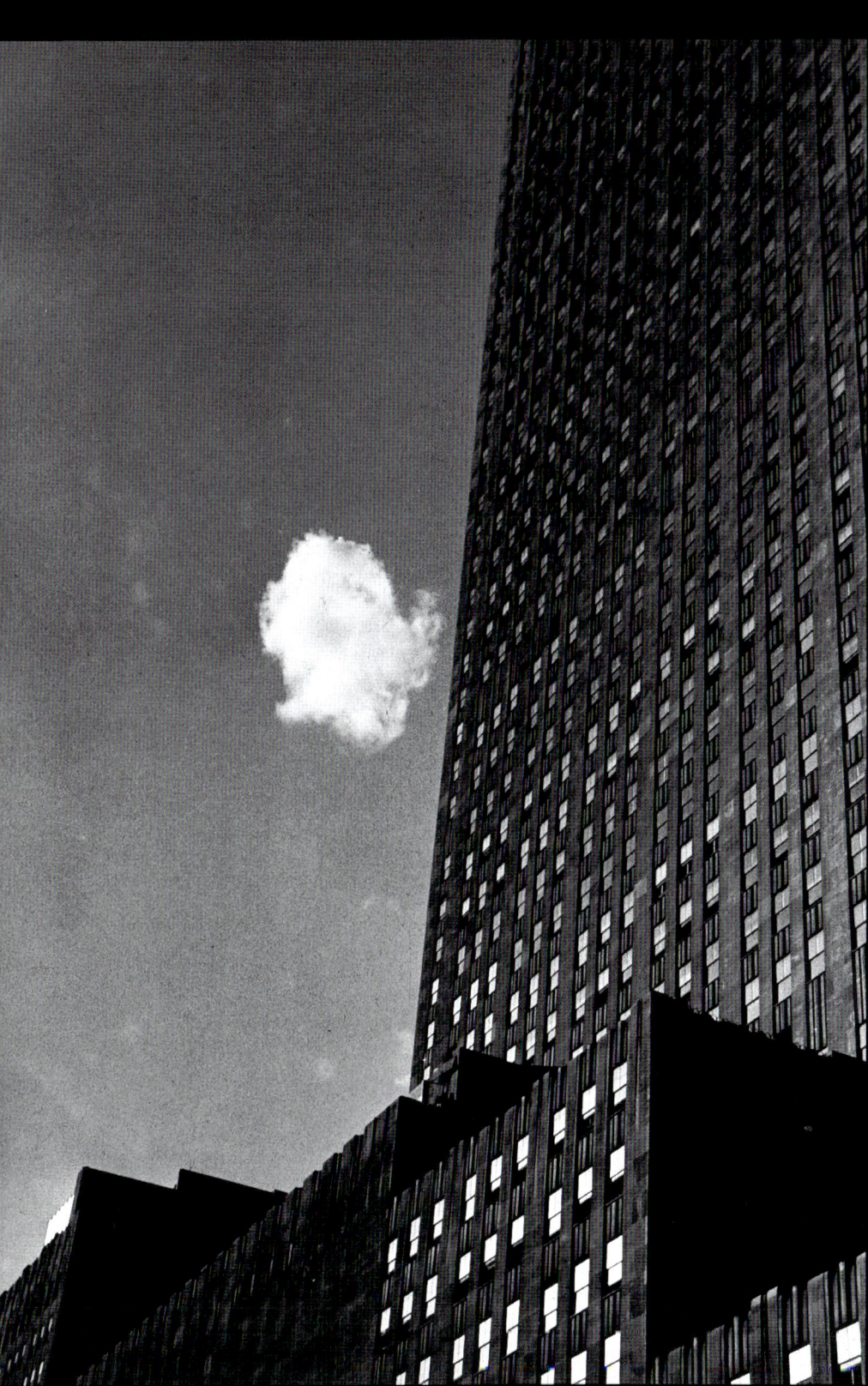

andreas b. l. feininger in new york, 1939–45

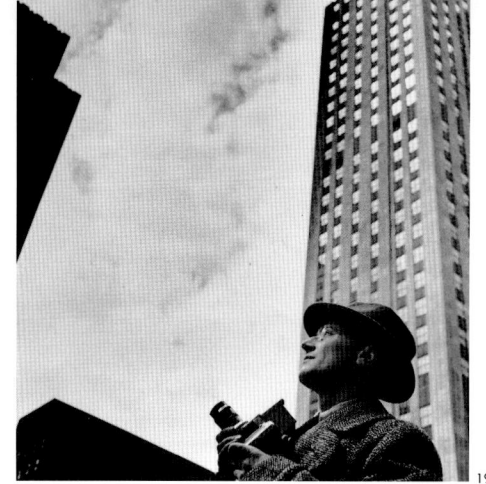

1906	born in Paris
1932	emigrates from Germany (Dessau) to France (Paris)
1933	immigrates to Sweden (Stockholm)
1939	immigrates to the U.S. (New York)

199
Andreas Feininger, 1941.

200
Andreas Feininger, *Solarized Nude*, 1941 (cat. no. 47).

When Andreas Feininger; his wife, Gertrud ("Wysse," née Hagg); and their young son, Tomas, disembarked from the steamer *Oslofjord* in New York on December 16, 1939, they had only three trunks of belongings. Among them were Rolliflex and Exacta cameras, an enlarger that Feininger had designed himself, and a nine-by-twelve-centimeter camera with a telephoto lens that he had constructed in Stockholm. Most important, however, was his American passport. Although born in Paris, Feininger obtained his citizenship from his American-born father, the painter Lyonel Feininger. Yet this was his first time on American soil.

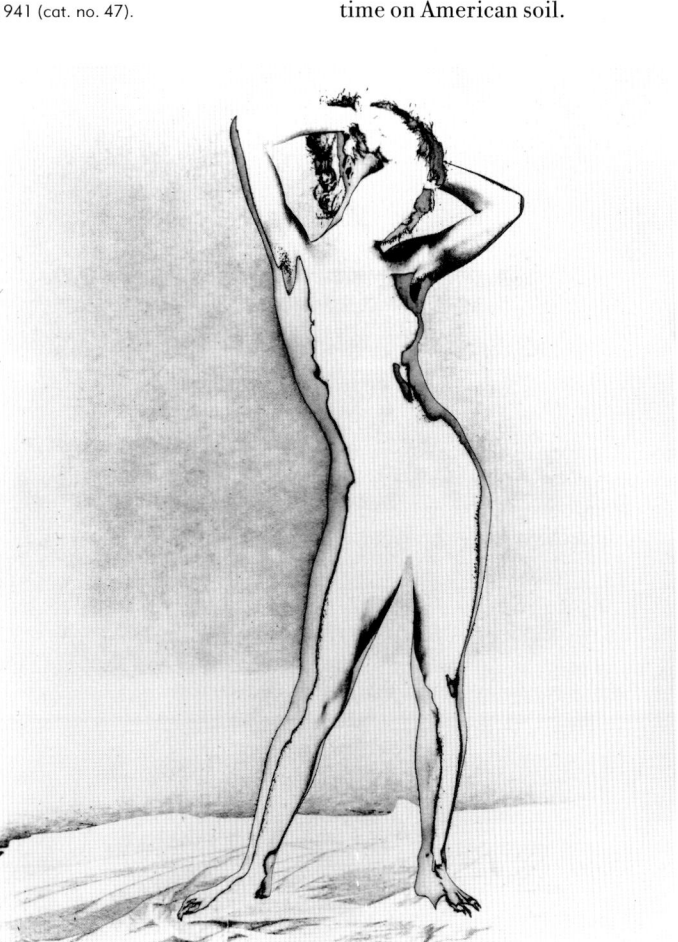

Feininger had been raised and educated in Germany but left there in 1932, at the age of twenty-six, to find work. For nine months he interned with Le Corbusier in Paris, but when his savings dwindled, he headed north to Stockholm with his future wife. There he found a city waiting to be photographed. Six years later, when Germany advanced into Finland, the Feiningers looked to America.

Feininger arrived in New York as a respected and widely published expert on modern photography, having written nine books on the medium, each illustrated with his own photographs.[1] His most recent book, *New Paths in Photography,* had been published in Boston only a few months prior to his emigration. The title of the book—which had been written in his native language, German, and translated into English—could be said to prefigure Feininger's future, for soon after his arrival he began his own new career path, working for the first time without restrictions, either political or economic. Nevertheless, he maintained his European perspective on the supremacy of style and attraction in his photography. This attitude is clearly stated at the beginning of *New Paths*: "I feel that I must urge my readers to free themselves from prejudices they may not have been aware of having, of which perhaps the strongest has ever been the assumption that a picture, photographic or otherwise, must need have another meaning than its own intrinsic beauty."[2]

All of the images chosen for *New Paths* were made in Sweden, and each was highly graphic, employing photographic techniques such as negative printing, solarization, and granulation, which emphasized linear elements

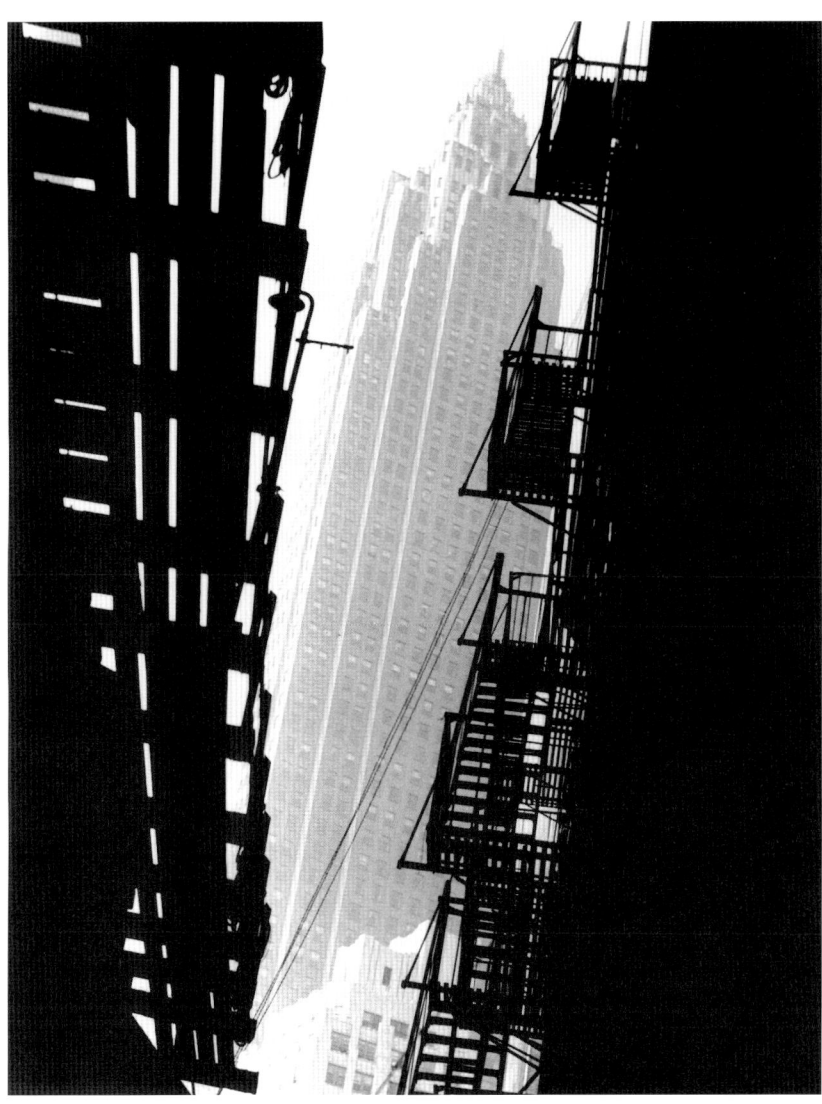

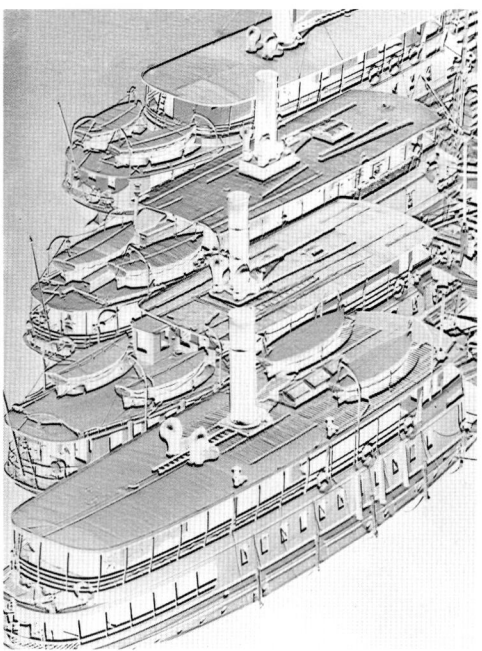

201
Andreas Feininger, *The Cities Service Building, Fire Escapes, and the El*, 1940 (cat. no. 42).

202
Andreas Feininger; *Stockholm—Lake Steamer*, 1937; solarized gelatin silver print; 9¼ x 7⅛ in (23.4 x 18 cm); Los Angeles County Museum of Art, Ralph M. Parsons Fund.

and pattern rather than the continuous-tone quality of a more traditional photographic rendering. Experimental, stylized images such as these would be part of Feininger's photographic repertoire for the next forty years. *Solarized Nude* (1941; fig. 200, cat. no. 47), made within the first two years of his arrival in New York, could be mistaken for *Standing Nude* (1933), in which he used the outline of a woman's lithe figure to illustrate his graphic virtuosity. The clear, purposeful arrangements of dark, linear elements against a light background in *The Cities Service Building, Fire Escapes, and the El* (1940; fig. 201, cat. no. 42) is reminiscent of the geometric landscape of a ship's bow in *Stockholm—Lake Steamer* (1937; fig. 202). Each is a study, an exercise in photographic composition, whose purpose is to provide aesthetic pleasure rather than information.

The sense of specificity or of the photograph as a medium of factual documentation was of lesser significance to a European sensibility than to an American one.[3] Feininger's titles are meant to identify the photograph rather than to elucidate the subject depicted, and we are given even less information about the nude than about the steamer or the urban vista. In an annotated chronology written in 1980, Feininger credits the photographic

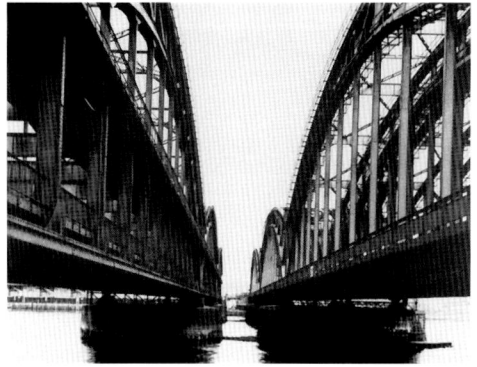

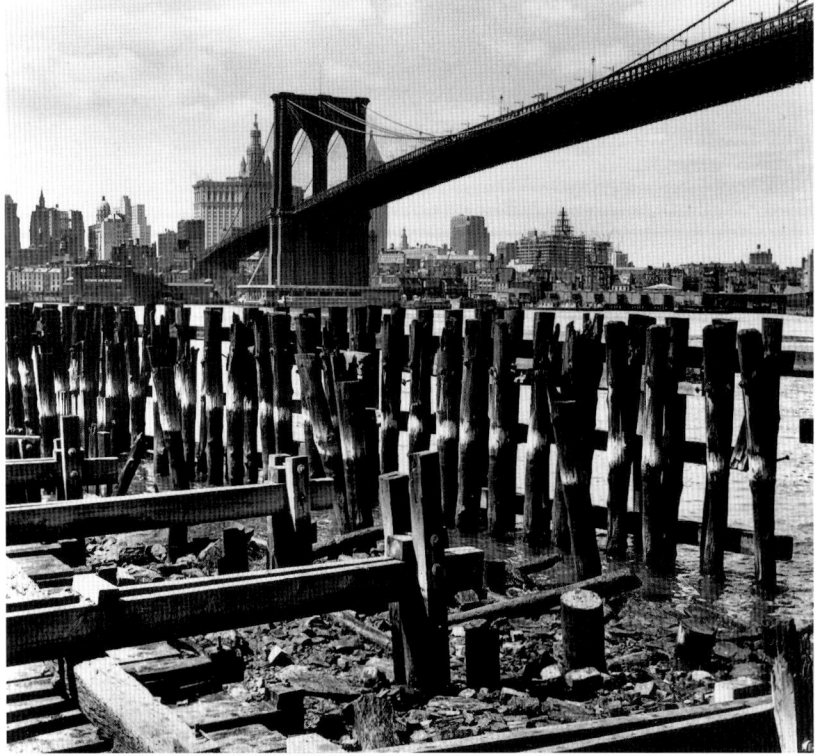

203
Albert Renger-Patzsch, *Railroad Bridge*, c. 1928.

204
Andreas Feininger, *N.Y.—Brooklyn Bridge from Brooklyn Shore*, 1940 (cat. no. 45).

methods of Germans Albert Renger-Patzsch (see fig. 203) and Paul Wolff, proponents of the photographic version of Neue Sachlichkeit (new objectivity) for this tactic, stating that he was attracted to "the boldness, clarity, and simplicity of their approach to *ordinary* subjects."[4]

Within three weeks of his arrival in New York, Feininger began working for the Black Star Picture Agency, at the rate of twenty dollars per week.[5] Almost immediately he was introduced to Wilson Hicks, *Life* magazine's executive editor, who, by 1940, was giving the photographer assignments and acquainting him with the burgeoning new genre of the picture story: a series of captioned photographs made specifically for the mass-produced American weekly magazine. It could be argued that this circumstance, coupled with the potency of the urban experience of New York itself, caused Feininger to elaborate his approach to the photographic image. While he never abandoned his belief in the primacy of technique, his graphic language, and his reliance on darkroom wizardry, the subject itself began to occupy a more prominent position in his oeuvre.

In works such as *Jewish Establishments on Manhattan's Lower East Side* (fig. 206, cat. no. 44) and *N.Y.—Brooklyn Bridge from Brooklyn Shore* (fig. 204, cat. no. 45), both from 1940, the graphic arrangements, pattern, and structure of the architectural elements are still essential to Feininger's photographic composition. Yet the imposing character of New York, the specificity of the place—communicated through the choice of a particular part of the skyline, as well as details such as the disintegrating supports of the pier and the presence of a distinctive person—signals a change, a meaning that goes beyond the subject's "own intrinsic beauty." *Elk's Rendezvous, a Harlem Night Club* (1940; fig. 205, cat. no. 43) reconfirms this shift in emphasis from the formal exercise to the exploration of place. The esteemed German emphasis on the "ordinary" subject has given way to a search for the uncommon, the more American preference for that which is "different." In describing his response to New York, Feininger defined his own shifting course from the aestheticized toward the wondrous:

> It was the most exciting city I'd ever seen in a way; it was dramatic. The most beautiful city was Stockholm, but New York was absolutely fabulous. It was

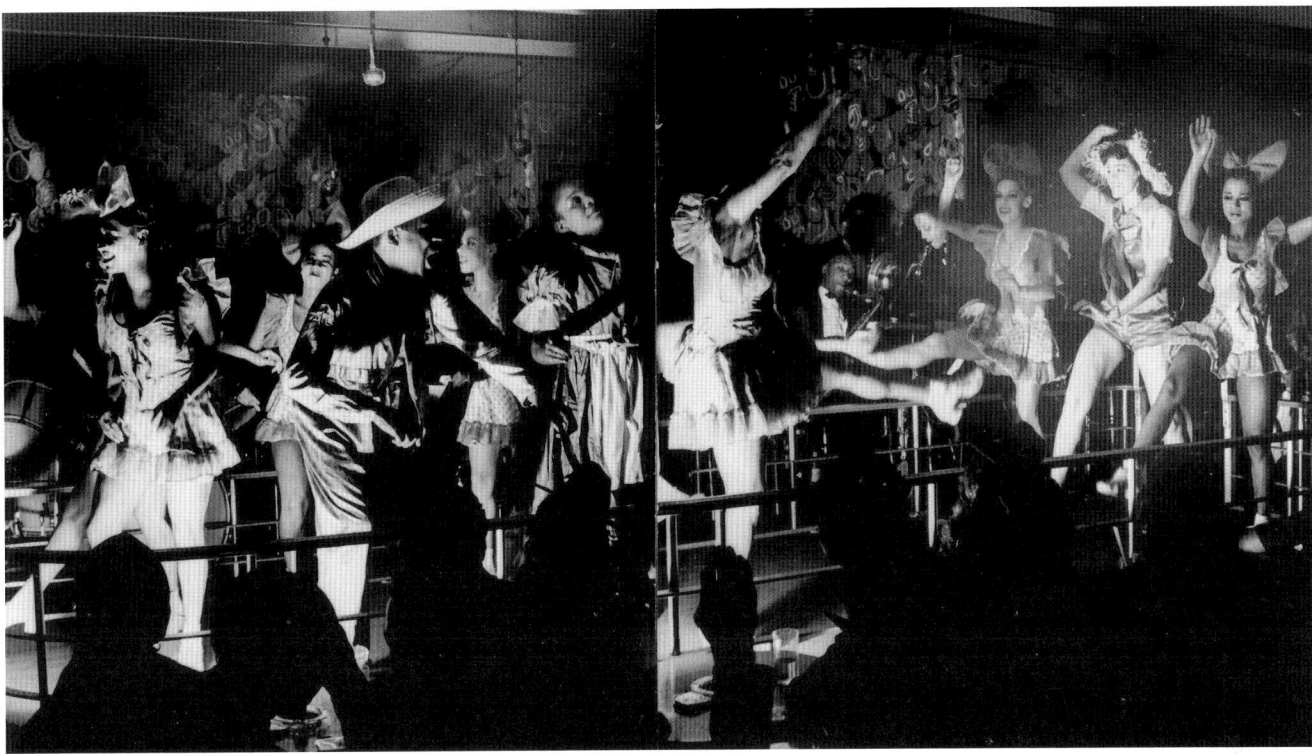

205
Andreas Feininger, *Elk's Rendezvous, a Harlem Night Club*, 1940 (cat. no. 43).

206
Andreas Feininger, *Jewish Establishments on Manhattan's Lower East Side*, 1940 (cat. no. 44).

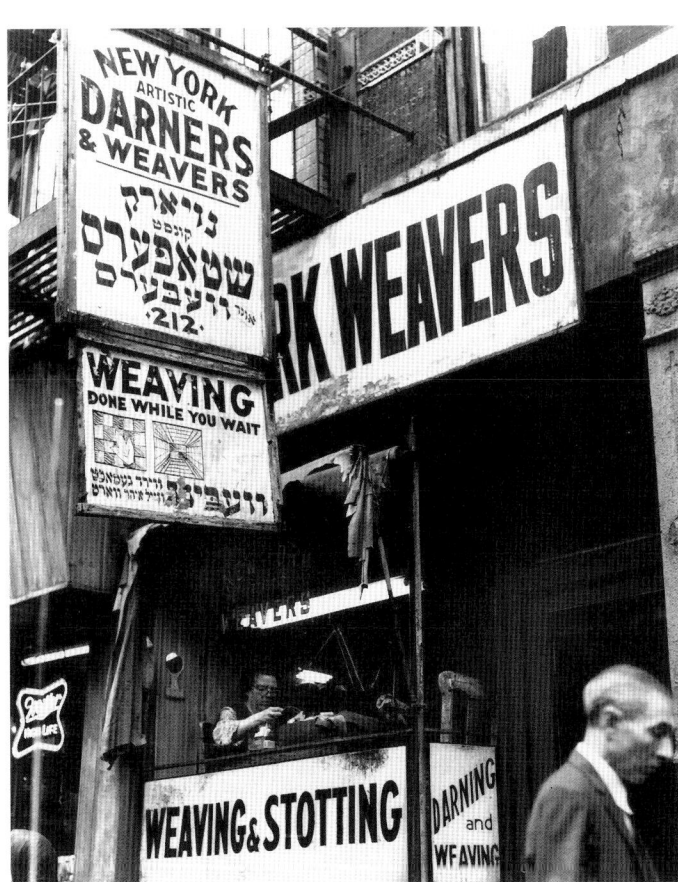

diversified.... There were skyscrapers and there were slums and there was a waterfront with ships and there were streets with traffic and there were all kinds of people ... black people. I'd never seen a black person before in my life. And there were whole sections with only one kind of people.... There was the Jewish quarter, and I loved the Hebrew writing in the little shops, and the Chinese quarter, and Yorkville was just as if it was taken out of Germany. The richness ... nothing like it existed in Europe."[6]

Although Feininger's career had been focused on photography for the page, either for his own books or for "picture stories," it is not surprising that by 1941 he had sold a photograph to the Museum of Modern Art. His documentary photographs confirmed the belief that subject and style could carry equal weight. That year he was accredited as a security-cleared correspondent for the Office of War Information, specializing in the photographic documentation of industry. Yet *Columbia Steel Company, Geneva, Utah* (1942), while a visual record of the war effort, appears even less informative, without the evidence of

andreas feininger 199

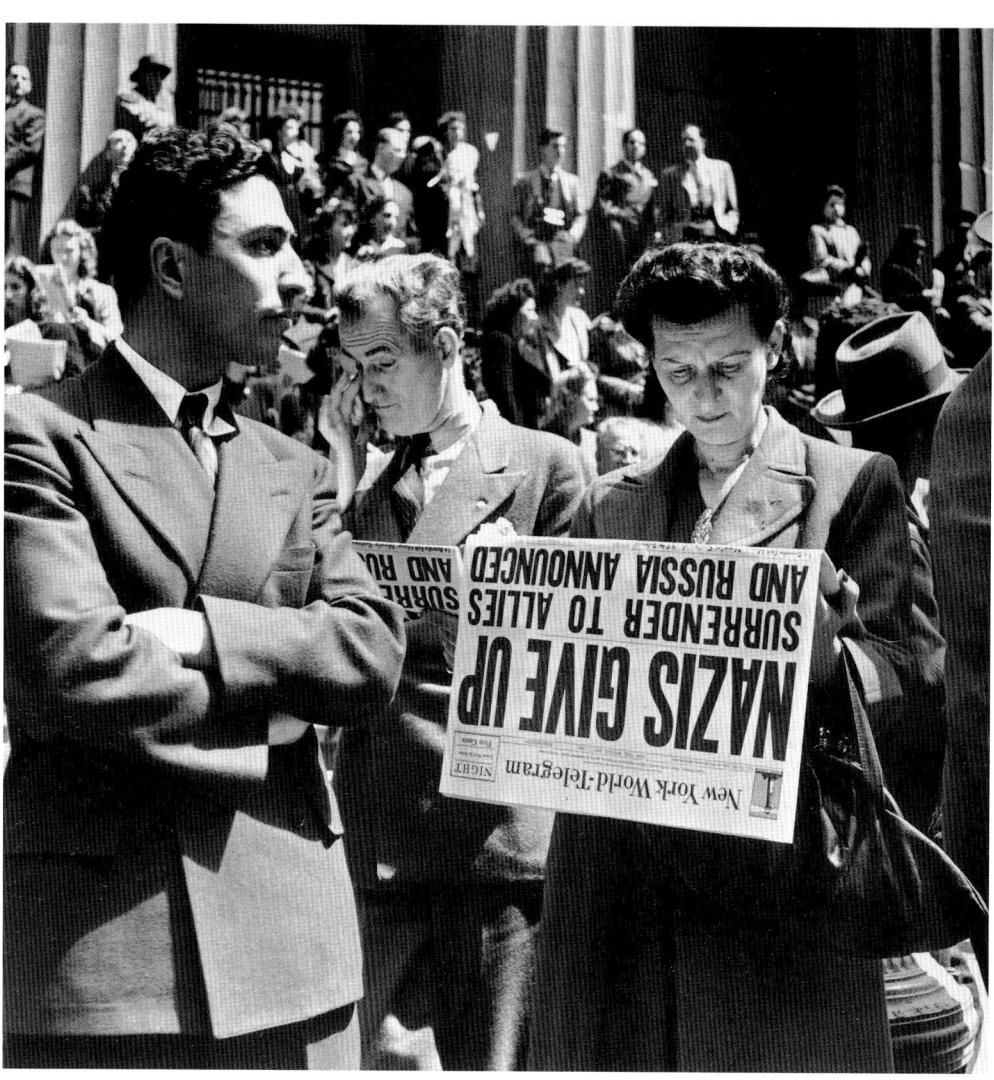

207
Andreas Feininger, *V-E Day Reaction*, 1945 (cat. no. 48).

Feininger's signature, that is, his elegant and usually prevalent formal concerns. One has the sense that the purpose of this picture was internal, that it was intended neither for the page nor the gallery wall. Conversely, in *V-E Day Reaction* of 1945 (fig. 207, cat. no. 48) Feininger's experiences and talents merge. The photograph, taken outside on a bright day, shows a man and a woman reading newspapers. The headline, "Nazis Give Up, Surrender to Allies and Russia Announced," is suspended upside down and serves as the focal point as well as the stand-in title of the photograph. The background, congested with chaotic swarms of people, is anchored in the exact center by a massive column. The entire image, illuminated by the strong raking light of a summer morning, reiterates the relief in the faces of the foreground figures. This is the work of an assimilated European photographer.

If Andreas Feininger had ever felt displaced in the United States, by 1941 such sentiments were well camouflaged in his work. By 1943 he could not have been more integrated into the cultural mainstream, receiving the coveted position of full-time staff photographer for *Life*. This appointment confirmed his command of the medium of photography and reaffirmed his citizenship, for *Life* in the 1940s and 1950s was more than a publication, it was an institution of American life, shaping a collective perception of events through photojournalism. Feininger published his pictures in *Life* for twenty years, and from this visible perch he attracted the attention of magazine and book publishers worldwide, enabling him to disseminate his pictorial philosophy in words and images and to instruct generations of photographers in the fundamentals of the medium.

Notes

1 See *Menschen vor der Kamera* (Harzburg: Herring, 1934); *Selbst entwickeln und kopieren* (Harzburg: Herring, 1935); *Aufnahmetechnik* (Harzburg: Herring, 1936); *Entwickeln, kopieren, vergrössern* (Harzburg: Herring, 1936); *Vergrössern leicht gemacht* (Harzburg: Herring, 1936); *Stockholm* (Stockholm: Bonniers, 1936); *Fotografische Gestaltung* (Harzburg: Herring, 1937); *Motive im Gegenlicht* (Harzburg: Herring, 1939); and *New Paths in Photography* (Boston: American Photographic Publishing, 1939).

2 Feininger, *New Paths in Photography*, 7

3 For further discussion of an "American" theory about photography and the abstracted image, see Beaumont Newhall on Edward Weston, in *The History of Photography from 1839 to the Present* (New York: Museum of Modern Art, 1982), 184–95.

4 Andreas B. L. Feininger, unpublished chronology, December 1980, 13 (emphasis mine). Biographical information was taken from this document. I would like to thank Andreas and Wysse Feininger and Bonni Benrubi for providing me with this and other material for this essay.

5 Interview with the author, 21 September 1994.

6 Ibid.

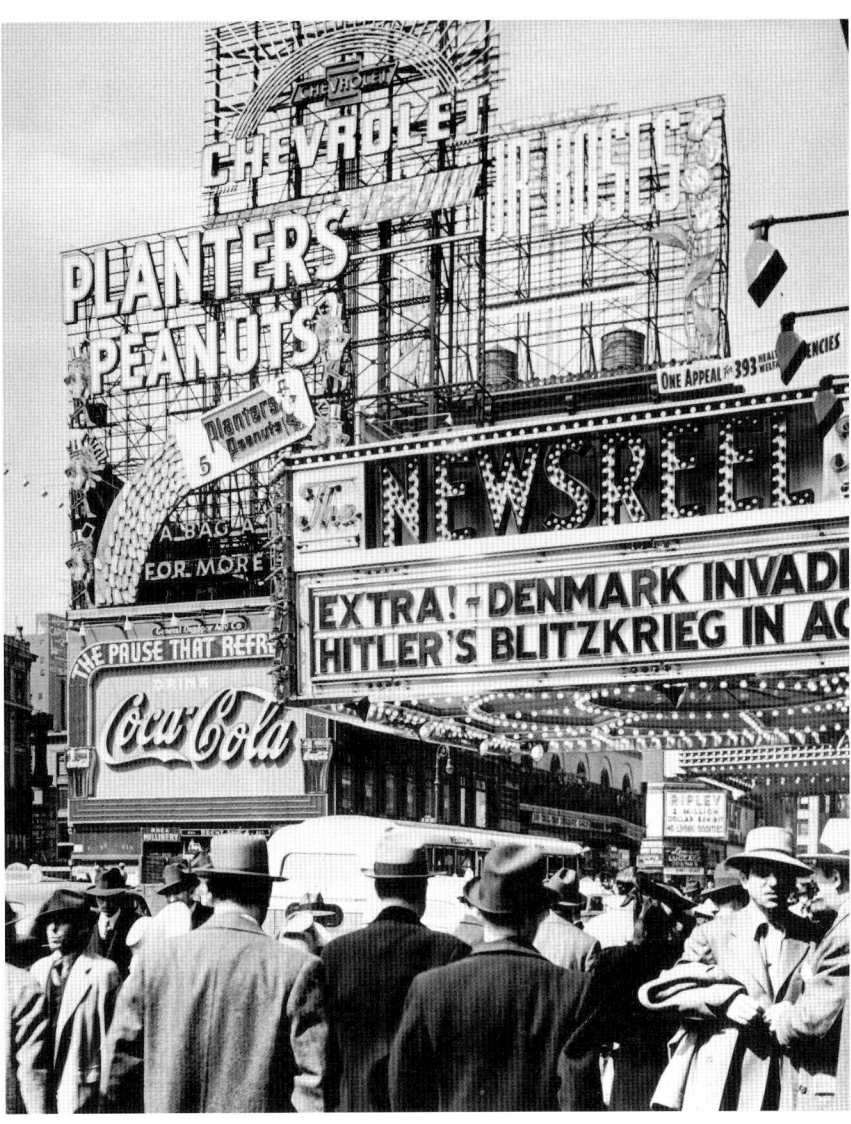

208
Andreas Feininger, *Times Square and Longacre Square*, 1940 (cat. no. 46).

andré kertész in new york, 1936–45

1894	born in Budapest
1936	emigrates from France (Paris) to the U.S. (New York)
1985	dies in New York

André Kertész's decision to leave Paris for New York in 1936 was neither obvious nor solitary. While his wife, Elizabeth, was a partner in the resolution to relocate, the photographer's brother Imre, writing from their native city of Budapest, urged Kertész to consider the invitation to work for the Keystone Photographic Company merely as a way to continue his creative work. Imre imagined that Kertész, with his Leica, would be able to fulfill his commercial assignments and create his personal work simultaneously. No agency, he wrote, especially an

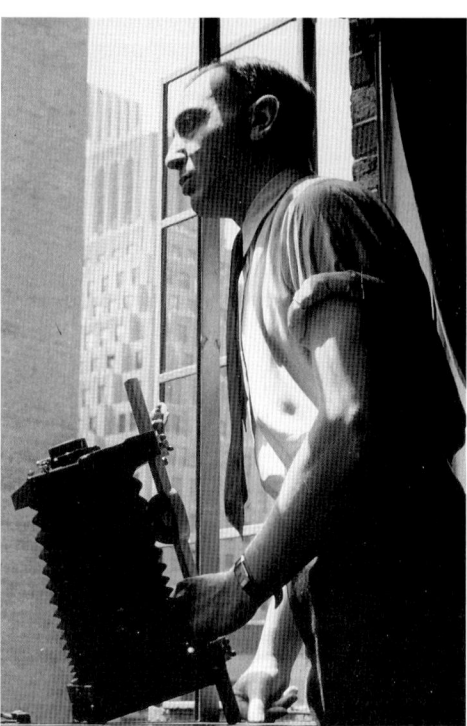

American one, could keep its contractors under continual supervision.[1] Imre's preconceptions certainly reinforced his brother's beliefs as well.

When Kertész arrived in New York in October, at the age of forty-two, his particular and original sensibility had already been noticed. What he was searching for in America was not only the recognition that he had received in Paris as an artist with an amalgamated surrealist and humanist vision but also the financial stability that had eluded him there. Even before he left Europe, he was arranging introductions for himself in New York to realize that aim. Within five weeks of his arrival he had an appointment with Julien Levy, who had already exhibited thirty-five of Kertész's works at his New York gallery in 1932. But other, more pragmatic, clearly commercial engagements graced his appointment calendar as well: visits to weekly publications, camera companies, and movie studios.[2] Curiously, as Kertész was crossing the Atlantic Ocean, Beaumont Newhall, the young curator of photography at New York's Museum of Modern Art, was seeking him out in Paris in order to include him in what would become the landmark exhibition *The History of Photography, 1839–1937*. Several weeks later Newhall found the emigré photographer in his New York hotel.[3]

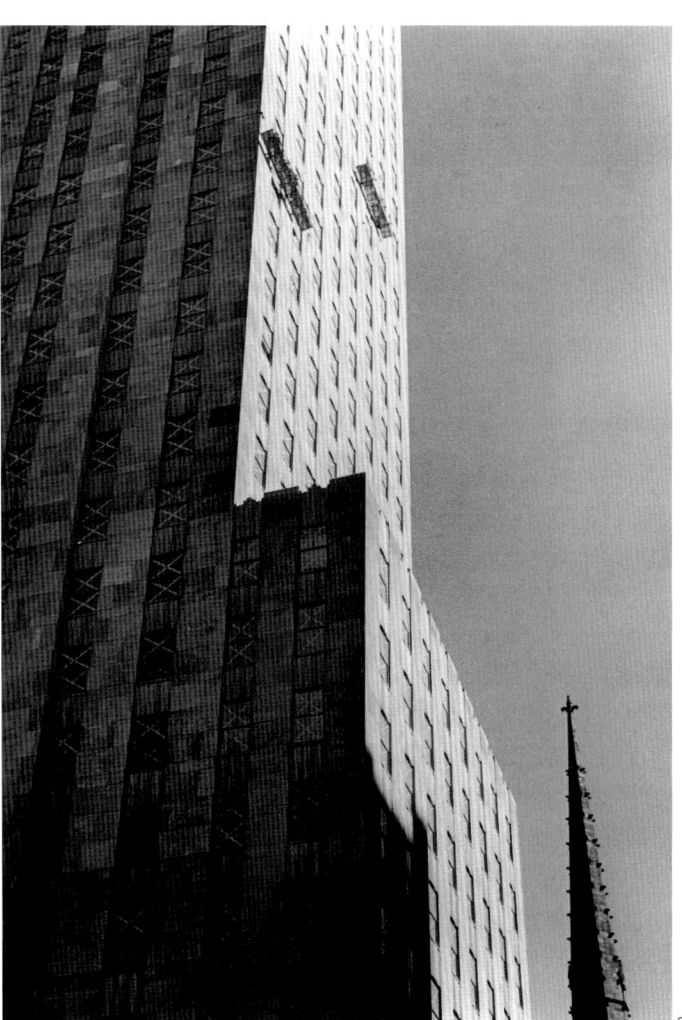

209
André Kertész, *Self-Portrait in the Hotel Beaux-Arts*, 1936 (cat. no. 76).

210
André Kertész; *Window Washing—Rockefeller Center*, 1937; gelatin-silver print; 9⅝ x 6¾ in. (24.6 x 17.3 cm); The J. Paul Getty Museum, Malibu, California. © Estate of André Kertész.

211
André Kertész, *Clothes Lines*, 1937 (cat. no. 78).

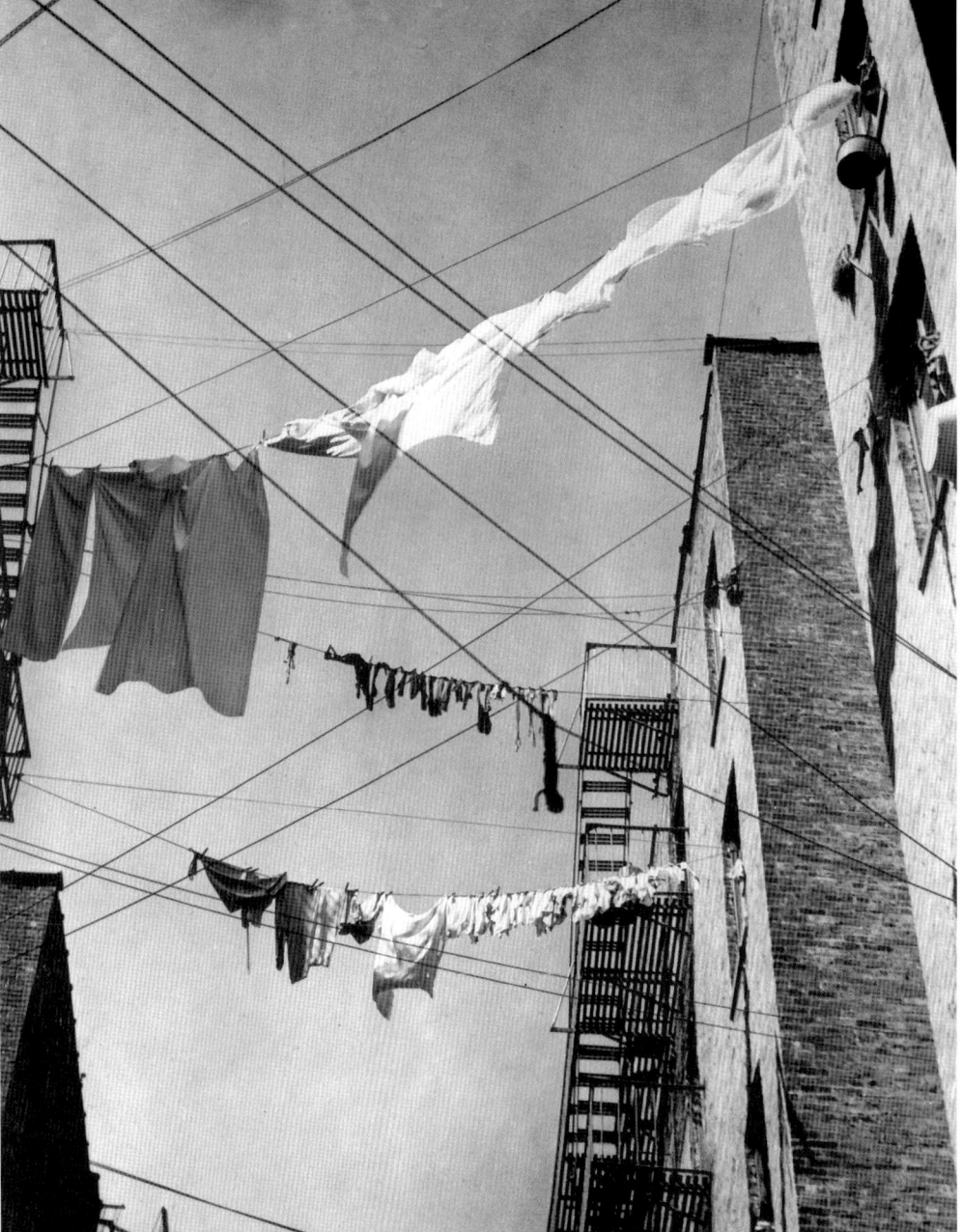

Self-Portrait in the Hotel Beaux-Arts (1936; fig. 209, cat. no. 76), taken in the morning hours of a sunny day in autumn, is a photograph filled with tentative anticipation. With his left hand on the tool of his trade and the right pressed against the window ledge, the photographer leans forward into the light skirting the open window. The variegated urban landscape beyond is the object of Kertész's fear and excitement. While the photographer's own body is equal in compositional mass to that of the city, his extended-view camera and the dark, curtained interior and window ledge surround him as if composing a protective frame. Presenting himself looking out, Kertész seems to be recording this image both as a personal, biographical document and as a study of explicit arrangements testifying to his stylistic inclination for capturing static forms together with dynamic ones.

The towering architecture of the city served as a recurring and unavoidable backdrop in several of Kertész's photographs from 1937. Views of monolithic skyscrapers against the sky are punctuated by inconsistencies of man and nature: laundry hung chaotically, window-washing scaffolding, and low-lying puffs of cumulus clouds are a poetic metaphor for the emigré photographer's sense of being overwhelmed

andré kertész   **203**

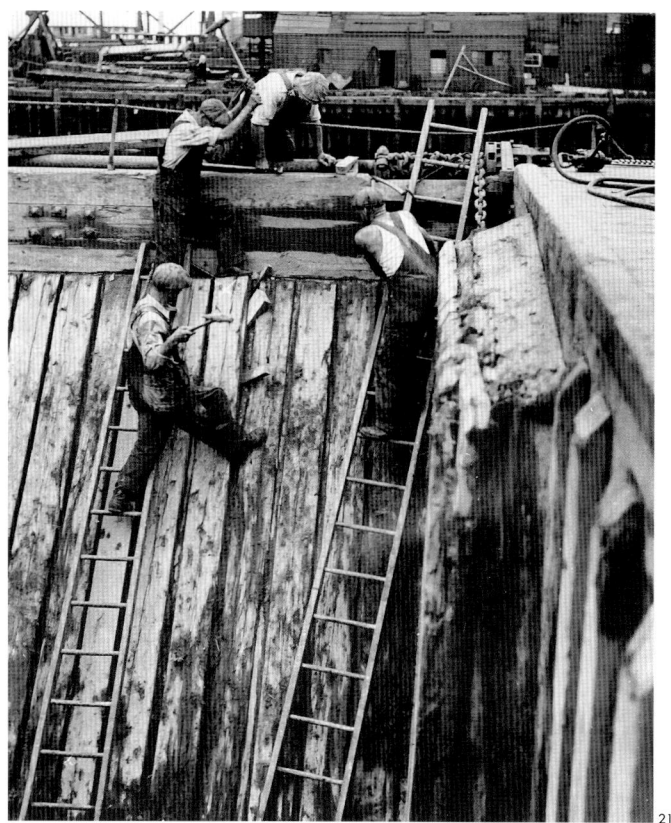

212

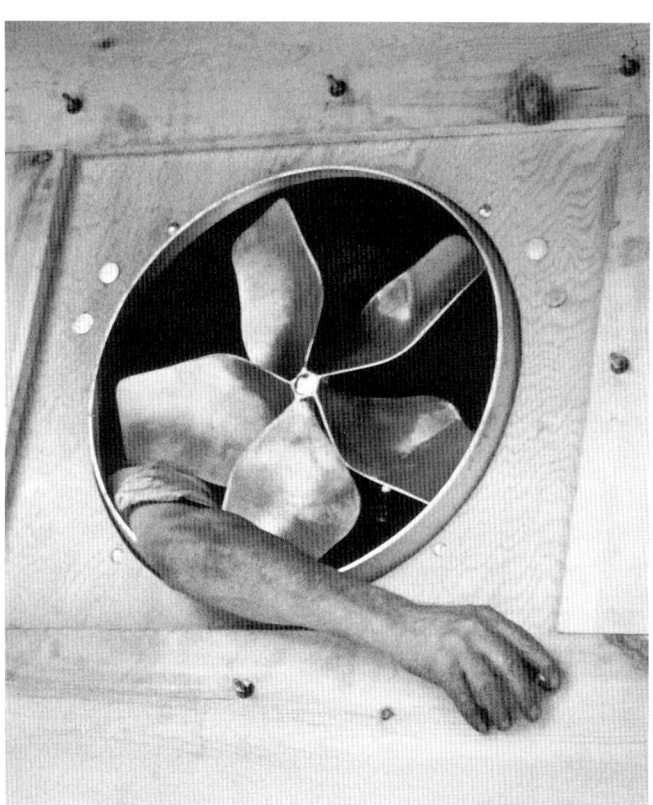

213

by his new, powerful surroundings. *Window Washing—Rockefeller Center* (1937; fig. 210), *Clothes Lines* (1937; fig. 211, cat. no. 78), and *Lost Cloud* (1937; fig. 198, cat. no. 80), as well as other images from this period, have been regarded as some of the most significant of the artist's career. Photographic historians have differed, however, on the reading of this work. While it seems that much of it was created for a book on New York proposed to the photographer by Imre Kertész, modeled on the 1934 publication *Paris vu par André Kertész* (Paris seen by André Kertész), some feel that, despite its subject matter, the work from this period is a nostalgic attempt to re-create the home left behind. Sandra Phillips has noted that the urgency and plethora of work from this period are reminiscent of a period ten years earlier, when Kertész first arrived in Paris. What he saw then on the streets of the French capital evoked memories of Hungary, and this led him to create some of his most enduring and important work.[4] Others see his New York output as the prototype of a distinctly urban vision, the birth of a street photography that would be associated forever aesthetically, if not actually, with the New York school of photographers. Jane Livingston recognizes the "peculiar mixture of toughness and romanticism" characteristic in the work of Louis Faurer, William Klein, Weegee, and others as part of the legacy of Kertész's work from this period.[5]

These interpretations of Kertész's early American period should not be regarded as contradictory. Ambivalence, nostalgia, and the excitement of discovering a new place coexist in this work. Consider *Workmen on the Waterfront* (c. 1938; fig. 212). Dungareed laborers—armed

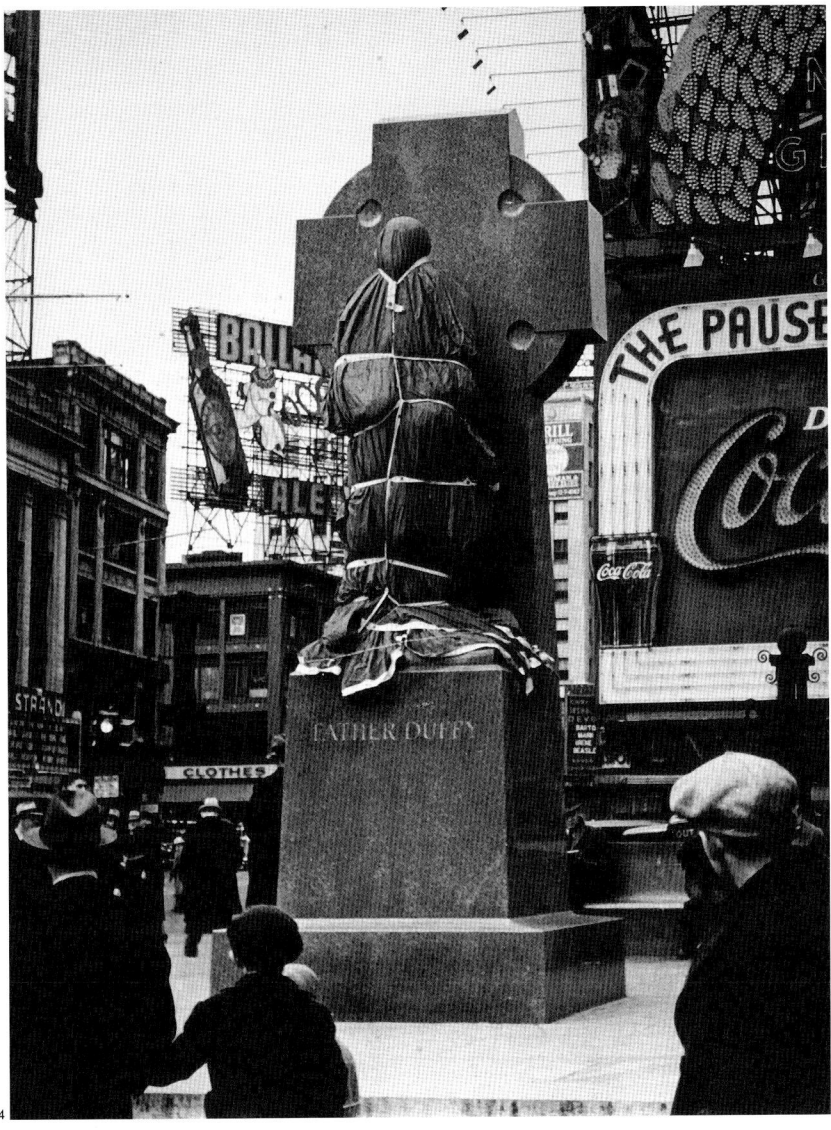

212
André Kertész; *Workmen on the Waterfront*, c. 1938; gelatin-silver print; 9⅜ x 7½ in. (23.8 x 19.0 cm); The Metropolitan Museum of Art, Purchase, Rogers Fund, The Elisha Whittelsey Collection, The Elisha Whittelsey Fund, Mary Livingston Griggs and Mary Griggs Burke Foundation and Mrs. Vincent Astor Gifts, 1984. © Estate of André Kertész.

213
André Kertész, *Arm and Ventilator*, 1937 (cat. no. 77).

214
André Kertész, *Father Duffy Monument, New York*, 1937 (cat. no. 79).

with metal cables, pickaxes, and pails—are actively building. Kertész certainly had to remain in the vicinity of this activity and be engaged by it to have succeeded in making this picture. Although it can be seen as a testament to the recovery of an economy that had been depressed for the previous ten years, this photograph cannot be read simply as a visual report on American current events. French artists such as Fernand Léger, once a subject of Kertész's camera, celebrated the workplace in their paintings. Wharves, boats, and ladders were codified as appropriate subject matter for the twentieth-century artist, and Léger's simple, flat forms, defined by powerful black lines, attest to the birth of a spirit of solidarity with ordinary working people which Kertész imported with him to the United States and transposed to the photographic image.

Kertész's mature vision—stimulated by new, unsettling circumstances and a radically different physical environment—engendered work that he believed should have earned him a position as a *Life* staff photographer. His elegantly structured, richly referential photography was perhaps seen as too European in its sensibility to be considered pure magazine reportage. His disappointment at being overlooked plagued him nearly fifty years after the fact: "At *Life* magazine they said, 'You're talking too much with your pictures. We only need documents. We have editors to write the text to go with it.' I don't want to go into details, but I felt cheated."[6] This great disappointment, this sense of being passed over, allowed Kertész to construct a role for himself as a defeated, unrecognized genius, one whose melancholy stemmed from both the physical and the emotional displacement of his life. In *Self-Portrait, November 18, 1939*, a depressed Kertész fondles the remainder of two shot glasses of liquor. Late afternoon light exaggerates the expression of dejection on his face, which is held aloft by his own hand. This photograph can be seen as a counterpart to the enthusiastic self-portrait made three years prior. But it is also possible that, in presenting himself as an artist suffering from mythic sorrow, Kertész was exploiting preconceptions about Eastern Europeans, creating a persona that has been misconstrued by American and Western European historians.[7]

From an examination of Kertész's career, it cannot be concluded that he was completely ignored. A solo exhibition at the P.M. Gallery in 1937 and a freelance career as a commercial photographer for some of the most recognized

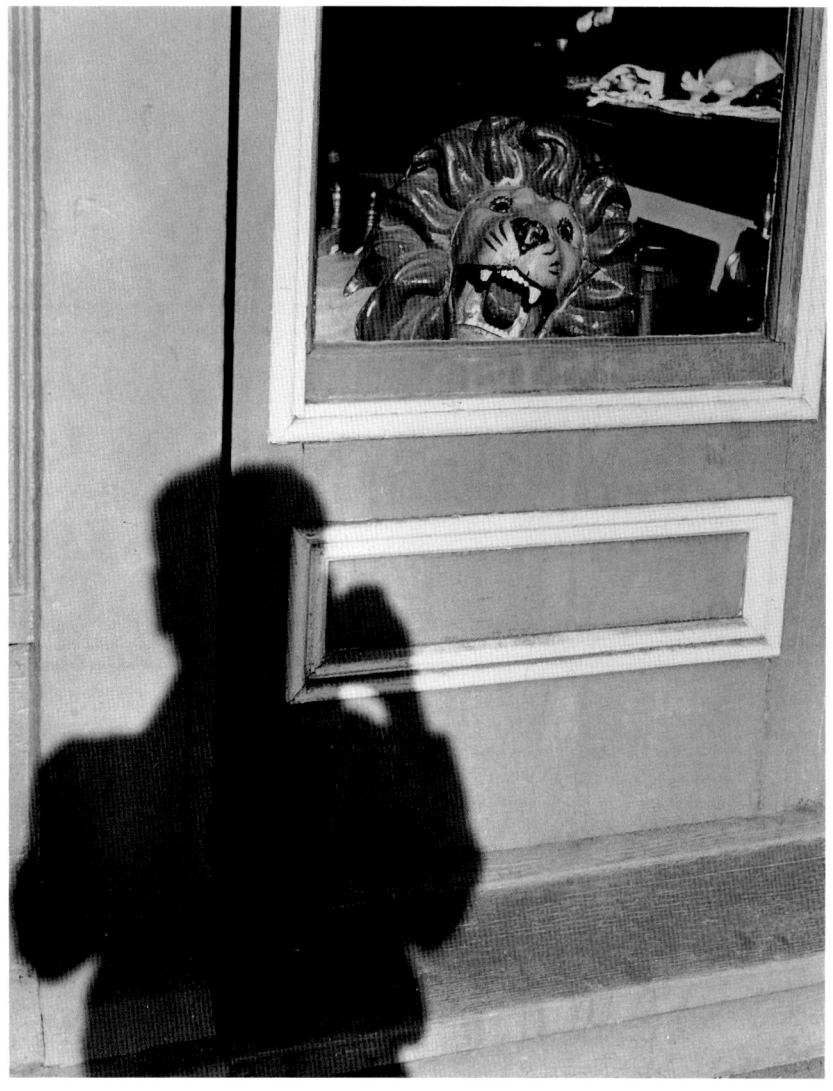

215
André Kertész, *Lion Seen through a Window*, 1942 (cat. no. 81).

magazines of the day—including *Town and Country, House and Garden,* and *Look*—allowed him to earn an income in the field of his choice. One unfortunate event that befell the photographer, however, was being declared an enemy alien by the United States government in 1941, when the country entered World War II. Until Japan surrendered in 1945, this status restricted him from photographing out of doors.

Thus, it is not surprising that photographs taken during these years are rare, and it is tempting to brand them as emotionally charged and biographical, especially in light of Kertész's Jewish ancestry. *Lion Seen through a Window* (1942; fig. 215, cat. no. 81) has elements of his surrealist-inspired humanist work—the fragments juxtaposed in the frame, the layering of dynamic and static forms. It is Kertész's familiar language, inspired as much by emotional status as by visual surprise. And since the shadowed form arrested on the paneled wall is that of the photographer himself, there is reason to read this image as a statement of an adjustment, an understanding of America after having lived in New York for six years as an immigrant. Kertész does not represent himself clearly in three dimensions; we no longer see the specific "André," but only a shadow of the man. And the stylized toy lion peeking through the window frame, the object of Kertész's gaze—is that "America" staring back at the man with a camera?

Imre Kertész proved to be correct in his brotherly advice. Kertész found both financial and artistic success by immigrating to the United States, albeit not within the time frame that both brothers envisioned. As photography began to receive greater recognition from American art institutions in the early 1960s, the recognition of Kertész as an important modern artist followed. A solo exhibition at the Museum of Modern Art in New York in 1964 confirmed his status. And while commercial success might have been more forthcoming to the photographer earlier in his career had his imagery been more neutral and less emotionally charged, surely he would not have found international acclaim as a unique artist of the twentieth century.

Notes

1 Imre Kertész to André Kertész, 17 April 1936, collection of the Mission du Patrimoine, Paris.
2 Entries from Kertész's date book for 1936, Archives of the Mission du Patrimoine, Paris.
3 André Kertész, *Kertész on Kertész: A Self-Portrait* (New York: Abbeville Press, 1985), 90.
4 Sandra Phillips, "Preface," in *André Kertész: Of Paris and New York,* exh. cat. (New York: Thames and Hudson, 1985), 12.
5 Jane Livingston, "The American Period (1936–1962): A Mutual Misunderstanding," in *André Kertész: His Life and Work,* ed. Pierre Borhan (Boston: Little, Brown, 1994), 229.
6 Kertész, *Kertész on Kertész,* 90.
7 Pierre Borhan writes: "Kertész himself was very selective in his memories, stories, and explications, and misled his interlocutors; he always chose melancholy, the sigh, and complaint" ("The International Period [1963–1985]," in *André Kertész: His Life and Work,* 274).

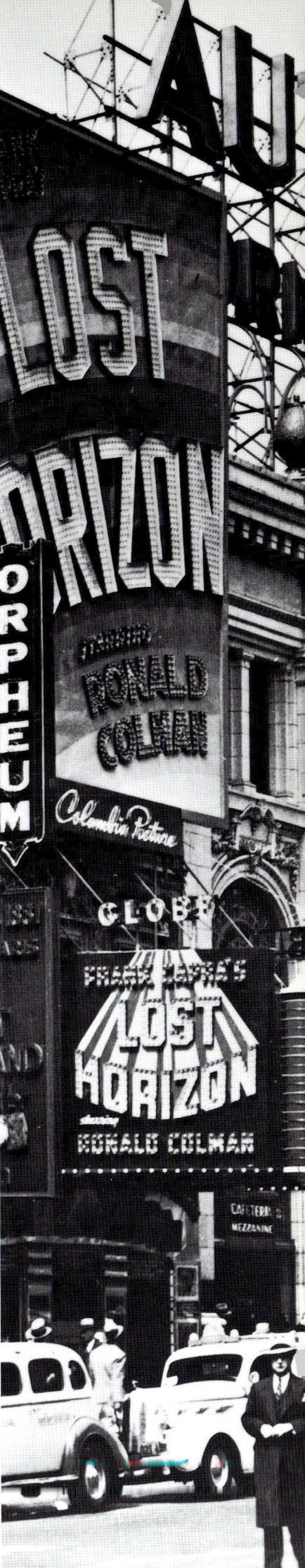

Overleaf left:
View of the west side of Broadway between Forty-seventh and Forty-eighth Streets, c. 1937.

Overleaf right:
A drawbridge, Chicago, July 1941; photograph by John Vachon.

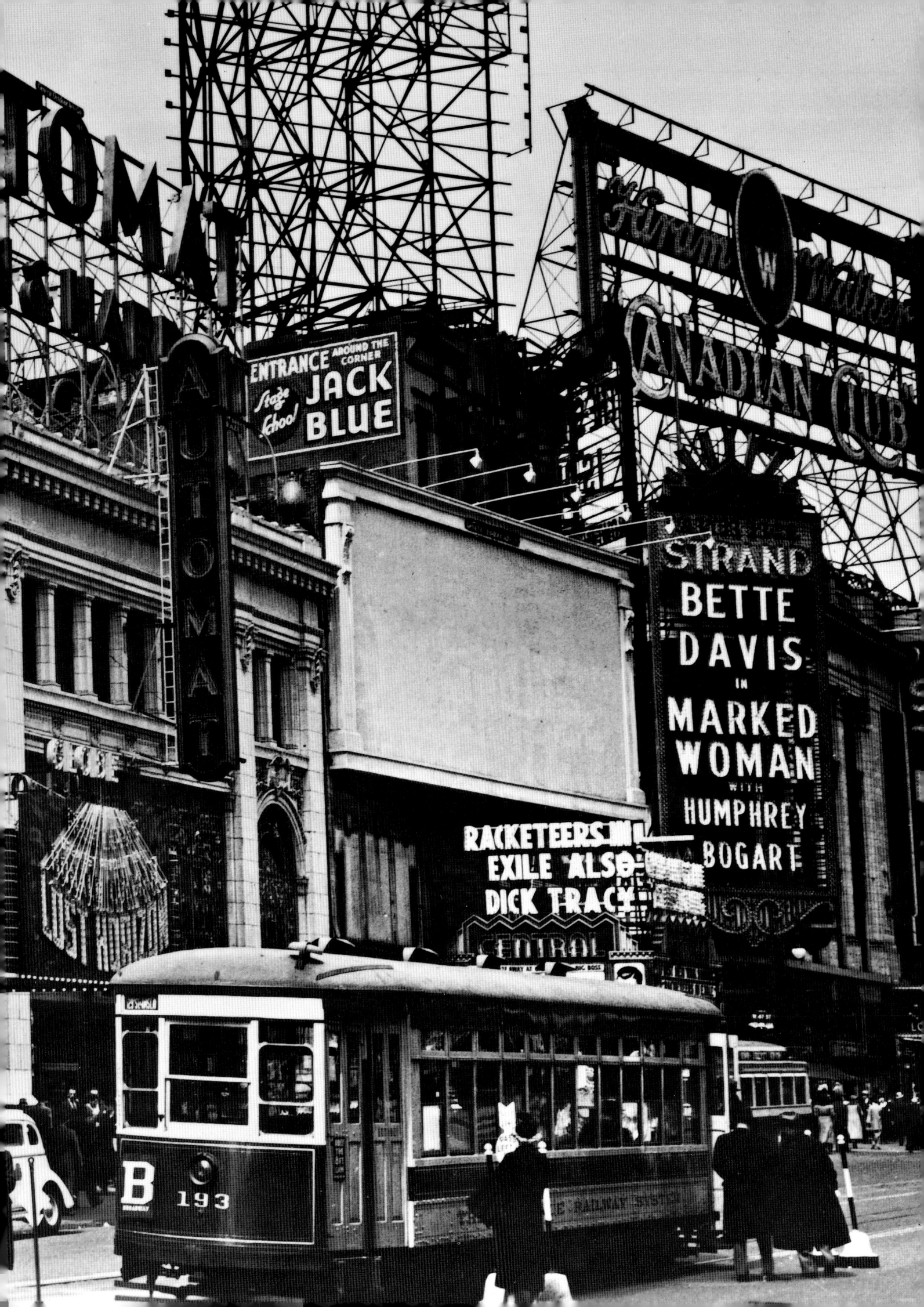

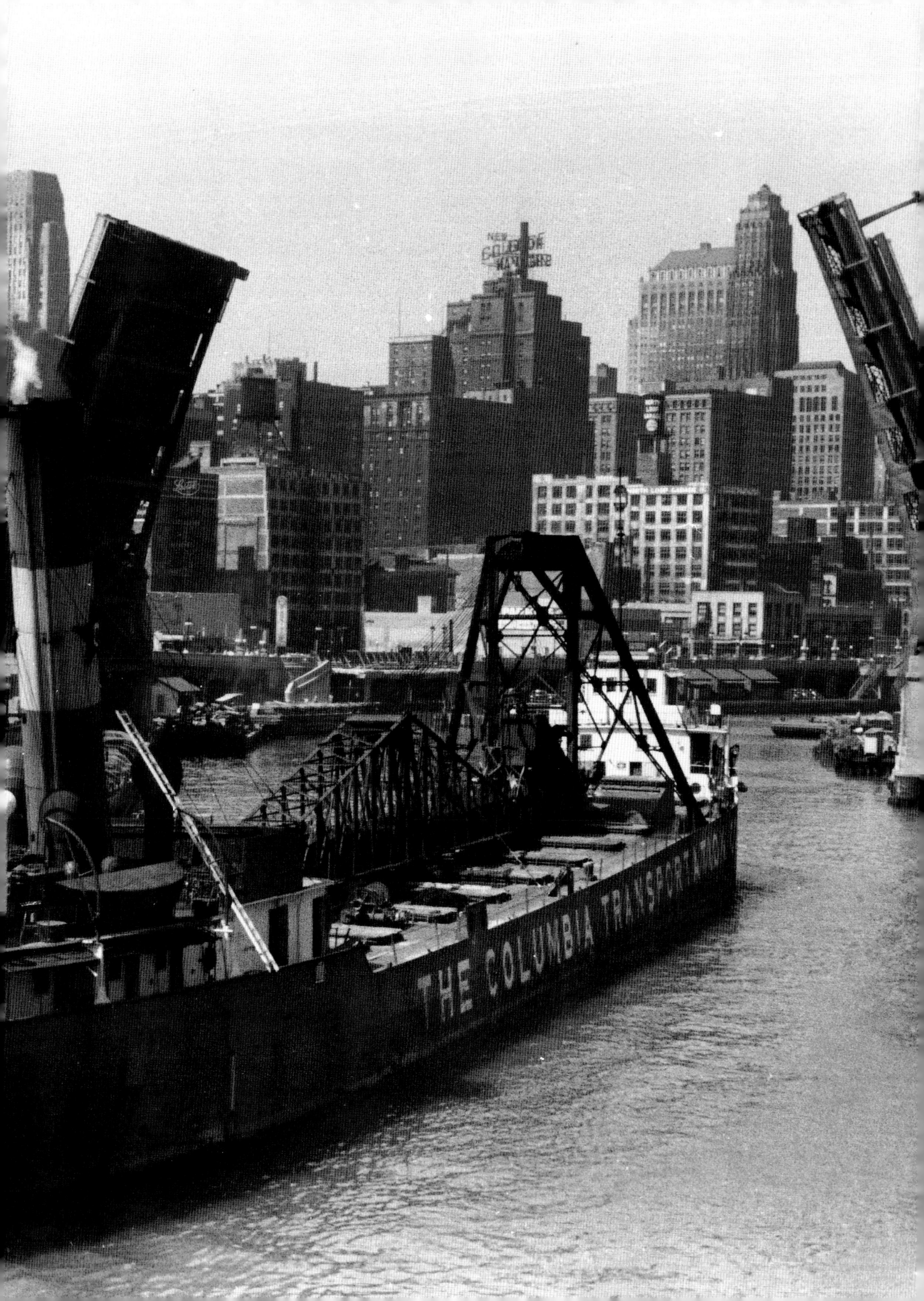

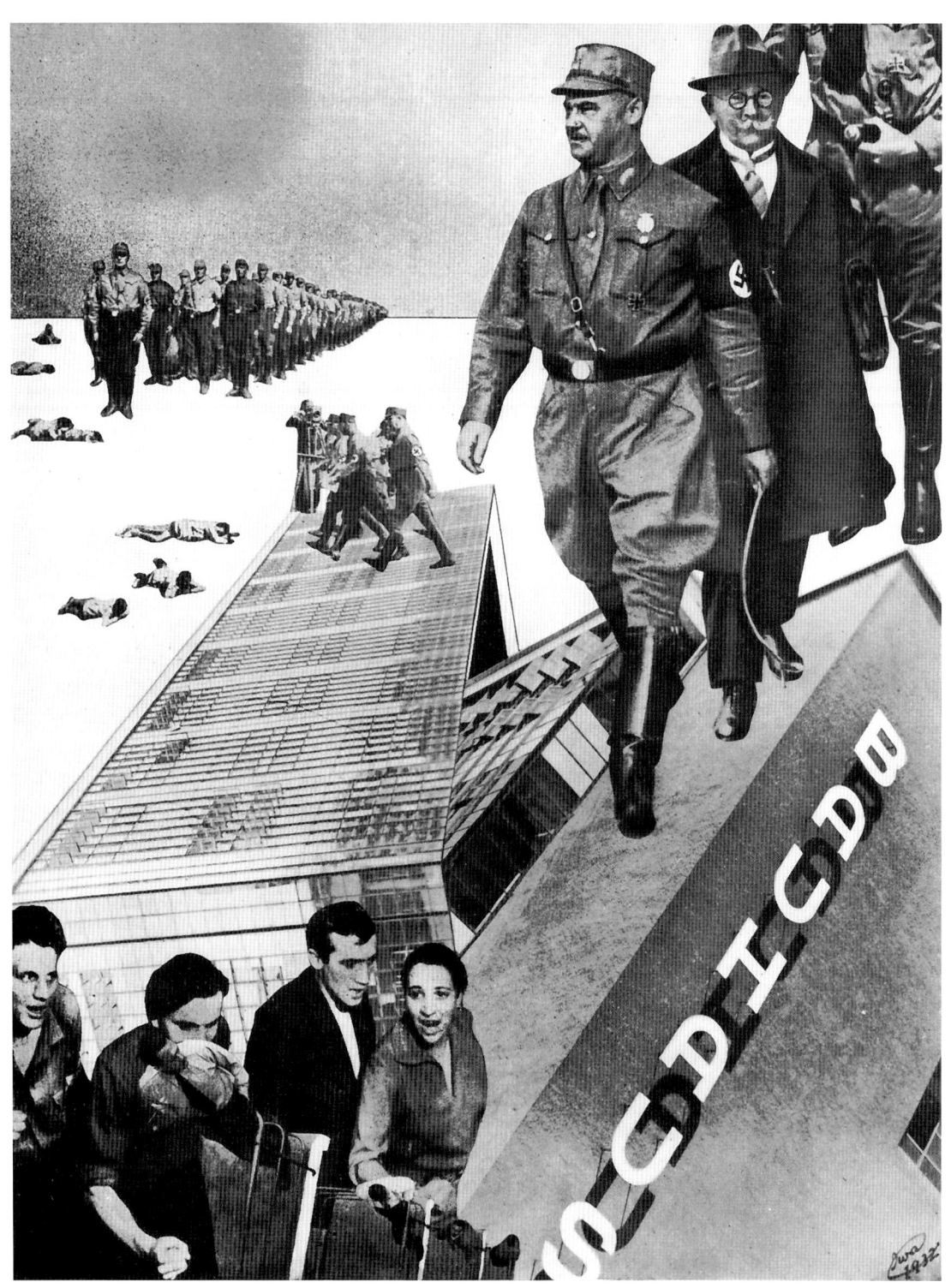

216
Iwao Yamawaki; *The Blow against the Bauhaus*, 1932; collage; present location unknown.

PETER HAHN

bauhaus and exile:
bauhaus architects and designers between the old world and the new

In the story of the impact of the Bauhaus, and of those modernist tendencies in design for which it stood, the fateful year 1933 represents a turning point. It cut short the promising development of what is probably Germany's most significant twentieth-century school of art and design, but Bauhaus ideas found a continuation in the influential work of its emigré members, most notably in the United States. In a dictum that became famous, the last director of the Bauhaus, Ludwig Mies van der Rohe, stated that the school had been successful primarily as an idea: "The Bauhaus...was not an institution with a clear program—it was an idea, and Gropius formulated this idea with great precision.... The fact that it was an idea, I think, is the cause of this enormous influence that the Bauhaus had on every progressive school around the globe. You cannot do that with organization; you cannot do that with propaganda. Only an idea spreads so far."[1]

Many of these commonly held notions about the Bauhaus require some qualification. Its demise as a teaching institution in April 1933 did not come as a bolt from the blue; nor was America unfamiliar with the Bauhaus or entirely unprepared for the consequences of the subsequent influx of Bauhaus architects and artists. In terms of politics (an unavoidable topic in any account of the movement of Bauhaus people from the Old World to the New), it is necessary to question the myth that the Bauhaus, or at least its leading members, went abroad when the Nazis took power—and that it therefore stands for the "better Germany" that returned from exile in 1945 to form the democratic basis for what became the Federal Republic.[2] This view was current in Germany after World War II, and to some extent it still is; in the United States, however, the transplantation of the Bauhaus tends to be seen in terms of immigration rather than of political exile.

The Dissolution of the Bauhaus

On April 11, 1933, the school building of the Berlin Bauhaus in the borough of Steglitz was surrounded and searched by police and storm troopers. A number of students were detained and taken away, to be released a few days later. Files were seized, the building was sealed, and police mounted guard over it during the months that followed.[3] This raid was certainly a political act, or at least an act with a political background. Earlier than other cultural institutions, or so it seems, the Bauhaus was swept away by the rising tide of repression in the nascent Third Reich. There is more to this, however, than the common supposition that the Nazis disliked the Bauhaus and simply liquidated it with a stroke of the pen.

In the last phase of the Bauhaus's existence, first in Dessau and then in Berlin, in 1932–33, the school was caught up in the crisis of the Weimar Republic. It felt the effects of economic hardship and political collapse. Enrollment dwindled, and so did budgets. The curriculum—particularly workshop practice and complementary general studies, both of which were always highly important at the Bauhaus—had to be drastically cut back. There were also internal conflicts, despite the determination of the new director, Mies van der Rohe (appointed in 1930 after the dismissal of Hannes Meyer), to impose order, if necessary, by disciplinary means.

In the Bauhaus literature these last years are often described as the "phase of disintegration," which is accurate only up to a point. Not only was Mies trying to cope with a genuine crisis, but he was developing an innovative teaching program at the same time as well. For example, he relaxed the hitherto rigorous and pivotal Bauhaus requirement that all students complete the preliminary course, waiving it for those who had completed comparable course work elsewhere. He also changed the format of the workshops, which had formerly included production activities, limiting them solely to teaching. Finally, under his direction the Bauhaus developed more and more into a professional school of architecture. It is hard to believe that economic and political circumstances alone enforced this reduction of the school's nonarchitectural curriculum. In Chicago a few years later, with incomparably superior material resources, Mies set up a training program for architects that closely resembled the one he had inaugurated, at least in outline, at the Bauhaus.[4]

In Germany events moved fast. The final phase of the Bauhaus began with a purely political process: the Saxony-Anhalt state elections of May 1932. These gave a majority to the Nazis, whose platform demanded "the cancellation of all expenditures for the Bauhaus" and inveighed against "Jewish Bauhaus culture."[5] The consequences were not long in coming. The closure of the Dessau Bauhaus in September 1932 was a foregone conclusion, despite vociferous protests in the press and among culturally aware segments of the public (see fig. 216).

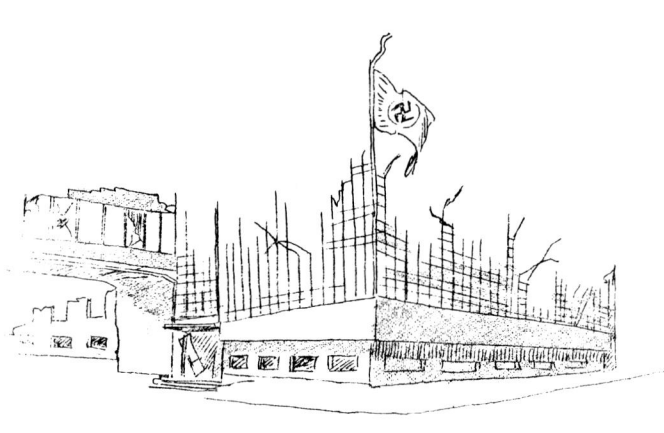

217
Caricature by a communist student group commenting on the situation at the Bauhaus in 1931; the caption translates as "fascism is official at this institution." From a mimeographed booklet, *Bauhaus* (November–December 1931).

After the Dessau experience Mies's courageous attempt to carry on the Bauhaus in Berlin, as a private school independent of public or municipal support, ended after six months with the police raid. Carried out under the pretext of looking for evidence in a case brought against former Dessau mayor Fritz Hesse, this raid (like many things in the early days of the Nazi regime) was, on the face of it, perfectly legal. In marked contrast to the Dessau closure in 1932, there were no protests to speak of—a clear sign of the change in the political climate. There was no word from the friends who had always stood by the Bauhaus in its numerous previous crises. Of course, a few weeks earlier even those at the Bauhaus had barely reacted to the Nazi "assumption of power," though this sensational event, complete with a torchlight procession celebrating the "national uprising," can hardly have escaped their notice.

As a private school the Bauhaus depended on fees for its cash flow; the sealing of the school doors by the police after the raid put it under crushing financial pressure. The pressure was political as well; there was a press campaign against the Bauhaus as a "germ-cell of Bolshevik subversion," against the "patrons and popes of the Arty German Empire of the Jewish Nation," and against the "soul silos" of modernist architecture.[6] At the same time there were attempts by Bauhaus students to keep the school going, both by making declarations of loyalty to the new masters and by proposing the appointment of a "reliable" (in the National Socialist sense) state commissioner.

The students were not the only ones who thought this way. Wassily Kandinsky, for instance, wrote painter Willi Baumeister on April 23, 1933, proposing that modernist artists join the Kampfbund für deutsche Kultur (Campaign for German culture), led by the Nazi ideologue Alfred Rosenberg. As Kandinsky told Bauhaus student Werner Drewes (who was later to immigrate to the United States), "Of course it is a matter of great regret to us, as 'modern' artists, that the new government misunderstands the new art. In Italy it's all quite different. There the new architecture and the new art [futurism] are recognized as Fascist art."[7]

This kind of thinking was quite common among artists and intellectuals in 1933; nor did it seem unreasonable, since in 1933 the fledgling dictatorship was not yet speaking with a single voice on cultural matters. One has only to think of the well-known rivalry between Rosenberg and Joseph Goebbels, whose propaganda ministry took charge of all cultural organizations from the end of 1933 onward. It is possible that the Bauhaus—like many other institutions, including the Deutscher Werkbund—might have continued to exist by accepting *Gleichschaltung,* assimilation into the status quo. (The Gestapo actually laid down its terms for this, which included the dismissal of Kandinsky and Ludwig Hilberseimer and their replacement by instructors loyal to the regime.)

There remained one overwhelming obstacle to the continued existence of the Bauhaus. In terms of cultural politics it stood for everything that the Nazis loathed. Or, in any event, that was what Rosenberg told Mies when the latter vainly sought permission to reopen the school. Several futile attempts later, there was nothing to do but shut down the Bauhaus for good. This was done on July 20, 1933. Significantly, Mies insisted that it be by decision of the faculty: a final act of defiance in an economically and politically hopeless situation. Or so he was to describe it in retrospect, in 1953, pointing out with pride that it was not the Nazis who closed down the Bauhaus but he himself, at a moment when he had the Gestapo's permit to reopen in his pocket. The faculty saluted the end of the Bauhaus with a friendly glass of champagne.[8]

The deeper causes of the Bauhaus's self-closure go beyond the mere facts of its existence in the early months of the Nazi regime. They lie in the curriculum, in the history of the Bauhaus itself, and, not least, in the good and bad publicity it attracted as the symbol and arbiter of modernism in architecture and design. It was one of its great claims to fame that it sought to bridge the gap between two strands of evolution that had long seemed irreconcilably antagonistic: the "classical" tradition, centered on the values of "fine art," in which training was to take place at the academy, and the more technological orientation represented by the civil and industrial engineer, whose values were sound construction, efficiency, and progress. The Bauhaus program of "the unity of art and technology" made enemies as well as friends. Conservatives loathed the way it undermined the obsolete academic structures of art education. More significantly still, after starting with a clarion call for a "return to craftsmanship," the Bauhaus moved toward the industrialization of design and art, thus laying the foundations of modern industrial design—a move for which it is now praised, but which at the time earned it the hostility of the same petit bourgeois elements that were the cradle of the Nazi movement.

Furthermore, throughout its existence the Bauhaus attracted nationalist hostility by virtue of the international composition of its faculty and student body. By comparison with other German art schools and academies, the Bauhaus employed a relatively large number of teachers from abroad, including some of its best-known figures: the Swiss Johannes Itten, who had first developed his preliminary course in Vienna; the German-Swiss Paul Klee; the Austrian Herbert Bayer; the Hungarian László Moholy-Nagy; two more Swiss, Hannes Meyer and Konrad Wittwer; the Dutchman Mart Stam; and the Czech Karel Teige. The proportion of foreigners among Bauhaus students was also higher than at comparable institutions.[9]

There was also a social dimension to the Bauhaus that made it even more suspect to its right-wing detractors: its interest in social responsibility in design and in the provision of "minimal housing for survival" (a central and politically explosive concern of modernist architects). Politically speaking, the Bauhaus had always been highly dependent on support from the center (or "center-left") of the democratic spectrum. When those forces lost ground to right-wing adversaries—as did the Social Democratic and Socialist state government of Thuringia in Weimar in 1924–25 and the democratic city council under Mayor Hesse in Dessau in 1932—the Bauhaus lost its power base.

In spite of all this, those who ran the Bauhaus always emphasized its "apolitical" character. "Uns trägt kein Volk," said Klee laconically: "There are no People behind us."[10] And it was not until 1954, twenty years after leaving Germany, that Walter Gropius felt himself to be "with the majority."[11] With the benefit of hindsight this may or not have been the case; for just as long as it existed, however, the Bauhaus was regarded as left-wing. The phrase "cathedral of socialism" made the rounds, and there were endless political attacks, including personal onslaughts on Gropius and Mies; the school's final phase was dominated by the recurrent smear of "cultural bolshevism."

The Bauhaus under National Socialism

In their attitudes toward the rise and eventual victory of National Socialism, Bauhaus people (as we have seen in the case of Kandinsky) were as liable to self-contradiction and compromising entanglements as other artists, not to mention the German population in general. Numerous Bauhaus alumni suffered persecution, especially those of Jewish origin and those who had been active communists.[12] Within the Nazi state and its component organizations, such as the Reichskulturkammer (Reich chamber of culture), any association with Bauhaus "cultural bolshevism" was not exactly an astute career move. Contrary to a widely held impression, no one seems to have been persecuted just for belonging to the Bauhaus, but Bauhaus people frequently experienced discrimination, professional setbacks, and virtual ostracism. To varying degrees, this happened to a number of Bauhaus teachers who stayed in the country, including the painters Oskar Schlemmer and Georg Muche and the sculptor Gerhard Marcks. All three were dismissed from their teaching posts when the Nazis took over (as were Kandinsky and Klee, who left the country), and they continued to be regarded with distrust.

Even so, Schlemmer was disappointed when he did not win a propaganda ministry competition to decorate the congress hall at the Deutsches Museum in Munich, having been the only entrant to try to depict the *Volksgemeinschaft* (national community). As late as February 1937 he could still detect clear parallels between the basic themes of his own art ("law, measure,

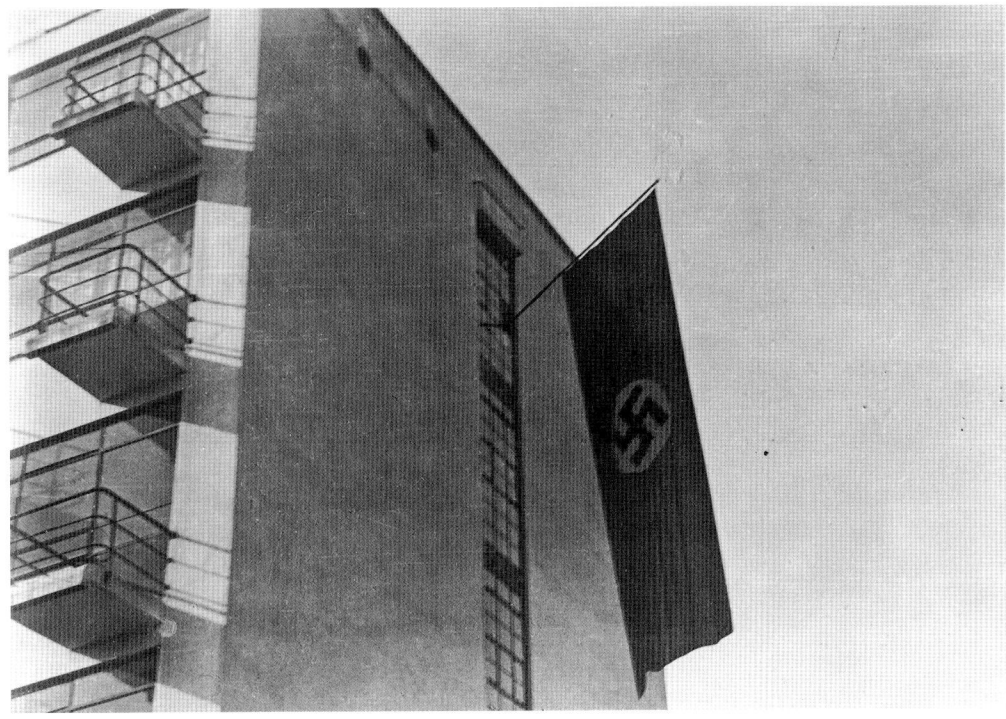

218
Swastika flag at the former studio building of the Bauhaus, Dessau, Christmas 1933.

and order") and the National Socialist state.[13] He cherished the forlorn hope of gaining recognition, even after a succession of humiliations that ranged from the destruction of his murals in the former Bauhaus building in Weimar (back in 1930) to vilification as a "degenerate" artist. Can he really have thought that these were all misunderstandings?

Muche was better at reading the signs of the perilous times; by the exercise of some cunning, he was able to ensure his personal and artistic survival and even to go on teaching. For his part, Marcks was able to appreciate "the good fundamental ideas of National Socialism," while remaining at a loss to understand its cultural policies.[14] In 1937, up to which point he had remained successful in commercial (i.e., sales) terms, he was horrified to find his work included in the exhibition *Entartete Kunst* (Degenerate art).

Thus, in dealing with the stereotype of the persecuted German artist, we need to draw some fine distinctions, and it is worth bearing in mind the curious, and by no means exceptional, ability of some artists to reconcile distaste for the National Socialist regime with (ultimately fruitless) efforts to gain its approval.

In some fields Bauhaus-trained designers and architects continued to find professional openings after 1933, and they made full use of them. It is worth noting that in general the Nazis, despite their routine tirades against the "cultural bolshevism" of the Bauhaus, tolerated its achievements and its former members wherever they could be useful to the regime, particularly in areas such as product design, graphic propaganda, and architecture (not the prestige architecture of official buildings, of course, but industrial structures). Thus, the Bauhaus-trained designer Wilhelm Wagenfeld was in charge of the Saxon state glassmakers, Vereinigte Lausitzer Glaswerke, from 1935 onward, and his work dominated the interior design that was done for the Nazis' Deutsche Arbeitsfront (German labor front), though he himself never yielded to pressure to become a party member. The graphic designer Herbert Bayer worked successfully as head of the Dorland agency in Berlin, both before and after 1933, and received a succession of official commissions to design propaganda exhibitions.

Bauhaus architects were also involved in Third Reich planning work; perhaps the most prominent of these was Ernst Neufert, author of an extremely successful treatise on building design (*Bauentwurfslehre,* 1936). Neufert, who had formerly worked for Gropius, was placed in charge of standardization by chief Nazi architect Albert Speer. Another former Gropius employee was Hanns Dustmann, chief architect to the Hitler Youth.[15] One Bauhäusler, Fritz Ertl, worked for the SS construction department, and in 1941 he was designing hutments to house Soviet prisoners of war at Auschwitz.[16]

Many other Bauhaus alumni scraped by as best they could, often in menial jobs far removed from their own inclinations and abilities. Very few refused to have anything to do with the Nazi state; among those who did was the painter Hans Thiemann, who practically starved. Many, if not most, adapted to circumstances and did their design work in modest obscurity, keeping fairly quiet about their past associations with the Bauhaus.

The Bauhaus in Exile

Those who went abroad included some of the most prominent Bauhaus teachers, the VIPs whose names were inseparable from the program and the work of the outlawed school. Foremost among these were the founder, Walter Gropius, and the last director, Ludwig Mies van der Rohe. (The second of the three directors, Hannes Meyer, had been ousted in 1930 and was working in the Soviet Union with a group of his former students.) Kandinsky and Klee left in 1933, for France and Switzerland, respectively. Lyonel Feininger and Itten went home (Feininger to the United States in 1937, Itten to Switzerland in 1938). Josef Albers, Marcel Breuer, Moholy-Nagy, and Bayer, all former members of the Bauhaus inner circle, left Germany either in 1933–34 or in 1937–38.

One can hardly speak of "exile" in the strict sense of the word in any of these cases, any more than one can of political resistance to the new regime in Germany, let alone antifascist struggle. Those concerned went mainly for professional reasons and because they believed that they would have better opportunities to put their artistic creed into practice outside Germany. This expectation turned out to be well founded. In America the VIPs, at least, found excellent career openings because the ideas and achievements of the Bauhaus were already known there and also, in all likelihood, because in some circles American architecture was perceived to be stagnating and the new arrivals promised to bring new ideas with them. Those ideas were a success. It is significant that hardly any of these Bauhaus personalities seriously considered returning to Germany after 1945.

The spectrum of motives for leaving extended far beyond the two categories of "exile" and "emigration": from normal job offers at one extreme (as when Albers was invited to teach at Black Mountain College in 1933) to downright persecution at the other (as in the case of the Bauhaus weaver Otti Berger, who fled to Yugoslavia; captured there some years later, she was murdered at Auschwitz). In assessing the exile issue and the individual careers of Bauhaus people—whether overall or in relation to the Nazi regime—we have to take one case at a time (and to exercise due caution with the self-serving revisions of history that we often encounter in connection with the Nazi years). This can be done here only in a few isolated instances.

Walter Gropius

In looking at Gropius's career, and at his relations with the Nazi state during the decisive period immediately before and after 1933, one is struck by a certain ambivalence in his attitude to German politics. On the one hand, he voted along with Martin Wagner and Wilhelm Wagenfeld against the National Socialists' *Gleichschaltung* of the Deutscher Werkbund in 1933,[17] and he protested the Nazis' campaign against modernist architecture in a letter to Eugen Hönig, the Nazi president of the Reichskammer der bildenden Künste (Reich chamber of fine arts): "Is this powerful new architectural movement, born in Germany, really to be lost to Germany? Must we be compelled to cease its creative development at the very time when the whole world has begun to respond to our stimulus?"[18] Gropius went on to refer to Marinetti and Italian Fascism.

On the other hand, this argument—though it testifies to Gropius's personal courage—also typifies the ultimately vain hope that the new state might follow the example of Italian Fascism and give recognition to modernist architecture and design. The same hope found expression in an architectural drawing from 1934, when Gropius and Rudolf Hillebrecht submitted an entry to the competition for a Haus der Arbeit (house of labor). The drawing shows a modernist structure liberally festooned with swastikas (see fig. 219). Nor did Gropius shrink from contributing to the exhibition *Deutsches Volk—deutsche Arbeit* (German nation—German labor, 1934; see fig. 220), for which he designed the nonferrous metals section (see fig. 221), again in a consistently modernist style, while seemingly oblivious to the overtly racist propaganda content of the exhibition as a whole. A number of other former Bauhaus people were also involved in that exhibition, notably Bayer, who designed the catalogue in the best Bauhaus manner. All of which goes to show that it was perfectly possible to combine Bauhaus modernism with Nazi-tainted subject matter—just so long as the client considered this useful.

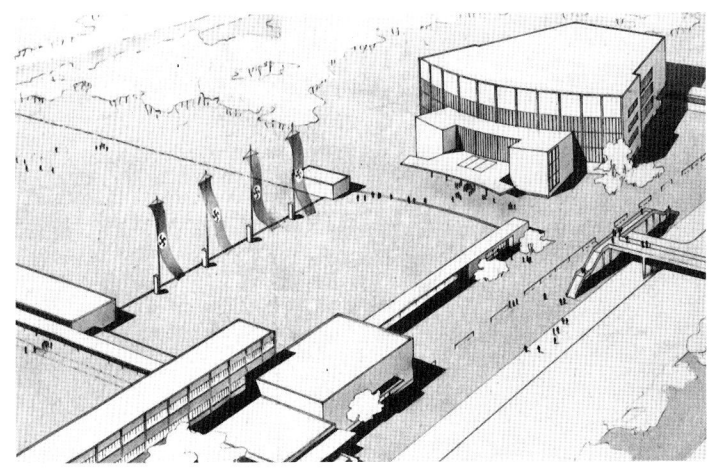

219
Walter Gropius and Rudolf Hillebrecht; competition entry for a "house of labor," 1934, bird's-eye view; Bauhaus-Archiv, Berlin.

220
Gustav Hassenpflug; hall of honor (*Ehrenhalle*) of the exhibition *Deutsches Volk—deutsche Arbeit*, Berlin, 1934; Bauhaus-Archiv, Berlin.

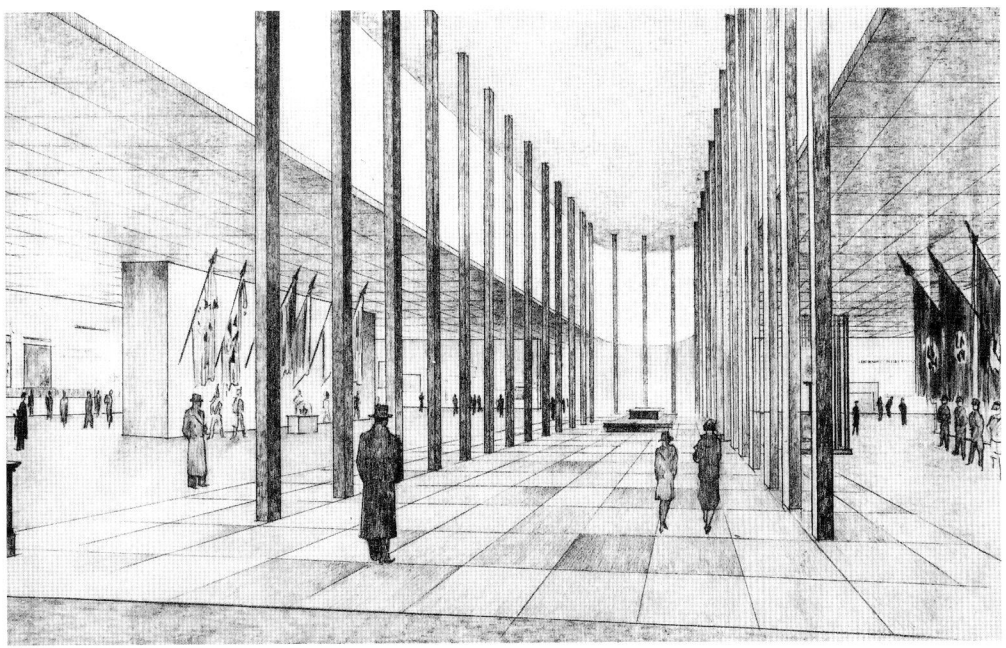

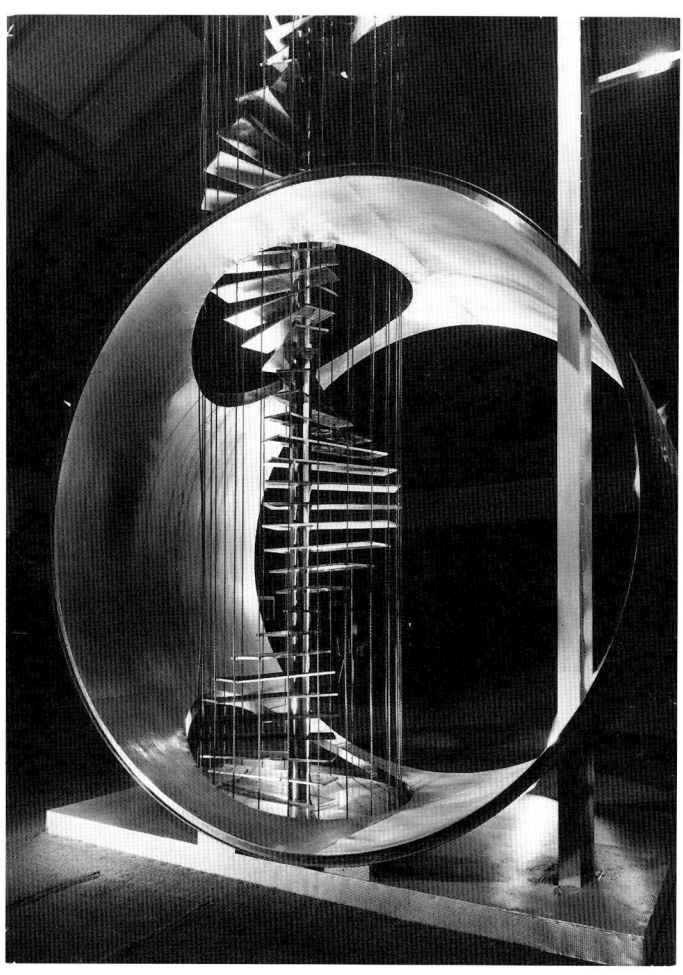

221
Walter Gropius and Joost Schmidt; nonferrous metals section of the exhibition *Deutsches Volk—deutsche Arbeit*, Berlin, 1934; Bauhaus-Archiv, Berlin.

Gropius had always argued in favor of an "apolitical" Bauhaus, and he stuck to this line even after he was safely out of the Nazis' reach. It is probable that he left Germany because of a shortage of commissions, rather than for any political reason. In 1934 he moved to England, having expressly sought and received permission from the relevant Nazi authority, the Reichskulturkammer. Gropius was thus neither a refugee nor an emigré. During his whole time in England he conducted himself as a loyal German citizen and took good care not to say or do anything that might compromise that loyalty. He kept clear of all initiatives and events critical of artistic and political developments in Germany[19] and took pains to avoid identification with those politically active artists who were in England at the same time, such as the members of the Oskar-Kokoschka-Bund. He declined to voice any criticism of events in Germany, telling the BBC's weekly journal *The Listener* in May 1936 that he was still a German citizen, working in Great Britain with the due consent of the German government, and made it clear that in his view the evolution of modern architecture had nothing to do with any political system whatsoever.[20]

Gropius was appointed to his chair at Harvard in 1937 (after once more securing the consent of the German authorities), and the appointment attracted favorable mentions in the docile German press. Once there he soon became a highly respected authority, and indeed an embodiment of modernism, but he still kept well away from politics. There is no trace of any public statement from him about events in Nazi Germany—not even the *Entartete Kunst* exhibition, held in the very year of his appointment, in which practically all of his Bauhaus artist friends were vilely defamed.

In 1939 it was decided that the New York World's Fair would include a "Freedom Pavilion," designed to draw attention to conditions in Nazi Germany by showing a democratic alternative. Ferdinand Kramer, a Bauhaus alumnus who had recently arrived in the United States, was commissioned to produce a design.[21] Supporters of the project included emigrés (such as Thomas Mann) and also American citizens of the most varied political views and religious affiliations. Gropius was invited to take part but declined.[22] In this, as in his general policy of keeping silent about events in the German Reich, he seems to have been influenced by the fact that he still had relatives and friends in Germany, including some from the Bauhaus, who might at any time be exposed to reprisals. Gropius was not alone in this concern; the Bauhaus painter Muche, who was still living in Germany, begged him to ensure that the proposed pavilion contain no work by any former Bauhäusler who had not expressly given consent. Plans for the pavilion eventually foundered on the opposition of the German Reich, which was not officially represented at the World's Fair (in itself a significant sidelight on the political situation shortly before the outbreak of World War II).

The impact of *Bauhaus, 1919–1928*—an exhibition organized by the Museum of Modern Art, New York, in 1938—on the American view of the Bauhaus can hardly be overstated. Held on safe territory, the exhibition provided an excellent platform for the dissemination of information, and yet, even there, the one and only critical reference to conditions in Germany was an implicit one. In his preface to the catalogue Alfred H. Barr Jr., the museum's director, wrote: "The work of many artists in this book is being shown without their consent. When the book was at the point of going to press it was considered advisable to delete the names of several of these artists."[23] Barr proposed that a reference to the closure of the Bauhaus by the Nazis be included in the touring version of the exhibition, but it is not known whether this ever actually appeared.[24] If we call to mind how clearly such emigrés as Thomas Mann and Albert Einstein spoke out against Hitler in speeches, articles, and statements of all kinds, such reticence is remarkable in itself.

Also remarkable was the time span that the organizers of *Bauhaus, 1919–1928* chose to cover. The exhibition was not about the Bauhaus as a whole, but exclusively about the Gropius era; the directorships of Meyer (1928–30) and Mies (1930–33) were both excluded. Gropius himself has sometimes been blamed for this—probably wrongly, since he was keen to include at least Mies in the show. Mies refused. In view of "the present official attitude," he wrote from Germany, there must be no account of his Bauhaus period so long as he was still in the country. He maintained this refusal even in 1938, when he was already in the United States and personally had nothing more to fear.[25] He explained this, in line with Gropius's attitude, as a measure to protect his former pupils still in Germany. It may well be that Mies's decision to stay out incorporated an element of rivalry with Gropius: it was all too plain that this was a promotional exhibition for the American debut of the newly appointed Professor Walter Gropius of Harvard, "Mr. Bauhaus." It is now known that Mies himself, who was skeptical enough in any case about Gropius's artistic standing as an architect, had been under consideration for the Harvard chair at one stage.[26]

Be that as it may, the 1938 exhibition was a turning point in the New World careers of several major Bauhaus architects and designers. Limited to the years 1919–28, it offered, so to speak, the pure Bauhaus doctrine as seen by the founder himself. Also prominently featured were Bayer (who was prompted by it to move to the United States), Breuer (who had followed Gropius to Harvard and for several years remained his most important architectural collaborator there), Albers (who had been teaching at Black Mountain College since 1933), Feininger (who had reluctantly returned to the United States in 1937), and Moholy-Nagy (who since 1937 had been in charge of the New Bauhaus in Chicago). For these individuals the exhibition was a great success, a breakthrough for the modern movement—or "our movement," as they called it in their letters to one another.

The exhibition could have at least been regarded as a moral victory over the Nazis, who had driven the Bauhaus and several of its leading exponents out of Germany and who had destroyed the Bauhaus vision in the land of its birth, but there is absolutely no indication that it was seen this way. The real issue, however, and quite probably the main motive for the offer of the Harvard chair to Gropius, was something quite different: the conflict between the modern movement and the Beaux-Arts. In this pairing, the Bauhaus was firmly on the modern side, and if the modern movement now triumphed over the Beaux-Arts principles

Bauhaus, 1919–1928

previously dominant in the United States, this represented a major victory for an idea that Bauhaus people had pursued together in Germany and that they had now brought to the New World.

All of this was expressly stated in the exhibition, which included a brief account of the continuation of Bauhaus teaching in the United States, both by Albers at Black Mountain and by Moholy-Nagy at the New Bauhaus. Moholy-Nagy's New Bauhaus, which existed under that name for just one year, in 1937–38, was the one and only direct successor institution to the Bauhaus, dedicated to the principle of maintaining its full curriculum.[27] In 1938, when Mies began teaching in Chicago, two very different Bauhaus concepts were represented in one city: the Gropius concept, as pursued (albeit in modified form) by Moholy-Nagy, and Mies's personal teaching of architecture at the Armour Institute of Technology (later Illinois Institute of Technology).

Ludwig Mies van der Rohe

In 1933 Mies's role as the last director of the Bauhaus—that hotbed of "cultural bolshevism"—undoubtedly rendered him suspect in the eyes of those in charge of Nazi cultural policy. Here, as in other cases, it is debatable whether there was any threat to his personal safety; he himself clearly did not think so. Like Gropius and the other leading exponents of architectural modernism, however, he could see that his career prospects had suffered. His competition entries got nowhere; his design for a new Reichsbank building, for instance, was praised and even received a prize, but the commission went to a design that had not been submitted in competition, an early executed example of the architecture of intimidation favored by the Nazis. For the German Pavilion at the Brussels world's fair of 1935 Mies submitted a consistently modernist design, emblazoned with swastikas as per specification (see fig. 229). This was never executed, because Germany withdrew from the exhibition on grounds of cost. But it shows that, as far as Mies was concerned, modernist design was perfectly compatible with nondemocratic content.

Within a few short years Mies had designed a communist memorial, an exhibition pavilion for the German Republic in Barcelona, and a propaganda building for the Nazis. He has accordingly been dubbed the "Talleyrand of architecture,"[28] though this analogy is only partly apt: unlike France's turncoat politician, Mies was largely uninterested in politics and in political ideas. In any case, he remained entirely consistent in pursuing his own artistic line without any concessions to political pressure. Nevertheless, his signing of a "Call to Creative Workers in the Arts" in the daily *Völkischer Beobachter* on August 18, 1934, soliciting votes for Hitler to succeed Hindenburg as head of state,[29] was pilloried as an act of opportunism even at the time. This dubious appeal, also signed by Wilhelm Furtwängler and Ernst Barlach among others, probably reflected a tactical initiative on Goebbels's part to secure the signatures of non-Nazi artists. In this case Mies was undoubtedly being opportunistic; at the time he was known to be angling for the Brussels world's fair commission.

Many colleagues who were already living in the United States also censured Mies for having left Germany so late, in 1938, and then only after securing a well-paid teaching post in Chicago. Sibyl Moholy-Nagy excluded Mies from the "diaspora of honorable emigrés," dismissing him with the scornful words: "He who lies down with dogs gets up with fleas."[30] The fact is that Mies was not really an emigré at all, in Sibyl Moholy-Nagy's sense, but an architect who was grimly determined to pursue nothing but the best conditions for the realization of his artistic ideas, wherever those conditions might be found. In any event, the future celebrated leader of the "Second Chicago School" of architecture was not prepared—any more than Gropius was—to make any effective protest against what went on in Nazi Germany.

The key to this conspicuous political restraint, both in Gropius and in Mies, does not lie entirely in their fear of endangering those relatives, friends, and colleagues who had remained within reach of the Nazi terror. These men did not see themselves as political refugees, as exiles of the kind who fled to the United States from Germany after 1933 and from other European countries invaded by Germany after 1939. Nor did they see themselves entirely as immigrants: people who had come to the New World, like so many others before them, to seek new careers and new lives, often in conditions of extreme hardship. As architects and as university professors, Mies and Gropius were the exponents and the ambassadors of a cultural movement: modernism. What mattered to them was their self-imposed task of evolving and establishing genuinely contemporary forms of architecture and design. When, much to their disappointment, political developments in their home country made this impossible, they found in the United States not only redress but vastly greater practical opportunities as well.

Bauhaus versus Beaux-Arts

In Germany there had long been a keen interest in the evolution of American architecture. The pivotal influence of Frank Lloyd Wright on the European avant-garde before World War I (Gropius, Mies, Le Corbusier) has often been described. And Gropius, for one, had been an admirer of American industrial architecture long before he founded the Bauhaus. In 1928, immediately after resigning the directorship of the Bauhaus, he traveled widely in the United States and not only studied the American construction industry but also made numerous contacts that were to be extremely valuable a few years later, when his Harvard appointment came up.[31]

In America European artistic achievements fell on fertile ground. The Bauhaus and its architecture were known there much earlier than is usually assumed.[32] Always controversial, and consequently always in the public eye, the school and its checkered career were closely observed in the United States. American scholars, artists, and architects visited the Bauhaus on many occasions. True, it was only in 1932 that the modernist architects of Germany and the United States were comprehensively surveyed in the Museum of Modern Art's *Modern Architecture: International Exhibition* and in its possibly even more influential accompanying book, *The International Style,* by Henry-Russell Hitchcock and Philip Johnson, but this was certainly not the first the American public had heard of Mies and Gropius. Even so, the exhibition was both a historic event and an eye-opener, and it gave both architects, for the first time, wide publicity and institutional backing.[33] Gropius, for his part, later firmly and consistently disavowed the expression "International Style" (which has remained popular to this day). The Bauhaus, he said, never set out to be a "style" or design formula; it was an active "movement."[34]

more than three-quarters of a century after the founding of the Bauhaus, the school's name has become something of a catchphrase throughout the world, at times taking on mythic proportions. It is associated primarily with the industrial design that originated there but also with the International Style of architecture and, last but not least, with the unique collaboration among artists, craftsmen, and architects that developed over a few years in Weimar, Dessau, and Berlin. This constellation was more or less forcibly destroyed by the National Socialists' assumption of power in Germany. Ironically the dissolution of the Bauhaus did not blunt the impact of its pedagogical and aesthetic ideas, at least when viewed from an international perspective. Indeed, the opposite is the case, for in exile—especially in American exile—these ideas made great forward strides. Should it be any surprise that the leaders of the Bauhaus are regarded today almost as legends? Has not the school's political fate, its closing in 1933 and the subsequent emigration of its most important personalities, contributed to the myth of the Bauhaus?

In this essay I have tried to look more closely at the emigration of Bauhaus ideas and personalities, questioning the notion that the school per se protected itself against entanglements with the Nazi state. The final phase of the Bauhaus forms the backdrop for the exodus of its leaders from the country of its origin. Not a few of the members of the Bauhaus were persecuted, and some were murdered. Yet a look at Bauhaus modernism during the National Socialist period makes it clear that, despite official defamation of the Bauhaus as representing "cultural Bolshevism" and "Jewishness," there existed throughout the period a certain degree of creative latitude for the ideas and artists of the Bauhaus. This is true, for example, in the areas of product design, graphic design, and industrial architecture—as long as the designs served the purposes of the new state. Modernist artists also strove, though in vain, for recognition from the Nazi state.

Thus, in considering the image of the ostracized Bauhaus member, one has to examine each individual case. The same is true of those architects and artists who continued their work in foreign lands. This is not meant to diminish the indisputable historical significance of men like Gropius, Mies, Albers, Bayer, Breuer, or Moholy-Nagy (to mention only the inner circle, those who established influential new careers in the United States). But among those who emigrated, political motives were not the rule. Certainly none of those named can be said to have had an affinity for National Socialist ideology, but at the same time one also cannot speak of political resistance. In most cases—and, indeed, on both sides of the Atlantic—it was a question of professional opportunities and, even more, of furthering the cause of modernism against an artistic tradition that was increasingly perceived as moribund.

Notes

1 Ludwig Mies van der Rohe, address on the seventieth birthday of Walter Gropius, Blackstone Hotel, Chicago, 15 May 1953; cited in Sigfried Giedion, *Walter Gropius: Work and Teamwork* (New York: Reinhold, 1954), 27.
2 Winfried Nerdinger, "Modernisierung, Bauhaus, Nationalsozialismus," in *Bauhaus-Moderne im Nationalsozialismus,* ed. Winfried Nerdinger (Munich: Prestel, 1993), 9.
3 The final closure of the Bauhaus is fully documented in Peter Hahn, ed., *Bauhaus Berlin* (Weingarten: Kunstverlag Weingarten, 1985).
4 See *Der vorbildliche Architekt: Mies van der Rohes Architekturunterricht 1930–1958 am Bauhaus und in Chicago,* exh. cat. (Berlin: Nicolaische Verlagsbuchhandlung, 1986).
5 Hahn, ed., *Bauhaus Berlin,* 41.
6 Ibid., 124, 140.
7 Wassily Kandinsky to Werner Drewes, 10 April 1933, in ibid., 126, 129–30.
8 Interview with Ludwig Mies van der Rohe, *North Carolina University, State College of Agriculture and Engineering, School of Design, Student Publication* 3, no. 3 (1953): 16–18.
9 Folke Dietzsch estimates the total number of Bauhaus students at 1,258 ("Die Studierenden am Bauhaus" [Ph.D. diss., Hochschule für Architektur und Bauwesen, Weimar, 1990], vol. 2, 113). Comparing the proportions of foreign students at selected German institutions of higher education between 1928 and 1933 with those at the Bauhaus, Dietzsch (336) finds the proportion at the Bauhaus to have been markedly higher.
10 Paul Klee, "Die bildnerischen Mittel," lecture at Jena, 1924, cited in Christian Geelhaar, *Paul Klee und das Bauhaus* (Cologne: DuMont, 1972), 19.
11 James Marston Fitch, *Walter Gropius* (New York: Braziller, 1960), 31. Gropius made a statement to this effect on a visit to Japan.

12 For the period 1933–45 Folke Dietzsch counts twenty-four arrests and internments, twenty periods of detention in concentration camps, and eight other terms of imprisonment. At least eight Bauhaus people were murdered in concentration camps ("Die Studierenden am Bauhaus," 322).
13 Magdalena Droste, "Bauhaus-Maler im Nationalsozialismus," in Nerdinger, ed., *Bauhaus-Moderne im Nationalsozialismus,* 131–32.
14 Magdalena Bushart, "Ein Bildhauer zwischen zwei Stühlen," in ibid., 103.
15 Winfried Nerdinger, "Bauhaus-Architekten im Dritten Reich," in ibid., 161.
16 Robert-Jan van Pelt, "Auschwitz: From Architect's Promise to Inmate's Perdition," *Modernism* 1, no. 1 (1994): 98.
17 Reginald Isaacs, *Walter Gropius: Der Mensch und sein Werk* (Berlin: Gebrüder Mann, 1984), vol. 2, 625.
18 Ibid., 650.
19 Ibid., 782.
20 Ibid., 780, 802.
21 *Ferdinand Kramer,* exh. cat. (Zurich: Museum für Gestaltung, 1991), 62.
22 Gropius to Georg Muche, 3 March 1939, cited in Hahn, ed., *Bauhaus Berlin,* 231–32. Gropius was answering an inquiry sent by Muche on February 10, 1939 (ibid.).
23 Alfred H. Barr Jr., preface to *Bauhaus, 1919–1928,* ed. Herbert Bayer, Walter Gropius, and Ise Gropius (New York: Museum of Modern Art, 1938), 9.
24 Barr to Gropius, 10 December 1938. In his letter Barr proposed the following wording: "In 1933 the Bauhaus was closed by the National Socialist Government. Because the Bauhaus had developed during the Social Democratic regime the National Socialists felt that it was politically related to the German Democracy and was therefore suspect." Ise Gropius added a handwritten note, in English: "The radical innovations took place in the field of art and education and were never related to any political party program" (Nachlass Walter Gropius, Bauhaus-Archiv, Berlin).

25 Gropius gives his account of Mies's attitude in a letter to Josef Albers, 7 October 1939 (Houghton Library, Harvard University).
26 Franz Schulze, *Mies van der Rohe: A Critical Biography* (Chicago: University of Chicago Press, 1988), 206.
27 Peter Hahn and Lloyd Engelbrecht, eds., *50 Jahre New Bauhaus: Bauhaus-Nachfolge in Chicago,* exh. cat. (Berlin: Bauhaus-Archiv; Argon, 1987).
28 Richard Pommer, "Mies van der Rohe and the Political Ideology of the Modern Movement," in *Mies van der Rohe: Critical Essays,* ed. Franz Schulze (New York: Museum of Modern Art, 1989), 97.
29 Hahn, ed., *Bauhaus Berlin,* 147–48.
30 Sibyl Moholy-Nagy, "The Diaspora," *Journal of the Society of Architectural Historians* 24 (March 1965): 24–25.
31 Isaacs, *Walter Gropius,* vol. 2, 499–500.
32 Margret Kentgens-Craig, *Bauhaus-Architektur: Die Rezeption in Amerika, 1919–1936* (Frankfurt am Main: P. Lang, 1993), 11.
33 Ibid., 123.
34 Isaacs, *Walter Gropius,* vol. 2, 836.

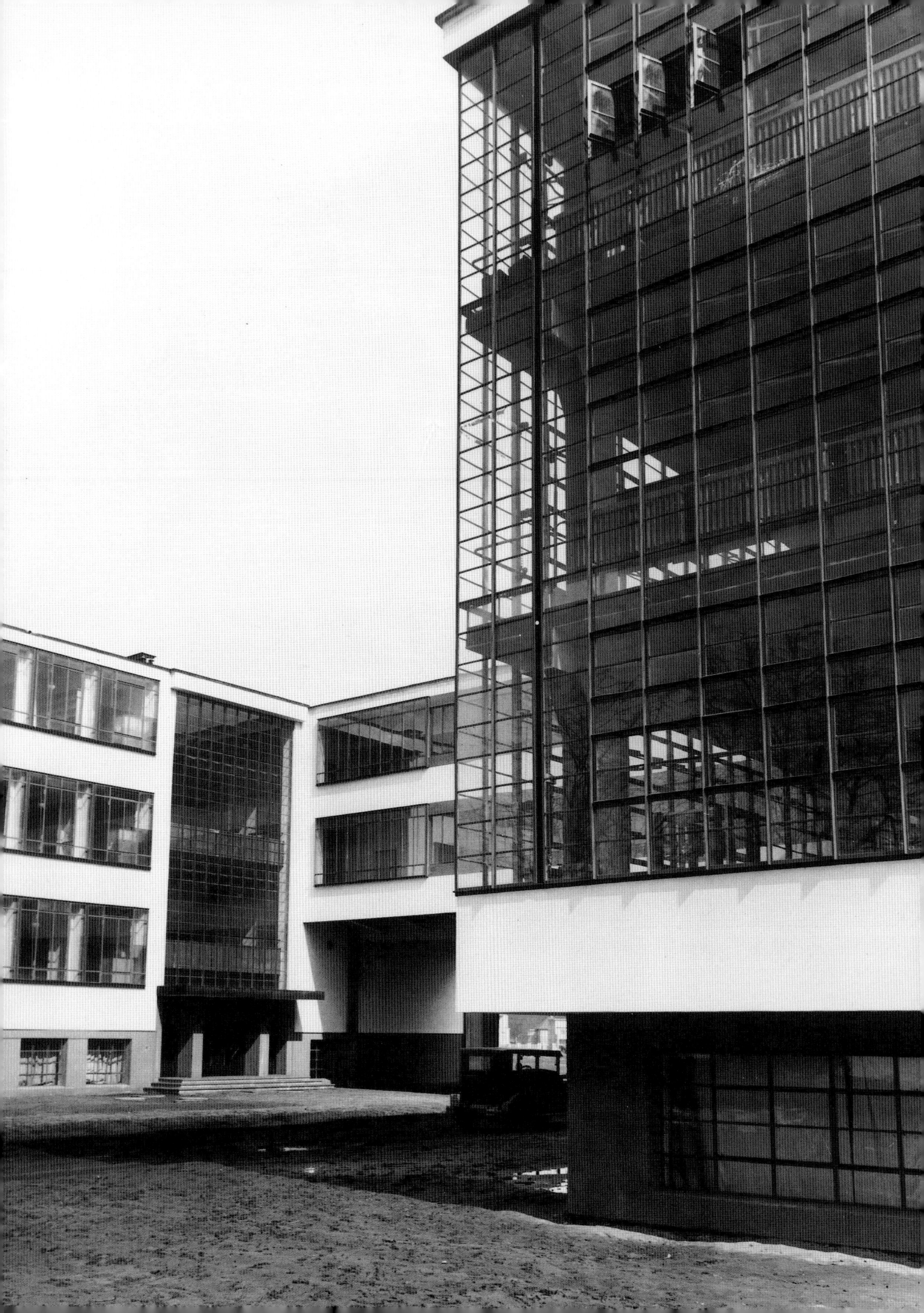

the bauhaus architects
and the rise of modernism in the united states

FRANZ SCHULZE

It is tempting to ascribe the rise of modernist architecture in the United States directly to the emigration of the leaders of the movement, most of them from Nazi Germany, not least because the facts support such an interpretation. In less than a single decade, the 1930s, Hitler turned Germany from a politically impotent nation famous for its wide-ranging artistic freedoms into a totalitarian state determined to repress most modernist experimentation in the arts. Reacting to a cultural and political climate that became increasingly inhospitable to the new architecture that had developed in the course of the 1920s, several of the chief representatives of the movement emigrated to the United States, where by the early 1940s they were not only putting up structures that objectified their point of view but were also teaching a generation of young Americans how to follow their example.

In two short years, 1937 and 1938, Marcel Breuer, Walter Gropius, Ludwig Hilberseimer, Ludwig Mies van der Rohe, László Moholy-Nagy, and Martin Wagner—a half dozen of the most illustrious architects, designers, and planners of Weimar Germany—arrived in the United States, each of them in the fullness of his creative years, each with a professional assignment awaiting him. The painter Josef Albers had come earlier, in 1933, and the architect Erich Mendelsohn came later, in 1941.[1]

Their situations were not typical. American immigration policies of the day were stringent, and refugees were far from automatically welcome. The artists, scholars, and scientists who succeeded in emigrating were in many, if not most, cases asked to come and, once here, eased into gainful positions. American conversion to the modernist cause, in short, was not the reaction to an unsolicited benison. A sympathy with the new architecture and even a measure of achievement in it were already sufficiently established on this side of the Atlantic to warrant the institutional invitations that enabled the European masters to find refuge here.

Americans studying the Weimar scene in the early 1930s were aware that the faculty of the Bauhaus included names known not just for their educational innovations but for their own creative efforts as well: Gropius, the school's founder; his close colleagues Breuer, Moholy-Nagy, and Albers; and the last director of the Bauhaus, Mies van der Rohe. Thus, the offers made to each of these men were stimulated by respect for their stature as artists and as educators together with the belief that their futures, which were likely to be bleak in Germany, would be far more fruitful in the United States.

It was a growing awareness in America of Gropius's reputation as both architect and educator that led Harvard University in 1937 to offer him a professorship and, a year later, make him head of its Graduate School of Design. Five years earlier the Museum of Modern Art in New York had staged *Modern Architecture: International Exhibition,* a display that

222
Walter Gropius and Adolf Meyer; the Bauhaus, Dessau, 1925; photograph by Lucia Moholy-Nagy.

drew widespread American professional and public attention for the first time to the new architecture as it had been practiced not only in Germany but also in most of Europe and, to a limited degree, even in the United States since the early 1920s. The show, which gave pride of place to Gropius, Mies van der Rohe, the Dutchman J. J. P. Oud, and the French-Swiss Le Corbusier as the leading figures of the movement, was the collaborative effort of three Harvard alumni: the museum's director, Alfred H. Barr Jr.; architectural historian Henry-Russell Hitchcock; and the museum's unsalaried curator Philip Johnson. Although these three men, thanks to several years of purposeful travel through Europe, had learned more about the new architecture than virtually any of their countrymen, their aesthetic biases led them to stress the stylistic importance of the movement at the expense of its social purposes. This formalist position was definitively expressed in the book *The International Style*,[2] which Hitchcock and Johnson cowrote at the time of the exhibition.

Although American builders of the late nineteenth century had pioneered new technologies, especially in the invention of the skyscraper, a return to historicism in the 1910s and 1920s had opened the way for the European designers to assume the vanguard, and their advances were apparent in built form as well as on the drawing board and the printed page. By the end of the 1920s the impact of the 1925 Paris *Exposition internationale des arts décoratifs et industriels modernes* was manifest in a growing number of American buildings executed in the "art deco" manner. An additional influence was the increasing volume of pertinent architectural literature. Le Corbusier's famous *Towards a New Architecture* of 1923 was read by students and designers alike following its translation into English in 1927.[3] Gropius himself was the author of *The New Architecture and the Bauhaus* (1935), while Nikolaus Pevsner's *Pioneers of the Modern Movement* (1936) and Walter Curt Behrendt's *Modern Building* (1937) were significant further additions to the literature. The career of the aging Frank Lloyd Wright, in something of a prolonged eclipse since the early 1920s, burst forth with renewed energy with the completion and quick renown of his Kaufmann House, Fallingwater, in 1936. In that building Wright seemed to many observers (though he loudly denied it) to have shifted his manner in the direction of the white architecture of the International Style.[4]

Modernism was more and more in the air, Depression or no Depression. In fact, the economic slowdown of the 1930s granted new freedom to the search for ways to revitalize the profession, not only in architecture offices but also in schools. The traditional Beaux-Arts system of education, with its emphasis on the application of the classical orders to the decoration of buildings based on axiality and symmetry of plan, had for decades been appropriate to an architecture whose construction methods were attuned to the time-honored forms of wall-bearing masonry. With the preeminence of steel and glass in an age increasingly informed by machine technology, however, the Beaux-Arts system seemed more and more irrelevant.

The importance of the Bauhaus in this context should not be underestimated. Its curriculum represented the clearest, readiest, most radical alternative to the Beaux-Arts. Gropius had encouraged the various arts to unite in their efforts to produce creative work that was derived, most prominently in the famous *Vorkurs* (preliminary course), from the nature of modern materials freely experimented with. Pictorialism gave way to abstraction, and historical styles, even history itself, came to be regarded more as a burden than a boon.

Gropius had already left Berlin for England in 1934, anticipating a new career. Breuer and Moholy-Nagy followed him to London in 1935, both with similar intentions. Mies remained longer in Germany, for different reasons, among them an antipathy to long-distance travel that made the prospect of emigration especially unappealing. More important, he was fundamentally indifferent to politics, an attitude that is reflected in his professional vita: he had designed a monument for communist clients (the Liebknecht-Luxemburg Memorial of 1926), a villa for wealthy capitalists (the Tugendhat House of 1930), and in 1934 a competition entry for the German Pavilion in the projected Brussels world's fair (see fig. 229). Of this last work he was willing to claim, in a statement to the German government jury, that it "correspond[ed] with the character of German production."[5] But in that same year, 1934, when Nazi opposition to modernism formally hardened and the jury rejected his Brussels project, Mies began at last to consider the possibility of pursuing his career—that is, making architecture, the art that absorbed him to the exclusion of all else, family as well as politics— in a foreign milieu.[6]

During the summer of 1936 the dean of the Harvard Graduate School of Design, Joseph Hudnut, was in Europe, seeking to learn whether one of the major modernists there might be tempted to bring the new gospel to America. Hudnut had consulted with Barr, who, remembering the 1932 *Modern Architecture* show, recommended that he approach Gropius, Mies, and Oud. There ensued a curious courtship of sorts between Hudnut and Gropius, in London, and Mies, in Berlin. (Oud, in Rotterdam, removed himself from consideration.) Hudnut appears to have asked both men if they were interested in a professorship at Harvard. Reginald Isaacs, Gropius's biographer, implying that Hudnut favored Gropius, wrote that the dean was actually "displeased with [Mies's] unmarried state and informal household."[7] (Mies was in fact married but had long been separated from his wife and children.) Whether this figured in the outcome of negotiations is uncertain, but Mies—upon hearing that Harvard was thinking not only of him but also of Gropius, with whom he had carried on a long and at times chilly professional rivalry in Germany—wrote Hudnut: "If you stand by your intention to submit several names to the President of the University, kindly omit mine."[8] Hudnut in effect did just that, and Mies never forgave Harvard for hiring Gropius, whose cultivated elegance he had long envied, but whose creative abilities he just as certainly regarded as overrated.

Gropius arrived in New York in March of 1937, prepared to assume his new duties at Harvard in the fall. He secured places on the faculty for Breuer, his former student at the Bauhaus and now a designer-architect of international note, later that year and for Martin Wagner, one of the more socially conscious architects of the pre-Hitler years, in 1938. In a further gesture of generosity that seems to have been characteristic of his professional conduct, Gropius persuaded a group of business leaders in Chicago to invite Moholy-Nagy to the United States to head a new school, the New Bauhaus.

Mies meanwhile decided to take more seriously the interest shown in him by Armour Institute of Technology (later Illinois Institute of Technology) in Chicago. Until Harvard walked away from him, he had kept Armour at arm's length. He knew little about Chicago's distinguished architectural history but just enough about its gritty reputation to presume that it could not match East Coast cities such as Boston for the sophistication to which he had grown accustomed in Berlin. Now, however, with his career languishing, he elected to overcome his distaste for travel. He accepted a commission for a vacation house in Wyoming and made the five-thousand-mile trip out there to work on it.[9] In the course of that trek he stopped in Chicago and talked with the administrators at Armour.

They were eager to listen. Like Harvard, Armour had long relied on the Beaux-Arts system but had lately grown uneasy about it; the prospect of hiring a major modernist to head a new program grew all the more attractive with Mies himself at the negotiating table. An agreement was struck: Mies would join the faculty subject to Armour's approval of a full-scale revision of the curriculum, on which he labored during the winter of 1937–38 and which Armour accepted directly. He also asked for and was granted the appointment of two old Bauhaus associates, the architect and city planner Ludwig Hilberseimer and photographer Walter Peterhans.

The warmth of the welcome these refugees encountered in their new homes during 1937 and 1938 varied from case to case, but as a whole the American public greeted them, especially the two most famous, Gropius and Mies, with a pronounced enthusiasm. In the first several months after Gropius arrived, he published his views about architectural education in *Architectural Record*,[10] addressed the Boston chapter of the American Institute of Architects and was awarded a standing ovation, and even began to build a house for himself in Lincoln, Massachusetts (see fig. 223), with money and on land given him by a wealthy local patron, Mrs. James Storrow. The Museum of Modern Art, in turn, lost no time in mounting an exhibition in 1938 called *Bauhaus, 1919–1928*, which was accompanied by a catalogue edited by Gropius; his wife, Ise; and former Bauhäusler Herbert Bayer.

223
Walter Gropius and Marcel Breuer; Gropius residence, Lincoln, Massachusetts, 1937–38, view from the north; photograph by Robert Damora.

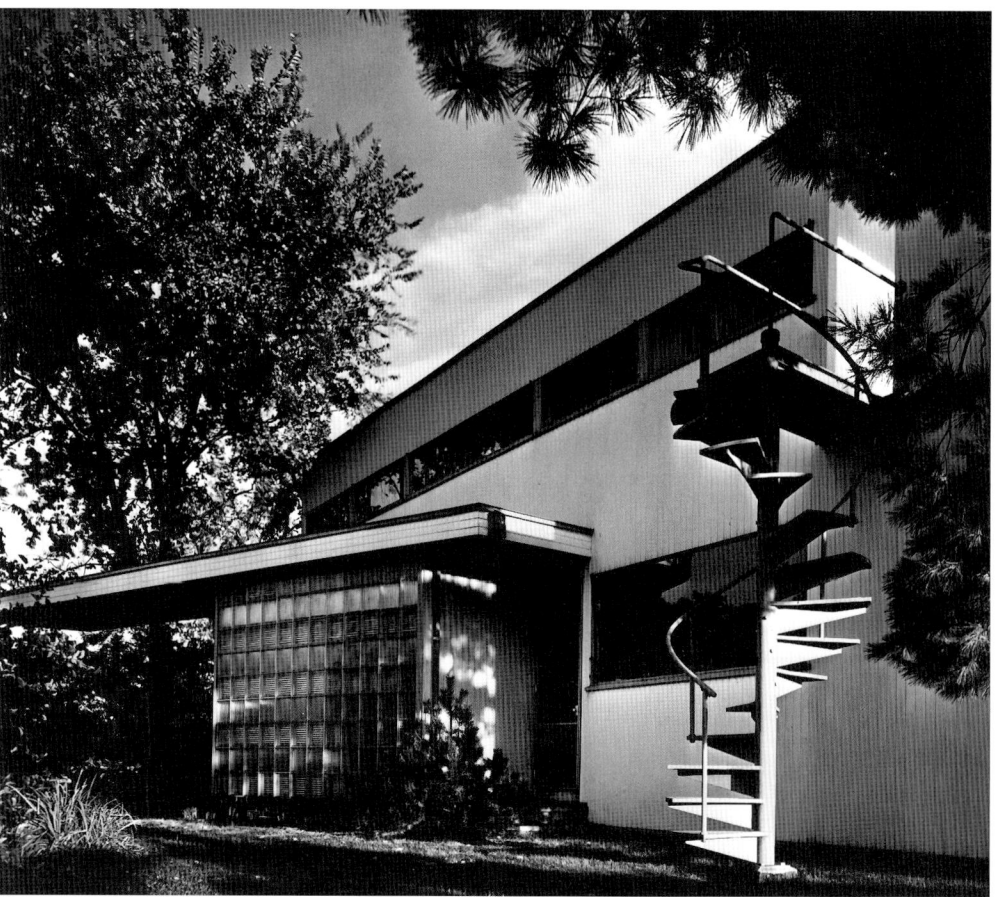

Mies was met no less cordially in Chicago. At a banquet staged in his honor in October 1938 at the Palmer House, the four hundred guests—including leading Chicagoans and architectural deans from around the country—were treated to a now famous introductory speech by Wright, who freely, and typically, acknowledged Mies's debt to him: "*I* give you Mies van der Rohe. But for me there would have been no Mies.... I admire him as an architect, respect and love him as a man."[11] A year later, in 1939, the Art Institute of Chicago exhibited models, photographs, and drawings of several of Mies's German works.

Moholy-Nagy at the New Bauhaus and Albers at Black Mountain College in North Carolina (where he sought to transplant the programs of the Bauhaus as early as 1933) encountered fiscal difficulties of a kind that Gropius and Mies were free from, but they kept their respective ships afloat and principles in place, Moholy until his death in 1946 and Albers until his move to Yale University in 1950. During that period, moreover, their reception by the American professional art world was steadily affirmative.

Nonetheless, if acclamation was the standard public response to most of these emigrés, with the passage of time their individual intentions and achievements, and the reactions to them, diverged. Gropius enjoyed the special good fortune that Harvard, among all American academic institutions, provided him. He could and did invite an assortment of the most celebrated architects, critics, historians, and scholars to Cambridge, thus advancing the education of students whose high level of talent and cultivation he could likewise take for granted. In the classroom and workshop he sought to activate his educational philosophy, the chief postulates of which were enunciated in the catalogue of the Museum of Modern Art's *Bauhaus* exhibition: "The Bauhaus believes the machine to be our modern medium of design and seeks to come to terms with it." Thus, by extension, technology, industry, and standardization—all products of the machine—were meant to replace traditional forms and images as the starting points of architectural design. This much accomplished, the "inner logic [of the building] will be radiant and naked, unencumbered by lying facades and trickeries." Such polemical language was aimed at the Beaux-Arts dependence on historical style vocabularies and formal allusions and associations. There was also a social dimension to Gropius's objectives: "Any industrially produced object is the result of countless experiments, of long systematic research," and thus must elevate "the common basis on which many individuals are able to create together a superior unit of work."[12]

As this system was practiced under Gropius and Breuer, students were encouraged to experiment with "pure" visual form and basic properties of materials, while at the same time comparing their findings with those of their fellows and together working toward a variety of common goals. Competition and collaboration became the dialectic of the Harvard method.

Gropius remained on the Harvard faculty until 1952. The list of graduates during his tenure includes some of the most renowned figures of the second half of the century: Edward Larrabee Barnes, Ulrich Franzen, John Johansen, Philip Johnson, I. M. Pei, Paul Rudolph, and Harry Seidler. Yet, despite the laurels laid on him in Cambridge, Gropius found himself working with a faculty that included some distinguished members, several of conservative stripe, who proved cooperative enough under their new leader but were not easily housebroken. In the last analysis Harvard was not the Bauhaus, and even the relations between Gropius and the man who hired him, Hudnut, eventually soured.

On the face of it, Mies's academic appointment would seem to have left him at a distinct disadvantage to Gropius. As an institute of technology, Armour had a modest national reputation but little more than that, and its architecture classes were conducted in makeshift ateliers in the attic of the Art Institute of Chicago. That put them four miles from the school's main campus on the city's South Side, a rather motley complex surrounded by a slum-ridden neighborhood. Mies's students, moreover, unlike Gropius's well-bred charges, were an earnest but unworldly lot drawn mostly from public high schools in Chicago and its suburbs.

Yet these drawbacks were quickly turned into blessings, due primarily to the coordinated efforts of several strategically situated people at Armour. The administration and the students there were eager and compliant, convinced that their dreams of a status the school didn't yet possess could be realized under the stewardship of a figure of world stature, one who, in any case, had no serious rivals among his new faculty colleagues. Armour trustee John Holabird, a partner at Holabird and Root, one of Chicago's oldest and most eminent architectural firms, was totally committed to Mies and willing to grant him any favors he could. Equally vital was Armour's newly appointed president, Henry Heald, who provided Mies with the single greatest stroke of luck of his early American career. Heald directed him to replace the old Armour campus with a new one of his own design, an assignment calculated to remake the institution's public image—and immediate physical environs—even as it challenged Mies's creative capacity on a scale he had never known.

While World War II did not foreclose Heald's grandiose project, it slowed it,[13] leaving Mies to spend the early 1940s developing an educational program that resembled Gropius's at Harvard in its reliance on modernist concepts, but in little else. Of the two former Bauhaus masters Mies brought to Armour, Peterhans was assigned a course in visual fundamentals roughly analogous to the Bauhaus's *Vorkurs,* while Hilberseimer was put in charge of classes in city and regional planning. Training in building materials was emphasized at both Harvard and Armour.

In other respects the two schools were driven by opposing impulses. Harvard students were permitted to design whole buildings relatively early in their training, reflecting Gropius's belief in freedom of expression and wide-ranging experimentation. Mies, contrarily, openly doubted the value of improvisation, at one point reportedly advising a student that she could satisfy her desire for self-expression by signing her name to her worksheet.[14] Even Peterhans's visual fundamentals course was devoted to the most exacting lessons in pencil drawing, and not until some mastery had been achieved in this could the student proceed to the business of carefully measuring, drawing, and laying courses in brick. Design came later, one modest room at a time, with actual building projects undertaken only in the student's fifth year.

Mies's approach was as autobiographical as it was authoritarian. He had first learned building as an adolescent bricklayer on construction sites in his native Aachen, then served as an apprentice draftsman in a local architecture studio, only later gaining employment as an assistant in a large Berlin office. He never attended an advanced architectural school, as had the young Gropius at the Technische Hochschule in Munich.

The stress Mies laid in Chicago on order, over and against license, seems traceable to his personal shift of values during the course of the 1930s. The commitment to freedom in architecture that he expressed even as late as 1933 (after Hitler's takeover), insisting on that "measure of freedom in spatial composition that we will not relinquish anymore,"[15] gave way to other priorities—was indeed "relinquished." Early in 1938, before starting work at Armour, he wrote to a friend: "In contrast to the extraordinary order apparent in [today's] technical and economic realms, the cultural sphere, moved by no necessity and possessed of no genuine tradition, is a chaos of directions.... It should be the natural responsibility of the university to bring clarity to this situation.... Things by themselves create no order. Order as the definition of the meaning and measure of being is missing today; it must be worked toward, anew."[16]

The ironies abound. In 1936 a former Bauhaus student, the American Michael van Beuren, had advised Mies: "It would be better for you in Chicago than in Boston. The people [in Chicago] have more initiative; they get more naturally and directly to the point of things.... At Armour... you could do what you want.... Boston is a proud, 'foin' city, which all in all does not love our century."[17] It was nevertheless Gropius, at Harvard, who proved to be the apostle of freedom and enemy of tradition as surely as Mies, in presumably less hidebound Chicago, became the strictest of taskmasters, dedicated to the pursuit not only of order but also of what he regarded as absolute "truth."

After the war the impact of the emigré architects on the arts of this country became the primary, overarching criterion of American judgment of them. They had clearly initiated a revolution in education that spread in the 1940s and 1950s, just as the whole modernist doctrine took command of the American approach to things in all the arts. And they produced work of their own, in the modernist idiom, that had a similar effect on American taste and the habits of American architects.

Where the reputations of individual emigrés are concerned, however, differences again began to overtake similarities. The three emigré architects most carefully watched by the profession were Mies, Breuer, and Gropius, an order consistent with the ranking in which they came to be held in the course of their American careers. In the years immediately following the war, Gropius was widely assessed—together with Wright, Le Corbusier, and Mies—as one of the four greatest designers of the century. By consensus he has since been dropped from that lofty company. Several of the products of his American partnership with Breuer, which lasted from 1937 to 1941, are still held in reasonably high esteem: his own house in Lincoln (1937–38), the Chamberlain House in Sudbury, Massachusetts (1939), and the Aluminum City Terrace housing in New Kensington, Pennsylvania (1941–42; see figs. 224, 242). Some of his more ambitious efforts at city planning and prefabricated building,

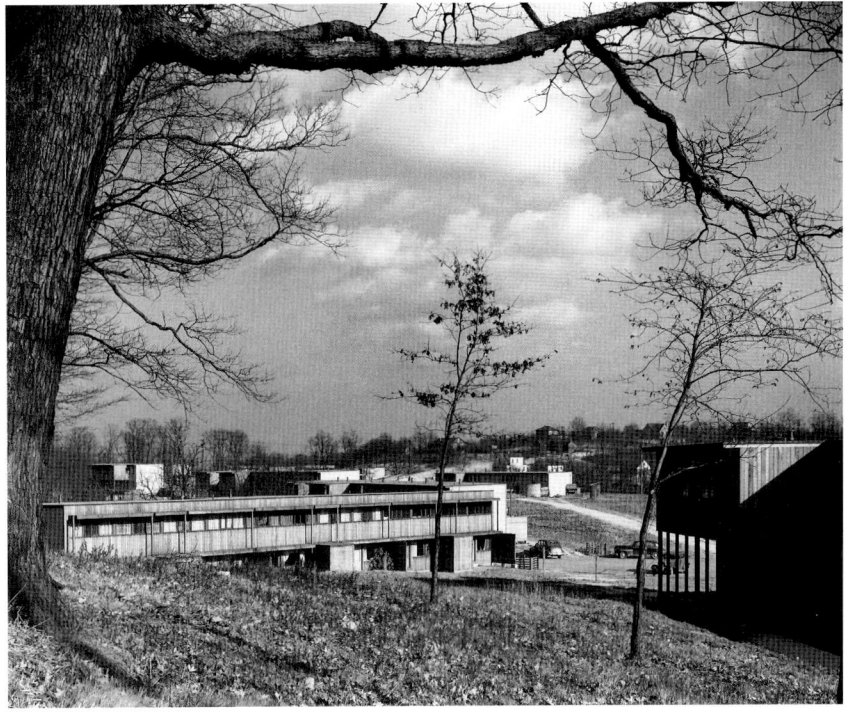

224
Walter Gropius and Marcel Breuer; Aluminum City Terrace, New Kensington, Pennsylvania, 1941–42; photograph by Gottscho-Schleisner, Inc.

however, such as the Michael Reese Hospital Campus on Chicago's South Side in the late 1940s and the Packaged House System done with fellow emigré Konrad Wachsmann in 1942, remained in large part frustrated and frustrating, more well intentioned in concept than successful in results. As a leading member of the Architects Collaborative (founded in 1946), a firm whose name was chosen to represent his work philosophy, he produced an abundance of building, most of which, however, did little or nothing to restore the reputation he had brought with him from Germany.

Breuer's prestige fared far better as the years passed. Some credit for this must go to a pragmatic nature that enabled him to make a creative adjustment to a foreign environment. Breuer's resourcefulness reflects his freedom from the bondage of theory. He was described as a "peasant mannerist" by Philip Johnson, a Harvard graduate of the 1940s who claimed to have learned more from Breuer's casual method of instruction than from Gropius's formal pedagogy.[18] It appears, moreover, that it was Breuer, more than Gropius, who, in their collaborative house designs of the late 1930s and 1940s, moved to temper the abstract austerities of the International Style with such devices as wood clapboard and natural stone, drawn from the New England vernacular. Indeed, Breuer had already employed regionalist elements to impart a greater warmth of material expression in England, notably in the rough masonry walls and flagstone terraces of the Gane Pavilion (with F. S. R. Yorke, 1936). This inclination to blend modernist form with local idiom was most happily achieved in the house he built for himself in 1947 in New Canaan, Connecticut, a work customarily regarded as the capstone of his American residential designs.

It was Mies whose reputation as an architect flourished in America at least as fully as it had in Europe. While his emphasis on discipline in his teaching might suggest a stiff-necked attitude toward the design of his own buildings, he adjusted to his new environment as surely as Breuer did and, if anything, with more impressive, certainly more influential, consequences. In the United States he enjoyed greater access to steel than he had in Germany, and he found that material especially compatible with his concept of order. Structure, to which steel lends itself with reductivist clarity, became the primary formative force in his American teaching and his American work, as such masterpieces as the Seagram Building (1954–58; see fig. 232) and the Farnsworth House (1946–51; see fig. 225) attest. "Structure," in architectural historian Kevin Harrington's words, "was a constant inner check which rewarded reason and punished willfulness.... With the plan founded on structure, Mies advanced his thinking about space, the most intangible and abstract of architectural elements, and structure, the most tangible and presumably most rational of elements, into a position of astringent reciprocity."[19] The unitary space of Crown Hall (1956), hung from its famous four plate girders, illustrates Harrington's argument.

Moreover, Mies's influence as a teacher in Chicago went a long way in producing a following close enough in its reliance on declarative structure to the works of the generation of Louis Sullivan and John Wellborn Root that it earned the label "Second Chicago School." Furthermore, it produced its own set of masters, including Jacques Brownson, Myron Goldsmith, Bruce Graham, and Gene Summers, all of whom worked in the 1950s and 1960s for the big Chicago commercial firms (e.g., Skidmore, Owings and Merrill, C. F. Murphy Associates) that added so effectively to the look of contemporary downtown Chicago.

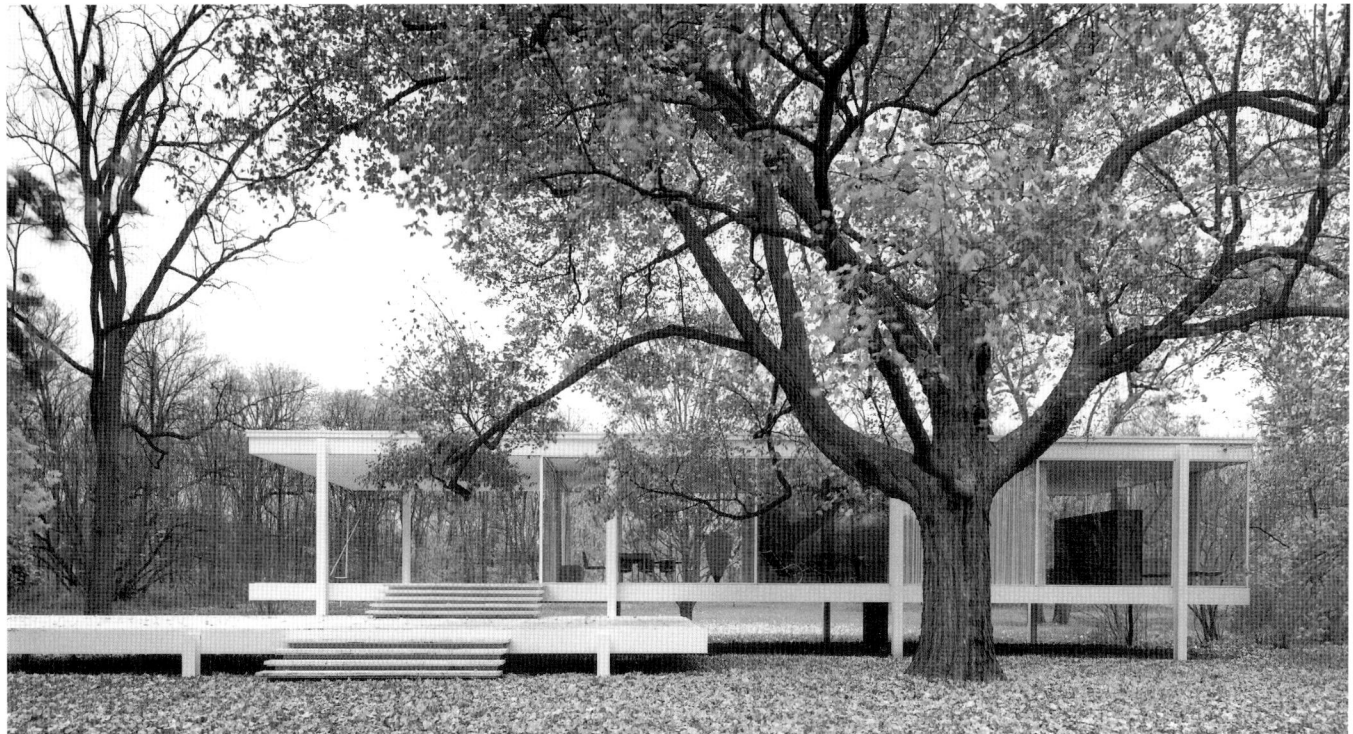

225
Ludwig Mies van der Rohe; Farnsworth House, Plano, Illinois, 1946–51; photograph by Jon Miller.

With the passage of two-thirds of a century since the arrival of the emigrés, it appears beyond argument that they were crucial to the qualitative change in American architecture and architectural education that occurred in the period surrounding World War II. Nevertheless, keeping in mind that the invitations extended by their sponsors were signs of a growing American interest in modernism, there is no way of measuring precisely the impact of the emigrés or of knowing how far or in what directions modernism would have gone in the United States without their intervention.

What seems most reasonable is to recognize the reciprocity of the encounter. Not only are the monuments built here by Mies, Gropius, Breuer, and other emigrés now an indelible part of American architectural history, but one can hardly discount the extent to which their disciples have acknowledged a direct debt to them. Yet the demonstrable change in the manners and outlooks of the Europeans once they had taken up residence in the United States attests to the effect of their new environment upon them. The impress of American technology and the composition of the American cityscape were surely central to the development of the Miesian highrise building and to its ready adoption by other architects, just as the form and materials of the traditional American house qualified postwar modernist versions of it. Similarly, if the teaching of architecture in the United States was affected by a philosophy traceable largely to the Bauhaus, it was negotiated not in the highly focused setting of a European-style academy, but in the more generalized atmosphere of the multidisciplined American university.

The final certainty in a record otherwise marked by uncertainties is that the immigration of these architects to the United States, like that of the multitude of other accomplished intellectuals driven from their homelands by the forces of Adolf Hitler, turned out to be a gift of historically unparalleled generosity—albeit one of grotesque and unwitting irony—from one enemy to another.

Notes

1   The last major figure of the architectural emigration, Mendelsohn is not remembered as an important architect in America, neither as a teacher of influence nor as a designer of great works. The modesty of his American record as a whole stands in sharp contrast to the brilliant career he had fashioned for himself during the Weimar period. He was obliged to wait until 1946 for his first major commission in the United States, a synagogue in Saint Louis (see fig. 226), the first of four completed houses of worship that together constitute his most serious American efforts. In each of them his expressive intention, to create a monumental form consonant with the spiritual significance of the synagogue, was ambitiously conceived but, in the view of most critics, never realized with the freshness or persuasive coherence that marked the best of his German output. He lived in San Francisco until his death in 1953. In his last years he taught for a time at the University of California, Berkeley, but he never established a theoretical position there comparable to those achieved by his Weimar fellows in Chicago and on the East Coast.

2   Henry-Russell Hitchcock and Philip Johnson, *The International Style: Architecture since 1922*, preface by Alfred H. Barr Jr. (New York: W. W. Norton, 1932).

3   Originally titled *Vers une architecture* and published by Editions Crès, Paris, the book was translated into English by Frederick Etchells and published by Architectural Press, London.

4   A counterinfluence from America to Europe is worth noting here, but, even so, it required the blessing of foreign authority before it affected American-educated designers. The Europeans were fascinated throughout the 1920s by the formal simplicity of the American grain elevator, and the Viennese architect Richard Neutra, who had come to America in 1923 to seek out Frank Lloyd Wright, published a book entitled *Amerika* (1930), in which he juxtaposed photographs of pueblo architecture with images of U.S. skyscrapers, factories, and industrial products. Rudolph Schindler, another Austrian, emigrated earlier still—also to work with Wright—and, like Neutra, practiced a vigorous modernism during the 1920s. Even so, these two men were atypical on the American scene, as were those native Americans, like Bertram Goodhue and Ralph Walker, who worked as early as the mid-1920s in forms similar to those that later came to be regarded as advanced.

5   Ludwig Mies van der Rohe, "Zu dem Vorentwurf für ein Ausstellungsgebäude...," 3 July 1934, Brussels Folder 6, Mies van der Rohe Archive, Museum of Modern Art.

6   It has been reported by numerous authorities that the rejection of the Brussels project was overseen, angrily, by Hitler himself. A year later, in 1935, Mies's project for a house for Ulrich Lange in Krefeld was judged "un-German" by the local building authorities, who agreed to its construction only on the condition that Mies erect a berm around it. It was at about this time that solicitations from foreign institutions began to arrive in his hands, the first from an American institution coming in 1935 from Mills College in Oakland. Mies turned it down, perhaps because he could not speak English, perhaps because he hoped to secure the commission to design a major textile exhibition for Berlin. See Jean-Louis Cohen, *Mies van der Rohe*, trans. Maggie Rosengarten (London: Spon, 1996).

7   Reginald Isaacs, *Gropius: An Illustrated Biography of the Creator of the Bauhaus* (Boston: Little, Brown, 1990), 217.

8   Franz Schulze, *Mies van der Rohe: A Critical Biography* (Chicago: University of Chicago Press, 1985), 207.

9   The commission came from Mr. and Mrs. Stanley Resor of New York City. Mies worked fitfully on the project until 1943, but it was never completed.

10   Walter Gropius, "Architecture at Harvard University," *Architectural Record* 81 (May 1937): 9.

11   Quoted in Schulze, *Mies van der Rohe*, 219.

12   Walter Gropius, "The Theory and Organization of the Bauhaus," in *Bauhaus, 1919–1928*, ed. Herbert Bayer, Walter Gropius, and Ise Gropius (New York: Museum of Modern Art, 1938), 25, 27, 28; translation of *Idee und Aufbau des Staatlichen Bauhauses Weimar* (Munich: Bauhausverlag, 1923).

13   Mies carried forward the design of the campus in earnest after 1945, completing twenty-two buildings before he retired from the faculty in 1958.

14   Conventional wisdom has it that the student was Elizabeth Wright Ingraham, in residence at IIT in the early 1940s and now an architect practicing in Colorado Springs. In a conversation with the author, 22 November 1995, she claimed that she could not recall the incident but allowed that it "quite possibly could have happened that way."

15   Ludwig Mies van der Rohe, "Was wäre Beton, was Stahl ohne Spiegelglas?" contribution to a prospectus of the Verein deutscher Spiegelglas-Fabriken, 12 March 1933; quoted in Fritz Neumeyer, *The Artless Word* (Cambridge: MIT Press, 1991), 217.

16   Mies van der Rohe, letter, unaddressed but probably written to Carl O. Schniewind, 31 January 1938; quoted in Schulze, *Mies van der Rohe*, 214.

17   Van Beuren to Mies van der Rohe, 21 October and 3 November 1936 (Mies van der Rohe Archive); quoted in Schulze, *Mies van der Rohe*, 207–8.

18   Philip Johnson, "Retreat from the International Style to the Present Scene," in *Writings* (New York: Oxford University Press, 1979), 85.

19   Kevin Harrington, "Order, Space, Proportion—Mies's Curriculum at IIT," in *Mies van der Rohe: Architect as Educator*, exh. cat., ed. Rolf Achilles, Kevin Harrington, and Charlotte Myhrum (Chicago: Illinois Institute of Technology, 1986).

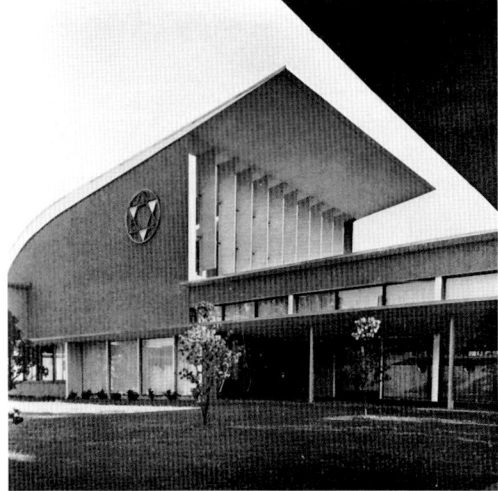

226
Erich Mendelsohn, B'nai Amoona Synagogue, Saint Louis, 1946–50.

227
Ludwig Mies van der Rohe; 860–880 North Lake Shore Drive from the west, Chicago, 1951; photograph by Hedrich-Blessing.

changing the agenda:
from german bauhaus modernism
to u.s. internationalism

KATHLEEN JAMES

ludwig mies van der rohe
walter gropius
marcel breuer

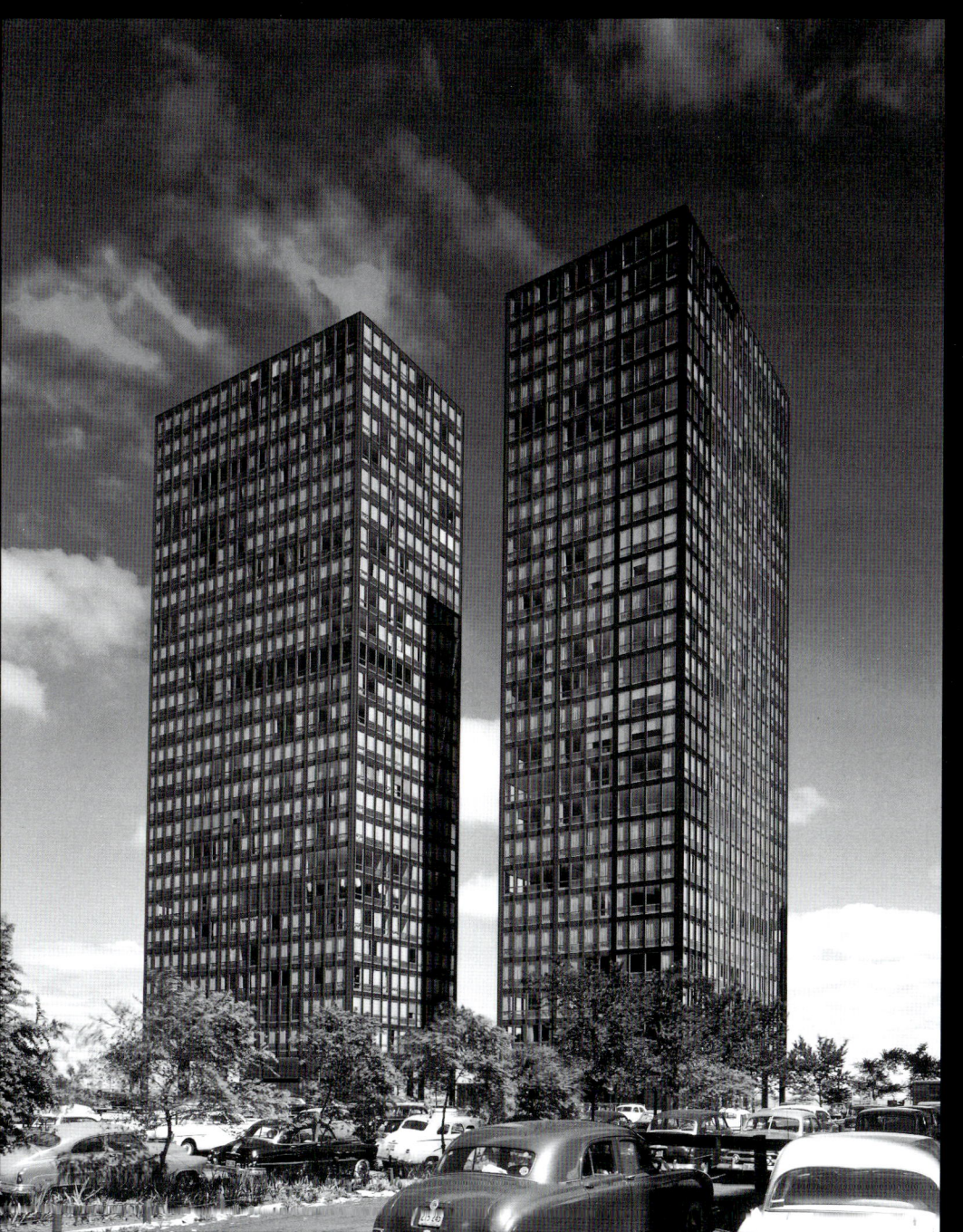

ludwig mies van der rohe
in chicago, 1938–45

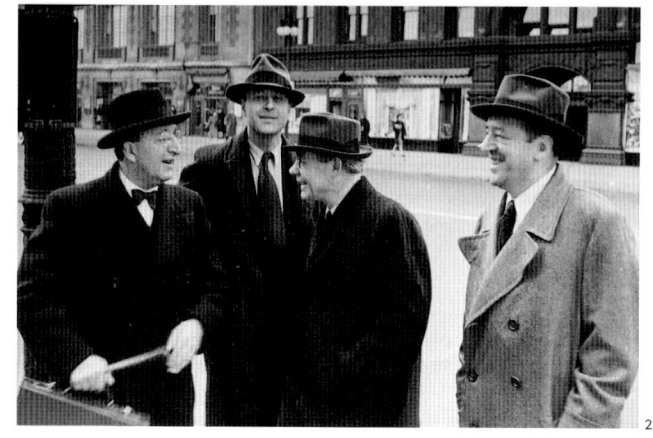

1886	born in Aachen, Germany
1938	immigrates to the U.S. (Chicago)
1969	dies in Chicago

First in Germany and then in the United States Ludwig Mies van der Rohe was at the geographical center of a movement whose formal content, despite the dislocations of emigration, proved for him to be remarkably consistent. Inspired already in the 1920s by the technology of American steel and reinforced-concrete frame construction, he was able in Chicago to design buildings that were simultaneously interpreted as the logical fulfillment of a cherished moment in American architectural history and as the realization of European utopian vision. This combination of German intellectual rigor and American know-how resulted in enormous success.

Mies was over fifty when he arrived in Chicago. In Germany only a handful of his designs, most of them for houses, had actually been built. In America, despite his late start, he quickly became the most important architect of his generation, entrusted with numerous commissions for high-rise apartment and office buildings as well as prestigious institutional buildings. His postwar work was widely interpreted as fulfilling the early promise of his adopted city's most famous commercial architects: Louis Sullivan, John Root, and Daniel Burnham.

Trained in the neoclassicism popular in Germany in the early years of the twentieth century, in maturity Mies united the abstract geometry of De Stijl and constructivist art with an impeccable attention to the material facts of construction in brick, steel, and glass. As the designer of a monument to the communist martyrs Rosa Luxemburg and Karl Liebknecht (1926), the organizer of the Weissenhof Siedlung (a housing exhibit of permanent dwellings which opened in Stuttgart in 1927), and the third director of the Bauhaus (1930–33), he was closely identified with the aspects of the modern movement most often attacked by right-wing opponents of the Weimar Republic. Nonetheless, he initially had reason to hope that he would be treated by Hitler's new government as one of the country's leading architects.

Lured by the hope of prestigious commissions, Mies did not oppose the new government, even when it successfully pressured him to shut down the Berlin Bauhaus. His was one of the winning entries in the Reichsbank competition (1933), in which a number of modernists participated; the following year a government official invited him to compete for the commission to design the German Pavilion for the 1935 Brussels world's fair (see fig. 229). Although never a member of the party, Mies did join several Nazi-sponsored organizations and in 1934 signed a petition in which artists and other cultural figures declared their support for Hitler.[1] By the end of that year, however, it was clear that, despite initial support for his architecture within one Nazi faction, he would in the future be allowed only minor private commissions.

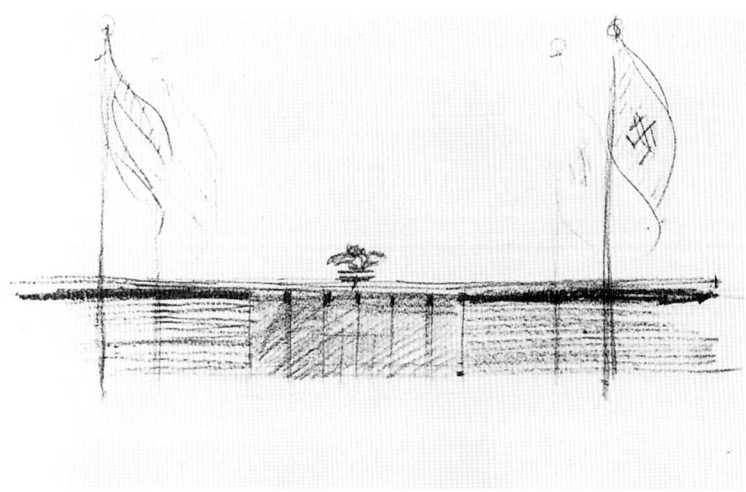

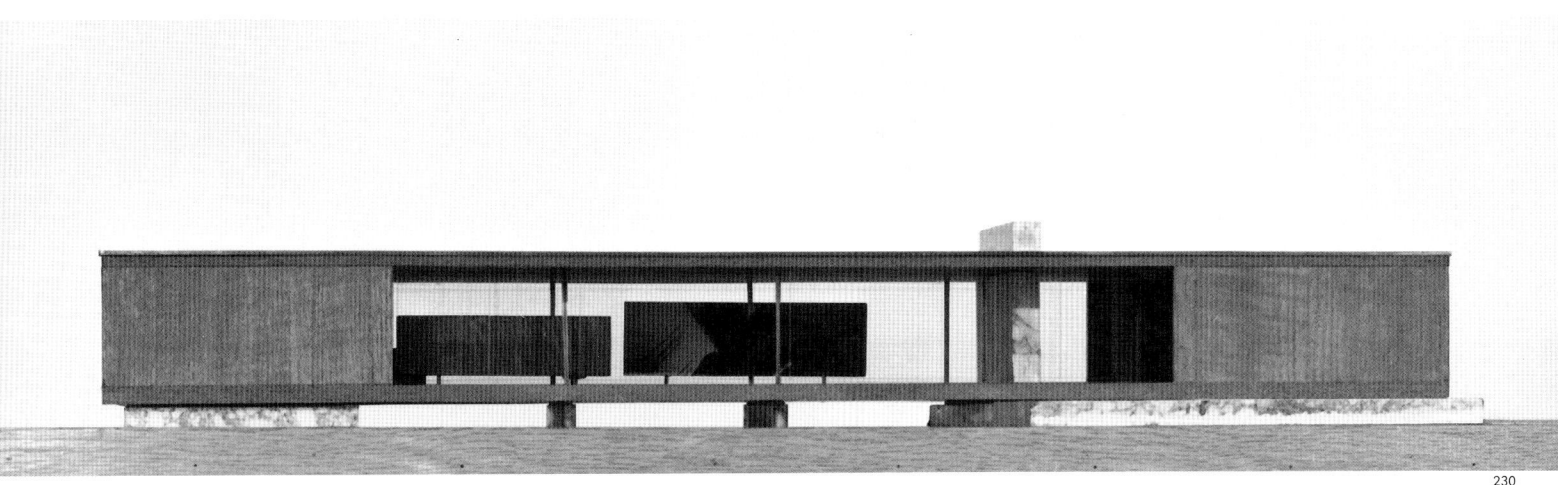

230

228
Ludwig Mies van der Rohe (right) with (from left) Erich Mendelsohn, Walter Peterhans, and Ludwig Hilberseimer across from Orchestra Hall and the Pullman Building, Chicago, c. 1940.

229
Ludwig Mies van der Rohe; project for the German Pavilion, Brussels world's fair, 1934; original sketch; collection of Dirk Lohan.

230
Ludwig Mies van der Rohe; Resor House project, Jackson Hole, Wyoming, 1938; model; The Mies van der Rohe Archive, The Museum of Modern Art, New York, special purchase fund.

Marginalized in Germany, Mies was increasingly celebrated in the United States. Much of the credit for this attention, and for his later success in the United States, can be attributed to the consistent support given him by the Museum of Modern Art's pioneering Department of Architecture and Design. Although he did not always hold the official title of curator, Philip Johnson, who had first met Mies in Berlin in 1930, was largely responsible for this advocacy. In the museum's exhibition *Modern Architecture: International Exhibition,* held in New York in 1932, Henry-Russell Hitchcock and Johnson singled out Mies, Le Corbusier, Walter Gropius, and J. J. P. Oud as the leaders of a new style that provided what they saw as the first alternative to decades of historicist eclecticism.[2] Fifteen years later Johnson curated an exhibition of Mies's work which challenged the view that to be accepted in the United States, modern architecture must be made more accessible, its original asceticism replaced, as in the first American houses by Gropius and Marcel Breuer, with the familiar textures of wood and stone.[3]

Three separate efforts, one of them spearheaded by Johnson, eventually encouraged Mies to immigrate to America.[4] In 1936 Joseph Hudnut seriously considered him as a candidate for the Harvard professorship eventually awarded to Gropius. The same year Chicago's Armour Institute of Technology (which became the Illinois Institute of Technology, or IIT, in 1940) contacted Mies in the hope that he could transform its relatively undistinguished architecture department into one of the nation's best. Meanwhile, Johnson arranged for him to design the Resor House in Jackson Hole, Wyoming (see fig. 230). Although never built, the commission brought Mies to the United States for the first time in a visit that lasted from August 1937 to March 1938. During these months he toured Chicago and met with Frank Lloyd Wright in Spring Green before finally accepting the Armour position.

After briefly returning to Berlin, Mies began work in Chicago on an entirely new architecture curriculum for the program he would direct until 1959.[5] Hiring Ludwig Hilberseimer and Walter Peterhans, with whom he had taught at the Bauhaus, he instituted a curriculum emphasizing the mastery of individual elements of design: composition, drawing, and materials. Ensuring a high level of competence rather than nurturing individuality, an IIT education remained distinct from both its Beaux-Arts-inspired predecessors and the new curriculum at Harvard, where Gropius stressed imaginative planning rather than Mies's meticulous attention to construction.

Mies was the most important architect to emigrate directly from Germany to the United States during the 1930s and the only one of such stature to settle in the Midwest. Untouched by the taste for the regional and the organic that pervaded the modern movement in the 1930s, he chose to acclimatize himself to his new home only to the degree—and it would prove quite considerable—to which its traditions could be integrated with his own formal predilections. The rise of the modern movement in Europe had elevated Sullivan, Root, and Wright to positions at the pinnacle of American architectural history and defined Chicago as a city whose businesslike efficiency had laid the foundation for architectural innovation on both sides of the Atlantic. By building on the same scale and with the same technology as the architects of Chicago's early office buildings, Mies inherited their new prestige, even as he proposed a far more radical relationship between construction and ornament, which would strip his buildings of overt references to history and to nature.

Mies's emergence as an important American architect was delayed, however, by the outbreak of World War II in 1939 and restrictions placed upon new construction following the entry of the United States into the conflict in 1941.

Photocollages, a technique with which he had first experimented two decades earlier, rather than actual buildings, illustrate two of his earliest reactions to his new surroundings.[6] A master plan for a new IIT campus (1939–41; fig. 18) and a project for a concert hall (1942; fig. 231) contrast his own startling abstraction with the Chicago neighborhood surrounding IIT and the clear span of Albert Kahn's Glenn L. Martin factory. Both designs are inconceivable without the interest Mies had already shown in Germany in the plans of Wright's Prairie houses. New, however, was his interest in reorganizing existing spaces, rather than merely inserting his buildings within them, as he experimented with finding his own place in a still largely unfamiliar architectural culture. He accomplished this in the concert hall simply by pasting pieces of paper, including an image of an Egyptian scribe, onto a photograph of the existing building, juxtaposing the opacity of his additions with the continuous openwork truss of the bomber factory's roof. In the plan for IIT, by contrast, the arrangement of individual buildings established a new spatial order independent of the surrounding city.

If the openness of the campus master plan seemed liberating at the time, an exacting module of twelve- and twenty-four-foot bays disciplined the steel-framed classroom and laboratory buildings Mies began to erect at IIT in 1943. It was only with the commission for 860–880 Lake Shore Drive (1948–51; see fig. 227), however, that he fully demonstrated the new focus upon the derivation of order from structure encouraged by his access to the American construction techniques so widely admired in Germany during the 1920s.[7] In these two slabs,

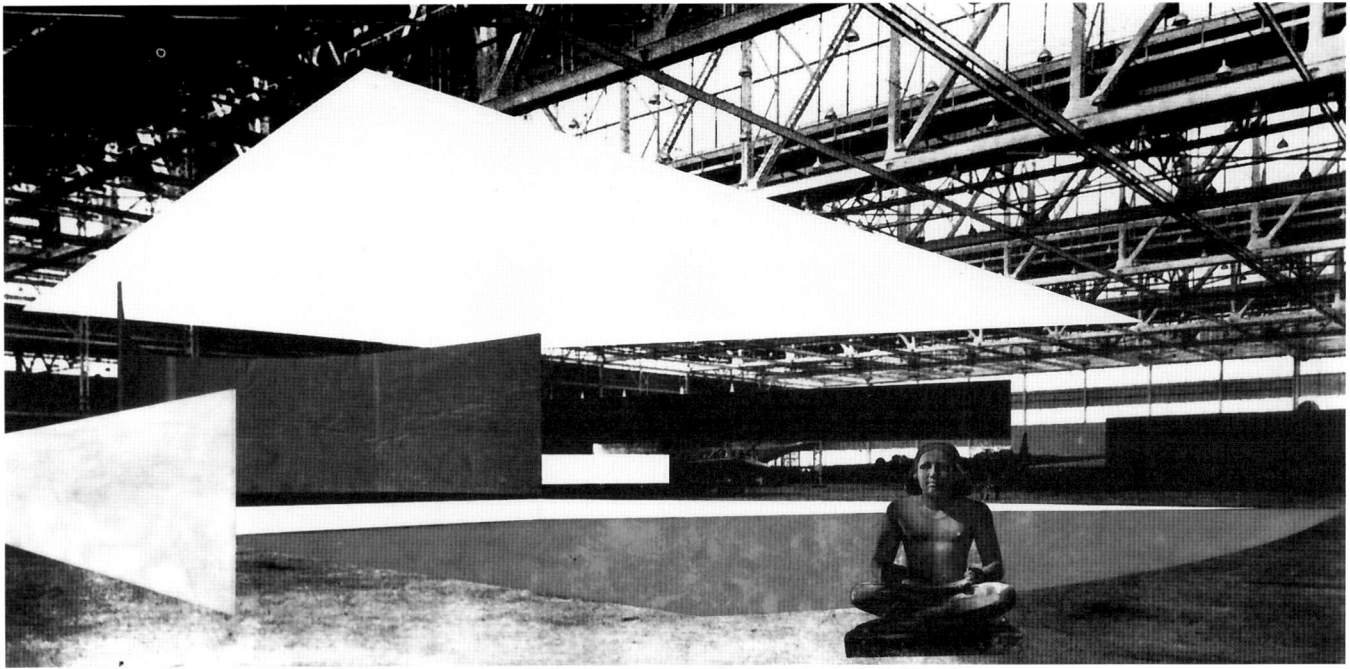

231
Ludwig Mies van der Rohe; *Concert Hall Project*, 1942; collage over photograph; 29½ x 62 in. (75 x 157.5 cm); The Mies van der Rohe Archive, The Museum of Modern Art, New York, gift of Mary Callery.

set perpendicular to each other, he drew upon Chicago's early high-rises and the skyscraper projects he had designed while still in Germany to create the most powerfully metaphoric of a series of contemporary American curtain-wall high-rises that also included Pietro Belluschi's Equitable Building in Portland (1948); the Secretariat of the United Nations in New York (1950), designed by a committee headed by Wallace Harrison; and Skidmore, Owings, and Merrill's Lever House (1952), also in New York.[8] Mies's use of steel I-beams as window mullions, although not in fact integral with the underlying steel frame, adhered to a rigid, constructionally based logic and indicated his renunciation of a trend toward enlivening modern architecture by dramatizing innovative structure.

No other new American building of the day was greeted with the same degree of admiration and enthusiasm accorded the Lake Shore Drive Apartments, and none so completely integrated what had until then been the two very different faces of modernity in architecture: the abstract approach to form pioneered in Europe during the 1920s and the efficient construction technologies developed during the same period in the United States. Almost immediately writers for the country's leading architecture magazines began to hail Mies as the worthy successor to Sullivan, who half a century earlier had been the city's premier advocate of the rational articulation of the steel skeletal frame.[9] Meanwhile real estate developers noted that, despite some complaints about excessive heat in the west-facing apartments, the towers cost less to build than more conventional masonry-faced apartment buildings and that by the end of 1952 the resale value of individual units was almost double the original purchase price. Rather than an artistic risk, modern architecture now appeared a sound investment—at least if one was building a skyscraper.[10]

Regardless of their actual function, the buildings Mies designed after his arrival in the United States almost all fall into one of two categories: towers (like the Lake Shore Apartments) and pavilions. Conceptually and structurally, the purest of the latter were the house Mies built for Dr. Edith Farnsworth in Plano, Illinois (1946–51; fig. 225), and the much later Neue Nationalgalerie in Berlin (1962–68). The first also illustrates the misunderstandings that even the most successful emigrés could encounter when their clients' assumptions were very different from their own.[11]

For Mies the Farnsworth commission presented the opportunity to create a meticulously detailed and perfectly proportioned object. Farnsworth was equally interested, however, in a usable—and affordable—weekend home.

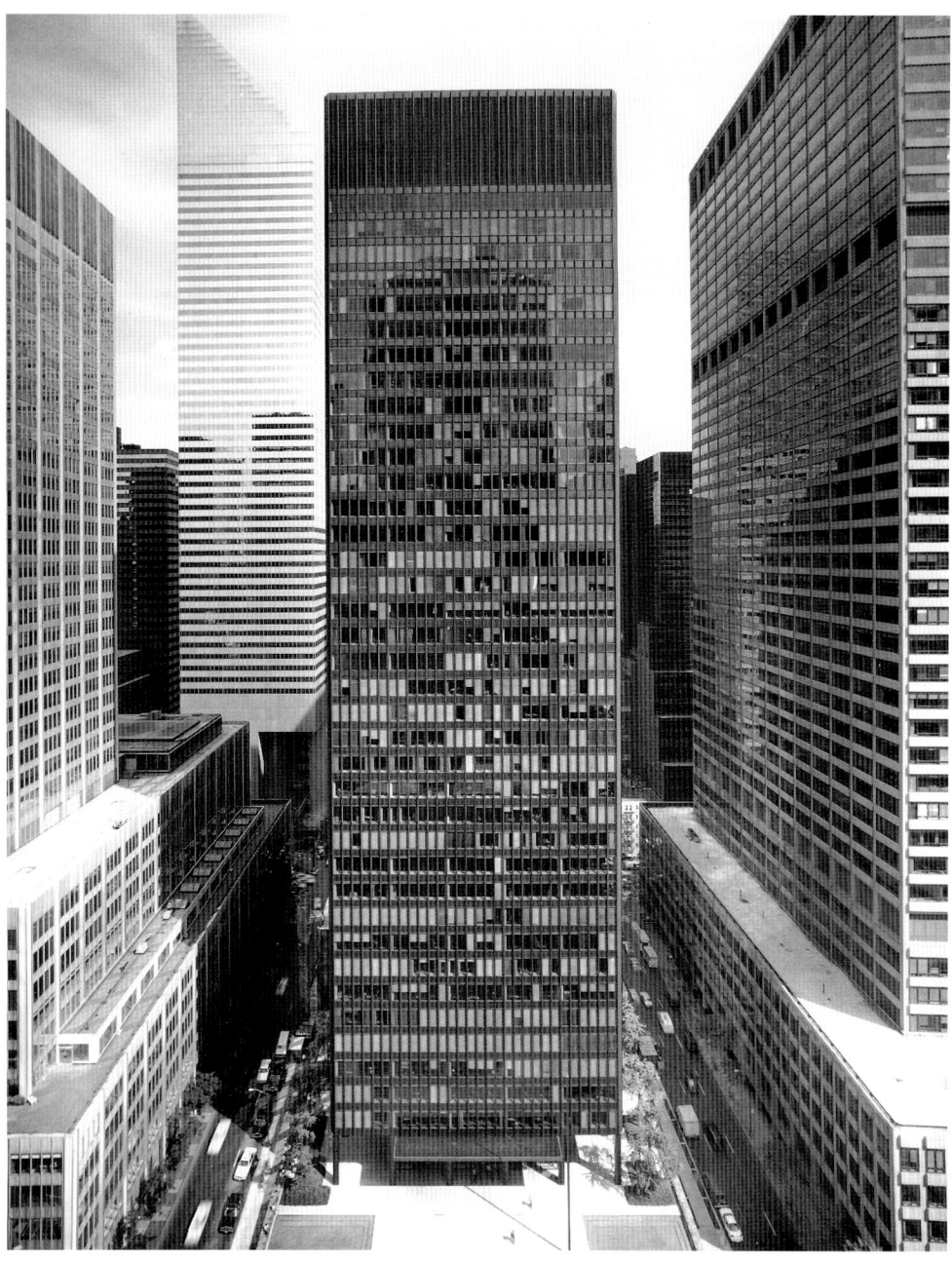

232
Ludwig Mies van der Rohe and Philip Johnson; Seagram Building, New York, 1954–58; photograph by Ezra Stoller © Esto. All rights reserved.

Despite widespread appreciation of the apparent simplicity of this travertine terrace and glass box framed by and supported on steel beams—Arthur Drexler described it as "a quantity of air caught between a roof and a floor"—Farnsworth sued for cost overruns (Mies had acted as his own contractor).[12] Although she lost, others understood her frustration. In an otherwise enthusiastic review a writer in *Architectural Forum* noted that the house "has little to say to those whose ideal is an informal setting for family living, or those who seek first to express the individual personality of a client, or finally to those who concentrate on devices of climate control and scientific management of the environment."[13]

Mies did not have time to rue his difficulties with the Farnsworth commission. Transposing the Lake Shore Drive Apartments into a single, far more luxurious tower—the Seagram Building in New York (1954–58; fig. 232), designed in partnership with Philip Johnson— he demonstrated an ability to integrate modern architecture and economic organization that had eluded him when he had first sought large commercial commissions, during the 1920s in Germany. Mies continued to practice until his death in 1969, and his final decade was the busiest of his entire career.

Notes

1 The most complete and balanced account of Mies's political views and their relationship to his architecture is Richard Pommer, "Mies van der Rohe and the Political Ideology of the Modern Movement in Architecture," in *Mies van der Rohe: Critical Essays,* ed. Franz Schulze (New York: Museum of Modern Art, 1989), 96–145. See also Lee Gray, "Addendum: Mies van der Rohe and Walter Gropius in the FBI Files," in ibid., 146, for documentation of Mies's oral objections to the Nazis, albeit uttered only after his arrival in the United States. On the Nazi flirtation with modern architecture, see Barbara Miller Lane, *Architecture and Politics in Germany, 1918–1945* (Cambridge: Harvard University Press, 1985), 169–84.

2 Although not literally the catalogue of this exhibition, Henry-Russell Hitchcock and Philip Johnson, *The International Style: Architecture since 1922* (New York: W. W. Norton, 1932), proved its most influential document.

3 Philip Johnson, *Mies van der Rohe* (New York: Museum of Modern Art, 1947), which appeared in conjunction with this exhibition, was the first monograph devoted to Mies's work.

4 Accounts of these can be found in Franz Schulze, *Mies van der Rohe: A Critical Biography* (Chicago: University of Chicago Press, 1985), 205–17, and Kevin Harrington, "Order, Space, Proportion—Mies's Curriculum at IIT," in *Mies van der Rohe: Architect as Educator,* ed. Rolf Achilles, Kevin Harrington, and Charlotte Myhrum (Chicago: Illinois Institute of Technology, 1986), 49–55.

5 Harrington, "Order, Space, Proportion," 55–67.

6 The earliest of these was his entry in the 1921 competition for a high-rise office building to be located on Berlin's Friedrichstrasse.

7 See, for example, Erich Mendelsohn, *Amerika: Bilderbuch des Architekten* (Berlin: Rudolf Mosse, 1926), and Richard Neutra, *Wie baut Amerika?* (Stuttgart: J. Hoffmann, 1927).

8 William Jordy, *American Buildings and Their Architects: The Impact of European Modernism in the Mid-Twentieth Century* (Garden City, N.Y.: Anchor Press, 1973), 221–77. See also "Our New Capital Towers," *Architectural Forum* 98 (February 1953): 142–45.

9 "Glass and Brick in a Concrete Frame," *Architectural Forum* 92 (January 1950): 70, and Henry-Russell Hitchcock, "The International Style Twenty Years After," *Architectural Record* 110 (August 1951): 96. See also Eero Saarinen, "The Six Broad Currents of Modern Architecture," *Architectural Forum* 99 (July 1953): 114, for a thoughtful evaluation of Mies's position in contemporary architecture.

10 "Mies van der Rohe," *Architectural Forum* 97 (November 1952): 96, 100, 102.

11 "Edith Farnsworth Sues Mies," *Architectural Forum* 95 (November 1951): 67.

12 Henry-Russell Hitchcock and Arthur Drexler, *Built in USA: Postwar Architecture* (New York: Museum of Modern Art, 1952), 21.

13 "This Is the First House Built by Ludwig Mies van der Rohe," *Architectural Forum* 95 (October 1951): 157.

walter gropius at harvard, 1937–45

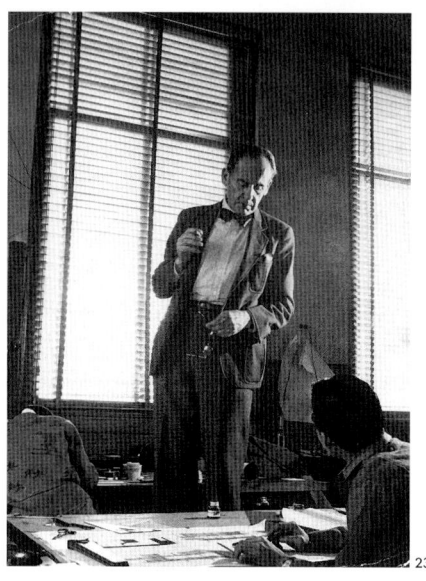

1883	born in Berlin
1934	immigrates to England (London)
1937	immigrates to the U.S. (Cambridge, Mass.)
1969	dies in Boston

Following World War I, Walter Gropius, a scion of a distinguished Prussian family of landowners and architects, emerged from the nationalist chrysalis that had inspired much of his early thinking about architecture to become the championed and despised advocate of the new styles, building types, and methods of construction associated with the Weimar Republic and the political left.[1] During the 1930s, as the republic collapsed and he moved first to Britain and then to the United States, he was torn between his patriotic attachment to his native country and his role as a leader in the creation of an approach to architecture often unappreciated by its new government. Although circumspect in public about the Nazis, he was welcomed abroad as a representative of the innovative culture Hitler had crushed.

His most creative years behind him, Gropius nonetheless continued to be among the most important architects of his generation. He had always been an able administrator and an effective spokesman, and his position as chair of the department of architecture at Harvard University enabled him to integrate many of his most radical accomplishments into the postwar mainstream. He continued to defend the importance of the Bauhaus, which he had founded and led, and the integration of planning, engineering, and construction with the teaching and practice of architecture. Leaving to others the Bauhaus's engagement in product design, he now focused on disseminating the architectural pedagogy he had begun to develop there and on the collaborative approach to architecture that had characterized his entire career.[2]

An early and enthusiastic supporter of the Weimar Republic, Gropius nonetheless initially imagined that he could work with Hitler's regime. During 1933 and 1934 he entered competitions to design the Reichsbank in Berlin and a prototypical Haus der Arbeit (house of labor) and participated in the design of the exhibition *Deutsches Volk—deutsche Arbeit* (German nation—German labor).[3] He also joined the Nazi-controlled arts organization, the Reichskulturkammer. Even after moving to London at the end of 1934, anxious to protect family members and property he had left behind and motivated by a respect for Germany that transcended the character of its government, he vacillated between private denunciation and public accommodation, refusing to allow his critical comments about the new regime to be quoted in the press.[4]

Gropius was nonetheless lionized in Great Britain and the United States, both for his directorship of the Bauhaus and his experiments with the efficient construction of inexpensive housing. His move to London, for instance, was prompted by an exhibition of his work at the Royal Institute of British Architects as well as a meeting of the Congrès internationaux d'architecture moderne (CIAM).[5] Despite his ambivalent stance toward the Nazi regime and his repeated denials of his refugee status, Gropius was regarded as a representative of the artistic expression suppressed by the Nazis. Perceived now as a symbol of democracy rather than of the unwelcome extremism of socialism, modern German art and architecture attracted new audiences in Britain and the United States.[6] For Gropius this attention culminated in the

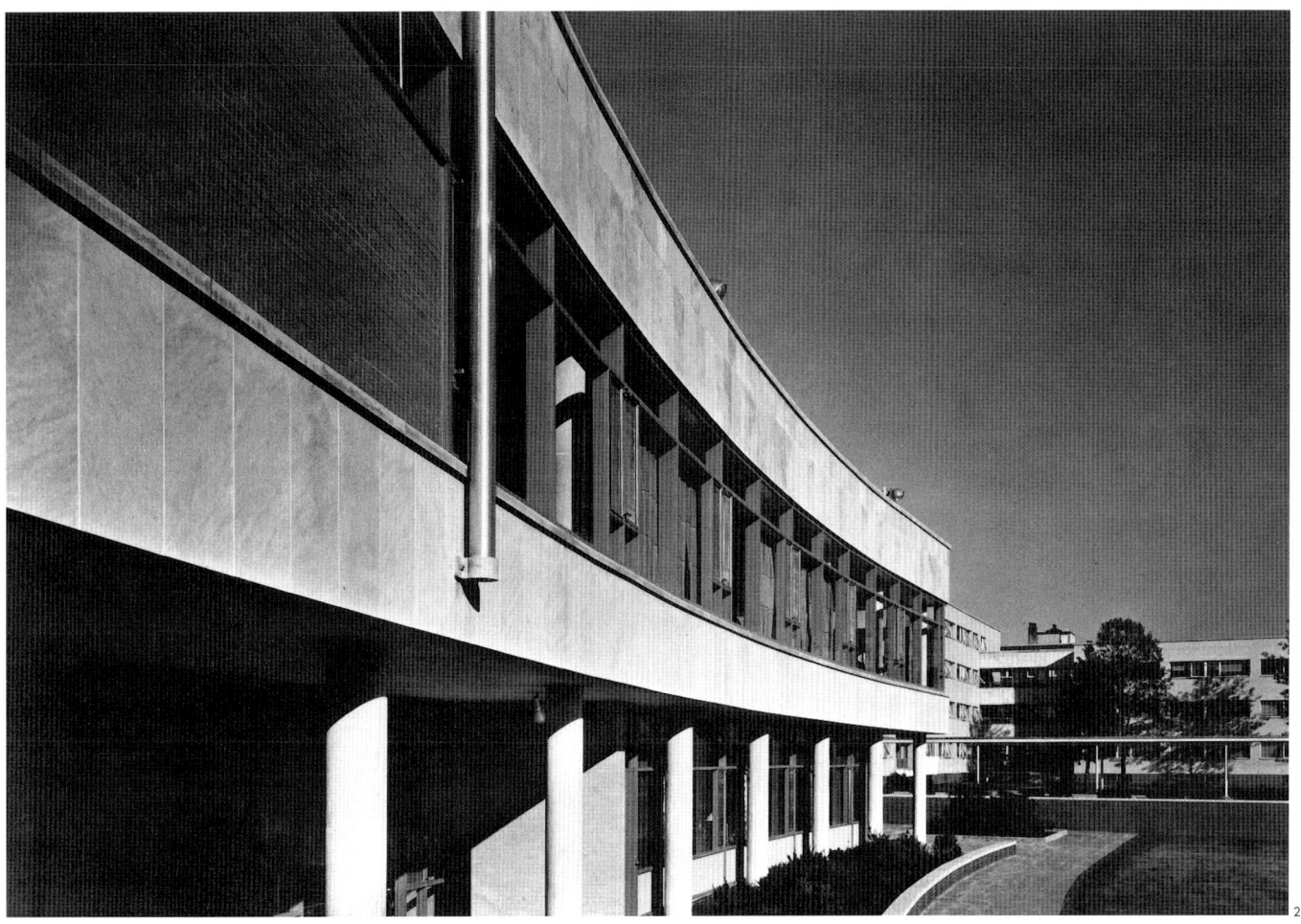

233
Walter Gropius, Harvard University, 1944; photograph by Ise Gropius.

234
Walter Gropius/The Architects Collaborative, Harvard Graduate Center, graduate commons and courtyard, 1948–50; photograph by Fred Stone.

invitation that Joseph Hudnut, the dean of the School of Architecture at Harvard University, issued him in 1937 to teach architecture there and his appointment the following year as chair of the department.[7]

Although hesitant to criticize Hitler openly, Gropius never wavered in his advocacy of modern architecture or in his efforts on behalf of its supporters. Even in London, where he and his wife endured real financial hardship, he did his best to assist others. In America he obtained teaching positions at Harvard for Marcel Breuer and for Martin Wagner, the former city architect of Berlin. Josef and Anni Albers, Herbert Bayer, László Moholy-Nagy, and many far less famous figures benefited from everything from extended periods of hospitality (Konrad Wachsmann, with whom Gropius developed a scheme for a mass-produced house, lived with the Gropiuses in Lincoln, Massachusetts, for months) and assistance in procuring work to the more general attention his proselytizing for the Bauhaus brought to their accomplishments.[8]

Exhibitions at the Museum of Modern Art and articles written by Gropius and by his wife, Ise, publicized his ideas and his accomplishments during the 1930s, but it was only in the United States that he was able to translate this fame into a comfortable standard of living and ample opportunities to build.[9] His brief partnership with the British architect Maxwell Fry resulted in only four completed commissions. None of these had the same impact upon architecture in Britain that the Gropius House in Lincoln had in the United States.

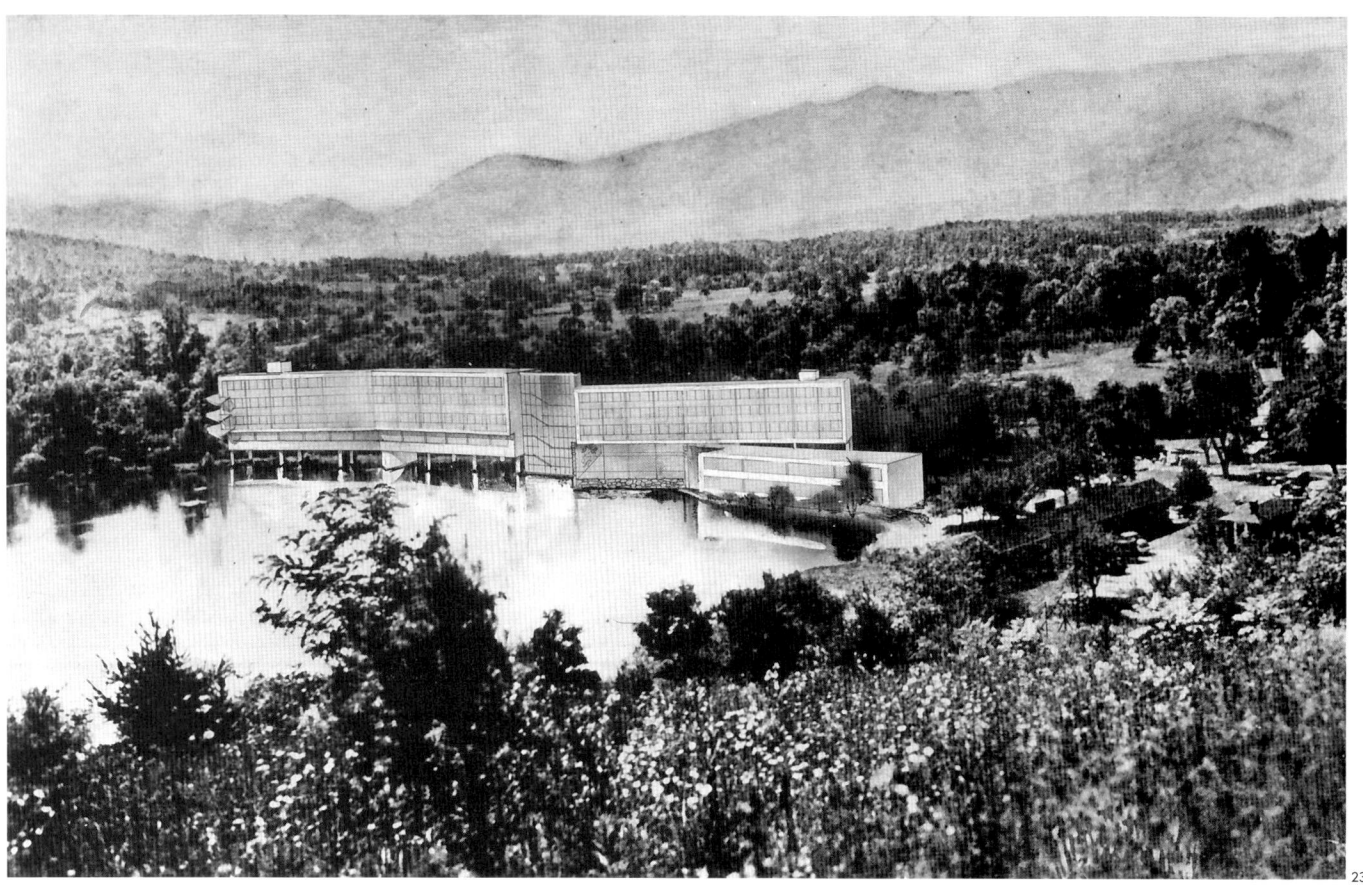

235
Walter Gropius and Marcel Breuer; *Black Mountain College*; collage element with ink and gouache over photograph; 12⅞ x 20 in. (32.8 x 50.9 cm); Busch-Reisinger Museum, Harvard University Art Museums, gift of Walter Gropius.

236
Gropius residence, Lincoln, Massachusetts, screen porch; photograph by Robert Damora.

Almost immediately upon his arrival at Harvard, Mrs. James Storrow offered Gropius land and funds to build a house that would demonstrate the suitability of his approach to his new American context. Her generosity was indicative of the respect accorded Gropius in America, which had often eluded him in Germany, even during the 1920s. For a quarter century already, his fascination with American building methods had been integral to his career as an architect. His publication in 1913 in the yearbook of the German Werkbund of a sheaf of photographs of American factories and grain silos had influenced an entire generation of European architects. A decade later his entry in the Chicago Tribune Tower competition, in which he had frankly expressed the skyscraper's skeletal frame construction, had garnered little attention in the United States but was widely admired in Europe. In 1928 he had toured the United States, paying particular attention to American construction.[10] Now, working in collaboration with Breuer, he shied away from fully exploiting the technological prowess he had long admired.[11]

Soon after his arrival Gropius praised America's "extraordinary building organization," which he claimed "provide[s] an instrument of such wonderful perfection that I think any architect would feel inspired and eager to take part in the task of developing the American architecture of the future." In the years that followed, however, he largely failed to avail himself of this precision tool.[12] Ironically, his best American buildings would instead be inspired in part by vernacular traditions that predated the industrial revolution. Although by American standards the Gropius House in Lincoln (1938; see fig. 236) was unusually modern, its wood-frame construction and redwood siding, which he painted white, were intended to harmonize with local colonial farmhouses. A flat-roofed box enlivened by projections such as a sun porch and an exterior spiral stair leading to the roof terrace, the modest building included a number of quotations from Gropius's German work, including the house he had built for himself near the Dessau Bauhaus, but was hardly an exercise in standardization.[13] Instead this became the first of a succession of houses he, his collaborators, and his students designed in which the geometry of the International Style was made more decorative for an American audience enamored of machine-age conveniences but unwilling to express them in the architecture of their homes.

An important exception to this move away from the overtly industrial character of much of his European work is a project for Black Mountain College (1938–39; see fig. 235). Had it been built, this string of dramatically glazed boxes, the most prominent of them raised on pilotis, would undoubtedly have been seen as a reincarnation of the Bauhaus on American shores. The experimental school—at which several Bauhaus alumni, including Josef and Anni Albers, taught—was never able, however, to raise enough funds to undertake the construction of this ambitious scheme.[14]

More typically, the goals as well as the style of Gropius's German architecture proved difficult to transfer to American shores. Neither Gropius's prestigious position at Harvard nor the adoption of characteristically American materials guaranteed the acceptance of designs that contrasted with middle-class preferences for detached, single-family houses. For instance, Gropius and Breuer's Aluminum City Terrace (1941–42; see figs. 224, 242), built by the Defense Housing Coordinators in New Kensington, Pennsylvania, was the subject of considerable controversy, despite the ample use its architects made of wood and, to a lesser degree, brick. Erected just outside Pittsburgh for the workers of an aluminum factory that was in fact never built, the complex met with strong local resistance, triggered as much by opposition to working-class neighbors as to its architecture. Early tenants were largely satisfied, however, with the row-house units, which the architects, in a sharp departure from the regularity of Gropius's German housing, arranged picturesquely in relation to the steep terrain, and the government was pleased by the cost of $3,098 a unit, which matched that of other DHC-built communities.[15]

His American experiences somewhat muted Gropius's earlier calls for standardization but did not alter his equally influential view of the architectural profession. Almost incapable of drawing, a skill usually integral to the career of an architect, he sought out unusually talented collaborators throughout his career and stressed engineering over the artistic dimension of architecture. At Harvard, where his students included Harry Cobb, I. M. Pei, and Paul Rudolf, he emphasized the integration of urban planning

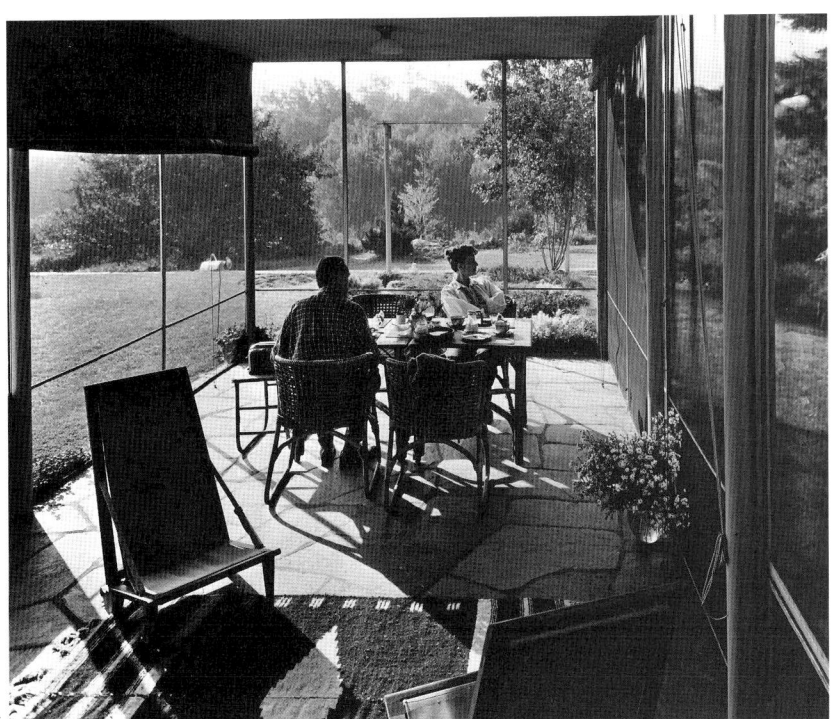
236

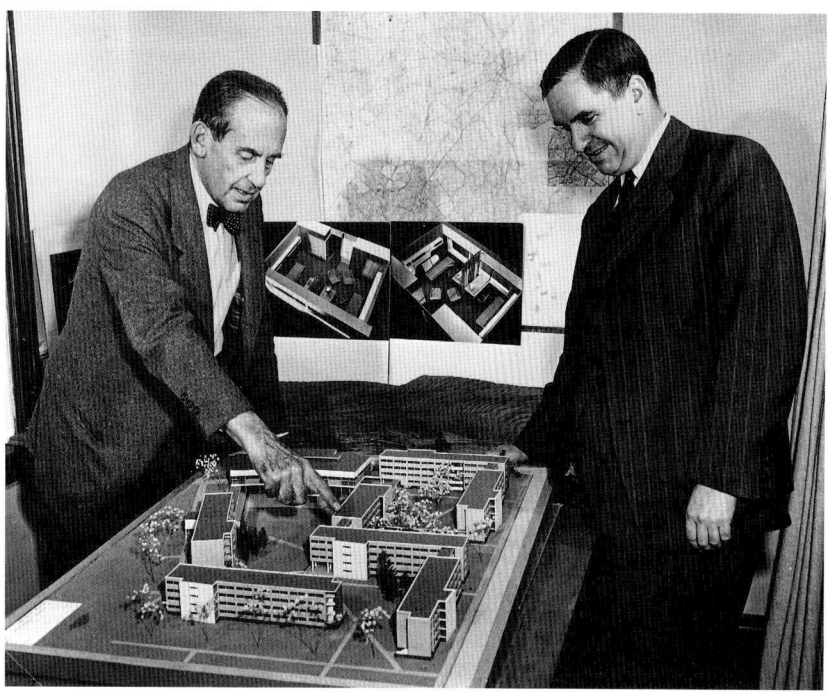

237
Walter Gropius and Dean Erwin Griswold with model of the Harvard Graduate Center, c. 1948; photograph by Walter R. Fleischer.

and architecture.[16] And in lectures delivered around the country in the early 1950s, Gropius repeatedly called upon the profession to eliminate the barriers separating the practice of architecture from its execution by builders, claiming that only once architects "build up a closely co-operating team together with the engineer, the scientist, and the builder, [would] design, construction and economy . . . again become an entity—a fusion of art, science and business."[17]

This attitude, as well as the dissolution of his partnership with Breuer, led him in 1945 to found the Architects Collaborative (TAC) in partnership with Jean Bodman Fletcher, Norman Fletcher, John Harkness, Sarah Pillsbury Harkness, Robert McMillan, Louis McMillen, and Benjamin Thompson. The firm's first major commission was for the Graduate Center at Harvard (1948–50; see figs. 234, 237). Its relationship to his earlier building for the Dessau Bauhaus defined Gropius's dilemma in exile as he struggled to invent an architecture appropriate to twentieth-century circumstances without relying, as he had in Germany, upon machine-age imagery.

TAC's client was now the nation's oldest university rather than a brash new school. Gropius chose to continue the campus's long tradition of courtyard-oriented brick housing, even as he completely rejected the colonial revival style that had flourished at Harvard for half a century. At the same time, however, he was hampered in his attempt to create the modern equivalent of the Graduate Center's imposing predecessors by his own defense of modern architecture as the logical result of rationalization. A reputation for economy was crucial to the postwar popularity of modern architecture but often led, as in this case, to disappointingly banal results. Constrained by a budget that—at a time of rapid inflation in construction costs—allowed only half the expenditure per student room of the prewar housing for undergraduates, TAC's dormitories and dining hall for students in the Law and Graduate Schools included the contributions of the Alberses, Bayer, Richard Lippold, and Joan Miró but not the delicately machined detailing and dynamic composition that had enlivened the Bauhaus. The architectural press lauded the Graduate Center as a demonstration of the widespread acceptance of modern architecture rather than as an innovative new building.[18]

Although Gropius was active in TAC until his death in 1969, his most important contribution in his later years was to architectural education and theory. Even after his retirement from Harvard in 1952 he continued, as one of modern architecture's most celebrated elder statesman, to promote the legacy of the Bauhaus and the efficacy of planning to a new generation of architects and students around the world. His influence was particularly profound in the Federal Republic of Germany, and through visits and letters he kept close track of the resurgence of Bauhaus influence there.

Notes

1 See Reginald Isaacs's biography, *Gropius: An Illustrated Biography of the Creator of the Bauhaus* (Boston: Little, Brown, 1990), for the architect's background. The roots of his early factory architecture in the troubled issue of German cultural identity are particularly clear in Reyner Banham, *A Concrete Atlantis* (Cambridge: MIT Press, 1986). For the political controversy that dogged the Bauhaus, see Barbara Miller Lane, *Architecture and Politics in Germany: 1918–1945* (Cambridge: Harvard University Press, 1985), 69–86.

2 The most complete appraisal of Gropius's career in exile and his impact upon American architecture can be found in William Jordy, "The Aftermath of the Bauhaus in America: Gropius, Mies, and Breuer," in *The Intellectual Migration: Europe and America, 1930–1960*, ed. Donald Fleming and Bernard Bailyn (Cambridge: Harvard University Press, 1969), 485–543.

3 This work and its context in the activities and similar attitudes of other Bauhäuslers, many of whom would also eventually emigrate, are detailed in Winfried Nerdinger, ed., *Bauhaus-Moderne im Nationalsozialismus* (Munich: Prestel, 1993).

4 Leslie Humm Cormier, "Walter Gropius: Emigre Architect: Works and Refuge, England and America in the '30s" (Ph.D. diss., Brown University, 1986), 22–24.

5 Ibid., 21.

6 For the American reception of Gropius and the Bauhaus up to the point of his arrival at Harvard, see Margret Kentgens-Craig, *Bauhaus Architektur: Die Rezeption in Amerika, 1919–1936* (Frankfurt: Peter Lang, 1993). In New York the activities of the Museum of Modern Art's fledgling department of architecture and design were particularly important. Gropius was one of four architects singled out for special attention in *Modern Architecture: International Exhibition*, mounted there in 1932. See Terence Riley, *The International Style: Exhibition 15 and the Museum of Modern Art* (New York: Rizzoli, 1992).

7 See "Gropius to Harvard," *Architectural Forum* 66 (March 1937): 14, and Walter Gropius, "Architecture at Harvard University," *Architectural Record* 81, no. 5 (1937): 8–10, for how this appointment was greeted by the American architectural press.

8 See, for instance, Gilbert Herbert, *The Dream of the Factory Made House: Walter Gropius and Konrad Wachsmann* (Cambridge: MIT Press, 1984), 212, 263–64.

9 Most important in this regard were Walter Gropius, *The New Architecture and the Bauhaus* (London: Faber and Faber, 1935), and Herbert Bayer, Walter Gropius, and Ise Gropius, eds., *Bauhaus, 1919–1928*, exh. cat. (New York: Museum of Modern Art, 1938). See also Ise Gropius, "The Dammerstock Housing Development: The House for Practical Use," *Architectural Forum* 53 (1930): 187–92; Walter Gropius, "The Small House Today," *Architectural Forum* 54 (1931): 266–78; and Ise Gropius, "A House in Wiesbaden," *Architectural Review* 78 (1935): 13–14. The last is an account of a house by Breuer.

10 For Gropius's relationship with American architecture up to the point of his emigration, see Winfried Nerdinger, *Walter Gropius* (Berlin: Gebrüder Mann, 1985), 9–28.

11 The most detailed accounting of the two men's individual responsibility for the work of this partnership can be found in Joachim Driller, "Marcel Breuer: Das architektonische Frühwerk bis 1950" (Ph.D. diss., Universität Freiburg, 1990), 120–25.

12 Walter Gropius, "Architecture at Harvard University," 9.

13 See Driller, "Marcel Breuer," 125–58.

14 Mary Emma Harris, *The Arts at Black Mountain College* (Cambridge: MIT Press, 1987).

15 The design was originally published in "House Types, One and Two Story, One to Three Bedrooms," *Architectural Forum* 75 (1941): 218–20, as part of a survey of defense housing. "Aluminum City Terrace Housing," *Architectural Forum* 81 (July 1944): 65–76, recounted neighborhood complaints about and surveyed tenant satisfaction with the project.

16 For a perceptive, if critical, account of Gropius's teaching at Harvard, see Klaus Herdeg, *The Decorated Diagram: Harvard Architecture and the Failure of the Bauhaus Legacy* (Cambridge: MIT Press, 1983).

17 "Gropius Appraises Today's Architect," *Architectural Forum* 96 (May 1952): 111.

18 "Harvard Builds a Graduate Yard," *Architectural Forum* 93 (December 1950): 61–71. Bainbridge Bunting, *Harvard: An Architectural History,* ed. Margaret Henderson Floyd (Cambridge: Harvard University Press, 1985), 210–29, places this housing within the context of the almost simultaneous transformation of the architectural curriculum and the campus at Harvard, both sponsored by President James Bryant Conant.

marcel breuer at harvard, 1937–45

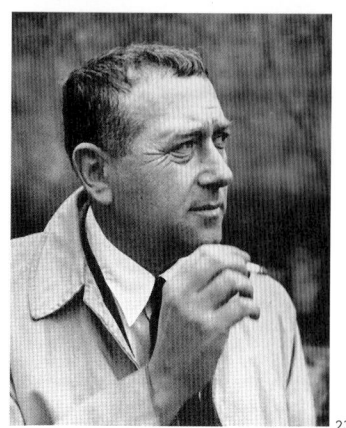
238

1902	born in Pécs, Hungary
1935	settles in England (London)
1937	immigrates to the U.S. (Cambridge, Mass.)
1981	dies in New York

Hungarian-born and trained at the Bauhaus, Marcel Breuer was just thirty when Hitler and the National Socialists seized power in Germany. A Jew who had converted to Protestantism in 1926, Breuer initially left Germany to work and travel. Already in 1931 the collapse of the German economy had caused him to close his architecture office in Berlin; for the next four years he divided his time between Budapest, Zurich, and study tours that took him as far as North Africa. Breuer's gradual transition into exile in Britain and the United States was eased by the royalties he continued to receive from his furniture patents and by the continuing encouragement of Walter Gropius, the former director of the Bauhaus. Young and flexible enough to adapt to rapidly changing circumstances, he emerged by the end of the 1930s as a leader among those architects ready to reinvent modernism. Tempering its founders' interest in social change and moderating its original industrial aesthetic, he emphasized texture and shape in ways that demonstrated his respect for vernacular traditions and accorded with American taste.

The 1930s were difficult years for architects across Europe. The economic crisis nearly brought new construction to a halt in the early years of the decade. Breuer initially used this lull to travel to Paris and around the Mediterranean, activities financed by the patents he held as the inventor of the tubular steel chair.[1] Having built only one house in Germany, he left little behind as he began collaborating with better-established architects abroad. In Hungary his brief partnership with Farkas Molnár and József Fischer generated no built work. He fared better in Zurich, where he aided Alfred and Emil Roth in the design of the Dolderthal Apartments (1934; see fig. 239), for whom the client was the architectural historian Sigfried Giedion, a friend and fellow member of the Congrès internationaux d'architecture moderne (CIAM).[2] Breuer's move to Britain at the end of 1935 was facilitated by F. R. S. Yorke, a young architect with whom he practiced for the next two years.[3]

In London exiles from the Continent and their local supporters were transforming an architectural community that had throughout the 1920s remained beyond the reach of modernism.[4] Although his buildings on the European continent were rather conventional examples of what Henry-Russell Hitchcock and Philip Johnson referred to as the International Style—white stucco boxes floating on pilotis (stilts)—in Britain Breuer became an important spokesman for a less threatening version of modern architecture.[5] Rejecting, for instance, claims that the new architecture was inherently socialist, he declared: "In spite of the undeniable influence of politics in every sphere of life and thought no one can deny that each of these spheres has a highly important unpolitical side to it, and that this side determines its nature. As an architect I am content to confine myself to analyzing and solving the various questions of architecture and city-planning which arise from their several psycho-physical, co-ordinating, and technical-economic aspects."[6]

In another transition that would enhance his eventual appeal to Americans, Breuer moved away from the industrial aesthetic epitomized by his steel chairs. Encouraged once again by Gropius, who had been his teacher and

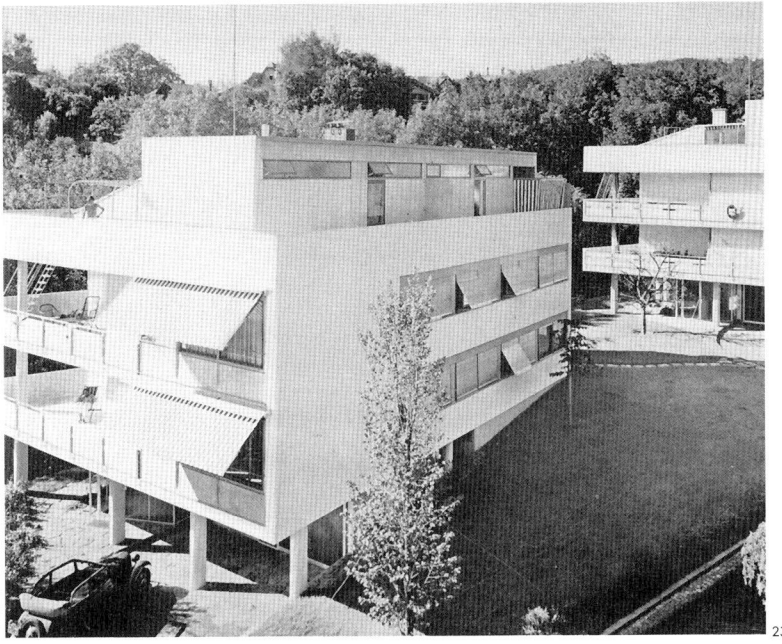

238
Marcel Breuer; photograph by Homer Page.

239
Marcel Breuer and Alfred and Emil Roth, Dolderthal Apartments, Zurich, Switzerland, 1934.

had entrusted him with the furniture workshop at the Bauhaus, Breuer experimented with designs for softly curved molded-plywood furniture during his stay in Britain. Like Gropius, Breuer lived at Lawn Roads Flats, an International Style apartment building erected at the instigation of Jack Pritchard. In 1935 Pritchard founded the Isokon Furniture Company to manufacture Breuer's designs. Fascinated by the peasant buildings he had seen during his travels, Breuer also began to use roughly textured materials such as fieldstone and plywood in his buildings and to site them directly on the ground.

Breuer's new direction paralleled, and was surely influenced by, the recent work of Alvar Aalto in Finland and Le Corbusier in France. For Breuer this approach was undoubtedly reinforced by the exercises in color and material he had undertaken as a student at the Bauhaus, even as it encompassed the rejection of the industrial aesthetic associated with the school's own architecture. In collaboration with Gropius he would introduce this openness to vernacular traditions and interest in exploring the texture of organic materials to an American context, where it would dovetail with prominent themes in the recently revived career of the country's most prominent modern architect, Frank Lloyd Wright. This less overtly revolutionary approach to modern architecture offered New Deal–era Americans interested in a modern middle-class regionalism a convincing alternative to the aristocratic pretensions of much of the historicism that dominated civic and domestic architecture in the United States during the 1920s.

In the summer of 1937 Breuer abandoned a promising career in Britain to travel for the first time to the United States. He came to explore new markets for his furniture but stayed when Gropius offered him an associate professorship at Harvard University. The two men also established an architecture office together. Although this arrangement lasted only until 1941, the prestige of his association with Gropius and with Harvard, where he taught for nine years, ensured Breuer's future success. Scholars disagree about how to apportion credit for the work of the partnership, but there is no doubt that each benefited from the other's expertise.[7] Breuer profited enormously from Gropius's renown as founder of the Bauhaus, particularly after the Bauhaus exhibition held at the Museum of Modern Art in 1938, which included Breuer's chairs.[8] Meanwhile, although he kept a discreet distance from the overt regionalism of West Coast architects like William Wurster and Pietro Belluschi and from Wright's highly individualistic oeuvre, Breuer's less rigid approach to modern architecture proved popular among Americans uncomfortable with the austerity of the Bauhaus.

Breuer was well aware of how fortunate he was. Little interested in politics, he nonetheless spent a great deal of time during his early years in the United States assisting friends and fellow architects in their efforts to escape Europe. He wrote countless letters in

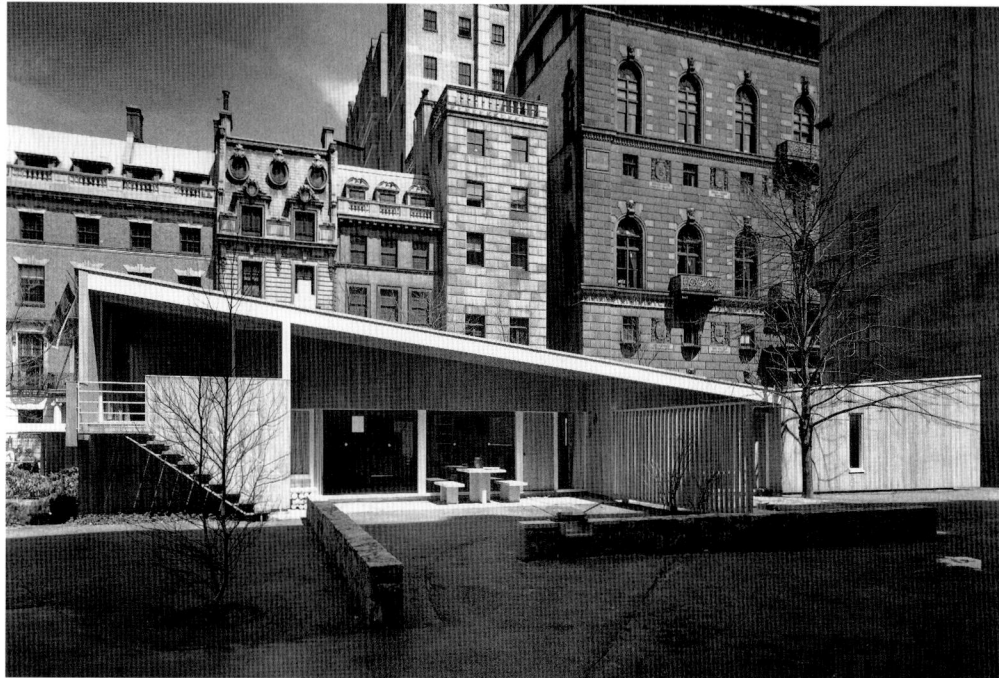

240
Marcel Breuer; exhibition house in the garden of the Museum of Modern Art, New York, 1949; photograph by Ezra Stoller © Esto. All rights reserved.

241
Marcel Breuer; Geller House, Lawrence, New York, 1945.

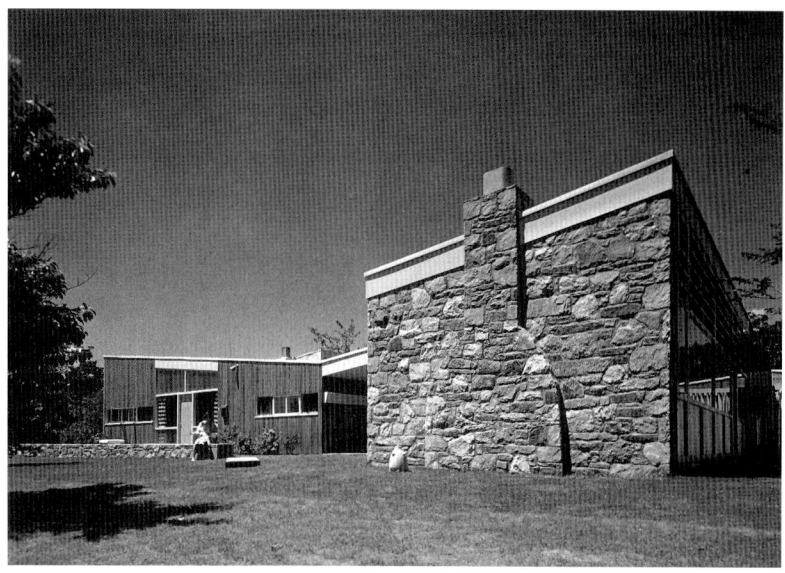

attempts to find jobs for everyone from José Luis Sert, an opponent of Franco who was also Spain's leading modern architect, to Hans Falkner, a Jewish ski instructor for whom Breuer had designed a hotel in the Tyrol, which, because of the German invasion of Austria, was never built.[9]

Breuer's decision to go into practice on his own paid off when his postwar houses in New England and the New York suburbs quickly attracted enormous attention. More than any of the other European architects who emigrated to the United States in the 1930s, he grasped the importance of the single-family home to his new compatriots and the increasing desire of even affluent Americans for a newly informal, up-to-date domesticity.

In his American houses he eschewed such European models as the repetitive blocks of workers' housing erected on the outskirts of many German cities during the 1920s and the austere houses of the Bauhaus faculty in Dessau. Instead he developed plans that offered conventional nuclear families both spacious, open living areas and entirely private bedrooms and that utilized affordably efficient but familiar materials and construction practices.

Breuer's first commission executed entirely independently of Gropius—the Geller House of 1945 in Lawrence, New York (see fig. 241)—demonstrated the reasons for this success. Juxtaposing vertically laid wooden siding with fieldstone walls (which he left exposed on the interior and also, through low parapets, stretched out to define the surrounding landscape), he presented a compelling image of suburban living. This house for a family with three young sons was also the first example of his characteristic binuclear plan. He emphasized this separation of the single-story house into two separate volumes—one for sleeping and the other for living activities—through the use of a butterfly roof, a motif he repeated in the detached garage and guest house. Enthusiastic critics stressed the house's suitability for young children, noting in particular such easily maintained surfaces as the playroom's stone floor.[10]

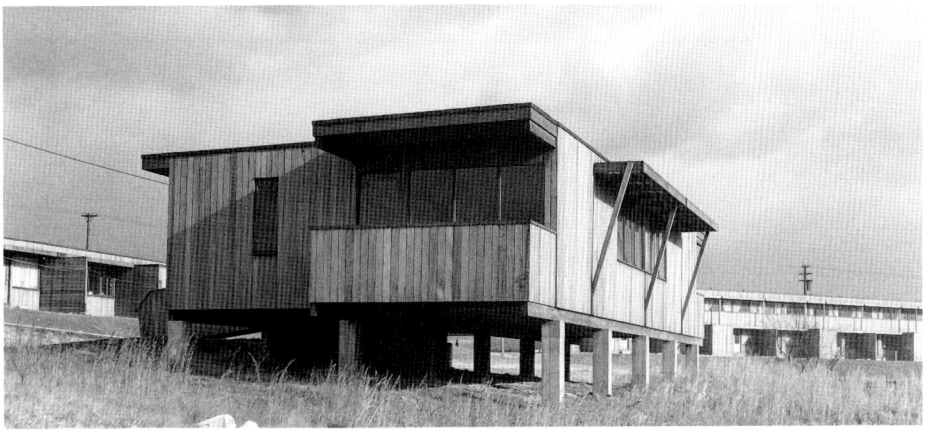

242
Walter Gropius and Marcel Breuer;
Aluminum City Terrace, New Kensington,
Pennsylvania, 1941; photograph by
Gottscho-Schleisner, Inc.

Although praised for its informality, the Geller House remained atypically luxurious. Few of the veterans who bought new, federally subsidized houses in the suburbs during the late 1940s and 1950s could afford the Geller House's maid's quarters, custom-designed furnishings, or enormous lot. In 1949, however, Breuer demonstrated the appeal to a less privileged audience of the ideas he had developed in the Geller House, when tens of thousands of people toured the exhibition house he temporarily erected in the garden of New York's Museum of Modern Art (see fig. 240). In this more modest dwelling, which the museum estimated could be built at a cost of $27,475, exclusive of land (or as little as $20,000 for a smaller version), the kitchen rather than the entrance hall linked what were now separate spaces for adults and children. Using the full height of the butterfly roof to place the parents' bedroom atop the living room, he located the children's sleeping and play areas in its counterpart, an arrangement that he extended out into the garden, where he gave each generation its own terrace.[11]

During the 1950s Breuer's practice expanded rapidly. In his first institutional commission, Ferry House, a dormitory at Vassar College in Poughkeepsie, New York (1949–51), he demonstrated that his modern approach to domestic architecture could accommodate even slightly unconventional programs. The building was the result of a gift by Dexter Ferry, whose daughter Edith Ferry Hooper was an alumna of the college and had become acquainted with Breuer's architecture while working at the Museum of Modern Art (Breuer would later design a house in Baltimore for her and her husband). Built to house twenty-eight students responsible for their own cooking and housekeeping, the T-shaped building consisted of a dormitory block raised on pilotis and, perpendicular to it, a single-story wing containing the lounge, dining room, and kitchen. Corrugated asbestos sunshades suspended from cables gave depth and shading to the principal dormitory façade. This high-tech accent was a lively antidote to the otherwise ordinary materials—cypress paneling and brick—that clad the building's steel frame as well as an indication of Breuer's sensitivity to the interlocking issues of site and climate.[12] Although both the architecture and the program of Ferry house were unquestionably progressive, its overall horizontality and the comfortable, if crisp, interiors tempered the challenge that the modern movement had initially posed to cozy domesticity.

Within a few years of the completion of Ferry House, much larger and more prestigious commissions—such as the UNESCO headquarters in Paris (1953–58; designed in association with Pier Luigi Nervi and Bernard Zehrfuss), Saint John's Abbey and University in Collegeville, Minnesota (1953–68), and the Whitney Museum of American Art in New York (1963–66)—demanded the bulk of Breuer's attention as he emerged from the rigors of exile to become one of the most esteemed architects of the 1950s and 1960s. In this context much of the attention to texture and scale that had distinguished his earliest work in the United States was replaced by an emphatically sculptural approach in keeping with the monumentalism that became increasingly characteristic of civic and religious architecture in the postwar years.

Notes

1. Breuer designed the Wassily chair in 1925, when still a student at the Bauhaus. From 1926 to 1928 he headed the school's furniture workshop. The Marcel Breuer papers at the George Arents Research Library for Special Collections, Syracuse University, Syracuse, New York, are full of correspondence from the 1930s regarding Breuer's furniture patents and the income he derived from them. See also Christopher Wilk, *Marcel Breuer: Furniture and Interiors* (New York: Museum of Modern Art, 1981).

2. Joachim Driller, "Marcel Breuer: Das architektonische Frühwerk bis 1950" (Ph.D. diss., Universität Freiburg, 1990), 25, 102–14, 191, 309–34.

3. Wilk, *Marcel Breuer*, 126–27.

4. For an account of British architecture during these years, see John Allan, *Berthold Lubetkin: Architecture and the Tradition of Progress* (London: RIBA Publications, 1992). The Russian-born Lubetkin had trained in Germany and France. Other prominent emigrants included Serge Chermayeff, Walter Gropius, and Erich Mendelsohn.

5. Henry-Russell Hitchcock and Philip Johnson, *The International Style: Architecture since 1922* (New York: W. W. Norton, 1932). The context of this shift is elaborated in William Jordy, "The Aftermath of the Bauhaus in America: Gropius, Mies, and Breuer," in *The Intellectual Migration: Europe and America, 1930–1960*, ed. Donald Fleming and Bernard Bailyn (Cambridge: Harvard University Press, 1969), 497–500.

6. Marcel Breuer, "Where Do We Stand?" *Architectural Review* 77 (1935): 135.

7. Winfried Nerdinger is particularly generous in crediting Breuer (*Walter Gropius* [Berlin: Gebr. Mann Verlag, 1985], 9–28), while Driller gives a more generous appraisal of Gropius's activity throughout "Marcel Breuer."

8. Herbert Bayer, Walter Gropius, and Ise Gropius, eds., *Bauhaus, 1919–1928*, exh. cat. (New York: Museum of Modern Art, 1938).

9. Copies of these letters and many more like them can be found among Breuer's papers at Syracuse.

10. The most prominent articles devoted to the house were "Tomorrow's House Today," pts. 1, 2, *House and Garden*, January, February 1947, 60–67, 56–59, 118–19, and "The Geller House, Lawrence, Long Island," *Progressive Architecture* 28 (February 1947): 50–66.

11. "House for the Growing Family," *Architectural Forum* 90 (May 1949): 96–101. The exhibition coincided with the publication of Peter Blake, *Marcel Breuer: Architect and Designer* (New York: Museum of Modern Art, 1949).

12. For the most comprehensive account of this building and of Breuer's role in the transplantation of European modernism to the United States, see William Jordy, *American Buildings and Their Architects: The Impact of European Modernism in the Mid-Twentieth Century* (Garden City, N.Y.: Anchor Press, 1973), 165–220.

243
László Moholy-Nagy, *Space Modulator*, 1939–45 (cat. no. 118).

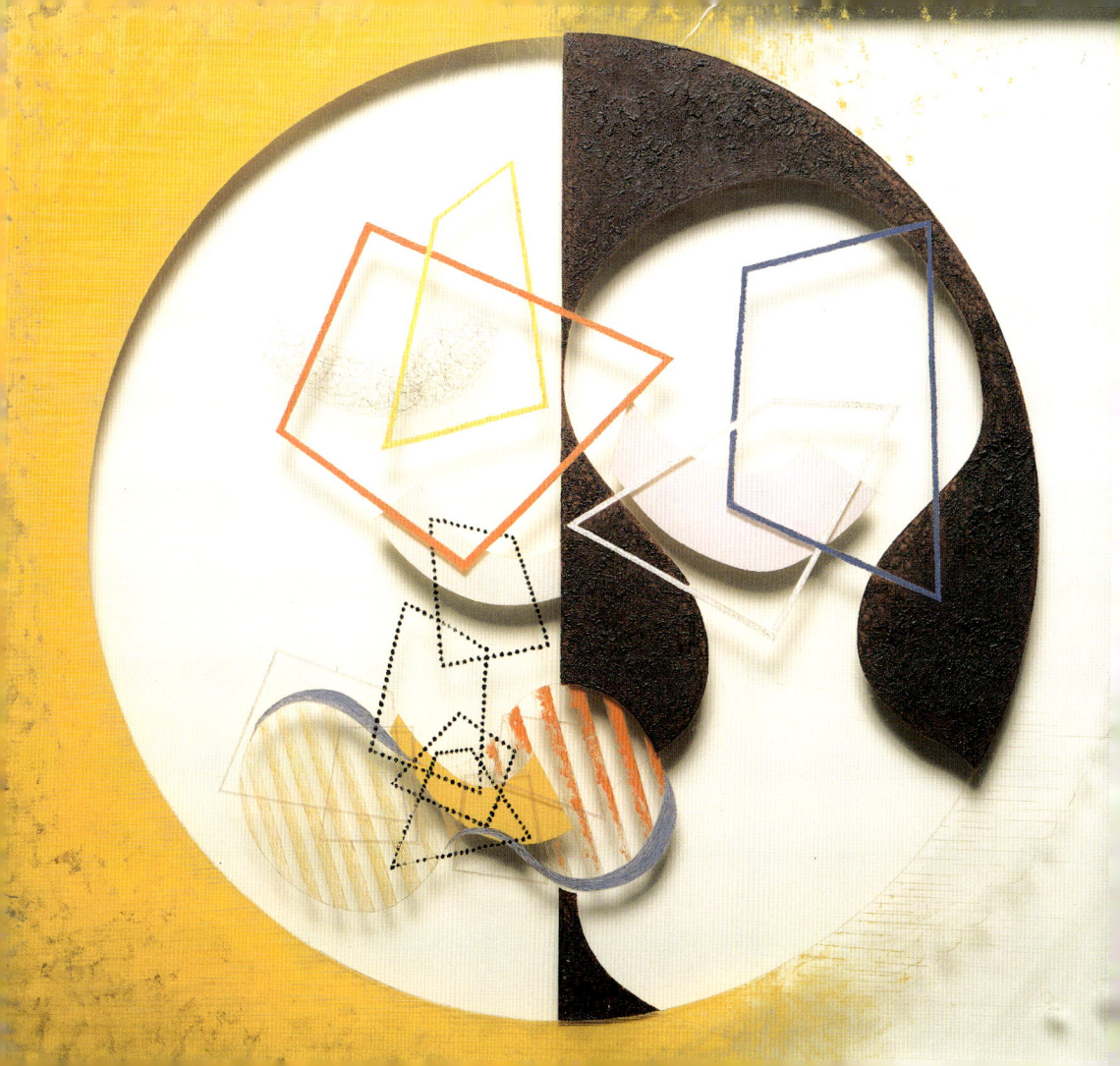

josef albers
at black mountain college,
1933–45

1888   born in Bottrop, Germany
1933   immigrates to the U.S. (North Carolina)
1976   dies in New Haven, Conn.

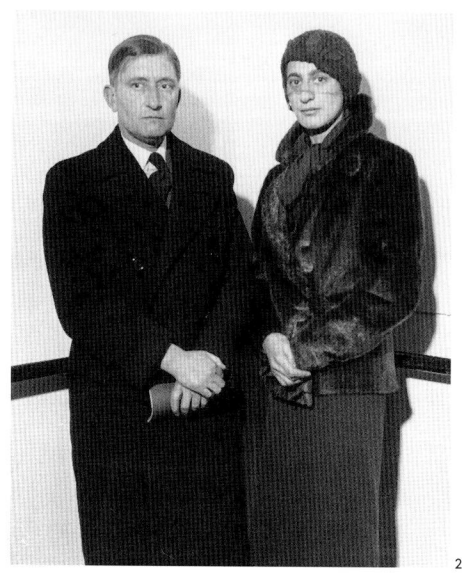

244

Josef Albers, who never referred to himself as an exile, was the first Bauhaus faculty member to immigrate to the United States.[1] In November of 1933 he and his wife, Anni Albers, an important textile artist also affiliated with the Bauhaus, arrived in New York on the SS *Europa*. They were en route to Black Mountain College in North Carolina, where Philip Johnson, curator of architecture at the Museum of Modern Art in New York, had secured teaching positions for them.

Despite their impassive appearance in a much-publicized immigration photograph (fig. 244), the Alberses' lives in Germany had been thrown off course following Hitler's appointment as chancellor in January of 1933 and his subsequent assumption of dictatorial power. In June of that year Josef Albers had received a threatening letter from the city council of Dessau, which terminated his contract and inaccurately accused him of engaging in "political activity" as a teacher at the Bauhaus, which the Nazis considered a "germ-cell of bolshevism."[2] The following month, Albers and the remaining Bauhaus faculty reluctantly voted to close the school under Nazi pressure. Albers's loss of employment after ten years on the Bauhaus faculty and the fact that Anni Fleischmann Albers, although a converted Protestant, was "in the Hitler sense, Jewish,"[3] clearly put his immediate interests at odds with those of the Nazis.

Yet, as noted in numerous American newspaper articles that announced the couple's arrival (under headlines such as "Noted German Leader Arrives in U.S."[4]), Albers maintained a staunchly apolitical stance and asserted his complete devotion to the production of abstract art free of political content or associations. His continued adherence to this stance as an emigré was reflected in his decision in 1934 to show his works at the Galleria del Milione in Milan, even though it was openly supported by the Italian Fascist government.[5] Also indicative was Albers's refusal to exhibit with the antifascist Freier Künstlerbund (Free league of artists), a group of exiled German and Austrian artists, in Paris in 1938, and his advice to the exhibition's organizers to focus on art and to refrain from "the publicizing of negative tendencies in Germany."[6] Ironically the "apolitical" Albers benefited from his transplantation to the United States, brought about expressly by political changes in Germany; he achieved greater professional success in his new home than he had ever attained at the Bauhaus. In the United States he found an environment in which he could produce art in accordance with his purist sensibilities, and he received recognition for this approach in numerous exhibitions—more than twenty solo shows between 1933 and 1945[7]—and prestigious teaching appointments.[8]

During his first decade and a half in the United States Albers experienced America primarily through the filter of Black Mountain College, founded by educational iconoclast John Andrew Rice just months before the Alberses' arrival. Sequestered in the hills of North Carolina, which the couple thought might be in the Philippines when they first received word of job opportunities there,[9] Black Mountain was a small, experimental

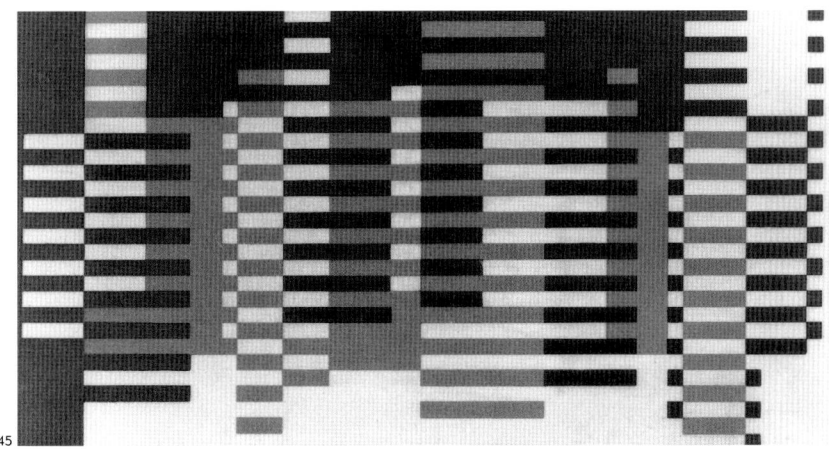

244
Josef and Anni Albers aboard the S.S. *Europa* upon their arrival in New York, November 25, 1933.

245
Josef Albers; *City*, 1928; sandblasted opaque flashed glass with black paint; 11 x 21⅝ in. (28 x 55 cm); Kunsthaus Zürich.

school built on alternative principles of self-government and communal living. Its instructors, many of them refugees, were committed to combating excessive specialization within education and "the spectator attitude of the day."[10] Consequently, they took a holistic approach to education, encouraging active learning as opposed to the rote memorization of facts. Art instruction was aimed less at training artists than at developing creative abilities within all individuals and was thus central to the school's curriculum. Above all else, Black Mountain fostered its own independence and self-sufficiency as a community. With no president, dean, or external governing body, the students and teachers together made administrative decisions and participated in every aspect of running the college, from repairing roads—a task overseen by Albers— to working on the school's farm, which by 1944 produced most of the food consumed there.[11]

Black Mountain College offered Albers greater security, authority, and autonomy than he had experienced at the Bauhaus. Although he spoke no English when he arrived, he was granted tenure in March of 1934 and even served as rector of the college for one year, in 1948. At the Bauhaus, where he headed the glass and furniture workshops and taught the preliminary course, Albers had always operated under the administrative supervision of the school's director, while at Black Mountain he was made the sole head of the art department. Along with the freedom to teach exactly what he wanted, Albers had fewer students and teaching responsibilities than he had had at the Bauhaus. As he later recollected: "Teaching had always been stealing from my painting before. These were fairly free years. I painted and painted. It was in some ways a very monkish life."[12]

Albers's art changed considerably during his initial years at Black Mountain. Whereas fellow emigré Piet Mondrian experienced America as a dynamic, urban metropolis, as reflected in his paintings, for Albers it was a simple, bucolic place where he became more sensitized to nature. In the United States Albers abandoned the production of hard-edged, rigidly structured glass paintings (see fig. 245), which had entailed a highly technical process of sandblasting at a professional foundry; instead he took up oil painting and began a series of sketchy, abstract studies called Free Forms. While this change can be attributed in part to the absence of glass foundries in the Black Mountain vicinity, it signaled a more profound shift in Albers's work in the mid-1930s, from a focus on technology to one on nature and from a reliance on mechanical processes to a direct, physical engagement with materials.[13] In paintings from the Free Forms series, such as *Evening (an Improvisation)* (1935; fig. 246), he applied

246

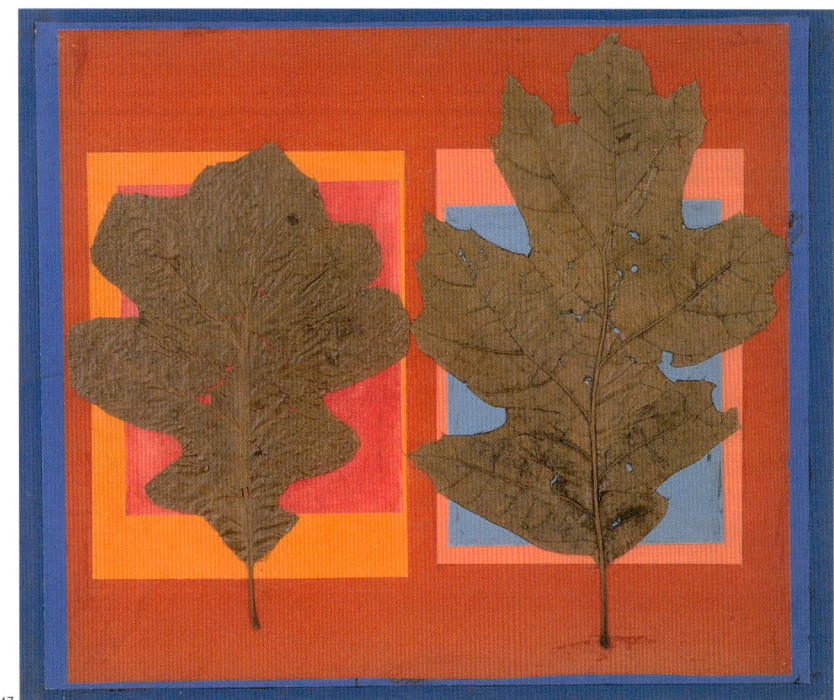

247

unmixed paint directly from the tube to create immediate, abstract impressions of the light and landscape. With their textured surfaces and appearance of spontaneity, these works proved antithetical in form and sensibility to his pristine, geometric constructions of the Bauhaus years.

As reflected in the titles of his paintings from this period—for example, *In Open Air* (1936), *Growing* (1940), and *Tierra Verde* (1940)—Albers's writings and teaching practices were infused with an unprecedented interest in nature and its processes. In his 1936 essay "Art as Experience" he called for artists to abandon scientific study and "[go] out of doors to get the events of life, the vital functions."[14]

Later he characterized teaching in organic terms, as a job aimed at "making ourselves and others grow."[15] This newfound approach, at odds with his own constructivist education at the Bauhaus, was also reflected in his suggestion that his Black Mountain students "try to see a chair apart from its functional characteristics, as a living creature."[16] He reportedly even took students into the surrounding woods to collect sticks, which they chewed and later used as brushes.[17] Numerous class projects, such as the leaf collages that he himself also produced (see fig. 247, cat. no. 6), required the incorporation of found natural materials. In Albers's first years at Black Mountain, then, producing art became entwined with accessing and emulating nature in its purest state.

Although Albers's self-proclaimed goal at Black Mountain was "to open eyes" and thus to cultivate a heightened sense of awareness among his students, his approach was aimed specifically at developing visual and tactile awareness and precluded other methodological approaches that might incorporate politics or history. In focusing, for example, on questions of opticality—the apparent likeness of disparate forms, as illustrated in *"Related" A* (1937; fig. 248, cat. no. 2), or the perceptual effects of placing particular colors next to each other—Albers drew attention to "timeless" formal relationships, which existed in an absolute present. In keeping with his belief that "we over accentuate the past,"[18] he rejected art history as mired in European, academic tradition and instead exhorted: "Let us be younger with our students. We ought to discuss movies and fashions, make-up and stationery. The pupil and his growing into his world are more important

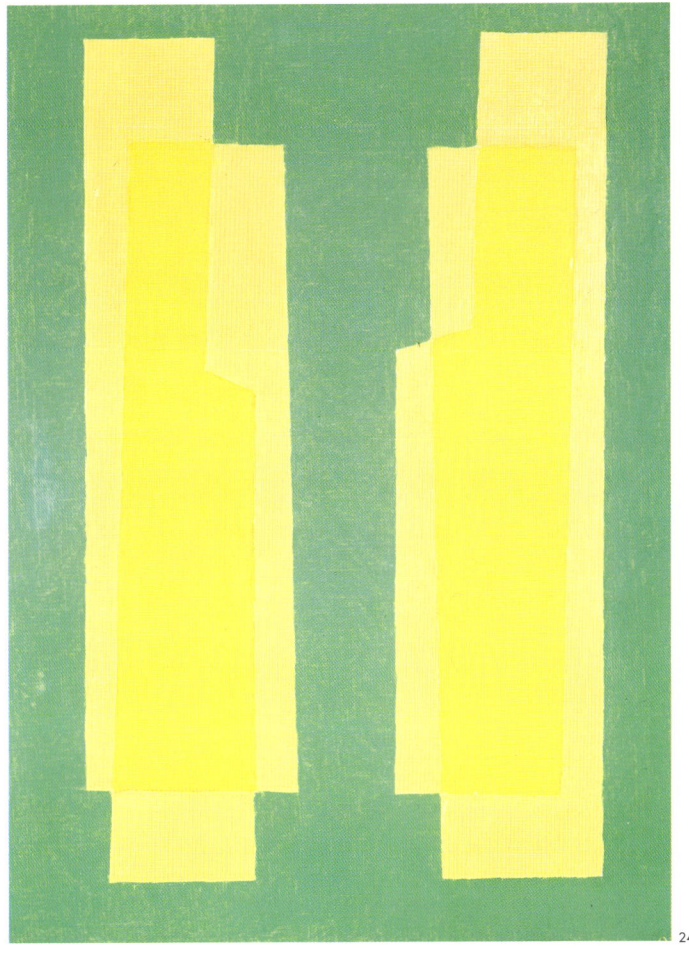

than the teacher and his background."[19] As this statement suggests, Albers brought a comparable rejection of the past to bear on his own history in claiming to shed his European, Bauhaus experience and "in this new part of the world … to start a new life on my own."[20] Although he made a similar break in 1920, when he left behind his provincial upbringing and academic training to enroll at the Bauhaus,[21] his dissociation from his cultural roots after emigration and his subsequent claim to have descended directly "from Adam"[22] had a particular significance in light of negative American perceptions of Germany at the time.

246
Josef Albers; *Evening (an Improvisation)*, 1935; oil on Masonite; 11 x 12⅜ in. (28 x 31.5 cm); The Josef and Anni Albers Foundation.

247
Josef Albers, *Leaf Study IV*, c. 1940 (cat. no. 6).

248
Josef Albers, *"Related" A*, 1937 (cat. no. 2).

249
Josef Albers, *Cadence*, 1940 (cat. no. 4).

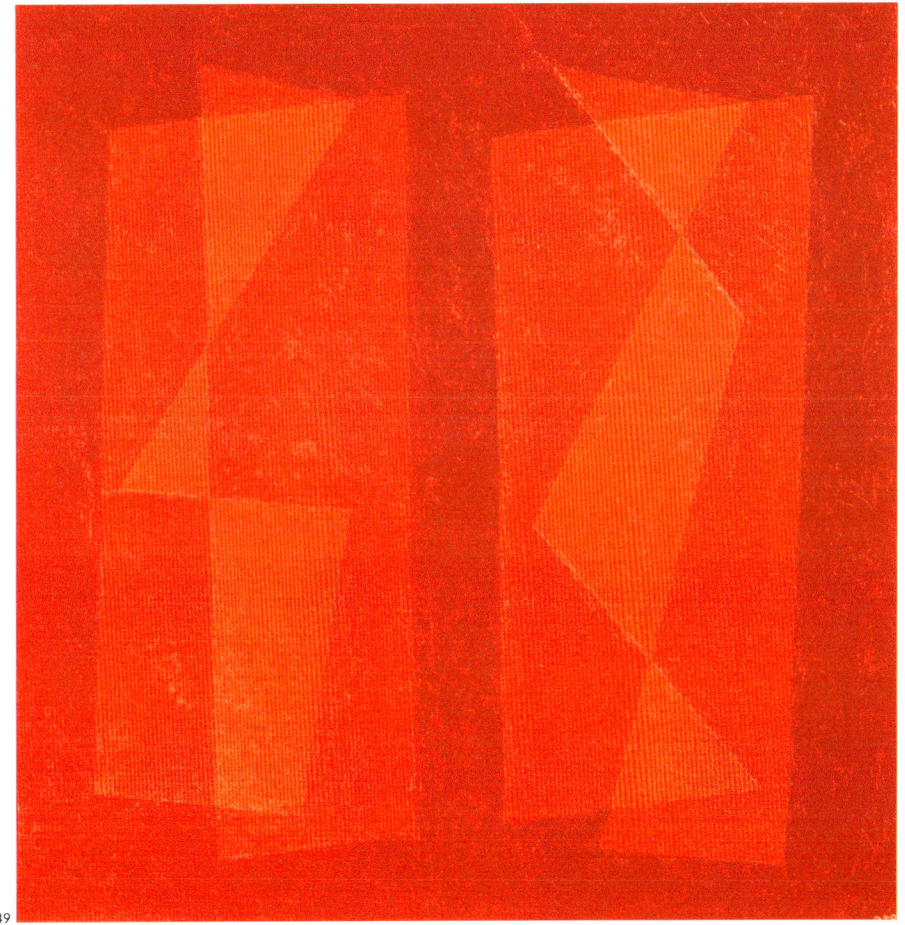

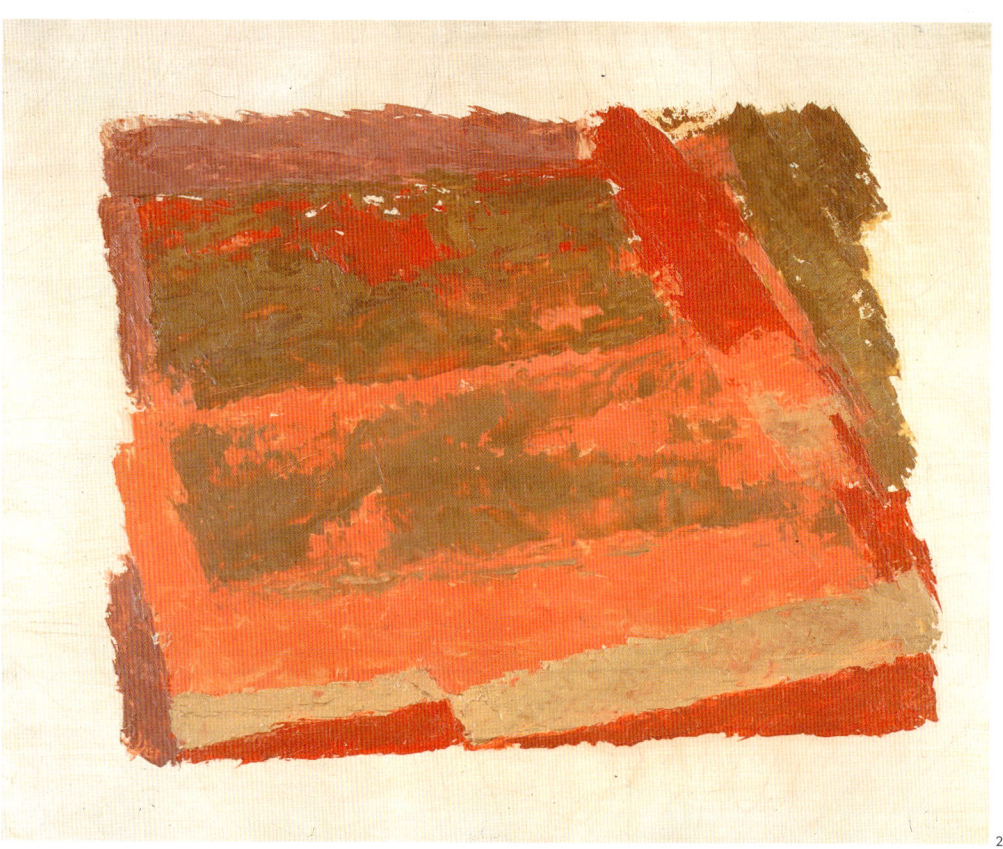

250

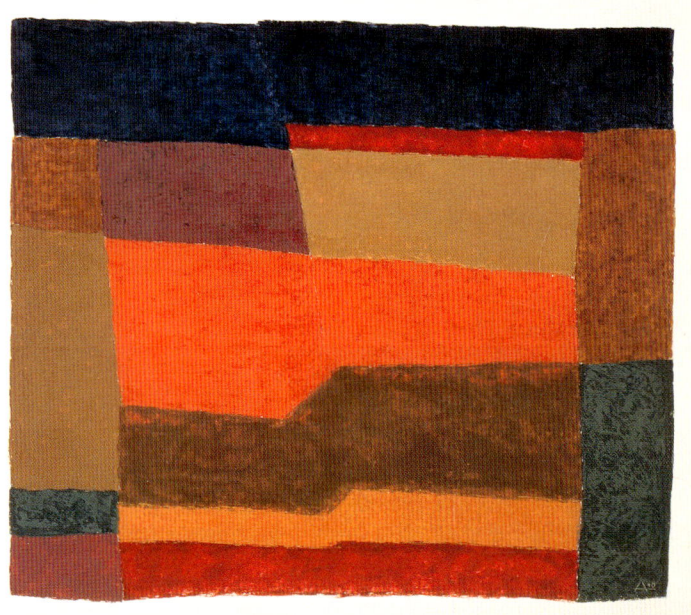

251

A manifestation of Albers's desire to separate himself from his own cultural heritage was his attachment to Mexico and his fascination with pre-Columbian art. After their first trip to Mexico in 1935 the Alberses returned there thirteen times, including an extended stay during a sabbatical from Black Mountain in 1940. Many of Albers's works from the period convey his immediate, perceptual responses to the places they visited. *Etude: Hot-Dry* (1935; fig. 250, cat. no. 1), for example, evokes the dusty, arid quality of the Mexican landscape. His photographs of the pyramids at Tenayuca reveal an appreciation for the abstract simplicity of the indigenous architecture, and numerous paintings and prints contain geometric designs inspired by ancient stonework. Yet a more profound level of signification is suggested in *Layered* (1940; fig. 251, cat. no. 5). With its patchwork of ruddy hues beneath a strip of indigo sky, this painting offers an abstract cross-section of the Mexican landscape, imagined as layered with the histories of ancient peoples. Anni Albers later echoed this conception of Mexico, asserting that it contained "layer upon layer of former civilization . . . waiting for excavation."[23] For the Alberses the culture of ancient Mexico remained inextricably bound to the landscape and as such held the key to a simpler way of life, which they nostalgically embraced as an antidote to their modernist heritage. The Alberses' extensive collection of pre-Columbian objects—more that one thousand in all—attests to their

250
Josef Albers, *Etude: Hot-Dry*, 1935 (cat. no. 1).

251
Josef Albers, *Layered*, 1940 (cat. no. 5).

252
Josef Albers, sketch on Hotel Villa Montaña stationery, n.d.; ballpoint ink on paper; 5³⁄₈ x 4¹⁄₈ in. (13.7 x 10.5 cm); The Josef and Anni Albers Foundation.

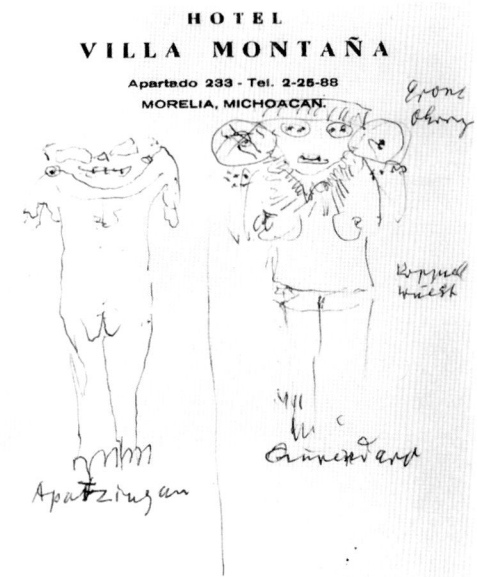

252

desire to internalize what they viewed as timeless[24] lessons of the "primitive" peoples of Mexico.

Cultural theorist Marianna Turgovnick has written, "The condition of exile or cultural estrangement and the consequent desire to 'go home' turn up as grounding conditions for interest in the primitive."[25] This assertion seems particularly apt in the case of Josef Albers, whose strong affinity for pre-Columbian art developed simultaneously with his dissociation from Europe as a cultural emigré and his effort to construct a new identity in America. His sketch of two Chupìcuaro figurines from the Alberses' collection (fig. 252) illuminates the psychological function of the category "primitive" for him. In this drawing Albers emphasized the primal quality of the figurines as opposed to their stylized form. The male-female pair can be viewed as the uncivilized, aboriginal alter egos of the reserved and highly proper couple in the photo of the Alberses on their arrival from Europe. Ultimately Albers's conceptualization of Mexican culture and of the United States itself as closer to nature were informed by the same primitivist impulse: to conceive of an unfamiliar culture as a new point of origin for oneself, in opposition to the culture one has left behind.

Yet the Alberses, like most participants in the discourse of primitivism, never fully immersed themselves in either Mexican or North American culture during these years and retained, if unconsciously, a sense of European superiority and distance. For example, Anni Albers's assertion that, although the Mexicans they encountered may have "smelled a bit like cattle, to me it was a wonderful, wonderful smell,"[26] reveals an underlying attitude of condescension, specifically toward contemporary people, who were not as easily abstracted and idealized as were ancient civilizations and their artifacts. Josef Albers revealed an equally patronizing attitude toward Americans in his statement to fellow emigré Walter Gropius that "the people here are very hungry for a culture" and that Europeans should "show them what they have not yet achieved and convince them that such achievement has its value."[27] The Eurocentric, elitist assumptions inherent in this statement ran counter to Albers's own, Bauhaus-informed critique of "high" culture and his valorization of non-European art forms.

Albers's continuing respect for hierarchy and order, a product of both his European background and his inherently authoritarian personality, prevented his adoption of a more carefree sensibility in the unstructured, natural environment of Black Mountain College. As a teacher he continued to stress discipline

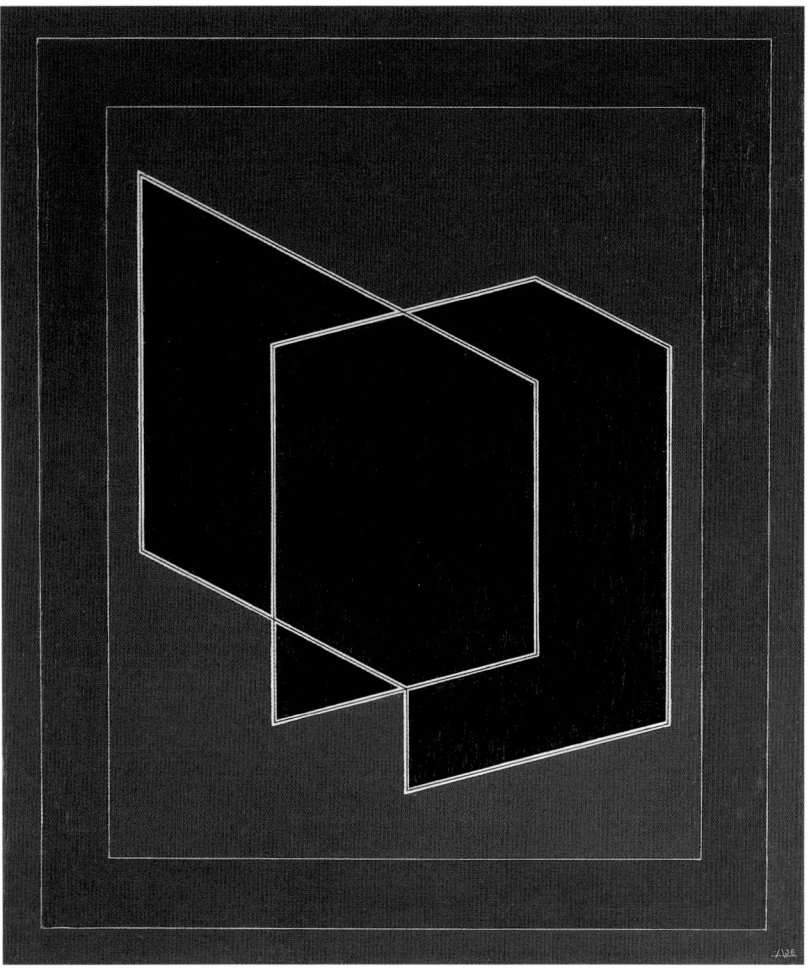

253
Josef Albers, *Penetrating (A)*, 1938 (cat. no. 3).

and restraint and did not, for example, permit students to begin painting until they had systematically completed more than half a year of theoretical exercises with colored paper.[28] Ultimately it was his frustration with the participatory, democratic process adhered to at Black Mountain—"There are things that you don't discuss with babies," he complained. "That's the same parallel to education"[29]— that led to his resignation from the college in 1949. Two years later he accepted a position at a far more traditional, hierarchical institution, Yale University, where he served as chairman of the Department of Design during the subsequent decade.

Principles of order and control also assumed an increasingly central role in Albers's art production in America. By the late 1930s the inchoate quality of his Free Forms series gave way to an elimination of painterly surfaces and a tighter, more linear structure, as reflected in *Penetrating (A)* (1938; fig. 253, cat. no. 3). With paintings such as *Bent Black (A)* of 1940

Albers began to meticulously calculate the surface area of his paintings to ensure that he used precisely equal amounts of different colors. The same controlling impulse that inspired this practice, also evident in his remark at the age of seventy-seven that he wanted his colors "to *behave*; to do what *I* want, not what they want,"[30] eventually informed his notoriously fixed and uniform series Homage to the Square, which he worked on from 1950 until his death in 1976.

The two principal forces governing Albers's work in America from 1933 to 1945— his newfound interest in nature and the primitive, on the one hand, and his enduring respect for order and control, on the other—initially appear antithetical. Yet both are indicative of his retreat from the chaos and complexity of contemporary life in favor of a pursuit of pure, timeless fundamentals. His works from this period attest to this purist stance. That Albers was able to effectuate such a retreat and retain a purist approach to art, even during the war years, was due largely to the seclusion and independence of the Black Mountain College environment.

Notes

1 Albers became a U.S. citizen in 1939.

2 Dessau city council to Albers, Berlin, 15 June 1933; translated in Hans M. Wingler, *The Bauhaus*, ed. Joseph Stein, trans. Wolfgang Jabs and Basil Gilbert (Cambridge and London: MIT Press, 1969), 188. The city council of Dessau was still obligated to pay Bauhaus salaries after the school moved from Dessau to Berlin in 1932.

3 Quoted in Nicholas Fox Weber, *The Woven and Graphic Arts of Anni Albers* (Washington, D.C.: Smithsonian Institution Press, 1985), 20.

4 *Omaha World-Herald*, 2 December 1933. See also, for example, "Famous German Art Instructor in City," *Charlotte Observer*, 23 January 1934, sec. 2; "German Professor to Go to Black Mt. College," *New York Herald Tribune*, 10 December 1933; and "Germans on Faculty at Black Mountain School," *Asheville (N.C.) Citizen*, 5 December 1933.

5 *Silographie recenti di Josef Albers e di Luigi Veronesi*, Galleria del Milione, Milan, 23 December 1934–10 January 1935. Kandinsky, Klee, Léger, and Picasso also exhibited at the Galleria del Milione.

6 Albers to Frau Dr. Herta Wescher, 1 July 1938 (Bundesarchiv Potsdam, Nachlaß Eugen Spiro, Akte 3, Bl. 64). In the same letter Albers nevertheless wishes the Freier Künstlerbund success with the exhibition, and he attributes his decision not to exhibit with the group to concern for the safety of relatives still in Germany.

7 Albers had solo shows in New York at J. B. Neumann's New Art Circle (1936, 1938, 1945) and the Nierendorf Gallery (1941), both of which featured works by emigré artists, and in such other cities as Cambridge, Mass. (1936), Chicago (1937), Baltimore (1942–43), San Francisco (1940), and Los Angeles (1941). He also exhibited with American Abstract Artists, beginning with the group's first exhibition, in 1937. For a selected history of exhibitions and reviews, see *Josef Albers: A Retrospective*, exh. cat. (New York: Solomon R. Guggenheim Foundation, 1988), 297–301.

8 Albers periodically offered lectures and seminars as a guest professor at the Graduate School of Design at Harvard University, headed by former Bauhaus director Walter Gropius, from 1936 to 1940, and taught basic design and color there while on sabbatical from Black Mountain College in 1941.

9 Nicholas Fox Weber, "The Artist as Alchemist," in *Josef Albers: A Retrospective*, 31.

10 "Cooperative Work at Black Mountain," *New York Times*, 1 September 1935, sec. 10.

11 For a comprehensive study of Black Mountain College, see Mary Emma Harris, *The Arts at Black Mountain College* (Cambridge and London: MIT Press, 1987), and Martin Duberman, *Black Mountain: An Exploration in Community* (New York: E. P. Dutton, 1972). For a contemporary account, see Louis Adamic, "Education on a Mountain: The Story of Black Mountain College," *Harper's*, April 1936, 516–30.

12 Quoted in Neil Welliver, "Albers on Albers," *Art News* 64 (January 1966): 51.

13 See Josef Albers, "The Educational Value of Manual Work and Handicraft in Relation to Architecture," in *New Architecture and City Planning*, ed. Paul Zucker (New York: Philosophical Library, 1944), 688–94.

14 Josef Albers, "Art as Experience," *Progressive Education* 12 (October 1935): 391.

15 Unpublished lecture given at the Black Mountain College Meeting at the Museum of Modern Art, New York, 9 January 1940 (Josef Albers Papers, Yale University Library, New Haven); reprinted in Harris, *The Arts at Black Mountain College*, 53.

16 Albers, "Art as Experience," 391–92.

17 See Harris, *The Arts at Black Mountain College*, 17.

18 Albers, "Art as Experience," 391.

19 Ibid., 392.

20 Quoted in "Josef Albers: March 1965 Interview," in Melvin Lane, ed., *Black Mountain College: Sprouted Seeds: An Anthology of Personal Accounts* (Knoxville: University of Tennessee Press, 1990), 37.

21 Anni Albers made a comparable break from her past, in her case from an affluent background, in joining the Bauhaus in 1922.

22 Quoted in Weber, "The Artist as Alchemist," 15.

23 Anni Albers, *Pre-Columbian Mexican Miniatures: The Josef and Anni Albers Collection* (New York: Praeger Publishers, 1970), unpaginated.

24 As Anni Albers later recalled, "Perhaps it was this timeless quality in pre-Columbian art that first spoke to us, regardless of our ignorance of the special significance it must have had to a contemporary community" (ibid.).

25 Marianna Turgovnick, *Gone Primitive: Savage Intellects, Modern Lives* (Chicago and London: University of Chicago Press, 1990), 187.

26 Quoted in Nicholas Fox Weber, preface to Karl Taube, *The Albers Collection of Pre-Columbian Art* (New York: Hudson Hills Press, 1988), 11.

27 Albers to Gropius, 11 October 1937, Walter Gropius Papers, Harvard University; cited in Harris, *The Arts at Black Mountain College*, 53.

28 See "Concerning Art Instruction," *Black Mountain College Bulletin*, no. 2 (June 1934); revised edition with an illustrated cover, November 1944.

29 Albers interview in Lane, ed., *Black Mountain College*, 40.

30 Cited in *Josef Albers: The American Years*, exh. cat. (Washington, D.C.: Washington Gallery of Modern Art, 1965), 23.

lászló moholy-nagy in chicago, 1937–45

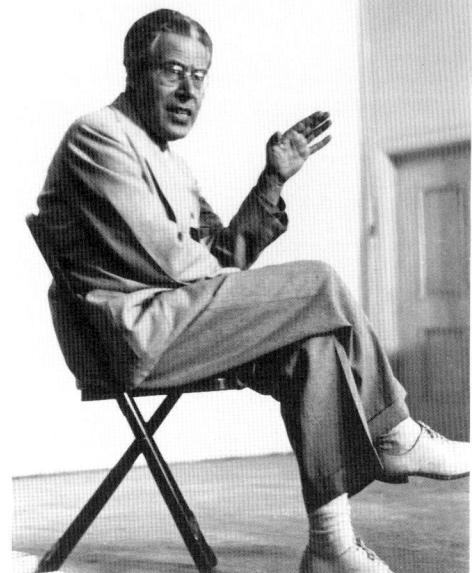

1895	born in Bacsbarsód, Hungary
1934	emigrates from Germany (Berlin) to the Netherlands (Amsterdam)
1935	immigrates to England (London)
1937	immigrates to the U.S. (Chicago)
1946	dies in Chicago

Yes, . . . I want to remain in America. There's something incomplete about this city [Chicago] and its people that fascinates me. Everything seems still possible. The paralyzing finality of European disaster is far away. I love the air of newness, of expectation around me.[1]

László Moholy-Nagy's initial impression of America as a place of limitless potential for innovation, expressed in letters to his wife, Sibyl, clinched his decision to leave Europe permanently in 1937. In immigrating to the United States at the age of forty-two, the Hungarian-born Moholy was entering his third and final phase of self-imposed exile in search of creative freedom and stimulus. He had first fled an oppressive cultural climate in Hungary following the Revolution of 1918 and had settled in Germany; after establishing himself as an important avant-garde artist and a central figure at the Bauhaus in the 1920s, he was compelled in 1935 by the rise of National Socialism to relocate to London, where he worked primarily on design commissions and tried unsuccessfully to garner support for a new Bauhaus.[2] When the Association of Arts and Industries (AAI) in Chicago invited him, at the recommendation of Walter Gropius,[3] to establish a school of design based on Bauhaus principles, he enthusiastically accepted. Chicago seemed to offer an unfettered and lively environment in which "to produce something positive again."[4]

Moholy did realize some of his most significant professional aspirations in Chicago, namely, the founding of his own teaching institution and the writing of his definitive text, *Vision in Motion*.[5] Nevertheless, the nine years that he spent in the Midwest before his death from leukemia in 1946, at the age of 51, proved frustrating in many respects, leading him to decry Chicago in 1945 as a place where "creative people don't seem to thrive," because "there is no stamina, . . . no convictions."[6]

At first Moholy and his anticipated New Bauhaus received a good deal of positive press. Local and national newspapers heralded him as a "brilliant Hungarian" and "capable genius, . . . who has already proved himself in the eyes of the men who know," welcoming his "broad and bold" program as "an outstanding asset to Chicago."[7] Speaking before a crowd of eight hundred in September 1937, he expressed in broken English his convictions that "everyone is talented" and that creative pursuits are integral to the balanced life of all individuals,[8] convictions that undoubtedly appealed to American democratic sensibilities.

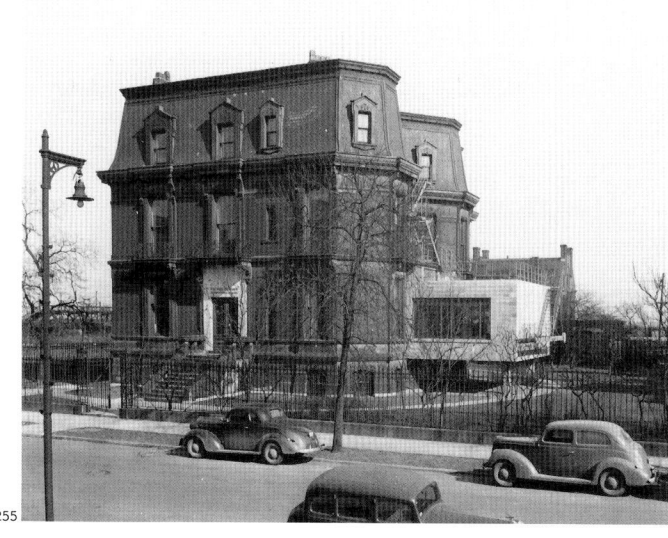

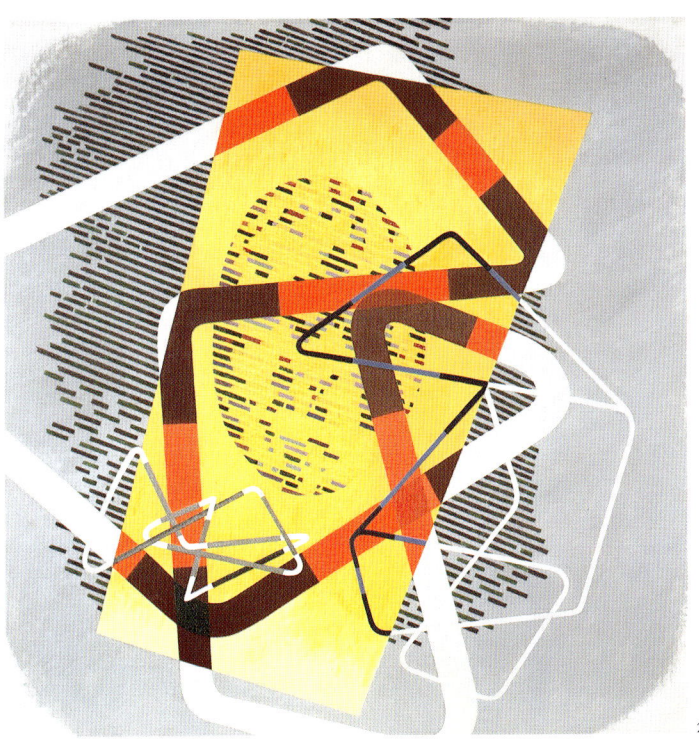

256

254
László Moholy-Nagy, c. 1945; photograph by Arthur Siegel.

255
New Bauhaus, c. 1938; photograph by Henry Holmes Smith.

256
László Moholy-Nagy, *Space Modulator*, 1938–40 (cat. no. 117).

Despite the initial fanfare, however, the New Bauhaus, which opened in October 1937 with a class of thirty-five students, almost immediately engendered rancor. By the summer of 1938 the AAI's board of directors, composed of leading Chicago businessmen and industrialists, had decided to close the school. Although the board publicly claimed financial insolvency, a court dispute disclosed allegations that Moholy "lacked 'poise, balance, diplomacy, patience, and teaching experience', 'alienated people, firms, and corporations', and 'undermined' the school's effectiveness."[9] These claims suggest that, in addition to questions regarding his character and abilities, there were profound ideological objections to Moholy's utopian ideals, which were informed by his avant-garde, collectivist affiliations in Hungary and Germany. The ideological differences between the local community and Moholy were manifested in the jarring contrast between the lavish mansion donated by the Marshall Field family to house the AAI's new school and the austere, boxlike structure that Moholy added on to it (see fig. 255). Clearly his call for "clarity, brevity, and precision"[10] in design clashed with bourgeois conventions and tastes. More fundamentally, his quest for societal transformation through artistic enlightenment was at odds with the American business community's demand for an institution to train effective product designers.

Moholy did succeed in reopening the school in 1939 and in keeping it afloat at a new location without the involvement of the AAI, but this achievement owed much to his pragmatic modification of the New Bauhaus curriculum to address the needs, values, and concerns of Middle America. First, he changed the school's name to the School of Design, thereby eliminating foreign—and, specifically, German—associations. Second, he expanded the evening program for working professionals and geared it more toward practical design training. Until 1942 the day-school curriculum was modeled on that of the Dessau Bauhaus, with a hands-on preliminary course aimed at awakening individual creativity (to which he added academic course work in the sciences[11]), six specialized workshops, and a final concentration in architecture. By the early 1940s Moholy was compelled by the educational "market" to make the day curriculum less general and more professionally oriented, specifically toward design. Other alterations were made when the United States entered the war in December 1941 and he lost many of his staff and students and faced shortages of art supplies. At that time he secured accreditation in camouflage training,[12] developed a rehabilitation course in art therapy for wounded soldiers, and oversaw the development of

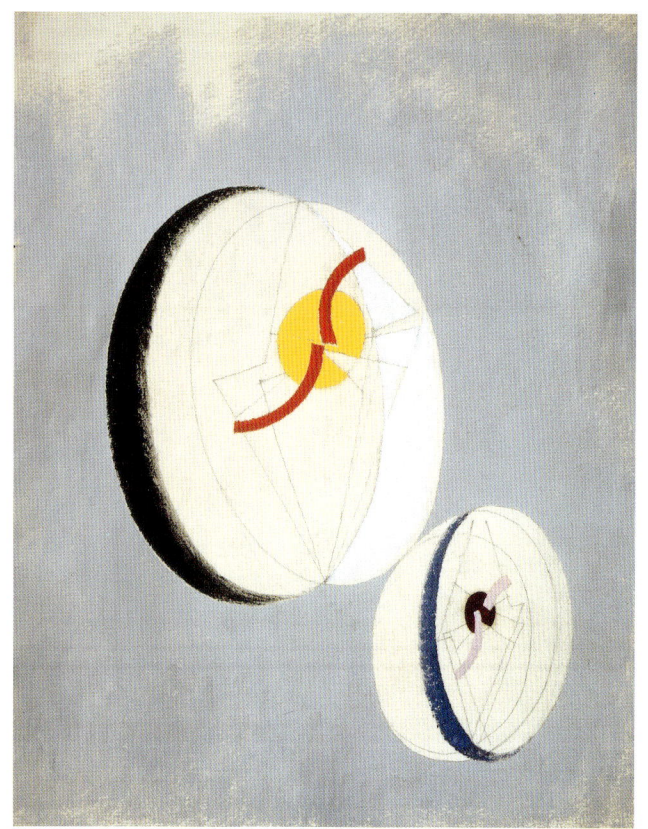

257

products using new materials, such as wood-spring mattresses,[13] to minimize the domestic consumption of steel. Largely as the cumulative result of these pragmatic actions, the School of Design, which in 1944 became the Institute of Design and gained a prominent board of directors, attracted a growing body of students and supporters.[14]

Perhaps the pivotal factor in the school's success, however, was Moholy's ability to harness the resources of corporate America on its behalf. For, unlike the German Bauhaus, which was funded by the Thuringian state government in Weimar and by the municipal government in Dessau, its American offshoot received no public support and thus was dependent on private funding. Recognizing that he had to "be the advertisement" for his school,[15] Moholy made two road trips around the country, in 1938 and 1939, to solicit funds from private business. These and subsequent efforts resulted not only in monetary commitments from large corporations such as Kodak but also in considerable donations of equipment and materials from midsize businesses. By far his closest and most effective corporate ally was

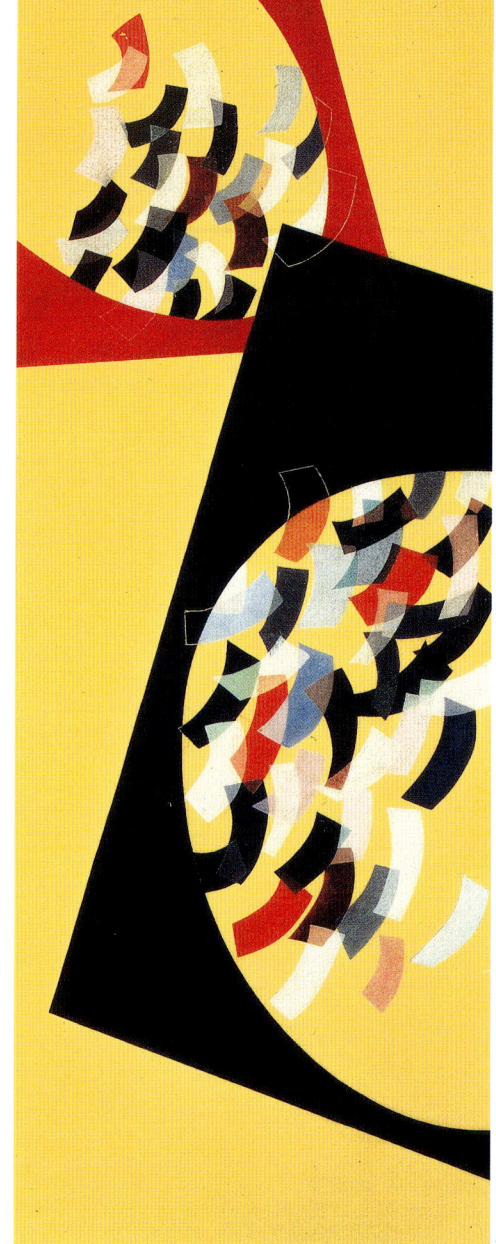

258

257
László Moholy-Nagy, *Composition*, 1942 (cat. no. 120).

258
László Moholy-Nagy, *Space Modulator*, 1942 (cat. no. 121).

259
László Moholy-Nagy, patent design for a fountain pen for the Parker Pen Company (filed February 11, 1946; patented May 20, 1947).

260
László Moholy-Nagy, *Photogram*, 1943 (cat. no. 122).

Walter Paepcke, president of the Chicago-based Container Corporation of America and vanguard promoter of modern art in the service of advertising.[16] The only member of the AAI board to stand by Moholy after the split, Paepcke contributed funds that enabled the school to reopen in 1939; attracted important gifts from fellow executives; donated a country house, which served as a summer school; and became director of the newly reorganized Institute of Design in 1944, after convincing Moholy to relinquish his administrative duties.

Although Moholy affectionately dedicated *Vision in Motion* to Paepcke and his wife, at times he regarded him as just another businessman to whom artists in the United States were beholden. Following what he called a "nightmarish" celebration of the Container Corporation's landmark exhibition *Modern Art in Advertising* in 1945, Moholy reflected that he and Fernand Léger, whose work was featured in the exhibition, were "ashamed in a strange sort of way that none of us had protested.... The

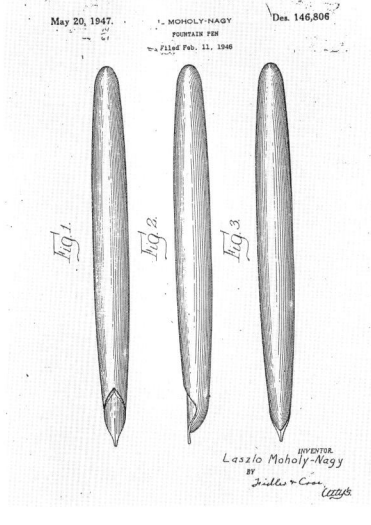

provocative statement of modern art is constantly annulled by checkbook and cocktail party. Am I on the same way?"[17] Here Moholy uneasily acknowledged the ideological leap he had made from being an artist affiliated with the political left in Europe to a figure with close corporate ties in the United States.

As further evidence of this change, Moholy channeled much of his creative energy in America into product design and other commercial activities. Although design work and even advertising had been components of his artistic practice in Germany, in keeping with his Bauhaus belief in the integration of art into society, these activities took on a much greater role once he left Germany in 1934. His earlier, vanguard experiments in film, for example, were discontinued in the United States, and his avant-garde work in stage design was replaced by window displays and showroom renovations for clothing stores such as Simpson's Picadilly in London and Lanz in Chicago. This shift was initially driven by financial need (in 1938–39 Moholy's $10,000 salary as the art adviser to the Chicago mail-order firm Spiegel, for example, enabled him to support his family and to open the School of Design), but eventually his commercial work came to assume a more central role in his artistic practice. In 1945 he became art adviser to the Parker Pen Company in Janesville, Wisconsin, serving as a consultant on production issues and designing posters, stationery, inkstands, and pens, some of which were patented (see fig. 259).

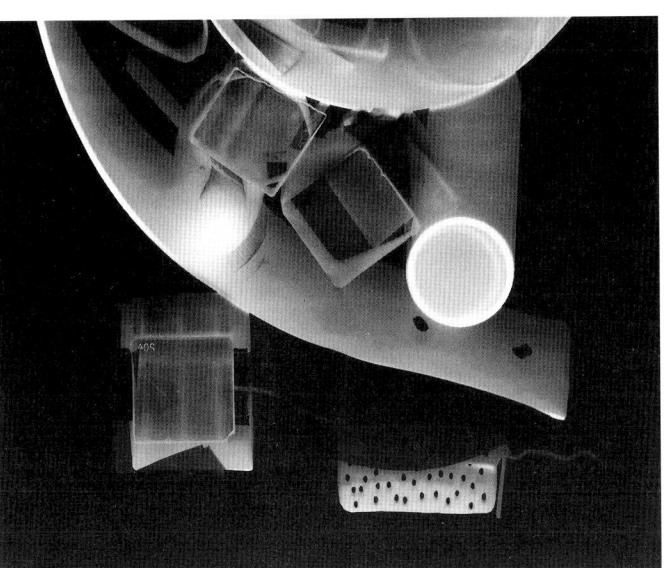

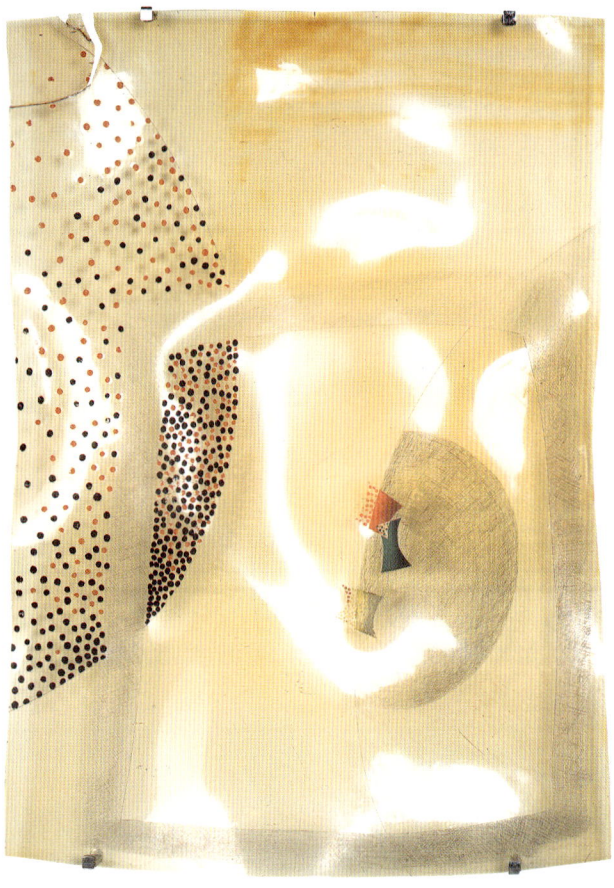

261

261
László Moholy-Nagy, *Composition*, 1938 (cat. no. 116).

262
László Moholy-Nagy, *CH B4*, 1941 (cat. no. 119).

263
László Moholy-Nagy; *A II*, 1924; oil on canvas; 45¼ x 53¾ in. (115 x 136.5 cm); The Solomon R. Guggenheim Museum, New York.

264
László Moholy-Nagy, *Space Modulator*, 1945 (cat. no. 123).

Moholy continued to produce works of art throughout his years in America, primarily in the evenings and on weekends. Although Sibyl Moholy-Nagy contended that "in Moholy the designer and the painter were one, and the elements of his vision were subject to the same laws . . . and carriers of the same message,"[18] there were, in fact, significant distinctions between his commercial designs and his private artwork from this period. Simply put, Moholy consistently valued process over product in his art and did not tailor it for the market. His cryptic, whimsical, and organic-looking *Composition* (1938; fig. 261, cat. no. 116), for example, stands in stark contrast to the standardized and highly readable designs he produced for Spiegel chain saws and Parker pens. Created in rhodoid,[19] a material that warps and yellows over time, *Composition* testifies to Moholy's belief in uninhibited experimentation for its own sake, which he promoted freely at the New Bauhaus and, more diplomatically, at the School of Design.

Just as the open-ended and unstructured teaching philosophy Moholy espoused at the New Bauhaus was not readily embraced by practical-minded Americans, neither were his experimental works of art. Already an internationally recognized and exhibited artist when he immigrated to the United States, Moholy did not have his first major solo exhibition in America until 1946, shortly before his death.[20] This show, organized by the Modern Art Society of Cincinnati, "was not a popular success and nothing was sold."[21] The fact that Moholy did not have a dealer no doubt affected his sales.[22] Many of his American works wound up in the collections of his colleagues at the School of Design, and some were purchased by the industrialists who enlisted his services.

Despite the frustrations he experienced in America, Moholy's works from this period convey a sense of relief at having gained distance from the political situation in Germany and from the rigid ideologies that had informed his European work. Energized by what he described as "American buoyancy," he said that he was "happy to paint again, with stronger colors than ever before."[23] The Space Modulator paintings of 1938–45 (see figs. 243, 256, 258, 264, cat. nos. 117–18, 121, 123)—with their vibrant hues and dynamic, diagonal compositions—attest to this change in outlook. So, too, do works such as *CH B4* of 1941 (fig. 262, cat. no. 119), whose lyrical qualities and expressive, irregular imagery signal a notable departure from Moholy's depersonalized constructivist vocabulary of the 1920s (see fig. 263).

Moholy continued to produce photograms through a process he had pioneered in the 1920s (see fig. 260, cat. no. 122), but his

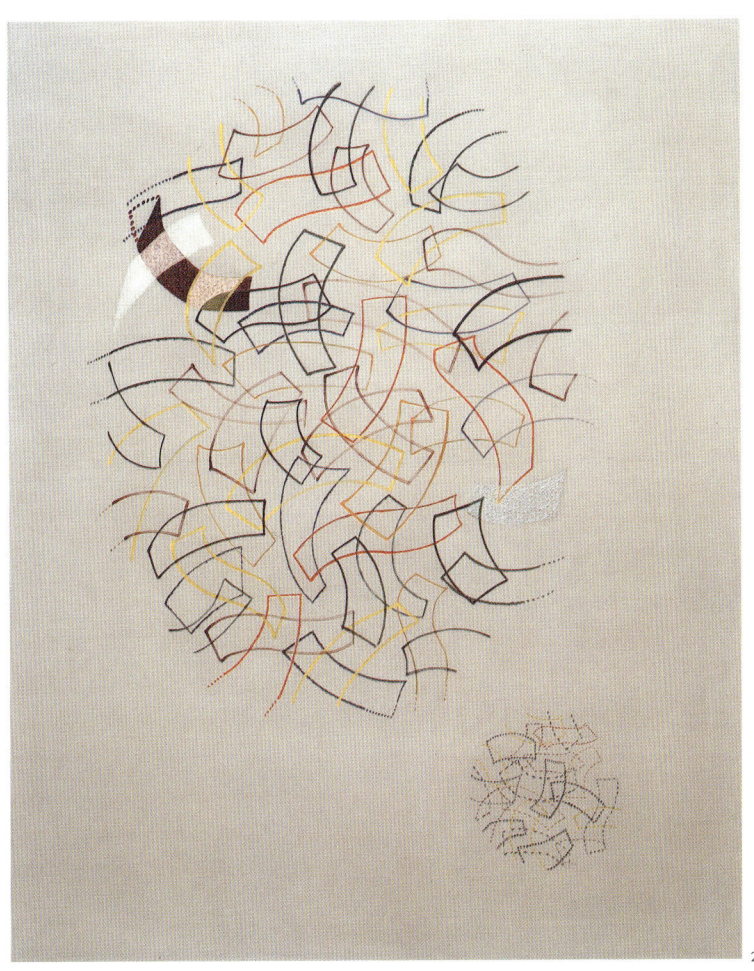

262

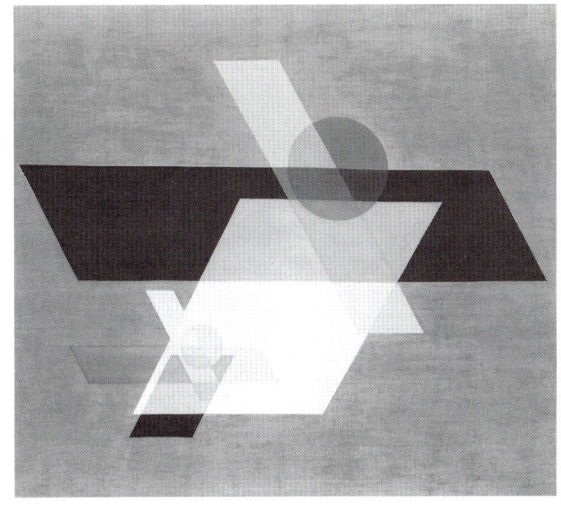

263

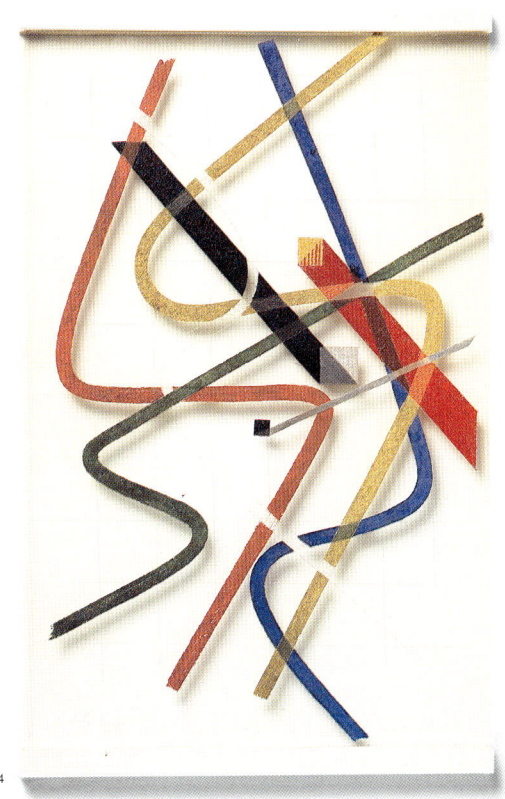

264

most inventive work in America involved experimentation with new plastics. Having already worked for many years with unconventional materials, including aluminum and glass, he began to experiment with the plastics galalith and rhodoid in London around 1935. Plastic did not become his central focus, however, until 1937, when the company Rhom and Haas began manufacturing the durable cast resin Plexiglas and donated quantities of it to Moholy's school.[24] Some of the Space Modulator paintings were made by incising and painting abstract designs directly on Plexiglas sheets, which were then mounted at a slight distance from a plain wooden background so that the designs cast complex, floating shadows.[25] Moholy created clear, undulating sculptures such as *Spirals* (1946; fig. 265, cat. no. 124) by heating pieces of Plexiglas in his kitchen oven, molding them with his bare hands, enlisting the help of family members to hold them as they cooled, and immersing them in water.[26] Because these works were created

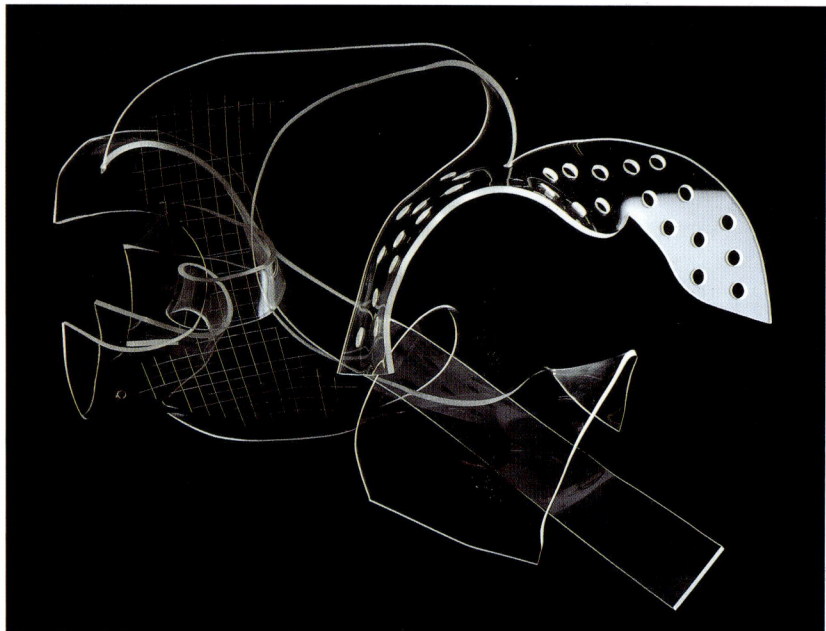

265
László Moholy-Nagy, *Spirals*, 1946 (cat. no. 124).

with cutting-edge materials, they necessitated a process of trial and error, which Moholy consistently embraced both as an artist and as a teacher.

The availability of Plexiglas and other new plastics enabled Moholy to achieve the effect of creating "glass architecture," which he had first sought as a young artist drawn to utopian art of the Russian and German avant-gardes. Yet in America he used new materials to different ends. Whereas his experiments in Germany fell in line with an avant-garde tradition of working with unconventional materials to critique bourgeois society and to build a new social order, in America they were devoid of these leftist associations and simply served to maximize his capacity for individual artistic expression. Moholy, who had once declared himself a communist as young man, was in essence fully compliant with the American political and economic system as a middle-aged artist and teacher. Although he had to compete in the capitalist market to promote his school and to sell his designs, the United States offered him the freedom in his art to eschew politics and the cataclysmic events of his day and to escape instead to a realm of personal creative exploration.

Notes

1   Moholy-Nagy to Sibyl Moholy-Nagy, Chicago, 8 August 1937; quoted in Sibyl Moholy-Nagy, *Moholy-Nagy: Experiment in Totality* (New York: Harper and Brothers, 1950), 145.
2   Moholy also spent brief interim periods in Vienna (in 1919) and Amsterdam (in 1934), prior to moving to, respectively, Berlin and London.
3   The AAI had first made an offer to Gropius himself, who declined the invitation and suggested Moholy instead. Gropius subsequently joined the faculty at Harvard University.
4   Moholy-Nagy to Gropius, London, 13 June 1937 (Walter Gropius Papers, Houghton Library, Harvard University); translated by Alain Findeli in "Design Education and Industry: The Laborious Beginnings of the Institute of Design in Chicago in 1944," *Journal of Design History* 4, no. 2 (1991): 98.
5   László Moholy-Nagy, *Vision in Motion* (Chicago: Paul Theobald, 1947).
6   Moholy-Nagy to Sibyl Moholy-Nagy, 11 May 1945; quoted in S. Moholy-Nagy, *Experiment in Totality*, 218.
7   "New School of Industrial Design," *Christian Science Monitor*, 6 November 1937; Eleanor Jewett, "School for Design Will Open Oct. 18," *Chicago Tribune*, 11 October 1937. See also "America Imports Genius," *New York Times*, 12 September 1937, sec. 4.
8   The substance of this lecture at the Knickerbocker Hotel on September 13, 1937, is recounted in S. Moholy-Nagy, *Experiment in Totality*, 148–50. The lecture is summarized in László Moholy-Nagy, "Why Bauhaus Education?" *Shelter*, March 1938, 7–21.

9 Files of the Circuit Court of Cook County; cited in C. L. Morrison, "Chicago Dialectic," *Artforum* 16 (February 1978): 32.

10 László Moholy-Nagy, *Malerei-Photographie-Film*, Bauhausbücher, no. 8 (Munich: A. Langen, 1925); quoted in S. Moholy-Nagy, *Experiment in Totality*, 38.

11 Moholy had taught the preliminary course, or *Vorkurs,* at the Bauhaus in Weimar and Dessau. At the School of Design he and a staff composed of Americans and recent emigrés, including his Hungarian colleague from the Bauhaus Gyorgy Kepes, taught all visual arts courses. Academic courses were taught by faculty from the University of Chicago, such as professor of philosophy Charles W. Morris. Moholy listed Morris's classes at the School of Design under the heading "Intellectual Integration"; see the course catalogue of the School of Design (1939–40), 2 (Institute of Design Papers, University of Illinois at Chicago).

12 While optics specialist Gyorgy Kepes taught the camouflage course, Moholy himself was appointed to the Chicago mayor's committee to develop methods of camouflaging Chicago from the air. See James Sloan Allen, "Marketing Modernism: Moholy-Nagy and the Bauhaus in America," in *The Romance of Commerce and Culture: Capitalism, Modernism, and the Chicago-Aspen Crusade for Cultural Reform* (Chicago: University of Chicago Press, 1983), 65, and Findeli, "Design Education and Industry," 100–101.

13 Patented in 1942.

14 Alain Findeli discusses the issue of Moholy's pragmatism in terms of his pedagogy—specifically his indebtedness as an art educator to John Dewey's pragmatic philosophy—in "The Methodological and Philosophical Foundations of Moholy's Design Pedagogy in Chicago (1937–1946)," *Design Issues* 7 (Fall 1990): 13–14. By the 1945–46 academic year there were four hundred students enrolled. For a detailed analysis of the changes in the School of Design from 1937 to 1946, see Findeli, "Design Education and Industry," 97–113.

15 S. Moholy-Nagy, *Experiment in Totality*, 213.

16 See James Sloan Allen, "Modernist Marketing: The Consumer Revolution and the Container Corporation of America," in *The Romance of Commerce*, 3–34.

17 Moholy-Nagy to Sibyl Moholy-Nagy, 26 April 1944; quoted in S. Moholy-Nagy, *Experiment in Totality*, 215–16.

18 Ibid., 209.

19 Rhodoid, a form of plastic, was used in the cockpits of fighter jets in World War II. I am grateful to Eugene Bielawski for this information.

20 Other exhibitions during his American years include a solo show at the Katharine Kuh Gallery in Chicago (1939), a group exhibition of School of Design work at the Mills College Art Gallery (1940), and *European Artists Teaching in America* (1941) at the Addison Gallery of American Art, Andover, Mass.

21 S. Moholy-Nagy, *Experiment in Totality*, 225.

22 In 1944 Karl Nierendorf, a German emigré who was an important dealer for emigré artists, offered to represent Moholy, but he declined the offer. Nierendorf had wanted the exclusive right to sell Moholy's work in New York, and Moholy thought this would compromise his relationship with the Museum of Non-Objective Painting. See Moholy-Nagy to Nierendorf, 11 October 1944; quoted in S. Moholy-Nagy, *Experiment in Totality*, 207–8.

23 Quoted in *European Artists Teaching in America,* exh. cat. (Andover, Mass.: Addison Gallery of American Art, Phillips Academy, 1941), 39.

24 Interview with former School of Design instructor Eugene Bielawski, 18 May 1996.

25 Moholy's experimentation with incising and painting plastic is described in his essay "Abstract of an Artist" (1944), which was first published in 1947 as an introduction to the fourth edition of his 1928 book *The New Vision* (New York: Wittenborn Schultz, 1947). The essay is reprinted in Krisztina Passuth, *Moholy-Nagy* (New York: Thames and Hudson, 1985), 360–64, 381–83.

26 This process is described in S. Moholy-Nagy, *Experiment in Totality*, 191.

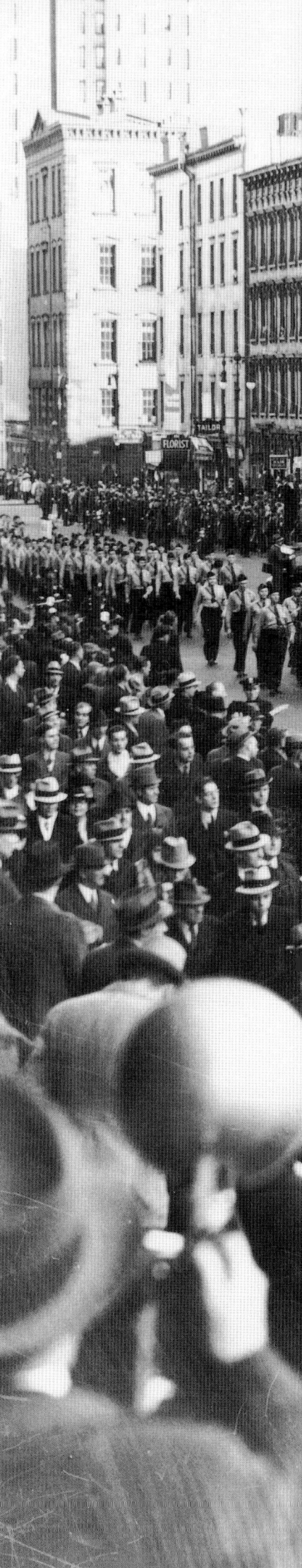

Overleaf left:
Nazi parade, East Eighty-sixth Street, October 30, 1937.

Overleaf right:
Anti-Nazi demonstration, Madison Square Garden, March 15, 1937.

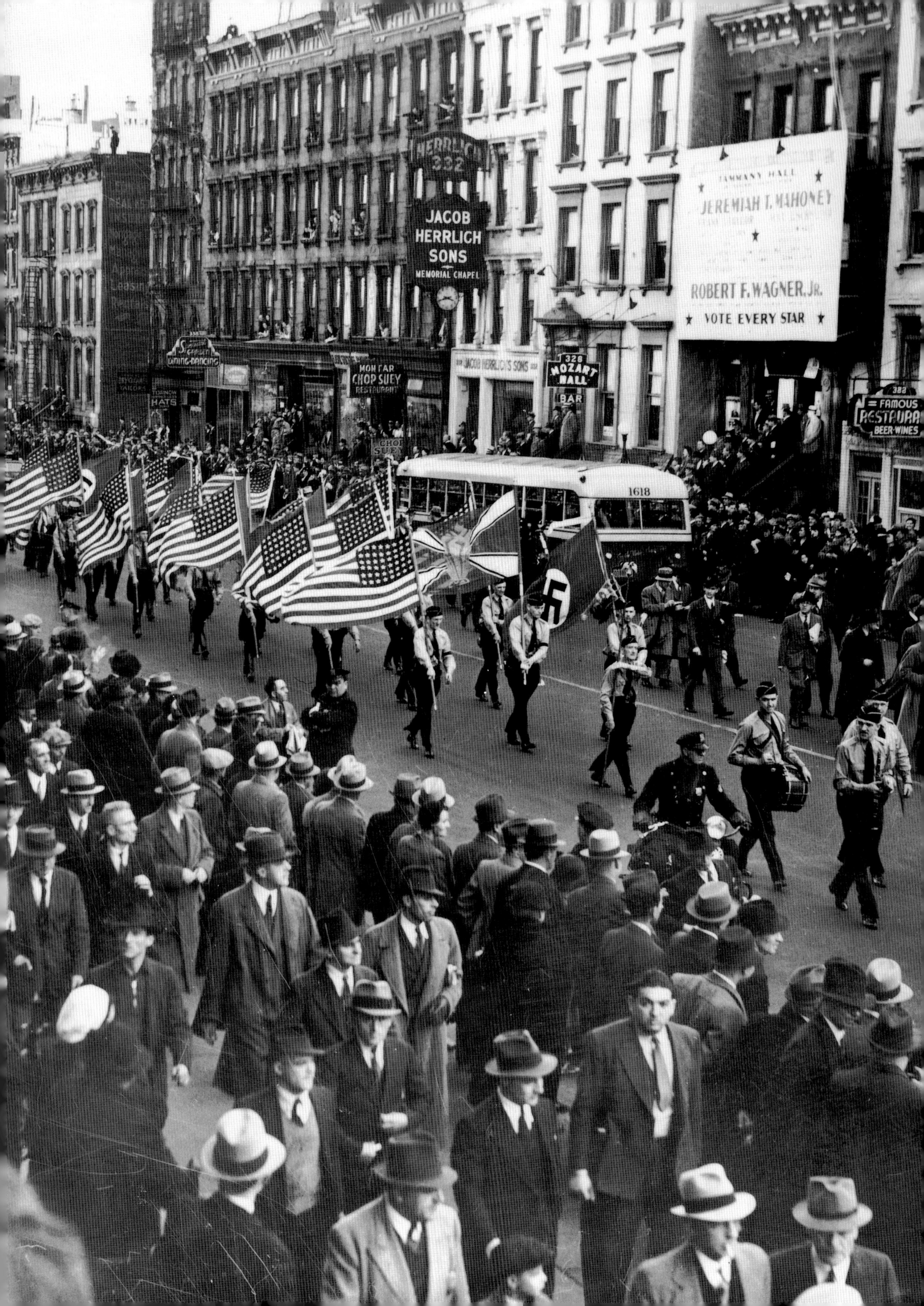

BOYCOTT NAZI GERMANY

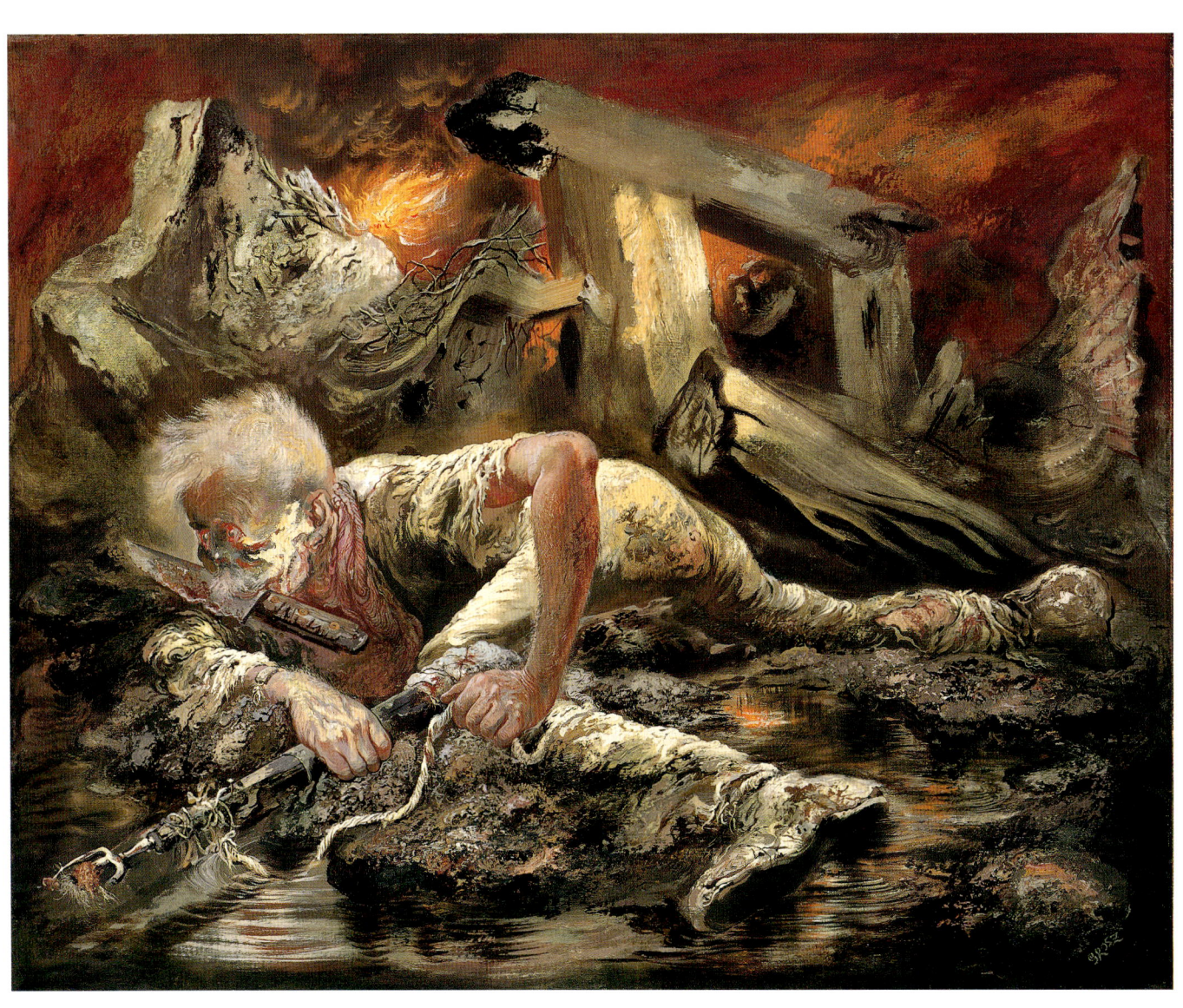

banned german art:
reception and institutional support of modern german art in the united states, 1933–45

VIVIAN ENDICOTT BARNETT

modern German art has always appealed to a limited audience in the United States and has been overshadowed by comparisons with art from other countries, especially France. Yet, in the words of Alfred H. Barr Jr., the first director of the Museum of Modern Art and the organizer of its influential 1931 exhibition *German Painting and Sculpture,* "many people believe that German painting is second only to the School of Paris, and that German sculpture is at least equal to that of any other nation."[1] During the 1930s the perception of German art changed as the National Socialists came to power and increasingly curtailed the freedom of artists. In June 1933 the first issue of the *Bulletin of the Museum of Modern Art* reported on the closing of the Bauhaus: "The Bauhaus has been closed by the National Socialists. This school, where Klee and Kandinsky taught, had been for more than a decade the most famous school of modern architecture and applied arts in the world.... In April, 1933, the Nationalist Socialist Storm Troopers forcibly removed the students and faculty from the old factory where they had been holding classes. No explanation of this move has been issued by the Government."[2]

Between October 15, 1933, when Hitler laid the cornerstone of the Haus der deutschen Kunst (House of German art) in Munich, and July 1937, when works of "degenerate" art that he had ordered purged from German museums were exhibited in Munich, the Nazis' political motives with regard to art and artists became increasingly apparent. Subsequent sales of confiscated works of art resulted in their acquisition by American museums and collectors. Moreover, between 1937 and 1939 a growing number of artists fled Germany.

By 1933 German artists as different as Josef Albers and George Grosz had already immigrated to the United States. The previous summer Grosz had taught at the Art Students League and established ties to the New York art world.[3] In the case of Albers, after the faculty voted to dissolve the Bauhaus on July 20, 1933, he and other professors of diverse nationalities decided to leave Germany. Lyonel Feininger had never given up his American citizenship; the Swiss-born Klee and the Russian-born Kandinsky, however, were German citizens. Albers was first invited by Philip Johnson, head of the Department of Architecture at the Museum of Modern Art, and by Edward M. M. Warburg to teach at Black Mountain College in North Carolina. As Warburg explained in a letter written on August 31 to Barr, his friend from their days at Harvard University: "I cannot help but feel that getting Albers into this country would be a great feather in the cap of the Museum of Modern Art. His summer vacations would be, so to speak, free, and I am sure he would be interested in working at that time with us on anything that we might have in mind. With Albers over here we have the nucleuos [*sic*] for an American Bauhaus! What do you think of the whole scheme?"[4] Barr had, of

266
George Grosz, *The Survivor*, 1944
(cat. no. 58).

course, visited the Bauhaus in December 1927, when he and his roommate Jere Abbott traveled to Germany following the advice of the emigré art dealer J. B. Neumann.

In analyzing the institutional support and critical reception of modern German art in the years from 1933 to 1945, this essay will focus on institutions where German art had been exhibited and collected during the previous decade. Not only museums in New York but also those in Boston and Cambridge, Detroit, Chicago, Saint Louis, Los Angeles, and the San Francisco Bay Area will be considered.

As its name implies, the Germanic Museum at Harvard University was dedicated to promoting interest in German art as well as the artistic production of what it considered "related countries."[5] By the mid-1930s sculptures by Ernst Barlach, Georg Kolbe, and Gerhard Marcks had been acquired by the museum, and in 1934–35 "a splendid collection of contemporary German watercolors and drawings" by Otto Dix, Feininger, Grosz, and Karl Hofer was added. In the autumn of 1935 the museum's curator, Charles L. Kuhn, organized the exhibition *Watercolors and Drawings by George Grosz*. At that time, in a letter written to the collector Erich Cohn, Kuhn expressed his reservations about including Grosz's decidedly anti-Nazi political drawings "since the Germanic Museum so far has been able to escape the accusation of being on one side of the fence or the other."[6] In her review of the show, however, Dorothy Adlow observed: "Like many of the best contemporary artists, Mr. Grosz has left Germany. One has but to glance at the pictures to know the reason."[7]

On the West Coast the efforts of Emmy "Galka" Scheyer in conjunction with William H. Clapp of the Oakland Museum resulted in numerous exhibitions of German art in the late 1920s and early 1930s. Since 1924 Scheyer had represented the "Blue Four" artists—Feininger, Alexej von Jawlensky, Kandinsky, and Klee—in the United States. From 1926 on, she organized exhibitions of their work in Los Angeles as well as San Francisco, although her influence diminished after 1933.[8] During the summer of 1935 paintings and watercolors from the collection of Josef von Sternberg were presented at the Los Angeles County Museum of Science, History, and Art. Arthur Millier, writing in the *Los Angeles Times*, compared works from the School of Paris with those of the German expressionists, singling out works by Dix, Grosz, Hofer, Kandinsky, Oskar Kokoschka, Emil Nolde, Max Pechstein (see fig. 267), and Karl Schmidt-Rottluff. He concluded: "The distinguishing feature of this collection is its representation of that outburst of expressionistic art which took place in Germany between 1907 and the rise of Hitler. It might be regarded as the last cry of individualism before the inevitable march of collectivism."[9]

In 1935 Alfred Neumeyer left Germany to become a professor of art history at Mills College in Oakland, and in the same year Grace McCann Morley became the director of the San Francisco Museum of Art. It was Neumeyer who

267
Max Pechstein; *Sunlight*, 1921; oil on canvas; 47¼ x 36 in. (120 x 91.4 cm); Los Angeles County Museum of Art, gift of Josef von Sternberg.

invited Feininger to teach at Mills in 1936 and who, together with Morley, organized a Feininger show for that summer in Oakland and San Francisco.[10] The following year the San Francisco Museum of Art presented paintings and prints by Klee, a Hofer exhibition, the Henle collection of contemporary German watercolors, and a selection of paintings from the Lilienfeld collection of German art as well as another Feininger exhibition, in September–October 1937.

Also in 1937 William R. Valentiner, director of the Detroit Institute of Arts since 1924, opened a solo show of Ernst Ludwig Kirchner's art in January and added Schmidt-Rottluff's painting *Rain Clouds, Lago di Garda* (1927) to the museum's growing collection of German art. In February the Art Institute of Chicago exhibited modern German prints; in February and March the Cleveland Museum of Art presented a Kandinsky retrospective, which had been organized by the College Art Association and Karl Nierendorf (see fig. 268). In Pittsburgh the 1937 Carnegie International Exhibition of Paintings took place in the autumn, and the German section included works by Dix, Max Ernst, and Pechstein as well as Kokoschka, who was awarded an honorable mention. The Midwest's large population of Americans with German ancestry probably accounted for the growing interest in exhibiting and collecting German art in the region.

The year 1937 was crucial for the reception of German art. Even before the Nazis confiscated works from German museums and exhibited them as *entartete Kunst* (degenerate art), prominent dealers such as Nierendorf and Curt Valentin (see fig. 269) had moved to New York. In February 1937 *Art News* reported: "The opening of the Nierendorf Gallery in New York, one of the backbone galleries of modern art in Germany, promises to make America more familiar with the great figures in experimental Germany.... The gallery is filled with the work of German expressionists, beginning with several of the pioneers, Heckel and Nolde." The article went on to praise Barlach's bronze *Monks Reading* (1932) as well as sculptures by Kolbe, Wilhelm Lehmbruck, and Marcks.[11] Two months later Nierendorf showed works by Feininger in his gallery at 20 West Fifty-third Street, across from the Museum of Modern Art. Valentin's first exhibition, *Sculpture by Barlach, Kolbe, Lehmbruck, Marcks, and Sintenis,* took place from March 18 to April 17, 1937, at the Buchholz Gallery at 3 West Forty-sixth Street. A review of his subsequent exhibition of German expressionist art began: "German art of the twentieth century is gradually becoming more familiar to the American public which has directed its attention almost excessively towards modern France. Such an extensive and well selected exhibition as the one current at the Buchholz Gallery is an important link in this season's chain of events sponsoring German art."[12]

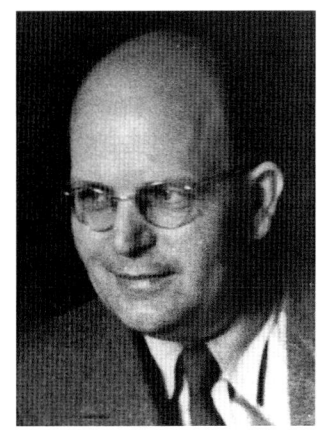

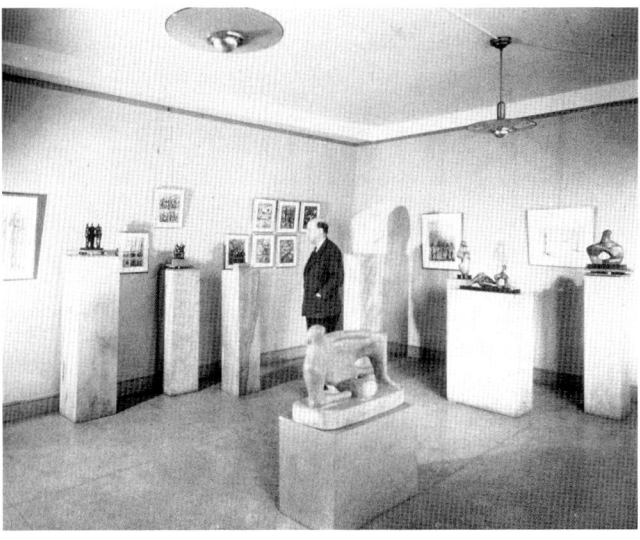

268
Karl Nierendorf, 1940s.

269
Curt Valentin at the Buchholz Gallery, New York City.

At the beginning of 1938 Harvard's Germanic Museum presented a Lovis Corinth exhibition, which was organized by the Westermann Gallery in New York, followed by *Modern German Sculpture,* which included loans from the Buchholz, Nierendorf, and Weyhe Galleries in New York. Soon thereafter, in the annual report to the trustees of Harvard

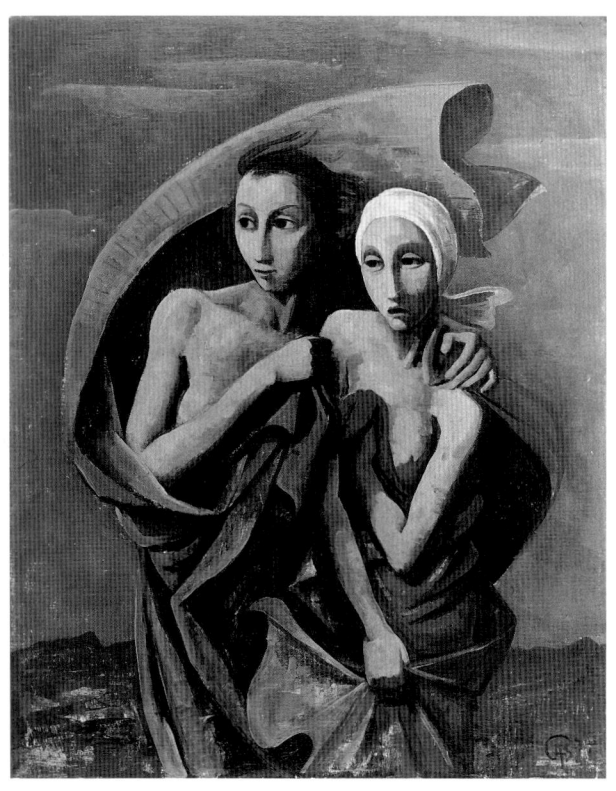

270
Karl Hofer; *The Wind*, 1937; oil on canvas; 48 x 38¾ in. (121.9 x 98.4 cm); The Detroit Institute of Arts, gift of Mrs. George Kamperman in memory of her husband, Dr. George Kamperman.

University, Kuhn stated: "In my report for the year 1936–37, I suggested that the Germanic Museum might better benefit the University and the country by becoming a research institute rather than remaining a museum of art. Since writing that report, political events in Europe have made the need for such an institute even more apparent."[13] Exhibitions were suspended almost entirely between June 1938 and February 1940.

Nevertheless, other American museums featured modern German art in 1938. That year, for the first time, a German artist won first prize in the Carnegie International Exhibition in Pittsburgh; Hofer, who received the award for his painting *The Wind* (1937; fig. 270), had been given a second prize in 1934. In June 1938 the City Art Museum of Saint Louis presented its first exhibition of paintings by Max Beckmann, which was organized by the Buchholz Gallery. At the end of the year *George Grosz: A Survey of His Art from 1918–1938* opened at the Art Institute of Chicago, the *Ernst Barlach Memorial Show* took place at the Buchholz Gallery in New York, and the Museum of Modern Art presented a major exhibition devoted to the Bauhaus.

Bauhaus, 1919–1928, which was organized by Bauhaus founder Walter Gropius and installed by former Bauhaus master Herbert Bayer, brought together a vast amount of material and engendered strong criticism in the press because of its content as well as its installation (see fig. 271). An article in the *New York Times* on December 4, 1938, was headlined "Nazi-Banned Art Is Exhibited Here," and in another article, published on December 11, Edward Alden Jewell quoted Barr as saying: "By no means, was the present exhibition planned as a memorializing wreath laid 'upon the tomb of brave events, important in their own day but now of primarily historical interest.... The Bauhaus is not dead; it lives and grows through the men who made it, both teachers and students.'"[14] In an undated memo entitled "Notes on the Reception of the Bauhaus Exhibition," Barr explained:

> As the period covered by the exhibition proper closed in 1928 and the Bauhaus itself in 1933, we had little expectation that there would be much controversy about the exhibition. Indeed we were very doubtful whether the exhibition would be a popular success because of the complexity and difficulty of the subject and its comparative lack of popular elements and the fact that circumstances prevented any advance publicity of any kind. To our surprise we were completely mistaken. We have had a far larger attendance at the exhibition than at any previous show in our present quarters and the controversy aroused has been more violent than almost any exhibition that the Museum has had.[15]

It was during 1938 that works of art that had been seized by the National Socialists from German museums began to find their way to the United States. Valentin, who had worked for Karl Buchholz in Berlin from 1934 until 1937, acquired many works and offered them to American museums and private collectors. In a letter written on September 19, 1938, to Hilla von Rebay, curator of Solomon R. Guggenheim's collection, Valentin explained that he had tried to get in touch with her in Paris because "the German Government wants to sell most of the modern pictures belonging to German museums. I just had a cable from Berlin that I could buy all these pictures.... I thought you might be interested in some of the pictures by Klee, Kandinsky and Franz Marc. Since I heard that you were in Germany yourself, it may be that you got in touch with the museums directly."[16] Although Rebay appears not to have replied, Guggenheim had already purchased a Kandinsky painting from Gutekunst und Klipstein in Bern in February, *Study for Landscape with Tower* (1908). The Swiss artist Otto Nebel assisted Guggenheim and Rebay in acquiring more than one group of paintings from Klipstein in the spring of 1939.[17]

In September 1938 an article by Carlyle Burrows entitled "German Art outside the Nazi State" was published in the *New York Herald Tribune*:

> Although the German government has declined to participate in the New York World's Fair next year, the possibility of a large exhibition of German art being shown here at that time is being discussed with interest in art circles. Few details of the venture are known as yet, except that friends of German art in England and America are interested in bringing a show to New York, and that it will be composed principally of so-called banned German art—the paintings and sculpture of artists either disapproved or exiled by the Nazi regime in Germany. Perhaps the plan, as at present constituted, will fail to materialize, for there are those on the side of the suppressed artists who frankly doubt the advisability of such a show being held here.... What constitutes authentic German art today has already been determined for Germany by the dictators of culture in the Nazi state. The question was first officially clarified in Munich in the summer of 1937.[18]

Burrows went on to review the Kokoschka show on view at the Buchholz Gallery, whose owner, Valentin, was probably one of the sources of the above information.

In 1939 there was no official German presence at either the Golden Gate Exposition in San Francisco or the World's Fair in New York. Numerous examples of German art could

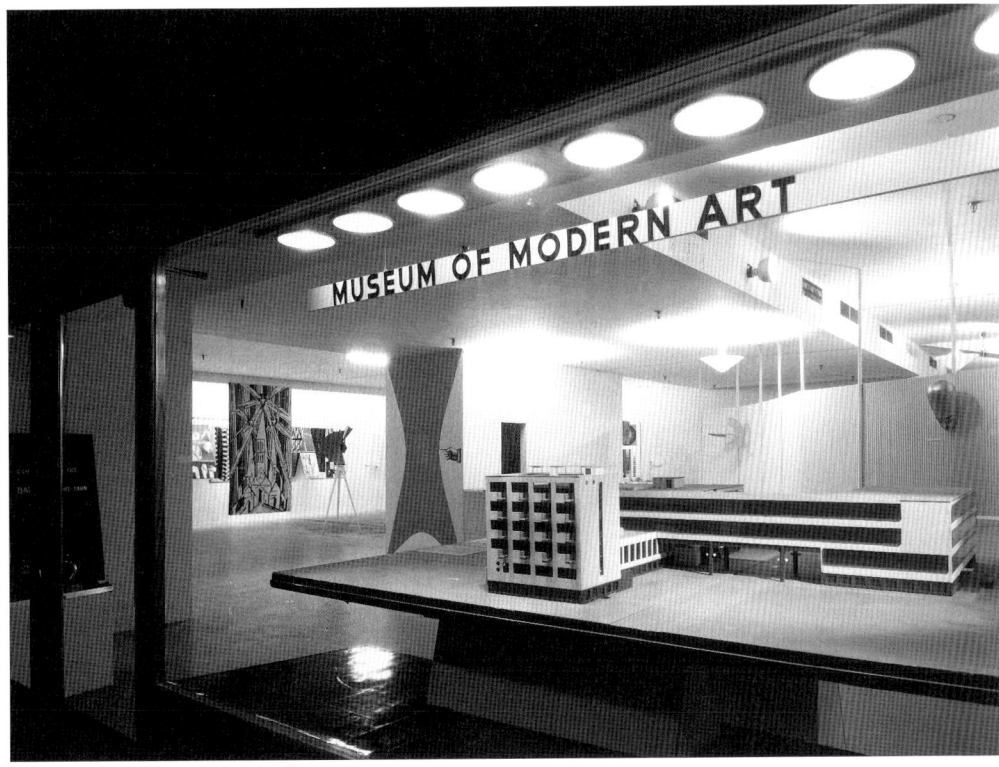

271
The exhibition *Bauhaus, 1919–1928* at the Museum of Modern Art, 1938.

be seen, however, in the section of the Golden Gate Exposition devoted to contemporary European art from American collections. The jury, whose chairman was Daniel Catton Rich, director of the Art Institute of Chicago, awarded first prize to Beckmann's triptych *Temptation* (1936–37; fig. 272), lent by the Buchholz Gallery, and second prize to Karl Hofer's *Early Hour,* lent by the Portland Art Association.[19]

In addition, various plans were under way for exhibitions of banned German art to take place in 1939. In New York a committee chaired by Frank Kingdon was organized for the Freedom Pavilion at the World's Fair, where "a great exhibition of the work of leading Germans thrown out of Germany for their race, religion, or politics" was planned but was vetoed by businessmen and politicians.[20] Incidentally William Valentiner, who was in charge of a panoramic survey of European art through 1800, also commissioned Feininger to design the murals for the Marine Transportation Building and the Masterpieces of Art Building at the fair.[21] To coincide with the World's Fair, the Museum of Modern Art celebrated its tenth anniversary with the exhibition *Art in Our Time* from May to September. At the same time, on East Fifty-fourth Street, Solomon R. Guggenheim's collection of nonobjective painting was publicly shown as *Art of Tomorrow*. The emphasis was clearly on nonobjective art, and there was no mention of German art, although pictures by Kandinsky and László Moholy-Nagy—both exiled from Germany—were included.[22]

Among the works exhibited in *Art in Our Time* were Kirchner's *Street, Berlin* (1913; fig. 273) and Lehmbruck's *Kneeling Woman* (1911); both had been lent anonymously but had formerly been in the collection of the Nationalgalerie in Berlin. Before the closing of the exhibition, the museum announced that it had purchased through the Buchholz Gallery five works that had belonged to German museums. *Art Digest* featured *Kneeling Woman* on the cover of the issue dated September 1 and stated in an article entitled "Exiled Art Finds

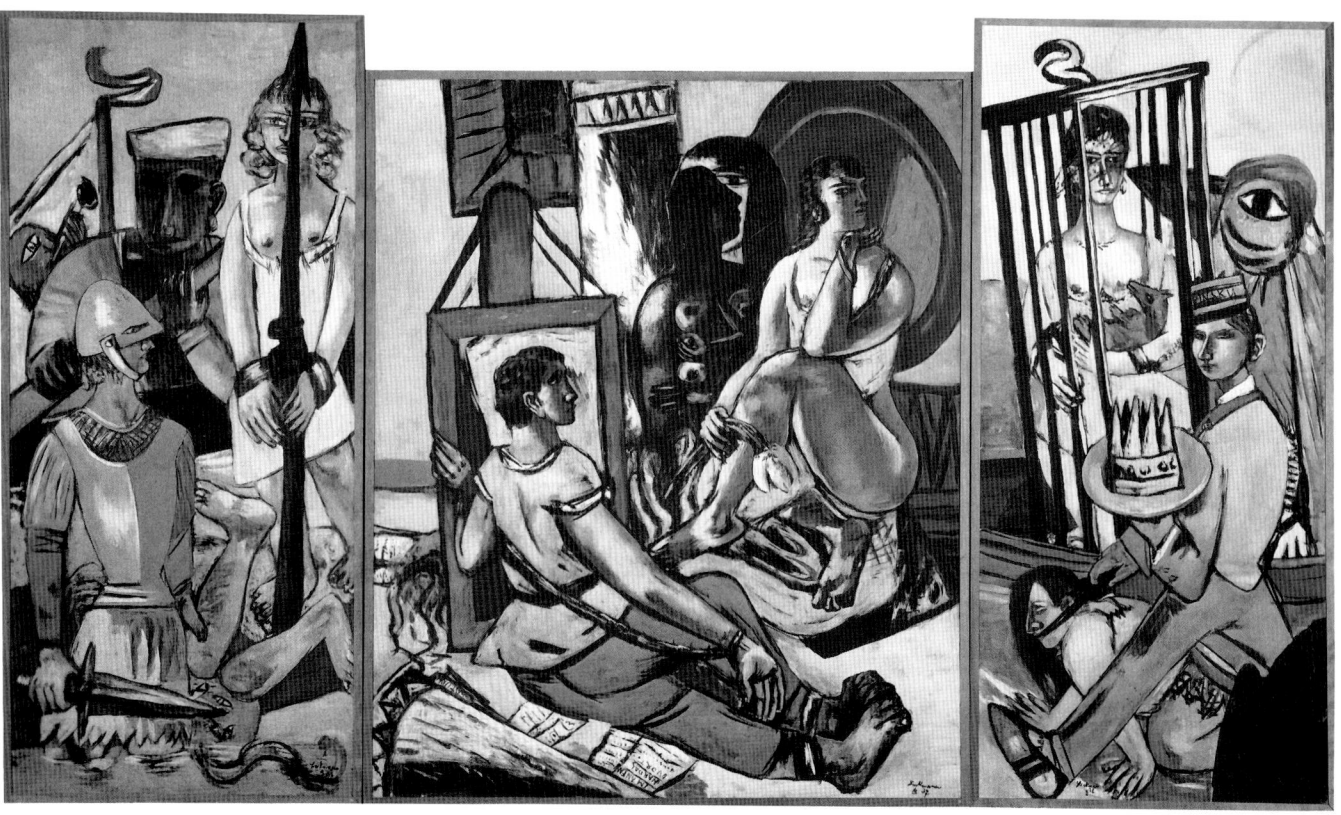

272
Max Beckmann; *Temptation*, 1936–37; oil on canvas; middle panel: 78¾ x 67⅛ in. (200 x 170.5 cm); side panels: 84⅞ x 39⅜ in. (215.5 x 100 cm) each; Bayerische Staatsgemäldesammlungen, Munich.

Haven in Modern Museum" that these works "were not excluded from German museums on racial grounds. Two of the artists, Lehmbruck and Kirchner, are Aryan Germans; two, Derain and Matisse, are Frenchmen; and Klee, though a native of Switzerland, was long a resident of Germany." Barr was quoted as saying that "the Nazi opposition to modern art seems in fact to be due to Hitler's personal taste rather than to any racial or political factors." He observed: "The museum is very fortunate in having acquired these works of art.... The only good thing about the exile of such fine works of art from one country is the consequent enrichment of other lands where cultural freedom still exists."[23] Likewise, *Art News* reported: "None of these works were excluded from Germany on racial grounds" and emphasized that "the Museum, like other European and American collections, by acquiring them, gives the strongest condemnation to the policies which barred these and similar artistic expressions."[24]

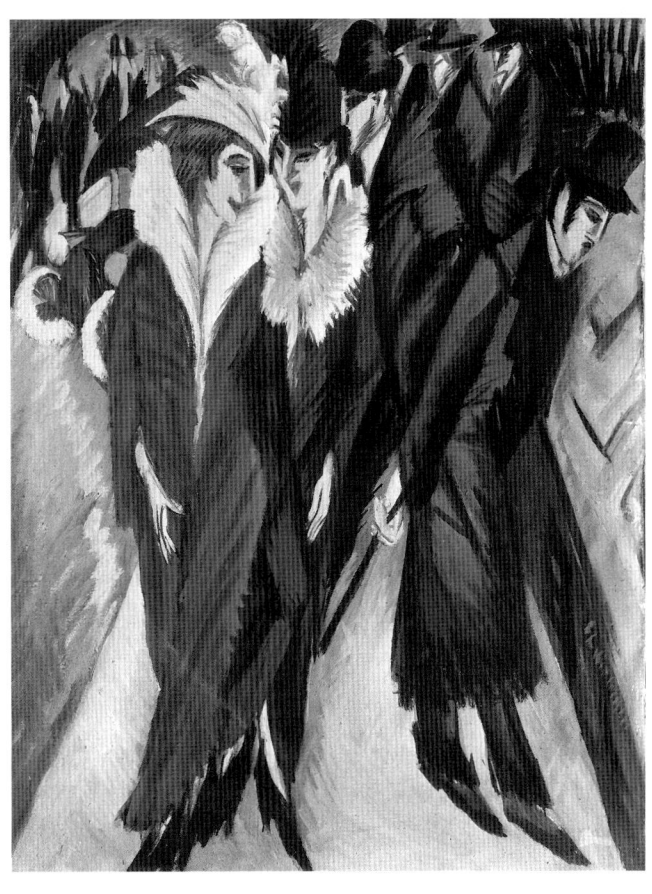

273
Ernst Ludwig Kirchner; *Street, Berlin*, 1913; oil on canvas; 47½ x 35⅞ in. (120.6 x 91.1 cm); The Museum of Modern Art, New York, purchase.

Moreover, efforts were made to bring a portion of the New Burlington Galleries' *Exhibition of Twentieth Century German Art* from London to the States, where it was shown in June 1939 at the Milwaukee Art Institute.[25] Soon afterward the director of the Smith College Museum of Art, Jere Abbott, wrote to his old friend Alfred Barr: "Some time ago we contracted to show the exhibition which was held in England and is now being routed in this country by Blanche [Byerley], of German deposed art.... I am now, because of what I have subsequently heard, getting a little cold feet about the exhibition, not by any political consideration but because I hear that the works in it are really not representative of the men. If this is the case, the show would do more harm than good because it would give people the opportunity to say, quite rightly, that the pictures were not worth hanging in museums."[26] Subsequently, on October 5, Barr related in a letter to the Cincinnati collector Paul E. Geier: "As you may know, our Museum bought some months previous to the [Galerie Fischer] auction several other works from German museums. As a result we had planned to organize a small exhibition of the very highest quality" at the Museum of Modern Art, which would open on January 15, 1940, after a larger show at the Institute of Modern Art in Boston. Barr continued: "I should add that the reason we are doing this is that we have heard—this is confidential—that there is a large exhibition of German art, rather badly chosen, touring museums. It seems to be doing a lot of harm so far as the reputation of German painting is concerned and is even causing people who are not in sympathy with modern art to say, with a certain relief, that Hitler is right. The purpose of our carefully selected small show would be in part to correct this state of affairs."[27] The New York exhibition did not take place as planned, although there were two significant presentations of German art in Massachusetts.

In fact, in January 1939 the Springfield Museum of Fine Arts showed ninety-four works by major artists—including Albers, Barlach, Beckmann, Dix, Ernst, Heckel, Hofer, Kirchner, Klee, Kolbe, Lehmbruck, Marc, Paula Modersohn-Becker, Nolde, and Pechstein—

which were lent by American collectors such as Katherine S. Dreier and Erich Cohn as well as by the Germanic Museum at Harvard, the Nierendorf Gallery, Weyhe Gallery, and especially the Buchholz Gallery. In the preface to the catalogue the museum's director, John Lee Clark Jr., stated:

> Of the thousands of exhibitions hung and taken down each year in this country, a surprisingly few of them deal with 20th century German art. Not since 1931, when the Museum of Modern Art staged a most important exhibition of painting and sculpture has there been a comprehensive show east of the Alleghenies. What Carnegie, Detroit and the far western Museums have done to display and evaluate modern German art, only a few dealer galleries in New York have done in the East during the last seven years. This is all the more remarkable, when one considers that in sculpture, Germany has been second to none and in painting only second to, and sometimes equaling, the achievements of modern French painting.[28]

The review in *Art News* repeated the above text, referring to the political and cultural events of 1933 to 1938 in Germany and emphasizing that several of the artists were already living in the United States.[29]

The exhibition *Contemporary German Art,* which opened at the Institute of Modern Art in Boston on November 2, 1939, included works from the Germanic Museum, the Art Institute of Chicago, the Detroit Institute of Arts, the Museum of Modern Art, J. B. Neumann, Karl Nierendorf, Curt Valentin, and other New York dealers. Valentiner lent a recently acquired painting by Nolde, *Christ among the Children* (1910), from his own collection, and Perry Rathbone, who was then a curator at the Detroit Institute of Arts under Valentiner, lent a bronze by Marcks. Works that had formerly belonged to German museums were prominently indicated in the catalogue. In the foreword—written by the museum's director, James S. Plaut, and by Mary C. Udall—the 1931 exhibition at the Museum of Modern Art was cited, and specific references were made to the "Day of German Art" proclaimed by the Third Reich in 1933, to the Nazi decree excluding works of "degenerate" artists from German museums, and to subsequent sales of works at auction. The organizers explicitly stated: "It is largely from among these [works] that the present exhibition has been chosen."[30]

Reinhold Heller has contrasted the attitudes of Barr and Plaut in presenting German art in New York and Boston, respectively.[31] Whereas Barr's insistence on formalist doctrines resulted in the denial of the political and racial implications of Nazi cultural policies even as late as 1939, Plaut clearly recognized the political context of his exhibition *Contemporary German Art*. Writing in *Art News* in November, Udall observed: "The Nineteen-Thirties stand as a milestone in German art. The last seven years have witnessed a considerable upheaval with many headlines but, in the United States at least, almost no exhibitions to show what was happening." Again, she compared the Institute of Modern Art exhibition with the one that had taken place in New York, noting that "a startling change has taken place since 1931." That change was clearly political and not art historical.[32]

When Albers arrived in the United States in 1933, according to the *New York Times*: "He made it plain that he had left Germany of his own volition, because of the closing of the Bauhaus and because of the offer of a position in America arranged through Philip Johnson.... Professor Albers further explained that the closing of the Bauhaus was due to economic rather than political considerations."[33] Such denials of the political and racial aspects of the German government's art policies had become harder to sustain by the late 1930s. In the American press the terms *Aryan* and *non-Aryan* appeared more frequently in articles about artists and art dealers. These distinctions were implicit, however, in earlier accounts where, for example, Grosz was inevitably described as blond and Aryan.

The question of nationality, which had always been puzzling, became more ambiguous and contradictory with the advent of war. The small catalogue accompanying the Grosz exhibition organized by the Museum of Modern Art in 1941, which circulated to other museums, identified the artist as: "Now one of the most brilliant American masters of watercolor."[34] The case of Feininger is indicative. In 1933 he was widely considered to be German or at least the son of German parents.[35] In 1938, during the preparation of the Bauhaus exhibition, he felt compelled to write the following to the Museum of Modern Art:

> Although I lived and worked for many years as an artist in Germany, I am an American, born of American parents, in the City of New York, and have never given up my nationality. My case is doubtless exceptional, so far as the fact of my having lived in *Germany* is concerned; but many American artists live in France or Italy, whose nationality is never called into doubt or questioned. My ancestors were, naturally, as is the case with *all* white Americans, born in foreign countries. I trace my descendance from German, Italian and French forbears [*sic*]. I am desirous of clearing all doubts as to my American nationality, so please put the above statement in your files where they will have authoritative value.[36]

When Grosz became an American citizen, in late November 1938, there was extensive press coverage. Curiously Max Ernst, who had earlier been considered German, was now identified as French in exhibitions in the United States.

As the war expanded in Europe in late 1939 and early 1940, German works of art continued to be sold by the Nazi regime, and the Buchholz Gallery was the chief conduit to the United States. On December 20, 1939, Valentin wrote to Galka Scheyer: "By the way, it is not too difficult to get pictures from Europe. I received shipments from Switzerland, from France, from England and even from Klee himself."[37] In the 1940s, however, there were markedly fewer exhibitions of German art in the United States. After Klee died in June 1940, several museums and galleries presented memorial exhibitions (Klee was, of course, not German by birth).

Max Beckmann emerged as probably the most widely exhibited and admired German artist. In 1940 he was invited by the Art Institute of Chicago to teach at its summer school but was unable to obtain a visa to go there. Later that year, when his work was shown in Cambridge, William Germain Dooley wrote in the *Boston Transcript*: "If ever an artist reflected with merciless eloquence a brief but agonizing experiment in world history, it is Max Beckmann whose first large exhibition in this country has just opened at the Germanic Museum."[38] Soon after the show closed, the museum purchased Beckmann's self-portrait of 1927 from the Buchholz Gallery.

The proliferation of exhibitions of modern German art which occurred in 1938–39 ended in the early 1940s as the war spread in Europe. Travel and commerce became more restricted. Significantly the Carnegie International Exhibition of Paintings showed only

American art throughout the 1940s. As European countries declared war on Germany, many American museums shifted their policies and focused on art of the Americas. Barr's "Report of the Director" in the Museum of Modern Art's annual report for the year ending July 1, 1940, included a section devoted to "The Museum and the World Crisis":

> But far more serious questions confronted the Museum in the terrible month of June, 1940. The catastrophe in Western Europe suddenly created an emergency toward which the Museum, profoundly concerned with the preservation of cultural freedom, could not remain indifferent. "The Museum studied its program in relation to a sense of new and wider responsibility. It studied the question of American morale. Could not the American's pride in his own civilization be confirmed by pointing to achievements in the arts?... Long before the fateful month of June the Trustees had been interested unofficially in the national effort to further cultural relations with Latin America.... The Museum also studied the problem of the artist in the world crisis: how to help the American artist confronted by dwindling government support and a public distracted by threat of war; and how to help salvage European art menaced by Nazi tyranny which as the year closed had laid hold of Paris, thereby creating a new wave of refugee artists whose experimental art and anti-Nazi sympathies put them in hazard."[39]

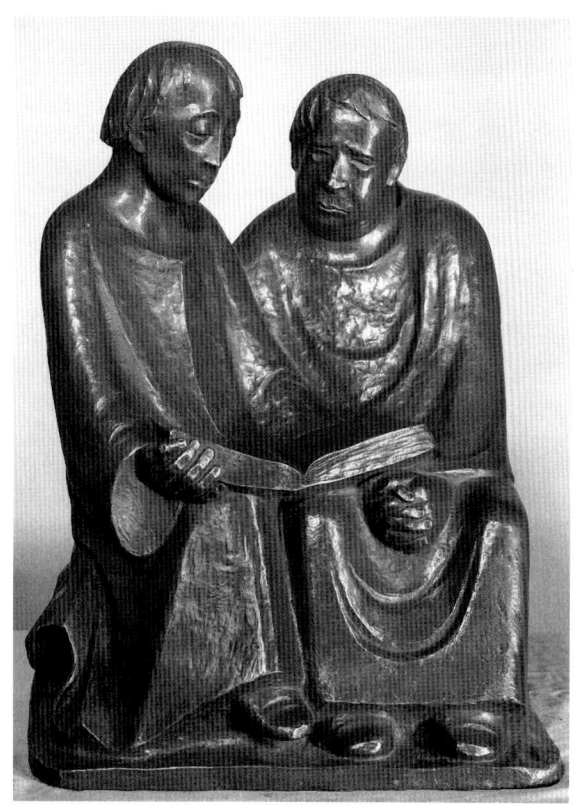

274
Ernst Barlach; *Monks Reading*, 1932; bronze; h: 23½ in. (59.7 cm); The Art Institute of Chicago, Samuel P. Avery Fund, 1938.1166.

As the *New York Times* reported during the exhibition *Landmarks in Modern German Art* at the Buchholz Gallery: "Slowly but steadily the modern 'degenerate' art that the Nazis drove out of Germany appears to be finding new permanent homes in America. Curt Valentin, director of the Buchholz Gallery, mentions that within the last year paintings once belonging to German museums have been acquired by the Museum of Modern Art in New York, the Chicago Art Institute and the Rhode Island School of Design in Providence."[40] In 1940 the Art Institute of Chicago purchased Barlach's *Monks Reading* (1932; fig. 274) and was given a Lehmbruck sculpture, *Bust of Kneeling Woman* (1911).[41] Since 1938 the director of the Rhode Island School of Design had been Alexander Dorner, previously director of the Provinzialmuseum (now the Landesmuseum) in Hannover. After becoming director of the City Art Museum of Saint Louis in 1940, Perry Rathbone acquired Feininger's picture *The Glorious Victory of the Sloop Maria* (1926; formerly in the Staatsgalerie, Dresden) from the Buchholz Gallery. The following year he added to the collection Kokoschka's painting *Harbor of Marseilles* (1925), Käthe Kollwitz's bronze *Self-Portrait* (1926–36), and Klee's *Polyphonic Architecture* (1936). In the museum's annual report he observed, "These three works of high aesthetic importance in themselves afford the added satisfaction that we in America have the liberty to enjoy what has been branded as 'degenerate' by the Nazis and erased from German museums."[42]

During the summer of 1942 the Museum of Modern Art displayed *New Acquisitions: Free German Art*, which included Beckmann's triptych *Departure* (1932–35), purchased from Valentin, and Barlach's *Head* (1927), given by Edward M. M. Warburg.[43] Phrases such as "Nazi ban," "verboten art," "forbidden art," and its converse, "free art," were used in newspaper articles. On June 28, 1942, the *New York Times* quoted a statement issued by Barr:

> Among the freedoms which the Nazis have destroyed, none has been more cynically perverted, more brutally stamped upon, than the Freedom of Art. For not only must the artist of Nazi Germany bow to political tyranny, he must also conform to the personal taste of that great art connoisseur, Adolf Hitler.... But German artists of spirit and integrity have refused to conform. They have gone into exile or slipped into anxious obscurity. Of all the painters and sculptors who made the pre-Nazi German school second in Europe only to that of Paris, almost none is now honored and few are tolerated in Germany today. Their paintings and sculptures, too, have been hidden or exiled, even those that were once the pride of German museums. But in free countries they can still be seen, can still bear witness to the survival of a free German culture.[44]

It was in the spring of 1943 that Feininger, reflecting upon the previous year, wrote to Scheyer: "To speak of the events of the past winter, the outstanding one was perhaps the award for, and purchase of, my 'Gelmeroda' by the Metropolitan [Museum of Art]... It is our fate for all of us, to be outcasts from Europe; our works are scattered away, most of them here now; and with their dispersal, gone is the 'aura' of our reputations."[45]

In 1942–43 the American involvement in World War II and resultant expressions of patriotism were reflected in museum exhibitions as well as press releases. Moreover, museum schedules were sharply curtailed as many museum directors and curators took leaves of absence to serve in the military. During the war years German art was not shown in American museums,[46] and the New York dealers encountered greater difficulty in selling works. After the United States declared war on Germany, the status of German citizens shifted as their country officially became the enemy. Ironically Hilla von Rebay, still a German citizen, was detained as an enemy alien in the autumn of 1942, although she and Solomon Guggenheim had helped bring Rudolf Bauer and Hans Richter to the States.[47] In contrast, Grosz showed in the Whitney Annuals during the war years and was awarded second prize in the Carnegie Annual in 1945 for his painting *Survivor* (1944; fig. 266, cat. no. 58).

After the war in Europe ended, Nierendorf presented the exhibition *Forbidden Art in the Third Reich,* which traveled subsequently to the Institute of Modern Art in Boston (see fig. 275).[48] It was only then, in October 1945, concurrent with Nierendorf's show, that Barr's articles on art in the Third Reich were published in *Magazine of Art*.[49] The point was not lost that the essays had been written in May 1933, after his stay in Stuttgart, but were published only after the defeat of the Nazis. In his prefatory comments Jacques Barzun recalled that he too had been in Germany around 1933–34 and observed that Hitler's concern with art was part of his political plan. Barzun concluded: "The moral is plain:... 'In times of revolution, art follows politics as the convict follows the guard.'"[50]

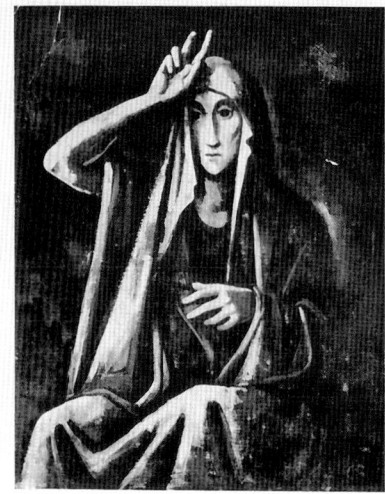

275
Cover of the exhibition catalogue for *Forbidden Art in the Third Reich*, 1945. Karl Hofer's *Cassandra* is illustrated.

Notes

1 Alfred H. Barr Jr., *German Painting and Sculpture*, exh. cat. (New York: Museum of Modern Art, 1931), 14. The first major exhibition of modern German art in the United States took place in New York in October 1923; see W. R. Valentiner, *A Collection of Modern German Art*, exh. cat. (New York: Anderson Galleries, 1923), and Penny Joy Bealle, *Obstacles and Advocates: Factors Influencing the Introduction of Modern Art from Germany to New York City, 1912–1933: Major Promoters and Exhibitions* (Ann Arbor, Mich.: UMI Press, 1990).

2 *Bulletin of the Museum of Modern Art* 1 (June 1933): 4.

3 M. Kay Flavell, *George Grosz: A Biography* (New Haven and London: Yale University Press, 1988), 72–105.

4 Warburg to Barr, 31 August 1933 (Archives of American Art [hereafter AAA]: 2164; 1209). For a fascinating account of Barr's friendships and the Harvard Society for Contemporary Art, see Nicholas Fox Weber, *Patron Saints: Five Rebels Who Opened America to a New Art, 1928–1943* (New York: Alfred A. Knopf, 1992).

5 Peter Nisbet and Emilie Norris, *The Busch-Reisinger Museum: History and Holdings* (Cambridge: Harvard University Art Museums, 1991), 21–22.

6 Kuhn to Cohn, 29 October 1935 (Busch-Reisinger Museum, file for Grosz exhibition).

7 *The Christian Science Monitor*, 2 December 1935.

8 See Sara Campbell, ed., *The Blue Four Galka Scheyer Collection: Norton Simon Museum of Art at Pasadena* (Pasadena, Calif.: Norton Simon Museum of Art, 1976).

9 *Los Angeles Times*, 23 June 1935.

10 Neumeyer to Scheyer, 20 January 1936 (Norton Simon Museum of Art, Blue Four Galka Scheyer Archive). See also Peter Selz, "The Impact from Abroad," in "California: The Modernist Impulse, 1900–1950" (unpublished ms., AAA), 20–24.

11 M. D., "A New Gallery Opens with a Show of Moderns," *Art News* 35 (27 February 1937): 15.

12 M. D., "German Twentieth Century Expressionists," *Art News* 35 (15 May 1937): 15.

13 *Annual Report* (Cambridge: Germanic Museum, Harvard University, 1938)

14 *New York Times*, 11 December 1938.

15 Museum of Modern Art Archives, registrar's file for *The Bauhaus, 1919–1928* (exhibit #82).

16 Valentin to Rebay, 19 September 1938 (Hilla von Rebay Archive, Solomon R. Guggenheim Museum). Among Valentin's papers at the Museum of Modern Art, there is virtually no correspondence before 1946.

17 August Klipstein to Rebay, 20 April and 22 May 1939 (Hilla von Rebay Archive), and accession records (registrar's office, Solomon R. Guggenheim Museum).

18 *New York Herald Tribune*, 25 September 1938.

19 *Golden Gate International Exposition: Contemporary Art*, exh. cat. (San Francisco: San Francisco Bay Exposition Company, 1939), 6–10. See also *Art Digest* 13 (15 March 1939): 15–47.

20 Laura Z. Hobson, "Freedom Pavilion," *Nation* 148 (29 April 1939): 492–98.

21 Margaret Sterne, *The Passionate Eye: The Life of William R. Valentiner* (Detroit: Wayne State University Press, 1980), 251–58.

22 *Art of Tomorrow: Fifth Catalogue of the Solomon R. Guggenheim Collection of Non-Objective Paintings*, exh. cat. (New York: Solomon R. Guggenheim Foundation, 1939). In this and other catalogues Rebay differentiated between nonobjective works and paintings with objects. The latter were listed in the back and not illustrated.

23 "Exiled Art Finds Haven in Modern Museum," *Art Digest* 13 (1 September 1939): 8.

24 "New York: Exiled Europeans," *Art News* 37 (16 September 1939): 16.

25 A brochure entitled *Exhibition of 20th Century (Banned) German Art* was published, listing seventy-six works and stating that the exhibition was circulated by Blanche A. Byerley. See also "Nazi-Banned Art Comes to American Shores," *Art Digest* 13 (15 May 1939): 19, and "Milwaukee: The German 'Degenerate' Art Show on Tour," *Art News* 37 (10 June 1939): 18.

26 Abbott to Barr, 23 August 1939 (AAA: 2165; 697). A similar point of view was expressed in the minutes of the meeting of the trustees of the Institute of Modern Art in Boston on October 19, 1939 (Archives in the director's office, Institute of Contemporary Art, Boston).

27 Barr to Geier, 5 October 1939 (Museum of Modern Art Archives 11.1/90, circulating exhibition file).

28 *Modern German Art*, exh. cat. (Springfield, Mass.: Springfield Museum of Fine Arts, 1939).

29 "Springfield: A Distinguished Showing of Modern German Art," *Art News* 37 (14 January 1939): 18–19.

30 *Contemporary German Art*, exh. cat. (Boston: Institute of Modern Art, 1939), 5–8.

31 Reinhold Heller, "The Expressionist Challenge: James Plaut and the Institute of Contemporary Art," in *Dissent: The Issue of Modern Art in Boston*, exh. cat. (Boston: Institute of Contemporary Art, 1985), 28–29, 31–32.

32 Mary C. Udall, "German Museums' Nazi-Verboten Art Exhibited in Boston," *Art News* 38 (11 November 1939): 13, 18.

33 *New York Times*, 29 November 1933.

34 *Paintings, Drawings, Prints by George Grosz*, exh. cat. (New York: Museum of Modern Art, 1941), 1.

35 When Feininger's work was included in the exhibition *Paintings by Nineteen Living Americans* at the Museum of Modern Art in 1929, a controversy arose. See Alfred H. Barr Jr., in *Lyonel Feininger—Marsden Hartley*, exh. cat., ed. Dorothy Miller (New York: Museum of Modern Art, 1944), 12–13.

36 Feininger to Janet M. Henrich, 26 September 1938 (Museum of Modern Art Archives, registrar's file for *The Bauhaus, 1919–1928*).

37 Valentin to Scheyer, 20 December 1939 (Norton Simon Museum of Art, Blue Four Galka Scheyer Archive).

38 *Boston Transcript*, 16 November 1940.

39 *Annual Report to the Board of Trustees and Members, 1939–1940* (New York: Museum of Modern Art, 1940), 10–11.

40 *New York Times*, 5 April 1940.

41 Dorothy Odenheimer, "Lehmbruck and Barlach," *Art Institute of Chicago Bulletin* 34 (1940): 41–42.

42 Perry T. Rathbone, "Report of the Director," *Annual Report, 1941–1942* (Saint Louis: City Art Museum of Saint Louis, 1942), 20.

43 No catalogue was published, but information about the eighteen works is found in the June 24, 1942, issues of the *New York Times*, *New York Herald Tribune*, and *New York World-Telegram*.

44 *New York Times*, 28 June 1942.

45 Feininger to Scheyer, 9 May 1943 (Houghton Library, Harvard University: bMS Ger 146.1; 2445).

46 An exception was the San Francisco Museum of Art, where both an exhibition of works by Josef Scharl and a Kokoschka show took place in 1944.

47 Joan M. Lukach, *Hilla Rebay: In Search of the Spirit in Art* (New York: George Braziller, 1983) 163–66, 173–74.

48 The catalogue was subtitled "Paintings by German Artists Whose Work Was Banned from Museums and Forbidden to Exhibit."

49 Alfred H. Barr Jr., "Art in the Third Reich—Preview, 1933," *Magazine of Art* 38 (October 1945): 212–22. The essays were written in 1933 in Ascona, Switzerland, after his experiences in Stuttgart, Germany.

50 "Editorial and a Memorandum from Jacques Barzun," *Magazine of Art* 38 (October 1945): 221.

276
George Grosz, *The Wanderer*, 1943 (cat. no. 57).

the loss of homeland and
cultural identity

SABINE ECKMANN   george grosz
lyonel feininger

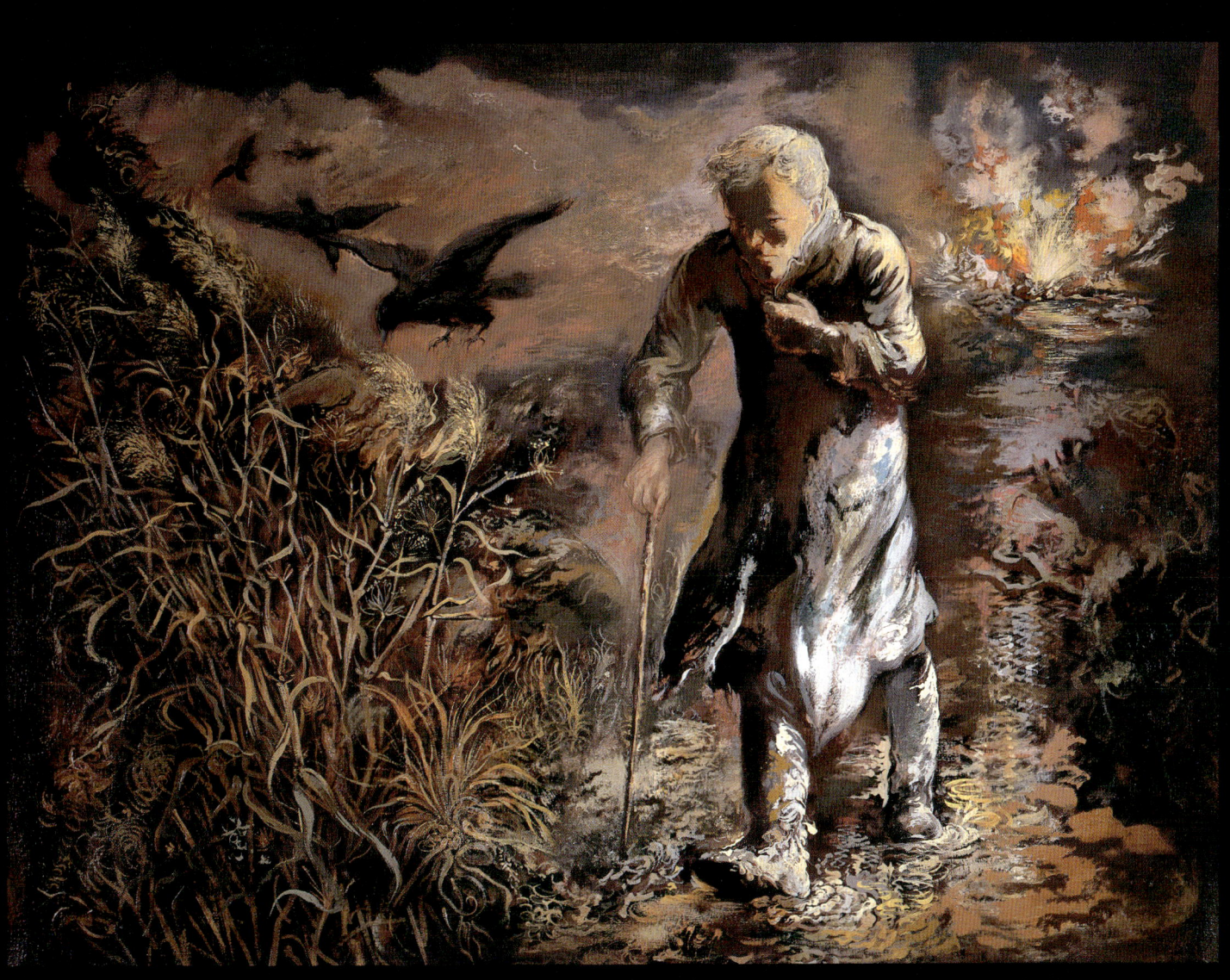

george grosz in new york, 1933–45

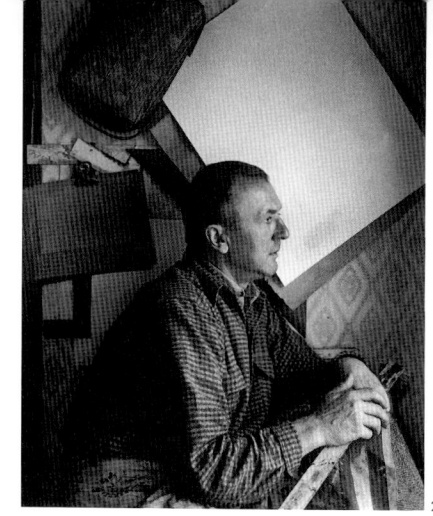

277

1893	born in Berlin
1933	immigrates to the U.S. (New York)
1959	returns to Germany (West Berlin)
1959	dies in West Berlin

I really haven't brought it off. I can never become a genuine American. Thus, I am after all, nothing more—yes, than a demoralized and forgotten German.[1]

Like many of his contemporaries in Weimar Germany, George Grosz had had a strong fascination with the New World since childhood. After he finally immigrated to the United States in 1933, however, his absorption with his German heritage—in particular, with contemporary German political, social, and cultural life—proved so strong that he was unable to sever his ties to his homeland. More important than his new culture was his complicated and contradictory struggle with Germany's past and present as well as his goal of redefining his role as a topical, politically conscious German artist.[2]

Grosz decided to emigrate after he had gained some experience of American life while teaching a summer class at the Art Students League in New York City in 1932. He and his wife arrived in New York on January 23, 1933,[3] just days before Hitler assumed power. According to Grosz's letters of 1933, he decided to leave Germany primarily because of the increasing power of the National Socialists and his deep disappointment with the failure of the socialist opposition parties.

In 1931 Grosz had published an article on the subject of German tradition in which he plainly stated his allegiance to Germany and its culture: "Certainly we live in a transitional period.... Whatever the case may be, I regard Germany now as the most interesting and most puzzling country in Europe."[4] In light of this comment it seems surprising that he left Germany two years later, even before the National Socialists had come to power and selected him as a prime target of persecution.[5] Yet the ambivalence inherent in his rejection of Germany through emigration and his continuing obsession with his home country would prove to be paradigmatic for his years spent in exile.

For more than a decade Grosz had identified with a circle of radical left-wing intellectuals and artists who were among the most incisive critics of German society. This group was supported by the German workers' movement and the German Communist party (KPD), and its intellectual discourse was informed by the belief that the realization of socialism, the establishment of a communist society, would end the class struggle and usher in a more just and humane society. Yet already in the early 1920s, after a visit to the Soviet Union in 1922, Grosz had become suspicious of communism and tried to redefine his leftist political agenda.

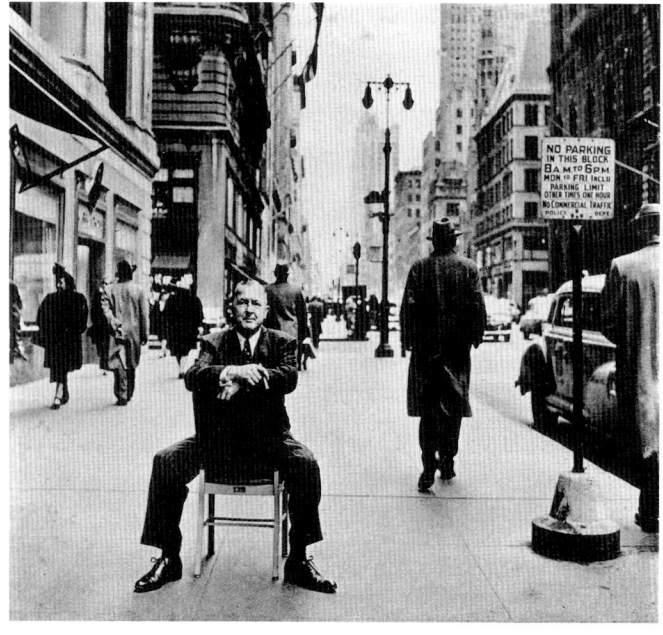

278

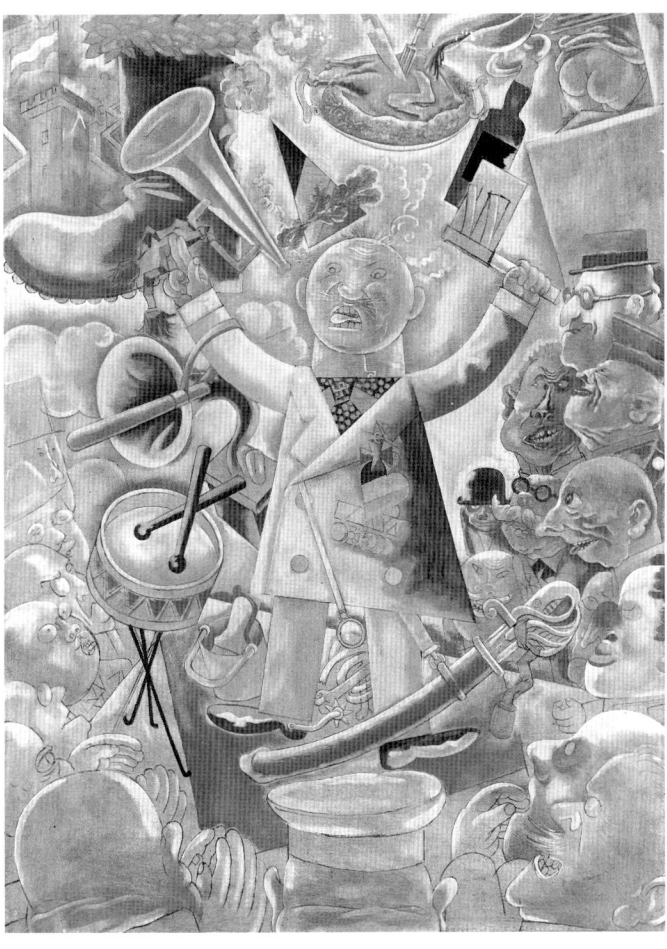

279

277
George Grosz, Bayside, New York, 1942; photograph ©1942 Arnold Newman.

278
George Grosz on Fifth Avenue, New York City.

279
George Grosz; *Rabble Rouser*, 1928; oil on canvas; 42½ x 31⅞ in. (108 x 81 cm); Stedelijk Museum, Amsterdam.

In sharp contrast to some of his friends—such as John Heartfield, Bertolt Brecht, Wieland Herzfelde, and Erwin Piscator—Grosz gradually distanced himself from the German communist movement during the late 1920s and concentrated on aggressively criticizing dogmatism of any kind, whether aligned with ideologies of the right or the left. In paintings such as *Rabble Rouser* of 1928 (fig. 279) he had denounced Adolf Hitler, whose attributes of a bucket and a brush clearly identify him as the *Anstreicher* (house painter or painter). Hitler is depicted as a manipulative ideologue who uses military devices and the radio to seduce the masses.

Even prior to his exile, however, Grosz had begun to question the effectiveness of political art and was trying to alter his well-established identity as a politically active artist on the left. Following his emigration he not only faced the problem of assimilating into a new culture but also had to gain control over his emergent identity, for in America his reputation still rested on his Weimar activities as a moralist and caustic social critic.

His need to forge a new identity was one reason why Grosz committed himself to addressing America and becoming an American.[6] In 1931 he had criticized America by rejecting pure materialism, the American work ethic, and capitalism and by expressing skepticism about the merits of technical progress.[7] Only one year later, during the summer he spent in New York, he defended his new country by evoking clichés, thereby contradicting his earlier critique. In his letters to Herzfelde, Otto Schmalhausen, Max Herrmann-Neisse, and Brecht, among others, Grosz addressed each of them in a different voice, adjusted to suit their individual personalities and points of view. He not only emphasized the cultural diversity of New York City but also described his fascination with advanced technology, for which he used the skyscrapers and the energetic pace of city life as metaphors.[8] In a letter to the KPD-aligned Herzfelde he lauded America for its "childish," "laughing," "energetic," and "youthful" qualities, terms often used in tourist brochures to promote the American dream,[9] which were most effective in provoking and alienating his correspondent. It is striking that, in criticizing the German Socialist movement, Grosz drew upon this popular discourse, which he also used to justify his new life and to paint a picture of a happy, born-again, Americanized Grosz. Yet he also relied on these and similar

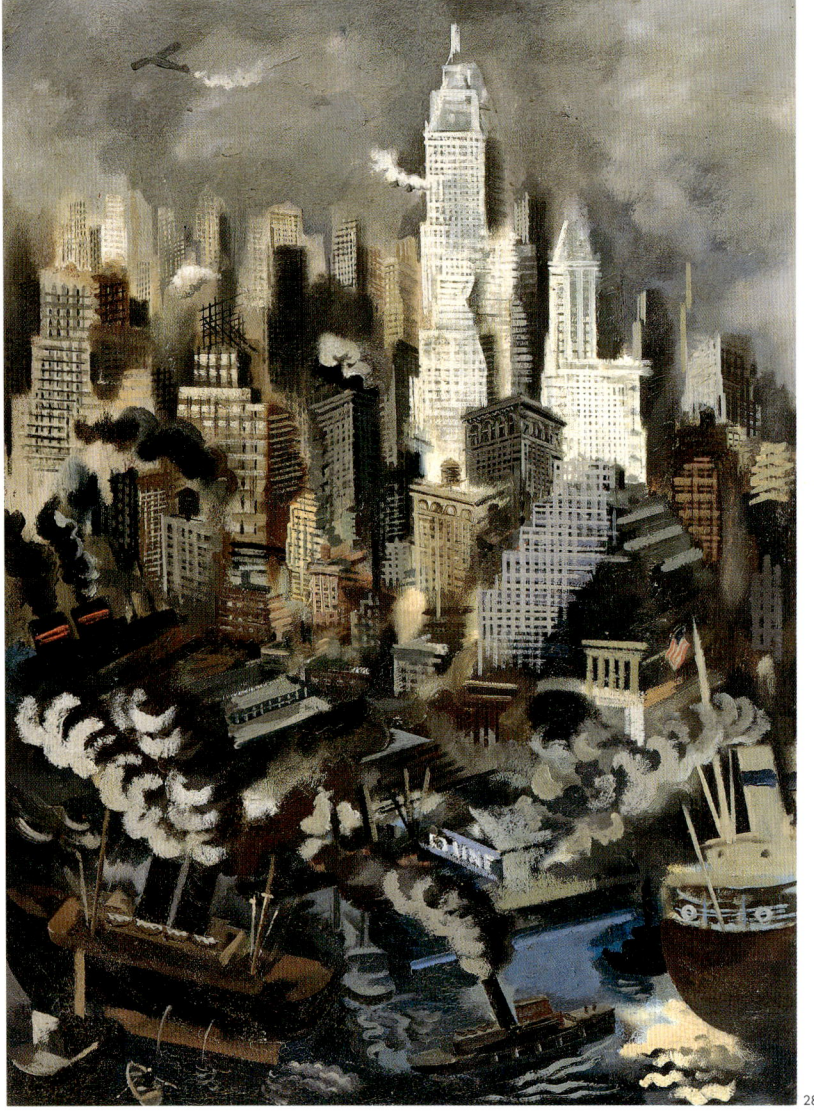

280
George Grosz, *Lower Manhattan*, 1934 (cat. no. 53).

281
George Grosz; *"Hit Him Once More at the Collar, Comrade,"* c. 1935; watercolor; present location unknown.

282
George Grosz, *The Mighty One on a Little Outing Surprised by Two Poets*, 1942 (cat. no. 55).

stereotypes—such as the notion of America as a young, colonial country—to compare his adopted country with Germany in order to expose the ossified and fractured social and political structures of his homeland. Therefore, the main point of these early observations was not, as is often stated,[10] to idealize the United States. I interpret them instead as willful readings in the service of Grosz's objectives of criticizing Germany, provoking his fellow Marxist artists (which resulted in his intellectual isolation), and redefining his own identity by means of negation.

In the light of the Nazi regime, however, Grosz was certainly serious when he claimed that America embodied real democracy: "It is a 'free' country with a 'true democratic' tradition."[11] This view of his new country and his alienation from his earlier leftist affiliations forced him—in contrast to his former position as a critic of German society—to establish an affirmative relationship with the United States. Like many other exiles, he tried to conform to the American norm.

In his depictions of America Grosz often played the role of a quasi-objective illustrator.[12] With the exception of his 1936 portfolio Interregnum, published in a small edition, most of the works he exhibited and published between 1933 and 1939 were watercolors depicting traditional subjects such as landscapes, nudes, and American street scenes. Some of these works, however, such as *Lower Manhattan* (1934; fig. 280, cat. no. 53), are ambivalent. The busy and colorful harbor scene—with cardboardlike skyscrapers symbolizing the young, energetic city—is overshadowed by a dark, ominous sky. It prefigures the apocalyptic allegories that he painted between 1937 and 1945. The defeat in Vienna of the civil uprising against Austrofascism in early 1934 as well as the murder of his friend the leftist writer Erich Mühsam in the concentration camp of Oranienburg in the same year were among the important contemporary political events that Grosz alluded to in this and other paintings that convey a sense of gloom and foreboding.[13] He addressed these themes more directly in social realist drawings such as *"Hit Him Once More at the Collar, Comrade"* (c. 1935; fig. 281) and in many of the works in the Interregnum portfolio.[14] Thus, his critical energies were directed solely toward European politics, specifically Fascism and National Socialism.

Even though Grosz made politically critical art during this period, he usually turned

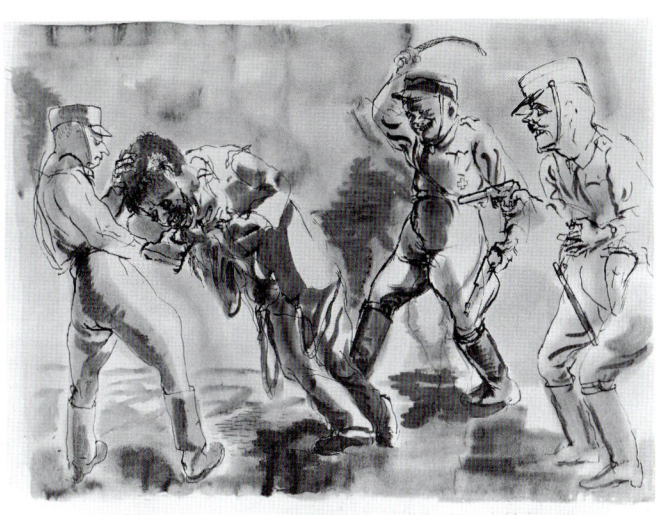

281

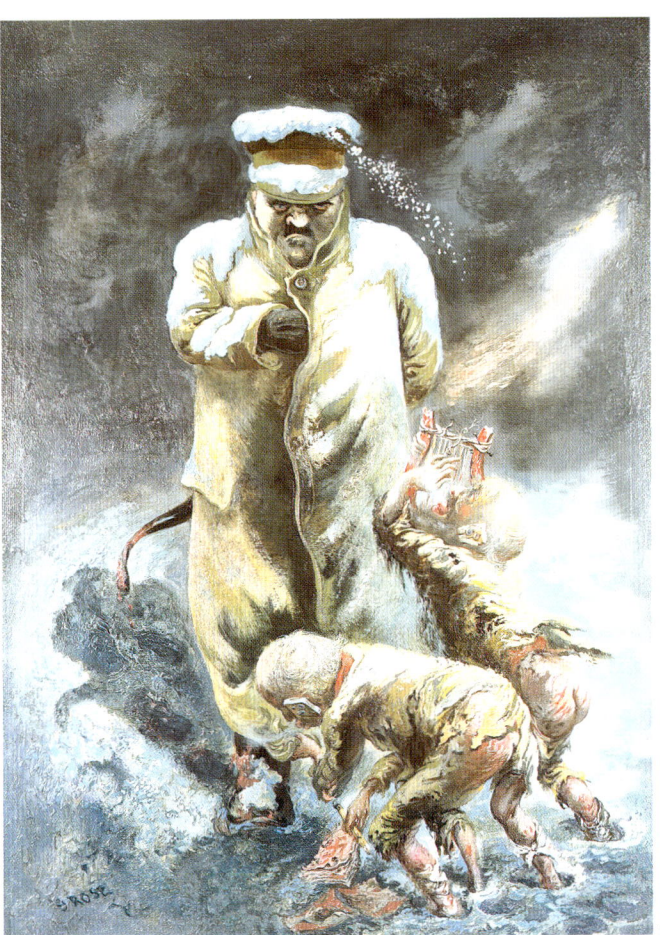

282

down requests to produce work on behalf of political causes. He wrote to Herzfelde: "Before I could still see meaning in my art; today I don't know anymore... one gets rid of visions. I don't show my works to anyone.... For proletarians optimistic cinema and photo are the best."[15] While most German exiles in the 1930s promoted the concept of a better Germany[16] and for a time believed that the National Socialist regime would be short lived, Grosz eschewed German idealism and utopias and countered these beliefs with nihilism. He also refused to join American groups affiliated with the leftist agenda of the American Artists' Congress.[17] *The Mighty One on a Little Outing Surprised by Two Poets* (1942; fig. 282, cat. no. 55), depicts two conformist artists serving a Nietzschean[18] Übermensch (Hitler or Stalin). In this allegory of political oppression Grosz harshly criticizes the concept of art as propaganda for a state ideology by depicting the artists as distorted, dehumanized figures who have completely lost their self-determination.

Grosz tried to stay abreast of events in Germany by carrying on an extensive correspondence and reading exile publications as well as American newspapers. Sometimes he addressed his homesickness—for example, in a letter to Herrmann-Neisse, who was in exile in London—by calling up memories of German food, social intercourse, and costumes. At the same time, however, he showed his disgust for German traditions.[19] This ambivalence not only reflects his disdain for National Socialism but also reveals the problem of the inauthenticity of the immigrant.[20] Like many other immigrants, Grosz lost his sense of authenticity through his physical displacement from his

283
George Grosz, *Remembering*, 1937 (cat. no. 54).

284
George Grosz; *Self-Portrait*, 1937; charcoal on paper; 24⅞ x 18⅞ in. (63.2 x 48.0 cm); Hirshhorn Museum and Sculpture Garden, Smithsonian Institution, gift of Joseph H. Hirshhorn, 1966.

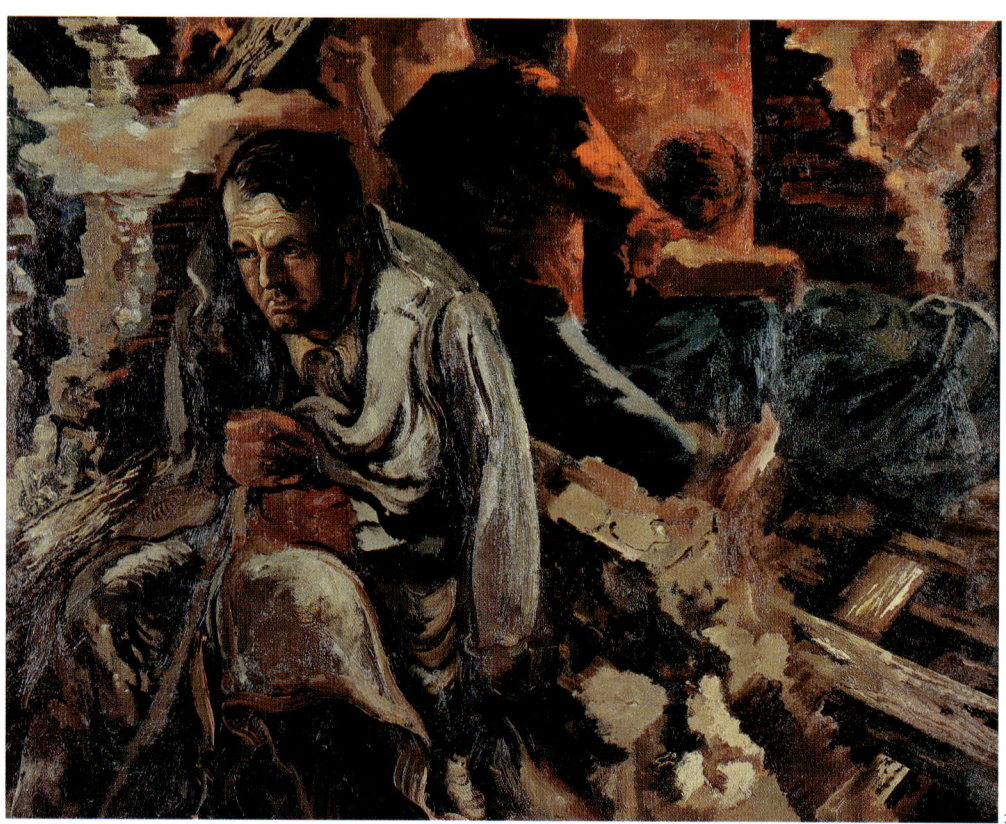

home country, which brings with it a certain estrangement, and also through his failure to assimilate fully into his new culture or to identify with a synthesis of both cultures. He thus wavered between deviation from and conformity to a new norm. The contexts to which he referred were constantly shifting, as were the signs and meanings. This also caused a temporal vacillation between past and present, as thematized by Grosz in his self-portrait *Remembering* (1937; fig. 283, cat. no. 54). A man (Grosz) in the background of the painting carries someone out of a burning house, while in the foreground he is depicted as a refugee in a raincoat. In *The Wanderer* (1943; fig. 276, cat. no. 57) we see him trying to escape from a burning world, heading to an unknown destination. Self-portraiture, with its inherent notions of individualism and authenticity, also played a major role in Grosz's attempt to come to terms with his identity as an artist, an immigrant, and an exile from Nazi Germany. The mirror and the canvas in *Self-Portrait* (1937; fig. 284) symbolize his struggle to manage refracted multiple identities.

Although Grosz stated on several occasions that film and photography are the modern mass media that speak to large audiences,[21] he rejected the use of these and other popular modes for his own artistic practice, even though he had employed such everyday materials in his Dada photomontages of

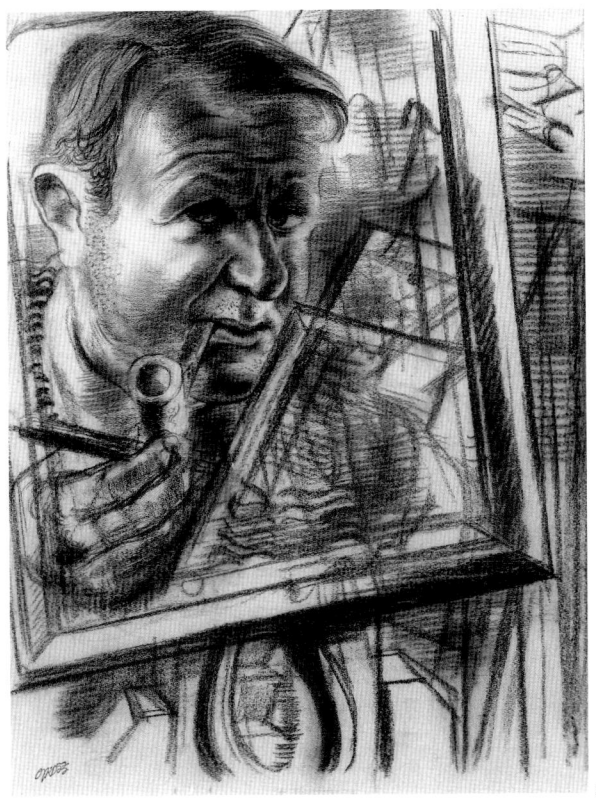

284

1919–20. One reason for this was that his experiences of Nazi Germany and Soviet Russia had given rise to serious misgivings about the efficacy of addressing the masses. He wrote Brecht: "*Mann Bert!* For the stupid, idolatrous masses, one needs neither a Brecht nor a Grosz nor a Heartfield."[22] Nevertheless, in light of his long-standing fascination with American popular culture, it is puzzling that he did not commit himself to the employment of popular images and media. Yet it once more demonstrates Grosz's deep absorption in the German leftist discourse. His use of mass media would most likely have been misinterpreted as enlisting his art as propaganda for the communist political agenda. He denied a request by Max Horkheimer: "I don't think that I am the right man for these propaganda works.... to be generally understood, one has to get down to the so-called mass level. For some years now I have been moving away from that."[23]

Instead Grosz withdrew and attempted to revive other German traditions: "Let us tear down the storehouse of ready-mades and all the manufactured junk and show the ghostly nothing behind them.... Why not return to our ancestors and set forth a German tradition?"[24]

This other tradition was the art of the Danube school, namely artists such as Albrecht Altdorfer and Wolf Huber, and also that of painters of the Dutch school, such as Hieronymus Bosch and Pieter Breughel. As his new artistic mode Grosz chose allegory,[25] which was also adopted by other German and Austrian modernists—including Otto Dix, Oskar Kokoschka, and Rudolph Schlichter—in response to Nazism. Allegory had been foregrounded as an important concept by Walter Benjamin in his *Ursprung des deutschen Trauerspiels* (The origin of German tragic drama), which was first published in 1928, and was subsequently applied to modernism by Theodor W. Adorno, Jürgen Habermas, and Peter Bürger. Benjamin emphasized allegory as an antiaesthetic principle within art itself in which decay and disintegration are thematized. It is especially common during periods when the relationship between sign and meaning is ambiguous.[26] In the practice of allegory Grosz found an artistic mode that allowed him both to maintain his Weimar belief that "art is not a matter of aesthetics"[27] and to distance himself from social realism.

In addition to expressing despair over political events in Nazi Europe, Grosz embraced irrational beliefs. At a time when Fascism, National Socialism, and also communism were employing ritualistic methods to seduce the masses, Grosz became convinced of the futility of using reason to refute these political ideologies. Instead he engaged himself with artworks that responded to dehumanizing political events with irrational images that cynically challenge the notion of an enlightened humanity, often to the point of fatalism.

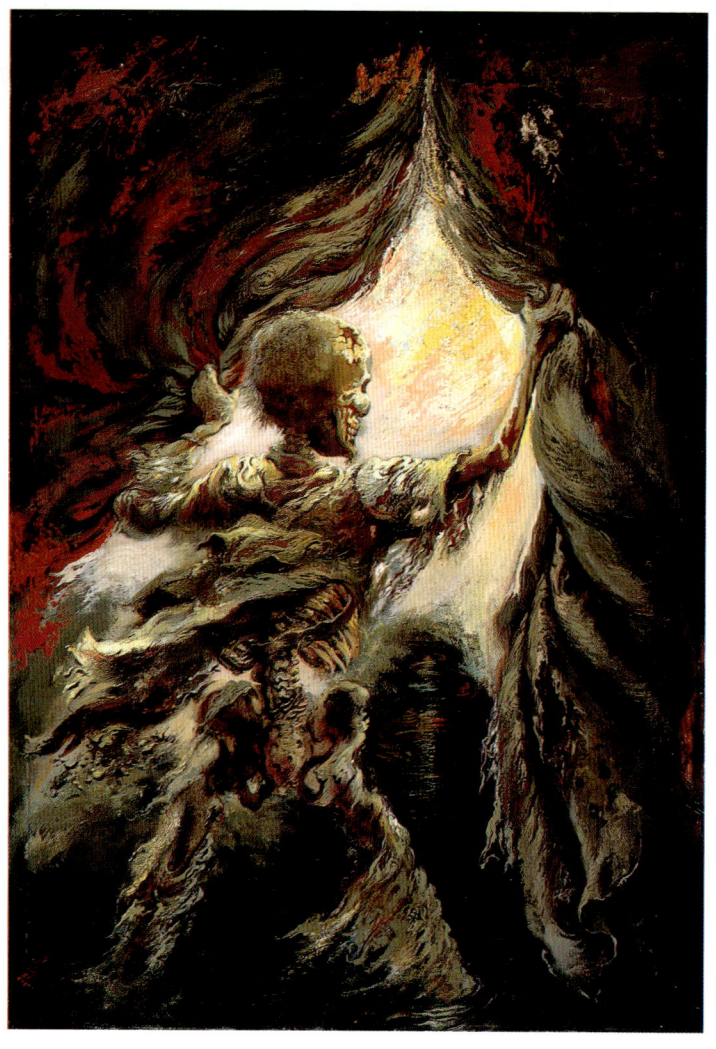

He was drawn to Francisco de Goya's Disasters of War series, for example, which was available to him at New York's Metropolitan Museum of Art, and he tried to follow Goya's example in his own work. In his writings Grosz also emphasized his disbelief in enlightenment. He claimed that he was attracted to the premodern conception of a world ruled by menacing and unpredictable gods: "And, if necessary, I will make the bogeymen and fetishes and medicines myself."[28]

Thus, in political allegories such as *"I'm Glad I Came Back"* (1943; fig. 285, cat. no. 56), which exposes the triumph of death, or *Cain or Hitler in Hell* (1945; fig. 286, cat. no. 59), in which Nazism is identified with the archetypal

285
George Grosz, "I'm Glad I Came Back," 1943 (cat. no. 56).

286
George Grosz, *Cain or Hitler in Hell*, 1945 (cat. no. 59).

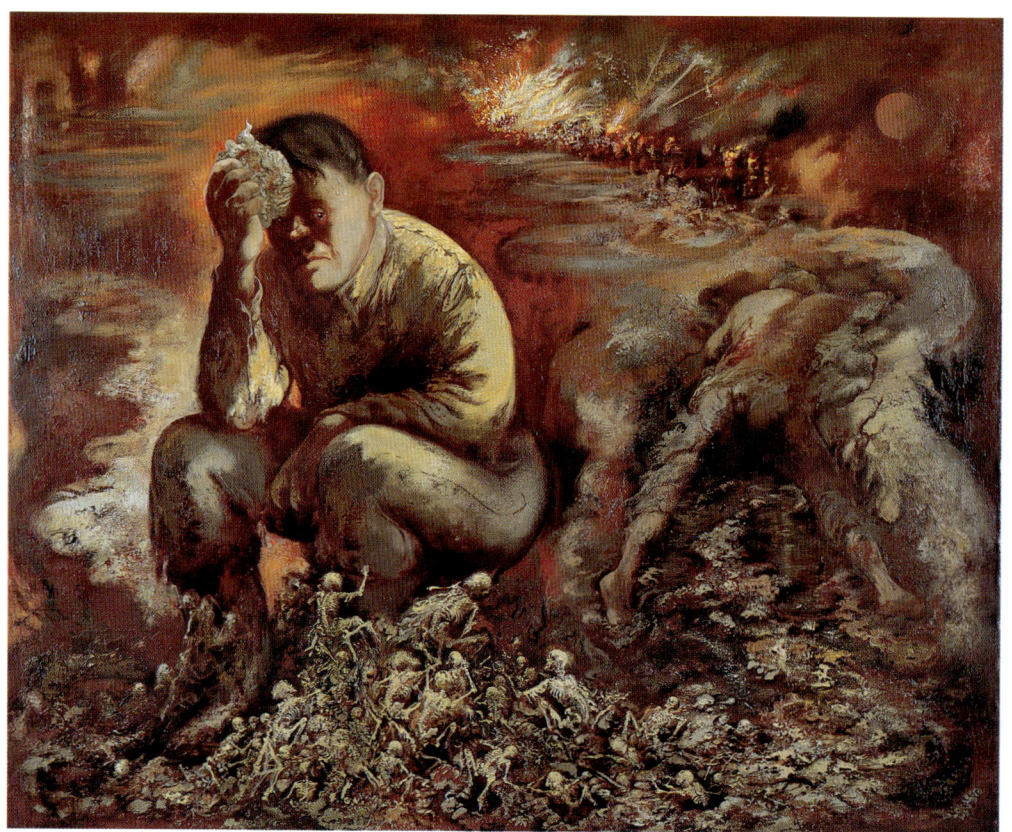

287

George Grosz; *The Painter of the Hole I*, 1948; oil on canvas; 30⅛ x 22⅛ in. (76.5 x 56.2 cm); Hirshhorn Museum and Sculpture Garden, Smithsonian Institution, gift of Joseph H. Hirshhorn, 1966.

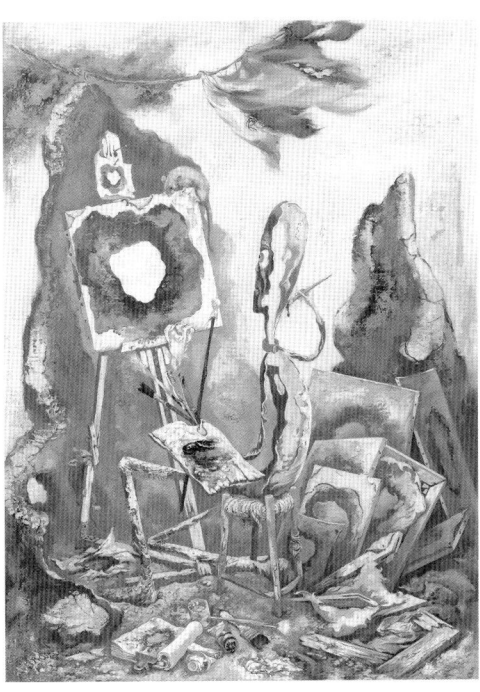

fratricide, Grosz not only leaves the viewer alone in an empty, demoralized world but also likens Nazism to a supernatural force beyond human control. Grosz demonstrates allegory's capacity for multivalence in *The Survivor* (1944; fig. 266, cat. no. 58). We do not know whether the survivor is a victim or a representative of Nazism or Soviet communism, but in either case he is a dehumanized creature.

Although Grosz continued to focus on the relationship between individuals and society during his exile, his work showed no trace of the Weimar moralist who had put forth his commitment to the struggle for a better society through caustic satire. In the end his bitter accusations against National Socialism, and despotic ideologies in general, reveal a senseless world and point beyond it, to irrational beliefs. He thematized this vacuity by using the metaphor of boredom.[29] (Here he was also taking up a German tradition represented by the literary work of Georg Büchner, in particular *Danton's Death*.) Boredom and emptiness are underscored in such images as *The Painter of the Hole I* (1948; fig. 287), not only in the subject matter itself but also in the lack of temporal structure and a traditional aesthetic form.

It was exactly because of the absence of a moralizing quality, rather than, as often noted, because of his retreat from political themes that American critics dismissed Grosz's work. Malcolm Cowley reproached the Interregnum portfolio for being too negative for American taste and lacking a constructive point of view. He stated that "the logical answer—the only logical answer that Grosz can give—is for the modern world to be blown apart by airline bombs."[30] Elizabeth McCausland underpinned this by attacking Grosz for not assuming a moralist stance: "It is not enough to express one's own emotions, one must express the larger truths and enduring goals of human life. Otherwise, [the artist] supports those who trade in death...the potential fascists of all countries."[31] And in 1941 the College Art Association journal *Parnassus* published an unsigned critique in which the reviewer even veered toward the Nationalist Socialist critical vocabulary in dismissing Grosz's work: "This is decadent art, an art which is permeated by a deep-rooted bitterness, which sees in landscape decay and obscenity."[32]

Despite these devastating critiques of his political works of the 1930s and 1940s—mainly the allegories—Grosz was also praised for his earlier achievements as one of the foremost satirists of Weimar Germany, for example, by the Museum of Modern Art in New York on the occasion of his retrospective there. But even Alfred H. Barr Jr., after focusing on Grosz's past as a harsh moralist, noted that "in recent years...his assaults upon human baseness have become less and less apparent." In the face of National Socialism, however, and his newfound conviction that art could not affect society, moralist satire was no longer an option for Grosz.

Because of his grounding in realist traditions, Grosz was considered an outsider by the modern art world. Thomas Craven saw him as an antimodernist,[33] and Clement Greenberg—the advocate of abstract, pure painting—never even mentioned Grosz in his writings of this period. The institutional support he received varied. On the one hand, he built a reputation as a painter of traditional themes in watercolor[34] and participated in group shows of contemporary American art, including the annual exhibitions of the Whitney Museum of American Art and the Carnegie Institute. On the other hand, he was supported as a German exile and famous Weimar satirist. It was due to this latter role that the German emigré dealer J. B. Neumann represented him and that he received a Guggenheim fellowship in 1937 and was the subject of solo shows in 1939 at the Art Institute of Chicago and in 1941 at the Museum of Modern Art (the latter show traveled to ten American cities). These exhibitions did not, however, improve Grosz's prospects on the American art market. On the contrary, his most recent work became more and more difficult to sell.

To interpret George Grosz in American exile, one has to respect a multifold and refracted personality who struggled with his previous German identity and finally adopted a nihilistic, fatalist stance. Yet during the same years he simultaneously tried to become assimilated into American culture. His inability to free himself from or reconcile himself with his German past is also reflected in his apparent devotion to American capitalism, which seems to have been motivated primarily by a perverse desire to shock his former comrades in the socialist movement. Following Boris Groys's argument that "money is in our society the universal sign of inauthenticity,"[35] one might also decode Grosz's attitude toward capitalism as an index of his inauthenticity as an immigrant, especially as it became apparent to him that there was no possibility of establishing a credible identity in America.

Notes

1   George Grosz, in Ulrich Becher, *Der grosse Grosz und eine grosse Zeit* (Reinbeck bei Hamburg: Rowohlt, 1962), 17; translated in Beth Irwin Lewis, *George Grosz: Art and Politics in the Weimar Republic* (Princeton: Princeton University Press, 1991), 233.

2   Grosz's exile in the United States is addressed in Hans Hess, *George Grosz* (New York: Macmillan, 1974); Eva Ingersoll, in *George Grosz,* exh. cat. (Huntington, N.Y.: Heckscher Museum, 1977); Kay M. Flavell, *George Grosz: A Biography* (New Haven and London: Yale University Press, 1988); and, most recently, in Christine Fischer-Defoy, "Der amerikanische Grosz—eine Spurensuche"; Barbara McCloskey, "George Grosz in den USA: Kunst und Anti-Stalinismus in den dreißiger Jahren"; Birgit Möckel, "'A Little Yes and a Big No': George Grosz in Amerika," in *George Grosz: Berlin—New York,* exh. cat., ed. Peter-Klaus Schuster (Berlin: Staatliche Museen zu Berlin—Preußischer Kulturbesitz; Ars Nicolai, 1994).

3   His two sons, Martin and Peter, followed their parents about six months later. Grosz and his wife first settled in Manhattan; later the family lived in the Bayside and Douglaston areas of Queens. Grosz supported his family by teaching at the Art Students League from 1933 to 1936 and again after 1940.

4   George Grosz, "Among Other Things, a Word for German Tradition," in *The Weimar Republic Sourcebook,* ed. Anton Kaes, Martin Jay, and Edward Dimendberg (Berkeley, Los Angeles, and London: University of California Press, 1994), 499; originally published in *Das Kunstblatt* 15, no. 3 (1931): 79–84.

5   Grosz was deprived of his German citizenship in March 1938. His studio and his apartment had already been searched in the spring of 1933 by the Gestapo, however, and his name was published in a list of enemies of the National Socialist regime.

6   Grosz obtained his American citizenship in November 1938.

7   Grosz, "Among Other Things," 500.

8   Grosz to Schmalhausen, 14 July 1932, in Herbert Knust, ed., *George Grosz: Briefe, 1913–1959* (Reinbeck bei Hamburg: Rowohlt, 1979), 148.

9   Grosz to Herzfelde, 23 August 1932, in ibid., 157.

10   See, for example, Möckel, "'A Little Yes and a Big No,'" 283ff.

11   Grosz to Walter Mehring, 17 September 1933, in Knust, ed., *Briefe,* 185.

12   See Möckel, "'A Little Yes and a Big No,'" 284.

13   Grosz to Herzfelde, 30 June 1934, and Grosz to Ulrich Becher, 17 August 1934, in Knust, ed., *Briefe,* 199, 201.

14   Interregnum, published in October 1936 by Black Sun Press, includes sixty-four reproductions of black-and-white drawings executed between 1918 and 1936, in which Grosz criticized the political ideologies of Nazi Germany and Soviet Russia as well as social injustice in a more general sense. One print, for example, deals with Erich Mühsam's murder. The portfolio includes an introduction by John Dos Passos.

15   Grosz to Herzfelde, 30 June 1934, in Knust, ed., *Briefe,* 199.

16   See Keith Holz's essay in this catalogue.

17   For a discussion of Grosz's relationship to the American left, see McCloskey, "George Grosz in den USA," 276–82; see also Flavell, *George Grosz,* 144–55.

18   The painting is dedicated to the German philosopher (Schuster, ed., *George Grosz: Berlin—New York,* 377).

19   Grosz to Herrmann-Neisse, 12 May 1934, and Grosz to Hermann Borchardt, 7 October 1935, in Knust, ed., *Briefe,* 194, 222ff.

20   For a discussion concerning the appearance of inauthenticity as a characteristic of the immigrant, see Boris Groys, "Der Asylant in ästhetischer Hinsicht," in *Deutschsein? Eine Ausstellung zum Fremdenhaß und Gewalt,* exh. cat. (Düsseldorf: Kunsthalle, 1993), 92–97.

21   For example, in the letter to Herzfelde of 30 June 1934 (see note 15); see also Flavell, *George Grosz,* 54ff., 190ff.

22   Grosz to Brecht, 23 May 1935, in Knust, ed., *Briefe,* 217.

23   Grosz to Max Horkheimer, 15 February 1945, in ibid., 344.

24   Grosz, "Among Other Things," 501–2.

25   Allegory is a mode of representation in which abstract, often religious content is visualized through images of emblems, personifications, or deeds. While baroque or nineteenth-century historicist allegories were based on common connotations, modernist allegories often rely on the hermetic subjectivity of an individual artist.

26   In earlier periods, however, allegories did point to a transcendent referent, usually Christian redemption, while those of modern enlightened societies often testify to a "metaphysical homelessness" (Nietzsche) and despair.

27   George Grosz, "Kurzer Abriss (Brief Summary)" (1924), in Uwe M. Schneede, *George Grosz: His Life and Work* (New York: Universe Books, 1979), 82.

28   Grosz to Brecht, 23 May 1935, in Knust, ed., *Briefe,* 216. There are parallels between Grosz's critique of rationality and his embrace of irrationality (in opposition to modern enlightenment) and Max Horkheimer and Theodor W. Adorno's *Dialectic of Enlightenment,* written in 1940 during their exile in Los Angeles and first published in 1947. Horkheimer and Adorno, both philosophers of the Frankfurt School, show the close connection between progressive enlightenment and barbarism.

29   See, for example, his letter to the painter Arnold Rönnebeck of 30 March 1945, in ibid., 347–48.

30   Malcolm Cowley, "Hymn of Hate," *New Republic,* 23 December 1936, 250. In this review of Interregnum Cowley misrepresents the portfolio insofar as he dates it entirely to 1928–32, thus neglecting to inform the reader that major parts of it were executed between 1932 and 1936 while Grosz was already living in the United States.

31   *Springfield (Mass.) Sunday Union and Republican,* 26 March 1939.

32   "Death of an Artist," *Parnassus* 13 (May 1941): 194.

33   Thomas Craven, *Modern Art: The Men, the Movement, the Meaning* (London: Williams and Norgate, 1935), 204–18.

34   See, for example, his 1935 *Exhibition of Watercolors (1933–1934)* at An American Place, New York, or *Painting of the Nude,* Walker Art Galleries, New York, April 1941.

35   Groys, "Der Asylant in ästhetischer Hinsicht," 94.

lyonel feininger in new york, 1937–45

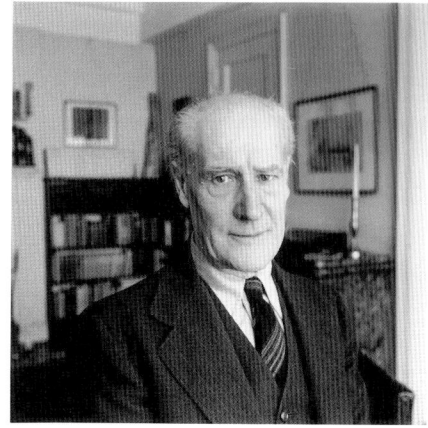

1871 born in New York
1937 emigrates from Germany (Berlin) to the U.S. (New York, Stockbridge, Mass.)
1956 dies in New York

Lyonel Feininger, American by birth and citizenship, went to Germany at age sixteen and established a career as an independent modernist artist with ties to German expressionism and the Bauhaus. His 1931 retrospective at the Nationalgalerie in Berlin, which coincided with his sixtieth birthday, testifies to the significance of his position there. After the National Socialist takeover in 1933, Feininger cautiously observed the transformation of German cultural life. As late as 1935 he was still anticipating that the situation might improve, writing to his wife, Julia: "I still think it is best to preserve silence. I will only say that I am hopeful. (Hopeful! In a hopeless period of cultural history, in a land where all vital cultural elements are systematically persecuted, one is hopeful only for one's own endeavors.)"[1] This statement illuminates Feininger's philosophic and artistic agenda insofar as it stresses his highly individualistic and autonomous approach as well as his conception of the creation of art as a spiritual, transcendent act, removed from the material and political worlds. It is not surprising that he was disinclined to participate in antifascist protests and instead aimed to remain detached and to preserve his privacy.

Although his wife's Jewish ancestry and his own modernist affiliations made him vulnerable to Nazi persecution, Feininger was wary about the prospect of returning to America and even hesitated over an invitation from Mills College in Oakland to teach a summer class in 1936.[2] This was to be his first encounter with the United States in forty-nine years. In addition to his age and his successful German career, Feininger's dedication to German culture also contributed to his reluctance to seek asylum in the United States. He envisioned his prospective artistic life there as a "spiritual death,"[3] a statement that exposes his very European prejudice against the United States as a country where culture had yet to be established. His experiences with the National Socialist regime, however—which included official accusations of being Jewish, a demand by the Reichskulturkammer (Reich chamber of culture) that he prove his Aryan descent, a house search by storm troopers, and the removal of about 378 of his paintings from German museums—must finally have persuaded him.[4] Just days before he left Germany, he acknowledged his appreciation for the democratic cultural policy of the United States. "I feel twenty-five years younger knowing that I will move to a country where fantasy in the arts and abstraction aren't considered absolute crimes, as they are here."[5] On June 11, 1937, he and his wife left Germany for America. Only one month later he was pilloried in the *Entartete Kunst* (Degenerate art) exhibition, which included eight paintings, one watercolor, and thirteen woodcuts by Feininger.

Feininger was not very well known in America. It is true that one of William R. Valentiner's first acquisitions for the Detroit Institute of Arts in 1921 was Feininger's 1913 painting *Sidewheeler,* that Feininger was featured in the Museum of Modern Art's exhibition *Nineteen Living Americans* in 1929, and that in the 1920s Galka Scheyer had promoted him on the West Coast as a member of the Blue Four (along with Alexej von Jawlensky, Wassily Kandinsky, and Paul Klee). Nevertheless, Feininger was perceived by Americans primarily as a German artist, and thus neither cultural

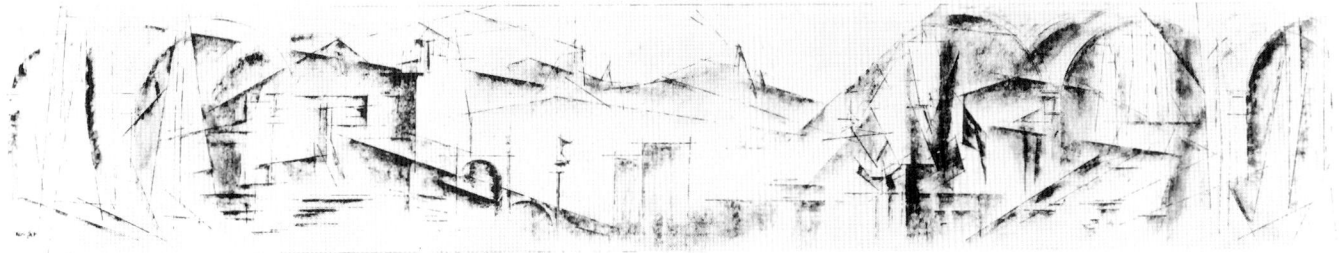

289

288
Lyonel Feininger, 1943; photograph by Josef Breitenbach.

289
Lyonel Feininger; *Landscape with Hills* (design for one of three murals in the Masterpieces of Art Building, New York World's Fair), 1939; pen and ink and watercolor; 9¼ x 50 in. (23.5 x 127 cm); present location unknown.

institutions nor the art market was particularly interested in him. Like other German exile artists, he had to rely on emigré supporters such as Alfred Neumeyer, Alois J. Schardt, and Curt Valentin or on dealers and curators who were at times sympathetic to German art, such as Marian Willard and Alfred H. Barr Jr., the first director of the Museum of Modern Art. It was through Valentiner, who served as director of the art exhibition for the New York World's Fair, that Feininger obtained in 1938–39 his first American commissions, designs for murals for the fair's Marine Transportation Building and Masterpieces of Art Building. In 1941 Valentin and Willard took him under contract, guaranteeing him a monthly income of two hundred dollars.[6] But only in 1944, with the major Feininger retrospective at MoMA, which traveled to ten American cities, was his reputation in the American art world secured.

The transition to American life wasn't easy for the sixty-six-year-old artist, as he admitted to Jawlensky: "Until now I have still not done any painting here. The break was too tremendous to heal easily. . . . Over there: a cemetery of dearest memories; here: impressions that cannot be assessed without a resolute grasp and persistent struggle."[7] In the press release for the MoMA retrospective he described his experience: "I had to readjust myself in every respect and sometimes felt my very identity had shriveled within me." Feininger's solution, however, was not to attempt to synthesize both cultures or rediscover the American one, but to find refuge in his inner world.[8] Only in November of 1939 did he take up painting again. He continued to explore the same themes that had occupied him throughout most of his artistic career—such as Gothic architecture, coastal landscapes, seascapes, and German village scenes—which reflected his attachment to German romanticism, especially the work of Caspar David Friedrich.

In his 1939 watercolor design for the mural of the Masterpieces of Art Building (fig. 289), Feininger emphasized his past by depicting motifs such as sails, boats, viaducts, dunes, the ocean, village church towers, and abstracted architectural compositions. These elements are rendered as prismatic units in a style similar to that he had practiced in Germany. On the one hand, they symbolize his devotion to German spiritualism; on the other, they allowed him to indulge in nostalgic memories. Thus, this work can be read as a narrative of the artist's involuntary journey. The architectural elements on the right and left allude to his past in Germany and his present in the United States, while the seascape in the center suggests his journey by boat from one world to the other.

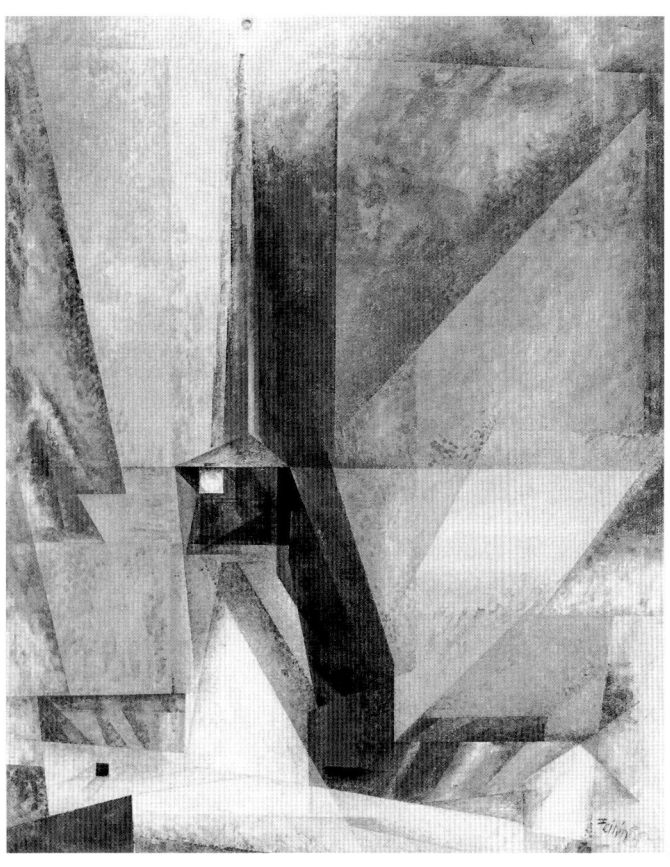

290
Lyonel Feininger; *Church at Gelmeroda (Gelmeroda XIII)*, 1936; oil on canvas; 39½ x 31⅝ in. (100.3 x 80.3 cm); The Metropolitan Museum of Art, George A. Hearn Fund, 1942 (42.158).

291
Lyonel Feininger, *Manhattan II*, 1940 (cat. no. 49).

292
Lyonel Feininger, *Manhattan, Night*, 1940 (cat. no. 50).

According to Roland März, it was "the feeling of an element of longing for the places of the past that made Feininger into a modern Romantic." This element of longing also informed the artist's affection for Germany, which, considering that his early years were spent in the United States, also reveals a typically American attitude toward Europe's centuries-old cultural traditions. He employed the Gothic cathedral as a "paradigm of his inner vision," in contrast to romantic architect and painter Karl Friedrich Schinkel, who used it as a "patriotic symbol."[9] Friedrich also practiced art on a spiritual level but used it to express his hopes for a future society. Whereas the romantic painter condensed reality into images of endlessness and solitude symbolizing his desire for a unified German nation, Feininger, by contrast, dissolved the material world in order to subordinate it to his highly individualized artistic concerns. The romantic trope of the crystalline,[10] which shaped the notion of an ideal society evidently possible only in the realm of art, is visualized in many of Feininger's paintings, such as *Church at Gelmeroda (Gelmeroda XIII)* (1936; fig. 290). In his conception, however, it reveals a dismantled reality and emphasizes an independent artistic practice based on transcendental abstraction and spiritual utopianism.[11] In short, whereas the romantic intellectuals of the nineteenth century believed in an aesthetic utopia that would anticipate a future society, Feininger adhered to a utopia of aesthetics— one not directed toward the material world— a belief also shared at times by other German modernists, such as Kandinsky and Franz Marc. Thus, Feininger stripped the romantic concept of its political topicality.

Feininger's spiritualism required a harmony of life and art which he had encountered in Germany and its culture. In America, however, he could not establish a relationship between his surroundings and his inner self.[12] In 1940 he started work on a series inspired by his fascination with the skyscrapers of New York: "The strands of Manhattan were a wonderful play, colossal boats, forests of masts and cross masts."[13] But he now wanted to depict them "without symbolism, with only the structure and interpenetration, abstract dematerializations, excluding anything episodic."[14] Yet *Manhattan II* (1940; fig. 291, cat. no. 49) still draws on his concept of interspersed flat and

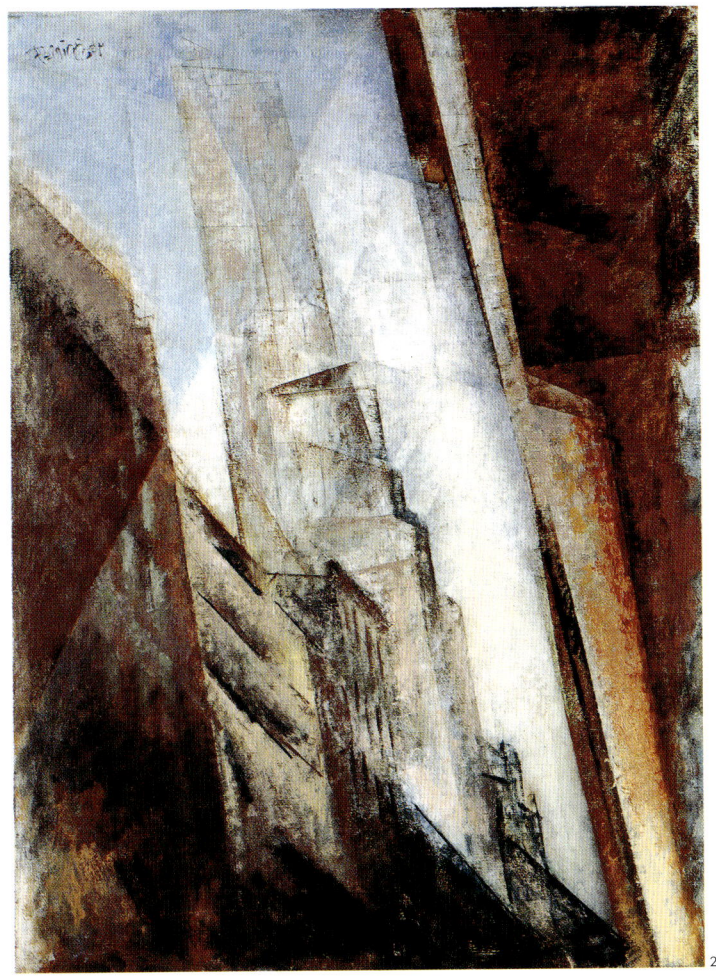
291

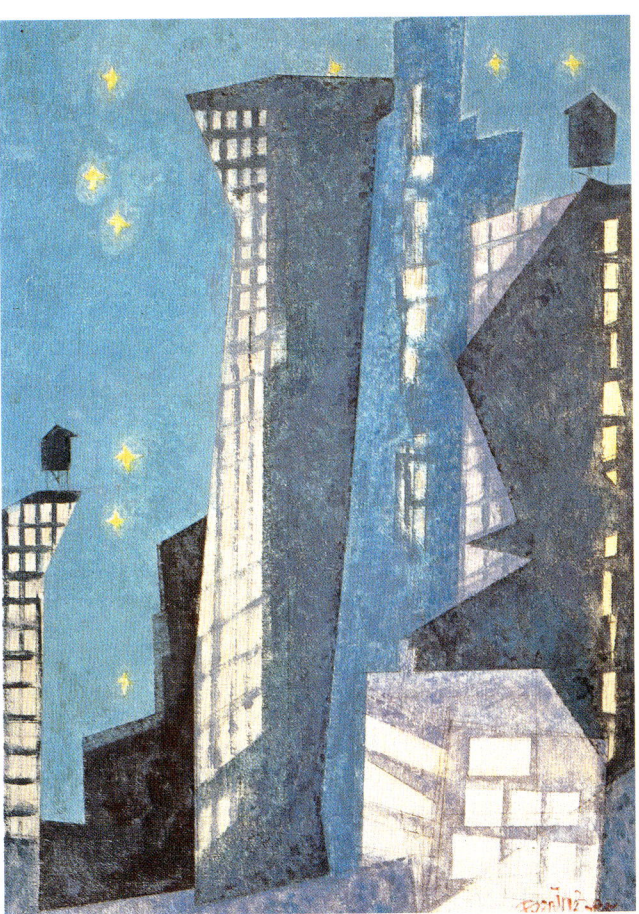
292

transparent planes in vertical orientation, which, as employed in *Church at Gelmeroda,* transcend architectural representation in order to symbolize his inner visions. In the strongly colored *Manhattan, Night* (1940; fig. 292, cat. no. 50), however, the skyscrapers resemble cardboard boxes, effecting not only a dematerialization but also a demonumentalization. In *Manhattan, the Tower* (fig. 293, cat. no. 52) and *Manhattan, Dawn* (fig. 294, cat. no. 51), both of 1944, Feininger offers a new concept. Color and linearity are introduced as independent qualities, with the graphic mode dominant. The skyscrapers are inscribed with thin, barely noticeable pencil scratches—picking out just a few figurative details, such as window frames, roofs, or the outline of buildings— against a background on which almost transparent color is applied expressively.

In a letter of 1942 to Schardt, the former director of the Berlin Nationalgalerie and the Städtisches Museum für Kunst und Kunstgewerbe in Halle, who was then living in Los Angeles, Feininger commented on his altered visual concept and the impact of his new environment, hinting at the liberating political circumstances. "I am working just now on a series of architectural 'visions.'... I had to come to America to free myself of the severe constraint of the straight and rigid line."[15] Adopting the notion of America as a free country in terms of both its political system and its expansive spaces, which allow for more personal freedom, Feininger relinquished volume and mass, thereby eliminating architectural monumentality. In contrast to his monumentalization of German village churches as "crystalline sound-color-pictures"

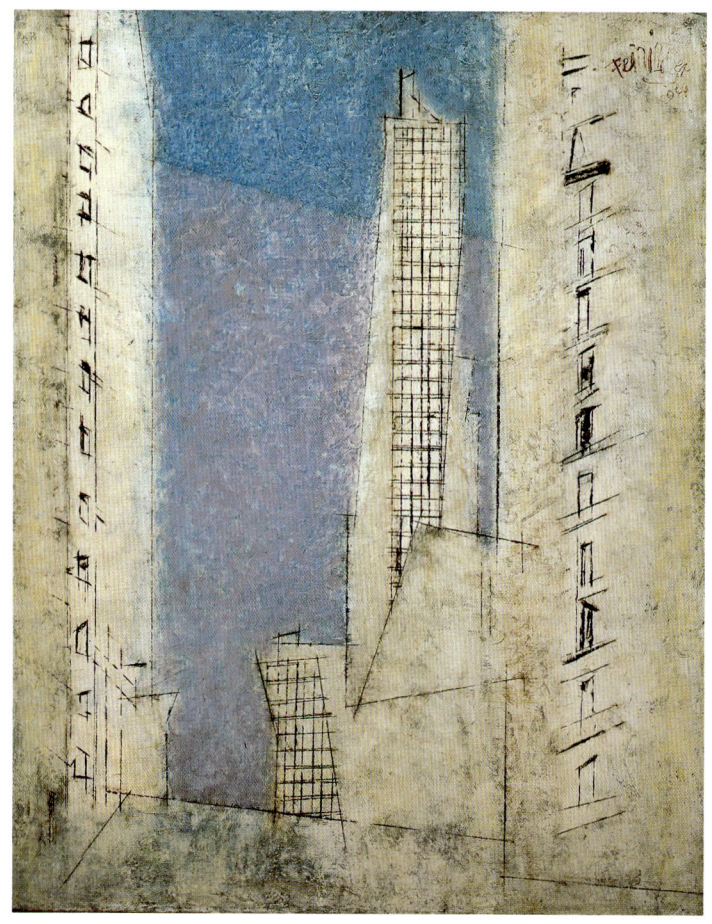

293
Lyonel Feininger, *Manhattan, the Tower*, 1944 (cat. no. 52).

294
Lyonel Feininger, *Manhattan, Dawn*, 1944 (cat. no. 51).

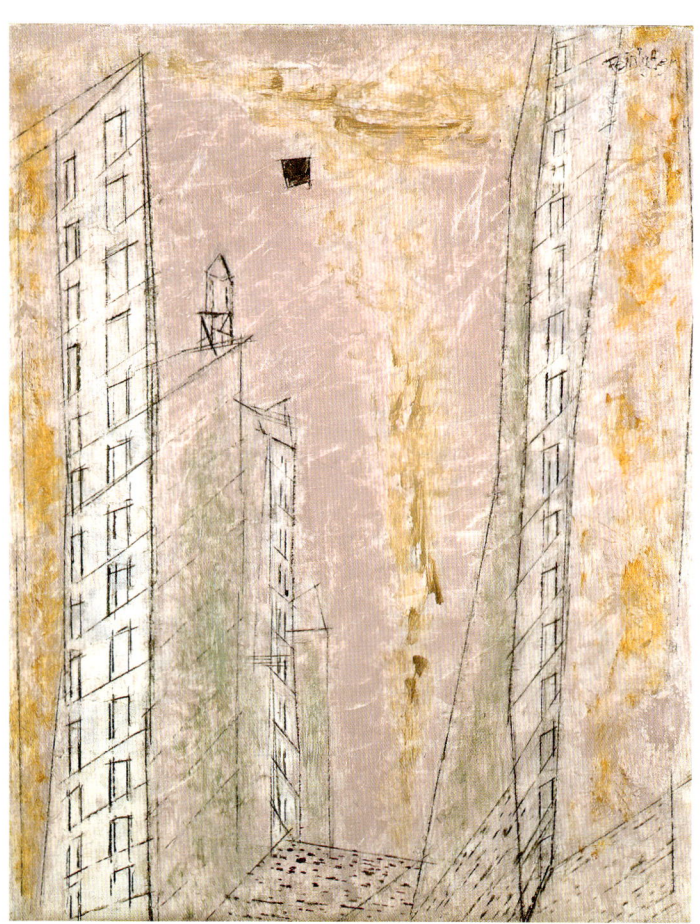

emblematic of his transcendental ideals, he transformed New York's skyscrapers into "dissolved color-light-spaces."[16] They appear humanized and, in comparison to their older German counterparts, uninhabited by metaphysics.[17] The latter quality can be attributed to the fact that Feininger never did find a visualization of his inner world in America. "What I really miss is drawing after nature, making *Notizen* [sketches] at the Baltic, in Deep, or in the villages around Weimar. Somehow I have no satisfaction from the subjects hereabouts; they form too little of my own, inner preference and result only in naturalistic efforts."[18]

Feininger's reception in America was thoroughly positive, even if it fell short of the acclaim he had received from the German art world. Clement Greenberg's assessment was typical: "Feininger always paints with honesty and grace. He is not important in a large sense, but he has a very definite and secure place in contemporary painting."[19] Feininger was regarded by the American press as a "painter of memories"[20] and enchanting pictures,[21] "an architect in the land of beauty."[22] Moreover, the musical affinities in his art were appreciated, and he gained popularity in more conservative circles because his art did not resemble "ultra-modernist" abstract painting. Although the decorative effects of his painting were considered very appealing, there was little interest in his intellectual background.[23]

Both Schardt and Neumeyer tried to clarify Feininger's artistic concept for American audiences, positioning him within the modern movement. On the occasion of Feininger's 1937 exhibition at Mills College, Neumeyer, a former professor of art history in Berlin who taught at Mills after his emigration, took a didactic approach, first introducing his audience to abstract painting in general in order to make Feininger's abstraction more palatable. To explain why Feininger's art was "independent of exterior sensation," he asserted that formal analysis of reality had become the definitive task of modern painting. He further anchored Feininger in modernism by emphasizing the technical precision of his paintings while linking the emotions that they elicit to a sublime or remote world. As the most important elements of Feininger's art, Neumeyer distinguished the "crystalline shapes," embodying the artist's interest in "the infinite and the relationship of matter with the infinite."[24] He thus underscored Feininger's search for higher truth, which is removed from present-day struggles.

Schardt's interpretation was also based on the insight that art, in distancing itself from the material world, can manifest freedom by illuminating a higher truth. He addressed the topical question of "how the individual responds to forces beyond the individual" in reference to Feininger's engagement with the isolation of modern man. According to Schardt, Feininger visualized this as a struggle between vertical and horizontal, or ascending and descending, forces, which ultimately rise upward to the realm of idealized freedom. Feininger had resolved this conflict in the late 1910s by creating paintings that symbolize man's ability to unite opposing forces. His recent American works were "variations of the same theme: creative forces." His art had thus become "a symbol of man's striving toward security and freedom."[25]

Both Germans alluded to Feininger's involvement with German intellectual thought and, by focusing on his search for "higher truth," they implicitly defended his apolitical stance. They also demonstrated their own attachment to the spiritual, which in their view transcended current political circumstances, and, in particular, revealed their belief in a utopia of aesthetics. Barr, by contrast, in the catalogue of the MoMA retrospective, aimed to demonstrate that Feininger was an American artist who was completely indebted to the American tradition. He asserted that Feininger's childhood experiences shaped his art fundamentally: "And so before he left America at the age of sixteen, . . . Feininger seems to have absorbed in New York many of the essential elements of his art." Barr further argued that Feininger had always thought of himself as an American, quoting from a letter written in 1924 to Julia Feininger: "My American childhood had got to me and I became acutely conscious of the poisonous atmosphere

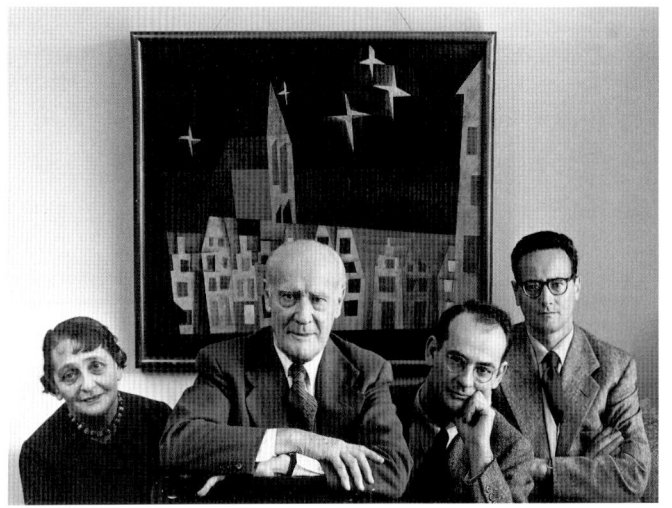

295
Lyonel Feininger with his wife, Julia, and sons Andreas and Lux, New York City, 1951. Photograph ©1951 Arnold Newman.

in which one is living here and that I... am a free American."²⁶ Barr couldn't even discern a resemblance between Feininger and German modernism, be it expressionism or new objectivity. He also pointed out that Kandinsky and Klee, two artists with whom Feininger had been affiliated both as a teacher at the Bauhaus and as a member of the Blue Four, were, respectively, of Russian and Swiss descent.

It is obvious that Barr's promotion of Feininger as an American was politically motivated. In 1944 even the director of New York's Museum of Modern Art could not get away with honoring a German artist with a retrospective exhibition while the rest of the nation was engaged in defeating Germany in World War II. So Barr, who on many other occasions had strongly advocated internationalism, entangled himself in a strange kind of nationalist discourse by confusing the artist's birth country with his intellectual identity, which in the twentieth century is very often related to a different country than that of one's birth. Feininger's intellectual affiliation was certainly with the German romantic movement, with which he shared thematic parallels such as the Baltic landscape and Gothic cathedrals, and with those aspects of German modernism that were invested in the spiritual. But in the end politics caught up with Feininger again in America. Ironically for this artist so devoted to the spirit, the major exhibition that provided his necessary breakthrough on the American art market had to pay its dues to the political realities of the day by promoting him as an American national.

Although Feininger was able to establish himself after a few years as a successful and popular artist, his American exile was marked by alienation from his new environment, which didn't inspire his art as had the German surroundings. As a voluntary resident of Germany, the American-born Feininger came to identify with his adopted country's culture, as did, for example, the Russian-Jewish artist Marc Chagall with France. Both mourned after they were forced into exile in America and indulged in nostalgic memories. Whereas Chagall continued to explore Jewish and Russian themes in his work while embracing French culture, Feininger seems to have suppressed his American heritage, perhaps in order to be able to identify more completely with German intellectual traditions. He even adopted the common European notion of America as lacking a "sophisticated" culture. Feininger's loss exemplifies what Edward Said has called the "rhetoric of belonging."²⁷ Moreover, the events surrounding Feininger's exile made it impossible for him to succeed in his attempt to find refuge in the realm of art as an autonomous domain. Neither the devastating political events in Germany nor America's wartime cultural policies allowed for a retreat; it was repeatedly demonstrated to him that art cannot be practiced outside the material and political world.

Notes

1   Lyonel Feininger to Julia Feininger, 29 March 1935, in June L. Ness, ed., *Lyonel Feininger,* Documentary Monographs in Modern Art (New York: Praeger, 1974), 238.
2   Alfred Fischer, "Lyonel Feininger in Amerika, 1937–1956," in *Lyonel Feininger: Natur-Notizen: Skizzen und Zeichnungen aus dem Busch Reisinger Museum, Harvard University,* exh. cat., ed. Andrea Firmenich and Ulrich Luckhardt (Cologne: Wienand, 1993), 30.
3   T. Lux Feininger, "Lyonel Feininger's 'East German Pictures,'" in *Lyonel Feininger,* exh. cat. (New York: Acquavella Galleries, 1985).
4   Fischer, "Lyonel Feininger in Amerika," 30.
5   Feininger to T. Lux Feininger, 31 May 1937; quoted in *Lyonel Feininger: Städte und Küsten: Aquarelle, Zeichnungen und Druckgraphik,* Ausstellung zum 200. Jubiläum der Albrecht Dürer Gesellschaft (1792–1992) (Marburg: Hitzeroth, 1992), 256 (all translations are by the author).
6   A copy of this contract is in the Curt Valentin Papers at the Museum of Modern Art, New York.
7   Feininger to Alexej von Jawlensky, 27 July 1938, quoted in *Lyonel Feininger: Städte und Küsten,* 256.
8   Press release, Museum of Modern Art Archives, New York.
9   Roland März, "The Cathedral of Romanticism: Gothic Visions of Architecture: Lyonel Feininger and Karl Friedrich Schinkel," in *The Romantic Spirit in German Art, 1790–1990,* exh. cat., ed. Keith Hartley, Henry Meyric Hughes, Peter-Klaus Schuster, and William Vaughan (Edinburgh: Scottish National Gallery of Modern Art; London: Hayward Gallery, South Bank Centre, with the assistance of the Nationalgalerie, Berlin, 1994), 164.
10 In my discussion of Feininger's affinities to nineteenth-century German romanticism and its notion of the crystalline, I have relied primarily on März, "The Cathedral of Romanticism," and Tilmann Osterwold, "Ichperspektive-Bildperspektive-Weltperspektive: Am Beispiel Caspar David Friedrich und Lyonel Feininger," in *Romantik und Gegenwart: Festschrift für Jens Christian Jensen zum 60. Geburtstag,* ed. Ulrich Bischoff (Cologne: DuMont, 1988), 175–83.
11 Osterwold, "Ichperspektive-Bildperspektive-Weltperspektive," 176ff.
12 Fischer, "Lyonel Feininger in Amerika," 32.
13 Feininger to Theodore Spicer-Simson, 18 September 1937, in *Lyonel Feininger: Städte und Küsten,* 256.
14 Quoted in Ulrich Luckhardt, *Lyonel Feininger* (Munich: Prestel, 1989), 46.
15 Quoted ibid., 156.
16 Stephan E. Hauser, in *Lyonel Feininger: Städte und Küsten,* 32.
17 See also März, "The Cathedral of Romanticism," 169, and Alfred Fischer, "Lyonel Feininger in Amerika," 33.
18 Feininger to T. Lux Feininger, 6 October 1953; quoted in Luckhardt, *Lyonel Feininger,* 166.
19 Clement Greenberg, "Review of Exhibitions of Marc Chagall, Lyonel Feininger, and Jackson Pollock," *Nation,* 27 November 1943; reprinted in Clement Greenberg, *The Collected Essays and Criticism,* ed. John O'Brian, vol. 1, *Perceptions and Judgments, 1939–1944* (Chicago: University of Chicago Press, 1986), 165.
20 *San Francisco Chronicle* (East Bay ed.), 22 June 1936 (scrapbook, Mills College Archives).
21 Elizabeth Sacartoff, "Feininger's Pictures Enchant," *P.M.,* 16 March 1941 (Curt Valentin Papers, Museum of Modern Art, New York).
22 Unidentifiable San Francisco newspaper, 17 July 1937 (scrapbook, Mills College Archives).
23 Carlyle Burrows, "Romantic Abstraction," *New York Herald Tribune,* 16 March 1941 (Curt Valentin Papers, Museum of Modern Art, New York).
24 Alfred Neumeyer, "The Art of Lyonel Feininger," typescript of 1937 lecture, 4, 2 (San Francisco Museum of Modern Art Archives).
25 Alois J. Schardt, "Lyonel Feininger," in *Lyonel Feininger—Marsden Hartley,* exh. cat., ed. Dorothy Miller (New York: Museum of Modern Art, 1944), 15, 17.
26 Alfred H. Barr Jr., "Lyonel Feininger—American Artist," in Miller, ed., *Lyonel Feininger—Marsden Hartley,* 8–9, 10.
27 Edward Said, "Reflections on Exile," in *Out There: Marginalization and Contemporary Cultures,* ed. Russell Ferguson et al. (New York: New Museum of Contemporary Art; Cambridge and London: MIT Press, 1990), 359.

transfer and transformation:
the german period in american art history

KAREN MICHELS

In both Britain and the United States generous gestures of welcome were made to art historians driven out of Germany and Austria by the National Socialist regime. British colleagues gave up part of their own salaries to fund aid programs for the refugees, and the transfer of the Warburg Library from Hamburg to London was regarded as a valuable gift. In the United States, which opened its borders by issuing "nonquota" visas, one of the institutions that benefited most from the influx of refugees gave thanks with a wisecrack: "Hitler shakes the tree," said Walter Cook, director of New York University's Institute of Fine Arts, "and I pick up the apples."

The forced migration of German and Austrian art historians to the United States is now seen as the most momentous transmission process in the history of twentieth-century scholarship, comparable in its effects only to the migration of sociologists and psychologists.[1] The conventional wisdom is that the influx of leading talents so advanced the evolution of art historical study in America—where it was still in its infancy—that within a few years it had attained full international parity and in some specialties had taken the lead. In this view the pragmatism and openness of American society, together with the clarity and economy of argument enforced by the use of the English language, detectably influenced the emigré scholars' work for the better, so that they were later able to bring a renewed stimulus to the (now somewhat retarded) practice of the discipline in the countries they had left behind.

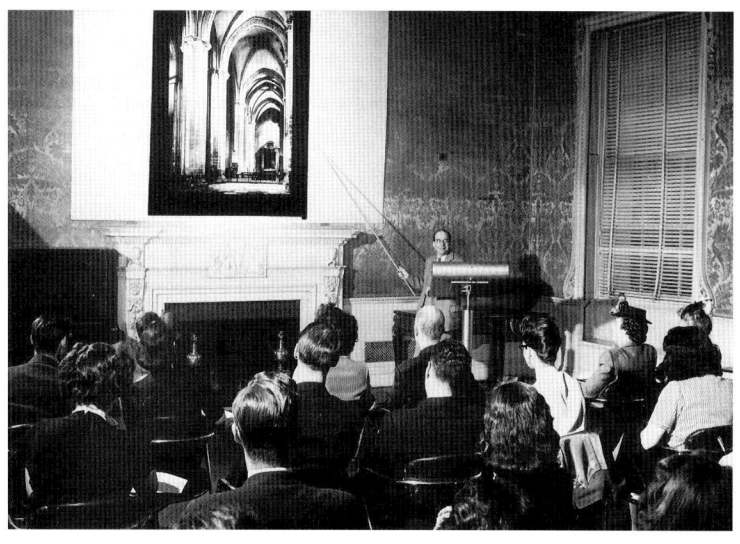

296
Erwin Panofsky lecturing at the Institute of Fine Arts, New York, 1940s.

To this day, nevertheless, there remain problems of communication and mutual comprehension between "American" and "European" or "German" art history—so much so that one has to ask whether this transplant of a whole academic tradition was really so smooth and successful, so irreversible in its outcome, as it might seem. The process has not yet been analyzed in all its complexity; nor have the conditions under which it took place been examined. Only by inquiring into the composition of the emigré group; its modes of access to the American academic scene; the varying receptivity of different regions and institutions; the kinds of career patterns that resulted; the differing situations in teaching, research, and museum work, respectively; and the attendant degrees of social acculturation, can we establish the true nature of what Colin Eisler has called "*Kunstgeschichte* American style."[2]

According to the statistics presently available, art history was one of the disciplines hardest hit by the consequences of National Socialist policy. Some 250 individuals, around one quarter of the total of art history specialists, were dismissed from their posts or prevented from continuing their studies or from working in a freelance capacity. Almost all of these were forced to emigrate. In most cases the reason given was the Jewish ancestry of those concerned or of their spouses, their adherence to Judaism, or—less frequently—their "political unreliability." At least five non-Jewish art historians resigned their posts in protest.

The preferred initial destinations were in Europe, mostly Italy, France, or Switzerland—countries that many emigrés knew from past study trips. More than one-third of the persecuted art historians moved to Great Britain,[3] where one important German art historical institution had already found a home. The transfer of the Kulturwissenschaftliche Bibliothek Warburg, or Warburg Library, to London, though privately funded, serves as an indicator of the solidarity shown by British art historians with their German colleagues. Not only did the Courtauld Institute in London offer support in the form of teaching and research assignments, but periodicals such as the respected *Burlington Magazine* offered the emigré scholars a platform. As an appeal published in the *Burlington* in 1939 reveals, these gestures of solidarity were not based on the infrastructure of a long-standing professional connection. For art history, unlike some other disciplines, had "no home…in which to exercise the hospitality that we should like to extend to art historians no less than to chemists and philologists."[4]

Where the British state was concerned, the welcome was less warm. Work permits were rarely issued, and—at least by the time of the wholesale internment measures taken in 1940—many emigrés came to regard Great Britain merely as a stopping-off point. Among those scholars who did settle there, the two who assimilated most successfully were Ernst H. Gombrich, who served as director of the Warburg Institute from 1959 until 1976, and Nikolaus Pevsner, who became a professor at Birkbeck College, University of London. Pevsner, in particular, became a major cultural influence in his adopted country both as an authority on modern architecture and design and as the editor of two series of books, the Buildings of England and the Pelican History of Art, in which he succeeded in matching standards first set in Germany (the prototypes here being the Dehio-Gall Handbuch der deutschen Kunstdenkmäler and the Handbücher der Kunstwissenschaft). In no small measure both he and Gombrich owed their acceptance to a conscious effort on their part to cross the barriers that often separated the German scholar from the general, nonspecialist public.

What gave Gombrich his unique popularity was his belief that art history needed to be looked at from outside, by considering psychological, sociological, and philosophical factors. Even earlier, however, the Warburg Institute, under its first directors, Fritz Saxl and Gertrud Bing, had deployed a variety of imaginative devices to communicate with the British public. Among these were public lectures and traveling exhibitions, including *Indian Art* (1940), *English Art and the Mediterranean* (1941), and *Portrait and Character* (1943). Though the exhibitions relied exclusively on photographic images, they attracted a large audience at a time when the London museums were closed, their contents having been evacuated.

Perhaps the clearest sign of an incipient process of assimilation was the joint publication, from 1940 onward, of the *Journal of the Warburg and Courtauld Institutes*. In numerous research projects methodologies that had been developed in the German-speaking countries were applied to the study of works of art held in Britain. The title of Pevsner's celebrated book *The Englishness of English Art*,[5] published in 1956, clearly reflects the combination of detachment and intimacy that typified so much of this work.

Two scholars who became itinerants, and thus mediators between British and American culture, were Hugo Buchthal and Edgar Wind, both of whom moved from Hamburg to London, spent years there as university teachers, and then went on to the United States before eventually returning to Great Britain. Buchthal taught Byzantine studies at the Institute of Fine Arts in New York for ten years; Wind went to Smith College before being invited in 1955 to occupy Oxford University's first-ever professorial chair in art history.

Despite its openness to German and Austrian influences when it came to the interpretation of art, British society had no interest in the contemporary art of either country. Alfred Flechtheim, the celebrated art dealer from Berlin, was unsuccessful in promoting German expressionist art in Britain.[6] The art historian Rosa Schapire, who was a committed advocate of the Brücke artists and had managed to get part of her Schmidt-Rottluff collection from Hamburg to London, found herself unable to carry on with her previous work; instead she worked for Pevsner on the Buildings of England.

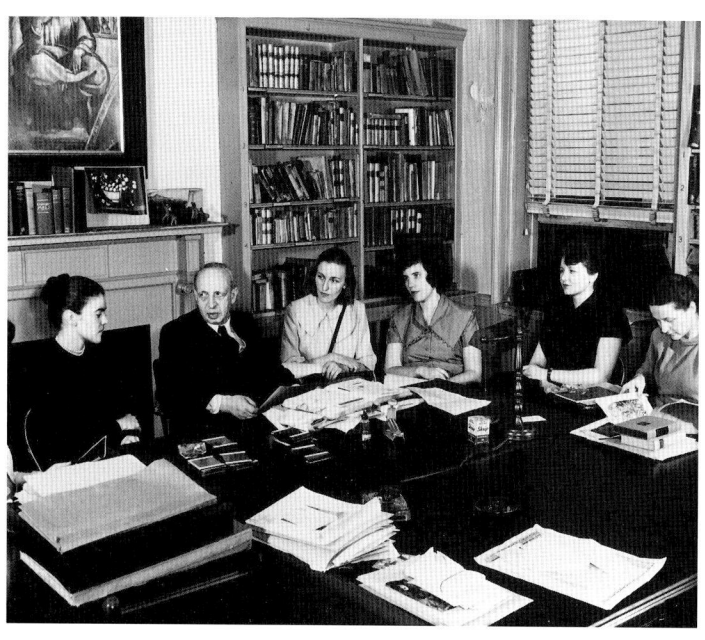

297
Walter Friedlaender conducting a seminar at the Institute of Fine Arts, New York.

By far the largest contingent of refugee art historians found a home in the United States, where many were guaranteed entry under the system of nonquota visas for college faculty members. The group consisted of some 130 people in all, made up as follows: 35 percent university teachers, 25 percent museum workers, 10 percent freelance scholars, and 30 percent recent graduates. The university teachers included just two full professors in the German sense (departmental heads with the title of *ordinarius*): Paul Frankl from Halle and Erwin Panofsky from Hamburg (see fig. 296).[7] The fact is that in art history only 10 percent of these exalted posts—three out of thirty—had been occupied by scholars of Jewish origin.[8] Both Frankl and Panofsky were distinguished figures in the German-speaking world, but they were not among those internationally known art historians—such as Adolph Goldschmidt, Wilhelm Worringer, and, above all, the members of the Vienna School, including Max Dvořák, August Schmarsow, and Josef Strzygowski—whose reputations had already reached the United States. Though well known in Germany for his work on mannerism, Walter Friedlaender (see fig. 297), an untenured (or "extraordinary") professor from Freiburg whose Jewish origins had robbed him of promotion to *ordinarius* rank, arrived in the United States only to be mistaken for his far more celebrated namesake, Max J. Friedländer, director of the Berlin Museum.[9] Panofsky owed his invitation to New York to a recommendation from Goldschmidt, as did a number of others, including Arthur Haseloff, a manuscript specialist from Kiel, who, like Panofsky, was a regular guest professor at New York University but who, unlike Panofsky, ultimately returned to Germany.

Along with those just named, the overwhelming majority of those who are counted today among the "important art historians...[who] turned their backs on Germany...Rudolf Wittkower, Richard Krautheimer, Charles de Tolnay, Alfred Neumeyer, Ernst Kris, Emil Kaufmann, Alexander Dorner, Justus Bier, Paul Zucker, William Suida, Edgar Wind, Rudolf Arnheim"[10]—and to this list should be added Adolf Katzenellenbogen, Ernst Kitzinger, Horst W. (Peter) Janson, William S. Heckscher (see fig. 298), Wolfgang Stechow, Julius Held, and Max Raphael—enjoyed no prior international reputation on their arrival in America. Nor, indeed, should we underestimate the number of emigrés who never did gain such a reputation but who spent their lives teaching at small colleges or pursuing other occupations, beyond the ken of the specialist world.

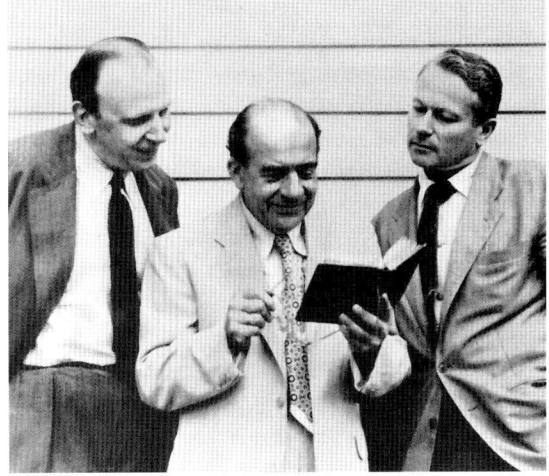

In gaining entry to the American academic world, the art historians most hampered by this relative obscurity were those who were just beginning their careers. Access to the American universities was controlled by the major aid organizations and foundations,[11] which powerfully influenced the placing of exiled scholars through the financing of temporary teaching posts. In accordance with the principle of "enriching our national education," these agencies applied criteria that favored established, middle-aged specialists and experienced instructors. The Emergency Committee for Displaced Foreign Scholars expressly demanded evidence of three years' teaching experience immediately prior to the date of emigration.

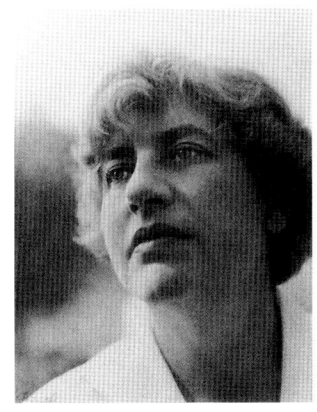

For the relatively large group of beginners with no record of academic recognition, it was not possible to supply the necessary references. Nevertheless, they found support in an intercollegiate network that operated on the margins of the official aid system, partly in conjunction with it and with comparable efficiency. This network counted among its members such leading American-born art historians as Alfred H. Barr Jr., Walter S. Cook (exceptionally active in this connection), Charles R. Morey, and Paul J. Sachs, as well as a number of Germans who had been in the United States for years, notably William R. Valentiner. They were joined, eventually, by those emigrés who became established figures in their own right, such as Panofsky, Krautheimer, and Wilhelm Köhler. Those who (like Panofsky and Köhler) had initially come to America as invited guests enjoyed an enhanced social status that gave them authority within the ranks of the profession.[12]

298
Horst Janson (left), Erwin Panofsky, and William S. Heckscher.

299
Lotte Brand Philip

Where a number of adverse factors—such as unimpressive testimonials, excessive age, or too late an emigration date—coincided, would-be immigrants were sometimes turned away. Older scholars who had not previously held a steady position, and those who arrived after 1935, often waited in vain for a permanent post. By 1940 the American universities had become less receptive, most of the posts had been filled, and the aid organizations had exhausted their funds.

Women, as well as specialists in marginal areas of the discipline, were among those who found it hardest to break into the American job market. For instance, it took seventeen years for Lotte Brand Philip (see fig. 299), a promising student of Panofsky's from Hamburg who immigrated to the United States in 1941, to find a position that matched her qualifications.

After working for years as a jewelry designer, she was engaged as a lecturer at Queens College in 1958. Sabine Gova, who had submitted a doctoral dissertation in Freiburg on Friedrich Schinkel's Altes Museum in Berlin, had intended to write a professorial dissertation (*Habilitation*) based on the spectacular source material that she had discovered. In America she spent years as a cleaning woman before gradually regaining a foothold in art history through lectures and private courses; eventually, in the late 1950s, she became an assistant professor at Fordham University in New York. Max Raphael, who had been something of an outsider in Germany but had carved out a niche for himself in adult education, now found himself totally isolated, an "exile in exile." In 1952 he took his own life.

Even in these marginal groups, however, there were many art historians who successfully vaulted into teaching posts. With around 110 employment initiatives,[13] the American colleges and universities, many of them suffering the effects of the Depression, showed an impressive readiness to absorb the newcomers, which they did on grounds of humanitarian feeling, cultural policy, and also sheer financial necessity. Initially the salaries of most of the emigrés were funded by aid organizations or foundations, so that schools were able to enrich their own teaching programs without burdening their often already tight budgets. A geographical survey of the schools that took in emigré art historians shows a marked concentration in the eastern states, with more than three-quarters of the posts located there. In the Midwest and South, where there were fewer colleges, nineteen art historians were appointed; on the West Coast, twelve.

The great Ivy League institutions remained notably aloof, offering little beyond positions on the periphery of academic life and occasional invitations to lecture—or else waiting until the emigrés had long since been established elsewhere. Columbia University appointed an emigré art historian, Adolf Placzek, to head the Avery Library; Julius Held was appointed professor at its women's school, Barnard College; Rudolf Wittkower was appointed only in 1956. In 1950 Princeton University belatedly awarded a full professorship to Kurt Weitzmann (who was neither a Jew nor, in his own view, a "refugee"). Harvard, with its Germanophile traditions, appointed Jakob Rosenberg to the Fogg Art Museum and Köhler, a non-Jew who had been a visiting professor there before 1933, to the A. Kingsley Porter chair; from 1941 onward Ernst Kitzinger, from Munich, taught at the associated Dumbarton Oaks Institute. Yale, Pennsylvania,[14] and Brown employed no German emigré art historians. All of this certainly reflects xenophobic and anti-Semitic tendencies,[15] as well as a conservative allegiance to the tradition of connoisseurship within American art history.

It was a very different story at the Institute of Fine Arts (IFA) in New York, a young institution, unfettered by tradition, which had been engaging visiting professors from Europe since 1930. It was during his spell as a guest at the institute that Panofsky was notified of his dismissal from the government service in Hamburg. Cook launched a fund-raising campaign to endow an "emergency professorship" at the institute, which Panofsky gratefully accepted. This was financed by the Rockefeller Foundation and by a number of private individuals, so that he found himself in the awkward and (for a formerly tenured German public employee) entirely unfamiliar situation of having to regard his salary as a donation from individuals personally known to him. Nor did he enjoy the new sensation of being drafted as (in his view) the "workhorse" of the institute, whose courses were required to attract as large a paying audience as possible.

It was on Panofsky's initiative that the IFA engaged Walter Friedlaender, who, despite his advanced age, became a more influential teacher in the United States than he had ever been in Germany. With the appointments of Richard Ettinghausen, Robert von Heine-Geldern, Karl Lehmann-Hartleben, Alfred Salmony, Guido Schoenberger, Martin Weinberger, and, on an occasional basis, Held and Krautheimer, the institute emerged as an art historical center with a markedly European bent; in 1938 half of its faculty were emigrés. In spite of the attractiveness of the teaching program, voices were raised (especially after the United States entered the war in 1941) criticizing Cook's employment policy and warning that the institute was in danger of being swamped by "Teutonic" influences. In the late 1940s the New York University administration stepped in to curb his freedom of action.[16]

Only one other institution had a comparable employment record: the Institute for Advanced Study in Princeton, founded in 1930 with the avowed object of giving opportunities to Jewish scholars.[17] There Panofsky was appointed one of five permanent members of the School of Humanistic Studies. He had been recommended for the post by Princeton University art historian Charles R. Morey, who saw Panofsky's expertise in late medieval and early Renaissance art as an ideal complement to that of his own faculty members. Others appointed to long-term posts were the former *ordinarius* at Halle, Paul Frankl, and a former lecturer from Hamburg, Charles de Tolnay. In addition, the institute employed Hugo Buchthal, William Heckscher, Adolf Katzenellenbogen, and Hanns Swarzenski (see fig. 300)—younger art historians, some of them former students of Panofsky's, who thus gained a foothold in the American academic world. A policy that had initially been an emergency relief measure for scholars driven out of Germany was to turn the Princeton institute into a link between European and American forms of scholarly discourse. Eventually—from the late 1950s onward—this became the place where younger scholars from the Federal Republic made contact with their exiled colleagues and learned firsthand how their discipline had evolved in America.[18]

Vassar College, which had been a pioneer in the introduction of art history into the curriculum, was one established institution that lost no time in engaging a number of highly original talents: Krautheimer, Katzenellenbogen, and the orientalist Salmony. Smith College, too, when it took on Edgar Wind (as late as 1944), chose a brilliant scholar with a strong interest in methodology. In some instances even scholars with little or no established reputation—such as Johannes Gaertner, who had been a bookseller in Peru after leaving Germany but was appointed to teach at Lafayette College in 1947—were given not only short-term contracts but the opportunity to build new art history departments as well.

Away from the East Coast this sort of pioneer work was the rule—the one great exception being the University of Chicago. There policy reforms instituted by an ambitious president, Robert M. Hutchins, brought in Otto von Simson, the orientalist Ludwig Bachhofer, and Ulrich Middeldorf, who, as a long-serving department chairman, enjoyed an administrative career of his own. Ernst Scheyer (Sceyer), formerly a curator at the Schlesisches Museum in Breslau, took up a tenured post at Wayne State University, as did Clemens Sommer, a former lecturer at Greifswald, at the University of North Carolina. Krautheimer

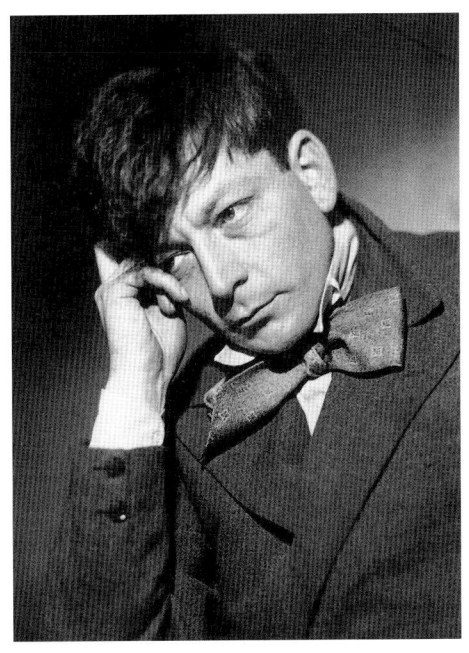

300
Hanns Swarzenski, 1931.

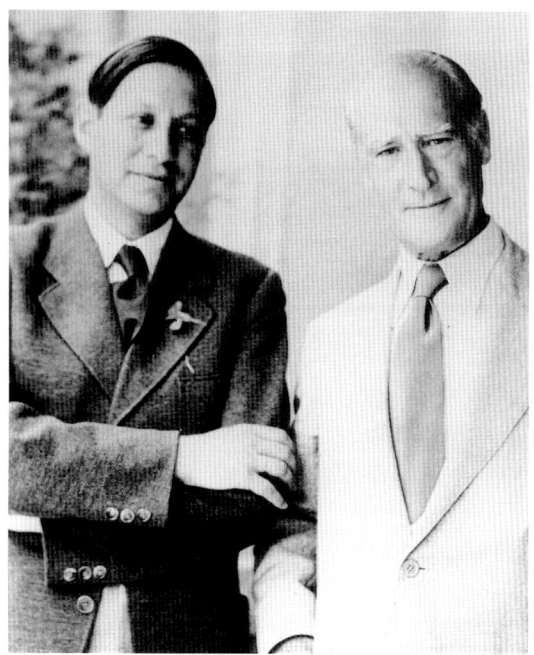

did a year's pioneer work at the University of Louisville, as did Janson at the University of Iowa—"the first real, live art historian anyone there had ever set eyes on."[19] Setting up the scholarly infrastructure of an art library and slide collection was an unfamiliar challenge, one that often distracted the emigrés from their own scholarly work.

By the time it reached the American West, the wave of work-hungry art historians had spent much of its force. The writer and art historian Alfred Neumeyer set his mark on the teaching of art history at Mills College in Oakland from 1935 through 1966 (see fig. 301). Notably it was in his hands that the college's museum acquired a more than regional status, with a distinguished collection focusing on modern prints and drawings. He had a strong personal commitment to artists whose work had been banned in Germany, such as Max Beckmann, Lyonel Feininger, Oskar Kokoschka, and Emil Nolde. Like other scholars in similar positions, Neumeyer considered his new job, "although not quite comparable to my former occupation, interesting and satisfactory."[20] What they all missed was an intellectual milieu, but they kept in touch through visiting professorships at major American universities and in Europe.

301
Alfred Neumeyer and Lyonel Feininger at Mills College, 1936; photograph by Rondal Partridge.

302
Karl With

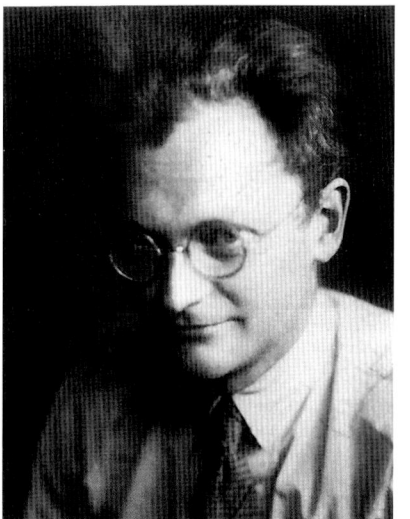

Another scholar who taught at Mills College for a time, in the late 1930s, was art historian and librarian Edgar Breitenbach, who would have known Neumeyer from their time together at the Bibliothek Warburg in Hamburg. In 1938 a further representative of the "Hamburg School" reached California in the person of Walter Horn, who had the task of building an art history department for the University of California, Berkeley, complete with a photographic collection and a library that would later become famous.

Stephen (Salli) Kayser, who had worked in publishing before leaving Germany, lectured at Berkeley from 1941 through 1944, occupying a post funded by the Emergency Committee. Later, after three years at San Jose State College, he went on to be director of the Jewish Museum in New York. The University of California, Los Angeles, employed Helmut Hungerland as a specialist in "art, art history, psychology, and sport"—an odd combination, especially by European standards. He was followed in the late 1940s by the former director of the Kunstgewerbemuseum in Cologne, Karl With (see fig. 302), whose first American post had been at the California Graduate School of Design, Pasadena. Paul Laporte (Heilbronner), a Munich graduate, was another who taught in the Los Angeles area, at Immaculate Heart College. Laporte's multiple expertise as painter, photographer, and art historian reflected a versatile type that was in great demand in the West. There educational needs and policies differed markedly from those in the East: the demand was not so much for intellectualism as for a broad spectrum of knowledge and practical skills.

This outline of the geographical distribution of emigré employment suggests two conclusions. First—outside such exceptional institutions as the Institute of Fine Arts—emigré art historians were relatively evenly distributed over the colleges and universities of the country. Their notion of scholarship, their knowledge of the original monuments, and their methodical approach produced an effect, however briefly, even in comparatively small and isolated schools. Second, the regions differed in their requirements and therefore in their recruitment policies. The East Coast, with its traditional allegiance to European standards, managed recruitment accordingly. The West Coast took a more independent line; there thinking about art was much more closely bound up with the practice of art, and there was greater demand—as also at the smaller colleges in the East and Midwest—for generalists. Anyone who could combine theory with practice found openings of a kind that would have been unthinkable in the German-speaking countries. In the western states, especially, those scholars whose interests extended beyond the narrow confines of their own profession—and who would consequently have been marginalized in their native culture—were able to take advantage of a far more open career structure while continuing to teach art history.

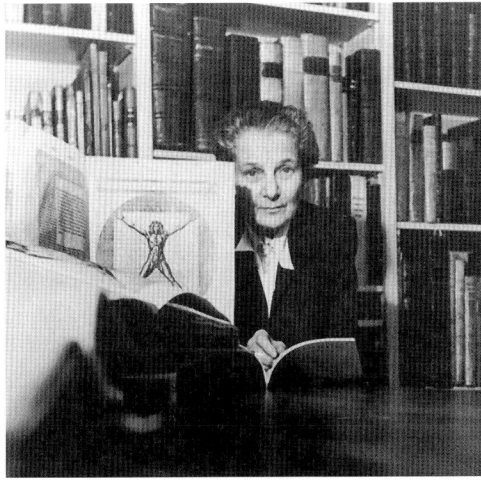

303
Kate Steinitz

One notable example was the writer and artist Kate Steinitz (see fig. 303), a member of the Hannover Dada circle who had studied art history in Germany for only a few semesters and who initially made a living in the United States as a book-jacket designer and translator. Kurt Schwitters put her in touch with a Los Angeles physician, Elmer Belt, who commissioned her to set up a large private library on Leonardo da Vinci. When the library was handed over to the University of California, Los Angeles, Steinitz was appointed honorary curator. In parallel with the scholarly work of building up the library, which also entailed the editing of publications and a considerable lecture program, Steinitz kept working as an artist; she also became a champion of contemporary art and wrote on Schwitters and Paul Klee, among others.

This sense of greater openness beyond the East Coast is confirmed on a more general level. It not only led to more flexible individual career patterns but also widened the scope of even traditional professional activities. The many public art collections that were affiliated with institutions of higher learning allowed a number of scholars, such as Justus Bier at Louisville and Wolfgang Stechow at Oberlin, to hold both teaching and curatorial posts simultaneously. In almost every case the emigrés regarded this as a benefit.

The emigrés' influence was widespread, extending into the remotest parts of the country, but on the whole they did not rise to senior, administrative, or policy-making positions. A few important exceptions—such as Panofsky's appointment at the Institute for Advanced Study, or those of Middeldorf and Wittkower, already mentioned, or that of Janson as chairman of the Fine Arts Department of New York University—prove the rule.[21] After Panofsky it was certainly Janson who, through his teaching and above all through his publications, exerted the greatest influence within and even beyond the institutional world of art history. He was chairman of the College Art Association from 1970 to 1972. Another emigré, the architectural historian Paul Zucker, who taught at the New School for Social Research and at Cooper Union for the Advancement of Science and Art, was president of the Society of Architectural Historians from 1946 to 1950. As a rule, however, the university careers of emigré art historians were confined within the scale that rises from lecturer or assistant professor to associate professor and then to full professor. In the organization of university studies, so different from that in Germany, and in the shaping of American education as a whole, their influence remained slight. Public proposals for reform, such as Panofsky's suggestion of setting up model schools conforming to the standards of the German gymnasium, came to nothing.[22]

The emigrés' influence was exerted within the existing structure of American university life. The organization of the courses mostly remained the same; it was the content that was radically changed. "The bottles," said Krautheimer, "were the old ones, but the wine was new every year."[23] The existing facades labeled "antiquity, Middle Ages, Renaissance" now served to front courses on mannerism; Early Christian, Late Gothic, and baroque art; and on specifically German themes. As a consequence, published lecture programs started to get noticeably more specific: in place of global topics covering broadly defined movements or schools in art history, the lists now included such titles as "Old Saint Peter's" (Krautheimer at Vassar), "From Rococo to Realism" (Friedlaender at the IFA), "Dürer" (Panofsky at the IFA), and—to my knowledge, the first appearance of the word *iconography* on any American curriculum—"Iconography of the Renaissance," a course given by Wind at the IFA in 1940. Panofsky's IFA course "Gothic and Late Medieval Illuminated Manuscripts" was given at the Pierpont Memorial Library, using the material available there.

Contemporary art, which never appeared on any syllabus in Germany until after World War II, played no major role in the emigrés' work. Such exceptions as Panofsky's essay "On Movies," Neumeyer's writings on contemporary art, and Paul Wescher's paper on Man Ray were certainly inspired by the cultural climate of the host country.[24] There was rather more evidence of interest in eighteenth- and nineteenth-century North American painting, American collections, and Latin American art. In general, however, emigré art historians explored no new themes; they labored to adapt their existing, basic stock-in-trade to American circumstances—and, not least, to the new language.

Unmistakably, however, the emigrés themselves were changed by the impact of America. They not only took advantage of the pithiness of the English language but—as exemplified by the conferences on museology held by Rosenberg at Harvard and by Martin Weinberger and Hans Huth in New York—learned new modes of training and communication as well. The fundamental differences between the two academic systems, which many of them did not immediately recognize, bore on highly sensitive issues of educational practice. The American educational ideal placed the responsibility for success on teachers rather than on students; in German universities, by contrast, learning depended on the students' motivation. Teaching in America was directed toward specific educational objectives; the teaching offered in Germany, in the tradition established by Wilhelm von Humboldt, was closely allied to the scholar's own research, independent of demand pressures and largely self-legitimizing. American universities passed on authenticated knowledge; German-speaking universities prized the transmission of methodological skills.

Supply and demand were thus out of kilter, and the emigré teacher could remedy the situation only by deviating from those Germanic standards of scholarship that were based on the idea of the unity of teaching and research and of freedom in both teaching and learning. Additionally they had to accept that they were dealing with a less self-reliant, less educated type of student. "We expected," Krautheimer remembers, "among our audience the preparation we were used to in graduates of a German *Gymnasium*; a knowledge of the monuments gained in situ, of the geographical situation, of European history, and of languages."[25] Scholars now found themselves having to replace theoretical concerns with the imparting of facts, to structure their material more strongly, and to define chronological and geographical categories more broadly. In many cases the emigrés themselves have pointed out that this pressure to adapt had positive consequences for their own work; among its tangible results were new modes of publication, such as Krautheimer's *Rome: Profile of a City*, the first art historical monograph on a city, or Panofsky's *Albrecht Dürer*.[26] The latter followed an American pattern by dispensing with the "showers of footnotes"[27] that Eisler counts among the most notable imports brought by the German emigrés. One of the most successful products of the acculturation process is Janson's *History of Art*;[28] having arrived in the United States as a student, he benefited from a training that spanned both cultures.

One incontrovertibly positive consequence of the influx is to be found in the groups of pupils or disciples who owed allegiance to individual emigré scholars. To name just a few: Marilyn Aronberg-Lavin and Irving Lavin were influenced by both Janson and Panofsky. (The latter also counted Harry Bober among his direct pupils, but because of his irregular teaching activity, Panofsky's influence was generally more diffuse.) James S. Ackerman, John Coolidge, Kenneth Donahue (later director of the Los Angeles County Museum of Art), Richard Pommer, Howard Salaman, and Leo Steinberg were pupils of Krautheimer. The school of Walter Friedlaender includes Jane Costello, S. J. Freedberg, Frederick Hartt, Donald Posner, John Shearman, Craig Hugh Smyth, and Robert Rosenblum (who also regards himself as deeply indebted to Frances Gray-Godwin [Franziska Grabkowitz]). Seymour Slive was a pupil of Stechow and of Rosenberg, who also influenced Sydney Freedberg. John Walsh (now director of the J. Paul Getty Museum) was a student of Held, as was Elizabeth Sears of William Heckscher. Wittkower was a major influence on Howard Hibbard, Douglas Frazer, and Colin Rowe; Herbert L. Kessler was a pupil of Kurt Weitzmann.

From the emigrés' point of view the assimilation process had its negative consequences: not only the loss of status, which was painful for many of them, but also the added burden of work outside the classroom and, even worse, the marked reduction in the stimulus received from students. As Panofsky complained in a letter to the Hamburg philologist Bruno Snell, American students during their university years were "essentially receptive," and even after that, they were "instantly reabsorbed into a teaching or museum post," so that the relationship was not "*mutually* fruitful to the same degree" that it had been in his experience in Hamburg.[29]

In the museum field the contrasts between German and American culture were even more marked than in academia. For the most part privately funded and dependent on foundations, the museums—or at least those in provincial centers—were organized neither for systematic collection nor for the scholarly study of their holdings. "I arrived at just the right moment," wrote Elisabeth Moses soon after joining the staff of the De Young Memorial

Museum in San Francisco, "when Dr. [Walter] Heil [the museum's German-American director] made up his mind to turn this Wild West museum, an amusing assortment of plaster figures, stuffed giraffes, Rococo chests of drawers, Indian baskets, and life-size photographs of pioneers, into a proper museum. A constructive labor that was or is far more attractive and many-sided than working in our more or less finished European museums. Also rather more difficult, because here you have to know just as much about Peru or Mexico as about French Gothic or Egyptian prehistory."[30]

In the United States it was not customary for museum staff to have academic training; it was more important for them to have a strong foothold in the stratum of society from which potential donors were recruited. Emigrés, foreigners, with their German accents and their lack of organizational experience, were hardly the best people to act as fund-raisers. No wonder that, of the twelve or so art historians who managed to secure museum posts, only two achieved leading positions: Alexander Dorner at the Art Museum of the Rhode Island School of Design and Gertrude Rosenthal[31] at the Baltimore Museum of Art. Dorner, the former director of the Provinzialmuseum in Hannover, had made his reputation as one of the most innovative museum directors of the Weimar Republic and as an uncompromising advocate of abstract art, before resigning his post in protest over National Socialist art policies. In Rhode Island his successful formula of trying to reach the public by going beyond aesthetics and classification to present art in evolutionary terms, within the context of its age, was adapted to American requirements. This lasted just three years, before he fell out with his administrative superiors. By an ironic chance he was able to buy for the Rhode Island museum two paintings by Franz Marc that he himself had originally acquired for Hannover; the National Socialists had put them in the *Entartete Kunst* (Degenerate art) exhibition and subsequently sold them to an American collector.[32]

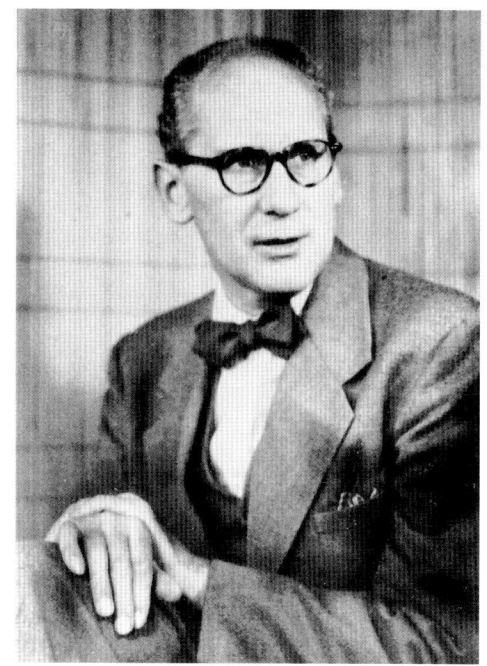

304
Paul Wescher

Rosenberg, too, was able to acquire expressionist art for the Fogg Art Museum at favorable prices and endow it with an important collection of twentieth-century prints and drawings. Held succeeded in forming a large private collection by using a few Beckmann drawings that he brought to the United States as the basis for a succession of trades.

It is clear that in museum work, as in teaching, the emigré specialists were most effective in situations where they were permitted to work within the system but precluded from interfering with its structures. Thus, Georg Swarzenski, the former director of the Städelsches Institut in Frankfurt, became a research fellow at the Museum of Fine Arts in Boston, where he was able to set up an important department of medieval studies. The activity of the Art Institute of Chicago was similarly enriched and deepened by the work of Oswald Goetz, Harold Joachim, and (intermittently) Hans Huth, all of whom held curatorial posts. Paul Wescher (see fig. 304), formerly on the print-room staff of the Staatliche Museen in Berlin, was appointed curator of the newly founded J. Paul Getty Museum in 1954. He owed the appointment to Valentiner, who had come to America from Berlin in 1908 to work at the Metropolitan Museum of Art in New York, later served as director of the Detroit Institute of Arts and the Los Angeles County Museum, and was placed in charge of setting up the Getty Museum.

A widespread shift in visual perception took place in the United States, which was the doing not only of museum people and perceptual psychologists but also of the whole community of emigré art historians, whether they worked as lecturers, as antique or art dealers, or in adult education. Their efforts resulted in new modes of access, new themes, new issues, transformed ways of dealing with art—both in the training of the next generation of academics and in the education and culture of society at large.

As far as the discipline itself was concerned, it is probably an undisputed fact—not only from a European but also from an American perspective—that the emigré scholars acted as catalysts for the professionalization and internationalization of art-historical study. The more we see of the forces at work in the process, however, the less we can sustain such simplistic interpretations as that of a one-way, transatlantic transfer of learning. The idea that everything that counted for anything in German art history went into exile along with its "leading talents" requires a great deal of qualification. Only a few of those who came to this country after 1933 had enough of a prior reputation to be regarded as "leading talents," and only a minority went on to acquire that status.

Among those who did were scholars who devised new methodologies that broke through the fossilized confines of the discipline—those who, like Rudolf Arnheim in the psychology of art and Arnold Hauser[33] in the sociology of art, developed models of contextualization. The most successful German import of all was iconology, which had been practiced in Germany by a partly Jewish (and thus peripheral) group of specialists; the United States gave it a platform from which it achieved worldwide acceptance. As can also be shown in the fields of nuclear physics and molecular genetics, a new academic context, with permeable lines of demarcation, released creative energies that unfolded freely in the uncramped spaces of the discipline as practiced in America.[34]

Like all imported science and learning, however, iconology underwent a sea change in adapting to American conditions. It is worth inquiring whether its subsequent ossification and schematization—as recorded by its principal champions, among others—might be interpreted as a reaction to an environment in which the method could be absorbed but its organizational framework could not. Iconographic and iconological method was transplanted into an academic milieu markedly different from that in which it was devised—one that had different academic and social objectives and therefore produced a different structure of application and response. The result was that an initial phase of amalgamation with the "alien" milieu was followed by a phase of distancing, after which iconology gained new life through its adoption by other disciplines, such as anthropology, semiotics, and the field known as *l'histoire de mentalité* (the history of mentality).

This process may well encapsulate in miniature the wider outcome of the migration of German art historians, as seen from today's viewpoint. That is to say that the transfer of knowledge and methods, and the transplantation of the individuals who carried them, has brought American art history to an aggregate state in which the work of individuals reflects the assimilation of imported scholarship, but the entity as a whole displays an increasingly well-defined autonomy. The emigrés served as catalysts for an evolutionary process whose present state can no longer be described as "*Kunstgeschichte* American style," but as "art history *mit deutschem Beigeschmack*"—art history with a German flavor.

Notes

1   I am grateful to numerous American institutions and their staffs for their generous support and to many American colleagues, as well as to the emigrés themselves, for supplying information. My particular thanks go to Martin Warnke, Irving Lavin, Kurt W. Forster, Meyer Schapiro, William S. Heckscher, and Wolfgang Kemp.
  The basic study is still Colin Eisler's "*Kunstgeschichte* American Style: A Study in Migration," in *The Intellectual Migration: Europe and America, 1930–1960*, ed. Donald Fleming and Bernard Bailyn (Cambridge: Charles Warren Center for Studies in American History, Harvard University, 1969), 544–629, together with Anthony Heilbut, *Exiled in Paradise: German Refugee Artists and Intellectuals in America from the 1930s to the Present* (New York: Viking Press, 1983).

2   See Eisler, "*Kunstgeschichte* American Style." (*Kunstgeschichte* is German for "art history.")

3   Peter Lasko, "Der Einfluß der deutschen Kunstgeschichte in England," in *Die Emigration der Wissenschaften nach 1933: Disziplingeschichtliche Studien*, ed. Herbert A. Strauss (Munich: K. G. Saur, 1991). On this whole topic, see also *Kunst im Exil in Großbritannien, 1933–1945*, exh. cat. (Berlin: Neue Gesellschaft für bildende Kunst, Orangerie des Schlosses Charlottenburg, 1986).

4   "Commentary—Art Historians in Exile," *Burlington Magazine* 74 (March 1939): 137.

5   Nikolaus Pevsner, *The Englishness of English Art* (London: Architectural Press, 1956).

6   See Cordula Frowein, "Alfred Flechtheim im Exil in England," in *Alfred Flechtheim, Sammler, Kunsthändler, Verleger*, exh. cat. (Düsseldorf: Kunstmuseum, 1987), 59–63.

7   The third exiled *ordinarius* was Adolph Goldschmidt, of Berlin, who settled in Switzerland.

8   I am grateful to Ulrike Wendland for permitting me to consult her thesis, "Verfolgung und Vertreibung deutschsprachiger Kunsthistoriker/innen im Nationalsozialismus: Ein biographisches Handbuch" (Hamburg University, 1995).

9   Meyer Schapiro, conversation with the author, 28 November 1990.

10   Udo Kultermann, *Geschichte der Kunstgeschichte* (Frankfurt am Main: Ullstein, 1981), 373.

11   The principal ones were: in Britain, the Society for the Protection of Science and Learning and, in the United States, the Emergency Committee for Displaced Foreign Scholars and the Rockefeller and Carnegie Foundations.

12   Even later both Weitzmann and Panofsky were at pains to stress that they had not come to the country as refugees. See Erwin Panofsky, "Three Decades of Art History in the United States: Impressions of a Transplanted European," in *Meaning in the Visual Arts: Papers in and on Art History* (Garden City, N.Y.: Doubleday, 1955), 322.

13   By "employment initiative" I mean a decision on the part of any institution to offer one (temporary or permanent) position; many schools did this on a multiple basis, whether concurrently or serially.

14   Martin Weinberger taught at the University of Pennsylvania but only on a temporary basis.

15   See David O. Levine, *The American College and the Culture of Aspiration, 1915–1940* (Ithaca, N.Y.: Cornell University Press, 1986), 136ff., and Leonard Dinnerstein, *Antisemitism in America* (New York: Oxford University Press, 1994), esp. 85–91. Especially in the 1920s and 1930s many colleges and universities used quotas to limit the enrollment of Jewish students. Kevin Parker, too, in his lecture, "The Jewish Body and the Liberal Eye: Panofsky Goes to America," points to the underrepresentation of Jewish students and teachers at American colleges and universities in the 1920s and 1930s; see also his essay in this catalogue. I am grateful to him for allowing me to consult his work. In philology William M. Calder III has shown how it was only the appointment of distinguished refugee specialists from Europe that broke the (unwritten) law against the appointment of Jews to senior university posts; cited in Eisler, "*Kunstgeschichte* American Style," 621–22.

16   New York University Archives, Harry W. Chase Administration, Box 42.

17   *Bulletin of the Institute for Advanced Study*, no. 7 (1938).

18   See Willibald Sauerländer, "Zersplitterte Erinnerung," in *Kunsthistoriker in eigener Sache: Zehn autobiographische Skizzen*, ed. Martina Sitt (Berlin: Dietrich Reimer, 1990), 314ff.

19   Lise Lotte Möller, "Horst Woldemar Janson, 4. Oktober 1913–30. September 1982," *Zeitschrift für Kunstgeschichte* 46 (1983): 469.

20   Neumeyer to Academic Assistance Council, 11 December 1938 (Archive of the Academic Assistance Council / Society for the Protection of Science and Learning, Department of Western Manuscripts, Bodleian Library, Oxford).

21   I have disregarded those appointments as chairman that took place at a late date and often for a brief period, such as that of Walter Horn at Berkeley.

22   Erwin Panofsky, *Bulletin of the Institute for Advanced Study*, no. 7 (1938): 344.

23   Richard Krautheimer, *Ausgewählte Aufsätze zur europäischen Kunstgeschichte* (Cologne: DuMont, 1988), 16.

24   See Erwin Panofsky, "On Movies," *Bulletin of the Department of Art and Archaeology of Princeton University* 3 (1936): 5–15; Alfred Neumeyer, *Die Kunst in unserer Zeit: Versuch einer Deutung* (Stuttgart: H. Goverts, 1961); published in English as *The Search for Meaning in Modern Art*, trans. Ruth Angress (Englewood Cliffs, N.J.: Prentice-Hall, 1964); and Paul Wescher, "Man Ray as Painter," *Magazine of Art* 46 (January 1953): 341–50.

25   Richard Krautheimer, "And Gladly Did He Learn and Gladly Teach," in *Rome: Tradition, Innovation, and Renewal: A Canadian International Art History Conference, 8–13 June 1987, Rome, in Honor of Richard Krautheimer and Leonard Boyle* (Victoria, B.C.: University of Victoria Press, 1991), 106.

26   Richard Krautheimer, *Rome: Profile of a City, 312–1308* (Princeton: Princeton University Press, 1980); Erwin Panofsky, *Albrecht Dürer* (Princeton: Princeton University Press, 1943).

27   Eisler, "*Kunstgeschichte* American Style," 619.

28   Horst W. Janson and Dora Jane Janson, *History of Art: A Survey of the Major Visual Arts from the Dawn of History to the Present Day* (New York: Harry N. Abrams, 1962).

29   Panofsky to Snell, 27 March 1952 (Staatsarchiv Hamburg, Hochschulwesen, Dozenten- und Personalakten, IV, 1204).

30   Moses to Alexander Dorner, 30 August 1937 (Archives of the Fogg Art Museum, Harvard University).

31   Rosenthal stands out as one of the few women emigrés to attain a high-level position. After completing her dissertation in Cologne in 1931, she worked as a journalist until 1933. There is no record of her activities between 1933 and 1939, the year she went to England, where she spent one year as a research assistant at the Courtauld Institute. In 1940 she immigrated to the United States, where she became art librarian and lecturer at Goucher College in Baltimore (1940–45). She became a research assistant at the Walters Art Gallery, Baltimore, in 1943. Two years later she moved to the Baltimore Museum of Art, first as director of research and then as general curator (1949–56).

32   Eisler, "*Kunstgeschichte* American Style," 594.

33   Hauser had initially gone to Britain; he taught in the United States from 1952 onward.

34   See, especially, Klaus Fischer, "Wissenschaftsemigration und Molekulargenetik," in Strauss, ed., *Die Emigration der Wissenschaften*, 105–35.

art history and exile:
richard krautheimer and erwin panofsky

KEVIN PARKER

The academic practice of art history in the United States was essentially founded by German-Jewish and Austrian-Jewish exiles in the 1930s. Against tremendous odds, including the financial turmoil of universities in the post-Depression era and a vigorously anti-Semitic environment, able administrators such as Walter Cook of New York University and Charles R. Morey of Princeton University seized upon world-historical circumstances and found the means to establish the discipline of art history in the United States.[1]

Most of the emigré art historians were from Jewish families who had been assimilated for at least one generation. Despite the fact that Wilhelmine society placed occasional roadblocks in their way because of their ethnicity, these scholars were strongly German identified. Many of them fought for their country in World War I, and all of them paid rather conspicuous obeisance to German spiritual and philosophical traditions in their work. Their loyalty to Germany is further explained by their propitious class affiliations. These were the sons of the fathers of the so-called free professions, often the scions of banking families who had absorbed the ideals of German *Kultur* and who were wealthy enough to countenance a career ministering to them. These economically elite Germans had every reason to be confident in the social contract; their families enjoyed a historic rise in prosperity in the 1910s, and it appeared that the kind of discrimination suffered by their ancestors had reached its final ebb. Thus, their betrayal by Germany in the early 1930s came as a great shock, and for the better part of the decade many of them held out for the possibility that reason, if not the "German spirit," might prevail over the temporary aberration of National Socialism.

Although these scholars were summarily excused from their academic posts at German universities in 1933 and barred from most archives, art collections, and museums in Germany and Italy, and although, most importantly, their lives and the lives of their families were placed in peril in Germany from the mid-1930s onward, the topic of exile was almost never raised by them publicly, even in the decades after the war. The reasons for their scrupulous avoidance of the topic are various and complex, but foremost among them is the delicate situation they faced being both German and Jewish in American academia in the 1930s.

With a few notable exceptions American universities in the 1930s did not welcome Jewish scholars onto their faculties. In some cases, such as that of Harvard, anti-Semitic admissions and hiring policies were stated openly, while at other prestigious universities, especially in the Northeast, more subtle discriminatory practices militated against the appointment of German-Jewish academics seeking refuge from Hitler's Germany.[2] It is difficult for us today to imagine how thoroughly anti-Semitism pervaded American academia sixty years ago. Although the situation for Jewish men, both students and faculty, improved quickly after World War II, the 1920s and 1930s were arguably the worst decades in terms of anti-Semitic discriminatory admissions and hiring practices. In 1927 the faculties of Yale, Princeton, Johns Hopkins, and the Universities of Chicago, Georgia, and Texas each included one Jew. Berkeley and Columbia each had two Jewish faculty members, and Harvard had three.[3] In sum, although Jews faced considerable impediments to their advancement in German universities, the situation was still considerably better there than it was in the United States before Hitler's rise to power.[4]

For many of these scholars the same upper-class background that played a role in their decisions to pursue a career in art history in Germany brought suspicion upon them in the United States. From the 1910s on a principal target of the most powerful strain of American anti-Semitism was the international Jewish banker.[5] On both sides of the Atlantic members of the Warburg family, brothers, in fact, of the famous art historian and founder of the Warburg Institute, Aby Warburg, were publicly accused of compromising their loyalty to their respective home countries.[6] In Germany Max Warburg was scapegoated for selling out Germany at Versailles, even though he implored his government not to accept the harsh reparation terms demanded by the Allies.[7] In the United States Paul Warburg was elected to the Federal Reserve Board in 1914 and faced continuous scrutiny and harassment from the press and the Congress about his loyalties until President Wilson finally sacrificed him on the altar of politics, firing him 1918.[8] Throughout the 1920s Jewish bankers, particularly German-Jewish bankers, were frequently targeted by powerful anti-Semites such as Henry Ford, who bought the myth of an international Jewish banking conspiracy lock, stock, and barrel and saw to it that it was well publicized.[9] It was not the more recent Jewish refugees from the Russian pogroms who poured into East Coast cities at the turn of the century who were suspected of international treachery and duplicity by these powerful Jew baiters, but affluent German Jews like the Warburgs. This particular brand of anti-Semitism persisted through the 1930s; the collapse of the stock exchange, the malaise of the Depression, and Roosevelt's New Deal (dubbed by some the "Jew Deal"), continued to fan the flames of an anti-Semitism focused upon affluent and educated European Jews.[10] The emigré art historians therefore had every reason to lie low upon their arrival in the United States.

If these art historians chose not to call attention to the topic of exile, their practice was nonetheless profoundly affected by it. They generally took extreme care to winnow out any ideological inflection from their work. They were well practiced in the techniques of neutrality as a result of their experiences in Germany. There they had already begun to direct their research and methods away from the ideologically tainted techniques of style analysis, judgments of beauty, and the more intolerably chauvinistic and "unscientific" aspects of Hegelian historiography.[11] They favored instead an emphasis on iconographic research, the study of cultural adaptation, and a politically benign approach to history as "context." But upon their arrival in the United States, where the problems of difference and assimilation were compounded, they steered art history in an even more austere and ideologically chaste direction. That direction, established amid the dire circumstances of exile, continues to influence mainstream art history. This essay will consider the effect of exile on two of the most influential of the art historian emigrés, Richard Krautheimer (1897–1994) and Erwin Panofsky (1892–1968).

richard Krautheimer's half century of teaching and writing in the United States has left an indelible imprint on the practice of art history, especially architectural history. His students, mostly from the Institute of Fine Arts of New York University, where he began to offer seminars in the late 1930s, disseminated the methods and agenda for the study of architectural history in the years of academic expansion following the war. By the 1960s they could be found at virtually every major university or college in North America. None of these students could be charged with simply reduplicating the work of their teacher, especially in terms of their areas of specialization, but they generally maintained a certain methodological constant. That constant entailed, and continues to entail for subsequent generations of Krautheimer's intellectual progeny, a fastidious devotion to the physical description of the artifact or building in question and a careful and always "objective" weighing of contextual detail. "Context," for Krautheimer and his followers, typically runs through the registers of building technology, patronage, and social and religious function. But it is important to point out that Krautheimer's methodological template never allows context to upstage its monument, nor does it ever indulge in what he would call abstract and potentially partisan speculation about the nature of the work of art's demand for a context. He and other art historians of the intellectual migration frequently circumvented such issues by calling them "German," suggesting that the precision of the English language and the pragmatic demands of the American academy did not, thankfully, permit such indulgences.[12] But *German,* in this context, is a code word for something else, and that is *politics,* such as the racist politics that had compromised the scholarship of many of his former colleagues who remained in Germany. As a liberal mandarin steeped in the Kantian myth of the possibility of disinterested scholarship, Krautheimer apparently believed that it was possible to avoid politics by eschewing discussions of method.[13] At the same time, and given the ideological constraints of his exile, he really had little choice but to continue operating according to this belief.

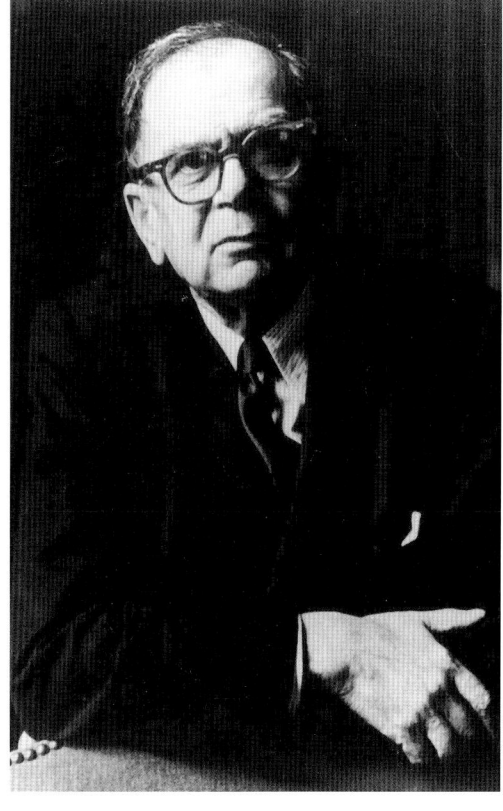

305
Richard Krautheimer

Krautheimer was born in Bavaria in 1897, at the dawn of the so-called Golden Era of the German-Jewish bourgeoisie.[14] As was befitting his social standing, he attended gymnasium and entered the University of Munich when he was fifteen, intending to study law. But on the advice of a friend he attended the lectures of Heinrich Wölfflin and was won over. He abandoned his study of the law and turned full-time to art history, also coming into contact with Paul Frankl. If Wölfflin is to be credited with luring Krautheimer into the discipline, it was Frankl who set his orientation and scholarly temper. In contrast to Wölfflin's style-based approach and emphasis on all visual media, Frankl specialized in architecture and encouraged Krautheimer to think about "extrinsic" factors bearing on the meaning of a building, factors such as religious and social function. Before pursuing his graduate work, Krautheimer entered the military and fought for two years "in the blood and dirt" of the trenches for the kaiser. Thereafter he went to Halle, where Frankl had been appointed chair, to finish his Ph.D. An indicator of Krautheimer's economic standing in the early 1920s is that, after his marriage in the spring of 1924, he was sent by his family to Italy for a honeymoon of sorts lasting a year and a half. His economic situation in the Weimar years would soon stand in sharp contrast to that of his exile. If the years of rampant inflation did not eat up his family's resources, the obstacles to transferring funds out of Germany must have left him and his wife, Trude, comparatively impoverished upon their arrival in the United States.

Krautheimer's most substantial published preemigration work is the thesis he submitted in 1927 for his habilitation as a *Privatdozent* at the University of Marburg, *Mittelalterliche Synagogen* (Medieval synagogues).[15] In light of the historical situation the book is interesting from a couple of perspectives. Unlike his more antiquarian works of the 1930s, it is organized around a problem. The problem was this: If Diaspora Jews of the Middle Ages maintained relative autonomy in many aspects of their culture, why is their synagogue architecture so stylistically inconsistent? Although Krautheimer did not frame his study in conspicuous opposition to a European, anti-Semitic tradition that argues that the Jew is not capable of artistic invention, it would be naive to claim, as some have, that his Jewishness had nothing to do with his selection of the topic or the form of his argument.[16] What is most interesting about the study, which consists largely of sober, if not dry, archaeological description, is that its argument amounts to an assimilation allegory in terms of both its approach to the problem and its solution. Wölfflinian style-based analysis was of no use to Krautheimer for his treatment of these buildings. He drew instead on the functionalist model of his teacher Frankl, solving the problem of the hybridity of medieval synagogue architecture by arguing that the building type's function was not only ecclesiastical but also legal and educational. Thus, medieval synagogues drew their vocabularies from both religious and secular buildings (Gothic and Romanesque halls). Krautheimer's solution was brilliant. The medieval synagogue, as a cultural expression of the Diaspora, could not be understood using a method developed for the description of national styles, but required a more specific understanding of the function of a building and of its historical context.

Following his dismissal from his position at Marburg in the spring of 1933, Krautheimer moved to Italy. It was then that he began work on his lifelong project, *Corpus basilicarum christianarum Romae*, with the support of the few friends there who risked association with him, since, in his words: "All the rest dropped us like a hot potato. The American Academy [in Rome] was no exception."[17] His resources in Italy down to nothing, Krautheimer obtained a position at the University of Louisville in Kentucky with the assistance of the Emergency Committee in Aid of Displaced German Scholars, based in New York City.

Generally speaking, city-sponsored universities maintained more open admissions and hiring policies in the 1930s with respect to Jews than their private counterparts. Notwithstanding its racist segregation policies, this was true of the University of Louisville. Indeed, Krautheimer was invited to a city with a long tradition of German and Jewish settlement. Louisville's first German immigrants had fled Germany following the revolution of 1848 because they feared reprisal as Jews or revolutionaries. Following the Civil War, however, owing to antinativist harassment, most of the city's prominent Jewish families, including the Strausses and Kuhns, moved to the Northeast, but some, like the Brandeises, remained, continuing a Jewish cultural presence there into the twentieth century.

Upon his arrival in Louisville in 1935 Krautheimer was charged with starting a new Department of Fine Arts. Previously the university had offered a single course in art appreciation; its studio component consisted of jewelry making. He spoke virtually no English, the library owned few books relating to art history, possessed no slides or photographic materials, and a new museum provided, according to Krautheimer, exactly one painting worthy as a teaching resource. One can only wonder at the culture shock he must have experienced as a highly trained, haute bourgeois Wilhelmine gentleman charged with the cultural edification of the children, in his words, of "Russian-Jewish, Polish, Irish, Italian immigrants; Southern Baptist and Methodists who had never seen a religious painting."[18] He made the best of it, so to speak, obtaining a grant from the Carnegie Foundation for $10,000 to buy slides and books for the department and even winning the admiration of students once they were able to cut through his accent. His most promising student at Louisville was Kenneth Donahue, who later became director of the Los Angeles County Museum of Art.

In two years time Krautheimer obtained a position at an institution more amenable to his professional and class outlook. In the fall of 1937 he arrived at Vassar College, where he was asked to train not scholars, but "intelligent, broad-minded, politically and socially active citizens—an élite," for, his memoir continues, "every society needs one."[19] At Vassar Krautheimer also benefited from the resources of universities and museums in nearby New York City. It was not long before Walter Cook asked him to offer periodic seminars on architecture at the Institute of Fine Arts. Thus, in 1938, Krautheimer began his relationship with the institute, a relationship that was solidified in 1952, when the newly appointed director, Craig Smyth, asked him to join the full-time faculty.

By any other standard Krautheimer was very productive during the first decade of his exile, but not when compared with the prodigious output of his postwar years at the institute. From 1935 through the war years he produced several articles, mostly excerpts from his work on the *Corpus basilicarum christianarum Romae,* and a number of book reviews. He completed the first installment of the magisterial, five-volume *Corpus* in 1937.[20] Considering the difficulties he faced in the first decade of his exile—including the loss of his sister and his wife's parents to the Holocaust, adaptation to new professional and cultural situations, inflated prewar course loads, and a short period working for the Office of Strategic Services (forerunner of the Central Intelligence Agency) in Washington in the 1940s—it is remarkable that he accomplished as much as he did.

The difference between Krautheimer's work in the first decade of his exile and pre-emigration works such as *Mittelalterliche Synagogen* consists in the avoidance of problems of interpretation that might have raised questions of identity or politics. Of course, any representation of the past requires interpretation, and in a restricted sense Krautheimer engaged in it, but never in a way that might call undue attention to the relationship between his present and the past he represented. Hence, the *Corpus* and the articles he prepared from 1935 to 1945 amount to carefully crafted, objective, and comprehensive descriptions of early Christian churches in Rome. Never is the work from this period keyed to a historiographic problem with the potential political stakes of his preemigration interpretation of the medieval synagogue. Krautheimer's emphasis on "objective" historical scholarship must be understood within the historical terms dictated by his exile. These terms do not exist for art historians working in the United States today, yet the humanist myth of disinterested historical representation propounded by Krautheimer and his generation is still very much with us.

Without a doubt the most influential of the emigré art historians was Erwin Panofsky. His "iconological method," which emphasizes the historical nature of the transformation of symbols in art, continues to guide much contemporary research. Panofsky's emigration went more smoothly than those of most of his compatriots. Indeed, he tended to downplay the fact of his exile, pointing out that his professional relationship with Princeton and the Institute of Fine Arts began two years before his dismissal from the University of Hamburg in 1933.[21] Nonetheless, there is no question that the direction his work took after his bridges to Germany had been burned was shaped by his exile in America.

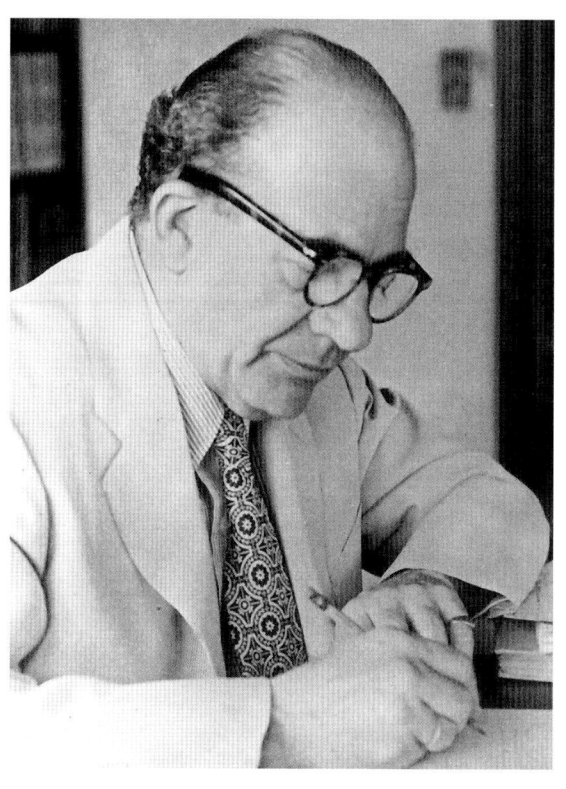

306
Erwin Panofsky

The iconological method was custom-designed for the American academy; it lent itself perfectly to workmanlike scholarship, inspired or not, and avoided the troubling nationalistic and racial issues raised by style-based analysis. The study of iconology also suited Panofsky in the difficult years leading up to World War II because it did not place as high a premium on the close inspection of the work of art as did other approaches. From the mid-1930s through the war years Panofsky's access to Renaissance paintings and archival resources was severely restricted; thus, his approach was adjusted to complement his erudition rather than his powers of inspection and description.

Panofsky came from a Berlin banking family, attended gymnasium, and matriculated at Freiburg University, the institution that was so famously swept into the Nazi orbit by Martin Heidegger in the 1930s. He did most of his graduate work there under Wilhelm Vöge and, after completing his dissertation, went to Berlin to study with Adolph Goldschmidt as a *Privatgelehrter,* or independent scholar. In 1920 Panofsky obtained a position as the first *Privatdozent* in art history at the new University of Hamburg. While in Hamburg he became affiliated with the famous Kulturwissenschaftliche Bibliothek Warburg, or Warburg Library, and was influenced by Aby Warburg's interest in the problem of the symbol and his broad, interdisciplinary approach. More significant perhaps was Panofsky's encounter with the neo-Kantian philosopher Ernst Cassirer, soon to serve as the university's rector, and the senior and best-known member of the Warburg Library group. The title of Panofsky's most theoretically daring work from his Hamburg period, "Perspektive als 'symbolische Form'" (Perspective as "symbolic form"), honors Cassirer's influence, since the phrase "symbolic form" is derived from the title of the first published volume of Cassirer's three-volume study on the philosophy of the symbol.[22] Panofsky's study of perspective has only recently been translated into English, which is indicative of the difficulty with which it would have been received in the United States before the war. It consists of a wild adaptation of Hegel's dialectic which inscribes the discovery of linear perspective as the penultimate episode in reason's quest for autonomy. Although the liberal convictions that so openly underpin the perspective study persist in Panofsky's American publications, never again would they be so plainly couched in German philosophical terms.

Panofsky was first called to the United States in 1931 by New York University. To a certain extent the way had been prepared for him by his association with Goldschmidt in Berlin.

Goldschmidt frequently hosted American art historians when they visited Germany and had himself spent a couple of semesters as a guest lecturer in the United States in the 1920s.[23] Thus, the relays were in place for Panofsky to be invited to teach in the United States at a time when a transition to American academia was not yet an obligatory proposition. He accepted the invitation and proceeded to shuttle back and forth from Hamburg to New York University and Princeton University for two years, until his dismissal from Hamburg in 1933. In 1935, upon the recommendation of Princeton's Charles R. Morey, Panofsky was invited by Abraham Flexner to join the faculty of the recently founded Institute for Advanced Study in Princeton, New Jersey. He was the first professor hired in the "humanistic sciences" at an institution that is famous for its scientists; its first recruit, in 1932, was Albert Einstein.

The Institute for Advanced Study was founded with an endowment from a wealthy Jewish New Jersey family, the Bambergers, who owned the fourth-largest department store in the United States and were fortunate enough to sell it to Macy's before the stock market crashed.[24] The Bambergers hired Flexner based upon his searing critique of higher education, *The American College,* and an influential study he conducted for the Carnegie Foundation on medical training in the United States. The family's original idea for the institute was that it be a medical school for Jewish students, who were finding it increasingly difficult to gain admission to schools of medicine in the late 1920s. Flexner insisted that anti-Semitism did not affect the chances of Jewish applicants to medical school and proposed that the institute address a different kind of pursuit, what he called "advanced research."[25] The offer from the Institute for Advanced Study must have been especially appealing to Panofsky. Not only would he be freed of undergraduate teaching responsibilities, but the institute was located near Princeton University, with its libraries, photographic resources, and iconography index; it allowed him to pursue difficult research projects; and it paid well.[26]

In Panofsky's brief professional memoir, "Three Decades of Art History in the United States," he tells of his dismissal from Hamburg. It came in the form of a telegram, sealed with a green strip of paper that bore the inscription, "Cordial Easter Greetings, Western Union."[27] Aside from the ironically light tone of the greeting, I am sure that the Christian presumptuousness of its message was not lost on him. But if Panofsky could joke about this telegram in 1953, effectively deflecting the gravity of its contents, there is little question that his framing of his famous introduction to the iconological method in 1939 reflects a response to his exile. In the face of a world coming apart at the seams, and in the lap of exile, Panofsky composed an introduction that is perhaps the most overdetermined humanistic defense of moderation and reason ever conceived.

Familiar to every student of art history is the example Panofsky uses in his "Introductory" to his *Studies of Iconology* to distinguish the three levels of the iconological method: "When an acquaintance greets me on the street by lifting his hat."[28] Panofsky proceeds to describe the difference between the formal and iconographic components of the gesture of the man lifting his hat, between the shape and color of the perceived gesture, and the iconographic recognition of the man and the hat and the gesture, all tallying up to a greeting. Next comes the punch: "However, my realization that the lifting of the hat stands for a greeting belongs in an altogether different realm of interpretation. This form of salute is peculiar to the Western world, and is a residue of medieval chivalry: armed men used to remove their helmets to make clear their peaceful intentions and their confidence in the peaceful intentions of others."²⁹

Granted, Panofsky is merely offering an illustration of an interpretive process that may be transposed to the study of a painting, but one cannot help but be struck by the civility of his example. Hats were rife with significance in 1939. This was the golden age of noir detective fiction, in which the fedora was the private dick's existential badge, but the high-crowned wedge of the Nazi officer's cap, which could be seen in newspaper photos of events such as Kristallnacht of 1938, must have made an impression as well. One is also reminded of Freud's boyhood memory of his father's yarmulke being knocked off his head and destroyed by thugs and of a comment made by Max Warburg in 1933. Warburg explained that he had stopped tipping his hat to people on the streets of Hamburg because he didn't want to trouble his acquaintances, who would otherwise have to cross the street in order to avoid association with him as a prominent Jew and Nazi assassination target.³⁰ It is impossible to believe in the innocence of Panofsky's example. Its difficulty lies in its confidence in the precepts of humanism at a time when evidence of their vitality was in very short supply. Why should this hat be about chivalric trust and not about ethnicity, class, or gender? Because Panofsky, in his ivory tower, continued to believe that history progresses by overcoming difference—never mind that it almost did, but not by lifting its hat.

richard Krautheimer and Erwin Panofsky were but two of some 250 art historians and museum curators exiled from Hitler's Germany.³¹ Like Krautheimer and Panofsky, many of them found permanent positions at universities and museums in the United States. A few returned after the war, and some, like Ernst Kris, moved on to make their mark in other academic fields. But the emigrés who exercised the most influence on the fledgling discipline of art history in the 1930s were those who were able to divest their work of a discernible politics. Krautheimer did it by adopting a kind of archaeological antimethod, thus eschewing the difficult and ideologically challenging topics of his preemigration work. Panofsky did it by withdrawing from the kind of methodological debate he engaged in so avidly in Hamburg in the 1920s, effectively deflecting questions of ideology with his consummate American performance as the perennial humanist and scholar.

If Krautheimer and Panofsky had not adopted these tactics, it is unlikely that they would have played significant roles in the formation of art history in the United States. What is so fascinating about their position in a German art historical tradition stretching back to Winckelmann is that they completely transformed a discourse that had always been intimately identified with politics into one that was not. The hard-won German Enlightenment ideal that "disinterestedness" in judgments of beauty and history might underpin a political claim to self-determination had, of course, become outmoded by the twentieth century. In the hands of Krautheimer and Panofsky, however, "disinterestedness" was used to divert attention away from politics and from questions of difference, including the one raised by the impossibility of reconciling the circumstances of their exile with their confidence in humanistic ideals.

Notes

1 An excellent source of information on the migration of German and Austrian art historians to the United States is Colin Eisler's "*Kunstgeschichte* American Style," in *The Intellectual Migration: Europe and America, 1930–1960*, ed. Donald Fleming and Bernard Bailyn (Cambridge: Charles Warren Center for Studies in American History, Harvard University, 1969), 544–629.

2 Marcia Graham Synnott, "Anti-Semitism and American Universities: Did Quotas Follow the Jews?" in *Anti-Semitism in American History*, ed. David A. Garber (Urbana: University of Illinois Press, 1986), 233–74; Lewis S. Feuer, "The Stages of Social History of Jewish Professors in American Colleges and Universities," *American Jewish History* 71 (June 1982): 455; Susanne Klingenstein, *Jews in the American Academy, 1910–1940* (New Haven: Yale University Press, 1991), xi.

3 Leonard Dinnerstein, *Antisemitism in America* (New York: Oxford University Press, 1994), 87.

4 For a history and politics of German academia in the first decades of the twentieth century, see Fritz K. Ringer, *The Decline of the German Mandarins: The German Academic Community, 1890–1933* (Cambridge: Harvard University Press, 1969).

5 Dinnerstein, *Antisemitism in America*, 80–114; Nathan C. Belth, *A Promise to Keep: A Narrative of the American Encounter with Anti-Semitism* (New York: Times Books, 1979), 58–114; Myron I. Scholnick, *The New Deal and Anti-Semitism in America* (New York: Garland, 1990).

6 Ron Chernow, T*he Warburgs: The Twentieth-Century Odyssey of a Remarkable Jewish Family* (New York: Random House, 1993).

7 Ibid., 209–18.

8 Ibid., 186–89.

9 Belth, *A Promise to Keep*, 75–86.

10 Scholnick, *The New Deal and Anti-Semitism*, 62, 73.

11 Style analysis powered the grand narratives of nineteenth-century German art history, which most often took the familiar form of Hegelian *Geistesgeschichte* (intellectual history), with the usual complement of chauvinistic reifications (of class, obviously, but also of the superiority of occidental over oriental cultures). By the turn of the century, however, art historical narratives stemming from stylistic analysis and classification began to take on racist overtones, since they were easily appropriated by art historians propounding overtly nationalistic agendas. Some, such as the Viennese anti-Semite Josef Strzygowski, were especially aggressive in their promotion of such agendas, but it was not unusual for even the most highly regarded and influential art historians to lapse into race-based interpretation, as Alois Riegl did in 1902, when he explained that "the innate striving for grandeur in every Latin" prevented Italian painters from achieving balance in their art (*Das Holländische Gruppenporträt* [1902], reprinted under the supervision of K. M. Svoboda [Vienna: Österreichische Staatsdruckerei, 1939], 17. Riegl provides an especially significant example because Panofsky promoted his work; see Erwin Panofsky, "Der Begriff des Kunstwollens," *Zeitschrift für Ästhetik und allgemeine Kunstwissenschaft* 14 [1920]: 321–39). Obviously the classification of artists, cultural regions, or periods based on stylistic differences and affinities is not in itself ideologically charged, but any interpretation of such a classification would be, and that is why this approach fell out of favor among liberal German art historians in the late 1920s and early 1930s.

12 See, for example, Richard Krautheimer, "And Gladly Did He Learn and Gladly Teach," in *Rome: Tradition, Innovation, and Renewal: A Canadian International Art History Conference, 8–13 June 1987, Rome, in Honor of Richard Krautheimer and Leonard Boyle* (Victoria: University of Victoria Press, 1991), 93–126; Erwin Panofsky, "Three Decades of Art History in the United States: Impressions of a Transplanted European," in *Meaning in the Visual Arts: Papers in and on Art History* (Garden City, N.Y.: Doubleday, 1955), 329–30.

13 "Mandarin" here derives from Ringer, *The Decline of the German Mandarins*.

14 Biographical details are taken from Krautheimer's memoir, "Gladly."

15 Richard Krautheimer, *Mittelalterliche Synagogen* (Frankfurt: Verlags-Anstalt, 1927).

16 For a discussion of the European stereotype of the cultural impoverishment of the Jew, see Paul Lawrence Rose, *Revolutionary Antisemitism in Germany from Kant to Wagner* (Princeton, N.J.: Princeton University Press, 1990). James Ackerman claims that "any deep personal engagement with Judaism he might have felt would have been sufficient reason to avoid [the *Medieval Synagogues*] project" ("Richard Krautheimer: An Homage," in *Rome: Tradition, Innovation, and Renewal*, 82–83).

17 Krautheimer, "Gladly," 99.

18 Ibid., 100.

19 Ibid., 102.

20 Richard Krautheimer, *Corpus basilicarum christianarum Romae*, vol. 1 (Vatican City: Vatican, 1937).

21 Panofsky, "Three Decades," 321.

22 Erwin Panofsky, *Perspective as Symbolic Form*, trans. Christopher S. Wood (Cambridge: MIT Press, 1991); Ernst Cassirer, *The Philosophy of Symbolic Forms*, vol. 1, *Language*, trans. Ralph Manheim (New Haven: Yale University Press, 1953).

23 Kurt Weitzmann provides details about the connections between Goldschmidt and American art history in his *Sailing with Byzantium from Europe to America: The Memoirs of an Art Historian* (Munich: Editio Maris, 1994).

24 On the founding of the Institute for Advanced Study, see Ed Regis, *Who Got Einstein's Office?* (Reading, Mass.: Addison-Wesley Publishing, 1987), 3–38.

25 Flexner, a Southern Jew, may have been reacting to the role he played in the restriction of Jews from medical schools in the 1920s. Marcia Graham Synnott writes: "Following the publication of Abraham Flexner's 1910 report on 'Medical Education in the United States and Canada,' that exposed the 'enormous over-production of uneducated and ill-trained medical practitioners,' inferior commercial medical schools were eliminated, thereby reducing from 162 to 76 the number of those accredited. In order to ensure places for native-born, white, Protestant applicants, medical school admissions officers added religious and social criteria to academic qualifications. The obvious targets of restriction or exclusion were Jews, Catholics, Negroes, and women."

26 Regis, *Who Got Einstein's Office?* 6.

27 Panofsky, "Three Decades," 321.

28 Erwin Panofsky, "Iconography and Iconology: An Introduction to the Study of Renaissance Art," in *Meaning in the Visual Arts*, 26. Panofsky's use of the hat-lifting example has an interesting history. It made an earlier appearance in a 1932 article on the problem of description and interpretation in art ("Zum Problem der Beschreibung und Inhaltsdeutung von Werken der bildenden Kunst," *Logos* 21 [1932]: 103–19), where it was used to illustrate a theoretical distinction, first made by Karl Mannheim in 1922, between "objective" and "expressive" meaning. In this first use of the hat-lifting example, Panofsky effectively neutralized the class complications of Mannheim's original argument, which entailed the example of two men encountering a beggar on the street (Karl Mannheim, "Beiträge zur Theorie der Weltanschauungs-Interpretation," *Jahrbuch für Kunstgeschichte* 1 [1921–22]: 236–74). Panofsky's complete revision of Mannheim's example and the theoretical distinction it represents occurs finally in his most influential methodological statement, the classic "Introductory," in *Studies in Iconology: Humanistic Themes in the Art of the Renaissance* (New York: Oxford University Press, 1939), later retitled and reprinted over and over again as "Iconography and Iconology: An Introduction to the Study of Renaissance Art." It is here that Panofsky offers his extended interpretation, and overwrought humanistic allegory, of the gesture's origins in chivalric practices. It is also significant that he did not feel compelled to cite Mannheim in this permutation of the example; for an excellent discussion of Panofsky's relationship to the Hungarian-Jewish sociologist and fellow exile, see Joan Hart, "Erwin Panofsky and Karl Mannheim: A Dialogue on Interpretation," *Critical Inquiry* 19 (Spring 1993): 534–66.

29 Panofsky, "Iconography and Iconology," 27.

30 Chernow, *The Warburgs*, 373–74.

31 For a more detailed overview of the art historical migration, see Karen Michels's essay in this catalogue. I would also like to thank Michels for her helpful comments on this essay.

the german migration:
is there a figure in the carpet?

MARTIN JAY

no student of the forced migration from Germany to the United States during the Nazi era can fail to be impressed by the extent of its impact on the cultural life of the country to which its members fled. Of the somewhat more than one hundred thousand refugees who arrived between January 1933 and December 1941, almost eight thousand were academics and probably another fifteen hundred or so were artists, cultural journalists, or free-floating intellectuals.[1] Although some grudging attention has been paid to the silent majority of emigrés with no claim to membership in the *Bildungsbürgertum* (cultural bourgeoisie) or the artistic avant-garde,[2] the lion's share of scholarly research has focused on elite intellectuals, whose often poignant stories have special resonance for historians, who can so easily identify with them.

As a result there is now a dauntingly large volume of literature on the intellectual migration, whose sheer magnitude is perhaps indicated by the fact that the most ambitious attempt to summarize it all, the French scholar Jean-Michel Palmier's *Weimar en exil* (Weimar in exile), published in 1988, needed more than one thousand pages to tell its story.[3] Amid all of this scholarship there are many accounts dealing with individual disciplines and groups but few attempts to grasp patterns in the whole. This reluctance is not surprising, given the variety of fields affected and the divergent experiences of those who came. No general narrative or even ideal typical reconstruction can hope to do justice to the bewildering tangle of individual stories—some triumphant, others tragic—that make up the migration.

And yet it has been hard to refrain from trying to find at least one intelligible figure in this remarkably complex carpet. If a plausible pattern in the German intellectual migration has been sought, one frequent candidate has been its political configuration. From the very beginning, after all, the intellectual migrants knew that they were chased from Germany for political reasons and that their histories would therefore have an inevitable political dimension. And so for those scholars eager to do more than present yet another laundry list of distinguished intellectuals who invigorated this discipline or deprovincialized that one or muse about the perils of acculturation or the benefits of cross-fertilization, it has made sense to focus on the political implications of the migration, including its subtle impact on American politics.

As a result, a political reading of the migration's impact has frequently informed, at least tacitly, much of the previous literature. It is now in fact time, I would argue, to stand one remove from the migration and examine instead the pattern of politicization in the histories of the migration themselves. My real subject, in other words, is less the politics of the migration per se than its subsequent interpretation on the part of historians who have drawn out of it lessons for more contemporary purposes. By focusing on the subtle ways in which the history of the migration has served as an occasion for post facto political allegorization, we can understand something about the period that followed it, a period that extends to the present day.

If, as has frequently been noted, the political quarrels of the Weimar Republic were often carried on far into the period of exile, then it should be no surprise that the historiography following the end of the exile period remained deeply divided. Although *Exilforschung* (exile studies), as it has become known, is now so extensive that any generalization about its contours must be taken as provisional and open to many counterexamples, certain broad patterns can be discerned, which reflect, either explicitly or implicitly, deep political investments. Let me try to sketch them, first in the German literature on the migration and then in the American.

The two postwar Germanies, tensely divided along political lines, struggled to appropriate the legacy of the migration for purposes of legitimation.[4] Only the internal German resistance, relatively weak and splintered, could vie with it for the role of representing the "other Germany," that subordinate tradition of enlightened, Western-oriented liberalism, moderate socialism, or nonauthoritarian conservatism which might serve as a touchstone for a post-Nazi future.[5] In the immediate aftermath of the war the emigrés remained, to be sure, a problematic subject in the areas controlled by the Western powers, where the so-called inner emigrés, who had remained in Germany, resisted their claim to moral superiority. From their point of view, at least the non-Jewish emigrés were somehow "deserters" or even "traitors," who had abandoned their country in its time of need and returned, if they did at all, wearing the uniforms of the enemy's army. Here the classic episode was the controversy over Thomas Mann's provocative and insulting contention that the writings of all those who remained in Nazi Germany should be pulped because "a stench of blood and disgrace clings to them."[6] Mann (see fig. 307) was vilified by Otto Flake, Walter von Molo, Frank Thiess, and others who sought to justify their accommodations to the Third Reich as a form of passive resistance.

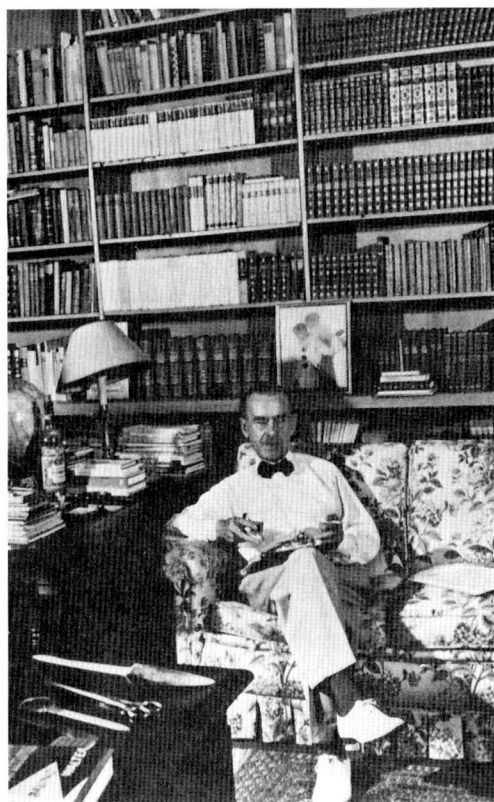

307
Thomas Mann at his home in the Pacific Palisades section of Los Angeles, 1946.

Once the dust settled in 1950s, however, it was apparent that the relative victors were the Manns, who had "run away," rather than the moral pygmies who defensively claimed that they had "stayed at their posts." Postwar German literature did not, of course, simply revert to the stylistic or substantive preferences of the migrants; a more existentially inflected, politically skeptical alternative, which had developed in POW camps around journals such as *Der Ruf*, was more in tune with the times than the typical emigré's humanist pathos.[7] And as late as 1964 a survey of schoolbooks in Bavaria showed that inner emigrés and even Nazi-approved writers were represented twenty times more frequently than those who fled Hitler.[8] But on the whole the tide was running in the emigrés' favor.

Mann himself, to be sure, did not live long enough to enjoy a true reconciliation with his countrymen, and his progressive commitments were all but forgotten when he was elevated into a depoliticized classic of German literature. This amnesia, it must be noted, was not entirely unmotivated. Mainstream West German scholarship in the years that followed sought, by and large, to valorize those emigrés who rejected both Nazism and its putative totalitarian twin to the left, communism. They lauded intellectuals who had rejected extremes and embraced the liberal, democratic, market-oriented system whose virtues many had come to appreciate firsthand during their exile. Anti-utopianism, skepticism about planning, a sober adoption of allegedly value-neutral American social-scientific techniques were all attributes of the emigrés most admired in the initial West German reading of their legacy. In fact, according to one historian, the neo-liberal underpinnings of the German *Wirtschaftswunder* owed a great deal to the return of such ideas from exile, even if their defenders often still remained citizens of the countries to which they had fled.[9]

In the much more rapidly launched scholarship of the newly created German Democratic Republic, the emigrés, as might be expected, were viewed through a very different ideological lens. Those whose "antifascist" credentials were deemed beyond reproach were lauded as forerunners of the new communist order. Broadly conceived in a manner that recalled the Popular Front strategy of the 1930s, these included writers and intellectuals who were bourgeois "progressives"—Lion Feuchtwanger (see fig. 308), Leonard Frank, and Heinrich Mann, for example—as well as militants of the proletarian cause such as Bertolt Brecht and Hanns Eisler. A number of these figures were in fact lured back to the GDR and

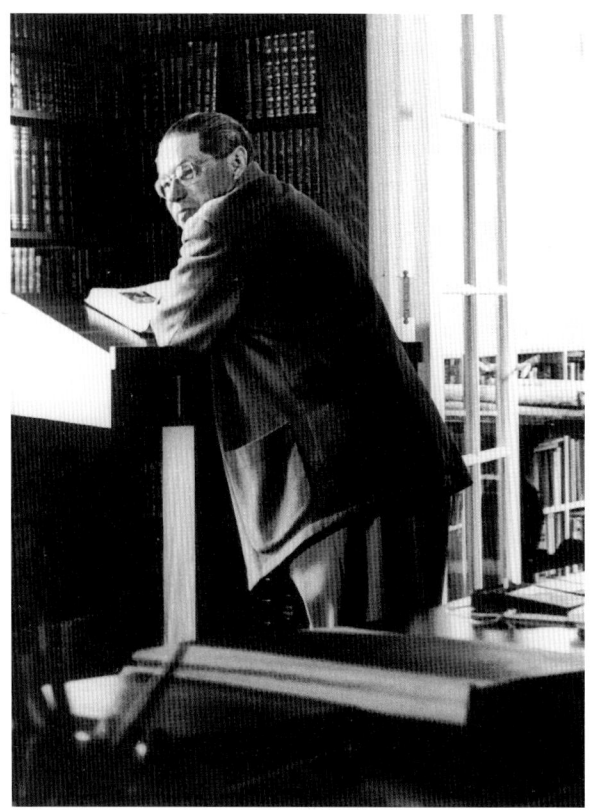

308
Lion Feuchtwanger in his study at Villa Aurora, Pacific Palisades, c. 1949; photograph by Morris P. Kagan.

given an honored status. Not surprisingly, those who were ignored or even pilloried were the former communist renegades—including Arthur Koestler, Willi Münzenberg, Manès Sperber, and Karl August Wittfogel—whose careers were generally admired in the alternative West German narrative of emigré deradicalization. Also forgotten were those who emigrated to the Soviet Union and became victims of the purges, among them Carola Neher, the original Polly Peachum of Brecht's *Three-Penny Opera*, who had been shot as a "Trotskyist." The category of "exile literature," moreover, was reserved primarily for those who were forced to leave for political reasons, while that of "emigration literature" was for those who allegedly fled ethnic persecution alone, an often dubious distinction that fit well with the general communist refusal to stress the centrality of anti-Semitism in its analysis of German fascism.[10]

By the mid-1960s, however, the blatantly Cold War spin put on divided Germany's reading of the emigré legacy began to slow down and in a certain respect was even reversed. In the West the former leftist backgrounds of some of the emigrés were rediscovered by a new generation eager to learn the lessons they might still teach. Virtually forgotten figures such as Ernst Bloch, Karl Korsch, and Siegfried Kracauer became objects of more than mere historical inquiry as their ideas were marshaled for contemporary purposes. The members of the Frankfurt School, several of whose leading figures had returned to Germany, were elevated into reluctant mentors of a New Left whose practical application of the school's critical theory they in fact deeply distrusted. Rather than serving as a source of legitimation for the Federal Republic, the emigrés, or at least some of them, could now be used by those who sought its radical restructuring.

In East Germany a somewhat less direct softening of the Cold War line can also be discerned. In journals such as *Sinn und Form* emigré writers who were once damned as decadent formalists, such as Hermann Broch, were paid new attention, and dissident Marxists such as Theodor W. Adorno and Walter Benjamin were given a cautious hearing. As the flabby humanist pieties of Popular Front cultural politics lost their hegemonic status, it was possible to appreciate the virtues of writers who did more than compose exemplary historical narratives in a socialist or critical realist style. Some refugees who had returned to the East, most notably the philosopher Ernst Bloch, became disillusioned and sought exile again in the West. By the 1980s, according to Ernst Loewy, a convergence between the two Germanies' receptions of the emigrés was in the works, preparing the way for a paradigm shift in the wake of the recent reunification.

Now, with the Cold War behind them, German scholars can perhaps begin to examine the political implications of the migration with comparatively fresh eyes. Although, as the *Historikerstreit* (historians' dispute) of the late 1980s showed, it is still too early to normalize the Nazi past, some historians now feel it may at least be time to reconsider the postwar politicization of the emigré legacy. Although there is a danger that such a reconsideration may also degenerate into a simple reversal of earlier celebrations—the filmmaker Hans Jürgen Syberberg's 1990 diatribe against the allegedly baleful influence of returning emigrés is an ominous sign of this possibility[11]—there is no reason to assume that this pattern will be widely followed by historians themselves.

Can the same pattern of politicization and nascent depoliticization be found in the American reception? Is a similar new paradigm of post–Cold War reassessment on the horizon? Here, of course, the initial stakes were very different from those in the two Germanies, as there was no postwar government that needed to borrow legitimation from those who fled or resisted the previous regime. Nor was there the problem of inner emigrés justifying themselves at the cost of those who had left. Still, in the American reception of the emigrés, political undertones are not hard to find. From the beginning of the migration itself, it was clear to those who came with strong political allegiances that they would have to modify their positions or keep them hidden from public scrutiny. Unwilling to jeopardize their newfound but still tenuous security, uncertain about the vagaries of American politics, focused more on events in Europe than on those on these shores, they were understandably reluctant to speak out in provocative ways. As has often been remarked, President Roosevelt became an adored icon for them, despite his shamefully weak effort to help refugees, which has been revealed only by subsequent scholarship.[12]

When America entered World War II, many emigrés eagerly joined the war effort and sought to influence American policy toward a defeated Germany. Even a number of the once-militant Marxists in the Institute of Social Research remained in government service for a while after the war.[13] But the McCarthy era—when some emigrés (for example, Brecht, Eisler, and Mann) returned to Europe and others (such as Ruth Fischer, Hede Massing, and Karl August Wittfogel) cooperated with the witch-hunters—had a chilling effect, to say the

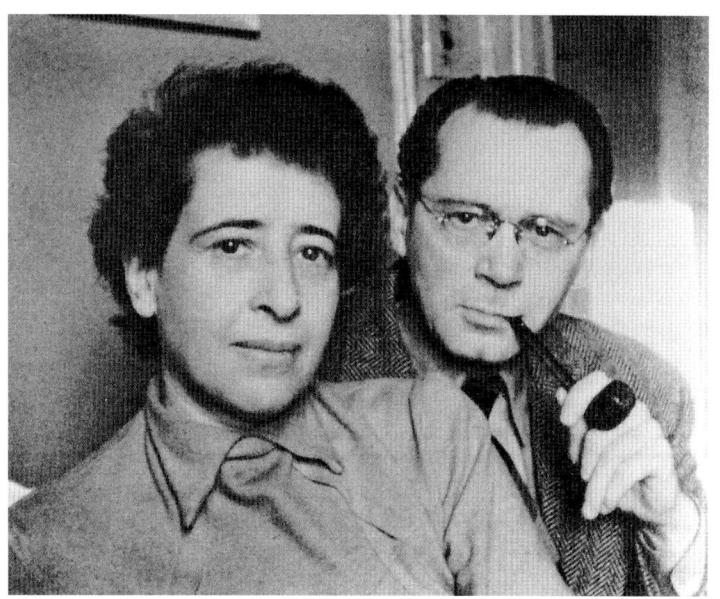
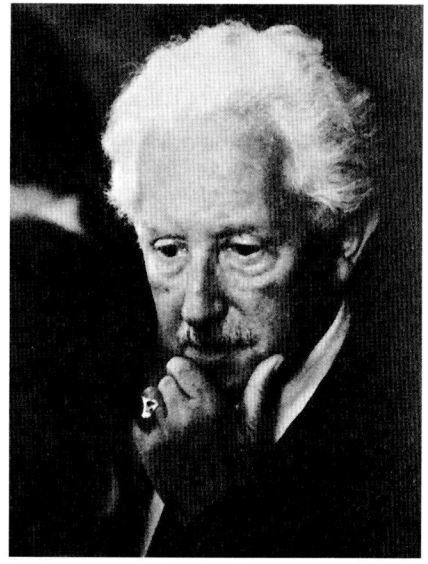
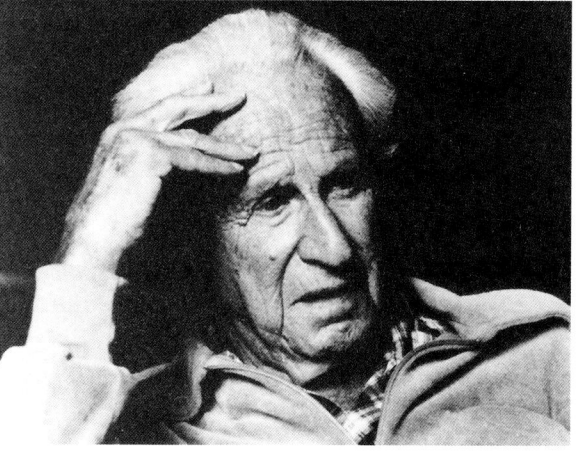

309
Hannah Arendt and her husband, Heinrich Blücher, in New York, c. 1950.

310
Erik H. Erikson; photograph by Olive Pierce.

311
Herbert Marcuse, 1978.

least, on emigré political activism. Only in the 1960s, during the Vietnam era, did indignant voices with thick German accents—like those of Hannah Arendt (see fig. 309), Erik Erikson (see fig. 310), Herbert Marcuse (see fig. 311), and Hans Morgenthau—feel comfortable enough to challenge mainstream American political thought and official governmental policy.

It was in fact during the late 1960s that the emigrés first became an object of serious historical study in this country.[14] Following the efforts of John Spalek, Guy Stern, and Joseph Strelka, the Modern Language Association organized an ongoing group on the migration, which later led to an international Society for Exile Studies and a substantial yearbook.[15] Laura Fermi's *Illustrious Immigrants* appeared in 1968, as did a volume of *Perspectives in American History* entitled *The Intellectual Migration: Europe and America, 1930–1960*; *Salmagundi*'s special issue *The Legacy of the German Refugee Intellectuals* was published in the following year.[16] In the 1970s such works as Robert Cazden's *German Exile Literature in America, 1933–1945,* H. Stuart Hughes's *The Sea Change,* Egbert Krispyn's *Anti-Nazi Writers in Exile,* and my own study of the Frankfurt School added to the general awareness of the exiles' importance.[17] During the 1980s scholarly interest remained strong, with synthetic treatments such as Anthony Heilbut's *Exiled in Paradise* and Lewis Coser's *Refugee Scholars in America*; monographs such as Peter Rutkoff and William Scott's *New School,* Russell Jacoby's *The Repression of Psychoanalysis,* and Barry Katz's *Foreign Intelligence*;

biographies of prominent exiles, including Elisabeth Young-Bruehl's *Hannah Arendt: For Love of the World* and Katz's *Herbert Marcuse and the Art of Liberation*; and essay collections such as Jarrell Jackman and Carla Borden's *The Muses Flee Hitler* and my own *Permanent Exiles*.[18] In addition, Reinhard Bendix, Felix Gilbert, Leo Lowenthal, and other eminent refugee scholars wrote extended memoirs, which counterposed the testimony of participants to the reconstructions of historians.[19] The 1990s opened with a volume devoted to refugee historians, edited by Hartmut Lehmann and James Sheehan for the new series of publications launched by the German Historical Institute in Washington, D.C., to which others were added a few years later, on the political philosophers Arendt and Strauss and on the experiences of women refugees.[20] In addition, a little-known corner of the migration was illuminated by Gabrielle Simon Edgcomb, who told the often moving story of refugees who taught at historically black colleges (for example, the sociologist Ernst Borinski, who taught at Tougaloo).[21]

A common theme of many of these accounts is the progressive deradicalization of most of the emigrés. No history of the Bauhaus fails to comment on its transition from a builder of workers' housing to an inspiration for International Style corporate headquarters. No commentator on Kurt Weill ignores his evolution from a militant collaborator with Brecht to a successful composer for the commercial Broadway stage. No critic of the once-radical artist George Grosz neglects what one called the "unseemly haste"[22] of his adjustment to the money ethic of American society.

Among social scientists the transformation is no less frequently remarked. To take a typical example, Rutkoff and Scott described the erstwhile socialist circle of political economists around Emil Lederer, the dean of the University in Exile at the New School for Social Research (see fig. 312), as experiencing a "politics of disillusionment." By the time it was complete, they write, "the New School emigrés had provided American intellectuals with the basis for a postwar ideological consensus that identified Nazism and communism as variants of totalitarianism.... For the members of the Graduate Faculty, the horror of 1933 had destroyed the idealism of 1918. In 1918 these intellectuals had seen themselves as a vanguard. By the late 1930's they considered themselves a rearguard, committed to a desperate defense of Enlightenment humanism." Or as the disillusioned Marxist Henry Pachter put it, "the great discovery of the 'thirties was that the dividing line is not between Left and Right but between decent people and political gangsters, between tolerant people and totalitarians."[23]

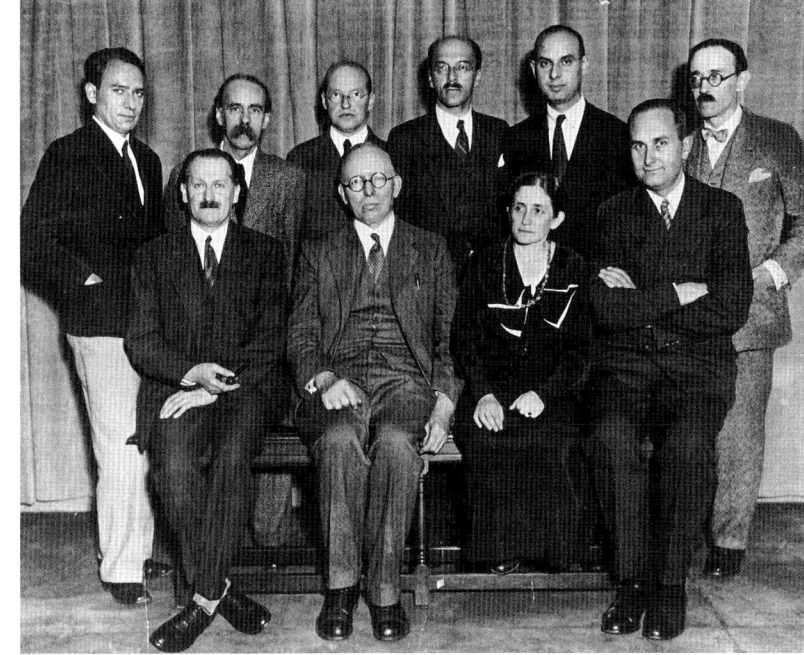

312
Faculty of the University in Exile of the New School for Social Research (left to right, seated: Emil Lederer, Alvin Johnson, Frieda Wunderlich, Karl Brandt; standing: Hans Speier, Max Wertheimer, Arthur Feiler, Eduard Heimann, Gerhard Colm, E. von Hornbostel); published in the *New York Times*, 4 October 1933.

What differs, however, in the accounts of this process of deradicalization and accommodation is the way in which it is plotted. For some the story is largely a triumphalist saga of salutary maturation. Lewis Coser's synoptic account of some fifty refugee scholars identifies the path to "success" with acculturation to dominant American values, albeit qualified by a modicum of marginal distance that permits a residual critical edge. Thus, in his reconstruction, insiderness and academic recognition become virtually the sole measure of an emigré's achievement. In the cases of the sociologist Paul Lazarsfeld and the political theorist Franz Neumann, for example, the result is that Coser emphasizes their influence on American social science while minimizing the loss of their former political allegiance. Comparing the fates of two major emigré psychoanalysts, Coser characteristically contends, "While [Erik] Erikson, with his many-faceted involvement in a great number of networks, made contributions to American culture at large, [Wilhelm] Reich, encapsulated in a cocoon of self-chosen disciples, developed esoteric themes that could never have been accepted by the culture in general, though they did stimulate the imaginations of active minorities in revolt against the main tenets of American culture." And as for the often politically embittered community of emigré writers in Hollywood, who refused to accommodate easily to American mass culture, he claims that the "gilded ghetto" in which they isolated themselves became a "ship of fools" where they were condemned to "artistic sterility."[24]

Although Coser recognizes that in certain cases, most notably that of Paul Tillich, the easy passage from critical outsider to mainstream insider had its costs in the banalization of their work, he by and large celebrates the success of the emigrés, a success built on, among other things, the loss of their often radical pasts. He even manages to applaud Adorno and Max Horkheimer for coming to take "a more benign and reformist outlook on American cultural phenomena"[25] in the 1940s, at virtually the same time they were in fact formulating a ruthlessly intransigent critique of the "culture industry" in their *Dialectic of Enlightenment*.

Subtly different interpretations are evident in the work of other scholars of the migration. Hughes, for example, claims that, exceptions such as Hannah Arendt aside, most exiles resisted the easy identification of communism and Nazism as variants of a single model of totalitarianism.[26] A colleague of a number of the more radical emigrés who served in the Office of Strategic Services during the war, he stresses their continuing resistance to the complete embrace of mainstream American values. Admiring their fierce ethical commitment, he praises Erikson for refusing to sign the notorious loyalty oath at the University of California in the early 1950s and Neumann for resisting Cold War pressures to turn political theory into an exercise in Machiavellian accommodation to the reigning order. Tacitly siding with the more radical members of the Frankfurt School in their debate with Erich Fromm, Hughes contends that their critique of mass society remained rooted in a Marxism that was never completely undermined by their newer American experience. For Hughes the emigrés' "sea change" was rarely so complete as to cancel out the critical edge they brought with them. Although he agrees that some loss of militancy occurred, he refuses to read the results as a wholesale capitulation to the politics of cautious moderation.

A similar appreciation of the adversarial energy of the migration as a whole is evident in Heilbut's magisterial *Exiled in Paradise*. Even in the films made by emigré directors, he senses a defiance of accepted norms, whether it be in the unfashionable attention paid to race relations by Fritz Lang and Otto Preminger or the bitter exposé of popular culture in Billy Wilder's *Sunset Boulevard*, which he calls a "dramatic deconstruction of the American dream in its contemporary incarnation, which was Hollywood itself."[27] Heilbut's account fittingly ends with a chapter entitled "Heroes of the 1960's," which details the contribution made by figures originally from very disparate political backgrounds to the disaffection of that generation: Arendt, Erikson, Marcuse, and Morgenthau. Although he acknowledges the importance of emigrés such as Bruno Bettelheim and Henry Kissinger, who played a very different role, it is clear that Heilbut identifies with those who remained in some sense "enemy aliens" rather than becoming fully assimilated Americans.

Even more eager to read the migration politically, but coming to less sanguine conclusions than Hughes or Heilbut about the survival of the emigrés' critical impulse, is Russell Jacoby. His study of Otto Fenichel and the small group of Freudian leftists who came to America is an unrestrained lament over the domestication of psychoanalysis in its new home. The pressures to accommodate produced by demands for professionalization, the prohibition of lay analysis, and the omnipresent threat of deportation for political reasons led Fenichel and his friends to confine their radical beliefs to privately circulated *Rundbriefe*, while in public they became stalwart defenders of classical Freudianism at its most unpolitical. As a result, Jacoby ruefully concludes, the field was open for the socially oriented neo-orthodox revisionism espoused by other emigrés, such as Fromm and Karen Horney, whose watered-down version of psychoanalysis lacked any radical power.[28]

A similar lament over the sapping of the emigrés' critical energies can be found in Mike Davis's widely read history of Los Angeles, *City of Quartz*. Although he acknowledges that European observers of that bewildering city had long been appalled by its apparent superficiality, he stresses the Weimar diaspora's "collective melancholy" and feelings of impotence in the face of a phenomenon they didn't really understand. "With few exceptions," Davis writes, "they complained bitterly about the absence of a European (or even Manhattan) *civitas* of public spaces, sophisticated crowds, historical auras and critical intellectuals. Amid so much open land there seemed to be no space that met their criteria of 'civilized urbanity.'" With Los Angeles as the "crystal ball of capitalism's future, they experienced all the more painfully the death agony of Enlightenment Europe." Their justifiable feelings of alienation, he suggests, were shared, despite all appearances, by those who seemed to prosper: "Even the most suntanned of the exiles, including [Thomas] Mann and [Max] Reinhardt, woke up to the fact that behind the Mediterraneanized affluence lurked exploitation and militarism."[29]

In the work of historians such as Hughes, Heilbut, Jacoby, and Davis—and I would have to add my own name to this list—the migration has thus been interpreted as a vital source of resistance, either potential or actual, to the dominant intellectual and cultural assumptions of the America to which the emigrés fled. As George Mosse grandiloquently put it in his essay on the "socialist humanism" of emigré novelists such as Alfred Döblin and Lion Feuchtwanger, "this heritage of German refugee intellectuals is of importance to our age."[30] Although there is almost universal agreement that some accommodation to American intellectual and cultural values was healthy, of the commentators mentioned above, only Coser has argued for a relative balance between the two traditions, however they may be understood. Whereas Jacoby is the most extreme in his denunciation of compromises, political and theoretical, he is not alone in worrying about the costs of the acculturation process. In short, for historians who discovered the migration during the 1960s, and who deplored the reversals of the subsequent decades, the migration has tended to be allegorized into a moment of brief and tenuous resistance to the dominant ideologies, political and scholarly, of American life. The fear that this moment may also have been ephemeral is captured in Hughes's observation in the early 1980s that, "as a younger generation of Americans who had no direct knowledge of the emigration came of age, its lessons began to be forgotten. Witness the current recrudescence of positivism in social science. Witness the renewed tendency to slice up the study of society into clearly demarcated disciplines and subdisciplines."[31]

Thus, it can be said that the reception of the migration by American scholars has been as politically charged in its own way as those in the two postwar Germanies. Whereas there it served in the struggle to legitimate or undermine the new regimes, here it could be marshalled by those who either celebrated the resiliency of American culture or bemoaned its ability to domesticate anything that might call it into serious question. Can it also be argued that a paradigm shift is in the works here with the end of the Cold War? If so, it seems to me less evident than the one Ernst Loewy sees for contemporary Germany, partly because no new major accounts of the migration have appeared since the collapse of Soviet communism. But one change does seem to be in the wind, which concerns the controversial impact of French theory on the American academy. Although by no means universally welcomed, it has served in certain quarters to dilute the impact of the exiles. No longer is the dominant debate in, say, psychoanalysis between the ego psychology of Erik Erikson, Heinz Hartmann, and Ernst Kris; the neo-orthodox revisionism of Erich Fromm and Karen Horney; and the Freudo-Marxism of Herbert Marcuse and Wilhelm Reich, but rather between the followers of a French version of Freud associated mostly with Jacques Lacan and those of an English one derived largely from the object-relations theory of W. R. D. Fairbairn and D. W. Winnicott. No longer is the Marxist humanism of many of the emigrés as powerful a guiding star for critical theory as an eclectic brew of poststructuralist and hermeneutic ideas, whose political implications are anything but clear. No longer is the cutting edge of aesthetic controversy the battle between modernism and realism, as it was for many of the emigrés, but rather a conflict between modernism and a postmodernism whose multifarious sources rarely include anything from the migration itself. And, finally, no longer is the issue of gender, to which the migration, understandably preoccupied with race and class, contributed relatively little,[32] marginal to our concerns.

Thus, with the passage of time and the gradual disappearance of the exiles themselves from our cultural life, other intellectual currents have emerged to supplant those they transplanted to American soil. And *pace* Hughes, these have not been predominantly positivist in tone, nor have they restored the disciplinary boundaries that existed before the migration. In political terms, moreover, they have tended to retain much of the critical, irreverent tone many historians have found so congenial in the migration, even if they lack the utopian hopes that at least some emigrés never entirely abandoned.[33]

In fact, a certain continuity between what we can crudely call German and French critical theory can be discerned precisely in their shared adversarial pathos. Or, at least, so their common enemies have argued.[34] Perhaps the most significant example can be found in Allan Bloom's best-selling jeremiad, *The Closing of the American Mind,* which blames the ills of the academy largely on intellectual subversion from abroad. But rather than focusing on the poststructuralist corrupters of the young, the French "left Nietzscheans," whose work he seems to know only by rumor, Bloom points a finger at what he calls "the German connection." Reversing Jacoby's lament about the domestication of the exiles' radicalism, he contends that they succeeded all too well in spreading the evils of European thought at its most nihilistic.

In his dyspeptic screed against the rise of irrationalism and relativism, Bloom sees Freud and Weber as the stalking horses for Heidegger and Nietzsche and argues that their popularity in the American academy was due to "a mix of German refugees from Hitler and of Americans who had either studied in Germany prior to Hitler or who had learned from these emigres."[35] The insidious infiltration of their ideas bore fruit in the 1960s, when excessive value relativism led to its opposite, the value certainty of self-styled radicals intent on remaking the world. Although it may have seemed that these young militants were drawing on a native heritage, Bloom thinks otherwise: "After the war, while America was sending out its blue jeans to unite the young of all nations, a concrete form of democratic universalism that has had liberalizing effects on many enslaved nations, it was importing a clothing of German fabrication for its souls, which clashed with all that and cast doubt on the Americanization of the world on which we had embarked, thinking it was good and in conformity with the rights of man. Our intellectual skyline has been altered by German thinkers even more radically than has our physical skyline by German architects."[36]

Bloom's sloppy diatribe cannot, of course, be taken as a serious consideration of the migration's impact; he makes only a few passing snide comments about selected emigrés, including Arendt, Fromm, Marcuse, and Adorno (whose first name, symptomatically, he misspells). And worse still, he disingenuously neglects to acknowledge that he is often merely parroting the conservative ideas of another prominent exile, his teacher Leo Strauss, whose influence on political theory and, indirectly, on political practice in this country has been extraordinary. What the pivotal place of the emigrés in *The Closing of the American Mind* does suggest is that the political allegorization of the migration has by no means ended. We have not yet reached a point of Olympian detachment in which it is possible to avoid identifying with the positions of one emigré or another.

It is precisely the ease with which the migration can be allegorized politically—at times as an emblem of America's genius for moderating extremism, at other times as a sign of our intolerance for critical ideas, at still others as a warning against foreign contamination—that bespeaks its continuing importance for us. For it shows that the experiences and ideas of those who sought refuge from Hitler in America strike a deep chord in our contemporary culture as well, even if the actual refugees have virtually passed from the scene. Although the Cold War may have ended and the German reception of the emigration can be said to have entered a new phase, the so-called culture wars of the recent American past show no sign of abating. Their noisier battles, to be sure, are waged over different issues—minority discourse, multiculturalism, the timelessness of the Western canon, and so on—but important skirmishes are still being fought over the political lessons to be drawn from that extraordinary influx of intellectual talent that changed the American cultural landscape forever.

Notes

1 The number of German and Austrian refugees arriving in America from 1933 to 1941 has been put at 104,098, of whom some 7,622 were academics. See Donald Peterson Kent, *The Refugee Intellectual: The Americanization of the Immigrants of 1933–1941* (New York: Columbia University Press, 1953), 15, and Helge Pross, *Die deutsche akademische Emigration nach den Vereinigten Staaten, 1933–1941* (Berlin: Duncker und Humblot, 1955), 45. About half of the total refugee population settled in New York City, but the academics were more widely scattered.

2 See, for example, Herbert Strauss, "Zur sozialen und organisatorischen Akkulturation deutsch-jüdischer Einwanderer der NS-Zeit in den USA," in *Leben in Exil: Probleme der Integration deutscher Flüchtlinge im Ausland, 1933–1945*, ed. Wolfgang Frühwald and Wolfgang Schieder (Hamburg: Hoffman und Campe, 1981), and Steven M. Lowenstein, *Frankfurt on the Hudson: The German-Jewish Community of Washington Heights* (Detroit: Wayne State University Press, 1989). One conclusion that they draw was that the identity of the nonintellectuals was often more Jewish than German, which was not usually the case with the more assimilated elite. The former also came less frequently from large urban centers such as Berlin or Frankfurt.

3 Jean-Michel Palmier, *Weimar en exil: Le destin de l'émigration intellectuelle allemande antinazie en Europe aux Etats-Unis* (Paris: Payot, 1988). To be fair, Palmier needed so much space because he dealt with the European as well as the American migration. He would have needed even more if he had treated emigrés who went elsewhere in the world.

4 For a recent overview, see Ernst Loewy, "Zum Paradigmenwechsel in der Exilliteraturforschung," *Exilforschung: Ein internationales Jahrbuch* 9 (1991): 208–17. Palmier also gives a summary in *Weimar en exil*, 14ff., and provides a full bibliography of relevant texts.

5 The historical reconstruction of the resistance, it should be noted, was no less politically charged, the role of the communists, for example, being minimized in the Federal Republic and that of the Catholic conservatives being underplayed in the GDR. A similar account can be given of the commemoration of the concentration camps, which began in the GDR with Buchenwald in 1958 and in the Federal Republic with Dachau in 1965. Here too a deliberate pattern of politically motivated selective memory was at work.

6 Mann to Dolf Sternberger, 19 March 1946, cited in Nigel Hamilton, *The Brothers Mann: The Lives of Heinrich and Thomas Mann, 1871–1950 and 1875–1955* (New Haven: Yale University Press, 1978), 335. The entire episode is usefully summarized in this book. For another account, see Egbert Krispyn, *Anti-Nazi Writers in Exile* (Athens: University of Georgia Press, 1978).

7 For an account, see Krispyn, *Anti-Nazi Writers in Exile*, chap. 11.

8 Lionel Richard, *Le nazisme et la culture* (Paris: Maspero, 1978), 167–71.

9 Joachim Radkau, *Die deutsche Emigration in den USA: Ihr Einfluss auf die amerikanische Europapolitik, 1933–1945* (Düsseldorf: Bertelsmann Universitätsverlag, 1971). It was largely the ideas of Austrian economists, who were schooled in neoclassical theories, rather than German ones, who tended to be from the historical school, which had an impact after the war.

10 In the West German literature, by contrast, *exile* referred to those who were forced to leave, for whatever reason, whereas *emigré* referred to those who left by choice. Thus, those who remained after 1945—more than 80 percent by some estimates—turned from exiles to emigrés. See, for example, the usage in Benita Luckmann, "New School—Variantan der Rückkehr aus Exil und Emigration," in *Exil, Wissenschaft, Identität: Die Emigration deutscher Sozialwissenschaftler, 1933–1945*, ed. Ilja Sruber (Frankfurt: Suhrkamp, 1988). A similar distinction sometimes appears in the American literature; see, for example, Lewis A. Coser, *Refugee Scholars in America: Their Impact and Their Experiences* (New Haven: Yale University Press, 1984), 11. He uses the category of "refugee" to embrace both groups.

11 Hans Jürgen Syberberg, *Vom Unglück und Gluck der Kunst in Deutschland nach dem letzten Krieg* (Munich: Matthes und Seitz, 1990).

12 See, for example, Arthur D. Morse, *While Six Million Died: A Chronicle of American Apathy* (New York: Random House, 1967); David S. Wyman, *Paper Walls: America and the Refugee Crisis, 1938–1941* (Amherst: University of Massachusetts Press, 1968); idem, *The Abandonment of the Jews: America and the Holocaust, 1941–1945* (New York: Pantheon, 1984); Henry L. Feingold, *The Politics of Rescue: The Roosevelt Administration and the Holocaust, 1938–1945* (New Brunswick, N.J.: Rutgers University Press, 1970); and Saul S. Friedman, *No Haven for the Oppressed: United States Policy towards Jewish Refugees, 1938–1945* (Detroit: Wayne State University Press, 1973).

13 Their story is told in Barry M. Katz, *Foreign Intelligence: Research and Analysis in the Office of Strategic Services, 1942–1945* (Cambridge: Harvard University Press, 1989).

14 There were, to be sure, isolated earlier studies, such as Maurice R. Davie et al., *Refugees in America: Report of the Committee for the Study of Recent Immigration from Europe* (New York: Harper, 1947); Stephen Duggan and Betty Drury, *The Rescue of Science and Learning: The Story of the Emergency Committee in Aid of Displaced Foreign Scholars* (New York: Macmillan, 1948); Franz Neumann et al., *The Cultural Migration: The European Scholar in America* (Philadelphia: University of Pennsylvania Press, 1953); William K. Pfeiler, *German Literature in Exile: The Concern of Poets* (Lincoln: University of Nebraska Press, 1957), as well as the personal memoirs of participants such as Varian Fry (*Surrender on Demand* [New York: Random House, 1945]), but the field as a whole did not really develop until the late 1960s.

15 The yearbook *Exilforschung: Ein internationales Jahrbuch* began publication in Munich in 1983. The society, whose president since 1986 has been Michael Winkler, also publishes an annual newsletter, which contains exhaustive bibliographical material on the migration as well as reports of scholarly conferences. Both are published almost entirely in German, however, which reflects the society's main constituency of specialists in German literature in Germany and America.

16 Laura Fermi, *Illustrious Immigrants: The Intellectual Migration from Europe, 1930–1941* (Chicago: University of Chicago Press, 1968); *The Intellectual Migration: Europe and America, 1930–1960*, special issue of *Perspectives in American History* 2 (1968), republished as Donald Fleming and Bernard Bailyn, eds., *The Intellectual Migration: Europe and America, 1930–1960* (Cambridge: Harvard University Press, 1969); *The Legacy of the German Refugee Intellectuals*, special issue of *Salmagundi* 10–11 (Fall 1969–Winter 1970); republished as Robert Boyers, ed., *The Legacy of the German Refugee Intellectuals* (New York: Schocken Books, 1972).

17 Robert E. Cazden, *German Exile Literature in America, 1933–1945: A History of the German Press and Book Trade* (Chicago: American Library Association, 1970); H. Stuart Hughes, *The Sea Change: The Migration of Social Thought, 1930–1945* (New York: Harper and Row, 1975); Krispyn, *Anti-Nazi Writers in Exile*; Martin Jay, *The Dialectical Imagination: A History of the Frankfurt School and the Institute of Social Research, 1923–1950* (Boston: Little, Brown, 1973).

18 Elisabeth Young-Bruehl, *Hannah Arendt: For Love of the World* (New Haven: Yale University Press, 1982); Barry Katz, *Herbert Marcuse and the Art of Liberation: An Intellectual Biography* (London: Verso, 1982); Jarrell C. Jackman and Carla M. Borden, eds., *The Muses Flee Hitler: Cultural Transfer and Adaptation, 1930–1945* (Washington, D.C.: Smithsonian Institution Press, 1983); Anthony Heilbut, *Exiled in Paradise: German Refugee Artists and Intellectuals in America from the 1930s to the Present* (New York: Viking Press, 1983); Russell Jacoby, *The Repression of Psychoanalysis: Otto Fenichel and the Political Freudians* (New York: Basic Books, 1983); Coser, *Refugee Scholars in America*; Peter M. Rutkoff and William B. Scott, *New School: A History of the New School for Social Research* (New York: Free Press, 1986); Katz, *Foreign Intelligence*; and Martin Jay, *Permanent Exiles: Essays on the Intellectual Migration from Germany to America* (New York: Columbia University Press, 1985).

19 Felix Gilbert, *A European Past: Memoirs, 1905–1945* (New York: W. W. Norton, 1988); Reinhard Bendix, *From Berlin to Berkeley: German-Jewish Identities* (New Brunswick, N.J.: Transaction, 1986); Leo Lowenthal, *An Unmastered Past: The Autobiographical Reflections of Leo Lowenthal*, ed. Martin Jay (Berkeley: University of California Press, 1987). For a recent discussion of their significance, see Barry Katz, "The Accumulation of Thought: Transformations of the Refugee Scholar in America," *Journal of Modern History* 63 (December 1991): 740–52.

20 Hartmut Lehmann and James J. Sheehan, eds., *German Speaking Refugee Historians in the United States, 1933–1970's* (Cambridge: Cambridge University Press, 1991); Peter Graf Keilmansegg, Horst Mewes, and Elisabeth Glaser-Schmidt, eds., *Hannah Arendt and Leo Strauss: German Emigres and American Political Thought after World War II* (Cambridge: Cambridge University Press, 1995); Sybille Quack, ed., *Between Sorrow and Strength: Women Refugees of the Nazi Period* (Cambridge: Cambridge University Press, 1995).

21 Gabrielle Simon Edgcomb, *From Swastika to Jim Crow: Refugee Scholars at Black Colleges* (Malabar, Fla.: Krieger, 1993).

22 Heilbut, *Exiled in Paradise*, 137. He notes that the former dadaist now chose Norman Rockwell as his model popular illustrator!

23 Rutkoff and Scott, *New School*, 127; Henry Pachter, "On Being an Exile," *Salmagundi* 10–11 (Fall 1969–Winter 1970): 14.

24 Coser, *Refugee Scholars in America*, 62, 234–35.

25 Ibid., 97.

26 Hughes, *The Sea Change*, 241.

27 Heilbut, *Exiled in Paradise*, 255. For a recent account that tries to soften the picture of emigrés in Hollywood bitter about their experience, see Helmut G. Asper, "Hollywood—Hölle oder Paradies? Legende und Realität der Lebens- und Arbeitsbedingungen der Exilanten in der amerikanischen Filmindustrie," *Exilforschung: Ein internationales Jahrbuch* 10 (1992): 187–200.

28 Jacoby's critique echoes the earlier one of Marcuse and Adorno, which also informed his *Social Amnesia: A Critique of Conformist Psychology from Adler to Laing* (New York: Basic Books, 1975). In his widely remarked *The Last Intellectuals: American Culture in the Age of Academe* (New York: Basic Books, 1987), Jacoby's analysis of the deradicalization of psychoanalysis was broadened into a nostalgic critique of the transformation of genuine intellectuals, who sit in worldly European cafés, into mere academics, who populate college cafeterias in late twentieth-century America.

29 Mike Davis, *City of Quartz: Excavating the Future in Los Angeles* (London and New York: Verso, 1990), 47, 48, 52.

30 George L. Mosse, "The Heritage of Socialist Humanism," *Salmagundi* 10–11 (Fall 1969–Winter 1970): 138.

31 H. Stuart Hughes, "Social Theory in a New Context," in Jackman and Borden, eds., *The Muses Flee Hitler*, 120.

32 The nonfeminist character of the exiles' impact may not be solely a product of their adherence to traditional European models of patriarchy. Jacoby argues, for example, that a decline in the role of women in the psychoanalytic community occurred with the transfer to America, where the requirement for medical training proved a significant obstacle.

33 See, for example, Lowenthal, *An Unmastered Past*.

34 Not only their enemies have seen a continuity. Mike Davis, for example, writes that "the contemporary 'adventures in hyperreality' of Eco and Baudrillard in Southern California, which have caused such a stir, strictly follow in these earlier footsteps" (*City of Quartz*, 50).

35 Allan Bloom, *The Closing of the American Mind* (New York: Simon and Schuster, 1987), 148.

36 Ibid., 152.

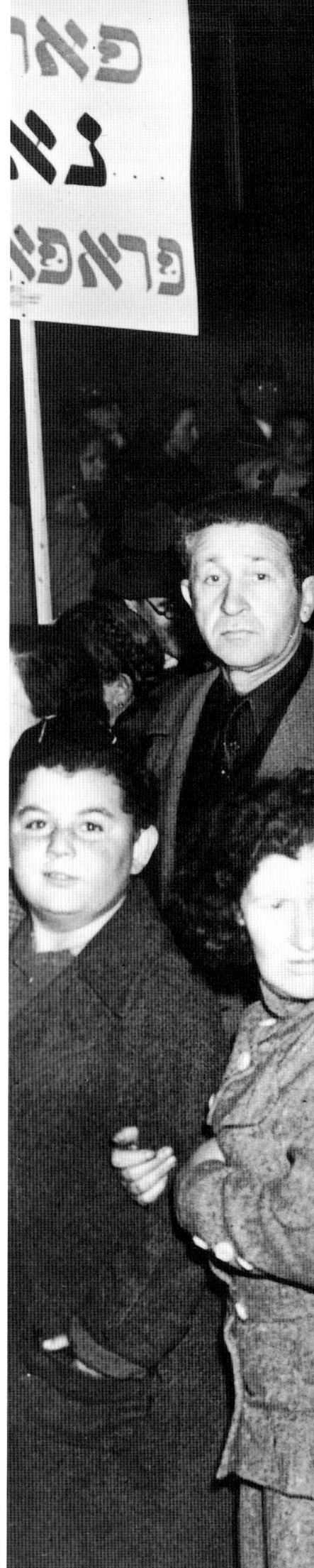

Overleaf left:
Demonstration in Los Angeles urging boycott of German goods, November 24, 1938.

Overleaf right:
Long view of Hollywood Boulevard, from the air, c. 1941, with Grauman's Chinese Theatre in the foreground and, across the street on the far side, the Hollywood Hotel.

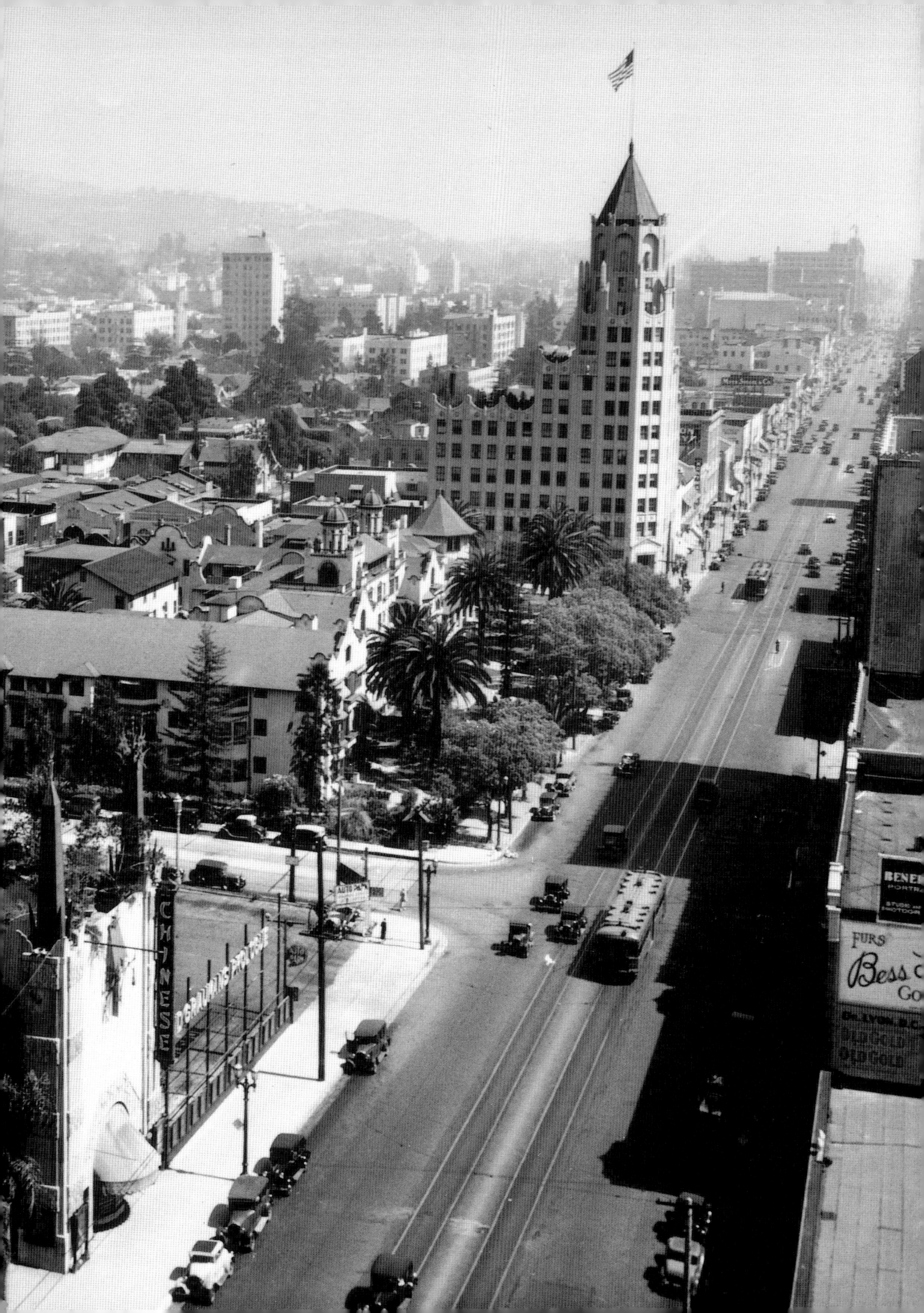

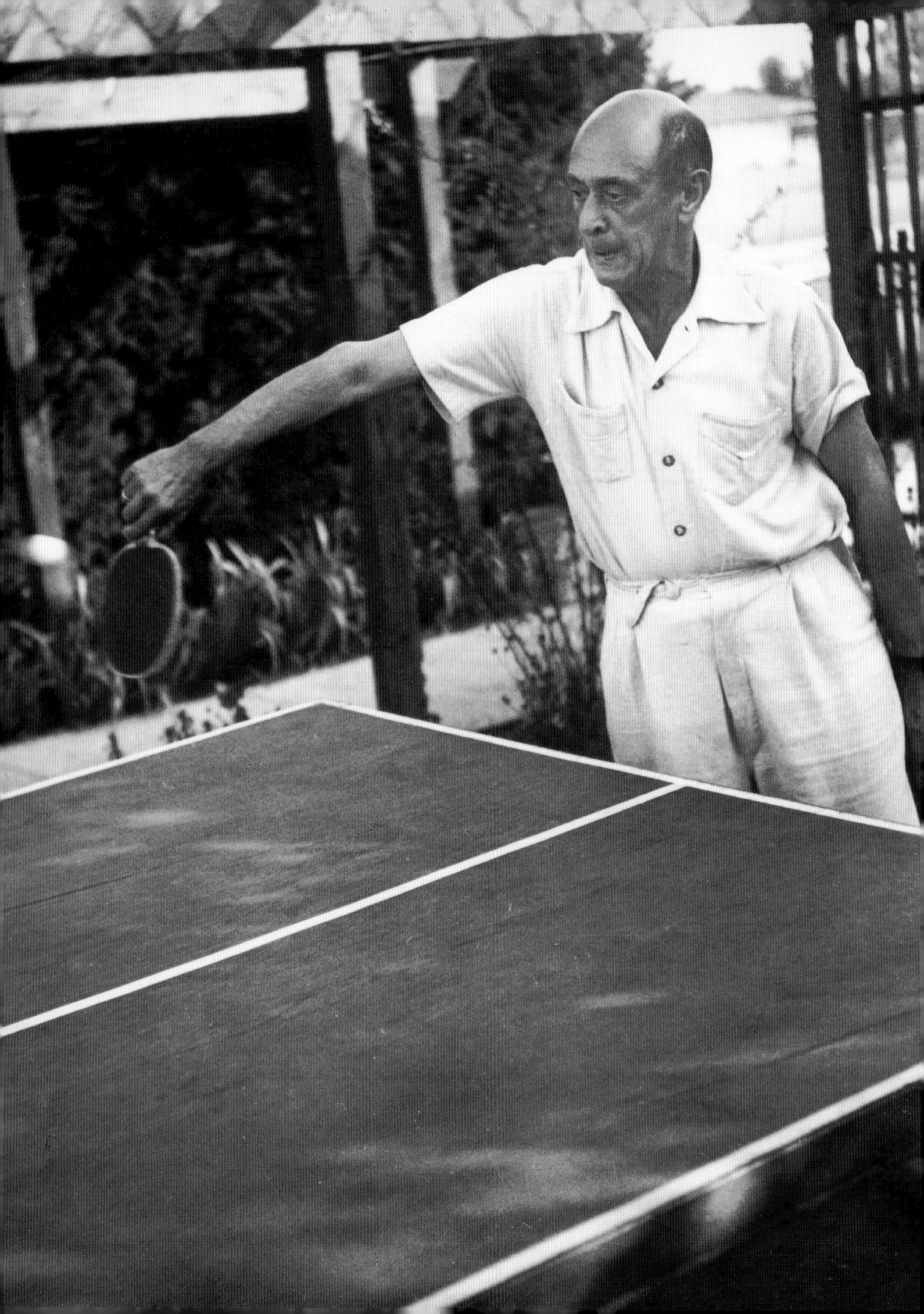

paradise:
the southern california idyll of hitler's cultural exiles

LAWRENCE WESCHLER

during the late 1950s Mrs. Arnold Schoenberg, the widow of the composer, used to entertain visitors on the front lawn of their home on Rockingham, just off Sunset, in the Brentwood section of West Los Angeles. (I know; I was one of them. My mother, the daughter of another emigré composer, Ernst Toch, had herself been a childhood friend of Schoenberg's daughter Nuria.) Every half hour or so, a huge tour bus would wheel round, all of its passengers craning their necks the other way, gazing out across the street. The metallic voice of the tour guide would squawk, "And on the left you can see the house where Shirley Temple lived in the days when she was filming..." And then they'd be gone. Mrs. Schoenberg would smile indulgently, whimsy (or so I inferred at the time) masking pain. Who knows what she'd make nowadays of the buses lurching by on their way to O. J. Simpson's notorious digs, just a few houses up the road? Or what the tourists inside those buses would make of news of her. But, oh, there was a time.

Well, the following section of this catalogue is for Mrs. Schoenberg. It's for Schoenberg and Igor Stravinsky, Bertolt Brecht and Charles Laughton, Thomas Mann and Heinrich Mann, Lion Feuchtwanger and Franz Werfel, Alma Mahler-Werfel and Salka Viertel, for Richard Neutra and Rudolf Schindler, Theodor Adorno and Max Horkheimer, Ernst Toch and Erich Korngold, Hanns Eisler and Mario Castelnuevo-Tedesco, Bruno Walter and Otto Klemperer, Fritz Lang and Jean Renoir, Christopher Isherwood and Aldous Huxley... for the scores of emigrés who, fleeing the upsurge of European fascism, during the 1930s and the 1940s and tapering off into the 1950s, briefly transformed Los Angeles into one of the capitals of world culture and then were gone, having left no trace, having left some trace, having profoundly altered the horizons of the Southern California experience.

The manna of creative intensity, as has often been noted, seems to float through history from one locale to another, and in the late 1920s that manna hovered over Berlin. During those last years of the Weimar regime, Berlin was the center for modernist music (both composition and performance), for expressionist art, theater, and film. With Hitler's seizure of power that vibrant glow of aesthetic productivity was suddenly extinguished. In some ways Los Angeles during the 1930s and early 1940s may be seen as its afterglow, the image that persists for a few moments when you've been forced to shut your eyes.

Not all of the emigrés we will be considering came from Berlin, although most of them had spent a good deal of time there during the previous decade. And not all of them arrived as political refugees; some who were already here in the late 1920s and early 1930s (the architects Neutra and Schindler, for example, and many of those who worked in the film industry, including Ernst Lubitsch, Berthold and Salka Viertel, and Paul and Frederick Kohner) were

313
Arnold Schoenberg playing ping-pong at his home in the Brentwood section of Los Angeles.

The Manns at the Viertels'

Perhaps the most evocative memoir of life in the emigré community is Salka Viertel's marvelously affecting *The Kindness of Strangers* (1969), now sadly out of print. Mrs. Viertel, the wife of the great Viennese and Weimar director Berthold Viertel, had herself been a significant actress back in Europe and became a notably successful scenarist in Hollywood, particularly associated with her friend Greta Garbo, for whom she wrote, among other scripts, *Queen Christina*. The Viertel home on Mabery Road, in Santa Monica, was one of the mainstays of emigré social life, the site, for example, of frequent Sunday morning brunches whose regulars, she reports, included the Arnold Schoenbergs, the Otto Klemperers, the Bertolt Brechts, the Aldous Huxleys, Christopher Isherwood, Bronislow Kaper, Oscar Levant, Max Reinhardt, Charles Laughton… and Johnny Weissmuller.

It was also the site of one of the more significant evenings in L.A. emigré history, a dinner held in 1941 to celebrate Heinrich Mann's seventieth birthday. Salka Viertel's account of the event affords a sense of the tone of her whole book:

Heinrich Mann's seventieth birthday was approaching and the "German writers in exile" felt that some notice should be taken of this event. Unfortunately, on the same day in March, 1941, Thomas Mann was to receive an Honorary Doctor's degree from the University of California in Berkeley. Immediately afterward he had a commitment for lectures and would not return to Los Angeles until the end of April. After long diplomatic negotiations, the dinner had to be postponed until May. A major disagreement ensued as to whether it should take place in a restaurant or a private home. I called Berthold in New York and asked him whether I should not offer our house for the celebration. He was all for it. Lion Feuchtwanger and Liesl Frank were both delighted and promised to give me a list of guests, which had to be accepted by Nelly [Heinrich Mann's wife]. She and Alma Mahler-Werfel were feuding and Nelly disapproved of everyone who was friendly with the Werfels. Finally the Feuchtwangers succeeded in arranging a truce and forty-five persons were invited. I set a long table in the living room; it could be removed quickly after the dinner was over. Decorated with flowers and candles it looked very festive.

Heinrich sat on my right and Thomas Mann on my left, Nelly was opposite us, towering over the very small Feuchtwanger on her right; on her left was Werfel. Everyone else was seated strictly according to age and prominence. I had begged Berthold to send me a telegram which would welcome Heinrich Mann, and I hoped to get it before dinner. Good, faithful Toni Spuhler took over the kitchen and managed very well, in spite of the many refugees who, awed by the importance of the evening, had insisted on giving her a hand, and also helping Walter and Hedy to serve. For them Heinrich and Thomas Mann, Alfred Neumann, Franz Werfel, Alfred Polgar, Lion Feuchtwanger, Alfred Doeblin, Walter Mehring, Ludwig Marcuse, Bruno Frank represented the true Fatherland to which in spite of Hitler they adhered, as they adhered to the German language.

We finished the soup and as the telegram had not arrived I made a speech, which had the virtue of being very brief. Bruno Frank and Feuchtwanger were to speak after the main course and I motioned to Walter to go on serving but he discreetly pointed to Thomas Mann, who had risen and was putting on his spectacles. Then, taking a sizeable manuscript out of the inner pocket of his tuxedo, he began to read. I assumed it was at least fifteen pages long and I was right, because many years later Thomas Mann mentioned this speech in a letter to his son Klaus, offering it as an essay for the periodical *Decision*. It was a magnificent tribute to the older brother, an acknowledgement of Heinrich's prophetic political wisdom, his far-sighted warnings to their unhappy country, and a superb evaluation of his literary stature.

We hardly had time to drink Heinrich Mann's health before he rose, also put on his glasses and also brought forth a thick manuscript. First he thanked me for the evening then, turning to his brother, paid him high praise for his continuous fight against fascism. To that he added a meticulous literary analysis of Thomas Mann's oeuvre in its relevance to the Third Reich. I no longer remember all the moving and profound thoughts expressed in both speeches. It gave one some hope and comfort at a time when the lights of freedom seemed extinguished in Europe, and everything we had loved and valued buried in ruins. At the open door to the pantry the "back entrance" guests were listening, crowding each other and wiping their tears.

The roast beef was overdone and Toni was upset, but the guests were elated and hungry and did not mind. Bruno Frank's and Lion Feuchtwanger's speeches were brief and in a lighter vein. The dessert, my chocolate cake, a "specialty of the house," was served and disappeared rapidly. Toward the end of the dinner Marta Feuchtwanger spontaneously offered a toast, "To Nelly, who saved Heinrich Mann's life, practically carrying him in her arms on their rough trek through the Pyrenees. She supported him with her loving strength and gave courage to us all."

Nelly hid her face in her hands when we surrounded her to clink glasses and then, screaming with laughter, pointed to her red dress, which had burst open revealing her bosom in a lace bra.

Berthold's telegram was handed to me after we had left the table. I read it aloud and Heinrich Mann suggested that all the guests send a greeting to the absent host. While everyone gathered to sign his name, I said to Bruno Frank how touched I was by the wonderful homage the brothers had paid each other.

"Yes," said Bruno. "They write and read such ceremonial evaluations of each other, every ten years."

From Salka Viertel, *The Kindness of Strangers* (New York: Holt Rinehart, 1969), 250–51. ©1969 by Salka Viertel. Reprinted by permission of Henry Holt & Co., Inc.

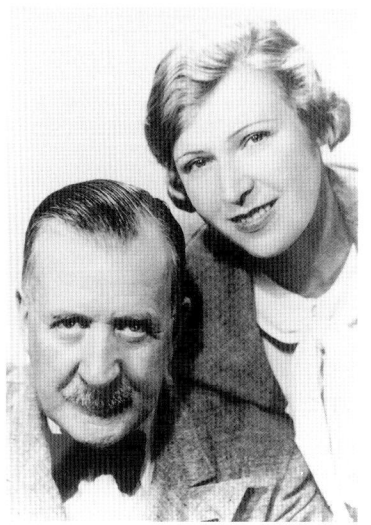

314
Heinrich and Nelly Mann, late 1930s.

transformed into instant refugees when safe return to their homeland was suddenly denied them. Nor did they all arrive immediately. Many first attempted to carve out shelter in Czechoslovakia or Austria or Poland or France (some indeed were Czech or Austrian or Polish or French), but one by one, as these havens collapsed before the spreading Nazi terror, they were forced to flee once again. (To cite one particularly curious such way station, an unusually large number of the L.A. emigrés—including the Feuchtwangers, the Thomas Manns, the Heinrich Manns, the Bruno Franks, Alma Mahler-Werfel and Franz Werfel, Aldous Huxley, and during the summers Bertolt Brecht and Arnold Zweig—initially congregated in the hills surrounding the French Mediterranean fishing village of Sanary, from which many of them presently had to escape, in some cases by foot over the Pyrenees, following the fall of France in 1940.)

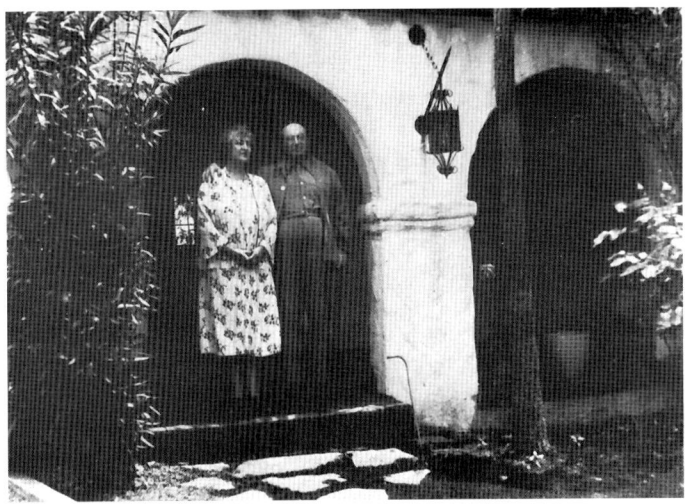

315
Franz Werfel and Alma Mahler-Werfel in front of their house on Los Tilos Road in Hollywood, 1941.

The emigrés congregated in Southern California for many reasons. To begin with, there was the Mediterranean climate, the same balmy ambiance that for centuries had exercised its hypnotic attraction on the imaginations of Northern Europeans, luring them south each year, away from their long, bleak, low-skyed winters. (Although clearly not on *all* such Northern Europeans: Hannah Arendt, visiting Los Angeles from her own transplanted base in New York, wrote to her husband that "the climate alone is enough to turn people meshuge.") In any case, that climate could have been found elsewhere as well, but Los Angeles also offered Hollywood, with its vast opportunities for lucrative employment. After a certain point, however, the primary reason for these emigrés' gathering in Southern California may have been the fact that so many others had already settled there; they had achieved a vital mass that began to exert its own magnetic pull.

The usual account of their life in L.A. casts the emigrés as a group of Continental geniuses utterly victimized by the philistine cultural environment to whose backwaters an ill tide of history had relegated them. "Wherever I go," Brecht wrote in a poem, "they ask me 'Spell your name!' / And, oh, that name was once accounted great." When it came to names, the eminently proud Max Reinhardt, perhaps the greatest stage director of his time back in Berlin and Vienna, had to accustom himself to the back-slapping informalities of presumptuous glad-handers who routinely addressed him as "Max!" Or, in a similar vein, there's the old story about the rich society hostess at Ira Gershwin's one evening who (in John Russell Taylor's telling) "tried to rope Schoenberg into the after-dinner entertainments with 'Give us a tune, Arnold.'"

The reality of the situation, however, was considerably more complicated or, at any rate, nuanced than such tales suggest. Many of the arriving professionals were indeed forced

An Evening with the Werfels

"S. N. Behrman described a dinner party at the home of Franz Werfel, then married to the widow of Gustav Mahler. Alma Mahler Werfel, as she called herself—following Werfel's death it became Alma Werfel Mahler—regaled the guests, who included Arnold Schoenberg, with tales of her conquests: the painter Oskar Kokoschka had been so in love with her that he took a life-sized model of her on his travels; Alban Berg had dedicated *Wozzeck* to her; the architect Walter Gropius was a devoted slave. Coming to the end of the list, she looked straight at Werfel and said: 'But the most interesting personality I have known—was Mahler!' Her current husband nodded in fervent agreement, and the party ended with Mme Werfel producing the lock of Beethoven's hair which the Vienna Symphony had presented to Mahler on his departure to America."

From John Baxter, *The Hollywood Exiles* (New York: Taplinger, 1976), 216–17.

to downgrade their vocations (stories abound of lawyers and musicians becoming chauffeurs and caterers, concert pianists becoming piano tuners). Still, one must take into account the "dachshund effect." ("Two dachshunds," the story goes, "meet out on the palisade in Santa Monica, and one assures the other, 'Here, it's true, I'm a dachshund; but in the old country I was a Saint Bernard!'") There inevitably was a good deal of idealization going on with regard to putative prior incarnations. But even this line of thinking misses the single most trenchant point, which is that for all their displacement and disorientation, an extraordinary number of emigrés in Southern California were living quite well indeed. For starters, just look at *where* they were living: Beverly Hills, Pacific Palisades, Santa Monica, the West Side . . .

(Of all the destinies suggested by the accompanying map, perhaps the most incongruous is that of the sublime Marxist critic Theodor W. Adorno gazing out sourly upon the dismaying vistas of unredeemably bastardized American pop culture from his humble redoubt on Kenter, just south of Sunset. It's still something of a leap to picture him there, painstakingly dissecting the *Los Angeles Times*'s astrology column in preparation for his exhaustive—and exhausting—essay "Stars down to Earth," noting, for example, how "inasmuch as the social system is the 'fate' of most individuals independent of their will and interest, it is projected upon the stars in order to thus obtain a higher degree of dignity and justification in which the individuals hope to participate themselves. At the same time, the idea that the stars, if only one reads them correctly, offer some advice mitigates the very

Steak Tartare and a Sardine Sandwich

At a news conference during an American concert tour in the early 1930s, my grandfather, the Viennese-born modernist composer Ernst Toch, gently urged his interlocutors to open themselves to new sounds. He warned them of the consequences of trying to force such sounds into preexisting mental compartments such as the preclassical or the baroque or the romantic. "In such a case," he explained, "either the music remains outside of you, or else you force it with all of your might into one of those compartments, even though it does not fit. And that hurts you, and you blame the music. But in reality it is you who are to blame, because you forced it into a compartment into which it did not fit, instead of calmly, passively, quietly, and without opposition, helping the music to build a compartment for itself." The assembled reporters absorbed this lesson impassively and then asked a few more mundane questions, such as the composer's favorite food, to which Toch replied "Steak tartare." Predictably, the next morning, the local paper's headline trumpeted the news conference's most significant revelation: "AUSTRIAN COMPOSER EATS RAW MEAT!"

If Americans often had a hard time fitting the emigrés into their own preexisting compartments, the emigrés, for their part, frequently displayed an obverse tendency. Toch's daughter (my mother) Franzi used to tell a story about how several years later, in the late 1940s, she and her close friend, Schoenberg's daughter Nuria, went on a double date. In fact, this was to be the seventeen-year-old Nuria's first such outing. When Franzi and the two escorts arrived at the front door of the Schoenberg manse on Rockingham, a tense but proper Schoenberg was there to present his daughter. Sternly he inquired, "What time will Nuria be home?" "Well," replied one of the young men, "let's see, the opera downtown will end around eleven, and then there's the ride back"—remember, this was in the days before the existence of the Santa Monica Freeway—"and we'll probably go out for a snack—we should be back by about one-thirty." "Oh," frowned Schoenberg. "Do you have to go out for a snack? Couldn't I give you a sardine sandwich to take along?"

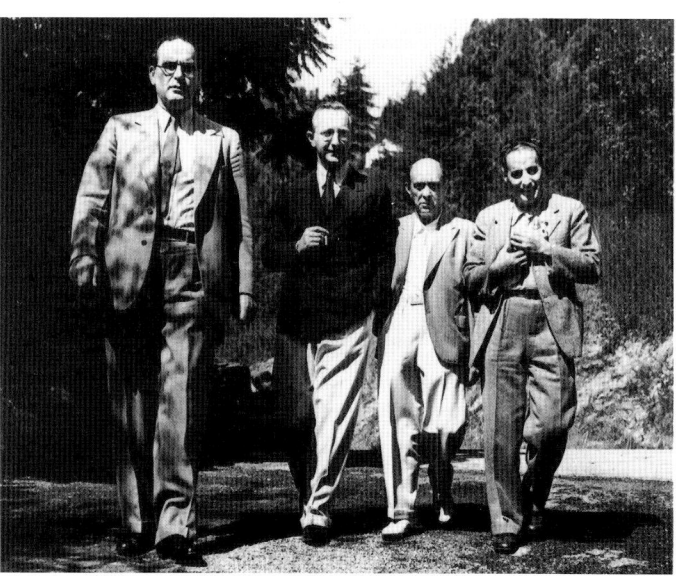

316
Otto Klemperer (left), Prince Hubertus zu Löwenstein, Arnold Schoenberg, Ernst Toch, 1937.

same fear of the inexorability of the social processes the stargazer himself creates." And so on. If there were clearly some things about America Adorno way over-interpreted and others he just plain never got—for instance, jazz—there were, at the same time, among his writings moments of startling aphoristic lucidity: "The triumph of advertising in the culture industry is that the consumers feel compelled to buy and use its products even though they see through them." Such that: "Mass culture is unadorned make-up." And though he obviously disdained pretty much everything about his California interlude—and returned to Frankfurt as soon as he was able, in 1949—even he admitted: "Reflections of this sort are hardly conceivable without American experiences. It is scarcely an exaggeration to say that a contemporary consciousness that has not appreciated the American experience, even in opposition, has something reactionary about it.")

Indeed, we will not begin to plumb the true despair of these outcasts until we comprehend that they were, as they themselves often noted, Exiled in Paradise (the title, incidentally, of Anthony Heilbut's magisterial volume subtitled *German Refugee Artists and Intellectuals in America from the 1930s to the Present*). How painfully incongruous must lazy palms on breezy evenings have seemed to people whose homeland was being bombed to smithereens. "Here everything blooms in violet and grape colors that look rather made of paper," Thomas Mann wrote a friend in June of 1941, soon after settling in Pacific Palisades, "and because one can't quite appraise them, one can't praise them. But I can praise the oleander; it blooms very beautifully. Only I have a suspicion that it may do so all year round." Their continual anxiety over the fate of loved ones was compounded by a nagging sense of guilt at their own safety. "Day after day," Brecht recorded in a poem entitled "Summer 1942," "I see the fig trees in the garden / The rosy faces... / The chessmen on the corner table / And the newspapers with their reports / Of bloodbaths in the Soviet Union." The exiles were continually launching into fierce political disputes concerning the proper course for postwar Germany, as if the very intensity of such disputations could mask their irrelevance. "Where I am, there is Germany," Thomas Mann is often quoted as having proclaimed, and many of his friends were advancing his name for the presidency of the postwar German republic. But what they thought, as they sat secure on the benign side of a distant continent, was pretty much beside the point. Surely they must have sensed this, and it must have contributed to their frustration.

Although many of the personnel had been salvaged—L.A. really constituted a second Weimar—the esprit never quite revived; it was a shadow Weimar. What the emigrés perhaps missed most was the sense of resonance that had supported their activities on the Continent.

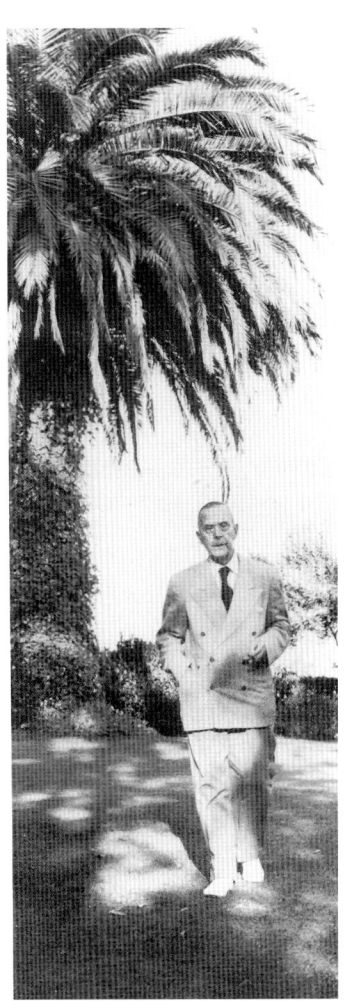

A Walk on the Beach

From Thomas Mann's diary:

Thursday, April 14 [1938]; Beverly Hills

Got to sleep late, Phanadorm. Drank coffee. Wrote a page and was stimulated. Outing to the beach with the Huxleys, the weather clearing rapidly and becoming warmer, where we got out and took a rather long walk along the glistening blue-and-white ocean at ebb tide. Many condoms on the beach. I did not see them, but Mrs. Huxley pointed them out to Katia.

From Thomas Mann, *Diaries, 1918–1939*, ed. Hermann Kesten, trans. Richard and Clara Winston (New York: Harry N. Abrams, 1982).

317
Thomas Mann in the Pacific Palisades section of Los Angeles, 1947.

Back there a rich tradition of popular immersion in the arts, coupled with a thriving structure of support (there were, for example, four year-round, top-notch orchestras in Berlin and dozens of live theaters), provided a continuous context of anticipation. Their ongoing work was charged with pressing and immediate significance. Not only would audiences experience that work, but they would spend hours arguing about it. Now, by contrast, as composer Ernst Krenek once complained, the emigrés were confronted with "the echolessness of the vast American expanses." Conductor Henri Temianka cited the primary characteristics of Southern California as "unlimited indifference and passive benevolence toward anything and anybody."

And yet this was a time when benign indifference was proving fatal not only to the spirit but also in terms of actual lives. One chief way in which the emigrés came into contact with the locals was through the scramble for affidavits. Their desperate efforts to save relatives and friends still trapped behind Nazi lines were immeasurably complicated by a U.S. government requirement that every entering refugee had to be sponsored by some individual who could submit an affidavit and accompanying financial statement guaranteeing economic support of the refugee for a period, if necessary, of up to five years. The same collateral funds could not be used twice, so there emerged a feverish quest to find new sponsors, usually Americans, who would be willing to post the required bond on behalf of people they didn't even know. The search became more complicated after Pearl Harbor, when the German emigrés were ironically classified as "enemy aliens" and had all their foreign royalties and accounts impounded (they were also required to observe a strict curfew throughout the war).

Outside their various affidavit and employment contacts the emigrés appear to have lived a fairly insular existence. They culled one another for friendship and even transplanted enmities intact. (Stravinsky and Schoenberg, for example, lived within several miles of each other but appear to have preserved the same arch distance they had maintained in Europe when the one reigned over Paris and the other over Berlin.)

It was entirely possible to go weeks without having to dust off one's faulty English. (Gottfried Reinhardt tells a wonderful story about visiting the Clover Club, a casino on Sunset Boulevard, one evening in the company of Otto Preminger. As it happened, they were the only two non-Hungarians at the roulette table, and the agglutinative language of their neighbors steadily grated on Preminger's nerves until finally "he brought his fist down on the baize, shouting, 'Goddamnit, guys, you're in America! Speak German!'") "We live our by now deeply habituated waiting room days," Thomas Mann wrote a friend, "among our

---

Mann, Schoenberg, and Doctor Faustus

The emigré scene in Los Angeles tended to grow quite inbred and was occasionally given over to bizarre eruptions of scandalous enmity. Perhaps the most famous of these involved the 1948 publication of Thomas Mann's novel *Doctor Faustus*. The protagonist of Mann's complex allegory of the demonic rise of Adolf Hitler and the selling of Germany's soul was a spectacularly brilliant composer named Adrian Leverkuhn, whose increasingly feverish explorations—he was, in addition, apparently suffering from some sort of venereal disease—culminated in his creation of a twelve-tone system remarkably like Arnold Schoenberg's. (During the composition of the novel Mann had indeed received extensive guidance on the intricacies of Schoenberg's method from Adorno.)

At any rate, soon after the book's publication (and, according to several accounts, considerably goaded on by a slyly meddling Alma Mahler-Werfel), Schoenberg grew beside himself with fury—or rather with two seemingly contradictory furies. On the one hand, he was enraged that his own role as the actual creator of the twelve-tone method had not been acknowledged in the body of the text (he invoked the anxious fantasy of some 1988 edition of an *Encyclopedia Americana* in which Mann would be credited as the system's creator and he himself dismissed as a pathetically false claimant and "a nobody"). On the other, he was just as frenziedly mortified that readers might actually assume that he was the model for Leverkuhn. Marta Feuchtwanger used to tell a story about a disconcerting chance meeting with the composer at the Brentwood Country Mart one afternoon around that time, when, reaching for a grapefruit, she was suddenly confronted by Schoenberg himself, on the far side of the aisle, shouting (though thankfully in German), "Lies, Frau Marta, lies! You have to know, *I never had syphilis!*"

The Max Reinhardt Workshop

"My father fell in love with the landscape, the climate, the openness of the inhabitants," Gottfried Reinhardt, the son of Max Reinhardt, arguably the greatest stage director of his era in Vienna and Berlin, wrote of his father's years in Southern California. "This love, which lasted the rest of his life... remained largely unrequited."

Though not entirely so: Reinhardt père's lush 1934 production of *A Midsummer Night's Dream*, in the Hollywood Bowl, with Mickey Rooney in the role of Puck, was an unqualified smash—it's just that its success proved sadly ephemeral.

"It is wonderful here on the Pacific, and life is a thousand times better than in New York," the father wrote his son in 1942. "But I grew up on the fourth balcony of the Burgtheater."

And indeed, by 1942, Gottfried Reinhardt's father was scraping together most of his livelihood running a school for young actors, the Max Reinhardt Workshop. "What my father did not understand," Reinhardt *fils* reports,

was why every member of [the emigré community] considered himself happy to be invited to his house under the Pacific palms for dinner, for conversation, and for the best of memories, when hardly anyone came to see his performances at his Workshop. The Max Reinhardt Workshop curiously was no center of attraction to the [emigré] ghetto. Its activities took place behind closed doors.

I think it might interest you to see a modern version of *Jedermann*, the final production this semester; it introduces a good many talented young people. I would be very happy if you and Mrs. Lubitsch could come today, tomorrow or the day after. Warmest regards, Max Reinhardt

A draft for a telegram to Lubitsch to be typed by my father's secretary. Similarly to Greta Garbo:

Please come to the Workshop today or tomorrow and take a look at the old *Everyman* in a modern version with a number of young talents. It would make me very happy to see you again. Cordially yours, Max Reinhardt

Identical messages were drafted for Charlie Chaplin, Sam Goldwyn, Harry and Jack Warner, Joe Schenck, Darryl Zanuck, Aldous Huxley, James Hilton, Harold Lloyd, Cecil B. De Mille, Joe Pasternak, Frank Capra, Walt Disney, Walter Wanger, Norma Shearer, Charles Boyer, Bette Davis and many, many others: "I would not dare impose on your precious time..."

All to no avail. As Reinhardt's son concludes, "The Europeans would rather wallow in a rich Reinhardt past than enjoy a more modest Reinhardt present (of the sort that so many of them had demanded of him back home)."

From Gottfried Reinhardt, *The Genius: A Memoir of Max Reinhardt* (New York: Knopf, 1979), 304–5.

318
Max Reinhardt's production of *A Midsummer Night's Dream* at the Hollywood Bowl, 1934. Reinhardt is standing behind his Puck, Mickey Rooney (center).

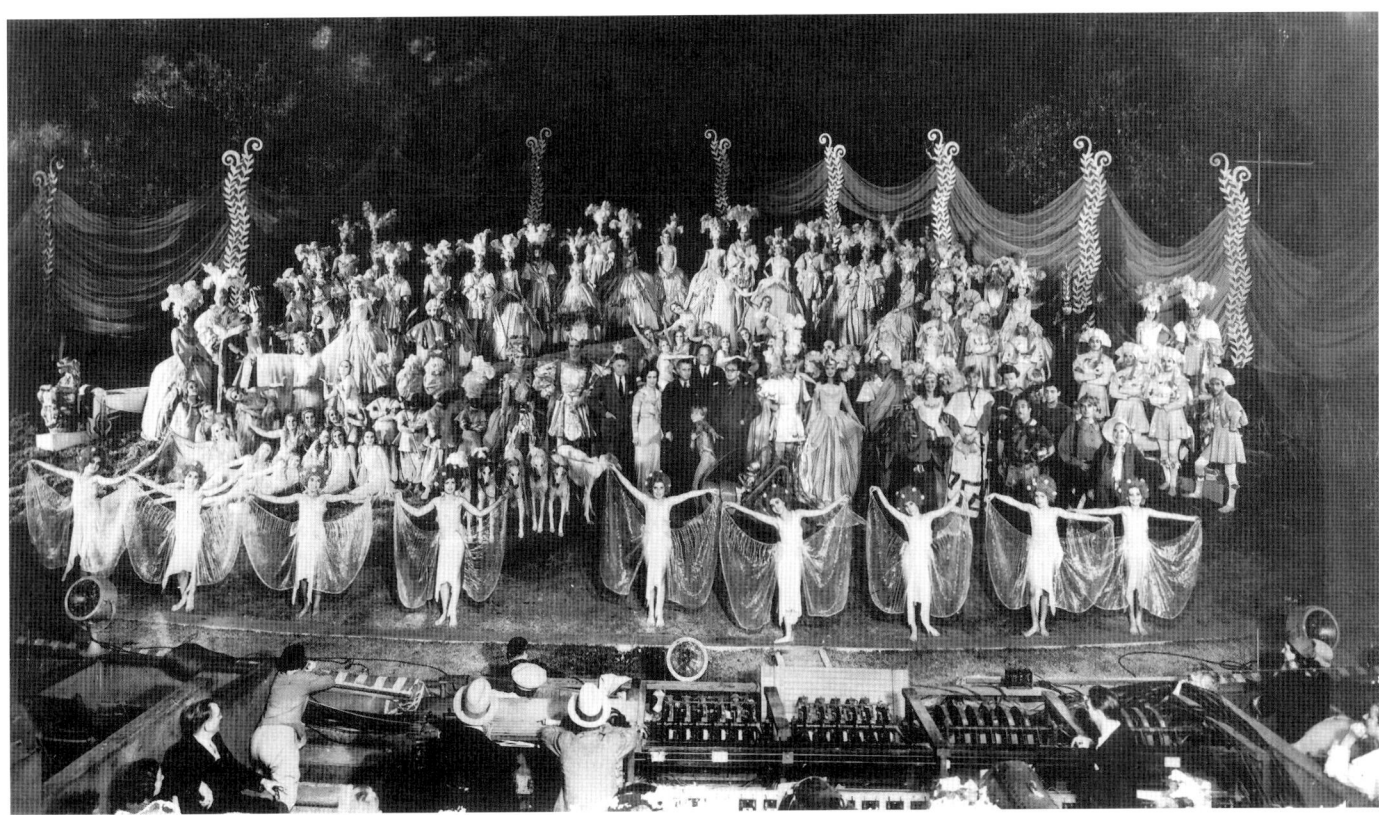

Discovering the Barbed Wire

Constance Collier was actually a distinguished *English* stage actress who was active in Hollywood during the 1930s, but her 1935 letter to her friend Hugh Walpole anticipated the feelings many of the other emigrés would be experiencing during the years to come:

Hugh, this place is just like Donington Hall [which, during World War I, had apparently served as a POW camp for captured enemy soldiers]. When the German prisoners first went there they were amazed by its splendor and beauty. 'Aren't the English fools!' they said. 'Why, it's better to be prisoner than free.' Then after walking in the grounds for a few days, they discovered the barbed wire. A month later all they did was to walk on the same track up to the barbed wire and back again.

Quoted in John Russell Taylor, *Strangers in Paradise: The Hollywood Emigrés, 1933–1950* (London: Faber and Faber, 1983), 91.

palms and lemon trees, in sociable intercourse with the Franks, Werfels, Dieterles, Neumanns—always the same faces, and if occasionally an American countenance appears, it is as a rule so strangely blank and amiably stereotyped that one has had quite enough for some time to come." In reviewing the emigrés' letters and memoirs, it is startling how often one finds them drifting into a common metaphorical conceit: they're always likening themselves to Roman nobility in the rustic provinces, Horace and Virgil exchanging visits from one hilltop villa to the other. They could be as stubbornly patronizing and aloof as the locals were sometimes naive and gauche. They were inbred, cliquish, and caste conscious, and yet this brash American town gradually began to exercise a fascination over them.

Many emigrés did secure employment in one form or another in Hollywood. The European Film Fund—spearheaded by, among others, Ernst Lubitsch, Paul Kohner, Salka Viertel, Wilhelm Dieterle, and Bruno and Liesl Frank—was instrumental in locating studio jobs for dozens of individuals, notably including Leonhard Frank, Wilhelm Speyer, Walter Mehring, Hans Lustig, Heinrich Mann, and Alfred Döblin (the latter two of whom had truly been Saint Bernards back in the old country). But there were many horror stories; for one thing, many of those thus benefited were merely given make-work assignments, if that, at low salaries and even then only for one year, after which they were cut loose and forced to scramble. Bertolt Brecht, perhaps the greatest playwright of this century,

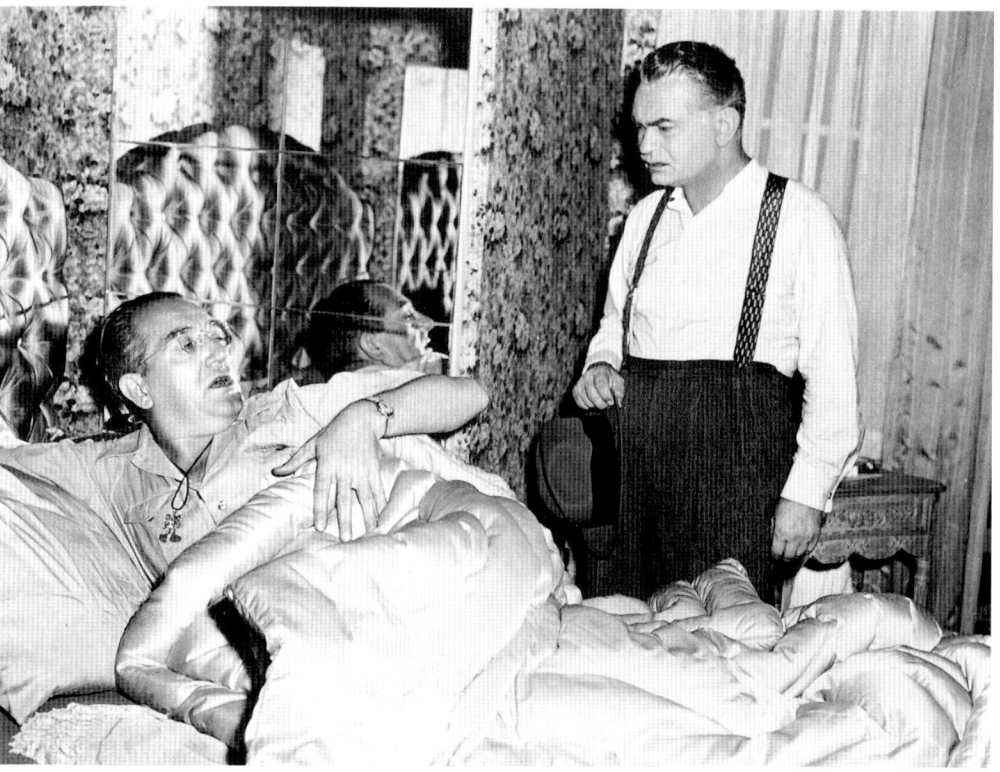

319
Producer-director Fritz Lang, standing in for actress Joan Bennett, offers tips to Edward G. Robinson during a rehearsal for Universal's *Scarlet Street* (1945).

was repeatedly unsuccessful in his attempts at placing screenplays. (During his six years in Los Angeles he authored only one completed film, Fritz Lang's *Hangmen Also Die*, and he subsequently disowned that.) One of his poems from the period, entitled "Hollywood," consists in its entirety of the following lines:

> Every morning to earn my bread
>
> I go to the market where lies are bought.
>
> Hopefully
>
> I line up with the sellers.

Brecht didn't make it easy, however; Gottfried Reinhardt, Max's son and an unusually sympathetic intermediary at the studios, reports that on one occasion the playwright came to his office and "in his unadulterated Bavarian accent, fascinated me for an hour and a half with a proposal for a film about the production, distribution and consumption of bread," a proposal that, as Reinhardt notes wryly, "had as much chance of being accepted by MGM as *Gone with the Wind* would have had of being put on by Brecht's Berliner Ensemble." Ernst Toch, a fine modernist composer back in Berlin, was quickly typecast as a specialist in chase scenes and eerie effects (that's what the studio executives made of Germany's *Neue Musik*). He used to complain to Oscar Levant that musical

---

Hell

A particularly trenchant surveyor of the barbed-wire perimeter of Hollywood's lotus prospects was, of course, Bertolt Brecht. Consider the following typically sour entry from his diary, dated August 9, 1941:

i feel as if i had been exiled from our era, this is tahiti in the form of a big city; at this very moment i am looking out onto a little garden with a lawn, shrubs with red blossom, a palm tree and white garden furniture, and a male voice is singing something sentimental to piano accompaniment—it's not a wireless. they have nature here, indeed, since everything is so artificial, they even have an exaggerated feeling for nature, which becomes alienated. from dieterle's house you can see the san fernando valley; an incessant, brilliantly illuminated stream of cars thunders through nature; but they tell you that all the greenery is wrested from the desert by irrigation systems. scratch the surface a little and the desert shows through: stop paying the water bills and everything stops blooming. the butchery 15,000 kilometres away, which is deciding our fate right across europe at its broadest point, is only an echo in the hubbub of the art-market here.

<small>From Bertolt Brecht, *Journals*, ed. John Willet, trans. Hugh Rorrison (New York: Routledge, 1993), 159.</small>

He elaborated on several of these themes across an extended series of poems. For example, in one of them, "On Thinking about Hell," he began by noting how just as London had been hell for Shelley, so L.A. seemed hell to him:

> In Hell too
> There are...
>   fruit markets
> With great heaps of fruit, albeit having
> Neither smell nor taste. And...
> Jolly-looking people [who] come
>   from nowhere and are
>   nowhere bound.
> And houses, built for happy
>   people, therefore standing
>   empty
> Even when lived in.
>
> The houses in Hell, too, are not
>   ugly.
> But the fear of being thrown on
>   the street
> Wears down the inhabitants of
>   the villas no less than
> The inhabitants of shanty towns.

Or consider another of Brecht's variations on the theme, this time from a poem called "Hollywood Elegy":

> The village of Hollywood was
>   planned according to the
>   notion
> People in these parts have of
>   heaven. In these parts
> They have come to the conclu-
>   sion that God
> Requiring a heaven and a hell,
>   didn't need to
> Plan two establishments but
> Just the one: heaven. It
> Serves the unprosperous,
>   unsuccessful
> As hell.

<small>From Bertolt Brecht, *Poems, 1913–1956*, ed. John Willet and Ralph Manheim (New York: Methuen, 1976), 367, 380.</small>

320
Otto Klemperer at the Bel Air Bay Club with son Werner and daughter Lotte, 1935.

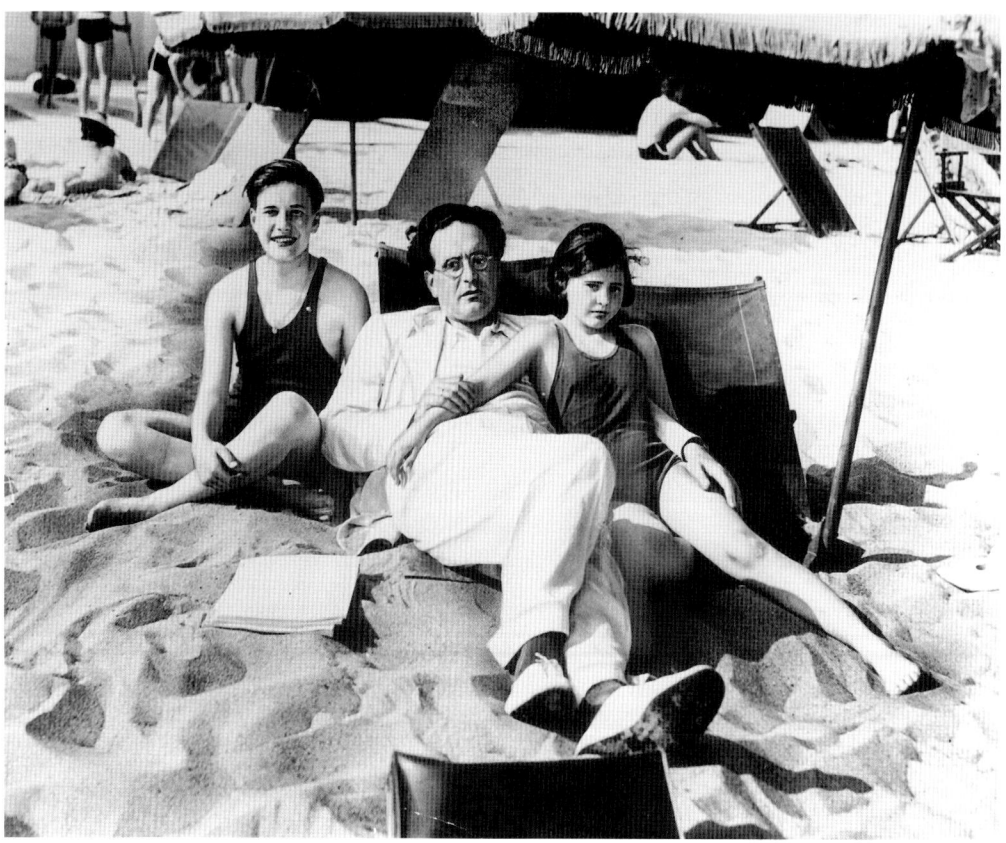

directors would often economize in recording his scores by simply eliminating the upper staves. ("No serious composer writes for the motion pictures for any other than money reasons," Hanns Eisler wrote in 1947, summing up his own experiences in his book *Composing for the Films*, written in collaboration with Adorno. Eisler goes on to excoriate the kind of stupid, mindless music that constitutes "the sort of melodrama for which the German language has no specification but which the English word 'tune' expresses quite accurately.")

Such comments and stories, which perpetuate the image of Hollywood as the very incarnation of crass Americanism, in one sense obscure the real drama, which was that many of the studio moguls were themselves European emigrants from the immediately prior generation, usually from the "backward" steppes of Eastern Europe, and that what was in fact being played out, at least in part, was a ritual of class revenge. Back in Europe the highbrow cultural figures of Vienna and Berlin had looked upon these peasants and shopkeepers with disdain, and now they were getting a touch of their own treatment. Furthermore, horror stories notwithstanding, from emigré ranks emerged some of the most successful careers in Hollywood, including those of agent Paul Kohner, composer Erich Korngold, scenarist Georg Froeschel, and directors William Dieterle, Ernst Lubitsch, William Wyler, Billy Wilder, and Otto Preminger—to name just a few and not even to mention the

---

Schoenberg's Father

The memoirs of Thomas Mann's wife, Katia, *Unwritten Memories* (based on taped interviews), tend to get a bit catty, especially in comparison with those of Salka Viertel (of which Marta Feuchtwanger once remarked that "perhaps the most admirable and lovable thing about Salka's book are all the things that she left out"), but her book too includes some wonderful scenes. One of the more poignant of these starts out by noting the great pride Schoenberg took in the tennis prowess of his son Ronald, who starred in many of his school's tournaments:

But one day [Arnold Schoenberg] and his wife went for a walk, and on the way a young couple came toward them. The young woman whispered something to her husband, and they both looked at Schönberg very closely as they went by. Schönberg stopped and turned around to look at the young couple, who had also stopped and turned around. He was just able to catch the young wife saying to her husband, "That was Schönberg's father."

From Katia Mann, *Unwritten Memories* (New York: Alfred A. Knopf, 1975), 125.

Emigré Rap

Back in Germany, in 1930, my grandfather Toch had invented a kind of spoken music (a sort of precursor, I suppose, of rap), "The Geographical Fugue," an a cappella choral work made up entirely of the names of various towns, lakes, and places, splayed out in contrapuntal syncopation: "Ratibor! und der Fluß Mississippi und die Stadt Honolulu und der See Titicaca…" He'd considered the exercise something of a lark and proceeded more or less to forget about it. Soon after his arrival in Los Angeles in 1934, however—or so my grandmother used to like to recount—there came a knocking at the door and a young man inquiring after Dr. Toch. After my grandfather presented himself, the young man asked whether he was indeed the author of the marvelous "Geographical Fugue," premiered in Berlin in 1930. Toch acknowledged his authorship of the work but assured his young interlocutor that the piece had been but a joke and was of no particular importance. The young man insisted that, on the contrary, it was very important and asked for permission to see to its widest possible dissemination, which Toch grudgingly granted. (The piece has indeed gone on to become his most regularly performed work.) The young man in question was John Cage (Los Angeles High School, class of 1928). (Years later Cage used to complain to me how my grandfather had made such a brilliant breakthrough with the "Geographical Fugue" and some of his other experiments but then had gone on to waste the rest of his life on string quartets and the like.)

Anyway, although Toch spoke virtually no English when he first arrived in America, he gradually acquired an astonishing command of the vernacular, which he proceeded to display, many years later (in 1961) in his "Valse for Spoken Chorus," a throwback to his "Geographical Fugue" idiom in which he contrived to marshal dozens of cocktail party clichés to 3/4 meter, so that the various choral protagonists indulge in such badinage as: "What a pity—Oh, no, never ever—My, how super dooper—Hold your tongue, you strapper—Let's behave not like children but grown-ups—She is right—Oh, I am so happy that I have this little dance with you—Oh, I am so happy that I have this little *chance* with you—Ain't it wonderful, ain't it beautiful?—I should say it is—I am beside myself, completely mad—SO WHAT!"

Ernst Krenek, for his part, composed another spoken chorus piece, "The Santa Fe Timetable" (1947), fashioned entirely out of the train schedule for the run between Albuquerque and Los Angeles.

---

countless actors and actresses (many of whom, incidentally, achieved considerable renown for their perennial roles as Nazi villains).

Nor was the emigrés' influence confined to Hollywood. Their teaching at local universities was often seminal (in the field of musical composition, for example, Schoenberg at UCLA and Toch at USC and in the philosophy of science Hans Reichenbach and subsequently Rudolf Carnap at UCLA). Their contributions in the field of musical performance (Otto Klemperer's tenure at the helm of the L.A. Philharmonic, alongside concert master Bronislaw Gimpel; Stravinsky's patronage of Peter Yates's legendary Evenings on the Roof chamber concerts, where no fewer than twelve of his pieces received their world premiere; the catalytic presences of Gregor Piatigorsky, Jascha Heifetz, Artur Rubinstein, and Jakob Gimpel, Bronislaw's pianist brother) were legion. The musical sophistication of the city—already surprisingly substantial owing to the high concentrations of players tied to the studio orchestras—was immeasurably deepened through the presence of the emigrés, many of whom joined those orchestras or took on orchestra members or other locals as private students, both in composition and in performance.

Curiously the emigré impact on the purely visual arts was considerably more attenuated, but this was in part because most of the emigré visual artists remained on the East Coast, where many of the great European dealers (including Curt Valentin, Karl Nierendorf,

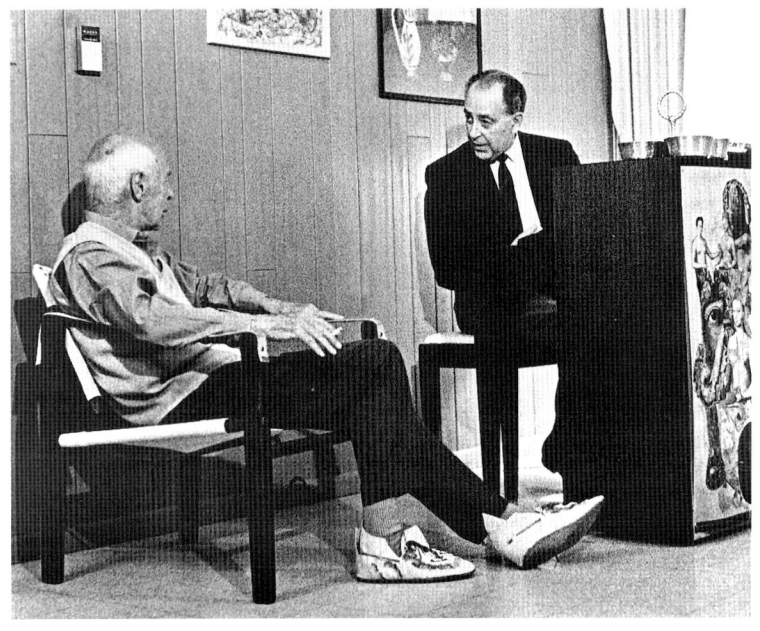

321
Jakob Gimpel (right) and Henry Miller at Miller's home in Pacific Palisades, 1968, at a celebration of Miller's seventy-seventh birthday; from the documentary film *The Henry Miller Odyssey*, directed by Robert Snyder.

Pierre Matisse, and J. B. Neumann) had congregated. In Los Angeles the European artistic presence primarily took the form of museum people (notably William R. Valentiner, out of Berlin by way of Detroit, at the Los Angeles County Museum of Art, from 1946 to 1954, and then as the first director of the Getty, though 1956) and collectors, in particular Galka Scheyer, with her uncanny Blue Four concentration, and Kate Steinitz, with her marvelous Kurt Schwitters collection. The American expatriate Man Ray ricocheted for a time, after the fall of France, into a Hollywood apartment on Vine Street (from the window of which he could probably spy the Griffith Park Observatory, an eerie echo, perhaps, of his emblematic 1936 painting of those mammoth, sky-floating lips). In 1946 he and a briefly visiting Max Ernst celebrated a double wedding with their respective brides, Juliet Browner and Dorothea Tanning, at the home of the great collectors Walter and Louise Arensberg. But Man Ray returned to Paris in 1951, and some years later the Arensbergs could find no L.A. institution interested in taking their astonishing collection of seminal surrealist masterworks (which, for that reason, can now be found at the Philadelphia Museum of Art). (Scheyer's collection was eventually folded into what became the Norton Simon Museum in Pasadena; Steinitz's papers are at UCLA.)

Gidget

Gidget, the beach nymph and quintessential California girl, was in fact the creation of emigré Frederick Kohner, whose 1957 novel of that name was inspired by his daughter's surfing exploits along Malibu Beach.

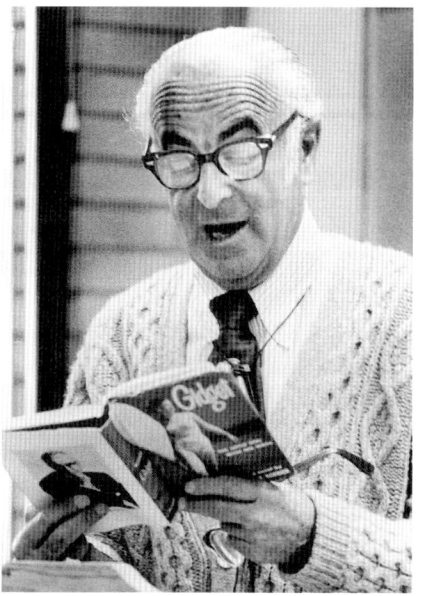

322
Frederick Kohner at a reading at the Max Kade Institute, University of Southern California, 1976.

Whereas the emergence of abstract expressionism in New York in the immediate aftermath of the war can be said to have had everything to do with the presence of the European surrealists and other modernists who'd earlier sought refuge there, the California art scene emerged from the war largely untouched by such influences; indeed, a virtually complete innocence of any such historical baggage (and hence an ability to see New York's abstract expressionist achievement entirely afresh) would prove a distinctive feature of the upwelling of modernist art in Southern California—ranging from Ed Kienholz's grungy assemblages through Robert Irwin's pearlescent perceptual wonders—a generation later.

(Curiously the generation immediately preceding the so-called Ferus group of the late 1950s—artists like Lorser Feitelson, Helen Lundeberg, and the young Philip Guston and possibly even Jackson Pollock—had somewhat more direct exposure to emigré traditions by way of the Arensberg collection. That collection also made a huge impact on the young Walter Hopps, who went on to cofound the Ferus Gallery with Kienholz and, in the following decade, even curated the first Marcel Duchamp retrospective ever mounted anywhere, at the Pasadena Art Museum. Some have argued that the whole California assemblage movement—as exemplified, say, by Kienholz and Wallace Berman—was a fusion between the European modernist tradition and a native predilection for beachcombing and bricolage. But it's more likely the case—and was certainly so with Kienholz—that California assemblage was a homegrown eruption that received a kind of high art validation from the likes of Hopps, with his deep awareness of European precedents. Meanwhile, as for direct artistic influences, the

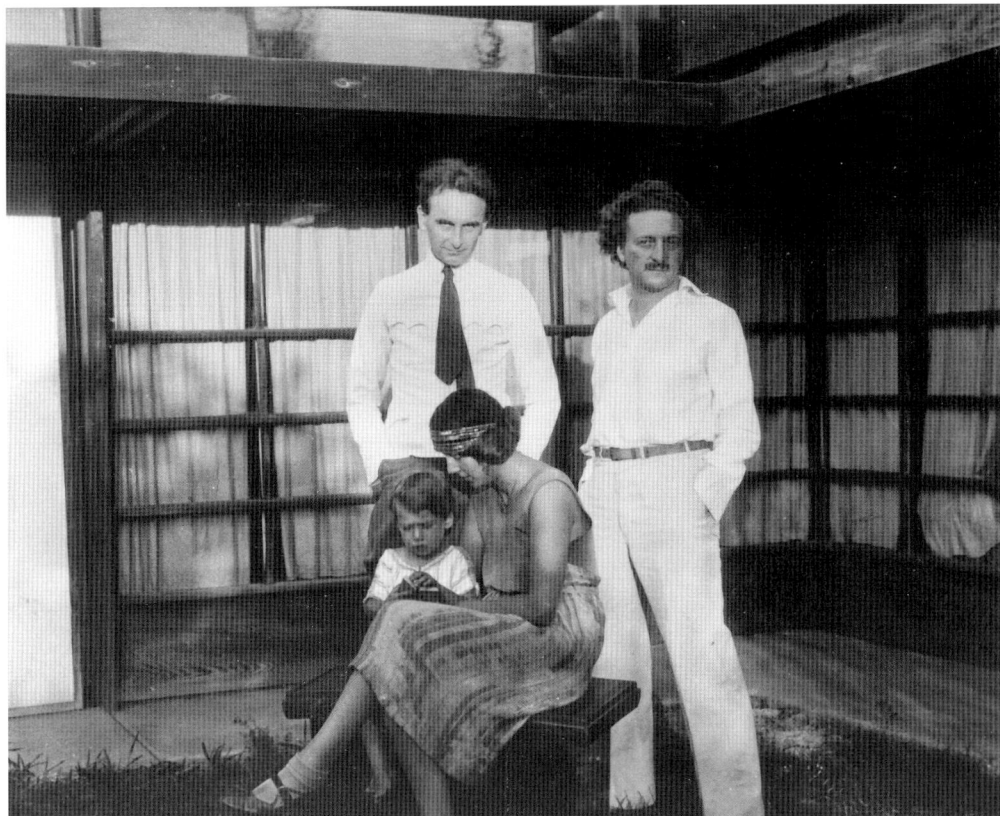

323
Richard Neutra (left), Rudolf M. Schindler, Dione Neutra and son Frank Lloyd (seated).

neo-cubists Rico Lebrun and Hans Burkhardt had both arrived in the United States, from Italy and Switzerland, respectively, well before the period focused upon in these pages. In any case, their imprint, particularly by way of local art schools, while relatively widespread, proved remarkably shallow. Among the core group of exiles considered here, it is rather Oskar Fischinger—the great emigré abstract filmmaker, who never quite clicked in Hollywood but nevertheless exerted a remarkable influence on a subsequent generation of California avant-garde filmmakers—who provides the exception that proves the rule.)

Considerably more immediate and far reaching, however, was the imprint the emigrés left on Southern California architecture. The path-breaking work of Richard Neutra and Rudolf Schindler during the 1930s and 1940s (both of them, as noted, had arrived well before the post-Hitlerian influx) in adapting a Viennese modernist aesthetic to the California landscape virtually defined the possibilities for home and office design in the region for generations to come. (Mrs. Neutra was fond of telling the story of how one day, shortly after the war, she was chauffeuring her husband around, as was their wont, when suddenly he ordered her to stop the car. He didn't remember having built a house on *that* lot: they'd happened upon one of the first of many, many subsequent Neutra knockoffs.) And Victor Gruen is said to have invented the shopping plaza (with its cluster of department stores facing in and parking spaces massed outside) because he was trying to re-create the Austrian village marts of his youth.

Nor, of course, must one forget psychiatry, eventually one of the very emblems of the Southern California lifestyle, which originally arrived on the scene on the couches of fleeing emigrés. But, of course, that's a whole other story.

Emigré Wives

"Refugee wives were often years younger than their husbands. This alone accounted for a certain social resilience, as did their apparent linguistic superiority: a man who taught English to refugees says the women invariably scored higher on language exams. Refugee wives also acquired independence because they got jobs first.... The women knew—from menial jobs, from trips to supermarkets, from PTA meetings—the requirements of American discourse. As a rule, they valued a direct and economical mode of expression, in contradiction to the often windy literary styles favored by their husbands."

From Anthony Heilbut, *Exiled in Paradise: German Refugee Artists and Intellectuals in America from the 1930s to the Present* (New York: Viking, 1983), 69.

Galileo and the Little Man at the Back of the Hall

For several months in 1945 Charles Laughton's mansion perched above the Pacific Coast Highway just north of Chatauqua served as the site for one of the most extraordinary collaborations in the history of the theater. Bertolt Brecht was wasting away, his gift virtually unrecognized in Hollywood. But Laughton, at the peak of his own acting career, had heard of Brecht's 1938 *Galileo* and became intoxicated with the prospect of incarnating the lead role. Brecht spoke obstinately little English; Laughton understood no German. But there at the Laughton mansion, day after day, the two convened—the small playwright in his leather jacket, chewing on the perennial stub of his cigar; the huge actor in his bulging robe, the Bible and Shakespeare in opposite pockets—and through a special language of gesture and empathy, with occasional recourse to the dictionary, they spun out the English translation. Brecht subsequently memorialized the collaboration in a poem:

Still your people and mine were
   tearing each other to pieces
   when we
Pored over those tattered
   exercise books...
While the housefronts crashed
   down in our capitals—
The façades of language gave
   way....
Again and again I turned actor,
   demonstrating
A character's gestures and tone
   of voice, and you
Turned writer. Yet neither I nor
   you
Stepped outside his profession.

   From Bertolt Brecht, *Poems, 1913–1956*, ed. John Willet and Ralph Manheim (New York: Methuen, 1976), 405.

Joseph Losey (himself under Brecht's direction) supervised the 1947 premiere production with Laughton at the docket of the tiny Coronet Theater on La Cienega. The audiences were legendary; the reviews lukewarm.

One person who haunted the rehearsals of the production was a young starlet named Shelley Winters. She'd been offered a small role as a nun, but her studio, Universal, wouldn't let her out of the Western to which she'd been assigned, so instead (as she herself subsequently recalled in her memoir, *Shelley*):

Whenever possible, I would dash from Universal, not even stopping to take off my long blonde wig, and sit in the third or fourth row at the Coronet Theater and watch the rehearsals. Joe Losey, the director, was very nice to me and never objected to my sitting there, but I began to feel that my long platinum hair was distracting the actors, so I moved to the back.

One day I noticed a little man, who seemed to need a shave and who was wearing greenish coveralls, hovering around the back of the theater, picking up pieces of paper and putting them in the trash basket. I assumed he was the janitor and asked him for a program, which he went and got for me. He had a heavy German accent, and I asked him if he was a refugee. He said he was. We sat together and watched the rehearsal. He didn't seem to understand English too well and the rehearsals often put him to sleep.

He always looked lonely and hungry, so one Friday afternoon I invited him home for the Sabbath meal—my mother still made glorious chicken soup—and to meet my father and mother, who also spoke German. The little man gratefully accepted and enjoyed my parents so much I left him there playing pinochle with my father. For several months after that, he was there every Friday night.

The next few times I went to rehearsals Joe Losey, John Houseman and Charles Laughton seemed quite upset—they wanted rewrites and were having trouble as the playwright seemed to have disappeared. In all innocence I just sat there and watched what went on and wondered myself where this irresponsible playwright had gone.

Plummer Park is about ten blocks from where my parents lived, and senior citizens still go there on lovely days to play pinochle, klaberjass, chess and boccie. By that time my father was so busy taking care of my career and finances that he had retired, so every morning he and the German refugee janitor would walk to Plummer Park and talk endlessly about their experiences as young men. Pop had never told anybody about his troubles with the New York judicial system and the racketeering in the men's garment union in both New York and Los Angeles. But in German he was able to tell this little man all about it; for some reason, in that language he could reveal his agonies.

When my daughter graduated from Harvard recently, she and I and her father, Vittorio Gassman, saw Al Pacino do *Arturo Ui*, another of Bertolt Brecht's great plays. It was about gangsters in the Chicago unions and the characterizations were parallel to Hitler and his henchmen. Vittorio, who is very familiar with Brecht's work, told me that probably while the playwright was playing klaberjass with my father, he was no doubt confirming his research on this the most American of his plays.

But I didn't discover Brecht's identity until after my father's death, when I was living in New York with my mother and very young daughter and went to see *Brecht on Brecht* in an Off-Broadway theater in Greenwich Village. When the curtain went up, to the right of the stage, hanging from the top of the set, was an enormous picture of my father's pinochle partner. I said to my companion, "What the hell is that picture of my father's friend doing up there?"

He turned to me in amazement. "That's Bertolt Brecht." I started to give him an argument, but the people around shushed me. As the play progressed, I began to remember where and under what circumstances I had met this little man. After the play, which was another extraordinary work, I went home in a daze and took out a huge book of Brecht's plays. My mother had awakened and was making us tea. I asked her if she remembered the little German janitor who was a friend of Daddy's in about 1950. "Oh, yes, Mr. Brechstein. Did you know, Shelley, after everything Hitler did, that man went back to Germany. Maybe he went to look for his family."

"Mother," I said, showing her the book, "that man's name was Bertolt Brecht, and he wrote all these plays. He's famous all over the world."

With a pitying look my mother said, "Shelley, don't be silly. He was a costume jeweler."

"Mom, why do you think that?"

"Well, once Daddy asked him what he did in the old country, and he told us he made jewels for poor people." I didn't argue.

   From Shelley Winters, *Shelley: Also Known as Shirley* (New York: Morrow, 1980), 310–12. Reprinted by permission of the author.

the community of European emigrés in western Los Angeles crested during the mid-1940s. During the first years after the Nazi surrender, many of them expired, as much from exhaustion as anything else—Bruno Frank, Franz Werfel, Heinrich Mann, Arnold Schoenberg. In this period the satisfactions of victory were further tempered by a pervasive sense of anxiety as America lurched from its external war against fascism into an internal obsession with communism. The very broadcasts and papers in which these emigrés had cried out against Nazism from its earliest festerings were suddenly being cited as evidence of long-standing "communist sympathies." The witch-hunt focused on Hollywood and, by implication, on the emigré influence. Brecht was the eleventh of what would eventually become known as the Hollywood Ten and in 1947 faced interrogation by a House Un-American Activities Committee that included freshman congressman Richard Nixon. Brecht turned in a wily, faux-lunkheaded performance before skipping the country altogether (this on the virtual eve of the Broadway premiere of the English-language version of *Galileo,* which he'd painstakingly crafted with Charles Laughton and which they'd premiered at the Coronet Theater on La Cienega Boulevard only a few months earlier). Many of the emigrés found themselves subject to official harassment: In 1953 Salka Viertel was denied a passport and was thus unable to visit her ailing husband, Berthold, on his sickbed back in Vienna or even, subsequently, to attend his funeral. Clear up through his death in 1958 Lion Feuchtwanger, the historical novelist (who, among other things, had focused his Continental sensibility in celebration of the triumphant events surrounding the American Revolution in his best-selling *Proud Destiny*), was repeatedly denied American citizenship, owing to the (and this was the official charge) "premature antifascism" he'd evinced by, among other things, penning an antiwar poem (Germany's first) in 1915 and then composing the first anti-Hitler satirical novel, as early as 1927. (In 1948 Feuchtwanger also wrote a play, *The Devil in Boston,* which used the Salem witch-hunts as a figure for the gathering Red Scare, thereby anticipating by several years Arthur Miller's appropriation of the same

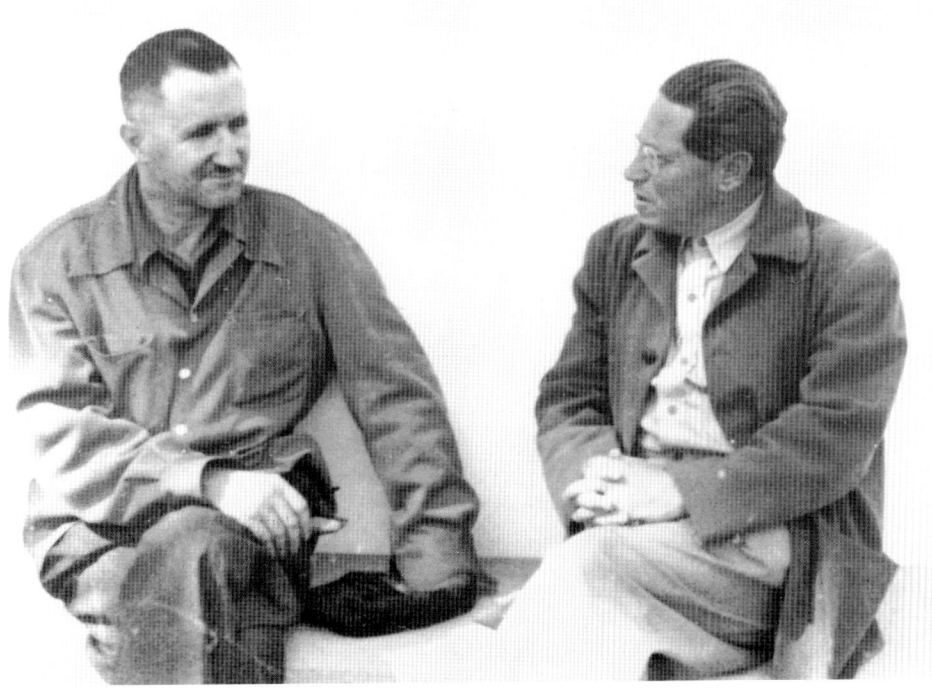

324
Bertolt Brecht and Lion Feuchtwanger, Pacific Palisades.

metaphor in *The Crucible*). Other emigrés fell into other sorts of disfavor: Neutra's extraordinary project for innovative public housing in Elysian Park, within walking distance of downtown Los Angeles, was suddenly canceled upon discovery of its putative socialist connotations (instead L.A. got Dodger Stadium in Chavez Ravine). Still others, including Thomas Mann, simply left in disgust.

The so-called Weimar colony in Los Angeles for all intents and purposes thus ceased to exist as a cohesive entity after the early 1950s. Of the creative artists who did not flee the McCarthyite mania, a few survived into the 1960s, but most of the remainder died during that decade. Many, however, were survived by their families, and today, on the western slopes of Los Angeles, the shadow community of Weimar is itself shadowed by the persistence of children, grandchildren... and *their* children.

An earlier version of this essay appeared in the *L.A. Reader* of November 17, 1978, under the title *Exiles' Paradise*. The author would like to acknowledge the invaluable research assistance of Deborah Young in the current version's amplification.

Thomas Mann, American

In 1944 Thomas Mann and his wife, Katia, became American citizens after passing the usual civics tests. When asked under oath whether he thought Thomas Mann would make a desirable citizen, Max Horkheimer, who served as one of the couple's witnesses, emphatically replied, "You bet!"

But within a few years Mann himself wasn't so sure—or at any rate he wasn't sure the United States, in its developing Cold War guise, was the sort of country of which he'd still want to remain a citizen. Very early on, and exceptionally forcefully, he publicly challenged the House Un-American Activities Committee, which was cutting a terrible swath through the emigré (and other liberal-minded) communities. In 1948, in the midst of the committee's investigations into communist infiltration of the film industry, Mann took to the radio airwaves to declare,

I have the honor to expose myself as a hostile witness. I testify that I am very much interested in the moving-picture industry, and that since my arrival in the United States nine years ago, I've seen a great many Hollywood films. If communist propaganda had been smuggled into any of them, I, for one, never noticed anything of the sort.

I testify, moreover, that to my mind, the ignorant and superstitious persecution of the believers in a political and economic doctrine which is, after all, the creation of great minds and great thinkers, I testify that that persecution is not only degrading for the persecutors themselves but harmful to the cultural reputation of this country. As an American citizen of German birth, I finally testify that I am painfully familiar with certain political trends. Spiritual intolerance, political inquisitions and declining legal security—and all in the name of an alleged "state of emergency"—that is how it started in Germany. What followed was fascism, and what followed fascism was war.

He stayed on a few more years, though with increasing wariness. In a 1950 letter he wrote that although he was "very much attached to our house, which is so completely right for me, and I also love the country and the people, who have certainly remained good-natured and friendly... the political atmosphere is becoming more and more unbreathable." A year later, in another letter, he wrote: "I myself am nothing but a bundle of nerves, trembling at every thought and word. Only yesterday I let myself break down and weep listening to the Lohengrin prelude—simply in reaction to the baseness. Have people ever had to inhale so poisoned an atmosphere, one so utterly saturated with idiotic baseness?"

Within a few months he had decided to immigrate once again, this time to Switzerland, where he would live out his last three years. Preparing to leave, he made reference in another of his letters to a story he'd heard about one friend who was sailing from New York to Europe while another was sailing in the opposite direction. As their ships pass on the high seas, they recognize each other, and both cry out in horror, simultaneously, "Have you gone crazy?"

Letters cited from *Letters of Thomas Mann, 1889–1955*, ed. and trans. Richard and Clara Winston (New York: Vintage Books, 1975).

SELECTED BIBLIOGRAPHY

Books

Adorno, Theodor W. *Minima Moralia*. London: Verso, 1978.

Bedford, Sybille. *Aldous Huxley: A Biography*. 2 vols. London: Chatto and Windus; Collins, 1973.

Boyers, Robert, ed. *The Legacy of German Refugee Intellectuals*. New York: Schocken, 1972. Reprint of Fall 1969–Winter 1970 issue of *Salmagundi*.

Brecht, Bertolt. *Poems, 1913–1956*. Edited by John Willet and Ralph Manheim. New York: Methuen, 1976.

———. *Journals, 1934–1955*. Edited by John Willet. Translated by Hugh Rorrison. New York: Routledge, 1993.

Cook, Bruce. *Brecht in Exile*. New York: Holt, Rinehart, 1982.

Crawford, Dorothy Lamb. *Evenings on and off the Roof: Pioneering Concerts in Los Angeles, 1939–1971*. Berkeley and Los Angeles: University of California Press, 1995.

Davis, Mike. *City of Quartz: Excavating the Future in Los Angeles*. London and New York: Verso, 1990.

Dunaway, David King. *Huxley in Hollywood*. New York: Harper and Row, 1989.

Fermi, Laura. *Illustrious Immigrants: The Intellectual Migration from Europe, 1930–1941*. Chicago: University of Chicago Press, 1968.

Fleming, Donald, and Bernard Bailyn, eds. *The Intellectual Migration: Europe and America, 1930–1960*. Cambridge: Harvard University Press, 1969.

Friedrich, Otto. *City of Nets*. New York: Harper and Row, 1986.

Gabler, Neal. *An Empire of Their Own: How the Jews Invented Hollywood*. New York: Crown, 1988.

Heilbut, Anthony. *Exiled in Paradise: German Refugee Artists and Intellectuals in America from the 1930s to the Present*. New York: Viking Press, 1983.

Heyworth, Peter. *Otto Klemperer: His Life and Times*. Vol. 2, *1933–1973*. New York: Cambridge University Press, 1996.

Hughes, H. Stuart. *The Sea Change: The Migration of Social Thought, 1930–1945*. New York: Harper and Row, 1975.

Isherwood, Christopher. *Prater Violet*. New York: Farrar, Strauss, 1945.

Lanchester, Elsa. *Elsa Lanchester, Herself*. New York: St. Martin's Press, 1983.

Loos, Anita. *Kiss Hollywood Goodbye*. New York: Viking Press, 1974.

Mann, Katia. *Unwritten Memories*. Edited by Elisabeth Plessen and Michael Mann. Translated by Hunter and Hildegarde Hannum. New York: Alfred A. Knopf, 1975.

Mann, Thomas. *Letters of Thomas Mann, 1889–1955*. Edited and translated by Richard and Clara Winston. New York: Vintage Books, 1975.

———. *Diaries, 1918–1939*. Edited by Herman Kesten. Translated by Richard and Clara Winston. New York: Harry N. Abrams, 1982.

Reinhardt, Gottfried. *The Genius: A Memoir of Max Reinhardt*. New York: Alfred A. Knopf, 1979.

Rolfe, Lionel. *Literary L.A.* San Francisco: Chronicle, 1981.

Schnauber, Cornelius. *Spaziergänge durch das Hollywood der Emigranten*. Zurich: Arche, 1992.

Taylor, John Russell. *Strangers in Paradise: The Hollywood Emigrés, 1933–1950*. London: Faber and Faber, 1983.

Viertel, Salka. *The Kindness of Strangers*. New York: Holt, Rinehart, 1969.

Exhibition Catalogues

One Way Ticket to Hollywood: Film Artists of Austrian and German Origin in Los Angeles (Emigration: 1884–1945). Los Angeles: Max Kade Institute, University of Southern California, 1986.

Merrill-Mirsky, Carol, ed. *Exiles in Paradise*. Los Angeles: Hollywood Bowl Museum and Los Angeles Philharmonic Association, 1991.

Stadler, Friederich, and Peter Weibel, eds. *Vertreibung der Vernunft: The Cultural Exodus from Austria*. Vienna and New York: Springer Verlag, 1995.

Other Sources

Oral histories of Gustav Arlt, Hans Burkhardt, Pia Gilbert, Marta Feuchtwanger, Dione Neutra, Alice Toch, and Gertrude Zeisl, Department of Special Collections, University of California, Los Angeles.

Sontag, Susan. "Pilgrimage." *New Yorker*, 21 December 1987.

a map to the homes of the emigrés

PACIFIC PALISADES

Hanns Eisler *689 Amalfi Dr.*
Lion Feuchtwanger *520 Paseo Miramar*
Christopher Isherwood *145 Adelaide Dr.*
Harry Horner *728 Brooktree Rd.*
Aldous Huxley *701 Amalfi Dr.*
Charles Laughton *14954 Corona Del Mar*
Emil Ludwig *701 Amalfi Dr. (1942);*
 303 Grenola St. (1944–45)
Thomas Mann *740 Amalfi Dr. (1941)*
Max Reinhardt *15000 Corona Del Mar*
Berthold and Salka Viertel *165 Mabery Rd.*

BRENTWOOD

Theodor Adorno *316 S. Kenter Ave.*
Vicki Baum *1461 Amalfi Dr.*
Max Horkheimer *13524 D'Este Dr.*
Thomas Mann *1550 San Remo Dr.*
Gregor Piatigorsky *400 S. Bundy Dr.*
Arnold Schoenberg *116 N. Rockingham Ave.*
Fred Zinnemann *1766 Westridge Rd.*

SANTA MONICA

Bertolt Brecht *817 Twenty-fifth St. (1941–42);*
 1063 Twenty-sixth St. (1942–47)
Heinrich Mann *2145 Montana Ave. (1948–50)*
Hans Reichenbach *469 Seventeenth St.*
Gottfried Reinhardt *12324 Montana Ave.*
Ernst Toch *811 Franklin St.*

BEL AIR

Oskar Homolka *10788 Bellagio Rd.*
Ernst Lubitsch *268 Bel Air Rd.*
Otto Klemperer *924 Bel Air Rd.*
Paul Kohner *901 Stone Canyon Rd.*
Otto Preminger *333 Bel Air Rd.*
Walter Reisch *420 Amapola Ln.*
William Thiele *1054 Chantilly Rd.*

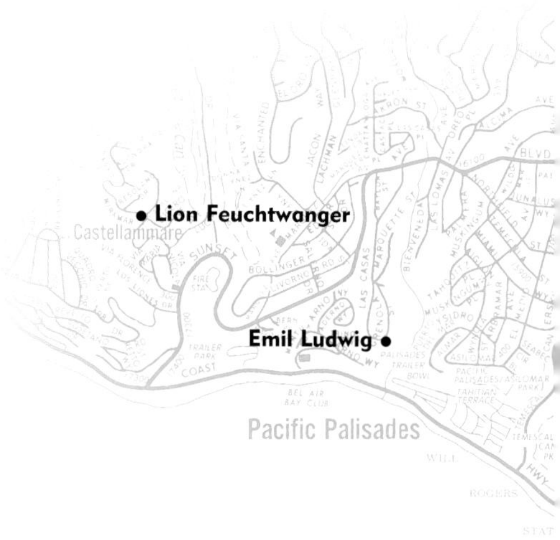

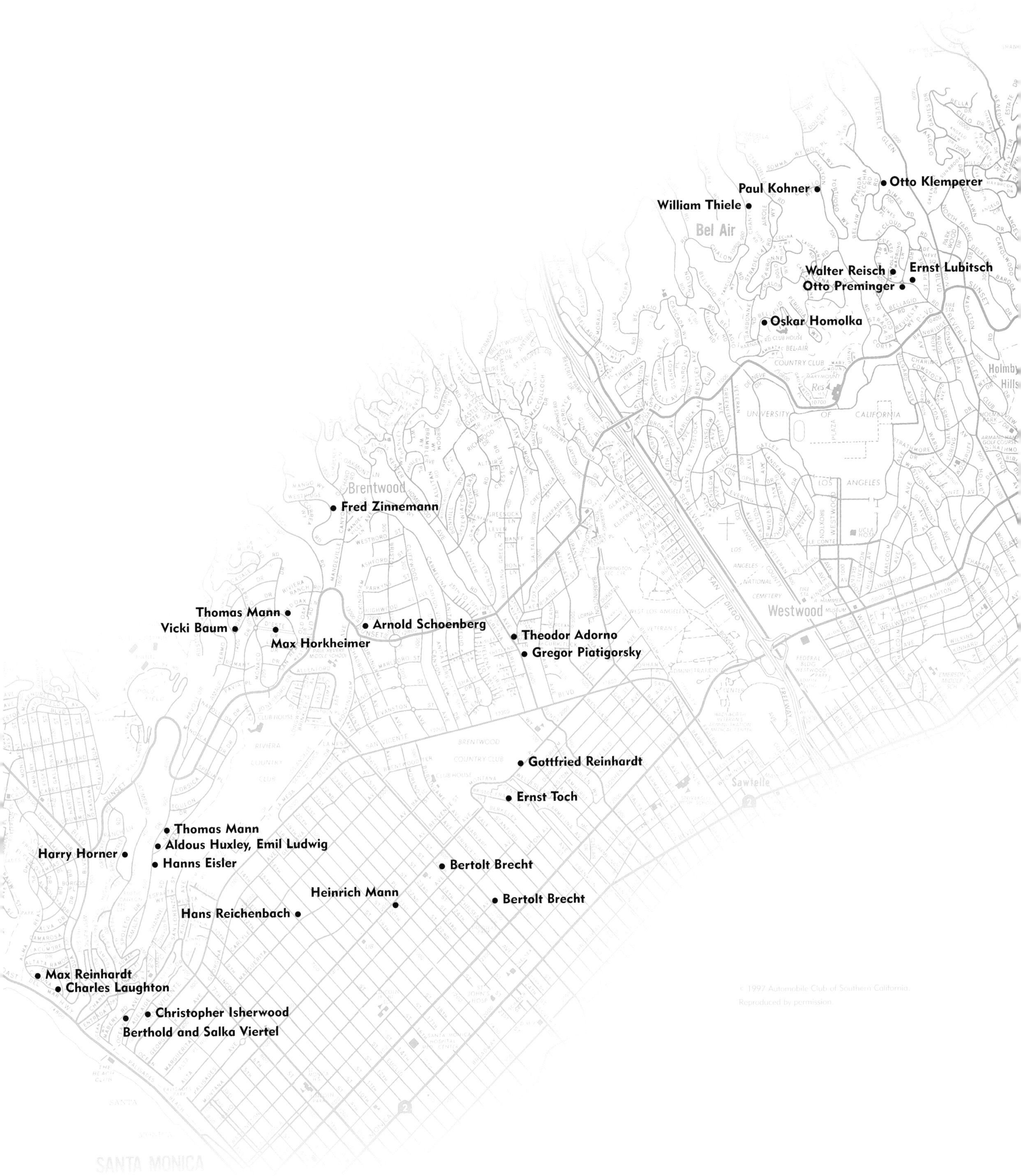
Otto Klemperer
Paul Kohner
William Thiele
Bel Air
Walter Reisch
Ernst Lubitsch
Otto Preminger
Oskar Homolka
Brentwood
Fred Zinnemann
Westwood
Thomas Mann
Vicki Baum
Arnold Schoenberg
Max Horkheimer
Theodor Adorno
Gregor Piatigorsky
Gottfried Reinhardt
Sawtelle
Ernst Toch
Thomas Mann
Aldous Huxley, Emil Ludwig
Harry Horner
Hanns Eisler
Bertolt Brecht
Heinrich Mann
Bertolt Brecht
Hans Reichenbach
Max Reinhardt
Charles Laughton
Christopher Isherwood
Berthold and Salka Viertel
SANTA MONICA
© 1992 Automobile Club of Southern California
Reproduced by permission

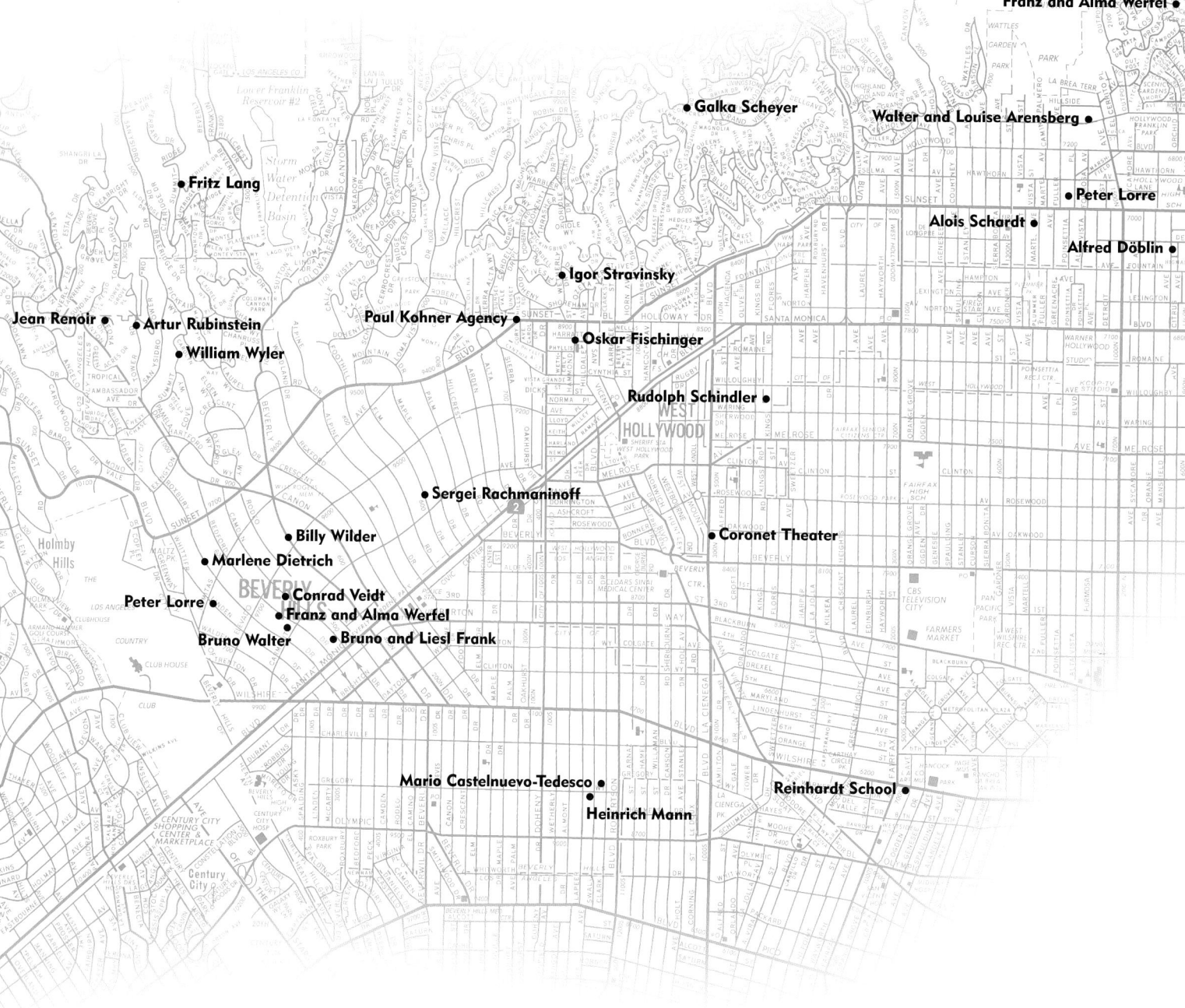

BEVERLY HILLS

Mario Castelnuevo-Tedesco *269 S. Clark Dr.*

Marlene Dietrich *822 N. Roxbury Dr.*

Bruno and Liesl Frank *513 N. Camden Dr.*

Fritz Lang *1501 Summitridge Dr.*

Peter Lorre *722 N. Linden Dr. (1939–42)*

Heinrich Mann *301 S. Swall Dr. (1942–48)*

Sergei Rachmaninoff *610 N. Elm Dr.*

Jean Renoir *1273 Leona Dr.*

Artur Rubinstein *1139 N. Tower Rd.*

Conrad Veidt *617 N. Camden Dr.*

Bruno Walter *608 N. Bedford Dr.*

Franz and Alma Werfel *610 N. Bedford Dr.*
   (after 1942)

Billy Wilder *704 N. Beverly Dr.*

William Wyler *1121 Summit Dr.*

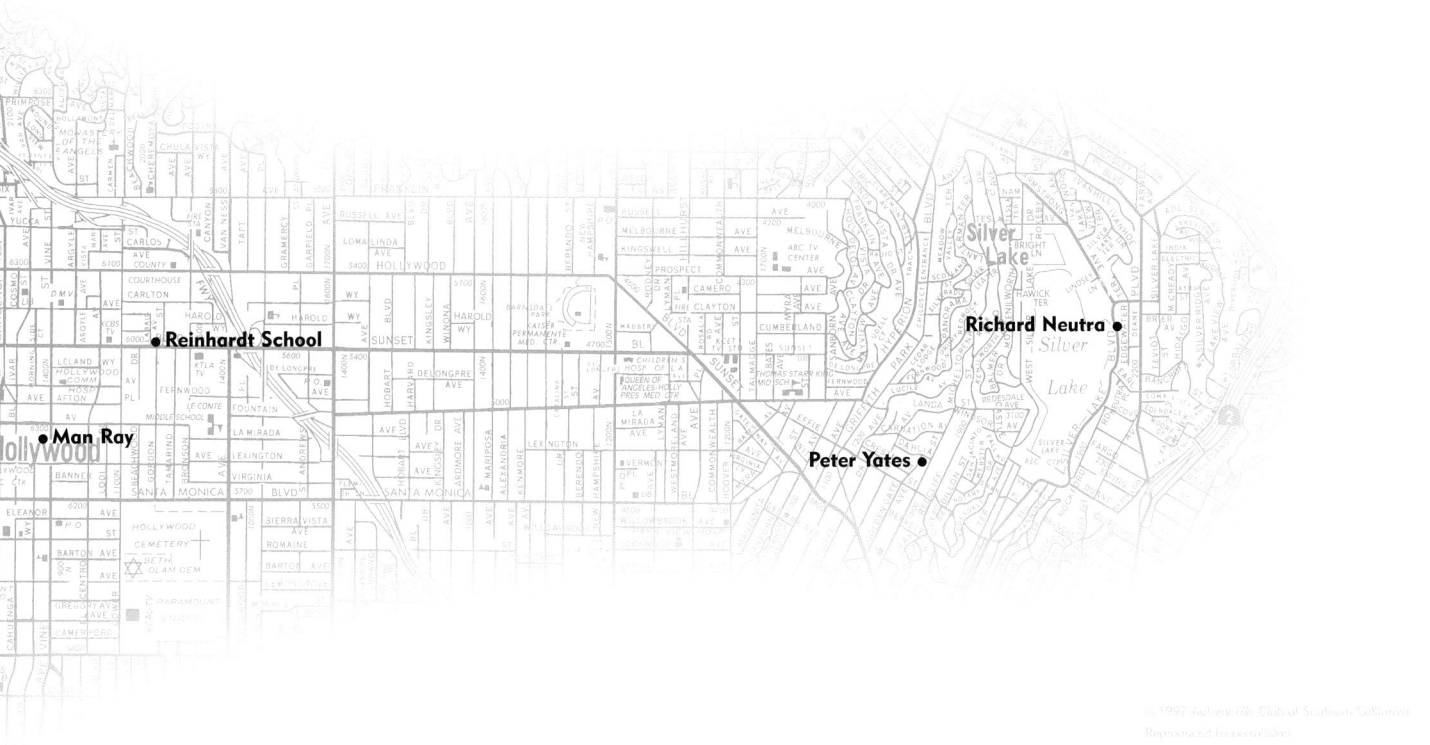

WEST HOLLYWOOD

Coronet Theatre *366 N. La Cienega Blvd.*
Oskar Fischinger *1010 Hammond St.*
Paul Kohner Agency *9169 Sunset Blvd.*
Galka Scheyer *1880 Blue Heights Dr.*
Rudolf Schindler *835 N. Kings Rd.*
Igor Stravinsky *1260 N. Wetherly Dr.*

MIRACLE MILE

Reinhardt School *6040 Wilshire Blvd.*

HOLLYWOOD

Walter and Louise Arensberg *7065 Hillside Dr.*
Alfred Döblin *1347 N. Citrus Ave.*
Hollywood Bowl *2301 N. Highland Ave.*
Peter Lorre *1545 N. Poinsettia Pl. (after 1942)*
Man Ray *1245 Vine St.*
Alois Schardt *1433 N. Martel Ave.*
Reinhardt School *5939 Sunset Blvd.*
Franz and Alma Werfel *6800 Los Tilos Rd.*
   (before 1942)

SILVER LAKE

Richard Neutra *2300 E. Silver Lake Dr.*
Peter Yates (Evenings on the Roof)
   1735 Micheltorena St.

paradise   361

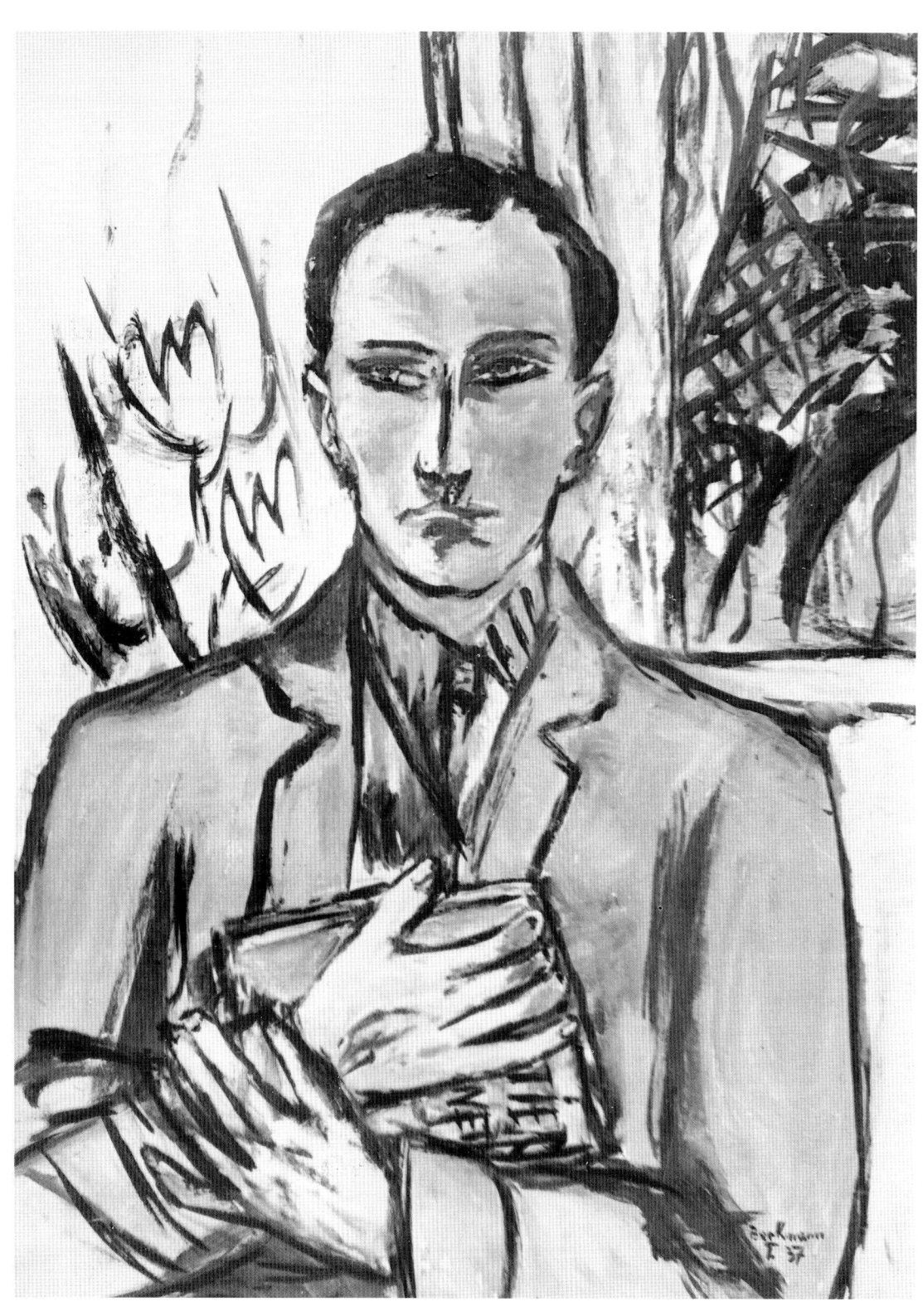

reflections on exile
in france and the united states

STEPHAN LACKNER

How can a refugee end the problems and tribulations of emigration? There are exactly three ways of finishing the unstable state of exile.

First, an emigré can return to his or her former homeland in reconciliation or even in triumph. Victor Hugo's homecoming to France comes to mind: After eighteen years in exile and after the fall of Emperor Napoléon III in 1870, the Parisians gave the returning writer a triumphal reception. Nothing of the kind was accorded to any anti-Nazi refugee after Hitler's demise. Thomas Mann, the most prominent returnee, encountered quite a bit of hostility, mixed with some adulation. He chose to reemigrate to Switzerland in 1952.

Second, the emigrant can become an immigrant, thus ending the provisional circumstances inherent in the concept of exile. To achieve this solution, the persona has to melt into the pot of new national characteristics and to shed many peculiarities brought over from the original country. Numerous Hollywood writers and directors chose this path, becoming successful and wealthy through adaptation.

Third, of course, one can die in exile, thereby ending the state of uncertainty.

Personally I have never made up my mind which of these three endings is appropriate for my own biography. So it will be a mélange of all three.

Let me emphasize that legally, politically, and philosophically I am an American with all my heart. Nevertheless, I wrote many works in German—novels, art books, plays, and short stories—and some of them were quite successful in the "old country." Am I, therefore, a German writer living in America? Definitely not. Several of my books were written first in English and translated later by me into German (such as my monograph on Max Beckmann). Sometimes I felt more comfortable proceeding the other way around. Anyway, since 1940 my domicile has been Santa Barbara; this is my hometown. And yet—and yet—

Let me quote Golo Mann, a son of Thomas Mann and an important historian: "Anyone who lived through the thirties and forties as a German can no longer completely trust his nation.... No matter how such a person may and should strive for trust, he will remain sad in the depths of his soul until he dies."

Perhaps I was predestined to be an emigré?

I was born in Paris in 1910. But in 1914, when World War I broke out, my German-Jewish father discovered his patriotism and returned with his whole family to Berlin to help the war effort. I went to school and universities in Germany, hoping from an early age to become a writer. I was the last "half-Jewish" student to receive a Ph.D. at Giessen University in 1933.

The decisive influence on my art and on my life was Max Beckmann. I remember vividly how, at age sixteen or seventeen, I was tremendously impressed by his paintings in the Städel

325
Max Beckmann; *Portrait of Stephan Lackner*, 1939; oil on canvas; 28¾ x 21¼ in. (73 x 54 cm); collection of Stephan Lackner.

Museum in Frankfurt. The expressionist way of seeing things seemed to open vistas on the future: all of a sudden, the spirit had the right to modify reality. I met Beckmann, probably in my last year of high school, at a party at a friend's house. The big, slow-moving man was somewhat intimidating, but he was nice to us students and amused by our excited questioning.

In June 1933 my brother and I wanted to visit a Beckmann exhibition in Erfurt. When we arrived, red strips were pasted across the posters: "Postponed." The museum officials told us that the propaganda ministry in Berlin had just notified them that this "degenerate" show was *verboten,* but the director let us view the forbidden paintings in a storage room.

I was overwhelmed by the new, almost classical figures. I telegraphed Beckmann in Berlin, asking whether I could buy his large *Man and Woman* of 1932. He agreed and wrote me on June 21, 1933, "I was delighted that a young man has the courage and energy to realize his feelings." A little later, when I visited him and "my" picture in Berlin, he told me that on the difficult day when his art was officially banned in Germany, my offer was the only sign of sympathy he received. From then on, until his death in 1950, we were friends.

Meanwhile my parents and two brothers had emigrated to Paris. For my father this was less painful than for many other refugees because he still had French friends and business connections from the time before World War I. He soon remade himself into a prosperous Parisian businessman. My mother had a harder time adjusting. She was a typical Protestant North German, taking life very seriously, and she could not adapt to the French lightness of manner and outlook. She loved my father and reacted to the Nazis' anti-Semitic diatribes with more anger and bitterness than her Jewish husband. My parents rented a nice villa in the Paris *banlieue,* and I lived with them for a while until I found an apartment with a view of the Seine and the Eiffel Tower. I hung newly acquired Beckmann paintings on my walls, which attracted art lovers and literati, and I continued writing.

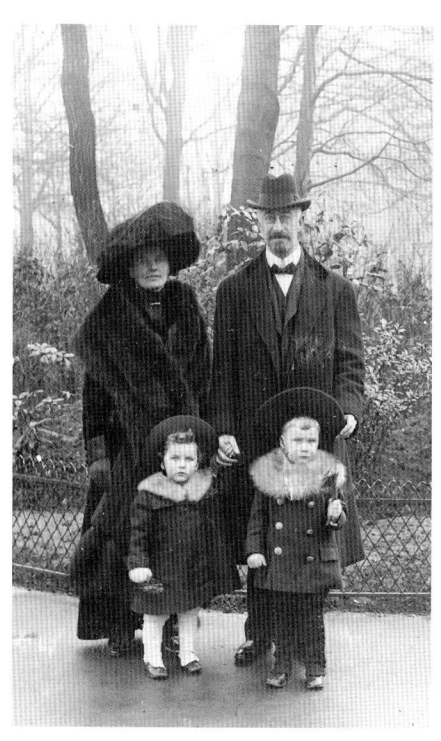

326
Sigmund and Lucie Morgenroth in Paris, January 1912, with their sons Henri and Ernest Gustave. The latter adopted the nom de plume Stephan Lackner in 1935.

In August 1935 I became a contributor to the German-language weekly *Das neue Tagebuch,* which was published in Paris. It was an influential paper, a gathering place for international antifascist voices, from Churchill to Trotsky, with many moderate emigrés in the middle. Most of the contributors, including the editor, had participated in the literary life of the Weimar Republic. It was quite an honor for a young author to be accepted in this company.

My first articles were think pieces, examining current events from the elevated standpoint of a philosophical observer. I wrote about "national characteristics" and the danger inherent in narrow definitions. *The* Italian, for instance, had turned from a mandolin-strumming leisure lover into a strutting imperialist, reclaiming ancient Roman glory, converting the old *mare nostrum* into a *nightmare nostrum.* And *the* German, once a dreamer and thinker, had become a glorifier of martial might. I derived some hope from the fact that the character of a given people can change again, that it is not predetermined once and for all.

The editor, Leopold Schwarzschild, called me into his office and told me that he liked my article very much but that the general themes should be reserved for the boss; he wanted me to write about actual occurrences. Nonetheless, when I handed him my second philosophical essay, he published it right away. Entitled "Die Tiefe" (Depth), it made something of a stir. In it I argued that the success of National Socialism among highly educated Germans was the result of its appeal to antirationalistic tendencies. This development had started with Nietzsche, who wrote: "The world is deep, deeper than was thought by the day." Spirit and soul were seen as antagonists. Alfred Rosenberg, the official Nazi philosopher, entitled his racist tome *The Myth of the Twentieth Century*. The appeal to subconscious forces made Hitler dangerously seductive.

Up to then anti-Nazis had explained the advent of fascism either as the culmination of an economic process—namely the mounting concentration of wealth and power in ever fewer hands, which they designated "the last phase of economic imperialism"—or, alternately, as the expression of the inborn, rude, aggressive German character. Neither of these contradictory explanations seemed sufficient to me. My article showed how the anti-intellectual forces in the collective unconscious of the 1930s and 1940s (such as Henri Bergson's *élan vital*) helped the Nazis achieve success and power.

My numerous subsequent articles in *Das neue Tagebuch,* written from 1935 to 1939, form a cool but not dispassionate analysis and chronicle of one of the most nefarious aberrations of the human spirit. Scanning all those pages, I don't find a single invective against the evil that was National Socialism; I kept my objectivity. I wrote on Sigmund Freud and Thomas Mann, on French Marxist thinkers. I compared Heinrich Heine's and Friedrich Nietzsche's Weltanschauungen, showing how Nietzsche took over Heine's thoughts on Christianity and Judaism almost verbatim. I reported on a fascinating theater festival in Moscow and Leningrad, which I attended in 1936, and also on the "character analysis" of Wilhelm Reich, with whom I had many oral and written discussions about sexual liberation and its (supposed) future benefits.

Our magazine had considerable influence, in spite of its modest circulation. Of course, it was forbidden and unobtainable in Naziland. The editor-in-chief told us under the seal of secrecy, however, that the German *Außenministerium* (foreign ministry) maintained twenty paid subscriptions and that German diplomats studied it avidly. We had readers in Austria (up to the Anschluss), in German-speaking parts of Switzerland and Czechoslovakia, in North America, and among refugees everywhere. The editors had clandestine sources of information about German rearmament and Nazi crimes, and we were proud about spreading the truth in an age of shameless mendacity.

Although I was never very close to Thomas Mann, he influenced my outlook on life. During my childhood my family read and discussed every new work that he published. *Tonio Kröger* and *The Magic Mountain* were seminal for my own writing.

My parents and brothers used to spend several weeks each winter in Saint-Moritz, in a pleasant family hotel called the Chantarella. In February of 1935 we saw Mann and his wife, Katia, wandering through the snow, and we were thrilled that the famous couple were staying at our hotel. Our host introduced us that evening after dinner. We had a lively conversation about Nietzsche, Jewish culture, traveling, and Mann's own work. He drank tea, half mint, half chamomile. Afterward my mother said to me, "Be glad."

"What about?"

"That you are still young and full of hope."

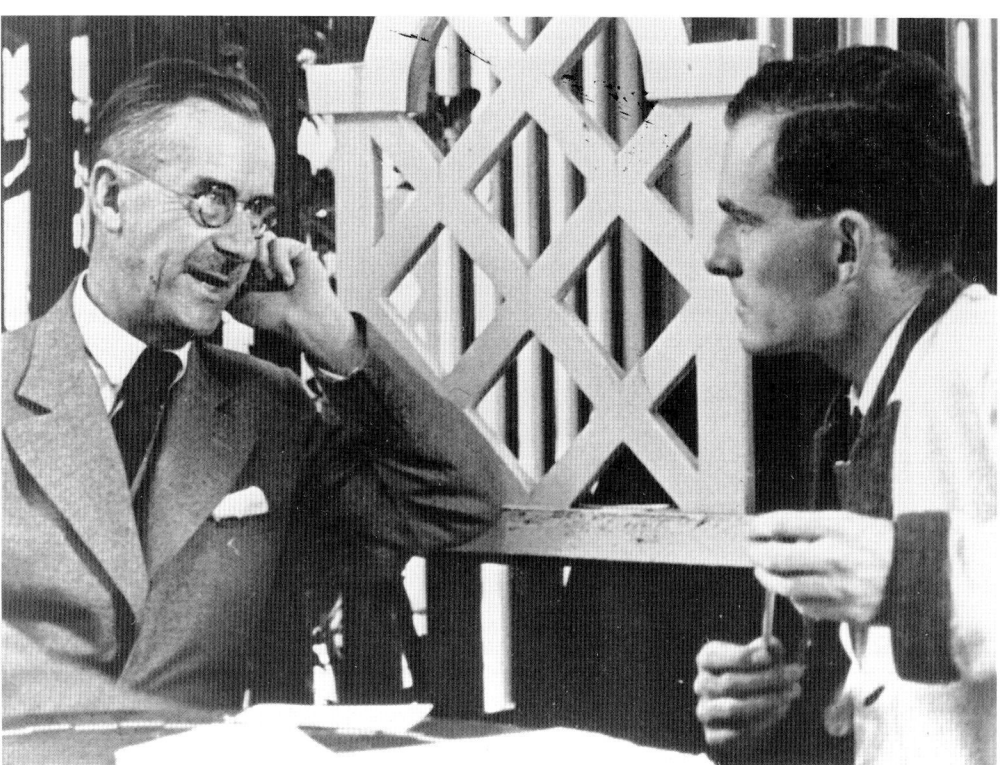

327
Thomas Mann being interviewed by Stephan Lackner at the Café Bazar in Salzburg, 1935.

While my friends and I were skiing, the Manns and my parents took long walks together. Mann told me that my mother reminded him of an austere sculpture by Ernst Barlach. Mother was charmed by his soulful eyes, with their slightly ironic twinkle.

He must have found me not uninteresting, for on March 30, 1935, he invited me for tea at his home in Küsnacht, near Zurich, where I was privileged to leaf through his work in progress, the third volume of his Joseph epic.

And then, in August 1935, I was granted an interview with him. This lengthy conversation took place on the terrace of the Café Bazar in Salzburg (see fig. 327), and I was pleased that I got the great man to talk freely about the recent changes in German civilization and mentality. You have to consider that Mann's books, even several years after Hitler and Goebbels took over, were still sold and read in Germany while the works of his brother, Heinrich Mann, of Bertolt Brecht, Lion Feuchtwanger, Freud, Erich Maria Remarque, Joseph Roth, Franz Werfel, and many others were removed from all libraries, bookstores, and publishing houses and burned. Reading any book by these "enemies of the Third Reich" was punishable by imprisonment in a concentration camp. Thomas Mann, although he had been vehemently attacked by Nazi scribes and academics, was still not *verboten,* perhaps with the tacit understanding that he would refrain from adding his voice to the chorus of antifascists.

Here are some short excerpts from that 1935 interview:

"The events of the last few years are not yet ripe for a valid depiction. Thus, the Great War had to slide back into the past for ten or twelve years before the first artful books about it could appear. I, myself, feel a far-reaching resignation concerning immediate experiences."

My question: whether he would not hope for a favorable influence of his words upon our times. He sits there quietly, thinking, eyebrows raised, the angular head pensively tilted to one side. "Art can put its stamp upon an epoch," he admits. "Works of art formulate people and epochs and, in turn, influence their models by lifting them into consciousness. Balzac's work was a reflection of French society, on one hand, and in a certain sense this society was also the work of Balzac. I myself have noticed that the diction of my *Buddenbrooks* and *Tonio Kröger* influenced everyday language."

I insist: "What influence do you expect from art in this epoch of fascism?"

"Insofar as human groups have become fascist, art has no influence. During fascist periods art and culture lose their importance. You may regret this, but it is justified, art does not have to come to the fore in every era. The solution of political and social questions may be more important. Of course, one would have to solve these questions in the right manner!"

"Do you think that a total renunciation is even feasible? Didn't fascism derive some of its slogans from important thinkers?"

"Certainly. Much of Nietzsche's substance has permeated our time, but in spoiled versions, not digested, not understood. It is a great fire sale of thoughts, a fast using-up of changing ideas. An unhappy state of affairs. The slogans were used only as weapons to bash in one another's heads."

Out of loyalty I sent the typed version of these rather tame utterances to Mann first, even though the editor of *Das neue Tagebuch* was eagerly waiting for the text of my interview. But Mann refused to give his imprimatur. He wrote me from Küsnacht on August 31, 1935: "All these years since the German upheaval I have kept silent on these matters, which your interview presents in tight and somewhat dry terms. I always had the mental reservation that one day I would come forward with my opinion about these happenings in a complete and, for me, decisive version. A preliminary, premature, and insufficient publication about this entire complex in form of an interview is distasteful to my soul."

Well, too bad. It would have been a pretty sensational scoop for a young writer.

Mann procrastinated until 1937, continuing his "appeasement" policy until he was officially deprived of his German citizenship and of his honorary doctorate from Bonn University. Then, indeed, he found a clear, decisive voice in denouncing the evils of Nazism.

during my first few years of exile I sometimes felt pangs of homesickness, particularly for Frankfurt and its stately cathedral, for the beautiful Main River, with its picturesque bridges, and for the nearby Taunus Mountains, which I had roamed as a boy. But I got over it, especially since I made friends with wonderful people in France. I played second violin in a string quartet with an excellent young musician who introduced me to her circle and family. They were French Protestants, and even though their own persecutions lay back four hundred years, they had an instinctive sympathy for other disadvantaged minorities. We visited a cousin of my violinist friend in a small village where he served as pastor and foster parent to a dozen orphans, tending goats, chickens, vegetables, and souls. The simple goodness of these folks touched me deeply.

The young violinist also brought me to her grandfather's rural estate. "Grandpère Sénateur" was an imposing politician with a walrus moustache. There were numerous family members with, it seemed to me, countless children playing, eating, and discussing on the terraces. Because I was the very first German refugee seen in these parts, many people asked me whether the Nazis were really as bad as was stated in the papers. My negative appraisal was

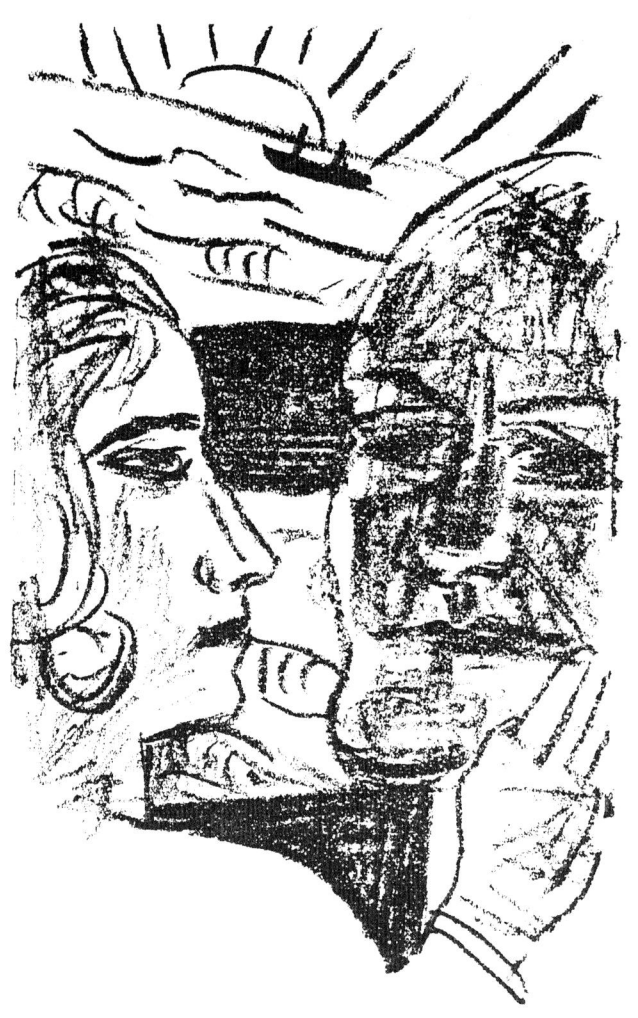

328
Max Beckmann; Untitled, from *Der Mensch ist kein Haustier*, 1937; lithograph; 8 5/8 x 5 3/8 in. (22 x 13.5 cm); collection of Stephan Lackner.

contradicted by some: perhaps Hitler was really good for his country, restoring its self-confidence and political unity. I gave a short speech: this moment in world history demanded not sharper emphasis on frontiers and national differentiation, but international understanding and collaboration. My friend applauded, as did several younger family members, and Grandpère Sénateur agreed, nodding his mighty head. Then we all jumped into the lake.

I was quite determined to enjoy my involuntary stay in Paris. Still, one always looked back over one's shoulder toward Germany, which loomed ever more menacingly over the horizon. I was lucky enough to find a charming French girlfriend to alleviate "the cold night of exile," as the poet Heine called it. I also made friends with expatriate literati, we held meetings of antifascist writers and journalists of many nationalities, and we signed high-minded resolutions. My most valuable friendship was with Walter Benjamin, a critic and philosopher who, posthumously of course, is now a cultural icon in Germany. In our many conversations his far-reaching thoughts and observations always emerged with the precision of printed words. He was pitifully poor, sometimes remaining in his tiny room for a day in order to preserve his dwindling monetary reserves. I was happy to help him and to invite him for dinner, where I listened eagerly to his challenging analyses of literary events. He seemed to know everything about Jewish mysticism, Marxism, and French and German literature. And he liked much of what I wrote. I appreciated his encouragement.

My first three books were published during my Parisian exile. The first one, *Die weite Reise* (The long journey), a collection of poems, came out in Zurich in 1936 and received some good reviews. The second book, a drama called *Der Mensch ist kein Haustier* (literally, "Man is not a domestic animal"; *Untamed* might be a better English title) appeared in Paris in 1937, with seven lithographs by Max Beckmann (see fig. 328). My third book was a novel, *Jan Heimatlos,* published in Zurich in 1938. It dealt with the fate of a nonconformist young man under the Nazis and in exile.

I think that of these three works the second one may be the most important. The three main characters in *Der Mensch ist kein Haustier* represent three basic endeavors of *Homo sapiens.* The freedom-loving, elitist Princess Louise loses her husband, palace, and treasures during a violent revolution. The rough-and-tumble revolutionary Peter falls in love with her but loses sight of her. The ice-cold rationalist Felix Faber builds up a strictly regulated, futuristic state where everything functions according to his theories. He calculates that he, the most valuable man, needs a child from the most accomplished woman, namely Louise. After a search through various continents Louise is lured back to her former homeland. But Peter and she discover that they are still in love. Even though she is pregnant with Felix's child, she flees with Peter. Peter is captured; Louise kills herself. Felix's impeccable intellect is converted into its opposite—madness.

I wrote this play in 1934. I showed it to Beckmann in 1936. He was surprised to find many parallels to his own Weltanschauung, and he proposed several changes in the text. In 1937, when the persecution of so-called degenerate art in Germany became unbearable, Beckmann and his wife, Quappi, emigrated to Amsterdam. Very soon thereafter he created the lithographs for my play. Only recently, fifty-six years after its publication, was it staged for the first time, in Tübingen, Germany.

When Beckmann left Berlin in 1937 (never to set foot on German soil again), he had been able to save his paintings and some belongings, but not his reputation as one of the foremost artists of his time. His art dealers had been forced to flee; German museums were forbidden to show or buy his works; critics could not write favorably about him. Hitler, in an infamous speech, threatened all expressionists, dadaists, and abstract artists with sterilization "in order to prevent the further inheritance of these horrible distortions of vision." In other countries Beckmann was not well known. It was an almost desperate situation. For three years I was his only collector. I managed to arrange exhibitions for him in Zurich, Basel, London, and Paris, but without much material success. I wrote essays about his art; one of them is now known as "the bible of Beckmann scholars" in Germany. It's all happening a little late!

In 1937 I commissioned Beckmann to paint my portrait (fig. 325). From time to time I reminded him that I would appreciate seeing it, but he replied: "You are not quite real yet." He finished the portrait in 1939, just as I was getting ready to leave for America. So I saw it only years later, after the war. It is still hanging in my house in Santa Barbara, a possession dear to my heart as a document of a wonderful union of two spirits.

t he Munich crisis of September 1938 gave us refugees quite a jolt. The Western powers sacrificed parts of Czechoslovakia to Hitler as payment for his promise of future nonaggression. Many French and British politicians still believed in the possibility of a durable peace; after all, the Germans had by now acquired Austria and the German-speaking regions of Bohemia, what more could they want? Indeed, if Hitler had stopped right there, *Großdeutschland* might have been a permanent reality. But *der Führer* remained insatiable. In March 1939 German troops conquered the rest of Czechoslovakia. My father felt that nothing could stop the Nazis anymore. He did not want to repeat his mistakes of 1914. With great determination my parents, brothers, and I prepared for our further emigration, this time to the United States.

We booked passage on the steamer *Paris* for April 19, 1939, and sent our belongings ahead to Le Havre. Half a day before we were to take the train from Paris to the harbor, we heard on the radio that the ship was burning at the pier. My hair stood on end: all my manuscripts, all my Beckmann paintings seemed lost. Many hours later we received word that, by some benign neglect, our crates were still standing in the rain on the quai. We took a later boat and arrived in New York on April 28, 1939.

Manhattan impressed me no end. Of course I had known its vistas from movies and newsreels, but to actually see hundreds of buildings reaching for the sky produced in me a dizzy kind of elation. And to look from a rooftop down on a cathedral was simply unbelievable; European cathedrals always dominated their cities. I admired the easygoing, mocking, tough New York way of speaking. I looked up every unknown word in my dictionary, kept it in mind, and recalled it exactly three minutes later so as to transfer it from short-term memory into my mental thesaurus. I hoped that I might soon become a writer of tolerable English.

Only twelve days after my arrival, contacting old friends from Europe, I met my future wife. "Puck," as she was called, was an Austrian girl who worked at the fashion house Lanz of Salzburg on Madison Avenue. She wore a light-blue dirndl in the middle of Manhattan's traffic roar. Her blond hair was flying in the breeze. She informed me that the skyscrapers around us did not represent the wave of the future at all, as I had surmised, and that a more humane kind of architecture was needed. I knew right away that I could learn a lot from her, especially because she had arrived in America half a year earlier than I. And I had not the slightest doubt that she was the loveliest woman on any continent. (By the way, we are still together fifty-seven years later.)

In Vienna she had read my novel *Jan Heimatlos* and some of my articles, and she was interested in my literary endeavors. I told her that I was working on a roman-fleuve, a series of novels set in Germany and France from World War I on, scheduled to take at least ten more years to finish. She was not dismayed by this quixotic project and said that I should stick with it as long as I could afford it. I moved to Long Island for the summer in order to work without distractions, and Puck visited me every weekend. I could not entice her to give up her job and live with me as a lover, but when I made it clear that I urgently needed a secretary, she joined me permanently and began typing. Over the years she typed thousands of pages for me.

Even though the political horizons became darker and darker, we felt a strong, private exhilaration. We were together, we were free, we would surely survive the Nazi nightmare. In the fall we drove along the Atlantic coast to Florida, where we rented a home for my parents and ourselves. But then Germany conquered its Western neighbors. It looked like Hitler might become the master of the world—"Morgen die ganze Welt" (Tomorrow, the whole world), as the Nazis were singing. Puck and I decided that a little more stability in our own lives might be useful, so we got married in June of 1940. In the autumn we traveled west, observing and admiring this still unfamiliar country. We finally settled in Santa Barbara.

I worked on a lemon ranch, driving a tractor, pruning trees, destroying weeds and gophers. At first my muscles ached, but I liked the fresh air and the visible, tangible results of my labor. On December 7, 1941, the Japanese attacked Pearl Harbor. Four days later Germany declared war on the United States. Hitler's hubris finally revealed itself as folly pure and simple.

Even newcomers could discern how the whole fabric of American life suddenly changed. An almost terrifying resolve gripped the country. Industry, agriculture, even teaching were focused on the war effort. The draft sucked up the youngsters around us. The iceman, who once a week delivered a big block of ice, asked me every time: "Are you still here? What's the matter with you?"

Even though I had been declared an enemy alien and was put under curfew and surveillance, I knew that I would have to become a soldier. After all, I had used my pen so much against National Socialism that it was only logical to continue the fight with other tools. I was not surprised when, in November 1943, I received greetings from the President of the United States ordering me to report for military duty.

I got my basic training in Fort Knox, Kentucky. On a questionnaire I had noted that I had been driving a tractor on a ranch, so I was classified as a tank driver. I enjoyed maneuvering the mighty M3 tank through the wilderness. Soon our Thirteenth Armored Division was transferred to Camp Bowie, Texas, where I gave many lectures to GIs and officers on the Wehrmacht and Nazi mentality.

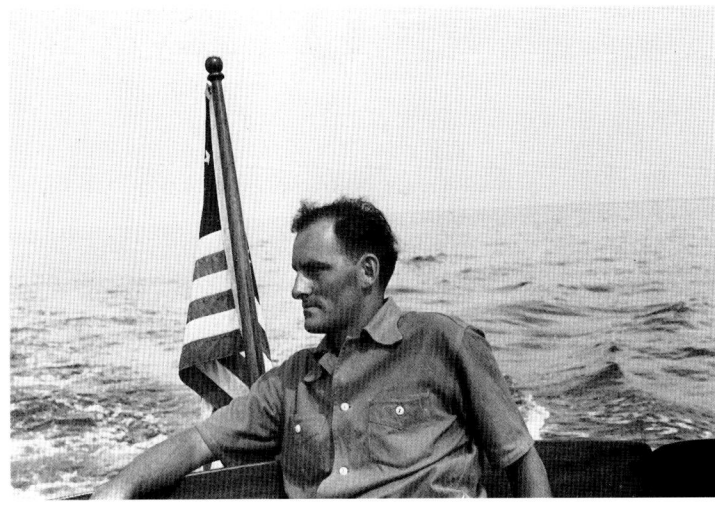

I saw action in Lorraine and the Ruhr pocket. It was an eerie feeling to return to Germany in American uniform: an archetypal dichotomy. My wife's brother was serving in Hitler's army; if I had encountered him, we would have tried to kill each other. As a reconnaissance soldier I constantly came into contact with the civilian population and German soldiers who gave up, and it was sometimes hilarious, sometimes tragic to overhear their conversations while they were unaware that I understood them. They griped against the American occupiers as well as the SS troops, who, by now, were thoroughly hated.

Burning cities, fleeing civilians, disoriented "displaced persons" seeking to regain their dignity, dead and maimed soldiers, hunger and hatred and misery everywhere. No, it was not a pleasant *Wiedersehen*.

On April 13, 1945, our division was made part of General Patton's Third Army, and we began a relentless drive southward. We reached the Inn River on May 2 and helped liberate the Ebensee concentration camp in Austria. Hundreds of emaciated corpses were stacked neatly in front of the ovens, each displaying a blue-penciled, four-digit number on its dirty-white chest to prove that the dispensers of death were really orderly people. The survivors kissed us, staggering around and crying; some of them died despite the best efforts of our army doctors and nurses.

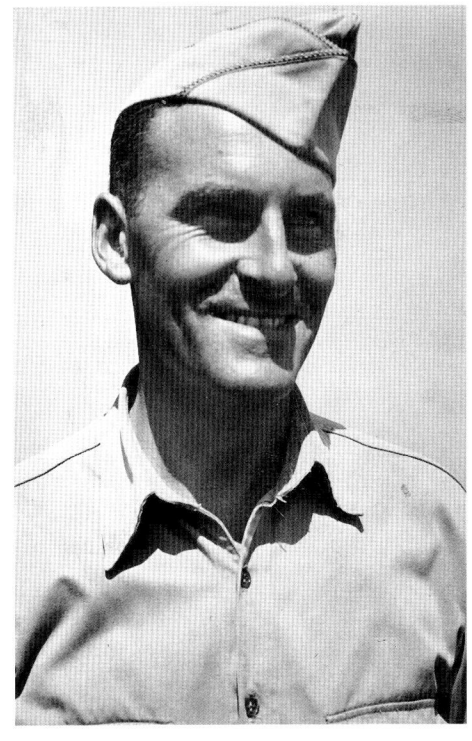

329
Stephan Lackner in Florida, 1940.

330
Stephan Lackner as an American soldier, Camp Bowie, Texas, 1944.

I was glad when I was shipped back to the United States. After a short reunion with my lovely wife and anxious parents, I started amphibious training at Camp Cooke (now Vandenberg Air Force Base) in California. It was clear that we were scheduled to participate in the invasion of the Japanese home islands. Then came the atomic destruction of Hiroshima and Nagasaki. We assembled in a recreation hall, the highest officers sitting on a dais, large-scale maps of Japan covering the walls. Our lieutenant colonel pointed out to us, with a certain regret, where the Forty-fifth Tank Battalion would have landed and advanced through the plain of Tokyo. Well, I wasn't much interested in seeing Japan anyway.

With all kinds of ribbons and commendations, I was discharged on December 7, 1945. When I put on civilian clothes and walked along State Street in Santa Barbara, I knew what a khaki-colored chrysalis must feel spreading rainbow wings and fluttering toward freedom.

already before the war Puck had a strong, natural desire to have children. Sometimes she stamped her foot: "Every cat can have kittens, why can't I have a baby?" I replied that, with Hitler in the same world, I did not want to engender a new human life. Now Hitler was gone, and we were in a hurry. The first of our three sons, Peter, was born on June 16, 1946.

I was extremely happy to return to my old desk and continue what I considered my life's task. I had started this roman-fleuve in 1937, and the first novel of the series was already half finished. Together the series would cover the years and events from 1914 to 1943. The main characters, Mathias and Marina, are a typically German engineer and a Jewish pianist. They embody the fruitful antithesis between the sober, mechanistic worldview and the artistic, romantic way of life. They marry and support each other in spite of Nazi terror and war; when their situation becomes insupportable, they commit suicide. I envisioned five or six volumes, with many figures and auxiliary plots depicting those adventurous times and changing moods and mores. I finished the first novel at the same time that we had our baby.

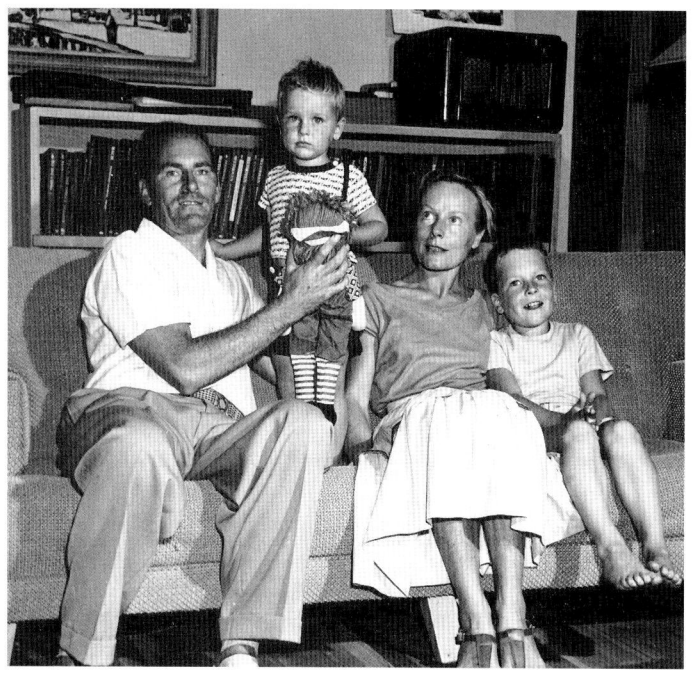

331
Stephan and Margaret ("Puck") Lackner in Santa Barbara with their sons Peter and Thomas, 1951.

Meanwhile a lively correspondence with Beckmann had developed. My friend and his wife had survived in Amsterdam. In spite of hunger, freezing cold, bombings, and Nazi persecution, he had painted about eighty pictures, four important triptychs among them. We sent him packages of delicacies that were still unobtainable in Holland. He had an ardent wish to come to America.

But first we traveled to Europe with our tiny son. We arrived in Paris on April 16, 1947, where we met Max and Quappi. It was the first time since the outbreak of the war that they had been able to leave the Netherlands, and we celebrated.

My former French girlfriend, Marcelle, had very cleverly hidden all the Beckmann paintings left in my apartment in an old brewery. Now she guided Beckmann and me through the labyrinthine building, where we found the canvases hidden behind huge copper kettles. Marcelle told us that the German occupation troops had confiscated every example of "degenerate" art they could find in Paris, even from private collections, and had destroyed them in a bonfire on the terrace of the Tuileries; so she had literally saved the Beckmanns for posterity. The artist and I separated the paintings that belonged to him from those that were mine. As soon as feasible, we had them all shipped to New York. Max and Quappi were able to sail to New York in August 1947.

We remained in Europe for a few more years. It never felt like a homecoming. Many Germans had a nasty resentment against emigrés—as if we had deserted and left them alone to cope with the tyrannical Nazis and Allied bombs. The most prominent literary society, the Gruppe 47, expressly excluded "Thomas Mann and such" from its membership. I tried very hard to find a publisher for the novel I had brought with me, to no avail. So we stayed mostly in Switzerland and Austria. Our second son, Thomas, was born in Switzerland.

Still haunted by what I had seen and done just a few years earlier, I wrote an antiwar play, *Doomsday minus One* (entitled in German *In letzter Instanz*). The Judge orders Man to justify his persecutions of his Brother over centuries. The dead Brother is summoned from his grave to testify. The enraged Man kills him again and is sentenced to death by means of an atomic rocket. But Woman sneaks into the rocket with him. The Judge, realizing that Woman is not guilty, commutes the sentence and directs the rocket to fly into space to explore other worlds and a peaceable future.

This play, written in late expressionist style, was received with some confusion and some enthusiasm. In 1950 it was first performed in Vienna, then in Frankfurt, Düsseldorf, Utrecht, Santa Barbara, and other cities. The problem of the drama is still as acute as it was half a century ago. I think it could profitably be rediscovered and staged in small theaters or even in churches.

In October 1950 we returned to America. By this time it couldn't be called exile any more. We were Americans with an accent; our existence was interwoven with Santa Barbara. Our third son, Lucas, was born here three years later. I started writing in English, and my book *Discover Your Self*, published in 1956, was successful, selling 120,000 copies in paperback.

I continued my work alternately in German and English. Three of my novels were published in Germany, as were many short stories and my 1988 autobiography. My biosophical tome *Peaceable Nature* (1984) was much discussed. My books on art usually came out in English and German editions.

We often visited Europe, spending many months in Vienna, Bavaria, Switzerland, finding wonderful new German friends, but never growing roots there again. Now, at eighty-six, I can't leave California anymore.

Occasionally I remember the most deeply touching verses in the *Odyssey*. The hero is stranded far from home, pining "to see just once again the smoke rising from Ithaka's hills and then to die." Even this last, modest pleasure was spoiled for me by Hitler's cohorts. The sight of smoke rising from a German chimney cannot evoke nostalgia, but only horror. And so—no last wish.

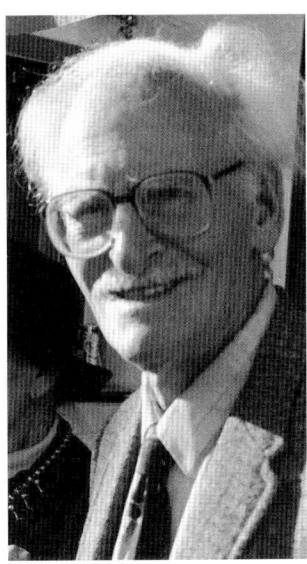

332
Stephan Lackner, 1995.

STEPHAN LACKNER: SELECTED BIBLIOGRAPHY

Die weite Reise. Zurich: Oprecht, 1937.

Der Mensch ist kein Haustier. Paris: Editions Cosmopolites, 1937.

Jan Heimatlos. Zurich: Liga, 1939.

Discover Your Self: A Practical Guide to Autoanalysis. New York: Merlin Press, 1956.

Max Beckmann: Memories of a Friendship. Coral Gables, Fla.: University of Miami Press, 1969.

Max Beckmann. The Library of Great Painters. New York: Harry N. Abrams, 1977.

Peaceable Nature: An Optimistic View of Life on Earth. San Francisco: Harper and Row, 1984.

Selbstbildnis mit Feder: Ein Tage- und Lesebuch: Erinnerungen. Berlin: Limes, 1988.

Max Beckmann. New York: Harry N. Abrams, 1991.

the great migration

HANS MAGNUS ENZENSBERGER

a map of the world. Swarms of blue and red arrows condense into eddies before scattering in opposite directions again. Underlying this diagram are curves which demarcate the color-tinted zones of varying air pressure, isobars, and winds. Such a weather chart looks pretty, but it cannot be accurately interpreted without previous knowledge. It is abstract. It has to represent a dynamic process by static means. Only a film could show what is really going on. The normal state of the atmosphere is turbulence. The same is true of the settlement of the earth by human beings.

Two passengers in a railway compartment. We know nothing about them, their origin, or their destination. They have made themselves at home and have commandeered the little tables, coat-hooks, and baggage-racks. Newspapers, coats, and bags lie around on the empty seats. The door opens and two new travelers enter. Their arrival is not welcomed. A distinct reluctance to move up, to clear the free seats and let the newcomers share them is evident. The original passengers, even if they do not know one another, behave with a remarkable degree of solidarity. They display a united front against the new arrivals. The compartment has become their territory, and they regard each new arrival as an intruder. Their consciousness is that of natives claiming the whole space for themselves. This view cannot be rationally justified. It appears all the more deeply rooted.

Nevertheless, matters rarely get to the point of open conflict. The passengers are subject to a system of rules that is not dependent on them. Their territorial instinct is curbed both by the institutional code of the railroad and by other unwritten norms of behavior such as courtesy. So only looks are exchanged and formulaic apologies muttered through clenched teeth. The new passengers are tolerated. One gets used to them. Yet they remain, even to a diminishing degree, stigmatized.

This harmless model is not without its absurd features. The railway compartment is itself a transitory domicile, a location which serves only to change locations. Fluctuation is its nature. The passenger is the negation of the sedentary person. He has traded real territory for a virtual one. Despite this, he defends his transient abode with sullen resentment.

Two new passengers open the compartment door. From this instant, the status of those who entered earlier changes. Only a moment ago, they were the intruders; now, all at once, they are natives. They belong to the sedentary clan of compartment-occupants and claim all the privileges the latter believe are due to them. The defense of an "ancestral" territory that was only recently occupied appears paradoxical. The occupants do not empathize with the newcomers, who have to struggle against the same opposition and face the same difficult initiation which they recently underwent. Curious, the rapidity with which one's own origin is concealed and denied.

A lifeboat is packed with survivors from a shipwreck. In the stormy sea around it there are other people in danger of going under. How should the occupants of the boat behave? Should they push away or hack off the hands of the next person who grabs the side of the boat? That would be murder. Pull him on? Then the boat would sink, taking all the survivors with it. The dilemma is part of the standard repertoire of casuistry. The moral philosophers and all the rest who discuss it usually pay no attention to the fact that they themselves are safely on dry land. Yet all abstract reflections founder on just this "as if," no matter what their conclusion. The best intention is frustrated by the coziness of the seminar room, because no one can credibly declare how he would behave in an emergency.

The parable of the lifeboat is reminiscent of the railway-compartment scenario. It is that model taken to its extreme. Here, also, travelers act as if they were property owners, with the difference that the ancestral territory they are defending is a drifting nutshell, and that it is no longer a matter of a little more comfort, but of life and death.

It is, of course, no accident that the image of the lifeboat recurs in the political discourse about immigration, usually in the form of the assertion, "The boat is full." That this sentence is factually inaccurate is the least that can be said about it. A look around is enough to disprove it. Those who make use of it know that too. They are not interested in its truthfulness, however, but in the illusion it conjures up, and that is an astonishing one. Evidently many West Europeans believe that their lives are in danger. They compare their situation with that of shipwreck survivors. The metaphor is turned upside-down, as it were. Suddenly those who have a roof over their heads imagine that they are fleeing *boat people,* emigrants sailing steerage, Albanians on an overcrowded ghost ship. The distress at sea which is hallucinated in this way is presumably intended to justify behavior which is only conceivable in extreme situations. From here it is not a very big step to the hacked-off hands in the parable.

There is something comforting about the railway compartment analogy, simply because the scene of the action is so restricted. Even in the terrifying image of the lifeboat, individual human beings can still be recognized—as in Géricault's painting, *The Raft of the "Medusa,"* where eighteen faces, actions, fates can be distinguished. Contemporary statistics, whether referring to the starving, the unemployed, or refugees, express everything in millions. Such numbers paralyze the imagination. The aid organizations and their campaign managers know that too, which is why they always show just one child with huge, pathetic eyes, so as to make the catastrophe commensurate with our compassion. But the terror of the big number is without eyes. Empathy breaks down before such excessive demand, and reason is made aware of its impotence.

> Superfluous, superfluous... an excellent word I've come up with. The deeper I plunge into myself and the closer I examine the whole of my past life, the more I am convinced of the harsh truth of that expression. Superfluous—precisely so. The word does not apply to other people.... People are good and evil, intelligent and stupid, pleasant and unpleasant; but superfluous?

It would not have occurred to Ivan Turgenev to regard the peasants on his estate, still less whole villages, regions, peoples, continents as superfluous. Although his hero Chulkaturin, in the novel *Diary of a Superfluous Man* (whose situation seems almost idyllic 150 years after his demise), talks in such terms of his landowning father with his country houses, and of himself—his boredom, his loneliness, and his disgust—"The word does not apply to other people," he thinks.

But he has been proved mistaken. Of course there have been great massacres and endemic poverty in every age. Enemies were enemies, and the poor were poor; yet only since history has become world history have whole peoples seen themselves condemned to superfluousness, and that by authors who remain strangely subjectless. The judges who pass this sentence go under the names of "colonialism," "industrialization," "technological progress," "revolution," "collectivization," "final solution," "Versailles," or "Yalta," and their decrees are pronounced openly and put into practice systematically, so that no one can be in any doubt what fate is intended for him: flight from the land or emigration, expulsion, or genocide.

State-organized crime continues to be widespread. The overarching, anonymous world market, however, appears ever more clearly as the instance which condemns increasingly large sections of mankind to superfluousness. It does so not through political persecution, by command of the Führer or party resolution, but spontaneously, by its own logic, so that more and more people fall out of it. The result is no less murderous, but the guilty are even less likely to be brought to book than before. In the language of economics that means: an enormously increasing supply of human beings is faced with a declining demand. Even in wealthy societies people are rendered superfluous daily. What should be done with them?

For a long time there was greater anxiety in Europe about the consequences of emigration than of immigration. This debate stretches back into the eighteenth century. The concept of population as wealth derives from the theories of mercantilism. In those days emigration was regarded as a hemorrhage, and the attempt was made to limit, even forbid it. Secret emigration, particularly recruitment for and the abetting of emigration, was subject to severe punishment in many states, a practice which communist states adhered to until very recently. Louis XIV had the French borders carefully watched in order to keep his subjects in the land, and in England there was a ban on the emigration of qualified artisans until the middle of the nineteenth century. The so-called Free or Departure Money, an emigration tax imposed on the estates of emigrants, was in force in Germany until 1817, and the Nazis reverted to this confiscatory procedure when they did not yet want to murder the Jews, only expel them.

Emigrants never represent a cross-section of the whole population, a fact which is of crucial importance to any estimation of the consequences. "It is the man of energy, of some means, of ambition, who takes the chances of success in the new country, leaving the poor, the indolent, the weak and crippled at home," wrote Richmond Mayo Smith. "It is maintained that such emigration institutes a process of selection which is not favorable to the home country."

This thesis is persuasive. The brain drain, a kind of demographic flight of capital, has had devastating effects on countries such as China, India, and the former Soviet Union. It was of considerable importance in the collapse of East Germany. A large proportion of the Iranian intelligentsia has emigrated in recent decades. The number of doctors from the Third World working in Western Europe exceeds the number of aid workers who are sent to Asia, Africa, and Latin America—where there is a shortage of trained doctors everywhere—from the states of the European Community.

The better qualified the immigrants, the fewer reservations they encounter. The Indian astrophysicist, the star Chinese architect, the Black African Nobel Prize-winner are welcome all over the world. The rich are also never mentioned in this context; no one questions their freedom of movement. For businessmen from Hong Kong the acquisition of a British passport is no problem. For immigrants from any country, Swiss citizenship, too, is only a matter of price. No one has ever objected to the color of the Sultan of Brunei's skin. Where bank accounts look healthy, xenophobia disappears as if by magic. But strangers are all the stranger if they are poor.

In this respect the drug and arms dealers, together with the banks which launder their money, put everyone else in the shade. They recognize no distinctions of race or nationality. These are probably the only people in the world who are quite without prejudice.

Black markets flourish everywhere there are restrictions. Like connecting vessels, they equalize pressure between supply and demand without regard for laws, regulations, and ethical norms. Since in the real world there are no completely closed systems, illegal transactions can be impeded by controls but never quite prevented. Market forces seek and find the smallest gap, the tiniest crack, and eventually slop through every barrier.

So an illegal trade in human beings has developed in all wealthy countries. However, whereas in classic black markets higher prices are always obtained than in legal trade, the black market in labor obeys the reverse logic. Lack does not rule here, but superfluity. Superfluous people are cheap. Clandestine immigration reduces the price of labor.

Each illegally employed immigrant presupposes an illegally operating entrepreneur. The shadow economy usually works hand in glove with the criminal gangs and networks that smuggle human beings. In the textile industry, parts of the service sector, and, above all, the building trade, practices dominate which are reminiscent of the slave markets of the past.

In some parts of the United States and in the Mediterranean countries of Europe, the shadow economy has so much political power that it is in a position to exert considerable pressure on the administration. In Germany also, the authorities often turn a blind eye to illegal employment. Regulations supposed to stem immigration are surreptitiously sabotaged, and curious forms of compromise arise.

Inevitably the size of these slave markets is unknown. No one has any interest in discovering it. The only certain thing is that the numbers involved are very large. In the United States, estimates suggest there are several million illegal immigrants, mostly from Mexico; in Italy, the figure must be well over a million. Wherever one looks closely it becomes evident that the officially proclaimed "policy towards foreigners" rests on a series of deliberate self-deceptions.

Asylum is an ancient convention of sacred origin. It owes its name to the Greeks, though the convention can also be demonstrated in other tribal societies, for example among the Jews. It also survived during the Middle Ages: criminals and debtors who had taken refuge in a church could be delivered up to secular justice only with the consent of the bishop. In more recent times, this custom has been increasingly restricted, first in the Protestant countries, and with the modern legal code it has disappeared altogether.

In international law, embassies were the first places of asylum, a tradition maintained until today, notably in Latin America. From the expanded concept of sovereignty, nation states derived the right to take in foreigners who were being politically persecuted in their homeland, and to refuse to surrender them. Yet asylum is not the individual right of the refugee but of the receiving state which admits him. Representative cases of this practice include the rebellious Poles, as well as revolutionaries such as Garibaldi, Kossuth, Louis Blanc, Bakunin, and Mazzini, who were regarded as criminals in their countries of origin but often celebrated as heroes in the countries that took them in.

The refugees, whom in Germany we call asylum-seekers or *Asylanten* (asylants), usually have little in common with such historical figures. Contemporary linguistic usage is influenced by a meaning the word assumed in the Victorian period: "The most frequently occurring asylums, the need for which makes itself felt chiefly in the great cities, are the following: I) for drunkards (inebriates' homes); II) for prostitutes (often called Magdalene Foundations); III) for released prisoners, who are lacking employment; IV) for poor women in childbed; V) asylums for the homeless." These are the antiquated expressions of a reference work from the turn of the century.

Such places of custody have nothing to do with the original meaning of asylum. They are intended not for foreigners, but for stigmatized locals. The only thing these people have in common is poverty.

The idea of asylum has always been ambiguous. Expediency and religiously determined ethics have become fused so that it is difficult to separate them again. In the beginning were robbery, murder, and killing. Within one's clan there was no other sanction but the endless chain of revenge, and whoever did not belong had no rights at all. Asylum—etymologically, the place where one was not robbed—was a makeshift, created in order to meet a need and to make communication and exchange beyond tribal boundaries possible.

The immunity of asylum necessarily held good for both guilty and innocent, criminals and victims alike, and the moral ambiguity is evident even to the present day. One only needs to think of figures such as Pol Pot in Peking, Idi Amin in Libya, Marcos in Hawaii or Stroessner in Brazil, to say nothing of the numerous Nazis, who, with the help of the Vatican, found refuge in Latin America. Originally this practice may have represented an attempt to provide overthrown rulers with the option of retreat, lessening the risk of civil war. As the Cambodian example shows, however, the granting of asylum can also serve the aim of keeping conflicts alive. At any rate, the "noble" asylum-seeker is a nineteenth-century idea. In historical perspective he is the exception.

Confusing the right to asylum with other questions of immigration and emigration has fatal consequences. The social and political expansion of the concept of asylum has made the muddle even greater. It is not clear why immigrants should be equated with overthrown dictators and criminals on the run, nor with alcoholics and tramps. The result is that "asylum-seeker" has become a discriminatory, negatively loaded term, a political football.

This deliberately engineered confusion, however, turns against those who practice it, because it contradicts the fundamental idea of asylum to separate the good from the bad according to the motto: I decide who is a "genuine" asylum-seeker and who is not. This is simply not possible, even with the best will in the world—which can hardly be assumed. The distinction between economic refugees and victims of political persecution has become an anachronism in many countries. A state of law which tries to make the distinction will inevitably be embarrassed, since it is increasingly difficult to deny that the impoverishment of whole continents has political causes, and that internal and external factors can no longer be clearly distinguished.

After all, the diffuse world war between winners and losers is carried out not only with bombs and automatic rifles. Corruption, indebtedness, flight of capital, hyper-inflation, exploitation, ecological catastrophes, religious fanaticism, and sheer incompetence can reach a level which provides just as solid reasons for flight as the direct threat of prison, torture, or shooting. All administrative procedures which aim to distinguish irreproachable from improper asylum-seekers must fail for that reason alone.

Germany is a country that owes its present population to huge movements of migration. Since earliest times there has been a constant exchange of population groups for the most diverse reasons. As a consequence of their geographical position alone, the Germans, like the Austrians, are a very mixed people. That blood- and race-ideologies became politically dominant here, of all places, can be understood as a form of compensation. The Aryan was never anything more than a risible construct. (To that extent German racism is different from Japanese racism, which appeals to the relatively high degree of ethnic homogeneity of the island population.) A cursory glance at a historical atlas is enough to show that the idea of a compact German population is unfounded. Its function can only be to prop up, by means of a fiction, an especially fragile national identity.

The recent history of the country bears witness to exactly that. The Second World War mobilized the Germans in more than one sense. Not only did the majority of the male population swarm out as far as the North Cape and the Caucasus (and, as prisoners of war, as far as Siberia and New England), and not only did fascism force substantial elements of the German elite and almost the whole Jewish population into emigration or to their deaths. During the war, nearly ten million forced laborers, a third of them women, were abducted to Germany from all over Europe, so that 30 percent of all jobs, and in the armaments industry more than half, were filled by foreigners. After the war, they were followed by millions of displaced persons; only a very few of them, however, remained in Germany.

Further large-scale migrations began at the end of the war. The number of refugees who, between 1945 and 1950, came into the four occupation zones is estimated at twelve million; in addition there were more than three million "resettlements" of people from Eastern Europe and the Soviet Union who were considered to be of German origin. Between 1944 and 1989, 4.4 million went to the West from the former East Germany. Then, in the mid-fifties, the systematic recruitment of labor migrants began, which is the principal reason for more than five million foreigners having their legal place of residence in Germany. (The proportion of foreigners is still well below the level of 10 percent which, if one includes the Poles from the Prussian eastern provinces, was recorded before the First World War.)

Until the eighties, the right to asylum was an infinitesimally minor factor in population movements. But from 1955 to 1986 between 400,000 and 600,000 Germans emigrated every year, a fact which, remarkably, is ignored in political debate.

It is puzzling that a population that has lived through such times can suffer from the delusion that the current migrations are an unprecedented phenomenon. It is as if Germans had fallen victim to the amnesia observed in the railway passenger scenario. To a large extent they are new arrivals, who themselves have only just secured a seat, but insist on enjoying the rights of those who have been there for ever. As is well known, the consequences go beyond a reluctance to move closer together in the first-class compartment. Since 1991 they have reached the dimensions of an organized manhunt.

Is xenophobia a specifically German problem? If that were so, it would be too good to be true—the solution would be obvious: isolate the Federal Republic, and the rest of the world would heave a sigh of relief. It would be easy to point to some neighboring countries where immigration is dealt with more rigorously and where entry quotas are lower than in Germany. But such comparisons are unproductive. Xenophobia is a universal phenomenon. The irrationality of the controversy is not specifically German, since nowhere does the subject seem accessible to reason. What, then, is so special about the Germans? Why has such an extreme polarization emerged here?

The historical guilt felt by the Germans, no matter how well founded, is not a sufficient explanation. The causes go further back. They lie in the precarious self-consciousness of the nation. It is a fact that Germans like neither each other nor themselves; the emotions which came to the surface with German unification leave no doubt about that. But someone who dislikes himself is going to find it difficult to love those who are not even his neighbors.

This is evident not only in the hostility towards foreigners, which, from the denial of obvious facts ("Germany is not a country of immigration") to the mobilization of gangs of thugs, has formed a continuum, but also from the opposition to it.

Nowhere is a universalist rhetoric more highly valued than in Germany. Immigrants are defended in a moralizing tone of utter self-righteousness: slogans such as "Foreigners, don't leave us alone with the Germans!" or "Never again Germany!" testify to a sanctimonious reversal of signs. The racist cliché appears in the negative. Immigrants are idealized in a manner reminiscent of philo-Semitism. Taken far enough, the inversion of prejudice can become discrimination against the majority. Self-hatred is projected onto others—notably in the insidious assertion "I am a foreigner," which numerous German celebrities have adopted.

A curious alliance between the remnants of the left and the clergy has emerged. (Similar alliances can also be observed in Scandinavia, which suggests that the stance has something to do with the political culture of Protestantism.) Preaching the Sermon on the Mount is surely a duty of the church. Ineffectiveness cannot be an objection in the context of religion. Professing it only becomes hypocrisy when it passes itself off as a political solution. Whoever calls upon his fellow citizens to offer shelter to the weary and wretched of the earth—often with reference to collective crimes stretching from the conquest of America to the Holocaust—without consideration of the consequences, without regard for political and economic mediations or whether such a project is realizable, loses all credibility. He becomes incapable of action. Deep-seated social conflicts cannot be abolished by sermons.

Evidently a disoriented left, in defiance of its classic texts and despite the disastrous consequences of years of self-deception, still clings to the superstition that a recalcitrant being will, after all, submit to correct consciousness if only it is drummed into people often enough. That a self-declared minority of the righteous wants a different nation for itself may correspond to its pedagogic ambition. But a change of heart will hardly be achieved through blackmail. To paraphrase Brecht, "Would it not be easier/In that case for the preachers/To dissolve the people/And elect another?"

From a subjective viewpoint, things look even worse. A readiness and capacity for integration can no longer be assumed in any country or group. The multicultural society remains a confusing slogan as long as the difficulties which it throws up, and fails to clarify, remain taboo. The wearisome dispute will never be resolved if no one knows, or wants to know, what culture means—"Everything that humans do and do not do" seems the most precise definition. For this reason alone, the debate is condemned to reproduce the contradiction between deliberate underestimation and denunciation, idyll and panic.

The experiences provided by large-scale migrations in the past are ignored in such discussions. The opponents of immigration deny the examples of success which could be found everywhere, from the Swedes in Finland to the Huguenots in Prussia and elsewhere, from the Poles in the Ruhr to the Hungarian refugees of 1956. The advocates will not hear of the risks. They refuse to take account of the civil wars in the Lebanon, in the former Yugoslavia and in the Caucasus, or the conflicts in the American cities. The idea of a multinational state has seldom proved durable. It is perhaps asking too much that anyone remember the disintegration of the Ottoman Empire or the Habsburg Monarchy. But as far as the former Soviet Union is concerned, no knowledge of history is required; a television is enough. The Soviet Union made great efforts to instill a sense of identity and of common goals in a "multicultural society." The result was implosion, with incalculable consequences.

Dangers can also be observed in the classic countries of immigration. New arrivals traditionally showed themselves extremely willing to adapt, even if it is doubtful that the famous "melting pot" ever existed. Most were well able to distinguish between integration and assimilation. They accepted the written and unwritten norms of the society which took them in, but they tended to hold on to their cultural tradition—and often also to their language and religious customs.

Today it is impossible to count on such an attitude among the old minorities or the new immigrants. More and more frequently common bonds are being renounced. Poverty and discrimination have led minorities, especially in the United States, but also in Great Britain and France, to adopt aggressive political ideologies. The excluded have turned the tables and are cutting themselves off. Ever more groups in the population are insisting on their "identity." It is by no means clear what this is supposed to mean. Militant spokesmen raise separatist demands. At times, the slogans fall back on the legacy of tribalism. There is talk of a black "nation" and an Islamic "nation." In England, Pakistani fundamentalists have set up a "Muslim Parliament" on the grounds that the Islamic population of the country constitutes a political system of its own. Conspiracy theories attract a mass following; many blacks in the United States believe that the drug trade is a calculated strategy of the whites with the aim of exterminating the black minority.

There are confrontations not only with the majority but also between the minorities. African-Americans fight against Jews, Latinos against Koreans, Haitians against local blacks, and so on. Social conflicts become nationalized. In some city districts there are virtual tribal wars. In extreme cases apartheid is claimed as a human right and the conversion of the ghetto into a separate state is elevated into an ultimate goal. Nevertheless, the spokesmen for these movements are demagogues without democratic legitimacy, and it does not look as though the masses which they supposedly represent stand behind them.

Certain Peculiarities concerning the Manhunt

Anyone who intervenes in the political discourses of German public life does so at his own risk. It is not so much the moral accusations usual in this sphere which are a deterrent (they draw on an established tradition and are a familiar feature of journalism); more serious are the intellectual risks taken by someone who participates in a media debate. He will almost inevitably be made to look foolish as soon as he makes a contribution. The reason is not hard to find: whoever submits to the premises of a chat show is already lost, and has only himself to blame. It is no secret where the rules, to which the participants more or less cheerfully subordinate themselves, come from.

Years ago, word got round the party headquarters that the occupation of ideas is strategically just as important as control of the apparatus of power. One has to admire the skill with which the political class, for which nothing is less congenial than an idea, has made this theory its own. One consequence is that political debate is becoming more and more of a media phantom; it evaporates on television, and especially television at its dreariest: the daily news report on political developments in Bonn. The discourse of the opposition is also restricted by such conditions: it contents itself by turning its opponent's slogans upside down.

Nowhere does this crude pattern emerge more clearly than in the "policy towards foreigners" and the "asylum debate." The very formulations are obviously products of the Bonn muck heap. Politicians have, however, managed to displace the argument onto two areas which can be arbitrarily interchanged as required. On the one hand, an abstract moralizing discussion of principles is instigated; on the other, it is possible, at any time, to fall back on issues of legal procedure as soon as the question of putting anything into practice is raised. With this double strategy, quite obvious questions, which the promoters are evidently not interested in asking, fall by the wayside.

I would like to raise one such question here, which though it is not central to the problem of the Great Migration, is, nevertheless, a matter of life and death for those who already live in Germany—whatever their passport or stamp or legitimacy. It is the question of whether the country is actually habitable. I call a place uninhabitable where a gang of thugs is free to attack people in the middle of the street or set fire to their homes.

One can disregard the question of who is and who is not supposed to be German, at least as long as it is not decided by having one group wear normal clothes, while the rest are forced by law to stick triangles, crosses, or stars on themselves. Since no one has so far proposed such laws, the distinction between natives and foreigners is irrelevant in this context. It is also superfluous, in this context, to distort sentimentally the status of the foreigner, for example, with the popular assertion which is being proclaimed by every would-be celebrity: "I am a foreigner."

Even the briefest glance reveals that swindlers and bores, louts and idiots are encountered among the native population with the same statistical frequency as among Turks, Tamils, and Poles. Being forced to live together with them without resorting to violence is an unreasonable demand, which in a civilized society everyone without exception has to put up with. Even those who do not want to accept it must, if necessary, be compelled to do so. For what is intolerable is the presence of people who undertake individual or organized manhunts.

The simple distinction has nothing to do with the so-called foreigners' problem. Neither does it have anything to do with new regulations for asylum procedures, still less with the misery of the Third World nor with the ubiquitous racism. At stake is the monopoly of force which the state claims for itself.

One can accuse the various governments of this republic of all kinds of things, but no one can say that they ever hesitated to make use of this monopoly if it seemed threatened. On the contrary, the executive has never shown itself lacking in enthusiasm in this respect. Federal Border Guards, secret services, security task forces, police mobile rapid response units, state and federal detective departments have always been on hand with hard- and software from computer dragnets to helicopter squadrons, from identikit pictures to armored personnel carriers. Nor has the legislature been any less diligent. It has been game to the point of irresponsibility, constantly breaking new legal ground from the construct of the "criminal association" to the law allowing bans on visits and letters to prisoners awaiting trial. As a result, the state has access to a terrifying arsenal of means of self-protection.

In recent months not even the least significant use has been made of these resources. Indeed, the apparatus of repression, from the police to the courts, has responded to the appearance on a massive scale of gangs of thugs in both parts of Germany with an unprecedented degree of restraint. Arrests have been the exception; where they have been carried out, the culprits have almost always been set free the following day. The Federal State Prosecutor's Office and the Federal CID, once omnipresent in the media, devoted to repelling any threats to the German people, have kept quiet, as if they had been temporarily retired.

The Federal Border Guards, which only a few years ago occupied every second crossroads, seem to have disappeared from the face of the earth.

As for the politicians, many of them have taken the stage in an unfamiliar role: as social workers. Their therapeutic efforts were not directed at the hunted—they were fobbed off with high-flown phrases—but at the very people who were engaged in the manhunt. Regrettable deficiencies in the education system, especially in the former GDR, have been mentioned; there have been pleas for an understanding of the harsh reality of unemployment; besides their immaturity, the killers' cultural disorientation was taken into account. All in all, we were dealing with "poor souls" who had to be treated with the utmost patience. It was hardly possible to expect such underprivileged persons to realize that setting fire to children is, strictly speaking, not permissible. Attention must be drawn all the more urgently to the inadequate supply of leisure activities available to the arsonists.

Such heartfelt sympathy is astonishing, when one remembers the pictures from Brokdorf (a power station which became the focus of antinuclear protest) and Startbahn West (a runway at Frankfurt Airport, intended primarily for U.S. military use, whose construction was delayed by years of protest). At that time, those in power did not appear to regard the rapid development of discotheques and youth clubs as providing the solution; evidently in the seventies, uncontested free access to the paradise of leisure society had not yet become an inalienable right. On the contrary, beating, kicking, and shooting were carried out with considerable vigor and, if I remember rightly, the state was quite prepared to take a couple of dead in its stride.

Is the sudden change of heart due to a conversion? Since the Enlightenment there have always been humanitarians who have assured us that criminal law is unsuitable as a solution to social problems. That can hardly be denied, given the condition in the jails and the high rate of recidivism, even if the reformers still owe us a convincing alternative. However, that does not explain the puzzling shift of the state apparatus towards sympathetic lenience for killers. Shoplifters and bank robbers, confidence tricksters and embezzlers, terrorists and extortionists are being sent down as they always have been; no political party has as yet advocated the abolition of the penal code or, even, a thorough reform of the penal system. We therefore have to turn to other explanations to understand the discrepancy between enthusiastic prosecution on the one hand, and *laissez faire* on the other.

Is it possible that the intensity of the effort depends on the interests which the law exists to protect? In the precedents already mentioned, it was a matter of the private ownership of real estate, of the right to enlarge airports, build motorways, and erect nuclear installations of every kind. In the attacks and arson of recent months, however, the lives of a few thousand inhabitants of the country have been at stake. Evidently the agencies of the state consider murder and manslaughter a mere breach of the law, while removal of a fence is a serious crime.

The circumstances also invite other interpretations. It is difficult to believe, but it cannot be quite excluded that there are politicians who sympathize with the murderous gangs roaming the country. Perhaps more likely is that many sit back and watch the manhunt impassively because they imagine that such an attitude could be politically advantageous. One does not, of course, like to believe in such a degree of idiocy, and only the absence of other plausible explanations justifies considering it.

Even the most stupid person should grasp one thing: renouncing the state's monopoly of force has consequences which may harm the political class itself. One result is a need for self-defense. If the state refuses to protect them, threatened individuals or groups will have to arm themselves. International trade will effortlessly meet the required demand. As soon as a resistance has been organized, there will be gang wars (a development that can already be observed in big cities like Berlin and Hamburg). Politically this may lead to conditions such as those Germany experienced towards the end of the Weimar Republic.

Furthermore, if mass terror on the streets has no effect, it will eventually turn against the political class. No personal security is perfect, and it would be an illusion to believe that all-German hit-squads will, in the long term, continue to reciprocate the paternal indulgence which is extended to them in many places. Such tolerance, which always favors the criminals and never the victims, is evidence of an excessive taste for continuity. Certain politicians clearly have difficulty breaking with it. That allows several conclusions, only one of which is surprising: the sense of self-preservation of these people is less pronounced than we think.

This essay is excerpted from "The Great Migration," in *Civil Wars: From L.A. to Bosnia* (New York: New Press, 1994). © 1993 by Hans Magnus Enzensberger; translation © 1994 by Martin Chalmers. Reprinted by permission of the New Press.

chronology

Items relating to emigration are in **bold** type.

CULTURAL

Ludwig Grote, director of the Anhaltinische Gemäldegalerie in Dessau, is dismissed, as is Carl Georg Heise, director of the Museum Behnhaus in Lübeck.

Bauhaus member Hajo Rose escapes to the Netherlands, where he works at Paul Citroen's Nieuwen Kunstschool.

Heinrich Campendonk immigrates to the Netherlands, where he is appointed director of the Amsterdam Imperial Academy.

Alois Schardt, director of the Städtisches Museum für Kunst und Kunstgewerbe in Halle, is named director of the Nationalgalerie in Berlin.

12 January
George Grosz leaves Germany for the U.S. He teaches at the Art Students League in New York (also 1934, 1935, and from 1941 on).

15 February
Käthe Kollwitz and Heinrich Mann are forced to leave the Prussian Academy of the Arts after signing a proclamation advocating the cooperation of the Socialist and Communist parties in the 1933 election campaign. Hans Poelzig resigns in protest. **Mann immigrates to France (Sanary-sur-Mer).**

13 March
Joseph Goebbels is named minister of public enlightenment and propaganda.

15 March
The German publishing trade journal, *Das Börsenblatt des deutschen Buchhandels*, publishes the first official blacklist in the fine arts.

31 March
Willi Baumeister and Max Beckmann lose their teaching posts at the Städelschule in Frankfurt. An exhibition of Beckmann's works to be held in Erfurt is canceled.

April
First exhibitions defaming modern art—such as *Regierungskunst von 1918 bis 1933* (Government art from 1918 to 1933), organized by Hans Adolf Bühler, and the *Schreckenskammer* (Chamber of horrors) exhibitions—are shown in Nuremberg, Dresden, and Dessau and travel throughout Germany in the years following.

Karl Hofer, Max Pechstein, Edwin Scharff, and Oskar Schlemmer are fired from their teaching positions in Berlin; Heinrich Campendonk, Paul Klee, and Oskar Moll are dismissed from theirs in Düsseldorf.

Jankel Adler flees to Paris.

In Amsterdam the first German exile publishing company, Querido Verlag, is founded by Fritz H. Landshoff and Emanuel Querido.

7 April
In Germany the Professional Civil Service Restoration Act (*Gesetz zur Wiederherstellung des Berufsbeamtentums*) is enacted, allowing university professors, museum directors, and museum

1933

POLITICAL

30 January
In Germany Adolf Hitler becomes chancellor by invitation of President Hindenburg, heading a coalition in which the National Socialist party has a minority of votes.

Hitler immediately initiates a campaign to purge Germany of its Jewish population by forcing its members to emigrate. About 525,000 Jews are affiliated with religious communities, and an additional 600,000 "non-Aryans" live in Germany. Up to 20,000 Jews from Eastern Europe, mainly Poland, are expelled from Germany this year.

17 February
The Prussian Interior Ministry permits shooting "enemies of the state" with impunity.

23 February
Homosexual rights groups proscribed.

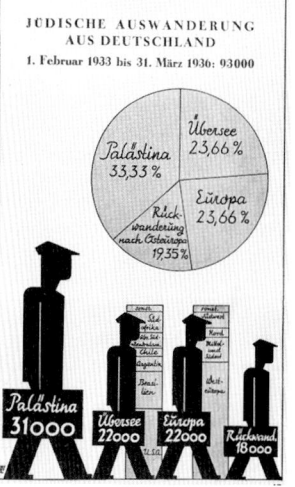

Above: Chart showing the destinations of Jews emigrating from Germany, 1933–36.

Right: A Jewish family leaving Germany, 1935.

27 February
In Berlin the Reichstag burns down; the Dutch communist Marinus van der Lubbe is arrested for this crime. The National Socialists start a campaign against communists and arrest many of them.

February–March
Violence against individual Jews and Jewish shops by members of the National Socialist party and the SA (*Sturmabteilung*, "storm troopers") results in the first wave of emigration from the Reich.

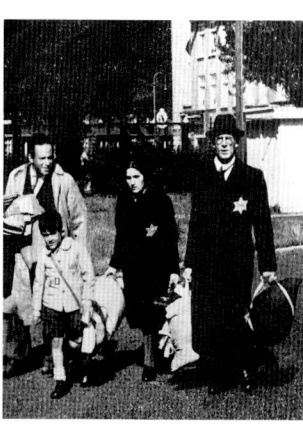

curators to be laid off and effecting the compulsory retirement of Jewish civil servants. Ernst Gosebruch (Essen), Gustav Hartlaub (Mannheim), Ludwig Justi (Berlin), Ernst Pauli (Hamburg), Max Sauerlandt (Hamburg), and Ernst Waldmann (Bremen) are among the museum directors dismissed.

8 April
Otto Dix is dismissed from the Dresden Academy.

11 April
The Bauhaus in Berlin, under the directorship of Ludwig Mies van der Rohe, is closed by the Nazis but is allowed to reopen after negotiations.

16–17 April
John Heartfield and his brother, Wieland Herzfelde, escape from Berlin to Prague. There Herzfelde reestablishes his publishing company, Malik Verlag.

25 April
The proportion of Jewish students in German schools and universities is limited to 1.5 percent.

In a letter to Goebbels, Schlemmer protests the defamation of artists in the *Schreckenskammer* exhibitions.

May
The Nazi student organization exhibits works by Ernst Barlach, Emil Nolde, Karl Schmidt-Rottluff, and others, making a strong case for expressionism as the official Nazi art.

The Deutsche Arbeitsfront (German labor front) is founded; one division, Kraft durch Freude (Strength through joy), oversees mass leisure activities and official cultural events.

The Jewish mural painter Hans Feibusch immigrates to England; photographer Gisèle Freund immigrates to Paris.

6 May
Max Hirschfeld's Institut für Sexualwissenschaften (Institute of sexual research) is ransacked, and its library is burned down.

7 May
Max Liebermann resigns from the Prussian Academy.

10 May
Goebbels attends book burnings at the Opernplatz in Berlin and later in other university towns. Works by Bertolt Brecht, Sigmund Freud, Heinrich Mann, and Kurt Tucholsky are among those burned.

20 June
500,000 books are confiscated in Berlin.

July
Andreas Feininger emigrates from France to Sweden; he had left Dessau for Paris in 1932.

20 July
In Berlin the Bauhaus finally closes, following a decision by the faculty to dissolve the school.

22 September
The Reichskulturkammer law, centralizing cultural production, is passed, creating seven chambers, one of which, the Reichskammer der bildenden Künste, is to oversee the fine arts. Goebbels heads the Reichskulturkammer.

October
Heinrich Mann is named honorary president of the Schutzverband deutscher Schriftsteller (Defensive league of German writers), an exile group that organizes 150 events in France.

4 October
The Editorial Law (*Schriftleitergesetz*) includes a paragraph excluding Jews from journalism.

November
U.S.: The Public Works of Art Project (PWAP) is established within the Department of the Treasury, under the direction of financier and painter Edward Bruce. It provides emergency relief work to artists, preferably those who work on American themes or paint in a representational mode. PWAP expires on 30 June 1934, but the Roosevelt administration continues to view patronage of the arts as a governmental function.

---

4 March
In the midst of the Great Depression Franklin Roosevelt is inaugurated president of the U.S. More than one-quarter of the working population is unemployed.

The U.S. immigration quota allows 25,957 Germans to enter the country each year. Special provisions for "nonquota" immigrants such as clergymen and university professors. All applicants are required to furnish proof of employment or financial support.

5 March
The National Socialists gain 44 percent of votes in a national election. With the support of the Nationalist and Center parties, they pass an enabling act, giving Hitler dictatorial power.

8 March
Interior Minister Wilhelm Frick announces the establishment of concentration camps.

21 March
The Malicious Practices Law (*Heimtückegesetz*) prohibits criticism of the regime.

April
French Interior Minister Camille Chautemps encourages his countrymen "to give to German refugees the same hospitality formerly offered in analogous circumstances to Italian, Spanish and Russian citizens." The alien population in France consists of around 3 million people. Great Britain declares, "We do not . . . admit that there is a 'right of asylum' but when we have to decide whether a particular political refugee is to be given admission to this country, we have to base our decision . . . on whether it is in the public interest that he be admitted."

1 April
Germany: Nationwide boycott of Jewish businesses, medical doctors, and lawyers.

30 June
U.S.: The legislative foundations of Roosevelt's New Deal have been laid. The National Industrial Recovery Act establishes the Public Works Administration and the National Recovery Administration. The first bill is intended to increase employment by funding the construction of roads and public buildings; the latter will stimulate competition.

15,000 refugees have arrived in the Netherlands.

July
The National Socialist party is the only legal party in Germany; trade unions and strikes have been outlawed, and 27,000 political prisoners are held in concentration camps.

15 July
Rome Pact, binding Britain, France, Germany, and Italy to the League Covenant, Locarno treaties, and Kellogg-Briand Pact.

September
10,000 German refugees have crossed into Switzerland.

14 October
Germany leaves the League of Nations and the Disarmament Conference.

30 November
The Gestapo (*Geheime Staatspolizei*, "secret state police") is created.

Four-fifths of the 65,000 Germans who left the country in 1933 were Jews; 40 percent went to France. Chautemps ends exceptional measures to receive refugees and restricts the entry of new exiles from Germany. 30,000 immigrants entered Palestine; most are from Poland, and about one-fifth are from Germany.

CULTURAL

15 November
The architect Eugen Hönig is named president of the Reichskammer der bildenden Künste. He will be replaced by the painter Adolf Ziegler in 1936.

Josef and Anni Albers arrive in the U.S.

December
The library of the Aby Warburg Institute is moved from Hamburg to London.

21 December
Wassily Kandinsky arrives in Paris.

23 December
Paul Klee returns to Switzerland.

January
László Moholy-Nagy immigrates to the Netherlands.

January–February
Renée Sintenis and Bruno Taut are dismissed from the Prussian Academy.

April
A caricature exhibition organized by the Manes artists' society in Prague is protested by Germany, Austria, and Italy. Seven photomontages by Heartfield, as well as works by František Bidlo and Bert (J. Justaz) are removed.

10 May
The Deutsche Freiheitsbibliothek (German library of freedom) is founded in Paris by Lion Feuchtwanger, Heinrich Mann, and others. It will collect literature that is banned in Germany.

10 July
The leftist writer Erich Mühsam is murdered in the Oranienburg concentration camp by Nazi storm troopers.

October
Oskar Kokoschka moves from Vienna to Prague.

Gert Arntz immigrates to the Netherlands, where he publishes *Das dritte Reich* (The Third Reich), a woodcut showing the pyramidal structure of Nazi society.

The literary monthly *Die Sammlung* is published in Amsterdam by Klaus Mann under the patronage of André Gide, Aldous Huxley, Heinrich Mann, and Querido Verlag.

The artist Hans Grundig is forbidden to practice his profession.

U.S.: The Artists' Union is organized in New York with local offices elsewhere to promote the creation of art projects for unemployed artists. Similar organizations include the Artists' Committee of Action and the Art Students' Council. Stuart Davis begins publishing *Art Front*, which becomes an official organ of the Artists' Union.

14 October
U.S.: The Treasury Section of Painting and Sculpture is established by Henry Morgenthau Jr., with Bruce as its director. It will commission public art projects.

Walter Gropius immigrates to London.

1934

POLITICAL

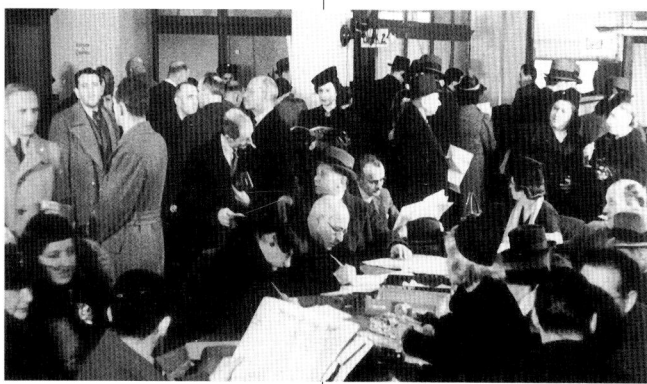
German Jews seeking to emigrate gather in the office for immigration to Palestine in Berlin, 1935.

January
Unemployment is high in France and Britain. **In the Netherlands foreigners are no longer given work permits because of high unemployment.**

26 January
Ten-year nonaggression pact between Germany and Poland signed.

February
Austrian Chancellor Engelbert Dollfuss moves sharply to the right, dissolving parliament and forming an alliance with Fascist Italy for protection. At Mussolini's urging, Dollfuss bans the Austrian Social Democrats. This is followed by a civil war, which is resolved with the help of the artillery and Viennese rightists active in the Heimwehr, the Austrian fascist party. **As a result, thousands of Austrians leave, many of them heading for Paris.**

17 March
Rome Protocols, binding Austria and Hungary to Italy. Mussolini guarantees Austrian independence.

30 June
"Night of Long Knives," during which the SS (*Schutzstaffel*, "elite guard") liquidates members of the SA, including its head, Ernst Röhm, and opponents.

In fiscal year 1933–34 4,392 Germans immigrated to the U.S., while 14,693 U.S. residents emigrated to Germany.

25 July
Dollfuss is murdered in a Nazi putsch in Vienna.

2 August
Death of President Hindenburg. Hitler becomes president, and the army swears an oath of allegiance to him. Two weeks later he appoints himself Führer and chancellor of the Reich.

27 September
Britain and France guarantee Austrian independence.

October–November
Germany: Nationwide arrests of homosexuals.

1,500 refugees from the Netherlands and 3,000 from France return to the Reich. In 1934 there were 42,000 immigrants to Palestine, of which one-fifth were from Germany.

The exhibition *Blut and Boden* (Blood and soil) opens in Munich. Hitler declares in his speech at the Nuremberg party congress that the eradication of modernism is a pressing goal.

Moholy-Nagy moves from Amsterdam to London.

24 April
The German press is required to conform to National Socialist ideology. Its members have to prove their Aryan ancestry.

6 June
U.S.: The Works Progress Administration (WPA) provides employment for artists, musicians, actors, writers, and scholars. It will continue its efforts until 1943.

21–25 June
In Paris the Communist-organized Congrès international des écrivains pour la défense de la culture (International congress of writers in defense of culture) emphasizes the necessity for socialist and bourgeois members to join in the fight against fascism.

Johannes R. Becher, Brecht, Max Brod, Jean Cassou, Feuchtwanger, Gide, Alfred Kerr, Egon E. Kisch, Heinrich Mann, and Klaus Mann are among the participants.

July
U.S.: The Treasury Relief Art Project is established under the directorship of painter Olin Dows to commission unemployed artists to provide small-scale decoration for public buildings.

August
U.S.: The WPA Federal Art Project (WPA/FAP) is established, with former museum curator Holger Cahill as director. In contrast to the Treasury's art programs, the WPA/FAP employs artists with a wide range of styles, sponsors more varied and experimental works, and has a substantial impact on subsequent American art movements.

3 August
Lyonel Feininger notes in a letter that Nolde had notified German officials that Pechstein was Jewish.

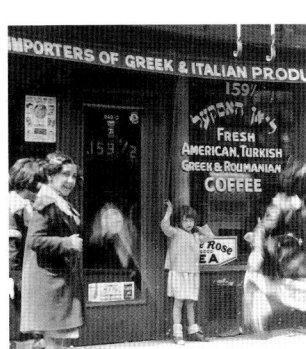

Article on the Dresden *Schreckenskammer der Kunst* exhibition, from the *Kölnische illustrierte Zeitung*, 17 August 1935.

26 September
In Paris antifascists meet under the direction of Heinrich Mann to discuss the possibility of a German Popular Front in exile.

23 November
Paris: The Kollektiv deutscher Künstler (Collective of German artists) is founded. Members include Max Ernst, Otto Freundlich, Hanns Kralik, Robert Liebknecht, Heinz Lohmar, Erwin Öhl, Eugen Spiro, Horst Strempel, Gert Wollheim, and writer Paul Westheim.

Marcel Breuer immigrates to London.

The American Abstract Artists group is founded in New York, with the aim of making the city a center of abstract art.

At the Museum of Modern Art in New York Alfred H. Barr Jr. organizes *Cubism and Abstract Art* (February–April) and *Fantastic Art, Dada, Surrealism* (December 1936–January 1937), which help familiarize the American public with European avant-garde art. Salvador Dali, Marcel Duchamp, Ernst, Grosz, Moholy-Nagy, and Yves Tanguy are among those represented.

1935

10,000 refugees who fled the Reich in 1933 return.

13 January
Saarland plebiscite results in reunification with Germany. **7,000 refugees—Social Democrats, Communists, and Jews—leave the area, which had been an important refuge for political dissidents fleeing Hitler. Most go to France. About 40 percent of the refugees are Jews.**

16 March
Germany repudiates the disarmament clause of the Treaty of Versailles. Reestablishment of German military service.

April
Jehovah's Witnesses are barred from employment in German civil service; members of the sect are arrested nationwide.

11–14 April
At a conference in Stresa, Italy, Britain, France, and Italy form the Stresa Front, reaffirming their opposition to German expansion.

6 May
U.S.: The Works Progress Administration (WPA) is initiated, putting millions of Americans to work.

May–August
Germany: Escalation of propaganda urging boycott of Jewish businesses.

30 June
During 1934–35 5,201 Germans arrived in the U.S., while 9,079 U.S. residents returned to Germany.

15 September
At the Nuremberg party conference Hitler announces the Nuremberg Laws, which assign Jews a lower class of citizenship, deprive them of many civil rights, and make marriages and extramarital sexual relations between Jews and Aryans crimes.

14 November
Jews are dismissed from public service.

1936

26 November
In Germany Gypsies and Negroes are included in the prohibition against racially mixed marriages.

December
A total of about 80,000 refugees have left the Reich. In 1935 62,000 Jews were admitted to Palestine, but only a small number were German Jews.

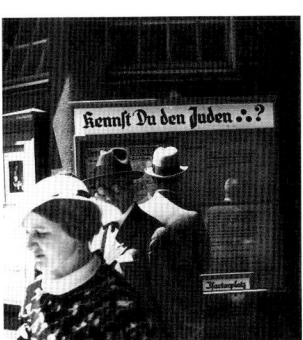

German street scene with poster reading "Kennst Du den Juden?" (Do you know the Jew?), Berlin, 1935; photograph by Varian Fry.

Jewish storefront, Lower East Side, New York, 1930s.

6 January
Mussolini leaves the Stresa Front in order to support Germany.

10 February
Gestapo actions are placed above the law.

March–April
German forces move into the demilitarized Rhineland; a plebiscite affirming Hitler's expansionist foreign policy follows.

chronology 389

CULTURAL

18 March
Curt Valentin opens the Buchholz Gallery in New York with the exhibition *Sculpture and Drawings*, including works by Barlach, Georg Kolbe, Wilhelm Lehmbruck, Gerhard Marcks, Richard Scheibe, and other German artists. In the years following Valentin will devote himself to promoting German art in New York.

25 April
Grundig is dismissed from the Reichskammer der bildenden Künste. He and his wife, Lea, are arrested for the first time.

26 May
The Reichskammer der bildenden Künste demands proof of "Aryan" ancestry from its members.

October
André Kertész immigrates to New York.

30 October
The modern section of the Berlin Nationalgalerie is closed by Minister of Education Bernhard Rust.

November
The Reichskulturkammer is declared "free of Jews."

The American Artists' Congress forms, demanding increased public aid to artists, protesting censorship and other attacks on civil liberties, and condemning Fascism in Italy and National Socialism in Germany.

24 November
The Nobel Prize for Peace for 1935 is awarded to left-wing journalist and social theorist Carl von Ossietzky. Hitler responds by forbidding Germans to accept the prize.

26 November
Goebbels bans all art criticism. Only the National Socialist party and the state have the right to decide whether a work of art mirrors the National Socialist concept of culture.

Gropius and Breuer emigrate from London to the U.S. Karl Nierendorf emigrates from Germany to the U.S.

Grosz receives a two-year Guggenheim Fellowship.

Eberhard Hanfstaengl and Alfred Hentzen are suspended from their jobs at the Berlin Nationalgalerie.

Barlach, Ludwig Gies, Ernst Ludwig Kirchner, and others "voluntarily" leave the Prussian Academy. In August Rudolf Belling follows their example. On 6 September Pechstein is dismissed.

In Paris the Freier Künstlerbund (Free league of artists), chaired by Eugen Spiro, is founded.

U.S.: Founding of the Defensive League of German-American Writers, chaired by Thomas Mann.

1 January
Kurt Schwitters leaves Germany for Norway.

March
The German caricaturist Fritz Alfred Behrendt immigrates to Amsterdam.

10 May
Exhibition of Beckmann, Hofer, Kirchner, Klee, Macke, Nay, Nolde, Scholz, Barlach, Kolbe, Marcks, Sintenis at Valentin's Buchholz Gallery in New York.

May–November
The Paris world's fair, *Exposition internationale des arts et techniques de la vie moderne* (International exposition of the arts and technologies of modern life), opens. Germany is represented by a pavilion built by Albert Speer, which wins a gold medal. Pablo Picasso's *Guernica* is shown in the Spanish pavilion.

June
Moholy-Nagy moves from London to Chicago.

11 June
Lyonel Feininger leaves Germany for the U.S.

1937

POLITICAL

26 March
Jews are no longer permitted to run pharmacies in Germany.

June
Women are banned from the legal profession in Germany.

30 June
During 1935–36 6,346 Germans entered the U.S.; 85 percent were Jewish.

Summer
With the new Popular Front government under Léon Blum in France, a liberal immigration policy is put into effect.

July
First Gypsies sent to Dachau.

17–18 July
Spanish army units proclaim a revolution against the Madrid government, which is headed by the leftist Popular Front. General Franco soon emerges as the leader of various conservative factions, and a civil war between the Republicans, on the left, and the Nationalists, on the right, breaks out. In August the U.S. announces that it will not interfere in this civil war, which signals to Mussolini and Hitler that the democracies are not ready to stand up against fascism.

28 August
Mass arrest of Jehovah's Witnesses in Germany.

19 October
Announcement of German four-year plan, designed to make German industry and agriculture entirely self-sufficient.

1 November
Rome-Berlin Axis is announced.

25 November
Germany and Japan sign the Anti-Comintern Pact, directed against the Third Communist International.

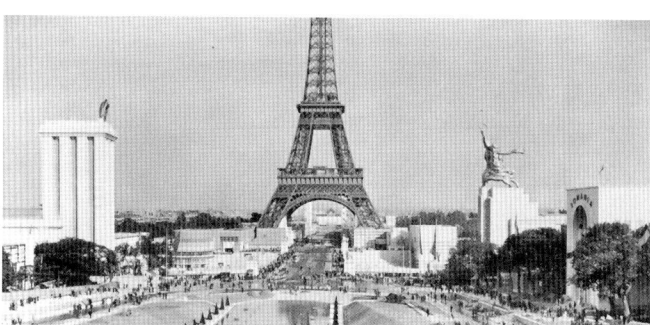

The Paris world's fair, 1937, with the German (left) and Russian (right) pavilions.

The British reduce Jewish immigration to Palestine; only 10,600 will enter the country this year.

20 January
Roosevelt begins his second term as president.

30 January
The Reichstag extends the enabling act four years.

26 April
The German Condor Legion, fighting on the side of the Nationalists, destroys the Basque town of Guernica.

23 June
Germany and Italy withdraw from the agreement for nonintervention in Spain. Germany signs a military cooperation treaty with Franco. The U.S. and Britain remain neutral.

30 June
The "degenerate art" campaign begins when Goebbels gives permission for Ziegler, the president of the Reichskammer der bildenden Künste, to confiscate artworks from German museums. Some 12,000 prints and 5,000 paintings and sculptures are removed from 101 German museums.

18 July
In Munich Hitler opens the *Große deutsche Kunstausstellung* (Great German art exhibition), which shows artworks endorsed by the Nazis and claims to cleanse Germany of "degenerate" art.

19 July
Ziegler opens the exhibition *Entartete Kunst* (Degenerate art) in the old gallery building in the Hofgarten arcades in Munich. Two million people see it in Munich. Thereafter it travels to Berlin, Leipzig, Düsseldorf, and Frankfurt.

Beckmann immigrates to Amsterdam.

Fall
In Prague the Oskar-Kokoschka-Bund is founded; its members include Hans Abarbanell, Theo Balden, Kurt Lade, Heinz Worner, and Johannes Wüsten. Its goals are to unite antifascist artists, to support democratic organizations in the fight against fascism, and to educate the local population about events in Nazi Germany.

18 October
Moholy-Nagy opens the New Bauhaus in Chicago.

Albert Speer is appointed general inspector of buildings for Berlin. Hitler publishes a directive on the redevelopment of German cities.

November
The exhibition *Die ewige Jude* (The eternal Jew) opens in Munich. It includes many works confiscated from public collections and purports to show the destructive influence of Jews on German culture.

Friedrich Vordemberge-Gildewart immigrates to Switzerland.

Jimmy Ernst, Amédée Ozenfant, and Mies van der Rohe arrive in the U.S. The latter will assume the directorship of the architecture department at Armour Institute (later Illinois Institute of Technology), Chicago. The artist Herbert Fiedler immigrates to Amsterdam.

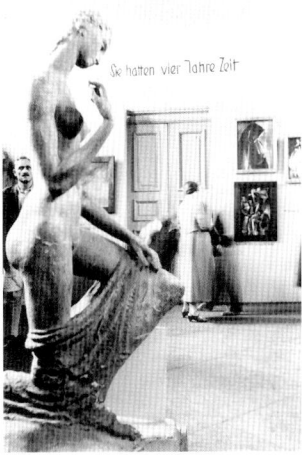

Visitors viewing the *Entartete Kunst* exhibition in Munich.

31 January
The exhibition *Cinq ans de régime Hitlerien* (Five years of Hitler's rule) opens in Paris. German left-wing exile artists such as Alfred Herrmann, Heinz Kiwitz, Hanns Kralik, Max Lingner, Heinz Lohmar, Erwin Öhl, and Fritz Wolff developed the show.

April
The German emigré art dealer Karl Nierendorf presents works by Kandinsky, Klee, and Fernand Léger in his gallery in New York.

May
The Gestapo starts confiscating artworks that belong to Jews in Vienna. After Kristallnacht the same practice will be applied in Germany.

Raoul Hausmann immigrates to Paris.

1938

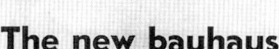

Announcement of the founding of the New Bauhaus in *Architectural Forum*, October 1937.

30 June
During 1936–37 10,895 Germans were received by the U.S. This is 70 percent more than in the year before.

July
U.S.: The WPA Alien Rule restricts employment by the WPA to U.S. citizens.

5 November
Hitler and his generals discuss plan for a future war (Hossbach Memorandum).

19 November
Lord Halifax indicates that Britain will tolerate nonviolent territorial expansion by Germany.

Out of a total of 135,000 Jewish refugees who left Germany in 1937, 100,000 went overseas, of whom 43,000 immigrated to Palestine. A report for the British Royal Institute of International Affairs lists a total of about 165,000 refugees from Germany.

About 30,000 refugees from Germany are in exile in the Netherlands.

12 February
Hitler and Austrian chancellor Kurt Schuschnigg meet at Berchtesgaden. Austria is forced to appoint the Nazi Arthur Seyss-Inquart interior minister, release Nazi prisoners, and subordinate the Austrian army to Germany's. Schuschnigg resigns and is succeeded by Seyss-Inquart.

11 March
German invasion of Austria. Annexation (Anschluss) of Austria followed by plebiscite on 10 April. Persecution of Jews in Austria follows the Anschluss, including compulsory "Aryanization" of many Jewish firms and expulsion of Jews into neighboring states.

13 March
Law for the reunification of Austria with the German Reich. Resignation of Austrian president Wilhelm Miklas.

A new wave of emigration takes place. Now the German Jewish and political refugees are joined by those fleeing Austria (there are about 190,000 Austrian Jews). In response Great Britain restricts immigration. By now about 8,000 refugees are in Great Britain; another 2,000 people await immigration. About 80 percent of the refugees are Jews.

France: After the collapse of the Popular Front, with its liberal policies toward refugees, the government of Edouard Daladier tightens procedures for entering France. A decree makes it difficult to obtain temporary residence permits and allows low-level frontier officials to summarily reject refugees. France declares that it is saturated by refugees and will try to denationalize certain aliens who had previously received French citizenship and to intern undesirables.

chronology 391

CULTURAL

15 June
In Switzerland Kirchner commits suicide; about six hundred of his works had been confiscated by the Nazis.

1 July
Karl Hofer and Kokoschka are dismissed from the Prussian Academy.

8 July
Opening of the *Exhibition of Twentieth Century German Art* at the New Burlington Galleries in London, curated by Herbert Read. Although conceived as a response to *Entartete Kunst*, the exhibition loses much of its critical thrust because of British appeasement policies. Most of the 270 works by German artists on view belong to German exiles in London. Beckmann gives a talk, "On My Painting," at the opening.

21 September
Piet Mondrian leaves Paris for London.

October
Kokoschka immigrates to London.

November
Grosz receives his American citizenship papers; his German citizenship had been revoked in March.

4 November
The protest exhibition *Freie deutsche Kunst* (Free German art) opens at the Maison de la Culture in Paris.

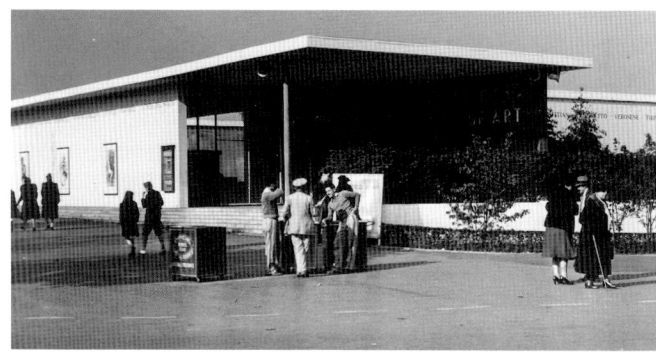

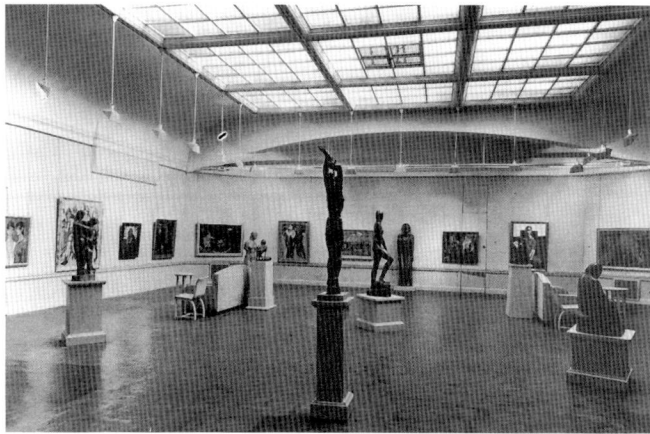

Above: Masterpieces of Art Building, New York World's Fair, 1939.

Left: Installation view of the exhibition *Contemporary German Art*, Institute of Modern Art, Boston, 1939.

Below: Jewish youths sent away from Germany by their parents after Kristallnacht, c. 1938–39.

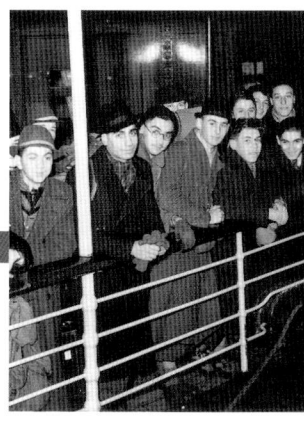

POLITICAL

9 June
Destruction of the synagogues of Munich.

15 June
In Germany 1,500 Jews are arrested and taken to concentration camps.

30 June
During 1937–38 the U.S. receives 17,199 refugees from Germany and Austria. According to official statistics, the total number of German immigrants for the period 1932–38 is 80,693. The quotas would have permitted 191,390 to immigrate legally. In the same period 20,445 aliens with permanent resident status left the U.S. for Germany.

6 July
After the annexation of Austria the refugee crisis becomes more pressing. Roosevelt establishes the Committee for Political Refugees and proposes an international conference, which takes place in Evian, France, and is chaired by U.S. representative Myron Taylor. The thirty-two participating nations are reassured that no country will be expected to receive a greater number of refugees than permitted by existing law. The refugee assistance programs are to be financed by private agencies. Moreover, Great Britain is assured that Jewish immigration to Palestine will not be discussed, and the U.S. declares that it will not increase immigration quotas. The conference fails to resolve the European refugee crisis. Great Britain will admit some Jews but won't open Palestine; the Netherlands and Denmark offer temporary asylum; and the U.S. agrees to admit the full legal quota of immigrants from Germany and Austria. The Dominican Republic offers to receive 100,000 Jews.

21 September
Czechoslovakia is persuaded by Britain and France to cede to Germany territory where more than half the population is German.

29–30 September
Munich Conference between Britain, France, Italy, and Germany. British Prime Minister Neville Chamberlain and French Prime Minister Daladier sign an agreement allowing Germany to take over the Sudetenland. They believe that this act of appeasement will guarantee peace. In the U.S. an October poll shows that only a minority of Americans disapprove of the accord. The Munich Agreement is followed by a wave of emigration from Germany and Central Europe. The Sudetenland has an estimated Jewish population of 25,000. Great Britain admits around 8,000 refugees from the Sudetenland.

7 October
The Gran Consiglio del Fascismo in Rome adopts racial laws along National Socialist lines. Jews are excluded from military service, teaching, banking, and civil service. Their right to own property is severely restricted.

26–28 October
17,000 Jews with Polish citizenship are expelled from the German Reich and transported to the Polish border.

9 November
Kristallnacht, the "night of broken glass," a nationwide pogrom against Jews. More than 100 Jews are killed, 191 synagogues are destroyed, almost all Jewish cemeteries are desecrated, and 7,500 Jewish shops are ransacked.

December
The painter Joseph Scharl immigrates to New York.

6 December
Heartfield and other German antifascists emigrate from Prague to London.

31 December
London: The Free German League of Culture forms. Its 100 members include visual artists Theo Balden, Heartfield, Kokoschka, Schwitters, Fred Uhlman, and Worner.

Goebbels establishes a commission for the disposal of "degenerate" art, which will sell confiscated artworks over the next four years.

Vordemberge-Gildewart emigrates from Switzerland to the Netherlands.

Leo Breuer, Heinrich Maria Davringhausen, Arthur Kaufmann, Johannes Molzahn, and Gert Wollheim immigrate to the U.S., as do Wieland Herzfelde, Thomas Mann, and Kurt Seligmann, who settle in or near New York City (Mann later moves to Los Angeles).

Max Ernst is interned as an *apatride* (stateless person) in Les Milles internment camp in southern France.

10 January
The Springfield (Mass.) Museum of Fine Arts opens the exhibition *German Art*, which presents art banned in Germany by the National Socialist government.

January–February
MoMA presents *Bauhaus, 1919–1928*, organized by Gropius and designed by Herbert Bayer.

20 March
The National Socialists burn 1,000 paintings and sculptures and 4,000 watercolors, drawings, and prints in the courtyard of the main fire station in Berlin.

23 April
Hitler gives a special order that all masterpieces of art in occupied territory be confiscated for a "world art museum" in Linz, Austria, which he plans to open after the National Socialist victory. Ultimately 8,000 of the most valuable artworks are kept in storage in Linz.

May–September
MoMA shows *Art in Our Time*, a celebration of the museum's tenth anniversary. Included in the exhibition, which coincides with the New York World's Fair, are many works banned by the Nazis.

31 May
Solomon R. Guggenheim's collection of nonobjective art, formed under the curatorial guidance of Hilla von Rebay, is presented in New York as *Art of Tomorrow*.

3 June
At the Wertheim Galleries in London the first group exhibition of the Free German League of Culture opens.

30 June
The Galerie Fischer in Lucerne auctions 125 paintings and sculptures purged from German museums.

Summer
The New York World's Fair opens. The planned exhibition *Germany of Yesterday, Germany of Tomorrow*, designed by German exile artists in Paris, is canceled.

The Ozenfant School of Fine Arts opens in New York; Ozenfant also teaches at the New School for Social Research and Cooper Union.

The Golden Gate Exposition is held in San Francisco. Beckmann is awarded first prize in the contemporary European section.

August
Ludwig Meidner immigrates to England; artist Rudolf Bauer, to New York.

1939

10–12 November
Mass arrest of Jewish men; 20,000 Jews are deported to concentration camps. **A new wave of Jewish emigration takes place. The Netherlands immediately takes another 1,700 Jews; the U.S. does not change its quota system but fills more places than in previous years.**

3 December
Compulsory Aryanization of Jewish businesses begins.

6 December
Anthony Eden, former foreign minister of Britain, protests the Munich Accord in a New York radio speech and warns that all democracies are threatened by the expanding fascist powers.

A French government report on Jewish refugees claims that 30,000 German and Austrian Jews are living illegally in France.

Great Britain liberalizes its immigration laws. It sends £4 million to Prague to assist refugees from areas taken by the Germans. Social Democrats from the Sudetenland are admitted en bloc to Great Britain. 10,000 children, mostly Jewish, are also admitted.

24 January
Hermann Göring instructs Interior Minister Frick to establish a Reich Central Office for Jewish emigration; Reinhard Heydrich is appointed director.

30 January
In the Reichstag Hitler warns that another war will mean the "extermination of the Jewish race in Europe."

15 March
German troops invade the rest of Czechoslovakia. Hitler divides the country into the German protectorates of Bohemia and Moravia and the state of Slovakia.

Spring
The British decide that the annual quota of Jews admitted to Palestine will be 10,000 for the next five years, plus another 25,000 refugees. Following this period, no more Jews are to be admitted without the agreement of the Arab states. Illegal Jewish immigration to Palestine becomes common.

450,000 Spanish Republican exiles arrive in France.

31 March
Britain and France guarantee Polish independence.

14 April
Roosevelt asks Hitler and Mussolini to guarantee a ten-year peace for Europe and the Middle East, yet Hitler revokes the nonaggression pact with Poland and the Anglo-German Naval Agreement.

30 April
In Nazi-occupied territories Jews are evicted from their homes and forced into designated Jewish accommodation.

30 June
In 1938–39 the U.S. admitted 33,515 immigrants from greater Germany.

1 July
U.S. Congress decides—after long debate—not to admit 20,000 refugee children from Germany (proposed Wagner-Rogers bill).

21 July
Adolf Eichmann is appointed head of the Jewish emigration office in Prague. At the outbreak of the war, despite their desperate attempts to leave, about 330,000 Jews remain in greater Germany.

1 September
German invasion of Poland and annexation of Danzig. More than 5 million Jews live in Poland.

A *Fortune* poll indicates that 83 percent of Americans disfavor admitting more refugees from Nazi Germany.

CULTURAL

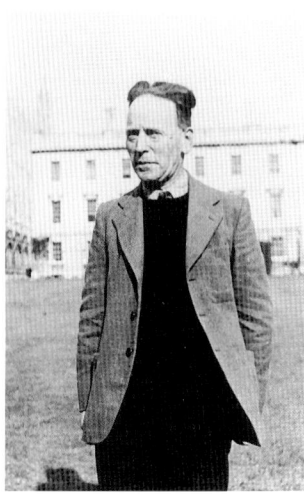

Above: John Heartfield in British internment camp, c. 1940.

Below: Refugees arriving in Paris, May 30, 1940.

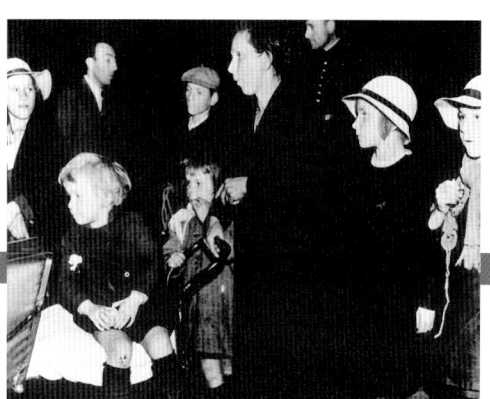

November
Alois Schardt immigrates with his family to the U.S. and settles in Los Angeles. Tanguy and Matta arrive in the U.S.

December
The New Bauhaus in Chicago is reconstituted as the School of Design; it will later be renamed the Institute of Design.

Andreas Feininger arrives in New York.

Between 1933 and 1939 about 10,000 German scientists emigrated.

4 December
In London the Arcade Gallery opens the Heartfield exhibition *One Man's War against Hitler*.

Thomas Mann makes the first of fifty-five antifascist speeches broadcast on British radio.

Beckmann is invited to teach at the School of the Art Institute of Chicago but is denied a visa by the American consul in Amsterdam. As a result he will remain in Amsterdam throughout the war and immigrate to the U.S. only in 1947.

6 February
The San Francisco Museum of Art presents the *Exhibition of Twentieth Century German Art*, which originated in 1938 at London's New Burlington Galleries.

March
In New York the surrealist-oriented magazine *View* publishes its first issue. It continues publication on a quarterly basis through 1947. The editor is the American Charles Henry Ford.

2 April
Landmarks in Modern German Art at Buchholz Gallery displays works formerly in the collections of eleven German museums. Included are works by Beckmann, Lyonel Feininger, Erich Heckel, Hofer, Kirchner, Klee, Kokoschka, Nolde, Schmidt-Rottluff, and others.

10 May
The Jewish painter Felix Nussbaum is arrested in his hiding place in Brussels and deported to the Saint-Cyprien camp in the South of France. Ernst, Hans Bellmer, Wollheim, and Wols are interned as enemy aliens in camps in the South of France.

June
The New School for Social Research invites the British printmaker Stanley William Hayter to move his print studio, Atelier 17, to the campus. Occasionally exiled artists such as Lipchitz, André Masson, and Matta work there.

1940

POLITICAL

3 September
Britain and France declare war on Germany. The U.S. declares neutrality. **An estimated 40,000 refugees from greater Germany are in France. About 55,000 refugees from Germany, Austria, and Czechoslovakia, 90 percent of them Jews, are in Great Britain.**

7 September
The German army overruns western Poland.

21 September
Polish Jews forced into ghettos. 30,000 Gypsies are moved from greater Germany to Poland.

September–November
Einsatzgruppen (special units) of the security police murder large numbers of Jews in occupied Poland. Mass deportations of Jews to Poland begin.

2 October
Secretary of State Cordell Hull states that the U.S. does not recognize the partition of Poland between Germany and the USSR but will maintain diplomatic relations with the Polish government in exile in Paris.

4 November
Roosevelt signs the Neutrality Act of 1939, allowing the sale of arms to warring parties, thereby asserting U.S. support for Britain, France, and their allies.

Between 1933 and 1939 about 215,000 Jews immigrated to Palestine, mostly from Poland. With the outbreak of the war Palestine stops admitting refugees from Poland.

January
Germany: First gassing of the mentally ill.

2–13 February
First deportation of Jews from Northern Germany, Vienna, Ostrava, and Teschen to Poland.

8 March
Mussolini agrees to join Germany and other Axis powers in the war against Britain.

9 April
Germany invades Denmark and Norway.

27 April
Himmler orders the establishment of a concentration camp at Auschwitz.

30 April
First enclosed Jewish ghetto, in Lodz.

April–May
2,500 Gypsies are deported from the Reich to Poland.

10 May
Germany attacks the Netherlands, Belgium, and Luxembourg. Winston Churchill succeeds Chamberlain as British prime minister.

Great Britain declares Austrian, Czechoslovak, German, and Italian emigrés enemy aliens and interns them. By June all available capacity is filled. 7,000 refugees are deported to Canada together with 6,500 German war prisoners and Nazi sympathizers. Most of the internees are released by December 1941.

15 May
Churchill asks Roosevelt for America's support and eventual participation in the war.

3 June
The U.S. War Department agrees to sell Britain surplus and outdated arms, munitions, and aircraft.

18 June
Schwitters arrives in Great Britain, where he is interned as an enemy alien on the Isle of Man for a year and a half.

25 June
In New York the Emergency Rescue Committee is founded as a private refugee organization. In August Varian Fry is sent to Marseilles to assist some 200 preselected intellectual refugees to escape to America. Over the next thirteen months, however, he saves about 2,000 endangered people persecuted for reasons of race, religion, or political or intellectual views.

8 August
Dali arrives in New York.

August–September
Man Ray returns to America from Paris. He settles in California.

September
With the help of Fry and the Emergency Rescue Committee Feuchtwanger, Heinrich Mann, Franz Werfel, and Alma Mahler-Werfel escape across the French-Spanish border near Marseilles, ultimately arriving in the U.S.

12 September
Procedure established to review applications of endangered refugee intellectuals seeking visas to enter the U.S. Their names must first be submitted to the President's Advisory Committee on Political Refugees.

3 October
Mondrian flees the German air raids over London and arrives in New York.

27 October
Walter Benjamin commits suicide at the French-Spanish border rather than face arrest and deportation by the Gestapo.

November
In the Jeu de Paume in Paris Göring inspects the art treasures confiscated by the Rosenberg unit from French public and private collections, especially the holdings of the Jewish Rothschild, Seligmann, and Wildenstein families. The artworks are transported to Germany, and some are kept by Goebbels for his collection.

Léger arrives in the U.S.

18 December
The U.S. State Department issues a statement regarding intellectual refugees. It explains that, because of the dire situation facing these refugees, the State Department will grant them emergency visitor's visas outside the quota system.

Mondrian becomes a member of American Abstract Artists; he completes his essay "Liberation from Oppression in Art and Life" (working title: "Art Shows the Evil of Nazi and Soviet Oppression").

Brecht, André Breton, Marc Chagall, Claude Lévi-Strauss, Jacques Lipchitz, Masson, and Ossip Zadkine arrive in the U.S.

January–March
Gordon Onslow Ford gives a series of lectures on surrealism at the New School for Social Research. A series of related exhibitions includes solo presentations of work by Giorgio de Chirico, Max Ernst, and Joan Miró. *Adventures in Surrealist Painting during the Last Four Years* features work by Victor Brauner, Paul Delvaux, Hayter, Matta, Wolfgang Paalen, Onslow Ford, and Seligmann.

Spring
Mondrian writes "Abstract Art" and "Toward the True Vision of Reality."

April
Baumeister is forbidden to exhibit in Germany.

May
The National Socialists burn 500 works of modern art in front of the Tuileries in Paris.

1941

5 June
German forces invade France, taking Paris by June 14. Two days later Philippe Pétain replaces Paul Reynaud as the head of the French government.

By U.S. executive order alien refugees must present unexpired passports or travel documents showing their origin and identity and valid visas in order to be admitted to the U.S.

18 June
In London General Charles de Gaulle pledges to carry on the fight for a free France.

22 June
Marshal Pétain signs an armistice with Germany and sets up the French government in Vichy. Article 19 requires that France extradite any German national the Gestapo demands. All German nationals are interned.

28 June
U.S. Congress passes the Alien Registration Act (Smith Act), requiring all aliens to register periodically to ensure internal security and to guard the U.S. from infiltration by enemy aliens who might be working on behalf of their governments.

29 June
U.S. Secretary of State Hull advises all diplomatic and consular officers to examine all applications for immigration visas with extreme care and states that no visa should be issued if there is any doubt whatsoever concerning the alien. This results in a drastic reduction in visas issued.

30 June
In 1939–40 21,520 emigrants from the Reich entered the U.S.; the total number of refugees from Europe was 70,756.

23 August
German blitz of Britain begins. When the Battle of Britain ceases at the end of October, the Germans will have failed to control British airspace.

3 September
Lend-Lease agreement: The U.S. agrees to give Britain fifty American destroyers and will in exchange have the right to build naval and air bases on British possessions in the Western Hemisphere. The agreement reveals U.S. intention to play an active role in the war. On 11 March 1941 the House of Representatives passes the Lend-Lease Act, and Roosevelt immediately signs it.

October
Residents of the Jewish ghetto in Warsaw are no longer allowed to leave. Before the war 600,000 Jews had been living in Warsaw.

14 November
Aliens in the U.S. are prohibited from leaving without an exit permit.

6 January
In his State-of-the-Union address Roosevelt defines the Four Freedoms as international social and political objectives: freedom of expression and religion, freedom from suffering and fear.

6 April
Germany invades Yugoslavia and Greece. On April 17 Yugoslavia capitulates.

14 May
3,600 Parisian Jews are arrested by the French police.

27 May
Roosevelt announces a state of unlimited national emergency.

5 June
The State Department orders the withholding of visas from aliens who have close relatives residing in German-controlled areas.

CULTURAL

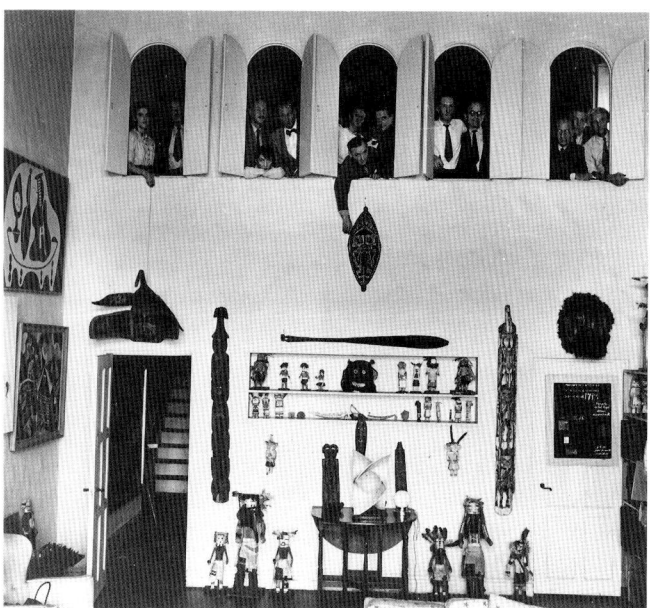

15 June
The exhibition *Works by Refugee Artists and Their English Friends*, organized by the Free German League of Culture and the Artists International Association (AIA), opens in London.

Above: The surrealists in Peggy Guggenheim's triplex, New York, fall 1941; photograph by Hermann Landshoff.

Right: The offices of the Centre Américain de Secours, Marseilles, 1941; photograph by YLLA.

Below right: The SS *Serpa Pinto*, on which many refugees traveled to the U.S., September 24, 1941.

14 July
Max Ernst and Peggy Guggenheim arrive in New York. The photographer Josef Breitenbach emigrates from Paris to New York.

23 August
Nolde is forbidden to paint.

September
The Addison Gallery of American Art, Andover, Mass., presents the exhibition *European Artists Teaching in America*. Most of the fourteen artists included are refugees.

Forced to leave Marseilles, Varian Fry returns to New York.

November
A special issue of *View* is devoted to surrealism. It includes the only American interview with André Breton, by Charles Henry Ford. Other contributors are Max Ernst, Georges Henein, Masson, Benjamin Péret, and Seligmann.

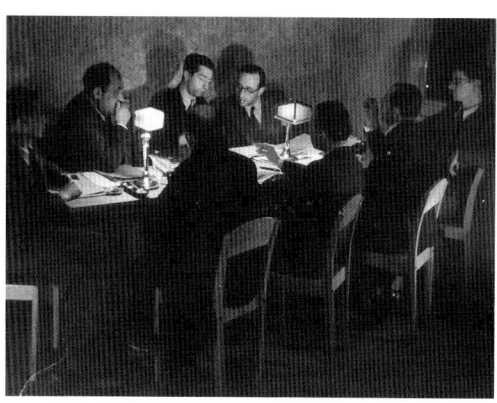

POLITICAL

16 June
Roosevelt orders that all German consulates in the U.S. be closed by 10 July. On 30 June all American consulates in Germany, Austria, Bohemia, Moravia, Belgium, occupied France, the Netherlands, and Italy close; the U.S. closes all Italian consulates by 20 July. It is no longer possible for Europeans to enter the U.S. through normal channels; the only exception is through the unoccupied South of France.

22 June
The Germans invade the Soviet Union.

30 June
51,776 immigrants from Europe came to the U.S. this past year.

1 July
U.S.: Applications for immigrant and nonimmigrant visas must be submitted to the State Department before they are referred to the consuls.

31 July
Göring gives Heydrich the task of finding a "comprehensive solution to the Jewish question." Himmler instructs the commandant of Auschwitz, Rudolf Hoess, to prepare the camp for the "final solution." Eichmann plans the deportation of Jews to death camps. The SS and police leader in Lublin, Odilo Globocnik, is ordered to annihilate the Polish Jews (Operation Reinhard).

14 August
Roosevelt and Churchill issue the Atlantic Charter: It sets forth eight goals for the world, including the renunciation of all aggression, the right of people to choose their own government, and the disarmament of aggressors. By 24 September fifteen anti-Axis nations—including the USSR—will endorse the Atlantic Charter.

September–November
The Germans build death camps at Chelmno, Belzec, Majdanek, and Auschwitz-Birkenau.

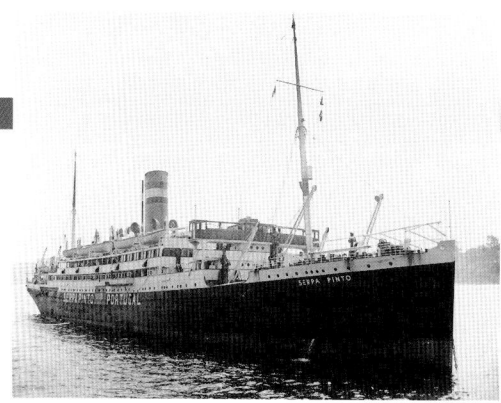

October–December
Battle for Moscow. On 16 October the Soviet government leaves Moscow. On 5 December the USSR launches a counteroffensive.

14 October
Mass deportations of Jews from the Reich to ghettoes in Kovno, Lodz, Minsk, and Riga.

23 October
Jewish emigration from German-controlled territory is forbidden by German law.

17 November
Roosevelt signs a bill that amends the Neutrality Act of 1939. U.S. merchant ships are now permitted to be armed and to call at ports of belligerents.

30 November
About 10,000 Jews are shot near Riga.

1 December
U.S.: The Interdepartmental Committee for Political Refugees is required to give all applications for immigration by enemy aliens (i.e., Jews and political refugees from Germany and Italy) to a specific reviewing committee. The applicant must fulfill security and desirability requirements.

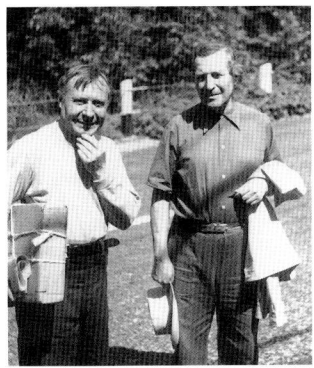

Above: André Masson and Marc Chagall in New Preston, Connecticut.

Below: Installation view of the exhibition *Allies inside Nazi Germany*, London, 1942.

Jean Arp escapes with his wife, Sophie Taeuber-Arp, from the South of France to Switzerland.

The Secret Life of Salvador Dali, the artist's autobiography, is published in New York.

February
Peggy Guggenheim commissions Frederick Kiesler to convert two tailoring shops at 50 West Fifty-seventh Street into the Art of This Century gallery, to present her permanent collection and art exhibitions. In October the gallery opens; Guggenheim also publishes a catalogue of her collection.

3 March
Artists in Exile opens at the Pierre Matisse Gallery; included are works by fourteen emigrés: Eugene Berman, Breton, Chagall, Ernst, Léger, Lipchitz, Masson, Matta, Mondrian, Ozenfant, Seligmann, Tanguy, Pavel Tchelitchev, and Zadkine.

May
Aspects of Modern Drawing is on view at the Buchholz Gallery; Beckmann, Chagall, Ernst, Grosz, Kokoschka, Léger, Lipchitz, Masson, Ozenfant, and Tanguy are among the European exiles represented.

June
Duchamp arrives in New York.

David Hare commences publication of the surrealist magazine *VVV*, with Breton, Duchamp, and Ernst as editorial advisers. The magazine continues publication through 1944 with two more issues.

6 June
In Germany the artist Fritz Schulze, active as an antifascist, is murdered after being arrested several times.

3 July
In London the exhibition *Allies inside Germany*, organized by the Free German League of Culture, opens.

October–November
Breton, Duchamp, and Sidney Janis organize *First Papers of Surrealism* at the Whitelaw Reid mansion, 451 Madison Avenue, under the auspices of the Coordination Council of French Relief Societies. Represented are both European artists and younger Americans. Duchamp uses one mile of string to decorate the gallery, creating a labyrinth that conceals the artworks.

December
Breton delivers a lecture at Yale University on surrealism between the two world wars.

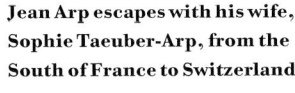

1942

7–8 December
The Japanese attack major targets in the Pacific, including Pearl Harbor, the U.S. naval base in Hawaii, sinking part of the U.S. Pacific fleet. The Japanese announce that they have declared war on the U.S. The U.S. declares war on Japan.

Enemy aliens are required to have a permit to travel within the U.S.; they are also subject to an 8 p.m.–6 a.m. curfew. No further enemy aliens are permitted to enter the U.S., but displaced persons (i.e., racial and political refugees who were already in other countries) are still considered.

11 December
Germany and Italy declare war on the U.S., and Congress declares war on Germany and Italy.

According to the American Jewish Joint Distribution Committee, Europe now has 335,000 stateless Jewish refugees.

1 January
Representatives of twenty-six nations, including the U.S., sign the declaration of the United Nations, affirming their cooperation against the Axis.

14 January
Roosevelt orders that all aliens in the U.S. register with the government. Most suspicions focus not on Germans or Italians, but on Japanese-Americans.

French transit camp at Gurs, c. April 1940.

20 January
At the Wannsee Conference in Berlin Heydrich proposes a "final solution" to the Jewish problem by forced labor and mass murder in concentration camps.

February
"Evacuation" of the Polish ghettoes begins; Jews are deported to death camps.

March
Deportation of south German Jews to Belzec begins. Transports of Jewish emigrants from Western Europe arrive in Auschwitz.

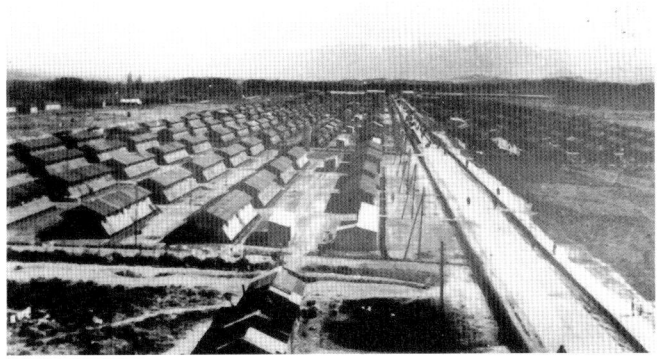

Introduction of the "yellow star" in occupied Western Europe.

June
The Germans begin the systematic mass murder of Jews in the gas chambers of Auschwitz.

6 June
Massacre of Lidice: The Germans murder the entire adult male population of this Czech village in reprisal for the assassination of Heydrich.

30 June
In 1941–42 there were 28,781 European immigrants to the U.S.

July
First deportations of Dutch Jews to Auschwitz; the French police arrest 13,000 stateless Jews in Paris, 9,000 of them (including 4,000 children) are immediately transported to Auschwitz. Mass transports from the Warsaw ghetto to Treblinka, where 60,000 Jews are gassed after their arrival. By September further mass deportations from Western Europe to Auschwitz.

chronology 397

CULTURAL

Germany: The sculptor Kurt Schuhmacher, who was active in the resistance, is executed.

Hans Richter, arriving in New York, becomes director of the Institute of Film Techniques at City College of New York.

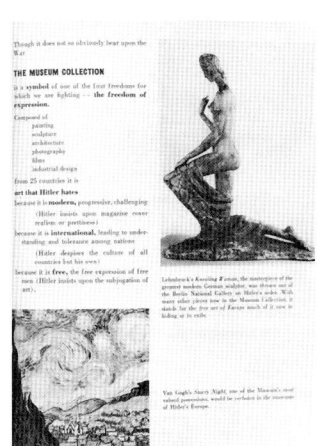

Special issue of the *Bulletin of the Museum of Modern Art* entitled *The Museum and the War*, October–November 1942.

January
In London Kokoschka gives the opening speech at the exhibition *The War as Seen by Children*.

23 February
Paul Klee, André Masson, and Some Aspects of Ancient and Primitive Sculpture opens at the Buchholz Gallery.

March
The Jewish artist Otto Freundlich is arrested in the Pyrenees by the Gestapo; he is deported to the Majdanek concentration camp in Poland, where he is murdered.

9 March
At the Pierre Matisse Gallery *War and the Artist* opens; included are works by Chagall, Ernst, Masson, Matta, Miró, Picasso, Georges Rouault, David Siqueiros, and Rufino Tamayo.

23 March
At the Institute of Modern Art, Boston, the exhibition *Europe in America* opens. On view are works by emigrés Berman, Chagall, Dali, Grosz, Hayter, Jean Hélion, Léger, Lipchitz, Masson, Matta, Moholy-Nagy, Mondrian, Mopp, Ozenfant, Seligmann, Tanguy, and Tchelitchev.

13 April
Oskar Schlemmer dies in Germany.

26 April
The German artist Johannes Wüsten dies of tuberculosis in Brandenburg Prison; he had been in exile in Prague and Paris and was arrested by the Gestapo in 1940 in Paris.

28 April
The German Jewish artist Bruno Gimpel commits suicide to avoid deportation.

October
In his last studio, at 15 East Fifty-ninth Street, Mondrian positions colored cards on the walls and constructs his own furniture; James Johnson Sweeney interviews him for a retrospective planned at MoMA, which opens in 1945.

23 November
The German sculptor Philipp Zöllner, active in the resistance, dies in the Sachsenhausen concentration camp.

November–December
The New Yorker profiles Grosz.

December
Julien Levy's exhibition *Through the Big End of the Opera Glass* presents works by Joseph Cornell, Duchamp, and Tanguy.

London: The German antifascist exhibition *We Accuse! Ten Years of Nazi-Fascism* opens. The German artist Julo Levin is murdered at Auschwitz.

The painter Rudolph Levy, who immigrated to Italy in 1933, is arrested by the Gestapo in 1943 in Florence and dies in a German concentration camp.

U.S.: With unemployment virtually eliminated, the WPA dissolves.

1943

POLITICAL

August
More than 200,000 Jews are gassed at Chelmno, Treblinka, and Belzec. Jews are arrested in Vichy France.

17 August
The first all-U.S. bombing raid is made on German positions around Rouen, France. (In 1943 the U.S. Air Force starts bombing targets in Germany.)

Fall
The Allies have reliable information about the death camps in Poland.

11–12 November
German occupation of Vichy France.

19–20 November
Soviet counterattack at Stalingrad cuts off most of the German forces. By November 25 the German army finds itself surrounded by the Russians. It will be February 2, 1943, when the last unit of the German Sixth Army surrenders. About 330,000 Germans have been killed or captured.

14–24 January
Conference in Casablanca, Morocco: Roosevelt, Churchill, and other Allied leaders participate. The decisions include the demand for the unconditional surrender of the enemy.

February
Germany: Arrest of Gypsies remaining in the Reich. On 27 February deportation of Jewish munitions workers from Berlin to Auschwitz.

April
Beginning of medical experiments in Auschwitz. End of mass murder in Chelmno; gas chambers are destroyed by SS. An uprising in the Warsaw Ghetto is suppressed; 50,000 Jews die.

30 April
Jews lose German citizenship.

11 June
Himmler orders the liquidation of all the Polish ghettoes.

19 June
Goebbels declares Berlin "free of Jews."

30 June
In 1942–43 23,725 immigrants from greater Germany entered the U.S.

July
A refugee conference takes place in Bermuda. Great Britain, the initiator, and the U.S. explain that the purpose of the conference is to "assist those who make their way to countries beyond German control."

10 July
British, American, Canadian, and French troops land in Sicily. With the taking of Messina on 17 August, Sicily falls to the Allies. The Gran Consiglio del Fascismo removes Mussolini from power on 25 July. King Victor Emmanuel III names as prime minister Marshal Pietro Badoglio, who immediately tries to get Italy out of the war. In August the Fascist party is dissolved.

August–September
Liquidation of Russian ghettoes; all residents are taken to death camps.

2 August
Prisoners' uprising in Treblinka; destruction of gas chambers.

3 September
Allied forces invade the mainland of Italy. The same day Badoglio signs a secret armistice with the Allies, agreeing to stop Italian military resistance on 8 September. Germany immediately treats Italy as an enemy and occupies northern Italy and Rome. On 13 October Italy declares war on Germany.

September–October
About 7,000 Danish Jews are smuggled to neutral Sweden.

19 October
End of Operation Reinhard.

28 November–1 December
Teheran Conference: Roosevelt and Churchill meet with Stalin and agree on the timing of the joint invasion of occupied Europe.

U.S.: 25,840 places for German immigrants allowed by the quota remain unfilled.

1 February
Mondrian dies.

The last issue of *VVV* appears, with a cover design by Matta.

June
London: The exhibition *Free German Art*, sponsored by the AIA, opens.

31 July
Nussbaum is deported to Auschwitz and gassed.

31 October
The exhibition *The Blue Four: Feininger, Jawlensky, Kandinsky, Klee* opens at the Buchholz Gallery.

November
Pillaged works of art are taken by the Germans to Austria and stored there in monasteries, castles, and mines.

8 December
Pierre Matisse presents the exhibition *Homage to the "Salon d'automne": Salon de la Libération*, which celebrates the end of oppression in Europe and the first presentation of free art in France, the 1944 *Salon d'automne*.

Sidney Janis organizes *European and American Pioneers in Twentieth-Century Art* for the Nierendorf Gallery, assembles *Abstract and Surrealist Art in America*—which travels to museums in Cincinnati, San Francisco, Denver, Seattle, Portland, and Santa Barbara—and publishes its catalogue.

The exhibition *Hayter and Studio 17* is on view at MoMA.

Richter starts making his film *Dreams That Money Can Buy*, with contributions by Alexander Calder, Duchamp, Ernst, Léger, and Man Ray.

Brecht, Oskar Maria Graf, Herzfelde, and Heinrich Mann found the Aurora publishing company in New York.

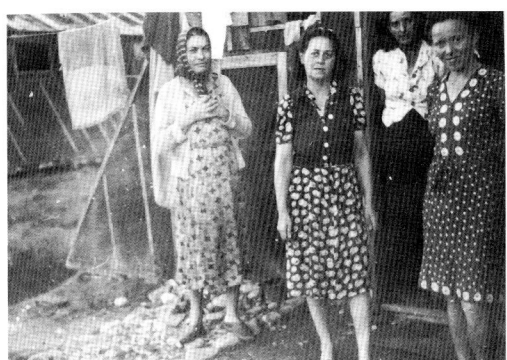

Above: Women prisoners standing in front of a barracks in Gurs transit camp in Vichy France, c. 1943; photograph by Alice Resch-Synnestredt.

Left: Prisoners being selected for extermination at the Birkenau concentration camp.

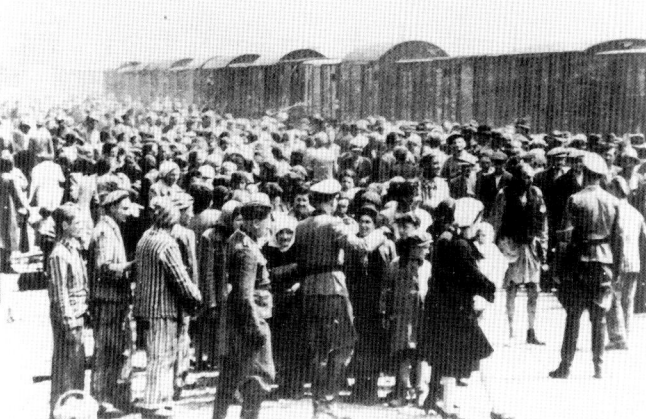

1944

January
Treasury Secretary Henry Morgenthau Jr. persuades President Roosevelt to set up a War Refugee Board "to take all measures within its power to rescue the victims of enemy oppression who are in imminent danger of death, and otherwise to afford such victims all possible relief and assistance consistent with the successful prosecution of the war." By this time, however, most of the European Jews are in death camps, and it is impossible to evacuate them from enemy territory.

6 March
660 U.S. bombers make the first raid on Berlin. This and the raids that follow almost daily on German cities will eventually weaken the Germans' will to resist.

April–July
After Hungary is forced to cooperate with Germany, the Hungarian Jews are ghettoized. 437,000 are deported to Auschwitz by July; 280,000 of them are gassed immediately.

6 June
D-Day: The largest invasion force in history lands on the Continent. It begins along a series of beaches in Normandy—between Cherbourg and Le Havre—with two U.S. airborne divisions, 4,000 invasion ships, 600 warships, 10,000 planes, and 156,000 Allied troops. Despite heavy losses on the side of the Allies, they eventually prevail.

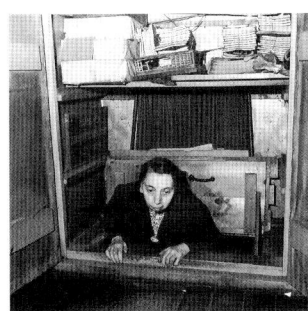

Jewish refugee woman in Amsterdam during World War II (photograph from Nazi files).

10 June
The Germans destroy the French village of Oradour and murder its population in reprisal for resistance activity.

30 June
In 1943–44 28,551 immigrants from Europe were admitted to the U.S.

6 July
General de Gaulle arrives in Washington, D.C., to seek U.S. support for his French forces fighting the Germans and his plans to govern France after the liberation.

20 July
Claus von Stauffenberg and conspirators try to assassinate Hitler but fail.

24 July
Soviet troops capture Lublin and discover the death camp at Majdanek, with few surviving inmates.

August
The Intergovernmental Committee on Refugees claims that there are between one and two million stateless individuals in the world.

11 August
Allies land in southern France.

25 August
Allied troops enter Paris. De Gaulle appears the next day and marches in a ceremonial parade.

21 October
Aachen is the first German city to be captured by the Allies on the Western Front.

23 October
Allies recognize the de Gaulle administration as the provisional government of France.

27 November
Himmler orders cessation of gassing at Auschwitz.

16 December
Germany begins the Ardennes offensive; Allied counteroffensive begins 3 January 1945.

CULTURAL

January
Drawing on early Dada and surrealist practices, Julien Levy organizes a chess game: world champion George Koltanowski plays simultaneously against Barr, Ernst, Kiesler, Levy, Tanning, and Gregory Zilboorg. Duchamp serves as the judge. This event opens Levy's show *Imagery of Chess*, for which Duchamp, Ernst, Dorothea Tanning, and others have designed and constructed chess figures.

12 January
The German antifascist artist Alfred Frank is executed.

11 February
The sculptor Joachim Karsch commits suicide in Berlin.

March
View devotes an issue to Duchamp, with articles by Breton, Robert Desnos, Harriet and Sidney Janis, and James Thrall Soby.

Publication of the second, enlarged edition of Breton's *Le surréalisme et la peinture*.

13 March
The Whitney Museum opens the encyclopedic show *European Artists in America*, which includes work by many artists who had come to the U.S. since 1938. Among them are Breton, Chagall, Dali, Duchamp, Ernst, Léger, Lipchitz, Masson, Matta, Mondrian, Ozenfant, and Tanguy.

22 April
Käthe Kollwitz dies in Germany.

October
Léger, Masson, and Zadkine return to France; they are followed by Breton in the spring of 1946.

Karl Nierendorf opens the exhibition *Forbidden Art in the Third Reich* at his gallery in New York. It travels to the Institute of Modern Art in Boston, where it opens on November 8

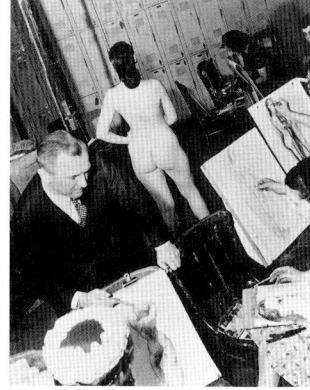

George Grosz teaching at the Art Students League, New York, 1947.

November
Sweeney's "Eleven Artists in America," published in the MoMA *Bulletin*, comprises interviews with Duchamp, Max Ernst, Masson, Seligmann, and Tanguy among others and functions as the catalogue for a traveling exhibition that opens at Vassar College.

1945

POLITICAL

27 January
Soviet troops liberate Auschwitz.

4–11 February
At the Yalta conference Churchill, Roosevelt, and Stalin plan the final phase of the Allied assault on Germany and discuss conditions for peace.

7 March
U.S. forces cross the Rhine at Remagen; by 25 March all German forces are driven east of the Rhine.

28 March
End of German offensive against Britain.

12 April
Roosevelt suffers a massive cerebral hemorrhage and dies. Vice President Harry S. Truman is sworn in as president.

13 April
Fall of Vienna.

20 April
Soviet troops reach Berlin.

21–28 April
Last gassing of concentration camp inmates at Ravenbrück and Mauthausen.

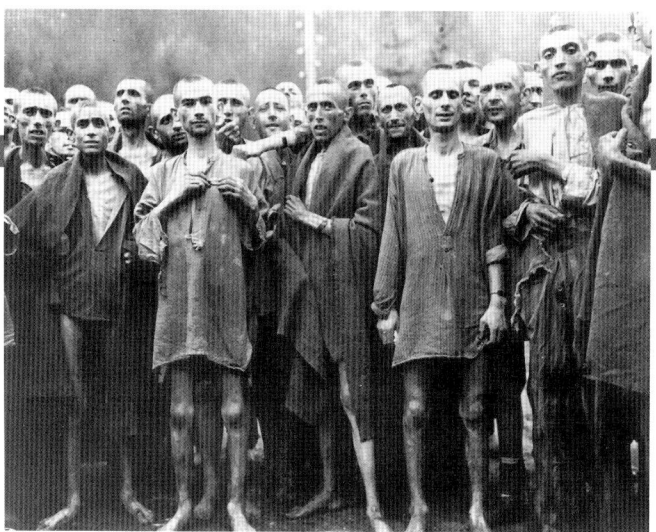

Liberated prisoners at the Ebensee concentration camp, May 7, 1945.

25 April
In Austria Karl Renner becomes chancellor, leading the provisional government. The Red Army has surrounded Berlin.

29 April
American troops occupy Dachau. Surrender of German forces in Italy.

30 April
Hitler commits suicide. Admiral Doenitz becomes head of Germany.

1 May
Goebbels commits suicide.

2 May
Surrender of Berlin.

7–9 May
Unconditional surrender of armed forces of Germany. After the U.S. drops atomic bombs on Hiroshima and Nagasaki (6–9 August) and the USSR declares war on Japan, Japan surrenders on August 14, and World War II ends. Among those murdered by the Germans are about 6.2 million Jews and 400,000 Gypsies.

5 June
Allied Control Commission assumes control over Germany.

There were about 1.6 million refugees from Germany and occupied Europe during Hitler's reign. Between 1933 and 1945 the U.S. admitted an estimated total of 318,000 refugees from Europe. About 250,000 were of Jewish descent. 132,000 refugees from greater Germany entered the U.S., including some 100,000 Jews (this excludes those refugees who entered the U.S. by visitor's visas). A total of about 278,000 German Jews emigrated worldwide. An estimated total of 500,000 people left Germany, Austria, and Czechoslovakia between 1933 and 1945, of whom 94 percent were Jewish.

checklist of the exhibition

Unless otherwise noted, the works listed here can be seen at all three venues of the exhibition. Exceptions are indicated as follows:

● Los Angeles
▲ Montreal
■ Berlin

Josef Albers

1. *Etude: Hot-Dry*, 1935
   Oil on Masonite
   12 3/4 x 15 3/4 in. (32.4 x 40 cm)
   The Josef and Anni Albers Foundation

2. *"Related" A*, 1937
   Oil on canvas
   23 7/8 x 17 3/4 in. (60.6 x 45.1 cm)
   Bill Bass, Chicago

3. *Penetrating (A)*, 1938
   Oil, casein, and tempera on Masonite
   30 x 26 in. (76.2 x 66 cm)
   The Josef and Anni Albers Foundation

4. *Cadence*, 1940
   Oil on Masonite
   28 7/16 x 28 3/16 in. (72.2 x 71.6 cm)
   Yale University Art Gallery, gift of the Josef and Anni Albers Foundation

5. *Layered*, 1940
   Oil on Masonite
   23 1/2 x 28 in. (59.7 x 71.1 cm)
   The Josef and Anni Albers Foundation

6. *Leaf Study IV*, c. 1940
   Collage of leaves on paper
   18 9/16 x 22 1/2 in. (47.2 x 57.2 cm)
   The Josef and Anni Albers Foundation

Max Beckmann

7. *Birth*, 1937
   Oil on canvas
   47 5/8 x 69 1/2 in. (121 x 176.5 cm)
   Staatliche Museen zu Berlin, Preussischer Kulturbesitz, Neue Nationalgalerie

8. *Birds' Hell*, 1938
   Oil on canvas
   47 1/4 x 63 3/16 in. (120 x 160.5 cm)
   Richard L. Feigen, New York
   ● ▲

9. *Death*, 1938
   Oil on canvas
   47 5/8 x 69 1/2 in. (121 x 176.5 cm)
   Staatliche Museen zu Berlin, Preussischer Kulturbesitz, Neue Nationalgalerie

10. *Self-Portrait with Horn*, 1938
    Oil on canvas
    43 5/16 x 39 3/4 in. (110 x 101 cm)
    Dr. and Mrs. Stephan Lackner, Santa Barbara
    ● ▲

11. *The Artists with Vegetable*, 1943
    Oil on canvas
    59 x 45 3/8 in. (149.9 x 115.3 cm)
    Washington University Gallery of Art, Saint Louis, university purchase, Kende Sale Fund, 1946

12. *The Architect (Two Men)*, 1944
    Oil on canvas
    23 5/8 x 15 3/4 in. (60 x 40 cm)
    Kurpfälzisches Museum der Stadt Heidelberg

13. *The Journey*, 1944
    Oil on canvas
    35 7/16 x 57 1/16 in. (90 x 145 cm)
    Private collection, Germany
    ■

14. *Double Portrait: Curt Valentin and Hanns Swarzenski*, 1946
    Oil on canvas
    51 1/2 x 29 3/4 in. (130.8 x 75.6 cm)
    Museum of Fine Arts, Boston, gift of Hanns Swarzenski

15. *The Prodigal Son*, 1949
    Oil on canvas
    39 3/8 x 47 1/4 in. (100 x 120 cm)
    Sprengel Museum, Hannover

16 *The Argonauts*, 1949–50
    Oil on canvas
    Middle panel: 81 x 48 1/16 in.
    (205.8 x 122 cm)
    Side panels: 72 1/2 x 33 1/2 in.
    (184.1 x 85.1 cm)
    National Gallery of Art, Washington,
    D.C., gift of Mrs. Max Beckmann

17 *Hotel Lobby*, 1950
    Oil on canvas
    56 x 35 in. (142.2 x 88.9 cm)
    Albright-Knox Art Gallery, Buffalo,
    Room of Contemporary Art Fund, 1950
    ■

18 *Self-Portrait*, 1950
    Oil on canvas
    54 15/16 x 36 in. (139.5 x 91.5 cm)
    The Saint Louis Art Museum, bequest of
    Morton D. May

19 *The Town (City Night)*, 1950
    Oil on canvas
    64 15/16 x 75 3/16 in. (165 x 191 cm)
    The Saint Louis Art Museum, bequest of
    Morton D. May

Marc Chagall

20 *Ghetto* (renamed *Resistance*), 1937–48
    Oil on canvas
    66 1/8 x 40 9/16 in. (168 x 103 cm)
    Musée National d'Art Moderne, Centre
    Georges Pompidou, Paris, on loan to
    Musée National Message Biblique
    Marc Chagall, Nice

21 *Resurrection*, 1937–48
    Oil on canvas
    66 1/4 x 42 3/8 in. (168.3 x 107.7 cm)
    Musée National d'Art Moderne, Centre
    Georges Pompidou, Paris, on loan to
    Musée National Message Biblique
    Marc Chagall, Nice

22 *Liberation*, 1937–52
    Oil on canvas
    66 1/8 x 34 5/8 in. (168 x 88 cm)
    Musée National d'Art Moderne, Centre
    Georges Pompidou, Paris, on loan to
    Musée National Message Biblique
    Marc Chagall, Nice

23 *Persecution*, c. 1941
    Gouache on paper
    21 7/8 x 14 7/8 in. (55.6 x 37.8 cm)
    Herta and Paul Amir

24 *Obsession*, 1943
    Oil on canvas
    29 15/16 x 42 5/16 in. (76 x 107.5 cm)
    Musée National d'Art Moderne, Centre
    Georges Pompidou, Paris, permanent
    loan to the Musée de Nantes

25 *Yellow Crucifixion*, 1943
    Oil on canvas
    55 1/8 x 39 3/4 in. (140 x 101 cm)
    Musée National d'Art Moderne, Centre
    Georges Pompidou, Paris

Salvador Dali

26 *Honey Is Sweeter than Blood*, 1941
    Oil on canvas
    20 x 24 in. (50.8 x 61 cm)
    Santa Barbara Museum of Art, gift of
    Mr. and Mrs. Warren Tremaine

27 *Ruin with Head of Medusa*, 1941
    Oil on canvas
    14 3/16 x 10 in. (36 x 25.4 cm)
    Collection Juan Abelló
    ● ▲

28 *Allegory of an American Christmas*, 1943
    Oil on canvas
    15 15/16 x 12 in. (40.5 x 30.5 cm)
    Private collection, Switzerland

29 *The Apotheosis of Homer*, 1944
    Oil on canvas
    25 1/16 x 45 15/16 in. (63.7 x 116.7 cm)
    Bayerische Staatsgemäldesammlungen,
    Munich, Staatsgalerie moderner Kunst
    ● ■

30 *Dream Caused by the Flight of a Bee
    around a Pomegranate a Second before
    Awakening*, 1944
    Oil on panel
    20 1/16 x 15 15/16 in. (51 x 40.5 cm)
    Fundación Colección Thyssen-
    Bornemisza, Madrid
    ■

31 *Melancholy Atomic and Uranic Idyll*,
    1945
    Oil on canvas
    26 x 34 5/8 in. (66 x 88 cm)
    Museo Nacional Centro de Arte Reina
    Sofía, Madrid

32 *Portrait of Isabel Styler-Tas
    (Melancholy)*, 1945
    Oil on canvas
    25 13/16 x 33 7/8 in. (65.5 x 86 cm)
    Staatliche Museen zu Berlin, Preussischer
    Kulturbesitz, Neue Nationalgalerie

Max Ernst

33 *Napoleon in the Wilderness*, 1941
    Oil on canvas
    18 1/4 x 15 in. (46.3 x 38.1 cm)
    The Museum of Modern Art, New York,
    purchase and exchange, 1942

34 *Stolen Mirror*, 1941
    Oil on canvas
    26 3/4 x 59 1/16 in. (68 x 150 cm)
    Ms. Dallas Ernst

35 *Painting for Young People*, 1943
    Oil on canvas
    24 1/8 x 30 1/8 in. (61.4 x 76.6 cm)
    The Menil Collection, Houston

36 *Painting for Young People*, 1943
    Oil on canvas
    24 x 30 in. (61 x 76.2 cm)
    The Ulla and Heiner Pietzsch Collection,
    Berlin
    ●

37 *The Eye of Silence*, 1943–44
    Oil on canvas
    42 1/2 x 55 1/2 in. (108 x 141 cm)
    Washington University Gallery of Art,
    Saint Louis, university purchase,
    Kende Sale Fund, 1946
    ● ▲

38 *An Anxious Friend*, 1944
    Bronze
    26 3/16 x 14 1/16 x 16 5/8 in.
    (66.5 x 35.7 x 42.3 cm)
    A: Mr. and Mrs. James A. Nathan,
    Los Angeles
    ● ▲
    B: Wilhelm Lehmbruck Museum,
    Duisberg
    ■

39 *Moonmad*, 1944
    Bronze
    36 3/4 x 13 x 12 3/8 in.
    (93.3 x 33 x 31.4 cm)
    Hirshhorn Museum and Sculpture
    Garden, Smithsonian Institution,
    Washington, D.C., gift of Joseph H.
    Hirshhorn, 1966

40 *The Cocktail Drinker*, 1945
    Oil on canvas
    45 11/16 x 28 9/16 in. (116 x 72.5 cm)
    Kunstsammlung Nordrhein-Westfalen,
    Düsseldorf
    ●

41 *Euclid*, 1945
    Oil on canvas
    25 5/8 x 23 1/4 in. (65.1 x 59.1 cm)
    The Menil Collection, Houston

Andreas Feininger

42 *The Cities Service Building, Fire Escapes, and the El*, 1940 (printed later)
Gelatin-silver print
14 x 11 in. (35.6 x 27.9 cm)
Courtesy Bonni Benrubi Gallery, New York

43 *Elk's Rendezvous, a Harlem Night Club*, 1940 (printed later)
Two gelatin-silver prints
A: 11 5/8 x 10 9/16 in. (29.6 x 26.8 cm)
B: 11 3/4 x 10 5/8 in. (29.9 x 26.9 cm)
Center for Creative Photography, the University of Arizona

44 *Jewish Establishments on Manhattan's Lower East Side*, 1940 (printed later)
Gelatin-silver print
14 x 11 in. (35.6 x 27.9 cm)
Courtesy Bonni Benrubi Gallery, New York

45 *N.Y.—Brooklyn Bridge from Brooklyn Shore*, 1940
Gelatin-silver print
8 x 9 in. (20.3 x 22.9 cm)
Courtesy Bonni Benrubi Gallery, New York

46 *Times Square and Longacre Square*, 1940 (printed later)
Gelatin-silver print
14 x 11 1/4 in. (35.6 x 28.6 cm)
Center for Creative Photography, the University of Arizona

47 *Solarized Nude* (negative version), 1941
Gelatin-silver print
10 x 8 in. (25.4 x 20.3 cm)
Courtesy Bonni Benrubi Gallery, New York

48 *V-E Day Reaction*, 1945 (printed later)
Gelatin-silver print
10 7/8 x 10 1/4 in. (27.6 x 26 cm)
Time Life Syndication, New York

Lyonel Feininger

49 *Manhattan II*, 1940
Oil on canvas
38 x 28 3/8 in. (96.5 x 72 cm)
Collection of the Modern Art Museum of Fort Worth, purchase made possible by anonymous contributions, 1946

50 *Manhattan, Night*, 1940
Oil on canvas
24 x 17 in. (61 x 43.2 cm)
Carl D. Lobell

51 *Manhattan, Dawn*, 1944
Oil on canvas
35 x 28 in. (88.9 x 71.1 cm)
The Art Institute of Chicago, gift of Mr. and Mrs. Andreas Feininger

52 *Manhattan, the Tower*, 1944
Oil on canvas
39 1/2 x 31 3/4 in. (100.3 x 80.6 cm)
San Francisco Museum of Modern Art, gift of Mrs. Drew Chidester

George Grosz

53 *Lower Manhattan*, 1934
Oil on cardboard
24 x 18 in. (61 x 45.7 cm)
The Fine Arts Museums of San Francisco, gift of Dalzell Hatfield

54 *Remembering*, 1937
Oil on canvas
28 3/4 x 36 5/8 in. (73 x 93 cm)
George Grosz estate

55 *The Mighty One on a Little Outing Surprised by Two Poets*, 1942
Oil on canvas
28 x 20 in. (71.1 x 50.8 cm)
Hofstra Museum, Hofstra University, Hempstead, New York

56 *"I'm Glad I Came Back,"* 1943
Oil on cardboard
28 x 20 in. (71.1 x 50.8 cm)
Arizona State University Art Museum, Tempe, gift of Oliver B. James

57 *The Wanderer*, 1943
Oil on canvas
30 x 40 in. (76.2 x 101.6 cm)
Memorial Art Gallery of the University of Rochester

58 *The Survivor*, 1944
Oil on canvas on Masonite
31 3/4 x 39 1/4 in. (80.6 x 99.7 cm)
The Robert Gore Rifkind Collection, Beverly Hills

59 *Cain or Hitler in Hell*, 1945
Oil on canvas
39 x 49 in. (99 x 124.5 cm)
George Grosz estate

John Heartfield

60 *Freedom Calling: The Story of the Secret German Radio*, 1939
Photomontage (design for book cover)
14 3/16 x 9 7/8 in. (36 x 25.1 cm)
Stiftung Archiv der Akademie der Künste, Berlin, Kunstsammlung (Heartfield-Archiv)
● ▲

61 *Kaiser Adolf: The Man against Europe*, 1939
Cover of *Picture Post*, 9 September 1939
13 11/16 x 10 1/4 in. (34.7 x 26 cm)
Stiftung Archiv der Akademie der Künste, Berlin, Kunstsammlung (Heartfield-Archiv)
● ▲

62 *Reservations: Jews Driven like Cattle*, 1939
Photomontage (design for *Reynolds News*, December 1939)
22 1/16 x 15 3/8 in. (56 x 39 cm)
Stiftung Archiv der Akademie der Künste, Berlin, Kunstsammlung (Heartfield-Archiv)
■

63 *Burdens of War*, 1940
Cover of *Inside Nazi Germany*, March 1940
10 13/16 x 8 1/4 in. (27.5 x 21 cm)
Stiftung Archiv der Akademie der Künste, Berlin, Kunstsammlung (Heartfield-Archiv)
■

64 *Hitler's War Machine*, 1941
Book jacket
8 11/16 x 12 11/16 in. (22.1 x 32.2 cm)
Stiftung Archiv der Akademie der Künste, Berlin, Kunstsammlung (Heartfield-Archiv)

65 *Five Minutes to Twelve*, 1942
Photomontage
19 3/16 x 15 7/8 in. (48.8 x 40.3 cm)
Stiftung Archiv der Akademie der Künste, Berlin, Kunstsammlung (Heartfield-Archiv)
● ▲

66 Untitled, 1942
Cover of *Freie deutsche Kultur*, no. 3 (March 1942)
10 1/16 x 8 in. (25.5 x 20.3 cm)
Stiftung Archiv der Akademie der Künste, Berlin, Kunstsammlung (Heartfield-Archiv)

67 *And Yet It Moves!* 1943
Photomontage (design for pamphlet cover)
15 3/8 x 10 9/16 in. (39 x 26.8 cm)
Stiftung Archiv der Akademie der Künste, Berlin, Kunstsammlung (Heartfield-Archiv)
■

68 *Soviet Financial System*, 1945
Photomontage (design for pamphlet cover)
8 7/16 x 11 7/16 in. (21.4 x 29 cm)
Stiftung Archiv der Akademie der Künste, Berlin, Kunstsammlung (Heartfield-Archiv)
■

69 *American Melting Pot*, 1946
Photomontage (design for book illustration)
24 11/16 x 19 15/16 in. (62.7 x 50.6 cm)
Stiftung Archiv der Akademie der Künste, Berlin, Kunstsammlung (Heartfield-Archiv)
● ■ ▲

Wassily Kandinsky

70 *Balancing Act*, 1935
Oil with sand on canvas
32 x 39 1/8 in. (81.3 x 99.5 cm)
Lent anonymously
● ▲

71 *Brown with Supplement*, 1935
Oil on canvas
31 7/8 x 39 3/8 in. (81 x 100 cm)
Museum Boymans-van Beuningen, Rotterdam

72 *Grouping*, 1937
Oil on canvas
57 1/2 x 35 1/16 in. (146 x 89 cm)
Moderna Museet, Stockholm
● ▲

73 *Moderation*, 1940
Oil and enamel on canvas
39 1/4 x 25 3/8 in. (99.7 x 64.5 cm)
The Solomon R. Guggenheim Museum, New York

74 *Tempered Elan*, 1944
Oil on cardboard
16 9/16 x 22 13/16 in. (42 x 58 cm)
Musée National d'Art Moderne, Centre Georges Pompidou, Paris

75 *Unfinished Painting*, 1944
Oil on cardboard
16 9/16 x 22 13/16 in. (42 x 58 cm)
Musée National d'Art Moderne, Centre Georges Pompidou, Paris

André Kertész

76 *Self-Portrait in the Hotel Beaux-Arts*, 1936
Gelatin-silver print
6 1/2 x 9 5/8 in. (16.5 x 24.4 cm)
Estate of André Kertész

77 *Arm and Ventilator*, 1937 (printed later)
Gelatin-silver print
6 11/16 x 9 1/8 in. (17 x 23.2 cm)
Estate of André Kertész

78 *Clothes Lines*, 1937 (printed later)
Gelatin-silver print
7 11/16 x 9 1/2 in. (19.5 x 24.1 cm)
Estate of André Kertész

79 *Father Duffy Monument, New York*, 1937
Gelatin-silver print
7 9/16 x 9 11/16 in. (19.2 x 24.6 cm)
Estate of André Kertész

80 *Lost Cloud*, 1937 (printed later)
Gelatin-silver print
8 1/2 x 5 3/8 in. (21.6 x 13.7 cm)
Courtesy Howard Greenberg Gallery, New York, and the estate of André Kertész

81 *Lion Seen through a Window*, 1942
Gelatin-silver print
9 5/8 x 7 3/4 in. (24.4 x 19.7 cm)
Jane Corkin Gallery, Toronto

Oskar Kokoschka

82 *Thomas Garrique Masaryk*, 1936
Oil on canvas
37 x 50 3/8 in. (94 x 128 cm)
Carnegie Museum of Art, Pittsburgh, Patrons Art Fund, 1956

83 *Polperro II*, 1939
Oil on canvas
23 13/16 x 33 7/8 in. (60.5 x 86 cm)
The Tate Gallery, London, presented by Dr. Edvard Beneš, president of Czechoslovakia, 1941

84 *Loreley*, 1941–42
Oil on canvas
25 x 30 1/16 in. (63.5 x 76.4 cm)
The Tate Gallery, London, presented by Mrs. Olda Kokoschka, the artist's widow, in honor of the directorship of Sir Alan Bowness, 1988

85 *"Anschluss"—Alice in Wonderland*, 1942
Oil on canvas
25 x 30 1/16 in. (63.5 x 76.3 cm)
Wiener Städtische Allgemeine Versicherung AG
● ▲

86 *Marianne-Maquis*, 1942
Oil on canvas
25 x 29 15/16 in. (63.5 x 76 cm)
The Tate Gallery, London, presented by Mrs. Olda Kokoschka, the artist's widow, in honor of the directorship of Sir Alan Bowness, 1988
▲ ■

87 *Family of Jugglers*, 1946
Oil on canvas
19 11/16 x 24 in. (50 x 61 cm)
Dr. Peter Hahn, Berlin

Fernand Léger

88 *The Divers II*, 1941–42
Oil on canvas
90 x 68 in. (228.6 x 172.8 cm)
The Museum of Modern Art, New York, Mrs. Simon Guggenheim Fund, 1955
●

89 *The Divers*, 1942
Oil on canvas
50 x 58 1/16 in. (127 x 147.5 cm)
Sidney Janis Gallery, New York

90 *The Divers (Red and Black)*, 1942
Oil on canvas
50 1/8 x 58 1/8 in. (127.3 x 147.6 cm)
Dallas Museum of Art, Foundation for the Arts Collection, gift of the James H. and Lillian Clark Foundation, 1982

91 *Two Acrobats*, 1942–43
Oil on canvas
49 1/2 x 57 in. (125.7 x 144.7 cm)
Sidney Janis Gallery, New York
■

92 *Four Composition Studies (Rouses Point)*, 1943–45
Gouache on paper
8 7/16 x 11 5/8 in. (21.5 x 29.5 cm)
Martin S. James

93 *France Reborn*, 1945
Watercolor, gouache, and pencil on
paper, mounted on paperboard
26 1/16 x 21 7/8 in. (66.2 x 55.5 cm)
National Museum of American Art,
Smithsonian Institution, Washington,
D.C., gift of Container Corporation
of America

94 *Mechanical Fragments*, 1945
Gouache on paper
11 3/4 x 8 3/4 in. (29.8 x 22.2 cm)
Martin S. James

Jacques Lipchitz

95 *Flight*, 1940
Bronze
H: 14 1/2 in. (36.8 cm)
Nicholas A. Polsky

96 *Arrival*, 1941
Bronze
H: 21 in. (53.3 cm)
Des Moines Art Center Permanent
Collection, purchased with funds from
Rose F. Rosenfield

97 *Mother and Child II*, 1941–45
Bronze
51 1/2 x 51 1/2 x 32 in.
(130.8 x 130.8 x 81.2 cm)
Art Gallery of Ontario, Toronto, gift of
Sam and Ayala Zacks, 1970

98 *The Prayer*, 1943
Bronze
H: 42 1/2 in. (108 cm)
Philadelphia Museum of Art, gift of
R. Sturgis and Marion B. F. Ingersoll

99 *Prometheus Strangling the Vulture*, 1943
Bronze
H: 18 3/4 in. (47.6 cm)
Private collection, courtesy Phyllis Hattis
Fine Arts

André Masson

100 *The German Soldier*, 1941
Oil on canvas
20 1/16 x 16 1/8 in. (51 x 41 cm)
Private collection, Europe

101 *Curtain for a Ceremony*, 1942
Oil on canvas
22 7/8 x 50 in. (58 x 127 cm)
Collection Philippe Cazeau

102 *The Germ of the Cosmos*, 1942
Gouache and pastel on canvas
40 x 33 in. (101.6 x 83.8 cm)
San Diego Museum of Art, gift
of Mrs. Saidie A. May

103 *The Night*, 1942
Gouache and pastel on paper
26 x 19 1/2 in. (66 x 49.5 cm)
Private collection, Los Angeles

104 *The Seeded Earth*, 1942
Oil on canvas
30 x 40 in. (76.2 x 101.6 cm)
Detroit Institute of Arts, gift
of W. Hawkins Ferry

105 *Pasiphaë*, 1943
Oil and tempera on canvas
39 3/4 x 50 in. (101 x 127 cm)
Private collection, Winnetka, Illinois
● ▲

106 *Oradour*, 1944
Oil on canvas
32 1/4 x 38 3/16 in. (82 x 97 cm)
Comité André Masson, Paris

107 *The Resistance*, 1944
Oil on canvas
69 1/4 x 54 3/4 in. (175.9 x 139.1 cm)
Musée National d'Art Moderne, Centre
Georges Pompidou, Paris
▲ ■

Matta Echaurren

108 *Theory of Nature's Strategy
(Polypsychology)*, c. 1939
Crayon on paper
19 1/4 x 25 in. (48.9 x 63.5 cm)
Los Angeles County Museum of Art,
gift of Barbara Poe Levee

109 Untitled, 1940
Graphite and crayon on paper
15 x 22 in. (38.1 x 55.9 cm)
Acquavella Contemporary Art, New York

110 *Invasion of the Night*, 1941
Oil on canvas
38 x 60 1/8 in. (96.5 x 152.7 cm)
San Francisco Museum of Modern Art,
bequest of Jacqueline Marie Onslow Ford

111 *Locus Solus*, 1941–42
Oil on canvas
29 5/16 x 37 5/8 in. (74.5 x 95.5 cm)
The Ulla and Heiner Pietzsch Collection,
Berlin
●

112 *The Disasters of Mysticism*, 1942
Oil on canvas
38 3/8 x 51 3/8 in. (97.5 x 130.5 cm)
Private collection

113 *The Year 1944—the Putting to Death of
the Father*, 1942
Oil on canvas
38 3/16 x 50 in. (97 x 127 cm)
Staatliche Museen zu Berlin, Preussischer
Kulturbesitz, Neue Nationalgalerie

114 *The Thought of a Permanent Table*, 1945
Graphite and crayon on paper
14 1/2 x 23 in. (36.8 x 58.4 cm)
Acquavella Contemporary Art, New York

115 *A Grave Situation*, 1946
Oil on canvas
55 x 77 1/8 in. (139.7 x 195.9 cm)
Museum of Contemporary Art, Chicago,
promised gift of Mary and Earle Ludgin
Collection

László Moholy-Nagy

116 *Composition*, 1938
Oil and incisions on rhodoid
32 1/2 x 23 3/8 in. (82.5 x 59.3 cm)
Eugene Bielawski
●

117 *Space Modulator*, 1938–40
Oil on composition board
47 x 47 in. (119.4 x 119.4 cm)
Whitney Museum of American Art,
New York, gift of Mrs. Sibyl Moholy-Nagy
● ▲

118 *Space Modulator*, 1939–45
Oil on incised plastic, wooden rails,
plywood backing
24 7/8 x 26 in. (63.2 x 66 cm)
The Solomon R. Guggenheim Museum,
New York

119 *CH B4*, 1941
Oil on canvas
50 3/16 x 40 3/8 in. (127.5 x 102.5 cm)
Courtesy Annely Juda Fine Art, London

120 *Composition*, 1942
Oil and pencil on paper
17 15/16 x 14 1/16 in. (45.5 x 35.7 cm)
Private collection

121 *Space Modulator*, 1942
Oil on Formica (with yellow background)
60 5/8 x 23 5/8 in. (154 x 60 cm)
Hattula Moholy-Nagy

122 *Photogram*, 1943
Photogram
8 x 10 1/16 in. (20.4 x 25.6 cm)
Bauhaus-Archiv, Museum für
Gestaltung, Berlin

123 *Space Modulator*, 1945
Oil on incised Plexiglas
18 x 12 in. (45.7 x 30.5 cm)
Alberta Parker Horn

124 *Spirals*, 1946 (replica)
Plexiglas
19 5/16 x 14 3/4 x 15 3/4 in.
(49 x 37.5 x 40 cm)
Hattula Moholy-Nagy

Kurt Schwitters

125 *Small Flower Picture*, 1941
Collage
8 x 6 1/2 in. (20.2 x 16.5 cm)
Private collection

126 *The Double Picture*, 1942
Assemblage
25 15/16 x 21 7/8 in. (65.9 x 55.6 cm)
Galerie Gmurzynska, Cologne

127 *W. C. Fields*, 1942
Collage
19 3/4 x 15 1/4 in. (50.2 x 38.7 cm)
Helge Achenbach, Düsseldorf

128 *The Wounded Hunter*, 1942
Collage
8 x 10 1/4 in. (20.3 x 26 cm)
Private collection

129 *Collage (Herbert Read)*, 1944
Collage
7 1/16 x 10 1/4 in. (18 x 26 cm)
Collection of David and Paria Brandt, New York

130 *The Hitler Gang*, c. 1944
Collage
13 5/8 x 9 5/8 in. (34.7 x 24.5 cm)
Private collection

Yves Tanguy

131 *The Earth and the Air*, 1941
Oil on canvas
45 x 36 in. (114.3 x 91.4 cm)
Baltimore Museum of Art, bequest of Saidie A. May

132 *Indefinite Divisibility*, 1942
Oil on canvas
40 x 35 in. (101.6 x 88.9 cm)
Albright-Knox Art Gallery, Buffalo, Room of Contemporary Art Fund, 1945

133 *Slowly toward the North*, 1942
Oil on canvas
42 x 36 in. (106.7 x 91.4 cm)
The Museum of Modern Art, New York, gift of Philip Johnson, 1943

134 *The Prodigal Son Never Returns II*, 1943
Oil on canvas
11 x 9 1/16 in. (28 x 23 cm)
Galerie Jan Krugier, Ditesheim & Cie, Geneva
●■

135 *The Prodigal Son Never Returns III*, 1943
Oil on canvas
11 x 9 1/16 in. (28 x 23 cm)
Galerie Jan Krugier, Ditesheim & Cie, Geneva
●■

136 *Through Birds, through Fire, but Not through Glass*, 1943
Oil on canvas
40 x 35 in. (101.6 x 88.9 cm)
Minneapolis Institute of Arts, gift of Mr. and Mrs. Donald Winston in tribute to Richard S. Davis

Surrealist Portfolios

137 *Brunidor Portfolio Number 1*, 1947

Max Ernst
Dangerous Relations, 1947
Etching and drypoint
11 3/4 x 8 13/16 in. (29.8 x 22.4 cm)

Stanley William Hayter
Virtual Personage, 1947
Etching and engraving
11 3/4 x 8 7/8 in. (29.9 x 22.5 cm)

Wifredo Lam
Quetzal, 1947
Color lithograph
16 1/2 x 13 in. (42 x 33.1 cm)

Matta Echaurren
I Want to See It to Believe It, 1947
Color lithograph
16 3/8 x 12 7/8 in. (41.6 x 32.7 cm)

Kurt Seligmann
Acteon, 1947
Etching
11 3/4 x 8 13/16 in. (29.8 x 22.4 cm)

Yves Tanguy
Rhabdomancie, 1947
Color etching and monoprint
11 11/16 x 8 13/16 in. (29.7 x 22.4 cm)

The Museum of Modern Art, New York

138 *VVV Portfolio*, 1942 (selections)

André Breton
I Saluted at Six Paces Commander Lefebvre des Noettes, 1942
Collage of chromolithograph postcard, paper, colored thread, sequins, metallic ink, and black ink on brown paper
18 x 14 in. (45.8 x 35.6 cm)

Marc Chagall
Eiffel Tower, 1943
Etching
10 7/8 x 8 in. (27.6 x 20.2 cm)

Max Ernst
The Bird People, 1942
Black crayon frottage with colored crayon on orange paper
18 x 14 in. (45.7 x 35.6 cm)

Matta Echaurren
Untitled, c. 1942
Colored inks and graphite
16 3/4 x 13 3/4 in. (42.6 x 34.8 cm)

Kurt Seligmann
Phantom of the Past, 1942
Etching and aquatint
17 1/2 x 13 3/8 in. (44.6 x 34.1 cm)

A: The Baltimore Museum of Art, gift of Saidie A. May
●

B: Philadelphia Museum of Art, Louise and Walter Arensberg Collection
▲■

Architectural Models, Plans, and Drawings

Marcel Breuer
Geller House, Lawrence, New York, 1945: plans with elevation studies
Pencil on paper
18 1/4 x 19 1/2 in. (46.4 x 49.5 cm)
George Arents Research Library for Special Collections, Syracuse University

Walter Gropius and Marcel Breuer
Gropius House, Lincoln, Massachusetts: model, 1938
Wood, plaster, and other materials, with gouache
8 1/2 x 24 1/2 x 34 in.
(21.6 x 61.6 x 86.4 cm)
Busch-Reisinger Museum, Harvard University Art Museums, gift of Walter Gropius

Walter Gropius and Marcel Breuer
Black Mountain College Project, North Carolina, 1938–39
Collage element with ink and gouache over photograph
12 7/8 x 20 in. (32.8 x 50.9 cm)
Busch-Reisinger Museum, Harvard University Art Museums, gift of Walter Gropius

Walter Gropius/The Architects Collaborative
Graduate Center, Harvard University: site plan, 1948–50
Contemporary print
14 1/4 x 19 3/4 in. (36.2 x 50.2 cm)
Art Collection, Harvard Law School

Frederick Kiesler
Eight drawings related to Art of This Century gallery, c. 1942
Ink and gouache on paper
Various dimensions
Estate of Frederick Kiesler

Ludwig Mies van der Rohe
Concert Hall Project, 1942
Collage over photograph
29 1/2 x 62 in. (75 x 157.5 cm)
The Museum of Modern Art, New York, The Mies van der Rohe Archive, gift of Mary Callery

Ludwig Mies van der Rohe
Farnsworth House, Plano, Illinois: plan, 1946–51
Ink on illustration board
30 x 40 in. (76.2 x 101.6 cm)
The Museum of Modern Art, New York, The Mies van der Rohe Archive, gift of the architect

Architectural Reconstructions

Piet Mondrian's 15 East 59th Street studio, New York City, 1944
(1996 reconstruction by Paul Lubowicki and Susan Lanier)
Oroboard, plywood veneer, basswood, honeycomb panels, paint
128 x 132 x 37 in. (325.1 x 335.3 x 94 cm)
Reproductions of works by Mondrian courtesy of Mondrian Estate/Holtzman Trust

Surrealist Gallery of Peggy Guggenheim's Art of This Century gallery, 1942
(1996 reconstruction by Paul Lubowicki and Susan Lanier)
Oroboard, plywood veneer, basswood, honeycomb panels, paint
H: 36 in. (91.4 cm); W: 70 in. (177.8 cm); L: 240 in. (609.6 cm)

Marcel Breuer
Geller House, 1945
(1996 reconstruction by Brian O'Neill)
Wood, slate, cement, plastic
H: 8 in. (20.3 cm); W: 40 in. (101.6 cm); L: 60 in. (152.4 cm)

Walter Gropius and Marcel Breuer
Black Mountain College project, 1938–39
(1996 reconstruction by Brian O'Neill)
Basswood
H: 8 in. (20.3 cm); W: 36 in. (91.4 cm); L: 48 in. (121.9 cm)

Ludwig Mies van der Rohe
Lake Shore Drive Apartments, 1948–51
(1996 reconstruction by Brian O'Neill)
Wood and acrylic
H: 18 in. (45.7 cm); W: 24 in. (61 cm); L: 24 in. (61 cm)

Documentary Film

America and the Exiles: U.S. Immigration Policy and the European Refugee Crisis, 1996
15 min.
Directed by Chana Gazit
Steward/Gazit Productions

Historical Documents

Exiles and Emigrés: The Flight of European Artists from Hitler included representative examples of letters, exhibition catalogues, brochures, posters, official documents, photographs, newspaper and magazine clippings, architectural models, reconstructions, and film and video footage, divided into six thematic sections. "The European Centers of Exile: Paris, Amsterdam, and London, 1933–45" contained material related to the activities of the Kollektiv deutscher Künstler and exhibitions mounted in Paris and London in response to the 1937 *Entartete Kunst* show in Munich. "Escape to the United States, 1938–45" included documents related to the Emergency Rescue Committee and American immigration policy. "The Cultural Infrastructure in the United States, 1940–45" contained letters, catalogues, and brochures from the Museum of Modern Art, New York, and the Busch-Reisinger Museum, Harvard University, as well as from gallery exhibitions devoted to artists in exile. "Exiles from Paris in New York, 1940–45" displayed copies of the surrealist publications *VVV* and *View* as well as documents related to the Pontigny summer colloquia at Mount Holyoke College. "Exiles as Teachers in America, 1933–45" included material from Black Mountain College, the Institute for Advanced Study in Princeton, the Institute of Fine Arts, New York University, and Mills College. "The Reception of Banned German Art, 1933–45" traced the numerous exhibitions mounted in New York and Boston featuring German artists.

selected bibliography

HISTORY AND SOCIETY

Primary Sources

Allport, G. W., J. S. Bruner, and E. M. Jandorf. "Personality under Social Catastrophe: Ninety Life-Histories of the Nazi Revolution." *Character and Personality* 10 (September 1941): 1–22.

Arbeitsgemeinschaft der deutschen Emigranten in Frankreich. *Berichte über die "Internationale Konferenz deutscher Emigranten."* Paris, 1936.

———. *Memorandum zur Flüchtlingshilfe November 1935*. Paris, 1935.

Benjamin, Robert Spiers, ed. *I Am an American, by Famous Naturalized Americans*. New York: Alliance, 1941.

Bentwich, Norman De Mattos. *The Refugees from Germany: April 1933 to December 1935*. London: George Allen and Unwin, 1936.

Bliven, Bruce. *The Jewish Refugee Problem*. (Bound with Grover C. Hall. *The Egregious Gentile Called to Account*.) New York: League for Industrial Democracy, 1939.

Davie, Maurice R. *Refugees in America: Report of the Committee for the Study of Recent Immigration from Europe*. New York and London: Harper and Brothers, 1947.

Franck, Wolf. *Führer durch die deutsche Emigration*. Phoenix Bücher, no. 4. Paris, 1935.

Greber, Johannes. *A Plan for the Solution of the Problem of the German Refugees*. New York: American Welfare League, 1939.

Jaksch, Wenzel. *England and the Last Free Germans: The Story of a Rescue*. London: Lincolns-Prager, 1940.

Kalnay, Francis, ed. *The New American: A Handbook of Necessary Information for Aliens and New Citizens*. New York: Greenberg, 1941.

Koessler, Max. "Enemy Alien Internment." *Political Science Quarterly* 57 (March 1942): 98–127.

Neilson, William Allan, ed. *We Escaped: Twelve Personal Narratives of the Flight to America*. New York: Macmillan, 1941.

Ragatz, Lowell Joseph. *The German Refugees in France*. London: A. Thomas, 1934.

Saenger, Gerhart. *Today's Refugees, Tomorrow's Citizens: A Story of Americanization*. New York: Harper and Brothers, 1941.

Simpson, Sir John Hope. *The Refugee Problem: Report of a Survey*. London and New York: Oxford University Press, 1939.

Stern, Erich. *Die Emigration als psychologisches Problem*. Boulogne-sur-Seine: Stern, 1937.

Tartakower, Aryeh, and Kurt R. Grossman. *The Jewish Refugee*. New York: Institute of Jewish Affairs, 1944.

Wise, Stephen S., ed. *Never Again! Ten Years of Hitler: A Symposium*. New York: Jewish Opinion Publishing Corp., 1943.

Secondary Sources

Aaron, Daniel, and Robert Bendiner, eds. *The Strenuous Decade: A Social and Intellectual Record of the 1930s*. Garden City, N.Y.: Anchor, 1970.

Altmann, Peter, Heinz Brüdigam, Barbara Mausbach-Bromberger, and Max Oppenheimer. *Der deutsche antifaschistische Widerstand, 1933–1945: In Bildern und Dokumenten*. Frankfurt am Main: Roderberg, 1975.

Anderson, Benedict. *Imagined Communities: Reflections on the Origins and Spread of Nationalism*. London: Verso, 1983.

Azéma, Jean-Pierre. *De Munich à la Libération, 1938–1944*. Paris: Editions du Seuil, 1979. (Translated by Janet Lloyd, under the title *From Munich to the Liberation, 1938–1944*. Cambridge and New York: Cambridge University Press, 1984.)

Badia, Gilbert, et al. *Les bannis de Hitler: Accueil et luttes des exilés allemands en France (1933–1939)*. Paris: Études et Documentation Internationales; Vincennes: Presses Universitaires de Vincennes, 1984.

Behrendsohn, Walter A. *Probleme der Emigration aus dem Dritten Reich (Aus Politik und Zeitgeschichte: Beilage zu "Das Parliament")*. Bonn: Bundesregierung, 1956.

Berghahn, Marion. *German-Jewish Refugees in England: The Ambiguities of Assimilation*. New York: St. Martin's, 1984.

Bonte, Florimond. *Les antifascists allemands dans la résistance française*. Paris: Editions Sociales, 1969.

Bracher, Karl Dietrich, Manfred Dunke, and Hans-Adolf Jacobsen, eds. *Deutschland, 1933–1945: Neue Studien zur nationalsozialistischen Herrschaft*. Düsseldorf: Droste, 1992.

Cohen, Marcel, et al. *Les camps en Provence: Exil, internement, déportation, 1933–1944.* Aix-en-Provence: Alinéa et L.L.C.G., [1984].

Dallek, Robert. *Franklin D. Roosevelt and American Foreign Policy, 1932–1945.* New York: Oxford University Press, 1979.

Diekmann, Helmut. *"Erdbebenjahre": Von der Volksfrontpolitik bis zum finnisch-sowjetischen Winterkrieg: Aspekte der späten dreissiger Jahre im Spiegel der deutschen Exilpresse und Exilliteratur.* Stockholm: Almqvist and Wiksell, 1994.

Divine, Robert A. *American Immigration Policy, 1924–1952.* New Haven: Yale University Press, 1957.

Dokumentationsarchiv des österrichischen Widerstandes. *Österreicher im Exil: Großbritannien, 1938–1945: Eine Dokumentation.* Intro. Wolfgang Muchitsch. Vienna: Österreichischer Bundesverlag, 1992.

Eckert, Brita. *Die jüdische Emigration aus Deutschland, 1933–1941: Die Geschichte einer Austreibung: Eine Ausstellung der Deutschen Bibliothek, Frankfurt am Main, unter Mitwirkung des Leo Baeck Instituts, New York.* Frankfurt am Main: Buchhändler-Vereinigung, 1985.

Eitner, Hans-Jürgen. *Hitlers Deutsche: Das Ende eines Tabus.* Gernsbach: Casimir Katz, 1990.

Feingold, Henry L. *The Politics of Rescue: The Roosevelt Administration and the Holocaust, 1938–1945.* New Brunswick, N.J.: Rutgers University Press, 1970.

Fontaine, André. *Le camp d'étrangers des Milles: 1939–1943.* Aix-en-Provence: Edisud, 1989.

Foot, M. R. D., ed. *Holland at War against Hitler: Anglo-Dutch Relations, 1940–45.* London: Waanders Uitgevers, 1990.

Friedman, Saul S. *No Haven for the Oppressed: United States Policy toward Jewish Refugees, 1938–1945.* Detroit: Wayne State University Press, 1973.

Frings, Paul. *Das internationale Flüchtlingsproblem, 1919–1950.* Frankfurt am Main: Verlag der Frankfurter Hefte, [1951].

Fritsch-Estrangin, Guy. *New York entre de Gaulle et Pétain: Les français aux Etats-Unis de 1940 à 1946.* Paris: Table Ronde, [1969].

Frühwald, Wolfgang, and Wolfgang Schieder, eds. *Leben im Exil: Probleme der Integration deutscher Flüchtlinge im Ausland, 1933–1945.* Hamburg: Hoffman und Campe, 1981.

Grandjonc, Jacques, ed. *Emigrés français en Allemagne, émigrés allemands en France, 1685–1945: Une exposition....* Paris: Institut Goethe; Ministère des Relations Extérieures, 1983.

Grandjonc, Jacques, and Theresia Grundtner. *Zone d'ombres, 1933–1944: Exil et internement d'allemands et d'autrichiens dans le sud-est de la France.* Aix-en-Provence: Alinea, 1990.

Grossmann, Kurt R. *Emigration: Geschichte der Hitler-Flüchtlinge, 1933–1939.* Frankfurt am Main: Europäische Verlagsanstalt, 1969.

Hirschfeld, Gerhard, ed. *Exile in Great Britain: Refugees from Hitler's Germany.* Atlantic Highlands, N.J.: German Historical Institute, 1984.

Jong, Louis de. *The Netherlands and Nazi Germany.* Cambridge: Harvard University Press, 1990.

Kantorowicz, Alfred. *Exil in Frankreich.* Bremen: Carl Schoenemann, [1971].

Koebner, Thomas, Wulf Köpke, and Claus-Dieter Krohn, eds. *Politische Aspekte des Exils.* Vol. 8 of *Exilforschung: Ein internationales Jahrbuch.* Munich: Text und Kritik, 1990.

Koebner, Thomas, Wulf Köpke, Claus-Dieter Krohn, and Sigrid Schneider, eds. *Das jüdische Exil und andere Themen.* Vol. 4 of *Exilforschung: Ein internationales Jahrbuch.* Munich: Text und Kritik, 1986.

Koebner, Thomas, Wulf Köpke, and Joachim Radkau, eds. *Erinnerungen ans Exil: Kritische Lektüre der Autobiographien nach 1933 und andere Themen.* Vol. 2 of *Exilforschung: Ein internationales Jahrbuch.* Munich: Text und Kritik, 1984.

Krohn, Claus-Dieter, Erwin Rotermund, Lutz Winckler, and Wulf Köpke, eds. *Exil und Remigration.* Vol. 9 of *Exilforschung: Ein internationales Jahrbuch.* Munich: Text und Kritik, 1991.

Langkau-Alex, Ursula. *Volksfront für Deutschland?* Vol. 1 of *Vorgeschichte und Gründung des "Ausschusses zur Vorbereitung einer deutschen Volksfront," 1933–1936.* Frankfurt am Main: Syndikat, 1977.

Levering, Ralph B. *The Public and American Foreign Policy, 1918–1978.* New York: William Morrow, 1978.

Lixl-Purcell, Andreas, ed. *Women of Exile: German-Jewish Autobiographies since 1933.* New York and Westport, Conn.: Greenwood, 1988.

Marrus, Michael R. *The Unwanted: European Refugees in the Twentieth Century.* New York: Oxford University Press, 1985.

Morse, Arthur D. *While Six Million Died: A Chronicle of American Apathy.* New York: Random House, 1967.

Offner, Arnold A. *American Appeasement: United States Foreign Policy and Germany, 1933–1938.* New York: W. W. Norton, 1969.

Pech, Karl Heinz. *An der Seite der Résistance: Zum Kampf der Bewegung Freies Deutschland für den Westen in Frankreich (1943–1945).* Berlin: Militärverlag der Deutschen Demokratischen Republik, 1974.

Quack, Sibylle, ed. *Between Sorrow and Strength: Women Refugees of the Nazi Period.* Cambridge and New York: Cambridge University Press, 1995.

Radkau, Joachim. *Die deutsche Emigration in den U.S.A.: Ihr Einfluß auf die amerikanische Europapolitik, 1933–1945.* Düsseldorf: Bertelsmann Universitätsverlag, 1971.

Röder, Werner. *Die deutschen sozialistischen Exilgruppen in Großbritannien: Ein Beitrag zur Geschichte des Widerstandes gegen den Nationalsozialismus.* Hannover: Verlag für Literatur und Zeitgeschehen, 1968.

Rothchild, Sylvia. *Voices from the Holocaust.* Foreword by Elie Wiesel. New York: NAL Books, 1981.

Schapiro, Michael. "German Refugees in France." *Contemporary Jewish Record* 3 (March–April 1943): 134–40.

Schmitt, Hans A. *Lucky Victim: An Ordinary Life in Extraordinary Times, 1933–1946.* Baton Rouge: Louisiana State University Press, 1989.

Schoumans, Jan. *The Great Silent Battle.* New York: Vantage, 1991.

Schramm, Hanna. *Menschen in Gurs: Erinnerungen an ein französischen Internierungslager (1940–1941).* Worms: Georg Heintz, 1977.

Shirer, William L. *Twentieth-Century Journey: A Memoir of the Life and the Times.* Vol. 2, *The Nightmare Years, 1930–40.* Boston: Little, Brown, 1984.

Spalek, John M. *Guide to the Archival Materials of the German-Speaking Emigration to the United States after 1933.* 2 vols. Charlottesville: University Press of Virginia, 1978–92.

Steinhoff, Johannes, Peter Pechel, and Dennis Showalter. *Voices from the Third Reich: An Oral History.* Washington, D.C.: Regnery Gateway, 1989.

Strauss, Herbert A., ed. *Jewish Immigrants of the Nazi Period in the U.S.A.* 6 vols. New York and Munich: K. G. Saur; Detroit: Gale Research, 1978–92.

Trommler, Frank, and Joseph McVeigh, eds. *America and the Germans: An Assessment of a Three-Hundred-Year History.* Vol. 2, *The Relationship in the Twentieth Century.* Philadelphia: University of Pennsylvania Press, 1985.

Tutas, Herbert, E. *NS-Propaganda und deutsches Exil, 1933–1939.* Meisenheim and Glan: A. Hain, 1973.

Voigt, Klaus, ed. *Friedenssicherung und europäische Einigung: Ideen des deutschen Exils, 1939–1945.* Frankfurt am Main: Fischer-Taschenbuch, 1988.

Warmbrunn, Werner. *The Dutch under German Occupation, 1940–1945*. Stanford: Stanford University Press, 1963.

Wyman, David S. *The Abandonment of the Jews: America and the Holocaust, 1941–1945*. New York: Pantheon, 1984.

Zentner, Kurt. *Illustrierte Geschichte des Dritten Reiches*. 2 vols. Cologne: Lingen, [c. 1966].

_____. *Illustrierte Geschichte des Widerstandes in Deutschland und Europa, 1933–1945*. Munich: Südwest, 1966.

VISUAL ARTS AND CULTURE

Primary Sources

Artists in Exile. Exh. brochure. New York: Pierre Matisse Gallery, 1942.

Barr, Alfred H., Jr. "Art in the Third Reich—Preview, 1933." *Magazine of Art* 38 (October 1945): 212–22.

Bihalji-Merin, Oto [Peter Theone]. *Modern German Art*. Translated by Charles Fullman. Harmondsworth: Penguin, 1938.

Breton, André. *La situation du surréalisme entre les deux guerres*. Paris: Editions de la Revue Fontaine, 1945.

Coordinating Council of French Relief Societies. *First Papers of Surrealism: Hanging by André Breton: His Twine, Marcel Duchamp, 14 October–7 November 1942*. Exh. cat. New York: Coordinating Council of French Relief Societies, 1942.

Duggan, Stephen, and Betty Drury. *The Rescue of Science and Learning: The Story of the Emergency Committee in Aid of Displaced Foreign Scholars*. New York: Macmillan, 1948.

Europe in America: Berman, Chagall, Dali, Ernst, Grosz, Hayter, Hélion, Léger, Lipchitz, Masson, Matta, Moholy-Nagy, Mondrian, Mopp, Ozenfant, Seligmann, Tanguy, Tchelitchew, March 27–April 24, 1943. Exh. brochure. Boston: Institute of Modern Art, 1943.

European Artists in Exile. Exh. cat. New York: Whitney Museum of American Art, 1945.

European Artists Teaching in America. Exh. cat. Andover, Mass.: Addison Gallery of American Art, Phillips Academy, 1941.

Exhibition of Twentieth-Century German Art. Exh. brochure. London: New Burlington Galleries, 1938.

"57th Street." *Fortune* 34 (September 1946).

Forbidden Art in the Third Reich: Paintings by German Artists Whose Work Was Banned from Museums and Forbidden to Exhibit. Exh. brochure, Institute of Modern Art, Boston; Nierendorf Gallery, New York. [New York]: n.p., 1945.

Fry, Varian. *Surrender on Demand*. New York: Random House, 1945.

German Art. Exh. brochure. Springfield Museum of Fine Arts. N.p., 1939.

Gerry, Philippa. "German Painting." *American Magazine of Art* 29 (December 1936): 795–805.

Greenberg, Clement. "Surrealist Painting." Parts 1, 2. *Nation* 159 (12–19 August 1944): 192–93, 219–20.

Gropius, Walter. *Rebuilding Our Communities*. Chicago: Paul Theobald, 1945.

Guggenheim, Peggy. *Out of This Century: The Informal Memories of Peggy Guggenheim*. New York: Dial, 1946.

_____, ed. *Art of This Century: Objects—Drawings—Photographs—Paintings—Sculpture—Collages, 1910 to 1942*. New York: Art of This Century, 1942.

Hoffmeister, Adolf. *The Animals Are in Cages, Written and Drawn by Hoffmeister*. New York: Greenberg, 1941.

Janis, Sidney. *Abstract and Surrealist Art in America*. New York: Reynal and Hitchcock, 1944.

_____. "School of Paris Comes to U.S." *Decision: A Review of Free Culture* 2 (November–December 1941): 86–95.

Johnson, Alvin. "The Refugee Scholar in America." *Survey Graphic* 30 (April 1941): 226–28.

Kirstein, Lincoln. "Art in the Third Reich—Survey, 1945." *Magazine of Art* 38 (October 1945): 223–42.

Lazareff, Pierre. "French Spirit vs. Nazi Peace." *Decision: A Review of Free Culture* 1 (March 1941): 27–33.

Mann, Heinrich, Wystan H. Auden, Max Ascoli, Karin Michaelis, and Frank Kingdon. "Symposium." *Decision: A Review of Free Culture* 1 (January 1941): 44–49.

Mann, Klaus. "Surrealist Circus." *American Mercury* 56 (February 1943): 174–81.

Pinthus, Kurt. "Culture inside Nazi Germany." *American Scholar* 9 (4 October 1939): 483–98.

Read, Herbert. *The Politics of the Unpolitical*. London: Routledge, 1943.

Stein, Nina. "Plans for a Post-War World: A Survey." *Decision: A Review of Free Culture* 1 (February 1941): 48–57.

Sweeney, James Johnson. "Eleven Europeans in America." *Bulletin of the Museum of Modern Art* 13, no. 4–5 (1946).

Whiting, Philippa. "Speaking about Art: Germany Sharpens Her Noblest Weapon." *American Magazine of Art* 28 (July 1935): 435–38.

"Who Teaches Who? This Is What European Artists Have Been Doing in America." *Art News* 40 (15–31 October 1941): 18–19.

Wüsten, Ernst. "Künstler im Exil." *Bildende Kunst* 1 (1947): 29–32.

Secondary Sources

Abadie, Daniele, Hélène Seckel, and Alfred Pacquement. *Paris—New York: 1908–1968*. Rev. ed. Paris: Editions du Centre Pompidou; Editions Gallimard, 1991.

American Artists' Congress, New York. *Artists against War and Fascism: Papers of the First American Artists' Congress*. New Brunswick, N.J.: Rutgers University Press, 1986.

American Center for Students and Artists, Paris. *Artistes en exil, 1939–1946, U.S.A.: Exposition du 16 mai au 6 juin 1968*. Exh. cat. Paris: American Center for Students and Artists, 1968.

Amishai-Maisels, Ziva. *Depiction and Interpretation: The Influence of the Holocaust on the Visual Arts*. Oxford and New York: Pergamon, 1993.

Art in Britain, 1930–40, Centered around Axis, Circle, Unit One. Exh. cat. London and New York: Marlborough Fine Art, 1965.

Ateliergemeinschaft Klosterstraße Berlin, 1933–1945: Künstler in der Zeit der Nationalsozialismus. Exh. cat., Akademie der Künste. Berlin: Edition Hentrich, 1944.

Bammer, Angelika, ed. *Displacements: Cultural Identities in Question.* Bloomington and Indianapolis: Indiana University Press, 1994.

Barron, Stephanie, et al. *"Degenerate Art": The Fate of the Avant-Garde in Nazi Germany.* Los Angeles: Los Angeles County Museum of Art; New York: Harry N. Abrams, 1991.

Bendix, Reinhard. *From Berlin to Berkeley: German-Jewish Identities.* New Brunswick, N.J.: Transaction, 1986.

Bentwich, Norman De Mattos. *The Rescue and Achievement of Refugee Scholars: The Story of Displaced Scholars and Scientists, 1933–1952.* The Hague: M. Nijhoff, 1953.

Berghaus, Günter, ed. *Theatre and Film in Exile: German Artists in Britain, 1933–1945.* Oxford and New York: Oswald Wolff; St. Martin's, 1989.

Berthold, Werner, and Brita Eckert, eds. *Der deutsche PEN-Club im Exil, 1933–1948: Eine Ausstellung der Deutschen Bibliothek Frankfurt am Main.* Frankfurt am Main: Buchhändler-Vereinigung, 1980.

Berthold, Werner, Brita Eckert, and Frank Wende. *Deutsche Intellektuelle im Exil: Ihre Akademie und die "American Guild for German Cultural Freedom": Eine Ausstellung des Deutschen Exilarchivs 1933–1945 der Deutschen Bibliothek, Frankfurt am Main.* Munich: K. G. Saur, 1993.

Bertrand Dorléac, Laurence. *L'art de la défaite, 1940–1944.* Paris: Editions du Seuil, 1993.

———. *Histoire de l'art, Paris, 1940–1944: Ordre national, traditions et modernités.* Paris: Publications de la Sorbonne, 1986.

Betz, Albrecht. *Exil und Engagement: Deutsche Schriftsteller im Frankreich der dreissiger Jahre.* Munich: Text und Kritik, 1986.

Bhabha, Homi K. *The Location of Culture.* London and New York: Routledge, 1994.

Blatter, Janet, and Sybil Milton. *Art of the Holocaust.* New York: Routledge, 1981.

Blesh, Rudi. *Modern Art U.S.A.: Men, Rebellion, and Conquest, 1900–1956.* New York: Knopf, 1956.

Bluhm, Lothar. *Das Tagebuch zum Dritten Reich: Zeugnisse der inneren Emigration von Jochen Klepper bis Ernst Jünger.* Bonn: Bouvier, 1991.

Blum, John Morton. *V Was for Victory: Politics and American Culture during World War II.* New York: Harcourt Brace Jovanovich, 1976.

Bogner, Dieter, ed. *Friedrich Kiesler: Architekt, Maler, Bildhauer, 1890–1965.* Vienna: Locker, 1988.

Bolle, Michael, ed. *Stationen der Moderne: Die bedeutenden Kunstausstellungen des 20. Jahrhunderts in Deutschland.* Berlin: Berlinische Galerie, Museum für moderne Kunst, Photographie, und Architektur, 1988.

Boxer, Adam J., ed. *The New Bauhaus School of Design in Chicago: Photographs, 1937–1944.* Exh. cat. New York: Banning and Associates, 1993.

Boyers, Robert, ed. *The Legacy of the German Refugee Intellectuals.* New York: Schocken, 1972.

Britain and the Refugee Crisis, 1933–1947. London: Imperial War Museum, Department of Sound Records, 1982.

Cassel, Wolf van. "Wolfgang Frommel (1902–1986): Ein Humanist im holländischen Exil." *Exil* 9, no. 1 (1989): 82–87.

Castleman, Riva, ed. *Art of the Forties.* New York: Museum of Modern Art; Harry N. Abrams, 1991.

Chambers, Iain. *Migrancy, Culture, Identity.* London and New York: Routledge, 1994.

Chappell, Connery. *Island of Barbed Wire: Internment on the Isle of Man in World War Two.* London: Robert Hale, 1984.

Codrescu, Andrei, and Terence Pitts. *Points of Entry: Reframing America.* Exh. cat., Center for Creative Photography. Albuquerque: University of New Mexico Press, 1995.

Coke, David, ed. *Hans Feibusch: The Heat of Vision.* London: Lund Humphries; Pallant House Gallery Trust, 1995.

Cone, Michèle C. *Artists under Vichy: A Case of Prejudice and Persecution.* Princeton: Princeton University Press, 1992.

Dobson, Zuleika, and Monica Bohm-Duchen. *Art in Exile in Great Britain 1933–45.* Exh. cat. London: Camden Arts Centre, 1986.

Fermi, Laura. *Illustrious Immigrants: The Intellectual Migration from Europe, 1930–1941.* Chicago: University of Chicago Press, 1968.

Findeli, Alain. "Design Education and Industry: The Laborious Beginnings of the Institute of Design in Chicago in 1944." *Journal of Design History* 4, no. 2 (1991): 97–113.

Fleming, Donald, and Bernard Bailyn, eds. *The Intellectual Migration: Europe and America, 1930–1960.* Cambridge: Harvard University Press, 1969.

Flying Tigers: Painting and Sculpture in New York, 1939–1946. Exh. cat. Providence: Bell Gallery, Brown University, 1985.

Frank, Volker. "Europäische Plastik in den U.S.A.: Aspekte internationaler Kunstprozesse von 1930 bis 1946." *Bildende Kunst*, no. 4 (1986): 170–73.

Fulton, Jean, et al. *A History of the Renaissance Society: The First Seventy-Five Years.* Chicago: Renaissance Society at the University of Chicago, 1994.

Gillen, Eckhart, and Yvonne Leonard, eds. *Amerika: Traum und Depression, 1920/40.* Berlin: Neue Gesellschaft für bildende Kunst, 1980.

Golomstock, Igor. *Totalitarian Art in the Soviet Union, the Third Reich, Fascist Italy, and the People's Republic of China.* Translated by Robert Chandler. London: Collins Harvill, 1990.

Goodman, Cynthia. "Frederick Kiesler: Design for Peggy Guggenheim's Art of This Century Gallery." *Arts* 51 (June 1977): 90–95.

Grimm, Reinhold, and Jost Hermand, eds. *Exil und innere Emigration: Third Wisconsin Workshop.* Frankfurt am Main: Athenäum, 1972.

Grunewald, Michel, ed. *Die deutsche Literaturkritik im europäischen Exil (1933–1940).* Bern and New York: Peter Lang, 1993.

Grunewald, Michel, and Frithjof Trapp, eds. *Autour du "Front Populaire Allemand": Einheitsfront, Volksfront: Etudes.* Bern and New York: Peter Lang, 1990.

Guida-Laforgia, Patrizia. *Invisible Women Writers in Exile in the U.S.A.* Bern and New York: Peter Lang, 1995.

Guilbaut, Serge. *How New York Stole the Idea of Modern Art: Abstract Expressionism, Freedom, and the Cold War.* Chicago: University of Chicago Press, 1983.

Haftmann, Werner. *Verfemte Kunst: Bildende Künstler der inneren und äußeren Emigration in der Zeit des Nationalsozialismus.* Cologne: DuMont, 1986. Translated by Eileen Martin, under the title *Banned and Persecuted: Dictatorship of Art under Hitler.* Cologne: DuMont, 1986.

Hahn, Ulla. "Der Freie deutsche Kulturbund in Großbritannien: Eine Skizze seiner Geschichte." In *Antifaschistische Literatur*, vol. 2, ed. Lutz Winkler, 131–95. Kronberg/Taunus: Scriptor, 1977.

Heilbut, Anthony. *Exiled in Paradise: German Refugee Artists and Intellectuals in America from the 1930s to the Present.* New York: Viking, 1983.

Heller, Gerhard. *Un allemand à Paris: 1940–1944.* Paris: Editions du Seuil, 1981.

Hermsdorf, Klaus, Hugo Fetting, and Silvia Schlenstedt. *Exil in den Niederlanden und in Spanien*. Frankfurt am Main: Roderberg, 1981.

Heuberger, Georg, ed. *Expressionismus und Exil: Die Sammlung Ludwig und Rosy Fischer, Frankfurt am Main*. Exh. cat., Jüdisches Museum, Frankfurt am Main. Munich: Prestel, 1990.

Hirschfeld, Gerhard, and Patrick S. Marsh, eds. *Collaboration in France: Politics and Culture during the Nazi Occupation, 1940–1944*. Oxford and New York: Berg, 1989.

Hoffmann, Ludwig, et al., eds. *Exil in der Tschechoslowakei, in Großbritannien, Skandinavien, und Palästina*. Leipzig: Reclam, 1981.

Hohendahl, Peter Uwe, and Egon Schwarz, eds. *Exil und innere Emigration II: Internationale Tagung in St. Louis*. Frankfurt am Main: Athenäum, 1973.

Holborn, Mark. *Josef Breitenbach: Photographer*. New York: Temple Rock, 1986.

Holz, Keith. *Modern German Art and Its Public in Prague, Paris, and London, 1933–40*. Ann Arbor, Mich.: University Microfilms, 1992.

Jackmann, Jarrell C., and Carla M. Borden, eds. *The Muses Flee Hitler: Cultural Transfer and Adaptation, 1930–1945*. Washington, D.C.: Smithsonian Institution Press, 1983.

Janda, Annegret, and Jörn Grabowski, eds. *Kunst in Deutschland 1905–1937: Die verlorene Sammlung der Nationalgalerie im ehemaligen Kronprinzen-Palais*. Exh. cat., Staatliche Museen zu Berlin. Berlin: Gebrüder Mann, 1992.

Jewish Experience in the Art of the Twentieth Century. Exh. cat. New York: Jewish Museum, 1976.

Johnson, Alvin. *Pioneer's Progress: An Autobiography*. New York: Viking, 1952.

Karlstrom, Paul J. "Los Angeles in the 1940s: Post-Modernism and the Visual Arts." *Southern California Quarterly* 69, no. 4 (1987): 301–28.

Kent, Donald Peterson. *The Refugee Intellectual: The Americanization of the Immigrants of 1933–1941*. New York: Columbia University Press, 1953.

Kentgens-Craig, Margret. *Bauhaus-Architektur: Die Rezeption in Amerika, 1919–1936*. Frankfurt am Main and Berlin: Peter Lang, 1993.

Koebner, Thomas, Wulf Köpke, Claus-Dieter Krohn, and Sigrid Schneider, eds. *Vertreibung der Wissenschaften und andere Themen*. Vol. 6 of *Exilforschung: Ein internationales Jahrbuch*. Munich: Text und Kritik, 1988.

Koller, Gabriele, and Gloria Withalm. *Die Vertreibung des Geistigen aus Österreich: Zur Kulturpolitik des Nationalsozialismus*. Vienna and Salzburg: Zentralsparkasse und Kommerzialbank; Hochschule für angewandte Kunst, 1985.

Krohn, Claus-Dieter, Erwin Rotermund, Lutz Winckler, and Wulf Köpke, eds. *Aspekte der künstlerischen inneren Emigration, 1933–1945*. Vol. 12 of *Exilforschung: Ein internationales Jahrbuch*. Munich: Text und Kritik, 1994.

———. *Frauen und Exil*. Vol. 11 of *Exilforschung: Ein internationales Jahrbuch*. Munich: Text und Kritik, 1993.

———. *Künste in Exil*. Vol. 10 of *Exilforschung: Ein internationales Jahrbuch*. Munich: Text und Kritik, 1992.

Krug, Hartmut, and Michael Nungesser, ed. *Kunst im Exil in Großbritannien, 1933–1945*. Exh. cat. Berlin: Frölich und Kaufmann; Neue Gesellschaft für bildende Kunst, 1986.

Lader, Melvin P. "Howard Putzel: Proponent of Surrealism and Early Abstract Expressionism in America." *Arts* 56 (March 1982): 85–96.

———. *Peggy Guggenheim's Art of This Century: The Surrealist Milieu and the American Avant-Garde, 1942–1947*. Ann Arbor, Mich.: University Microfilms, 1981.

Lader, Melvin P., and Fred Licht. *Peggy Guggenheim's Other Legacy*. Exh. cat. New York: Solomon R. Guggenheim Foundation, 1987

Levine, Bruce, et al. *Who Built America? Working People and the Nation's Economy, Politics, Culture, and Society*. New York: Pantheon, 1989.

Levy, Julien. *Memoir of an Art Gallery*. New York: Putnam, 1977.

Loewy, Ernst, ed. *Exil: Literarische und politische Texte aus dem deutschen Exil, 1933–1945*. 3 vols. Frankfurt am Main: Fischer Taschenbuch, 1981–82.

Luckmann, Benita. "Exil oder Emigration: Aspekte der Amerikanisierung an der 'New School of Social Research' in New York." In *Leben im Exil: Probleme der Integration deutscher Flüchtlinge im Ausland 1933–1945*, edited by Wolfgang Frühwald and Wolfgang Schieder, 227–35. Hamburg: Hoffmann und Campe, 1981.

Maurois, André. *Memoirs, 1885–1967*. New York: Harper and Row, 1970.

McCabe, Cynthia Jaffee. *The Golden Door: Artist-Immigrants of America, 1876–1976*. Exh. cat., Hirshhorn Museum and Sculpture Garden. Washington, D.C.: Smithsonian Institution Press, 1976.

———, ed. *The American Experience: Contemporary Immigrant Artists*. New York: Independent Curators; Philadelphia: Balch Institute for Ethnic Studies, 1985.

Merrill-Mirsky, Carol, ed. *Exiles in Paradise*. Exh. cat. Los Angeles: Hollywood Bowl Museum, Los Angeles Philharmonic Association, 1991.

Middell, Eike, et al. *Exil in den U.S.A.: Mit einem Bericht, Schanghai, eine Emigration am Rande*. Leipzig: Reclam, 1979.

Milton, Sybil. "Is There an Exile Art or Only Exile Artists?" In *Exil: Literatur und die Künste nach 1933*, edited by Alexander Stephan, 83–89. Bonn: Bouvier, 1990.

Mittag, Gabriele, ed. *Gurs: Deutsche Emigrantinnen im französischen Exil*. Berlin: Argon, [1991].

Möller, Horst. *Exodus der Kultur: Schriftsteller, Wissenschaftler, und Künstler in der Emigration nach 1933*. Munich: C. H. Beck, 1984.

Morris, Lynda, and Robert Radford. *The Story of the AIA (Artists International Association), 1933–1954*. Exh. cat. Oxford: Museum of Modern Art, 1983.

Müller, Henning, ed. *Exil-Asyl: Tatort Deutschland: Texte von 1933 bis Heute—Eine literarische Anthologie*. Gerlingen: Lambert Schneider, 1994.

Myers, John Bernard. "Surrealism and New York Painting, 1940–1948: A Reminiscence." *Artforum* 15 (April 1977): 55–57.

Nessen, Susan Weil. *Surrealism in Exile: The Early New York Years, 1940–1942*. 2 vols. Ann Arbor, Mich.: University Microfilms, 1986.

Nettelbeck, Colin W. *Forever French: Exile in the United States, 1939–1945*. New York: Berg, 1991.

Neumann, Franz L., Henri Peyre, Erwin Panofsky, Wolfgang Köhler, and Paul Tillich. *The Cultural Migration: The European Scholar in America*. Philadelphia: University of Pennsylvania Press, 1953.

Nicholas, Lynn H. *The Rape of Europa: The Fate of Europe's Treasures in the Third Reich and the Second World War*. New York: Knopf, 1994.

Noël, Bernard. *Marseille—New York: Une liaison surrealiste/A Surrealist Liaison*. Marseilles: André Dimanche, 1985.

Olbrich, Harald. "Antifaschistische Kunst in der Emigration." *Wissenschaftliche Zeitschrift der Ernst-Moritz-Arndt Universität, Greifswald: Gesellschafts- und Sprachwissenschaftliche Reihe* 15, no. 4 (1966): 431–46.

Onderdelinden, Sjaak, ed. *Interbellum und Exil*. Amsterdam and Atlanta: Rodopi, 1991.

Palmier, Jean-Michel. *Weimar en exil: Le destin de l'émigration intellectuelle allemande antinazie en Europe et aux Etats-Unis*. Paris: Payot, 1988.

Pauli, Hertha Ernestine. *Der Riss der Zeit geht durch mein Herz: Ein Erlebnisbuch.* Vienna and Hamburg: Paul Zsolnay, 1970.

Pfanner, Helmut F. *Kulturelle Wechselbeziehungen im Exil/Exile across Cultures.* Bonn: Bouvier, 1986.

———, ed. *Der Zweite Weltkrieg und die Exilanten: Eine literarische Antwort/World War II and the Exiles: A Literary Response.* Bonn: Bouvier, 1991.

Phillips, Lisa. *Frederick Kiesler.* Exh. cat. New York: Whitney Museum of American Art; W. W. Norton, 1989.

Plessner, Monika. "Die deutsche 'University in Exile': New York und ihr amerikanischer Gründer." *Frankfurter Hefte* 19 (1964): 181–86.

Pross, Helge. *Die deutsche akademische Emigration nach den Vereinigten Staaten.* Berlin: Duncker und Humblot, 1955.

Radford, Robert. *Art for a Purpose: The Artists' International Association, 1933–1953.* Winchester, Hampshire: Winchester School of Art Press, 1987.

Raeithel, Gert. *Geschichte der nordamerikanischen Kultur.* Vol. 3, *Vom New Deal bis zur Gegenwart, 1930–1988.* Weinheim and Berlin: Quadriga, 1989.

Röder, Werner, and Herbert A. Strauss, eds. *International Biographical Dictionary of Central European Emigrés, 1933–1945.* Vol. 2, *The Arts, Sciences, and Literature.* Munich and New York: K. G. Saur, 1980–83.

Roters, Eberhard, and Gisela-Ingeborg Bolduan. *Aus Berlin emigriert: Werke Berliner Künstler, die Deutschland nach 1933 verlassen mußten.* Exh. cat. Berlin: Berlinische Galerie, 1983.

Rudenstine, Angelica Zander. *Peggy Guggenheim Collection, Venice: The Solomon R. Guggenheim Foundation.* New York: Harry N. Abrams; Solomon R. Guggenheim Foundation, 1985.

Rüger, Maria, ed. *Kunst und Kunstkritik der dreissiger Jahre: 29 Standpunkte zu künstlerischen und ästhetischen Prozessen und Kontroversen.* Dresden: Verlag der Kunst, 1990.

Said, Edward W. *Identity, Authority, and Freedom: The Potentate and the Traveller.* [Cape Town]: University of Cape Town, 1991.

———. "Reflections on Exile." In *Out There: Marginalization and Contemporary Cultures,* edited by Russell Ferguson, 357–66. New York: New Museum of Contemporary Art; Cambridge: MIT Press, 1990.

———. *Representations of the Intellectual.* New York: Pantheon, 1994.

Sanders, Marion K. *Dorothy Thompson: A Legend in Her Time.* Boston: Houghton Mifflin, 1973.

Sawin, Martica. *Surrealism in Exile and the Beginnings of the New York School.* Cambridge and London: MIT Press, 1995.

Schaber, Will. *Aufbau: Reconstruction.* New York: Overlook, 1972.

Schiller, Dieter. "Der 'freie Künstlerbund 1938': Eine antifaschistische Kulturorganisation im Pariser Exil." *Bildende Kunst,* no. 11 (1987): 485–87.

Schiller, Dieter, et al. *Exil in Frankreich.* Frankfurt am Main: Röderberg, 1981.

Schmidt, Diether, ed. *In letzter Stunde, 1933–1945.* Dresden: Verlag der Kunst, 1964.

Schmidt, Georg. *Die Malerei in Deutschland, 1918–1955.* Königstein im Taunus: K. R. Langewiesche Nachfolger, 1960.

Schoenberger, Gerhard, ed. *Artists against Hitler: Persecution, Exile, Resistance.* Translated by Patricia Crampton. Bonn: Inter Nationes, 1984.

Selz, Peter. "The Impact from Abroad: Foreign Guests and Visitors." In *On the Edge of America: California Modernist Art, 1900–1950,* ed. Paul J. Karlstrom. Berkeley: University of California Press, 1996.

Shedletzky, Itta, and Hans Otto Horch. *Deutsch-jüdische Exil- und Emigrantenliteratur im 20. Jahrhundert.* Tübingen: Max Niemeyer, 1993.

Silver, Kenneth E., and Romy Golan. *The Circle of Montparnasse: Jewish Artists in Paris, 1905–1945.* Exh. cat., Jewish Museum, New York. New York: Universe Books, 1985.

Smyth, Craig Hugh, and Peter M. Lukehart. *The Early Years of Art History in the United States: Notes on Departments, Teaching, and Scholars.* Princeton: Department of Art and Archeology, Princeton University, 1993.

Spiritual Resistance: Art from Concentration Camps, 1940–1945: A Selection of Drawings and Paintings from the Collection of Kibbutz Lochamei HaGhettaot, Israel. New York: Union of American Hebrew Congregations, 1978.

Steinweis, Alan E. *Art, Ideology, and Economics in Nazi Germany: The Reich Chambers of Music, Theater, and the Visual Arts.* Chapel Hill: University of North Carolina Press, 1993.

Strauss, Herbert A., Tilmann Buddensieg, and Kurt Düwell. *Emigration: Deutsche Wissenschaftler nach 1933: Entlassung und Vertreibung: List of Displaced German Scholars 1936: Supplementary List of Displaced German Scholars 1937: The Emergency Committee in Aid of Displaced Foreign Scholars: Report 1941.* Berlin: Technische Universität Berlin, 1987.

El surrealismo entre viejo y nuevo mundo. Exh. cat. Sala de Exposiciones de la Fundacion Cultural Mapfre Vida. Las Palmas de Gran Canaria: Cabildo Insular de Gran Canaria, Centro Atlantico de Arte Moderno, 1989.

Susman, Warren, ed. *Culture and Commitment, 1929–1945.* New York: Braziller, 1973.

Ta'arukhat zikaron: Omanium yehudim she-nispu ba-sho'ah/ Memorial Exhibition: Jewish Artists Who Perished in the Holocaust. Tel Aviv: Tel Aviv Museum, 1968.

Tashjian, Dickran. *A Boatload of Madmen: Surrealism and the American Avant-garde, 1920–1950.* New York: Thames and Hudson, 1995.

Taylor, John Russell. *Strangers in Paradise: The Hollywood Emigrés, 1933–1950.* London: Faber and Faber, 1983.

Tschirner, Manfred. *Kurt Lade, 1905–1973: Exil in Prag und London.* Exh. cat. Berlin: Staatliche Museen zu Berlin, Hauptstadt der DDR, Nationalgalerie, 1985.

Venema, Adriaan. *Kunsthandel in Nederland, 1940–1945.* Amsterdam: Arbeiderspres, 1986.

Wechsler, Jeffrey. *Surrealism and American Art, 1931–1947.* Exh. cat. New Brunswick, N.J.: Rutgers University Art Gallery, 1976.

Weld, Jacqueline Bograd. *Peggy: The Wayward Guggenheim.* New York: Dutton, 1986.

Werner, Klaus Ulrich. *Exil im Archiv: "Das Deutsche Exilarchiv 1933–1945" der Deutschen Bibliothek.* Herzberg: Traugott Bautz, 1992.

Westheim, Paul. *Kunstkritik aus dem Exil.* Hanau am Main: Müller und Kiepenheuer, 1985.

Widerstand statt Anpassung: Deutsche Kunst im Widerstand gegen den Faschismus, 1933–1945. Exh. cat., Badischer Kunstverein, Karlsruhe. Berlin: Elefanten Press, 1980.

Würzner, Hans, and Karl Kröhnke, eds. *Deutsche Literatur im Exil in den Niederlanden, 1933–1940.* Amsterdam and Atlanta: Rodopi, 1994.

Zwischen Widerstand und Anpassung: Kunst in Deutschland, 1933–1945. Exh. cat. Akademie-Katalog 120. Berlin: Akademie der Künste, 1978.

ARTISTS

Josef Albers

Albers, Josef. "Art as Experience." *Progressive Education* 12 (October 1935), 391–93.

———. "The Educational Value of Manual Work and Handicraft in Relation to Architecture." In *New Architecture and City Planning: A Symposium*, ed. Paul Zucker, 688–94. New York: Philosophical Library, 1944.

Duberman, Martin. *Black Mountain: An Exploration in Community*. New York: Dutton, 1972.

Feeney, Kelly. *Josef Albers: Works on Paper*. Exh. cat. Alexandria, Va.: Art Services International, 1991.

Harris, Mary Emma. *The Arts at Black Mountain College*. Cambridge: MIT Press, 1987.

Lane, Mervin, ed. "Josef Albers (Faculty 1933–49): March 1965 Interview." In *Black Mountain College: Sprouted Seeds: An Anthology of Personal Accounts*, 33–41. Knoxville: University of Tennessee Press, 1990.

Nordland, Gerald. *Josef Albers: The American Years*. Exh. cat. Washington, D.C.: Washington Gallery of Modern Art, 1965.

Spies, Werner. *Albers*. New York: Harry N. Abrams, 1970.

Weber, Nicholas Fox. *Josef Albers: A Retrospective*. Exh. cat. New York: Solomon R. Guggenheim Foundation, 1988.

Wissmann, Jürgen. *Josef Albers*. Recklinghausen: Aurel Bongers, 1971.

Max Beckmann

Barker, Walter. "Max Beckmann in America." In *Max Beckmann*, edited by Siegfried Gohr, 111–31. Exh. cat. Cologne: Josef-Haubrich-Kunsthalle, 1984.

Beckmann, Mathilde Q. *Mein Leben mit Max Beckmann*. Munich: R. Piper, 1985.

Beckmann, Max. *Tagebücher, 1940–1950*. Munich: Albert Langen; Georg Müller, 1955.

Buenger, Barbara C. *Max Beckmann's Artistic Sources*. Ann Arbor, Mich.: University Microfilms, 1981.

———, ed. *Max Beckmann: Self-Portrait in Words: Collected Writings and Statements, 1903–1950*. Chicago: University of Chicago Press, 1996.

Clark, Margot Orthwein. *Max Beckmann: Sources of Imagery in the Hermetic Tradition*. Ann Arbor, Mich.: University Microfilms, 1977.

Göpel, Erhard, and Barbara Göpel. *Max Beckmann: Katalog der Gemälde*. 2 vols. Bern: Kornfeld, 1976.

Lackner, Stephan. *Ich erinnere mich gut an Max Beckmann*. Mainz: Florian Kupferberg, 1967. Published in English as *Max Beckmann: Memories of a Friendship*. Coral Gables: University of Miami Press, 1969.

Maur, Karin von, ed. *Max Beckmann: Meisterwerke, 1907–1950*. Exh. cat. Staatsgalerie Stuttgart. Stuttgart: Gerd Hatje, 1994.

Max Beckmann in America. Exh. cat. New York: Catherine Viviano Gallery, 1969.

Schulz-Hoffmann, Carla, and Judith C. Weiss, eds. *Max Beckmann: Retrospective*. Exh. cat., Saint Louis Art Museum. Munich: Prestel, 1984.

Marcel Breuer

Blake, Peter, ed. *Marcel Breuer: Sun and Shadow: The Philosophy of an Architect*. New York: Dodd, Mead, 1956.

Herdeg, Klaus. *The Decorated Diagram: Harvard Architecture and the Failure of the Bauhaus Legacy*. Cambridge: MIT Press, 1983.

Jordy, William. *American Buildings and Their Architects*. Garden City, N.Y.: Doubleday, 1970.

Masello, David. *Architecture without Rules: The Houses of Marcel Breuer and Herbert Beckhard*. New York: W. W. Norton, 1993.

Wilk, Christopher. *Marcel Breuer: Furniture and Interiors*. Exh. cat. New York: Museum of Modern Art, 1981.

Marc Chagall

Abel, Raymond. "An Interview with Marc Chagall." *League* 14 (April 1942): 7.

Amishai-Maisels, Ziva. "The Artist as Refugee." *Studies in Contemporary Jewry* 6 (1990): 111–48.

Chagall, Marc. "Marc Chagall nous parle de l'Amérique." *Voix de France*, 15 May 1942, 8.

———. "Message de Marc Chagall aux peintres français." *Spectateur des arts*, no. 1 (December 1944): 3.

———. *Poèmes*. Translated by Assia Lassaigne and Philippe Jaccottet. Geneva: Cramer, 1968.

———. "Unity Is the Soul of Culture." *Jewish Life* 2 (suppl.) (November 1947): 3–5.

Haggard-Leirends, V. *My Life with Chagall: Seven Years of Plenty with the Master, as Told by the Woman Who Shared Them*. New York: Donald Fine, 1986.

Kagan, Andrew. *Marc Chagall*. New York: Abbeville, 1989.

Meyer, Franz. *Marc Chagall: Leben und Werk*. Cologne: DuMont Schauberg, [1961]. Translated by Robert Allen, under the title *Marc Chagall*. New York: Harry N. Abrams, 1964.

Sweeney, James Johnson. "An Interview with Marc Chagall." *Partisan Review* 11 (Winter 1944): 88–93.

Salvador Dali

Abadie, Daniel, et al., eds. *Salvador Dali: Retrospective, 1920–1980*. Exh. cat. Paris: Centre Georges Pompidou, [1980].

Catterall, Lee. *The Great Dali Art Fraud and Other Deceptions*. Fort Lee, N.J.: Barricade Books, 1992.

Dali, Salvador. *Hidden Faces*. Translated by Haakon M. Chevalier. New York: Dial, 1944.

———. *The Secret Life of Salvador Dali*. Translated by Haakon M. Chevalier. New York: Dial, 1942.

Descharnes, Robert, and Gilles Néret. *Salvador Dali, 1904–1989: The Paintings*. 2 vols. Cologne: Benedikt Taschen, 1994.

Etherington-Smith, Meredith. *The Persistence of Memory: A Biography of Dali*. New York: Random House, 1992.

Gallwitz, Klaus, ed. *Salvador Dali*. Exh. cat. Frankfurt: Städtische Galerie and Städelsches Kunstinstitut, 1974.

Maur, Karin von. *Salvador Dali, 1904–1989*. Exh. cat. Staatsgalerie Stuttgart. Stuttgart: G. Hatje; Heiden: A. Niggli, 1989.

Sandoz, Maurice. *Fantastic Memories: Illustrations by Salvador Dali*. Garden City, N.Y.: Doubleday, Doran, 1944.

Soby, James Thrall. *Salvador Dali*. Exh. cat. New York: Museum of Modern Art, 1941.

Max Ernst

Cowling, Elizabeth. "The Eskimos, the American Indians, and the Surrealists." *Art History* 1 (December 1978): 484–500.

Ernst, Max. *Beyond Painting and Other Writings by the Artist and His Friends*. New York: Wittenborn Schultz, 1948.

———. *Ecritures*. Paris: Gallimard, 1970.

Lake, Johannes auf der. *Skulpturen von Max Ernst: Ästhetische Theorie und Praxis*. Frankfurt am Main and New York: Peter Lang, 1986.

Max Ernst: A Retrospective. Exh. cat. New York: Solomon R. Guggenheim Foundation, 1975.

Patyk, Urs. *Max Ernst und Paul Delvaux: Bildstruktur und Erzählmodi in den Bildern zwischen 1938 und 1960*. Frankfurt am Main and New York: Peter Lang, 1988.

Spies, Werner. *Max Ernst, Collagen: Inventar und Widerspruch*. Cologne: DuMont Schauberg, 1974.

———, ed. *Max Ernst: Oeuvre Katalog*. Vol. 5, *Werke 1939–1953*. Houston: Menil Foundation; Cologne: DuMont Schauberg, 1975.

———. *Max Ernst: Retrospective zum 100. Geburtstag*. Exh. cat. Munich: Prestel, 1991.

Andreas Feininger

Feininger, Andreas. *Andreas Feininger: A Retrospective.* Exh. cat. New York: International Center of Photography, 1976.

———. *Andreas Feininger, Photographer.* New York: Harry N. Abrams, 1986.

———. *Feininger on Photography.* Chicago: Ziff-Davis, 1949.

———. *New Paths in Photography.* Boston: American Photographic, 1939.

Hattersley, Ralph. *Andreas Feininger.* Dobbs Ferry, N.Y.: Morgan and Morgan, 1973.

Lyonel Feininger

Büche, Wolfgang, ed. *Lyonel Feininger: Gelmeroda: Ein Maler und sein Motiv.* Exh. cat., Staatliche Galerie Moritzburg, Halle. Stuttgart: G. Hatje, 1995.

Büche, Wolfgang, Andreas Huneke, and Peter Romanus, eds. *Lyonel Feininger: Die Halle Bilder.* Exh. cat., Staatliche Galerie Moritzburg, Halle. Munich: Prestel, 1991.

Exhibition Lyonel Feininger. Exh. cat. New York: Acquavella Galleries, 1985.

Firmenich, Andrea, and Ulrich Luckhardt, eds. *Lyonel Feininger, Natur-Notizen: Skizzen und Zeichnungen aus dem Busch-Reisinger Museum, Harvard University.* Exh. cat. Cologne: Wienand, 1993.

Hauser, Stephan E., ed. *Feininger and Tobey: Years of Friendship, 1944–1956: The Complete Correspondence.* New York: Achim Möller Fine Art, 1991.

Hess, Hans. *Lyonel Feininger.* New York: Harry N. Abrams, [1961].

Luckhardt, Ulrich. *Lyonel Feininger.* Munich: Prestel, 1989.

Lyonel Feininger, Städte und Küsten: Aquarelle, Zeichnungen, Druckgrafik. Exh. cat., Kunsthalle, Nuremberg. Marburg: Hitzeroth, 1992.

Miller, Dorothy C., ed. *Lyonel Feininger, Marsden Hartley.* Exh. cat. New York: Museum of Modern Art, 1944.

Ness, June L., ed. *Lyonel Feininger.* New York: Praeger, 1974.

Prasse, Leona E. *Lyonel Feininger: Das graphische Werk: Radierungen, Lithographien, Holzschnitt/ A Definitive Catalogue of His Graphic Work: Etchings, Lithographs, Woodcuts.* Berlin: Gebrüder Mann; Cleveland: Cleveland Museum of Art, 1972.

Walter Gropius

Bayer. Herbert, Walter Gropius, and Ise Gropius, eds. *Bauhaus, 1919–1928.* Exh. cat. New York: Museum of Modern Art, 1938.

Cormier, Leslie Humm. "Walter Gropius, Emigré Architect: Works and Refuge: England and America in the 30s." Ph.D. diss., Brown University, 1986.

Gropius, Walter, et al., eds. *The Architects Collaborative, 1945–65.* New York: Architectural Book Publishing, 1966.

Herbert, Gilbert. *The Dream of the Factory-Made House: Walter Gropius and Konrad Wachsmann.* Cambridge: MIT Press, 1984.

Isaacs, Reginald R. *Walter Gropius: Der Mensch und sein Werk.* Berlin: Gebrüder Mann, 1983–84. Published in English as *Gropius: An Illustrated Biography of the Creator of the Bauhaus.* Boston: Little, Brown, 1991.

Jordy, William. "The Aftermath of the Bauhaus in America: Gropius, Mies, and Breuer." In *The Intellectual Migration: Europe and America, 1930–1960,* ed. Donald Fleming and Bernard Bailyn, 485–543. Cambridge: Harvard University Press, 1969.

Nerdinger, Winfried. *Walter Gropius.* Exh. cat., Bauhaus-Archiv, Berlin; Busch-Reisinger Museum, Cambridge, Mass. Berlin: Gebrüder Mann, 1985.

———, ed. *Bauhaus-Moderne im Nationalsozialismus: Zwischen Anbiederung und Verfolgung.* Munich: Prestel, 1993.

———. *The Walter Gropius Archive: An Illustrated Catalogue of the Drawings, Prints, and Photographs in the Walter Gropius Archive at the Busch-Reisinger Museum, Harvard University.* 4 vols. New York: Garland; Cambridge: Harvard University Art Museums, 1990–91.

George Grosz

Baur, John I. H. *George Grosz.* Exh. cat. New York: Whitney Museum of American Art, 1954.

Dückers, Alexander. *George Grosz: Das druckgraphische Werk.* Frankfurt am Main: Propylaen, 1979.

Flavell, M. Kay. *George Grosz: A Biography.* New Haven: Yale University Press, 1988.

Gatling, Eva Ingersoll. *George Grosz: Works in Oil.* Exh. cat. Huntington, N.Y.: Heckscher Museum, 1977.

Grosz, George. *Erste Landung, New York 1932: A Portfolio of Ten Photographs.* New York: Kimmel/Cohn, 1977.

———. *A Small Yes and a Big No: The Autobiography of George Grosz.* New York: Dial, 1946.

Hess, Hans. *George Grosz.* New York: Macmillan, 1974.

Huder, Walter, and Karl Riha, eds. *New York/George Grosz.* Siegen: Machwerk, 1985.

Knust, Herbert, ed. *Briefe 1913–1959/George Grosz.* Reinbek bei Hamburg: Rowohlt, 1979.

Lewis, Beth Irwin. *George Grosz: Art and Politics in the Weimar Republic.* Madison: University of Wisconsin Press, 1971.

Nisbet, Peter, ed. *The Sketchbooks of George Grosz.* Exh. cat., Busch-Reisinger Museum. Cambridge: Harvard University Art Museums, 1993.

Riha, Karl, ed. *George Grosz, Hans Sahl: So long mit Händedruck: Briefe und Dokumente.* Hamburg: Luchterhand, 1993.

Schneede, Uwe M. *George Grosz: Der Künstler in seiner Gesellschaft.* Cologne: DuMont, 1975.

Schuster, Peter-Klaus, ed. *George Grosz: Berlin, New York.* Exh. cat., Neue Nationalgalerie, Berlin. Berlin: Ars Nicolai, [1994].

John Heartfield

Evans, David. *John Heartfield: AIZ, Arbeiter-Illustrierte Zeitung: Volks-Illustrierte, 1930–38.* New York: Kent Fine Art, 1992.

Honnef, Klaus, and Hans-Jürgen von Osterhausen. *John Heartfield, Dokumentation: Reaktionen auf eine ungewöhnliche Ausstellung.* Cologne: DuMont, 1994.

März, Roland, ed. *John Heartfield: Der Schnitt entlang der Zeit: Selbstzeugnisse, Erinnerungen, Interpretationen: Eine Dokumentation.* Dresden: Verlag der Kunst, 1981.

Pachnicke, Peter, and Klaus Honnef, eds. *John Heartfield/ Idee und Konzeption.* Cologne: DuMont, 1991. Published in English as *John Heartfield.* New York: Harry N. Abrams, 1992.

Siepmann, Eckhard, ed. *Montage, John Heartfield: Vom Club Dada zur Arbeiter-Illustrierten Zeitung: Dokumente, Analysen, Berichte.* Exh. cat. Berlin: Elefanten Press Galerie, 1977.

Taylor, Brandon. "Montage and Its Comedies." *Oxford Art Journal* 16, no. 2 (1993): 91–97.

Uhlman, Fred. *The Making of a German Englishman.* London: Gollancz, 1960.

Wassily Kandinsky

Barnett, Vivian Endicott. *Kandinsky Watercolours: Catalogue Raisonné.* 2 vols. Ithaca: Cornell University Press, 1992.

Beutler, Christian, ed. "Zwölf Briefe von Wassily Kandinsky an Hans Thiemann, 1933–1939." *Wallraf-Richartz-Jahrbuch* 37 (1976): 155–66.

Derouet, Christian, ed. *Correspondence avec Zervos et Kojève: Vasily Kandinsky.* Translated by Nina Ivanoff. Paris: Editions du Centre Pompidou, 1992.

Hahl-Koch, Jelena. *Kandinsky.* Translated by Karin Brown, Ralph Harratz, and Katharine Harrison. New York: Rizzoli, 1993.

Kandinsky in Paris, 1934–44. Exh. cat. New York: Solomon R. Guggenheim Foundation, 1985.

Kandinsky, Nina. *Kandinsky und Ich*. Munich: Kindler, 1976.

Lindsay, Kenneth C., and Peter Vergo, eds. *Kandinsky: Complete Writings on Art*. 2 vols. Boston: G. K. Hall, 1982.

Overy, Paul. *Kandinsky: The Language of the Eye*. New York: Praeger, 1969.

Picon, Gaëtan, Rose-Carol Washton, and Nina Kandinsky. *Kandinsky: Parisian Period, 1934–1944*. New York: M. Knoedler, 1969.

Roethel, Hans K., and Jean K. Benjamin. *Kandinsky: Catalogue Raisonné of the Oil Paintings*. 2 vols. Ithaca: Cornell University Press, 1982–84.

André Kertész

Borhan, Pierre, ed. *André Kertész: His Life and Work*. Boston: Little, Brown, 1994.

Kertész, André. *Kertész on Kertész: A Self-Portrait*. New York: Abbeville, 1985.

Naef, Weston J. *André Kertész: Photographs from the J. Paul Getty Museum*. Malibu: J. Paul Getty Museum, 1994.

Philips, Sandra S., David Travis, and Weston J. Naef. *André Kertész of Paris and New York*. Exh. cat. Chicago: Art Institute of Chicago.

Oskar Kokoschka

Calvocoressi, Richard. *Kokoschka: Paintings*. New York: Rizzoli, 1992.

Holzner, Johann. "Ästhetik als Kundgebung gegen die Drosselung der Humanität: Über Oskar Kokoschka." In *Exil: Literatur und die Künste nach 1933*, edited by Alexander Stephan, 40–47. Bonn: Bouvier, 1990.

Hülsewig-Johnen, Jutta, ed. *Oskar Kokoschka, Emigrantenleben: Prag und London, 1934–1953*. Exh. cat., Kunsthalle, Bielefeld. Bielefeld: Kerber, 1994.

Kokoschka, Oskar. *Briefe*. Vol. 3, *1934–1953*. Düsseldorf: Claassen, 1986.

———. *Letters, 1905–1976*. Edited by Olda Kokoschka and Alfred Marnau. London and New York: Thames and Hudson, 1992.

Oskar Kokoschka, 1886–1980. Exh. cat. New York: Solomon R. Guggenheim Foundation, 1986.

Radford, Robert. "Kokoschka's Political Allegories." *Art Monthly*, no. 97 (June 1986): 3–6.

Spielmann, Heinz. "Kokoschka in Prag." *Drehscheibe Prag: Zur deutschen Emigration in der Tschechoslowakei 1933–1939*, ed. Peter Becher and Peter Heumos, 87–95. Munich: R. Oldenbourg, 1992.

Fernand Léger

De Francia, Peter. "Léger and the U.S.A." In *Fernand Léger*, 107–36. New Haven: Yale University Press, 1983.

James, Martin S. "Léger at Rouses Point, 1944: A Memoir." *Burlington Magazine* 130 (April 1988): 277–82.

Kotik, Charlotta. "Léger and America." *Fernand Léger: An Exhibition*, 41–59. Exh. cat. Buffalo: Albright-Knox Art Gallery; New York: Abbeville, 1982.

Léger, Fernand. "Un art nouveau sous le ciel californien." *Voix de France*, 15 November 1941, 8.

———. "Découvrir l'Amérique." *Voix de France*, 15 May 1942, 9.

———. *Mes voyages, avec un poème d'Aragon et des lithographies de l'auteur*. Facsimile eds. Paris: Editeurs Français Réunis, 1960; Geneva: Edito-Service, [1976].

———. "New York–Paris, Paris–New York." *Voix de France*, 15 September 1941, 10.

Warnod, André. "L'Amérique, ce n'est pas un pays, c'est un monde, dit Fernand Léger." *Arts*, no. 49 (4 January 1946): 1–2. (Translated by Charles Porter under the title "America Isn't a Country—It's a World." *Architectural Forum* 84, no. 4 [April 1946]: 50, 54, 58, 62.)

Willmoth, Simon. "Léger and America." *Fernand Léger: The Later Years*, ed. Nicholas Serota, 43–54. Exh. cat. Munich: Prestel; London: Whitechapel Art Gallery, 1987.

Jacques Lipchitz

The Drawings of Jacques Lipchitz. Exh. cat. New York: Curt Valentin, 1944.

Hammacher, A. M. *Jacques Lipchitz*. Translated by James Brockway. New York: Harry N. Abrams, 1975.

Lipchitz, Jacques, and H. H. Arnason. *My Life in Sculpture*. New York: Viking, 1972.

Patai, Irene. *Encounters: The Life of Jacques Lipchitz*. New York: Funk and Wagnalls, 1961.

Sweeney, James Johnson. "An Interview with Jacques Lipchitz." *Partisan Review* 12 (Winter 1945): 83–89.

Warnod, André. "Jacques Lipschitz [sic]." *Art*, no. 95 (29 November 1946): 5.

Wilkinson, Alan G. *Jacques Lipchitz: A Life in Sculpture*. Exh. cat. Toronto: Art Gallery of Ontario, 1989.

André Masson

Ades, Dawn. *André Masson*. New York: Rizzoli, 1994.

André Masson, 1925–1945. Exh. cat. New York: Arnold Herstand, 1984.

André Masson: Second Surrealistic Period, 1937–43. Exh. cat. New York: Blue Moon Gallery; Lerner-Heller Gallery, 1975.

Birmingham, Doris A. "André Masson in America: The Artist's Achievement in Exile 1941–1945." Ph.D. diss., University of Michigan, 1978.

———. "Masson's Pasiphae: Eros and Unity of the Cosmos." *Art Bulletin* 69 (June 1987): 279–94.

Brownstone, Gilbert, ed. *Vagabond du surréalisme: André Masson*. Paris: Editions Saint-Germain-des-Prés, 1975.

Clébert, Jean-Paul. *Mythologie d'André Masson*. Geneva: Pierre Cailler, 1971.

Levaillant, Francoise, ed. *Les années surréalistes: Correspondance 1916–1942: André Masson*. Paris: Manufacture, 1990.

Masson, André. *Entretiens avec Georges Charbonnier*. Paris: R. Julliard, [1958].

Rubin, William, and Carolyn Lanchner. *André Masson*. Exh. cat. New York: Museum of Modern Art, 1976.

Matta Echaurren

Ferrari, Germana. *Entretiens morphologiques: Notebook no. 1, 1936–1944*. London: Sistan, 1987.

Kozloff, Max. "An Interview with Matta." *Artforum* 4 (September 1965): 23–26.

Matta. Exh. cat. Paris: Editions du Centre Pompidou, 1985.

Matta: Drawings, 1937–1946. Exh. cat. New York: Acquavella Contemporary Art, 1990.

Matta: The First Decade. Exh. cat. Waltham, Mass.: Rose Art Museum, Brandeis University, 1982.

Rubin, William. "Matta." *Bulletin of the Museum of Modern Art* 25, no. 1 (1957).

Schmied, Wieland, ed. *Matta*. Exh. cat. Hypo-Kulturstiftung, Kunsthalle, Munich. Tübingen: Wasmuth, 1991.

Simon, Sidney. "Concerning the Beginnings of the New York School, 1939–1943: An Interview with Peter Busa and Matta." *Art International* 11, no. 6 (1967): 17–20.

Ludwig Mies van der Rohe

Achilles, Rolf, Kevin Harrington, and Charlotte Myhrum, eds. *Mies van der Rohe—Architect as Educator*. Exh. cat. Chicago: Illinois Institute of Technology, 1986.

Drexler, Arthur, ed. *The Mies van der Rohe Archive: An Illustrated Catalogue of the Mies van der Rohe Drawings in the Museum of Modern Art*. Part 2, *1938–1967: The American Work*. Vols. 7–20. New York and London: Garland, 1986–92.

Hitchcock, Henry-Russell, and Philip Johnson. *The International Style: Architecture since 1922*. New York: W. W. Norton, 1932.

Hochman, Elaine S. *Architects of Fortune: Mies van der Rohe and the Third Reich*. New York: Wiedenfeld and Nicolson, 1989.

Johnson, Philip C. *Mies van der Rohe*. Exh. cat. New York: Museum of Modern Art, 1947.

Mertins, Detlef, ed. *The Presence of Mies*. New York: Princeton Architectural Press, 1994.

Schulze, Franz. *Mies van der Rohe: A Critical Biography*. Chicago: University of Chicago Press, 1985.

———, ed. *Mies van der Rohe: Critical Essays*. New York: Museum of Modern Art, 1989.

László Moholy-Nagy

Allen, James Sloan. "Marketing Modernism: Moholy-Nagy and the Bauhaus in America." In *The Romance of Commerce and Culture: Capitalism, Modernism, and the Chicago-Aspen Crusade for Cultural Reform*, 35–77. Chicago: University of Chicago Press, 1983.

Caton, Joseph Harris. *The Utopian Vision of Moholy-Nagy*. Ann Arbor: UMI Research Press, 1984.

David, Catherine, and Corinne Diserens. *László Moholy-Nagy*. Exh. cat., Musée Cantini Marseille. [Marseilles]: Musées de Marseille; Paris: Réunion des Musées Nationaux, 1991.

Findeli, Alain. *L'esthétique pédagogique de László Moholy-Nagy et son rôle dans la transplantation du Bauhaus à Chicago*. Montreal: Faculté de l'Aménagement, Université de Montréal, 1989.

Hahn, Peter, and Lloyd Engelbrecht, eds. *50 Jahre New Bauhaus: Bauhausnachfolge in Chicago*. Exh. cat. Berlin: Bauhaus-Archiv; Argon, 1987.

Kaplan, Louis. *László Moholy-Nagy: Biographical Writings*. Durham, N.C.: Duke University Press, 1995.

Kostelanetz, Richard, ed. *Moholy-Nagy*. New York: Praeger, 1970.

Lusk, Irene-Charlotte. *Montagen ins Blaue: László Moholy-Nagy Fotomontagen und -collagen, 1922–1943*. Giessen: Anabas, 1980.

Moholy-Nagy, László. *The New Vision* (4th rev. ed.) and *Abstract of an Artist*. New York: Wittenborn, 1947.

———. *Vision in Motion*. Chicago: Paul Theobald, 1947.

Moholy-Nagy, Sibyl. *Moholy-Nagy: Experiment in Totality*. Cambridge: MIT Press, 1950.

Passuth, Krisztina. *Moholy-Nagy*. London: Thames and Hudson, 1985.

Suhre, Terry, ed. *Moholy-Nagy: A New Vision for Chicago*. Exh. cat. Springfield: Illinois State Museum, 1990.

Weitemeier, Hannah. *Licht-Visionen: Ein Experiment von Moholy-Nagy*. Berlin: Bauhaus-Archiv, 1972.

Piet Mondrian

Blotkamp, Carel. *Mondrian: The Art of Destruction*. New York: Harry N. Abrams, 1995.

Bois, Yve-Alain. "Piet Mondrian, *New York City*." In *Painting as Model*, 157–309. Cambridge: MIT Press, 1990.

Champa, Kermit Swiler. "Broadway Boogie-Woogie." In *Mondrian Studies*, 127–38. Chicago: University of Chicago Press, 1985.

Henkels, Herbert. "'There Is Too Much Old in the New': Mondrian's Late Work, a Sketch." In *Mondrian in New York*, 12–43. Exh. cat. Tokyo: Galerie Tokoro, 1993.

Holty, Carl. "Mondrian in New York: A Memoir." *Arts* 31 (September 1957): 17–21.

Masheck, Joseph. "Mondrian the New Yorker." *Artforum* 13 (October 1974): 58–65.

Mondrian, Piet. *The New Art—The New Life: The Collected Writings of Piet Mondrian*. Translated by Harry Holtzman and Martin James. Boston: G. K. Hall, 1986.

Mondrian: Zeichnungen, Aquarelle, New Yorker Bilder.../Drawings, Watercolors, New York Paintings. Stuttgart: Staatsgalerie, 1980.

Rudenstine, Angelica Zander, ed. *Piet Mondrian, 1872–1944*. Exh. cat., National Gallery of Art, Washington, D.C. Milan: Leonardo Arte, 1994.

Troy, Nancy. *Mondrian and Neo-Plasticism in America*. Exh. cat. New Haven: Yale University Art Gallery, 1979.

Welsh, Robert. "Landscape into Music: Mondrian's New York Period." *Arts* 40 (February 1966): 33–9.

Wiegand, Charmion von. "Mondrian: A Memoir of His New York Period." *Arts Yearbook* 4 (1961): 57–65.

Kurt Schwitters

Dietrich, Dorothea. *The Collages of Kurt Schwitters: Tradition and Innovation*. Cambridge and New York: Cambridge University Press, 1993.

Elderfield, John. *Kurt Schwitters*. London: Thames and Hudson, 1985.

Kurt Schwitters. Exh. cat. Paris: Editions du Centre Pompidou, 1994.

Kurt Schwitters in Exile: The Late Work, 1937–1948/Kurt Schwitters im Exil: Das Spätwerk, 1937–1948. Exh. cat. London: Marlborough Fine Art, 1981.

Schmalenbach, Werner. *Kurt Schwitters*. New York: Harry N. Abrams; London: Thames and Hudson, 1970.

Schwitters, Kurt. *Kurt Schwitters: Das literarische Werk*. Ed. Friedhelm Lach. 5 vols. Cologne: DuMont Schauberg, 1973–81.

Themerson, Stefan. *Kurt Schwitters in England*. London: Gaberbocchus Press, 1958.

Yves Tanguy

Breton, André. *Yves Tanguy*. Translated by Bravig Imbs. New York: Pierre Matisse Editions, 1946.

Matisse, Pierre. *Yves Tanguy: Un recueil de ses oeuvres/A Summary of His Works*. New York: Pierre Matisse, 1963.

Penrose, Roland. *Yves Tanguy: A Retrospective*. Exh. cat. New York: Solomon R. Guggenheim Foundation, 1983.

Schmidt, Katharina, ed. *Yves Tanguy*. Exh. cat. Baden-Baden: Kunsthalle; Munich: Prestel, 1982.

Soby, James Thrall. *Yves Tanguy*. Exh. cat. New York: Museum of Modern Art, 1955.

Suther, Judith. "Separate Studios: Kay Sage and Yves Tanguy." In *Significant Others: Creativity and Intimate Partnership*, edited by Whitney Chadwick and Isabelle de Courtivron, 136–53. London and New York: Thames and Hudson, 1993.

"Yves Tanguy." *View* 2 (May 1942).

Yves Tanguy. Exh. cat. New York: Acquavella Galleries, 1974.

Yves Tanguy: Das druckgraphische Werk/L'oeuvre gravé/The Graphic Work. Exh. cat., Wolfgang Wittrock Kunsthandel. Düsseldorf: Wittrock, 1976.

acknowledgments

as an art history student in New York in the late 1960s and 1970s, I had the privilege of studying with and attending lectures by several refugees from Nazi Europe, including Robert Goldwater, Julius S. Held, and John Rewald. Along with Meyer Schapiro, with whom I studied as an undergraduate, these scholars had a profound effect on my development. I am also grateful to the late curator Cynthia Jaffee McCabe, whose pioneering exhibition *The Golden Door: Artist-Immigrants of America, 1876–1976* I saw at the Hirshhorn Museum and Sculpture Garden more than twenty years ago; it made a deep impression on me and contributed to my early interest in this topic.

The conception, creation, and presentation of *Exiles and Emigrés: The Flight of European Artists from Hitler* has taken more than five years. It has been a complex undertaking, and I am grateful to the trustees, President and Chief Executive Officer Andrea L. Rich, and Director Graham W. J. Beal of the Los Angeles County Museum of Art for enthusiastically supporting the plans for this exhibition and for their confidence in its execution.

It is difficult today to plan such an ambitious exhibition and publication without corporate sponsorship. We are grateful for the government support we received for this project, from the National Endowment for the Arts and the National Endowment for the Humanities, as well as for an indemnity from the Federal Council on the Arts and the Humanities. The Federal Republic of Germany has also provided crucial financial assistance. The early and critically important grant received from Peter and Helen Bing was instrumental in the research phase of the project and in many of the educational programs. We are pleased that the Villa Aurora, Los Angeles, the former home of exiled writer Lion Feuchtwanger and now a center for exile studies, has joined us in sponsoring a symposium. Educational programs have been made possible in part through the support of Daniel Greenberg and Susan Steinhauser.

I am indebted to the Getty Research Institute for the History of Art and the Humanities for the opportunity to enjoy scholar privileges during 1995–96; I was afforded a refuge from the daily rigors of museum curatorship and had the opportunity to read, think, and write in the surroundings of the center. My thanks to Herb Hymans, Tom Reese, and Gretchen Trevisan for making this possible.

We were very pleased that at an early stage the Montreal Museum of Fine Arts, and the Neue Nationalgalerie, Berlin, expressed keen interest in presenting the exhibition after its showing in Los Angeles. It has been a pleasure to work with Pierre Théberge, director, and Mayo Graham, chief curator, of the Montreal Museum of Fine Arts, and with Wolf-Dieter Dube, director general of the Staatliche Museen zu Berlin, Preussischer Kulturbesitz; Peter-Klaus Schuster, director, Alte Nationalgalerie; and Angela Schneider, senior curator of the Neue Nationalgalerie, Berlin.

This project could not have been mounted without the rigorous scholarship and excellent archival work of the research team. My first and most heartfelt thanks go to my collaborator, Sabine Eckmann, who joined the project in 1993. In addition to contributing to the catalogue, she traveled to Berlin; Cambridge,

Massachusetts; Chicago; New York; Paris; Washington, D.C.; and other cities to conduct much of the primary research on which this exhibition is based. She has worked closely with me on all phases of the exhibition, catalogue, and installation. I am deeply grateful to her for her dedication and professionalism.

Our team included research assistant Sheri Bernstein, who joined the project in 1995; in addition to contributing to the catalogue and doing archival research in the San Francisco Bay Area, she has been indefatigable in tracking down archival photographs, securing complicated permissions, and attending to countless details with meticulous professionalism. Catalogue author Keith Holz, who joined our team during the summer of 1994, has provided invaluable assistance, particularly in planning the European section of the exhibition. He is also the chief architect of our two-day symposium, "Artists from Nazi Germany and the Enigma of Exile," with scholarly participation from Europe and America. In addition, Lisa Klotz (1992–93), Rebecca Cramer (1994–95), Lois Sein (1995–97), and Roz Leader (1996–97) assisted with various stages of research on the project, and I am grateful for their efforts. Catalogue author Kathleen James advised us on architecture. I thank Peter Guenther for his preliminary work on several of the artists in the exhibition.

At the Los Angeles County Museum of Art we are indebted to Susan Trauger, collection librarian of the Robert Gore Rifkind Center for German Expressionist Studies, and to Anne Diederick, program specialist in the Mr. and Mrs. Alan C. Balch Research Library, for assistance in locating many important sources and for help with countless interlibrary loans.

The lenders, without whom it would of course have been impossible to realize such a project, are listed on pages 422–23. We are especially grateful to colleagues at several museums who went out of their way to assist us: Nicholas Serota of the Tate Gallery, London; Lisa Dennison of the Solomon R. Guggenheim Museum, New York; Kirk Varnedoe and Cora Rosavear of the Museum of Modern Art, New York; Germain Viatte and Didier Schulman of the Musée National d'Art Moderne, Centre Georges Pompidou, Paris; James Burke of the Saint Louis Art Museum; Joseph Ketner of Washington University Gallery of Art, Saint Louis; and Earl A. Powell III of the National Gallery of Art, Washington, D.C.

The 1994–95 retrospective of works by Piet Mondrian, which included a comprehensive presentation of the artist's extraordinarily fragile New York paintings, made it impossible to secure a representative selection of those works for another three-venue show. Accordingly, we decided to represent Mondrian through a large-scale model of his last New York studio, with photo and film documentation of its contents. Similarly, the Fernand Léger retrospective—planned by the Musée National d'Art Moderne, Paris, and the Museum of Modern Art, New York, for mid-1997—explains why certain Léger works from the New York years were unavailable or could be shown only in Los Angeles.

During the research phase we were guided by the assistance, leads, and suggestions offered by many generous people. In addition to help given by our catalogue authors and those colleagues mentioned above, we would like to extend our thanks to the following: Petra Albrecht, Patricia Albright, Hildegard Bachert, Ehrhard Bahr, Timothy Baum, Collene Becker, Mayen Beckmann, Ilse Berg, Eugene Bielawski, Julia Bloomfield, Matthias Böckl, Olive Bragazzi, Barbara Brecht-Schall, Eugenie Candau, Janice Capecci, Sharon Chickanzeff, Richard Cohn, Christel Converse, Eva Crider, Catherine Crum, Bernard Crystal, Aaron Dabbah, Britta Eckert, Janis Ekdahl, Andreas Feininger, Karen Fiss, Gordon Onslow Ford, Judi Freeman, Cordula Frowein, Barbara Göpel, Peter Grosz, Marie-Luise Hahn, Diana Haskell, Stephan E. Hauser, Margaret Hedrich, Julius S. Held, Tom Hines, Walter Hopps, Isabelle Hyman, Jarell C. Jackman, Martin S. James, Caroll Janis, Ralph Jentsch, Peter C. Jones, Joop Joosten, Florian Karsch, Terry Keenan, Lillian Kiesler, Petra Kipphoff, Olda Kokoschka, Michael Krejsa, Stephan and

Puck Lackner, Melvin Lader, Irving Lavin, Natalie Leleu, Marvin Liberman, Adrien Maeght, Eline Magaz, Nadia Margolis, Guite and Diego Masson, Maria-Gaetana Matisse, Karin von Maur, James Mayor, Carol Merrill-Mirsky, Franz Meyer, Meret Meyer, Elizabeth Miller, Steven R. Miller, Sibyl Milton, Hattula Moholy-Nagy, Isabelle Monod-Fontaine, Susan Morgenstern, Weston Naef, Francis Naumann, Arnold Newman, Peter Nisbet, Norbert Nobis, Emily Norris, Karin Orchard, Jürgen Pech, Karin Pickel, Rona Roob, Norman Rosenthal, David Ross, Angelica Zander Rudenstine, Bart Ryckbosch, Martica Sawin, Carla Schulz-Hoffmann, Arturo Schwartz, Peter Selz, Werner Spies, Alfred Stendhal, Linda Stewart, Catherine Thieck, Nancy Troy, Rosemary Tudge, Carole Vail, Martin Warnke, Nicholas Fox Weber, Adam Weinberg, Sarah Wilson, Wolfgang Wittrock, Erdmut Wizisla, Christa Wolf, Deborah Young, Virginia Zabriskie, and John Zukowsky.

As the exhibition developed, it expanded to include not only the reconstruction of Mondrian's New York studio but also a model of the Surrealist Gallery of Peggy Guggenheim's Art of This Century. We are very pleased that architects Paul Lubowicki and Susan Lanier were able to work with us to realize these ambitious undertakings. Architect Brian O'Neill created models of buildings designed by Breuer, Gropius, and Mies. To explore the complex issues surrounding American immigration policy in the 1930s and early 1940s, it was necessary to turn to the film medium. We commissioned filmmaker Chana Gazit to create a fifteen-minute documentary, complete with archival footage and interviews with eyewitnesses, to examine more directly this pivotal aspect of our theme. In addition to more than 130 works of art, the show contains approximately two hundred documents—posters, letters, pamphlets, broadsides, newspaper and magazine articles, programs, invitations, and other ephemera—which enrich the presentation of this subject.

An extraordinary series of related events will take place throughout Los Angeles during the twelve weeks that the exhibition is on view here. We are grateful to our colleagues at institutions that have planned relevant collateral programming: Tom Reese, Leda Ramos, and Karen Stokes of the Getty Research Institute for the History of Art and the Humanities; Marianne Heuwagen, Volker Skierka, and Dagmar Spira of the Villa Aurora; Claudia Volkmar Clark of the Goethe Institut; Susan Solt and David Rosenboom of the California Institute of the Arts; Gordon Davidson of the Mark Taper Forum; Madeleine Puzo of the Ahmanson Theater; Sian Winship of the Society of Architectural Historians; Gerald Margolis of the Museum of Tolerance; and Cornelius Schnauber of the University of Southern California.

At the Los Angeles County Museum of Art Dorrance Stalvey, head of music programs, planned two concerts featuring music composed by exiles. Tony Kaes of the University of California, Berkeley, organized two film series, "Hollywood and the Nazis" and "The Experience of Exile," in collaboration with the museum's head of film programs, Ian Birnie.

Once again I was fortunate to work with distinguished architect Frank O. Gehry, who found time in his busy schedule to design the installation. He and architect Greg Walsh were sensitive to issues raised by the show, and they have created a powerful and inspiring setting for it.

This publication, which will be the lasting record of the exhibition, was exceptionally well designed by Scott Taylor of the museum's graphic design department. No curator could ask for a more dedicated, enthusiastic, and talented designer. Scott's solutions to complicated design and curatorial concerns produced a visually rich book. He was also responsible for the exhibition graphics, working sensitively with architects Gehry and Walsh to arrive at the design that will accompany the show on its international tour. All catalogue photography was ably coordinated by museum photographer Barbara Lyter. Editor Karen Jacobson brought her unfailingly sharp intelligence, comprehensive grasp of the material, grace with authors, and elegant style to bear on a range of texts, and I am profoundly grateful to her for her dedication and thoroughness. Thomas Frick, museum associate editor, provided valuable assistance at a crucial phase of the project. I am indebted to Mitch Tuchman, the museum's editor in chief, for overseeing the book's production and for negotiating with the publishers of the French and German editions. Jim Drobka, head graphic designer, was always available to offer helpful suggestions. I was delighted to work with Paul Gottlieb and his staff at Harry N. Abrams, Inc., on the copublication of this volume in English.

As always, I relied upon a team of colleagues at the museum to budget, mount, and oversee the tour of the exhibition: Mark Mitchell, budget manager; Leslie Greene Bowman, assistant director, exhibitions; Beverley Sabo, head, exhibitions; the late John Passi, former head, exhibitions; and Art Owens, assistant director, operations. Each enthusiastically contributed to the successful presentation of *Exiles and Emigrés*. Elvin Whitesides, program specialist, audio-visual department, creatively contributed to our installation team. Melody Kanschat, vice-president of external affairs; Tom Jacobson, head of grants and foundation giving; and Greg Murphy, corporate sponsorship coordinator, are to be commended for their efforts in preparing the proposals that led to funding for the show. Registrar Renee Montgomery and associate registrar Tamra Yost worked tirelessly to arrange the smooth collecting, packing, shipping, insurance, and touring of the works in the exhibition. Conservators Joe Fronek, Gini Rasmussen, and Victoria Blyth-Hill all helped to oversee the handling of the works of art. Barbara Pflaumer and Stefanie Salata deftly handled publicity. In the education department, under the direction of Jane Burrell, Nina Holland coordinated the collateral programming, and Susan Hoffman contributed many of the text panels.

To create an exhibition and a catalogue of this magnitude requires travel and time away from the museum. I am appreciative of my colleagues in the twentieth-century art department—curators Howard N. Fox, Carol Eliel, and Lynn Zelevansky and secretary Nina Berson—for their encouragement, advice, and understanding during the years of this project's gestation. Departmental Coordinator Eric Pals has worked tirelessly with me throughout this project. His excellent computer skills streamlined our work; his attention to detail rescued us from many an error; and his organizational skills inspired us all. He has my deep thanks.

A project of this magnitude takes on a life of its own: it occupies one's thoughts on weekends and evenings; it requires countless trips away from home for research and to secure loans; contemplation and writing demand closed doors and long hours. I thank my son, Max, for his understanding and patience during the time I spent planning and working on this exhibition, its catalogue, and the associated educational events.

Ultimately my thanks go to the exiles themselves, whose lives inspired me to undertake this project. A number of years ago I read from cover to cover the volume of the *International Biographical Dictionary of Central European Emigrés, 1933–1945* devoted to the arts, sciences, and literature. I was convinced that in their stories lay the germ of a powerful exhibition, and I am proud that *Exiles and Emigrés: The Flight of European Artists from Hitler* has finally come to fruition. Many of the issues facing the exiles during those turbulent twelve years continue to haunt us today.

STEPHANIE BARRON

Vice President of Education and Public Programs
Senior Curator of Twentieth-Century Art

lenders to the exhibition

Acquavella Contemporary Art, Inc.
Albright-Knox Art Gallery, Buffalo
Annely Juda Fine Art, London
Arizona State University Art Museum, Tempe
Art Gallery of Ontario, Toronto
The Art Institute of Chicago
The Baltimore Museum of Art
Bauhaus-Archiv, Museum für Gestaltung, Berlin
Bayerische Staatsgemäldesammlungen, Staatsgalerie moderner Kunst, Munich
Bonni Benrubi Gallery, New York City
Busch-Reisinger Museum, Harvard University, Cambridge
Carnegie Museum of Art, Pittsburgh
Cavaliero Fine Arts, New York
Center for Creative Photography, the University of Arizona
Comité André Masson, Paris
Dallas Museum of Art
Des Moines Art Center
The Detroit Institute of Arts
The Fine Arts Museums of San Francisco
Fundación Colección Thyssen-Bornemisza, Madrid
Galerie Gmurzynska, Cologne
Galerie Jan Krugier, Ditesheim & Cie, Geneva
George Arents Research Library for Special Collections, Bird Library, Syracuse University
The Getty Research Institute for the History of Art and the Humanities, Los Angeles
George Grosz Estate
Harvard Law School Art Collection

Hirshhorn Museum and Sculpture Garden, Smithsonian Institution, Washington, D.C.
Hofstra Museum, Hofstra University, Hempstead, New York
Howard Greenberg Gallery, New York
Illinois Institute of Technology, Paul V. Galvin Library, Chicago
Indiana University/Purdue University, Oram Collection, Ruth Lilly Special Collections and Archives, Indianapolis
Institute for Advanced Study, Princeton
The Institute of Contemporary Art, Boston
Institute of Fine Arts, New York University
Jane Corkin Gallery, Toronto
The Josef and Anni Albers Foundation
Estate of André Kertész
Kunstsammlung Nordrhein-Westfalen, Düsseldorf
Kurpfälzisches Museum der Stadt Heidelberg
Los Angeles County Museum of Art
Memorial Art Gallery of the University of Rochester
The Menil Collection, Houston
Mills College Art Gallery, Oakland, California
The Minneapolis Institute of Arts
Moderna Museet, Stockholm
Modern Art Museum of Fort Worth
Mount Holyoke College Archives and Special Collections, South Hadley, Massachusetts
Municipal Archives, Amsterdam
Musée de Nantes
Musée National d'Art Moderne, Centre Georges Pompidou, Paris
Musée National Message Biblique Marc Chagall, Nice

Museo Nacional Centro de Arte Reina Sofia
Museum Boymans-van Beuningen, Rotterdam
Museum of Contemporary Art, Chicago
Museum of Fine Arts, Boston
The Museum of Modern Art, New York
National Gallery of Art, Washington, D.C.
National Museum of American Art,
    Smithsonian Institution,
    Washington, D.C.
New School for Social Research
The Omnibus Gallery, Aspen
Philadelphia Museum of Art
The Saint Louis Art Museum
San Diego Museum of Art
San Francisco Museum of Modern Art
Santa Barbara Museum of Art
Sidney Janis Gallery, New York
The Solomon R. Guggenheim Museum,
    New York
Sprengel Museum, Hannover
Staatliche Museen Preussischer Kulturbesitz,
    Neue Nationalgalerie, Berlin
Stiftung Archiv der Akademie der Künste,
    Berlin
The Tate Gallery, London
Time Life Syndication, New York
Washington University Gallery of Art,
    Saint Louis
Wellesley College Library
Whitney Museum of American Art, New York
Wiener Städtische Allgemeine Versicherung
    Aktiengesellschaft
Wilhelm Lehmbruck Museum, Duisburg
Yale University Art Gallery

Juan Abelló
Helge Achenbach, Düsseldorf
Herta and Paul Amir
Bill Bass, Chicago
Eugene Bielawski, Richmond, California
David and Paria Brandt, New York
Philippe Cazeau
Hugo Dachinger, London
Ms. Dallas Ernst
Richard L. Feigen, New York
Dr. Peter Hahn, Berlin
Gert Jan Hemmink, Amstelveen
Alberta Parker Horn
Martin S. James
Mrs. Lillian Kiesler, New York
Dr. and Mrs. Stephan Lackner, Santa Barbara
Carl D. Lobell
Hattula Moholy-Nagy
Mr. and Mrs. James A. Nathan, Los Angeles
Arnold Newman
The Ulla and Heiner Pietzsch Collection,
    Berlin
Nicholas A. Polsky
The Robert Gore Rifkind Collection,
    Beverly Hills
Miriam Wosk, Los Angeles
Several private collections

index

Numbers in **boldface** refer to pages with illustrations.

Abbott, Berenice, **135**
Abbott, Jere, 274, 279
Adler, Jankel, 13, 386
Adorno, Theodor W., 291, 295n. 28, 329, 332, 335; in Los Angeles, 28, 344–45, 346, 358
AIZ (periodical), 18, 76
Albers, Josef, 243, **254**, 273, 280–81, 388; and Freier Künstlerbund, 47; at Black Mountain College, 24, **25**, 220, 229, 254–61; in *Bauhaus, 1919–1928* exhibition, 219
Albers, Josef, works by: *Bent Black*, 260; *Cadence*, **257**; *City*, **255**; *Etude*, **258**; *Evening*, 255, **256**; *Growing*, 256; *In Open Air*, 256; *Layered*, **258**; *Leaf Study*, **256**; *Penetrating A*, **260**; "*Related*" *A*, 256, **257**; sketch, **259**; *Tierra Verde*, 256
American Academy in Rome, 320
American Friends of German Freedom, 101, 102
Arendt, Hannah, 24, **330**, 331, 332, 333, 335, 343
Arensberg, Walter and Louise, 132, 352, 361
Arnheim, Rudolf, 24, 307, 315
Arp, Jean, 68, 70, 80, 102, 103, 397
Art Institute of Chicago, 275, 282, 314; and Beckmann, 281; and Grosz, 276, 294; and Mies, 229, 230
Artists International Association, 18, 50, 74, 82, 92
Artists' Refugee Committee, 50, 74
Art of This Century, 21, **22**, 132, 134, 140, **141**, 178, 397. *See also* Guggenheim, Peggy
Ashton, Dore, 36
Austin, A. Everett "Chick," 20, 143, 170

Balden, Theo, 50, 89, 391, 393
Barlach, Ernst, 12, 220, 274, 276, 387, 390
Barlach, Ernst, works by: *Head*, 282; *Monks Reading*, 275, **282**
Barr, Alfred H., Jr., **20**, 26, 143, 279, 282, 283, 307, 400; and the Bauhaus, 219, 223n. 24, 276; and Lyonel Feininger, 297, 301, 302; and Fry, 102, 105; and Grosz, 294; and Peggy Guggenheim, 132; and Tanguy, 170; exhibitions organized by, 226, 227, 273, 389
Bauer, Rudolf, 283, 393
Baumeister, Willi, 14, 32, 213, 386, 395
Bayer, Herbert, 243; and *Bauhaus, 1919–1928* exhibition, 21, 219, 228, 276, 393; and Nazi propaganda, 13, 215, 217; at the Bauhaus, 214, 216
Beckmann, Max, **27**, 31, 33, 47, 49, 53, 58–67, 276, 281, 386; in *Exhibition of Twentieth Century German Art*, 48–49, 392; in the Netherlands, **17**, 58, 372, 391
Beckmann, Max, works by: *The Architect*, **58**; *The Argonauts*, 27, 65, **66**; *The Artists with Vegetable*, **61**; *Birds' Hell*, 17, 59, **60**; *Birth*, **59**; *Café*, 63; *Death*, **59**, 60; *Departure*, 282; *Double Portrait*, **61**; *Hotel Lobby*, **62**, 63; *The Journey*, **64**; *Man and Woman*, 364; *Portrait of Stephan Lackner*, **362**, 369; *The Prodigal Son*, 27, **64**; *Self-Portrait*, **67**; *Self-Portrait with Horn*, 48, **49**, 57; *Still Life*, **62**; *Temptation*, **16**, **278**; *The Town*, 64, **65**; untitled lithograph, **368**; *Young Men by the Sea*, 65

Bellmer, Hans, 15, 158, 394
Bendix, Reinhard, 331
Benjamin, Walter, 291, 329, 368, 395
Berman, Eugene, **136**, 146n. 35, 397, 398
Bier, Justus, 307, 311
Bilbo, Jack, 82, 83
Bloch, Ernst, 328, 329
Bloom, Allan, 334–35
Borinski, Ernst, 331
Brandt, Karl, **331**
Brauner, Victor, 106, 108, 112n. 39, 395
Brecht, Bertolt, 389, 395; in Los Angeles, 342, 343, 345, 348–49, 354, **355**, 358
Breton, André, **21**, 35, 142, 395; and Dali, 149, 154; and Duchamp, 128, 138; and Emergency Rescue Committee, 105, **106**, **107**, 108; and Peggy Guggenheim, 132, 133, **135**; and Matta Echaurren, 177, 181; and Tanguy, 145n. 10, 171, 172; and *View* magazine, 137–38, 146n. 35, 396; in *Artists in Exile* exhibition, **136**, 397; in France, **106**, **107**
Breton, André, works by: *Portrait of the Actor A. B.*, 141; *Young Cherry Trees*, 138
Breuer, Marcel, 35, 225, 232, 389, 390; and the Bauhaus, 216; at Harvard, 25, 227, 229, 243, **248**, 249–52; Geller House, **250**, 251; in *Bauhaus, 1919–1928* exhibition, 219
Breuer, Marcel, and Alfred and Emil Roth: Dolderthal Apartments, 248, **249**
Broch, Hermann, 329
Bucher, Jeanne, 44, 70
Buchholz, Karl, 58, 61, 276

Buchholz Gallery, **275**, 278, 280, 281, 282, 390, 394, 398, 399; and Kokoschka, 277; and Lipchitz, 121–22, 125n. 3; and Masson, 166
Buchthal, Hugo, 306, 309
Burlington Magazine, 305

Cage, John, 351
Calas, Nicolas, **21**, 138, 149, 171, 172
Campendonk, Heinrich, 13, 17, 386
Carnegie Foundation, 316n. 11, 321, 323
Carnegie Institute, 275, 276, 281; and Grosz, 283, 294
Carrington, Leonora, **135**, 139
Casals, Pablo, 103, 105, 109
Cazden, Robert, 330
Chagall, Marc, 102, **103**, 302, 398, 400; and Masson, **397**; in *Artists in Exile* exhibition, **136**, 397; in New York, 22, 24, **114**, 115–19, 130–31, 143;
Chagall, Marc, works by: *The Crucified*, **116**; *Ghetto* (renamed *Resistance*), 22, **118**; *Liberation*, **119**; *The Martyr*, **116**; *Obsession*, **117**; *Persecution*, 22, **115**; *Resurrection*, **117**; *The Soul of the City*, **116**; *War*, 116; *White Crucifixion*, **114**, 115; *Yellow Crucifixion*, **113**, 115
Chanel, Coco, 140
Charoux, Siegfried, 50, 85n. 8
Cohen, Gustave, 142, 146n. 54
Cohn, Erich, 274, 280
Colm, Gerhard, **331**
Container Corporation of America, **187**, 188, 265
Cook, Walter S., 304, 307, 308, 309, 317, 321
Coordinating Council of French Relief Societies: *First Papers of Surrealism* exhibition, 21, 116, 134, 137, 138, **180**, 397
Corbusier, Le, 196, 226, 237, 249
Corinth, Lovis, 275
Coser, Lewis, 330, 331, 332
Courtauld Institute, 305
Cowley, Malcolm, 293, 295n. 30
Craven, Thomas, 294

Dali, Salvador, 389, 398, 400; in New York and California, 138–40, **148**, 149–55
Dali, Salvador, works by: *Allegory*, **151**, 154; *The Apotheosis of Homer*, **152**; *Birth of a Nation*, 154; *Dream Caused by the Flight of a Bee*, **155**; *Dream of Venus*, **139**, 140; *The Enigma of Hitler*, 154; *Face of War*, **148**, 153; *Hidden Faces*, 151; *Honey Is Sweeter*, **152**, 153; *Melancholy Atomic*, **150**; *Poetry of America*, **151**, 153, 154; *Portrait of Isabel Styler-Tas*, **148**; *Ruin with Head of Medusa*, **153**, 155n. 8; *Slave Market*, **149**; *Soft Self-Portrait*, **150**
Davis, Mike, 333
Detroit Institute of Arts, 275, 280, 296
Deutsche Arbeitsfront, 215, 387
Deutscher Künstlerbund. See Freier Künstlerbund
Deutscher Werkbund, 213, 217, 244
Deutsches Kulturkartell, 43, 47, 49
Dix, Otto, 14, 32, 274, 275, 279, 291, 387
Dominguez, Oscar, 106, 108, 112n. 39, 163n. 12
Dorner, Alexander, 14, 282, 307, 314
Dreier, Katherine S., 80, 132, 177, 280
Drummond, Lindsay, 76, 78
Duchamp, Marcel, 106, 112n. 37, 389, 398, 400; and Peggy Guggenheim, 132, **135**, 142; in *First Papers of Surrealism* exhibition, **21**, 138, **180**, 397; in France, 106, 112n. 37
Duchamp, Marcel, works by: *The Box in a Valise*, 128, **129**, 141, 145n. 5; cover for *Young Cherry Trees*, 138, **139**

Ecole Libre des Hautes Etudes, 142, 143, 146n. 48, 189n. 10
Edgcomb, Gabrielle Simon, 331
Ehrlich, Georg, 50, 89, 95n. 23
Eisler, Hanns, 24, 328, 329, 358
Eluard, Paul, 105, 108
Emergency Committee for Displaced Foreign Scholars, 23, 307, 316n. 11
Emergency Committee in Aid of Displaced German Scholars, 111n. 15, 320
Emergency Rescue Committee, 19–20, 99–112, 395; and Ernst, **106**, 108, 163n. 1; and Lipchitz, 120; and Masson, 105, **106**, 108, 164
Entartete Kunst exhibition, **14**, 314, **391**; and Ernst, 163n. 1; and Lyonel Feininger, 296; and Kokoschka, 86, 87; and Muche, 215; reaction to, 15, 16, 26, 43, 46, 47
Entretiens de Pontigny, 144
Erikson, Erik H., **330**, 332, 333, 334
Ernst, Max, 15, 50, 281, 393, 394, 399, 400; and Dali, 139; and Emergency Rescue Committee, 102, 103, **106**, **107**, 108; and Peggy Guggenheim, 108, 130, 132, 133, **135**, 139, 156, 157, 158, 163n. 1, 396; and Kollektiv deutscher Künstler, 15, 389; and Mondrian, 190; and New School, 24, 395; in *Artists in Exile* exhibition, **136**, 397; in Los Angeles, 352; in New York, **156–57**, 158–63
Ernst, Max, works by: *An Anxious Friend*, **162**; *The Barbarians*, **160**; *The Cocktail Drinker*, **157**; *Day and Night*, **158**, 161; *Euclid*, **158**; *Europe after the Rain II*, 22, **156**, 157, 158, 159; *The Eye of Silence*, 22, 158, **159**, 160, 161; *Moonmad*, **163**; *Napoleon*, **10**, 22, 158, 159, 160; *Painting for Young People*, **161**, 162; *Stolen Mirror*, **160**; *Surrealism and Painting*, **162**; *Totem and Taboo*, 158, **159**, 160; *Vox Angelica*, 158, 162
European Film Fund, 348

Feiler, Arthur, **331**
Feininger, Andreas B. L., 23, 387, 394; in New York, **196**, 197–201, **302**
Feininger, Andreas B. L., works by: *The Cities Service Building*, **197**; *Columbia Steel Company*, 199; *Elk's Rendezvous*, 198, **199**; *Jewish Establishments*, 198, **199**; *N.Y.–Brooklyn Bridge*, **198**; *Solarized Nude*, **196**, 197; *Standing Nude*, 197; *Stockholm*, **197**; *Times Square*, **201**; *V-E Day Reaction*, **200**
Feininger, Lyonel, 14, 27, 31, 37, 389; at Mills College, 26, 216, 273, 274, 275, **310**; in *Bauhaus, 1919–1928* exhibition, 219, 281; in New York, 23, 278, **296**, 297–301, **302**, 303, 390, 394
Feininger, Lyonel, works by: *Church at Gelmeroda*, 283, **298**, 299; *The Glorious Victory*, 282; *Landscape*, **297**; *Manhattan*, 298, **299**; *Manhattan, Dawn*, 299, **300**; *Manhattan, Night*, **299**; *Manhattan, the Tower*, 299, **300**; *Sidewheeler*, 296
Felixmüller, Conrad, 32
Fenichel, Otto, 333
Fermi, Laura, 34, 35, 330
Feuchtwanger, Lion, 388, 389; and Emergency Rescue Committee, 102, 106, 395; in Los Angeles, 28, **328**, 333, 342, 343, **355**, 358
Fiedler, Herbert, **61**, 62, 391
Fischer, Ruth, 329
Fischer, Theodor, 26, 29n. 19
Flake, Otto, 327
Flexner, Abraham, 323, 325n. 25
Focillon, Henri, 131, 142, 143, 146n. 51
Forbes, Malcolm, 24
Forbidden Art in the Third Reich exhibition catalogue: cover for, **283**
Ford, Charles Henry, 137, 146n. 35, 394, 396
Frank, Bruno, 342, 343, 355, 360
Frank, Leonard, 328
Frankl, Paul, 306, 309, 319
Free Austria Movement, 88, 89, 92
Free German League of Culture, 16, 396, 397; and Heartfield, 18, 74, 76, 77; and Kokoschka, 50, 87, 88, 91

Freie deutsche Kunst exhibition, 47, **87**, 392
Freier Künstlerbund, 15, 46, 48, 390; and Albers, 254, 261n. 6; and Beckmann, 49, 59; and Kokoschka, 50
Freundlich, Otto, **42**, 54, 71; and Fry, 108, 109, 112n. 39; and Kollektiv deutscher Künstler, 15, 44, 45, 389; *Composition*, 45, **46**
Friedlaender, Walter, **306**, 309, 312, 313
Friends of the German People's Front, 75
Fromm, Erich, 24, 332, 333, 334, 335
Frommel, Wolfgang, **61**, 62, 65
Frommhold, Erhard, 32
Frost, Rosamund, 136, 157, 181
Fry, Varian, 19–20, 99–112, 395, 396; photographs of, **100**, **103**, **106**, **108**

Galerie Fischer, 26, 279, 393. *See also* Fischer, Theodor
Galerie "Mai," 114, 115, 119n. 1
Galleria del Milione, 70, 254
Germanic Museum, 274, 275, 280
Germany of Yesterday exhibition, 43, **44**, 49
Gide, André, 103, 388, 389
Gilbert, Felix, 331
Gimpel, Jakob, **351**
Golden Gate Exposition, 277, 278, 393
Goldschmidt, Adolph, 306, 316n. 7, 322, 323, 325n. 23
Göpel, Erhard, 58, 61
Greenberg, Clement, 132, 143; and Dali, 138; and Ernst, 156; and Lyonel Feininger, 300; and Masson, 168, 169n. 17; and Matta Echaurren, 181
Gropius, Walter, 31, 32, 35, 343, 388, 390; and Moholy-Nagy, 262; and National Socialists, 13, 217, 218; at the Bauhaus, 211, 214, 216, 221; at Harvard University, 225, 227, 229, 231, 238, **242**, 243–45, **246**, 247; in *Bauhaus, 1919–1928* exhibition, 21, 219, 228, 276, 393; in *Modern Architecture* exhibition, 226, 237

Gropius, Walter/The Architects Collaborative: Harvard Graduate Center, **243**, 246
Gropius, Walter, and Marcel Breuer, 229, 248, 249; Aluminum City Terrace, **231**, 245, 251; Black Mountain College, **244**, 245; Gropius residence, **228**, 232, 237, 244, **245**
Gropius, Walter, and Rudolf Hillebrecht: "house of labor," **217**, 242
Gropius, Walter, and Adolf Meyer: the Bauhaus, Dessau, **224**
Gropius, Walter, and Joost Schmidt: contribution to *Deutsches Volk*, **218**, 242
Grosz, George, 13, 27, 37, 276, 281, 331, 389, 390; and Kokoschka, 51; in *Europe in America* exhibition, 398; in New York, 26, 273, **286**, 287–95, 386, **400**
Grosz, George, works by: *Cain or Hitler in Hell*, 27, **292**; "Hit Him Once More," 288, **289**; "I'm Glad I Came Back," **292**; *Lower Manhattan*, 288; *The Mighty One*, **289**; *The Painter*, **293**; *Rabble Rouser*, **287**; *Remembering*, 27, **290**; *Self-Portrait*, **291**; *The Survivor*, **272**, 283, 293; *The Wanderer*, **285**, 290
Group of the German Opposition, 75
Grundig, Hans, 31, 388, 390
Guggenheim, Peggy, 20, 133–35, 142; and Ernst, 108, 130, 139, 156, 157, 163n. 1, 177; group photographs at apartment of, 134, **135**, **396**. *See also* Art of This Century
Guggenheim, Solomon R., 133, 277, 278, 283, 393. *See also* Museum of Non-Objective Art
Guilbaut, Serge, 36

Haftmann, Werner, 33
Hanfstaengl, Eberhard, 58, 390
Hanfstaengl, Ernst, 83, 84, 85n. 7
Hare, David, 157, 397
Hartmann, Heinz, 334
Harvard University, 25, 143, 308, 317. *See also* Germanic Museum
Hassenpflug, Gustav, drawing by, **217**
Haus der deutschen Kunst, 273
Hauser, Arnold, 315, 316n. 33

Hausmann, Raoul, 81, 391
Hayter, Stanley William, 24, **135**, 394, 395, 398
Heartfield, John, 13, 387, 388, 393; and Free German League of Culture, 18, 44, 50, 54, 89; and Kokoschka, 51–53; in England, 16, 18, **74**, 75–79, **394**
Heartfield, John, works by: *American Melting Pot*, **78**; *And Yet It Moves!* **77**; *Burden of War*, **76**; *Five Minutes to Twelve*, 18, 76, **77**; *Freedom Calling*, **52**, 75; *Hitler's War Machine*, **76**; *Kaiser Adolf*, **75**; *Reservations*, **75**; *Soviet Financial System*, **78**; untitled journal cover, **79**
Heckel, Erich, 14, 275, 279, 394
Heckscher, William S., **307**, 309, 313
Heilbut, Anthony, 330, 332, 333
Held, Julius, 307, 308, 309, 313, 314
Heimann, Eduard, **331**
Hélion, Jean, 70, 105, 129, 131, 142, 398
Hermann, Alfred, 50, 391
Hérold, Jacques, 106, 108, 112nn. 38, 39
Herrmann-Neisse, Max, 287, 289
Herzfelde, Wieland, 13, 287, 289, 387, 399
Hilberseimer, Ludwig, 25, 213, 225, 228, 230; with Mies, **236**, 237
Hitchcock, Henry-Russell, 143, 221, 226, 237, 248
Hofer, Karl, 14, 274, 275, 279, 392, 394
Hofer, Karl, works by: *Cassandra*, **283**; *Early Hour*, 278; *The Wind*, 276
Hoffmann, Eugen, 50, 89
Holty, Carl, 129, 190
Holtzman, Harry, 190, 193, 194n. 8
Horkheimer, Max, 28, 291, 295n. 28, 332, 358
Hornbostel, E. von, **331**
Horney, Karen, 334
Hudnut, Joseph, 227, 229, 237, 243
Hughes, H. Stuart, 330, 332, 333, 334
Hutchins, Robert M., 29n. 9, 309
Huth, Hans, 312, 314

Institute for Advanced Study, 23, 309, 311, 323
Institute of Fine Arts, 308, 311; Krautheimer at, 309, 319–21; Panofsky at, **304**, 308, 309, 312, 322–23
Institute of Modern Art, 27, 280, **392**, 398
Itten, Johannes, 214, 216

Jackman, Jarrell C., and Carla M. Borden, 34, 331
Jacoby, Russell, 330, 333, 335, 337nn. 28, 32
Janis, Sidney, 134, 178, 181, 399, 400
Janson, Horst W., **307**, 310, 311, 313
Jewell, Edward Alden, 168, 276
Johnson, Alvin, 24, 29n. 9, 102, **331**
Johnson, Philip, 35, 221, 226, 232, 237, 248; and Albers, 24, 254, 273
Jordy, William H., 34, 35
Julien Levy Gallery, 398, 400; and Ernst, 156; and Kertész, 23, 202; and Matta Echaurren, 178. *See also* Levy, Julien

Kahnweiler, Daniel-Henry, 164, 166
Kandinsky, Wassily, 53, 216, 273; and Emergency Rescue Committee, 103; and Kampfbund für deutsche Kultur, 213; in Paris, **17**, **42**, **68**, 69–73, 388
Kandinsky, Wassily, works by: *Balancing Act*, 68, **69**; *Brown with Supplement*, 68, **69**; *Dominant Violet*, 72; *Each for Himself*, 45, **46**; *Grouping*, **70**, 71; *Moderation*, **71**; Study for "Landscape with Tower," 277; *Tempered Elan*, **72**; *Unfinished Painting*, 72, **73**
Katz, Barry, 330, 331
Katzenellenbogen, Adolf, 307, 309
Kertész, André, 390; in New York, 23, 202–7
Kertész, André, works by: *Arm and Ventilator*, **204**; *Clothes Lines*, **203**, 204; *Father Duffy Monument*, **205**; *Lion Seen through a Window*, **206**; *Lost Cloud*, **195**, 204; *Self-Portrait in the Hotel Beaux-Arts*, **202**, 203; *Self-Portrait, November 18, 1939*, 205; *Window Washing*, **202**, 204; *Workmen on the Waterfront*, **204**

Kiesler, Frederick, **135**, 400; gallery designed by, 21, **22**, 140, **141**, 397
Kirchner, Ernst Ludwig, 14, 275, 390, 394; *Street, Berlin*, 278, **279**
Kitzinger, Ernst, 307, 308
Klee, Paul, 14, 216, 273, 281, 388; and Art of This Century, 141; and Freier Künstlerbund, 47; at the Bauhaus, 214; *Polyphonic Architecture*, 282
Klemperer, Otto, 24, 28, 342, **344**, 351, 358
Klingender, Francis, 51, 74, 78
Koestler, Arthur, 328
Koffler, Camilla (YLLA), 105, 106
Köhler, Wilhelm, 307, 308
Kohner, Frederick, 341, **352**
Kokoschka, Oskar, 31, 33, 52, 54, 343, 388, 392, 398; and Free German League of Culture, 50, 51, 393; and Freier Künstlerbund, 48; in London, 17, **18**, **86**, 87–95
Kokoschka, Oskar, works by: "Anschluss," 17, **90**, 92; *The Crab*, 94n. 17; *Family of Jugglers*, **93**; *Harbor of Marseilles*, 282; *Loreley*, **18**, **89**; *Marianne-Maquis*, **89**; *Polperro*, **88**; *Portrait of Ambassador Ivan Maisky*, 94n. 17; *Portrait of Michael Croft*, **88**; *Portrait of Robert Freund*, **87**; *Prague*, 52, **53**; *The Red Egg*, **52**, 53, 89, 94n. 17; *Self-Portrait as a Degenerate Artist*, **86**; *Thomas Garrigue Masaryk*, **87**; *What We Are Fighting For*, 17, **86**, 90, **92**, 93
Kolbe, Georg, 274, 275, 279, 390
Kollektiv deutscher Künstler, 15, 44, 45, 46, 389
Kollwitz, Käthe, 31, 386, 400; *Self-Portrait*, 282
Korsch, Karl, 328
Kracauer, Siegfried, 328
Kralik, Hanns, 45, 389, 391
Krautheimer, Richard, 307, 309, 312, 313, **319**, 320–21
Kris, Ernst, 24, 307, 324, 334
Krispyn, Egbert, 330
Kuhn, Charles L., 26, 274
Kulturwissenschaftliche Bibliothek Warburg. *See* Warburg Library

Lade, Kurt, 50, 391
Lam, Wifredo, 106, **108**, 112n. 39
Lang, Fritz, 332, **348**, 360
Lazarsfeld, Paul, 332
Lederer, Emil, **331**
Léger, Fernand, 35, 142; and Kandinsky, 70; and Kertész, 205; and Moholy-Nagy, 265; in *Artists in Exile* exhibition, **136**, 397; in New York, 22, 128, **135**, 137, **184**, 185, **186**, 187–89
Léger, Fernand, works by: *Adieu New York*, 188; *Composition with Two Parrots*, **184**, 185; *The Divers*, 185, 186, **189**; *Four Composition Studies*, **186**, 187; *France Reborn*, **187**, 188; *Mechanical Fragments*, **186**; *Two Acrobats*, **188**; *La ville*, 189n. 8; *The Women Cyclists*, **185**, 186
Lehmann, Hartmut, and James Sheehan, 331
Lehmbruck, Wilhelm, 275, 279, 390; *Bust of Kneeling Woman*, 282; *Kneeling Woman*, 278
Lévi-Strauss, Claude, 24, 131, 142, 395
Levy, Julien, 20, 132, 143, 400; and Dali, 140; and Kertész, 202; and Matta Echaurren, 177; and Tanguy, 131, 145n. 10, 174. *See also* Julien Levy Gallery
Lingner, Max, 45, 391
Lipchitz, Jacques, 103, 130, 398, 400; in *Artists in Exile* exhibition, **136**, 397; in New York, 22, 24, **120**, 121–25, 394, 395
Lipchitz, Jacques, works by: *Arrival*, 120, **121**; *David and Goliath*, **122**; *Flight*, **120**, 121; *Mother and Child*, 121, **122**; *The Pilgrim*, 124; *The Prayer*, **124**; *Prometheus*, 122, **123**; *Rape of Europa*, 123
Loewy, Ernst, 329, 334
Lohmar, Heinz, 45, 50, 389, 391
Low, David, caricature by, **91**
Lowenthal, Leo, 331

MacLeish, Archibald, 134
Magnelli, Alberto, 70, 71, 108
Mahler-Werfel, Alma, 342, **343**, 346, 395
Mann, Heinrich, 386; and Emergency Rescue Committee, 102, 106, 395; and exile groups, 328, 387, 388, 389; in Los Angeles, 28, 342, 343, 348, 355, 358, 360
Mann, Klaus, 22, 29n. 9, 101, 133, 138, 388, 389
Mann, Thomas, 218, 219, 363, 372, 390, 394; and Emergency Rescue Committee, 101, 102; in Los Angeles, 28, **327**, 333, 342, 343, **345**, 346, 356, 358, 393; Lackner interview with, 365, **366**, 367; portrait of, 48, **49**
Man Ray, 352, 361, 395, 399
Marc, Franz, 279, 298, 314
Marcks, Gerhard, 14, 214, 274, 275, 280, 390
Marcuse, Herbert, **330**, 333, 335
Marinetti, Filippo Tommaso, 70, 217
Maritain, Jacques, 29n. 9, 102, 131, 142
Massing, Hede, 329
Masson, André, 31, 35, **136**, 137, 394, 395; and Emergency Rescue Committee, 105, 106, 108; at Mount Holyoke College, 26, 164; in Connecticut, 22, 130, **164**, 165–69, **397**
Masson, André, works by: *Curtain for a Ceremony*, **147**; *The German Soldier*, **165**; *The Germ of the Cosmos*, **167**; *Le jeu de Marseille*, 106; *Leonardo da Vinci and Isabella d'Este*, 169n. 12; *The Night*, 167, **168**; *Novalis*, **107**; *Oradour*, 22, 162, **165**; *Pasiphaë*, 167, **168**; *Praying Mantis*, 165; praying mantis design, **166**; *The Resistance*, **166**; *The Seeded Earth*, **167**; *Street Singer*, 169n. 12; *There Is No Finished World*, **164**, 165, 166
Matisse, Henri, 63, 103, **104**, 140, 279

Matisse, Pierre, 20, **21**, 132, 136; and Breton, 141; and Chagall, 116; and Matta Echaurren, 177, 178; and Tanguy, 170. *See also* Pierre Matisse Gallery
Matta Echaurren, Roberto Sebastián, **21**, 22, 29n. 14, 35, 399; in New York, **136**, **176**, 177–82, 394
Matta Echaurren, Roberto Sebastián, works by: *The Bachelors*, 180; *Being With*, 180; *The Disasters*, **180**; *The Earth Is a Man*, **178**, 179; *A Grave Situation*, 180, **181**; *The Great Transparent Ones*, **177**; *Invasion*, **178**; *Locus Solus*, **179**; *Theory of Nature's Strategy*, **176**; *The Thought of a Permanent Table*, 180, **182**; *The Year 1944*, **179**; Untitled, **177**
May, Saidie A., 164, 166, 170
McBride, Henry, 140, 166
Meidner, Ludwig, 14, 29n. 3, 393
Mendelsohn, Erich, 225, 234n. 1, **236**; B'nai Amoona Synagogue, **234**
Meyer, Hannes, 212, 214, 216, 219
Middeldorf, Ulrich, 309, 311
Mies van der Rohe, Ludwig, 32, 35; at the Bauhaus, 58, 211, 212, 213, 216, 226, 387; in Chicago, 220–21, 227–32, **236**, 237–41, 391
Mies van der Rohe, Ludwig, projects by: Concert Hall Project, **239**; Farnsworth House, 232, **233**, 239; German Pavilion, **236**; Institute of Technology, **25**, 238; North Lake Shore Drive Apartments, **235**; Resor House, 234n. 9, **237**
Mies van der Rohe, Ludwig, and Philip Johnson: Seagram Building, 232, **240**
Miller, Henry, **351**
Mills College: and Lyonel Feininger, 26, 275, 296, 301, **310**; and Mies, 234n. 6; and Neumeyer, 14, 26, 274, **310**
Milton, Sybil, 36
Miró, Joan, 68, 395, 398
Mittenzwei, Werner, 31
Mittig, Hans-Ernst, 32
Moholy-Nagy, László, 35, 216, 227, 243, 388, 389; and Mondrian, 190; in Chicago, 24, **25**, 219, 220, 229, **262**, 263–69, 390, 391

Moholy-Nagy, László, works by: *A II*, **267**; *CH B4*, 266, **267**; *Composition* of 1938, **266**; *Composition* of 1942, **264**; patent design, **265**; *Photogram*, **265**; Space Modulator paintings, **253**, **263–64**, **267**; *Spirals*, 267, **268**; *Vision in Motion*, 265
Molo, Walter von, 327
Mondrian, Piet, 22, 400; in New York, 22, 129, **135**, **136**, 137, 145n. 31, **190**, 191–94, 255, 395, 398
Mondrian, Piet, works by: *Broadway Boogie-Woogie*, 137, 186, **190**, **192**, 193; *Composition*, **190**, 191; *New York City*, **191**, 192, 193; *Victory Boogie-Woogie*, 137, **183**, **192**, 193
Mopp, Carl, 87, 398
Morey, Charles R., 307, 309, 317, 323
Morley, Grace McCann, 274, 275
Mosse, George, 333
Mount Holyoke College, 23, 26, 143, 146n. 54, 164
Muche, Georg, 214, 215, 218
Mühsam, Erich, 288, 295n. 14, 388
Münzenberg, Willi, 328
Museum of Modern Art, 128, 132–33, 400; and Albers, 273; and Beckmann, 63; and Breuer, 249, 251; and Chagall, 116; and Dali, 140, 153–54; and Andreas Feininger, 199; and Lyonel Feininger, 27, 281, 284n. 35, 302; and Gropius, 243; and Grosz, 281, 293, 294; and Kertész, 202, 206; and Léger, 185; and Masson, 169n. 12; and Matta Echaurren, 177; and Mies, 237; and Mondrian, 193, 398; and Schwitters, 81; and Tanguy, 170
Museum of Modern Art exhibitions: *Art in Our Time*, 278–79, 393; *Bauhaus, 1919–1928*, 21, 219, 228, 229, 276, **277**, 393; *Cubism and Abstract Art*, 389; *Fantastic Art*, 389; *German Painting and Sculpture*, 273, 280; *Hayter and Studio 17*, 399; *The History of Photography*, 202; *Modern Architecture*, 221, 225, 237, 247n. 6; *New Acquisitions*, 282; *Nineteen Living Americans*, 296

Museum of Non-Objective Art, 132, 269n. 22. *See also* Guggenheim, Solomon R.

Neher, Carola, 328
Neumann, Franz, 332
Neumann, J. B., 61, 261n. 7, 280, 294
Neumeyer, Alfred, 14, 274, 312; and Lyonel Feininger, 297, 301, 310
Neutra, Richard, 234n. 4, 341, **353**, 356, 361
New Bauhaus, 24, **262**, 263–66, **391**, 394
New Burlington Galleries: *Exhibition of Twentieth Century German Art*, **16**, 17, 18, 47, 48, 58, 74, 81, 279, 392
Newhall, Beaumont, 23, 105, 202
New School for Social Research, 23, 24, 111n. 15, 142, 394; University in Exile, 24, **331**
New York University, 322, 323. *See also* Institute of Fine Arts
Nierendorf, Karl, 20, 26, 269n. 22, **275**, 390, 391
Nierendorf Gallery, **26**, 261n. 7, 280, **283**, 399, 400
Nolde, Emil, 12, 31, 274, 387, 389, 394; *Christ among the Children*, 280
Nungesser, Michael, 31, 33

Oberlaender Trust, 23
Olbrich, Harald, 32
Onslow Ford, Gordon, 24, 142, 395
Oram, Harold, 102, 105, 106
Oskar-Kokoschka-Bund, 50, 87, 218, 391
Otto, Christian F., 35
Oud, J. J. P., 226, 227, 237
Ozenfant, Amédée, 129, 131, **135**, 142, 391; in *Artists in Exile* exhibition, **136**, 397; school of, 26, 146n. 46, 393
Paalen, Wolfgang, 145n. 7, 395
Pachter, Henry, 331
Palmier, Jean-Michel, 326
Panofsky, Erwin, 306, **307**, 313, 316n. 12, **322**; at Institute for Advanced Study, 309, 311, 323–24; at Institute of Fine Arts, **304**, 308, 312
Pechstein, Max, 275, 279, 389, 390; *Sunlight*, **274**
Penrose, Roland, 50, 82
Péret, Benjamin, 105, 106, 108, 396

Peterhans, Walter, 228, 230, **236**, 237
Pevsner, Nikolaus, 226, 305, 306
Philip, Lotte Brand, **307**
Picasso, Pablo, 84, 102, 103, 105, 109, 398
Pierre Matisse Gallery, 21, 398, 399; and Masson, 166; and Tanguy, 171; *Artists in Exile* exhibition, 116, 134, 135, **136**, 397. *See also* Matisse, Pierre
Piscator, Erwin, 24, 287
Plaut, James S., 26, 27, 280
Pollock, Jackson, 35, 163n. 18, 176, 352
Professional Civil Service Restoration Act, 12, 386
Putzel, Howard, 29n. 18, 132

Radio Libre, 131
Radziwill, Franz, 31
Raphael, Max, 307, 308
Rathbone, Perry, 26, 63, 280, 282
Read, Herbert, 71, 82, **83**, 392
Rebay, Hilla von, 276–77, 283, 393
Reich, Wilhelm, 24, 332, 365
Reichenbach, Hans, 351, 358
Reichskammer der bildenden Künste, 58, 217, 387, 388, 390, 391
Reichskulturkammer, 12, 214, 218, 242, 296, 387
Reid, Whitelaw, 134
Reinhardt, Max, 333, 342, 343, 347, 358, 361
Renger-Patzsch, Albert: *Railroad Bridge*, **198**
Rockefeller Foundation, 23, 111n. 15, 308, 316n. 11
Roosevelt, Eleanor, 29n. 9, 111n. 16, 146n. 54
Rose, Hajo, 16, 386
Rosenberg, Harold, 117
Rosenberg, Jakob, 308, 312, 313, 314
Roters, Eberhard, 32
Rutkoff, Peter, and William Scott, 330, 331

Sage, Kay, 131, 145n. 10, **170**
Said, Edward, 37, 302
San Francisco Museum of Art, 274, 275, 284n. 46, 394
Sawin, Martica, 36
Schardt, Alois J., 297, 299, 301, 361, 394
Scharl, Josef, 284n. 46, 393
Scheyer, Emmy "Galka," 274, 281; and Lyonel Feininger, 283, 296; in Los Angeles, 352, 361
Schiaparelli, Elsa, 134, 140
Schindler, Rudolph, 234n. 4, 341, **353**, 361
Schlemmer, Oskar, 14, 214, 387, 398
Schmidt-Rottluff, Karl, 14, 274, 387, 394; *Rain Clouds*, 275
Schoenberg, Arnold: in Los Angeles, **340**, 342, 343, **344**, 346, 351, 355, 358
Schwitters, Kurt, 31, 33; and Free German League of Culture, 18, 393; in England, 16, 18, 50, **80**, 81–85, 395
Schwitters, Kurt, works by: *Collage*, **83**; *The Double Picture*, 84, **85**; *Heavy Relief*, 84; *The Hitler Gang*, 18, 83, **84**; *Portrait of Fred Uhlman*, **80**; *Small Flower Picture*, **81**; *W. C. Fields*, **82**; *The Wounded Hunter*, 18, **82**, 83
Seligmann, Kurt, 105, **135**, **136**, 393
Smith College, 306, 309
Soby, James Thrall, 20, 132; and Dali, 140, 153; and Duchamp, 400; and Matta Echaurren, 29n. 14, 181; and Tanguy, 173
Spalek, John, 330
Speier, Hans, **331**
Sperber, Manès, 328
Spiro, Eugen, 44, 46, 54, 105, 389, 390; *Thomas Mann*, 48, **49**
Springfield Museum of Fine Arts, 279, 393
Stechow, Wolfgang, 307, 311, 313
Steinitz, Kate, 80, **311**, 352
Stern, Guy, 330
Stravinsky, Igor: in Los Angeles, 346, 351, 361
Strelka, Joseph, 330
Strempel, Horst, 45, 389
Swarzenski, Hanns, **61**, **309**
Sweeney, James Johnson, 132, 138, 156, 172, 398, 400
Syberberg, Hans Jürgen, 329

428

Taeuber-Arp, Sophie, 68, 80, 103, 397
Tanguy, Yves: in *Artists in Exile* exhibition, **136**, 397; in Connecticut, 130, 131, 145n. 10, 170–75; photographs of, **170–71**
Tanguy, Yves, works by: *The Earth and the Air*, 170, **171**, 173; *Indefinite Divisibility*, **171**; *Mama, Papa Is Wounded*, 170; *Nonessential Lights Off*, 170; *The Prodigal Son*, **173**; *Slowly toward the North*, 172, 173; *Through Birds, through Fire, but Not through Glass*, 173, **174**; *View* magazine cover design, **172**
Tashjian, Dickran, 36
Tchelitchev, Pavel, 29n. 14, **136**, 146n. 35, 171, 398
Themerson, Stefan and Franciska, 82, 83
Thiess, Frank, 327
Tillich, Paul, 332
Toch, Ernst, **344**, 349, 351, 358
Tolnay, Charles de, 307, 309

Uhlman, Diana Croft, 50, 74
Uhlman, Fred, 50, 74, **80**, 89, 393
University of California, Berkeley, 234n. 1, 310, 318
University of California, Los Angeles, 310, 311, 351, 352
University of Chicago, 23, 309, 318

Valentin, Curt, 14, **275**, 276, 277, 281, 282, 390; and Beckmann, **61**; and Lyonel Feininger, 297; and Lipchitz, 121, 125n. 3; and Masson, 166
Valentine Gallery, 190, 191, 193
Valentiner, William R., 26, 275, 280, 307, 314, 352; and Lyonel Feininger, 278, 296
Vassar College, 23, 251, 309, 312, 321, 400
Viertel, Salka, 28, 341, 342, 348, 355, 358
Vordemberge-Gildewart, Friedrich, 17, 61, 62, 391, 393
VVV magazine, 21, 137, 146n. 35, 157, 397, 399

Wachsmann, Konrad, 232, 243
Wagenfeld, Wilhelm, 215, 217
Wagner, Martin, 217, 225, 227, 243
Warburg, Aby, 318, 322
Warburg, Edward, M. M., 24, 273, 282
Warburg, Max, 318, 324
Warburg Institute, 318
Warburg Library, 15, 304, 305, 322
Weinberger, Martin, 309, 312, 316n. 14
Weitzmann, Kurt, 308, 313, 316n. 12
Werfel, Franz, 28, 102, 106, **343**, 355, 360, 361, 395
Wertheimer, Max, 24, **331**
Wescher, Paul, 312, **314**
Westheim, Paul, 15, 46, 48, 50, 89, 389
Whitney Museum of American Art, 132, 251, 283, 294, 400
Wind, Edgar, 306, 307, 309, 312
With, Karl, **310**
Wittfogel, Karl August, 328, 329
Wittkower, Rudolf, 307, 308, 311, 313
Wollheim, Gert, 15, 45, 47, 389, 394
Wols, Otto, 112n. 39, 394
world's fairs: of 1935, in Brussels, 227, 234n. 6, **236**; of 1937, in Paris, 70, 132, **390**; of 1939, in New York, 43, **44**, 49, **139**, 140, 218, 277, 278, **297**, **392**, 393
Worner, Heinz, 50, 89, 391, 393
Wright, Frank Lloyd, 221, 226, 229, 237, 238, 249
Wunderlich, Frieda, **331**
Wüsten, Johannes, 50, 391, 398

Yale University, 143, 260, 318
Yamawaki, Iwao: *The Blow against the Bauhaus*, **210**
YLLA. *See* Koffler, Camilla
Yorke, F. R. S., 232, 248
Young-Bruehl, Elisabeth, 331

Zadkine, Ossip, **136**, 395, 400
Zervos, Christian, 69, 70, 71
Zucker, Paul, 307, 311

photography credits

Works by Josef Albers, Max Beckmann, Lyonel Feininger, John Heartfield, Max Pechstein, Alfred Renger-Patzsch, Kurt Schwitters © ARS, New York/Bild-Kunst, Bonn. Works by Marc Chagall, Marcel Duchamp, Wassily Kandinsky, Fernand Léger, Matta Echaurren © ARS, New York/ADAGP, Paris. Works by Max Ernst, André Masson, László Moholy-Nagy, Yves Tanguy © ARS, New York. Works by Salvador Dali © ARS, New York/Demart, Paris. Works by Oskar Kokoschka © ARS, New York/Pro Litteris, Zurich. Works by Piet Mondrian courtesy of the Mondrian Estate/Holtzman Trust/Licensed by MMI, New York. Works by George Grosz © Estate of George Grosz/Licensed by VAGA, New York. Works by Jacques Lipchitz © Estate of Jacques Lipchitz/Licensed by VAGA, New York, courtesy of Marlborough Gallery, New York. Most other photographs in this volume have been supplied by the owners or custodians as listed in the captions and checklist. Every effort has been made by the publishers to trace copyright holders. Any unacknowledged claimants should notify the publishers for recognition in future editions.

The following additional photo credits apply to the figure or page numbers indicated:

Berenice Abbott/Commerce Graphics Ltd., Inc.: fig. 121
American Jewish Historical Society: p. 389 center
AP/Wide World Photos: figs. 9, 123, 244, 271; pp. 95–97, 125–27, 394 bottom, 396 bottom
Archives of American Art, Smithsonian Institution: figs. 117, 159 (George Platt Lynes Papers); 269 (Jane Wade Papers)
Ernst und Hans Barlach GBR: fig. 274
Bauhaus-Archiv, Berlin: figs. 17, 216–18, 222, 233, 255, 259; p. 391 left
Mayen Beckmann: figs. 7, 20, 32
© Bildarchiv Preussischer Kulturbesitz: pp. 39–40, 388, 391 right
Mrs. Tone Bjørn, courtesy Sprengel Museum, Hannover: fig. 65
Elisa Breton Collection: fig. 11
Busch-Reisinger Museum, Harvard University Art Museums: fig. 234 (Gift of Ise Gropius); figs. 223, 236 (Gift of Walter Gropius)
Center for Creative Photography, University of Arizona: fig. 288; figs. 6, 16, 22, 25, 47, 77 (Josef Breitenbach Archive, © 1986 The Josef Breitenbach Trust, New York); fig. 199 (Andreas Feininger Archive)
Chicago Historical Society: figs. 227, 254
Alan Clarke: fig. 82

Columbia University, Rare Book and Manuscript Library: figs. 92, 95, pp. 4–5, 98, 396 center (Varian Fry Papers)
Corbis-Bettmann: figs. 337–38
Dr. Wolfgang Elfe: fig. 89
© Andreas Feininger: figs. 200, 201, 204–6, 208
S. Fischer Verlag, Frankfurt: fig. 307
Annette Fry Collection: fig. 2, p. 389 bottom
Galerie Leiris: fig. 152
Harvard Law School Art Collection: fig. 237
© Hedrich-Blessing: fig. 225
Bruce Henstell Archives: p. 339
© Ingeborg & Dr. Wolfgang Henze-Ketterer, Wichtrach/Bern: fig. 273
Hollywood Bowl Museum: fig. 318
Howard Greenberg Gallery, New York: fig. 198
Institute for Advanced Study, Princeton University: fig. 306
The Institute of Contemporary Art, Boston: fig. 275
Institute of Fine Arts, New York: figs. 296, 297, 305
Martin S. James: fig. 188
Florian Karsch, Nierendorf Gallery, Berlin: figs. 19, 268
Dr. F. Karsten: p. 224
© Estate of André Kertész: figs. 210–15
Lillian Kiesler: figs. 13, 121
Walter Klein: fig. 136
Oskar Kokoschka-Archiv, Vienna: figs. 8, 74
Kunsthaus Zürich, © The Estate of Fritz Glarner: figs. 193, 196
Stephan Lackner: figs. 326–32

Library of Congress: fig. 14, pp. 269–70 (New York World Telegram and Sun Collection); figs. 224, 242 (Gottscho-Schleisner Collection); p. 209 (U.S. Farm Security Administration); p. 392 top
Dr. Ulrich Luckhardt, Hamburger Kunsthalle: fig. 289
Max Ernst Kabinett, Brühl: p. 396 top
Michael Werner Gallery: fig. 68
Mills College Art Gallery: fig. 301
Musée National d'Art Moderne, Centre Georges Pompidou, Paris: fig. 21 (Kandinsky bequest)
The Museum of Modern Art, New York: figs. 10, 86, 88, 90 (gift of Annette Fry); fig. 120 (gift of Julian Levy); figs. 18, 228, 230 (The Mies van der Rohe Archive); fig. 271, p. 398
Nederlands Fotoarchief/Cas Oorthuys: p. 399 bottom
William Nettles Photography: fig. 157
New School for Social Research: fig. 15
The New York Public Library, United States History, Local History, and Genealogy Division, Astor, Lenox and Tilden Foundations: pp. 207–8
The New York Times/NYT Pictures: fig. 312
Photograph by Tim Nighswander: figs. 246, 252, 253
Österreichische Gesellschaft für Zeitgeschichte, Vienna: p. 41
The Plaza Hotel, New York: fig. 41
Port Franc, Geneva: fig. 129
Sally Ritts: fig. 243
Dr. Cornelius Schnauber Collection: figs. 314, 319, 323

Ronald and Barbara Schoenberg, courtesy Hollywood Bowl Museum: fig. 313
Robert Snyder: fig. 321
Solomon R. Guggenheim Foundation: fig. 243
Werner Spies: p. 396 top
Lee Stalsworth: figs. 284, 287
Stiftung Archiv der Akademie der Künste, Berlin: figs. 55, 278; p. 400 top (George-Grosz-Archiv); p. 394 top (John-Heartfield-Archiv); p. 397 center (Heinz-Wörner-Archiv)
Syracuse University Library: fig. 241 (Marcel Breuer Papers)
Tate Gallery Archives: fig. 5 (Ewan Phillips Papers)
Prof. Gunther Thiem, Stuttgart: p. 389 top
Time Life Syndication: fig. 207
United States Holocaust Memorial Museum: pp. 2–3 (Hiram Bingham Collection); fig. 94 (Dyno Lowenstein Collection); figs. 87, 91 (Cynthia Jaffee McCabe Collection)
United States Holocaust Memorial Museum Photo Archives: p. 388 (© Bildarchiv Preussischer Kulturbesitz); p. 392 bottom (Rijksinstitut voor Oorlogsdocumentatie); p. 397 bottom (Jack Lewin); p. 399 top (Hanna Meyer-Moses)
University of California, Los Angeles, Music Library, Special Collections, courtesy Hollywood Bowl Museum: fig. 316 (Ernst Toch Archive)
University of California, Los Angeles, Research Libraries, Special Collections: fig. 317

University of Southern California Libraries, Department of Special Collections, courtesy Hollywood Bowl Museum: fig. 320 (Hearst Los Angeles Examiner Collection); figs. 308, 324 (Feuchtwanger Library)
University of Southern California, Max Kade Institute Archives: fig. 322
Warburg-Archiv, Hamburg: fig. 298
Simon Wiesenthal Center Archives, Los Angeles: fig. 3, p. 399 center (courtesy Oswiecim State Museum Archives); p. 400 bottom (courtesy U.S. Army Signal Corps Archives)
Mrs. Michiko Yamawaki: fig. 216

County of Los Angeles

Board of Supervisors, 1997

Zev Yaroslavsky
Chair

Michael D. Antonovich
Yvonne Brathwaite Burke
Don Knabe
Gloria Molina

David E. Janssen
Chief Administrative Officer

Los Angeles County Museum of Art

Andrea L. Rich
President and Chief Executive Officer

Graham W. J. Beal
Director and Executive Vice President

Board of Trustees, Fiscal Year 1996–97

Robert F. Maguire III
Chair

William A. Mingst
President

James R. Young
Secretary/Treasurer

William H. Ahmanson
Daniel N. Belin
Mrs. Lionel Bell
Dr. George N. Boone
Donald L. Bren
Gerald Breslauer
Eli Broad
Mrs. Willard Brown
Mrs. B. Gerald Cantor
Mrs. William M. Carpenter
Mrs. Edward W. Carter
John F. Cooke
Robert A. Day
Jeremy G. Fair
Michael R. Forman
Mrs. Camilla Chandler Frost
Julian Ganz, Jr.
Herbert M. Gelfand
Arthur Gilbert
Stanley Grinstein
Robert H. Halff
Mrs. Dwight M. Kendall
Cleon T. Knapp
Mrs. Harry Lenart
Herbert L. Lucas, Jr.
Steve Martin
Mrs. David H. Murdock
Mrs. Barbara M. Pauley Pagen
Mrs. Stewart Resnick
Dr. Richard A. Simms
Michael G. Smooke
Mrs. Jacob Y. Terner
Walter L. Weisman
David L. Wolper

Honorary Life Trustees

Mrs. Howard Ahmanson
Robert H. Ahmanson
Robert O. Anderson
The Honorable
    Walter H. Annenberg
Mrs. Anna Bing Arnold
R. Stanton Avery
Mrs. Freeman Gates
Felix Juda
Joseph B. Koepfli
Eric Lidow
Mrs. Lucille Ellis Simon
Mrs. Lillian Apodaca Weiner

Past Presidents

Edward W. Carter
1961–66

Sidney F. Brody
1966–70

Dr. Franklin D. Murphy
1970–74

Richard E. Sherwood
1974–78

Mrs. F. Daniel Frost
1978–82

Julian Ganz, Jr.
1982–86

Daniel N. Belin
1986–90

Robert F. Maguire III
1990–94